DIGITAL TECHNOLOGY
PRINCIPLES AND PRACTICE

DIGITAL TECHNOLOGY

PRINCIPLES AND PRACTICE

Virendra Kumar
MSc, Physics
(Indian Civil Service)

Publishing Globally

NEW AGE INTERNATIONAL (P) LIMITED, PUBLISHERS
LONDON • NEW DELHI • NAIROBI
Bangalore • Chennai • Cochin • Guwahati • Hyderabad • Kolkata • Lucknow • Mumbai
Visit us at www.newagepublishers.com

Published by New Age International (P) Ltd., Publishers
First Edition: 1992
Second Edition: 2015
Reprint: 2019

GLOBAL OFFICES

- **New Delhi** **NEW AGE INTERNATIONAL (P) LIMITED, PUBLISHERS**
  7/30 A, Daryaganj, New Delhi-110002, (INDIA)
  Tel.: (011) 23253771, 23253472, **Telefax:** 23267437, 43551305
  E-mail: contactus@newagepublishers.com • Visit us at www.newagepublishers.com
- **London** **NEW AGE INTERNATIONAL (UK) LTD.**
  27 Old Gloucester Street, London, WC1N 3AX, UK
  E-mail: info@newacademicscience.co.uk • Visit us at www.newacademicscience.co.uk
- **Nairobi** **NEW AGE GOLDEN (EAST AFRICA) LTD.**
  Ground Floor, Westlands Arcade, Chiromo Road (Next to Naivas Supermarket)
  Westlands, Nairobi, KENYA, **Tel.:** 00-254-713848772, 00-254-725700286
  E-mail: kenya@newagepublishers.com

BRANCHES

- **Bangalore** 37/10, 8th Cross (Near Hanuman Temple), Azad Nagar, Chamarajpet, Bangalore- 560 018
  Tel.: (080) 26756823, **Telefax:** 26756820, **E-mail: bangalore@newagepublishers.com**
- **Chennai** 26, Damodaran Street, T. Nagar, Chennai-600 017, **Tel.:** (044) 24353401, **Telefax:** 24351463
  E-mail: chennai@newagepublishers.com
- **Cochin** CC-39/1016, Carrier Station Road, Ernakulam South, Cochin-682 016, **Tel.:** (0484) 2377303
  Telefax: 4051304, **E-mail: cochin@newagepublishers.com**
- **Guwahati** Hemsen Complex, Mohd. Shah Road, Paltan Bazar, Near Starline Hotel, Guwahati-781 008,
  Tel.: (0361) 2513881, **Telefax:** 2543669, **E-mail: guwahati@newagepublishers.com**
- **Hyderabad** 105, 1st Floor, Madhiray Kaveri Tower, 3-2-19, Azam Jahi Road, Near Kumar Theater, Nimboliadda Kachiguda, Hyderabad-500 027, **Tel.:** (040) 24652456, **Telefax:** 24652457
  E-mail: hyderabad@newagepublishers.com
- **Kolkata** RDB Chambers (Formerly Lotus Cinema) 106A, 1st Floor, S N Banerjee Road, Kolkata-700 014
  Tel.: (033) 22273773, **Telefax:** 22275247, **E-mail: kolkata@newagepublishers.com**
- **Lucknow** 16-A, Jopling Road, Lucknow-226 001, **Tel.:** (0522) 2209578, 4045297, **Telefax:** 2204098
  E-mail: lucknow@newagepublishers.com
- **Mumbai** 142C, Victor House, Ground Floor, N.M. Joshi Marg, Lower Parel, Mumbai-400 013
  Tel.: (022) 24927869, **Telefax:** 24915415, **E-mail: mumbai@newagepublishers.com**
- **New Delhi** 22, Golden House, Daryaganj, New Delhi-110 002, **Tel.:** (011) 23262368, 23262370
  Telefax: 43551305, **E-mail: sales@newagepublishers.com**

ISBN: 978-81-224-3663-1

C-19-01-11814

Printed in India at Ajit Printing Press, Delhi.
Typeset at In-house, Delhi.

NEW AGE INTERNATIONAL (P) LIMITED, PUBLISHERS
7/30 A, Daryaganj, New Delhi-110002
Visit us at **www.newagepublishers.com**
(CIN: U74899DL1966PTC004618)

TO

MOTHER

Preface to the Second Edition

Except for the correction of a few printer's errors which in spite of best care and attention had crept in the final print, the amplification of the rubric as necessary & the slight change in size, the print edition is a reprint of the first. The publisher is thankful to the esteemed readers for ready acceptance of the book. We would be accepting further suggestions from the students and teachers with heartiest thanks for further improvement.

(Publishers)

Preface to the First Edition

Invention of the transistor was an epoch-making event in the field of electronics. However, significant technologies which followed the bipolar transistor have immensely advanced our understanding and application of electronics in numerous fields. Perhaps the most important being our appreciation of the fact that signals can be processed more efficiently by digital than by analog techniques, resulting in far more advanced devices than was possible at that time. While most signals in nature are of the analog variety, much of the processing of signals is now being done by digital techniques. There is hardly any engineering discipline now, where digital techniques not only play an important role, but are almost indispensable in many fields of application. Admittedly, digital techniques find wide application in computers; but there are equally important areas such as process control, electronic instrumentation, communication, consumer electronics, etc., which depend largely or digital techniques.

Not long after the advent of the transistor followed the development of integrated circuits, which have in many ways influenced our approach to the design of digital systems and this has, in no small measure, brought about significant changes in teaching methods relevant to digital technology. It is no longer necessary now to think of designing and building from scratch using discrete components, as integrated circuits combine within a very small space much of the circuitry formerly required to be assembled using discrete devices. It is far more important now to understand the capabilities of a very large variety of integrated circuits and the manner in which they can be interconnected to meet specific design requirements.

Consequently, for a student of digital electronics, it is of as much importance to get a firm grounding in the basic principles of digital electronics, as it is to acquire knowledge of ICs required to perform complex digital functions. This will help a serious student of this science in optimizing design of digital systems, with a view to provide the best compromise between cost, requirements of power, space and speed of operation.

This book is, therefore, intended to fulfil the urgent need to bridge the gap between digital principles and practice, to enable the student of digital electronics to be able to apply his knowledge, in finding solutions to digital design problems, and is structured to impart to students knowledge of fundamental concepts in digital technology and simultaneously to introduce him to the use and practical applications of a large variety of integrated devices. To make the second objective more meaningful, a chapter in the book deals exclusively with the design of some digital equipments. While dedicated integrated chips are now available to perform many specific functions, it was considered more useful to consider the building blocks required for each device, so that the students has a better grasp of the design, operation and performance of the equipment as a whole.

This book has been written to meet the requirements of students of technical institutes and college students at the undergraduate level, and combines both theory and practice in adequate scope and depth to meet this objective. It presupposes no knowledge of electronics or semiconductor circuit analysis. The only prerequisite is knowledge of algebra and an understanding of electric circuits. Keeping these requirements in view, the discussion of topics has been so designed as to make difficult ideas and concepts easy to comprehend. The contents of chapters in this book have been reviewed below to convey an idea of the scope and depth of the subjects dealt with in various chapters.

Chapter 1 introduces the students to the basics of different numbering systems and their interrelationship. Conversion from one numbering system to another has been considered in detail, as well as calculations involving the various systems. The hexadecimal numbering system has received special attention, as it will be of considerable help to students in computers and microprocessors. The application of an algorithm has been considered for the conversion of one number system to another. Several codes in common use in digital circuits have also received attention, as well as conversion from one coding system to another system. Complement numbers have been considered and arithmetic operations using complement numbers have been discussed.

Chapter 2 deals with the basic concepts of digital electronics and it will enable the student to acquire familiarity with several types of logic gates and their functioning. Particular attention has been paid to XOR and XNOR gates in such applications as equality comparator, parity checker, parity generator, data transmission, error detection and error correction.

Bipolar, MOS, and advanced logic families have been covered in Chapters 3, 4 and 5. Open collector and three-state devices and input and output profiles of logic families have received adequate attention as well as interfacing problems within the same logic family and between logic devices of different families have also been considered. In discussing advanced logic families, attention has been paid to emitter-coupled logic and integrated injection logic.

Postulates of Boolean algebra and their application in the solution of problems is the subject of Chap. 6. Sum-of-products and product-of-sums logic expressions have been considered and methods have been discussed for translating logic circuits to algebra and vice versa. Attention has also been paid for developing a truth table from a logic circuit, with a view to analyzing its performance. Conversely, the derivation of a logic circuit from a truth table has also been discussed. As it is sometimes necessary to convert AND/OR to NAND/NOR logic, procedures have been discussed for this purpose.

In Chap. 7, we have considered the application of Karnaugh map techniques for the reduction of Boolean expressions as well as the application of this method in the design of some logic systems. The application of this technique has also been considered in relation to the product-of-sums and sum-of-products functions. The importance of don't care states in the minimization process has received attention. Procedures for combinational logic circuit design have been described and some design examples have been, discussed to illustrate the procedures. Since the mapping method of minimization is not suitable for computerization, the tabular method of Quine McClusky has been discussed.

The subject of bistable multivibrators has been considered in Chap. 8, which discusses all types of flip-flops as well as their excitation characteristics, which are helpful in the design of sequential devices. Astable and monostable multivibrators have been covered in Chap. 9. The use of 555 timer as a multivibrator and its application as a Schmitt trigger has also been discussed. The application of monostables for pulse generation, timing and sequencing operations has been discussed.

While logic design techniques using Karnaugh maps and other devices were very important in earlier stages; however with the development of MSI devices, simpler methods using function capsules in MSI form such as decoders, encoders, multiplexers, demultiplexers, code converters and numerous other devices, the design emphasis has shifted to the use of MSI devices and it has become all the more important to understand their application in system design as well as design simplification. Chapter 10, therefore, pays considerable attention to the function and application of some of the MSI devices. Programmable logic arrays provide another very important tool for custom design of complicated systems in the smallest possible space. PLAs have therefore, been discussed in adequate detail in this chapter. Since multiplexers and demultiplexers also play an important part in system design and larger capabilities are required than are available in some MSIs, the design of multiplexer and demultiplexer trees has been discussed.

Shift registers which perform very important sequential functions in logic design have been discussed in Chap. 11. Their operation and characteristic features have been examined and some MSI devices which perform specific shift register functions have been discussed.

The subject of counters which constitute a versatile sequential system, have been taken up for consideration in Chap. 12. There is hardly any device which does not depend on some kind of counter for its operation. In this chapter, we have taken up in some detail the use, performance characteristics and application of counters. Modulus counters is another class of counters, the design procedures for which have been considered in this chapter and examples have been given illustrating the design techniques for modulus counters. Design procedures for both synchronous and asynchronous counters have been discussed and illustrated with examples. The problem of lock out in counter design has been discussed and design procedures suggested to avoid this problem. The application of some counter ICs has been discussed for using them as scalers and modulo counters and procedures outlined or implementing these functions. The subject of Ring and Johnson counters has also been discussed and procedures examined to incorporate self-starting and self-correcting capabilities in these counters. The Ring counter and its application as a frequency divider, sequence generator and feedback counter, to achieve a larger cycle length has been examined.

Logic circuits for carrying out arithmetic operations have been considered in depth in Chap. 13. The student is introduced to signed and unsigned binary numbers. Logic circuits for addition and subtraction in 1's and 2's complement notation have been discussed as well as addition and subtraction in the BCD code. Serial and Parallel addition procedures as also binary multiplication and logic implementation of these operations have been discussed. A section has been devoted to the arithmetic logic unit and its application in arithmetic and logic operations examined.

Since memory devices are an essential requirement of many digital systems, particularly computers and microprocessors, the topic of memory devices has been covered in sufficient depth. The chapter begins with a discussion of ROMs and lays emphasis on ROM memory expansion and their application. This is followed by a discussion of static and dynamic RAMs, cell structures, switching characteristics and serial and parallel expansion of RAM memories. Static and dynamic sequential shift register memories have also been taken up for consideration. Magnetic disk memories and tape data storage systems have been examined and this is followed by a discussion of charge-coupled devices and magnetic bubble memories.

In view of the importance of analog-digital conversions in the field of computers, microprocessors, process control equipment, etc. the design, operation and performance criteria of A–D converters have been adequately covered in Chap. 15.

Chapter 16 covers the subject of digital equipment to enable students to become familiar with basic building blocks required for most digital equipments and goes on to discuss the design of systems in common use. The subject of digital recording and reproduction has also been discussed in sufficient detail.

Virendra Kumar

Contents

1 Numbering Systems

1.1 INTRODUCTION

Basically we deal with two types of signals in electronics, analog and digital. When we refer to a voltage or current as being analog in nature, we mean that the voltage or current, as the case may be, varies smoothly and continuously. A digital signal is one which does not vary continuously or smoothly. A digital signal on the other hand is a series of pulses of rapidly changing levels of voltage or current, in which change in level occurs in discrete steps or increments.

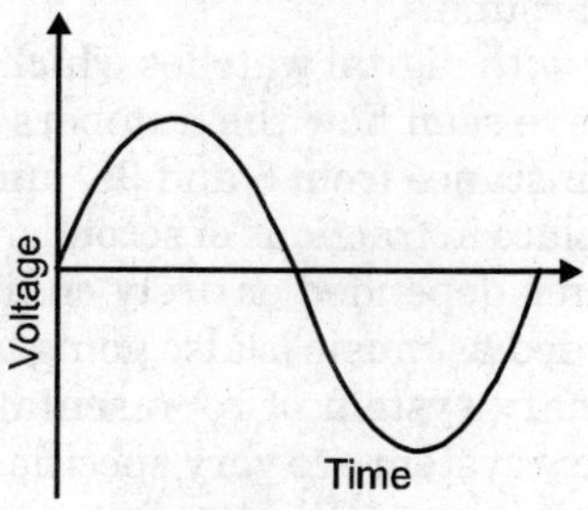

Fig. 1.1(a) Sine wave

Figure 1.1 (a) shows a sine wave which is an example of an analog signal. You will notice that voltage, which the sine wave represents, is varying smoothly and continuously. Another example of an analog signal is a dc voltage or current as shown in Fig. 1.1 (b), where the voltage level is maintained at the same level without change. Even if there are fluctuations in the voltage or current level of a dc source, it will still be analog in nature.

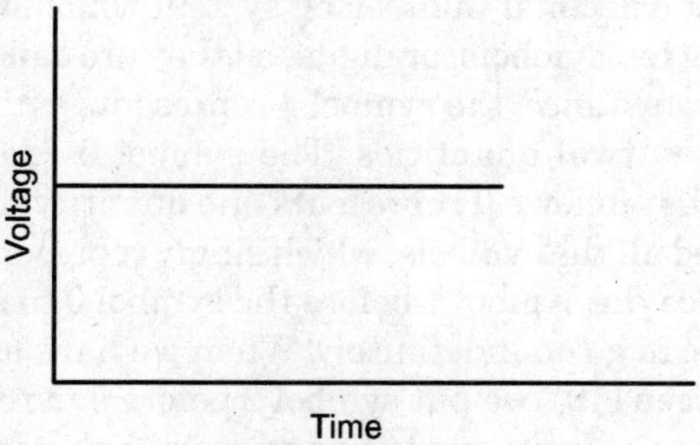

Fig. 1.1 (b) D.C. voltage

Voltmeters and current meters which indicate the value of voltage and current by the movement of a pointer against a calibrated scale are examples of analog devices. In these instruments the pointer moves smoothly and continuously until the pointer stops at the correct reading. Another example of a very good analog device is an electric bulb, the brightness of which can be changed continuously by manipulating the regulator. However, if you use a switch to switch on or switch off the bulb, it becomes a digital device. The bulb, thus, has two distinct states 'off' and 'on'. The bulb is, therefore, binary in nature; that is it has two distinct states. When the switch is 'on', current flows into the bulb; but when the switch is 'off', no current flows into the bulb. These two states can be represented diagrammatically as shown in Fig. 1.2.

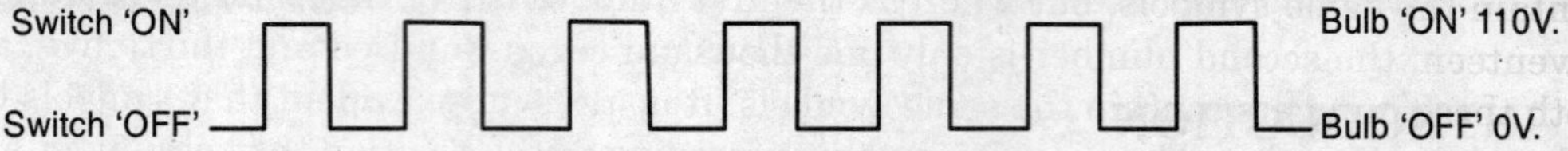

Fig. 1.2 Digital signal

You will notice that the voltage in this case switches between two distinct levels, 110V and 0V. We have referred above to the term 'binary'. This term indicates any two-state device or signal and can be represented as 'on' or 'off', 'closed' or 'open', 'true' or 'false'. It is most common to represent the binary nature by '0' or '1'. Depending on the convention adopted, any meaning can be assigned to '0' and '1'. If '0' is assumed to be the 'off' state, '1' is automatically the 'on' state, or it may be the other way around.

You must already be familiar with digital watches which use numbered displays for indication of time and date. You must have seen how the numbers indicating seconds keep changing from one number to the next, for instance from 8 and 9s, jumping from 8 to 9, skipping all the intermediate changes which take place in fractions of seconds. There are now digital multimeters and many devices which at one time depended entirely on linear technology are going digital. Even discs are now digitally recorded as music is also going digital.

In digital electronics the binary system of representation has become common, mainly because the two states in the binary system are very specific and therefore convenient to adopt from a design point of view. This leads us to the binary system of representation; but before we go into the details of this system it will lead to a better understanding of the binary system if we devote some time to the decimal system of representing quantities, which we widely use today in our calculations.

1.2 DECIMAL NUMBERING SYSTEM

All of us are familiar with the decimal numbering system which we have been using for ages. This numbering system uses ten symbols, or digits, as they are called 0, 1, 2, 3, 4, 5, 6, 7, 8, 9 for representing quantities. For instance, the symbol 4 represents • • • • (four) quantities, just as the symbol 2 represents • • (two) quantities. The symbol 0 represents the absence of any quantity and each symbol that follows 0 represents one quantity more than the previous symbol. When we have exhausted all the symbols, which singly represent only up to nine quantities, what we have to do is to place the symbol 1 before the symbol 0 to represent more than nine or 10 quantities. This process can go on indefinitely. When we have again exhausted all the symbols by counting up to nineteen (19), we put symbol 2 before 0 to represent twenty (20) quantities. Thus we can represent very large quantities by using only ten elementary symbols.

Another noteworthy feature of this system is that these symbols by themselves mean very little unless they are part of a number system, when they acquire a point of reference. Let us take a specific example. Consider a whole number (called integer) 5505. As we all know the number to the extreme right is in the 'units' position which means five quantities. It also serves as a point of reference which fixes the values of the other digits in this number. The digits 5 in the extreme left is in the thousands position and represents five thousand quantities and not five, which is the value of the digit to the extreme right. Similarly the digit five, which is next to the digit in the thousands position, is in the hundreds position and represents only five hundred quantities. Also notice that the tens position is vacant and it has no digit which could represent ten quantities. So you must have realized that a digit acquires weight according to the position it occupies in a number.

Let us take another example. Consider the numbers 5317 and 1735. Both these numbers contain the same symbols, but whereas the first number is five thousand three hundred and seventeen, the second number is only one thousand seven hundred and thirty five, although both these numbers contain the same symbols. It is, thus quite evident that symbols by themselves have no value. They acquire a value according to the position they occupy in a number and have a point of reference.

We will consider the same number 5505 again and mention against each number the weight of its position and the position of each digit in the number, as follows in Fig. 1.3.

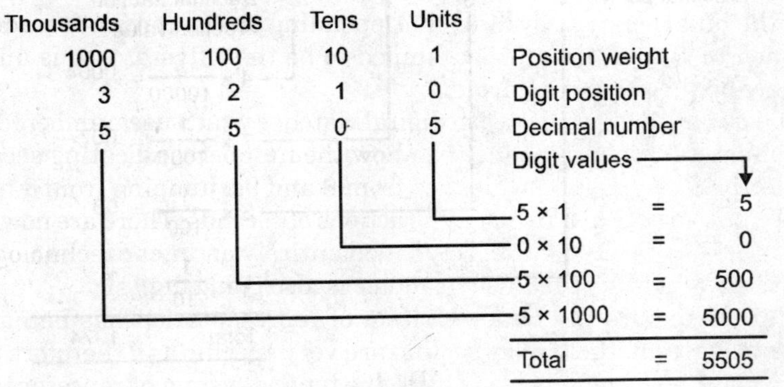

Fig. 1.3

You will notice from the diagram that just above the decimal number the position of each digit in the number has been mentioned. The digit in the extreme right is in the 0 digit position and the digit positions of the other digits are 1, 2 and 3. Thus in all there are four positions in this number. Above the digit positions we have mentioned the position weight of each position. If you multiply each digit by its position weight, as has been done in this diagram, you will come back to the original number 5505. This exercise has been done only to indicate that if each digit is multiplied by its position weight, the result is the original number.

You will notice from this diagram that as you proceed from the digit at the extreme right to the left, the value of each position increases by a factor of 10. Thus the weight of position 1 is ten times the weight of position 0. Likewise the weight of position 2 is ten times the weight of position 1 and so on. We can, thus express position weights in powers of ten for the same number as follows:

10^3	10^2	10^1	10^0	Weight in powers of 10
3	2	1	0	Digit position
5	5	0	5	Decimal number

As you already know

$$10^0 = 1$$
$$10^1 = 10$$
$$10^2 = 100$$
and
$$10^3 = 1000$$

It is not a coincidence that position weights are in powers of 10. Since there are ten digits in the decimal numbering system the position weights are in powers of ten. Ten is called the radix of the decimal system just as 2 is the radix of the binary system and 8 is the radix of the octal system. The weights of all numbering systems can be expressed in powers of the radix of those systems.

We have so far considered whole numbers or integers expressed in the decimal system. We will now consider fractions in the decimal system. Let us take up the decimal fraction .1374 and study the position weights of the different positions. You may refer to Fig. 1.4., which gives the decimal fraction along with digit positions and position weights.

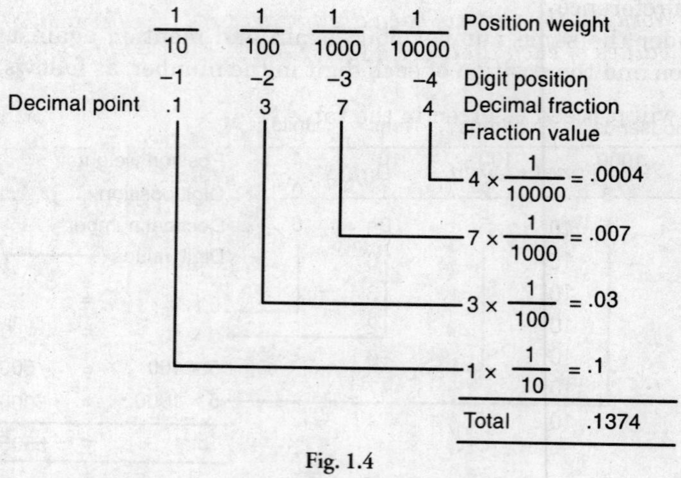

Fig. 1.4

The diagram shows the decimal fraction, above which are mentioned the digit positions and against each position the digit weight is mentioned. If each digit is multiplied by its position weight, as has been shown in the diagram, we get back to the original fraction. As before, position weights can be expressed in powers of ten, but in the case of fractional parts, the powers are negative powers of ten as shown below:

	10^{-1}	10^{-2}	10^{-3}	10^{-4}	Position weights
	–1	–2	– 3	– 4	Digit position
Decimal point	.1	3	7	4	Decimal fraction

As you already know

$$10^{-1} = .1$$
$$10^{-2} = .01$$
$$10^{-3} = .001$$
$$10^{-4} = .0001$$

You must already have noticed that in the case of a decimal fraction the value of a digit decrease by a factor of 10 whenever a digit moves one position to the right. It may also be mentioned that it is customary to use a decimal point to separate integers (whole numbers) from fractions. All numbering systems follow this. A complete picture of a decimal number with integers and fractions is given in Fig. 1.5.

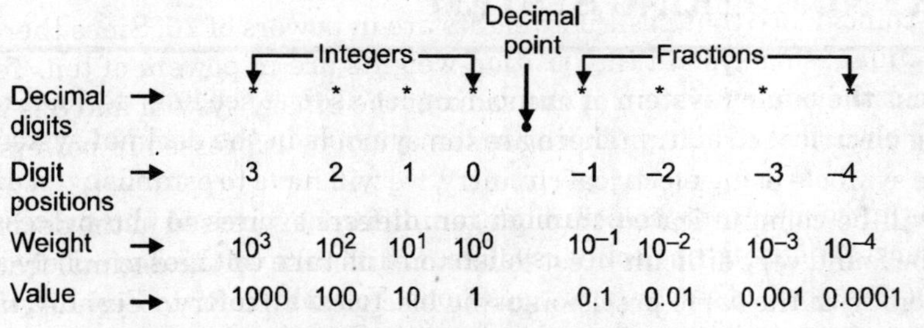

Fig. 1.5 Positional weights and values of decimal numbers

Example 1.1: *Work out the value of each digit of decimal number 5032.074 and show that when the positional values of each digit are added up the result tallies with the given decimal number.*

Solution: We will proceed as given in the table below:

Digit position	*Positional weight*	*Digit*	*Value*		*Total*
3	10^3	5	5 × 1000	=	5000
2	10^2	0	0 × 100	=	0
1	10^1	3	3 × 10	=	30
0	10^0	2	2 × 1	=	2
–1	10^{-1}	0	0 × .1	=	0.0
–2	10^{-2}	7	7 × .01	=	0.07
–3	10^{-3}	4	4 × .001	=	0.004
				Total	5032.074

As expected the result tallies with the original number.

In this chapter, we will consider other number systems also, as decimal systems are not convenient to use in digital circuits for reasons which will be explained shortly. The other systems in use, as well as the symbols they employ, and their radix numbers, are given in Table 1.1.

Table 1.1 Number systems and their symbols

Number system	*Radix*	*Symbols*
Binary	2	0, 1
Octal	8	0, 1, 2, 3, 4, 5, 6, 7
Decimal	10	0, 1, 2, 3, 4, 5, 6, 7, 8, 9
Hexadecimal	16	0, 1, 2, 3, 4, 5, 6, 7, 8, 9, A, B, C, D, E, F

When numbers other than decimal numbers are used, it is usual to mention the radix as a subscript to the number to avoid confusion. Thus, for an octal number, we will write the number as follows: 531.542_8. It is also, at times, convenient to mention the decimal number with a subscript 10 to avoid any mix up when numbering systems having a radix greater than 10 are in use.

1.3 BINARY NUMBERING SYSTEM

Before we discuss the binary system of numbering let us first see how decimal numbers can be processed using electrical circuitry. There are ten symbols in the decimal system and if we are to process these symbols using electrical circuitry, we will have to establish ten different voltage levels, which will be communicated through ten different wires to the processing circuit. In practice it will be found very difficult to establish ten different voltages precisely and also be able to recognize them with the same precision using electrical circuitry. Secondly, if noise voltages are present, as they always are, it will be very difficult to maintain these voltage levels, resulting in unwanted change of voltage levels, which will upset circuit function.

The most convenient arrangement for processing numbers would be a two-digit system which can be conveniently represented by simple on-off circuits. The binary numbering system, which involves only two digits 0 and 1, would appear to be the simplest numbering system for processing by electrical circuits. We can assign the binary 1 state to the system when it is conducting, and binary 0 state to the system when it is not conducting. Alternatively, we can assign binary 0 state to the system when it is conducting and binary 1 state to the system when it is not conducting. Both assignments can be used at the same time depending on convenience of design.

Let us consider a 4-bit (Bit is a contraction from Binary digit) binary number and see how weights are assigned to different digit positions. Notice that the least significant bit (LSB) is in the 1s position and the most significant bit (MSB) is in the 8s position. You have noticed earlier that in the decimal system of numbering the value of each position increases by a factor of 10, for each digit position it is moved to the left. Likewise, in the binary system, if we move left from the bit in the extreme right position, that is the LSB, the weight of a binary digit increases by a factor of 2 for each digit position it is moved to the left.

	MSB			**LSB**
Binary digits	*	*	*	*
Digit positions	3	2	1	0
Weight in powers of 2	2^3	2^2	2^1	2^0
Position value	8	4	2	1

You will notice from the above representation that positions are numbered from 0 to 3 (from right to left) as in the decimal system. Below digit positions, weights are given in powers of 2. In the last row, position values are mentioned. Let us work out the numerical value of a binary number 1011. We write below each bit its position value and the total value of all bit positions.

Binary number	1	0	1	1	
Position value	8×1	4×0	2×1	1×1	$= 8 + 2 + 1$
					$= 11$

Table 1.2 gives the decimal equivalent of 4-bit binary numbers. The maximum value that a 4-bit binary number can have is 1 1 1 1. Its value in decimal numbers is 8 + 4 + 2 + 1 or 15 as the following table shows.

Table 1.2

Decimal count	*Binary count*			
	2^3	2^2	2^1	2^0
	8s	*4s*	*2s*	*1s*
0	0	0	0	0
1	0	0	0	1
2	0	0	1	0
3	0	0	1	1
4	0	1	0	0
5	0	1	0	1
6	0	1	1	0
7	0	1	1	1
8	1	0	0	0
9	1	0	0	1
10	1	0	1	0
11	1	0	1	1
12	1	1	0	0
13	1	1	0	1
14	1	1	1	0
15	1	1	1	1

You will notice from the binary counting sequence 0000 0001 0010 0011 given in the table above that it follows the numerical values 0, 1, 2, 3, etc. This 4-digit natural binary code is generally used to represent decimal digits and is referred to as the 8 4 2 1 code. As you must have realized it is a weighted code; but there are other weighted and non-weighted codes which we will consider later.

It is also possible to express fractions in binary form as we saw with decimal numbers. A four bit binary fractional part is given below along with digit positions, positional weights and position values.

Binary • point	1	0	1	1	Binary number
	–1	–2	–3	–4	Digit position
	2^{-1}	2^{-2}	2^{-3}	2^{-4}	Position weight
	0.5	0.25	0.125	0.0625	Position value

Fraction value

1 × 0.0625 — 0.0625
1 × 0.125 — 0.125
0 × 0.25 — 0.0
1 × 0.5 — 0.5

Total 0.6875

A complete representation of a binary number with integers and fractions is given in Fig. 1.6. In this binary number there are 8 integers and four fractions. Digit weights are given below the digit positions. The digit positions are numbered from 7 to 0 and, after the binary point (equivalent to a decimal point), from –1 to –4. The weights of each position are given in the third row in powers of 2. Notice that the fractions are given in negative powers of 2, same as with the decimal fractions. The weights of the digit in the 0 digit position is 2^0 which is equal to 1. The last row gives the value of each digit position in decimal numbers. You will notice that every time a digit moves one position to the left its value increases by a factor of 2, that is it doubles itself. On the other hand, every time a digit moves one position to the right it loses weight by a factor of 2, that is its value goes down by half.

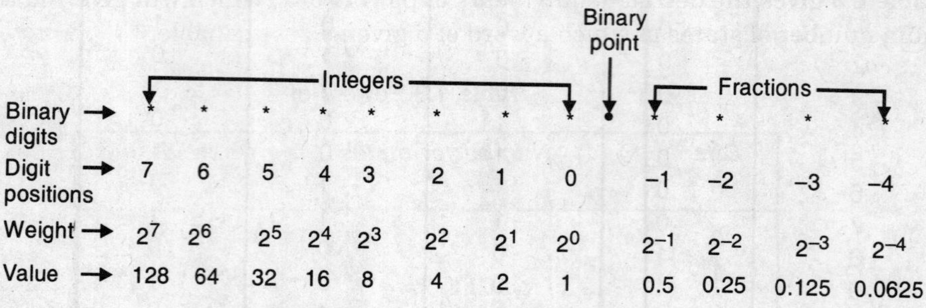

Fig. 1.6 Positional weights and values of binary numbers

1.3.1 Binary Words

The term binary word is commonly used instead of the term binary number. However, both mean the same thing. A string of four bits, which is a 4-bit word, is called a nibble, and a string of 8-bits, which is an 8-bit word, is called a byte.

Table 1.2 gives many examples of 4-bit binary words. You will also notice from this table that the maximum number a 4-bit binary word can accomodate is decimal 15. If you refer to Fig. 1.6, and leave aside the fractional part, you will find that the word size is 8-bits. If all the bits in this 8-bit binary word are binary 1, you can calculate the total number of states of the binary word by adding up the values of all the positions. The total works out to 256. This is the maximum number of states that can be represented by an 8-bit binary word. The size of the word determines the magnitude of the number that the binary word can represent. If there are 'n' bits in a binary word, the total number of states that it can represent is given by the following equation.

$S = 2^n$ where S is the total number of states.

Thus, an 8-bit word will represent

$S = 2^8$ states

Since one of the states is represented by 0, the maximum number that an 8-bit word can represent is given by the following equation.

$N = 2^n - 1$

For an 8-bit word

$N = 2^8 - 1 = 255$

Digital equipments generally use a word of a fixed size. As you have seen, the size of the word determines the maximum number that the word can represent. If you know the maximum number that is required to be represented, you can determine the size of the binary word from the following equation:

$B = 3.32 \log_{10} N$, where B is the number of bits,
and N is the maximum number

If the maximum number required to be represented is 64 K or 64000, the number of bits required is

$$\begin{aligned} B &= 3.32 \log_{10} 64000 \\ &= 3.32 \times 4.8 \\ &= 15.9 \text{ bits} \end{aligned}$$

You will therefore have to use a 16-bits word size.

Presently microcomputers use a 16-bit word size which gives them a memory capability 64K or 65,536 bytes.

Table 1.3 gives the decimal equivalents of powers of 2, which will give you an idea of the maximum number of states of which a word of a given size is capable.

Table 1.3 Powers of 2

Bits *n*	*Number of states* 2^n	*Abbreviation*
0	1	
1	2	
2	4	
3	8	
4	16	
5	32	
6	64	
7	128	
8	256	
9	512	
10	1,024	1 K
11	2,048	2 K
12	4,096	4 K
13	8,192	8 K
14	16,384	16 K
15	32,768	32 K
16	65,536	64 K

1.3.2 Binary Conversions

Sometimes we need to convert binary words into decimal numbers and decimal numbers into binary words.

The following procedure may be followed:

Binary to Decimal Conversion

The following method can be adopted:

1. Multiply each digit of the binary number by its positional weight and then add up the result.
2. If any digit is 0, its positional weight is not to be taken into account.

Example 1.2: *Convert binary number 11011110 into its decimal equivalent.*

Solution: Write the value of each digit position under the binary number as follows and add up the values.

1		1		0		1		1		1		1		0		
128	+	64	+	~~32~~	+	16	+	8	+	4	+	2	+	~~1~~	=	222

Decimal to Binary Conversion

The following method can be adopted:

1. Divide the decimal number by 2 producing a quotient and a remainder. This remainder is the LSB (least significant bit of the desired binary number).
2. Again divide the quotient obtained above by 2. This produces another quotient and remainder. The remainder is the next digit of the binary number.
3. Continue this process of division until the quotient becomes 0. The remainder obtained in the final division is the MSB (most significant bit of the binary number).

Example 1.3: *Convert decimal number 76 into its binary equivalent.*

Solution: Proceed as follows:

Quotient		**Remainder**
76 ÷ 2 = 38	Yielding a remainder of	0 LSB
38 ÷ 2 = 19	Yielding a remainder of	0
19 ÷ 2 = 9	Yielding a remainder of	1
9 ÷ 2 = 4	Yielding a remainder of	1
4 ÷ 2 = 2	Yielding a remainder of	0
2 ÷ 2 = 1	Yielding a remainder of	0
1 ÷ 2 = 0	Yielding a remainder of	1 MSB

The equivalent binary number is 1001100. If there is a mixed number, for instance 76.7, first convert 76 into its binary equivalent as above, and then proceed as follows to convert 0.7 into its binary equivalent:

Product	**Fraction**		**Carry**
0.7 × 2 = 1.4	= 0.4	and a carry of	1
0.4 × 2 = 0.8	= 0.8	and a carry of	0
0.8 × 2 = 1.6	= 0.6	and a carry of	1
0.6 × 2 = 1.2	= 0.2	and a carry of	1
0.2 × 2 = 0.4	= 0.4	and a carry of	0
0.4 × 2 = 0.8	= 0.8	and a carry of	0
0.8 × 2 = 1.6	= 0.6	and a carry of	1
0.6 × 2 = 1.2	= 0.2	and a carry of	1

The equivalent binary number is 1001100. 10110011. If necessary this process can be continued further where greater accuracy is desired.

1.3.3 Binary Calculations (Unsigned Binary Numbers)

When you are dealing with data which is either all positive or all negative you can ignore the plus and minus signs and think only of the magnitude (absolute value) of the numbers, while carrying out arithmetic operations. If you are dealing with 4-bit binary data the range will be as follows:

0 0 0 0 to 1 1 1 1

or decimal 0 15

If it is 8-bit data the range will be from

0 0 0 0 0 0 0 0 to 1 1 1 1 1 1 1 1

or decimal 0 255

If the numbers you are dealing with are within these limits you will not encounter any problem. However, if the numbers lie outside this range problems are bound to arise as there are bound to be overflows which you will have to ignore as they will be outside the range.

Binary Calculations

Binary numbers can be added, subtracted, multiplied and divided. Procedures are as follows:

Binary Addition

Rules for binary addition are as follows:

1. 0 + 0 = 0
2. 0 + 1 = 1
3. 1 + 0 = 1
4. 1 + 1 = 10 (or 0 with a carry of 1 to the left)
5. 1 + 1 + 1 = 11 (follows from rule 4)

If you find rule 4 confusing, remember that binary 1 + 1 equals decimal 2 and binary 10 equals decimal 2. Thus binary 1 + 1 equals binary 10.

Example 1.4: *Add binary numbers 110101 and 100101.*

Solution: Proceed as follows:

Decimal equivalent		
53	1 1 0 1 0 1	Augend
57	1 0 0 1 0 1	Addend
	0	carry 1 to the left
	1	no carry
	0	carry 1 to the left
	1	no carry
	1	no carry
	0	carry 1 to the left
	1	
90	1 0 1 1 0 1 0	Sum

It is not necessary to mention the decimal equivalents.

Binary Subtraction

The rules for binary subtraction are as follows:

1. 0 – 0 = 0
2. 1 – 0 = 1
3. 1 – 1 = 0
4. 10 – 1 = 1

Rule 4 follows the same reasoning as rule 4 for binary addition. Since binary 10 equals decimal 2, 10 – 1 is obviously equal to 1. We will now consider some examples of binary subtraction.

Example 1.5: *Subtract 001 from 101.*

Solution:

```
  101
– 001
```

Step 1 From column 1; 1 – 1 = 0

2 From column 2; 0 – 0 = 0

3 From column 3; 1 – 0 = 1

```
  101   Minuend
– 001   Subtrahend
  100   Difference
```

Example 1.6: *Subtract 001 from 110.*

Solution:

```
  110
– 001
```

Step 1. In the 1st column, since 1 cannot be subtracted from 0, borrow 1 from column 2. Column 2 will become 1 – 1 = 0 and column 1 will become 10 as shown alongside. Now subtract as follows:

```
    0 1
  1 1̸ 0
– 0 0 1
```

Step 2. From column 1; 10 – 1 = 1

3. From column 2; 0 – 0 = 0

4. From column 3; 1 – 0 = 1

```
      1
  1 0 0
– 0 0 1
  1 0 1
```

Example 1.7: *Subtract 001 from 100.*

Solution:

```
  1 0 0
– 0 0 1
```

Step 1. Since column 2 is 0 borrow from column 3. After borrowing from column 3, column 3 becomes 0 and column 2 becomes 10 as shown alongside.

```
  0 1
  1̸ 0 0
– 0 0 1
```

2. Now borrow 1 from column 2. Column 2 becomes 10 – 1 = 1, and column 1 becomes 10 as shown alongside. Now subtract as follows.

```
  0 1̸ 1 1
  1̸   0̸ 0
– 0    0 1
```

3. From column 1; 10 – 1 = 1

4. From column 2; 1 – 0 = 1

5. From column 3; 0 – 0 = 0

```
      1
  0 1 0
– 0 0 1
  0 1 1
```

Subtraction by 2's Complement Method

In this method first the 1's complement of a binary number is determined by replacing 1s by 0s and 0s by 1s as follows:

1 1 0 1 binary number
0 0 1 0 1's complement

By adding 1 to the 1's complement, the 2's complement of the binary number is obtained as shown below.

0 0 1 0	1's complement
1	Add 1
0 0 1 1	2's complement of the binary number

When carrying out a subtraction by this method the following procedure is followed:

1. Convert the subtrahend *B* to its 2's complement.
2. Add minuend, *A*, to the 2's complement of *B*.
3. The left-most digit serves only as an indication whether the answer is positive or negative. If the left-most digit is 1, the answer is positive in which case the left-most digit is dropped and the answer is read from the remaining digits.
4. If the left-most digit is 0, the answer is in the negative. To get the final answer in this case the 0 is dropped and the remainder is converted to its 2's complement. This represents the final answer.

Example 1.8: (*Both numbers are positive*)

1 1 0 1 Minuend A
1 0 0 1 Subtrahend B

Solution: The first step requires the subtrahend to be converted to its 1's complement, for which each bit requires to be complemented. The complement of 0 is 1 and the complement of 1 is 0. A binary number can also be considered to have a complement. The 1's complement of a binary number is determined by taking the complement of each bit of the binary number. Thus the 1's complement of 1 0 0 1 is 0 1 1 0. The 2's complement is obtained by adding 1 to the 1's complement. Thus, the 2's complement of 1 0 0 1 is 0 1 1 1. This procedure is summarized below:

Binary number	1 0 0 1
1's Complement	0 1 1 0
	+ 1
2's Complement	0 1 1 1

In order to subtract *B* from *A* we now add *A* to the 2's complement of *B* as follows:

A	1 1 0 1
2's complement of *B*	0 1 1 1
Sum	1 0 1 0 0

Since the left-most digit is 1 the final number is positive and it is, therefore 0 1 0 0.

Example 1.9: *Subtract 0 1 1 1 from 0 1 0 0.*

Solution: Minuend A 0 1 0 0

Subtrahend B 0 1 1 1

l's complement of B 1 0 0 0

\+ 1

2's complement of B 1 0 0 1

To subtract B from A add A to the 2's complement of B

A 0 1 0 0

1 0 0 1

2's complement of B * 1 1 0 1 Total

Since there is no carry from the most significant digit where the asterisk mark is, it indicates that the correct answer can be obtained by taking the 2's complement of the total as follows:

l's complement of 1101 is 0 0 1 0

\+ 1

2's complement of 1101 is 0 0 1 1

A 0 carry also indicates that the answer is in the negative. The correct answer, therefore, is –3.

We can consider another example where the result is positive. Subtract 1 0 1 1 from 1 1 0 0

1 1 0 0 Minuend

2's complement of 0 1 0 1 1 0 1 1 Subtrahend

1 0 1 1 1

In this example since, there is a carry of 1 from the most significant digit the answer is positive and besides to arrive at the correct answer it is not necessary to take the 2's complement of the total for the final result. The answer therefore is 7.

Binary Multiplication

Rules for binary multiplication are as follows:

1. 0 × 0 = 0
2. 0 × 1 = 0
3. 1 × 0 = 0
4. 1 × 1 = 1

Example 1.10: *Multiply 1 1 0 1 by 1 0 1 0.*

Solution:

```
        1 1 0 1
        1 0 1 0
---------------
        0 0 0 0
      1 1 0 1
    0 0 0 0
  1 1 0 1
---------------
1 0 0 0 0 0 1 0   Total
```

Binary Division

Binary division is very similar to decimal division. Some examples of binary division are following.

Example 1.11: *Divide 1 1 0 0 1 by 1 0 1.*

Solution:

```
          1 0 1
1 0 1 | 1 1 0 0 1
        1 0 1
        -----
        0 0 1 0 1
            1 0 1
            -----
            0 0 0
```

Example 1.12: *Divide 1 0 0 0 1 1 by 1 1 1.*

Solution:

```
              1 0 1
1 1 1 | 1 0 0 0 1 1
          1 1 1
        -------
          0 0 1 1 1
              1 1 1
              -----
              0 0 0
```

Example 1.13: *Divide 1 0 1 1 0 1 0 by 1 1 0.*

Solution:

```
              1 1 1 1
1 1 0 | 1 0 1 1 0 1 0
          1 1 0
        -------
          1 0 1 0
            1 1 0
          -------
            1 0 0 1
              1 1 0
            -------
              0 1 1 0
                1 1 0
              -------
                0 0 0
```

1.4 BINARY CODED DECIMAL (BCD)

The binary-coded-decimal (BCD) code is a weighted code. This code is found very convenient for representing digits. Each group of four bits is used to represent one decimal digit. For instance, decimal number 259 can be represented as 0010 0101 1001 in the BCD code. More precisely, it may be referred to as the 8 4 2 1 BCD code. This nomenclature represents the weighting of each bit in the 4-bit code. There are other weighted BCD codes, but the 8421 BCD code is usually referred to as the BCD code. The other weighted BCD codes always mention the weightage to distinguish them from the 8421 BCD code. As you will see later the 8421 BCD code is rather incovenient for computer arithmetic operations and that is one reason, why other 4-bit weighted codes were evolved.

Table 1.4 gives the BCD equivalents of decimal numbers from 0 through 9.

Table 1.4 8421 BCD code

Decimal digit	*BCD*			
	8s	*4s*	*2s*	*1s*
0	0	0	0	0
1	0	0	0	1
2	0	0	1	0
3	0	0	1	1
4	0	1	0	0
5	0	1	0	1
6	0	1	1	0
7	0	1	1	1
8	1	0	0	0
9	1	0	0	1

Since, there are other codes using the binary bits, the binary numbers that we have discussed in Section 1.3 are referred to as pure binary numbers. Pure binary numbers, if they are very long, are difficult to interpret mentally. For instance the binary word 10010011 represents a number 147; but you will take quite some time to work out the decimal value of this binary word. The pure binary has therefore, given way to an arrangement referred to as Binary-Coded-Decimal or BCD. If you look at Table 1.4 you will find that a group of only four binary digits can represent a decimal number from 0 through 9. By using groups of four binary digits we can represent any desired number, each group of four digits representing a number from 0 through 9. Thus, decimal number 147 can be represented as follows in the BCD system:

1	4	7
0001	0100	0111

As long as you know that you are using the BCD system, the four digit group of words can be combined together as follows:

000101000111

You can mentally separate them into groups of four and calculate the decimal equivalent mentally in a matter of seconds. You must, however, remember that this number is not a pure binary number. The only disadvantage is that, we use a larger number of digits to represent the number. Thus, we trade off efficiency for convenience.

1.4.1 BCD Conversions

Decimal to BCD

Example 1.14: *Convert decimal number 137.409 to BCD.*

Solution: Convert each decimal digit to BCD form as follows:

1	3	7	.	4	0	9
0001	0011	0111	.	0100	0000	1001

BCD to Decimal

Example 1.15: *Convert BCD number.*

1001 0011 . 0101 0100 1000 to decimal number.

Solution: Change each 4-bit number to its equivalent decimal number as follows:

1001	0011	.	0101	0100	1000
9	3	.	5	4	8

The equivalent decimal number is 93.548.

BCD to Binary

The following method can be adopted:

1. Break up the BCD number into groups of four bits and convert to decimal form.
2. Convert the decimal number to binary form as in Example 1.3.

Example 1.16: *Convert BCD number 1000 1001 . 0110 to binary form.*

Solution: Convert the BCD number to decimal form as follows:

1000	1001	.	0110
8	9	.	6

Convert the integer part of the decimal number into binary form by successive division as follows:

Quotient		Remainder
89 ÷ 2 = 44	yielding a remainder of	1 LSB
44 ÷ 2 = 22	yielding a remainder of	0
22 ÷ 2 = 11	yielding a remainder of	0
11 ÷ 2 = 5	yielding a remainder of	1
5 ÷ 2 = 2	yielding a remainder of	1
2 ÷ 2 = 1	yielding a remainder of	0
1 ÷ 2 = 0	yielding a remainder of	1 MSB

Thus decimal 89 is equal to binary 1011001.

Convert the fractional part of the decimal number into binary form by successive multiplication as follows:

Product	Fraction		Carry
0.6 × 2 = 1.2	0.2	and a carry of	1
0.2 × 2 = 0.4	0.4	and a carry of	0
0.4 × 2 = 0.8	0.8	and a carry of	0
0.8 × 2 = 1.6	0.6	and a carry of	1
0.6 × 2 = 1.2	0.2	and a carry of	1

The equivalent binary number is, therefore, as follows.

1011001 . 10011

If greater accuracy is desired the process of successive multiplication can be continued further.

Binary to BCD

This can be accomplished easily by first converting the binary number to decimal form and the later to BCD form.

Example 1.17: *Convert binary number 11011.101 to BCD form.*

Solution: Convert the binary number to decimal form and thereafter convert the decimal number to BCD form as shown below:

1	1	0	1	1	.	1	0	1	Binary
16	8	0	2	1	.	0.5	0	.125	Decimal
		2	7		.	0.625			Decimal
		0010	0111		.	0110	0010	0101	BCD

Thus, the equivalent BCD number is as follows:

0010 0111 . 0110 0010 0101

1.4.2 BCD Addition

The rules of binary addition which we have already considered earlier are no longer applicable to addition in the 8 4 2 1 BCD code. The rules for addition in the BCD format can be stated as follows:

1. The digits are added in the same manner as in the binary form starting with the LSB.
2. If this addition of the four digits results in a carry out of 1, or if the result of addition results in an illegal code proceed as follows:
3. Add 6 (0110) to the resultant sum and add the carry to the next most significant bit.

Example 1.18: *Add 9 5 6 and 4 9 2 in 8421 BCD code.*

Solution: In binary form, the addition will be as follows:

1 0 0 1 0 1 0 1 0 1 1 0
0 1 0 0 1 0 0 1 0 0 1 0

We will first add the 4 bits at the extreme right.

0 1 1 0
0 0 1 0
1 0 0 0 Sum

Since, there is no carry out and the resultant code is acceptable, we will proceed to the next four bits.

0 1 0 1
1 0 0 1
1 1 1 0 Sum

Since this code is not acceptable, we will add 6(0110) to the resultant sum.

1 1 1 0
0 1 1 0
1 0 1 0 0 Sum

Since there is carry of 1, we will have to add it to the next most significant bit.

```
       1
 1 0 0 1
 0 1 0 0
 -------
 1 1 1 0  Sum
```

Since this again is an unacceptable code, we will again add 6(0110) to the sum

```
  1 1 1 0
  0 1 1 0
 ---------
1 0 1 0 0  Sum
```

The final answer is	1	0100	0100	1000
In decimal terms	1	4	4	8

The representation of numbers in BCD form has a certain advantage, mainly because BCD numbers and decimal numbers are easily interconvertible. Another important consideration is that processing equipment has to encode signals from a keyboard using the decimal system and must also output information on a decimal display.

While there are decided advantages in the choice of BCD numbers over natural binary numbers, we use as few digits as possible in natural binary encoding, whereas we lose this advantage in going on for BCD representation. The choice of the system to be preferred will depend largely on the input-output interface requirements and the speed of operation.

1.5 OCTAL NUMBERING SYSTEM

The octal numbering system uses the digits from 0 to 7 (0, 1, 2, 3, 4, 5, 6, 7) and as such its radix is eight. Table 1.5 shows octal numbers along with the equivalent decimal and binary numbers. You will notice that the octal system numbers from 0 through 7 are the same as in the decimal system and, therefore, they have the same physical meaning as the decimal numbers. You will also notice that it skips numbers 8 and 9 and the next number after 7 is 10. This is because its radix is 8. A comparison with binary numbers will show that the octal system numbers can be represented by only three binary bits from 000 to 111. The octal system is, therefore, a valuable accessory to the binary system. To avoid any confusion, when octal system is used, the subscript 8 should always be used to identify an octal number.

Table 1.5 Octal numbering system

Decimal	*Octal*	*Binary*
0	0	0
1	1	1
2	2	10
3	3	11
4	4	100
5	5	101
6	6	110
7	7	111
8	10	1000

9	11	1001
10	12	1010
11	13	1011
12	14	1100
13	15	1101
14	16	1110
15	17	1111
16	20	10000
17	21	10001
18	22	10010
19	23	10011
20	24	10100

Refer now to Fig. 1.7 which is a complete representation of an octal number. If has been drawn on the same basis as Figs. 1.5 and 1.6 for decimal and binary numbers. Row 1, in this diagram shows the octal digit positions and the row below shows the weight of the integer part in powers of 8. You will notice that every time a digit moves one position to the left, it gains weight by a factor of 8. Values of integers are given in the decimal numbers below weights. On the right of the octal point is the fractional part. You will observe that every time a digit moves one position to the right it loses weight by a factor of 8. Therefore, weights are given in negative powers of 8. Values of the digit positions are given in decimal numbers in the last row. Although; more than 8 digits can be used in the octal system, the normal practice is to use the first eight digits only, as that is found most convenient.

	Integers				Octal point	Fractions			
Octal digits →	*	*	*	*	•	*	*	*	*
Digit positions →	3	2	1	0		−1	−2	−3	−4
Weight →	8^3	8^2	8^1	8^0		8^{-1}	8^{-2}	8^{-3}	8^{-4}
Value →	512	64	8	1		0.125	0.015	0.0019	0.0002

Fig. 1.7 Positional weights and values of octal numbers

1.5.1 Binary Coded Octal System

This system uses only the first eight digits of the octal system, which can be conveniently represented by only three bits of the binary system. The binary coded octal (BCO) system uses groups of the three binary bits (Table 1.6), starting from the octal point and working bothways i.e., left and right.

Table 1.6 Binary coded octal digits

Octal	*Binary*
0	000
1	001

2	010
3	011
4	100
5	101
6	110
7	111

Thus, a binary coded octal number may appear as follows:

$$100\ 101\ 011\ .\ 010\ 110_{BCO}$$

Interpreted, this will mean an octal number as;

$$4\ 5\ 3\ .\ 2\ 6_8$$

In binary form, this number will appear as;

100101011.010110

When separated into groups of 3 this will appear as shown above. The binary coded octal system eliminates the long string of 1's and 0's and is simple to interpret.

1.5.2 Octal Conversions

Procedures for conversion are described below :

Binary to Octal

1. Begin at the binary point and separate the binary number into groups of three digits both towards the left as well as the right of the binary point.
2. Add binary digit 0 at each end, if necessary, to complete a group of three digits.
3. Replace each group of three digits with its octal equivalent.

Example 1.19: *Convert binary 11011 . 01 to its octal equivalent.*

Solution: Begin by breaking the binary number into groups of three digits both towards the left as well as the right of the binary point as follows. Add 0's where necessary

Binary number	11011	.01				
When broken up	011	011	.	010		
Octal equivalent	3	3	.	2	or	33.2

Octal to Binary

1. For each octal digit write the corresponding binary digit.
2. The same procedure is to be followed to convert fractional parts also.

Example 1.20: *Convert octal 45 to its binary equivalent.*

Solution:	4	5
	100	101

The binary equivalent number is 100 101. The binary number may be written without a gap as it is easy to represent it in octal form.

Example 1.21: *Convert 4 5 . 3 1 2_8 into binary form.*

Solution: 4	5	.	3	1	2_8
100	101	.	011	001	010

The number in binary form is 100 101 . 011 001 010

Octal to Decimal

1. Multiply each digit of the octal number by its positional weight and add up the result.
2. Another method is to convert an octal number to its equivalent binary number, which is then converted to its decimal equivalent.

Example 1.22: *Convert 237_8 to its decimal equivalent.*

Solution: Digits 2 3 7

Weight 8^2 8^1 8^0

Value $2 \times 8^2 + 3 \times 8^1 + 7 \times 8^0$

$= 128 + 24 + 7$

$= 159_{10}$

Example 1.23: *Convert the same number 237_8 to its decimal equivalent by the second method.*

Solution:

Octal		2			3			7	
Binary	0	1	0	0	1	1	1	1	1
Decimal	0	128	0	0	+16	+8	+4	+2	+1
	=	159							

Decimal to Octal

1. For conversion of the integer part of the decimal number, use the method of successive division by 8. First divide the number by 8 and place the remainder in the units position of the octal number. Again divide the quotient obtained above by 8 and place the remainder in the position of the next digit to the left of the first remainder. This process is to be continued until quotient becomes 0. The last remainder from the final division forms the MSB (most significant bit).

Example 1.24: *Convert decimal number 127_{10} to its octal equivalent.*

Solution:

	Quotient		
127 ÷ 8	15	yields a remainder of	7 LSB
15 ÷ 8	1	yields a remainder of	7
1 ÷ 8	0	yeilds a remainder of	1 MSB

The equivalent octal number is 177.

2. If there is a decimal number with a fractional part, the number is to be multiplied by 8 according to the following procedure. Multiply the decimal fraction by 8 and place the carry into the integer position. Multiply the fractional part again by 8 and follow the same procedure as above.

Example 1.25: *Convert decimal .35 into octal fraction.*

Solution:	Product	Fraction	Carry of
.35 × 8	2.8	.8	2

.8 × 8	6.4	.4	6
.4 × 8	3.2	.2	3

The octal fraction is $.263_8$. The process can be continued further if greater accuracy is desired.

1.5.3 Octal Calculations

The following octal table (Table 1.7) will be useful in carrying out octal additions, subtractions and multiplications.

Table 1.7 Octal addition

+	0	1	2	3	4	5	6	7
0	0	1	2	3	4	5	6	7
1	1	2	3	4	5	6	7	10
2	2	3	4	5	6	7	10	11
3	3	4	5	6	7	10	11	12
4	4	5	6	7	10	11	12	13
5	5	6	7	10	11	12	13	14
6	6	7	10	11	12	13	14	15
7	7	10	11	12	13	14	15	16

Octal Additions

For instance if octal 4 is to be added to 6, the sum will be indicated by the number at the intersection of corresponding column and row. The two intersect at 12. Therefore, the sum of these two octal numbers is 12.

Example 1.26: *Add 12_8 and 15_8.*

Solution:

$$\begin{array}{r} 12 \\ 15 \\ \hline 27_8 \end{array}$$

Example 1.27: *Add 45_8 and 24_8.*

Solution: 1 Carry

$$\begin{array}{r} 45 \\ 24 \\ \hline 71_8 \end{array}$$

According to Table 1.7, 5 added to 4 yields 11. The sum is 1 and there is a carry of 1. 1 added to 4 yields 5 and 5 added to 2 yields 7. Therefore, the result of addition is 71.

Example 1.28: *Add 234_8 and 447_8.*

Solution: 1 1 Carries.

$$\begin{array}{r} 2\ 3\ 4 \\ 4\ 4\ 7 \\ \hline 7\ 0\ 3_8 \end{array}$$

According to Table 1.7, when 4 is added to 7 the sum is 13. Therefore, there is a carry of 1. Similarly, 1 + 3 + 4 yields 10. Therefore, there is again a carry of 1. The sum of the next column is 7.

Octal Subtraction

Let us go back to Table 1.7. If 7 is added to 6 the result is 15. Therefore obviously 15 – 7 is 6. Now suppose we have to subtract 7 from 15. We will look up the column for 7 and read down to number 15 and look up the number against it in the first column. It is 6 and that is the answer.

Example 1.29: *Subtract 57_8 from 66_8.*

Solution:

Balance	5	1	borrow
	6	6	
	5	7	
	0	7_8	

In order to subtract 7 from 6, we have to borrow 1 from the previous column. Now subtracting 7 from 16 yields 7 according to Table 1.7. The result of subtraction is 7, as 5 minus 5 yields 0.

Example 1.30: *Subtract $2\,4\,6\,1_8$ from $4\,3\,5\,2_8$.*

Solution:

	1	1		Borrow
4	3	5	2	
2	4	6	1	
1	6	7	1	

Subtracting 1 from 2 yields 1. Since 6 is larger than 5 we have to borrow 1 from the previous column. Subtracting 6 from 15 yields 7. The remainder in the previous column is now 2 instead of 3. Therefore, we have to borrow 1 from the previous column. Subtracting 4 from 12 yields 6. In the next column subtracting 2 from 3 leaves 1. The result is $1\,6\,7\,1_8$.

Octal Multiplication

The following procedure is to be followed:

1. Multiply the two octal numbers in the same way as you multiply decimal numbers.
2. Now take the above product and divide it by 8.
3. If this division yields a quotient of *A* and a remainder of *B*, the octal product of the two numbers would be *AB*.
4. Alternatively, you may refer to an octal multiplication table which follows:

Example 1.31: *Multiply octal 7 by 6.*

Solution: $7 \times 6 = 42$

$42 \div 8 =$ Quotient 5 and Remainder 2

The product is therefore 52 octal.

When larger octal numbers are involved it is more convenient to use an octal multiplication table (Table 1.8) given below.

Table 1.8 Octal multiplication

×	0	1	2	3	4	5	6	7
0	0	0	0	0	0	0	0	0
1	0	1	2	3	4	5	6	7
2	0	2	4	6	10	12	14	16
3	0	3	6	11	14	17	22	25
4	0	4	10	14	20	24	30	34
5	0	5	12	17	24	31	36	43
6	0	6	14	22	30	36	44	52
7	0	7	16	25	34	43	52	61

Example 1.32: *Multiply 42_8 by 23_8.*

Solution:

```
    4 2
    2 3
   -----
  1 4 6
1 0 4
-------
```

According to Table 1.8, multiplying 2 by 3 yields 6, and multiplying 4 by 3 yields 14. So the first partial product is 146.

Multiplying 2 by 2 yields 4 and multiplying 4 by 2 yields 10 according to Table 1.8. So the next partial product is 1 0 4.

Now we have to do the following addition to arrive at the final result of multiplication.

```
            4 2
Carry  1    2 3
           -----
          1 4 6
      1 0 4
      ---------
      1 2 0 6₈
```

In the second column adding 4 and 4 yields 10 (and not 8). So the sum of the second column is 0 and there is a carry of 1. The third column adds up to 2 and the fourth column is obviously 1.

1.6 HEXADECIMAL NUMBERING SYSTEM

The hexadecimal numbering system uses 16 digits to represent all the numbers. Thus, it has a radix of 16. The digits used are 0, 1, 2, 3, 4, 5, 6, 7, 8, 9, A, B, C, D, E and F. Table 1.9 gives the hexadecimal numbers and their equivalents in decimal and binary forms.

Table 1.9 Hexadecimal numbering system

Decimal	*Hexadecimal*	*Binary*
0	0	0000
1	1	0001

2	2	0010
3	3	0011
4	4	0100
5	5	0101
6	6	0110
7	7	0111
8	8	1000
9	9	1001
10	A	1010
11	B	1011
12	C	1100
13	D	1101
14	E	1110
15	F	1111

You will notice from Table 1.9 that; a hexadecimal digit can be represented by a group of four binary bits and it can represent decimal numbers from 0 through 15. A hexadecimal number is formed by grouping binary bits in groups of four bits each. For instance the hexadecimal number FF3C can be represented in binary form as follows:

1111 1111 0011 1100

In decimal form this will represent a number 65340. The largest decimal number that a group of four hexadecimal digits can represent is 65,535 which is the same as saying FFFF in hexadecimal language. You will notice how small the number is in hexadecimal form and how easy it is to remember it. A group of four hexadecimal digits, 0000 to FFFF, can represent any decimal number up to 65,535. For this reason hexadecimal numbers are extensively used in microcomputers. A microcomputer is capable of storing a maximum of 65,536 bytes. In binary form, their addresses will be from

0000 0000 0000 0000

to 1111 1111 1111 1111

and in hexadecimal form; from 0000 to FFFF. This represents a memory of 64 K, which is equivalent to 65, 536 hexadecimal addressed from 0000 to FFFF. The first eight bits are referred to as the upper bytes (UB) and the next eight bits are called the lower bytes (LB). Consider the binary digits given below and their hexadecimal equivalents:

	Upper	Byte	Lower	Byte
Binary	1110	1001	1100	1101
Hexadecimal	E	9	C	D
In short	E9CD			

1.6.1 Hexadecimal Digit Position Weights

A complete representation of hexadecimal digit positions, position weights and values is given in Fig. 1.8. The representation follows the same pattern as it was adopted earlier for binary and octal digits. You will notice from this representation that every time a digit moves one position to the left the digit gains weight by a factor of 16. When a digit moves one position to the right it loses weight by a factor of 16. It so happens because the radix of the hexadecimal numbering system is 16.

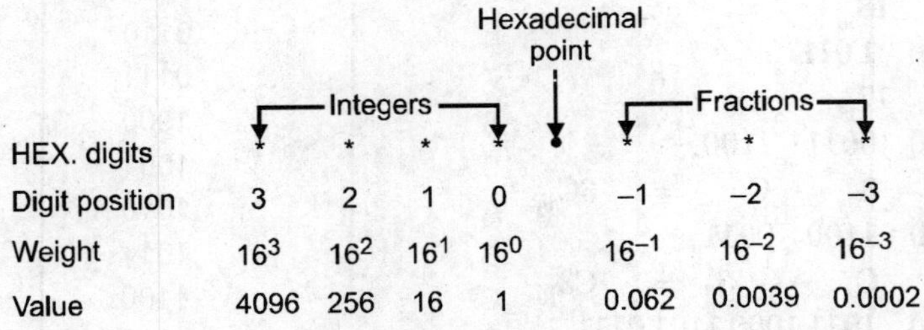

Fig. 1.8 Positional weights and values of hexadecimal numbers

1.6.2 Hexadecimal Conversions

Hexadecimal to Binary

The following procedure may be adopted:

1. Convert each hexadecimal number to its equivalent 4-bit binary number.
2. Refer to Table 1.9 to find the equivalent binary number.

Example 1.33: *Convert the following hexadecimal numbers to binary form:*

(a) *A 3 F E* (b) *C B 4 D*

Solution: (a) A 3 F E
1010 0011 1111 1110

The groups of bits are combined to form the binary number as follows 1010001111111110_2 equivalent binary number

(b) C B 4 D
1100 1011 0100 1101
1100101101001101_2 equivalent binary number

Fractional Hexadecimal to Binary

Example 1.34: *Convert hexadecimal. F C to binary.*

Solution: .F C
.1111 1100

The equivalent binary number is $.111111_2$

Binary to Hexadecimal

Example 1.35: *Convert the following binary numbers to their hexadecimal equivalents.*

(a) *11000*
(b) *10111*
(c) *0011 1100*
(d) *1100 0011*

(e) *1011 1000 1101 0111*

(f) *1100 0101 1111 1001.*

Solution: (a) $1\,1000_2$

18_{16}

(b) $1\,0111_2$

17_{16}

(c) $0011 \quad 1100_2$

$3 \quad C \quad = \quad 3C_{16}$

(d) $1100 \quad 0011_2$

$C \quad 3 \quad = \quad C3_{16}$

(e) $1011\,1000\,1101\,0111_2$

$B \quad 8 \quad D \quad 7 \quad = B\,8\,D\,7_{16}$

(f) $1100\,0101\,1111\,1001_2$

$C \quad 5 \quad F \quad 9 \quad = C\,5\,F\,9_{16}$

Fractional Binary to Hexadecimal

Example 1.36: *Convert binary 10 0101 . 0111 1000 to hexadecimal.*

Solution: $10 \quad 0101 \quad . \quad 0111 \quad 1100_2$

$2 \quad 5 \quad . \quad 7 \quad C \quad = \quad 25.7C_{16}$

Hexadecimal to Decimal

1. Consult with Section 1.6.1 to determine the weight of each hexadecimal digit.
2. Multiply each hexadecimal digit by its weight and add up the resultant values of all the digits.

Example 1.37: *Convert hexadecimal number C F 3 D to its decimal equivalent.*

Solution: Proceed as follows:

$$C \times 16^3 \quad F \times 16^2 \quad 3 \times 16^1 \quad D \times 16^0$$
$$= 12 \times 4096 + 15 \times 256 + 3 \times 16 + 13 \times 1$$
$$= 49152 + 3840 + 48 + 13$$
$$= 53053$$

Example 1.38: *Convert the following hexadecimal fraction into decimal equivalent: 241.*

Solution: Proceed as follows:

$$2 \times 16^{-1} + 4 \times 16^{-2} + 1 \times 16^{-3}$$
$$= 2 \times 0.062 + 4 \times 0.0039 + 1 \times .0002$$
$$= 0.124 + .0156 + .0002$$
$$= 0.1398$$

Decimal to Hexadecimal Conversion

1. A simple method of conversion is to convert decimal number to its equivalent binary number and the latter to its equivalent hexadecimal number.
2. Another method is successive division by 16 as illustrated in the following example:

Example 1.39: *Convert decimal number 3580 to hexadecimal number.*

Solution: Divide successively by 16 as follows:

	Quotient	*And a remainder of*
3580 ÷ 16	223	12 = C
223 ÷ 16	13	15 = F
13 ÷ 16	0	13 = D

The equivalent hexadecimal number is DFC_{16}.

1.6.3 Hexadecimal to Decimal Conversion Table

Microcomputers typically use 16-bit memories and; are thus, capabale of storing 65,536 bytes of information. Their binary addresses are from

	Upper	Byte	Lower	Byte
	0000	0000	0000	0000
to	1111	1111	1111	1111
and in hexadecimal from	0	0	0	0
to	F	F	F	F

If you have many conversions to make from one system to other, you will find it more convenient to do the conversions with the help of Table 1.10.

The upper half of the Table 1.10 lists the conversion values for the upper bytes and the lower half lists the conversion values of the lower bytes. The conversion is easily accomplished as follows:

Example 1.40: *Convert $7\,3\,2\,5_{16}$ to its decimal equivalent.*

Solution:

$$7 = 2\,8\,6\,7\,2_{10}$$
$$3 = 7\,6\,8_{10}$$
$$2 = 3\,2_{10}$$
$$5 = 5_{10}$$
$$7\,3\,2\,5_{16} = 2\,9\,4\,7\,7_{10}$$

Table 1.10 can also be used for converting decimal numbers to hexadecimal numbers.

Table 1.10 Hexadecimal to decimal conversion

Decimal	*Hex*	*Binary*		*Hex*	*Decimal*
		Upper	*Byte*		
0	0	0000	0000	0	0
4096	10	0001	0001	01	256
8192	20	0010	0010	02	512
12288	30	0011	0011	03	768
16384	40	0100	0100	04	1024
20480	50	0101	0101	05	1280
24576	60	0110	0110	06	1536
28672	70	0111	0111	07	1792
32768	80	1000	1000	08	2048
36864	90	1001	1001	09	2304

40960	A0	1010	1010	0A	2560
45056	B0	1011	1011	0B	2816
49152	C0	1100	1100	0C	3072
53248	D0	1101	1101	0D	3328
57344	E0	1110	1110	0E	3584
61440	F0	1111	1111	0F	3840
		Lower	***Byte***		
0	00	0000	0000	00	0
16	10	0001	0001	01	1
32	20	0010	0010	02	2
48	30	0011	0011	03	3
64	40	0100	0100	04	4
80	50	0101	0101	05	5
96	60	0110	0110	06	6
112	70	0111	0111	07	7
128	80	1000	1000	08	8
144	90	1001	1001	09	9
160	A0	1010	1010	0A	10
176	B0	1011	1011	0B	11
192	C0	1100	1100	0C	12
208	D0	1101	1101	0D	13
224	E0	1110	1110	0E	14
240	F0	1111	1111	0F	15

1.6.4 Hexadecimal Calculations

With the help of Table 1.11, which follows, both hexadecimal additions and subtractions can be easily carried out.

Table 1.11 Hexadecimal addition

+	0	1	2	3	4	5	6	7	8	9	A	B	C	D	E	F
0	0	1	2	3	4	5	6	7	8	9	A	B	C	D	E	F
1	1	2	3	4	5	6	7	8	9	A	B	C	D	E	F	10
2	2	3	4	5	6	7	8	9	A	B	C	D	E	F	10	11
3	3	4	5	6	7	8	9	A	B	C	D	E	F	10	11	12
4	4	5	6	7	8	9	A	B	C	D	E	F	10	11	12	13
5	5	6	7	8	9	A	B	C	D	E	F	10	11	12	13	14
6	6	7	8	9	A	B	C	D	E	F	10	11	12	13	14	15
7	7	8	9	A	B	C	D	E	F	10	11	12	13	14	15	16
8	8	9	A	B	C	D	E	F	10	11	12	13	14	15	16	17
9	9	A	B	C	D	E	F	10	11	12	13	14	15	16	17	18
A	A	B	C	D	E	F	10	11	12	13	14	15	16	17	18	19
B	B	C	D	E	F	10	11	12	13	14	15	16	17	18	19	1A
C	C	D	E	F	10	11	12	13	14	15	16	17	18	19	1A	1B
D	D	E	F	10	11	12	13	14	15	16	17	18	19	1A	1B	1C
E	E	F	10	11	12	13	14	15	16	17	18	19	1A	1B	1C	1D
F	F	10	11	12	13	14	15	16	17	18	19	1A	1B	1C	1D	1E

Example 1.41: *Add B A F 1$_{16}$ and C 4 9 D$_{16}$.*

Solution:

	1			Carry
	B	A	F	1
	C	4	9	D
1	7	F	8	E

Example 1.42: *Add 1 F A E 9 and 5 C D F 4.*

Solution:

1	1	1			Carries
1	F	A	E	9	
5	C	D	F	4	
7	C	8	D	D	

Subtractions

The hexadecimal addition table (Table 1.11) can also be used for carrying out subtractions.

Example 1.43: *Subtract 2 B 8$_{16}$ from 2 3 5 4$_{16}$.*

Solution:

	1	1		Borrow
2	3	5	4	
	2	B	8	
2	0	9	C	

Since, 8 does not go in 4, borrow 1 from the previous column. According to Table 1.11, 14 – 8 = C. Again borrow 1 to subtract B from 4 (which is the balance after borrowing 1). Now 14 – B yields 9 from the table. The rest is obvious.

1.7 CONVERSION ALGORITHM

An algorithm is a special method of solving a problem. We will consider an algorithm for converting one number system to another. Mathematically it can be stated as follows for converting integers as well as fractions:

$$Y = d_n \times r^n + d_{n-1} \times r^{n-1} + d_{n-2} \times r^{n-2} + \ldots + d_0 \times r^0 \quad \text{(integers)}$$

$$d_{-1} \times r^{-1} + d_{-2} \times r^{-2} + \ldots + d_{-m} \times r^{-m} \quad \text{(fractions)}$$

where Y represents the value of the number
d_n represents the value of the nth digit
r represents the value of the radix
d_{-m} represents the value of the mth fraction of the digit

The procedure to be followed for converting one number system to another can be started as follows. Let us suppose that decimal number 2496 is to be converted to the equivalent octal number.

1. Each decimal digit is converted to the equivalent digit. For instance 2 and 4 in decimal are the same as 2 and 4 in octal. However, 9 in decimal is equivalent to 11 in octal.

2. The digits are then multiplied by the radix (which should be expressed in terms of the new system) and then raised to a power. Since the radix of the decimal system is 10, in the octal system it will be equivalent to 12.
3. Finally, the results of converting the digits are added up to give the number in the required number system.

Example 1.46 shows how a decimal number can be converted to an octal number.

Binary to Decimal Conversion (Integers)

Example 1.44: *Convert 1 1 0 1 1_2 to decimal.*

Solution:

$$Y = d_4 \times r^4 + d_3 \times r^3 + d_2 \times r^2 + d_1 \times r^1 + d_0 \times r^0$$
$$11011_2 = 1 \times 2^4 + 1 \times 2^3 + 0 \times 2^2 + 1 \times 2^1 + 1 \times 2^0$$
$$= 16 + 8 + 0 + 2 + 1$$
$$= 27_{10}$$

Binary to Decimal Conversion (Fractions)

Example 1.45: *Convert .0 1 1 1_2 to decimal.*

Solution:

$$Y = d_{-1} \times r^{-1} + d_{-2} \times r^{-2} + d_{-3} \times r^{-3} + d_{-4} \times r^{-4}$$
$$.0111_2 = 0.0 \times 2^{-1} + 1 \times 2^{-2} + 1 \times 2^{-3} + 1 \times 2^{-4}$$
$$= 0.0 + 0.25 + 0.125 + 0.0625$$
$$= 0.4375_{10}$$

Decimal to Octal Conversion

Example 1.46: *Convert 2496_{10} to octal.*

Solution:

$$Y = d_3 \times r^3 + d_2 \times r^2 + d_1 \times r^1 + d_0 \times r^0$$
$$2496_{10} = 2 \times 12_8^3 + 4 \times 12_8^2 + 11_8 \times 12_8^1 + 6 \times 12_8^0$$
$$= 2 \times 1750_8 + 4 \times 144_8 + 132_8 + 6$$
$$= 3720_8 + 620_8 + 132_8 + 6$$
$$= 4700_8$$

Octal to Decimal Conversion

Example 1.47: *Convert 5763_8 to decimal.*

Solution:

$$Y = d_3 \times r^3 + d_2 \times r^2 + d_1 \times r^1 + d_0 \times r^0$$
$$5763_8 = 5_{10} \times 8_{10}^3 + 7_{10} \times 8_{10}^2 + 6_{10} \times 8_{10}^1 + 3_{10} \times 8_{10}^0$$
$$= 2560_{10} + 448_{10} + 48_{10} + 3_{10}$$
$$= 3059_{10}$$

Hexadecimal to Decimal Conversion

Example 1.48: *Convert B C 7_{16} to decimal.*

Solution:

$$Y = d_2 \times r^2 + d_1 \times r^1 + d_0 \times r^0$$
$$BC7_{16} = 11_{10} \times 16_{10}^2 + 12_{10} \times 16_{10}^1 + 7_{10} \times 16_{10}^0$$
$$= 11_{10} \times 256_{10} + 192_{10} + 7_{10}$$
$$= 2816_{10} + 192_{10} + 7_{10}$$
$$= 3015_{10}$$

1.8 GRAY CODE

The BCD code give in Table 1.4 is a weighted code as each bit position has been assigned a definite weight. On the other hand, the Gray code is a non-weighted code as no weights are assigned to the bit positions. A comparison of the Gray code given in Table 1.12 and the binary code brings out a very important point. Take the Gray code for any two consecutive decimal numbers, when you will notice a change in only one bit position. Now consider the binary numbers for decimal numbers 3 and 4. You will notice that there is a change in three bit positions. This greatly enhances the chances of error. Whereas in the Gray code, since only one bit position changes between decimal numbers 3 and 4, the chances of error are reduced. You will notice this feature between any two consecutive numbers. Besides, as it takes a finite time for changes in bit positions to take place, the Gray code circuitry can operate at higher speeds.

Table 1.12 Gray code

Decimal	*Gray code*	*Pure binary*
0	0000	0000
1	0001	0001
2	0011	0010
3	0010	0011
4	0110	0100
5	0111	0101
6	0101	0110
7	0100	0111
8	1100	1000
9	1101	1001
10	1111	1010
11	1110	1011
12	1010	1100
13	1011	1101
14	1001	1110
15	1000	1111

The disadvantage with the Gray code is that it cannot be used in arithmetic operations. Wherever you have to add, subtract, etc., the Gray code cannot be used. Before using the Gray code in arithmetic operations the Gray code must be changed to binary form.

1.8.1 Gray Code to Binary Conversion

The conversion of gray code to binary and binary to Gray code using Exclusive OR (XOR) gates has been discussed in a later chapter. For the present we will consider how this can be achieved without any electronic aid.

We will show how a Gray code can be converted to binary system by using simple arithmetic. The method used has been shown diagrammatically in Fig. 1.9 which demonstrates how Gray code 1 0 1 1 can be converted to its binary equivalent.

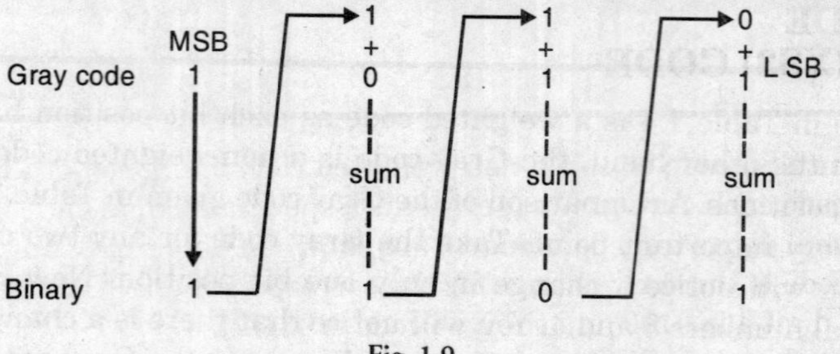

Fig. 1.9

The rules for conversion can be stated as follows:

1. The MSB in the Gray code is the same as in the binary number.
2. Add the MSB to the bit immediately on its right and record the sum. If there is a carry it should be ignored.
3. Continue adding bits to bits immediately to their right until all bits have been added and the LSB is reached.
4. The final sum will be the binary equivalent which will have the same number of bits as the Gray code.

Let us now see how these rules are applied in the present case. Since, there is no change in the MSB it is recorded as it is and represents the MSB of the binary number. The MSB of the binary number is then added to the Gray code bit immediately on its right. The sum is 1 + 0 = 1. This represents the next bit of the binary number and is recorded below. This bit is then added to the next bit which is 1. Since 1 + 1 = 10, the carry of 1 is ignored and 0 is taken down as the next bit of the binary number. 0 is then added to 1 of the LSB and the sum is 1 which now forms the LSB of the binary number. The result of conversion is binary number 1 1 0 1.

1.8.2 Binary to Gray Code Conversion

The method of conversion is shown in Fig. 1.10

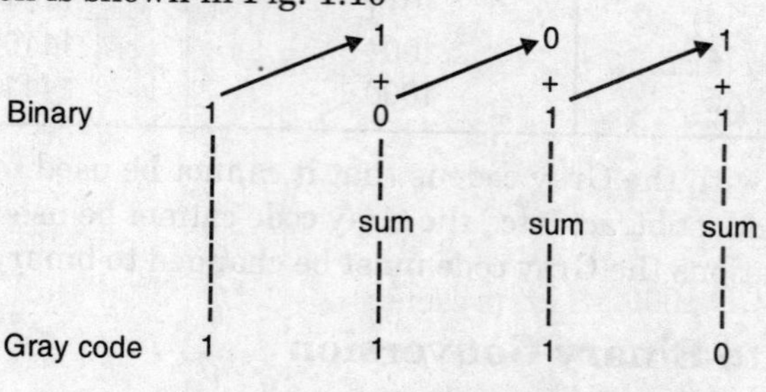

Fig. 1.10

The rules for conversion are very much the same as for the Gray code to binary conversion. The MSB in both is the same, so the MSB of the binary number is taken down as such, which will represent the MSB of the Gray code. The MSB of the binary number is then added to the next bit to its right. The sum will represent the next bit of the Gray code. The process is carried on until the LSB is reached. You will notice that 1 + 1 in the LSB column adds up to 10. The carry of 1 is to be neglected and 0 is taken down as the LSB of the binary code. Thus 1 1 1 0 represents the equivalent of the binary number 1 0 1 1.

1.9 EXCESS-3 (XS3) CODE

Like the Gray code the XS3 code is also a non-weighted code and is generally used with BCD numbers. In the XS3 code each 4-bit group represents a specific decimal digit. The XS3 code and the BCD code for decimal digits from 0 through 9 are shown in Table 1.13. For any decimal digit the value of the XS3 code is three more than for the corresponding BCD code. For instance the BCD code for decimal digit 4 is 0100 and the XS3 code is 0111.

The XS3 code has found application in arithmetic operations as it greatly simplifies the process. Later on, we will also consider some weighted codes which are equally useful in arithmetic operations.

Table 1.13 Excess-3 code

Decimal digit	*BCD code*	*XS3 code*
0	0000	0011
1	0001	0100
2	0010	0101
3	0011	0110
4	0100	0111
5	0101	1000
6	0110	1001
7	0111	1010
8	1000	1011
9	1001	1100

1.9.1 XS3 Conversions

Decimal to XS3

To convert any decimal number to XS3 form add 3 to the decimal number and then represent it in BCD form.

Example 1.49: *Convert decimal number 5 to XS3 form.*

Solution: Decimal number 5

Add 3 3

Sum 8

Convert to BCD 1000 XS3 representation

Example 1.50: *Convert decimal 62 to XS3 form.*

Solution: Add 3 to each decimal digit and convert to BCD form.

Decimal number 6 2

Add 3 3 3

Sum 9 5

Convert to BCD 1001 0101 XS3 representation.

Example 1.51: *Convert decimal 48 to XS3 form.*

Solution: Decimal number 4 8

Add 3 3 3

Sum 7 11

While converting 11 to BCD form, although it represents a number exceeding 9(1011), it is not necessary to carry the excess to the next column. Convert to BCD form as follows:

	7	11
XS3 form	0111	1011

XS3 to Decimal

Example 1.52: *Convert XS3 number 1011 to Decimal.*

Solution:

XS3 number	1011
Subtract 3	– 0011
Difference	1000
Decimal	8

1.10 COMPLEMENT NUMBERS

Since, computers can recognize only the magnitude of numbers, some device has to be incorporated to enable computers to distinguish between positive and negative numbers. To facilitate, negative numbers are often stored in complemented form. In this section, we will look into some of these aspects and also consider how additions and subtractions can be carried out.

The general rule for deriving the complements of numbers can be stated as follows:

1. In any number system the 'Radix minus 1' complement of a number is obtained by subtracting each digit of the number from 'Radix minus 1'.
2. In any number system the 'true complement' of a number is obtained by adding 1 to the LSB of the 'Radix minus 1' complement of the number.

1.10.1 Binary Number Complements

We will explain the application of the above rules by applying it to obtain the complements of the binary numbers. In the binary number system the 'Radix minus 1' complement is commonly referred to as the 1's complement. The 'true complement' of a binary number is called the 2's complement. Complements of binary numbers have been dealt with in Chapter 11. Here we will simply explain the application of the general rule for complementing binary numbers.

1's Complement

We will first consider how the rule stated above can be applied to the case of binary numbers. Let us consider binary number 1 0 0 1 and derive its 1's complement. Since, the radix is 2 for binary numbers, subtracting 1 from 2 gives 1. Now all that we have to do is to subtract each digit of the number from 1 as follows:

Radix –1	1 1 1 1
Binary number	1 0 0 1
Difference 1's complement	0 1 1 0

You must have noticed that the 1's complement of a binary number can be easily obtained by complementing each bit, that is changing all 0's to 1's and all 1's to 0's.

2's Complement

The 2's complement of binary number 1 0 0 1 can be easily obtained by adding 1 to the LSB of the 1's complement as follows:

1's complement	0 1 1 0
Add 1 to LSB	1
2's complement	0 1 1 1

1.10.2 Decimal Number Complements

In the decimal system the two complements are known as the 10's complement and 9's complement.

9's Complement

The 9's complement of a decimal number is obtained by subtracting each digit of the number from 9(10–1). For instance the 9's complement of 82 is 17 (99 – 82) and the 9's complement of 75 is 24 (99 – 75).

10's Complement

The 10's complement is obtained by adding 1 to the LSB of the 9's complement. Thus, the 10's complement of 82 is 18 (17 + 1) and the 10's complement of 75 is 25 (24 + 1).

1.10.3 Subtraction in 10's and 9's complements

Just as 1's and 2's complements are found useful in binary arithmetic operations, as you will see in a later chapter, 10's and 9's complements are useful in decimal subtraction. We will consider some examples to explain the procedure.

Subtraction in 10's Complements

Example 1.53: *Subtract 29 from 76.*

Solution:

Decimal subtraction	10's complement subtraction	
76	76	Minuend
–29	+71	10's complement of 29 is added
47	147	Since there is a carry the result is positive and the carry is dropped
	47	Answer

Example 1.54: *Subtract 4 from 8.*

Solution: Express the subtrahend in 9's complement and add

8 :	1 0 0 0	
– 4	0 1 0 1	9's complement
	1 1 0 1	

As this is invalid in the BCD code, add 0 1 1 0 to the result of addition as follows:

```
        1 1 0 1
Add     0 1 1 0
      ---------
      1 0 0 1 1
```

Now add the EAC (end-around-carry) to the LSB to get the final result

```
  1 0 0 1 1
  ↑------1 (End-around-carry)
  ---------
    0 1 0 0
```

Since, there was an EAC the result is positive +4.

Example 1.55: *Subtract 2 from 9.*

Solution: Proceed as follows

```
 9 :      1 0 0 1
–2 :      0 1 1 1   9's complement of 2
        ---------
        1 0 0 0 0   (Invalid)
Add:      0 1 1 0
        ---------
        1 0 1 1 0
        ↑-------1   Add EAC
        ---------
          0 1 1 1
```

Since, there is an end-around-carry the result is positive that is +7.

Example 1.56: *Subtract 7 from 5.*

Solution: Express the subtrahend in 9's complement form and add

```
 5 :  0 1 0 1
–7 :  0 0 1 0   9's complement
      -------
      0 1 1 1
```

Since, there is no EAC the result is negative and the final answer is the 9's complement with a minus sign, that is –2.

Before considering further examples of subtractions using the 9's complement method, we will sum up our conclusions as follows:

If adding the minuend to the 9's complement produces an invalid code, add decimal 6 (0 1 1 0) and th end-around-carry to the sum. The result will be a positive number representing the sum.

When the sum of the minuend and 9's complement of the subtrahend represents a valid BCD code, the result will be negative and it will be in the 9's complement form.

Example 1.57: *Subtract 86 from 51.*

Solution:

Decimal subtraction	10's complement subtraction	
51	51	Minuend
–86	+14	10's complement of 86
–35	65	

Since, there is no carry, the result is negative. The result is 10's complement with a minus sign.

–35 10's complement. Answer

Subtraction in 9's Complement

We will consider the same examples as before and see how it works out in 9's complement form.

Example 1.58: *Subtract 29 from 76.*

Solution:

Decimal subtraction	9's complement subtraction	
76	76	Minuend
–29	+70	9's complement of 29
47	146	Since, there is a carry, the difference is positive. The carry is added to the least significant digit as shown here.
	→1	
	47	Answer

Example 1.59: *Subtract 86 from 51.*

Solution:

Decimal subtraction	9's complement subtraction	
51	51	Minuend
–86	+13	9's complement of 86
–35	64	Since, there is no carry, the result is negative. The final answer is the 9's complement with a minus sign.
	–35	9's complement Answer

1.11 WEIGHTED BCD CODES

We have earlier considered two non-weighted BCD codes, that is the Gray code and the XS3 code. We will now consider some of the weighted codes. As you already know decimal numbers are frequently represented by the 8421 BCD code. The numbers 8 4 2 and 1 represent the weights of the digit positions. There are at the same time other weighted codes like 4 2 2 1, 2 4 2 1, which are also used to represent decimal digits as shown in Table 1.14.

Table 1.14

Decimal digit	Weighted BCD codes				Non-weighted code
	8421	4221	2421	5211	XS3
0	0000	0000	0000	0000	0011
1	0001	0001	0001	0001	0100
2	0010	0010	0010	0011	0101
3	0011	0011	0011	0101	0110
4	0100	1000	0100	0111	0111
5	0101	0111	1011	1000	1000

6	0110	1100	1100	1010	1001
7	0111	1101	1101	1100	1010
8	1000	1110	1110	1110	1011
9	1001	1111	1111	1111	1100

Since, 16 binary representations are possible with 4-bit codes, it is possible to use different combinations of the four binary digits to represent the same decimal digit. You will also notice that the weights assigned to the various digits are not the same in each code. A unique binary representation is used for each decimal digit.

We have also incorporated the XS3 code in Table 1.14, although it is not a weighted code, for the simple reason that in some ways it has the same advantage in representing 9's complement numbers as the other weighted codes. BCD codes can be classified into two categories, (1) sequential and (2) reflective.

Sequential Codes

You will observe that in the 8421 BCD code and the XS3 code each succeeding code has one binary number more than the preceding code.

Reflective Code

If you analyze codes 2421, 4221, 5211 and the XS3 code, you will notice a significant property associated with these codes. Consider the 1's complement of the binary representation for decimal number 2 in the 4221 code. This is 1101. Table 1.14 shows that 1101 represents decimal number 7, which is the 9's complement of decimal number 2. In short in all reflective codes the 1's complement of the binary representation of a decimal number will produce the corresponding 9's complement of the decimal number.

Let us now consider decimal number 4 in the XS3 code.

Decimal No	4	
Binary equivalent in XS3code	0111	
Its 1's complement	1000	
This represents decimal number	5	which is the 9's complement of 4

You will find this unique feature in all the codes shown in Table 1.14 except the 8421 BCD code. It is worth nothing that just as 1's and 2's complement numbers are found useful in carrying out binary subtractions, 9's and 10's complements are found useful in decimal subtractions.

1.12 ASCII CODE (PRONOUNCED ASK-EE)

The American Standard Code for Information Interchange, in short called the ASCII code, is extensively used for data communication and in digital computers. As it is a 7-bit code, it can represent 2^7 or 128 different characters. It can represent decimal numbers from 0 to 9, and letters of the alphabet, both upper and lower case. It is also used for controlling computer peripheral devices with the help of special characters which are incorporated in the code. Explanations of the special control functions incorporated in the code are given at the end of Table 1.15. There is a 7-bit code for each symbol and control function which is made up of a 3-bit group followed by a 4-bit group as shown in Fig. 1.11.

3-bit group			4-bit group			
X_6	X_5	X_4	X_3	X_2	X_1	X_0

Fig. 1.11

The 3-bit and 4-bit groups which will represent any desired character can be easily located from Table 1.15. For instance, if you want to indicate 'start of text' look for STX column 0 and row 2. The code for this is, therefore 0000010. If you have to decipher the code 0111001, look for 011 in the appropriate column and you will find 1001 in row 9. Where the row and columns meet you will find the character which is represented by this code. They meet at decimal number 9 which is represented by this code.

Table 1.15 ASCII character code

	Column	**0**	**1**	**2**	**3**	**4**	**5**	**6**	**7**
Row	**Bits** $X_3X_2X_1X_0$	$X_6X_5X_4$							
		000	**001**	**010**	**011**	**100**	**101**	**110**	**111**
0	0000	NUL	DLE	SPACE	0	@	P		P
1	0001	SOH	DC1	!	1	A	Q	a	q
2	0010	STX	DC2	"	2	B	R	b	r
3	0011	ETX	DC3	#£	3	C	S	c	s
4	0100	EOT	DC4	$	4	D	T	d	t
5	0101	ENQ	NAK	%	5	E	U	e	u
6	0110	ACK	SYN	&	6	F	V	f	v
7	0111	BELL	ETB	'	7	G	W	g	w
8	1000	BACK SPACE	CAN	(	8	H	X	h	x
9	1001	HOR TAB	EM	)	9	I	Y	i	y
10	1010	LINE FEED	SUB	*	:	J	Z	j	z
11	1011	VERT TAB	ESCAPE	+	;	K	[	k	{
12	1100	FORM FEED	FS	,	<	L	\	l	∫
13	1101	CARRIAGE RETURN	GS	—	=	M	]	m	} ALT MODE
14	1110	SHIFT OUT	RS	.	>	N	^(↑)	n	~
15	1111	SHIFT IN	US	/	?	O	—	o	DEL (RUB OUT)

Control Functions

NUL	NULL
SOH	Start of Heading
STX	Start of Text
EOT	End of Transmission
ENQ	Enquiry
ACK	Acknowledge
BELL	Bell (Audible signal)
BACK SPACE	
HORIZONTAL TABULATION (Punched Card skip)	
LINE FEED	
VERTICAL TABULATION	
FORM FEED	
CARRIAGE RETURN	
SHIFT OUT	
SHIFT IN	
SPACE BLANK	
DLE	Data Link Escape
DC1	Device Control 1
DC2	Device Control 2
DC3	Device Control 3
DC4	Device Control 4
NAK	Negative acknowledge
SYN	Synchronous Idle
ETB	End of Transmission
CAN	Cancel
EM	End of Medium
SUB	Substitute
ESCAPE	
FS	File Separator
GS	Group Separator
RS	Record Separator
US	Unit Separator
DEL	Delete

1.13 EBCDIC CODE (PRONOUNCED EB-SI-DIK)

This is another alphanumeric code, EBCDIC, known as the Extended Binary-Coded-Decimal Interchange code (Table 1.16), which is widely used by large computers for communicating alphanumeric data. Since this is an 8-bit code it has more variations and characters than the ASCII code. This code is very closely related to punch card codes.

Table 1.16 EBCDIC code

HEX LSD	*Hexadecimal MSD*															
	0	*1*	*2*	*3*	*4*	*5*	*6*	*7*	*8*	*9*	*A*	*B*	*C*	*D*	*E*	*F*
0	NUL	DLE	DS		SP	&							[	]	\	0
1	SOH	DC1	SOS				/		a	j	~		A	J		1
2	STX	DC2	FS	SYN					b	k	s		B	K	S	2
3	ETX	DC3							c	l	t		C	L	T	3
4	PF	RES	BYP	PN					d	m	u		D	M	U	4
5	HT	NL	LF	RS					e	n	v		E	N	V	5
6	LC	BS	EOB	UC					f	o	w		F	O	W	6
7	DEL	IL	PRE	EOT					g	p	x		G	P	X	7
8		CAN							h	q	y		H	Q	Y	8
9		EM							i	r	z		I	R	Z	9
A	SMM	CC	SM		¢u	!	|	:								
B	VT				.	$	,	#								
C	FF	IFS		DC4	<	*	%	@								
D	CR	IGS	ENQ	NAK	(	)	—	'								
E	SO	IRS	ACK		+	;	>	=								
F	SI	IUS	BEL	SUB	|	¬	?	"								

Problems

1.1 What decimal numbers do the following sums represent?

(*a*) $(3 \times 10^4) + (7 \times 10^1) + (8 \times 10^3) + (9 \times 10^2)$

(*b*) $(2 \times 10^{-1}) + (3 \times 10^{-3}) + (6 \times 10^{-2})$

(*c*) $(3 \times 10^2) + (5 \times 10^{-1}) + (2 \times 10^0) + (7 \times 10^{-2})$

1.2 What weighted decimal symbols when added up will represent the following decimal numbers?

(*a*) 10071 (*b*) 100.035 (*c*) 0.00247

1.3 How many binary states can be represented by

(*a*) an 8-bit binary word

(*b*) a 16-bit binary word?

1.4 What is the largest decimal number that can be represented by

(*a*) an 8-bit binary word

(*b*) a 16-bit binary word?

1.5 What size of binary word will be required to express the following decimal numbers?

(*a*) 64,000 (*b*) 250

1.6 Convert the following binary numbers to decimal numbers

(*a*) 010011 (*b*) 100110

(*c*) 100101 (*d*) 1101101

1.7 Convert the following decimal numbers to binary form:

(*a*) 205 (*b*) 101

(*c*) 99 (*d*) 105

1.8 Express the following decimal numbers in BCD form:
(*a*) 93 (*b*) 204
(*c*) 4590 (*d*) 2347

1.9 Perform the following additions of binary numbers and check your result using the decimal numbers in place of binary numbers:
(*a*) 10101 + 11101
(*b*) 1001 + 0111
(*c*) 111011 + 11100
(*d*) 10101 + 1101
(*e*) 1111 + 1111
(*f*) 110101 + 11101

1.10 Perform the following binary subtractions and verify your result by using decimal numbers:
(*a*) 11011 – 10101
(*b*) 011101 – 001100
(*c*) 1111 – 0101
(*d*) 100110 – 111001
(*e*) 00011 – 11100
(*f*) 110011 – 101100

1.11 Perform the following subtractions of binary numbers by the 2's complement method:
(*a*) 11010 – 10101
(*b*) 10110 – 01001
(*c*) 111011 – 011011
(*d*) 10101 – 11010
(*e*) 000111 – 101011
(*f*) 010111 – 101001

1.12 Multiply the following binary numbers and check your result using the decimal multiplication:
(*a*) 1110 × 1001
(*b*) 101 × 010
(*c*) 11011 × 011011
(*d*) 0011 × 11100
(*e*) 10101 × 01110
(*f*) 1101 × 1110

1.13 Perform the following division of binary numbers and verify your result using decimal numbers:
(*a*) 11011 ÷ 11
(*b*) 101010 ÷ 111
(*c*) 110111 ÷ 101
(*d*) 11011100 ÷ 1011

1.14 Express the following decimal numbers in BCD form:
(*a*) 93 (*b*) 204 (*c*) 4590 (*d*) 2347

1.15 Convert the following BCD numbers into their decimal equivalents:
(*a*) 0010 1001 0111 0011 (*b*) 0011 0001 0000 1000
(*c*) 0111 0000 1000 1001 (*d*) 0010 0101 1001 0001

1.16 Convert the following BCD numbers to binary form:
(*a*) 1001 0010 . 1001 (*b*) 0110 0101 . 0110
(*c*) 1000 0001 . 0010 (*d*) 0001 1000 . 0111

1.17 Convert the following binary numbers to BCD form:
(*a*) 11010 . 0100
(*b*) 10111 . 1000
(*c*) 10100 . 1100
(*d*) 10001 . 1000

1.18 Perform the additions of the following BCD numbers.

(*a*)
```
  1001  1000  0110
  1001  0101  0100
  ----------------
```
(*b*)
```
  0110  1001  1001
  1001  0001  0111
  ----------------
```

1.19 Add the following numbers in 8421 BCD code:
(*a*) 42 and 35 (*b*) 67 and 81
(*c*) 91 and 43 (*d*) 73 and 57

1.20 Convert the following octal numbers to binary numbers:
(*a*) 20 (*b*) 17 (*c*) 367
(*d*) 14 (*e*) 16 (*f*) 354

1.21 Convert the following binary numbers to octal numbers:
(*a*) 1101 (*b*) 10110
(*c*) 10111 . 011 (*d*) 1011 . 101

1.22 Convert the following octal numbers to decimal numbers:
(*a*) 547 (*b*) 734 (*c*) 231 (*d*) 623

1.23 Convert the following decimal numbers to octal numbers:
(*a*) 327 (*b*) 754 (*c*) 1473 (*d*) 1001

1.24 Convert decimal 0.45 into octal fraction.

1.25 Add the following octal numbers.
(*a*) 14 and 12 (*b*) 35 and 14
(*c*) 224 and 435 (*d*) 346 and 123

1.26 Carry out the following octal subtractions:
(*a*) 54 – 43 (*b*) 95 – 76
(*c*) 4221 – 3471 (*d*) 5221 – 4372

1.27 Perform the following octal multiplications:
(*a*) 7 × 6 (*b*) 6 × 4
(*c*) 12 × 12 (*d*) 12 × 12 × 12

1.28 Convert the following hexadecimal numbers to binary numbers:
(*a*) C35A (*b*) 4DFA
(*c*) 7BF3 (*d*) 73AC

1.29 Convert the following hexadecimal numbers to binary form:
(*a*) F .F 4 (*b*) D. 4CD

1.30 Convert the following binary numbers to hexadecimal numbers:
(*a*) 1011 (*b*) 1101
(*c*) 1100 (*d*) 0101
(*e*) 1101 1001 (*f*) 1110 1011

1.31 Convert the following hexadecimal numbers to decimal numbers:
(*a*) A3FC (*b*) 4BDA
(*c*) 54FA (*d*) F3DB

1.32 Convert the following decimal numbers to hexadecimal numbers:

(*a*) 2501 (*b*) 457

(*c*) 3387 (*d*) 3208

1.33 Convert the following binary number to hexadecimal:

(*a*) 101 0110 . 0101 1001 (*b*) 111 1010 . 0001 1011

1.34 Convert the following hexadecimal fractions to decimal fractions:

(*a*) .342 (*b*) .541

1.35 Use Table 1.10 to perform the following conversions:

(*a*) $0010\,0011_2$ to Decimal

(*b*) $0111\,1000_2$ to Decimal

(*c*) 12230_{10} to Binary

(*d*) 226_{10} to Binary

(*e*) $FE00_{16}$ to Binary

(*f*) $00CB_{16}$ to Binary

(*g*) 53249_{10} to Hexadecimal

(*h*) 3980_{10} to Hexadecimal

(*i*) $F2C4_{16}$ to Decimal

1.36 Perform the following hexadecimal additions:

(*a*) BCF2 and CD43 (*b*) F04E and F12C

(*c*) 1FF4C and 53F5E (*d*) 1CCDD and 1DDCC

1.37 Perform the following hexadecimal subtractions:

(*a*) $2C7_{16}$ from 3546_{10} (*b*) $3D4_{16}$ from 8430_{10}

1.38 Perform the following conversions using the conversion algorithm:

(*a*) $1\,0\,1\,1\,1_2$ to Decimal

(*b*) $0.0\,1\,0\,1_2$ to Decimal

(*c*) $3\,4\,7\,5_{10}$ to Octal

(*d*) $7\,5\,4\,4_8$ to Decimal

(*e*) $CB\,5_{16}$ to Decimal

1.39 Convert the following Gray codes to binary form:

(*a*) 0 1 1 1 (*b*) 1 1 0 1

(*c*) 1 0 0 1 (*d*) 1 0 0 0

1.40 Convert the following binary numbers to Gray code:

(*a*) 0 1 0 0 (*b*) 0 1 1 0

(*c*) 1 0 1 1 (*d*) 0 1 0 1

1.41 Convert the following BCD numbers to XS3 form:

(*a*) 0 0 0 1 (*b*) 0 1 1 0 (*c*) 0 0 1 1

1.42 Convert the following XS3 numbers to decimal form:

(*a*) 0 1 1 1 (*b*) 1 0 0 0

(*c*) 0 1 0 0 (*d*) 0 1 0 1

1.43 Convert the following decimal numbers into XS3 form:

(*a*) 45 (*b*) 63 (*c*) 55 (*d*) 48

1.44 Convert the following decimal numbers into their 9's complement form:

(*a*) 25 (*b*) 63 (*c*) 37 (*d*) 41

1.45 Convert the following decimal numbers into their 10's complement form:

(*a*) 18 (*b*) 39 (*c*) 67 (*d*) 22

1.46 Perform the following subtractions in 10's complement form:

(*a*) 83 – 25 (*b*) 76 – 22 (*c*) 31 – 13 (*d*) 41 – 14

1.47 Perform the same subtractions as in Example 1.46 in 9's complement form.

1.48 Subtract 67 from 25 in 10's complement form.

1.49 Subtract 85 from 38 in 9's complement form.

1.50 Encode the following into ASCII code:

(*a*) Delete para 2 (*b*) Group separator malfunction

1.51 Decode the following message in ASCII code:

0000110 1001101 1000101 1010011
1010011 1000001 1000111 1000101

2

Logic Gates

2.1 INTRODUCTION

Let us for a moment refer to an electrical switch with which you can light up a lamp or switch it off. This switch is a two-state device and it is either in the ON position or OFF position. In digital electronics two-state operation is common since transistors operate very reliably in the switching mode, when low and high signals can be clearly identified. Therefore, transistors are a common factor in all digital devices such as gates and even more complicated devices. In this chapter we will confine our dicussion to TTL (transistor-transistor logic) gates.

As an introduction to gates let us consider the mains switch in house wiring and a lamp switch. If the power supply from the mains is shut off, switching on the mains switch will not light up the lamp. The lamp will light up only if both the mains switch and the lamp switch are switched ON. These two switches together are working as an AND gate: that is both the mains switch and the lamp switch have to be ON to enable the lamp to light up.

There are other types of gates also which you will study later in this chapter. Gates are referred to as logic gates. In engineering terms the term 'logic' applies to AND, OR, NAND and NOR logic functions, although the term 'logic' refers to a much wider concept, meaning the science of correct reasoning, valid induction or deduction. Logic circuits, which employ logic gates, are used to perform mathematical operations, such as addition, subtraction, multiplication and division. Logic gates produce a HIGH or LOW (also referred to as TRUE or FALSE) condition at the output which is dependend on the condition of the inputs.

2.2 LOGIC CIRCUITS

Logic circuits fall into two main categories:

1. Decision-making logic circuits and
2. Logic circuits with memory.

In the first category come the gates, basically AND gates, OR gates and Inverters. Gates have two or more inputs and a single output. They accept binary inputs and, after processing the inputs, produce a binary output, which depends on the function it is intended for, and the information supplied at the inputs. Gates are therefore called decision-making logic circuits.

More complex decision-making logic circuits use a large number of gates and are called combinational circuits. Combinational logic circuits may have two or more inputs and one or more outputs. These combinational logic circuits still perform their basic decision-making function and in fact, it is difficult to imagine how complex operations, such as arithmetic operations, encoding, decoding, etc., could be performed without them.

Yet another type of logic circuit is one which has a memory. At the heart of a circuit with memory is a bistable flip-flop. As this circuit has two stable states, which may be designated as binary 0 and binary 1 states, it coluld be considered as a memory storage device. Each flip-flop can store a single binary bit. If many flip-flops are combined to form a memory bank, many binary bits of information can be stored in them.

As a next step, linking of memory storage units with combinational circuits, a more sophisticated memory storage system, called a sequential circuit, is formed. Shift-registers, counters, etc. are some common examples of sequential circuits. In this and in some of the following chapters we will be looking at these aspects of digital systems.

You must have seen electronic circuits, the circuit diagrams of which show transistors, resistors, capacitors, etc., to achieve the desired functional capability. Digital circuits, on the other hand, utilize symbols only. In digital systems it is more important to understand how a certain function is performed by a combination of digital gates and not how that functional capability is achieved by electronic circuitry. Digial systems represent a class of systems where it is more important to understand circuit organization than an understanding of circuit design. A typical diagram of a digital system will only have labelled gates (AND, OR, etc.) and flip-flops, etc. So you should concentrate on understanding how a certain function is performed and less attention need be given to circuit operation. By a combination of gates, flip-flops, schmitt triggers, etc., a system can be designed. It is not necessary to learn the electronic circuitry of the various black boxes which go into a system.

2.2.1 Logic Symbols

In order to be able to simplify, and lead to an intelligent understanding of digital systems, symbols have been devised to represent a circuit performing a specific function these are called logic symbols or diagrams. There are many kinds of symbols depending on the function they perform. In the absence of such symbols it would have been very confusing if the circuit details of every system had to be analyzed to understand the function they perform. Some of the symbols in common use are given in Table 2.1.

2.2.2 Logic Conventions

In addition to logic symbols there are some logic conventions which are observed in logic diagrams, which help to simplify logic diagrams and make it easier to follow logic systems. We will now deal with some of the commonly used conventions.

Logic polarity: It has been the usual practice to define the logic 1 signal as the more positive of the two logic signals; and the logic 0 signal as the more negative of the two signals. However, sometimes it is more convenient to define the more negative of the two logic signals as the logic 1 signal. The former is known as positive logic and the latter as negative logic. There may be some mixed systems which use both positive and negative logic. We will now see what this implies.

Positive logic: By and large most of the systems use positive logic. This implies that 0 V, represents binary 0 and +5 V represents binary 1 level. In practice, however, since it is difficult to achieve these voltages precisely, circuits are so designed that voltages less than 0.8 V (that is 0 – 0.8) are considered to be low (binary 0) and voltages exceeding +2.5 V are taken as HIGH (binary 1). The range from 0.8 to 2.5 V provides noise rejection.

Table 2.1

	Device	Abbreviation	Symbol
1.	Inverter		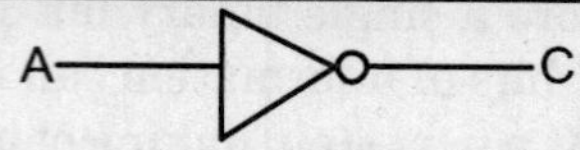
2.	Buffer		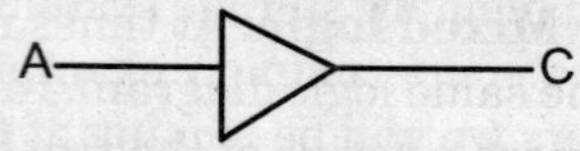
3.	AND Gate	AND	
4.	NAND Gate	NAND	
5.	OR Gate	OR	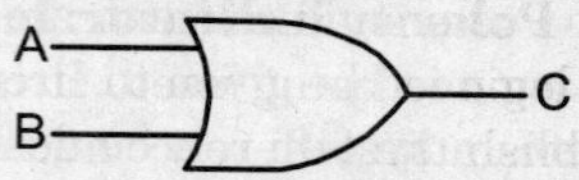
6.	NOR Gate (Not OR Gate)	NOR	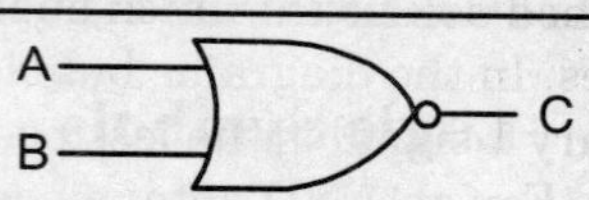
7.	Exclusive-OR Gate	XOR	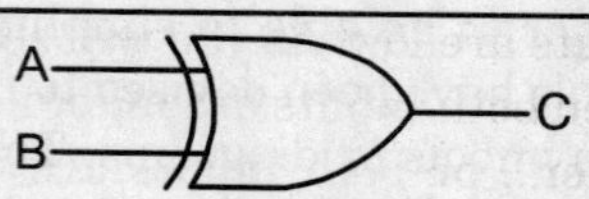
8.	Exclusive-NOR Gate	XNOR	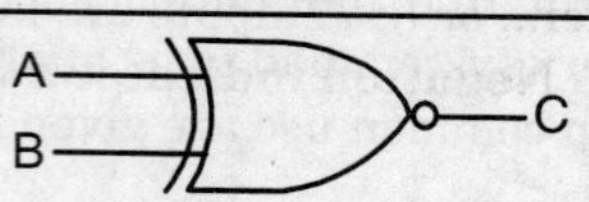

In any electrical system we have two voltage levels, one of which is more positive than the other, or you can say that one is more negative than the other. For instance, in a battery there is a positive and a negative terminal. The positive terminal is more positive than the negative terminal and the negative terminal is more negative than the positive terminal. If we assign the binary 1 state to the more positive of the two voltage levels, we conclude that positive logic is being used. Consider the following examples of positive logic (Table 2.2):

Table 2.2

Logic state	Voltage levels		
1	+ 5	+ 3.5	0
0	0	+ 0.4	– 5

Negative logic: If we assign the binary 1 state to the more negative of the two voltage levels we have a system which is using negative logic. The following are examples of negative logic (Table 2.3):

Table 2.3

Logic state	*Voltage levels*		
1	0	+ 0.4	– 5
0	+ 5	+ 3.5	0

Mixed logic: At times it is necessary to use both positive and negative logic assignments on the same logic diagram. In these diagrams, where positive logic is used, the binary 1 signal is the more positive of the two logic signals. Where negative logic assignment is used, the binary 1 signal is taken to be less positive of the logic signals.

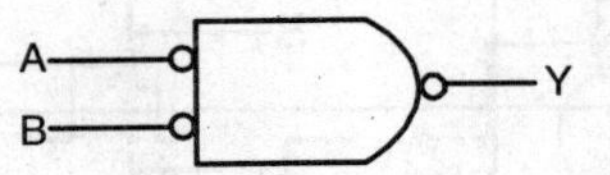

Fig. 2.1 (a) Symbol for AND gate used in negative logic

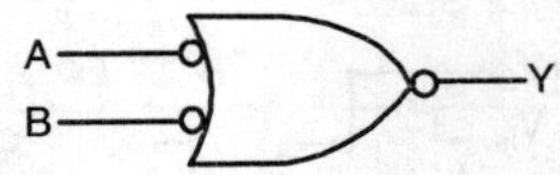

Fig. 2.1 (b) Symbol for OR gate used in negative logic

Polarity indicator: In diagrams using mixed logic, it is necessary to indicate when negative logic is being used. It is, therefore, necessary to use an indicator symbol which should establish the difference and simplify identification of positive and negative logic systems. The method used is the use of bubbles at the input and output lines as shown in Fig. 2.1 for AND, OR gates. In the diagrams bubbles at the input and output lines are indicative of the fact that the binary 1 signal is the less positive of the two signal voltages.

For an AND gate, when negative logic is being used, the output is low only when both inputs are low. As you will see later, the output of an AND gate with positive logic, is high only when both inputs are high. For an OR gate, when negative logic is used, the output is low when either... or both inputs are low. With positive logic the output of an OR gate is high when either... or both inputs are high.

Negation indicator symbol: Let us consider the symbols for an Inverter given in Fig. 2.2.

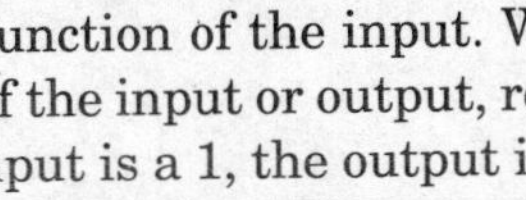

(a)

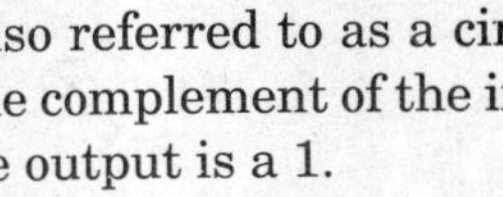

(b)

Fig. 2.2

You will notice that in Fig. 2.2 (a) there is a small bubble at the junction of the output. Sometimes the alternative symbol given in Fig. 2.2 (b) is also used. In the latter case the bubble is at the junction of the input. Whenever you see a bubble, also referred to as a circle, at the junction of the input or output, remember that the output is the complement of the input. That is if the input is a 1, the output is a 0; or if the input is a 0, the output is a 1.

Let us take the AND gate, the symbol for which is given in Fig. 2.3 (a). If we put a circle at the junction of the output it becomes a NAND gate (that is not AND). In other words, the output is negated as in Fig. 2.3(b).

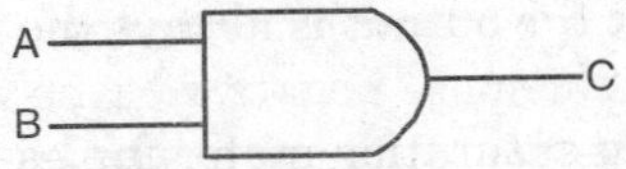

(a) AND gate

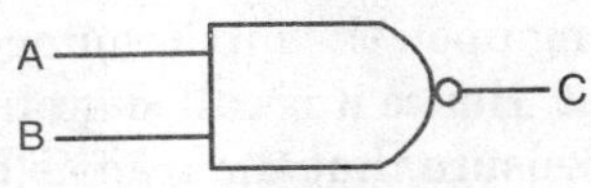

(b) NAND gate

Fig. 2.3

2.3 TRANSISTOR SWITCH

Transistors can work very efficiently as switches for switching on and switching off electrical currents in a device, which function they can perfom at very high speeds. Even though modern digital equipment is implemented with integrated circuits, it is at times quite necessary to use discrete components for special applications, such as logic level inversion, driving relays, etc. We will therefore devote some time to study the functioning of a transistor switch. Consider the circuit given in Fig. 2.4.

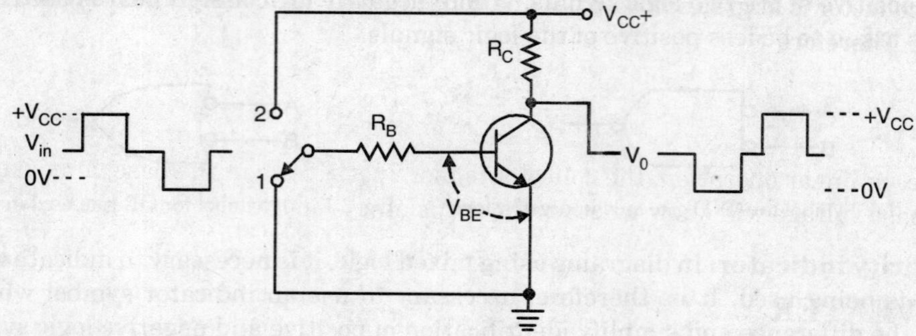

Fig. 2.4

The diagrams shows a transistor with a base resistor R_B and collector resistor R_C. If the free end of R_B is connected to terminal 1, which is at earth potential, it will make the input voltage V_{in} zero. The transistor will not conduct as there is no base bias. There will be a small collector leakage current, but it will be negligible. As the transistor is now cut off, the output voltage V_0 will be equal to V_{CC}, or it may be just a bit less than V_{CC}. That is when the input is LOW the output is HIGH. If you refer to the input and output waveforms, you will notice that when the input voltage is low the output voltage is high.

Let us now consider what happens to the output voltage when the free end of R_B is connected to terminal 2, which is connected to V_{CC}. The emitter-base junction becomes forward biased and collector current begins to flow. The voltage drop across R_C depends on the collector current, which in turn depends on the input voltage to the base, V_{in}. If V_{in} is small the transistor will be in the linear region of operation. If, on the other hand, V_{in} is large the transistor will operate in the saturation region with large collector current. The values of I_B, I_C and V_{out} will be as follows:

$$I_B = \frac{V_{in} - V_{BE}}{R_B} \approx \frac{V_{in}}{R_B}$$

$$I_C = I_B \times \beta_{dc}$$

$$V_{out} = V_{cc} - R_c I_c = V_{CE} \text{ sat.}$$

V_{CE} sat. will now drop to a few tenths of a volt. Thus when the input voltage is HIGH, the output voltage will be LOW. The transistor is thus either completely cut off or is hard saturated depending upon the input voltage, V_{in}. You will notice that the output is always the inverse of the input. Hence it is called an Inverter.

To ensure that the transistor is operating in the hard saturation state, the base current should be adjusted to saturate the transistor, so that the changes in temperature or variations in β_{dc} do not affect its performance. As voltage inverters find considerable application in digital circuits, we will consider the conditions under which a transistor can work satisfactorily as an Inverter. We know that

$$I_B = \frac{I_c}{\beta_{dc}}$$

Therefore if I_B is larger than I_c/β_{dc} the transistor will go into saturation. When this condition is satisfied V_{ce} will drop to a few tenths of a volt and the collector-base junction will become forward-biased. Since the base-emitter junction is already forward-biased, the base will be more positive than the collector. For practical purposes it may be assumed that in the saturation mode the collector is at ground potential and consequently the collector current is a function of V_{cc} and R_c. Therefore

$$I_c = \frac{V_{cc}}{R_c}$$

Since, in linear operation, the collector is more positive than the base, a measurement of collector-base voltage will show whether the transistor is operating in the linear or saturation mode.

2.4 INVERTER

In the previous section you have seen how a transistor functions as an Inverter. The Inverter is in fact a gate which has only one input and one output. The following are some of the important points to be noted about an Inverter:

1. A LOW input produces a HIGH output and a HIGH input produces a LOW output. This has been summarized in the following truth table (Table 2.4):

Table 2.4 Truth table for an inverter

Input	*Output*
V_{in}	V_0
Low	*High*
High	*Low*

or

Input	*Output*
A	$\overline{A}$
0	1
1	0

2. All gates are digital or two-state devices, since the input and output are either LOW or HIGH.
3. Also note that for an Inverter the output is always the complement of the input.
4. If the input to the Inverter is labelled A, the output is labelled $\overline{A}$ (called NOT A or A NOT). The bar over A indicates the complementary nature of the output. Since 0 and 1 are the only two possible values, it follows that "NOT 0" (written $\overline{0}$) must be 1 and "NOT 1" (written $\overline{1}$) must be 0.
5. **Truth table:** Table 2.4 shows the output which results from all possible combinations of input levels. For an Inverter there are only two input combinations binary 0 and binary 1. Input/output relationships for a given logic system are summarized in a truth table. The truth table gives in a tabular form the output levels derived from the various possible combinations of input levels.

HEX Inverter: I.C. 7404

Figure 2.5 shows the top view of IC 7404, which has six identical and independent Inverters. Note how the pins are numbered. The location of pin 1 is near the notch or dot. Pin numbering of all ICs follows the same sequence.

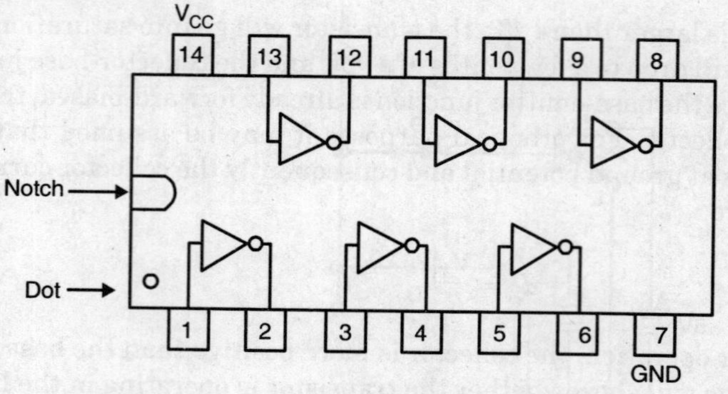

Fig. 2.5 Top View of IC 7404 : Hex inverter

2.5 BUFFER

If two Inverters are cascaded as shown in Fig. 2.6 (a) the circuit will behave as a non-inverting amplifier. In other words for a binary 1 input the output will also be binary 1 and for a binary 0 input the output will also be binary 0. An even number of Inverters in tandem act as a non-inverter (Buffer) and an odd number in tandem will invert the input signal. Buffers can also be implemented with AND gates as shown in Fig. 2.6 (b). The symbol for a Buffer is given in Fig. 2.6 (c).

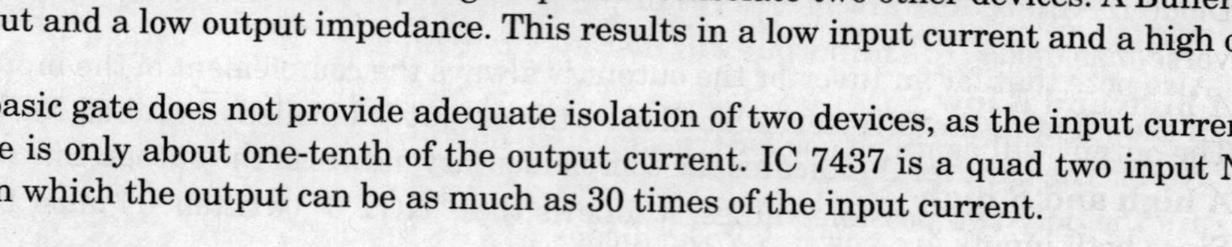

Fig. 2.6 Buffers

Buffers are used as non-inverting amplifiers to isolate two other devices. A Buffer has a high input and a low output impedance. This results in a low input current and a high output current.

A basic gate does not provide adequate isolation of two devices, as the input current of a TTL gate is only about one-tenth of the output current. IC 7437 is a quad two input NAND Buffer, in which the output can be as much as 30 times of the input current.

2.6 AND GATE

A brief reference was made to an AND gate in Section 2.1 when it was stated that unless the mains switch and the lamp switch are both ON the lamp will not light up. These two switches functioned as a 2-input AND gate. The AND gate is a logic circuit which can have two or more inputs, but there is only one output. The output of an AND gate is HIGH only if both inputs are HIGH. If either or all inputs are LOW the output will be LOW.

We will deal with a simple 2-input AND gate using diodes to verify the above statement. The circuit for a 2-input diode AND gate is given in Fig. 2.7.

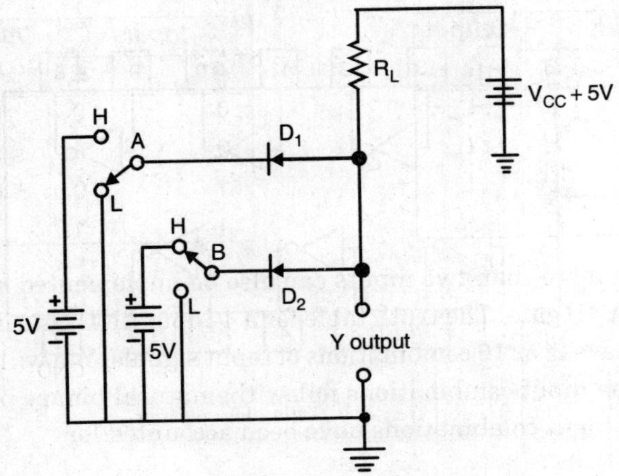

Fig. 2.7 Two input diode AND gate

The AND gate consists of two diodes to which input is applied at *A* and *B* and the output is *Y*. There is a load resistor R_L which is connected to a power supply of + 5V. Low and High inputs can be applied to the two diodes with the switching arrangement shown in the diagram. We will assume positive logic to analyze this circuit, so that 0 V input will be considered to be a Low input.

Since there are two inputs A and B, the total number of input combinations will be 2^2 or 4. With *n* inputs the total number of input combinations will be 2^n. We will now look at the output obtainable from each of the four input combinations.

1. ***A* low and *B* low**

   Both the diodes will conduct and, assuming a voltage drop 0.7 V across the diodes, the output voltage *Y* will be 0.7 V which can be considered low.

2. ***A* low and *B* high**

   Diode D_1 will be forward-biased resulting in low output at *Y*. The low output will reverse-bias diode D_2. The output will therefore remain low.

3. ***A* high and *B* low**

   The output will again be low for the same reason as in case 2.

4. ***A* high and *B* high**

   Since both inputs are now + 5 V the diodes will not conduct, there will be no current through R_L and the output will therefore be high and the same as the supply voltage.

Truth Table 2.5 summarizes the output available from a 2-input AND gate under all the four combinations of inputs. Table 2.6 is the binary representation of the same truth table.

Table 2.5 2-input AND gate

Inputs		*Output*
A	*B*	*Y*
L	*L*	*L*
L	*H*	*L*
H	*L*	*L*
H	*H*	*H*

Table 2.6 2-input AND gate (Binary form)

Inputs		*Output*
A	*B*	*Y*
0	0	0
0	1	0
1	0	0
1	1	1

An AND gate with more than two inputs can also be implemented by using diodes in the same way as a 2-input AND gate. The truth table for a 4-input AND gate is given in Table 2.7. A 4-input AND gate will have 2^4 or 16 combinations of input signals. You will notice from the truth table (Table 2.7) that the input combinations follow the natural binary progression. This is to ensure that all possible input combinations have been accounted for.

Table 2.7 Truth Table for 4-input AND gate

Inputs				*Output*
A	*B*	*C*	*D*	*Y*
0	0	0	0	0
0	0	0	1	0
0	0	1	0	0
0	0	1	1	0
0	1	0	0	0
0	1	0	1	0
0	1	1	0	0
0	1	1	1	0
1	0	0	0	0
1	0	0	1	0
1	0	1	0	0
1	0	1	1	0
1	1	0	0	0
1	1	0	1	0
1	1	1	0	0
1	1	1	1	1

You will notice from truth tables for AND gates that unless the input is 1 at all the inputs of an AND gate there will be no output. The output will be 1 only when all the inputs are 1.

AND gates may have two or more inputs. Symbols for AND gates with two and more inputs are shown in Fig. 2.8. When the number of inputs is large it is the usual practice to extent the input line to accommodate all the inputs.

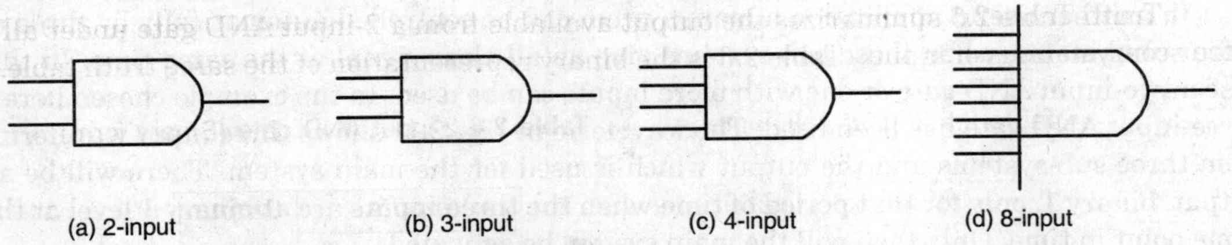

Fig. 2.8 AND gate symbols

When you come to the chapter on Boolean algebra you will acquire familiarity with symbols used in Boolean algebra. For the present it will suffice to mention that the output of an AND gate function in equation form can be written as:

$$\text{Output } = A \cdot B$$

A dot $(\cdot)$ or times sign $(\times)$ indicates a logical product or conjunction of two terms so connected. The operation is also frequently indicated without any symbol at all. Thus

$$\text{Output } = A \times B = A \cdot B = AB$$

These symbols are referred to as the AND operation and the terms so connected are said to be ANDed. This should not be confused with the algebraic expression $(\times)$ which denotes an algebraic product. Thus, A is not multiplied by B. They are ANDed.

2.6.1 Applications of AND Gates

The AND gate is an ideal control device as you will see from the following examples. Refer to the circuit diagram in Fig. 2.9, which shows an input signal at A and a control signal at B. The waveform of the input signal at A is as shown in Fig. 2.10 and the control signal is applied for a brief interval shown in the diagram. The output will then reproduce the input signal only for that period of time. Thus a control signal can allow the input signal to pass through to the output according to the requirements of the system being controlled by the output.

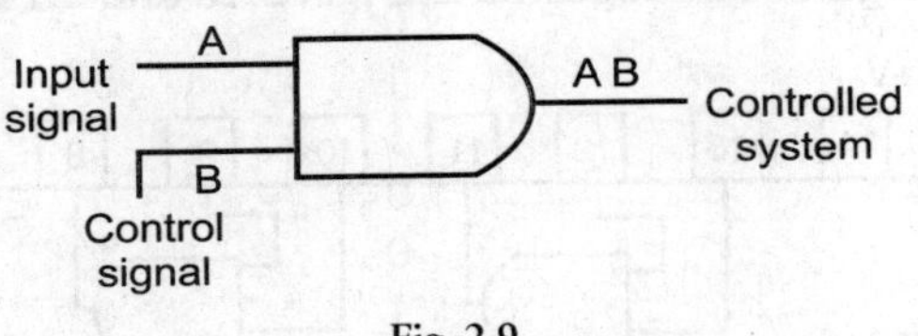

Fig. 2.9

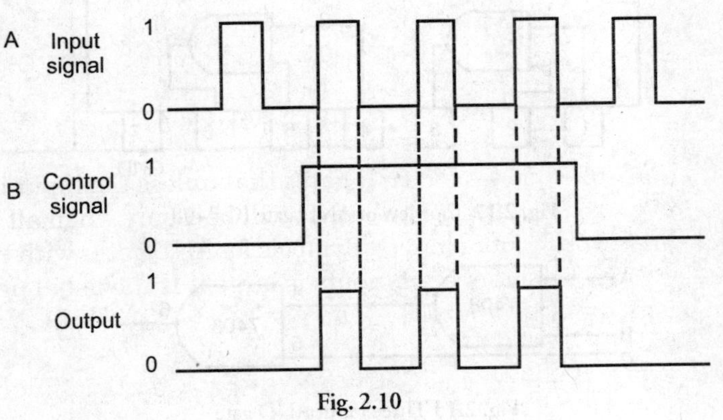

Fig. 2.10

In another useful application a main system can be controlled automatically by three or more sub-systems, when these sub-systems give an all-clear signal at the same time. In this case a two-input AND gate or one with more inputs can be used. In the example chosen here a three-input AND gate has been used. The waveform in Fig. 2.11 shows three input waveforms from three sub-systems and the output which is used for the main system. There will be an output, binary 1, only for that period of time when the three inputs are at binary 1 level at the same point in time. Only then will the main system be activated.

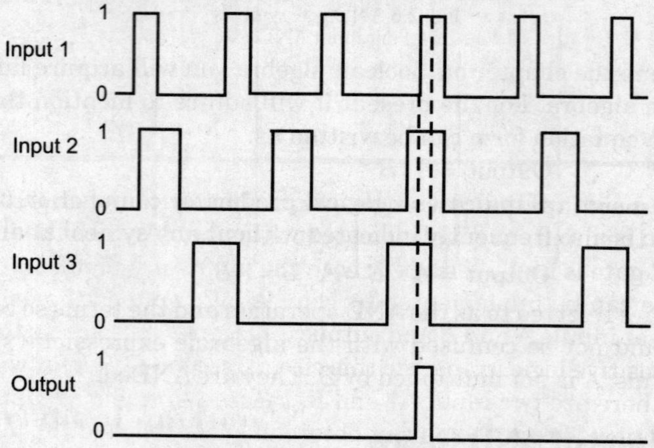

Fig. 2.11

T T L AND Gate : IC 7408

This IC contains four 2-input AND gates. A pinout diagram for this IC is given in Fig. 2.12. Pin 14 of the IC is required to be connected to +5 V and pin 7 to ground. TTL ICs containing 3-input and 4-input AND gates are also available. However, you can also implement 3-input and 4-input AND gates by using 2-input AND gates as suggested in Figs. 2.13 and 2.14.

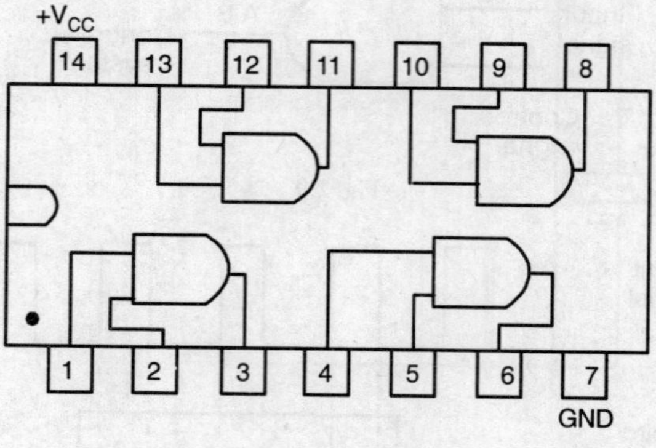

Fig. 2.12 Top view of AND gate IC 7408

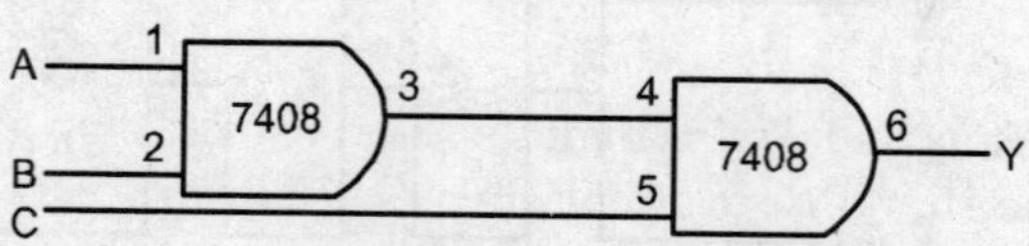

Fig. 2.13 Three input AND gate

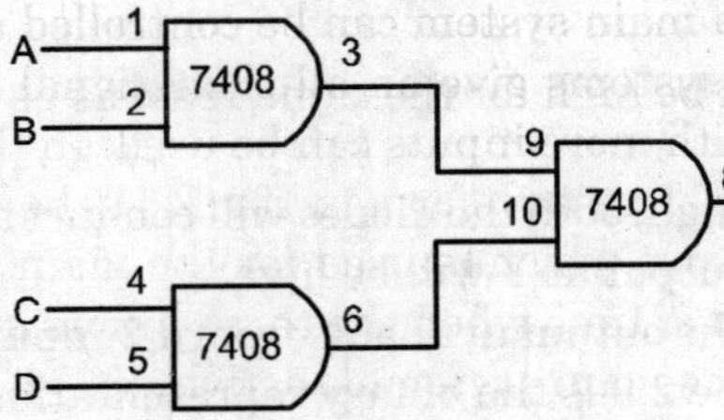

Fig. 2.14 Four input AND gate

2.7 OR GATE

An OR gate has two or more inputs and a single output. The output of an OR gate is high if any one of the inputs or all the inputs are high. The output is low only if all the inputs are low. The output of a 2-input OR gate is high if either or both the inputs are high.

A simple OR gate can be implemented by connecting two diodes as shown in Fig. 2.15. Input signal is applied at inputs *A* and *B* and output is obtained at *Y* across the load resistor R_L.

We will assume positive logic to analyze this circuit, so that 0 V input will be considered to be a low input. Since there are two inputs *A* and *B*, the total number of input signal combinations will be 4. We will now look at the output obtainable from each of the four input combinations.

1. *A low and B low*

   Since neither D_1 nor D_2 will conduct when inputs to these diodes are low, output *Y* will also be low.

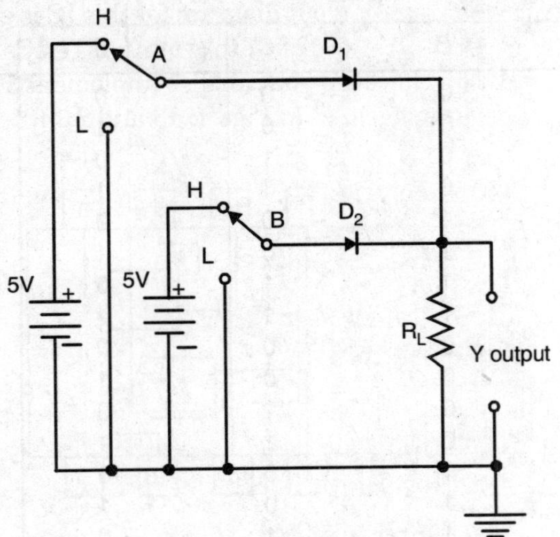

Fig. 2.15 Two input diode OR gate

2. *A low and B high*

   Diode D_2 will conduct as its input is high and this will develop a high voltage across the load R_L which will be +5 V if we overlook the voltage drop across the diode, or 4.3 V if we take into account the diode voltage drop. In either case diode D_1 will be reverse-biased. Therefore the output at *Y* will be high.

3. *A high and B low*
   The output at *Y* will again be high for the same reasons as in case 2.
4. *A high and B high*
   With both *A* and *B* inputs high, both the diodes will conduct as both of them are forward-biased and therefore the output at *Y* will be high.

Truth Table 2.8 summarizes the output available from a 2-input OR gate under all the four combinations of input signals. Table 2.9 is the binary representation of the same truth table.

Table 2.8 2-Input OR gate

Inputs		*Output*
A	*B*	*Y*
L	*L*	*L*
L	*H*	*H*
H	*L*	*H*
H	*H*	*H*

L – Low ; H – High

Table 2.9 2-input OR gate (Binary form)

Inputs		*Output*
A	*B*	*Y*
0	0	0
0	1	1
1	0	1
1	1	1

An OR gate with more than two inputs can also be implemented by using diodes in the same way as in a 2-input OR gate. The truth table for a 4-input OR gate is given in Table 2.10. With four inputs, 16 combinations of input signals will be possible as the truth table shows.

Table 2.10 Truth table for 4-input OR gate

Inputs				*Output*
A	*B*	*C*	*D*	*Y*
0	0	0	0	0
0	0	0	1	1
0	0	1	0	1
0	0	1	1	1
0	1	0	0	1
0	1	0	1	1
0	1	1	0	1
0	1	1	1	1
1	0	0	0	1
1	0	0	1	1
1	0	1	0	1
1	0	1	1	1
1	1	0	0	1
1	1	0	1	1
1	1	1	0	1
1	1	1	1	1

You must have noticed from the truth tables for OR gates that output is low only in one case and this happens when all the inputs are low. In all other cases at least one of the inputs is high and in all these cases the output is high.

OR gates, like AND gates, may have two or more inputs. Symbols for OR gates with two and more inputs are given in Fig. 2.16.

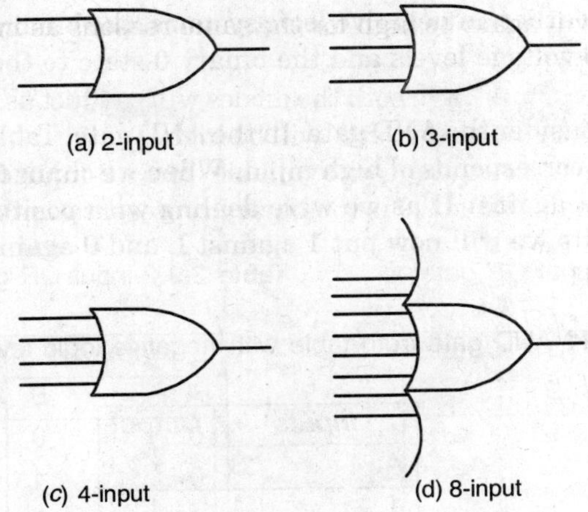

Fig, 2.16 OR gate symbols

The output of an OR gate is a function of A OR B. In equation form it is written as:

$$\text{Output} = A + B$$

The + sign is an indication, in logic terms, that the logical sum operation (called disjunction of terms so connected) has taken place. In engineering language we refer to it as the Inclusive-OR operation and the terms so connected are said to be ORed. You must remember that the symbol + here is not the same as the algebraic symbol for addition. The symbol AND and OR are some of the basic tools of logic and must be distinguished from algebraic symbols.

OR Gate IC 7432

There are four 2-input OR gates in this IC. Pin 14 of the IC should be connected to +5 V and pin 7 to ground. A pinout diagram of this IC is given in Fig. 2.17.

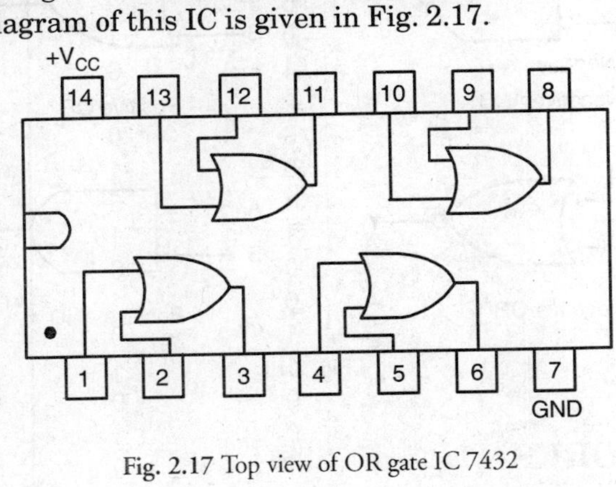

Fig. 2.17 Top view of OR gate IC 7432

2.8 DUAL CHARACTER OF LOGIC GATES

So far we have considered positive logic level assignments in evaluating the performance of AND and OR gates. We will now study the operation of these gates will negative logic level assignments.

As has been stated earlier, in negative logic systems, the binary 1 state is assigned to the more negative of the two voltage levels and the binary 0 state to the more positive of the two voltage levels.

We will first of all consider the AND gate. In the AND gate, Table 2.5, input L corresponds to low input and input H corresponds of high input. When we changed the table to binary form we put 0 against L and 1 against H as we were dealing with positive logic assignments. For negative logic assignments we will now put 1 against L and 0 against H. The resultant truth table is given in Table 2.11.

Table 2.11 AND gate truth table with negative logic level assignments

Inputs		*Output*
A	*B*	*Y*
1	1	1
1	0	1
0	1	1
0	0	0

If you compare this table with Table 2.9 for an OR gate using positive logic, you will find that the two tables are identical. This leads us to the conclusion that an AND gate using negative logic shows the same performance as an OR gate with positive logic. This demonstrates the dual nature of logic gates. AND logic gates can be made to perform AND or OR function, as the functioning depends on logic level assignments. Similarly you can prove that an OR gate using negative logic will perform like an AND gate. Using symbols we can say as follows (Fig. 2.18):

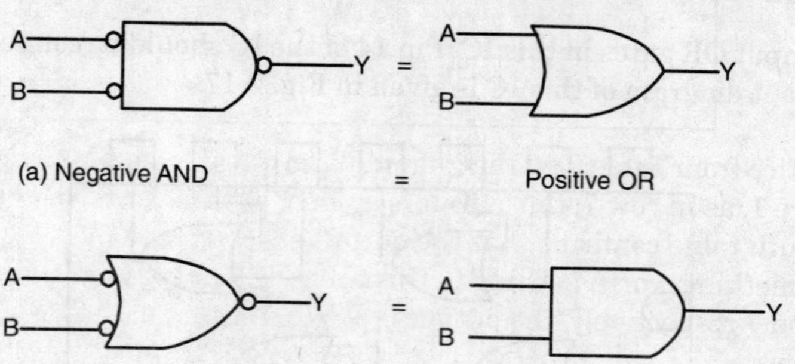

Fig. 2.18

2.9 GATE NETWORKS

The AND, OR gates and Inverters which we have discussed so far, as well as other gates which we will consider a little later, can be combined to form combinational logic circuits, which can be used to solve many logic problems. For the present we will confine our attention to logic networks using AND, OR gates and Inverters. A circuit using AND, OR gates, which occurs in many forms in logic networks, is called the AND-OR logic network and it takes the form shown in Fig. 2.19.

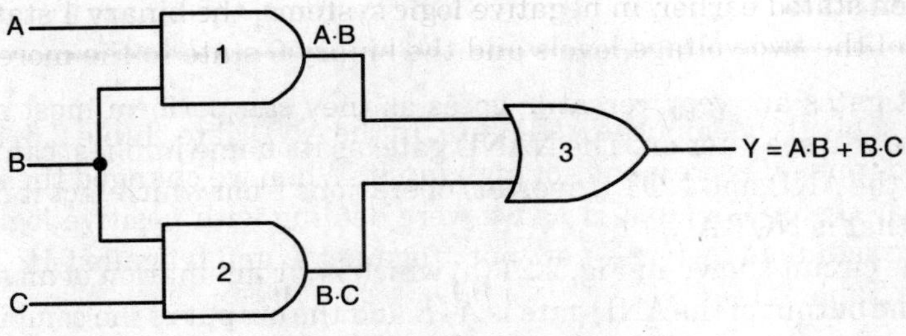

Fig. 2.19 AND-OR logic network

Since gates 1 and 2 are AND gates, their outputs will be $A \cdot B$ and $B \cdot C$ respectively. As gate 3 is an OR gate, its output will be $A \cdot B + B \cdot C$. The truth table for this network is given in Table 2.12. We will now consider this truth table to see whether it agrees with the expression for the output $Y = A \cdot B + B \cdot C$.

Table 2.12 Truth table for AND-OR network

Inputs			*Output*
A	***B***	***C***	***Y***
0	0	0	0
0	0	1	0
0	1	0	0
0	1	1	1
1	0	0	0
1	0	1	0
1	1	0	1
1	1	1	1

You will notice from Table 2.12 that when B and C are 1, as in row 4, the output is 1. Again when A and B are 1, as in row 7, the output is again 1. The last row restates the same position. Therefore the truth table confirms that the output expression $Y = A \cdot B + B \cdot C$ is correct.

There is something worth nothing in this table. If B is 1, as in row 4 and 7, and C or A are 1 as in rows 4 and 7 respectively, the output is 1. We can translate this observation into a logic equation as follows.

$$Y = B\,(A + C)$$

This point to the conclusion that the logic network of Fig. 2.20 will perform the same function as the AND-OR logic network of Fig. 2.19. As you will see later, logic networks can be reduced to simpler forms by using the laws of Boolean algebra and Kamaugh map techniques.

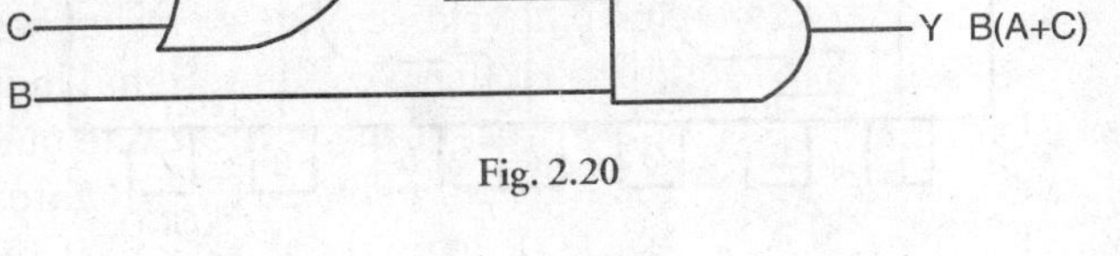

Fig. 2.20

2.10 NAND GATE

NAND and NOR gates are very versatile gates as they can perform most of the functions of other gates, as we will see later on. The NAND gate, as its name implies, can be looked upon as a combination of the AND and NOT (Inverter) operations from which fact it derives its classification of NAND that is NOT-AND.

Consider the circuit shown in Fig. 2.21 (a) which is a combination of an AND gate followed by an Inverter. The output of the AND gate is $A \cdot B$ and the output of the combination, that is the NAND gate, is $\overline{A \cdot B}$. Table 2.13 shows the output of the AND gate as well as the output of the NAND gate. You will notice from the table that for every combination of the input signals, the output of the NAND gate is the complement of the output of the AND gate.

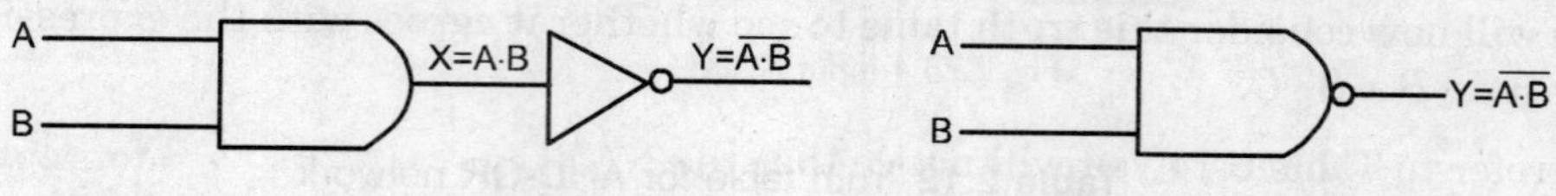

(a) Logic diagram of NAND function (b) Logic symbol for NAND gate

Fig. 2.21

Table 2.13

Input		*Output*	
A	*B*	*AND* $X = A \cdot B$	*NAND* $Y = \overline{A \cdot B}$
0	0	0	1
0	1	0	1
1	0	0	1
1	1	1	0

NAND Gate IC 7400

This IC contains four 2-input NAND gates. Pin connections for this IC are given in Fig. 2.22.

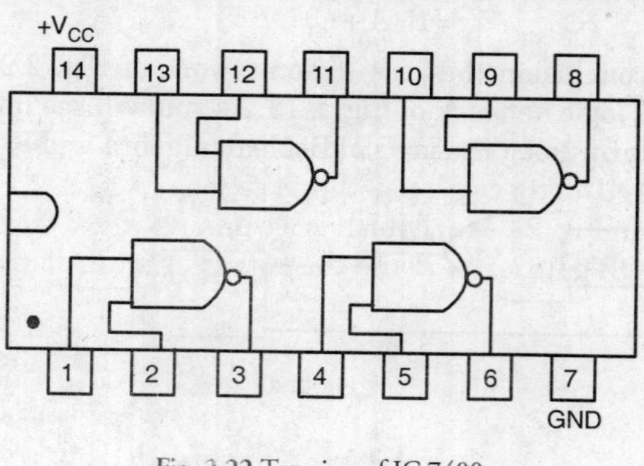

Fig. 2.22 Top view of IC 7400

A 3- input NAND gate is available as IC 7410 and a 4-input NAND gate as IC 7420. A 4-input NAND gate can also be assembled as shown in Fig. 2.23.

Table 2.14 gives the truth table for a 3-input NAND gate. You will notice from this table that when all the inputs are 1, the output is 0. This is quite the opposite of what happens with an AND gate. The NAND gate recognizes only those inputs in which at least one of the inputs is 0.

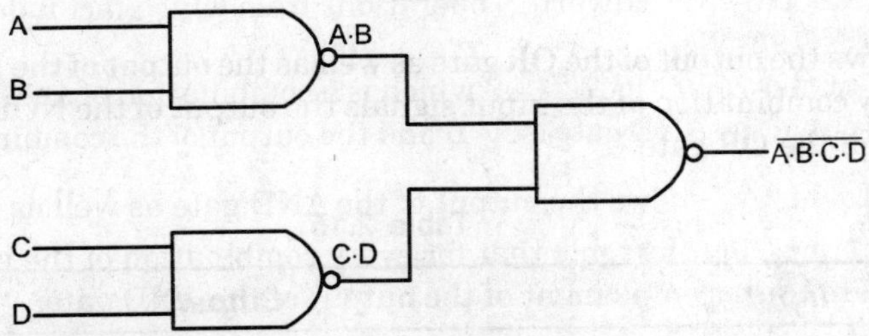

Fig. 2.23 4-input NAND gate

If you refer to Table 6.14 you will notice that the NAND gate can be used to implement Inverters, AND, OR, and negated-OR gates. NAND gates can also be used to implement XOR and XNOR gates. It is for this reason that the NAND gate is widely used in designing logic circuits. In a later chapter, we will consider how AND/OR logic can be converted to NAND/NOR logic.

Table 2.14 Truth table for a 3–Input NAND gate

Inputs			*Output*
A	*B*	*C*	$\overline{ABC}$
0	0	0	1
0	0	1	1
0	1	0	1
0	1	1	1
1	0	0	1
1	0	1	1
1	1	0	1
1	1	1	0

2.11 NOR GATE

NOR is a short form of the term Not-OR. A NOR gate combines the functions of an OR gate and an Inverter; just as the NAND gate combines the functions of an AND gate and an Inverter. Consider the circuit shown in Fig. 2.24 (a), which is a combination of an OR gate followed by an Inverter. The output of the OR gate is $A + B$ and the output of the combination, that is the NOR gate, is $\overline{A + B}$.

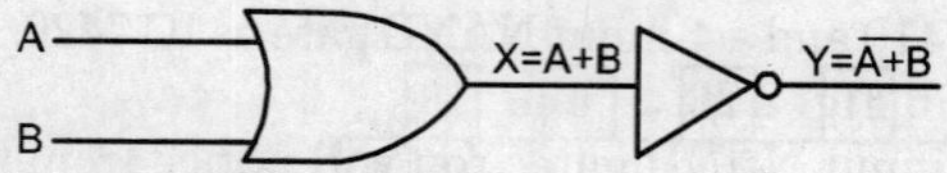

(a) Logic diagram of NOR function

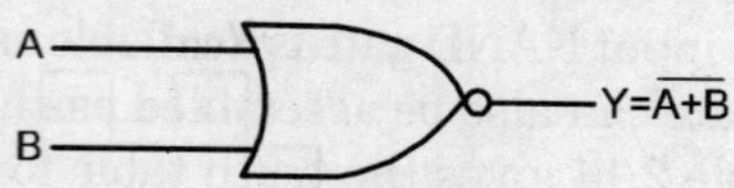

(b) Logic symbol for NOR gate

Fig. 2.24

Table 2.15 shows the output of the OR gate as well as the output of the NOR gate. The table shows that for every combination of the input signals the output of the NOR gate is the complement of the output of the OR gate.

Table 2.15

Input		*Output*	
A	*B*	*OR* $X = A + B$	*NAND* $Y = \overline{A + B}$
0	0	0	1
0	1	1	0
1	0	1	0
1	1	1	0

Let us consider the truth table (Table 2.16) for a 3-input NOR gate.

Table 2.16 Truth table for a 3-input NOR gate

Inputs			*Output*
A	*B*	*C*	$\overline{A + B + C}$
0	0	0	1
0	0	1	0
0	1	0	0
0	1	1	0
1	0	0	0
1	0	1	0
1	1	0	0
1	1	1	0

The truth table shows that the NOR gate recognizes only the input word whose bits are all 0s. It therefore follows that to get a high output all inputs must be low. If even a single input is high the output will be low.

NOR Gate IC 7402

This IC contains four 2-input NOR gates. Pin connections for this IC are given in Fig. 2.25.

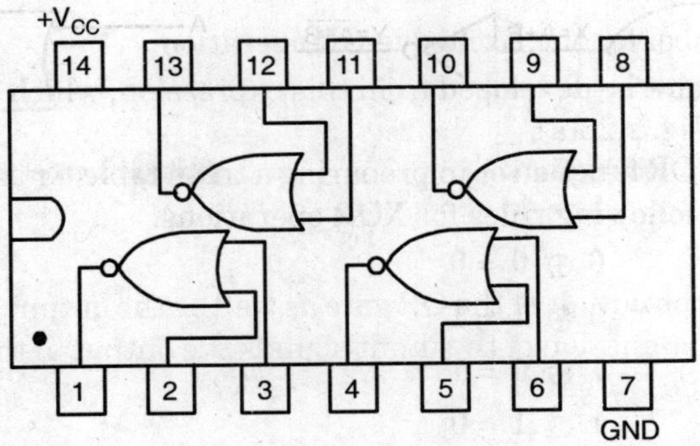

Fig. 2.25 Top view of IC 7402

2.12 EXCLUSIVE-OR (XOR) GATE

The OR gate with which you are already familiar is referred to as the Inclusive-OR gate. The Exclusive-OR gate is a special case of the general operation. In the Inclusive-OR operation either inputs A or B or both must be true (binary 1) in order that the OR function be true (binary 1).

The position is only slightly different in the Exclusive-OR (XOR) case. In the XOR operation either A or B, but not both, must be true (binary 1) for the function to be true. If both A and B are true (binary 1) at the same time the function will be false (binary 0).

Table 2.17, which is the truth table for a 2-input XOR gate, clearly shows the input-output relationship discussed above.

Table 2.17 Truth table for 2-input XOR gate

Input		*Output*
A	***B***	***Y***
0	0	0
0	1	1
1	0	1
1	1	0

If you compare this truth table with the truth table for a 2-input OR gate (Table 2.9) you will notice that the state of the output in the first three rows is the same as for an OR gate. When both the inputs are 1 as in the last row, the output of the XOR gate is 0, whereas the output of an OR gate is 1. We can, therefore conclude that the XOR gate is enabled with an odd number of 1s at the input, as in rows 2 and 3. Rows 1 and 4 of the truth table have an even number of 1s (0 and 2) which disables the XOR gate and a 0 appears at the output. The XOR gate can, therefore, be used an an odd-bits checker. From rows 2 and 3 of the truth table the following Boolean expression can be developed for the output of a 2-input XOR gate.

$$Y = \overline{A} \cdot B + \overline{B} \cdot A$$

or simply

$$Y = A \text{ XOR } B$$

or

$$Y = A \oplus B$$

Here ⊕ is the symbol for the Exclusive-OR operation.

A logic circuit can now be developed from this expression, which will function as a 2-input XOR gate, as shown in Fig. 2.26(a).

In simplifying an XOR function or in preparing a truth table for an XOR operation it will be useful to remember the following rules for XOR operations.

$$0 \oplus 0 = 0$$
$$0 \oplus 1 = 1$$
$$1 \oplus 0 = 1$$
$$1 \oplus 1 = 0$$

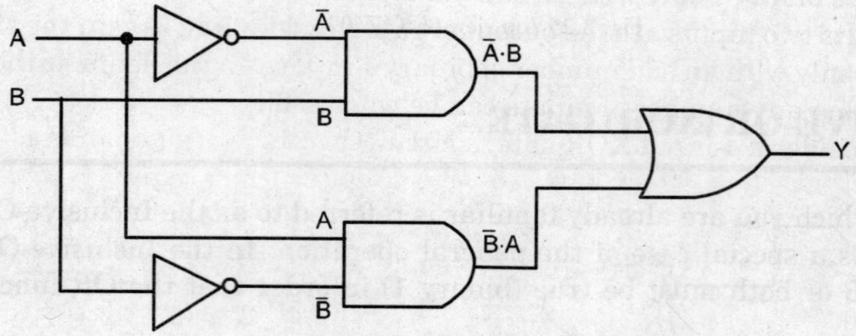

Fig. 2.26 (a) Two-input XOR gate

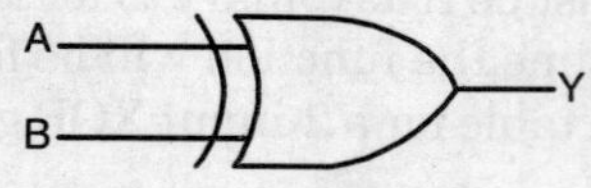

Fig. 2.26 (b) Symbol for XOR gate

We will now consider a 3-input XOR gate which can be implemented by using two XOR gates as shown in Fig. 2.27.

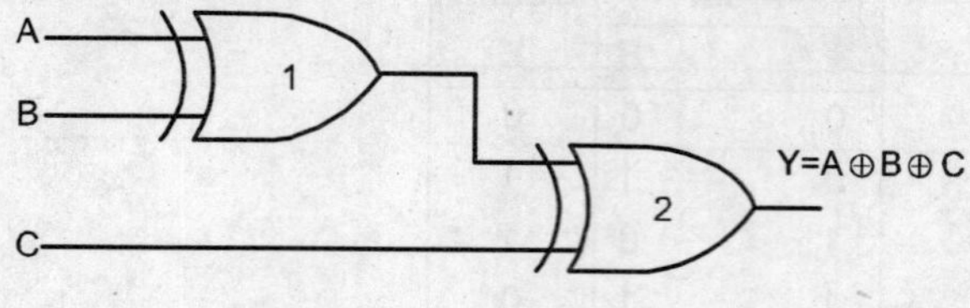

Fig. 2.27 Three-input XOR gate

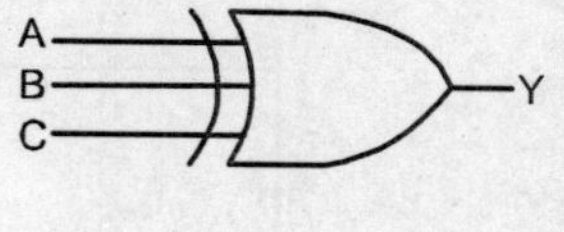

Fig. 2.28 Symbol for 3-input XOR gate

Table 2.18 gives the truth table for a 3-input XOR gate.

Table 2.18 Truth table for 3-input XOR gate

Inputs			*Output*	
A	***B***	***C***	***Y***	***Comment***
0	0	0	0	Even
0	0	1	1	Odd
0	1	0	1	Odd
0	1	1	0	Even
1	0	0	1	Odd

1	0	1	0	Even
1	1	0	0	Even
1	1	1	1	Odd

You will see from Table 2.18 that the output Y is 1 only with an odd number of binary 1 inputs. With an even number of binary 1 inputs the output is 0. The rule to remember is that an XOR gate, irrespective of the number of inputs, recognizes only those words which have an odd number of binary 1s.

The truth table has been worked out as follows. First we considered the output of gate 1 for different input combinations. The output should be the same as for a 2-input XOR gate. The output of gate 1 will be binary 1 only with an odd number of binary 1 inputs. Next we considered the output of gate 2. Its two inputs are the output of gate 1 and input C. Again the output of this gate will be binary 1 only with an odd number of binary 1 inputs. In this manner the truth table for an XOR gate having any number of inputs can be worked out.

We will now consider a 4-input XOR gate, a circuit for which is given in Fig. 2.29.

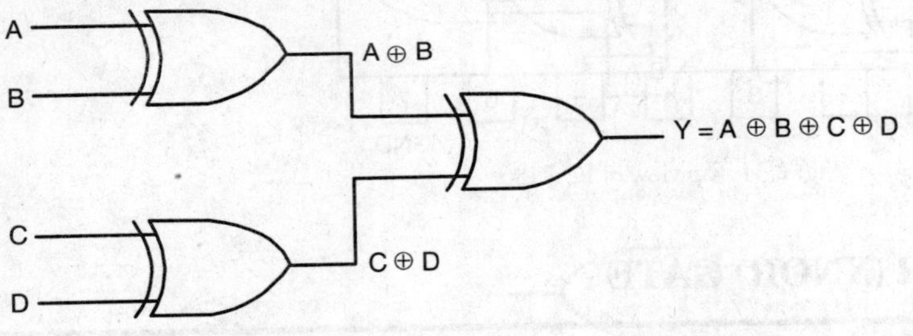

Fig. 2.29 Four-input XOR gate

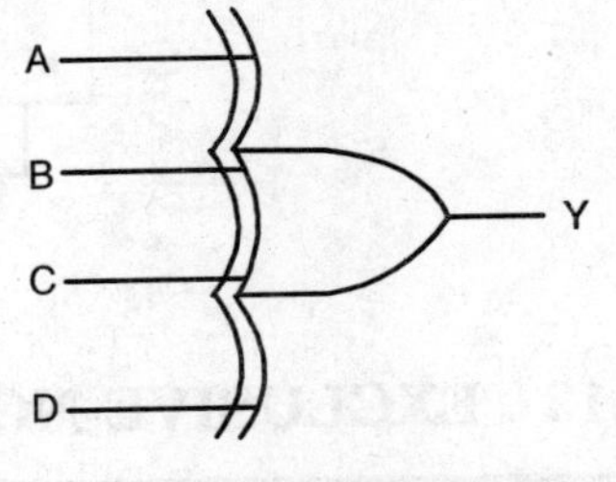

Fig. 2.30 Symbol for 4-input XOR gate

Table 2.19 gives the truth table for a 4-input XOR gate.

Table 2.19 Truth table for 4-input XOR gate

Input				*Output*
A	***B***	***C***	***D***	***Y***
0	0	0	0	0
0	0	0	1	1
0	0	1	0	1
0	0	1	1	0
0	1	0	0	1
0	1	0	1	0
0	1	1	0	0
0	1	1	1	1
1	0	0	0	1
1	0	0	1	0
1	0	1	0	0
1	0	1	1	1
1	1	0	0	0
1	1	0	1	1
1	1	1	0	1
1	1	1	1	0

A comparison of Tables 2.18 and 2.19 will show that with an even number of 1s the output is 0 and with an odd number of 1s the output is 1. This is so for all XOR gates irrespective of the number of gates used. This property of XOR gates is found very useful for data transmission as you will see a little later.

XOR Gate IC 7486

This IC contains four 2-input XOR gates. Pin connections for this IC are given in Fig. 2.31.

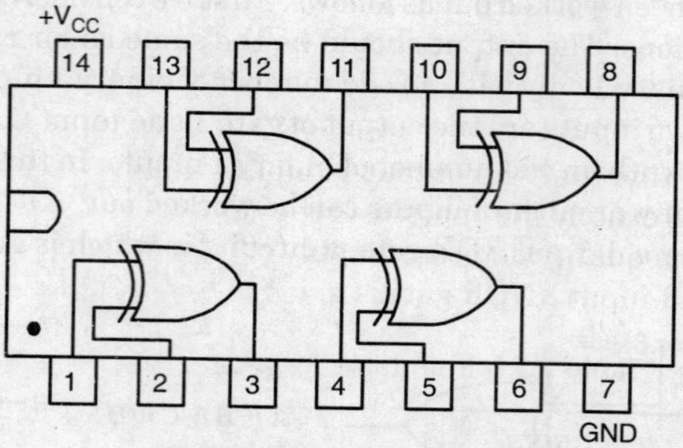

Fig. 2.31 Top view of IC 7486

2.13 EXCLUSIVE-NOR (XNOR) GATE

The Exclusive-NOR gate can be regarded as an XOR gate followed by an Inverter. In the XNOR operation either *A* and *B* should both be false (binary 0) or *A* and *B* should both be true (binary 1), in order that the XNOR function be true (binary 1). It follows, therefore that the XNOR gate functions like an XOR gate followed by an Inverter and can be implemented by the circuit shown in Fig. 2.32.

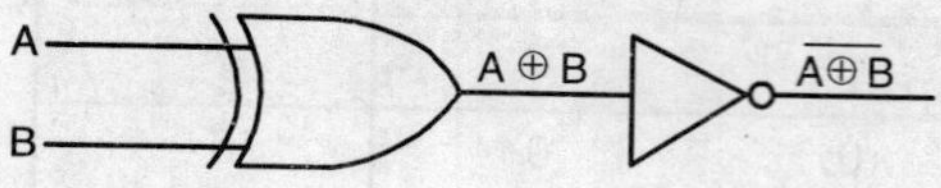

Fig. 2.32 XNOR gate

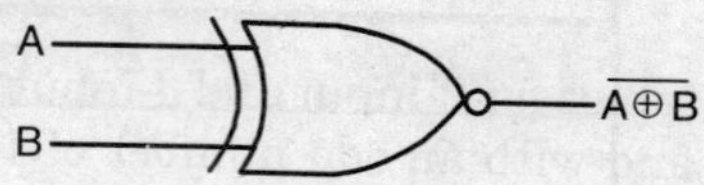

Fig. 2.33 Symbol for XNOR gate

The truth table for the XNOR gate is given in Table 2.20. If you compare it with Table 2.17, which is the truth table for the XOR gate, you will notice that the output of the XNOR gate is the complement of the output of the XOR gate.

Table 2.20 Truth table for 2-input XNOR gate

Input		*Output*
A	*B*	*Y*
0	0	1
0	1	0
1	0	0
1	1	1

A word equation for the XNOR operation can be written as follows:

$$Y = A \text{ XNOR } B$$

or as

$$Y = \overline{A \oplus B}$$

In simplifying an XNOR function or while preparing a truth table the following rules for the XNOR operation will be useful:

$$\overline{0 \oplus 0} = 1$$

$$\overline{0 \oplus 1} = 0$$

$$\overline{1 \oplus 0} = 0$$

$$\overline{1 \oplus 1} = 1$$

You will notice from this that the output is binary 1 only when both inputs are either binary 0 or binary 1. This is exactly the opposite of the rules for the XOR gate. This points to the use of an XNOR gate as an equality detector for only one bit of data.

The truth table for a 3-input XNOR gate is given in Table 2.21.

Table 2.21 Truth table for 3-input XNOR gate

Inputs			***Output***	
A	***B***	***C***	***Y***	***Comment***
0	0	0	1	Even
0	0	1	0	Odd
0	1	0	0	Odd
0	1	1	1	Even
1	0	0	0	Odd
1	0	1	1	Even
1	1	0	1	Even
1	1	1	0	Odd

Truth tables for 2-input and 3-input XNOR gates show that with an even number of 1s the output is 1 and with an odd number of 1s the output is 0. The property holds good for XNOR gates with any number of inputs.

Table 2.22 Input-output characteristics of gates

Gate	***Input***	***Output***
1. Positive AND 2. Negative OR	All inputs high	High
3. Positive OR 4. Negative AND	One or more inputs high	High
5. Positive NAND 6. Negative NOR	All inputs high	Low
7. Positive NOP 8. Negative NAND	One or more inputs high	Low
9. Positive XOR	Odd number of inputs high Even number of inputs high	High Low
10. Positive XNOR (2-inputs only)	Both inputs low or Both inputs high	High

2.14 EQUALITY COMPARATOR

The XNOR gate is ideally suited for comparing the equality of two words. A word comparator circuit is shown in Fig. 2.34. Registers *A* and *B* contain the two words which are required to be compared. Comparison is done by four 2-input XNOR gates, the output of which is fed to a 4-input AND gate. The top-most XNOR gate compares the bit A_0 with B_0 and if they are identical the output of this gate will be 1. Similarly the bit A_1 is compared with B_1, A_2 with B_2 and A_3 with B_3. If this comparison shown that the contents of register *A* are the same as the contents of register *B*, the outputs of all the XNOR gates will be 1. In that case the output of the AND gate will also be 1. This will show that the contents of register *A* and *B* are identical. If even a single bit of register *A* is different form the corresponding bit of register *B*, the output of the corresponding XNOR gate will be 0. Since the outputs are fed to an AND gate, the output of the AND gate will also be 0. This will indicate that the two words are not identical.

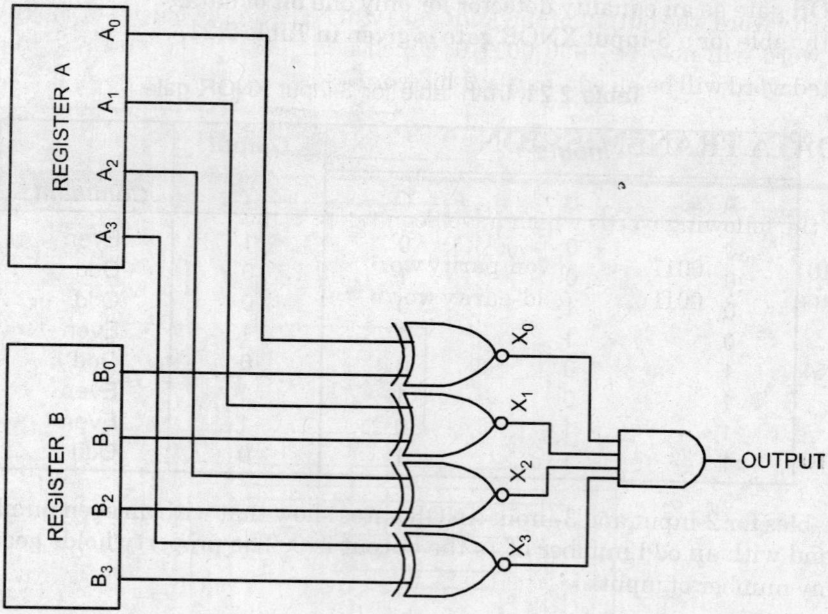

Fig. 2.34 Word comparator

2.15 PARITY CHECKER

There are some words which have an even number of 1s and they are called even parity words. There are other words which have an odd number of 1s and they are called odd-parity words. Tables 2.18 and 2.19 have many even and odd parity words. Consider the following 16-bit words:

1100	1010	1001	1011	Odd-parity word
1000	1100	1110	1100	Even-parity word

The first word has an odd number of 1s and it is, therefore, an odd-parity word. The second word has an even number of 1s and it is an even-parity word.

Exclusive-OR gates can easily check the parity of any word. For instance if you want to check the words listed above, apply these words at the input of a 16-bit XOR gate. The odd-parity word will produce an output of 1 and the even-parity word will produce an output of 0.

2.16 PARITY GENERATOR

It is sometimes considered desirable to transmit all words either as odd-parity words or as even-parity words. This is achieved by using a parity generator which adds an extra bit to make all words odd-parity or even-parity words. A circuit which will ensure that all words being transmitted have odd-parity is given in Fig. 2.35.

The word being transmitted also constitutes the input to the XOR gate. If this word is 1010 1111, which is an even-parity word, the output of the XOR gate will be 0 and the output of the Inverter will be 1. If the parity bit is added to the right of the units position, the new word will be 1010 1111 1, which is an odd-parity word. If the word being transmitted is 1000 0011, which is an odd-parity word, the output of the XOR gate will be 1 and the output of the Inverter will be 0. The new word will now be 1000 0011 0, which is an odd-parity word. So in either case the transmitted word will be an odd-parity 9-bit word.

2.17 DATA TRANSMISSION

Consider the following words which have been taken from the ASCII code.

101	0011	(even-parity word) stands for *S*
100	0011	(odd-parity word) stands for *C*

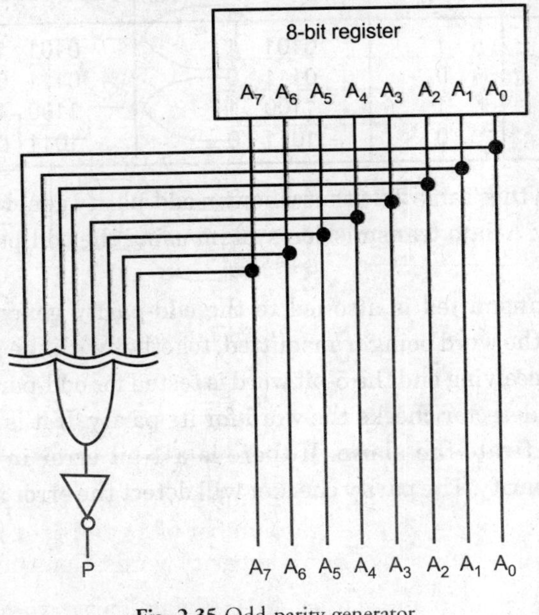

Fig. 2.35 Odd-parity generator

You will notice that between these two words there is a change in only one bit. Errors sometimes occur in transmission of data and it has been observed that they are usually one-bit errors. Therefore, it is not unlikely that *S* may be received as *C* or *C* may be received as *S*.

To avoid such errors it is the usual practice to transmit a parity bit along with the original word and test the received word for its parity. If an even-parity method is used, the parity generator ensures that the transmitted word has an even number of 1s. If the odd-parity method is used, the parity generator produces the required parity bit and all words are transmitted as odd parity words. Consider the following examples (Table 2.23) of transmission of all words an even-parity words.

Table 2.23

Original word	*Parity bit*	*Word transmitted*	*Word received*	*Parity*
0101	0	0101 0	0101 0	Even
0111	1	0111 1	0111 1	Even
1100	0	1100 0	1100 0	Even
1011	1	1011 1	1011 1	Even

You will see from Table 2.23 that all words have been transmitted and received as even-parity words. The parity generator shown in Fig. 2.35 can be modified to generate 'even-parity' by removing the Inverter.

If an odd-parity method of transmission is used the odd-parity generator shown in Fig. 2.35 can be used. Consider the following examples (Table 2.24) using the same words as in Table 2.23.

Table 2.24

Original word	*Parity bit*	*Word transmitted*	*Word received*	*Parity*
0101	1	0101 1	0101 1	Odd
0111	0	0111 0	0111 0	Odd
1100	1	1100 1	1100 1	Odd
1011	0	1011 0	1011 0	Odd

You will notice from this Table 2.24 that when an odd-parity generator is used all the words received have odd-parity. A data transmission system using the odd-parity method is shown in Fig. 2.36.

The word being transmitted is also fed to the odd-parity generator which generates a parity bit to ensure that the word being transmitted, together with the parity bit, constitutes an odd-parity word. At the receiving end the 5-bit word is tested for odd-parity by the parity checker and error detector. This detector checks the word for its parity. If it is an odd-parity word, the error output does not activate the alarm. If there is a 1 bit error in transmission, the word received will have even-parity. The parity checker will detect the error and the error output will sound an alarm.

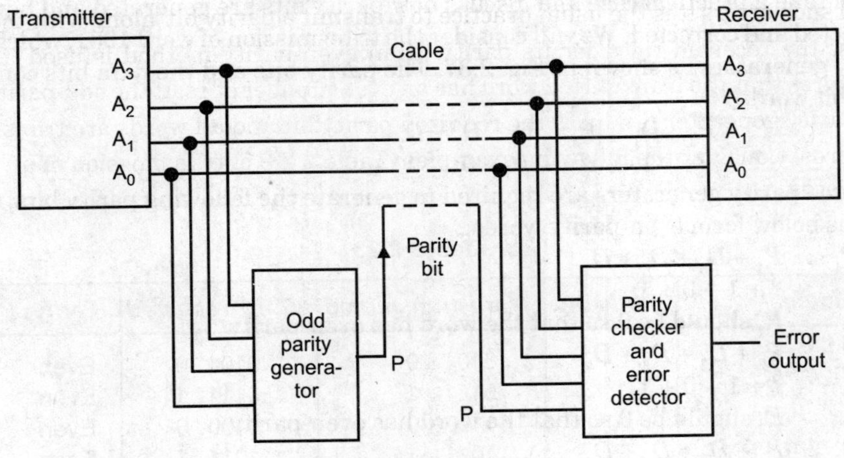

Fig. 2.36 Data transmitter

2.18 ERROR DETECTION AND CORRECTION

In Section 2.17, we have considered a method of data transmission which can detect 1-bit errors in the data received. However, this system cannot pinpoint the bit in error, nor can it correct the mistake. While many techniques have been developed for error detection and correction, we will consider here the coding techniques developed by Hamming, which makes it possible to detect and correct errors in transmission.

Although the technique developed by Hamming can be used with words of any length, we will restrict our discussion here to the application of the Hamming code for detection and correction of words in the 8421 BCD code. This method requires the addition of three parity bits to the 4-bit BCD code and thus the transmitted word has seven bits. The three parity bits P_1, P_2 and P_4 are interposed in the 4-bit BCD code as indicated below.

	Bit position						
	1	**2**	**3**	**4**	**5**	**6**	**7**
Data bits (8421)			D_3	D_4	D_5	D_6	D_7
Parity bits	P_1	P_2		P_4			
Composite 7-bit word	P_1	P_2	D_3	P_4	D_5	D_6	D_7

The parity bits are so generated that when they are combined with the groups of data bits shown below, the 4-bit words so formed have even-parity.

1. $P_1 D_3 D_5 D_7$ Even-parity word
2. $P_2 D_3 D_6 D_7$ Even-parity word
3. $P_4 D_5 D_6 D_7$ Even-parity word

At the receiving end the data bits and the parity bits are again combined in the same order as indicated above to check for even-parity. If any of the above combinations fails the test, one of the bits is in error.

We will take a practical case and discuss how parity bits are generated and how the bit in error is detected and corrected. We will consider the transmission of word 1001, which is also fed to the parity generators as shown in Fig. 2.37. The parity bits and the data bits constitute the following 7-bit word:

$$\begin{matrix} P_1 & P_2 & D_3 & P_4 & D_5 & D_6 & D_7 \\ ? & ? & 1 & ? & 0 & 0 & 1 \end{matrix}$$

The three parity generators are required to generate the following parity bits, so that the combinations below form even-parity words:

P_1 : $P_1 + D_3 + D_5 + D_7$
: $? + 1 + 0 + 1$
P_1 should be 0 so that the word has even-parity

P_2 : $P_2 + D_3 + D_6 + D_7$
: $? + 1 + 0 + 1$
P_2 should be 0 so that the word has even-parity

P_4 : $P_4 + D_5 + D_6 + D_7$
: $? + 0 + 0 + 1$
P_4 should be 1 so that the word has even-parity

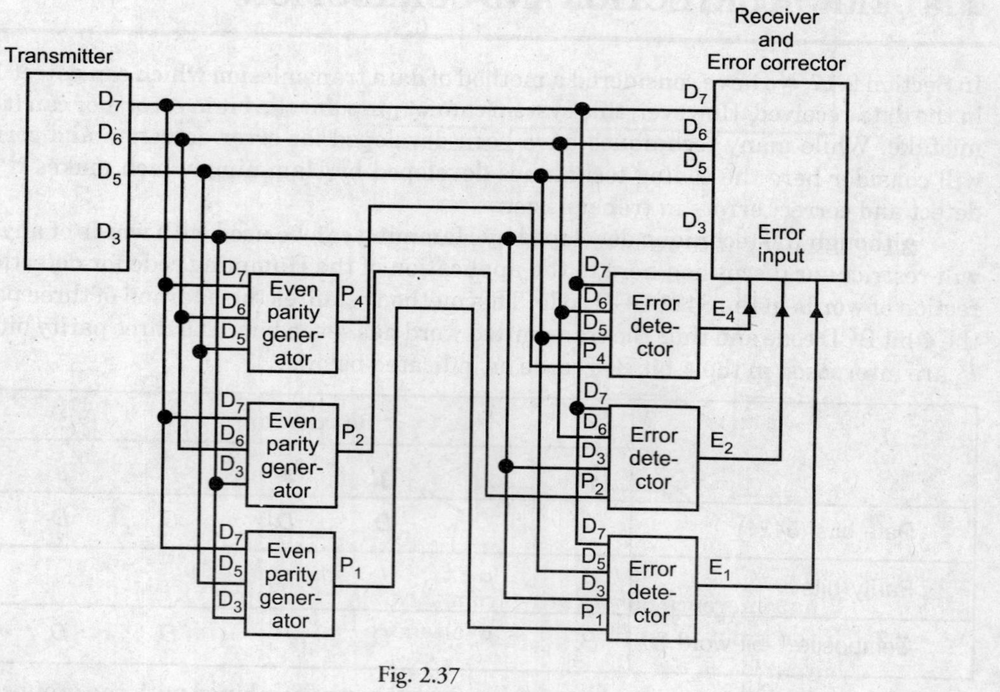

Fig. 2.37

The 7-bit word to be transmitted is now as follows:

0 0 1 1 0 0 1

Let us assume that the word received is as follows which indicates a 1-bit error in bit D_6:

0 0 1 1 0 1 1

At the receiving end the same parity checks are carried out by three error detectors as shown in Fig. 2.37. The result of parity checks are indicated given on next page.

1. $P_1 + D_3 + D_5 + D_7 = 0 + 1 + 0 + 1$: Even-parity : No eror : $E_1 = 0$
2. $P_2 + D_3 + D_6 + D_7 = 0 + 1 + 1 + 1$: Odd-parity : Error : $E_2 = 1$
3. $P_4 + D_5 + D_6 + D_7 = 1 + 0 + 1 + 1$: Odd-parity : Error : $E_4 = 1$

The bit in error is

$$\begin{matrix} E_4 & E_2 & E_1 & \\ 1 & 1 & 0 & \text{or bit } D_6 \end{matrix}$$

which is indeed the bit in error. The wrong bit is corrected at the receiving end by an error-correcting circuit. The position of the bit in error can be found out from Table 2.25, when the error output is known.

Table 2.25

Error output			*Position of the Bit in error*
E_4	E_2	E_1	
0	0	0	None
0	0	1	1
0	1	0	2
0	1	1	3
1	0	0	4
1	0	1	5
1	1	0	6
1	1	1	7

Problems

2.1 If the input to an Inverter is *A* what will be the output in the following cases?

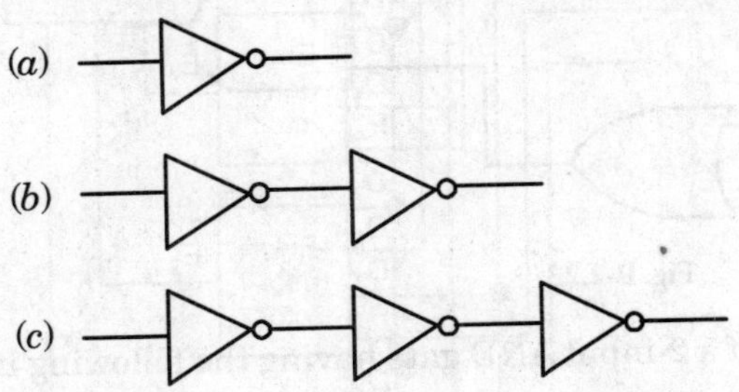

Fig. P-2.1

What inference do you draw from the above instances?

2.2 If the input to an inverter is a voltage level representing binary 0, what will be the output?

2.3 How will you assemble an Inverter by using a NAND gate or a NOR gate?

2.4 Assemble a Buffer using Inverters.

2.5 If the input to three Buffers connected in cascade is *A* what is the output?

2.6 How will you connect an AND gate to make a Buffer?

2.7 Is it possible to use NAND gates to make a non-inverting Buffer? If so how?

2.8 Assemble a Buffer using NOR gates.

2.9 Write the truth table for a 3-input AND gate.

2.10 Write the truth table for a 4-input AND gate.

2.11 How will you connect AND gates to make 3-input and 4-input AND gates?

2.12 Draw a circuit diagram for an AND gate using only NAND gates.

2.13 What is the symbol for an AND gate using negative logic? What gate is equivalent to a negative AND gate?

2.14 Write the truth table for a 3-input AND gate using negative logic.

2.15 What should be the state of the inputs of an AND gate using positive logic, if a high output is required? Does it resemble any gate using negative logic?

2.16 If you want to use an AND gate as an OR gate what logic assignments will you use?

2.17 What is the number of possible input combinations for a 4-input AND gate?

2.18 Write the truth table for the circuit of Fig. 2.26(a).

2.19 Sketch a circuit to implement the following equation:

$$X = \overline{A} \cdot B$$

and write the truth table.

2.20 Sketch a circuit to implement the equation given below:

$$X = A \cdot B + C \cdot D$$

2.21 What will be the output of the following circuit?

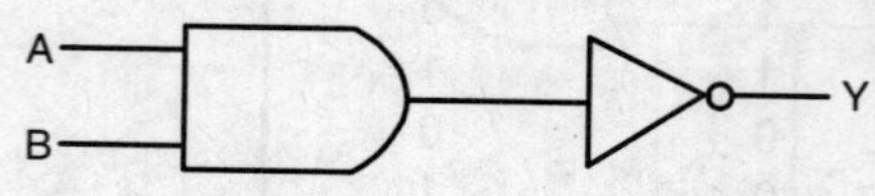

Fig. P-2.21

2.22 Write the truth table for the following circuit, indicating intermediate variables:

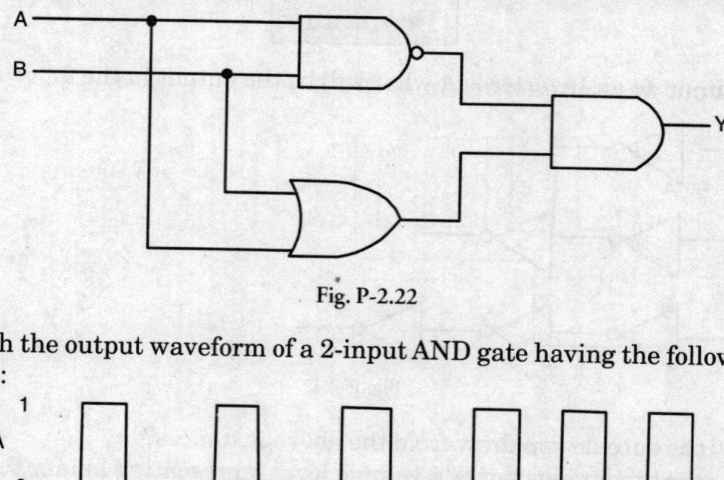

Fig. P-2.22

2.23 Sketch the output waveform of a 2-input AND gate having the following input waveforms:

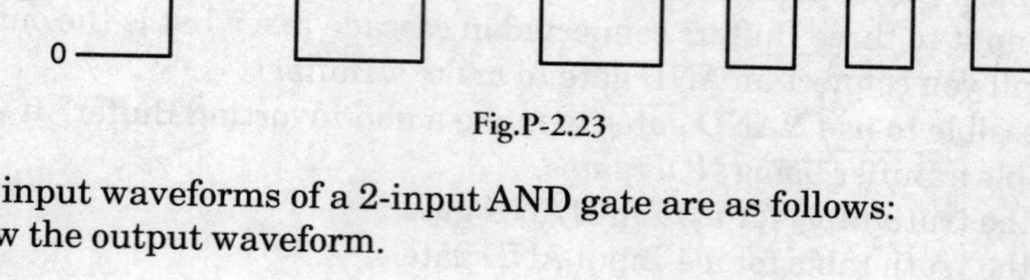

Fig.P-2.23

2.24 The input waveforms of a 2-input AND gate are as follows:
Draw the output waveform.

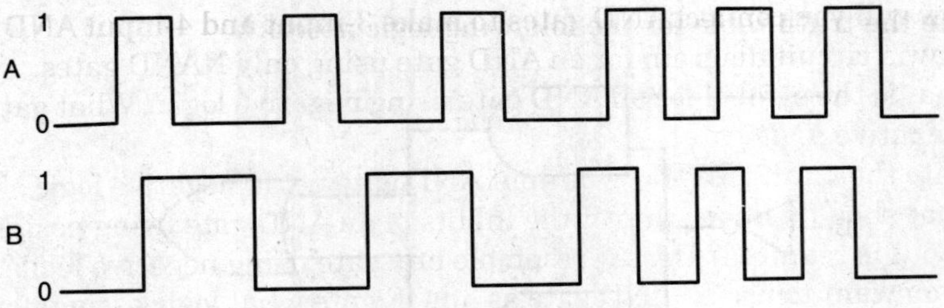

Fig. P-2.24

2.25 Write the truth table for a 3-input OR gate.

2.26 What should be the state of the inputs of an OR gate so that the output is binary 1?

2.27 Comment on the state of the output of an OR gate when negative logic assignments have been used.

2.28 Write the truth table for the following circuit indicating intermediate variables:

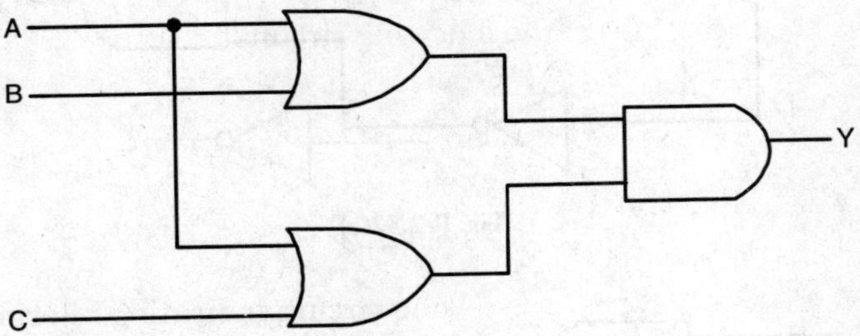

Fig. P-2.28

2.29 The input waveforms of a 2-input OR gate are as follows:

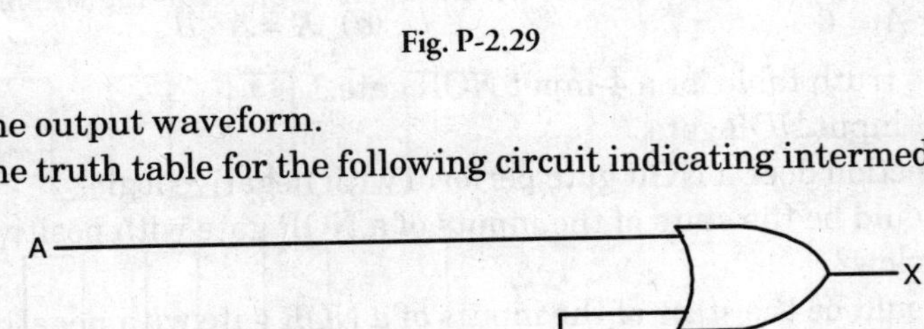

Fig. P-2.29

Draw the output waveform.

2.30 Write the truth table for the following circuit indicating intermediate variables:

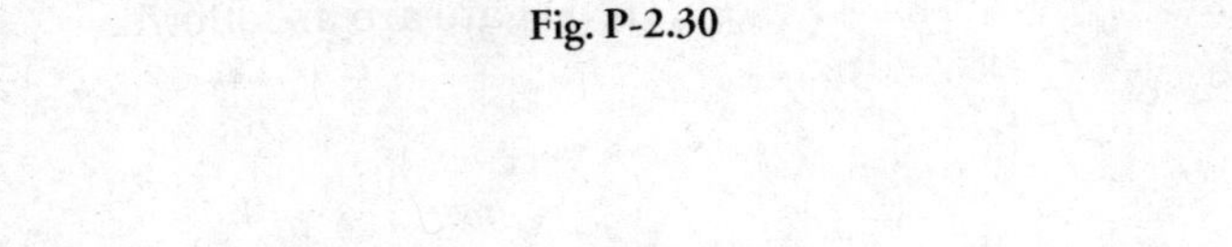

Fig. P-2.30

2.31 Write the truth table for the following logic network:

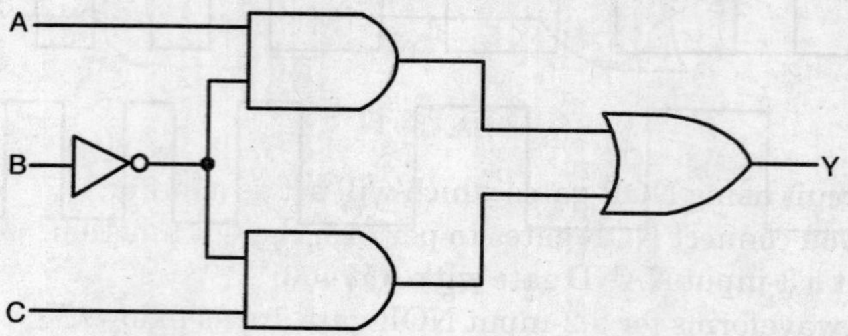

Fig. P-2.31

2.32 Simplify the following logic networks:

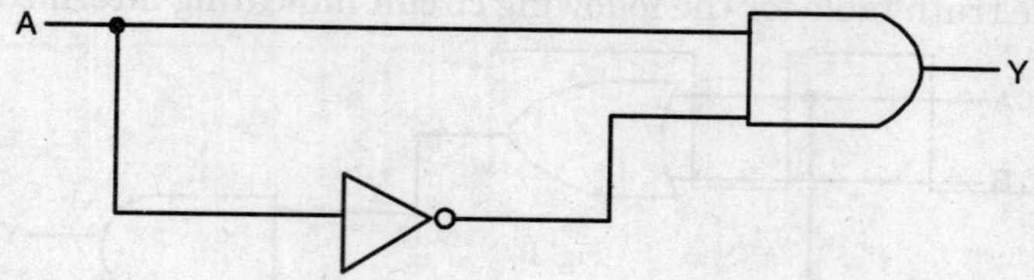

Fig. P-2.32(a)

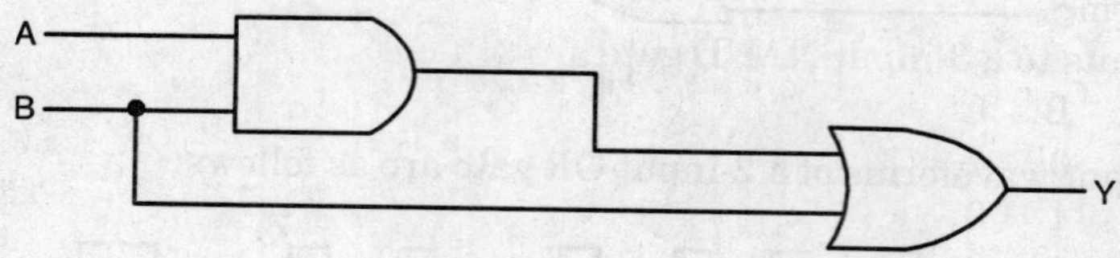

Fig. P-2.32(b)

(*c*) Logic circuit of Fig. P-2.28

2.33 State the logic functions being performed by the following equations:

(*a*) $X = A + B$ (*b*) $X = \overline{A \cdot B}$

(*c*) $X = \overline{A \cdot \overline{B}}$ (*d*) $X = A \cdot B$

2.34 Write the truth table for a 4-input NOR gate.

2.35 Draw a 3-input NOR gate

2.36 What function does a NOR gate perform with negative logic?

2.37 What should be the state of the inputs of a NOR gate with positive logic, so that the output is low?

2.38 What should be the state of the inputs of a NOR gate with negative logic so that the output is low?

2.39 Write the truth table of a 2-input NOR gate with negative logic.

2.40 What function does the following circuit perform?

Fig. P-2.40

2.41 Draw a circuit using NOR gates which will act as a buffer.

2.42 How will you connect NOR gates to perform the OR function?

2.43 Implement a 3-input NAND gate with IC 7400.

2.44 The input waveforms for a 2-input NOR gate are as follows:

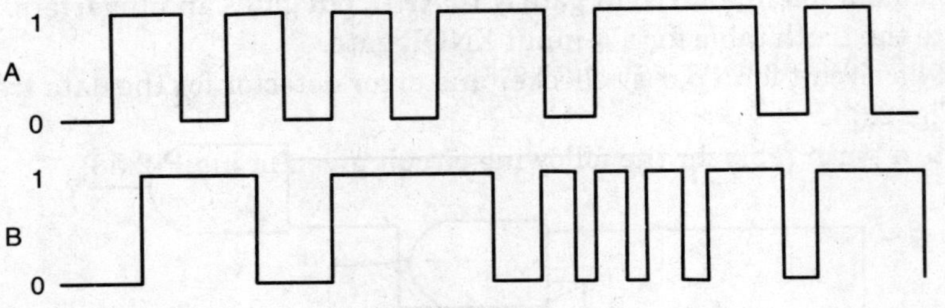

Fig. P-2.44

Draw the output waveform.

2.45 Write the truth table for a 3-input NAND gate with negative logic. What function does it perform?

2.46 The inputs to a 3-input NAND gate are as follows:

	A	B	C
(a)	1	0	1
(b)	1	1	0
(c)	0	1	0
(d)	0	0	0

What are the outputs?

2.47 Draw a circuit to perform as a 2-input AND gate using NAND gates.

2.48 The input wave-forms for a 2-input NAND gate are as follows:

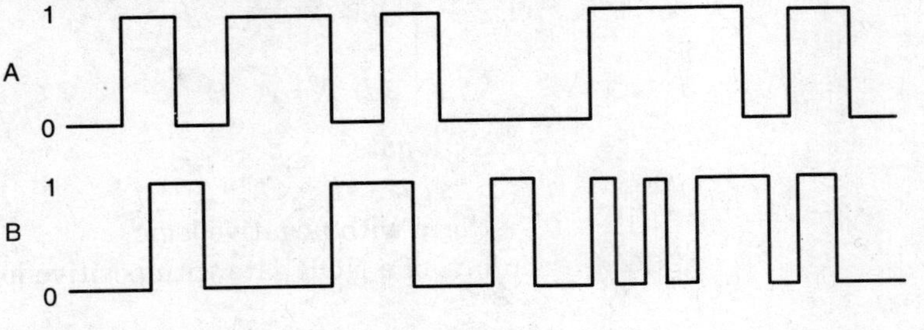

Fig. P-2.48

Draw the output waveform.

2.49 What should be the state of the inputs of a NAND gate using negative logic so that the output is low?

2.50 Implement a 2-input AND gate with IC 7400.

2.51 Draw a circuit diagram for a 6-input XOR gate.

2.52 For an XOR gate what should be the state of the inputs so that the output is high?

2.53 For a 2-input XNOR gate what should be the state of the inputs so that the output is high?

2.54 What function does the following circuit perform?

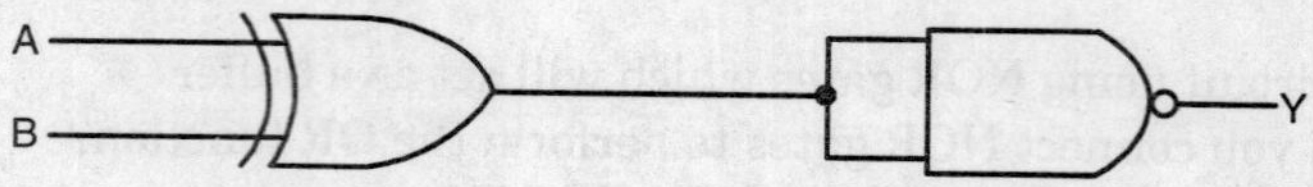

Fig. P-2.54

2.55 Implement a 2-input XNOR gate with AND, OR gates and Inverters.

2.56 Write the truth table for a 4-input XNOR gate.

2.57 Draw a circuit for a parity checker and error detector for the data transmitter given in Fig. 2.33.

2.58 Write a truth table for the following circuit given in Fig.P-2.58:

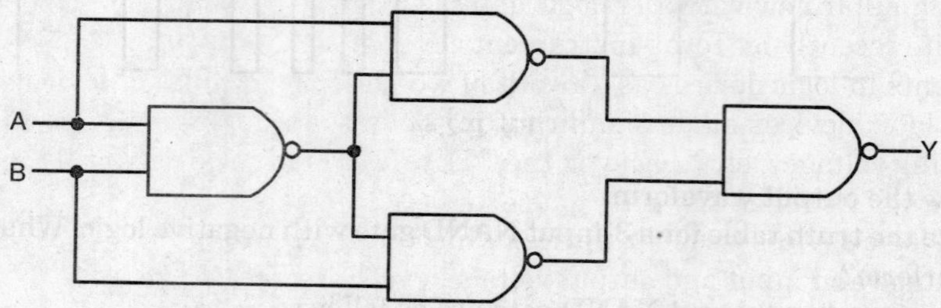

Fig. P-2.58

Does it resemble any truth table you are familiar with?

2.59 If you substitute NAND gates in Fig. P-2.58 by NOR gates what will be the equation for the output? What function will this circuit perform?

3

Bipolar Logic Family

3.1 INTRODUCTION

You must be quite familiar now with TTL logic gates. This very popular family of logic devices was introduced quite recently by Texas Instruments. Newer techniques, developed later, made further improvements in logic devices as a result of which other families of logic devices were introduced. These later devices made significant improvements in speed of operation, power dissipation, operating voltages, etc. However, the TTL family of logic devices still continue to be quite popular in view of its reliability, ease of use and cost considerations.

By a family of logic devices we mean devices which have compatibility within the family in terms of supply voltage and input and output voltage levels, so that it is possible to connect the output of one device to the input of another device of the same family.

These logic devices, called integrated circuits, use advanced photographic techniques which make it possible for a large number of electronic circuits containing transistors, diodes, resistors to be produced on a very small surface of a semiconductor material. They are very small in size, but still contain a large number of electronic gates. They can be classified broadly into the following categories.

SSI *Small scale integration* containing less than 12 gates on a single chip.

MSI *Medium scale integration* which contain between 12 and 100 gates. This enables the fabrication of a complete subsystem on a single chip.

LSI *Large scale integration* which contain more than 100 gates on a chip which enables the fabrication of a complete major subsystem or a system function on a chip.

VLSI *Very large scale integration*. These can incorporate 1000 or more gates and enable the fabrication of a complete system on a single chip.

3.2 LOGIC FAMILIES

Logic families can be broadly classified according to technologies in use today. Broadly speaking there are two main technologies known as 'bipolar' and 'MOS' technologies. Bipolar devices use both electrons and holes as current carriers and are, for this reason, referred to as bipolar devices. N-channel and P-channel MOSFETS are the products of MOS technology. In this chapter we will confine our discussion to bipolar devices and take up the MOS devices for consideration in the following chapter.

The bipolar family can be classified as follows:

1. DTL Diode-transistor logic
2. TTL Transistor-transistor logic
3. ECL Emitter-coupled logic
4. HTL High-threshold logic, also know as HNIL high noise immunity logic
5. IIL Integrated-injection logic.

3.3 TTL DEVICES

First we will take up for consideration the 74 series of TTL devices. The basic circuit of a TTL NAND gate is given in Fig. 3.1. In fact this circuit is the basic building block for all other gates. This circuit consits of three stages, the input, phase splitter and output stages. The input transistor has a multi-emitter input, each emitter acting like a diode and, therefore, along with R_1, acts as a 2-input AND gate. The rest of the circuit functions as an Inverter. A transistor is used in the input stage instead of diodes as higher speed of operation is achieved by using a transistor.

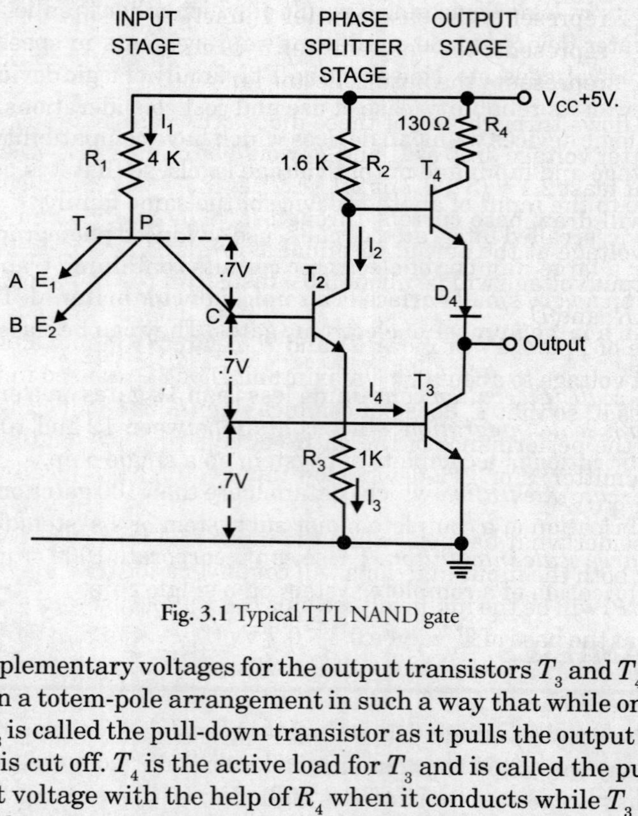

Fig. 3.1 Typical TTL NAND gate

T_2 provides complementary voltages for the output transistors T_3 and T_4, which are stacked one above the other in a totem-pole arrangement in such a way that while one of these conducts the other is cut off. T_3 is called the pull-down transistor as it pulls the output voltage down when it saturates while T_4 is cut off. T_4 is the active load for T_3 and is called the pull-up transistor, as it pulls up the output voltage with the help of R_4 when it conducts while T_3 is cut off.

We will now analyze the circuit in detail. In place of T_1 let us substitute three diodes which represent the following three junctions of T_1 as shown in Fig. 3.2.

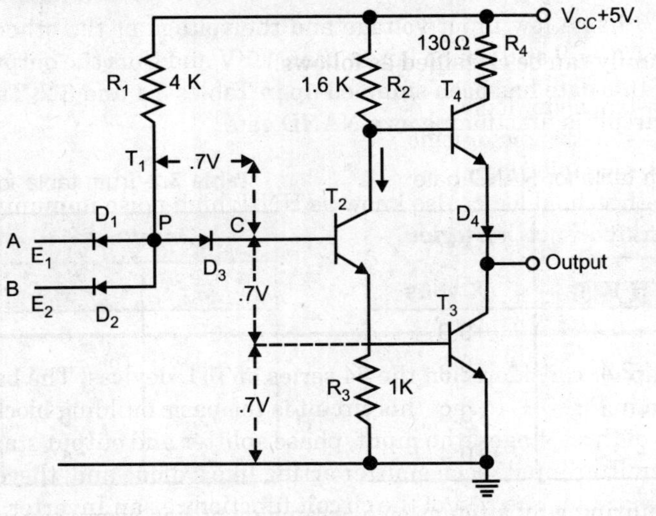

Fig. 3.2

D_1 represents the base-emitter 1 junction
D_2 represents the base-emitter 2 junction
D_3 represents the base-collector junction

When current flows through any of these diodes the voltage drop across them would be 0.7 V. The base-emitter voltage drop of T_2 and T_3 would be of the same order. Unless the voltage at the base of T_1 is at least 2.1 V (3 × 0.7 or 2.1 V). T_2 and T_3 will remain cut off. In that case the pull-up transistor will draw base current through R_2 and, acting as an emitter-follower, will develop an output voltage at the output terminal as while T_4 is turned on T_3 is cut off. When T_4 conducts, the output voltage will be about 3.9V instead of the full supply voltage, as there is voltage drop across R_4 and D_4.

When the base of T_1 is 2.1V or more, T_2 and T_3 begin to conduct and the latter saturates reducing the output voltage to about 0.4 V maximum. Diode D_4 is used in the circuit to develop a voltage drop across it, so that T_4 does not conduct when T_3 is conducting.

We can study the performance of the entire circuit with low and high input voltages at *A*(emitter 1) and *B*(emitter). For TTL devices low input voltage is typically 0.4 V and high input voltage is 2.4 V to 3.9 V.

Let is now consider what happens when the input at *A* or *B* or at both is 0.4 V or less. In that event either or both the input junctions will conduct as the case may be and the voltage at the base of T_1 (point *P*) will be the input voltage plus the voltage drop across D_1 or D_2. If the input is 0.4 V the voltage at the base of T_1 will be 0.4 + 0.7 V or 1.1V. Current will now flow through R_1 and E_1 or E_2, whichever has a lower input voltage. Since the voltage at the base of T_1 is less than that required to forward-bias T_2 and T_3, which is 2.1V, T_2 and T_3 will not conduct and, therefore, as stated earlier, the output voltage will be high, approximately between 2.4 V and 3.9 V. In conclusion we may say that a low input at either E_1 or E_2 or at both will produce high output.

When the input voltage at both *A* and *B* is high, that is not less than 2.1V, both the emitter-base diodes will be reverse-biased and, therefore, T_1 will not conduct. This will forward-bias T_2 and T_3 which will now conduct through R_1 while T_4 will be cut off. T_3 will now be saturated making the output voltage, that is the collector-voltage of T_3 approximately 0.4 V or less. This shows that with high inputs at both *A* and *B* the output will be low.

If either A or B has a low input voltage and the voltage at the other input is high, the voltage at the base of T_1 will still not be larger than 1.1 V and thus the output will still be high. The performance of this gate has been summed up in Tables 3.1 and 3.2. The above discussion will show that the circuit is functioning as a NAND gate.

Table 3.1 Truth table for NAND gate

Input		***Output***
A Volts	***B Volts***	***X Volts***
+ 0.4	+ 0.4	+3.9
+ 0.4	+2.4	+3.9
+ 2.4	+0.4	+3.9
+ 2.4	+ 2.4	+0.4

Table 3.2 Truth table for NAND gate

Input		***Output***
A	***B***	***X***
0	0	1
0	1	1
1	0	1
1	1	0

It is worth enquiring why a totem-pole arrangement has been used in the output stage. The reason is that with this configuration the output impedance is very low, both when the output is high and when it is low. A low output impedance is necessary to enable the output to change from low to high and high to low logic state in as short a time as possible and this means a faster switching speed.

3.3.1 Open-collector Output

The T T L NAND gate we have just discussed had a totem-pole output. In this section we will consider a modification of the same circuit with an open-collector output. If in the NAND gate circuit shown in Fig. 3.1, R_4 T_4 and D_4 are removed, it will still function as a NAND gate but with an open-collector output as in Fig. 3.3.

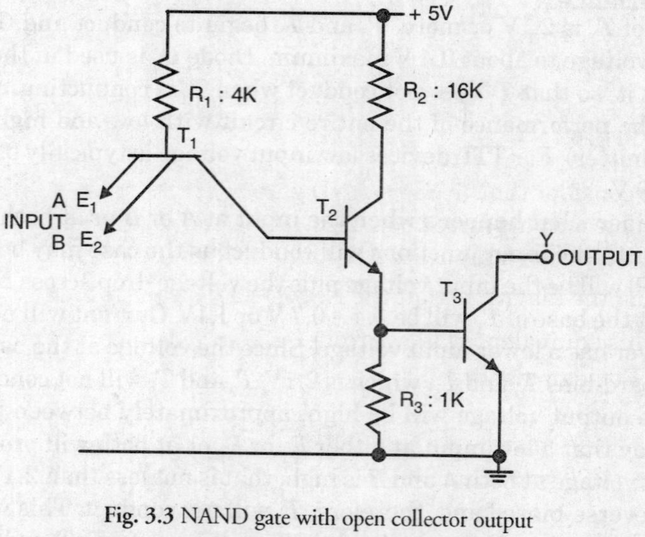

Fig. 3.3 NAND gate with open collector output

When either input A or B or both are low. T_1 is forward-biased, which cuts off T_2 and T_3, and the output is then an open circuit. When both inputs A and B are high, T_1 is reverse-biased which turns on T_2 and T_3 and the output goes low. Table 3.3 summarizes the circuit operation.

Table 3.3 Truth table for NAND gate with open collector output

Inputs		*Transistors*			*Outputs*
A	*B*	T_1	T_2	T_3	*Y*
0	0	ON	OFF	OFF	OPEN
0	1	ON	OFF	OFF	OPEN
1	0	ON	OFF	OFF	OPEN
1	1	OFF	ON	ON	0

The output of a gate with open collector requires an external pull-up resistor, which is connected to the output as shown in Fig. 3.4 (a). The open-collector output allows a wire-OR, also called wire-AND connection of the outputs, which is not possible with a gate having a totem-pole output. The advantage of a wire-OR connection is that the output of a number of gates can be combined by tying the outputs together without the need for a separate OR gate as shown in Fig. 3.4(b).

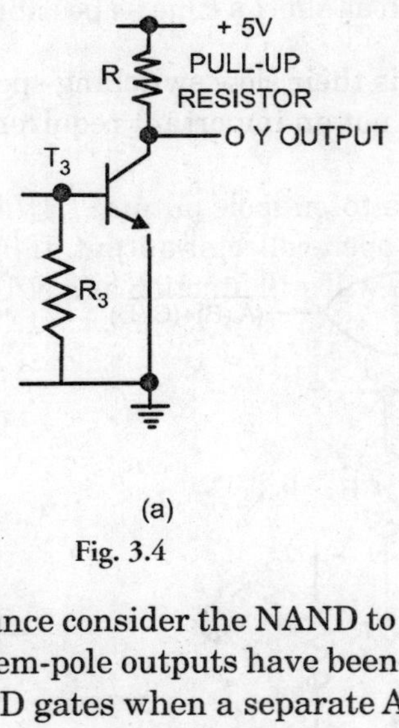

(a)

Fig. 3.4

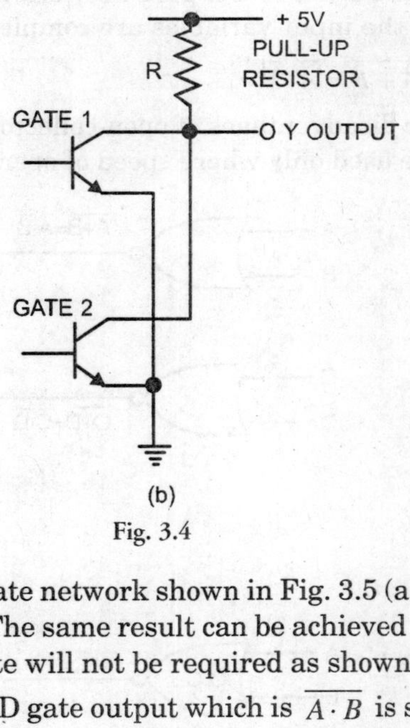

(b)

Fig. 3.4

For instance consider the NAND to AND gate network shown in Fig. 3.5 (a) where NAND gates with totem-pole outputs have been used. The same result can be achieved by using open-collector NAND gates when a separate AND gate will not be required as shown in Fig. 3.5 (b). You will notice from the diagrams that the NAND gate output which is $\overline{A \cdot B}$ is shown as being equal to $\overline{A} + \overline{B}$. This equivalence follows from De Morgan's theorem, which has been discussed in the chapter on Boolean algebra.

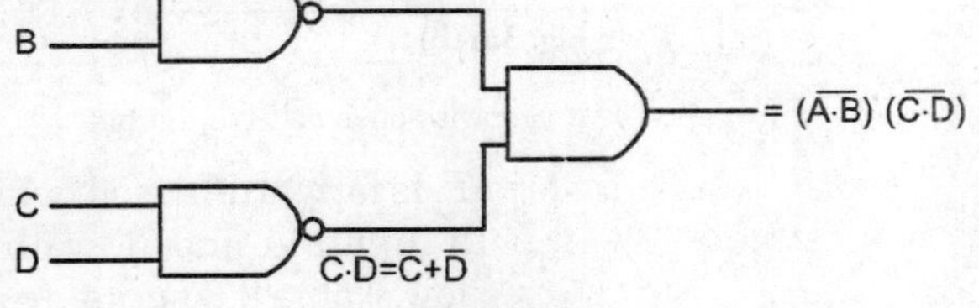

Fig. 3.5 (a)

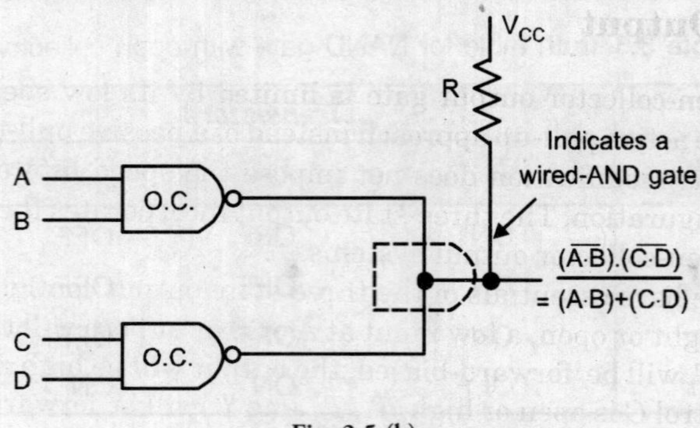

Fig. 3.5 (b)

Consider the NOR to OR gate network, where NOR gates with totem-pole output have been used as shown in Fig. 3.6(a). The same functional capability can be achieved by using NOR gates having open-collector output without the need for a separate OR gate at the output by tying the outputs of the NOR gates as shown in Fig. 3.6(b). The expression for the output indicates that the NOR to OR gate network functions as an AND to OR gate, with the only difference that the input variables are complemented. Note that it follows from De Morgan's theorem that $\overline{A+B} = \overline{A} \cdot \overline{B}$.

One of the disadvantages of open-collector gates is their slow switching speed and therefore they can be used only where speed of operation is not an important requirement.

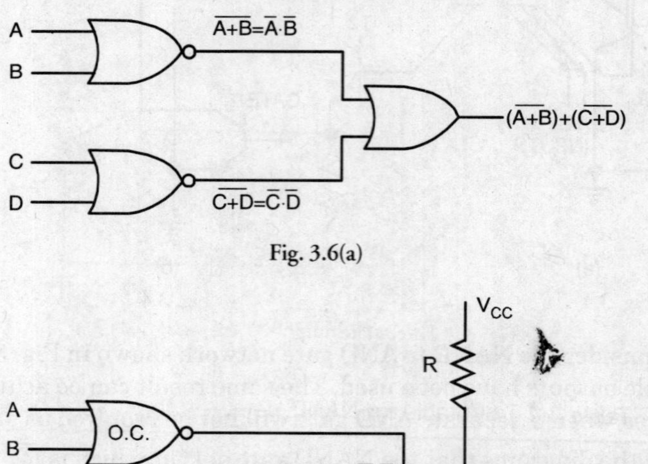

Fig. 3.6(a)

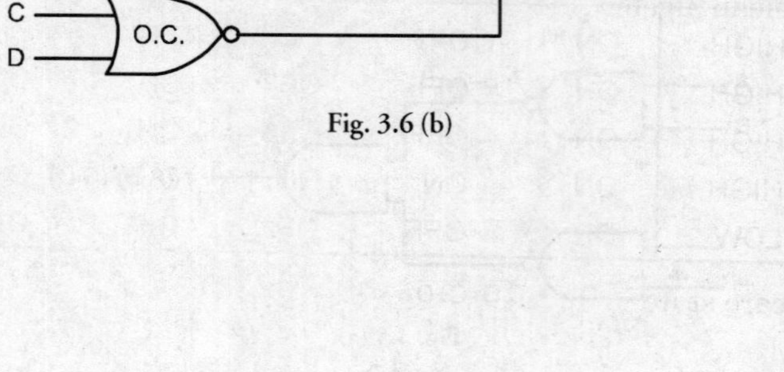

Fig. 3.6 (b)

3.3.2 Three-state Output

The usefulness of the open-collector output gate is limited by its low speed. The three-state output connection uses the active pull-up approach instead of a passive pull-up resistor, as in the open-collector output. This modification does not impose the speed limitation noticed in the open-collector output configuration. The three-state output incorporates the advantages of both the totem-pole and the open-collector output systems.

Figure 3.7 shows the bare essentials of the three-state output configuration for a NAND gate. When control C is hight or open, a low input at A or B or at both will cut off transistors T_2 and T_3; but since T_4 and T_5 will be forward-biased, the output will be high. When both inputs A and B are high, while control C is open or high. T_1, T_2, and T_3 will be forward-biased and T_4 and T_5 will be cut off. The output will therefore be low. When control C is low. T_1 will be forward-biased while T_2, T_3, T_4 and T_5 will be cut off. The output will be floating and, as you can see, the inputs A and B will have no effect on the output, which will remain open. A floating input is equivalent to an open switch. In other words, it indicates that output has no connection with the input. Table 3.4 summarizes the circuit operation.

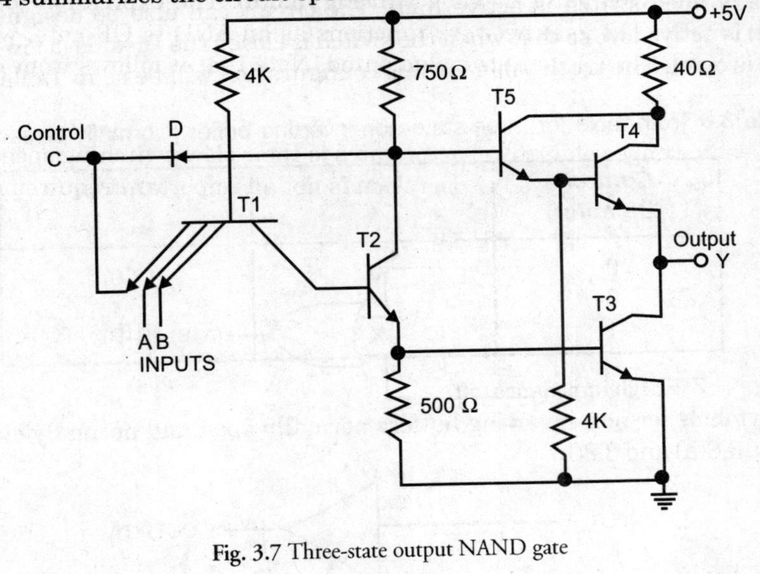

Fig. 3.7 Three-state output NAND gate

Table 3.4 Truth table for NAND gate with three state output

Inputs		*Control*	*Transistors*					*Output*
A	*B*	*C*	T_1	T_2	T_3	T_4	T_5	*Y*
0	0	HIGH	ON	OFF	OFF	ON	ON	1
0	1	HIGH	ON	OFF	OFF	ON	ON	1
1	0	HIGH	ON	OFF	OFF	ON	ON	1
1	1	HIGH	ON	ON	ON	OFF	OFF	0
X	X	LOW	ON	OFF	OFF	OFF	OFF	OPEN

X denotes don't care state

3.3.3 Application of Three-state Devices

This table shows that when control C is high the circuit functions as a NAND gate and when it is low the circuit acts as an open switch. This circuit can be modified for operation as a three-state non-inverting buffer, the truth table for which is given in Table 3.5.

Table 3.5 Truth table for three-state non-inverting buffer (Normally open switch)

Control (Enable)	*Input A*	*Output Y*
1	1	1
1	0	0
0	X	Z

Z = High impedance (off)

The normally open switch is active high. The circuit can also be designed so that the control (Disable) is active low, so that when the switch is closed the Disable is low and when it is high the switch is open. The truth table for this configuration will be as in Table 3.6.

Table 3.6 Truth table for three-state non-inverting buffer (Normally closed switch)

Control (Disable)	*Input A*	*Output Y*
0	0	0
0	1	1
1	X	Z

Z = High impedance (off)

The logic symbols for non-inverting buffers normally open and normally closed switches are given in Figs. 3.8(a) and 3.8(b).

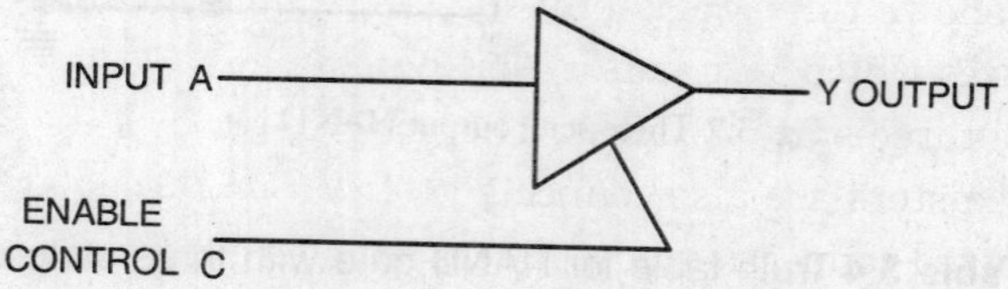

Fig. 3.8(a) Non-inverting Buffer normally open switch

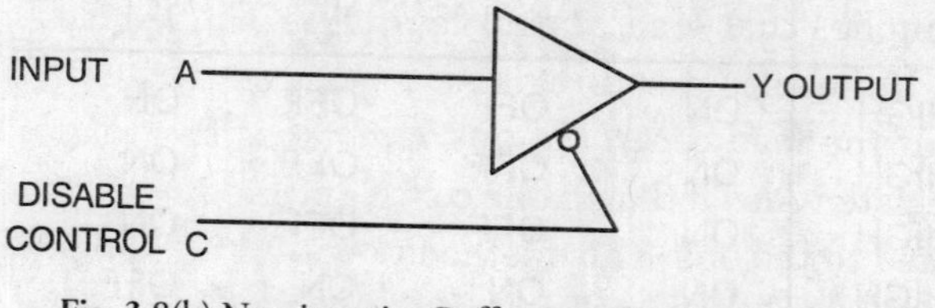

Fig. 3.8(b) Non-inverting Buffer normally closed switch

A TTL device 74125 which is a quad three-state buffer IC is available. The logic symbol for a single non-inverting buffer which is a normally closed switch is shown in Fig. 3.8(b). The IC package has four such buffers. The truth table for the buffers is as given in Table 3.6. The input data are passed without inversion when the control input is low. When the control input is high the output of the buffer goes to the high impedance state, which creates an open switch between the input *A* and the output *Y*. In this state the output floats to the voltage level of the data bus line to which it is connected.

Three-state buffers are normally incorporated into devices for interfacing them with data bus lines to which other devices like microcomputers, etc., are connected. Besides, there are peripheral interface devices. (PIAs) which incorporate, registers, latches, buffers and control lines for specific applications, which can meet the input and output need of a system.

The pin connections for IC 74125 are given in Fig. 3.8(c).

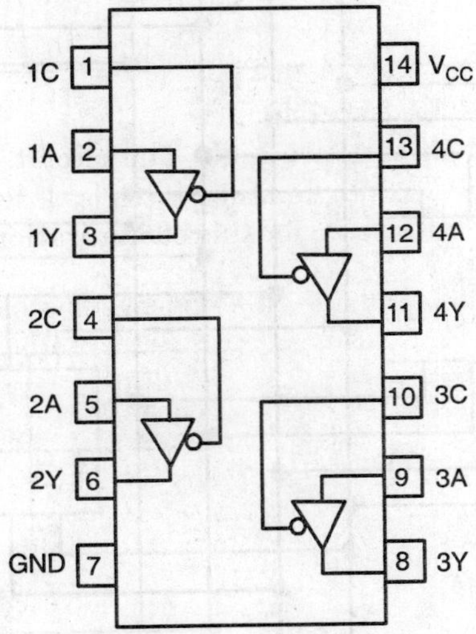

Fig. 3.8(c) Pin connections for quad 3-state Buffer IC 74125

Figure 3.9 (a) shows three registers *A*, *B* and *C*, the inputs and outputs of which are connected to four wires which transmit a 4-bit binary word and are referred to as a bus. The registers incorporate three-state switches. The registers receive their inputs from the bus and the outputs of the registers are also connected to the bus through three-state switches. This method of bus-organized connection of registers enables data to be loaded in any register and transmitted to any register connected to the bus.

All the three registers are driven by the same clock signal. All the registers have active high inputs which implies that load control inputs L_A, L_B, L_C must be held high to prepare a register for loading. If the output of a register is to be connected to the bus, its enable control must be held high. If the load control of any register is low the data on the bus will not be transferred to the register. Also if the enable control of any register is low, the data at its output will not be transmitted to the bus. This method of bus organization enables data appearing on the bus to be transmitted to any register to the exclusion of all other registers. It also enables the output of any register to be transferred to the input of any register via the bus.

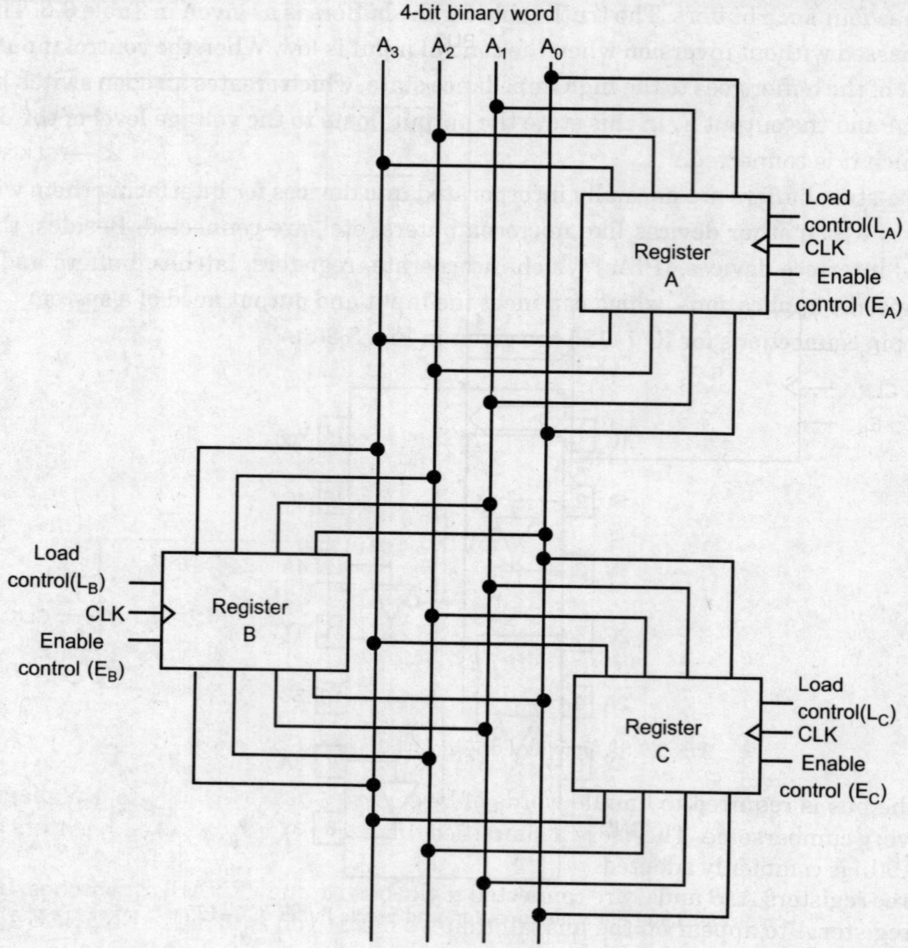

Fig. 3.9 (a) Bus-connected registers

Let us suppose that the data bit appearing on the bus has to be transmitted to register A only. This can be done by holding load control L_A high and load controls L_B and L_C low. If the data in register C has to be transferred to register B, enable control E_C must be held high and load control L_B must also be held high. When the controls have been set appropriately, the operation will be completed on the arrival of the next positive clock edge.

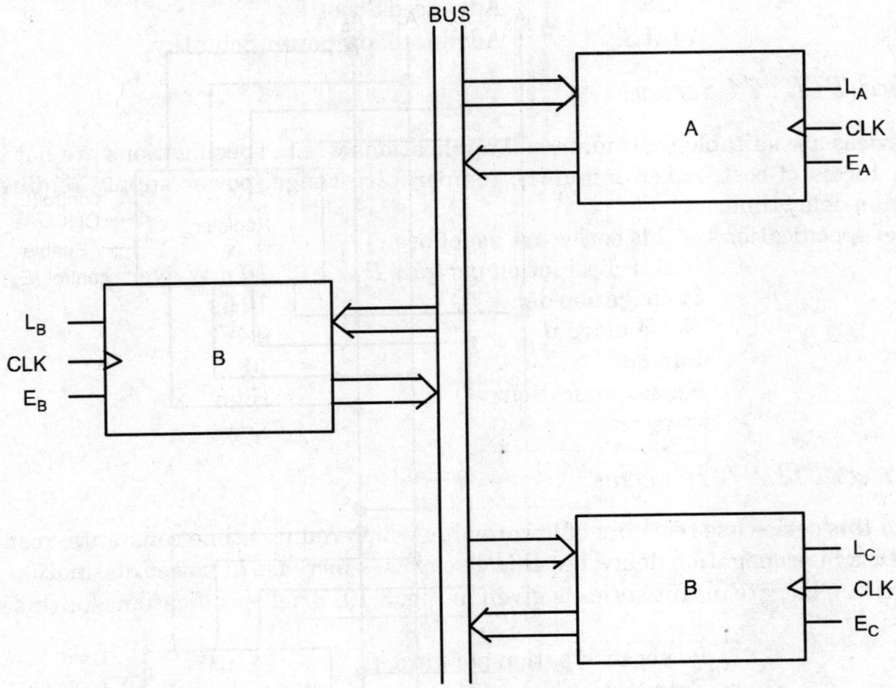

Fig. 3.9 (b) Simplified diagram of bus-connected registers

If the bus is required to handle words of larger size, 16 bits or 32 bits, the diagram may become very cumbersome. Therefore a simplified diagram of bus organized registers as shown in Fig. 3.9(b) is commonly adopted.

Three registers *A*, *B* and *C* are connected to the bus through ENABLE switches. If we want data in register *A* to appear on the bus, all that we have to do is to make ENABLE 1 high and ENABLES 2 and 3 low.

3.4 TTL INTEGRATED CIRCUITS : 74 SERIES

The 74 series of integrated circuits was introduced in 1964 by Texas instruments and it is still the most popular series of TTL circuits. All integrated circuits in this series work on a power supply range of 4.75V – 5.25V, although it is typically 5V. Devices in this series work over a temperature range of 0–70°C.

There is another series which is designated 54, which is primarily intended for military applications. Devices in this range work over a power supply range of 4.5 – 5.5V and a temperature range from –55°C to 125°C.

Currently many sub-families in the 74 series are available which are intended to meet the designer's requirements of power consumption, propagation delay, noise margin fan out, etc. We will consider here the characteristics of the following sub-families in this series:

74	Standard
74H	High power
74L	Low power
74S	Schottky
74LS	Low power Schottky

74AS	Advanced Schottky
74ALS	Advanced low power Schottky

Standard TTL : 74 Series

These devices are suitable for commercial applications where specifications are not very rigid, either in terms of cost, noise immunity, temperature range, power supply requirements or propagation delay time.

Brief specifications of this series are as follows:

Power dissipation per gate P_d	10 mW average
Propagation delay T_d	10 ns
Noise margin	0.4V
Fan out	10
Noise generation	High
Cost	Low

High Speed TTL : 74H Series

Devices in this series use resistors of lower value which reduces time constants, resulting also in a decrease in propagation delay; but this also causes increase in power dissipation. A typical circuit of a NAND gate in this series is given in Fig. 3.10. Brief specifications for this series are as follows:

Power dissipation per gate, P_d	22 mW
Propagation delay T_d	6 ns
Fan out	10

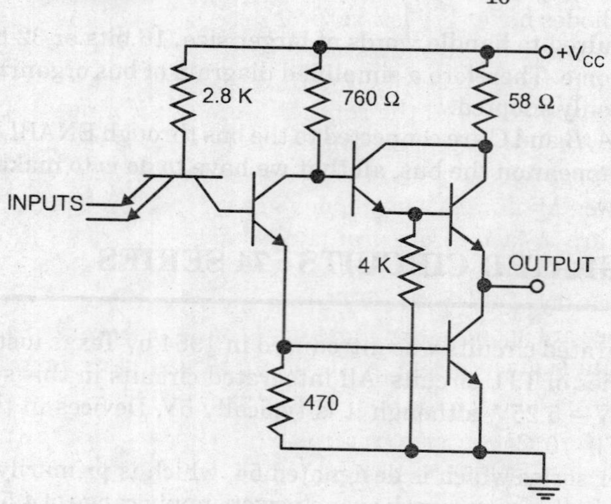

Fig. 3.10 TTL NAND gate; 74H series

Low Power TTL : 74L Series

Devices in this series are very useful, where very low power consumption and heat dissipation are critical parameters. This is achieved by using internal resistors of larger values, which reduces power dissipation to about one-tenth of the standard TTL series. However, you will notice from the specifications below that the propagation delay time of this series is 35 ns, which results from higher internal time constants and therefore they are considerably slower than standard TTL series. A diagram of a low power TTL NAND gate is given in Fig. 3.11.

Power dissipation per gate P_d	1mW
Propagation delay time T_d	35 ns

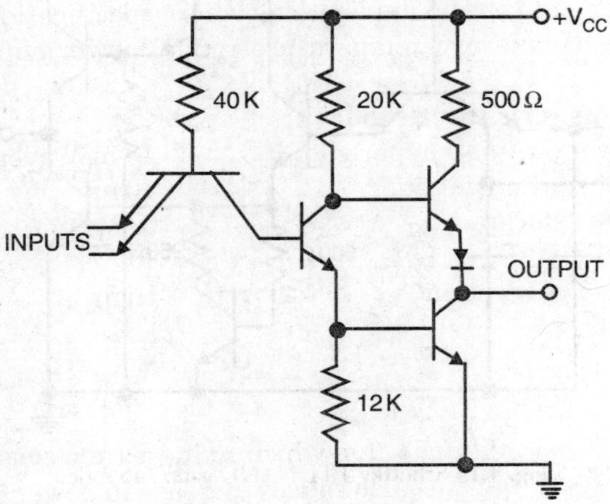

Fig. 3.11 TTL NAND gate: 74L series

Schottky TTL: 74S Series

The TTL series is known as the Schottky series, which gets its name from the inventer of the Schottky diode. Schottky diodes have very low saturation voltage of the order of 0.4 V. Transistors in a TTL logic circuit operate in the saturation mode. When a silicon transistor gets saturated, its base is at 0.7V and the collector is at 0.1V with respect to the emitter. When a Schottky diode is connected between the base and the collector as shown in Fig. 3.12 (a), the collector voltage does not fall below 0.4 V with respect to the base and, as a result, the Schottky diode clamps the collector to a voltage which prevents the transistor from being completely saturated. This reduces propagation delay time. These diodes are incorporated in each transistor of a Schottky TTL device and are in fact an integral part of every transistor in the circuit. These devices are capable of operating at very high switching speeds and perform reliably up to about 100 MHz. The internal circuitry of a Schottky TTL gate resembles that of a standard TTL gate. However, the resistor values are about half of those in a standard TTL gate. A circuit diagram of a Schottky TTL NAND gate is given in Fig. 3.13. Brief specifications for these devices are as follows:

Power dissipation per gate P_d	20 mW
Propagation delay T_d	3 ns

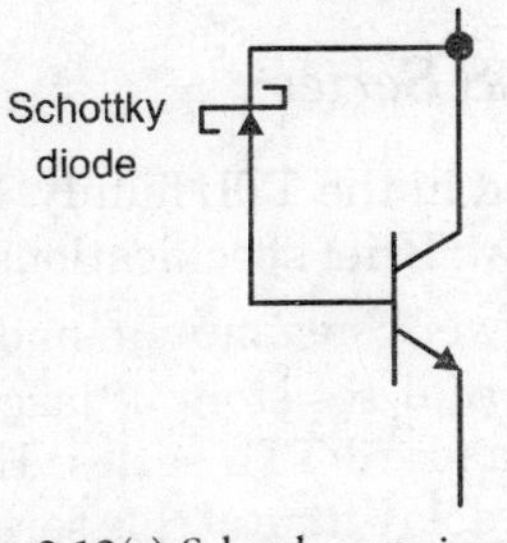

Fig. 3.12(a) Schottky transistor

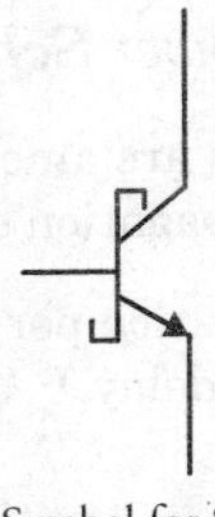

Fig. 3.12(b) Symbol for Schottky transistor

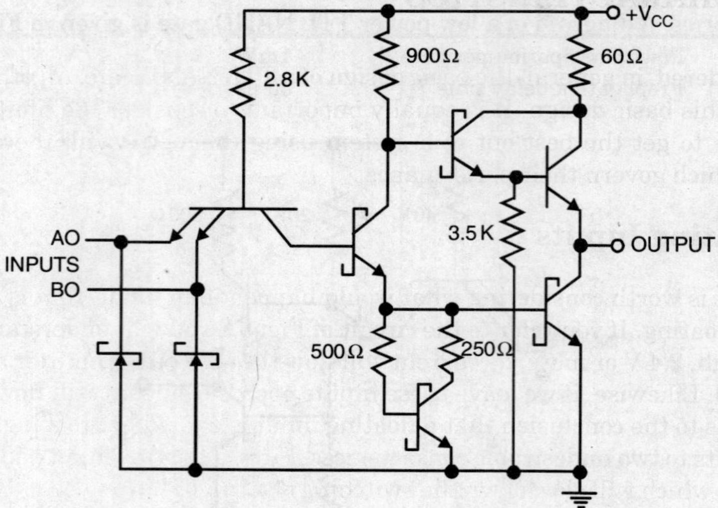

Fig. 3.13 Schottky TTL NAND gate: 74S series

Low Power Schottky TTL: 74LS Series

These devices use Schottky diodes and transistors as well as higher resistance values. This gives these devices the best compromise between higher switching speed and low dissipation. Current and power consumption are about one-fifth of the standard TTL series. The standard TTL series 74 and the low power Schottky series, 74LS are used more than other devices. Brief specifications for this series are as follows:

Power dissipation P_d	2mW
Propagation delay T_d	10 ns
Noise margin	0.3 V
Fan out	20

Advanced Schottky TTL : 74AS Series

Devices in this series are meant for those designers who want the highest speed attainable in TTL devices. These devices are of special value, where speed is a critical requirement and power consumption is not so material. Brief specifications are as follows:

Power dissipation P_d per gate	17mW
Propagation delay T_d	1.5 ns

Advanced Low Power Schottky TTL : 74ALS Series

Devices in this series are among the most advanced in the TTL family. Power consumption is very low and the propagation delay is reasonably low. Brief specifications are as follows:

Power dissipation per gate P_d	1mW
Propagation delay T_d	4 ns

3.5 TTL CHARACTERISTICS

We have considered, in general, the basic design of a TTL NAND gate. All other gates have been evolved from this basic design. It is equally important to consider the limitations of these devices, in order to get the best out of a system using them. We will, therefore, consider the parameters which govern their performance.

3.5.1 Floating Inputs

At this state it is worth considering what would happen if an input, that is not connected anywhere is left floating. If you refer to the circuit of Fig. 3.2 you will understand that if the input at *A* or *B* is high, 2.4 V or more, no current will flow through either emitter as D_1 and D_2 will be reverse-biased. Likewise, if we leave these inputs open, no current will flow through the emitters. This leads to the conclusion that a floating input is equivalent to a high input.

This points to two undesirable consequences. First, a floating input adds stray capacitance to a gate input which will slow down the switching of a gate. This will be particularly noticeable in circuits required to work at high speeds.

Secondly, a gate with a floating input will always be at logic 1 level. This will obviously affect the circuit performance. Besides, an open gate is always susceptible to pick up noise. A noise spike may pull the gate down to logic 0 level and this may happen intermittently, which will make it very difficult to trace the circuit fault.

It is, therefore, a common practice not to leave any inputs floating. Let us see what happens to an OR gate if a floating input acquires a logic 1 level. No matter what you do with the other gates, the output will remain stuck at logic 1. Similarly if an AND gate has an unused input which acquires a logic 0 level or is connected to earth, the output will get stuck at logic 0 level. The simple rule to follow is to so connect an unused input to a logic 1 or logic 0 level that the output does not get stuck.

We will now consider some practical examples to show how the unused gate input should be connected. We will first consider the OR and NOR gates. In both these cases the floating input may either be connected to an input in use or to earth if positive logic is in use as shown in Figs. 3.14 (a), (b), (c) and (d).

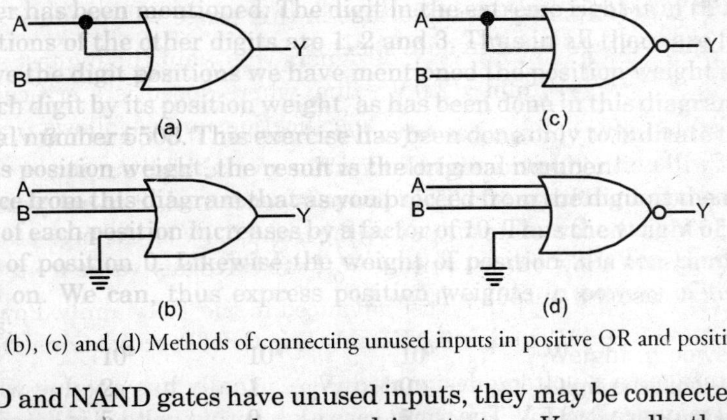

Fig. 3.14 (a), (b), (c) and (d) Methods of connecting unused inputs in positive OR and positive NOR gates

Where AND and NAND gates have unused inputs, they may be connected to the inputs in use. Another method is to connect the unused inputs to + V_{cc}, usually through a 1 K ohm resistor. The resistor protects the gate input against damage by supply-borne spikes. In fact up to 20 unused inputs may be connected to + V_{cc} through a single 1 K ohm resistor. These methods can be used for AND and NAND gates where positive logic is being used as shown in Figs. 3.15 (a), (b), (c) and (d).

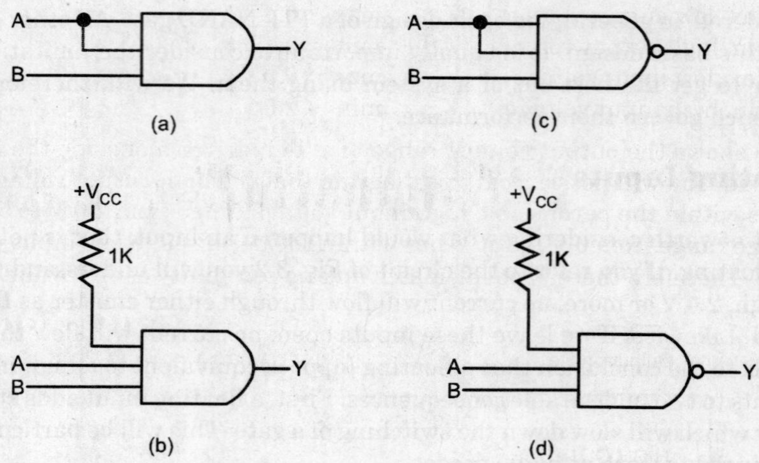

Fig. 3.15 (a), (b), (c) and (d) Methods of connecting unused inputs in positive AND and positive NAND gates

3.5.2 Logic Levels

We will now consider the input and output voltages of TTL devices measured under the worst conditions of voltage and temperature. Let us take the case of an Inverter. We will consider the output of an Inverter with logic 0 (low) and logic 1 (high) input voltages. A low input voltage for a TTL device, V_{IL} according to manufacturers' specifications is any voltage between 0 V and 0.8 V. Any input voltage in this range will produce a high output voltage. The low state input voltage can have any value up to 0.8 V. The data sheets list the worst case low input voltage as

$$V_{IL}\text{max} = 0.8 \text{ V}$$

If the low state input voltage exceeds this value, the output will be unpredictable.

Similarly, any input voltage from 5.0 V down to 2.0 V can be considered to be high input voltage, V_{IH}, for TTL devices. Any input voltage in this range will produce a low output. The worst case high input voltage listed in data sheet is

$$V_{IH}\text{min} = 2.0 \text{ V}$$

If the high state input voltage lies anywhere between 0.8 V and 2.0 V, the output will be unpredictable. It will neither produce a valid low nor a valid high output.

So far as the output voltage of a TTL device is concerned, it is not practical to attain an output voltage of 0 V as the low state output voltage, and 5.0 V as the high state output voltage. According to data sheets a low output voltage V_{OL}, can have any value from 0 V to 0.4 V. Data sheets list the worst case low output voltage as

$$V_{OL}\text{max} = 0.4 \text{ V}$$

The high state output voltage designated, V_{OH}, usually has a value which lies between 2.4 V and 3.9 V. It is typically 3.5 V. The worst case high output voltage is listed in data sheets as

$$V_{OH}\text{min} = 2.4 \text{ V}$$

The worst case input and output voltages have been listed below for convenience of reference.

Max. low output voltage	V_{OL}	max	0.4 V
Min. high output voltage	V_{OH}	min	2.4 V
Max. low input voltage	V_{IL}	max	0.8 V
Min. high input voltage	V_{IH}	min	2.0 V

Figure 3.16 shows the output voltage range of a TTL driver alongside the input voltage range of a TTL load. You will notice from this diagram that the high output voltage range from 2.4 V to 3.9 V lies within the permissible high input voltage range from 2.0 V to 5.0 V. Also the low output voltage range from 0 V to 0.4 V lies within the permissible low input voltage range from 0 V to 0.8 V. Therefore there is no mismatch and no possibility of an invalid output.

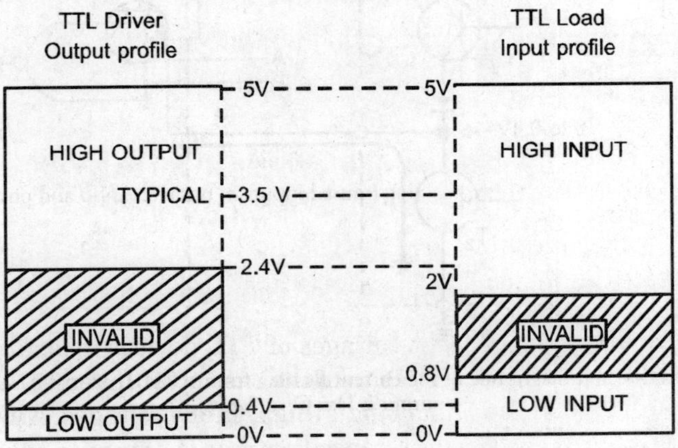

Fig. 3.16 Input and output profiles for a TTL gate

You will notice from this diagram that the maximum low output voltage for a TTL driver is less than the maximum low input voltage for a TTL load and the difference is 0.4 V.

$$
\begin{aligned}
V_{IL}\max - V_{OL}\max &= 0.8 - 0.4\text{ V}\\
&= 0.4\text{ V}
\end{aligned}
$$

Also the minimum high output voltage is more than the minimum high input voltage for a TTL load and the difference is again 0.4 V

$$
\begin{aligned}
V_{OH}\min - V_{IH}\min &= 2.4 - 2.0\text{ V}\\
&= 0.4\text{ V}
\end{aligned}
$$

Therefore the output of any TTL driver can be connected to the input of any TTL load. However, the output of a TTL driver cannot be directly connected to the input of a CMOS load. For this purpose a special device will have to be connected between two devices of different families. We can therefore say that there is compatibility between one TTL device and another.

3.5.3 Sourcing and Sinking of Current

When the output of a TTL driver is connected to the input of a TTL load, current flows from the driver to the load, or from the load to the driver, depending on the state of the output of the TTL driver. Figure 3.17 shows a TTL driver connected to a load and also shows the direction and the magnitude of the current when the driver output is low.

When the driver output is low, 0 to 0.4 V, current flows from the load to the driver. The maximum current in the worst case will not be more than 1.6 mA. According to the convention this is listed in data sheets as – 1.6 mA, as current is flowing from load, T_3, to the collector of T_2. Since T_2 is saturated, it acts like a current sink and is said to sink a current of 1.6 mA.

When the output of the driver is high, 2.4 V to 3.9 V, a current in the reverse direction of 40 μ A (worst case) flows from T_1 (driver) to T_3 (load), as shown in Fig. 3.18. In this case T_1 acts

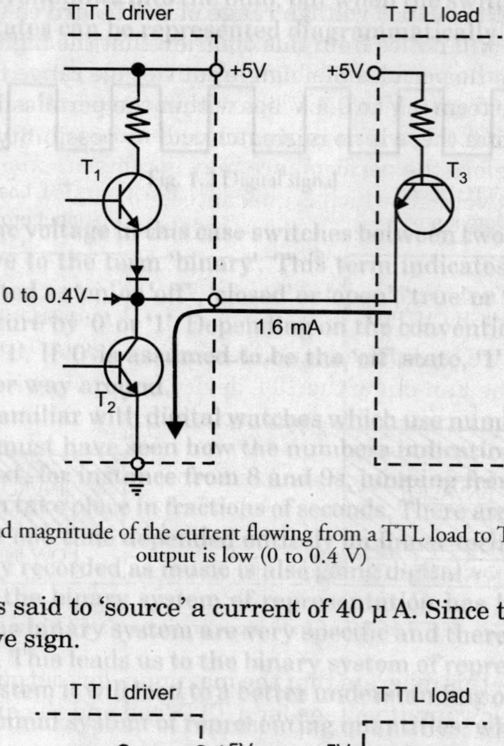

Fig. 3.17 Shows the direction and magnitude of the current flowing from a TTL load to TTL driver when the TTL driver output is low (0 to 0.4 V)

as current source and it is said to 'source' a current of 40 μ A. Since the current is flowing into the device, it has a positive sign.

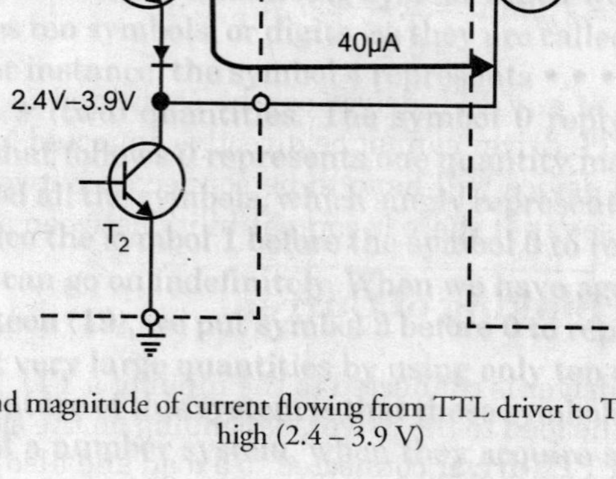

Fig. 3.18 Shows the direction and magnitude of current flowing from TTL driver to TTL load when the driver output is high (2.4 – 3.9 V)

A standard TTL device can sink up to 16 mA of current when its output is low (0–0.4V) and 'source' up to 400 μA of current when its output is high (2.4 – 3.9 V). These currents are listed in specification sheets as follows:

$$I_{OL} = 16 \text{ mA}$$
$$I_{OH} = -400 \text{ μA}$$

As before, according to convention, the minus sign indicates that the current is out of the device. In the earlier discussion you have seen that the low level input current, when a single load is connected to the driver, is 1.6 mA. The maximum current that a TTL driver can sink is ten times this current. Similarly, when the output level of the driver is high it can 'source' a current which is ten times the current of a single emitter (unit load).

If more than ten emitters (ten unit loads) are connected to the output of a TTL driver, the low state output voltage of 0.4 V, which is guaranteed under normal working conditions, may rise above 0.4 V and therefore the performance may become erratic. Also under similar conditions the high state output voltage, which is guaranteed to be 2.4 V or higher, may fall below the lower limit of 2.4 V and the high state operation may also become unreliable.

3.5.4 Fan-in and Fan-out

We have seen above that we can connect up to ten emitters (unit loads) to the output of a TTL driver. We may say that the Fan-out of the TTL device is ten. That is ten unit loads, comprising of one emitter each, can be connected to the output of a TTL device.

It a TTL load has two emitters, that is two unit loads, we may say that its fan-in is two. This means that only five loads of this type, in all constituting ten unit loads, can be connected to the output of a TTL device.

Our discussion above refers only to standard TTL devices. For other devices in the 74 series you will have to refer to data sheets to find out the fan-out of these devices.

3.5.5 Noise Margin

The maximum low level output of a TTL driver is 0.4 V and the maximum input voltage for a TTL load which can be regarded as a low level input is 0.8 V. This means that if a noise spike of up to 0.4 V is added to the driver, its output will still not be more than 0.8 V and it will be considered as a low level input, which will give a valid output. This, therefore, is the noise margin which can be absorbed by the system without upsetting its performance.

Also when the noise spike is in the opposite direction, the low level voltage will be 0.4 V – 0.4 V or 0 V. This is quite acceptable as low level voltage. These two situations have been shown in Fig. 3.19.

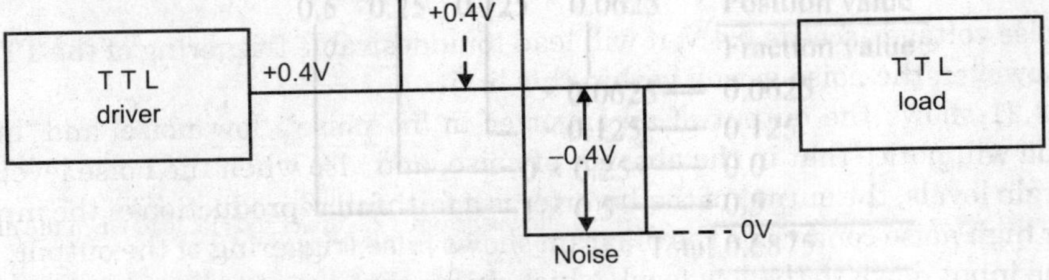

Fig. 3.19 Effect of noise on TTL driver output

We can now consider the effect of noise on the high level output of the driver. The minimum high level output of a TTL driver is 2.4 V. A noise spike of 0.4 – 4.0 will change the driver output to 2.4 V – 0.4 V or 2 V in the negative direction and 2.4 V + 0.4 V or 2.8 V in the positive direction. The minimum input voltage to a TTL load which can be considered as a high level voltage is 2 V. This situation is therefore quite acceptable. This is shown in Fig. 3.20. You will observe that the noise margin is the same in the low and the high level outputs.

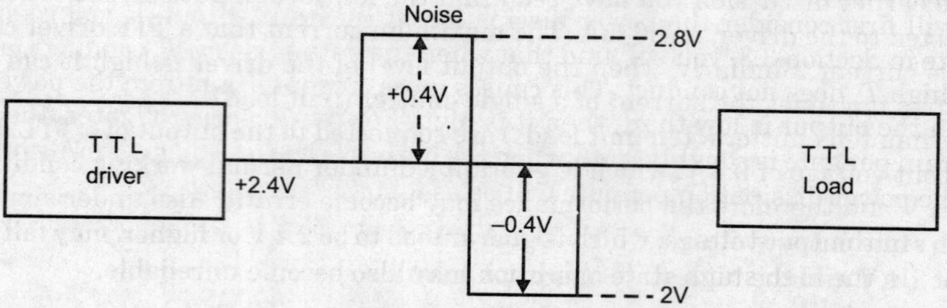

Fig. 3.20 Effect of noise on TTL driver output

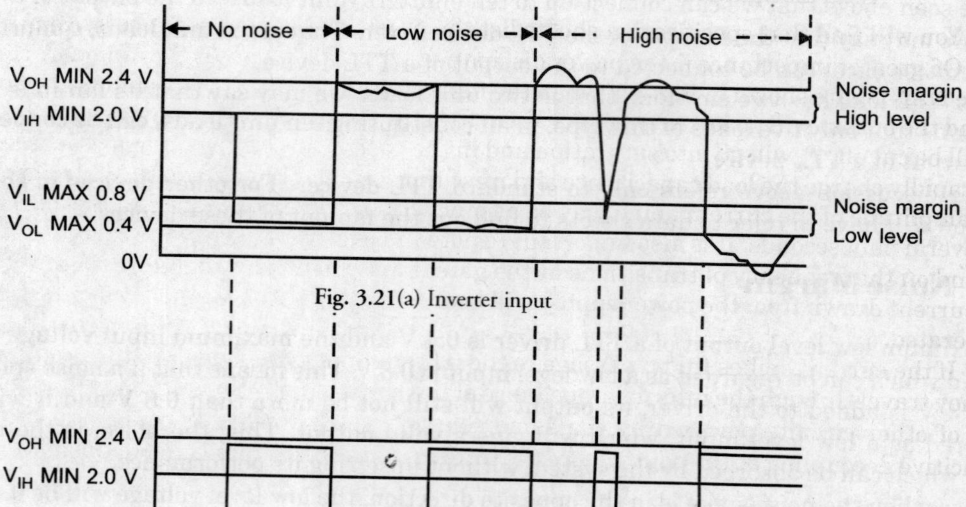

Fig. 3.21(a) Inverter input

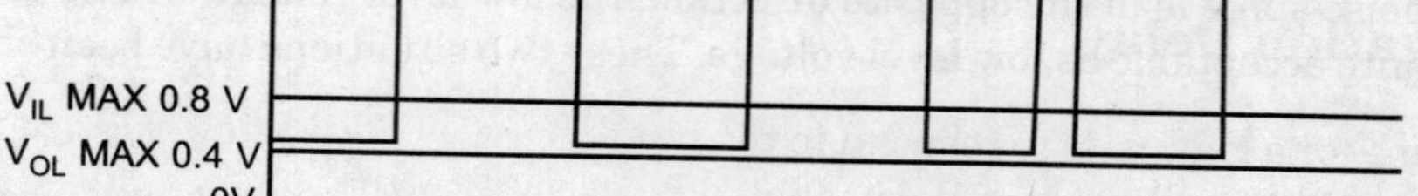

Fig. 3.21(b) Inverter output

If the noise voltage exceeds 0.4 V, it will lead to undesirable triggering of the TTL load. In most cases, however, the noise is well within this limit.

Figure 3.21 shows the output of an Inverter in 'no noise', 'low noise' and 'high noise' conditions. You will notice that in the absence of noise, and also when the noise level is within the noise margin levels, the output of the Inverter is a faithfull reproduction of the input digital signal. Under high noise conditions the diagram shows false triggering of the output, when the noise pulls the input down to the low level, which raises the output to the high level.

3.5.6 Power Dissipation

The power dissipation rating given in specification sheets is the average power dissipation at constant output. For instance, the power dissipation rating of a standard TTL gate of the 74 series is 10 mW per gate. However, in the active state, when the output is continuously changing, power dissipation increases and it must be taken into account where heat dissipation and power supply ratings assume importance.

We will first consider the power dissipation at constant output. If you refer to the TTL NAND gate in Section 3.3, you will find that when the output is low, T_2 conducts, and when the output is high T_2 does not conduct. This causes more current drain from the power supply per gate, when the output is low than when it is high. For the 74 series of gates, the steady state current drain per gate is roughly 3 mA when the output is low and about 1 mA when the output is high. The power dissipation per gate will be as follows:

In the low state : 5 V × 3 mA = 15 mW
In the high state : 5 V × 1 mA = 5mW

If we assume that the gate is on and off for equal time periods, the total dissipation per gate will be as follows:

Total dissipation : (15 + 5) ÷ 2 = 10 mW

You will find that specification sheets list the power dissipation per gate as 10 mW.

Of greater importance is the power dissipation when the output is continuously changing. In the NAND gate shown in Fig. 3.1, when the input is high, T_2 and T_3 will conduct, T_4 will be cut off and the output will go low to about 0.1 V. On the other hand, when the output goes low, T_2 and T_3 will be cut off, T_4 will go into saturation and in the process it will draw a heavy current which will rapidly charge the load capacitance and raise the output voltage from 0.1 V to roughly 3.5 V. The amplitude of the current spike may be as much as 40 mA. The duration of this current may be several nanoseconds. It is also important to note that the frequency of the current spikes will depend on the frequency of transitions at the gate input. Obviously, therefore, in this situation the current drawn from the power supply will bear a relation to the frequency at which the gate is operated.

If the current spikes find a passage to the power supply, they may produce voltage spikes as they travel through the internal impedance of the power supply and thereby affect the operation of other circuits powered by the same source. It is therefore, necessary to provide for capacitive decoupling at the point where the integrated circuit is connected to the power supply.

3.5.7 Propagation Delay

It takes a finite time for a logic gate to respond to the input signal. This is known as propagation delay. It is important that propagation delay should be as short as possible as this affects the speed of operation of a device. Digital signals also take time to change from a low to a high state and vice versa. Let us first consider the latter aspect referred to as 'rise time' and 'fall time'. The rise and fall times should also be as short as possible, since, if they are undesirably long, the logic device being driven may not respond appropriately to the input signal.

The rise time of a digital signal is the time taken for a change from the logic '0' to the logic '1' state. Similarly, the 'fall time' is a measure of the time a signal takes to change from the logic '1' to the logic '0' state. However, according to the convention the 'rise time' is a measure of the time it takes for a signal to change from the 10% level of the overall voltage to the 90% voltage level. Likewise the 'fall time' denotes the time a signal takes to fall from 90% voltage level to the 10% voltage level. This has been shown in Fig. 3.22.

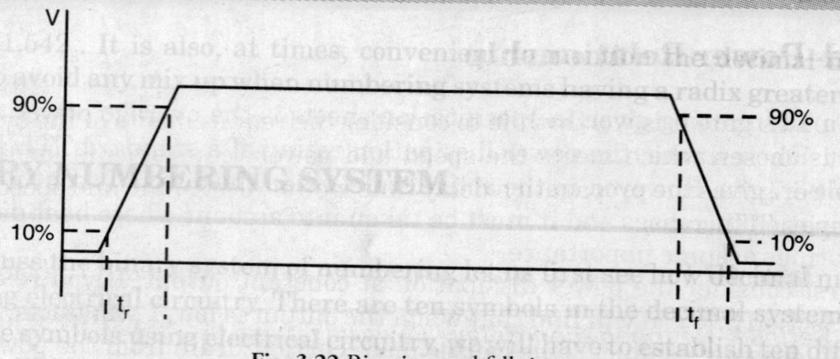

Fig. 3.22 Rise time and fall time

Propagation delay is a measure of the speed at which a logic circuit can operate and assumes great importance where the speed of operation is an important consideration. Propagation delay time is measured at 50% of the peak value as shown in Fig. 3.23, which shows the input and output of an Inverter. You will notice from the diagram that a change from logic 0 to 1 state at the input causes a change from logic 1 to logic 0 after a finite time. This is known as the propagation delay time and is measured at 50% of the peak value of the input and output signals. You will also notice that propagation delay time is not the same for the leading and trailing edges of the pulse. You must have also noticed that it takes the input and output pulses a finite time to reach the peak value. As pointed out earlier, this is also an important consideration in the design of logic circuits. The layout of a logic circuit must be planned carefully as the length of wiring also has a bearing on propagation delay time. Because of manufacturing tolerances, propagation delay time may also vary from the nominal indicated values. Besides, when a number of gates are cascaded, the propagation delay times add up.

It is important to remember that propagation delay is also influenced by capacitive loading and is also therefore a function of the fan out. The average propagation delay can be estimated as follows:

$$t_{pd} = 1/2[t_{pd}(\text{HL}) + t_{pd}(\text{LH})]$$

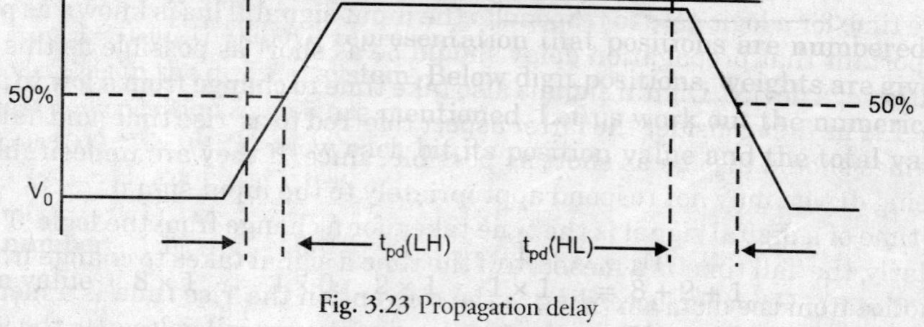

Fig. 3.23 Propagation delay

3.5.8 Speed–Power Relationship

While choosing a TTL gate it is worthwhile to consider the requirements of the system, so that the best device is chosen which meets the speed and power requirements for the particular application. Table 3.7 gives the propagation delay time, power dissipation and speed-power product for the 74 series TTL gates.

Table 3.7 Performance characteristics for the 74 series of TTL gates

Series	*Propagation delay time ns*	*Power dissipation mW*	*Speed-power product pj*
74	10	10	100
74H	6	22	132
74S	3	19	57
74LS	9.5	2	19
74AS	1.5	10	15
74ALS	4	1	4
74L	5	2	10

3.6 NOR AND OR GATES

The NAND gate schematic diagram given in Fig. 3.1 serves as the basic design for NOR and OR gates. To function as a NOR gate two transistors T_5 and T_6 are added to the basic NAND gate as shown in Fig. 3.24. Transistors T_1, T_2, T_3 and T_4 remain unchanged.

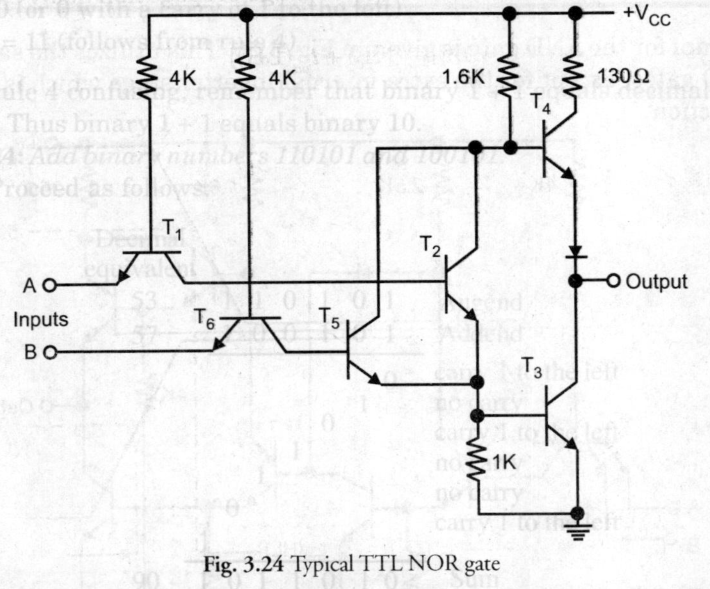

Fig. 3.24 Typical TTL NOR gate

You will notice from the diagram that T_5 and T_6 perform the same function as T_1 and T_2 in the NAND gate circuit. The addition of T_5 and T_6 enables the circuit to perform the ORing function. As it is essentially an inverter circuit, ORing is followed by inversion, which accounts for the NORing of the input.

When both inputs A and B are low, T_1 and T_6 are turned on and T_2 T_5 and T_3 and cut off, which saturates T_4 and the output goes high. When both the inputs are high, T_1 and T_6 are cut off, T_2 and T_5 are turned on which saturates T_3 and the output is pulled down to a low level. When one of the inputs is low and the other is high, the output is again low.

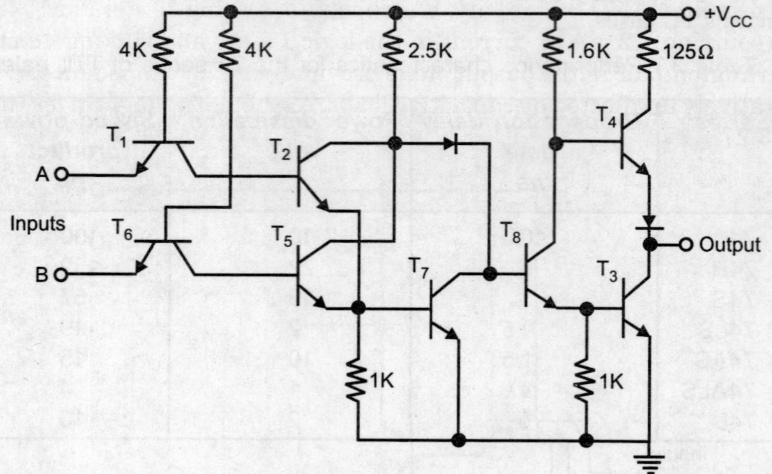

Fig. 3.25 OR gate

The OR gate circuit follows the same basic design except for the addition of an extra inverter stage before the totem—pole output, to obtain the OR logic function as in Fig. 3.25.

3.7 AND GATE

A schematic diagram for the AND gate is given in Fig. 3.26. This utilizes the same basic design features as NAND gates, except for the extra internal inverter stage which is added to obtain the AND logic function.

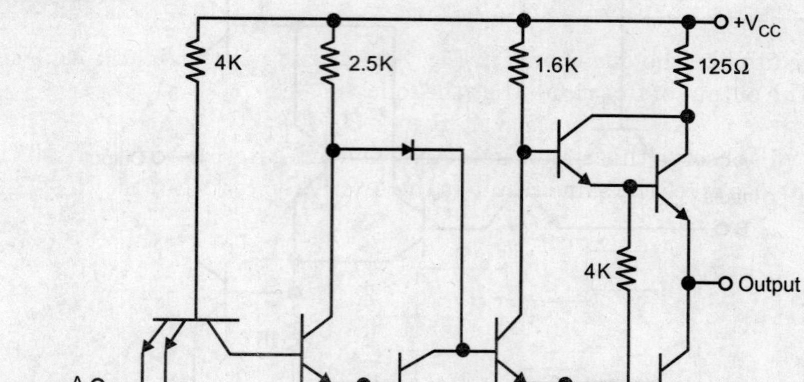

Fig. 3.26 TTL AND gate

3.8 NAND BUFFER GATE

Buffers are used when higher output currents are required much more than a standard TTL gate can source or sink. They are useful for driving clock lines and high capacitance loads. IC 7440 is a dual 4-input NAND Buffer gate. It is capable of driving 30 standard 74 inputs, which is equivalent to sourcing 1.2 mA or current in the logic 1 state and sinking 48 mA in the logic 0 state. The Darlington-pair in the output stage provides very low impedance in the logic 1 state and is comparatively unaffected by capacitive loads. A schematic diagram for this Buffer gate is given in Fig. 3.27.

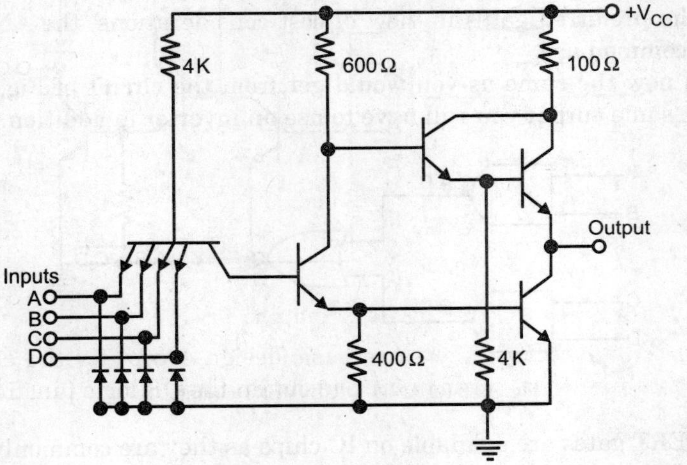

Fig. 3.27 NAND buffer gate

3.9 AND-OR-INVERT GATE

AND-OR circuits like the one shown in Fig. 3.28(a) occur very often in logic design in many variations. The output of this circuit has the following form:

$$Y = A \cdot B + C \cdot D$$

As you will observe this circuit uses AND and OR gates. A NAND-NAND network given in Fig. 3.28(b) also gives the same result as the AND-OR circuit; but the NAND-NAND circuit

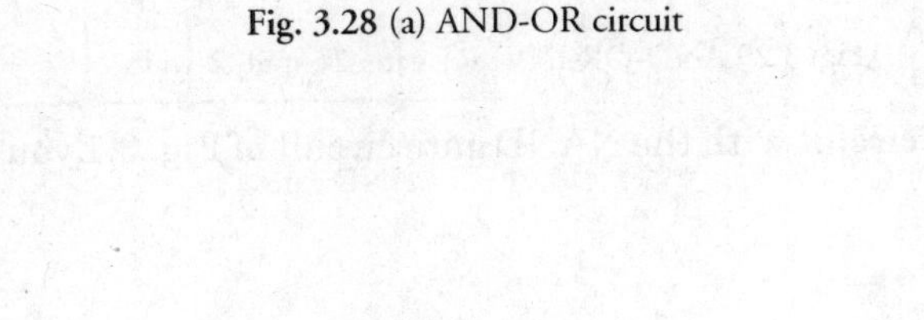

Fig. 3.28 (a) AND-OR circuit

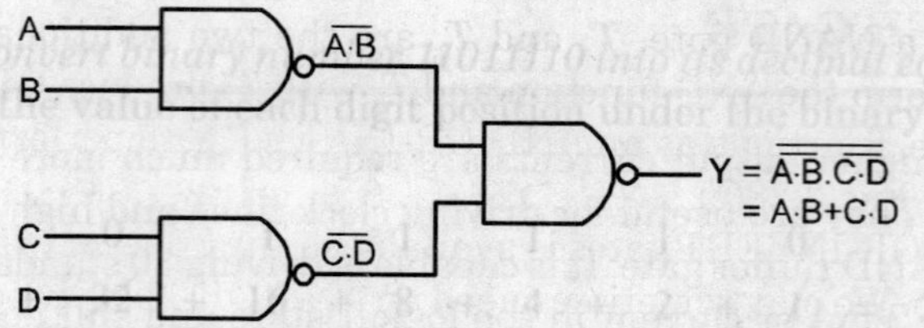

Fig. 3.28 (b) NAND-NAND circuit

cannot be easily derived from the basic NAND gate circuit. What can be easily derived from the basic NAND gate design is the AND-OR-INVERT configuration given in Fig. 3.28 (c). Since NAND gates are the preferred gates in view of cost considerations, the AND–OR–INVERT configuration is in common use.

The output is now the same as you would get from the circuit of Fig. 3.28 (a) as it is inverted. To get the same output you will have to use an inverter in addition.

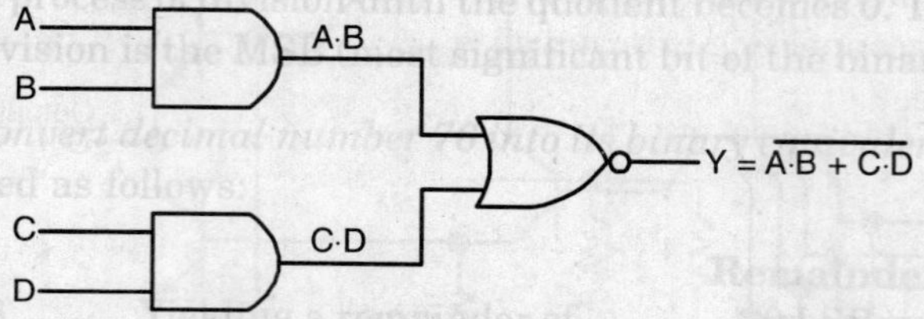

Fig. 3.28 (c) AND-OR-INVERT circuit

AND-OR-INVERT gates are available on IC chips as they are commonly used for implementing a variety of logic circuits. A schematic diagram of a 2-input, 2-wide AND-OR-INVERT gate is shown in Fig. 3.29. The expression '2-wide' refers to the number of AND gates, '2-input' refers to the number of inputs on each AND gate.

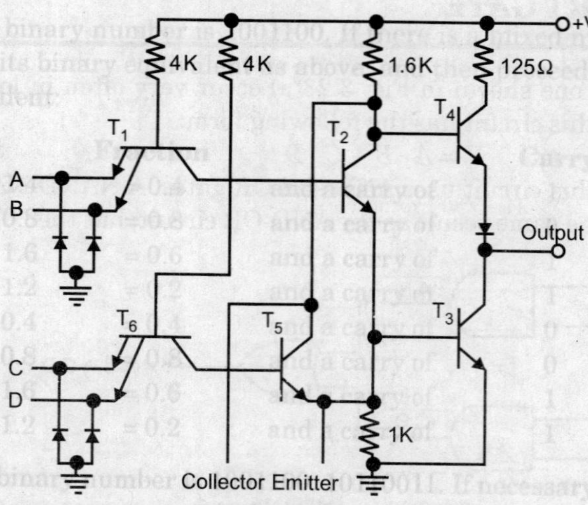

Fig. 3.29 AND-OR-INVERT gate: 2-input, 2-wide

If you compare this circuit with the NAND gate circuit of Fig. 3.1 you will notice the T_1, T_2,

T_3 and T_4 function as a NAND gate. T_5 and T_6 are the two additions to the basic circuit of Fig. 3.1. T_1 and T_6 perform the AND function and T_5 with T_2 produce ORing and inversion. The whole circuit, therefore, functions as an AND-OR-INVERT gate performing the same function as the circuit shown in Fig. 3.28(c).

A variety of AND-OR-INVERT gates is available in the 74 series. However, the widest gate available is only 4-wide. We may sometimes need an AND-OR-INVERT gate which is more than 4-wide (four AND gates) and has more than two inputs in some of the gates. The solution lies in the use of EXPANDABLE AND-OR-INVERT gates which we will discuss in the following section.

3.10 EXPANDABLE AND-OR-INVERT GATE

Figure 3.30 shows the schematic diagram of an expandable 2-wide, 2-input AND-OR-INVERT gate. If you compare this with the AND-OR-INVERT gate given in Fig. 3.29, you will notice that the only difference is that in the expandable version the collector and emitter, tie points of the phase-splitter are available outside the package. This provides access to T_2 and T_5 which provide the ORing function. By connecting external gates to these inputs we can expand the width of the AND-OR-INVERT gate.

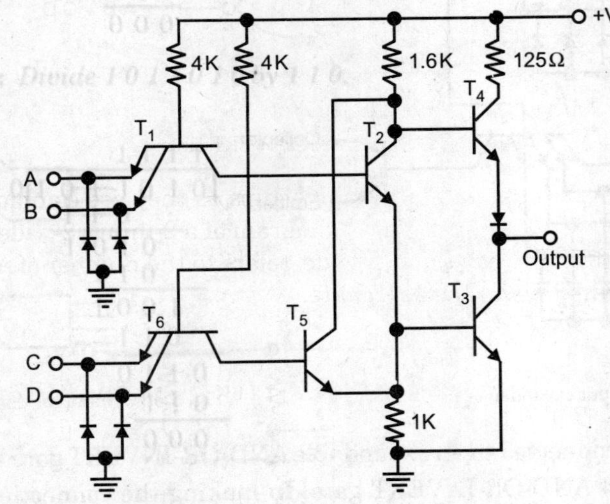

Fig. 3.30 Expandable AND-OR-INVERT gate

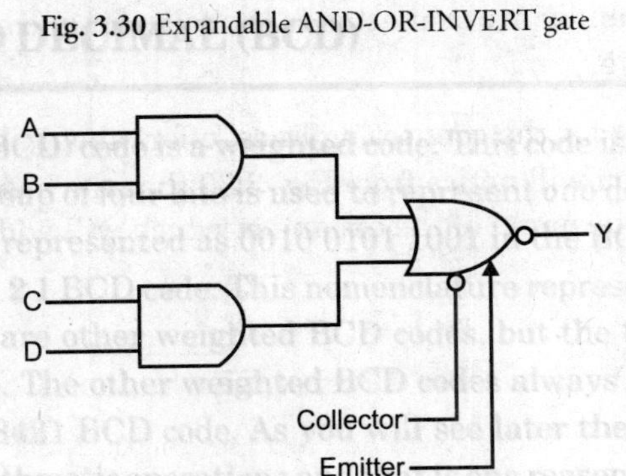

Fig. 3.31 Logic symbol for 2-wide, 2-input expandable AND-OR-INVERT gate

When AND-OR-INVERT gates which are more than 2-wide and have more than 2-inputs in the AND gates are required, a number of AND expanders may be connected to the NOR gate of the expandable AND-OR-INVERT gate given in Fig. 3.31. The 0-input threshold-voltage considerations dictate the number of AND gates that may be added, since the 0-input threshold voltage is decreased by about 20 mV for each Expander that is added. 7450 is a dual expandable 2-input 2-wide AND-OR-INVERT gate. It can take up to four 7460 expanders, which will make it a 2-2-4-4-4-4 input 6-wide AND-OR-INVERT gate, while still maintaining the DC noise margin.

Figure 3.32 gives the schematic diagram for a dual 4-input expander and Fig. 3.33 gives its logic symbol.

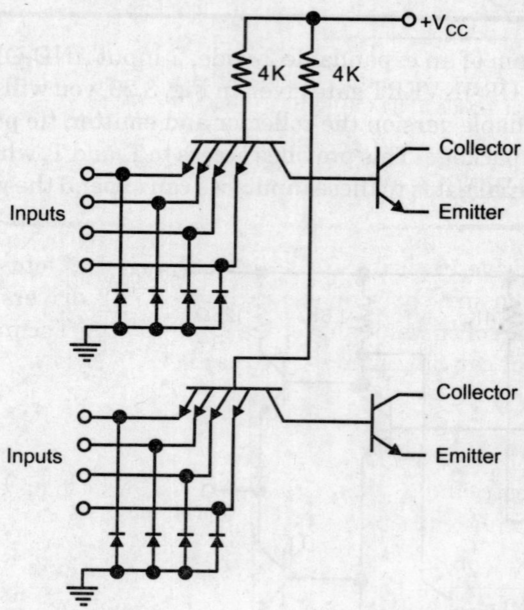

Fig. 3.32 Dual 4-input expander

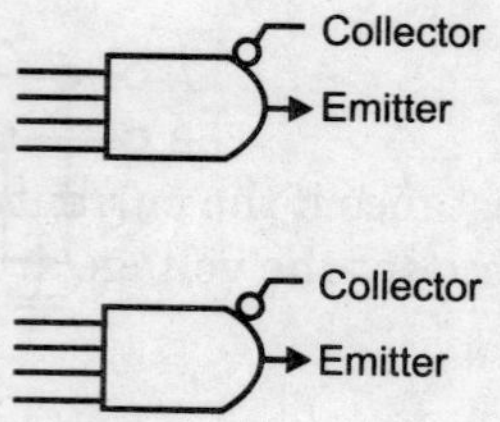

Fig. 3.33 Symbol for dual 4-input expander

This expander is connected to an expandable AND-OR-INVERT gate as shown in Fig. 3.34 to get a 4-wide, 2-2-4-4 AND-OR-INVERT gate. In making the connections the collector and emitter outputs of the expander are connected to the collector and emitter inputs of the expandable AND-OR-INVERT gate.

In preparing a layout for the connecting lines, effort should be made to minimize capacitance and noise pickup. You will notice from Fig. 3.30 that the base of the pull-up transistor is connected to the collector terminal of the expander, which will add to the stray capacitance.

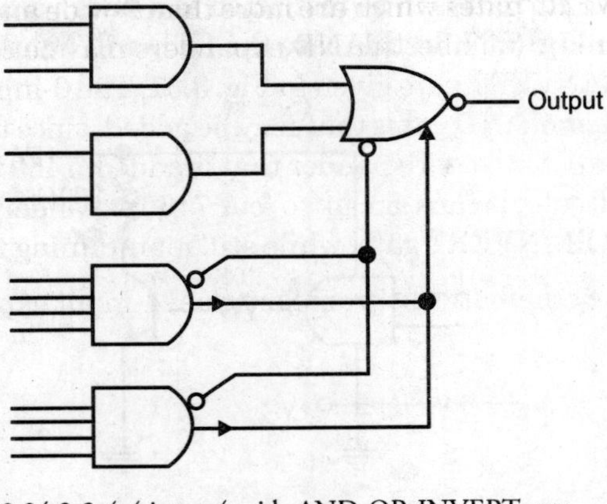

Fig. 3.34 2-2-4-4 input 4-wide AND-OR-INVERT gate

3.11 TTL DRIVERS FOR EXTERNAL LOADS

TTL drivers are sometimes required to drive external loads like LEDs, relays, etc. In such applications care should be exercised to ensure that current ratings of TTL drivers are not exceeded. A TTL driver can sink up to 16 mA of current and source up to 400 μA. The minimum value of a resistive load which a TTL driver can sink may be calculated as follows:

$$R_L = \frac{5\text{ V}}{16\text{ mA}} = 312\text{ ohm}$$

For instance if the current is to be restricted to 10 mA to drive an LED, it is necessary to take into account the voltage drop across it. R_L can now be calculated as follows:

$$R_L = \frac{5\text{ V} - 2\text{ V}}{10\text{ mA}} = 300\text{ ohm}$$

There are two ways of connecting an LED to a TTL gate used as a driver. If the driver is a NAND gate and it is required to light up an LED when the output is high, it should be connected as in Fig. 3.35. If the LED should light up when the NAND gate output is low, it should be connected as in Fig. 3.36.

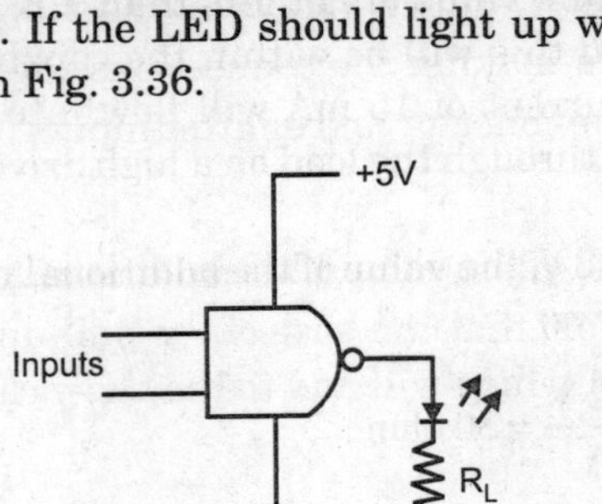

Fig. 3.35 LED lights up on high output

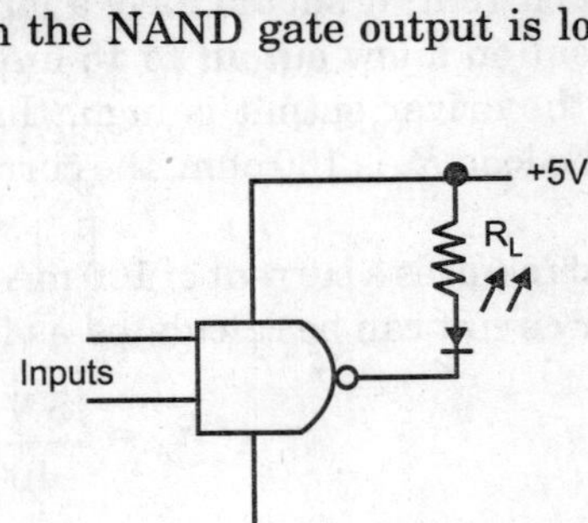

Fig. 3.36 LED lights up on low output

If the output drive current is to be restricted to a safer value, it is advisable to use a driver transistor as shown in Fig. 3.37. In this case the LED will light up when the output of the TTL driver goes high.

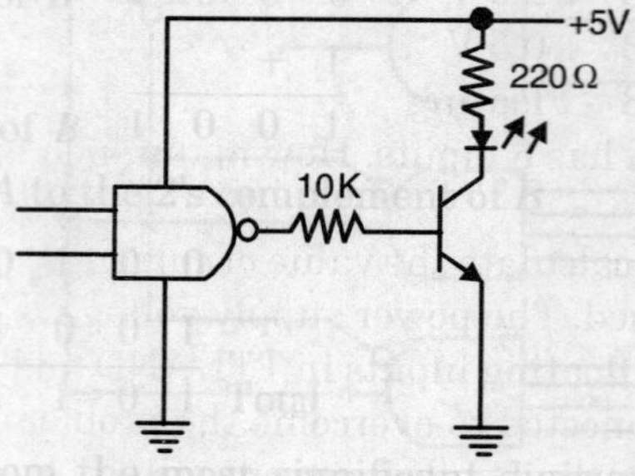

Fig. 3.37

If a load requires a higher drive voltage than + 5V, an open-collector TTL driver may be used to drive a transistor as in Fig. 3.38.

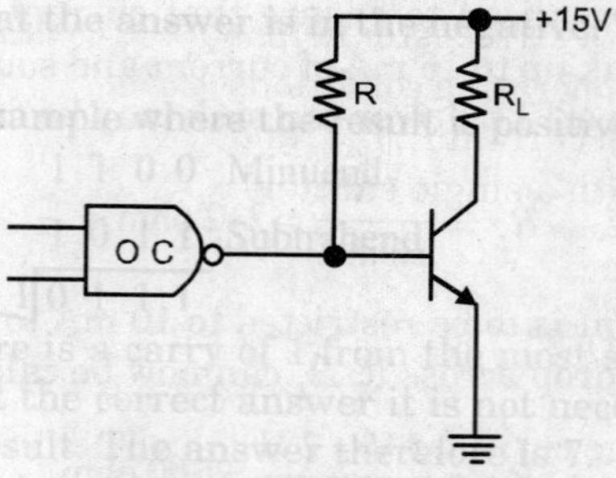

Fig. 3.38 Open-collector TTL driver

If the load requires a supply voltage of 15 V and since the TTL driver cannot sink more than 16 mA of current, R should have a minimum value of not less than 1 K ohm, which will limit the current on a low output to 15 mA and this will be within the capability of the TTL driver. When the driver output is high, this current of 15 mA will flow into the base of the transistor. If the load R_L is 150 ohm, the current through the load on a high driver output will be 100 mA.

If the load requires a current of 100 mA at 12 V, the value of the additional resistor required in the collector circuit can be calculated as follows:

$$R_A = \frac{15\text{ V} - 12\text{ V}}{100\text{ mA}} = 30\text{ ohm}$$

Problems

3.1 Draw a typical NAND gate circuit and explain how it works.

3.2 Four TTL gates are connected in cascade. The propagation delay time of each gate is 15 ns. What is the total delay?

3.3 What is the output of a standard 2-input TTL AND gate, if the inputs are as follows?

(*a*) A + 2.1V : B + 3.5 V
(*b*) A + 1.9 V : B + 2.4 V
(*c*) A + 1.9 V : B + 0.8 V
(*d*) A + 0.9 V : B + 2.0 V
(*e*) A +0 V : B + 0.5 V
(*f*) A +2.5 V : B Floating

3.4 A standard TTL load has 6 inputs. How many such loads can be connected to a standard TTL drive?

3.5 Refer to Fig. 3.1 and calculate the value of current I_1 if the voltage at the emitter E_1 is + 3 V and E_2 is earthed. The power supply voltage is + 5 V.

3.6 Explain the effect of floating inputs in TTL AND and OR gates. Suggest how floating inputs should be connected to overcome the problem.

3.7 A standard TTL driver can sink a current of 16 mA. How much current will it sink if 8 TTL loads are connected to the driver?

3.8 The output voltage of a standard TTL driver connected to a TTL load is + 0.2 V. The noise voltage varies from + 0.4 V to +0.8 V. In what way will it affect the output of the load?

3.9 A standard TTL driver can source a current of 400 μA. How many standard TTL unit loads can be connected to the driver?

3.10 Explain how a Schottky transistor helps to reduce power dissipation of a TTL device?

3.11 Under the following operating conditions a standard TTL driver has a logic 0 output. Calculate the value of current I_1, I_2, I_3 and I_4 as well as power dissipation of the device. (Consider Fig. 3.1 with a single emitter)

V_{CC}	=	+ 5.0 V
V_{BE}	:	As in Fig. 3.1
V_{CE} (sat), T_2	=	+ 0.2 V
V_{in}	=	+ 2.5 V
Leakage current	=	Negligible
R_1, R_2, R_3, R_4	:	As in Fig. 3.1

3.12 Under the same operating conditions as given in Problem 3.11, but with logic 0 input of 0.4 V, a TTL driver has a logic 1 output. Calculate the value of I_1 and the power dissipation of the device.

3.13 In Prob. 3.5 what would be the effect on current I_1 if both the emitters are at earth potential and the power supply is + 5V?

3.14 Explain how diode D_4 in Fig. 3.1 helps to maintain T_4 off while T_3 is conducting.

3.15 A noise voltage of 0.6 V is riding the high state output (3.9 V) of a standard TTL gate which is driving a standard TTL load. Will the performance be affected in any way by the noise voltage?

3.16 If the low level output of a standard TTL gate, driving a standard TTL load is 0.2 V, will a noise level of 0.4 V cause any problem?

3.17 During the high and low level outputs, the currents drawn by a standard TTL gate are I_{CCL} = 9.5 mA and I_{CCH} = 3.2 mA. Calculate the average device dissipation.

3.18 When open-collector gates are used, is there any limitation on the value of the pull-up resistor and the number of gates that can be connected to the output of the open-collector gate?

3.19 It is not possible to use TTL gates having totem-pole output in the wired-OR or wired-AND configuration? Explain, why?

3.20 Is it possible to implement the logic function Y = $B \cdot \overline{C}\,(\overline{A} + \overline{B})$ by the circuit given in Fig. P-3.20? If there are problems how would you implement it?

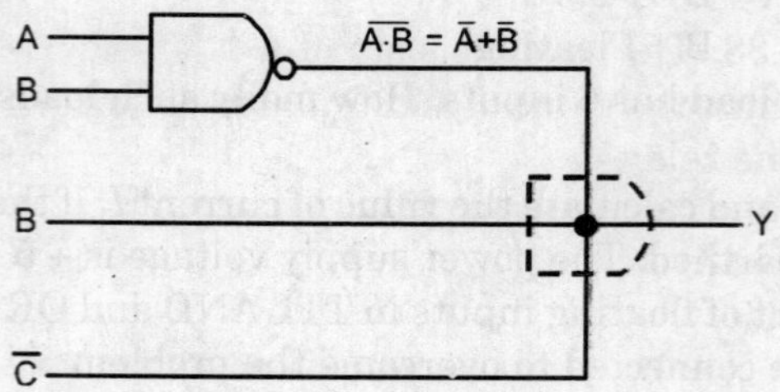

Fig. P-3.20

3.21 Refer to Fig. 3.7 and determine the state of the output under the following input conditions:

Input		*Control*	*Output*
A	***B***	***C***	***Y***
0	0	Low	
0	1	Low	
1	0	High	
1	1	Low	
1	1	High	

3.22 Refer to Fig. 3.9. You are required to transfer the contents of registers as indicated below:

From registers	*To Registers*		
	A	***B***	***C***
A	X	B	C
A	X	X	C
B	A	X	X
A	X	B	X
B	X	X	C
C	A	B	X

Determine the state of the Enable switches

3.23 Refer to Fig. 3.4 (b). If I_{OL} max is 16 mA and two gates are wire-ORed, what minimum value will you determine for the pull-up resistor to ensure that no device is damaged.

3.24 Refer to Fig. 3.35. The LED is required to light up on a high output and should not draw a current is excess of 15 mA. If the voltage drop across the LED is 2 V and the supply voltage is 5 V, what should be the minimum value of R_L?

3.25 Refer to Fig. 3.38. The load consists of a 9 V relay which has a current rating of 100 mA. Determine the value of additional resistance, if any required to be connected in series with the relay.

4

MOS Logic Family

4.1 INTRODUCTION

For very large integrated circuits we require very small logic gates. TTL devices which we have already considered in the last chapter do not substantially fulfil this requirement. Fortunately Metal Oxide Semiconductor FETs meet this requirement to a very large extent and at present these MOSFET devices are extensively used in pocket calculators, digital watches and in many other areas. They not only meet the requirement of small size but they are also very economical in cost and consume very little power although they are, at the moment, not as fast as TTL devices.

The category of MOS devices has the following families:

PMOS *P*-channel MOSFETS
NMOS *N*-channel MOSFETS
CMOS Complementary MOSFETS

Out of these MOS families the *P*-channel MOSFETS have almost become obsolete. Logic devices which use only *N*-channel MOSFETS, known as NMOS, are extensively used in large scale integrated circuits. The CMOS family, which uses complementary MOSFETS, that is both *N*-channel and *P*-channel enhancement type MOSFETS for implementing logic gates, has the advantage of low power consumption, high noise immunity and temperature stability. Besides, since they can work off low voltage power supplies, they dominate the portable equipment field.

4.2 PMOS, NMOS INVERTERS

An inverter circuit using a PMOS device is given in Fig. 4.1 and another inverter circuit employing an NMOS device is shown in Fig. 4.2. Notice the power supply polarity in these Inverter circuits.

When the T_2 gate input $-V_{DD}$ is high, T_2 is turned on, and as T_1 functions as a resistor, as shown in Fig. 4.2 (b), the output is low. When the gate input is 0 V, T_2 is turned off and the output voltage approaches $-V_{DD}$. The circuit functions as an Inverter. Since a resistive load is required for T_2 and it is more convenient to from another MOSFET than a resistor, a MOSFET is used as a load. It presents a resistance of about 10K to 100K ohm when gate is joined to drain. In diagrams sometimes T_1 is shown using the regular symbol and some manufactures show it as a resistor-plus-bar.

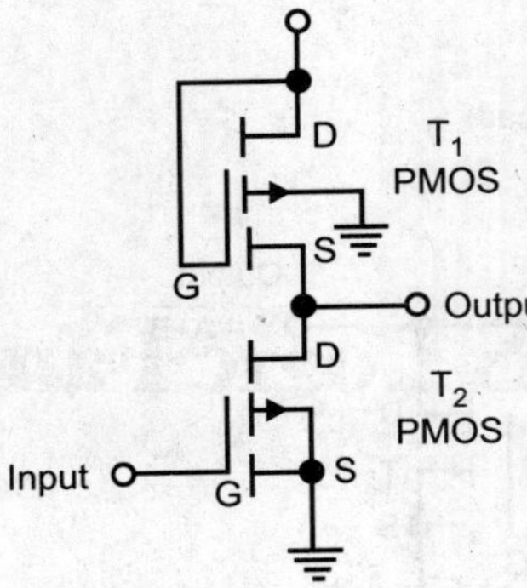

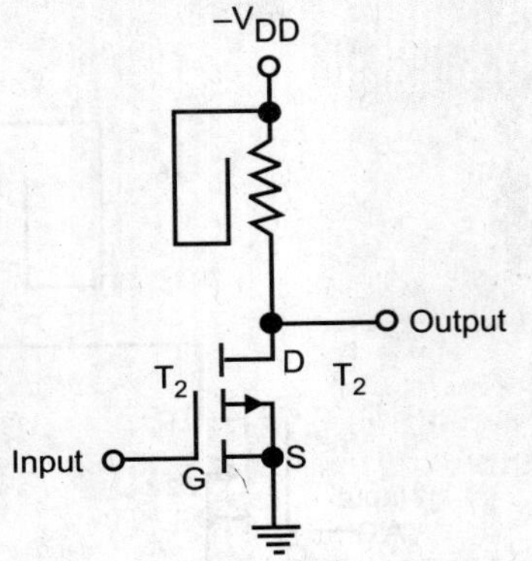

Fig. 4.1 (a) PMOS inverter (b) PMOS inverter: equivalent circuit

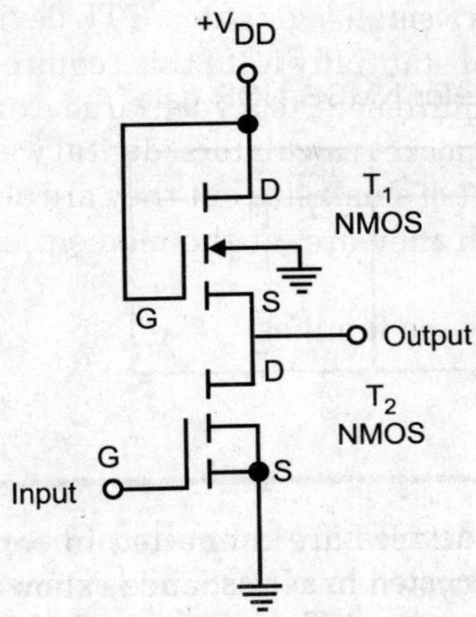

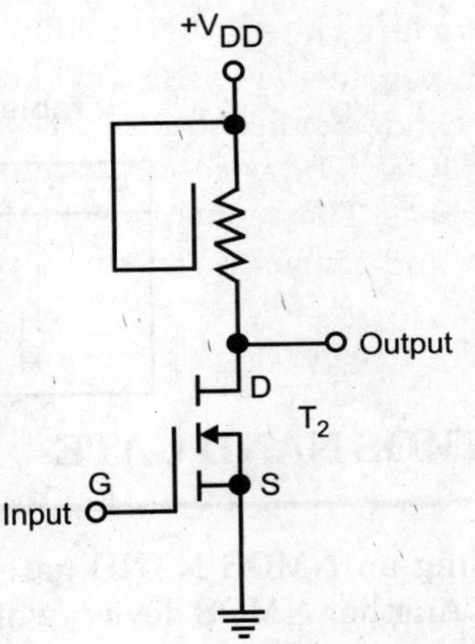

Fig. 4.2 (a) NMOS inverter, (b) NMOS inverter equivalent circuit

As in the PMOS device, transistor T_1 has its drain and gate tied together, so that it functions as a resistor. When the gate input $+V_{DD}$ is high, T_2 is turned on, the output goes low. When the gate input is 0 V, T_2 is cut off and the output goes high. It functions just like any inverter.

4.3 NMOS NOR GATE

A NOR gate can be fabricated following the same basic approach as in an Inverter. A simple design is given in Fig. 4.3. As before, the load consists of another NMOS transistor. The transistors which provide the input are connected in parallel. When the input, $+V_{DD}$, to any transistor is high, the output goes low. The output will go high only when inputs to both T_2 and T_3 are low, in which case both the transistors will be cut off.

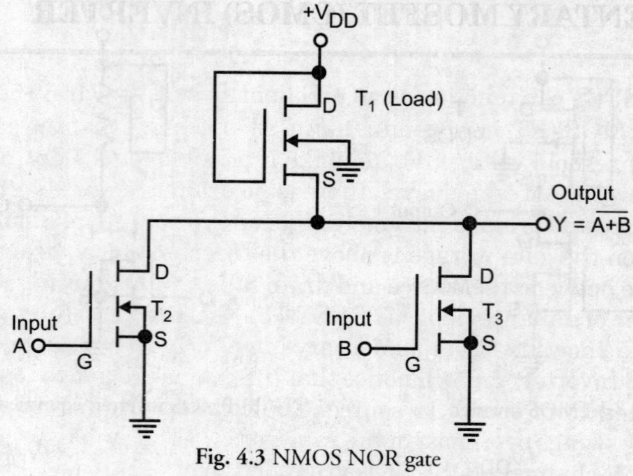

Fig. 4.3 NMOS NOR gate

Table 4.1 Truth table for NMOS NOR gate

A	*B*	*Y*
L	L	H
L	H	L
H	L	L
H	H	L

4.4 NMOS NAND GATE

In building an NMOS NAND gate, the NMOS devices are connected in series as shown in Fig. 4.4. Another NMOS device, which is also connected in series, and is shown as a resistor in the diagram, functions as the load. When the inputs at T_1 or T_2 or both are low, one of the transistors or both will be cut off as the case may be, and the output will be equal to V_{DD}. When inputs to both T_1 and T_2 are high, both transistors will be on, and the output will be nearly 0 V. Table 4.2 sums up the performance.

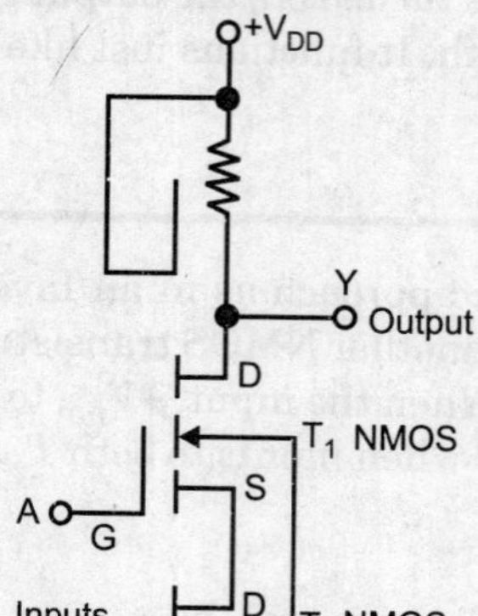

Fig. 4.4 NMOS NAND gate

Table 4.2 Truth table for NMOS NAND gate

A	*B*	*Y*
L	L	H
L	H	H
H	L	H
H	H	L

4.5 COMPLEMENTARY MOSFET (CMOS) INVERTER

The enhancement MOSFET can function as an excellent switch. The drain current characteristics of an enhancement MOSFET, in Appendix 1, Fig. AP-1.4, show that the gate-source voltage, V_{GS}, must exceed the threshold voltage, V_T, to make it possible for the drain current to flow. If the gate voltage is below the threshold level, there is no drain current, as a result of which the resistance between source and drain is extremely high, and closely approximates an open switch. On the other hand when the gate voltage is above the threshold level, drain current begins to flow, and the resistance between the source and drain falls, approximating a closed switch.

This characteristic of enhancement MOSFETS has been successfully utilized in building logic devices. Figure 4.5 shows two complementary MOSFETS, a *P*-channel and an *N*-channel device, to form a CMOS Inverter. You will notice that the drains are joined together and a supply Voltage V_{DD} is connected from source to source. The common drain connection provides the output and the input V_i swings over most of the range of V_{DD}. The supply voltage V_{DD} is positive, since the source of the *N*-channel MOSFET is grounded.

The *N*-channel MOSFET is turned on by a positive gate voltage and the *P*-channel MOSFET is turned on by a negative gate voltage. Therefore, when the gate voltage is positive, the NMOS transistor will be turned on and the PMOS transistor will be cut off. It will be just the reverse when the gate voltage in negative. MOSFETS connected in this manner bear a very close resemblance to two bipolar transistors in a complementary symmetry output stage, Fig. 4.5 (b), of an audio frequency amplifier.

When the gate input voltage, V_i, is exactly 1/2 V_{DD} the bias voltage at both T_1 and T_2 will be equal and they will, therefore, conduct equally. The output voltage will be 1/2 V_{DD}. If the input voltage is less than 1/2 V_{DD} the *N*-channel transistor will be cut off and the *P*-channel transistor will saturate. The output will therefore rise to V_{DD}. On the other hand, if V_i is larger than 1/2 V_{DD}, the *P*-channel transistor will be cut off and the *N*-channel transistor will saturate. The output voltage will drop down to almost 0 V.

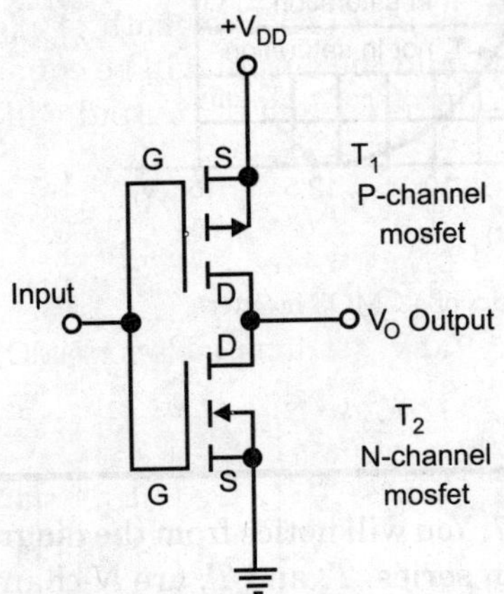

Fig. 4.5 (a) Complementary CMOS inverter

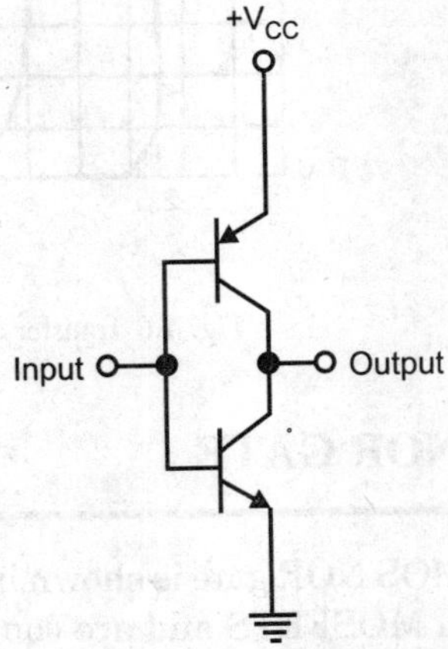

Fig. 4.5 (b) Bipolar complementary circuit

The switching characteristics of a CMOS inverter are shown in Fig. 4.6. The characteristics are shown for three supply voltages 5 V, 10 V and 15 V. You will also notice that the changeover from low to high or high to low is sharp and not gradual. The switching characteristics also show that the changeover point depends on the supply voltage. For instance when V_{DD} is 10V the changeover takes place at 5 V and when V_{DD} is 5 V the changeover occurs at 2.5 V.

There is no variation in switching characteristics due to temperature changes and these devices perform very reliably over a wide temperature range. CMOS inverters may show a little spread of switching voltage levels on eithr side of V_{DD} but on the whole you may take a low input voltage to be below 0.3 V_{DD} and high above 0.7 V_{DD}. The CMOS devices, therefore have a high noise immunity.

CMOS devices draw very little current since one of the transistors is always turned off. Therefore the standby power consumption is very small. Although hardly any current flows under static conditions, the situation is slightly different with an alternating input voltage at the gate. When the output changes from high to low or low to high both transistors are momentarily on and off. However, during the period of transition both of them may be on at the same time for a brief period and during this time some current will flow. Consequently, the power dissipation increases as the frequency of operation increases and may approach that of TTL devices at high operating frequencies.

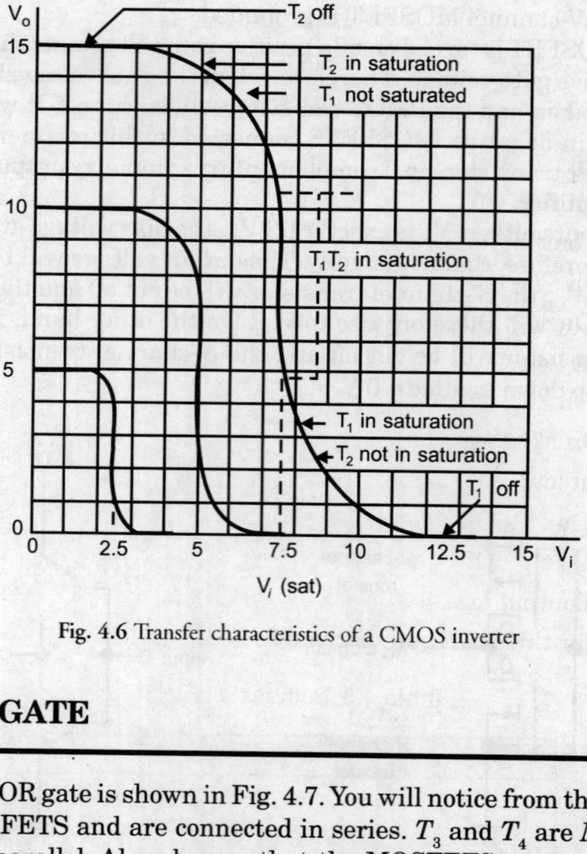

Fig. 4.6 Transfer characteristics of a CMOS inverter

4.6 CMOS NOR GATE

A circuit for a CMOS NOR gate is shown in Fig. 4.7. You will notice from the diagram that T_1 and T_2 are P-channel MOSFETS and are connected in series. T_3 and T_4 are *N*-channel MOSFETS and are connected in parallel. Also observe that the MOSFETS are so arranged that all are receiving voltages of the correct polarities. We shall study the output at *Y* with all possible input combinations at *A* and *B* as follows:

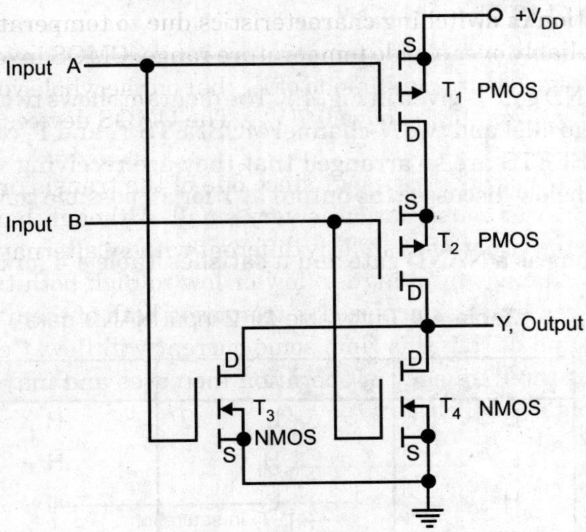

Fig. 4.7 CMOS NOR gate

1. A, Low : T_1, On : T_3, Off
   B, Low : T_2, On : T_4, Off
   T_1 and T_2 pull output high.
2. A, Low : T_1, On : T_3, Off
   B, High : T_4, On : T_2, Off
   T_4 pulls output low
3. A, High : T_2, On : T_1, Off
   B, Low : T_3, On : T_4, Off
   T_3 pulls output low
4. A, High : T_3, On : T_1, Off
   B, High : T_4, On : T_2, Off
   T_3 and T_4 pull output low.

The truth table for this NOR gate is given in Table 4.3.

Table 4.3 Truth table for NOR gate

A	*B*	*Y*
L	L	H
L	H	L
H	L	L
H	H	L

4.7 CMOS NAND GATE

A circuit for a CMOS NAND gate is given in Fig. 4.8. The diagram shows two *P*-channel MOSFETS, T_1 and T_2 connected in parallel and two *N*-channel MOSFETS T_3 and T_4 connected in series. You will notice that all MOSFETS are so arranged that they are receiving voltages of the correct polarities. The analysis below discusses the output at *Y* for all possible combinations of inputs at *A* and *B*.

This circuit functions as a NAND gate and it satisfies Table 4.4 for a 2-input NAND gate.

Table 4.4 Truth table for 2-input NAND gate

A	*B*	*Y*
L	L	H
L	H	H
H	L	H
H	H	L

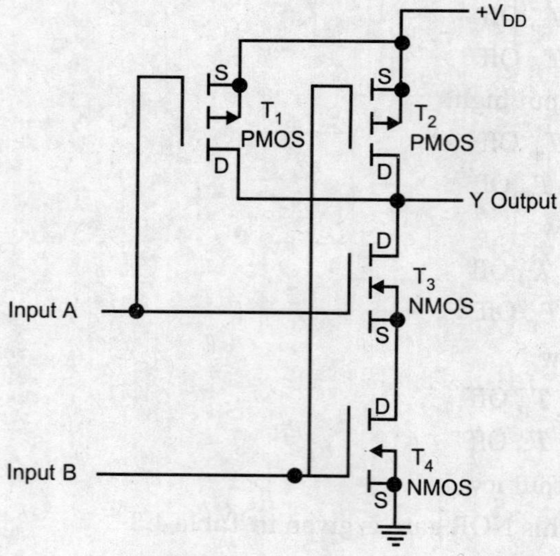

Fig. 4.8 CMOS NAND gate

Table 4.4 shows that the output will be low only when both the inputs are high. When both inputs *A* and *B* are high T_3 and T_4 will be on offering low resistance and T_1 and T_2 will be cut off offering high resistance. The output at *Y* will, therefore, be low. Analyzing the circuit further, you will see that when either or both inputs are low the output will be high.

4.8 BUFFERS AND LEVEL TRANSLATORS

Sometimes both CMOS and TTL integrated circuits are used in the same equipment. Since the logic level requirements of these two families of logic devices are different, special circuits are required which can translate CMOS logic levels to TTL logic levels. TTL circuits also require a current sinking capability of 1.6 mA per gate, which is beyond the capability of normal CMOS devices. Besides, TTL circuits require a power supply of 5 V, whereas CMOS devices can work on power supplies of 3 V to 15 V. CMOS Buffers and level translators meet this requirement when a CMOS device has to be interfaced with a TTL device. Figure 4.9 gives the schematic diagram of a CMOS inverting. Buffer which satisfies these criteria. Integrated circuit CD 4009 contains six such Buffer-translator-inverters in one package.

Figure 4.10 gives the schematic diagram of a non-inverting Buffer-level translator. Integrated circuit CD 4010 has six such non-inverting Buffer-level translators in a single package.

When it is desirable to use only one power supply which is suitable only for TTL devices, Buffers and level inverters type CD 4049 and CD 4050 will serve the purpose, as they are similar to CD 4009 and 4010, respectively and they are suitable for operation on a 5 V power supply.

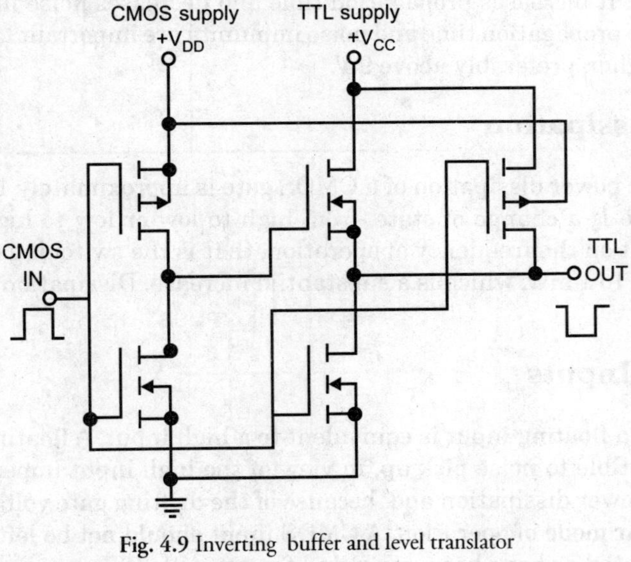

Fig. 4.9 Inverting buffer and level translator

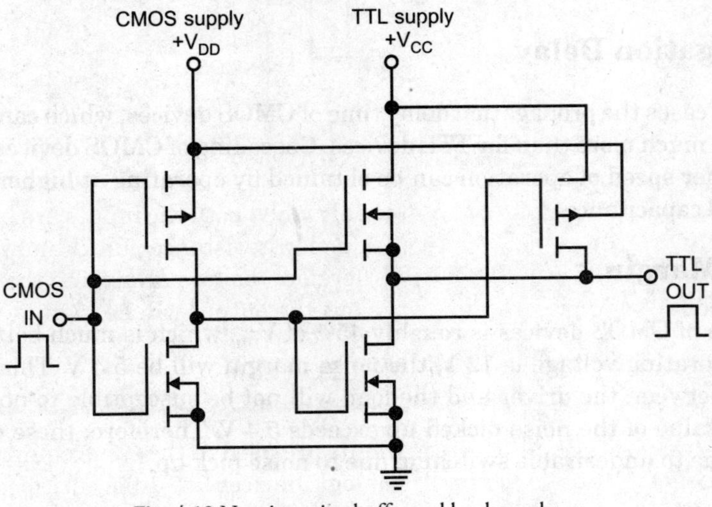

Fig. 4.10 Non-inverting buffer and level translator

4.9 CMOS CHARACTERISTICS

The characteristics of CMOS devices are naturally different from those of TTL devices; but the basic criteria are the same. Besides, it should be remembered that CMOS devices cannot be directly interfaced with TTL devices without special circuits.

4.9.1 Power Supply Requirements

Unlike TTL devices CMOS devices can work over a fairly wide voltage range, which extends from 3 V to 15 V. It should be remembered that the dissipation of a CMOS device increases with the supply voltage. Therefore, where power dissipation is an important consideration, CMOS devices should be operated at lower voltages. Operation at lower voltages is accompanied by some adverse effects. It increases propagation time and decreases noise immunity. Therefore, in applications where propagation time and noise immunity are important factors, the operation voltage should be higher, preferably above 9 V.

4.9.2 Power Dissipation

The average or static power dissipation of a CMOS gate is approximately 10nW. However, this increases when there is a change of state, from high to low or low to high. The quantum of increase is dependent on the frequency of operation, that is the switching speed. At 1MHz the dissipation increases to 1 mW, which is a substantial increase. Dissipation is also a function of the capacitive load.

4.9.3 Floating Inputs

As with TTL devices a floating input is equivalent to a high input. A floating input in a CMOS device is very susceptible to noise pick up, in view of the high input impedance of the device. This also increases power dissipation and, because of the drifting gate voltage, the CMOS gate may drift into a linear mode of operation. A CMOS input should not be left floating. The same methods may be adopted as have been suggested for use with TTL devices.

4.9.4 Propagation Delay

In the majority of cases the propagation delay time of CMOS devices, which can vary from about 25 ns to 100 ns, is much more than for TTL devices. Cascading of CMOS devices further adds up to the delay. Higher speed of operation can be obtained by operating at higher supply voltages and reducing load capacitance.

4.9.5 Noise Margin

The noise margin of CMOS devices is roughly 45% of V_{DD}, which is much better than for TTL devices. If the operating voltage is 12 V, the noise margin will be 5.4 V. This means that the connecting link between the driver and the load will not be susceptible to noise interference, unless the peak value of the noise picked up exceeds 5.4 V. Therefore, these devices are comparatively immune to undesirable switching due to noise pick up.

4.9.6 Sourcing and Sinking of Current

Just as TTL devices can source and sink current, so also the CMOS devices can source and sink current. The only difference is that, with CMOS devices the currents are very much smaller. Figure 4.11 shows a CMOS inverter driving a CMOS load. When the driver output is low, the driver sinks a current of 1 μA. It can also source a current of 1 μA when the driver output is high as shown in Fig. 4.12. Since the current is flowing out of the load when the driver output is low, I_{IL} max has a negative sign. Thus

$$I_{IL} \text{ max} = -1\,\mu\text{A}$$

As the current is flowing into the load when the driver output is high, I_{IH} max has a positive sign. Thus

$$I_{IH} \text{ max} = 1\mu\text{A}$$

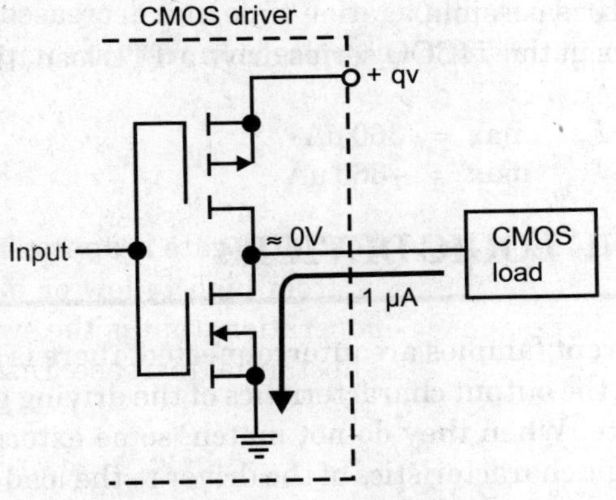

Fig 4.11 Shows direction and magnitude of current flowing from a CMOS load to a CMOS driver when the driver output is low (≈ 0 V)

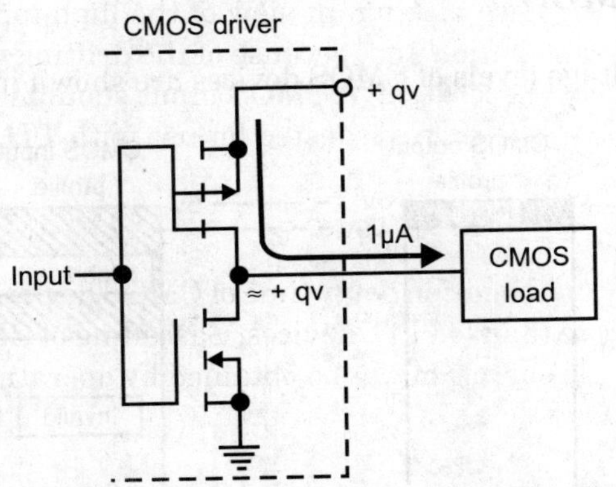

Fig. 4.12 Shows direction and magnitude of current flowing from a CMOS driver to a CMOS load when the driver output is high (≈ + 9 V)

4.9.7 Worst-case Voltages and Currents

We have considered earlier the worst-case voltages for TTL devices. Here we will consider the worst-case voltages and currents for CMOS devices in the 74COO series when operated from a 5 V supply.

The worst-case voltages are as follows:

$$V_{IH} \text{ min} = 3.5 \text{ V}$$
$$V_{IL} \text{ max} = 1.5 \text{ V}$$
$$V_{OH} \text{ min} = 4.9 \text{ V}$$
$$V_{OL} \text{ max} = 0.1 \text{ V}$$

Input and output currents for CMOS driving a CMOS load are as follows:

$$I_{IL} \text{ max} = -1 \text{ µA}$$
$$I_{IH} \text{ max} = 1 \text{ µA}$$
$$I_{OL} \text{ max} = 10 \text{ µA}$$
$$I_{OH} \text{ max} = -10 \text{ µA}$$

The worst-case voltages and currents show that when a CMOS driver is interfaced with a CMOS load, a fan out of 10 is possible.

When CMOS devices in the 74COO series drive a TTL load, the output currents are listed as follows in data sheets:

$$I_{OL} \text{ max} = 360 \text{ µA}$$
$$I_{OH} \text{ max} = -360 \text{ µA}$$

4.10 INTERFACING LOGIC DEVICES

When devices of two different families are interconnected, there is an interfacing problem; that is the need to ensure that the output characteristics of the driving gate match the input characteristics of the driven gate. When they do not match, some external circuitry may always be employed to match the logic characteristics of the driver to the load characteristics. We will now consider some interfacing problems and the methods normally employed in practice.

4.10.1 CMOS to CMOS

The output and input voltage levels of CMOS devices are shown in Fig. 4.13.

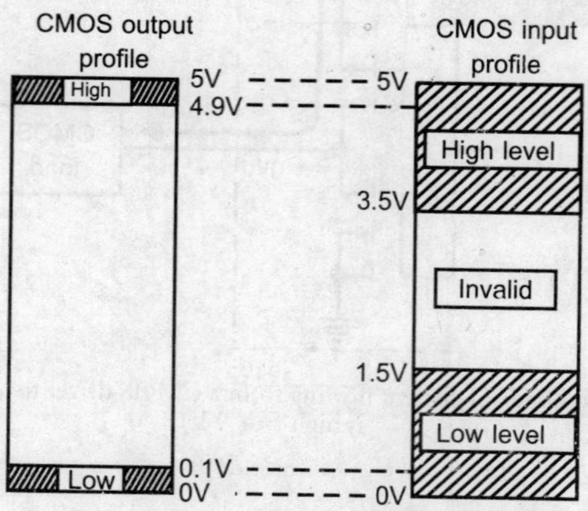

Fig. 4.13 CMOS output and input profiles

You will notice from the output and input profiles for CMOS devices that the high and low output logic levels fall within the acceptable high and low input voltage levels of a CMOS load. There is, therefore, no interfacing problem, and a CMOS driver can be directly connected to a CMOS load.

4.10.2 CMOS to NMOS and PMOS

Since the logic level and supply voltage requirements are the same for CMOS and NMOS devices, they can be interconnected directly.

PMOS devices can be operated from supply voltages of the order of 17 V to 24 V. When PMOS devices are operated on higher voltages than CMOS devices, it will be necessary to drop the high output voltage level of PMOS devices to somewhere below the supply voltage level of CMOS devices, so that it is compatible with CMOS input requirements. A resistor at the output of a PMOS device can be used for this purpose.

4.10.3 CMOS to TTL

In interfacing CMOS devices to TTL loads, we have to take into account the limiting values of voltage and current for CMOS and TTL devices. These have been listed below for CMOS drivers of the 74COO series and standard TTL loads, when both are operating on a 5 V supply.

CMOS Driver			TTL Load		
V_{OH}	min	: 4.9 V	V_{IH}	min	: 2.0 V
V_{OL}	max	: 0.1 V	V_{IL}	max	: 0.8 V
I_{OH}	max	: –360 μA	I_{IH}	max	: 40 μA
I_{OL}	max	: 360 μA	I_{IL}	max	: – 1.6 mA

The input and output profiles of a CMOS driver and a TTL load are shown in Fig. 4.14.

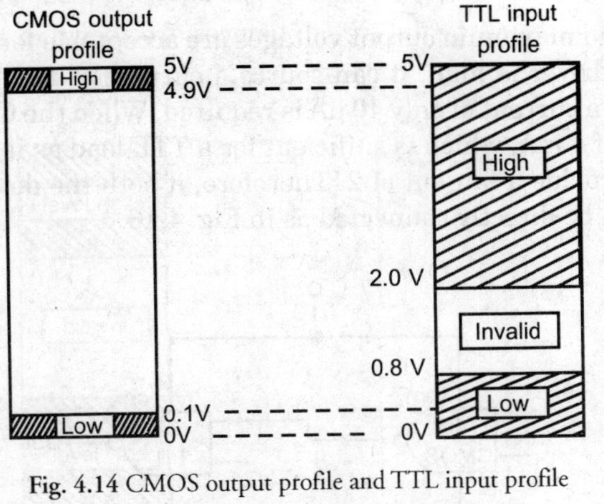

Fig. 4.14 CMOS output profile and TTL input profile

Since the high and low output logic levels of the CMOS driver fall within the permissible range of the high and low input levels of a TTL input, there is no problem so far as the logic voltage levels are concerned.

When the output is high, the CMOS driver can source a current of 360 μA, which is acceptable for a TTL load as the maximum current required is 40 μA. However, when the output of the CMOS driver is low, it can sink a current of only 360 μA, which is not adequate for a TTL load as the minimum current required is 1.6 mA.

We will consider how the interfacing problem can be solved. The simplest solution is to substitute a TTL load by a low power Schottky TTL load (74LS TTL series). The input current and logic level requirements are as follows:

I_{IH}	max	: 20 μA	V_{IH}	min	: 2.0 V
I_{IL}	max	: –360 μA	V_{IL}	max	: 0.8 V

V_{IH} min and V_{IL} max for the 74 LS TTL series are the same as for the 74 TTL series and so the logic levels present no interfacing problem. The current requirements are also within the permissible limits of CMOS drivers. If both devices are operating from a 5 V supply, they can be directly connected as shown in Fig. 4.15.

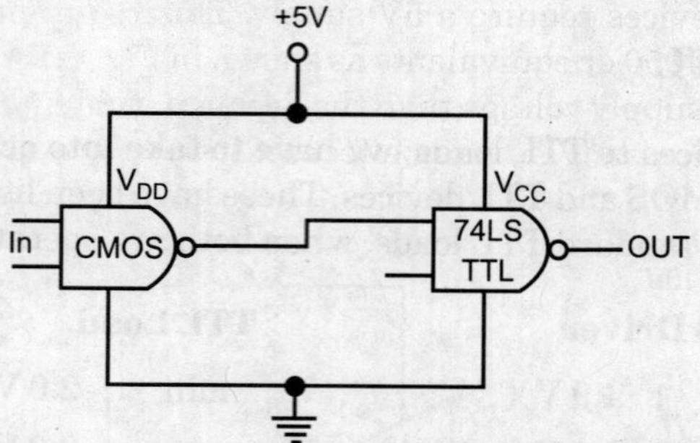

Fig. 4.15 CMOS driving a low power Schottky TTL

The other alternative is to use a CMOS driver of the 74 H series to drive a standard TTL load. The output currents and voltages for this CMOS series are as follows:

I_{OH}	max	: – 4.0 mA	V_{OH}	min	: 4.9 V
I_{OL}	max	: 4.0 mA	V_{OL}	max	: 0.1 V

The minimum and maximum output voltages are acceptable for the TTL series. When the output of the CMOS driver is high, it can source a current of 4 mA which is adequate for a standard TTL load, as a current of only 40 μA is required. When the CMOS driver output is low, it can sink a current of 4 mA, which is sufficient for a TTL load as it requires a current of only 1.6 mA. It can thus provide a fan-out of 2. Therefore, if both the devices are operating from a supply of 5 V, they can be directly connected as in Fig. 4.16.

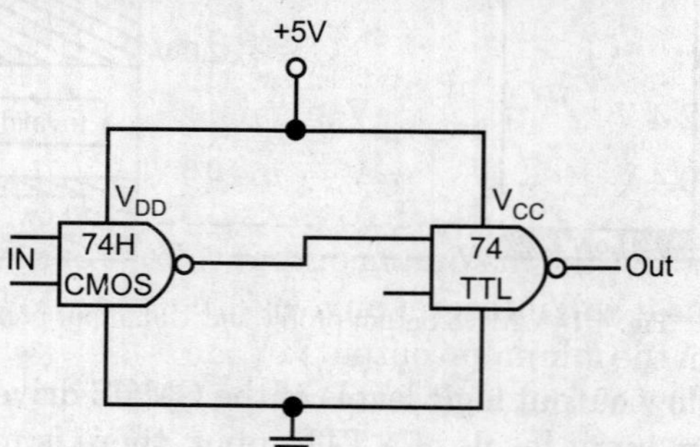

Fig. 4.16 CMOS 74 H driving a standard TTL

The other alternative is a CMOS inverting buffer CD 4049 or a non-inverting buffer CD 4050 or equivalents. These ICs, have six buffers in each package and each buffer can drive two TTL gates. If both the devices are operating from a 5 V supply, interfacing can be done as in Fig. 4.17.

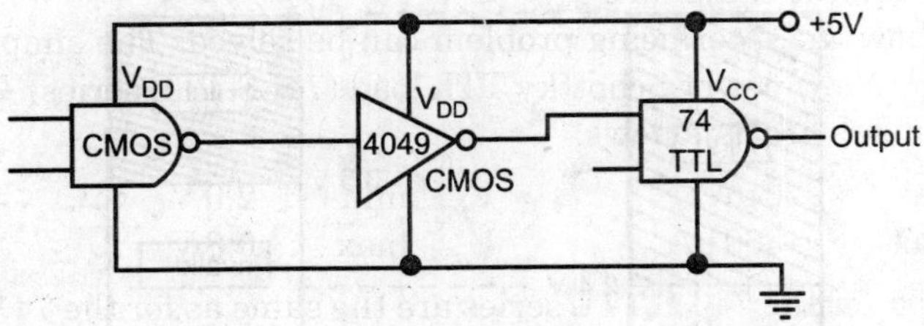

Fig. 4.17 CMOS to standard TTL interface through a buffer

CMOS devices give a better all round performance when they are operated at voltages around 9–12 V, while TTL devices require a 5V supply. This requirement can also be met by using buffers CD 4049 or CD 4050 or equivalents as shown in Fig. 4.18. Even though the CMOS buffer is operating on a lower supply voltage than the driver, it can handle input voltages greater than its supply voltage, without any adverse effect on its performance. In this case also the fanout will still be two.

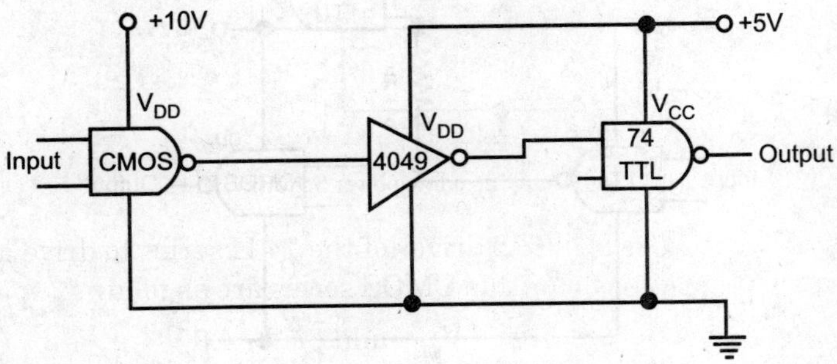

Fig. 4.18 Interfacing a CMOS driver to a TTL load when the supply voltages are different

4.10.4 TTL to CMOS

We will consider the worst-case output voltages of a TTL driver and the input voltages required for a CMOS load when both devices are operated from a 5 V supply. These are as follows:

TTL driver:	**CMOS load**
V_{OH} min : 2.4 V	V_{IH} min : 3.5 V
V_{OL} max : 0.4 V	V_{IL} max : 1.5 V

When the TTL output is low, the maximum output voltage of a TTL driver is 0.4 V, which is suitable for a CMOS load as it will interpret any voltage up to 1.5 V as a logic 0 input. When the TTL driver output is high, the minimum output voltage is 2.4 V, whereas the output voltage required for a CMOS load is 3.5 V. The high state output voltage of a TTL driver is, therefore, not adequate to drive a CMOS load.

The output profile of a TTL driver and the input profile of a CMOS load, as in Fig. 4.19, clearly show that there is an interfacing problem.

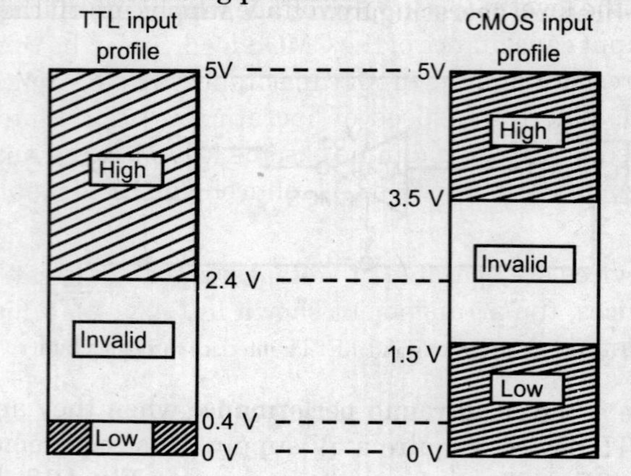

Fig. 4.19 Output profile of a TTL driver and input profile of a CMOS load

A simple solution to the problem lies in the use of a pull-up resistor which is connected beween the TTL driver and the CMOS load as shown in Fig. 4.20.

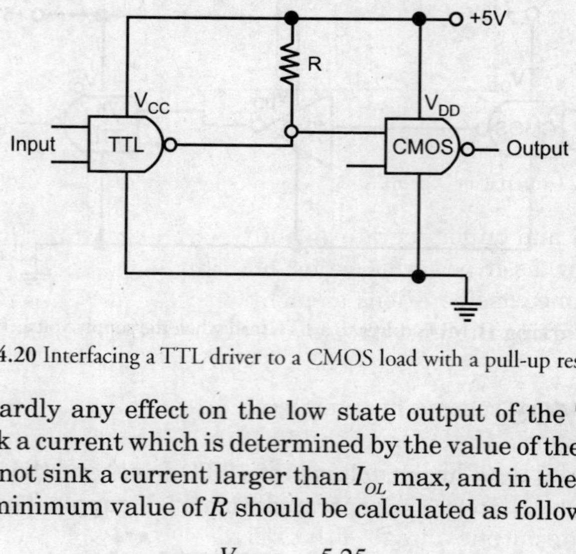

Fig. 4.20 Interfacing a TTL driver to a CMOS load with a pull-up resistor

Resistor R has hardly any effect on the low state output of the TTL driver. When the output is low it will sink a current which is determined by the value of the pull-up resistor. Since the TTL driver should not sink a current larger than I_{OL} max, and in the worst case V_{CC} may be as high as 5.25 V, the minimum value of R should be calculated as follows:

$$R_{\min} = \frac{V_{CC}}{I_{OL}\ \max} = \frac{5.25}{0.016} = 328 \text{ ohm}$$

There are two considerations in the choice of the maximum value of the pull-up resistor. In the first place it should allow a minimum sink current of 1.6 mA to flow through it. Therefore the maximum value of the pull-up resistor should not exceed.

$$R_{\max} = \frac{5.25}{1.6 \text{ mA}} = 3281 \textit{ or } 3.3 \text{ K ohm}$$

The upper limit of the pull-up resistor is a function of the input capacitance of the CMOS load. When the output of the TTL driver is high, roughly 2.4 V, the pull-up resistor raises it further and almost to the level of the supply voltage which cuts off the upper totem-pole transistor and charges the input capacitance of the CMOS load. Since the time constant depends on the values of the pull-up resistor and the input capacitance, a high value of the pull-up resistor will slow down the speed. Where the speed of operation is important, the value of the pull-up resistor can be reduced; but it should in no case be less than the minimum value of R, that is roughly 330 ohm. Normally a value of 1 – 3.3 K ohm should be adequate when the supply voltage is 5 V.

When CMOS devices are operated at voltages which are greater than the supply voltage required for TTL devices, the arrangement shown in Fig. 4.21, which uses an open collector/ Buffer, may be considered.

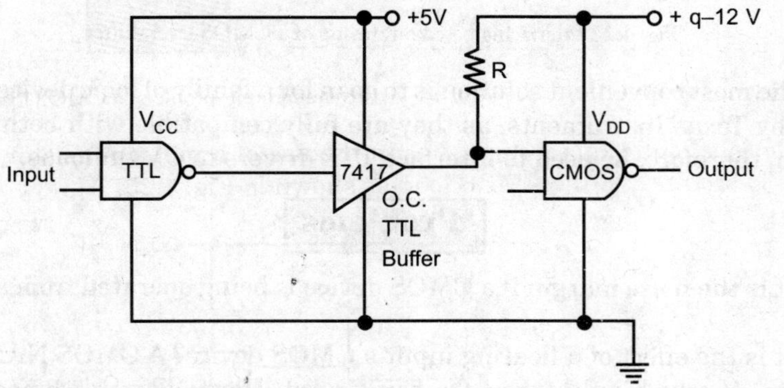

Fig. 4.21 Interfacing scheme using an open-collector non-inverting TTL buffer 7417

The TTL driver and buffer operate on a 5 V supply and the CMOS load is connected to a 9–12 V power supply, as it performs better on a higher voltage. The value of resistor R is calculated on the same considerations as mentioned earlier. The open-collector buffer in the diagram is a non-inverting Buffer, but an inverting buffer 7407 or their equivalents may also be used.

A more satisfactory scheme of interfacing depends on the use of a level shifter as in Fig. 4.22. In this scheme a CMOS level shifter is used. Its input side operates on a 5 V supply, which is the same as for the TTL device, and the output side operates on a supply of 12 V, which is the same as for the CMOS load. The value of the pull-up resistor connected to the TTL load pulls up the high state output voltage of the TTL driver to about 5 V, which is compatible with the requirement of the CMOS buffer. The output logic levels of the CMOS Buffer are compatible with the input requirements of the CMOS load.

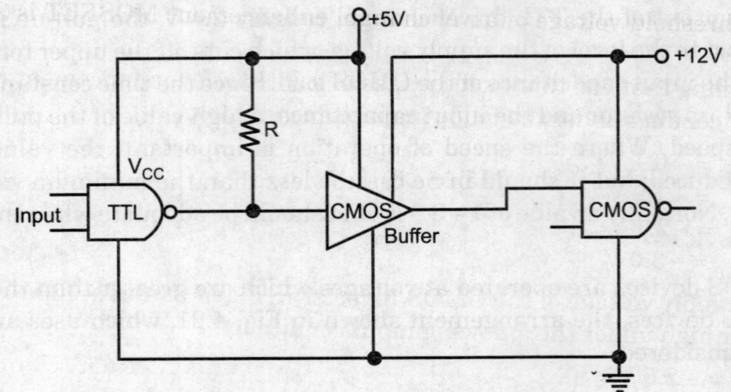

Fig. 4.22 Interfacing based on the use of a CMOS level shifter

Perhaps the most convenient solution is to go in for a family of logic devices, 54/74 HCTXX, manufactured by Texas Instruments, as they are fully compatible with both TTL and CMOS devices and can, therefore, be used to interface TTL drivers to CMOS loads.

Problems

4.1 What is the noise margin if a CMOS device is being operated from a power supply of +12 V?

4.2 What is the effect of a floating input a CMOS device? A CMOS NAND gate has four inputs, of which only three are being used. How will you connect the remaining input?

4.3 A CMOS device is being operated from a power supply of + 5V. What is the maximum value of the peak noise voltage which will not cause unwanted switching?

4.4 The values of V_{IL} max and V_{OH} min for CMOS loads are as follows, when the power supply voltage is + 5V:

V_{IL} max : + 1.5 V

V_{OH} min : + 3.5 V

What would be the output voltage of a 2-input CMOS AND gate in the following cases?

(*a*) A, + 0 V : B, + 3.5 V
(*b*) A, + 3.3 V : B, + 1.3 V
(*c*) A, + 3.7 V : B, + 1.2 V
(*d*) A, + 1.0 V : B, + 3.2 V
(*e*) A, + 3.0 V : B, + 1.5 V
(*f*) A, + 1.5 V : B, + 1.5 V
(*g*) A, + 1.5 V : B, + Floating
(*h*) A, + Floating B, + 3.7 V

4.5 Is it possible to directly interface a TTL driver to a CMOS load? Give reasons.

4.6 Explain the advantages and disadvantages of TTL and CMOS devices.

4.7 Refer to Fig. 4.5 (a). Which of the MOSFETS will be turned off if the input is at ground potential? What is the output?

4.8 How will you interface a CMOS NAND gate to a low power Schottky AND gate, if the power supply voltage is 5 V?

4.9 The threshold voltage of an *N*-channel enhancement MOSFET is 2 V. What does it signify?

4.10 Assuming that the threshold voltage of a *P*-channel enhancement MOSFET is –2 V, will it conduct under the following input conditions?

(*a*) $V_{GS} = -0.1$ V
(*b*) $V_{GS} = -1.9$ V
(*c*) $V_{GS} = -2.1$ V
(*d*) $V_{GS} = -3.0$ V

4.11 The supply voltage of the CMOS Inverter in Fig. 4.5 (a) is + 10 V. Will the output be low or high under the following input conditions?

(*a*) $V_i = +2.5$ V
(*b*) $V_i = +4.5$ V
(*c*) $V_i = +5.5$ V
(*d*) $V_i = +7.0$ V

4.12 Two CMOS devices are cascaded. If the propagation delay of one of these is 100 ns and that of the other 120 ns. What will be the total propagation delay?

4.13 A CMOS NAND gate is driving a standard TTL NAND gate and both are operating on a 5 V supply. What would be the noise margin when the output of the CMOS gate is high?

4.14 What logic function is performed by the circuit given in Fig. P-4.14? Draw up its truth table.

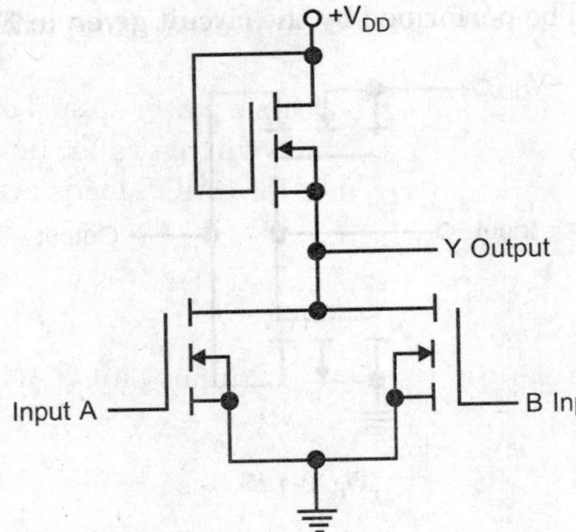

Fig. P-4.14

4.15 A TTL NAND gate is driving a CMOS inverter. Calculate the noise margin from the following data when the input to the inverter is low.

TTL	CMOS
V_{OL} max, 0.4 V	V_{IH} min, 3.5 V
V_{OH} min, 2.4 V	V_{IL} max, 1.0 V

4.16 Write the truth table for the circuit given in Fig. P-4.16 and draw the equivalent logic diagram.

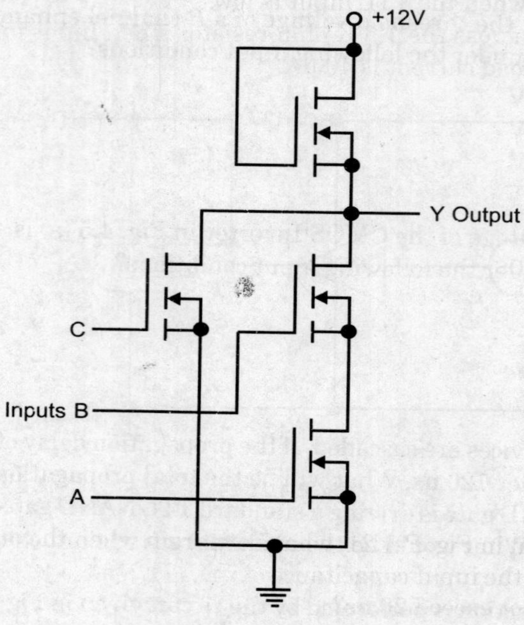

Fig. P-4.16

4.17 What function will be performed by the circuit given in Fig. P-4.17?

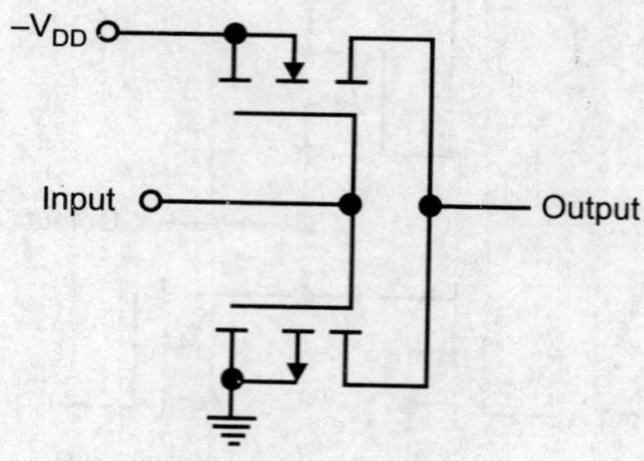

Fig. P-4.17

4.18 Refer to Fig. 4.20. If R is 3 K ohm and the supply voltage is 5 V, calculate the following:

(*a*) Sink current when the TTL output is low.

(*b*) Voltage drop across R if the input current of the CMOS load is 1 μA, when the TTL output is high.

4.19 Refer to Fig. 4.20 and calculate the pull-up time constant when R is 3 K ohm and the input capacitance of the CMOS load is 5 pF.

4.20 Refer to Fig. P-4.21. If R is 1800 ohm and the CMOS power supply is 10 V, calculate the current which the Buffer has to sink when input to the CMOS load is low.

4.21 Refer to Fig. P-4.21 and calculate the following:

(*a*) Sink current when the TTL input is low.

(*b*) Voltage drop across the 1.5 K ohm resistor when input to the TTL load is high and the TTL load current is 40 μA.

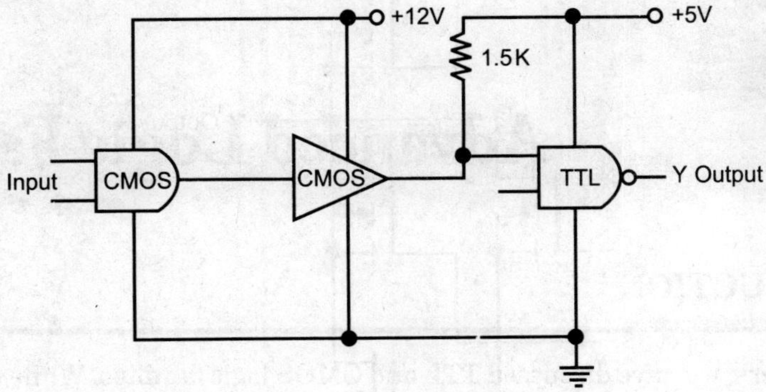

Fig. P-4.21

4.22 In the circuit given in Fig. P-4.21, what should be the limit on the maximum value of pull-up resistor if the input capacitance of the TTL load is 10 pF and the pull-up time constant should not exceed 20 ns?

5

Advanced Logic Families

5.1 INTRODUCTION

In previous chapters, we have discussed TTL and CMOS logic families. While these logic devices are very commonly used in the majority of cases, their limitations of speed and power dissipation are too obvious. There is a growing requirement for high speed logic devices consuming less power. Another important consideration is the number of gates that can be accommodated in a given area on a chip. While no logic device will fulfil all the requirements, there are some more advanced logic families which satisfy some of these needs. In this context we will consider the emitter-coupled logic (ECL) and integrated-injection logic (IIL).

The speed limitation of the logic families which we have already considered arises from the fact that transistors are driven into saturation to turn them ON and they are turned OFF when they come out of saturation. The time delay occurs because of the stored charge in the base region of tansistors, which has to be removed before the transistors can begin to turn off. Emitter-coupled logic devices overcome this problem by using a difference amplifier, which eliminates the need to use saturation as a means of turning on a transistor. Turning off a transistor presents no problem in the absence of saturation. While a higher speed of operation of about 0.3 ns can be achieved by using ECL gates, power dissipation will also be high, that is about 60 mW per gate.

As in integrated circuits, gates have to be packed very close together, heat generation is also an important consideration. A more appropriate criterion for the selection of a logic family for fabricating large integrated circuits is the speed-power product, pj, which we have considered in Section 3.5.8. The speed-power product for standard TTL gates is 100 (10 ns × 10 mW), which is a very high figure for large scale integrated circuits.

Another family of logic devices, known as integrated-injection logic (IIL or I^2L), which will also be discussed in this chapter, has a speed-power product of 0.1–0.7 pj. It appears to be very suitable for very large scale integrated circuits. Another advantage of this logic family is that, about 200 gates can be packed in an area of one square millimetre on a chip, whereas only 20 TTL gates can be accommodated in this space.

5.2 EMITTER-COUPLED LOGIC

Emitter-coupled logic gates consist of three sections, the difference amplifier, bias network and the output stage. The difference amplifier does away with the need to use saturation for turning on a transistor and the bias supply provides a reference voltage which fixes the logic levels. The output stage provides low-impedance emitter-follower outputs.

The basic circuit of a difference amplifier is given in Fig. 5.1.

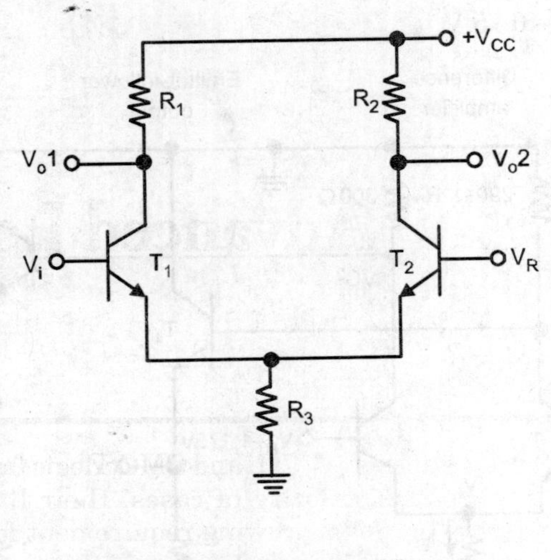

Fig. 5.1 Difference amplifier

Notice that the emitters of both the transistors are connected together, which gives this family of logic circuits the classification of emitter-coupled logic (ECL). Also observe that the two transistors function as emitter-followers, which introduces a measure of negative feedback, providing stability in the active region of operation.

When incorporated in an ECL gate, the base of T_2 is held at a fixed reference voltage, V_R and the input signal, V_i, is applied at the base of T_1. The resistance and the reference voltage are so chosen that the transistors function in the active region of their characteristics and not in the saturation mode.

As long as V_i is less positive than V_R with respect to ground T_1 will remain cut off and T_2 will be on. When $V_i = V_R$, the currents in the two transistors will be equal. When V_i exceeds V_R, the voltage across R_3 will rise, and since V_R is constant, T_2 will be cut off and T_1 will be turned on, which will now operate in the active region.

You will observe that increasing V_i from less than V_R to more than V_R switches the current from T_2 to T_1. On the other hand, when V_i decreases to a level below V_R, the current is switched back from T_1 to T_2 cutting off T_1 and switching on T_2. With this simple expedient, it is possible to switch on or switch off a transistor without the need to operate a transistor in the saturation mode.

5.3 ECL INVERTER

Figure 5.2, which represents an ECL Inverter, brings out some basic features of ECL gates. Transistors T_1 and T_2 constitute a difference amplifier. Input, V_i, is applied at A and outputs Y and $\overline{Y}$ are taken from the emitters of T_3 and T_4. A negative power supply of –5.2 V is used for the gate and, therefore, the collector resistors are grounded and the emitter resistors are connected to –5.2 V. We will be using positive logic assignments to analyze this inverter circuit when the logic levels will be as follows:

Logic 0 (low level) ; – 1.55V
Logic 1 (high level) ; – 0.75 V

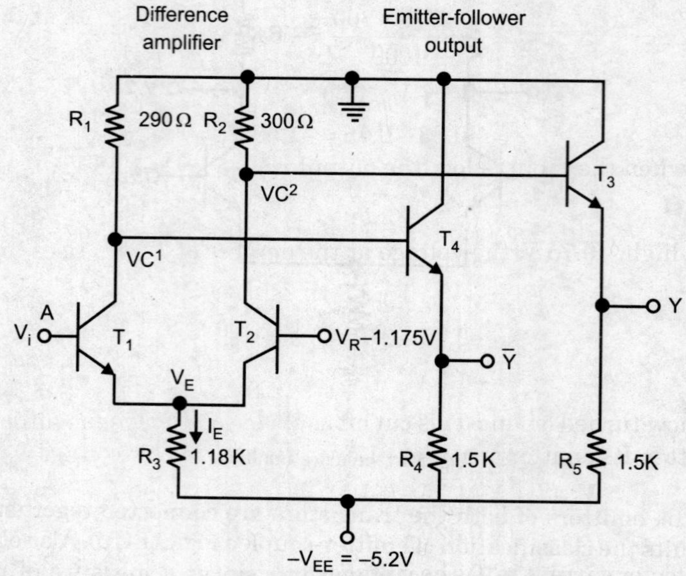

Fig. 5.2 ECL inverter

You will observe that the base of T_2 has been given a reference voltage $V_R = -1.175$ V, which is held constant. As the transistors will be operating in the active and not in the saturation mode, we will assume that in the active region $V_{BE} = 0.75$ V. We will now proceed to analyze the circuit.

Output *Y*(low output)

When the input to T_1, V_i is low, –1.55 V, the voltage V_E at its emitter will be as follows:

$$V_E = -V_R - V_{BE}(T_2)$$
$$= -1.175 - 0.75$$
$$= -1.925 \text{ V}$$

In this state T_2 will be turned on but T_1 will be cut off as the base of T_1 will not be sufficiently positive with respect to its emitter, as shown below:

$$V_{BE}(T_1) = V_i - V_E$$
$$= -1.55 - (-1.925)$$
$$= 0.375 \text{ V}$$

Now voltage across $R_3 = V_E - V_{EE}$

$$= -1.925 - (-5.2)$$
$$= 3.275 \text{ V}$$

$$I_E = \frac{V_E}{R_3}$$

$$= \frac{3.275}{1.18} = 2.775 \text{ mA}$$

T_2 collector voltage, $V_{C2} = -I_E \times R_2$

$$= -\frac{2.775 \times 300}{1000} = -0.83 \text{ V}$$

Output $Y = -V_{c2} - V_{BE}(T_3)$

$$= -0.83 - 0.75 = -1.58 \text{ V}$$

This shows that when the input is low, the output is also low, –1.58 V.

Output Y(high input)

When the input, V_i, is high, –0.75 V, the voltage at the emitter of T_1, V_E, rises to

$$V_E = -V_i - V_{BE}(T_1)$$
$$= -0.75 - 0.75$$
$$= -1.5 \text{ V}$$

Transistor T_1 is now turned on and T_2 is cut off as its base is no longer sufficiently positive with respect to its emitter. Its emitter is now at –1.5 V. Its base emitter voltage is now as follows:

$$V_{BE}(T_2) = -1.75 - (-1.5)$$
$$= 0.325 \text{ V}$$

As there is no collector current in T_2 the voltage drop across R_2 is negligible and, therefore, the voltage at the base of T_3 will be 0 with respect to ground. The output Y is, therefore, –0.75 V, that is the base-emitter voltage of T_3. If we apply a small correction for the voltage drop across R_2, the output at Y will be approximately –0.76 V. The analysis shows that the output at Y faithfully follows the input.

Output $\overline{Y}$ (low input)

We will now take up for consideration the output $\overline{y}$ at the emitter of T_4 when input V_i is low, –1.55 V (logic 0). As before T_1 will be cut off and T_2 will be turned on. The voltage V_{c1} at the collector of T_1 will be almost 0. The voltage at the emitter of T_4 will therefore be –0.75 V (logic 1). This shows that when the input is logic 0, the $\overline{Y}$ output is logic 1.

Output $\overline{Y}$ (high input)

When input V_i goes high, –0.75 V (logic 1), T_1 is turned on and the voltage at its emitter rises to –1.5 V as mentioned earlier. You will observe that the emitter voltage has gone positive with respect to its previous value and this decrease the base-emitter voltage of T_2, which is now cut off. Since in a differential amplifier the total current drawn by it remains nearly constant, the current of 2.775 mA which was formerly flowing through R_2, T_2 and R_3 will now flow through R_1, T_1 and R_3 without much change as T_2 is cut off and T_1 is turned on. The voltage drop across R_1 will be as follows:

$$\text{Voltage across } R_1 = \frac{290 \times 2.775}{1000} = -0.8 \text{ V}$$

Output $\overline{Y} = -0.8 - 0.75 = -1.55$ V

This shows that when the input is high (logic 1) the output $\overline{Y}$ is low (logic 0). Thus the output is inverted with respect to the input.

5.4 ECL OR/NOR GATE

ECL OR/NOR gates follow the same approach as an ECL inverter. In OR/NOR gates the number of transistors at the input is the same as the number of input variable. An ECL gate which can develop both OR and NOR outputs is shown in Fig. 5.3.

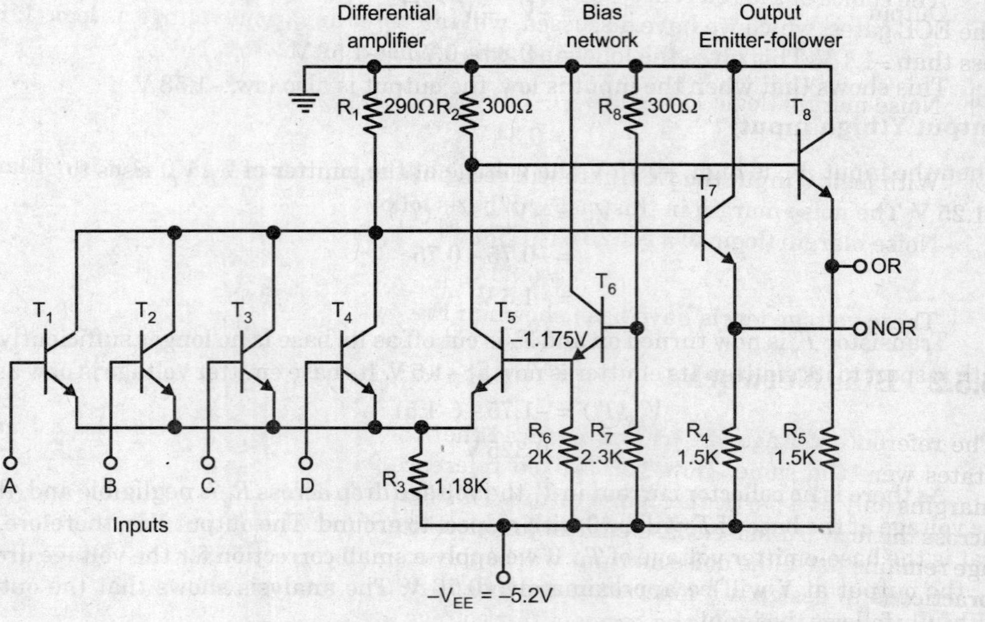

Fig. 5.3 Motorola MECL II emitter-coupled logic gate

The gate shown in the diagram is Motorola MECL II gate which develops both OR and NOR outputs, which resemble the Y and $\overline{Y}$ outputs of the inverter. The ECL gate has four inputs and it also incorporates a bias network which provides a bias voltage of –1.175 V for transistor T_5 of the differential amplifier portion of the gate. The rest of the circuit follows the same arrangement as the inverter circuit discussed earlier.

The circuit operates in the same way as the Inverter. When all the inputs are low, transistors T_1, T_2, T_3 and T_4 will be cut off and T_5 will be turned on and, as in the case of the Inverter, the OR output will be low (logic 0), –1.58 V. Also with all the inputs low, as in the case of the Inverter, the NOR output ($\overline{Y}$ in the case of the Inverter) will be high, –0.75 V (logic 1).

When any one of the inputs is high, that transistor will be turned on and T_5 will be cut off. Again, as in the case of the inverter, this will result in a high (logic 1) OR output and a low (logic 0) NOR output.

5.5 ECL CHARACTERISTICS

The characteristics of ECL devices naturally differ from those of other logic families. Their most useful feature is their speed of operation, which is very high and they consume substantially more power than other logic families. We will consider some of their important features.

5.5.1 Noise Margin

You will notice that the reference voltage of –1.175 V lies midway between the logic 1 and logic 0 input voltage levels of –0.76 V and –1.58 V.

$$1.17\text{ V} - 0.76\text{ V} = 0.41\text{ V}$$

and

$$1.58\text{ V} - 1.17\text{V} = 0.41\text{ V}$$

The choice of the reference voltage gives equal noise margins in logic 1 and logic 0 inputs. The ECL gates, which we have discussed, will interpret any input voltage as logic 1, if it is not less than –1.1 V. This gives the following logic 1 noise margin:

$$\text{Noise margin (logic 1)} = -0.76 - (-1.1) = 0.34\text{ V}$$

With logic 0 input the ECL gate will recognize any input as logic 0, if it is not larger than –1.25 V. The noise margin in this case will be as follows:

$$\text{Noise margin (logic 0)} = -1.25 - (-1.58) = 0.33\text{ V}$$

These voltage levels have been shown in Fig. 5.4.

5.5.2 Bias Network

The reference voltage of –1.175 V ensured that the noise margins in both logic 1 and logic 0 states were the same. However, a fixed reference voltage can ensure equality of the noise margins only at a particular temperature. This is so because in all transistors the voltage drop across the forward-biased base-emitter junction is temperature dependent. If the reference voltage remains fixed, the noise margins will be the same at a single temperature level. The normal practice is to design a temperature dependent reference voltage, which compensates for the temperature variation in the base-emitter voltage drop of transistor in the ECL gate and thus maintains the noise margin at a fixed level. A circuit commonly used for this purpose is shown in Fig. 5.5. You will notice from the diagram that a temperature-compensated voltage-divider network has been used.

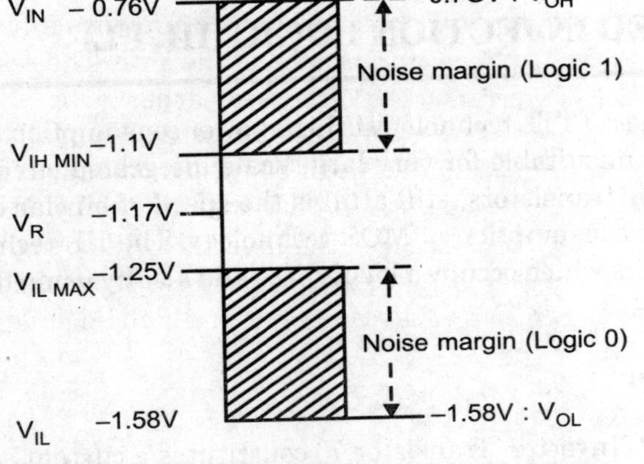

Fig. 5.4 Input and output logic levels for ECL OR gate

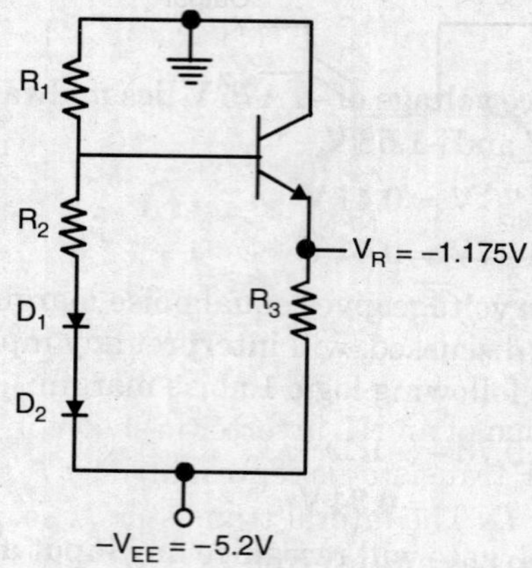

Fig. 5.5 Temperature compensated reference voltage

5.5.3 Fan-out

The gate is not required to supply any current to the driven gate when its output is at logic 0 level. Therefore the question of a limit on the fan-out does not arises. However, when the output of the gate is at logic 1 level –0.76 V, it has to furnish a drive current to the driven gate. As the number of driven gates increases, it will be accompanied by a corresponding fall in the output voltage, which will cause a reduction in the noise margin. The fan-out is, therefore, dependent on the acceptable level of the noise margin.

5.5.4 Propagation Delay

By far the most important characteristic of an ECL gate is its speed of operation. A speed of 1ns is not unusual while much higher speeds have also been attained. It is worth noting that the speed of operation is adversely affected by a capacitive load at the output, which should therefore be kept as low as possible.

5.6 INTEGRATED INJECTION LOGIC (III, I²L)

One of the disadvantages of TTL technology is high power consumption and low packing density, which makes it rather unsuitable for very large scale integrated circuits. The IIL technology, although it uses bipolar transistors, still attains the speed of bipolar devices and the packing density and low power consumption of MOS technology. The IIL technology achieves this by doing away with resistors which occupy a lot of space and also by using the same region on a chip for two or more devices.

5.6.1 IIL Inverter

Figure 5.6 shows an IIL Inverter. Transistor T_1 constitutes a current source and load while T_2 functions as an Inverter.

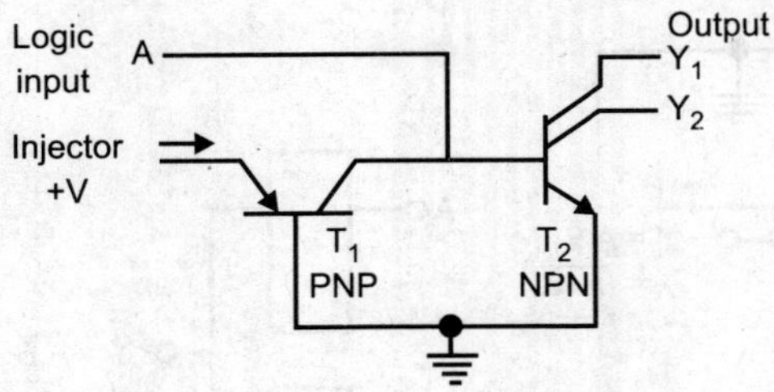

Fig. 5.6 (a) IIL inverter

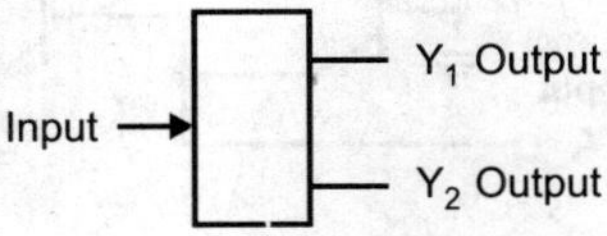

Fig. 5.6 (b) Logic symbol

The physical construction of an IIL inverter is shown in Fig. 5.7. You will notice from this diagram that the lateral PNP transistor is represented by T_1 in Fig. 5.6(a) and the vertical NPN transistor is represented by T_2. The lateral transistor T_1 serves as the current source and the vertical transistor T_2 functions as an Inverter.

The current injector injects a current into the device which may or may not pass through T_2, depending on the state of the logic input. In the absence of a logic input or when the logic input is high T_2 is turned on, resulting in the output going low. When the logic input is low, less than 0.7 V, the injector current is pulled away from T_2 which is cut off and the output goes high. The voltage swing between logic levels is about 0.6 V. Normally, since the logic input is open, the output is held low.

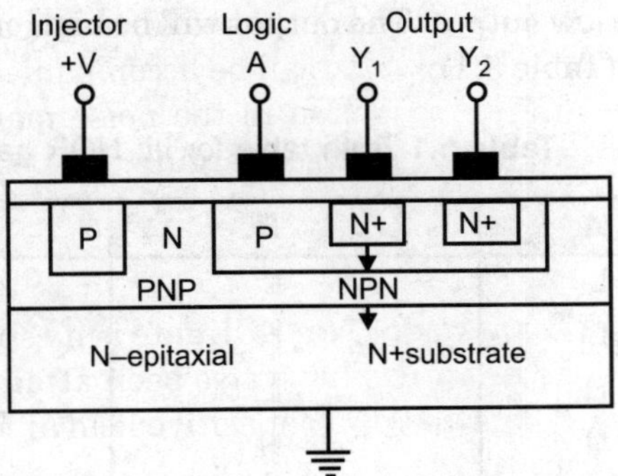

Fig. 5.7 Physical construction of IIL inverter

It is worth noting that although IIL gates have a single input, they have multiple outputs. Since IIL gate have open-collector outputs, the last collector is required to be connected to a supply voltage which can be as much as 10V through an external resistor. In this case the output voltage will be approximately 10 V. Outputs of IIL gates can be connected together, resulting in a wired–AND configuration. The IIL Inverter forms the basic unit, which can be used to implement other logic gates.

5.6.2 IIL NOR Gate

Figure 5.8 shows how two IIL Inverters can be used to implement a NOR gate.

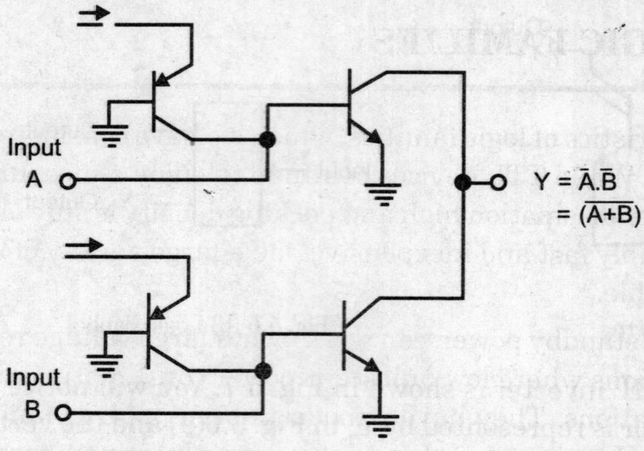

Fig. 5.8 (a) IIL NOR gate

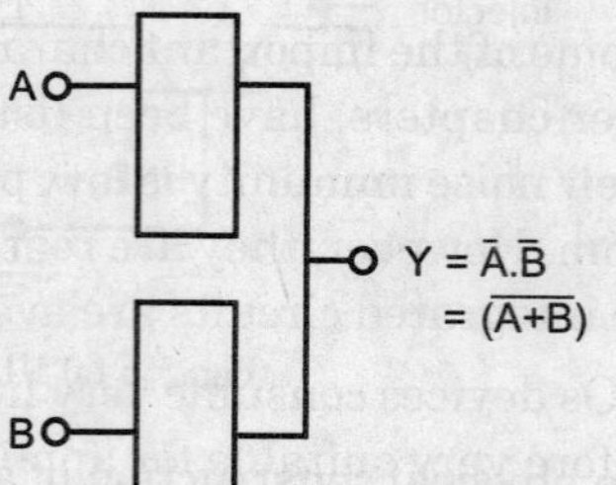

Fig. 5.8 (b) IIL NOR gate using IIL symbols

Since the outputs are wire-ANDed, the output takes the following form, using De Morgan's theorem:

$$Y = \overline{A}\,.\,\overline{B}$$

$$= \overline{(A + B)}$$

From this it follows that if either or both inputs are high, the output is low as one or both the transistors will provide a low output. The output will be high only when both inputs are low. The truth table is as follows (Table 5.1):

Table 5.1 Truth table for IIL NOR gate

A	*B*	*Y*
L	L	H
L	H	L
H	L	L
H	H	L

5.6.3 IIL OR Gate

Figure 5.9 shows how an OR gate can be implemented by adding another Inverter to the output of a NOR gate.

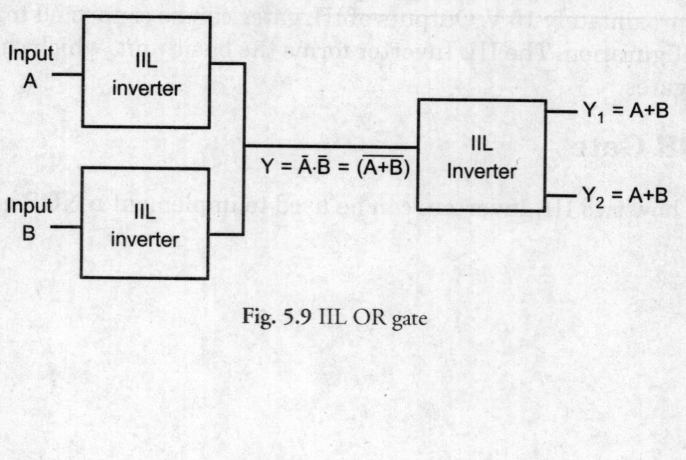

Fig. 5.9 IIL OR gate

5.7 RELATIVE MERITS OF LOGIC FAMILIES

In Table 5.2 some of the important characteristics of logic families, which we have considered in this and earlier chapters, have been listed. While TTL devices continue to enjoy a measure of popularity, their noise immunity is low, power dissipation high and packing density is only about 20 gates/sq. mm. However, they are reasonably fast and inexpensive and a large variety of TTL medium scale integrated circuits are available.

The CMOs devices consume very little standby power, can work over a large voltage range and are therefore very suitable for applications where low quiescent power consumption and a low voltage supply are important considerations. They have a modest speed, a large fan-out, high noise immunity and are inexpensive. However, an important point to be remembered is that power consumption increases as switching speed increases.

ECL devices have almost the highest speed of all the logic families and generate very little internal noise. However, they consume more power than devices of other logic families and are useful where the speed of operation is of primary importance.

The IIL logic family is very suitable for very large scale integrated circuits, as a large number of IIL gates can be packed in a very small area. They are fast and consume very little power; but they have yet to achieve a measure of standardization.

Table 5.2

Criteria	*STD TTL*	*CMOS*		*ECL*	*IIL*
		5 V	*10 V*		
1. Propagation delay per gate	3 ns	10 ns	7 ns	0.3 ns	1 ns
2. Power dissipation (quiescent)	10mW	10nw	10nW	60mW	60nW–70μW
3. Supply voltage	5 V	3–15 V		–5.2 V	1–15 V
4. Noise generation	High	Low-medium		Low-medium	—
5. Noise immunity	Low 1V	2V	4V	0.5 V	—
6. Logic voltage swing	5 V	5 V	10 V	0.8 V	0.6 V
7. Fan-out	10	50	50	5	—

Problems

5.1 Draw the circuit diagram of a 2-input ECL NOR gate incorporating a temperature-compensated bias network.

5.2 What would be the NOR outputs of the ECL gate shown in Fig. 5.3, when the inputs are as follows?

	A	*B*	*C*	*D*
(*a*)	0	0	1	0
(*b*)	1	0	1	0
(*c*)	1	1	1	1
(*d*)	0	0	0	0
(*e*)	0	0	0	1
(*f*)	1	1	1	0

5.3 Write the truth table for a 3-input ECL NOR gate.

5.4 Using IIL Inverters, draw a circuit diagram to implement a gate which will develop both OR and NOR outputs.

5.5 Draw the circuit diagram of a 3-input IIL NOR gate.

6

Boolean Algebra

6.1 INTRODUCTION

George Simon Boole, an Englishman, born in 1815, known today as the father of Boolean Algebra, published his 'Mathematical Analysis of Logic', which has found wide-spread application in the design of digital computers. Boolean Algebra is now the special language of digital logic circuits. In some ways, it is similar to the conventional algebra; but in many respects it has significant differences.

For expressing logic circuit functions, as well as for analyzing and designing logic circuits, Boolean algebra provides a mathematical basis which is almost essential for a proper understanding of digital circuits. In this chapter we will study the special rules of Boolean algebra and consider their application in the design of digital circuits.

6.2 BOOLEAN ALGEBRA SYMBOLS

We have discussed some of the symbols of Boolean algebra earlier; but so that you become thoroughly familiar with them, they are being restarted here. You must have used these symbols while dealing with problems of conventional algebra; but in Boolean algebra some of these symbols mean something different.

(a) Dot sign (·): A dot sign (·), which is also the same as (×) indicates a logical product of two terms so connected. A logical product of two terms A and B can be expressed as $A \times B$ and is read as "A and B". This logical product represents an AND operation and the terms so connected are said to be ANDed. It has to be differentiated from the '×' sign used in conventional algebra, where it represents multiplication of the terms so joined.

A system having two variables A and B will have a total of four states A, $\overline{A}$, B and $\overline{B}$ and the following AND combinations are possible:

1. $A \cdot B$ read as A and B
2. $\overline{A} \cdot B$ read as NOT A and B
3. $\overline{A} \cdot \overline{B}$ read as NOT A and NOT B

(b) Plus sign (+): The '+' sign indicates the logical sum of terms so connected. For instance $A + B$ represents a logical sum and is read as A or B. Here it is referred to as the inclusive -OR operation and the terms so joined are said to be ORed.

The following four OR combinations are possible in a system having two variables A and B.

1. $A + B$ read as A or B
2. $A + \overline{B}$ read as A or NOT B
3. $\overline{A} + B$ read as NOT A or B
4. $\overline{A} + \overline{B}$ read as NOT A or NOT B

(c) *Exclusive-OR (⊕):* This sign is used to indicate an exclusive-OR operation, which is expressed as $A \oplus B$ and is read as 'A exclusive -OR B'.

(d) *Overline '–':* This symbol serves a dual purpose.

(1) As a sign of operation it indicates that the terms so overlined are to be complemented, for instance $\overline{A}$ (read as NOT A).

(2) As a symbol of grouping it indicates that the terms grouped and overlined like $\overline{A + B}$ or $\overline{A \cdot B}$ are to be complemented together.

The term or terms overlined are said to be negated and the process of complementing is called negation.

(e) *Symbol of equality '=':* The sign of equality '=' has the same meaning as in conventional algebra. This sign between two quantities expresses a relationship of equivalence.

$A = B$ is read as A is equivalent to B.

(f) *Symbols of variables:* Letter symbols such as A, B, C, X, Y, Z, etc., are commonly used to represent variables.

(g) *Symbols of constants:* Since variables in digital electronics can exist in two states only, 0 and 1, these are the only numerals used in Boolean algebra. The result of a Boolean function can be only one of these two constants.

6.3 BOOLEAN POSTULATES

Boolean algebra is founded on postulates which originate from three basic logic functions. These functions are AND, OR and INVERT operations. The truth tables of these three basic logic functions are reproduced in Table 6.1 alongside the corresponding Boolean postulates.

Table 6.1

Logic function truth table			***Boolean postulate***
AND			Logical multiplication
A	B	C	
0	0	0	(1) 0 . 0 = 0
0	1	0	(2) 0 . 1 = 0
1	0	0	(3) 1 . 0 = 0
1	1	1	(4) 1 . 1 = 1

OR

A	B	C
0	0	0
0	1	0
1	0	1
1	1	1

Logical addition

(5) 0 + 0 = 0

(6) 0 + 1 = 1

(7) 1 + 0 = 1

(8) 1 + 1 = 2

Invert

A	$\overline{A}$
0	1
1	0

Logical complementation

(9) $\overline{0} = 1$

(10) $\overline{1} = 0$

6.4 BOOLEAN LAWS

Boolean laws have made it possible to design and analyze logic circuits mathematically. There are several laws of Boolean algebra which will be discussed in the following sections. In making a study of these laws we will refer frequently to truth table of AND, OR and INVERT logic functions as well as the Boolean postulates in Table 6.1.

6.4.1 Laws of Intersection

We will study the law as its applies to AND logic functions. The law is stated as follows:

1. $A \cdot 1 = A$

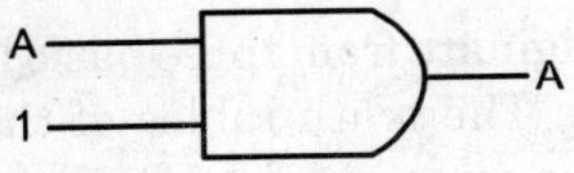

(a)

2. $A \cdot 0 = 0$

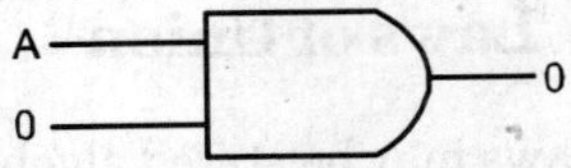

(b)

Fig. 6.1 (a) and (b)

Law 1: $A \cdot 1 = A$

This law states that if we apply a logic 1 signal to one of the two inputs of an AND gate and signal A to the other input, the output will be A. Since input A can be either logic 0 or logic 1, only two input combinations are possible which have been considered below:

From Postulate 2

When $A = 0$; $A \cdot 1 = 0 \cdot 1 = 0$ (same as A)

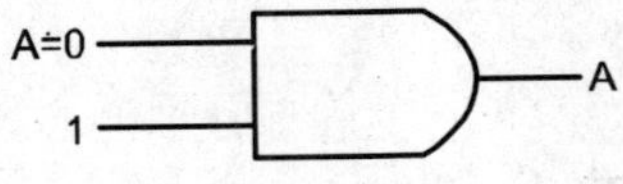

(a)

From Postulate 4

When $A = 1$; $A \cdot 1 = 1 \cdot 1 = 1$ (same as A)

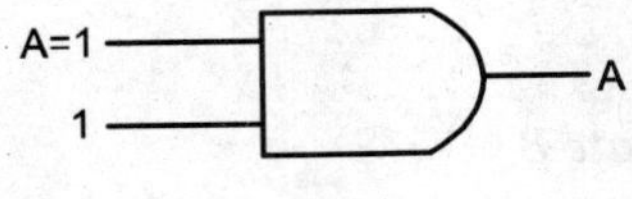

(b)

Fig. 6.2 (a) and (b)

You will notice that in both the cases output is the same as A.

Law 2 : $A \cdot 0 = 0$

The second law states that if we apply a logic 0 signal to one of the two inputs, when the other input is A, the output will be logic 0. The following two input combinations are possible:

From Postulate 1

When $A = 0$; $A \cdot 0 = 0 \cdot 0 = 0$

From Postulate 3

When $A = 1$; $A \cdot 0 = 1 \cdot 0 = 0$

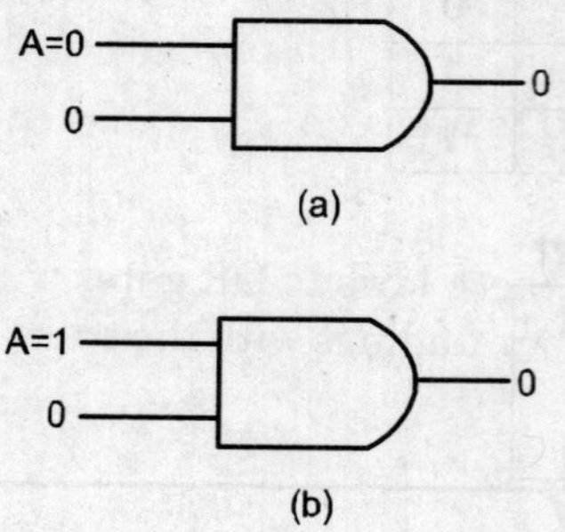

Fig. 6.3 (a) and (b)

This proves that if one of the two inputs of an AND gate is 0, the output will always be logic 0, irrespective of the logic state of the A input.

We can derive the following conclusions from these two laws:

(1) $A \cdot 1 = A$ for all values of A (A may be 0 or 1)

(2) $A \cdot 0 = 0$ for all values of A (A may be 0 or 1)

It is worth nothing that the laws of intersection are also applicable to AND gates having more than two inputs. For instance:

$$A \cdot B \cdot 1 = A \cdot B$$
$$A \cdot B \cdot 0 = 0$$

6.4.2 Laws of Union

These laws may be stated algebraically as follows:

1. $A + 1 = 1$

2. $A + 0 = A$

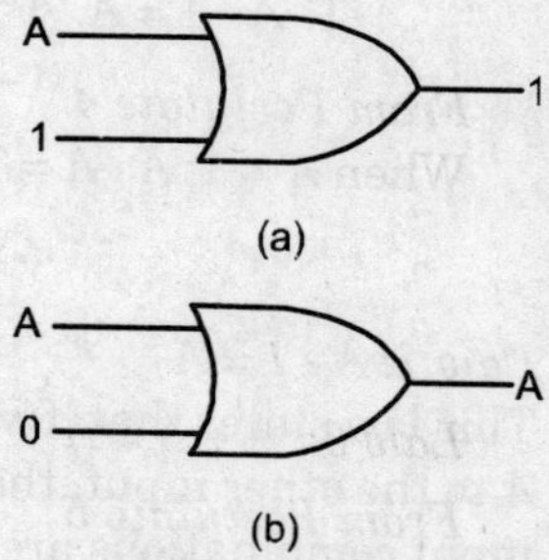

Fig. 6.4 (a) and (b)

Law 3: $A + 1 = 1$

From Postulate 6

When $A = 0$; $A + 1 = 0 + 1 = 1$

From Postulate 8

When $A = 1$; $A + 1 = 1 + 1 = 1$

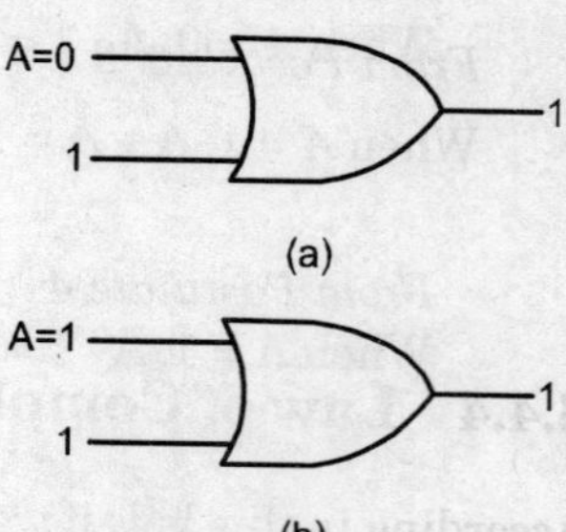

Fig. 6.5 (a) and (b)

Law 4 : $A + 0 = A$

From Postulate 5

When $A = 0$; $A + 0 = 0 + 0 = 0$ (same as A)

From Postulate 7

When $A = 1$; $A + 0 = 1 + 0 = 1$ (same as A)

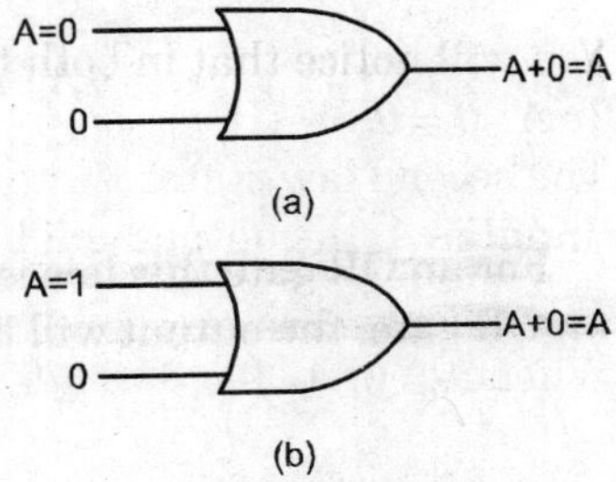

Fig. 6.6 (a) and (b)

Consider the application of these laws to OR gates with more than two inputs and draw your own conclusions. Compare your findings with the truth table of an OR gate with more than two inputs.

6.4.3 Laws of Tautology

These laws may be stated as follows:

1. $A \cdot A = A$

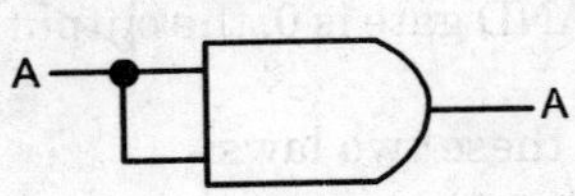

2. $A + A = A$

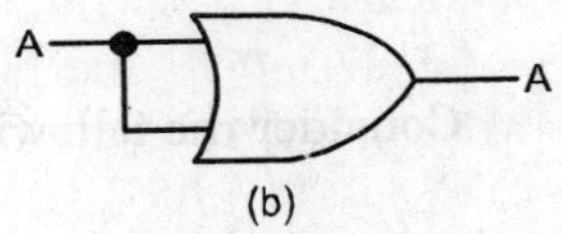

Fig. 6.7 (a) and (b)

These laws apply to both AND and OR gates. In short these laws imply that if the same signal is applied to all the inputs of a logic gate, the output will be the same as the input.

Law 5 : $A \cdot A = A$

From Postulate 1

When $A = 0$; $A \cdot A = 0 \cdot 0 = 0$ (same as A)

From Postulate 4

When $A = 1$; $A \cdot A = 1 \cdot 1 = 1$ (same as A)

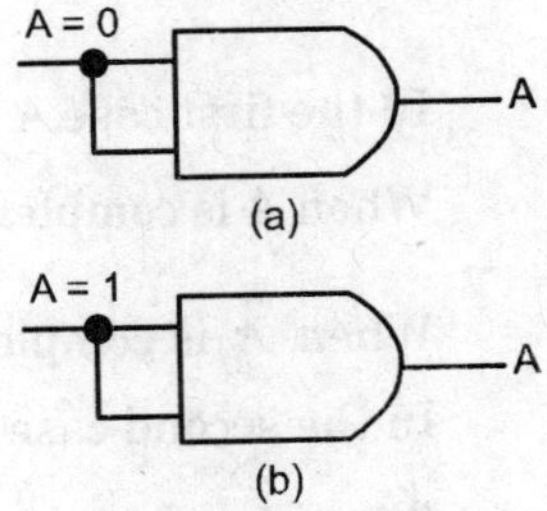

Fig. 6.8 (a) and (b)

Law 6 : $A + A = A$

From Postulate 5

When $A = 0$; $A + A = 0 + 0 = 0$ (same as A)

From Postulate 8

When $A = 1$; $A + A = 1 + 1 = 1$ (same as A)

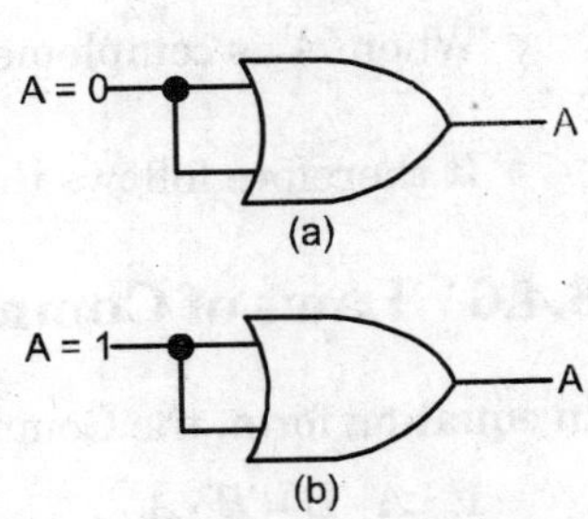

Fig. 6.9 (a) and (b)

6.4.4 Law of Complements

According to this law, if we apply a logic signal and its complement to an AND gate, the output will be logic 0. Stated algebraically it means that:

$$A \cdot \overline{A} = 0$$

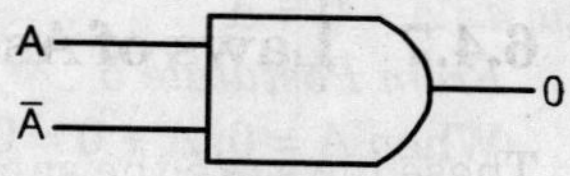

Fig. 6.10

For an OR gate this law is stated as follows: If we apply a logic signal and its complement to an OR gate, the output will be logic 1. Stated algebraically it means that:

$$A + \overline{A} = 1$$

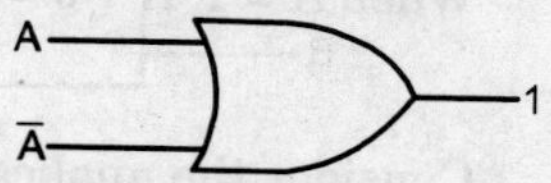

Fig. 6.11

6.4.5 Law of Double Negation

The law states that the complement of the complement of *A* is *A*. In equation form

$$\overline{\overline{A}} = A$$

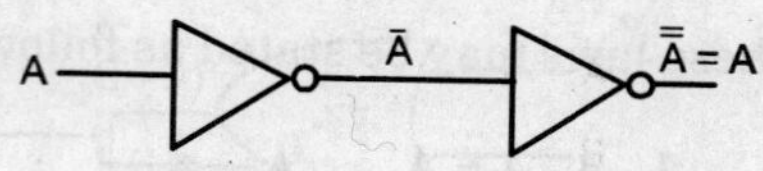

Fig. 6.12

Consider the following table:

	A	$\overline{A}$	$\overline{\overline{A}}$
1	0	1	0
2	1	0	1

In the first case $A = 0$

When A is complemented, $\overline{A} = \overline{0} = 1$, Postulate 9

When $\overline{A}$ is complemented, $\overline{\overline{A}} = \overline{\overline{0}} = \overline{1} = 0$, Postulate 10

In the second case $A = 1$

When A is complemented, $\overline{A} = \overline{1} = 0$, Postulate 10

When $\overline{A}$ is complemented, $\overline{\overline{A}} = \overline{\overline{1}} = \overline{0} = 1$, Postulate 9

It therefore follows that $\overline{\overline{A}} = A$ as shown in Table 6.9

6.4.6 Laws of Commutation

In equation form, the Commutation laws can be stated as follows:

1. $A \cdot B = B \cdot A$ Law 10
2. $A + B = B + A$ Law 11

6.4.7 Laws of Association

These laws are the same as for conventional algebra. They are stated below in equation form.

1. $(A \cdot B)\, C = A\, (B \cdot C)$ Law 12

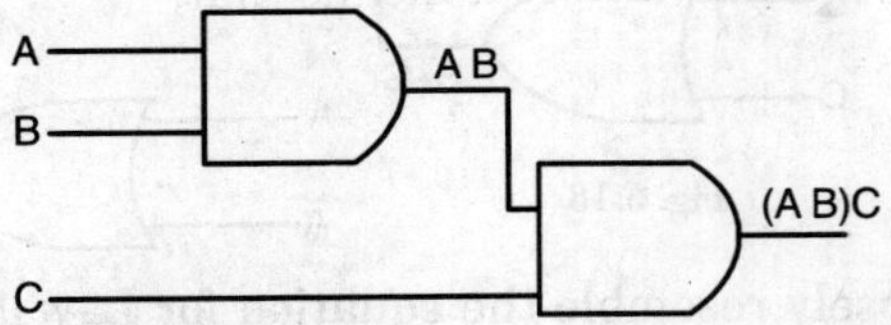

Fig. 6.13

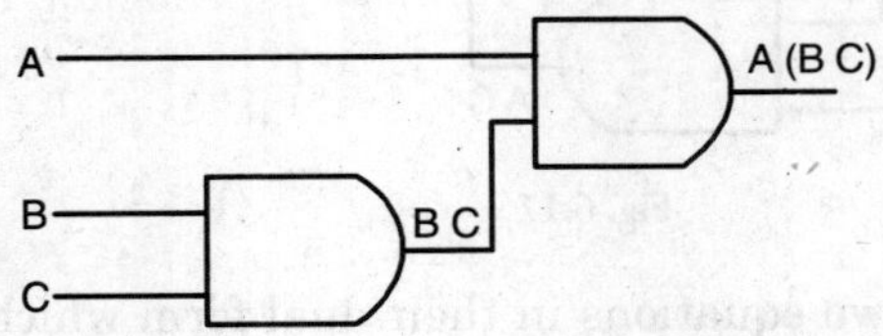

Fig. 6.14

2. $(A + B) + C = A + (B + C)$ Law 13

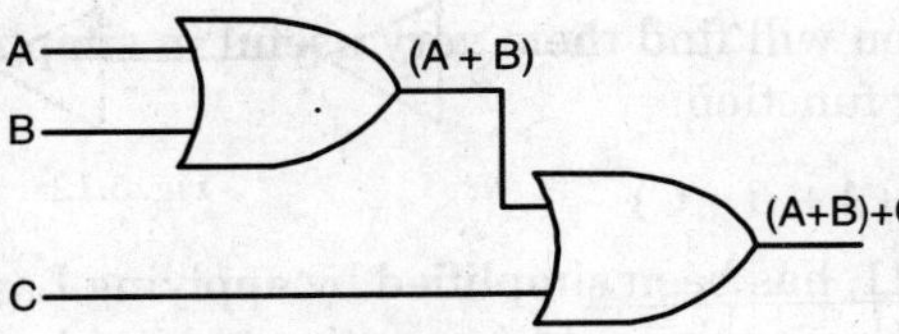

Fig. 6.15

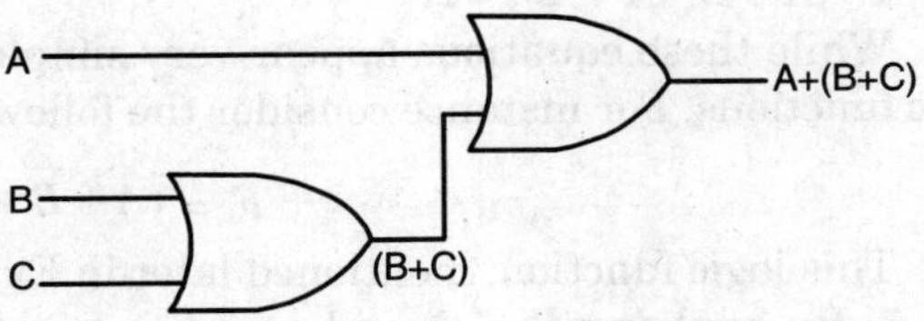

Fig. 6.16

6.4.8 Laws of Distribution

We will consider two typical example of the laws of distribution.

1. $A \cdot B + A \cdot C = A\, (B + C)$ Law 14

2. $(A + B)\, (A + C) = A + (BC)$ Law 15

In case 1 you will find that groups AB and AC, which are connected by like operators, that is '.', contain the same variable that 'A'. In case 2 you will again notice that groups $(A + B)$ and $(A + C)$, which are connected by like operators, that is '+', contain the same variable that is 'A'. The law of distribution states that in such cases, when a group of terms connected by the same operator have a commn variable, the variable may be removed from the terms and associated with them by appropriate sign of operation.

If you have a close look at the two cases cited above, you will notice that both of them satisfy the laws of distribution.

Law 14 : $AB + AC = A\, (B + C)$

Look at the diagrams given in Figs. 6.17 and 6.18, which represent the two sides of the equation for Law 14. You can prove their equality by drawing truth tables for these two circuits which will prove Law 14.

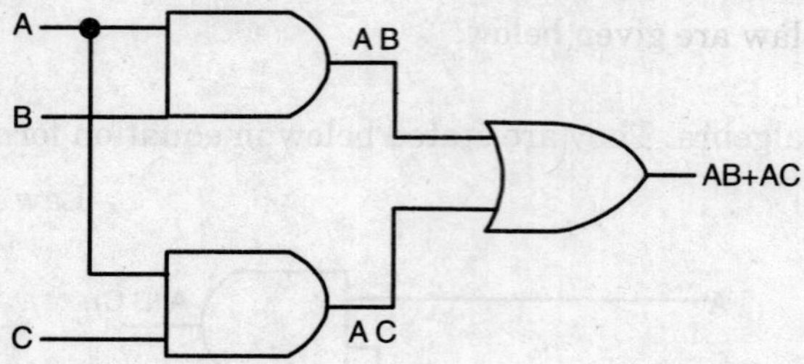

Fig. 6.17

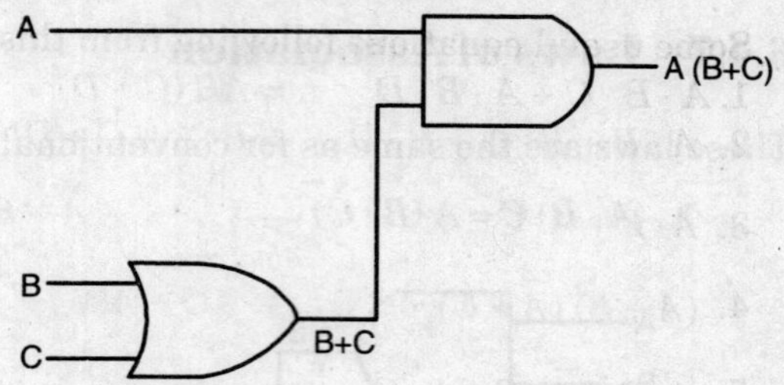

Fig. 6.18

Two equations in their dual form which closely resemble the equation for Law 14 given above are stated below:

1. $AB + A\overline{B} = A$
2. $(A + B)(A + \overline{B}) = A$

While these equations appear very simple, you will find them very useful in simplifying logic functions. For instance consider the following function:

$$F = (A + \overline{B} + \overline{C})(A + \overline{B} + C)$$

This logic function, mentioned later in Ex. 6.11, has been simplified by applying Laws 14 and 5. By applying the second equation given above, you could in no time write down its simplified form given below:

$$F = A + \overline{B}$$

Law 15: $(A + B)(A + C) = A + (BC)$

Logic circuits which represent the two sides of the following equation of Law 15 are given in Figs. 6.19 and 6.20:

$$(A + B)(A + C) = A + (BC)$$

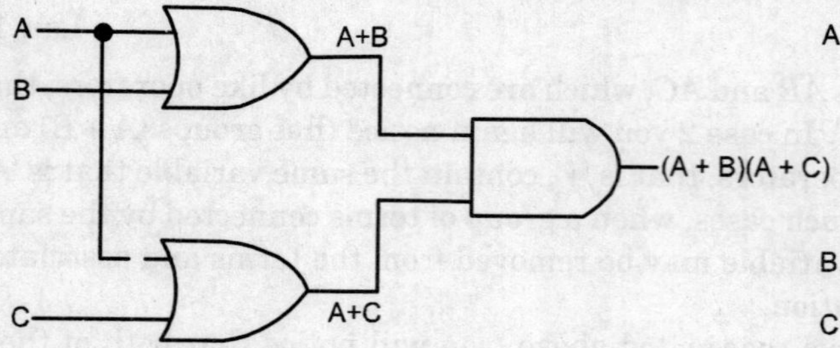

Fig. 6.19

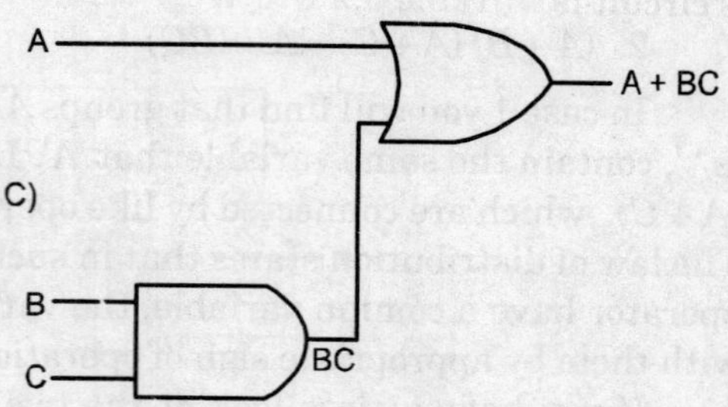

Fig. 6.20

Truth tables for these two circuits will show that they are performing identical functions which will prove Law 15. This law can also be proved as follows:

$$\begin{aligned}(A + B)(A + C) &= AA + AB + AC + BC \\ &= A(1 + B + C) + BC \\ &= A \cdot 1 + BC \\ &= A + BC\end{aligned}$$

Some useful equations following from this law are given below:

1. $A \cdot B \cdot C + A \cdot B \cdot D \quad = AB\,(C + D)$
2. $A \cdot B + B \cdot C + B \cdot D \quad = B\,(A + C + D)$
3. $A \cdot B + \overline{A} \cdot C \quad = (A + C)\,(\overline{A} + B)$
4. $(A + B)\,(\overline{A} + C) \quad = AC + \overline{A}B$
5. $A \cdot B + \overline{A} \cdot C + B \cdot C \quad = AB + \overline{A}C$
6. $(A + B)\,(\overline{A} + C)\,(B + C) = (A + B)\,(\overline{A} + C)$

You can verify the correctness of these equations by comparing the truth tables of the two sides of each equation.

6.4.9 Laws of Absorption

There are five versions of this law as follows:

1. $A(A + B) = A$ Law 16
2. $A + AB = A$ Law 17
3. $A(\overline{A} + B) = AB$ Law 18
4. $AB + \overline{B} = A + \overline{B}$ Law 19
5. $A\overline{B} + B = A + B$ Law 20

We will take up one of these laws at a time for consideration.

Law 16: $A(A + B) = A$

The equation is represented by the logic diagram given in Fig. 6.21, and the truth table for this circuit is in Table 6.2 which shows that $A\,(A + B) = A$

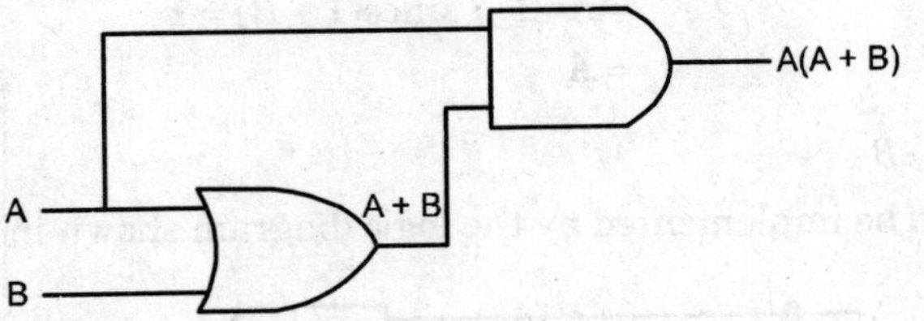

Fig. 6.21

Table 6.2

A	B	$A + B$	$A(A + B)$
0	0	0	0
0	1	1	0
1	0	1	1
1	1	1	1

This law can also be proved as follows:

$$\begin{aligned} A(A+B) &= A \cdot A + A \cdot B \\ &= A + A \cdot B \\ &= A(1+B) \\ &= A \end{aligned}$$

Law 17: $A + A \cdot B = A$

This function can be implemented by the logic circuit given in Fig. 6.22.

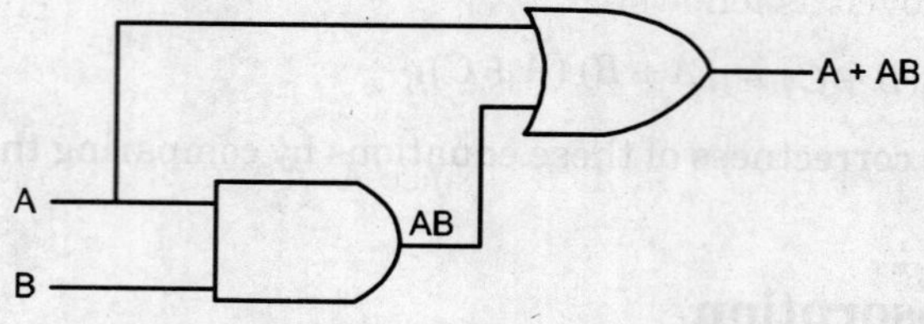

Fig. 6.22

The truth table for this circuit is given in Table 6.3. It shows that $A + A \cdot B = A$.

Table 6.3

A	*B*	*A* × *B*	*A* + *A* × *B*
0	0	0	0 + 0 = 0
0	1	0	0 + 0 = 0
1	0	0	1 + 0 = 1
1	1	1	1 + 1 = 1

This law can also be proved as follows:

$$\begin{aligned} A + A \cdot B &= A(1+B) \\ &= A \cdot 1 \quad \text{since}(1+B) = 1 \\ &= A \end{aligned}$$

Law 18: $A(\overline{A} + B) = A \cdot B$

This function can be implemented by the logic diagram shown in Fig. 6.23

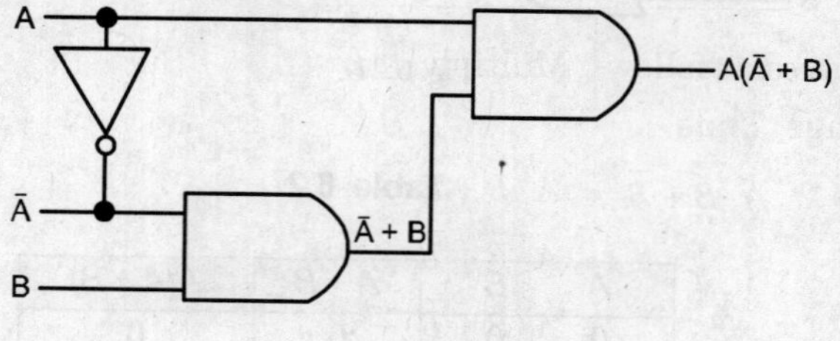

Fig. 6.23

The truth table for this circuit is given in Table 6.4. It shows that $A(\overline{A} + B) = A \cdot B$

Table 6.4

A	B	$\overline{A}$	$\overline{A}+B$	$A(\overline{A}+B)$	$A \times B$
0	0	1	1	0	0
0	1	1	1	0	0
1	0	0	0	0	0
1	1	0	1	1	1

This can also be proved as follows:

$$A(\overline{A}+B) = A \cdot \overline{A} + A \cdot B$$

$$= A \cdot B \quad \text{since } A \cdot \overline{A} = 0$$

Law 19: $A \cdot B + \overline{B} = A + \overline{B}$

The function is represented by the logic diagram shown in Fig. 6.24.

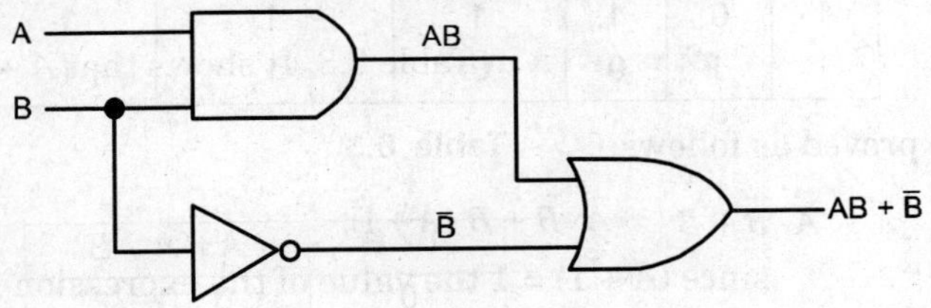

Fig. 6.24

The truth table for this circuit is given in Table 6.5. It shows that $AB + \overline{B} = A + \overline{B}$.

Table 6.5

A	B	$\overline{B}$	AB	$AB+\overline{B}$	$A+\overline{B}$
0	0	1	0	1	1
0	1	0	0	0	0
1	0	1	0	1	1
1	1	0	1	1	1

This can also be proved as follows: Multiply $\overline{B}$ by $(A+1)$. Since $(A+1) = 1$ and $\overline{B} \cdot 1 = \overline{B}$, the expression will not change. Thus

$$A \cdot B + \overline{B} = A \cdot B + \overline{B}\,(A+1)$$

$$= A \cdot B + \overline{B} \cdot A + \overline{B}$$

$$= A\,(B + \overline{B}) + \overline{B}$$

$$= A + \overline{B}$$

Law 20: $A \cdot \overline{B} + B = A + B$

The function can be implemented by the logic diagram shown in Fig. 6.25.

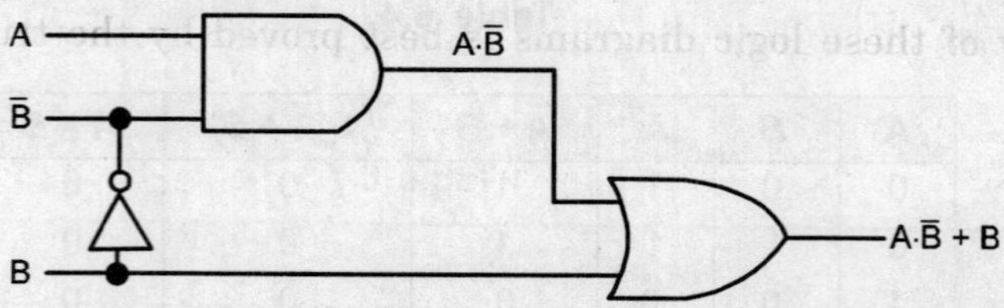

Fig. 6.25

The truth table for this circuit is given in Table 6.6. It shows that $A \cdot \overline{B} + B = A + B$

Table 6.6

A	B	$\overline{B}$	$A \times \overline{B}$	$A \times \overline{B} + B$	$A + B$
0	0	1	0	0	0
0	1	0	0	1	1
1	0	1	1	1	1
1	1	0	0	1	1

This can also be proved as follows:

$$A \cdot \overline{B} + B = A \cdot \overline{B} + B\,(A+1),$$

since $(A + 1) = 1$ the value of the expression remains unchanged

$$= A \cdot \overline{B} + A \cdot B + B$$

$$= A\,(\overline{B} + B) + B$$

$$= A \cdot 1 + B$$

$$= A + B$$

6.4.10 De Morgan's Theorem

There are two versions as follows:

1. $\overline{A + B} = \overline{A} \cdot \overline{B}$ Law 21
2. $\overline{A \cdot B} = \overline{A} + \overline{B}$ Law 22

Law 21: $\overline{A + B} = \overline{A} \cdot \overline{B}$

The two sides of the equation are represented by logic diagrams given in Figs. 6.26 and 6.27.

Fig. 6.26

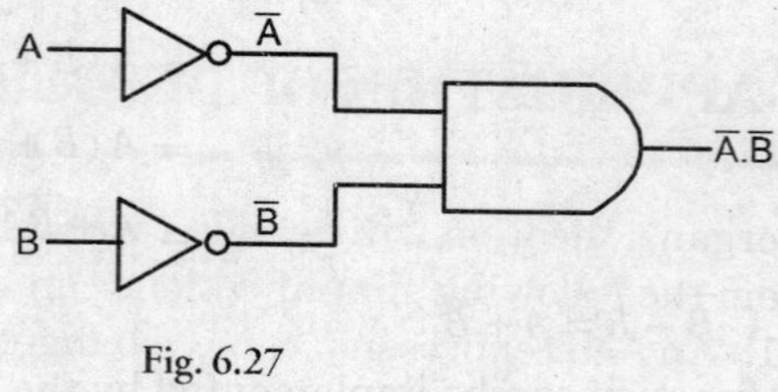

Fig. 6.27

The equality of these logic diagrams is best proved by the truth table given below (Table 6.7).

Table 6.7

Inputs		Intermediate values			Outputs	
A	B	$A+B$	$\overline{A}$	$\overline{B}$	$\overline{A+B}$	$\overline{A}\cdot\overline{B}$
0	0	0	1	1	1	1
0	1	1	1	0	0	0
1	0	1	0	1	0	0
1	1	1	0	0	0	0

Table 6.7 shows that $\overline{A+B}=\overline{A}\cdot\overline{B}$.

Law 22: $\overline{A\cdot B}=\overline{A}+\overline{B}$.

The two sides of the equation are represented by the logic diagrams in Figs. 6.28 and 6.29.

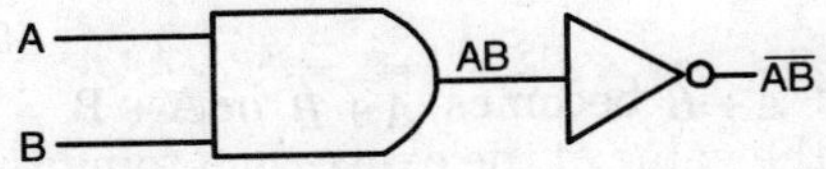

Fig. 6.28

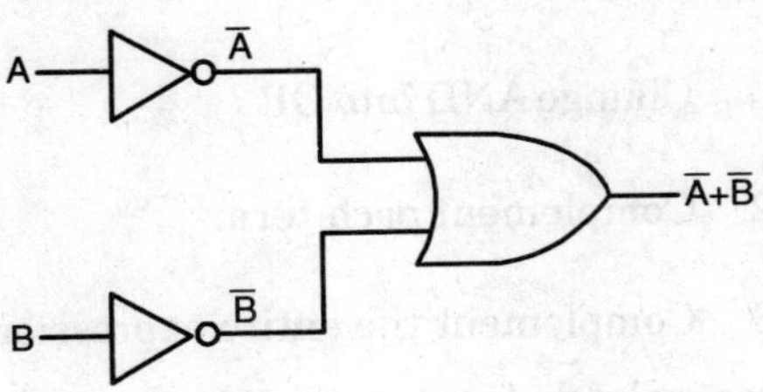

Fig. 6.29

The following truth table, Table 6.8, establishes the equality of the two expressions.

Table 6.8

Inputs		Intermediate values			Outputs	
A	B	$A\cdot B$	$\overline{A}$	$\overline{B}$	$\overline{A\cdot B}$	$\overline{A}+\overline{B}$
0	0	0	1	1	1	1
0	1	0	1	0	1	1
1	0	0	0	1	1	1
1	1	1	0	0	0	0

Table 6.8 shows that $\overline{A\cdot B}=\overline{A}+\overline{B}$.

6.5 APPLICATION OF DE MORGAN'S THEOREM

De Morgan's theorem will be found very useful in simplifying logic functions. By applying this theorem the following simplifications can be achieved.

1. An AND expression can be changed into an OR expression which makes further simplification easy. For example $\overline{A.\overline{B}}$ can be changed to $\overline{A}+\overline{\overline{B}}$.

2. A sum-of-products expression can be changed to a product-of-sums form. For example

$\bar{A}\cdot B+\bar{B}\cdot C$ can be changed to $\overline{(A+\bar{B})\,(B+\bar{C})}$.

If we follow the transformation from

$\overline{A+B}$ to $\bar{A}\cdot\bar{B}$

step by step, the process of transformation will appear simple.

Step 1. Change OR into AND : $\overline{A+B}$ becomes $\overline{A\cdot B}$

2. Complement each term : $\overline{A\cdot B}$ becomes $\overline{\bar{A}\cdot\bar{B}}$

3. Complement the entire expression : $\overline{\bar{A}\cdot\bar{B}}$ becomes $\overline{\overline{\bar{A}\cdot\bar{B}}}$

or $\bar{A}\cdot\bar{B}$

Now, following the same steps, let us transform

$\bar{A}\cdot\bar{B}$ into $\overline{A+B}$

Step 1. Change AND into OR : $\bar{A}\cdot\bar{B}$ becomes $\bar{A}+\bar{B}$

2. Complement each term : $\bar{A}+\bar{B}$ becomes $\bar{\bar{A}}+\bar{\bar{B}}$ or A + B

3. Complement the entire expression : $A+B$ becomes $\overline{A+B}$

The general rule for changing the form of an expression, following De Morgan's theorem, (better known as Demorganizing), can be stated as follows:

1. Change all OR(+) expression to AND (·) expression or the other way round as the case may be.
2. Complement individual terms that were ORed or ANDed.
3. Complement the entire expression.

Example 6.1: Prove that $\overline{A\cdot B}=\bar{A}+\bar{B}$ using the rule mentioned above.

Step 1. Change AND to OR : $\overline{A\cdot B}$ becomes $\overline{A+B}$

2. Complement each term : $\overline{A+B}$ becomes $\overline{\bar{A}+\bar{B}}$

3. Complement the entire expression : $\overline{\bar{A}+\bar{B}}$ becomes $\overline{\overline{\bar{A}+\bar{B}}}$

$\overline{\overline{\bar{A}+\bar{B}}}$ equal $\bar{A}+\bar{B}$

Example 6.2: Prove that $\overline{\bar{A}\cdot B}=A+\bar{B}$

Step 1. Change AND to OR : $\overline{\bar{A}\cdot B}$ becomes $\overline{\bar{A}+B}$

2. Complement each term : $\overline{\bar{A}+B}$ becomes $\overline{\bar{\bar{A}}+\bar{B}}$

3. Complement the entire : $\overline{\overline{\overline{A}}+\overline{B}}$ becomes $\overline{\overline{\overline{\overline{A}}+\overline{B}}}$

expression : $\overline{\overline{\overline{\overline{A}}+\overline{B}}}$ equals $A+\overline{B}$

De Morgan's theorem can also be used to simplify expressions having more than two terms by using the same procedure.

Example 6.3: Simplify $\overline{(\overline{A}\cdot B)\,(B\cdot\overline{C})\,(C\cdot\overline{D})}$

The best way to simplify this expression is to first expand each group, using De Morgan's theorem, and then to expand each term using the same procedure, as follows:

$\overline{(\overline{A}\cdot B)\,(B\cdot\overline{C})\,(C\cdot\overline{D})}$	given expression
$\overline{(\overline{A}\cdot B)}+\overline{(B\cdot\overline{C})}+\overline{(C\cdot\overline{D})}$	each group expanded by De Morgan's theorem
$(A+\overline{B})+(\overline{B}+\overline{C})+(\overline{C}+D)$	each term expanded by De Morgan's theorem
$A+\overline{B}+\overline{B}+\overline{C}+\overline{C}+D$	Law 13
$A+\overline{B}+\overline{C}+D$	Law 6

Example 6.4: Simplify $\overline{(\overline{A}\cdot B\cdot\overline{C})}+\overline{(A\cdot\overline{B}\cdot C)}$

$\overline{\overline{(\overline{\overline{A}}+\overline{B}+\overline{\overline{C}})}}+\overline{\overline{(\overline{A}+\overline{\overline{B}}+\overline{C})}}$	each group expanded
$=(A+\overline{B}+C)+(\overline{A}+B+\overline{C})$	Law 9
$=A+\overline{B}+C+\overline{A}+B+\overline{C}$	expanded by Law 13
$=A+\overline{A}+\overline{B}+B+C+\overline{C}$	expanded by Law 11
$=1+1+1$	Law 8
$=1$	

There is a simpler method to Demorganize expressions. It is simply stated as follows in a few words:

"BREAK THE LINE; CHANGE THE SIGN"

We will apply this method in those cases which we have already considered, to see how it works.

Example 6.5: Demorganize $\overline{A\cdot B}$

Step 1. Break the line $\overline{A}\cdot\overline{B}$

2. Change the sign $\overline{A}+\overline{B}$

Example 6.6: Demorganize $\overline{A\cdot\overline{B}}$

Step 1. Break the line $\overline{A}\cdot\overline{\overline{B}}$

2. Change the sign $\overline{A}+B$

Example 6.7: Simplify $\overline{(\overline{A}\cdot B)(B\cdot C)(C\cdot \overline{D})}$

Step 1. Break the line $\overline{(\overline{A}\cdot B)}\,\overline{(B\cdot C)}\,\overline{(C\cdot \overline{D})}$

2. Change the sign $\overline{(\overline{A}\cdot B)}+\overline{(B\cdot C)}+\overline{(C\cdot \overline{D})}$ each group expanded

3. Break the line $(\overline{\overline{A}}\cdot \overline{B})+(\overline{B}\cdot \overline{C})+(\overline{C}\cdot \overline{\overline{D}})$ each term separated

4. Change the sign $A+\overline{B}+\overline{B}+\overline{C}+\overline{C}+D$

$$A+\overline{B}+\overline{C}+D$$ simplified by Law 6

Example 6.8: $\overline{(\overline{A}\cdot B\cdot \overline{C})}+\overline{(A\cdot \overline{B}\cdot C)}$

Step 1. Break the line $(\overline{\overline{A}}\cdot \overline{B}\cdot \overline{\overline{C}})+(\overline{A}\cdot \overline{\overline{B}}\cdot \overline{C})$

2. Change the sign $\overline{\overline{A}}+\overline{B}+\overline{\overline{C}}+\overline{A}+\overline{\overline{B}}+\overline{C}$

$$A+\overline{B}+C+\overline{A}+B+\overline{C}$$ Law 9

$$A+\overline{A}+\overline{B}+B+C+\overline{C}$$ Law 11

$$1+1+1=1$$ Law 8

Table 6.9 Summary of Boolean algebra laws

Classification	*Algebraic definition*	*Law*
1. Laws of Intersection	$A \cdot 1 = A$	1
	$A \cdot 0 = 0$	2
2. Laws of Union	$A + 1 = 1$	3
	$A + 0 = A$	4
3. Laws of Tautology	$A \cdot A = A$	5
	$A + A = A$	6
4. Laws of Complements	$A \cdot \overline{A} = 0$	7
	$A + \overline{A} = 1$	8
5. Law of Double Negation	$\overline{\overline{A}} = A$	9
6. Laws of Commutation	$A \cdot B = B \cdot A$	10
	$A + B = B + A$	11
7. Laws of Association	$(A \cdot B)\, C = A \cdot (B \cdot C)$	12
	$(A + B) + C = A + (B + C)$	13
8. Laws of Distribution	$A \cdot B + A \cdot C = A \cdot (B + C)$	14
	$(A + B)\ (A + C) = A + (B \cdot C)$	15
9. Laws of Absorption	$A\,(A + B) = A$	16
	$A + A \cdot B = A$	17

	$A(\overline{A} + B) = AB$	18
	$A \cdot B + \overline{B} = A + \overline{B}$	19
	$A \cdot \overline{B} + B = A + B$	20
10. De Morgan's Theorem	$\overline{A+B} = \overline{A} \cdot \overline{B}$	21
	$\overline{A \cdot B} = \overline{A} + \overline{B}$	22

6.6 SIMPLIFICATION OF BOOLEAN ALGEBRAIC EXPRESSIONS

Simplification of Boolean Algebraic expressions leads ultimately to reduction of Boolean expressions. Since each logic operator represents a logic hardware, reduction of a Boolean expression means reduction in cost. A Boolean expression can be reduced by using Boolean algebraic laws which we have just considered. A stage may be reached when no further reduction is possible and that will represent the simplest form of logic circuitry which satisfies the Boolean expression.

Let us consider the function

$$F = A \cdot B + (B + C)$$

The logic diagram for this expression is given in Fig. 6.30.

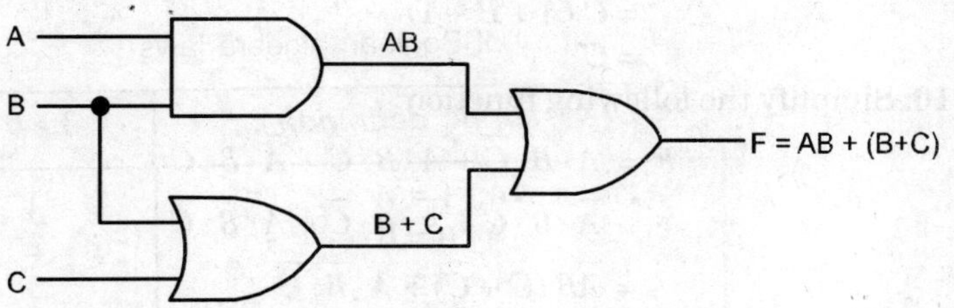

Fig. 6.30

Let us now simplify the expression

$$\begin{aligned} F &= A \cdot B + B + C \\ &= B(A + 1) + C && \text{Law 17} \\ &= B \cdot 1 + C && \text{Law 3} \\ &= B + C && \text{Law 1} \end{aligned}$$

The logic diagram which will represent this function is given in Fig. 6.31. You will notice the great simplification that has been achieved by using Boolean laws.

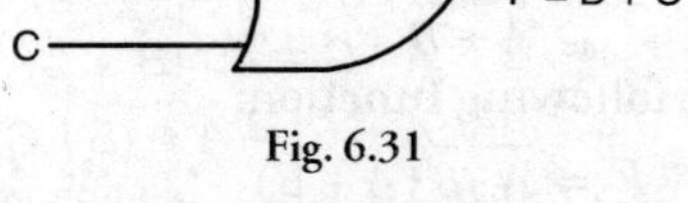

Fig. 6.31

To verify this you may draw up the truth tables for the two logic circuits. The truth tables for both the circuits are given in Table 6.10.

Table 6.10

A	B	C	$A \cdot B$	$B + C$	$A \cdot B + B + C$
0	0	0	0	0	0
0	0	1	0	1	1
0	1	0	0	1	1
0	1	1	0	1	1
1	0	0	0	0	0
1	0	1	0	1	1
1	1	0	1	1	1
1	1	1	1	1	1

You will notice from the above table that

$$B + C = A \cdot B + B + C$$

Example 6.9: Simplify the following function:

$F = C(B + C)(A + B + C)$

$= (CB + CC)(A + B + C)$ Law 14

$= (CB + C)(A + B + C)$ Law 5

$= C(B + 1)(A + B + C)$ Law 14

$= C(A + B + C)$ Law 3

$= CA + CB + CC$ Law 14

$= C(A + B + 1)$ Law 14

$= C$ Law 3

Example 6.10: Simplify the following function:

$F = A \cdot \overline{B} . \overline{C} + \overline{A} \cdot B \cdot \overline{C} + \overline{A} \cdot B \cdot C$

$= \overline{A} \cdot B \cdot C + \overline{A} \cdot B \cdot \overline{C} + A \cdot \overline{B} \cdot \overline{C}$ Law 11

$= \overline{A}B(C + \overline{C}) + A \cdot \overline{B} \cdot \overline{C}$ Law 14

$= \overline{A}B \cdot 1 + A \cdot \overline{B} \cdot \overline{C}$ Law 8

$= \overline{A}B + A \cdot \overline{B} \cdot \overline{C}$ Law 1

Example 6.11: Simplify the following function:

$F = (A + \overline{B} + \overline{C})(A + \overline{B} + C)$

$= AA + A\overline{B} + AC + \overline{B}A + \overline{B}\,\overline{B} + \overline{B}C + \overline{C}A + \overline{C}\,\overline{B} + \overline{C}C$ Law 14

$= A + A\overline{B} + AC + \overline{B}A + \overline{B} + \overline{B}C + \overline{C}A + \overline{C}\,\overline{B} + \overline{C}C$ Law 5

$= A(1 + \overline{B} + C + \overline{B} + \overline{C}) + \overline{B}(1 + C + \overline{C}) + 0$ Law 14

$= A \cdot 1 + \overline{B} \cdot 1$

$= A + \overline{B}$

Example 6.12: Simplify the following function:

$F = \overline{A \cdot B}(A + B)$

$= (\overline{A} + \overline{B})(A + B)$ Law 22

$= \overline{A} \cdot A + \overline{A} \cdot B + A \cdot \overline{B} + B \cdot \overline{B}$ Law 14

$$= 0 + \overline{A}\cdot B + A\cdot\overline{B} + 0 \qquad \text{Law 7}$$

$$= \overline{A}\cdot B + A\cdot\overline{B}$$

Example 6.13: Simplify the following function:

$$F = \overline{\overline{A\overline{(A\cdot B)}\cdot B\overline{(A\cdot B)}}}$$

$$= \overline{\overline{A\overline{(A\cdot B)}}} + \overline{\overline{B\overline{(A\cdot B)}}} \qquad \text{Law 22}$$

$$= A\overline{(A\cdot B)} + B\overline{(A\cdot B)} \qquad \text{Law 9}$$

$$= A(\overline{A} + \overline{B})) + B(\overline{A} + \overline{B}) \qquad \text{Law 22}$$

$$= A\cdot\overline{A} + A\cdot\overline{B} + B\cdot\overline{A} + B\cdot\overline{B} \qquad \text{Law 14}$$

$$= 0 + A\cdot\overline{B} + B\cdot\overline{A} + 0 \qquad \text{Law 7}$$

$$= A \oplus B$$

Example 6.14: Simplify the following function:

$$F = \overline{\overline{(A\cdot\overline{B})}\cdot\overline{(B\cdot\overline{A})}}$$

$$= \overline{\overline{(A\cdot\overline{B})}} + \overline{\overline{(B\cdot\overline{A})}} \qquad \text{Law 22}$$

$$= A\cdot\overline{B} + B\cdot\overline{A} \qquad \text{Law 9}$$

$$= A \oplus B$$

Example 6.15: Simplify the following function:

$$F = (A + \overline{B} + C)\,(A + B + C)\,(\overline{A} + B + C)\,(\overline{A} + \overline{B} + C)\,(\overline{A} + \overline{B} + \overline{C})$$

$$= (A + C)\,(\overline{A} + C)\,(\overline{A} + \overline{B} + \overline{C})$$

$$= C(\overline{A} + \overline{B} + \overline{C})$$

$$= C(\overline{A} + \overline{B})$$

6.7 LOGIC CIRCUITS

For various decision-making functions a combination of AND, OR and NOT logic gates is employed. The logic circuits so formed are known as combinational logic circuits. There are many types of combinational logic circuits which perform specific functions such as encoders, decoders, multiplexers, etc., which we will study later on. While these combinational logic circuits employ a variety of circuit configurations we will, for the present, restrict our discussion to two configurations, which occur frequently in combinational logic circuits. These circuits are referred to as

(*a*) Sum-of-products (SOP) and
(*b*) Product-of-sums (POS) circuits

Sum-of-products circuits

Figure 6.32 shows a circuit in which the output of two AND gates constitutes the input of an OR gate. The final output is thus (*AB* + *CD*).

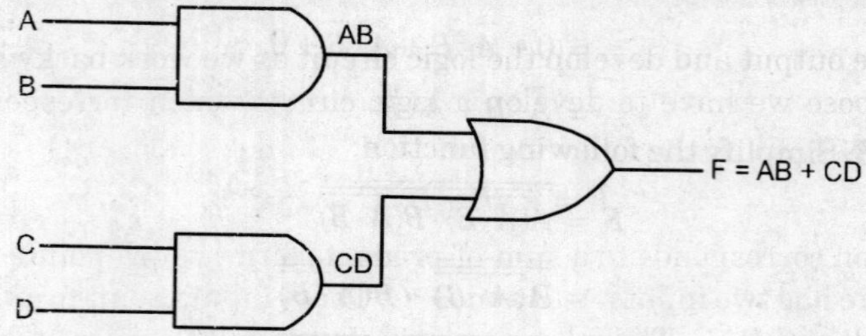

Fig. 6.32

You will observe that *AB* and *CD* are the two product terms and the output of the OR gate is a sum term (*AB* + *CD*), which is in the form of a sum-of-products. The distinguishing feature of this circuit is that, inputs are coupled to AND gates and the output is obtained from an OR gate.

We have considered a product term with two variables, but there may be a single variable product term or a logical product of several variables. It should also be noted that a sum-of-products expression may have more than two product terms such as (*AB* + *BC* + *CD*).

The sum-of-products circuit given in Fig. 6.32 is in the form of a two-level network, which means that the signal passes from input to output through two gates. There may, however, be SOP circuits which employ more than two levels.

Product-of-sums circuit

The other basic decision-making circuit is referred to as a product-of-sums circuit which, in its simplest form, is shown in Fig. 6.33.

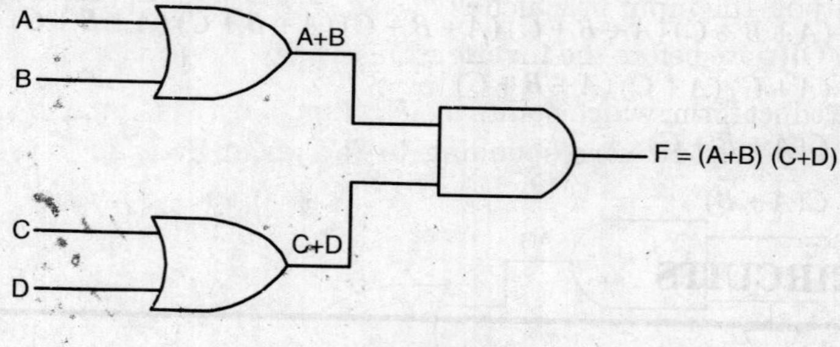

Fig. 6.33

In this type of circuit inputs feed OR gates and the output is derived from an AND gate. The expression for the output of this circuit is

$$F = (A + B)\,(C + D)$$

Like the SOP circuit this is also a two-level circuit, in which both the sum terms have two variables. However, a sum term may have a single variable or a sum of several variables. The POS circuit of Fig. 6.33 generates a product of two sum terms, but there may be POS expressions having several sum terms.

6.8 TRANSLATING ALGEBRA TO LOGIC

All logic diagrams are so drawn that the input is on the left hand side and the output is on the right hand side. To draw a logic diagram which corresponds to a given Boolean expression, we should begin at the output and develop the logic circuit as we work backwards from the output to the input. Suppose we have to develop a logic circuit which corresponds to the following Boolean expression:

$$F = A \cdot B + B \cdot C$$

The expression corresponds to a sum-of-products form, which points to an OR gate at the output. The OR gate has two inputs $A \cdot B$ and $B \cdot C$. These inputs point to an AND function which provide inputs $A \cdot B$ and $B \cdot C$. The following logic circuit will therefore correspond to the given Boolean expression:

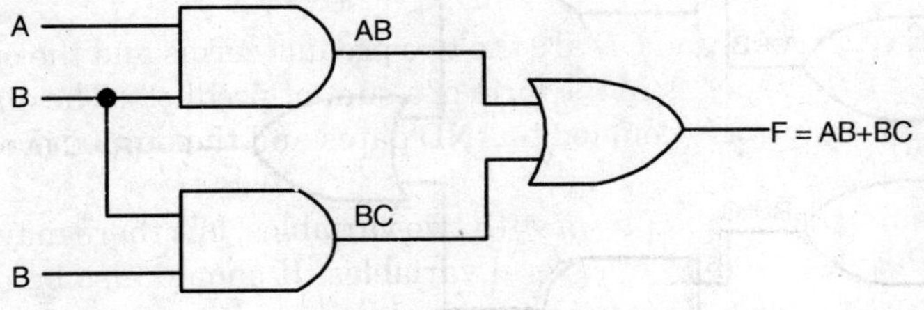

Fig. 6.34

Let us now consider the following Boolean expression:

$$F = \overline{A \cdot B + \overline{B} \cdot C}$$

and draw a corresponding logic circuit. The expression is a NOTed function which points to an inverter at the output, the input of which is $A \cdot B + \overline{B} \cdot C$. This is a sum-of-products function, which points to an OR gate before the Inverter. There are three input signals. The inputs to the OR gate are in a product form, which points to AND functions. The input $\overline{B}$ is realized by using an Inverter. The logic circuit corresponding to the given Boolean expression is given in Fig. 6.35.

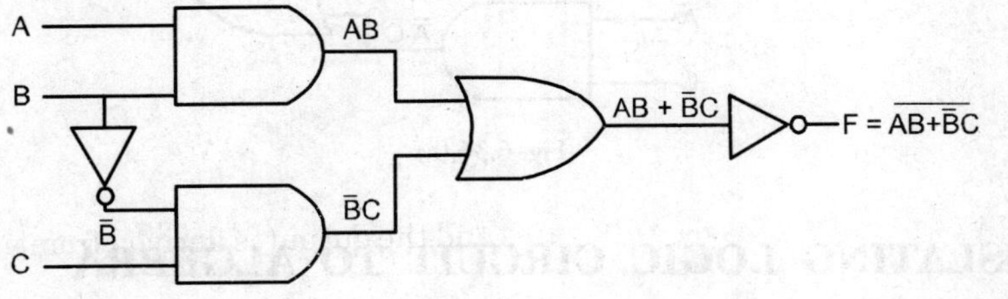

Fig. 6.35

We will now consider another expression involving more than two level changes as well as involving a combination of both product-of-sums and sum-of-product forms. The following expression is an example:

$$F = (A + \overline{C})(\overline{A} + B) + (\overline{B} + C)\,\overline{A} \cdot \overline{C}$$

This expression points to an OR gate at the output. It also suggests that the OR gate is fed by AND gates, which are preceded by OR gates and an AND gate. The entire circuit is given in Fig. 6.36 (a).

The Boolean expression was translated into a logic circuit without first simplifying it, and you will notice that in many cases considerable simplicity and saving in cost can be achieved by reducing an expression to its simplest form before translating it into a logic circuit, as you will see in this particular case. The Boolean expression which we have just considered can be reduced to the following form:

$$F = B(A + \overline{C}) + \overline{A} \cdot \overline{C}$$

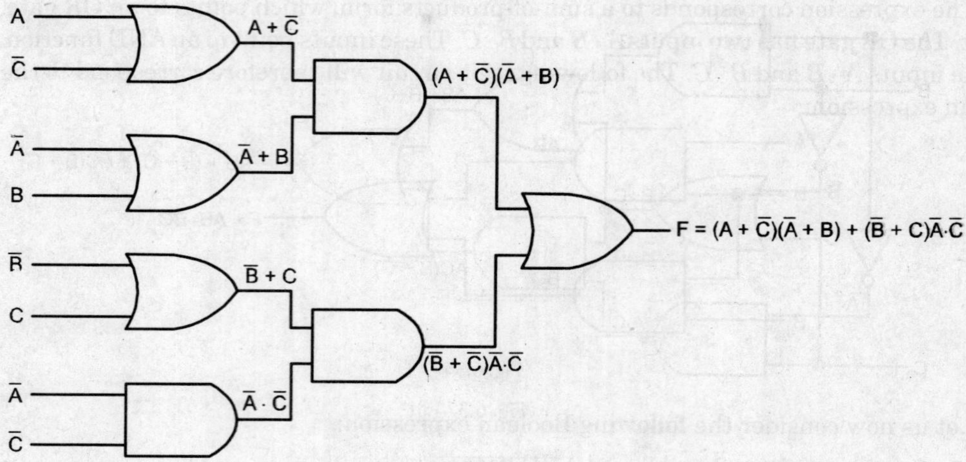

Fig. 6.36 (a)

This leads to a much simpler logic circuit as shown in Fig. 6.36 (b) which requires only four gates.

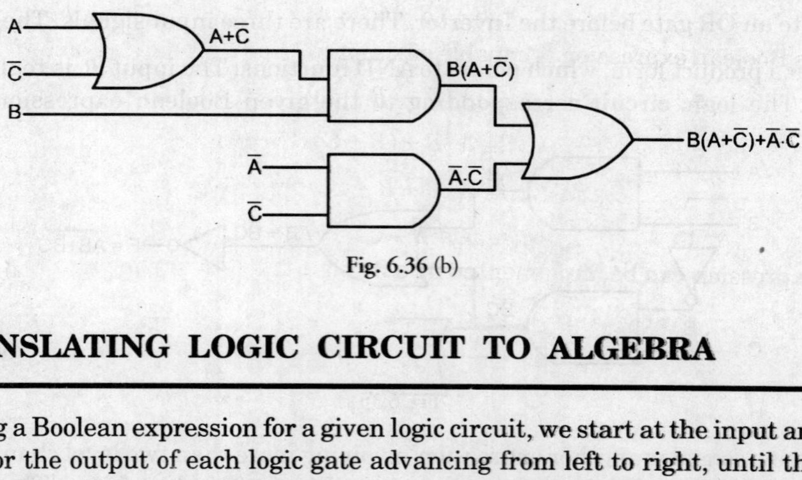

Fig. 6.36 (b)

6.9 TRANSLATING LOGIC CIRCUIT TO ALGEBRA

In developing a Boolean expression for a given logic circuit, we start at the input and develop an expression for the output of each logic gate advancing from left to right, until the output has been reached. We will consider the logic diagram given in Fig. 6.37 (a) and, after translating its function into a Boolean expression, we will attempt to simplify the Boolean expression and recreate a logic circuit which will perform the same function.

Steps

1. Inputs A and B feed AND gate 1, so its output is $A \cdot B$
2. Inputs $\overline{B}$ and C feed OR gate 2, so its output is $\overline{B} + C$

3. Inputs $\overline{A}$ and C feed AND gate 3, so its output is $\overline{A}\cdot C$
4. Outputs of gates 1 and 2 feed OR gate 4, so its output is

$$A\cdot B+(\overline{B}+C)$$

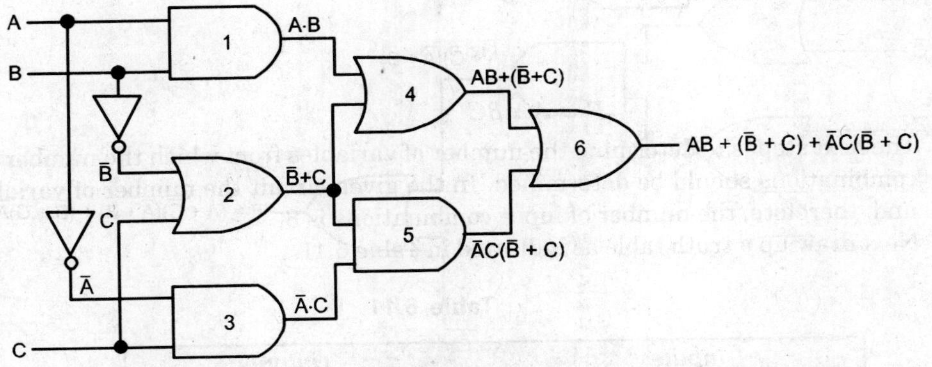

Fig. 6.37 (a)

5. Outputs of gates 2 and 3 feed AND gate 5, so its output is

$$\overline{A}\cdot C\,(\overline{B}+C)$$

6. Outputs of gates 4 and 5 feed OR gate 6, so the final output is

$$A\cdot B+(\overline{B}+C)+\overline{A}\cdot C\,(\overline{B}+C)$$

This Boolean expression is capable of simplification as indicated below:

$$\begin{aligned} F &= A\cdot B+(\overline{B}+C)+\overline{A}\cdot C\,(\overline{B}+C)\\ &= A\cdot B+(\overline{B}+C)\,(1+\overline{A}C)\\ &= A\cdot B+\overline{B}+C\\ &= A+\overline{B}+C \end{aligned}$$

This expression can be implemented by a 3-input OR gate as shown in Fig. 6.37(b).

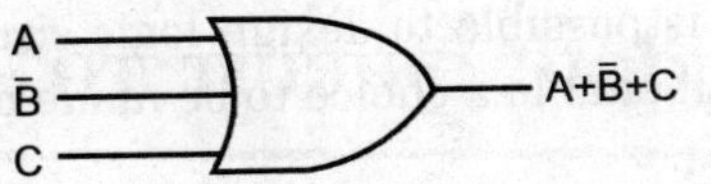

Fig. 6.37 (b)

6.10 TRUTH TABLE FROM LOGIC CIRCUIT

For analyzing the performance of a logic circuit, it is useful to develop a truth-table from which the output can be evaluated for all possible combinations of input values. We will analyze the performance of the logic circuit given in Fig. 6.38.

1. As a first step develop an output equation for the logic circuit following the guidelines given in Section 6.9. The output equation for the logic circuit of Fig. 6.38 is

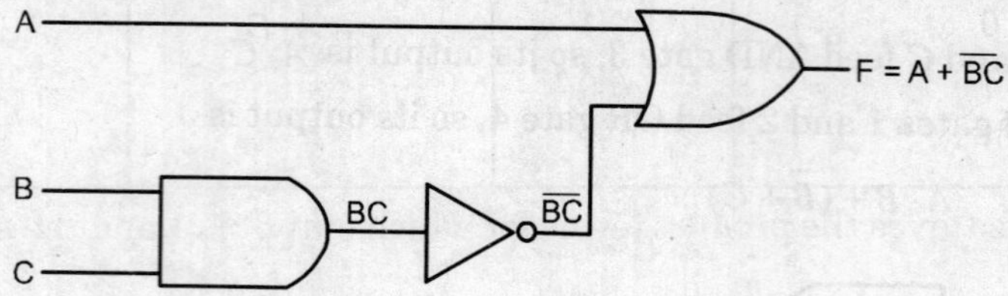

Fig. 6.38

$$F = A + \overline{BC}$$

2. The next step is to determine the number of variables from which the number of input combinations should be determined. In the given circuit the number of variables is 3 and, therefore, the number of input combinations is 8.
3. Next draw up a truth table as indicated in Table 6.11.

Table 6.11

Inputs			*Outputs*		
A	*B*	*C*	*BC*	$\overline{BC}$	$A + \overline{BC}$
0	0	0	0	1	0 + 1 = 1
0	0	1	0	1	0 + 1 = 1
0	1	0	0	1	0 + 1 = 1
0	1	1	1	0	0 + 0 = 0
1	0	0	0	1	1 + 1 = 1
1	0	1	0	1	1 + 1 = 1
1	1	0	0	1	1 + 1 = 1
1	1	1	1	0	1 + 0 = 1

You will notice from the truth table that the output is 0 only for one of the 8 combinations of the input variables.

6.11 LOGIC CIRCUIT FROM TRUTH TABLE

Starting from a truth table, it is possible to design logic circuits in the sum-of-products and product-of-sums forms. This will enable a choice to be made out of the simpler of the two logic circuits.

When we design a logic circuit, we know the number of inputs for which the circuit is to be designed and, according to the design criteria, we also know the output states for the various input combinations. Let us consider the following truth table for a 2-input logic circuit as given in Table 6.12.

Table 6.12

Input		*Output*	*Product terms*	*Sum terms*
A	*B*	*X*		
0	0	1	$\overline{A} \cdot \overline{B}$	

0	1	1	$\overline{A}\cdot B$	
1	0	0		$\overline{A}+B$
1	1	1	$A\cdot B$	

This table also gives the product terms for which output is 1 and the sum terms for which the output is 0.

Sum-of-products expression

For the sum-of-products expression, we only consider the product terms for the rows for which the output is 1. Output is 1 for rows 1, 2 and 4. The output of row 1 will be 1 only when both the inputs A and B are complemented. The output of row 2 will be 1 when A is complemented and B is not complemented. Likewise, for row 4 neither input is to be complemented. The product terms for the three output states will be $\overline{A}\cdot\overline{B}, \overline{A}\cdot B$ and $A\cdot B$. The logical sum of these three product terms will give the required SOP expression which will be as follows:

$$F = \overline{A}\cdot\overline{B}+\overline{A}\cdot B+A\cdot B$$

$$= \overline{A}+B$$

This leads to logic circuit given in Fig. 6.39.

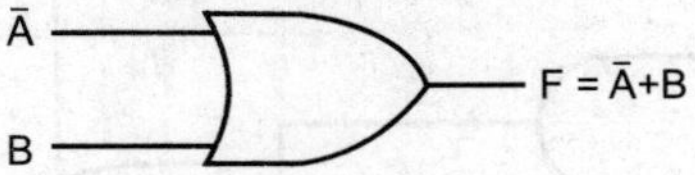

Fig. 6.39

Product-of-sums expression

For the product-of-sums expression, we need to consider the rows for which the output is 0. The output is 0 only for row 3 and what we require is the sum term for this row. The sum term for this row should, therefore, be $\overline{A}+B$, that is input A should be complemented and input B should remain as it is. If we had two sum terms, we would have taken the logical product of these two sum terms to give the required expression. However, since there is only one sum term, the expression will be given by

$$F = \overline{A}+B$$

This expression is the same as for the sum-of-products expression.

We now take up a circuit having three inputs, for which we will consider the truth table given in Table 6.13 and derive SOP and POS expressions for the required logic circuit.

Table 6.13

Inputs			*Output*	*Product terms*	*Sum terms*
A	*B*	*C*	*X*		
0	0	0	1	$\overline{A}\cdot\overline{B}\cdot\overline{C}$	
0	0	1	1	$\overline{A}\cdot\overline{B}\cdot C$	
0	1	0	1	$\overline{A}\cdot B\cdot\overline{C}$	

0	1	1	0		$A+\overline{B}+\overline{C}$
1	0	0	1	$A\cdot\overline{B}\cdot\overline{C}$	
1	0	1	1	$A\cdot\overline{B}\cdot C$	
1	1	0	0		$\overline{A}+\overline{B}+C$
1	1	1	0		$\overline{A}+\overline{B}+\overline{C}$

The sum-of-products expression will be as follows:

$$F = \overline{A}\cdot\overline{B}\cdot\overline{C}+\overline{A}\cdot\overline{B}\cdot C+\overline{A}\cdot B\cdot\overline{C}+A\cdot\overline{B}\cdot\overline{C}+A\cdot\overline{B}\cdot C$$

$$= \overline{A}\cdot\overline{B}(\overline{C}+C)+A\cdot\overline{B}\,(\overline{C}+C)+\overline{A}\cdot B\cdot\overline{C}$$

$$= \overline{A}\cdot\overline{B}+A\cdot\overline{B}+\overline{A}\cdot B\cdot\overline{C}$$

$$= \overline{B}+\overline{A}\cdot B\cdot\overline{C}$$

$$= \overline{B}+\overline{A}\cdot\overline{C}$$

The logic circuit required to implement this function will be as shown in Fig. 6.40.

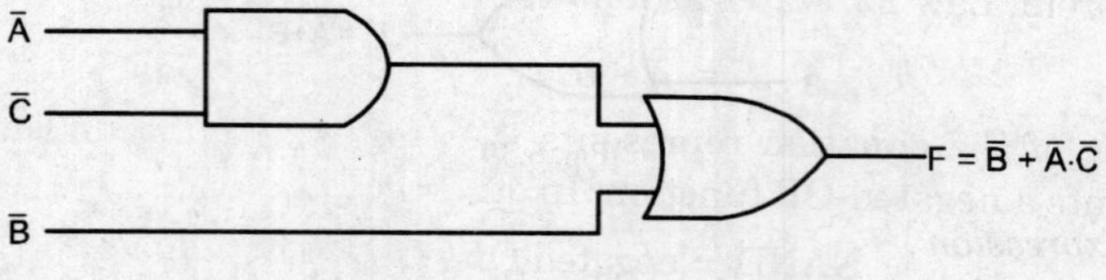

Fig. 6.40

The product-of-sums expression will be the product of the three sum terms as follows:

$$F = (A+\overline{B}+\overline{C})\,(\overline{A}+\overline{B}+C)\,(\overline{A}+\overline{B}+\overline{C})$$

$$= (A+\overline{B}+\overline{C})\,(\overline{A}+\overline{B})$$

$$= \overline{B}(A+\overline{A})+\overline{B}\,(1+\overline{C})+\overline{A}\cdot\overline{C}$$

$$= \overline{B}+\overline{A}\cdot\overline{C}$$

This expression happens to be the same as for the sum-of-products solution.

6.12 COMBINATIONAL CIRCUITS USING NAND/NOR GATES

We have so far considered AND, OR gates and inverters for implementing combinational logic circuits. However, NAND and NOR gates are more versatile, as they can be used to perform AND, OR and INVERT functions. In this section we will look into this aspect and later investigate how AND/OR/INVERT logic circuits can be converted to NAND/NOR logic.

6.12.1 NAND Logic

NAND used as Inverter

A NAND gate can be used as an Inverter by tying all inputs together. The summary of functions in Table 6.14 shows how a 2-input NAND gate can be used as an inverter.

When a NAND or NOR gate is used in a logic diagram, the symbol used in the diagram should represent the logic function being performed and not the NAND or NOR configuration. This is in accordance with the standards for logic symbols. Therefore, if a NAND or NOR gate is used as an Inverter, the logic diagram should show the Inverter symbol. Similarly when a NAND gate is used as a negated-OR, the symbol for negated-OR should be used. Also when a NOR gate is used as a negated-AND, the symbol for negated-AND should be used. You may refer to Tables 6.14 and 6.15 for these symbols.

NAND used as AND

If the output of a NAND gate is inverted by connecting an inverter at the output, the combination will function as an AND gate.

NAND used as Negated-OR

De Morgan's theorem, Law 22, states as follows:

$$\overline{A \cdot B} = \overline{A} + \overline{B}$$

The left side of the equation represents the NAND function and the right side of the equation represents a negated-OR function. In other words

NAND = negated-OR

In symbolic form

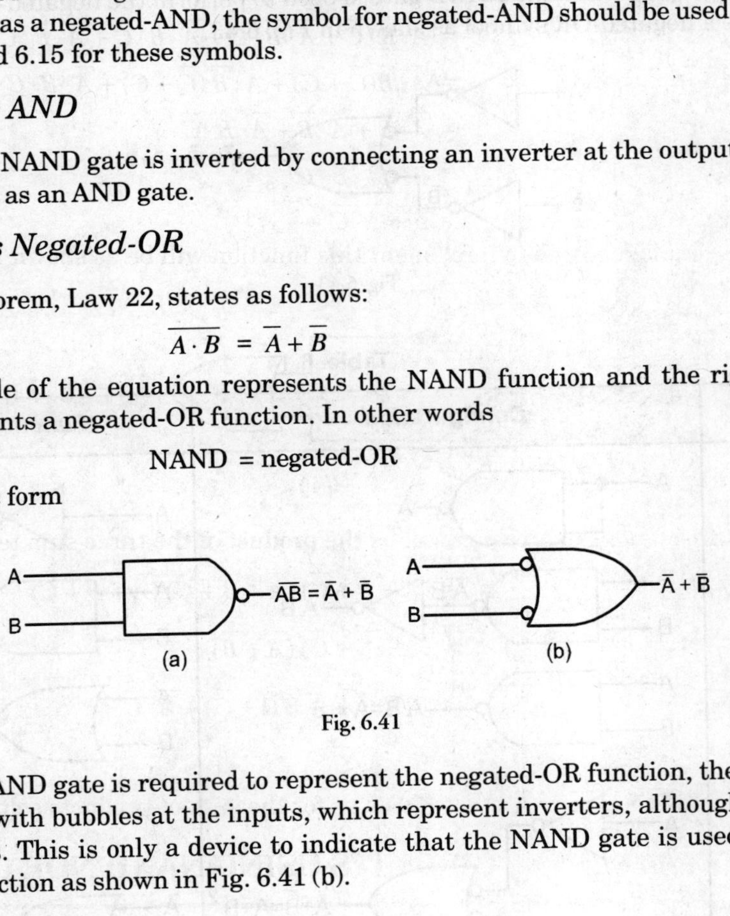

Fig. 6.41

When a NAND gate is required to represent the negated-OR function, the symbol used is the OR symbol with bubbles at the inputs, which represent inverters, although actually there are no inverters. This is only a device to indicate that the NAND gate is used to represent a negated-OR function as shown in Fig. 6.41 (b).

NAND used as OR

From the above discussion it will be obvious that a NAND gate will perform the OR function, if inverters are added ahead of the inputs of a NAND gate. The following diagrams (Figs. 6.42 and 6.43) will clarify the point:

By De Morgan's theorem

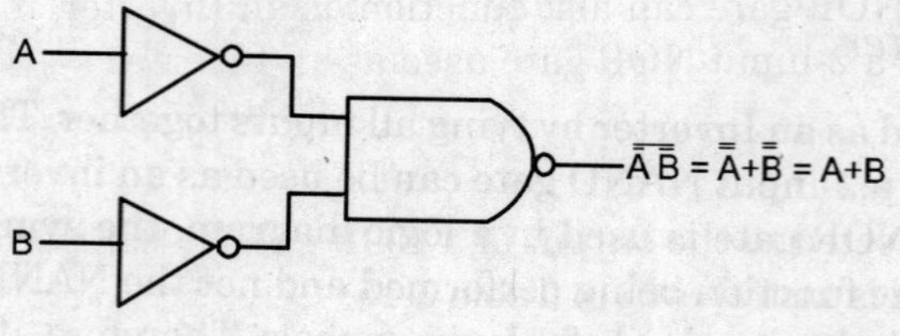

Fig. 6.42

Since in this application the NAND gate is used to perform the negated-OR function, it is desirable to use a negated-OR symbol as shown in Fig. 6.43.

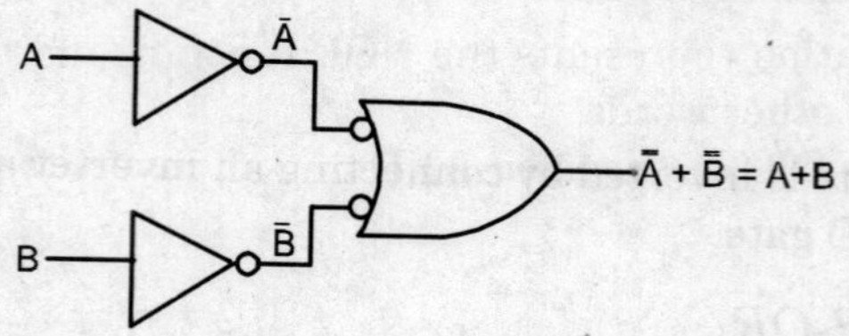

Fig. 6.43

Table 6.14

Function	*Configuration*	*Function symbol*
INVERTER	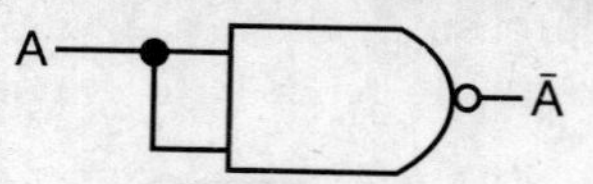	
AND	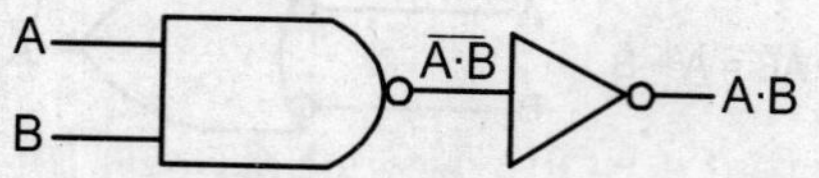	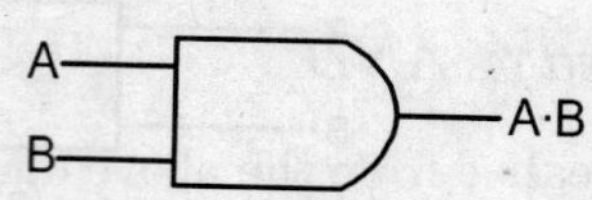
NEGATED-OR	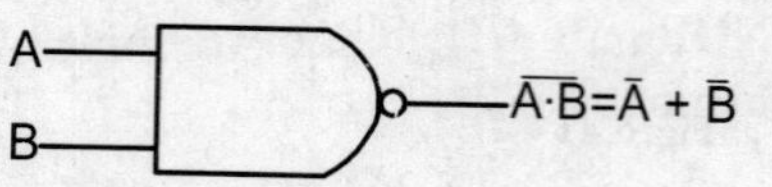	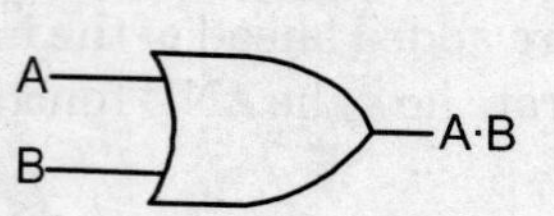
OR	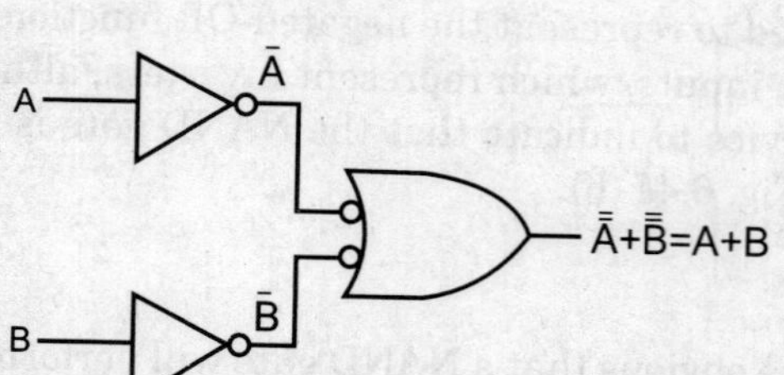	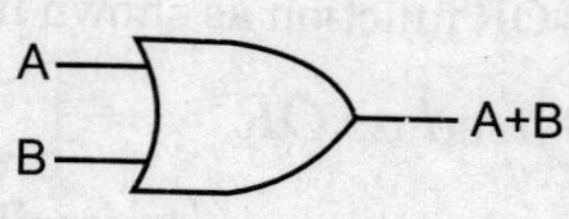

6.12.2 NOR Logic

The NOR gate is an versatile as the NAND gate and it can perform all logic functions.

NOR used as Inverter

Like the NAND gate, the NOR gate can also function as an Inverter, if all the inputs are tied together. Table 6.15 shows a 2-input NOR gate used as an Inverter.

NOR used as OR

If an Inverter is connected to the output of a NOR gate, it will perform the function of an OR gate. This combination is also shown in Table 6.15.

NOR used as negated-AND

De Morgan's theorem, Law 21, states as follows:

$$\overline{A+B} = \bar{A}\cdot\bar{B}$$

The left side of the equation represents the NOR function and the right side represents the negated-AND function. In other words

NOR = negated-AND

In symbolic form

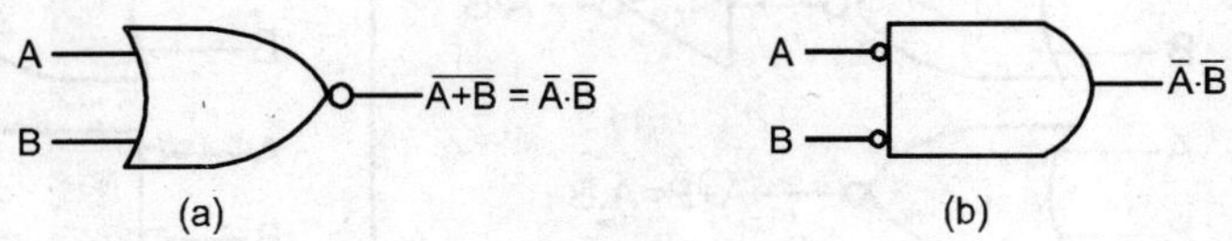

Fig. 6.44

When a NOR gate is required to represent the negated AND function, the symbol used is the AND symbol with bubbles at the inputs, which represent inverters, although actually there are no Inverters. This is only a device to indicate that the NOR gate is used to represent a negated-AND function.

NOR used as AND

You will realize from the above discussion that a NOR gate will perform the AND function, if Inverters are added ahead of the inputs of a NOR gate. The following diagrams (Figs. 6.45 and 6.46) illustrate how the AND function is performed.

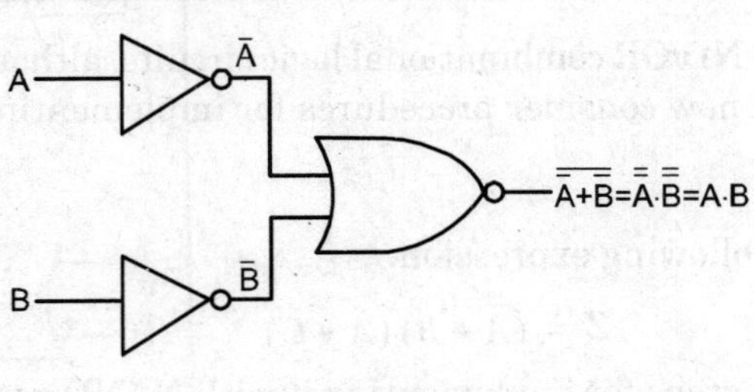

Fig. 6.45

Since in this application, the NOR gate is used to perform the negated-AND function, it is desirable to use the negated-AND symbol as shown in Fig. 6.46.

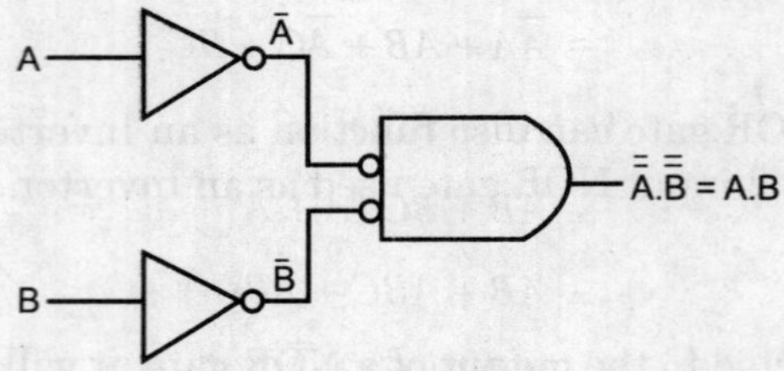

Fig. 6.46

Table 6.15

Function	*Configuration*	*Function symbol*
INVERTER	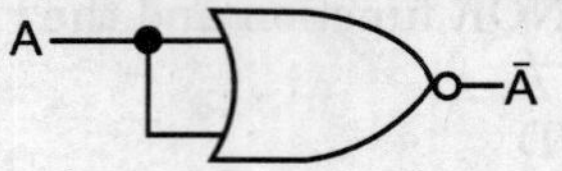	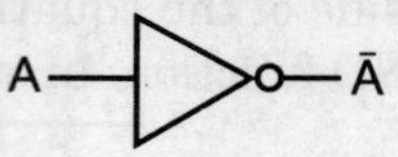
OR	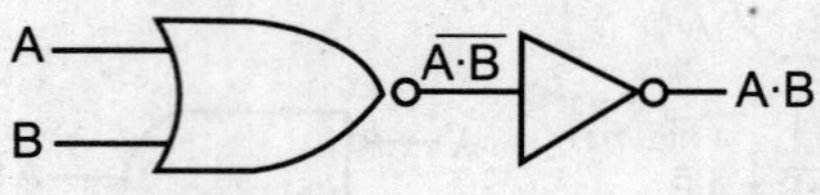	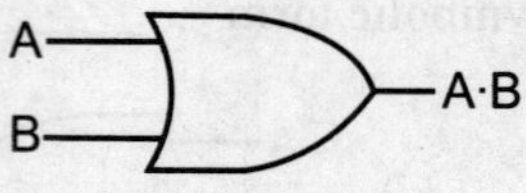
NEGATED-AND	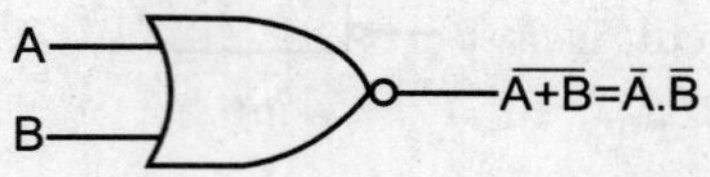	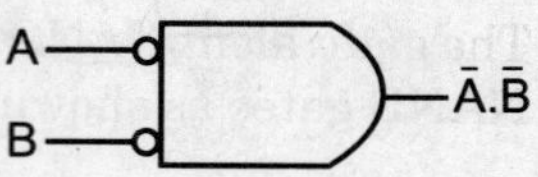
AND	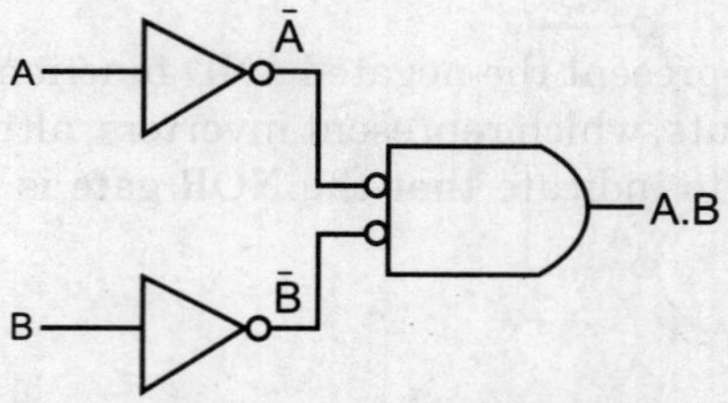	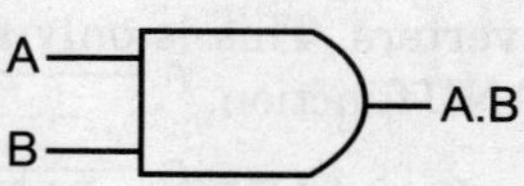

6.13 CONVERTING AND/OR TO NAND/NOR LOGIC

So far we have considered AND/OR combinational logic circuits, although NAND/NOR gates are far more versatile. We will now consider procedures for implementing Boolean expressions by using NAND/NOR gates.

NAND Logic

We will consider the following expression:

$$Z = (\overline{A} + B)\,(A + C)$$

and consider the necessary steps for implementing it with NAND gates.

1. For implementing the expression with NAND gates it should be changed to a sum-of-products form as indicated below:

$$Z = (\overline{A} + B)\,(A + C)$$

$$= \bar{A}A + AB + \bar{A}C + BC$$

$$= AB + BC + \bar{A}C$$

$$= AB + BC\,(A + \bar{A}) + \bar{A}C$$

$$= AB + ABC + \bar{A}BC + \bar{A}C$$

$$= AB(1 + C) + \bar{A}C\,(C + 1)$$

$$= AB + \bar{A}C$$

2. The next step is to draw a corresponding 2-level AND/OR configuration, as given in Fig. 6.47

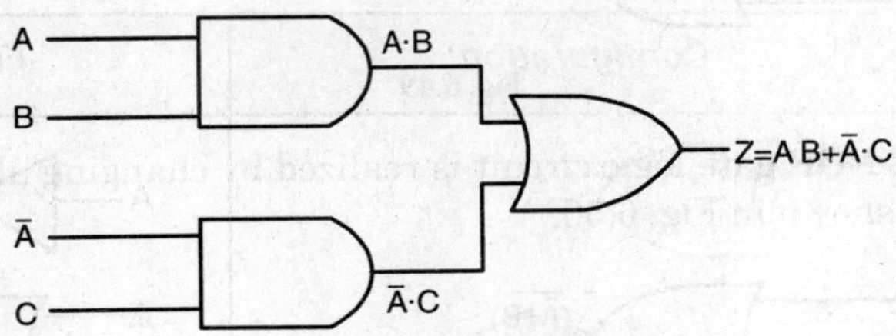

Fig. 6.47

3. The equivalent NAND gate logic circuit is obtained by changing all gates in Fig. 6.47 to NAND gates as shown in Fig. 6.48.

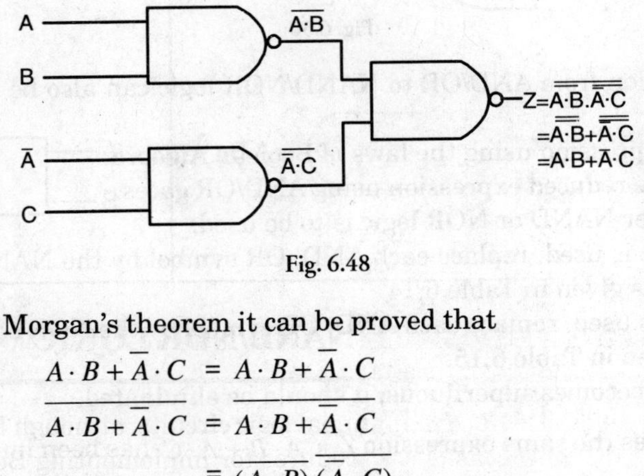

Fig. 6.48

By using De Morgan's theorem it can be proved that

$$A \cdot B + \bar{A} \cdot C \;=\; A \cdot B + \bar{A} \cdot C$$

$$\overline{A \cdot B + \bar{A} \cdot C} \;=\; \overline{A \cdot B + \bar{A} \cdot C}$$

$$= \overline{(A \cdot B)}\,\overline{(\bar{A} \cdot C)}$$

$$\overline{\overline{A \cdot B + \bar{A} \cdot C}} \;=\; \overline{\overline{(A \cdot B)}\,\overline{(\bar{A} \cdot C)}}$$

This proves that the logic circuit of Fig. 6.48 is equivalent to the logic circuit of Fig. 6.47.

NOR Logic

We will consider the same expression as before and discuss the various steps necessary for implementing it with NOR gates.

1. For implementing with NOR gates the expression has to be in the form of a product-of-sums. Since the expression under consideration

$$Z = (\overline{A} + B)\,(A + C)$$

is already in the S-O-P form, no transformation is required.

2. The next step is to draw a corresponding 2-level OR/ AND configuration as given in Fig. 6.49.

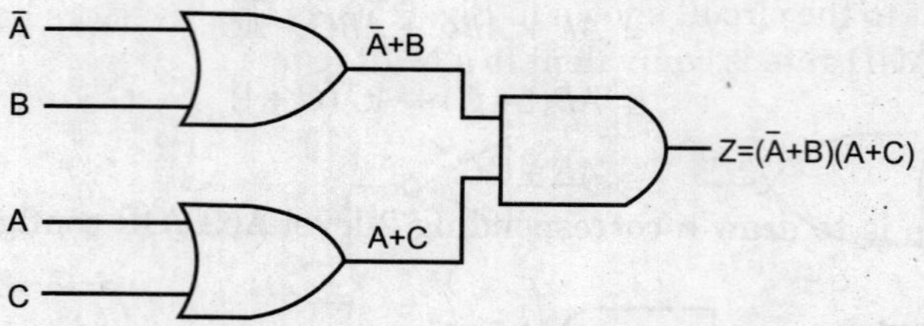

Fig. 6.49

3. The equivalent NOR gate logic circuit is realized by changing all gates in Fig. 6.49 to NOR gates, as shown in Fig. 6.50.

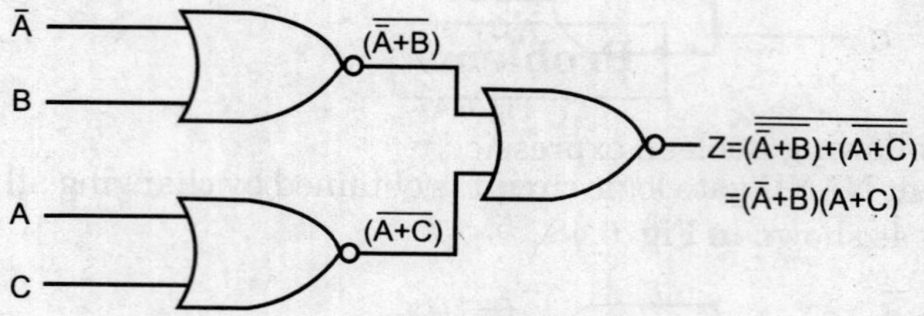

Fig. 6.50

The transformation from AND/OR to NAND/NOR logic can also be accomplished by the following procedure:

1. Reduce the expression using the laws of Boolean Algebra.
2. Implement the reduced expression using AND/OR gates.
3. Decide whether NAND or NOR logic is to be used.
4. If NAND logic is used, replace each AND, OR symbol by the NAND equivalent of the logic symbol as given in Table 6.14.
5. If NOR logic is used, replace each AND, OR symbol by the NOR equivalent of the logic symbol as given in Table 6.15.
6. If any symbol becomes superfluous, it should be eliminated.

Using NAND gates the same expression Z = $A \cdot B + \overline{A} \cdot C$ has been implemented as shown in Fig. 6.51. This circuit is equivalent to the circuit of Fig. 6.48, as the Inverters have become superfluous and the bubbled-OR gate is equivalent to a NAND gate.

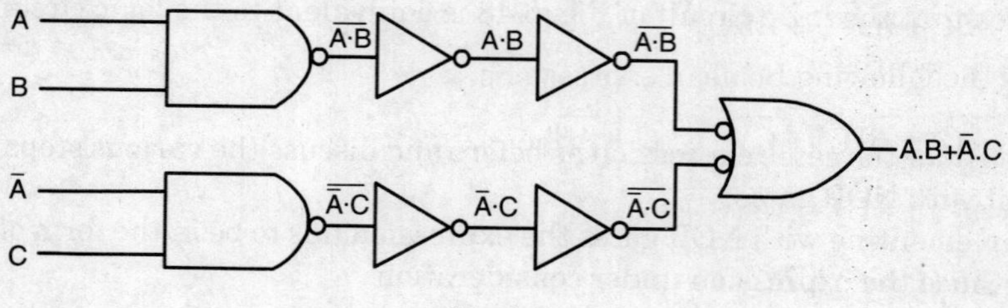

Fig. 6.51

Following this procedure the expression

$$Z = (\bar{A} + B)\,(A + C)$$

has been implemented using NOR gates for a product-of-sums expression, as shown in Fig. 6.52. This circuit is equivalent to the circuit shown in Fig. 6.50, as the Inverters have become superfluous and the bubbled AND gate is equivalent to a NOR gate.

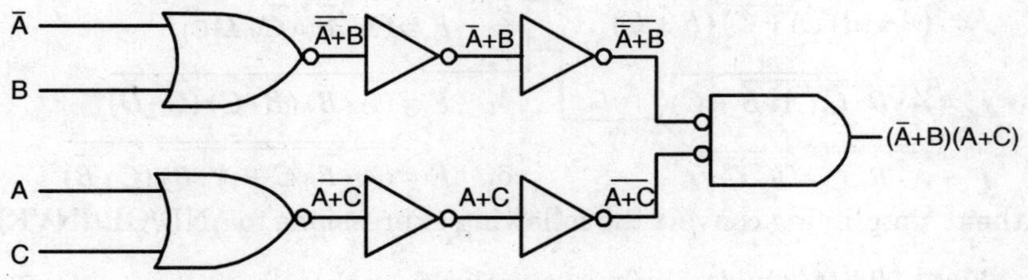

Fig. 6.52

Problems

6.1 Simplify the following Boolean expressions:

1. $F = A \cdot A \cdot 1$
2. $F = A \cdot B \cdot \bar{A}$
3. $F = A \cdot \bar{\bar{A}}$
4. $F = A \cdot \bar{A} \cdot \bar{\bar{A}}$
5. $F = A \cdot B \cdot \bar{\bar{A}} + \bar{A} \cdot B \cdot A$
6. $F = \bar{A} \cdot \bar{B} \cdot 1 + \bar{\bar{A}} \cdot \bar{B} \cdot \bar{A}$
7. $F = A \cdot \bar{B} \cdot \bar{\bar{A}} \cdot B + A \cdot B \cdot B$
8. $F = A \cdot B \cdot B \cdot C + A \cdot B \cdot \bar{\bar{C}} \cdot \bar{C}$

6.2 Simplify the following Boolean expressions:

1. $F = (A + \bar{B})\,(A + \bar{C})$
2. $F = (A + B + C)\,(A + \bar{B} + \bar{C})$
3. $F = A \cdot B\,(A + B)$
4. $F = (A + B)\,(A + C)$

6.3 Simplify the following Boolean expressions:

1. $F = A\,(A + B)\,(A + AB)$
2. $F = A(\bar{A} + B)\,(AB + \bar{B})$
3. $F = (A\bar{B} + B)\,(AB + \bar{B})$
4. $F = \bar{A}\,(AB + \bar{B})$

6.4 Simplify the following Boolean expressions:

1. $F = AB + A\bar{B} + B$
2. $F = A\bar{B} + \bar{A}C + A\bar{B}\,\bar{C}$
3. $F = \bar{A}BC + \bar{A}\,\bar{B}\,C + \bar{A}B\bar{C}$
4. $F = \bar{A}BCD + \bar{A}BC\bar{D} + ABC + BC\bar{D}$

6.5 Simplify the following Boolean expressions:

1. $F = \bar{A}\,(A + \bar{B})\,(A + \bar{C}) + \bar{C}\,(C + \overline{AB})$
2. $F = \bar{A}B\,(\bar{A} + C) + A\bar{B}\,(\bar{B} + C)$
3. $F = \bar{A}B\,(B + C) + BC\,(\bar{B} + \bar{A})$
4. $F = (AB + C)\,(AB + \bar{C})$

6.6 Simplify the following Boolean expressions:

1. $F=\overline{A\cdot\overline{B}}$
2. $F=\overline{\overline{A}\cdot\overline{B}\cdot\overline{C}}$
3. $F=\overline{\overline{A}\cdot B\cdot\overline{C}}$
4. $F=\overline{A\cdot\overline{B}\cdot C}+B\cdot C$

6.7 Simplify the following Boolean expressions:

1. $F=\overline{(\overline{A}+B)(\overline{A}+C)(B+C)}$
2. $F=\overline{\overline{\overline{(A\cdot\overline{B})}\cdot\overline{C}}\cdot D}$
3. $F=\overline{A\cdot B\cdot C}\,\overline{(\overline{A\cdot B}+C)}$
4. $F=\overline{(\overline{A}\cdot B)(\overline{B}\cdot C)(\overline{C}\cdot\overline{D})}$
5. $F=\overline{\overline{A}\cdot B\cdot C}+\overline{\overline{B}\cdot\overline{C}\cdot A}$
6. $F=\overline{\overline{(\overline{A}\cdot\overline{B}\cdot C+A\cdot B)}(C\cdot\overline{B})}$

6.8 Without simplifying convert the following expressions to AND/OR/INVERT logic:

1. $F=A\cdot B+\overline{A}\cdot C+D$
2. $F=\overline{A}\cdot B\cdot C+\overline{A}\cdot B\cdot\overline{C}+A\cdot\overline{B}\cdot C$
3. $F=\overline{A}\cdot B\cdot C\cdot D+A\cdot\overline{B}\cdot C\cdot D+A\cdot B\cdot\overline{C}$
4. $F=AB\,(C+\overline{D})+BC\,(A+D)$

6.9 Without simplifying convert the following expressions to AND/OR/INVERT logic:

1. $F=(A+\overline{B}\,(\overline{C}+D)$
2. $F=(AB+\overline{C})\,(\overline{A}C+B)$
3. $F=A(B+\overline{C})\,(\overline{A}+C)$
4. $F=AD(\overline{B}+D)$

6.10 Translate the following logic circuits to algebra and simplify the expression:
1. Logic circuit given in Fig. 6.7
2. Logic circuit given in Fig. 6.9
3. Logic circuit given in Fig. 6.10

6.11 Draw a logic circuit diagram from the following truth table:

Inputs			*Outputs*
A	B	C	F
0	0	0	1
0	0	1	0
0	1	0	0
0	1	1	0
1	0	0	1
1	0	1	0
1	1	0	0
1	1	1	0

6.12 Implement the following function with NAND/NOR logic:

$$F=(A+\overline{B})(\overline{C}+D)$$

6.13 Implement the following function with NAND/NOR logic:

$$F=AD(\overline{B}+D)$$

6.14 Simplify the following function and draw a logic circuit to implement the reduced logic expression:

$$F = \overline{[(\overline{A} + B)} + C] + BC$$

6.15 Prove that

$$(A + B)\,(\overline{A} + C)\,(B + C) \;=\; (A + B)\,(\overline{A} + C)$$

7

Karnaugh Map Techniques

7.1 INTRODUCTION

In Section 6.11, we have discussed Sum-of-products and Product-of-sums logic circuits. It was also explained how these logic circuits can be derived from truth tables.

However, before a logic equation can be translated into a logic circuit, it is necessary to reduce it to simplest possible form. For reducing logic expressions we have considered the application of Boolean laws in the preceding chapter. The application of these laws is sometimes inconvenient when the number of variables is large. Besides, at times, the application of these laws does not always lead to the simplest possible expression, which increases the chances of error. Fortunately there is not only a better system, but also a faster one, for reducing Boolean expressions. This is the Karnaugh map technique, which provides a graphical method for this purpose.

In this chapter, we will consider Karnaugh map technique for the reduction of Boolean expressions, as well as the application of this method in the design of some logic systems. We will also consider the reduction of Boolean expressions, which have more than four variables.

7.2 MINTERMS AND MAXTERMS

Before dealing with the graphical representation of a Boolean expression, it would be useful to acquire familiarity with some of the terms used in mapping techniques. One such term is referred to as 'Minterm'.

According to one of the theorems within the Boolean algebra, we can express any Boolean function as the sum-of-products of all the variables within the system. Let us consider Table 7.1 which shows the minterms (fundamental products) binary values and minterm designations of a three-variable logic system.

Table 7.1

Input			*Minterm*		*Output*
A	*B*	*C*	*Fundamental product*	*Designation*	
0	0	0	$\overline{A}\,\overline{B}\,\overline{C}$	m_0	1

0	0	1	$\overline{A}\,\overline{B}\,C$	m_1	1
0	1	0	$\overline{A}\,B\,\overline{C}$	m_2	1
0	1	1	$\overline{A}\,B\,C$	m_3	0
1	0	0	$A\,\overline{B}\,\overline{C}$	m_4	0
1	0	1	$A\,\overline{B}\,C$	m_5	1
1	1	0	$A\,B\,\overline{C}$	m_6	0
1	1	1	$A\,B\,C$	m_7	1

As has been explained in the previous chapter, the sum-of-products expression for the system having output values indicated in Table 7.1 can be written as follows, taking into account only those minterms (fundamental products for which the output is 1.

$$F = \overline{A}\,\overline{B}\,\overline{C} + \overline{A}\,\overline{B}\,C + \overline{A}\,B\,\overline{C} + A\,\overline{B}\,C + A\,B\,C \qquad ...(7.1)$$

You will notice from this expression that each minterm is a product of all the variables in the system. The same Boolean expression can be written as follows by using the minterm designations:

$$F = m_0 + m_1 + m_2 + m_5 + m_7$$

or as

$$F = \Sigma(0, 1, 2, 5, 7)$$

A related term which you may come across is referred to as 'Maxterm'. A maxterm is a sum of all the variables within a logic system. Just as we can determine an SOP expression from a sum of minterms, we can also derive a POS expression as a product of maxterms. You may refer to Table 7.2, which gives the maxterms and their designations for a three-variable system. We have retained the same output states as a Table 7.1, to obtain a logic expression in the POS form for the same logic system.

Table 7.2

Input			*Maxterm*		*Output*
A	*B*	*C*	*Expression*	*Designation*	
0	0	0	$A + B + C$	M_0	1
0	0	1	$A + B + \overline{C}$	M_1	1
0	1	0	$A + \overline{B} + C$	M_2	1
0	1	1	$A + \overline{B} + \overline{C}$	M_3	0
1	0	0	$\overline{A} + B + C$	M_4	0
1	0	1	$\overline{A} + B + \overline{C}$	M_5	1
1	1	0	$\overline{A} + \overline{B} + C$	M_6	0
1	1	1	$\overline{A} + \overline{B} + \overline{C}$	M_7	1

You will notice from this table that all the maxterms are formed by ORing of the inverted logic variables on that line. For the POS expression, we are only concerned with those maxterms for which the output is 0.

The POS expression for this logic system can be written as follows, taking into account only those maxterms for which the output is 0.

$$F = (A + \overline{B} + \overline{C})(\overline{A} + B + C)(\overline{A} + \overline{B} + C) \quad ...(7.2)$$

Using maxterm designations, the POS expression can also be written as follows:

$$F = M_3 \cdot M_4 \cdot M_6$$

or as

$$F = \Pi(3, 4, 6)$$

You will notice that minterms m_3, m_4 and m_6 are not present in the SOP equation. There is a complementary relationship between the SOP and POS expressions. It follows that if you have an expression in the SOP form, you can write the POS expression by giving maxterms, those subscripts which are not present in the SOP expression and vice versa.

7.3 EXPANSION OF BOOLEAN EXPRESSIONS

If you have to transfer a Boolean expression to a Karnaugh map, when every product term of the POS expression does not have all the variables of the relevant logic system, it will not be easy to do so unless the POS expression is expanded, so that each product term includes all the variables.

Example 7.1: *Expand the following expression:*

$$F = A + B\overline{C} \quad ...(7.3)$$

Solution: The expression has three variables. A is short of two variables and $B\overline{C}$ is short of one variable. The way to expand the terms is as follows:

1. Multiply A by all possible combinations of $B \cdot C$ and OR the product terms as follows:

   A becomes $A(\overline{B}\,C + B\,\overline{C} + \overline{B}\,\overline{C} + B\,C)$

   $$= A\,\overline{B}\,C + A\,B\,\overline{C} + A\,\overline{B}\,\overline{C} + A\,B\,C$$

2. Multiply $B\overline{C}$ by both the complemented and uncomplemented forms of A.

   $B\,\overline{C}$ becomes $B\,\overline{C}\,(A + \overline{A})$

   $$= A\,B\,\overline{C} + \overline{A}\,B\,\overline{C}$$

   The expanded expression is now as follows:

$$F = A\overline{B}C + AB\overline{C} + A\overline{B}\,\overline{C} + ABC + AB\overline{C} + \overline{A}B\overline{C} \quad ...(7.4)$$

$$= A\overline{B}C + AB\overline{C} + A\overline{B}\,\overline{C} + ABC + \overline{A}B\overline{C} \quad ...(7.5)$$

Since there are two identical product terms, $A\,B\,\overline{C}$, in Eqn. (7.4), one of them has been dropped from Eqn. (7.5). We can prove that Eqn. (7.5) has not changed in value from the original expression as follows:

$$F = A\overline{B}C + AB\overline{C} + A\overline{B}\,\overline{C} + ABC + \overline{A}B\overline{C}$$

$$= A\overline{B}\,(C+\overline{C}) + AB\,(\overline{C}+C) + \overline{A}\,B\,\overline{C}$$
$$= A\overline{B} + AB + \overline{A}B\overline{C}$$
$$= A(\overline{B}+B) + \overline{A}B\overline{C}$$
$$= A + \overline{A}B\overline{C}$$
$$= A(B\overline{C}+1) + \overline{A}B\overline{C}$$
$$= AB\overline{C} + A + \overline{A}B\overline{C}$$
$$= B\overline{C}\,(A+\overline{A}) + A$$
$$= A + B\overline{C}$$

Multiplying A by ($B\overline{C}$ + 1) does not change the value of the expression.

In the above reduction you must have noticed that most of the simplification has been carried out by the law of complements. For instance in the above simplification by this law

$A\overline{B}\,(C+\overline{C})$ becomes $A\overline{B}$

$AB(C+\overline{C})$ becomes AB

$A(\overline{B}+B)$ becomes A and

$B\overline{C}\,(A+\overline{A})$ becomes $B\overline{C}$

It follows that in this method of simplification the variables that change drop out, and the other variables of the product terms which do not change are retained and form a new product term. This is a very important conclusion and it forms the basis of reduction by the mapping technique.

For the purpose of reduction of a Boolean expression with the help of Karnaugh maps, it is the usual practice to place 1 in squares corresponding to the product terms of the Boolean expression. In doing so, it is found very convenient if the minterm designations of the product terms are known. The following example illustrates the procedure:

Example 7.2: *Write the following Boolean expression using minterm designations:*

$$F = \overline{A}\,B\,\overline{C}\,D + A\,\overline{B}\,\overline{C}\,D + A\,\overline{B}\,C\,\overline{D}$$

Solution:

Substitute 1s for uncomplemented letters and 0s for complemented letters	0 1 0 1 +	1 0 0 1 +	1 0 1 0
Decimal value	5	9	10
Express minterm designation using decimal value as subscript	m_5 +	m_9 +	m_{10}

$$F = m_5 + m_9 + m_{10}$$

7.4 KARNAUGH MAPS

The fundamental products of a logic function can be visually displayed on a Karnaugh map which is, in a way, an alternative to a truth table, as it can display in a visual form all the information contained in a truth table. Refer to a 2-variable Karnaugh map given in Fig. 7.1. The map has four squares which can display all the four fundamental products of a Boolean function with two variables.

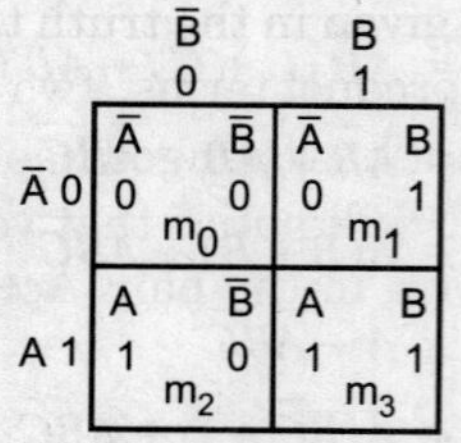

Fig. 7.1 Two-variable Karnaugh map

You will notice from the map that columns are assigned to variables $\bar{B}$ and B, and rows are assigned to variables $\bar{A}$ and A. Each square has been given an address which tallies with its location in the row and column. The addresses are 00, 01, 10 and 11. Each fundamental product has been assigned a square, which tallies with its address. For instance the fundamental product $\bar{A}B$ has been assigned a square, the address of which is 0 1, which tallies with its minterm designation. Also notice that in the same row only one variable changes. For instance in the top row $\bar{B}$ changes to B. In columns also, only one variable changes from the complemented to the uncomplemented form. This means that there is a change in only one digit, as you move vertically or horizontally (not diagonally) from one square to the adjacent square. Consequently, the full address differs by only one digit, from one square to the adjacent square.

You must have noticed that the Karnaugh map for two-variables has four squares that is 2^2 squares. A Boolean function with three variables will require 2^3 or 8 squares, so that there is one square for each of the eight product terms of a 3-variables function. Thus a Boolean function of 'n' variables will require 2^n squares. For a 4-variable function, there should be 16 squares to accommodate all the 16 product terms.

7.4.1 Two-variable Karnaugh Map

It has been pointed out earlier that a Karnaugh map may be regarded as an alternative to a truth table. To investigate this, we can consider the representation of the following logic function on a Karnaugh map:

$$F = \bar{A}\bar{B} + \bar{A}B \qquad ...(7.6)$$

The truth table for this function is given in Table 7.3 and the Karnaugh map representation is given in Fig. 7.2. The output values gives in the truth table have been entered in the Karnaugh map.

Table 7.3

Input		*Product term*	*Output*
A	*B*		*Y*
0	0	$\bar{A}\bar{B}$	1
0	1	$\bar{A}B$	1
1	0	$A\bar{B}$	0
1	1	AB	0

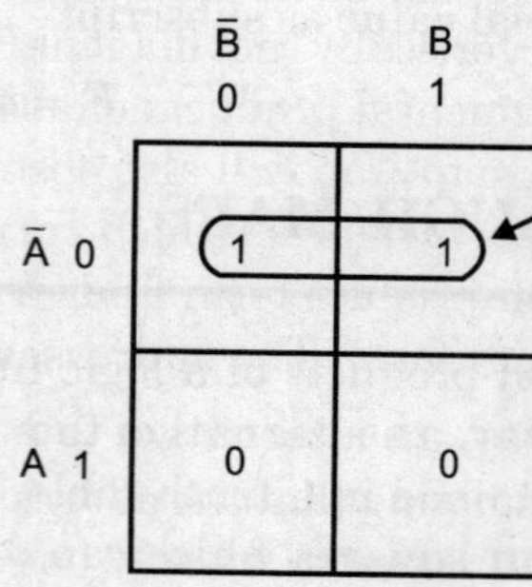

Fig. 7.2

In this map the output values given in the truth table have been entered in squares corresponding to the designations of the product terms. Two 1s which form a pair have been enclosed, and from this pair the variable B that has changed has been dropped and variable $\bar{A}$ which has not changed has been retained. You will notice that variable B has changed from the complemented to the uncomplemented form in the pair. According to the Karnaugh map reduction procedure, the reduced equation is

$$F = \bar{A}$$

Let us now reduce Eqn. (7.6) using Boolean laws:

$$F = \bar{A}\,\bar{B} + \bar{A}B$$

$$= \bar{A}\,(\bar{B} + B)$$

$$= \bar{A} \quad \text{by the law of Complements.}$$

We have arrived at the same result as before by using a Karnaugh map.

7.4.2 Three-variable Karnaugh Map

To accommodate the eight product terms of a three-variable function, we can have two squares in a row and four in each column, or four in each row and two is each column, which will in either case accommodate all the eight product terms. For our use the latter alternative as given in Fig. 7.3 will be adopted.

	$\bar{B}\bar{C}$ 00	$\bar{B}C$ 01	BC 11	$B\bar{C}$ 10
$\bar{A}$ 0	$\bar{A}\bar{B}\bar{C}$ 000 m_0	$\bar{A}\bar{B}C$ 001 m_1	$\bar{A}BC$ 011 m_3	$\bar{A}B\bar{C}$ 010 m_2
A 1	$A\bar{B}\bar{C}$ 100 m_4	$A\bar{B}C$ 101 m_5	ABC 111 m_7	$AB\bar{C}$ 110 m_6

Fig. 7.3

In this map the rows are labelled $\bar{A}$ and A, as a result of which when you move down from the top row to the row below in any column, only one of the variables that is $\bar{A}$ changes to A. The columns are also so labelled that only one variable is different between adjacent squares horizontally or vertically (not diagonally).

The fundamental products of a three-variables system given in Table 7.1 have also been entered in this map. You will also observe that the product terms in each square represent the product of three variables, which correspond to the row and column of their positions. Also notice that each product term finds a place in one of the squares and that each entry has an address in binary form. The addresses correspond to the binary representation of the product terms. For intance the address of the term $A\bar{B}C$ is 1 0 1 and the address of $\bar{A}B\bar{C}$ is 0 1 0.

It is worth noting that the address of every term differs from those of the adjacent terms in the same row and column by only one digit, which means that there is a change in only one of the variables in the product terms. You will also observe that the addresses of terms at the opposite extremities of the same row differ by only one digit. They can therefore be regarded to be adjacent as indicated below:

1. $\overline{A}\,\overline{B}\,\overline{C}$ and $\overline{A}\,B\,\overline{C}$ are adjacent

2. $A\,\overline{B}\,\overline{C}$ and $A\,B\,\overline{C}$ are adjacent

The output values of the product terms of the three-variable system given in Table 7.1 have been entered in the Karnaugh map shown in Fig. 7.4. In this map the minterm designations have been given for all the product terms. You will find that this map gives all the information contained in the truth table.

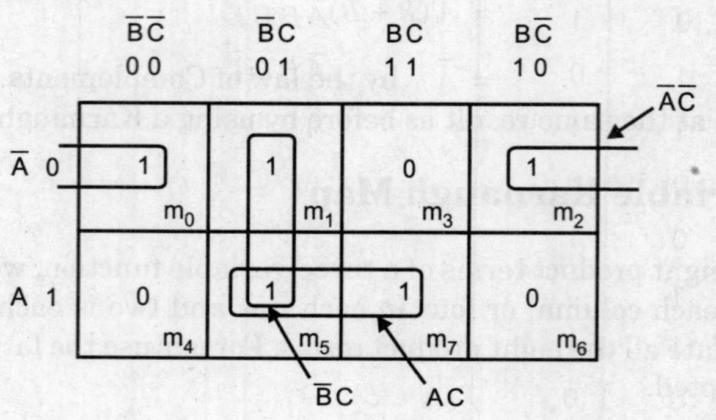

Fig. 7.4

In this map the following minterms are adjacent, which can be combined to form groups for the purpose of reduction of the Boolean function.

1. Minterms m_1 and m_5 are adjacent as only variable $\overline{A}$ changes to A. Variables $\overline{B}C$ do not change and so this group yields the product $\overline{B}C$.
2. Minterms m_5 and m_7 are adjacent and form a group yielding the product AC, as only variable $\overline{B}$ changes to B. The first and second groups overlap, but that is permissible.
3. Minterms m_0 and m_2 can be considered to be adjacent, although they are at the extreme ends of row, since only variable $\overline{B}$ has changed to B. This group yields a product $\overline{A}\,\overline{C}$.
4. Although minterm m_0 is adjacent to m_1 they have not been grouped, as grouping them does not cover any minterm which has not already been covered.

According to the Karnaugh map technique, the SOP expression is obtained by ORing all the reduced terms covering all the logic 1s on the map. Therefore the reduced function is

$$F = \overline{B}C + AC + \overline{A}\,\overline{C} \qquad ...(7.7)$$

Reduction of Eqn. (7.1) by using the laws of Boolean algebra will yield the same result.

7.4.3 Four-variable Karnaugh Map

We can now turn our attention to a four-variable Karnaugh map. A logic function with four variables will have 2^4 or 16 combinations of variables. Table 7.4 shows the fundamental products, binary values and minterm designations of a 4-variable logic system.

Table 7.4

Input				Minterm	
A	**B**	**C**	**D**	**Fundamental products**	**Designations**
0	0	0	0	$\bar{A}\bar{B}\bar{C}\bar{D}$	m_0
0	0	0	1	$\bar{A}\bar{B}\bar{C}D$	m_1
0	0	1	0	$\bar{A}\bar{B}C\bar{D}$	m_2
0	0	1	1	$\bar{A}\bar{B}CD$	m_3
0	1	0	0	$\bar{A}B\bar{C}\bar{D}$	m_4
0	1	0	1	$\bar{A}B\bar{C}D$	m_5
0	1	1	0	$\bar{A}BC\bar{D}$	m_6
0	1	1	1	$\bar{A}BCD$	m_7
1	0	0	0	$A\bar{B}\bar{C}\bar{D}$	m_8
1	0	0	1	$A\bar{B}\bar{C}D$	m_9
1	0	1	0	$A\bar{B}C\bar{D}$	m_{10}
1	0	1	1	$A\bar{B}CD$	m_{11}
1	1	0	0	$AB\bar{C}\bar{D}$	m_{12}
1	1	0	1	$AB\bar{C}D$	m_{13}
1	1	1	0	$ABC\bar{D}$	m_{14}
1	1	1	1	$ABCD$	m_{15}

A Karnaugh map for a four-variable function is given in Fig. 7.5. The map has four rows and four columns and it has in all 16 squares which can accommodate all the product terms of a 4-variable system. Notice that the rows are assigned to combinations of variables *A* and *B* and their complements in such a manner that there is a change in the nature of only one variable as you move from one row to the next in the same column. Columns have been assigned in a like manner to variables *C* and *D*.

	$\bar{C}\bar{D}$ 00	$\bar{C}D$ 01	CD 11	$C\bar{D}$ 10
$\bar{A}\bar{B}$ 00	$\bar{A}\bar{B}\bar{C}\bar{D}$ 0000 m_0	$\bar{A}\bar{B}\bar{C}D$ 0001 m_1	$\bar{A}\bar{B}CD$ 0011 m_3	$\bar{A}\bar{B}C\bar{D}$ 0010 m_2
$\bar{A}B$ 01	$\bar{A}B\bar{C}\bar{D}$ 0100 m_4	$\bar{A}B\bar{C}D$ 0101 m_5	$\bar{A}BCD$ 0111 m_7	$\bar{A}BC\bar{D}$ 0110 m_6
AB 11	$AB\bar{C}\bar{D}$ 1100 m_{12}	$AB\bar{C}D$ 1101 m_{13}	$ABCD$ 1111 m_{15}	$ABC\bar{D}$ 1110 m_{14}
$A\bar{B}$ 10	$A\bar{B}\bar{C}\bar{D}$ 1000 m_8	$A\bar{B}\bar{C}D$ 1001 m_9	$A\bar{B}CD$ 1011 m_{11}	$A\bar{B}C\bar{D}$ 1010 m_{10}

Fig. 7.5

As before, the product terms for each square are determined by their positions in rows and columns. For instance consider the minterm m_7. The product term in this square is $ABCD$. Also notice that as you move in any row or column from one square to the adjacent square, only one variable changes. Therefore, squares immediately above and below and to the right and left of any square in the map can be considered to be adjacent, as in these cases only one variable changes. This is a special feature of Karnaugh maps.

There is also a rather unique case of adjacencies in these maps. You will observe that between minterms m_0 and m_2, m_2 and m_{10}, m_{10} and m_8, m_8 and m_0 there is a change in only one variable, and they can therefore be considered to be adjacent. These minterms are in the four corners of the map.

If you fold the map to form a horizontal cylinder, the squares in the top row will appear to be adjacent to the corresponding squares in the bottom row. On the other hand, if you fold the map to form a vertical cylinder, the squares at the extreme right will appear to be adjacent to the corresponding squares on the extreme left. In short, we can generalized by saying that squares at the opposite ends of a row or column can be considered to be adjacent to corresponding squares. Thus m_3 is adjacent to m_{11} and m_{12} is adjacent to m_{14} and so on.

7.4.4 Implicants

There are a few basic terms, a knowledge of which will be found useful in working with Karnaugh maps. We will therefore, define these terms, before proceeding further with discussion on Karnaugh maps.

Implicant

One such term is referred to as an 'Implicant'. Product terms in a sum-of-products expression are referred to as 'Implicants'. On a Karnaugh map an implicant refers to a single entry or a group of adjacent entries. Figure 7.6 shows four circled groups, all of which are implicants of the logic function they represent. These groups can be rectangular or square and consist of a number of squares which is an integral power of 2, that is 1, 2, 4, 8, etc. On a Karnaugh map implicants are denoted by enclosures as in Fig. 7.6. It is not unusual for one implicant to overlap another implicant.

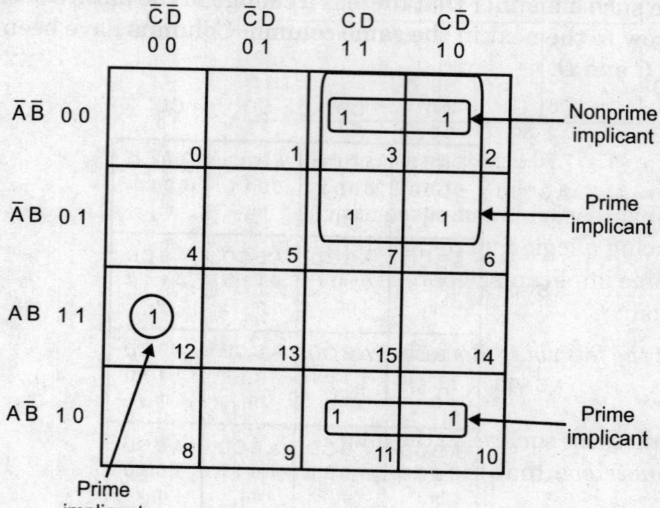

Fig. 7.6 Prime and nonprime implicants

Prime and Nonprime Implicants

There are two types of implicants, prime and nonprime. A prime implicant is one which cannot be enclosed by a larger implicant. The group of minterms 2, 3, 6 and 7 is a prime implicant, since these minterms cannot be enclosed by a larger enclosure. However, the group of minterms 2 and 3 is a nonprime implicant, as they can be enclosed by a larger group consisting of minterms 2, 3, 6 and 7 as shown in Fig. 7.6.

Essential and Nonessential Prime Implicants

Essential prime implicants consist of those groups of minterms which contain a minterm that does not form a part of any other group of minterms constituting a prime implicant. In Fig. 7.7 the group containing minterms 0, 1, 2 and 3 has two minterms 0 and 1, which do not form a part of any other group and it is therefore an essential prime implicant. For the same reason, the enclosure containing minterms 2, 3, 6 and 7 is an essential prime implicant. The group of minterms 13 and 15 constitutes an essential prime implicant, as minterm 13 cannot form a part of any other group, whereas the group of minterms 7 and 15 is a nonessential prime implicant, as both these minterms have already been covered by other essential prime implicants. A useful test to judge whether a prime implicant is essential, is to see whether it can be removed without leaving any minterm unenclosed.

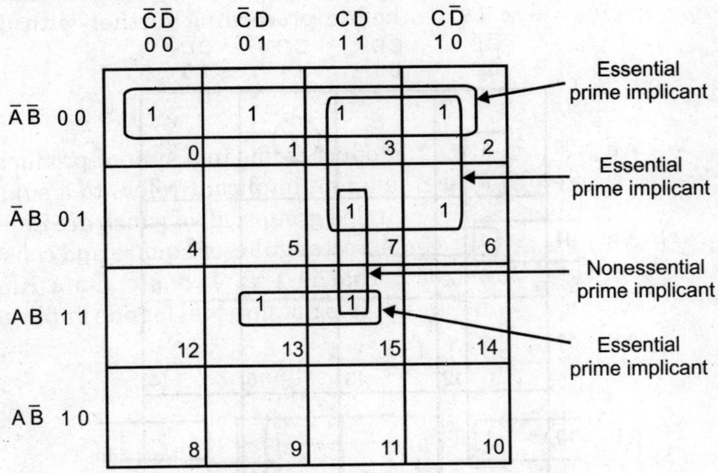

Fig. 7.7 Essential and nonessential prime implicants

A sum-of-products expression is composed of prime implicants and they completely define a logic function. In reducing a logic function with the help of Karnaugh maps, it is required to identify the essential prime implicants, whereas nonessential prime implicants are not required to identify a logic function.

Example 7.3: *Plot the following Boolean function on a map*:

$$F = \Sigma(0, 3, 4, 5, 6, 8, 10, 12)$$

Solution: Enter 1s in those squares in the map of Fig. 7.8, which correspond to the minterms of the function. It is understood that the empty squares correspond to logic 0 of the Boolean function.

You will notice that in this map 1s have been enclosed in groups. This has been done in accordance with the following rules for forming enclosures:

1. Enclosures may be rectangular or square and must group together 1s which are an integral power of 2, that is 1, 2, 4, 8, 16 and, in the last resort, if no groups can be formed, 1s may be enclosed singly.
2. Squares that do not appear to be adjacent on the map, but which exist at the opposite extremities of a row or column, are regarded as adjacent.
3. Diagonal squares are not regarded to be adjacent.
4. Any term may be covered more than once, but only if it helps to expand the enclosure to a larger number of squares.
5. Enclosures should be as large as permissible and as few as possible.
6. Begin by enclosing 1s in octets, quartets and pairs in that order, that is look for the bigger groups first and then go down enclosing 1s in pairs. If you are left with 1s which have not found a place in any group, enclose them singly.
7. If, after you have finished enclosing 1s in groups, you find any redundant group (non-essential prime implicant), remove them.
8. It will be helpful to remember that in a four-variable map, a pair eliminates one variable, a quartet two variables and an octet three variables. A single 1 not covered in any group will represent the AND function of all the variables.

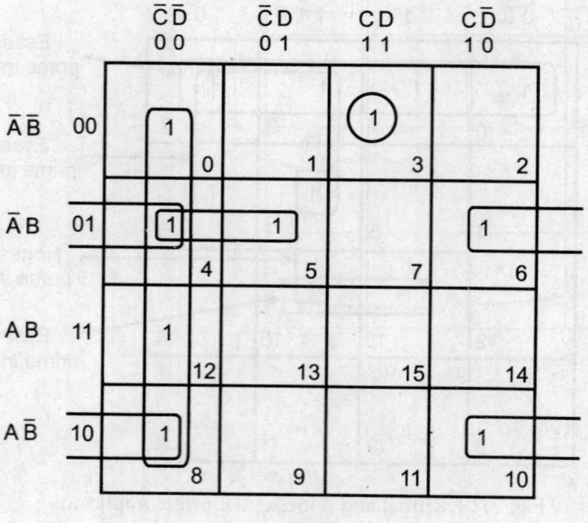

Fig. 7.8

9. The reduced SOP expression which corresponds to the logic 1s on the map is formed by ORing all the reduced variable terms covering all the logic 1s on the map.

After you have finished your grouping, study the map again, to make sure that you cannot improve upon your earlier groupings. Essentially check if a pair can be made into a quartet and a quartet into an octet. The larger the groups the greater is the reduction.

The groupings shown in Fig. 7.8 are indicated below along with the reduced terms:

1. m_3 $\overline{A}\,\overline{B}CD$
2. m_4, m_6 $\overline{A}B\overline{D}$

3. m_4, m_5 $\overline{A}B\overline{C}$

4. m_8, m_{10} $A\overline{B}\,\overline{D}$

5. m_0, m_4, m_{12}, m_8 $\overline{C}\,\overline{D}$

The reduced function in the SOP form will be as follows:

$$F = \overline{A}\,\overline{B}CD + \overline{A}B\overline{D} + \overline{A}B\overline{C} + A\overline{B}\,\overline{D} + \overline{C}\,\overline{D} \quad \text{...(7.8)}$$

7.4.5 Five-variable Karnaugh Map

A five-variable Karnaugh map is given in Fig. 7.9. Since a 5-variable function will require 32 squares to accommodate all the product terms, two blocks of 16 squares each have been used. The block on the left is used for those minterms in which A is 0 and the block on the right for those minterms in which A is a 1. Thus the block on the left has minterms from m_0 to m_{15} and the block on the right has minterms from m_{16} to m_{31}.

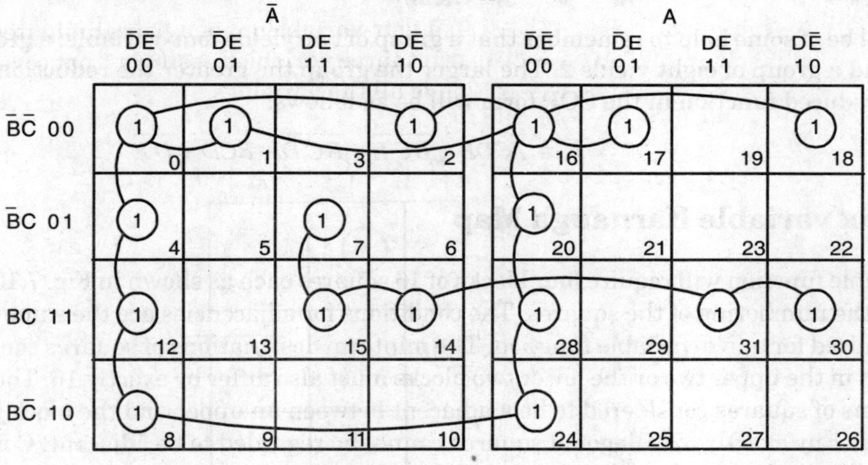

Fig. 7.9 Adjacencies in a 5-variable map

The minterms of a five-variable logic system given below have been entered in Fig. 7.9:

$$F = \Sigma(m_0, m_1, m_2, m_4, m_7, m_8, m_{12}, m_{14}, m_{15},$$
$$m_{16}, m_{17}, m_{18}, m_{20}, m_{24}, m_{28}, m_{30}, m_{31})$$

Groupings indicated in the map have been done on the basis of the following rules for adjacencies in a five-variable Karnaugh map:

1. When you place one block on top of the other or on its side, the squares which coincide with one another are considered to be adjacent, provided the following condition is also met.
2. The minterm designations of squares considered to be adjacent should differ exactly by 2^4 or 16.
3. The other requirements are the same as for other Karnaugh maps.

The groupings shown in the map are indicated below along with the reduced terms.

1. m_7, m_{15} $\overline{A}\,C\,D\,E$

2. $m_0,\ m_2,\ m_{16},\ m_{18}$ $\qquad \overline{B}\,\overline{C}\,\overline{E}$

3. $m_0,\ m_1,\ m_{16},\ m_{17}$ $\qquad \overline{B}\,\overline{C}\,\overline{D}$

4. $m_{14},\ m_{15},\ m_{30},\ m_{31}$ $\qquad BCD$

5. $m_0,\ m_4,\ m_{12},\ m_8$

   $m_{16},\ m_{20},\ m_{28},\ m_{24}$ $\qquad \overline{D}\,\overline{E}$

Minterms could also have been grouped as indicated below, but that would not have led to as much reduction as has been achieved by the above groupings. It is therefore necessary to explore all possible groupings.

1. $m_7,\ m_{15}$
2. $m_2,\ m_{18}$
3. $m_0,\ m_1,\ m_{16},\ m_{17}$
4. $m_{14},\ m_{15},\ m_{30},\ m_{31}$
5. $m_0,\ m_4,\ m_{12},\ m_8,\ m_{16},\ m_{20},\ m_{28},\ m_{24}$

It will be of some help to remember that a group of two yields four-variable: a group of four yields 3 and a group of eight yields 2. The larger the group the greater the reduction.

The reduced function in the SOP form will be as follows:

$$F = \overline{A}CDE + \overline{B}\,\overline{C}\,\overline{E} + \overline{B}\,\overline{C}\,\overline{D} + BCD + \overline{D}\,\overline{E} \qquad ...(7.9)$$

7.4.6 Six variable Karnaugh Map

A six-variable function will require four blocks of 16 squares each as shown in Fig. 7.10. Particularly note the numbering of the squares. The conditions for adjacencies are the same as for two blocks required for a five-variable function. The minterm designations of squares considered to be adjacent in the upper two or the lower two blocks must also differ by exactly 16. The minterm designations of squares considered to be a adjacent between an upper and the block just below it, must differ by exactly 32. Diagonal squares cannot be regarded to be adjacent. Consider the following adjacencies based on the above considerations:

1. $m_1,\ m_{17}$
2. $m_1,\ m_9$
3. $m_9,\ m_{25}$
4. $m_9,\ m_{41}$
5. $m_{18},\ m_{50}$
6. $m_{11},\ m_{27},\ m_{43},\ m_{59}$
7. $m_9,\ m_{11},\ m_{41},\ m_{43}$
8. $m_0,\ m_2,\ m_{16},\ m_{18}$

   $m_{32},\ m_{34},\ m_{48},\ m_{50}$

The minterms of a 6-variable logic system have been marked on the map and grouped in accordance with the rules of grouping mentioned above. The groups as well as the reduced terms have been listed below.

1. $m_{14},\ m_{30}$ $\qquad \overline{A}CDE\overline{F}$

2. $m_5,\ m_7,\ m_{21},\ m_{23}$ $\qquad \overline{A}CDF$

3. $m_{11},\ m_{27},\ m_{43},\ m_{59}$ $\qquad C\overline{D}EF$

4. $m_9,\ m_{11},\ m_{41},\ m_{43}$ $\qquad \overline{B}C\overline{D}F$

5. $m_{36}, m_{44}, m_{52}, m_{60}$ $\quad AD\overline{E}\,\overline{F}$

6. $m_{52}, m_{60}, m_{53}, m_{61}$ $\quad ABD\overline{E}$

7. m_0, m_2, m_{16}, m_{18}

$m_{32}, m_{34}, m_{48}, m_{50}$ $\quad \overline{C}\,\overline{D}\,\overline{F}$

The reduced function in the SOP form will be as follows:

$$F = \overline{A}CDE\overline{F} + \overline{A}\,\overline{C}DF + C\overline{D}EF + \overline{B}C\overline{D}F + AD\overline{E}\,\overline{F} + ABD\overline{E} + \overline{C}\,\overline{D}\,\overline{F} \qquad ...(7.10)$$

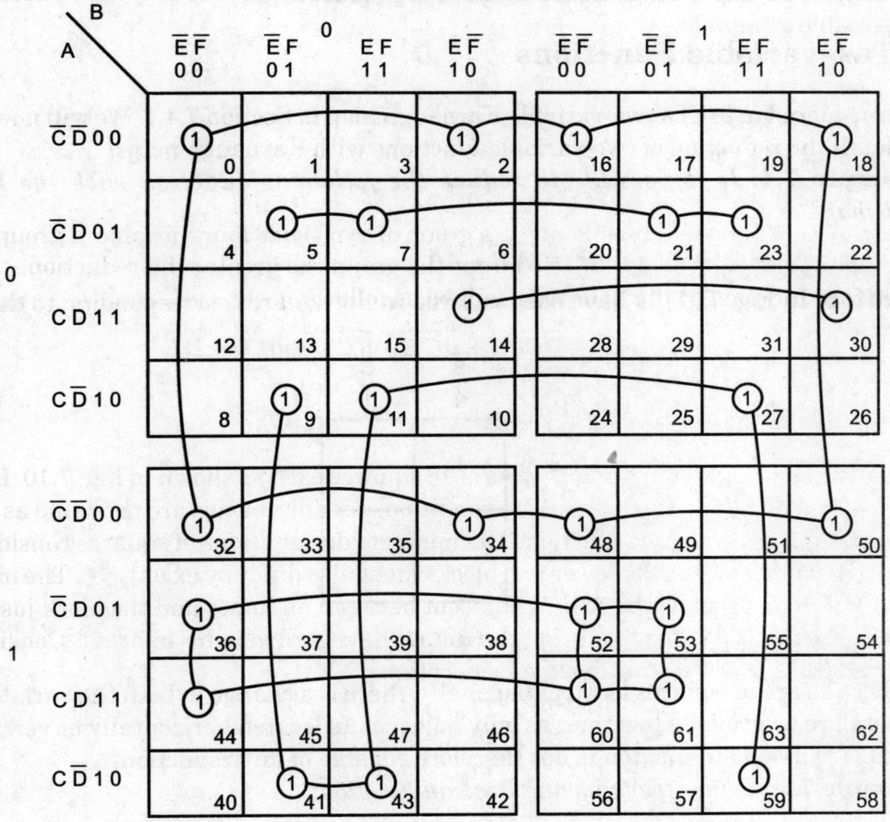

Fig. 7.10 Adjacencies in a 6-variable map

7.5 SUM-OF-PRODUCTS REDUCTION

Karnaugh maps will be found very useful in simplifying logic expressions before translating them into logic circuits. The starting point for designing a logic circuit is either a truth table or a Boolean equation. For a sum-of-products solution, we have to develop product terms for which we may proceed as follows:

1. If the starting point is a Boolean expression, examine if each term of the equation has all the variabes. If not expand the expression as explained in Section 7.3.

2. If the starting point is a truth table, develop all the product terms.
3. Construct an SOP expression containing those product terms which correspond to logic 1 state.
4. Now draw a Karnaugh map having 2^n squares, where 'n' is the number of variables and enter 1 in those square in the map, which correspond to the product terms.
5. Now form groups of 1s as has been explained already.
6. The next step is to take all the non-variables corresponding to the enclosures and write the SOP expression by ORing the reduced variable terms.

In this section, we will discuss reduction of Boolean expressions having two-to-six variables and form SOP expressions from the reduced product terms.

7.5.1 Two-variable Functions

We have considered in brief a two-variable Karnaugh map in Section 7.4.1. We will now consider in some detail the reduction of two-variable functions with Karnaugh maps.

Example 7.4: *Is it possible to reduce the following function with the help of a Karnaugh map?*

$$F = \overline{A}\,\overline{B} + AB$$

Solution: In Fig. 7.11, 1s have been entered in the squares corresponding to the product terms.

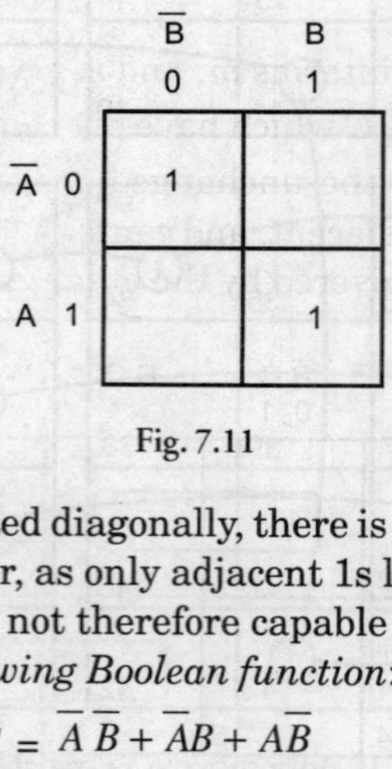

Fig. 7.11

As these 1s are in squares located diagonally, there is a change in both the variables. They cannot therefore be grouped together, as only adjacent 1s located horizontally or vertically can be grouped. The Boolean function is not therefore capable of any reduction.

Example 7.5: *Reduce the following Boolean function*:

$$F = \overline{A}\,\overline{B} + \overline{A}B + A\overline{B}$$

Solution: In Fig. 7.12, 1s have been entered in squares which correspond to the three product terms.

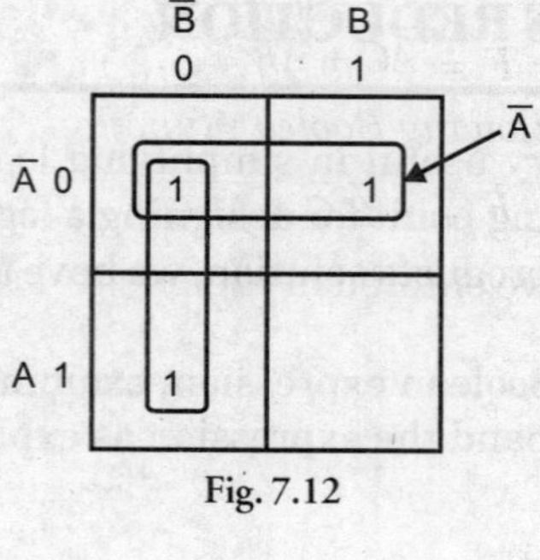

Fig. 7.12

There are two pairs of 1s and they can be enclosed as shown in the diagram. Notice that a 1 has been enclosed twice, as it is permissible to use the same 1 more than once. You can now drop those variables from each pair that have changed and retain those variables that have not changed and form an SOP equation by ORing them. This gives the following reduced function:

$$F = \overline{A} + \overline{B}$$

Rules for a two-variable Karnaugh map can be summed up as follows:

1. Any two adjacent logic 1s can be combined to form a pair. When so combined they will represent a single variable.
2. 1s located diagonally on a map cannot be considered to be adjacent.
3. A single logic 1 will represent the AND function of both the variables.
4. The SOP expression is obtained by ORing all the reduced terms in the map.

7.5.2 Three-variable Functions:

A few typical cases of three-variable functions have been considered in the following examples:

Example 7.6: *Reduce the following Boolean function:*

$$F = \overline{A}\,\overline{B}C + \overline{A}BC + ABC + AB\overline{C} \quad ...(7.11)$$

Solution: In Fig. 7.13 1s have been entered in squares, which correspond to the four product terms.

From the pair comprising of minterms m_1 and m_3, we can drop the variable $\overline{B}$ which has changed and retain variables $\overline{A}$ and C which have not changed. This gives the reduced product $\overline{A}C$. Similarly, from the other pair the unchanged product AB is retained. Also notice that, although minterms m_3 and m_7 are adjacent, and can form a pair, they have not been grouped, as these minterms have already been covered by the other groups. The reduced function is, therefore, as follows:

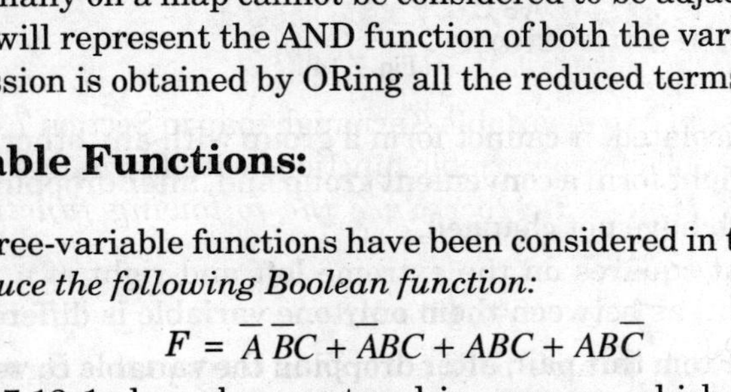

Fig. 7.13

$$F = \overline{A}C + AB$$

Example 7.7: *Reduce the following Boolean function:*

$$F = \overline{A}\,\overline{B}\,\overline{C} + \overline{A}B\overline{C} + AB\overline{C} + A\overline{B}C \quad ...(7.12)$$

Solution: In Fig. 7.14, 1s have entered in squares which corresponds to the product terms.

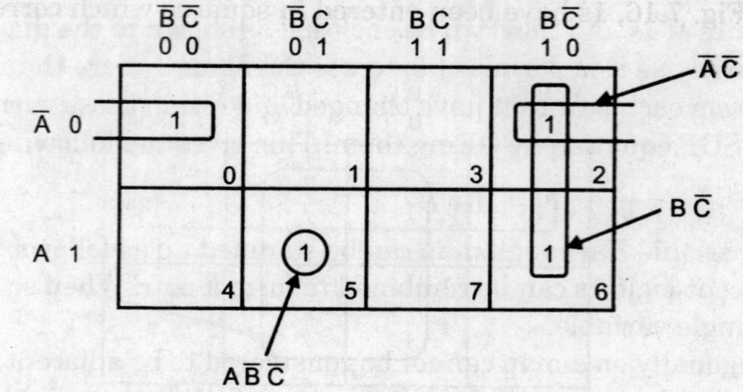

Fig. 7.14

As minterm m_5 is isolated, it cannot form a group with any other minterm. Minterms m_2 and m_6 on the extreme right form a convenient group and, after dropping the variable A, we are left with B and $\bar{C}$, which have not changed.

You will recall that squares on the extreme left and right of a row (or column) can be considered to be adjacent, as between them only one variable is different. Thus, minterms m_0 and m_2 can form a pair. From this pair, after dropping the variable B, we are left with $\overline{A}\,\overline{C}$. The reduced function is now as follows:

$$F = \overline{A}\,\overline{C} + B\,\overline{C} + A\overline{B}C \qquad ...(7.13)$$

Example 7.8: *Plot the following Boolean function on a Karnaugh map and reduce it:*

$$F = \overline{A}\,\overline{B}\,\overline{C} + \overline{A}\,\overline{B}\,C + \overline{A}BC + A\,B\,\overline{C} + A\,\overline{B}\,C + ABC \qquad ..(7.14)$$

Solution: The function has been plotted in Fig. 7.15

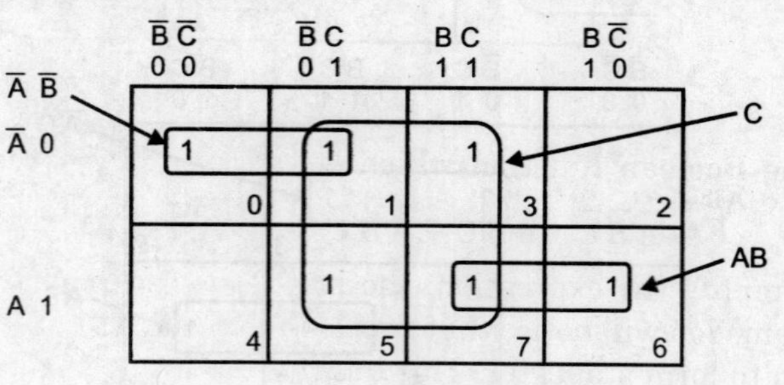

Fig. 7.15

Minterms m_1, m_3, m_5, and m_7 form a quartet. The variables in this are A and B and, after dropping them, we are left with only one variable that is C. Minterms m_0 and m_1 form one pair, which yield $\overline{A}\,\overline{B}$ and the other pair comprising of minterms m_6 and m_7 yields AB, after dropping the variable C. You will notice that two 1s which are part of a quartet, have been covered more than once, but that is permissible. The reduced function is as follows:

$$F = \overline{A}\,\overline{B} + AB + C \qquad ...(7.15)$$

Example 7.9: *Use a Karnaugh map to simplify the following Boolean function:*

$$F = \overline{A}\,\overline{B}\,\overline{C} + \overline{A}\,\overline{B}\,C + \overline{A}\,BC + \overline{A}\,B\,\overline{C} + A\,\overline{B}\,C + ABC \qquad ...(7.16)$$

Solution: In Fig. 7.16, 1s have been entered in squares which correspond to the product terms.

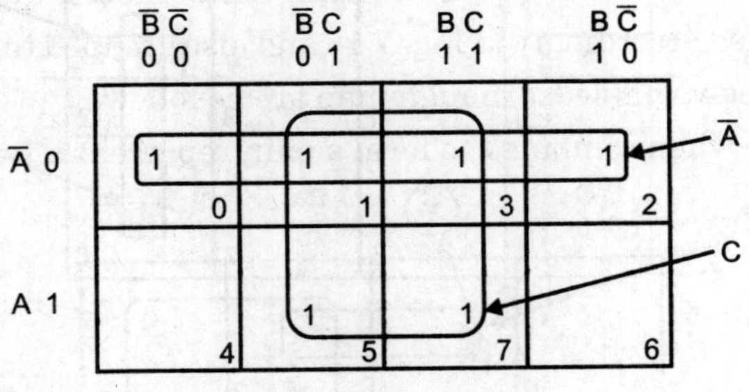

Fig. 7.16

You will notice from this diagram that the minterms have been covered by two quartets, one of which yields $\overline{A}$, and the other C. The reduced Boolean function is as follows:

$$F = \overline{A} + C$$

Example 7.10: *Write the Boolean function represented by the Karnaugh map of Fig. 7.17 and simplify it.*

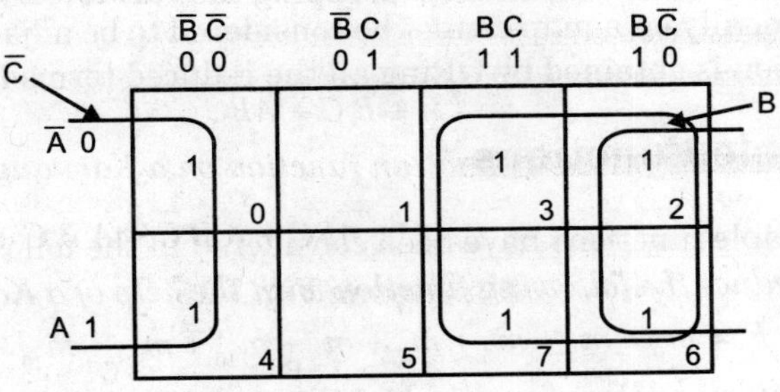

Fig. 7.17

Solution: The Boolean function which is represented by the diagram is as follows:

$$F = \overline{A}\,\overline{B}\,\overline{C} + \overline{A}\,B\,C + \overline{A}\,B\,\overline{C} + A\,\overline{B}\,\overline{C} + A\,B\,C + A\,B\,\overline{C} \quad ...(7.17)$$

In order to simplify the expression, the minterms can be enclosed by two quartets as shown in the diagram. You will notice that two 1s in the left column can be grouped with two 1s in the right column to form a quartet. This quartet has two variables A and B, which can be dropped and one nonvariable $\overline{C}$ which can be retained. The nonvariable yielded by the other quartet is B. The simplified function is as follows:

$$F = B + \overline{C}$$

Example 7.11: *Draw a Karnaugh map to represent the following Boolean function:*

$$F = A\overline{C} + \overline{A}C + B$$

Solution: The first product term has two nonvariables A and $\overline{C}$. Obviously the variable is B. Therefore, we should look for two squares for which the variable is B and nonvariables are A and $\overline{C}$. These squares are therefore squares 4 and 6. The other product term also points to two squares, for which the nonvariables are $\overline{A}$ and C, and variable is B. Two squares which satisfy this conditions are 1 and 3. The last term is a single nonvariable B, which points to a quartet for which the variables are A and C. The squares which satisfy this condition are 3, 2, 6 and 7. The squares have been marked accordingly in Fig. 7.18 and also grouped to show the reduced terms.

The rules for a three-variable Karnaugh map are as follows:

1. Two adjacent 1s when combined to form a pair, represent a two-variable term.

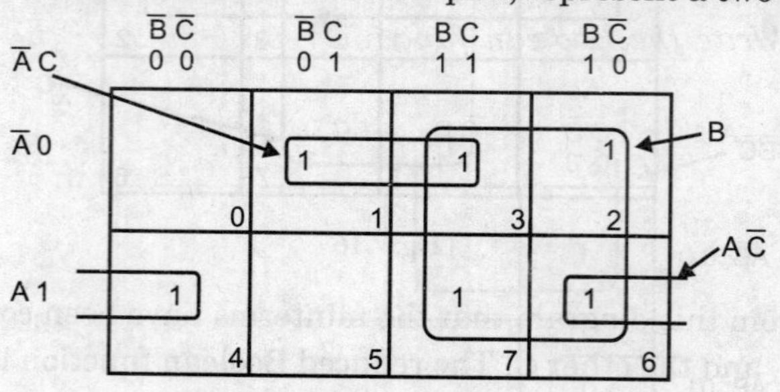

Fig. 7.18

2. Four adjacent 1s form a quartet and represent a single variable.
3. A single logic 1s will represent the AND function of all the three variables.
4. 1s located diagonally on a map cannot be considered to be adjacent.
5. The SOP function is obtained by ORing all the reduced terms in the map.

7.5.3 Four-variable Functions

Some cases of four-variable functions have been considered in the following examples:

Example 7.12: *Reduce the following function with the help of a Karnaugh map:*

$$F = m_0 + m_2 + m_5 + m_7 + m_8 + m_{10} + m_{13} + m_{15} \quad ...(7.18)$$

Solution: The minterms of this function have been plotted on a Karnaugh map (Fig. 7.19).

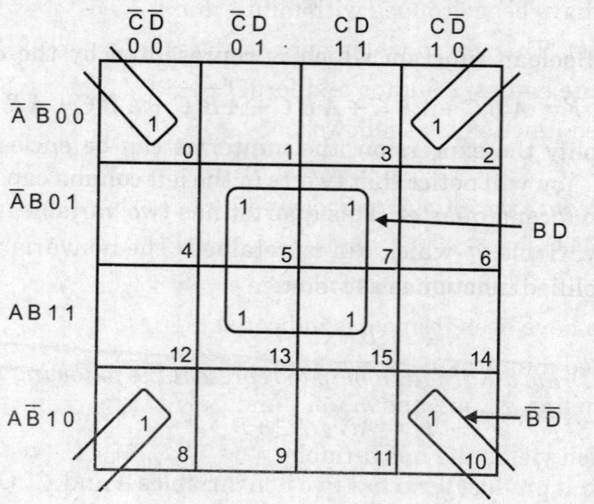

Fig. 7.19

Four 1s located in the four corners can be enclosed in one group, as they can be considered to be adjacent. From this group, we can eliminate two variables and their complements that is $A, \overline{A}, C$ and $\overline{C}$, and retain the nonvariables $\overline{B}$ and $\overline{D}$. Similarly, four 1s in the centre of the map can be enclosed, from which we can retain the nonvariables B and D. The reduced function will be as follows:

$$F = \overline{B}\,\overline{D} + BD \qquad ...(7.19)$$

Example 7.13: *Write the Boolean function represented by the map (Fig. 7.20) and simplify it.*

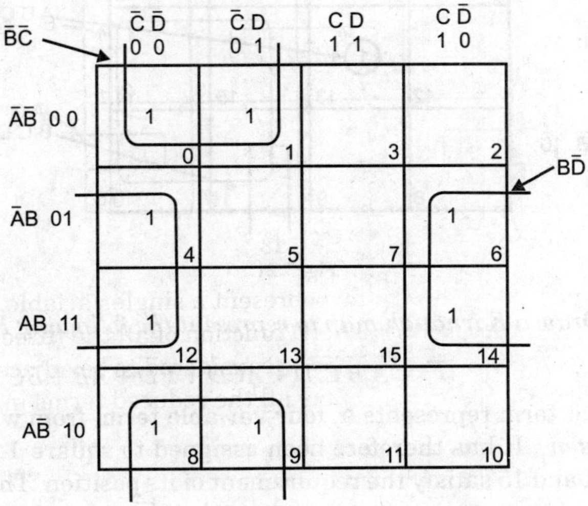

Fig. 7.20

Solution: The Boolean function represented by the map is as follows:

$$F = m_0 + m_1 + m_4 + m_6 + m_8 + m_9 + m_{12} + m_{14} \qquad ...(7.20)$$

Minterms m_0, m_1 have been grouped with minterms m_8, m_9 as they are at opposite ends of rows and form a quartet. This group yields nonvariables $\overline{B}\,\overline{C}$. Similarly, the remaining four minterms are at opposite ends of columns and form the other quartet. This group yields variables $B\overline{D}$. The reduced function is as follows:

$$F = \overline{B}\,\overline{C} + B\overline{D} \qquad ...(7.21)$$

Example 7.14: *Reduce the following Boolean function:*

$$F = m_0 + m_2 + m_3 + m_6 + m_7 + m_{13} + m_{11} \qquad ...(7.22)$$

Solution: In Fig. 7.21, 1s have been entered in squares which correspond to the minterms of the function. Groups have been formed as indicated in Fig. 7.21.

There is an isolated minterm m_{13} which represents the product of all the variables that is $AB\overline{C}D$. There are two pairs, m_0, m_2, and m_3, m_{11} and they yield the variables $\overline{A}\,\overline{B}\,\overline{D}$ and $\overline{B}CD$. There is a quartet which yields the nonvariable $\overline{A}C$. The reduced Boolean equation is as follows:

$$F = \overline{B}CD + \overline{A}\,\overline{B}\,\overline{D} + \overline{A}C + AB\overline{C}D \qquad ...(7.23)$$

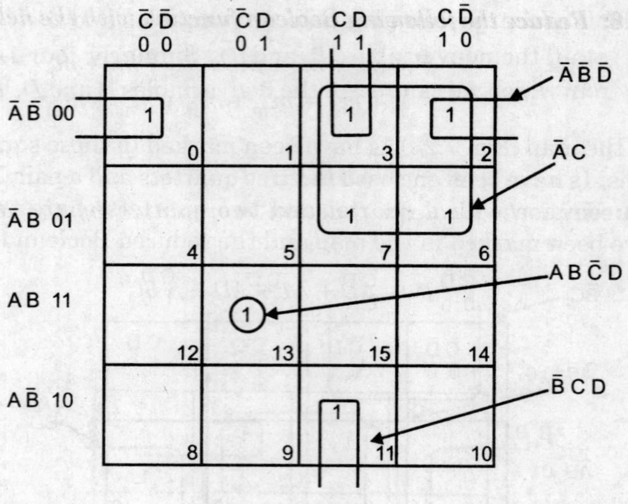

Fig. 7.21

Example 7.15: *Draw a Karnaugh map to represent the following Boolean function:*

$$F = \overline{A}\,\overline{B}\,\overline{C}\,D + ACD + B\overline{D} + AB + BC \qquad ...(7.24)$$

Solution: The first term represents a, four-variable term, from which it is clear that its minterm designation is m_1. It has therefore been assigned to square 1. The term *ACD* represents a pair. Squares 11 and 15 satisfy the requirement of its position. There are three quartets, each of which yields a product of two variables. The term $B\overline{D}$ points to squares 4, 6, 12 and 14. The nonvariables in the other quartet are *AB*, for which the proper squares are 12, 13, 14 and 15. The last quartet yields the product *BC*. Its proper position is in squares 6, 7, 14 and 15. The map (Fig. 7.22), is marked accordingly. The Boolean function before it was reduced should be as follows:

$$F = m_1 + m_4 + m_6 + m_7 + m_{11} + m_{12} + m_{13} + m_{14} + m_{15} \qquad ...(7.25)$$

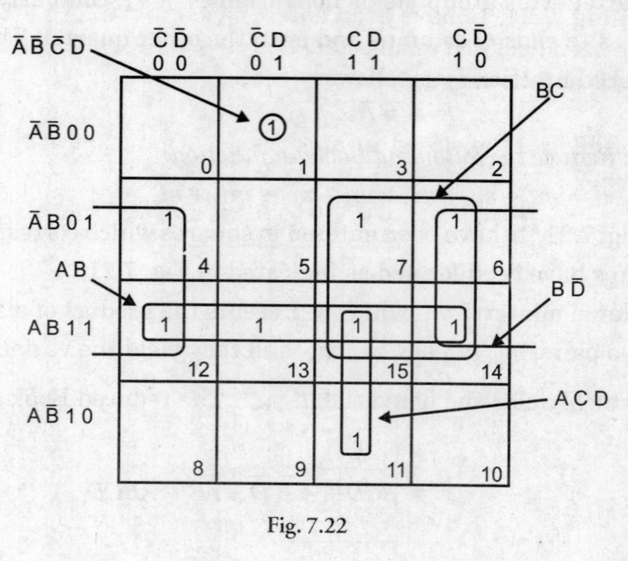

Fig. 7.22

Example 7.16: *Reduce the following Boolean function with the help of a Karnaugh map:*

$$F = m_1 + m_2 + m_3 + m_5 + m_7 + m_8 + m_9 + m_{10} + m_{11} + m_{12} + m_{14} \quad \text{...(7.26)}$$

Solution: In the map (**Fig. 7.23**) 1s have been marked in those squares which correspond to the product terms. 1s have been enclosed in three quartets and a pair. You will notice that one pair shares a 1 in common with a quartet and two quartets share two 1s in common. The reduced terms have been marked in the map and the reduced Boolean function is as follows:

$$F = A\overline{D} + A\overline{B} + \overline{A}D + \overline{A}\,\overline{B}C \quad \text{...(7.27)}$$

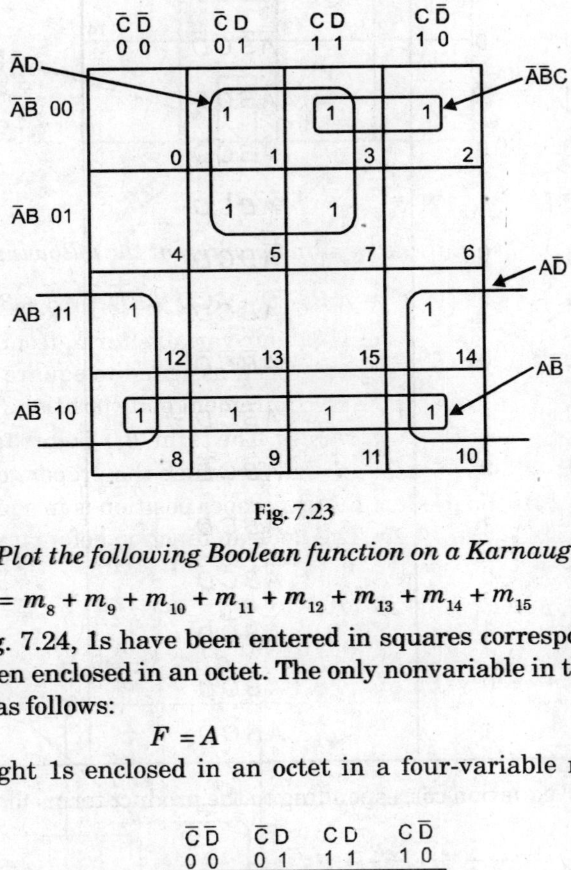

Fig. 7.23

Example 7.17: *Plot the following Boolean function on a Karnaugh map and simplify it.*

$$F = m_8 + m_9 + m_{10} + m_{11} + m_{12} + m_{13} + m_{14} + m_{15} \quad \text{...(7.28)}$$

Solution: In Fig. 7.24, 1s have been entered in squares corresponding to the minterms and all the 1s have been enclosed in an octet. The only nonvariable in the entire octet is A. The simplified function is as follows:

$$F = A \quad \text{...(7.29)}$$

Any group of eight 1s enclosed in an octet in a four-variable map will yield a single nonvariable.

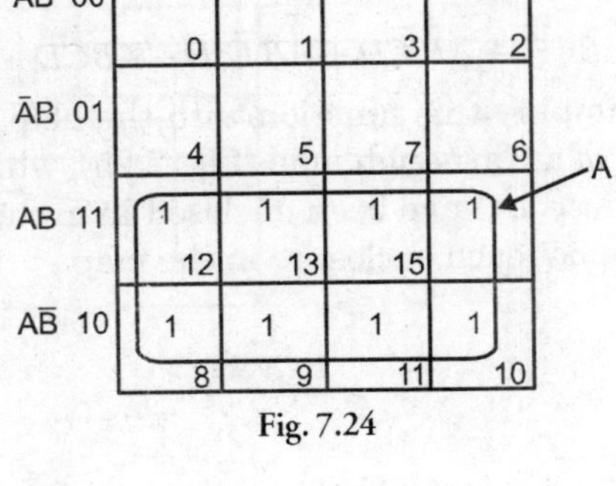

Fig. 7.24

Example 7.18: *Design a logic circuit to satisfy the truth table given in Table 7.5.*

Table 7.5

Input				Product term	Output
A	*B*	*C*	*D*		
0	0	0	0	$\overline{A}\,\overline{B}\,\overline{C}\,\overline{D}$	1
0	0	0	1	$\overline{A}\,\overline{B}\,\overline{C}D$	1
0	0	1	0	$\overline{A}\,\overline{B}C\overline{D}$	1
0	0	1	1	$\overline{A}\,\overline{B}CD$	1
0	1	0	0	$\overline{A}B\overline{C}\,\overline{D}$	1
0	1	0	1	$\overline{A}B\overline{C}D$	1
0	1	1	0	$\overline{A}BC\overline{D}$	1
0	1	1	1	$\overline{A}BCD$	0
1	0	0	0	$A\overline{B}\,\overline{C}\,\overline{D}$	0
1	0	0	1	$A\overline{B}\,\overline{C}D$	1
1	0	1	0	$A\overline{B}C\overline{D}$	0
1	0	1	1	$A\overline{B}CD$	0
1	1	0	0	$AB\overline{C}\,\overline{D}$	1
1	1	0	1	$AB\overline{C}D$	1
1	1	1	0	$ABC\overline{D}$	1
1	1	1	1	$ABCD$	0

Solution: The SOP equation corresponding to the product terms for which the output is 1 will be as follows:

$$F = \overline{A}\,\overline{B}\,\overline{C}\,\overline{D} + \overline{A}\,\overline{B}\,\overline{C}\,D + \overline{A}\,\overline{B}\,C\overline{D} + \overline{A}\,\overline{B}\,CD + \overline{A}B\overline{C}\,\overline{D} + \overline{A}\,B\,\overline{C}\,D$$

$$+\ \overline{A}BC\overline{D} + A\overline{B}\,\overline{C}D + AB\,\overline{C}\,\overline{D} + AB\overline{C}D + ABC\overline{D} \qquad \text{...(7.30)}$$

As it is much easier to simplify this function with the help of a Karnaugh map, 1s have been entered in those squares of a Karnaugh map (Fig. 7.25), which correspond to the product terms of the logic function. These 1s have been enclosed in groups as shown in the map. The nonvariables are indicated against each enclosure in the map.

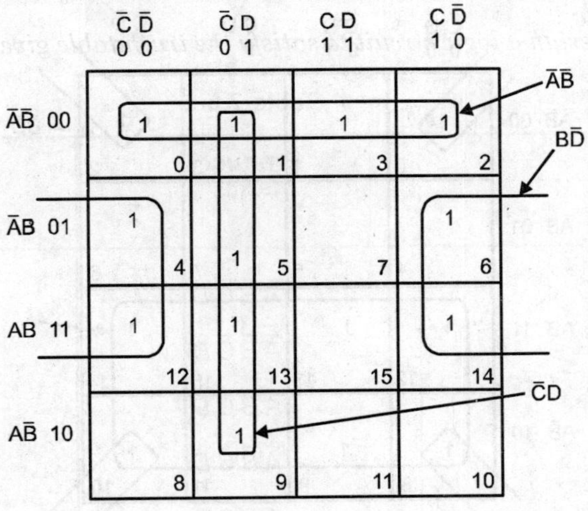

Fig. 7.25

The reduced logic function is as follows and it can be implemented by the logic circuit given in Fig. 7.26.

$$F = \overline{A}\overline{B} + B\overline{D} + \overline{C}D \qquad ...(7.31)$$

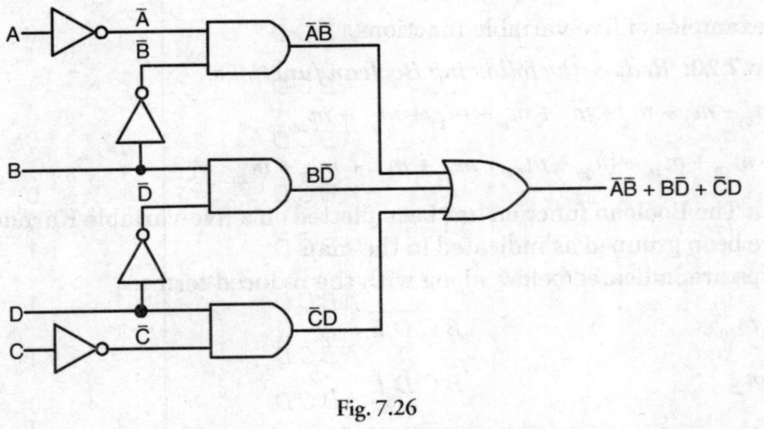

Fig. 7.26

Example 7.19: *Draw a Karnaugh map to represent the following Boolean function:*

$$F = A + \overline{BD} \qquad ...(7.32)$$

Solution: Since the first term is a single variable, it points to an octet in which the only nonvariable is *A*. The squares which satisfy this condition are from 8 to 15 as shown in the map (Fig. 7.27). The second term has two nonvariables, which points to a quartet. The squares in which $\overline{B}$ and $\overline{D}$ remain unchanged are 0, 2, 8 and 10, as shown in the map.

The Boolean function before reduction should be as follows:

$$F = m_0 + m_2 + m_8 + m_9 + m_{10} + m_{11} + m_{12} + m_{13} + m_{14} + m_{15} \qquad ...(7.33)$$

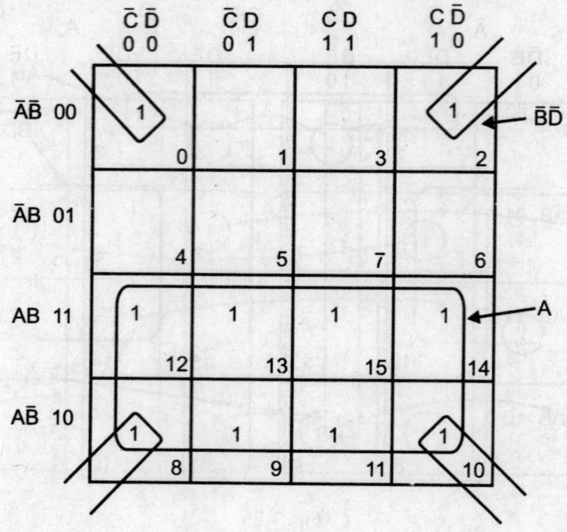

Fig. 7.27

7.5.4 Five-variable Function

Here are two examples of five-variable functions.

Example 7.20: *Reduce the following Boolean functions:*

$$F = m_0 + m_2 + m_4 + m_7 + m_8 + m_{10} + m_{11} + m_{13}$$

$$+ m_{16} + m_{18} + m_{20} + m_{22} + m_{23} + m_{24} + m_{26} + m_{29} \quad \text{...(7.34)}$$

Solution: The Boolean function has been plotted on a five-variable Karnaugh map (7.28). Minterms have been grouped as indicated in the map.

The groups are indicated below, along with the reduced terms.

1. m_4, m_{20} $\overline{B}\,C\,\overline{D}\,\overline{E}$
2. m_7, m_{23} $\overline{B}\,C\,D\,E$
3. m_{22}, m_{23} $A\,\overline{B}\,C\,D$
4. m_{10}, m_{11} $A\,B\,\overline{C}\,D$
5. m_0, m_2, m_{18}, m_{16}
   m_8, m_{10}, m_{24}, m_{26} $\overline{C}\,\overline{E}$

The reduced Boolean function is as follows:

$$F = \overline{B}C\overline{D}\,\overline{E} + \overline{B}CDE + A\overline{B}CD + AB\overline{C}D + \overline{C}\,\overline{E} \quad \text{...(7.35)}$$

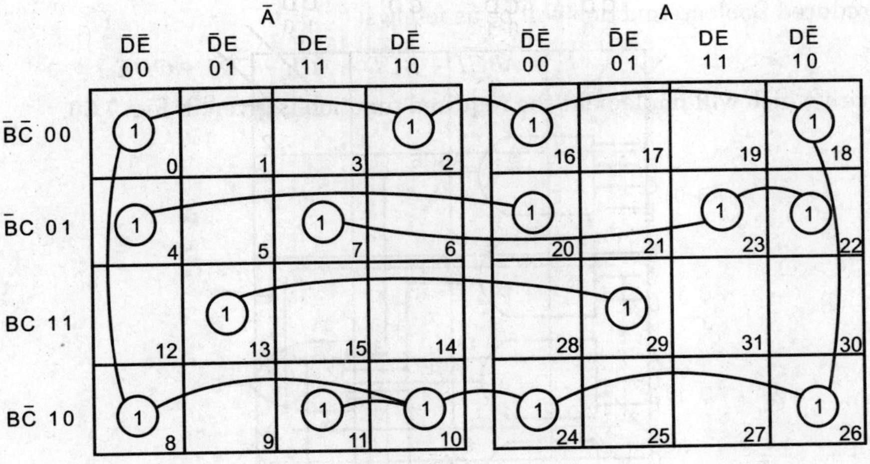

Fig. 7.28

Example 7.21: *Design an SOP circuit, which will output a 1 whenever the input is the binary equivalent of decimal 0, 1, 5, 7, 8, 10, 13, 15, 16, 17, 23, 24 and 31.*

Solution: In Fig. 7.29, 1s have been plotted in those squares which correspond to the minterm designations of these numbers. These 1s have been grouped as indicated below along with the corresponding reduced terms.

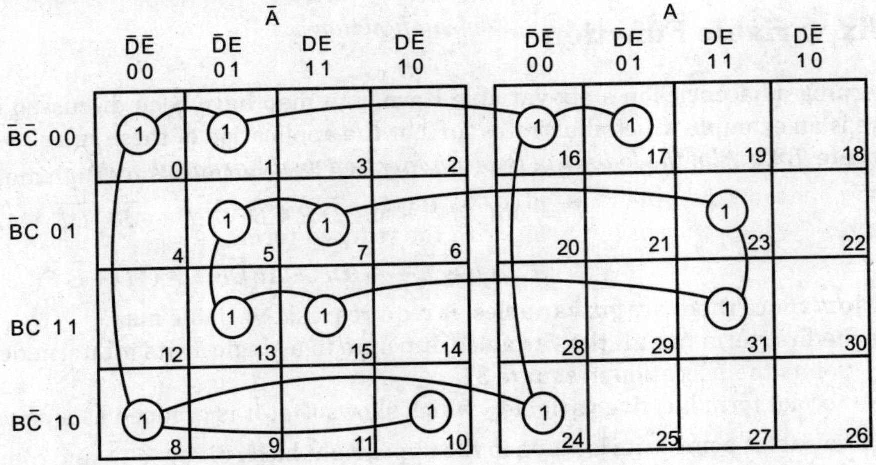

Fig. 7.29

1. $m_8,\ m_{10}$ — $\overline{A}\,B\,\overline{C}\,\overline{E}$
2. $m_0,\ m_1,\ m_{16},\ m_{17}$ — $\overline{B}\,\overline{C}\,\overline{D}$
3. $m_5,\ m_7,\ m_{13},\ m_{15}$ — $\overline{A}\,C\,E$
4. $m_7,\ m_{15},\ m_{23},\ m_{31}$ — $C\,D\,E$
5. $m_0,\ m_8,\ m_{16},\ m_{24}$ — $\overline{C}\,\overline{D}\,\overline{E}$

The reduced Boolean function will be as follows:

$$F = \bar{A}B\bar{C}\bar{E} + \bar{B}\bar{C}\bar{D} + \bar{A}CE + CDE + \bar{C}\bar{D}\bar{E} \qquad ...(7.36)$$

A circuit which will implement the required function is given in Fig. 7.30.

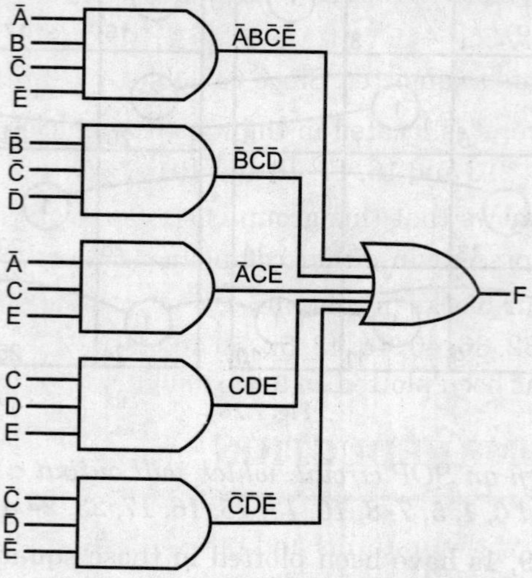

Fig. 7.30

7.5.5 Six-variable Function

Rules governing adjacencies in a six-variable Karnaugh map have been discussed in Section 7.4. 6. Here is an example which illustrates further the application of these rules.

Example 7.22: *Plot the following Boolean function on a Karnaugh map*:

$$F = \bar{A}BCDEF + \bar{A}BC\bar{D}\,\bar{E} + \bar{B}C\bar{D}EF + \bar{A}BC\,\bar{D}\bar{F} + A\bar{B}C\,\bar{D}F$$

$$+ \bar{A}\,\bar{B}\,\bar{C}\,\bar{E} + A\bar{C}DF + AB\bar{D}E + \bar{A}\,\bar{C}\,\bar{D} + \bar{E}\,\bar{F} \qquad ...(7.37)$$

Solution: Since there are six variables, it requires a six-variable map.

1. As the first term has all the variables, it points to a single 1. Its minterm designation m_{31} points to its location in square 31.
2. The second term has five variables, which shows that it is grouped as a pair. The first two variables point to its location in the upper right block in row $C\bar{D}$ and columns $\bar{E}\,\bar{F}$ and $\bar{E}F$. The squares which satisfy this condition are 24 and 25.
3. The third term is also a pair, as this also has five variables. Since variable A is not found in this term and B is complemented, this pair is to be found in the two blocks on the left hand side in column EF and rows $C\bar{D}$. This gives the location of the pair in squares 11 and 43.
4. The fourth and fifth terms are also pairs. They are located in squares 24, 26, and in 41 and 43.
5. The sixth term has four variables and it is therefore a quartet. As the first two variables are $\bar{A}\,\bar{B}$, it is located in the upper left block in squares 0, 1, 4 and 5.

6. Since variable A figures in the 7th term but not variable B, this quartet is located in two blocks at the bottom in row $\overline{C}D$ and columns $\overline{E}F$ and EF in squares 37, 39, 53 and 55.
7. The next term $AB\overline{D}E$ also points to a quartet. The variable AB in the term point to its location in the bottom block at the right in rows $C\overline{D}$ and $\overline{C}\,\overline{D}$ and columns EF and $E\overline{F}$ (squares 50, 51, 58, 59).
8. The term $\overline{A}\,\overline{C}\,\overline{D}$ points to an octet. Since variable $\overline{A}$ is present in the term and variable B does not figure, it is located in the upper two blocks in row $\overline{C}\,\overline{D}$. It therefore occupies squares 0, 1, 2, 3 and 16, 17, 18 and 19.
9. The last term $\overline{E}\,\overline{F}$ shows that this group is spread over 16 squares and, an neither variable A nor B is present in either complemented or uncomplemented form, it is spread overall the four blocks in columns $\overline{E}\,\overline{F}$ only. It therefore occupies squares 0, 4, 12, 8, 16, 20, 24, 28, 32, 36, 40, 44, 48, 52, 56 and 60.

The Boolean function has been plotted on a Karnaugh map (Fig. 7.31).

7.6 PRODUCT-OF-SUMS REDUCTION

In Section 7.2, we have dealt with minterms and maxterms and it was explained how a logic function expressed in minterms can be used to derive a logic expression using maxterms. In the previous section, we have discussed how an SOP expression can be derived using minterms. In the present section we will confine our attention to POS expressions from a knowledge of maxterms.

In Fig. 7.32, the minterms and maxterms of the following logic function have been entered in a Karnaugh map.

$$F = \overline{A}\,\overline{B}\,\overline{C}\,\overline{D} + \overline{A}\,\overline{B}\,\overline{C}\,D + \overline{A}\,\overline{B}\,CD + \overline{A}BC\,\overline{D} + \overline{A}\,B\,\overline{C}D + \overline{A}BCD \qquad ...(7.38)$$

The minterms have been entered as 1s and maxterms as 0s in squares which correspond to their designations. There is some difference in the numbering of minterms and maxterms, which will be clear from some examples is given below:

Location in square	Minterm	Maxterm
0	$\overline{A}\,\overline{B}\,\overline{C}\,\overline{D}$	
1	$\overline{A}\,\overline{B}\,\overline{C}D$	
3	$\overline{A}\,\overline{B}CD$	
2		$A+B+\overline{C}+D$
6		$A+\overline{B}+\overline{C}+D$
12		$\overline{A}+\overline{B}+C+D$

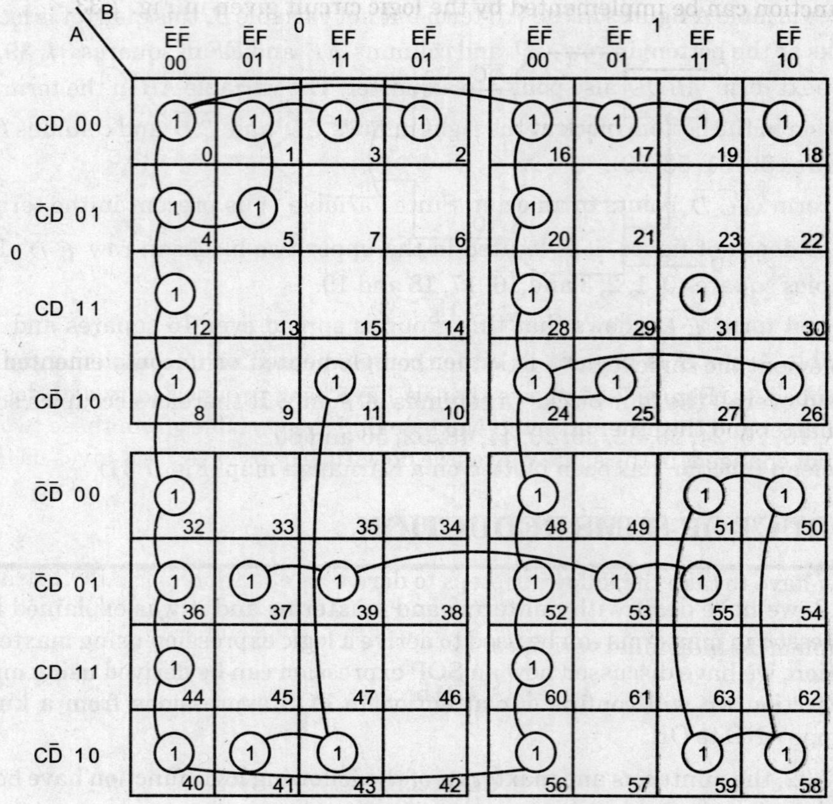

Fig. 7.31

1s have been grouped into two quatets. This leads to the following reduced equation in the SOP form.

$$F = \bar{A}\,\bar{C} + \bar{A}D \qquad \text{...(7.39)}$$

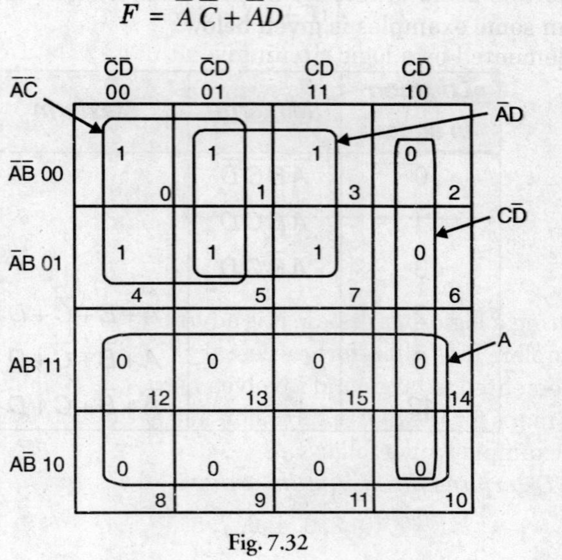

Fig. 7.32

This function can be implemented by the logic circuit given in Fig. 7.33.

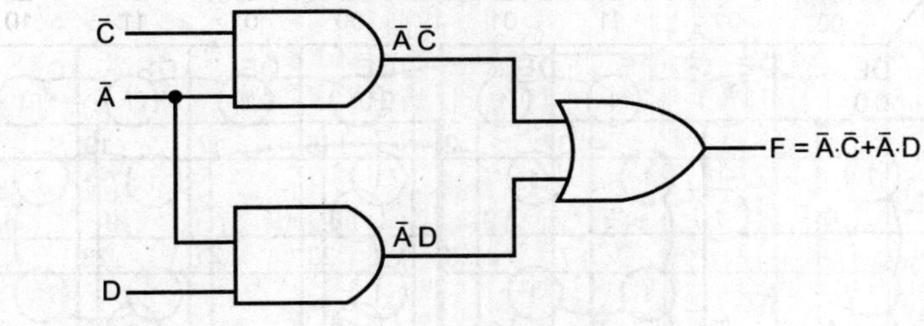

Fig. 7.33

To implement the same logic function in the POS form, a simple way is to group 0s just as we have grouped 1s. Figure 7.32 shows that 0s have been grouped in two enclosures, one of which is a quartet and the other an octet. Next we find the variables from these two enclosures, which have not changed, in the same way as we do with groups of 1s. This gives us the following two terms:

$$A, C\overline{D}$$

We now have to take the following steps to derive an equation in the POS form from these two terms.

1. Complement individual variables.

$$A, C\overline{D} \text{ becomes } \overline{A}, \overline{C}D$$

2. Change AND to OR

$$\overline{A}, \overline{C}D \text{ becomes } \overline{A}, (\overline{C} + D)$$

3. Form a product of these two terms

$$A, (\overline{C} + D) \text{ becomes } \overline{A}\,(\overline{C} + D)$$

4. The POS equation is now as follows:

$$F = \overline{A}\,(\overline{C} + D) \qquad \text{...(7.40)}$$

This can be implemented by a logic circuit given in Fig. 7.34.

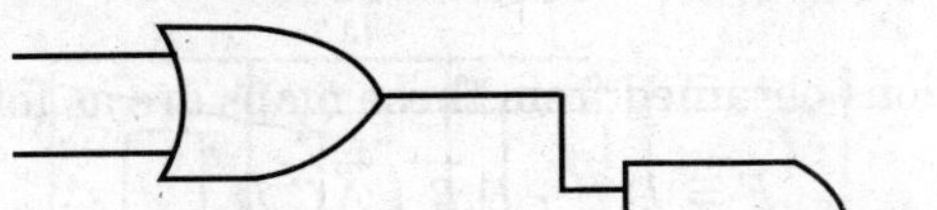

Fig. 7.34

When implementing a logic expression, it is advisable to ascertain whether the POS or the SOP form will be simpler. It is therefore necessary to work out both the forms. When the expression to be implemented is large and involves more than one map, it will be more convenient to use one set of maps for the SOP expression and the other set for the POS expression, as has been done in the example which follows.

Example 7.23: *Determine the minimum expression for the following function:*

$$F = \Sigma\,(0, 2, 3, 4, 6, 7, 8, 12, 14, 15, 16, 18, 19, 20, 22, 23, 24, 28)$$

Solution: To obtain the SOP expression, 1s have been entered in maps in Fig. 7.35, and for the POS expression, 0s have been entered in maps in Fig. 7.36.

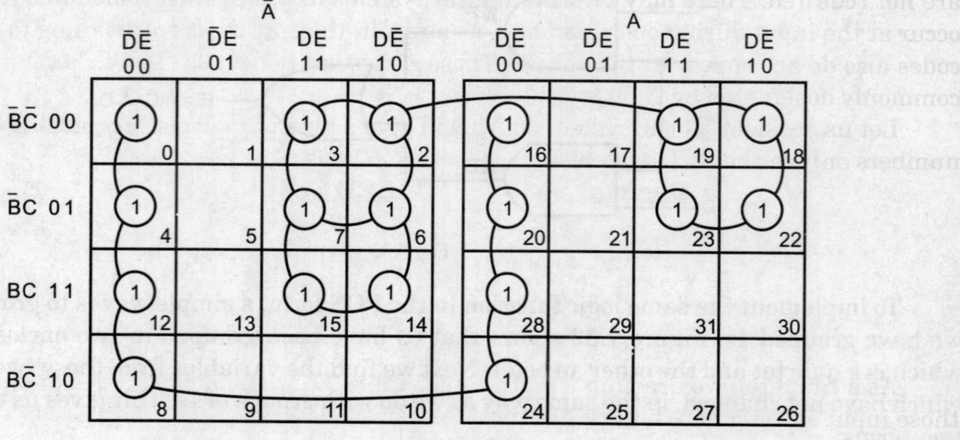

Fig. 7.35

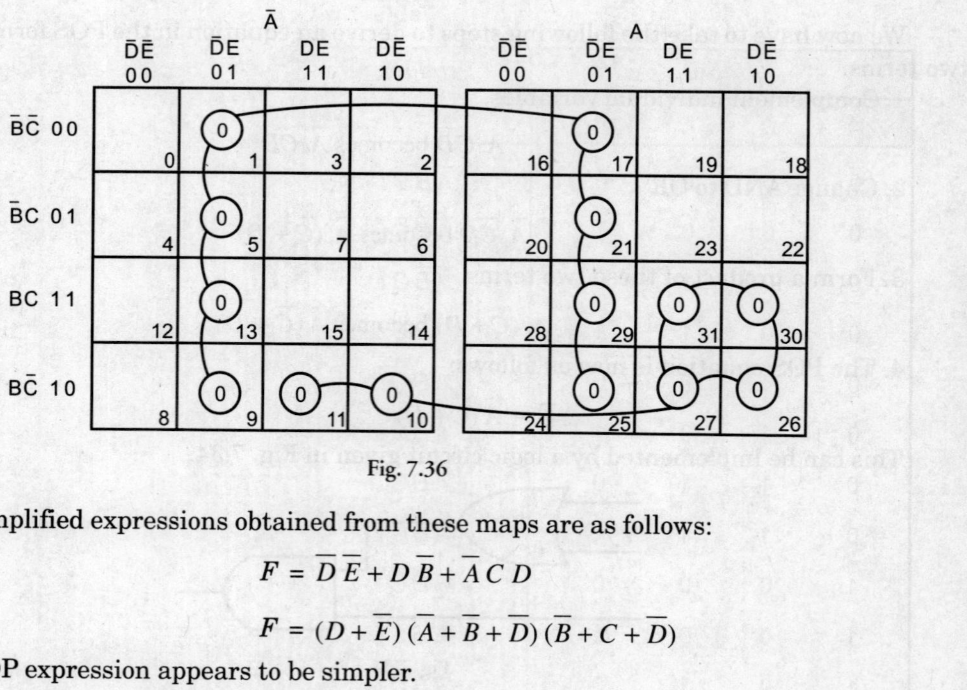

Fig. 7.36

The simplified expressions obtained from these maps are as follows:

SOP $F = \overline{D}\,\overline{E} + D\,\overline{B} + \overline{A}\,C\,D$

POS $F = (D + \overline{E})\,(\overline{A} + \overline{B} + \overline{D})\,(\overline{B} + C + \overline{D})$

The SOP expression appears to be simpler.

7.7 DON'T CARE STATES

Have a look at Table 1.2 for the decimal equivalent of binary numbers which uses a 4-bit code. Now look up Table 1.4 for the BCD system which also uses a 4-bit code; but the following codes are not used:

1010, 1011, 1100, 1101, 1110, 1111

Therefore, in a system using the BCD code, the above binary codes will never occur as they are not required. There may be other digital systems also, in which some binary codes do not occur at the input during operation and, as a result, the outputs corresponding to those binary codes also do not appear at the output. These states are known as "Don't Care" states and are commonly designated by '*X*' in truth tables.

Let us consider a logic system which will give a binary 1 output for the following decimal numbers only in the BCD systems:

Decimal No.	**BCD Code**
4	0100
5	0101
6	0110
7	0111
8	1000

As a first step we draw up a truth table. Table 7.6 with four variables and put 1 against those input states where binary 1 outputs is desired. 0 against those states where no output is desired, and *X* against those states which will not occur.

Table 7.6

Input				Product term	Decimal No.	Output
A	*B*	*C*	*D*			
0	0	0	0	$\bar{A}\bar{B}\bar{C}\bar{D}$	0	0
0	0	0	1	$\bar{A}\bar{B}\bar{C}D$	1	0
0	0	1	0	$\bar{A}\bar{B}C\bar{D}$	2	0
0	0	1	1	$\bar{A}\bar{B}CD$	3	0
0	1	0	0	$\bar{A}B\bar{C}\bar{D}$	4	1
0	1	0	1	$\bar{A}B\bar{C}D$	5	1
0	1	1	0	$\bar{A}BC\bar{D}$	6	1
0	1	1	1	$\bar{A}BCD$	7	1
1	0	0	0	$A\bar{B}\bar{C}\bar{D}$	8	1
1	0	0	1	$A\bar{B}\bar{C}D$	9	0
1	0	1	0	$A\bar{B}C\bar{D}$	10	X
1	0	1	1	$A\bar{B}CD$	11	X
1	1	0	0	$AB\bar{C}\bar{D}$	12	X
1	1	0	1	$AB\bar{C}D$	13	X
1	1	1	0	$ABC\bar{D}$	14	X
1	1	1	1	$ABCD$	15	X

SOP Function

In order to be able to decide which of the two functions, SOP and POS, would be more efficient, it is necessary to derive logic functions for both the cases. Let us first work out a function in the SOP form, as described below.

In the Karnaugh map, Fig. 7.37, enter 1s in squares corresponding to product terms for which the output is binary 1; 0s in squares corresponding to product terms for which the output is binary 0; and *Xs* in squares corresponding to product terms relating to 'Don't care' states. While forming enclosures, we can treat *Xs* as 0s or 1s according to convenience. Those *Xs* that ar not used are declared as 0s. For the purpose of the SOP function, we will ignore squares in which 0s have been entered.

Thus we have the following SOP function:

$$F = B + A\overline{D} \qquad \text{...(7.41)}$$

You will notice from the diagram that five *Xs* have been assumed to be 1s and this has helped the formation of an octet and a quartet.

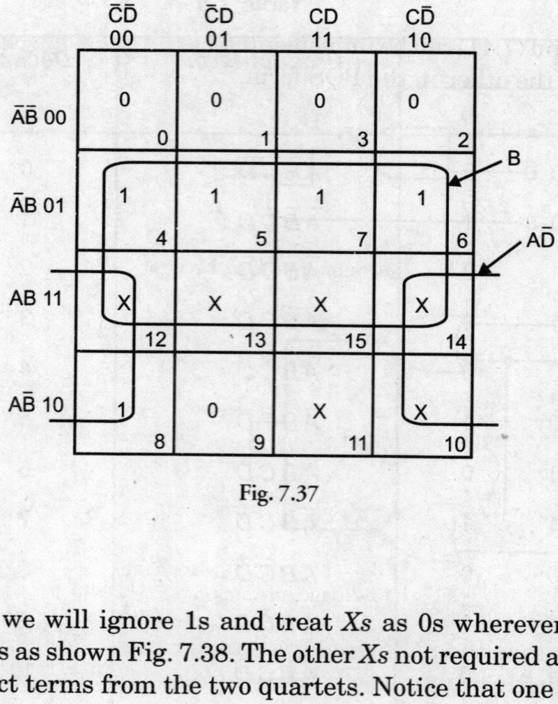

Fig. 7.37

POS Function

For the POS function, we will ignore 1s and treat *Xs* as 0s wherever convenient, and form enclosures along with 0s as shown Fig. 7.38. The other *Xs* not required are declared to be 1s. We get the following product terms from the two quartets. Notice that one *X* has been assumed to be 0.

$$\overline{B}D \text{ and } \overline{A}\,\overline{B}$$

These product terms can form the following function in the POS form:

$$F = (B + \overline{D})\,(A + B) \qquad \text{...(7.42)}$$

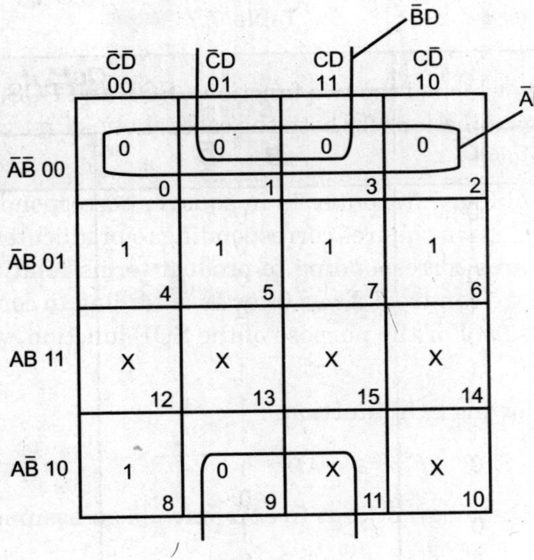

Fig. 7.38

Equations (7.40) and (7.41) can be implemented by the following logic circuits, one of which is in the SOP form and the other in the POS form.

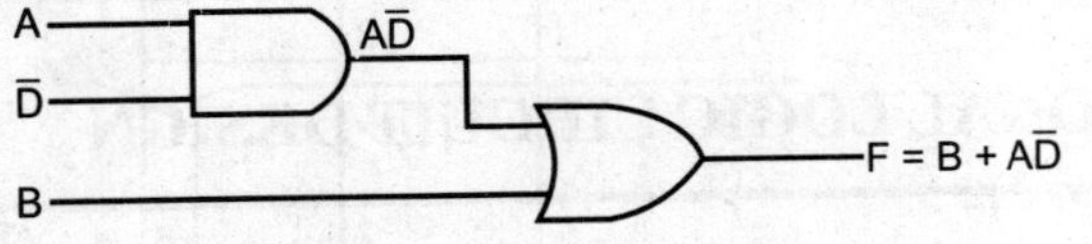

Fig. 7.39 Sum-of-product circuit (SOP)

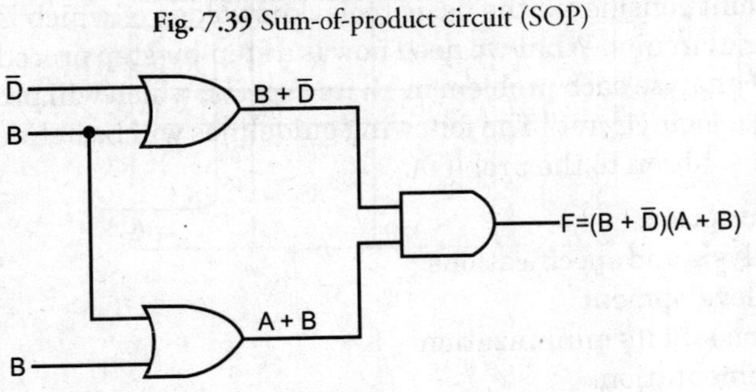

Fig. 7.40 Product-of-sums circuit (POS)

In this particular case the SOP circuit is simpler than the POS circuit as it uses fewer gates. It is a good practice to evaluate both forms, as it is likely that one of them will be simpler than the other.

Table 7.7 is a truth table for the circuits shown in Figs. 7.39 and 7.40. You will notice that the outputs of both the circuits are identical. However, there is one important point that needs some comment. You will notice that in those "Don't Care" states in which we had, for ease of grouping, assumed X to be 1, the output is 1 and where X was assumed to be 0, the output is 0. These are the states with which we were not concerned. The important point to remember about "Don't Care" states is that, we don't care whether the output is 0 or 1; but they have to be either 0 by 1, as these are the only two binary states.

Table 7.7

Input				Output	
				SOP	POS
A	B	C	D	$B + A\overline{D}$	$(A + B)(B + \overline{D})$
0	0	0	0	0	0
0	0	0	1	0	0
0	0	1	0	0	0
0	0	1	1	0	0
0	1	0	0	1	1
0	1	0	1	1	1
0	1	1	0	1	1
0	1	1	1	1	1
1	0	0	0	1	1
1	0	0	1	0	0
1	0	1	0	1	1
1	0	1	1	0	0
1	1	0	0	1	1
1	1	0	1	1	1
1	1	1	0	1	1
1	1	1	1	1	1

7.8 COMBINATIONAL LOGIC CIRCUIT DESIGN

We have up to this point considered the basic tools, knowledge of which is necessary in designing combinational logic circuits. What we need now is a step-by-step procedure which will enable us to understand and analyse each problem in all its aspects, which will provide us the necessary criteria for designing a logic circuit? The following guidelines will be helpful in analysing, evaluating and planning a solution to the problem:

1. Problem description
2. Problem analysis and specifications
3. Truth table development
4. Logic equation and its minimization
5. Design implementation.

1. Problem description

The most important part of the exercise is to understand the problem and thereafter prepare a written description of the application and functions required to be performed. If the problem is stated initially in mathematical terms, the task is simple and the truth table, logic equation and the design implementation can follow without difficulty.

The problem really arises when we have to proceed to tackle a problem from a verbal description of its application and functions. In this case the verbal description is likely to overlook some important input states and the related output events. It is, therefore, the circuit designer's task to visualise such situations and take note of them in circuit design.

2. Problem analysis and specifications

Afterall the implications have been thoroughly understood, you can proceed to analyse the problem. It must be determined if a fixed relationship exists between the inputs and outputs, as only then a combinational logic design will be possible. If that is not the case, perhaps the solution will lie in sequential logic, which we will consider in a later chapter.

Your problem description will help you to identify the number and types of input signals, the number of outputs required and the functions to be performed.

3. Truth table development

When the number of inputs and outputs have been determined, the next step is to draw up a truth table from the problem description. The truth table should show the input variables and under them all possible input combinations of the input variables. You can do this by listing all the binary numbers from 0 to the upper limit, which is a function of the number of input variables. For instance if the input variables are 4, the input combinations will be 2^4 or 16. If the input variables are '*n*', the number of input combinations will be 2^n.

In accordance with the problem description, determine the output state for each combination of the input variables and enter them in the truth table. Identify those input states that are not used, treat them as "don't care" states, and put an '*X*' mark against them in the output column, or list them separetly as invalid states. All the output states should be assigned a 0, 1 or *X* status, which should tally with the problem definition. In truth tables which have more than one output, each output bears a definite relationship with the input combination associated with it.

4. Logic equation and its minimization

After the truth table has been prepared, the rest of the exercise follows a well defined procedure. To prepare a logic equation in the SOP form, observe the outputs from the truth table for each output column and form a product term of the input variables for each input combination, where a binary 1 occurs in the output column. Reduce the equation to the simplest form with the help of Boolean algebra or Karnaugh maps. When the number of outputs are more than one, simplify each output equation before implementing it with logic gates.

5. Design implementation

It is often advisable to implement logic function using NAND gates. The procedure for this has been explained in an eariler chapter. It may be useful to explore both the SOP and POS forms, as one of these may be simpler and less costly than the other form.

Some examples of combinational logic design follow.

7.8.1 XS3 BCD Code to Standard 8421 BCD Code

Example 7.24: *Design a combinational logic circuit to convert the XS3 BCD code into the Standard 8421 BCD code.*

Solution: It is very clear from the problem definition that this will require four inputs and the same number of outputs, and that there will be ten discrete states from 0000 to 1100. It is also clear that, since there will be 16 input combinations, six of them will be don't care inputs. We can now draw up a truth table as shown in Table 7.8.

Table 7.8

Decimal number	XS3					BCD (8421)			
	Minterm designation	Input				Output			
		A	B	C	D	W	X	Y	Z
0	3	0	0	1	1	0	0	0	0
1	4	0	1	0	0	0	0	0	1
2	5	0	1	0	1	0	0	1	0
3	6	0	1	1	0	0	0	1	1
4	7	0	1	1	1	0	1	0	0
5	8	1	0	0	0	0	1	0	1
6	9	1	0	0	1	0	1	1	0
7	10	1	0	1	0	0	1	1	1
8	11	1	0	1	1	1	0	0	0
9	12	1	1	0	0	1	0	0	1

From the truth table we can write the four output equations in terms of the inputs as follows:

$$W = \Sigma(11, 12)$$

$$X = \Sigma(7, 8, 9, 10)$$

$$Y = \Sigma(5, 6, 9, 10)$$

$$Z = \Sigma(4, 6, 8, 10, 12)$$

The six don't care states are as follows:

$$m_0, m_1, m_2, m_{13}, m_{14}, m_{15}$$

The four output equations for outputs W, X, Y and Z have been plotted on four Karnaugh maps [Figs 7.41 (a), (b), (c) and (d)]. The don't care cells in the maps have been marked with X. The simplified equations, which have also been shown in the maps, are as follows:

$$W = AB + ACD$$

$$X = \overline{B}\,\overline{C} + \overline{B}\,\overline{D} + B\,C\,D$$

$$Y = \overline{C}D + C\overline{D}$$

$$Z = \overline{D}$$

The logic circuit to implement these equations is given in Fig. 7.42. It has been designed using NAND gates and an XOR gate. You may first implement it with AND gates and then convert the circuit to NAND logic.

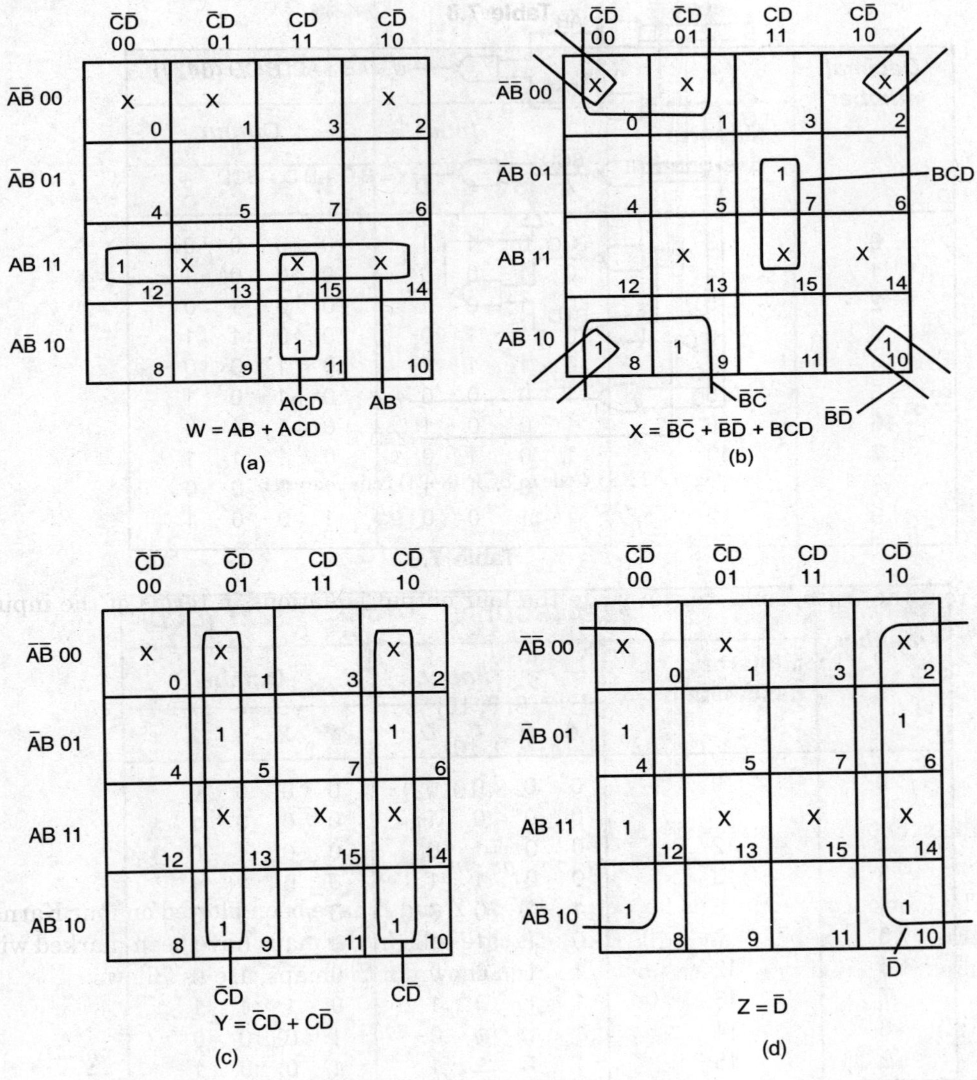

Fig. 7.41

7.8.2 4221 BCD Code to Standard 8421 BCD Code

Example 7.25: *Design a combinational logic circuit to convert the 4221 BCD code to the Standard 8421 BCD code.*

Solution: This problem is very similar to the one we have just considered and solution follows the same approach. There are four inputs and the same number of outputs. There are six don't care states. The truth table for this problem is given in Table 7.9.

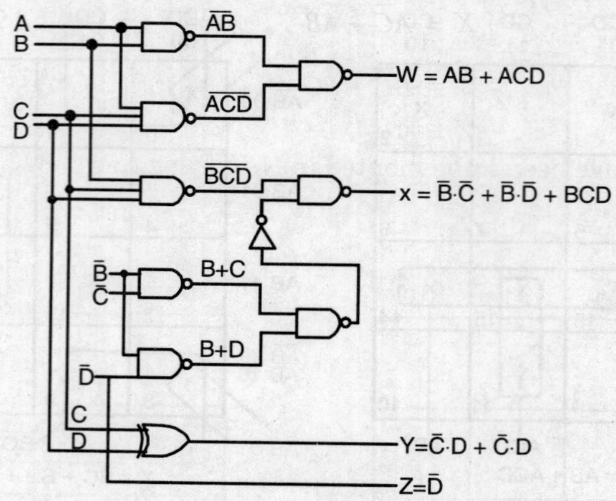

Fig. 7.42 XS3 Code to BCD (8421) code converter

Table 7.9

Decimal number	4221 (BCD)					8421 (BCD)			
	Minterm designation	Input				Output			
		A	B	C	D	W	X	Y	Z
0	0	0	0	0	0	0	0	0	0
1	1	0	0	0	1	0	0	0	1
2	2	0	0	1	0	0	0	1	0
3	3	0	0	1	1	0	0	1	1
4	8	1	0	0	0	0	1	0	0
5	7	0	1	1	1	0	1	0	1
6	12	1	1	0	0	0	1	1	0
7	13	1	1	0	1	0	1	1	1
8	14	1	1	1	0	1	0	0	0
9	15	1	1	1	1	1	0	0	1

The following output equations, in terms of the inputs, have been derived from the truth table:

$$W = (14, 15)$$
$$X = (7, 8, 12, 13)$$
$$Y = (2, 3, 12, 13)$$
$$Z = (1, 3, 7, 13, 15)$$

The six don't care states are as follows:

$$m_4, m_5, m_6, m_9, m_{10}, m_{11}$$

The above output equations for outputs W, X, Y and Z have been plotted on four Karnaugh maps in Figs. 7.43 (a), (b), (c) and (d). The don't care cells have been marked with X in all the maps. After simplification the following equations have been obtained for the four outputs.

$$W = AC$$

$$X = A\overline{C} + \overline{A}B$$

$$Y = B\overline{C} + \overline{B}C$$

$$Z = D$$

These equations have been implemented in NAND logic as shown in Fig. 7.44.

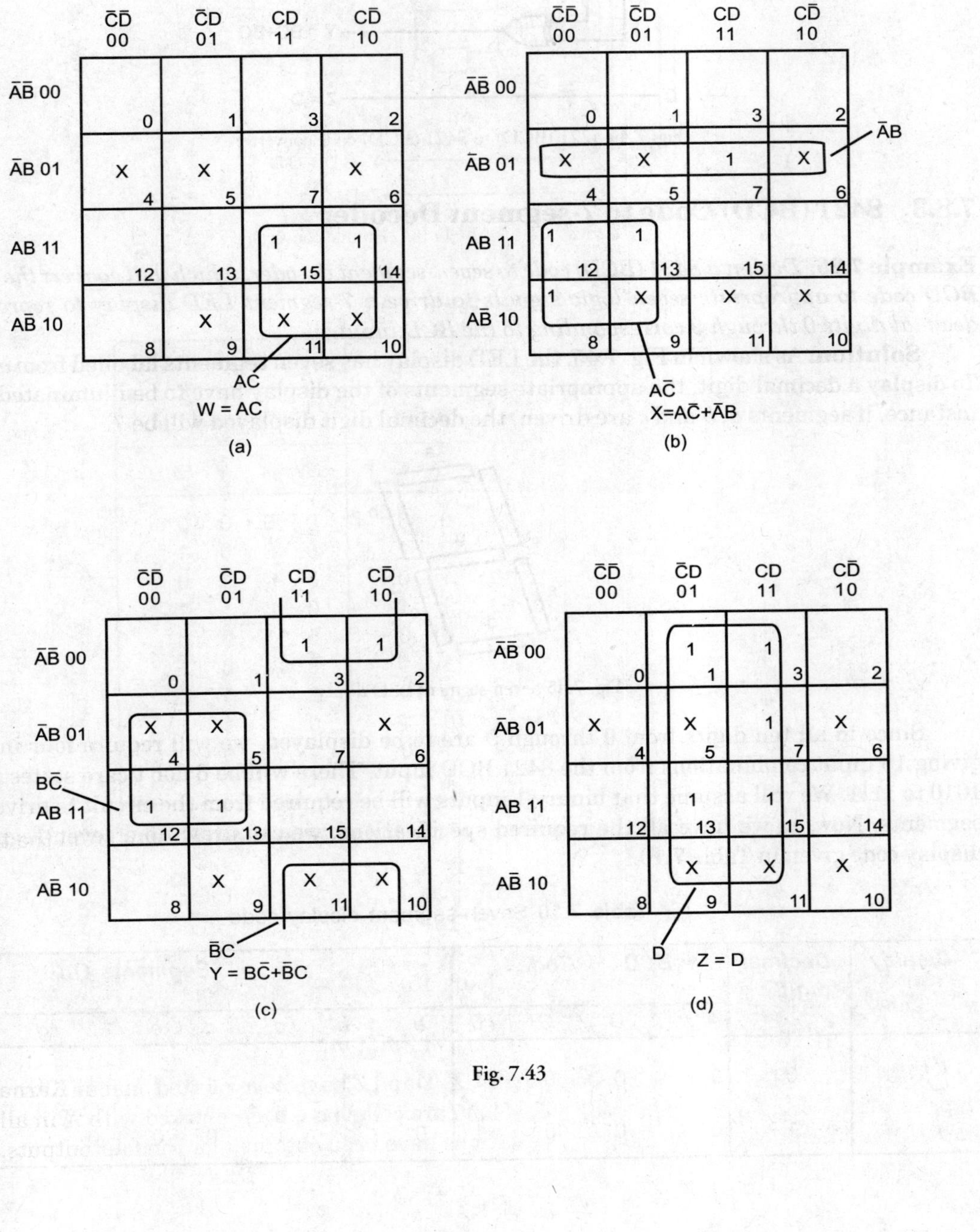

Fig. 7.43

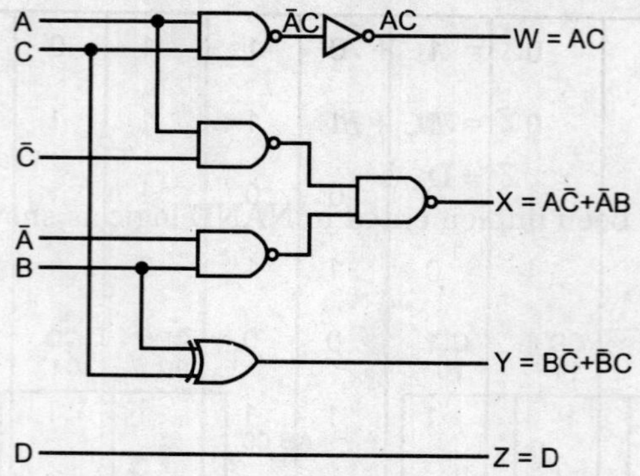

Fig. 7.44 4221 (BCD) to 8421 (BCD) code converter

7.8.3 8421 (BCD) Code to 7-segment Decoder

Example 7.26: *Design a 8421 (BCD) code to seven-segment decoder, which will convert the 8421 BCD code to appropriate seven logic signals to drive a 7-segment LED display to reproduce decimal digits 0 through 9 corresponding to the BCD input.*

Solution: As shown in Fig. 7.45, the LED display has seven segments labelled from a to g. To display a decimal digit, the appropriate segments of the display have to be illuminated. For instance, if segments a, b and c are driven, the decimal digit displayed will be 7.

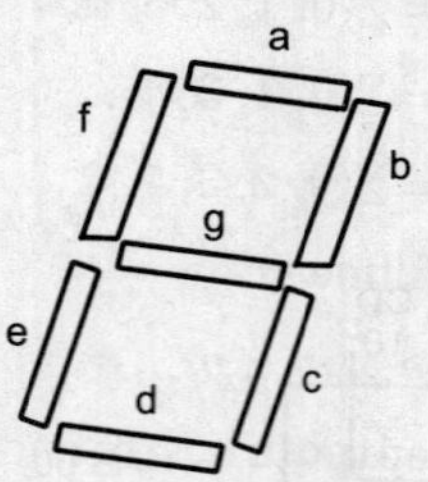

Fig. 7.45 Seven-segment LED display

Since in all ten digits from 0 through 9 are to be displayed, we will require four inputs giving 16 input combinations from the 8421 BCD input. There will be 6 don't care states from 1010 to 1111. We will assume that binary 1 inputs will be required from the circuit to drive the segments. Now, as we have all the required specifications, we can draw up a seven-segment display code given in Table 7.10.

Table 7.10 Seven-segment display code

Display	Decimal digit	BCD Code				Segments On						
		A	B	C	D	a	b	c	d	e	f	g
0	0	0	0	0	1	1	1	1	1	1	1	0
1	1	0	0	0	1	0	1	1	0	0	0	0

2	2	0	0	1	0	1	1	0	1	1	0	1
3	3	0	0	1	1	1	1	1	1	0	0	1
4	4	0	1	0	0	0	1	1	0	0	1	1
5	5	0	1	0	1	1	0	1	1	0	1	1
6	6	0	1	1	0	0	0	1	1	1	1	1
7	7	0	1	1	1	1	1	1	0	0	0	0
8	8	1	0	0	0	1	1	1	1	1	1	1
9	9	1	0	0	1	1	1	1	0	0	1	1

Note: The segments required to be illuminated for a particular digit are marked 1 and those not required to be illuminated are marked 0.

The following output equations, in terms of the BCD inputs, have been derived from the truth table, for segments a, b, c and d only:

$$a = \Sigma(0, 2, 3, 5, 7, 8, 9)$$

$$b = \Sigma(0, 1, 2, 3, 4, 7, 8, 9)$$

$$c = \Sigma(0, 1, 3, 4, 5, 6, 7, 8, 9)$$

$$d = \Sigma(0, 2, 3, 5, 6, 8)$$

The six don't care states are as follows:

$$m_{10}, m_{11}, m_{12}, m_{13}, m_{14}, m_{15}$$

The above output equations for outputs a, b, c and d have been plotted on four Karnaugh maps in Figs. 7.46 (a), (b), (c) and (d). The invalid states have been marked with X in all the maps. After simplification, the following equations have been obtained for the four outputs:

$$a = A + BD + CD + \overline{B}\,\overline{D}$$

$$b = A + \overline{B} + CD + \overline{C}\,\overline{D}$$

$$c = A + B + \overline{C} + D$$

$$d = \overline{B}C + \overline{B}\,\overline{D} + C\overline{D} + B\overline{C}D$$

The derivation of the outputs for the other segments as well as the design of the logic circuit have been left as an exercise for the student.

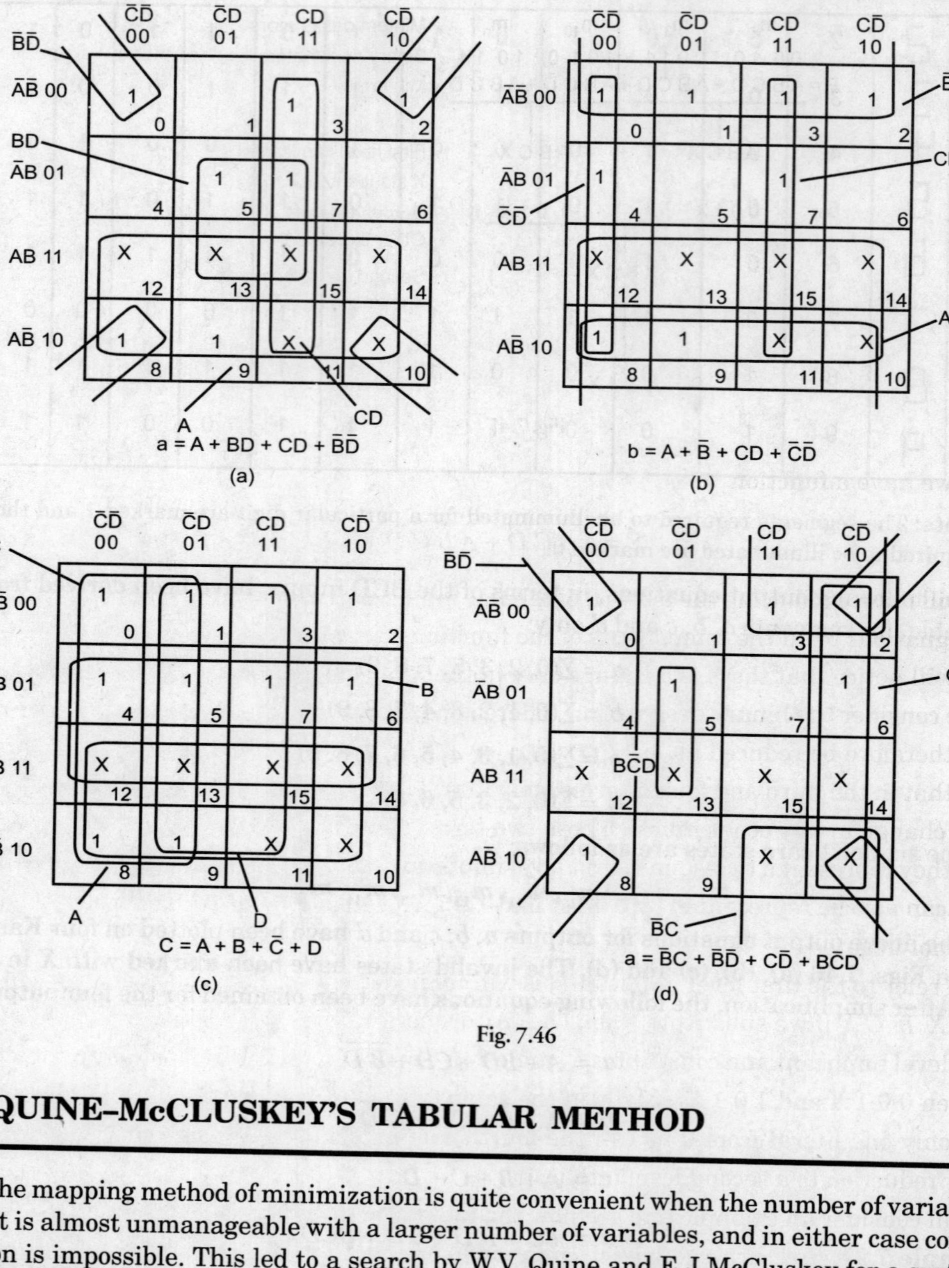

Fig. 7.46

7.9 QUINE–McCLUSKEY'S TABULAR METHOD

While the mapping method of minimization is quite convenient when the number of variables is small, it is almost unmanageable with a larger number of variables, and in either case computerization is impossible. This led to a search by W.V. Quine and E.J.McCluskey for a system of tabular minimization, which would make it possible to computerize the operation.

The minimization procedure shown in Fig. 7.47 highlights the basic principles of the tabular method.

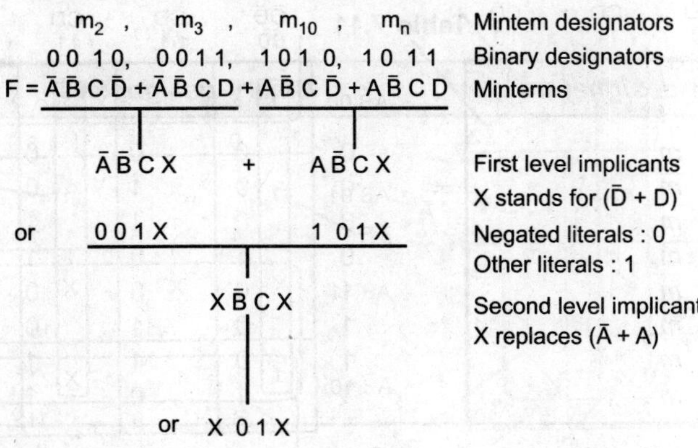

Fig. 7.47

Here we have a function

$$F = \overline{A}\,\overline{B}\,C\,\overline{D} + \overline{A}\,\overline{B}\,C\,D + A\,\overline{B}\,C\,\overline{D} + A\,\overline{B}\,C\,D$$

which we will reduce following the method of tabular minimization. The minterm as well as the binary designations of all the components of the function have also been given. In the first two terms you will notice that there is a change only in the first column, where $\overline{D}$ changes to D or 0 to 1, if we consider the binary designation. There is no change in any other literal. These two terms can therefore be reduced to $\overline{A}\,\overline{B}\,C(\overline{D} + D)$ or $\overline{A}\,\overline{B}C$, if we substitute $(\overline{D} + D)$ by X. You will notice that in the third and fourth terms, only literal in column one changes from 0 to 1 and there is no change in any other literal. These two terms can therefore be reduced to $A\overline{B}CX$ as before and they represent a two-square first level implicant. As shown in the diagram, these two implicants can also be represented by 0 0 1 X and 1 0 1 X, if we use 0 for negated literals and 1 for literals not negated.

If you refer to the first level implicants, it will immediately occur to you that they can be reduced to $X\ \overline{B}\ C\,X$ if we substitute X for $(\overline{A} + A)$ or more simply $\overline{B}\,C$. This term represents the second level implicant and constitutes a single four-square implicant. It is important to note that between 0 0 1 X and 1 0 1 X, X falls in the same column in both the terms and there is a change in only one literal from 0 to 1 in the fourth column. These two conditions have to be fulfilled for reduction to a second level implicant.

We will consider an example and see how the tabular method is applied in practice.

Example 7.27: *Reduce the following equation using the tabular method of minimization:*

$$F = m_0 + m_2 + m_3 + m_5 + m_8 + m_{10} + m_{11} + m_{13}$$

Solution: *Step 1:* Convert all minterm designators to binary designators as shown in Table 7.11.

Table 7.11

Minterm designators	*Binary designators*			
m_0	0	0	0	0
m_2	0	0	1	0
m_3	0	0	1	1
m_5	0	1	0	1
m_8	1	0	0	0
m_{10}	1	0	1	0
m_{11}	1	0	1	1
m_{13}	1	1	0	1

Step 2: Rearrange the binary designators in groups in order of the number of 1s in each binary designator and draw a line separating each group as shown in Table. 7.12.

Table 7.12

Minterm designator	*Binary designator*					*Number of 1s*
0	0	0	0	0	√	0
2	0	0	1	0	√	
8	1	0	0	0	√	1
3	0	0	1	1	√	
5	0	1	0	1	√	2
10	1	0	1	0	√	
11	1	0	1	1	√	
13	1	1	0	1	√	3

Step 3: Now proceed to compare every binary designator in each category of 1s with the next higher category of 1s. For instance you will compare each binary designator containing one 1 with those binary designators which have two 1s. If they differ in only one position, put an *X* in the position where they differ and put a check mark against the binary designators you have so checked.

For instance compare 0000 with 0010. They differ only in the 2s position, so we put a check mark against them and write 00*X* 0 for these binary designators, to denote that there is a change only in the 2s position. At the same time we write in Table 7.13 the minterm values of the binary designators compared and the resultant prime implicant which is a two-square implicant in this case.

Binary designator 0000 can also be compared with binary designator 1000, as they differ only in one position. We put a check mark against 1000 and write the designators compared, that is 0, 8 and the resultant prime implicant, *X* 000

Table 7.13 First level reduction

Minterms compared		*Primary implicant*	
0,	2	00*X*0	√
0,	8	*X*000	√
2,	3	001*X*	√
2,	10	*X010*	√
8,	10	10*X*0	√
3,	11	*X*011	
5,	13	*X*101	
10,	11	101*X*	√

Similarly, we will compare one 1s category with two 1s category. Binary designator 0010 can be compared with 0011. The resultant prime implicant is 001 *X*. We will write it down in Table 7.13 along with the minterms compared, that is 2 and 3. Minterm 2 can be compared with minterm 10, producing another prime implicant *X*010. We write it down in the table along with the minterms compared.

We can now proceed to compare two 1s category with three 1s category. The result of this comparison has been noted in Table 7.13. We now have eight first level prime implicants.

Step 4: We have now three categories of two-square prime implicants, as shown in Table 7.13. In this step we will identify four square prime implicants. To do this we have to compare each binary designator in every category. With binary designators in the next higher category of implicants; but the following conditions must be satisfied in this comparison.

(i) The two implicants must differ by only one 1.

(ii) Both implicants must have *X*s in the same column.

Table 7.14

Minterm designator	*Implicants compared*	*Resultant four-square implicant*
0, 2 and 8, 10	00*X*0 and 10*X*0	*X*0*X*0
0, 8 and 2, 10	*X*000 and *X*010	*X*0*X*0
2, 3 and 10, 11	001*X* and 101*X*	*X*01*X*

This comparison yields three four-square implicants (Table 7.14) but two of these are identical. The remaining terms *X*011 and *X*101 are prime implicants as they cannot be reduced any further; but we do not know which of these are essential. In the next step we will determine the essential prime implicants.

Step 5: As shown in Table 7.15, list all the minterms in columns and the prime implicants in rows, in a descending order of the squares covered.

Table 7.15

A	B	C	D	0	2	3	5	8	10	11	13
X	0	X	0	*	*			*	*		
X	0	1	X		*	*			*	*	
X	0	1	1			*				*	
X	1	0	1				*				*
				√	√			√	√		
						√				√	
							√				√

Against all the implicants put marks indicating the terms covered. The following conclusions can be drawn from this table:

(i) Implicant *X* 0*X*0 is an essential prime implicant, as no other implicant covers minterm 0. Indicate by check marks the minterms covered.

(ii) Implicant *X*01*X* is also an essential prime implicant. Put check marks under the minterms covered.

(iii) Prime implicant *X*011 is not an essential prime implicant, as minterms 3 and 11 have already been covered.

(iv) Prime implicant *X*101 is also essential, as it covers minterms 5 and 13, which have not been covered so far. Put check marks under minterms 5 and 13.

(v) All minterms have now been covered. The essential prime implicants are given below. Literals have been substituted for 1s and negated literals for 0s.

$$X0X0 \ldots \overline{B}\,\overline{D}$$

$$X01X \ldots \overline{B}\,C$$

$$X101 \ldots B\,\overline{C}\,D$$

The reduced function is now as follows:

$$F = \overline{B}\,\overline{D} + \overline{B}C + B\overline{C}D$$

Problems

7.1 Find the minterms for the following expressions:

1. $AB + \overline{B}C$ 2. $\overline{A}C + B\overline{C} + AC$

7.2 Find the minterms for the following expressions:

1. $\overline{A}B + A\overline{B}C$ 2. $A\overline{C} + AB\overline{C} + \overline{A}BC$

7.3 Find the minterms for the following expressions:

1. $A + B + \overline{C}$ 2. $AB + \overline{A} + C$

7.4 Determine the minterm designations for the followings:

1. $\overline{A}\,\overline{B}\,\overline{C}$ 2. $A\overline{B}C$ 3. $ABC\overline{D}$ 4. $A\overline{B}\,\overline{C}D$

7.5 Enter the following functions on a Karnaugh map.

1. $F = A + \overline{B}$ 2. $F = \overline{A}B + A\overline{B}$

7.6 Enter the following functions on a Karnaugh map:

1. $F = ABC + A\overline{B}C + AB\overline{C}$ 2. $F = \overline{A}B\overline{C} + \overline{A}BC + \overline{A}\,\overline{B}\,\overline{C}$

3. $F = A + \overline{A}C + B\overline{C}$ 4. $F = A + \overline{B}C + \overline{A}BC$

7.7 Enter the following functions on a Karnaugh map:

1. $F = \overline{A}BCD + A\overline{B}CD + AB\overline{C}D + ABC\overline{D}$

2. $F = \overline{A}B\overline{C}D + A\overline{B}C\overline{D} + \overline{A}BC\overline{D} + \overline{A}\,\overline{B}CD$

7.8 Write the S-O-P equations for the following Karnaugh maps:

	$\overline{B}\overline{C}$	$\overline{B}C$	BC	$B\overline{C}$
$\overline{A}$	1	1	1	1
A	0	1	1	1

Fig. P-7.8(1)

	$\overline{B}\overline{C}$	$\overline{B}C$	BC	$B\overline{C}$
$\overline{A}$	1	0	1	1
A	1	1	1	1

Fig. P-7.8 (2)

7.9 Simplify the following functions using Karnaugh maps:

1. $F = AB\overline{CD} + AB\overline{C}\,\overline{D} + ABCD + ABC\overline{D} + \overline{A}\,\overline{B}C\overline{D}$

2. $F = \overline{A}B\overline{CD} + \overline{A}B\overline{C}D + AB\overline{C}D + ABCD + ABC\overline{D} + A\overline{B}\,\overline{C}D$

7.10 Simplify the following functions using Karnaugh maps:

1. $F = m_0 + m_8 + m_9 + m_{10} + m_{12} + m_{13}$
2. $F = m_0 + m_2 + m_4 + m_7 + m_8 + m_{13} + m_{14}$

7.11 Draw a logic circuit to implement the following truth table:

Input			*Output*
A	*B*	*C*	
0	0	0	1
0	0	1	1
0	1	0	1
0	1	1	0
1	0	0	0
1	0	1	0
1	1	0	0
1	1	1	1

7.12 Express the following functions in POS form:

(a) $F = A + B\overline{C}$ (b) $F = \overline{A} + \overline{B}\,C$

7.13 Express the following 3-variable function in maxterms:

$$F = \Sigma\, m(1, 3, 5, 7)$$

7.14 Express the following 4-variable function in minterms:

$$F = \Pi\, M(0, 3, 5, 6, 8, 9, 11)$$

7.15 For a three-variable function

$$F = \Sigma\, m(1, 3, 6, 7)$$

express F and $\overline{F}$ in maxterms.

7.16 Reduce the following expressions using Karnaugh maps:

(*a*) $F = \Pi\, M(1, 5, 6, 8, 10, 12, 15)$ (*b*) $F = \Pi\, M\,(0, 3, 4, 6, 7, 8, 15)$

7.17 Reduce the following expression:

$$F = \Sigma\, m\,(0, 2, 3, 4, 6, 8, 9, 10, 12, 13, 14, 16, 20, 24, 28, 29)$$

7.18 Write the Boolean functions for the following Karnaugh maps:

(1)

	$\overline{C}\overline{D}$	$\overline{C}D$	CD	$C\overline{D}$
$\overline{A}\overline{B}$			1	1
$\overline{A}B$	1	1		1
AB	1			1
$A\overline{B}$		1	1	

Fig. P-7.18(1)

(2)

	$\overline{C}\overline{D}$	$\overline{C}D$	CD	$C\overline{D}$
$\overline{A}\overline{B}$		1	1	1
$\overline{A}B$		1	1	
AB		1	1	1
$A\overline{B}$	1			1

Fig. P-7.18(2)

7.19 Design a logic circuit which will generate an even parity bit for the 8421 BCD code.

7.20 Draw logic circuits to implement the following truth table in S-O-P and P-O-S forms:

Input				*Output*
A	*B*	*C*	*D*	
0	0	0	0	1
0	0	0	1	1
0	0	1	0	1
0	0	1	1	1
0	1	0	0	1
0	1	0	1	0
0	1	1	0	1
0	1	1	1	0
1	0	0	0	1
1	0	0	1	0
1	0	1	0	1

1	0	1	1	0
1	1	0	0	0
1	1	0	1	0
1	1	1	0	0
1	1	1	1	0

7.21 If in Problem 7.20 the last five states of the truth table are don't care states draw logic circuits in the SOP and POS forms to implement the truth table.

7.22 Refer to Problem 7.21 and derive the POS equation form the SOP equation, with the help of Boolean algebra.

7.23 Design a logic circuit which will detect whenever the binary input it from an 8421 BCD code is the binary equivalent of an even decimal number from 1 to 9.

7.24 A process control equipment receives inputs from four sensors of a four-input system. Design a logic circuit which will shut down the operation, when any three of the four inputs fail.

7.25 Design a logic circuit which will provide an output, when any three inputs from a four-input circuit are present.

7.26 Prepare Karnaugh maps for the *e*, *f* and *g* outputs of a BCD to 7-segment code converter and develop the logic diagram for these outputs.

7.27 Design a code converter to convert the 8421 BCD code to 2421 BCD code.

7.28 Design a code converter which will convert the 8421 BCD code to 5211 BCD code.

7.29 Design a logic circuit to convert the 8421 BCD code to XS3 code.

7.30 Develop logic functions which will provide an even parity bit for the 5211 BCD code.

7.31 Design a circuit which can detect invalid 8421 BCD codes.

8

Bistable Multivibrators (Flip-Flops)

8.1 INTRODUCTION

Multivibrators and logic gates constitute the two basic devices used in digital electronics. We have already dealt with logic gates and in this and the following chapter we will confine our attention to multivibrators. There are three types of multivibrators, astable, monostable and bistable. Multivibrators have two states which are complement of each other, that is if one of the outputs is logic 1 the other is logic 0. The output of an astable multivibrator keeps oscillating between logic 0 and logic 1. The monostable multivibrator has a stable and a quasistable state into which it can be triggered and remains in that state for a short period depending on the design.

The bistable multivibrator, which is appropriately called bistable, defines its most important characteristic and refers to the fact that it is a two state device and can be switched from one state to the other. Bistables are, therefore, known as flip-flops. A single flip-flop can store one bit of data, binary 1 or binary 0. This emphasizes the fact that the basic function of flip-flop is memory. A number of flip-flops put together constitute a register, which can store a multibit word. This property of the flip-flop makes it as basic an element in digital electronics as logic gates. Therefore, flip-flops find considerable application for data storage, counting and timing operations.

In this chapter, we will deal exclusively with bistable multivibrators and reserve our discussion of astable and monostable multivibrators for the next chapter.

8.2 *RS* NAND LATCH

Flip-flops, also known as latches, are bistable devices, that is they have two stable states. A latch will continue to be in one of the stable states into which it has been put, until it is triggered into another state. Latches can be built with NAND as well as with NOR gates. We will first consider a NAND latch for which a circuit is given in Fig. 8.1 (a) and its symbol in Fig. 8.1 (b).

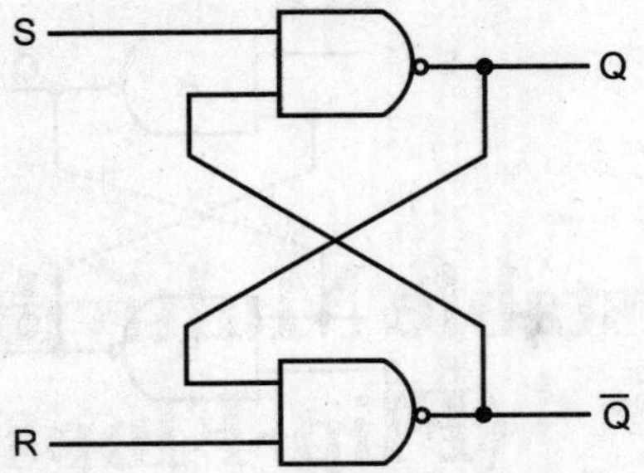

Fig. 8.1 (a) RS latch

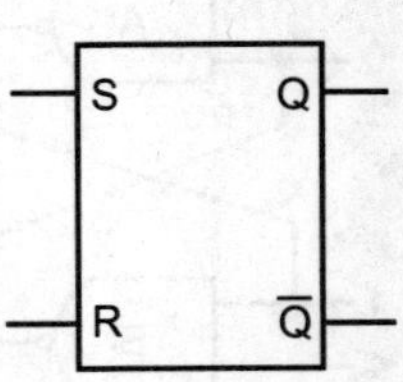

Fig. 8.1 (b) Symbol for RS latch

RS latches have two inputs, *S* and *R*. The *S* input is used to set the flip-flop and, when set, it is said to store a binary 1. *R* input resets the flip-flop and when it has been reset it is said to store a binary 0. Latches have two outputs *Q* (normal) and $\overline{Q}$ (complement). You can ascertain the state of a latch by looking at the *Q* (normal) output. If the logic level of the *Q* output is 1, the flip-flop is set and if it is 0, it is reset. This has been summarized in Table 8.1.

Table 8.1

	Output	
Latch	**Q**	$\overline{Q}$
Set	1	0
Reset	0	1

We will have a look at the functioning of a latch. For a NAND latch both inputs should be normally high, as high inputs do not affect the binary value, 0 or 1, stored in the latch. When the latch is required to be set or reset, short duration pulses are applied to reset or set the latch. We will study this more closely and see why NAND latch inputs should be held normally high.

We will now consider the output states of a NAND latch when both *S* and *R* inputs are open (high) and power is applied to it. The latch will either be set, as shown in Fig. 8.2 (a), or reset as shown in Fig. 8.2 (b). It is worth considering whether the high inputs at *S* and *R* have any effect on the state of the output. Let us first consider Fig. 8.2 (a). Since the output at *Q* is 1, both inputs at NAND gate *B* will be 1, and its output will be 0; but to start with it was already 0, as it is the

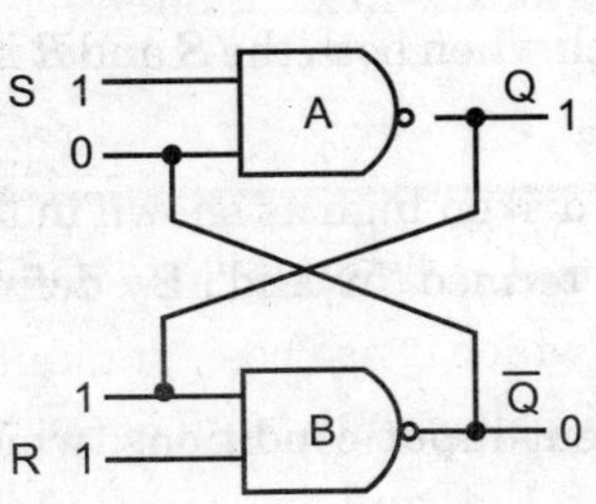

(a)

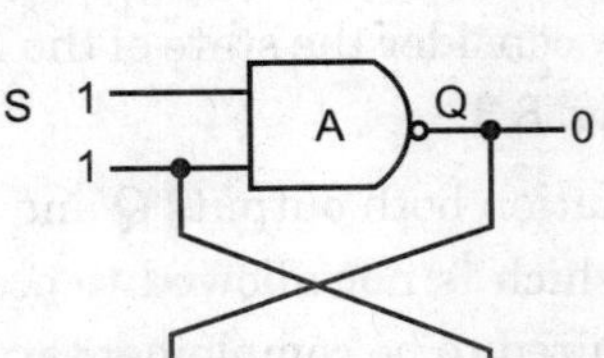

(b)

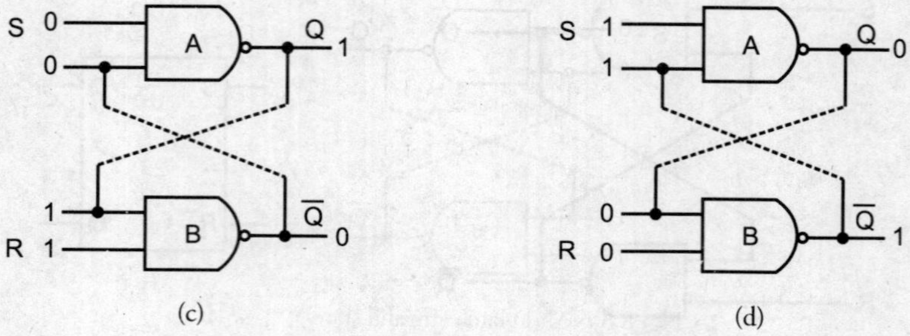

Fig. 8.2

complement of the output at Q. This makes one input of NAND gate $A = 0$ and, since the other input is already 1, the output of this NAND gate will be 1, which tallies with the initial output at Q. Therefore, high inputs at S and R have no effect on the output of the NAND latch.

For the same reasons, which we have considered in the above discussion, if the NAND latch is initially in the reset state, as shown in Fig. 8.2 (b), the high inputs at S and R will have no effect on the output of the latch.

We can conclude, therefore, that if a NAND latch is in the set or reset state, applying high inputs at S and R will not affect the state of the NAND latch.

Let us now consider the state of the output of a NAND latch with inputs as shown in Fig. 8.2 (c). For the present ignore the interconnection shown in dotted lines. With the inputs as shown, the outputs of NAND gates A and B will be binary 1 and 0, respectively. Since the output of NAND gate A, that is binary 1, is the same as one of the inputs of NAND gate B, they can be connected as shown by dotted lines. Also the output of NAND gate B is the same as one of the inputs of NAND gate A and so they can also be connected. This cross connection has not changed the output state of the NAND latch and so we can conclude that, with the inputs as shown, the latch is in a stable state, that is it is set. It will remain latched in this state unless input levels are altered or power is withdrawn.

If the inputs to the NAND latch are as shown in Fig. 8.2(d), the latch will be reset, which is the other stable state of the latch. We can argue, as above, that interconnection will not alter the state of the latch, that is it is in a stable state.

We can now consider the state of the NAND latch when both the S and R inputs are binary 0 as shown in Fig. 8.3.

In this situation both outputs Q and $\overline{Q}$ will be driven high as shown in the diagram, and this is a state which is not allowed to occur and is termed 'invalid'. By definition of a latch, outputs are required to be complementary.

The output states of a NAND latch for different input conditions, which we have just considered, have been summarized in Table 8.2.

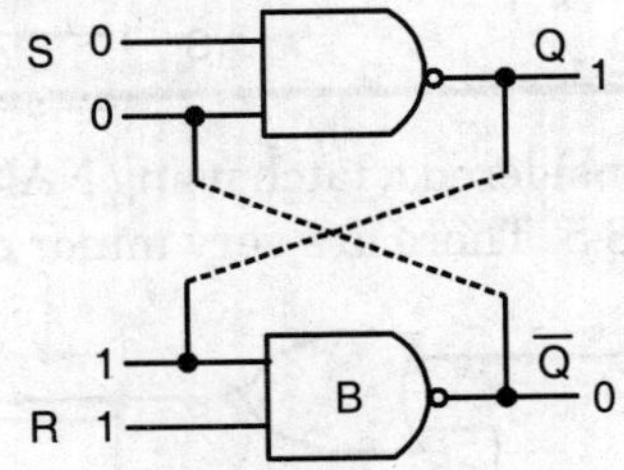

Fig. 8.3 NAND latch (Invalid state)

Table 8.2 Truth table for NAND latch

Input		*Output*		*Observation*
S	***R***	***Q***	$\overline{Q}$	
0	0	1	1	Invalid
0	1	1	0	Set
1	0	0	1	Reset
1	1	*X*	$\overline{X}$	No change, same as previous state set or reset

The timing diagram for a NAND latch, based on Table 8.2 is shown in Fig. 8.4 for various combinations of inputs. Compare the waveforms with the input and output values given in the diagram.

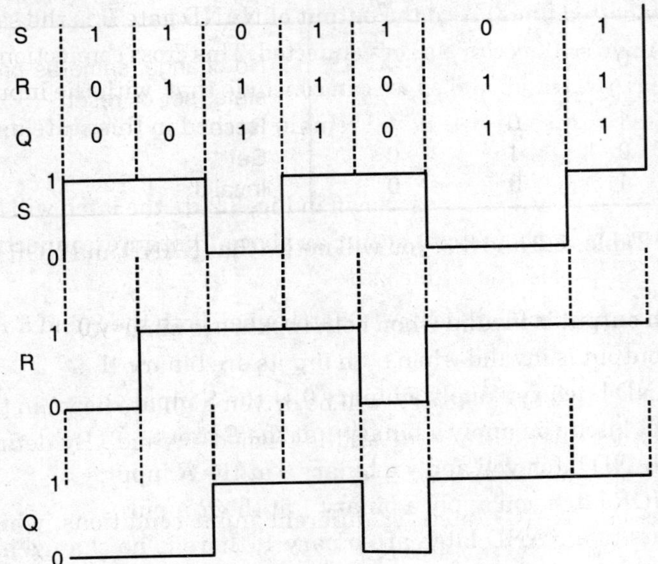

Fig. 8.4 Timing diagram for a NAND latch

8.3 *RS* NOR LATCH

In the previous section, we have considered a latch using NAND gates. A latch can also be made with NOR gates as shown in Fig. 8.5. There are very minor differences in their operation.

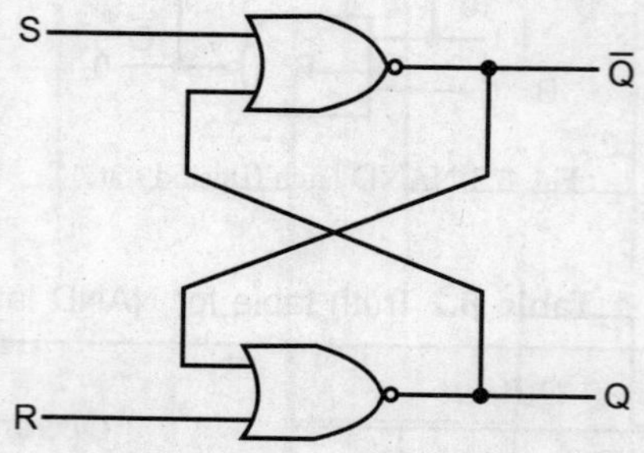

Fig. 8.5 NOR latch

If you compare the NOR latch with the NAND latch circuit given in Fig. 8.1(a), you will notice that the positions of the normal and complement outputs are reversed. The differences in the operation of the two latches will become evident if you refer to Table 8.3, which is the truth table for a NOR latch.

Table 8.3 Truth table for NOR latch

Input		*Output*		*Observation*
S	*R*	*Q*	$\overline{Q}$	
0	0	*X*	$\overline{X}$	No change, same as previous state, set or reset
0	1	0	1	Reset
1	0	1	0	Set
1	1	0	0	Invalid

If you compare Tables 8.2 and 8.3, you will notice that NAND and NOR latches differ in the following respects:

1. NAND latch output is invalid when both inputs are binary 0.
   NOR latch output is invalid when both inputs are binary 1.
2. To set a NAND latch you apply a binary 0 at the *S* input.
   To set a NOR latch you apply a binary 1 at the *S* input.
3. To reset a NAND latch you apply a binary 0 at the *R* input.
   To reset a NOR latch you apply a binary 1 at the *R* input.
4. If both inputs to a NAND latch are binary 1, there is no change in the output of the latch.
   If both inputs to a NOR latch are binary 0, there is no change in the output of the latch.

The timing diagram for a NOR latch, based on the Table 8.3 is given in Fig. 8.6.

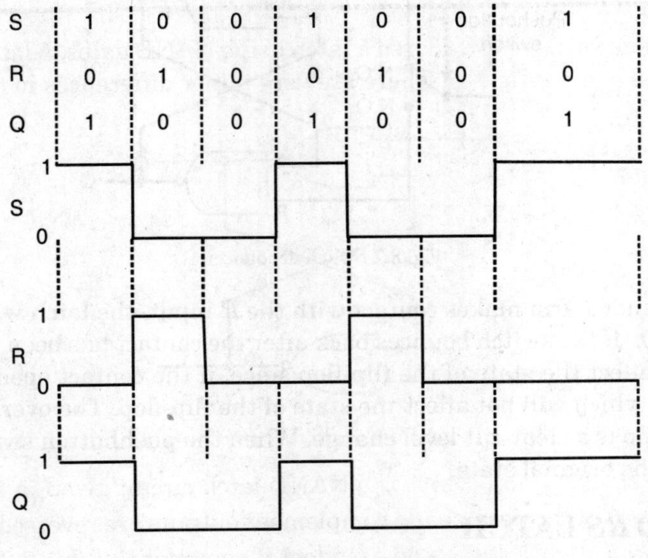

Fig. 8.6 Timing diagram for a NOR latch

8.4 CONTACT BOUNCE ELIMINATOR (SWITCH DEBOUNCER)

Pushbutton switches, which are normally used in digital equipments for making electrical contacts, open and close several times within a few milliseconds before a proper contact is made. When the pushbutton switch is released, the disconnection is not immediate. The switch opens and closes several times before final disconnection. This contact bounce produces pulses which can repeatedly trigger digital circuits and adversely affect their normal operation. As these switches generate a train of pulses, because of contact bounce, some device has to be incorporated to overcome this undesirable feature. Fortunately flip-flops offer a convenient solution. Flip-flops get set or reset on the very first contact of the switch and, as a result, subsequent contacts do not affect the state of the flip-flop.

Consider the flip-flop circuit shown in Fig. 8.7. The switch shown in the diagram is a momentary contact type SPDT pushbutton switch, which breaks contact before it makes one. When the switch is not depressed (normally closed, N.C.) its grounded arm is in contact with the S input of the flip-flop. Thus S is at binary 0 and R, being open, is at binary 1 and so the flip-flop is set, making the output at Q binary 1. When the switch is in the process of being depressed, it makes and breaks contact several times with the S input before final disconnection. When the contact is broken, both S and R inputs begin to float and thus go high. As you have seen earlier, this will not affect the state of the flip-flop. If it momentarily makes contact again with the S input, it will only result in setting the flip-flop, which is already in the set state and so no change will take place. When contact with the S input is finally broken, and before contact is made with the R input, both S and R inputs will be open (or high) and so the latch will remain set.

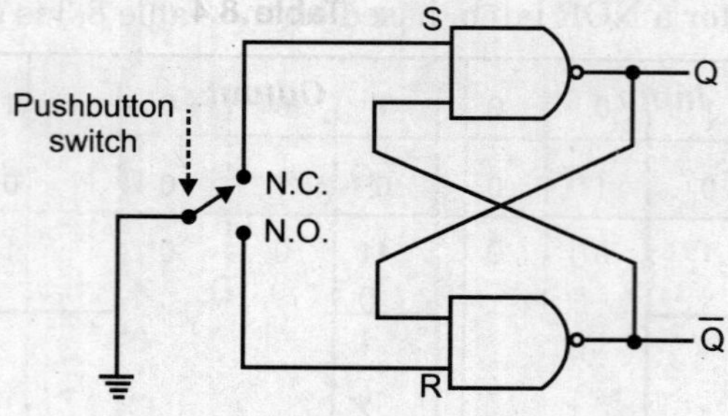

Fig. 8.7 Switch debouncer

When the grounded arm makes contact with the R input, the latch will reset making the output at Q binary 0. If the switch bounces back after the contact has been made with the N.O. contact, it will not affect the state of the flip-flop since, if the contact opens up, both S and R inputs will go high, which will not affect the state of the flip-flop. The overall result of using a switch with a flip-flop is a clear-cut level change. When the pushbutton switch is released, the flip-flop returns to the original state.

8.5 CLOCKED *RS* LATCH

In the latches which we have considered so far, the moment data is applied at the inputs, it influences the output condition. It is at times necessary to have a latch in which the output responds to the data input at some later time interval. This will ensure that only the required data at the input influences the output at a specific time interval, so that all other data that may be present at the inputs, at other points of time, do not influence the output. In an *RS* latch, this can be achieved by slightly modifying the *RS* latch as shown in Fig. 8.8 (a).

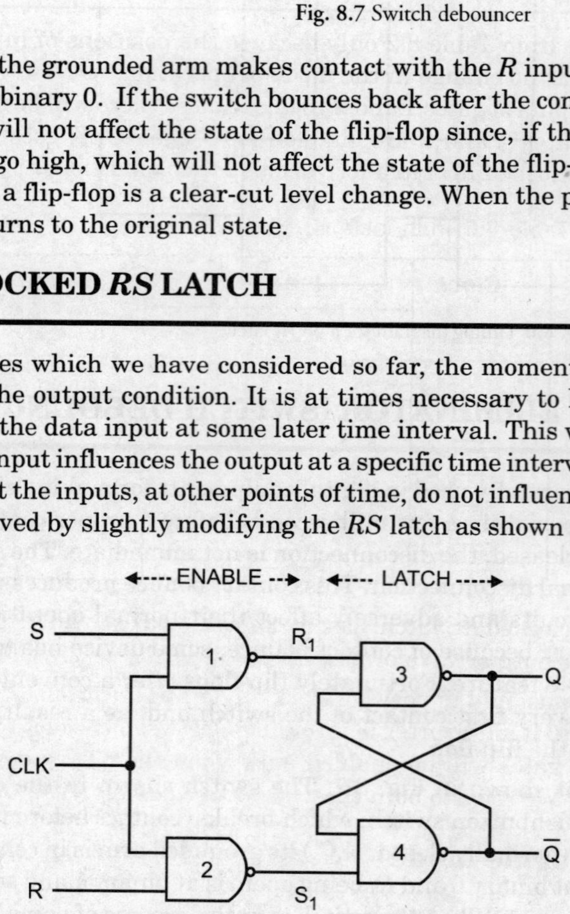

Fig. 8.8 (a) Clocked *RS* latch

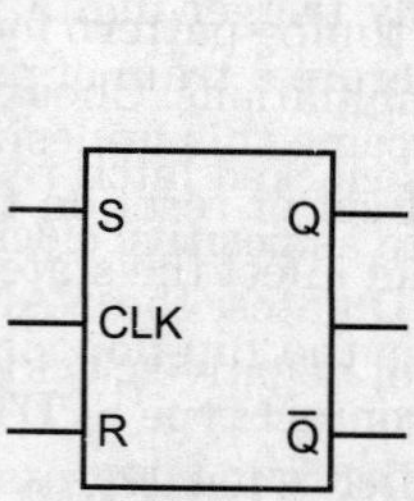

Fig. 8.8 (b) Symbol for clocked *RS* latch

You will notice that two NAND gates drive a NAND latch and there are two ENABLE gates, 1 and 2 with inputs S, R and CLK (short for CLOCK), the last of which supplies a square wave signal. The symbol for a clocked *RS* latch is shown in Fig. 8.8 (b). You will notice that NAND gates 3 and 4 constitute the *RS* latch. The location of inputs $S1$ and $R1$ is not the same as in Fig. 8.1 (a). This is to offset the inversion due to NAND gates 1 and 2. The operation of the NAND latch portion of the circuit has been summarized in Table 8.4.

Table 8.4

Input		*Output*		*Comment*
S1	***R1***	***Q***	$\overline{Q}$	
0	0	1	1	Invalid
0	1	0	1	
1	0	1	0	
1	1	X	$\overline{X}$	

This table looks different from Table 8.2 only because the positions of inputs $S1$ and $R1$ have been reversed, but there is no change in the mode of operation.

When CLK is low, the outputs of gates 1 and 2 go high and so there will be no change in the output of the NAND latch. Gates 1 and 2 are enabled only when CLK goes high. Table 8.5 summarises the output of the clocked RS latch for various input conditions.

Table 8.5 Truth table for clocked *RS* latch

Mode of operation	*Clock*	*Input*		*Output*
		S	***R***	***Q***
		X	$\overline{X}$	No change
Hold	0 ⎍	0	0	No change
Reset	⎍	0	1	0
Set	⎍	1	0	1
Invalid	⎍	1	1	$Q = \overline{Q} = 1$

The timing pattern for a clocked RS latch, based on Table 8.5 is shown in Fig. 8.9 for all the input combinations. Check the output waveforms with the input values given in the diagram.

This clocked latch responds only to positive clock signals and this clocking is, therefore, referred to as positive clocking. If an inverter is introduced between the clock and the input to the NAND gates, the NAND gates will be enabled only when the clock goes low. This is an example of negative clocking. We refer to both these as level clocking.

8.5.1 *RS* Flip-Flop (Toggle Mode)

If an RS flip-flop is connected as in Fig. 8.10 (a), the output will keep complementing itself in the presence of clock signals. The flip-flop shown in the diagram complements or toggles the output at the trailing edge of every clock pulse. The bubble at the clock input indicates that it responds to a low going clock signal.

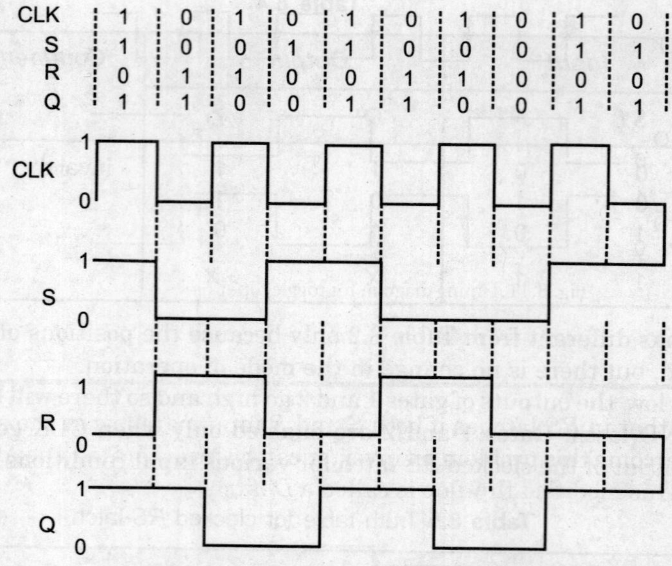

Fig. 8.9 Timing diagram for clocked *RS* latch

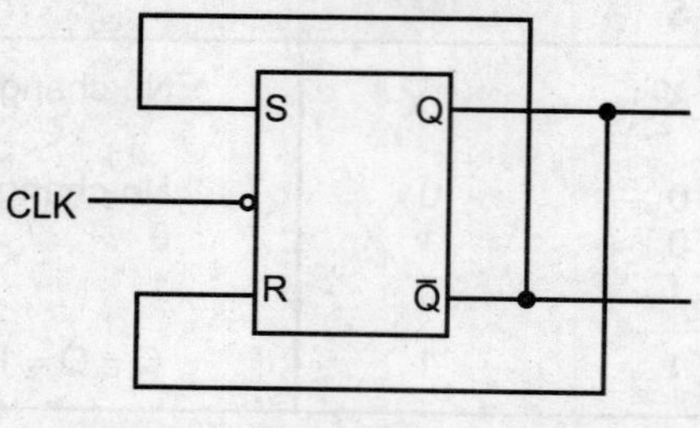

Fig. 8.10 (a) *RS* flip-flop wired in the toggle mode

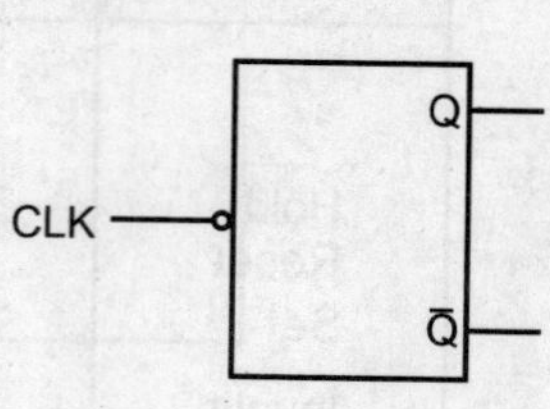

Fig. 8.10(b) Symbol for toggle flip-flop

Let us now look at the following sequence of operations of this flip-flop:

	Q	$\overline{Q}$	R	S
1. Initial state	1	0	1	0
2. After 1st clock pulse	0	1	0	1
3. After 2nd clock pulse	1	0	1	0
4. After 3rd clock pulse	0	1	0	1

You will notice from this table that to start with Q was 1 and R was 1. Therefore, after the trailing edge of the first clock pulse, the flip-flop was reset, Q became 0 and S became 1, and at the trailing edge of the second clock pulse the flip-flop was again set. This will go on as long as the clock pulses are applied.

The output waveform for this toggle flip-flop is shown in Fig. 8.11. You will observe that there is a change of state in the Q and $\overline{Q}$ outputs at every trailing edge of a clock pulse. You will also observe that for every two cycles of the clock pulse the Q output goes through only one cycle. In effect the output frequency is reduced by half. If a number of toggle flip-flops are cascaded, the output frequency can be reduced substantially.

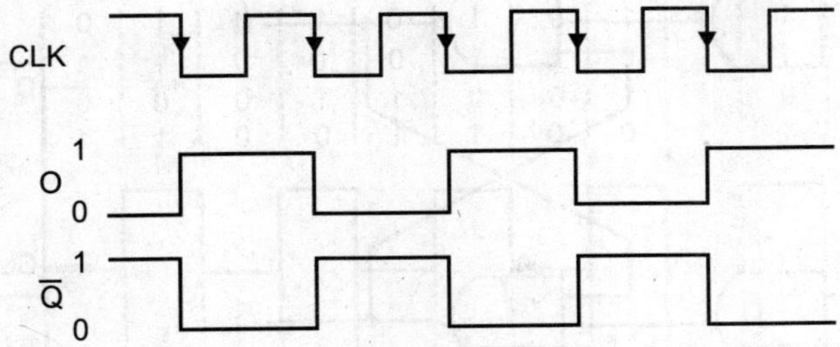

Fig. 8.11 Timing diagram for toggle flip–flop

8.6 *D* LATCH

You must have noticed that in *RS* latches if both *S* and *R* inputs are low at the same time, the output is invalid. To overcome this problem an inverter can be incorporated ahead of the *S* input as shown in Fig. 8.12. This modified flip-flop is called a *D* latch.

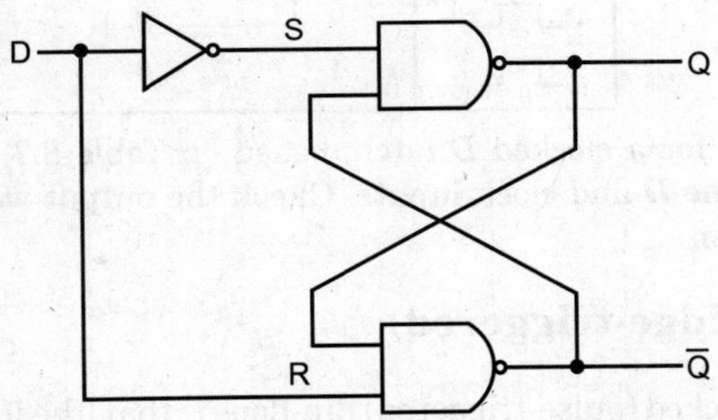

Fig. 8.12 *D* latch

The input at *D* drives the *R* input of the NAND latch and its complement drives the *S* input. When the input at *D* is 1, the *S* input is 0 and this sets the latch. When the *D* input is 0, the input at *R* is also 0 and this resets the latch. Since the *S* and *R* inputs are always in opposite states, the invalid state does not occur. The operation of the *D* latch has been summarized in Table 8.6.

Table 8.6 Truth table for D latch

Input	Output	
D	*Q*	$\overline{Q}$
0	0	1
1	1	0

8.6.1 Clocked *D* Latch

A clocked *D* latch is very similar to an *RS* latch and, besides, it does not produce an invalid state. A circuit for a clocked *D* latch is given in Fig. 8.13 and its symbol in Fig. 8.14. The truth table for this latch is in Table 8.7.

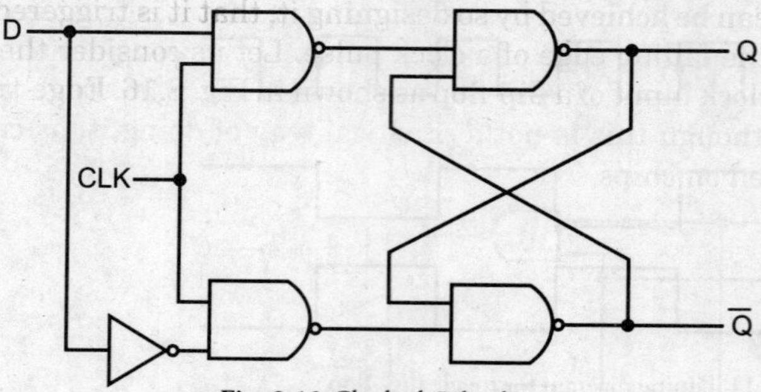

Fig. 8.13 Clocked *D* latch

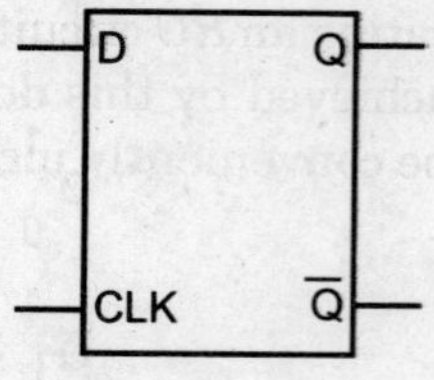

Fig. 8.14 Symbol for clocked *D* latch

Table 8.7 Truth table for clocked *D* latch

Clock	*Input*	*Output*
	D	***Q***
	X	No change
	0	0
	1	1

The timing diagram for a clocked *D* latch, based on Table 8.7 is given in Fig. 8.15 for various combinations of the *D* and clock inputs. Check the output waveforms with the input values given in the diagram.

3.6.2 *D* Flip-flop (Edge-triggered)

A disadvantage of level-clocked (pulse-triggered) flip-flops is that, the input to the flip-flop has to be held constant as long as the clock is active. If the input keeps changing while the clock is active, the output will also keep changing and this is obviously undesirable.

CLK	1	1	0	0	1	1	0	0	1	1
D	0	1	1	0	1	0	0	1	1	0
Q	0	1	1	1	1	0	0	0	1	0

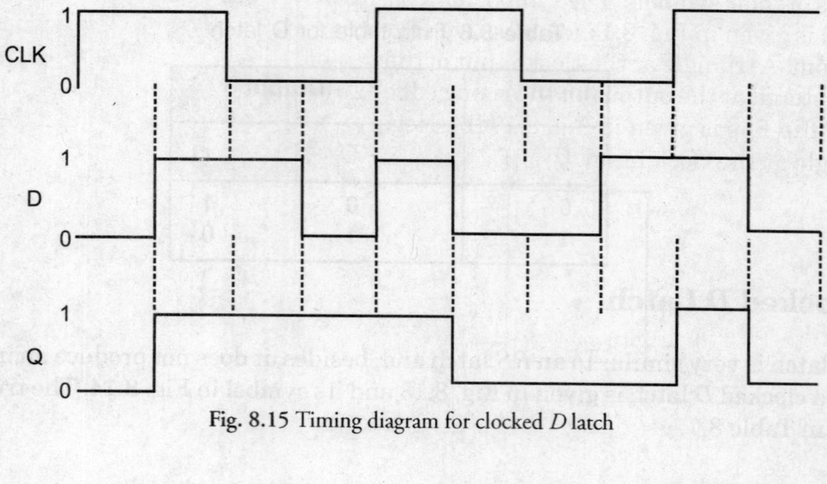

Fig. 8.15 Timing diagram for clocked *D* latch

Edge-triggering of a flip-flop can be achieved by so designing it, that it is triggered only for an instant either by the rising or the falling edge of a clock pulse. Let us consider the effect of incorporating an *RC* circuit at the clock input of a flip-flop as shown in Fig. 8.16. Edge-triggering can be achieved by this device, although this is not a practical way of doing it, as capacitors cannot be conveniently incorporated on chips.

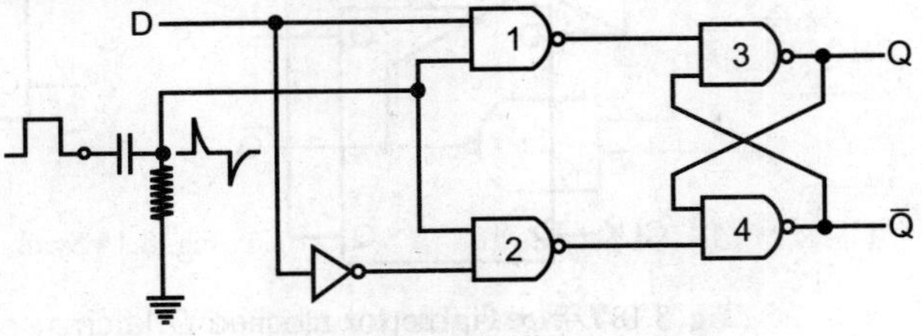

Fig. 8.16 *D* Flip–flop (Edge-triggered)

If the *RC* time constant is much smaller than the width of the clock pulse, the capacitor will get charged rapidly when the clock signal goes high and discharge equally rapidly when the clock signal goes low. Thus the leading edge of the clock pulse will produce a narrow positive voltage spike across the resistor and the trailing edge of the clock pulse will produce a narrow negative spike.

NAND gates 1 and 2 will be enabled by the positive voltage spike and the negative voltage spike will have no effect on the operation of the flip-flop. The input signal at *D* will be sampled by the flip-flop for only a small fraction of the time, during which the clock pulse is high. The important point to note is that change in the output of the flip-flop will occur only on the rising edge of the clock pulse. Thus the flip-flop will be set or reset depending on the nature of the input signal at *D*. This is an example of positive edge-triggering, as triggering takes place on the positive edge of the clock pulse, which is also the leading edge.

The important distinction between edge-triggering and pulse-triggering (level-clocking) is that, with pulse triggering the output can change as long as the clock is active (high or low), that is during an entire half cycle. On the other hand with edge-triggering the output can change only during the rising or falling edge of a clock pulse, and that too only at one point in time of the clock cycle.

We have considered a very simple device to explain edge-triggering but, as stated earlier, it is not practical to incorporate capacitors on chips. However, many edge-triggered circuits have been developed and edge-triggered flip-flops are commercially available.

As there are many types of flip-flops, it will be useful to acquire familiarity with the distinctive features of their symbols. The symbol for a positive edge-triggered *D* flip-flop (logic diagram in Fig. 8.16) is given in Fig. 8.17 (a). Positive edge-triggering is indicated by a small triangle at the clock input. A triangle at the clock input of the symbol should also remind you that the input at *D* will be stored at the output on the rising edge of the clock pulse. A symbol for negative edge-triggered *D* flip-flop is given in Fig. 8.17 (b). Negative edge- triggering is indicated by a bubble and a triangle at the clock input.

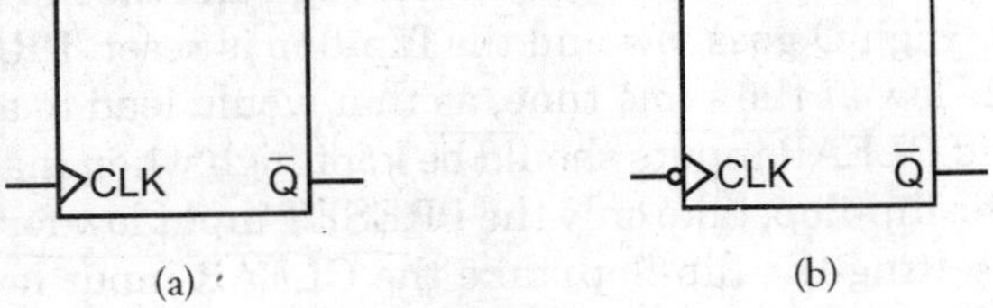

(a) (b)

Fig. 8.17

8.6.3 *D* Flip-flop (Toggle Mode)

The *D*-type flip-flop can also be used in the toggle mode, if it is connected as shown in Fig. 8.18.

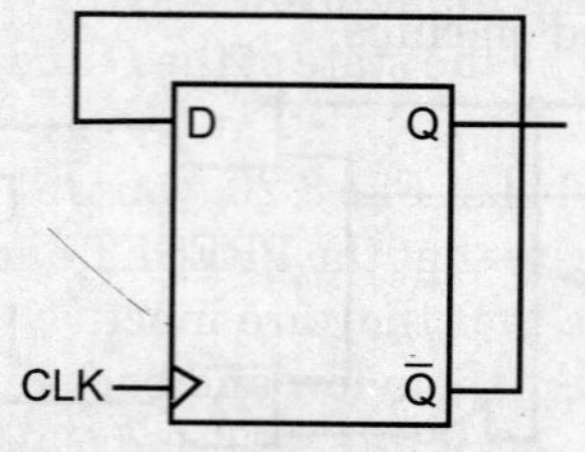

Fig. 8.18 *D*-type flip–flop (toggle mode)

8.6.4 Preset and Clear Functions

If we have to set or reset the flip-flop, we have considered so far, we have to use the inputs to the flip-flops. Since computers have a large number of flip-flops, it would be very inconvenient to set or reset each flip-flop independently. As flip-flops may come up in random states when power is switched on, it is necessary to use some method, whereby all flip-flops can be set or reset at the same time by a single switch. This is achieved by incorporating PRESET and CLEAR inputs in flip-flops which can override all other inputs.

A circuit incorporating PRESET, abbreviated as PR (same as set) and CLEAR, abbreviated as CLR (same as reset) inputs in a clocked *D* flip-flop is shown in Fig. 8.19(a). It is, however, not uncommon to use abbreviations SD (set direct) in place of PR and CD (clear direct) in place of CLR. The symbol for this flip-flop is shown in Fig. 8.19(b).

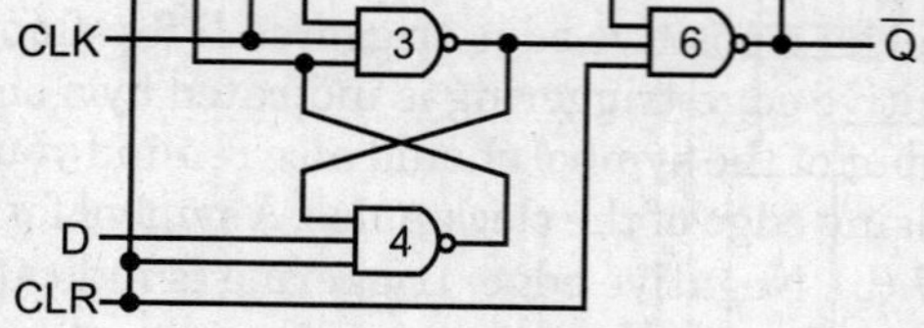

Fig. 8.19 (a) *D* flip–flop with PRESET and CLEAR inputs

Fig. 8.19 (b) Symbol for flip–flop of Fig. 8.19 (a)

When PRESET is low and CLEAR is high, *Q* goes high and the flip-flop is set. When CLEAR goes low and PRESET is high *Q* goes low and the flip-flop is reset. PRESET and CLEAR functions should not be made low at the same time, as that would lead to an invalid state. For this reason both PRESET and CLEAR inputs should be kept high when inactive.

If you have to set the flip-flop, take only the PRESET input low for a while and then return it to high. If you are resetting the flip-flop, take the CLEAR input low temporarily and then return it to high. Remember that unless the PRESET and CLEAR inputs are restored to high after presenting and clearing operations, the circuit will not operate.

The PRESET and CLEAR inputs have first priority and override all other inputs. For instance, if you have taken the CLEAR input to low and the flip-flop is thus reset, this reset state of the flip-flop will not be influenced by the state of the *D* and CLK inputs, as long as the CLEAR input stays low.

If you refer to the flip-flop symbol in Fig. 8.20, you will notice bubbles at the PRESET and CLEAR inputs. These bubbles indicate that the PRESET and CLEAR inputs have an active low state. In other words, it also means that they are inactive when high. To activate the CLEAR and PRESET inputs, you have to take them low and back high again.

The truth table for a *D* flip-flop with PRESET and CLEAR inputs is given in Table 8.8.

Table 8.8 Truth table for *D* flip–flop with PRESET and CLEAR inputs

Input				Output		
PR	*CLR*	*CLK*	*D*	*Q*	$\bar{Q}$	
0	1	X	X	1	0	
1	0	X	X	0	1	
0	0	X	X	1	1	Invalid
1	1	↑	1	1	0	
1	1	↑	0	0	1	

You will notice from the first three rows of this table that the output is determined by the asynchronous inputs and that the CLK and *D* inputs are ineffective. In the last two rows, when the asynchronous inputs have been disabled, the output is dependent on the synchronous input *D* and CLK so that the *Q* output follows the *D* input when the positive going edge of the clock pulse arrives.

Figure 8.20 gives the pin connections for TTL IC 7474, which is a dual *D*-type positive edge-triggered flip-flop.

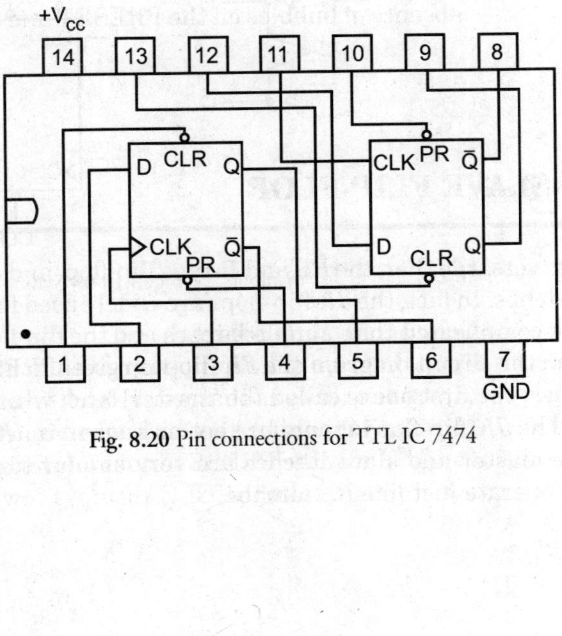

Fig. 8.20 Pin connections for TTL IC 7474

8.6.5 Symbols for *D*-type Flip-Flops

While on the subject of flip-flop symbols, have a look at Figs. 8.21, 8.22 and 8.23 for symbols of different types of flip-flops. These symbols are used here only to illustrate how flip-flop symbols should be interpreted.

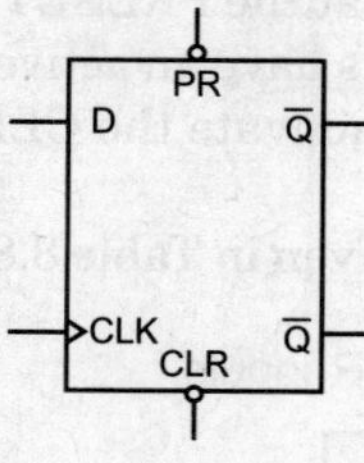

Fig. 8.21

Shows a symbol for positive edge-triggered *D* type flip-flop which responds to a rising clock edge with PRESET and CLEAR inputs which are active low. Notice the bubbles on the PR and CLR inputs.

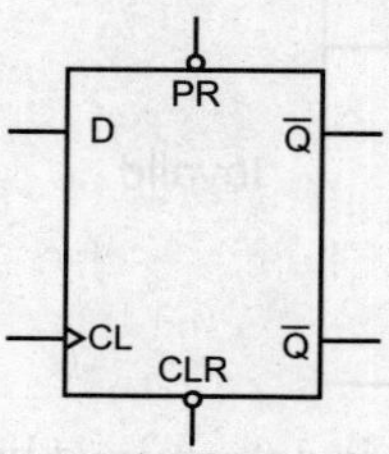

Fig. 8.22

Shows a symbol for negative edge-triggered *D*-type flip-flop which responds to a falling clock edge. Notice the bubble on the clock input. PRESET and CLEAR inputs are active low.

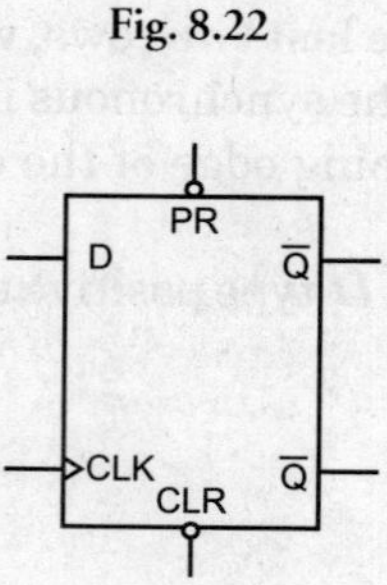

Fig. 8.23

Shows a symbol for level-sensitive *D*-type flip-flop which is enabled when clock is low. Notice the bubble on the clock input. The PRESET and CLEAR inputs are active high. Notice the absence of bubbles on the PRESET and CLEAR inputs.

8.7 *JK* MASTER-SLAVE FLIP-FLOP

JK flip-flops are far more versatile than the *RS* and *D*-type flip-flop, and can perform many more functions than simple latches. In fact, the *JK* flip-flops are widely used for storage of binary data and are, therefore, more complicated than simple latches.

As you will see from the circuit diagram of a *JK* flip-flop given in Fig. 8.24, it is a combination of two clocked latches, the first one is called the 'master' latch which feeds the second one, called the 'slave' latch. The *JK* flip-flop is therefore better known as *JK* master-slave flip-flop. You will notice that the master and slave latches are very similar to the *RS* latch shown in Fig. 8.8 (a). In fact they operate just like *RS* latches.

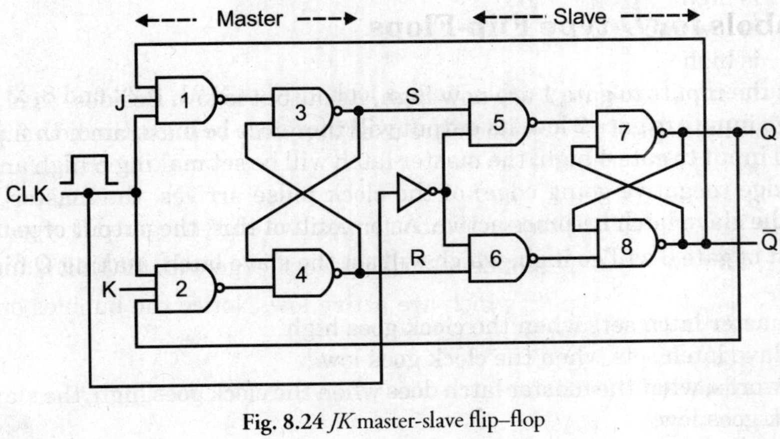

Fig. 8.24 *JK* master-slave flip–flop

The *JK* flip-flop shown in Fig. 8.24 is level-clocked and therefore the master latch is active when the clock is high. If changes occur in the *JK* inputs as long as the clock is high, this may affect the state of the flip-flop. This makes it necessary to keep the *J* and *K* inputs constant as long as the clock is high. To overcome this, edge-triggering of *JK* flip-flop has become common.

The master latch comprises of gates 3 and 4 and the input to the latch is controlled by gates 1 and 2, which, as you will see from the diagram, are positively clocked. The slave latch comprises of gates 7 and 8. It gets its input from the output of the master latch; but the transfer of the state of the master latch to the slave latch is controlled by gates 5 and 6, which are negatively clocked. When the clock signal goes negative, gates 5 and 6 are enabled because of the inverter and thus the output of the master latch is transferred to the slave latch. The output of the slave latch determines the output of the *JK* flip-flop. This arrangement of the clocking of the two latches leads to the following conclusions:

1. When the clock goes high, gates 1 and 2 will be enabled and so the master latch will become active. At the same time the output of the inverter will inhibit gates 5 and 6, as a result of which the slave latch will be disabled. In short when the master latch is active the slave latch in inactive.
2. When the clock goes low, gates 1 and 2 will be inhibited and so the master latch will be inactive. At the same time, the output of the inverter will enable gates 5 and 6, as a result of which the slave latch will become active. In short when the master latch is inactive the slave latch is active.

We can now consider the output states of the *JK* flip-flop for various combinations of inputs at *J* and *K*. The operation of the flip-flop can be said to have four modes—set, reset, toggle and the inhibit mode. We will consider these one by one.

1. Set Mode

We will assume that when the flip-flop is switched on it comes up in the reset mode, that is when

$$Q = 0 \quad \text{and}$$

$$\overline{Q} = 1$$

You will notice from Fig. 8.24 that output $\overline{Q}$ is coupled to one of the inputs of gate 1 and Q is coupled to one of the inputs of gate 2. We will now consider the output of the flip-flop when

J	is high
K	is low and
CLOCK	is high

Since all the inputs to gate 1 are now high, its output is low. Besides, as *K* and *Q* are low, this makes two inputs to gate 2 low, its output will therefore be high. Since this makes input to gate 3 low and input to gate 4 high; the master latch will be set making *S* high and *R* low. When the trailing edge (negative-going edge) of the clock pulse arrives, the master latch becomes inactive and the slave latch becomes active. As a result of this, the output of gate 5 will go low and the output of gate 6 will go high, which will set the slave latch, making *Q* high and $\overline{Q}$ low. Summing up

1. The master latch sets when the clock goes high.
2. The slave latch sets when the clock goes low.

In other words, what the master latch does when the clock goes high, the slave latch copies when the clock goes low.

2. Reset mode

We will now consider the output state of the flip-flop when the input and output are as follows:

Q	is high : $\overline{Q}$ is low (the flip-flop is set)
J	is low : K is high
CLOCK	is high

In this situation, as two inputs to gate 1 will be low, its output will be high and the output of gate 2 will be low. This will reset the master latch making *S* low and *R* high. When the clock goes low the slave latch will also be reset making *Q* low and $\overline{Q}$ high.

3. Toggle mode

If both *J* and *K* inputs are held high, the output of the master latch will be dependent on outputs Q and $\overline{Q}$. If the slave latch is set, that is when *Q* is high and $\overline{Q}$ low, the master latch will be reset when the clock goes high. When the trailing edge of the clock pulse arrives, the slave latch will also be reset, that is *Q* goes low and $\overline{Q}$ high. When the clock goes high again, the master latch will be set and this will set the slave latch when the clock goes low. The flip-flop will complement itself each time the clock switches from high to low. The flip-flop is said to toggle. The following output waveform of the flip-flop, shown in Fig. 8.25, shows the toggling state when the *J* and *K* inputs are held high.

From this waveform you will notice a very important relationship between the frequency of the clock and the output frequency. The output has a frequency which is half of the clock frequency. Thus when the flip-flop toggles, it divides the clock frequency by two. If the clock frequency is 100, the output frequency will be 50. If you use *n* flip-flops in cascade, the output frequency will be $f/2^n$ where *f* is the clock frequency.

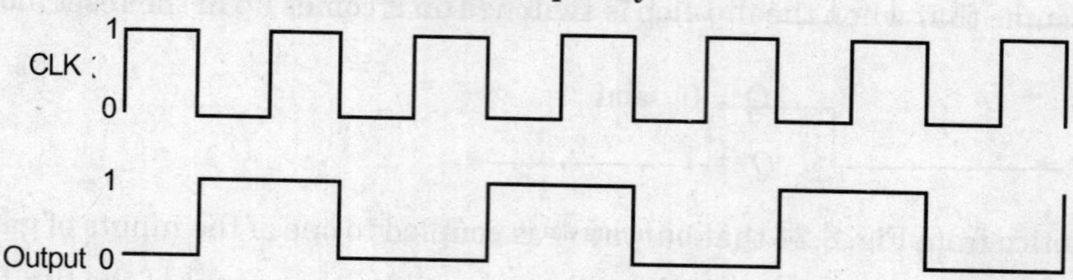

Fig. 8.25

4. Inhibit mode

When both J and K inputs are low, there will be no change in the output state of the flip-flop, even if the clock keeps changing all the time form high to low and low to high.

The four modes of operation have been summed up in Table 8.9. The table shows the state of the Q output prior to the arrival of the clock pulse (t) and at the end of one clock pulse ($t + 1$). X represents both the set and reset states.

Table 8.9 Truth table for *JK* flip–flop

Input		Output	
J	*K*	*Before clock pulse Q(t)*	*After clock pulse Q(t + 1)*
0	0	X	X No change
0	1	X	0
1	0	X	1
1	1	X	$\overline{X}$ Toggle

To sum up the operation of the flip-flop, if you have to reset the flip-flop, apply the following inputs:

$$J = 0$$
$$K = 1$$

and thereafter apply a clock pulse which will reset the flip-flop on the trailing edge.

To set the flip-flop apply the following inputs:

$$J = 1$$
$$K = 0$$

and then apply a clock pulse which will set the flip-flop on its trailing edge.

If you want the flip-flop to toggle, keep both J and K high and apply clock signals. If you have to inhibit the flip-flop keep both J and K inputs low.

The timing diagram for a *JK* flip-flop is given in Fig. 8.26. It has been assumed in the following discussion that the output of the flip-flop is low before the application of clock pulses.

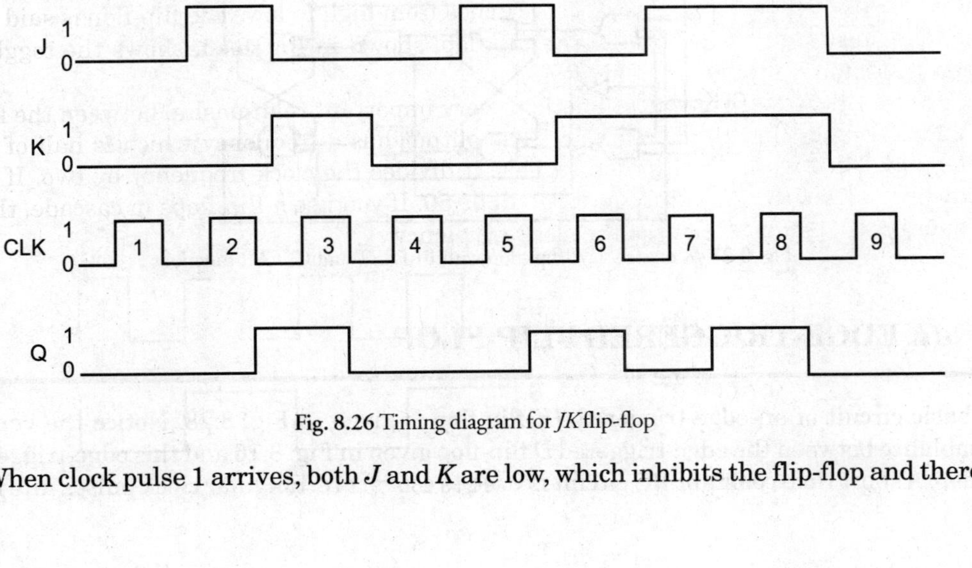

Fig. 8.26 Timing diagram for *JK* flip-flop

When clock pulse 1 arrives, both J and K are low, which inhibits the flip-flop and therefore no change takes place in its output. When pulse 2 arrives, *J* is high and *K* is low, and therefore on its trailing edge the flip-flop sets. When pulse 3 occurs *J* is low and *K* is high, and so the flip-flop resets on the trailing edge of the pulse. As *J* and *K* are both low when pulse 4 arrives, the flip-flop is inhibited and it remains in the reset state. On the arrival of pulse 5, *J* is high and *K* is low and so the flip-flop sets on its trailing edge. Pulse 6 finds *J* low and *K* high, which resets the flip-flop. Both *J* and *K* are high when pulse 7 arrives, and so the flip-flop toggles into the set state on the trailing edge. It toggles back into the reset state on the trailing edge of pulse 8. When pulse 9 arrives, both *J* and *K* are low, which inhibits the flip-flop and therefore it remains in the reset state.

PRESET and CLEAR functions can be incorporated in a *JK* master-slave flip-flop as shown in Fig. 8.27. Truth table for this flip-flop having PR and CLR functions is given in Table 8.10.

Table 8.10 Truth table for *JK* master-slave flip-flop having PRESET and CLEAR functions

Input					*Outputs*
Asynchronous		*Synchronous*			
PR	*CLR*	*CLK*	*J*	*K*	*Q*
0	0	*X*	*X*	*X*	Invalid
0	1	*X*	*X*	*X*	1
1	0	*X*	*X*	*X*	0
1	1	*X*	0	0	No change
1	1	⎍	0	1	0
1	1	⎍	1	0	1
1	1	⎍	1	1	Toggle

While the PR and CLR inputs are active, the synchronous inputs have no effect on the output. They are effective only when the PR and CLR inputs are held high.

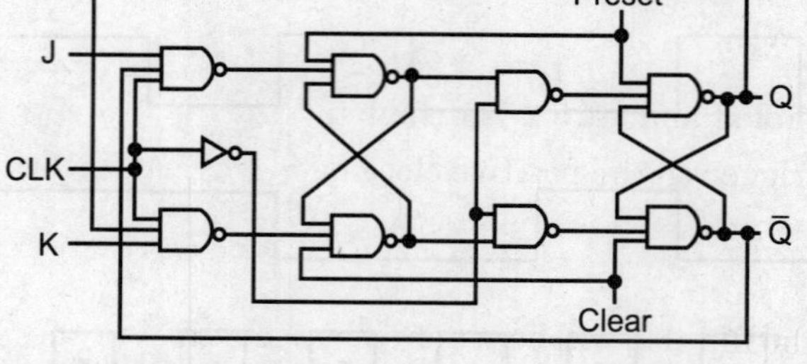

Fig. 8.27 *JK* master-slave flip–flop with PRESET and CLEAR functions

8.8 *JK* EDGE-TRIGGERED FLIP-FLOP

The basic circuit of an edge-triggered *JK* flip-flop is given in Fig. 8.28. Notice the very close resemblance between the edge-triggered *D* flip-flop given in Fig. 8.16 and this edge-triggered *JK* flip-flop. A short time constant RC circuit is used to convert rectangular clock pulses into narrow spikes, although this is not a convenient arrangement for use in IC devices. Many circuits have been developed which are suitable for fabrication on chips.

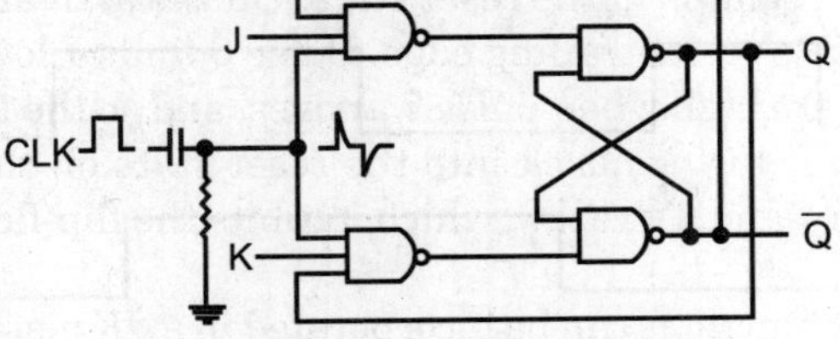

Fig. 8.28 Edge-triggered *JK* flip-flop

The circuit is triggered by the positive clock edge, which enables the inputs gates. The operation of the circuit has been summarised in Table 8.11.

Table 8.11

Inputs			*Outputs*
CLK	*J*	*K*	*Q*
X	0	0	No change
↑	0	1	0
↑	1	0	1
↑	1	1	Toggle

We will now look into the various modes of operation of this flip-flop:

1. $J = 0$
   $K = 1$

Since the upper gate 1 is disabled, the flip-flop cannot to set. However, it can be reset. If $Q = 1$ and $\overline{Q} = 0$, gate 2 is enabled and when the positive clock edge arrives gate 2 passes a reset trigger which resets the flip-flop.

2. $J = 1$
   $K = 0$

Now gate 1 is enabled and gate 2 is disabled. When $Q = 0$ and $\overline{Q} = 1$, gate 1, which is enabled, passes a set trigger on the positive clock edge which sets the flip-flop.

3. $J = 1$
   $K = 1$

In this situation the flip-flop will be set or reset depending on the state of the output. When Q is low, gate 1 passes a set trigger on the arrival of the positive clock edge. The opposite happens when Q is high. The flip-flop will complement itself on every positive clock edge.

Figure 8.29 shows the timing diagram for a positive edge-triggered *JK* flip-flop.

IC 7476 is a positive edge-triggered dual *JK* flip-flop, which also incorporates PRESET and CLEAR functions. Figure 8.30 gives the pin connections for this TTL IC.

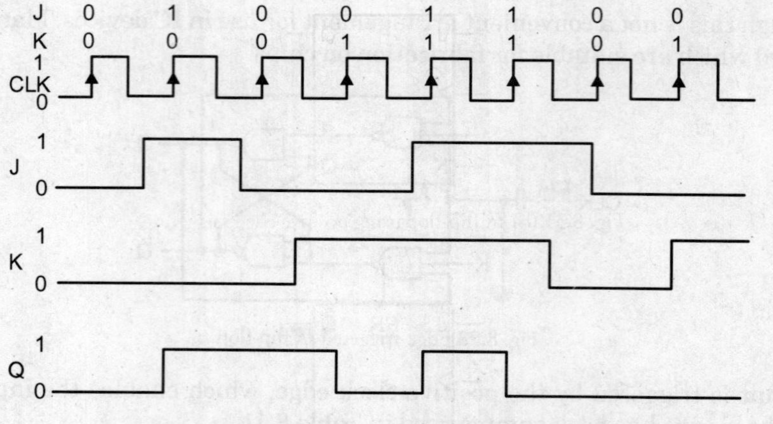

Fig. 8.29 Timing diagram for positive edge-triggered *JK* flip-flop

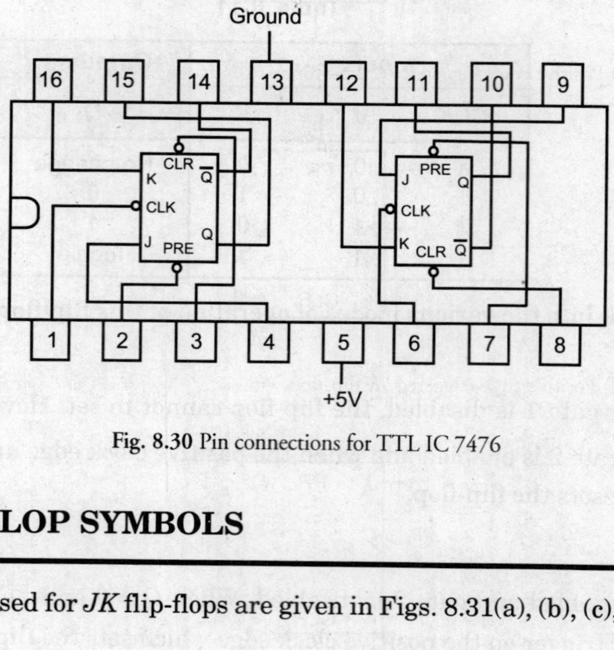

Fig. 8.30 Pin connections for TTL IC 7476

8.9 *JK* FLIP–FLOP SYMBOLS

Symbols commonly used for *JK* flip-flops are given in Figs. 8.31(a), (b), (c), (d) and (e).

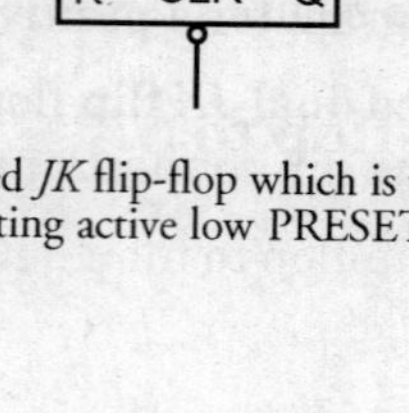

Fig. 8.31 (a) Level-clocked *JK* flip-flop which is triggered when the clock goes low, also incorporating active low PRESET and CLEAR controls

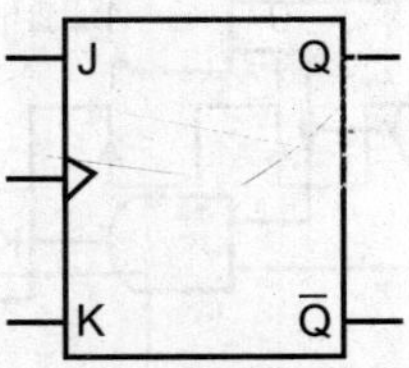

Fig. 8.31 (b) *JK* flip-flop using positive edge-triggering

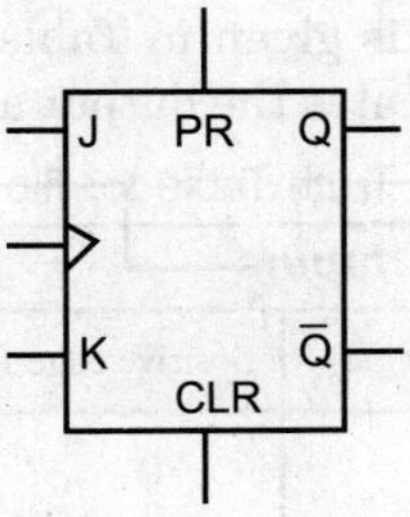

Fig. 8.31(c) Positive edge-triggered *JK* flip–flop with active high Preset and Clear controls

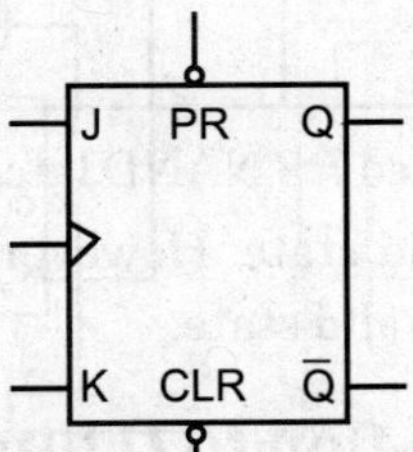

Fig. 8.31(d) Positive edge-triggered *JK* flip-flop with active low Preset and Clear controls

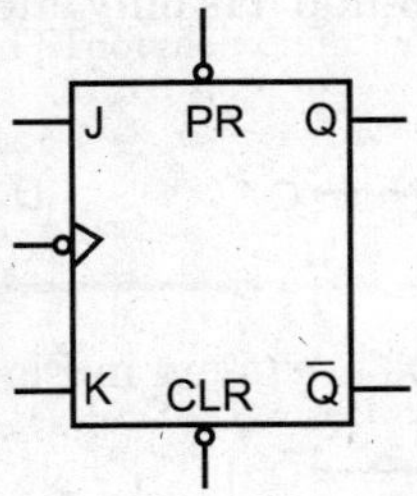

Fig. 8.31 (e) Negative edge-triggered *JK* flip-flop with active low Preset and Clear controls

8.10 CONVERTING *JK* FLIP-FLOP TO OTHER TYPES

With minor changes the *JK* flip-flop can be used to perform as an *SR*, *D* and *T* type flip-flops.

8.10.1 Conversion of *JK* flip-flop to *SR* flip-flop

A circuit diagram which enables a *JK* flip-flop to function as an *SR* flip-flop is given in Fig. 8.32.

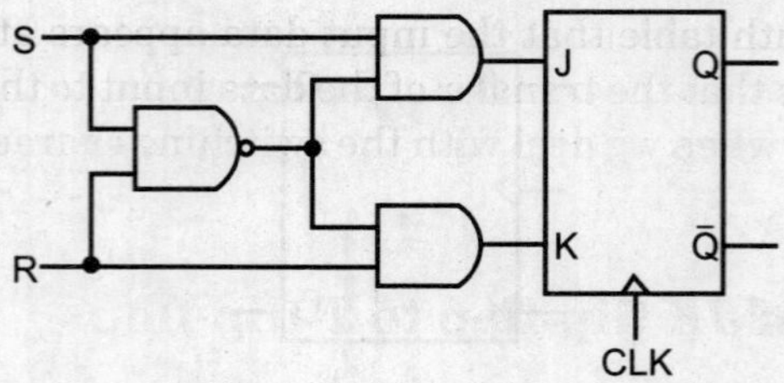

Fig. 8.32 Conversion of a *JK* flip-flop into an *SR* flip–flop

The truth table for this flip-flop is given in Table 8.12. In this table Q_n represents the output as it is at present and Q_{n+1} indicates the output are clock period later.

Table 8.12 Truth Table for flip-flop of Fig. 8.32

Inputs		***Outputs***
S	***R***	***Q_n+1***
0	0	Q_n
0	1	0
1	0	1
1	1	Q_n

If you refer to Table 8.5 for a clocked *RS* NAND latch, you will notice that when both S and R are 1, $Q = \overline{Q} = 1$; which is an invalid state. However, in the case of this flip-flop the state remains unchanged and there is no invalid state.

8.10.2 Conversion of *JK* flip-flop to *D* flip-flop

A *JK* flip-flop can perform as a *D* flip-flop by the arrangement shown in Fig. 8.33 (a). Its logic symbol is given in Fig. 8.33(b). This flip-flop has only one input *D* (data input).

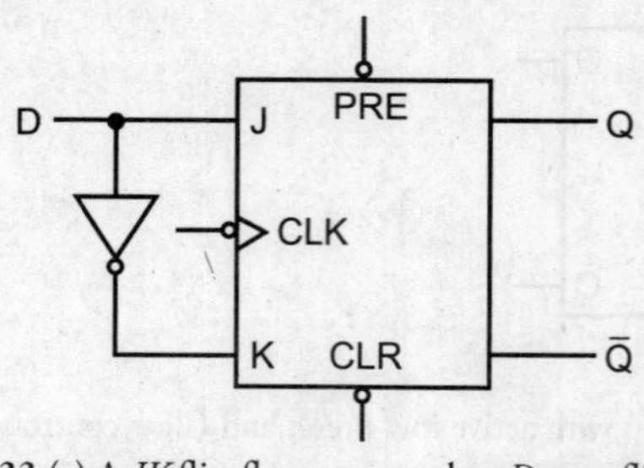

Fig. 8.33 (a) A *JK* flip-flop converted to *D*-type flip–flop

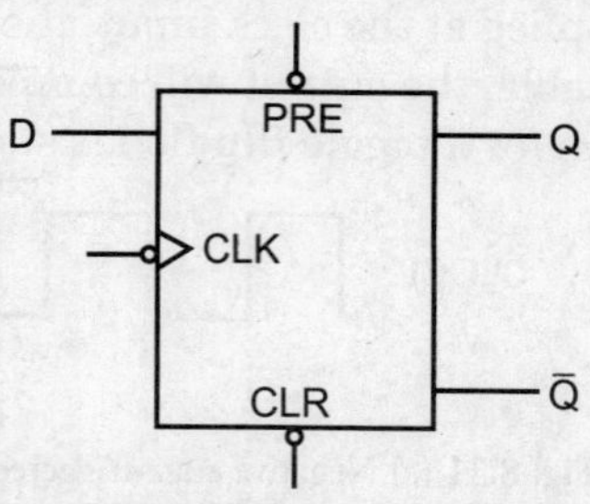

Fig. 8.33 (b) Symbols for flip–flop of Fig. 8.33 (a)

The truth table for this *D*-type flip-flop is given in Table 8.13, which shows that the output after the clock pulse $Q_n + 1$ is equal to the input D_n before the clock pulse.

Table 8.13 Truth table for flip–flop of Fig. 8.33 (a)

Input	***Output***
D_n	Q_{n+1}
0	0
1	1

It is clear from the truth table that the input data appears at the output after the clock, which in other words means that the transfer of the data input to the output is delayed. We will consider the aspect of delay when we deal with the switching characteristics of flip-flops a little later.

8.10.3 Conversion of *JK* flip-flop to *T* flip-flop

If the *J* and *K* inputs of a *JK* flip-flop are connected together, this results in a *T*-type flip-flop as shown in Fig. 8.34 (a) and its symbol is given in Fig. 8.34 (b). This flip-flop has only one input called the *T* input. The truth table for this flip-flop is given in Table 8.14.

Table 8.14 Truth table for *T*-type flip-flop

Input	*Output*
T_n	Q_{n+1}
0	Q_n
1	$\overline{Q}_n$

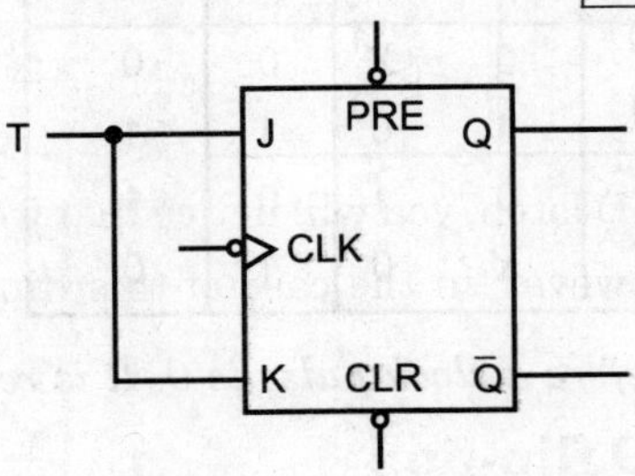

Fig. 8.34 (a) A *JK* flip-flop converted to *T*-type flip-flop

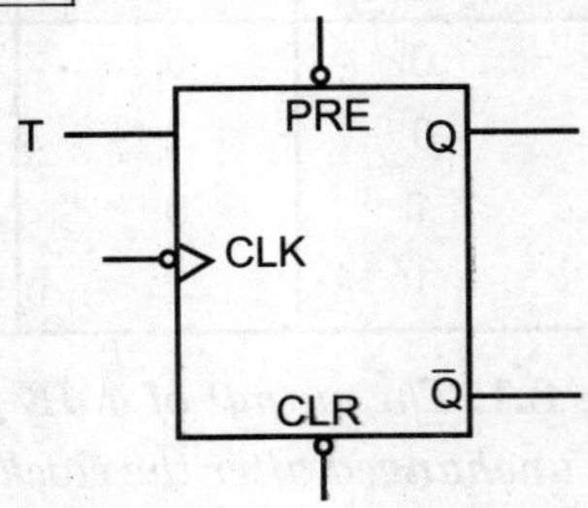

Fig. 8.34 (b) Symbol for *T*-type flip-flop

In a *JK* flip-flop wired as a *T*-type flip-flop, the *J* and *K* inputs are held high and when clock pulses are applied at the clock input, the flip-flop will simply toggle. As shown in the second row of the truth table, the output will complement itself every time the clock goes from high to low. The waveform for a toggle flip-flop is shown in Fig. 8.35.

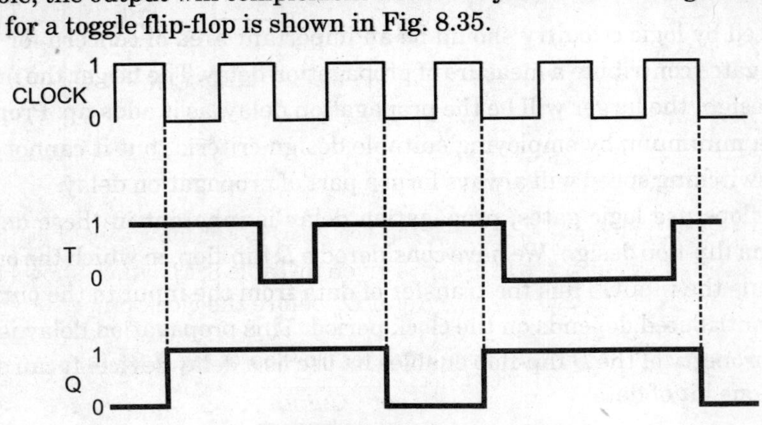

Fig. 8.35 Waveform for toggle flip-flop

8.11 EXCITATION OF FLIP-FLOPS

In designing sequential circuits, we have to deal with the 'present state' and the 'next state' of the circuit, as these are specified. Sequential circuits are implemented with flip-flops and we, therefore, have to determine the input conditions of flip-flops to achieve the desired transition from the present to the next state, that is before and after the clock pulse. In working out the proper input conditions, a tabulation of the input and output states, referred to as the excitation table (or the characteristic table) is very useful. The excitation table for *JK*, *SR*, *D* and *T* flip-flops is given in Table 8.15.

Table 8.15 Excitation table of flip-flops

Present state	*Next state*	*Flip-flops*					
		JK		*SR*		*D*	*T*
		J	*K*	*S*	*R*	D_n	T_n
0	0	0	*X*	0	*X*	0	0
0	1	1	*X*	1	0	1	1
1	0	*X*	1	0	1	0	1
1	1	*X*	0	*X*	0	1	0

Example 8.1: *The output of a JK flip-flop before a clock pulse is 0. It is required that it should remain unchanged after the clock pulse.*

Solution: It is seen from the excitation table that when $J = 0$ and $K = X$, the output is 0. It follows, therefore, that J has to be 0 and K may be 0 or 1.

8.12 SWITCHING CHARACTERISTICS

Delay contributed by logic circuitry should be an important area of concern for the circuit designer. All logic gates contribute a measure of propagation delay. The larger the number of gates in any circuit design, the larger will be the propagation delay, as it adds up. Propagation delay can be kept to a minimum, by employing suitable design criteria, but it cannot be completely eliminated, as switching speed will always form a part of propagation delay.

Since flip-flops use logic gates, propagation delay is inherent in these devices and will depend largely on flip-flop design. We have considered a *D* flip-flop, in which the output after the clock pulse equals the input. Thus the transfer of data from the input to the output is delayed and the delay contributed depends on the clock period. This propagation delay is illustrated in Fig. 8.36. This property of the *D* flip-flop enables its use as a delay device. It can also be used as a latch to store one bit of data.

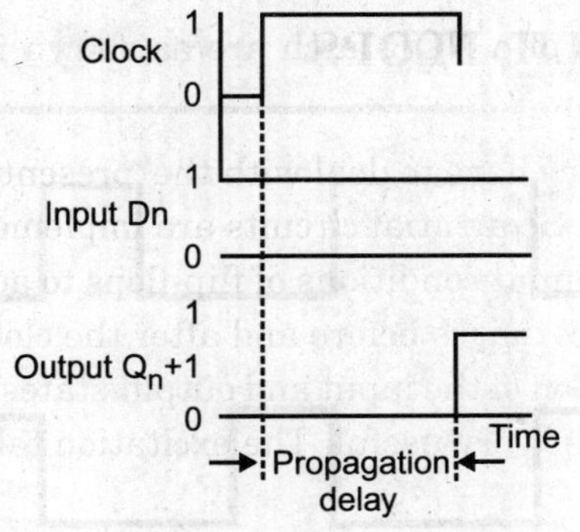

Fig. 8.36 Propagation delay in a flip-flop

Problems

8.1 What will be the state of the output of a NAND latch in the following cases?

(*a*) $S = 0; R = 1$ (*b*) $S = 0; R = 0$

(*c*) $S = 1; R = 1$ (*d*) $S = 1; R = 0$

8.2 In a NAND latch the following changes occur in the S and R inputs in the following order: What will be the state of the latch at each step?

(*a*) $S = 0; R = 1$ (*b*) $S = 1; R = 1$ (*c*) $S = 0; R = 1$ (*d*) $S = 1; R = 1$

8.3 The S and R input of a NAND latch are as given in Fig. P-8.3. Draw the output waveform.

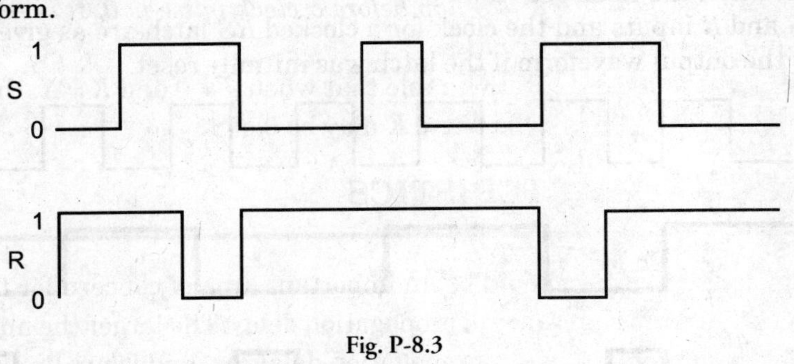

Fig. P-8.3

8.4 Both inputs to a NAND latch are low to begin with and first the R input goes high and shortly afterwards S also goes high. What is the state of the latch?

8.5 What will be the state of the output of a NOR latch in the following cases?

(*a*) $S = 1; R = 1$ (*b*) $S = 0; R = 1$

(*c*) $S = 0; R = 0$ (*d*) $S = 1; R = 0$

8.6 Both inputs to a NOR latch are low, then R goes high and shortly thereafter R goes low. What is the state of the output?

8.7 The S and R inputs of a NOR latch are as shown in Fig. P-8.7. Draw the output waveform.

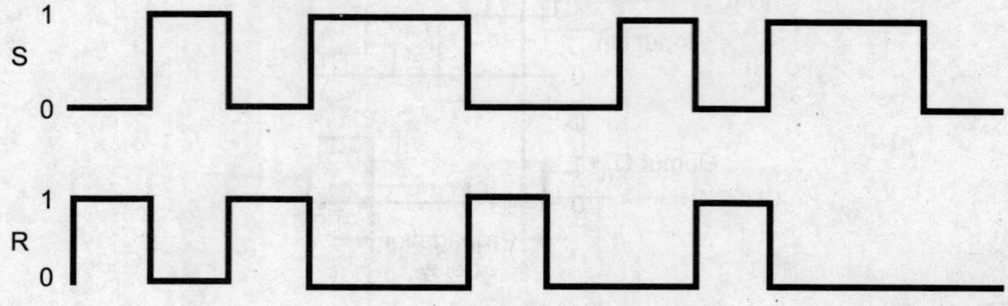

Fig. P-8.7

8.8 In a NOR latch both S and R inputs are high to begin with. First S goes low and then R also goes low. What is the state of the latch?

8.9 Draw a logic diagram of a single pulse generator using NAND gates.

8.10 Which flip-flop will you use if an invalid state is to be avoided?

8.11 Draw a diagram of a switch debouncer using inverters.

8.12 Draw a diagram of a switch debouncer using NOR gates.

8.13 What will be the state of the output of a clocked *RS* latch in the following cases?

(*a*) Clock high : $S = 0$; $R = 1$ (*b*) Clock low : $S = 1$; $R = 0$

(*c*) Clock high : $S = 0$; $R = 1$ (*d*) Clock low : $S = 1$; $R = 1$

8.14 If a clocked *RS* latch is set when the clock goes high, what will be the state of the output when the clock goes low?

8.15 The S and R inputs and the clock for a clocked *RS* latch are as given in Fig. P-8.15. Draw the output waveform if the latch was initially reset.

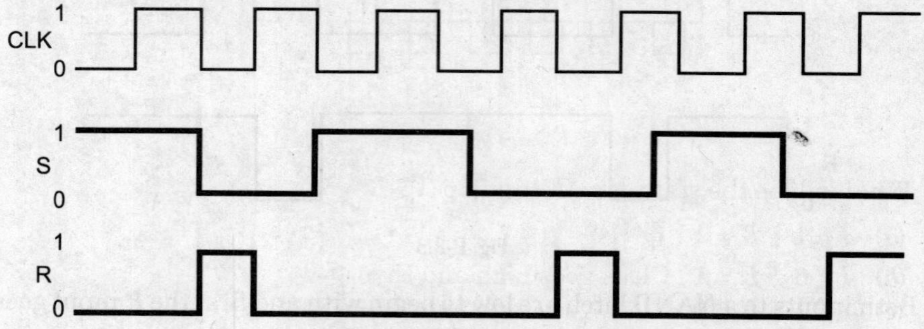

Fig. P-8.15

8.16 When a clocked *RS* latch is switched on and the clock is low, the latch comes up in the set state. What will be the state of the latch when the clock goes high and S and R inputs are low?

8.17 In the same latch if S remains low and R goes high and the clock is also high, what will be the state of the latch?

8.18 Write a truth table for the latch shown in Fig. P-8.18. Is it similar to any other latch with which you are familiar?

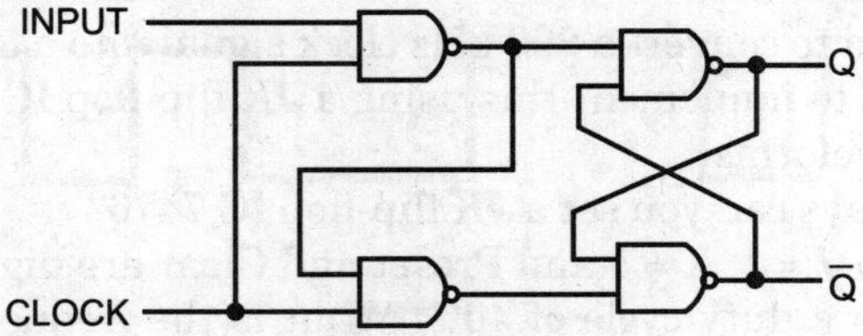

Fig. P-8.18

8.19 How will you connect a clocked D latch, so that it toggles when clock pulses are applied?

8.20 The output of a clocked D flip-flop is high. What happens when the clock goes high and then low?

8.21 In a single clocked D latch you can store any binary bit, depending on the input at D. Sketch a circuit using clocked D latches for storing any desired 4-bit binary word. (Use IC 7475, which has four clocked D latches. The top view of the IC is given in Fig. P-12.21)

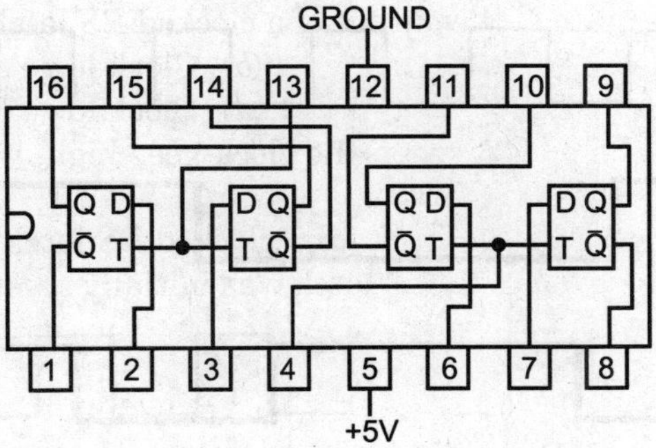

Fig. P-8.21 Top view of IC 7475

8.22 What will be the state of a JK flip-flop (IC 7476) in the following cases?

(*a*) $J = 1$; $K = 1$: $\overline{Q} = 0$

(*b*) $J = 0$; $K = 1$: Clock goes high and then low

(*c*) $J = 1$; $K = 0$: Clock goes high and then low

(*d*) $J = 1$; $K = 0$: Preset low

(e) $J = 0$; $K = 1$: Clear low

8.23 Draw the output waveform of a clocked D latch, when the inputs are as shown in Fig. P-8.23.

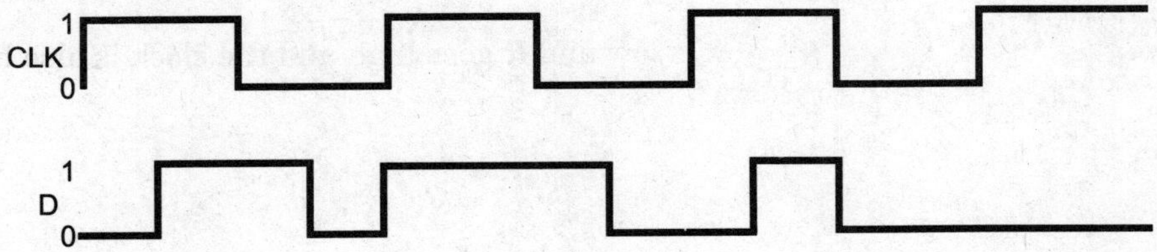

Fig. P-8.23

8.24 A *JK* flip-flop (IC 7476) is initially set and both *J* and *K* inputs are held low, while Preset and Clear inputs are held high. What will be the state of the flip-flop after the second clock pulse?

8.25 You are required to convert a 200 kHz clock signal into a 50 kHz clock signal. Draw a circuit diagram to implement this using a *JK* flip-flop IC 7476. Sketch the 100 kHz and 50 kHz waveforms.

8.26 In how many ways can you set a *JK* flip-flop IC 7476?

8.27 In a *JK* flip-flop $J = 1$, $K = 1$ and Preset and Clear are high. The clock frequency is 1 MHz and it has a duty cycle of 40%. What is the frequency and duty cycle of the output?

8.28 How many *JK* flip-flops will be required to generate a square wave of 125 kHz from a 1 MHz square wave?

8.29 How will you connect a *JK* flip-flop, so that it functions as a clocked *D* latch?

8.30 How many *JK* flip-flops will you require to store binary number 01101?

8.31 In a *JK* flip-flop (IC 7476), Preset and Clear held high while J and K are also held high. If the flip-flop was initially reset, what will be the state of the flip-flop after each clock cycle, when four clock pulses are applied?

8.32 How many *JK* flip-flops will be required to store decimal number 23 in binary form?

8.33 Draw the output waveform for a *JK* flip-flop with inputs as shown in Fig. P-8.33.

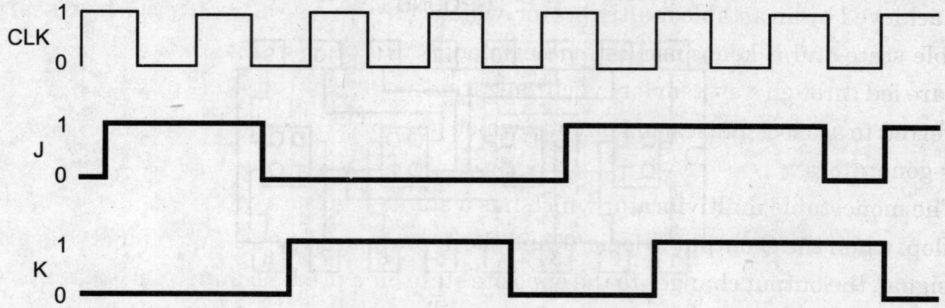

Fig. P-8.33

9 Astable and Monostable Multivibrators

9.1 INTRODUCTION

Sequential logic circuits, such as counters and shift registers, are dependent on a train of clock pulses for their operation. Clocks provide periodic signals for stepping logic circuits from one state to the next, so that they progress through their operating states. Quite often it is necessary to feed a number of circuits with clock pulses, so that their functions are coordinated. This can be achieved by an astable multivibrator, which can generate a train of clock pulses, as it has no stable state and it keeps oscillating between SET and RESET states at a fixed frequency, which are fed through a system for synchronization as well as for timing functions. These pulses are referred to as clock pulses and circuits which generate them are referred to as clock oscillators or generators.

The monostable multivibrator which has a stable state corresponding to the reset state of a flip-flop, when the Q output is logic '0' and the $\bar{Q}$ output is logic '1'. When it is triggered by an input signal, the output changes to the opposite state for a predetermined period, which depends on the time constant of the circuit. The monostable multivibrator finds numerous applications, which we will consider in this chapter. We will also consider how clock oscillators can be built using various elements, as well as pay some attention to wave shaping for which purpose Schmitt triggers are normally used.

9.2 CLOCK OSCILLATOR

Clock oscillator are required to generate a train of clock pulses, which may either be square or rectangular as shown in Fig. 9.1. Whatever the shape of these clock pulses, they must also meet some other requirements discussed below:

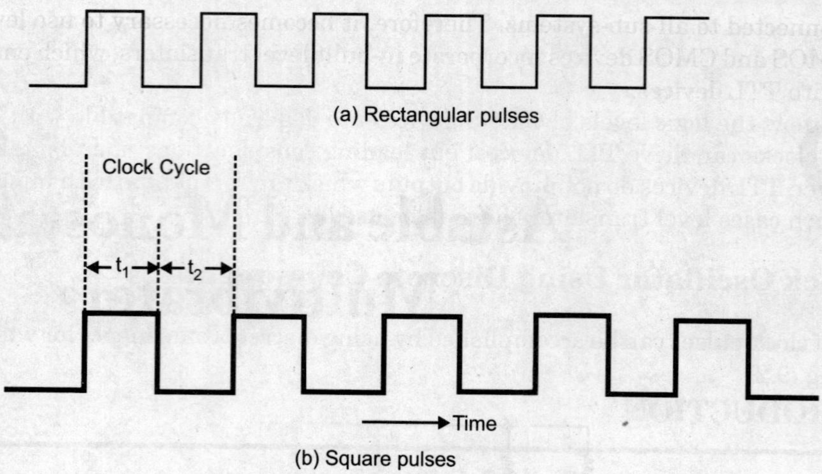

Fig. 9.1 Clock oscillator waveforms

If you refer to Fig. 9.1 (b) you will notice that the clock is 'on' for a time t_1 and 'off' for a time t_2. The total time period of one cycle is $t_1 + t_2 = t$ sec. The frequency of the clock pulses is

$$f = 1/t \text{ cycles per second.}$$

The duty cycle of the clock pulses is defined here as follows:

$$\text{Duty cycle} = \frac{\text{Pulse on time}}{\text{Clock cycle time}} = \frac{t_1}{t_1 + t_2}$$

One of the important considerations is the clock cycle time, that is the period of one clock waveform during which all logic elements in a system must complete their operations. If the time taken by some logic elements is more than the time taken by some others, the system functioning will be erratic. It is, therefore, equally important that the clock cycle time should remain constant. This also implies that the clock frequency should be stable over a period of time. The requirement of frequency stability over short periods can be met by using quartz crystals. If stability is required over longer periods, special circuits have to be used as well as temperature control systems.

It is also important that the clock output logic levels should maintain the required high and low logic levels and should remain steady over a period of time.

If you refer to Fig. 3.22 which shows the rise and fall time of waveforms, you will notice that it takes a finite time for a signal to rise and fall to the required levels. Preferably, therefore, the transition time required by a clock pulse to rise and fall to the required levels should be zero.

It is also desirable that clock pulses should be square in shape. This implies that the duty cycle of clock pulses should be 50%.

Another important consideration in designing a clock oscillator is the choice of logic elements used in it. Normally it is a good practice to use logic elements of the same family in the clock oscillator, as those used in the system for which it is required. Thus, both the clock oscillator and the device or system can be operated from the same supply voltage, which will ensure that the clock output is compatible with the input requirements of the device or system.

Compatibility becomes an important consideration, since many systems use more than one logic family. In such cases it is not possible to design a clock oscillator, so that its output can be directly connected to all sub-systems. Therefore, it becomes necessary to use level translators. Some PMOS and CMOS devices incorporate in-built level translators, which enables direct interfacing with TTL devices.

As you know the logic levels of CMOS devices are generally compatible with TTL inputs when CMOS clocks can drive TTL devices; but loading considerations must be taken into account. However, TTL devices do not provide outputs which are compatible with inputs of CMOS devices. In such cases level translators have to be used.

9.2.1 Clock Oscillator Using Discrete Components

Generation of clock pulses can be accomplished by using discrete components for which a circuit is given in Fig. 9.2.

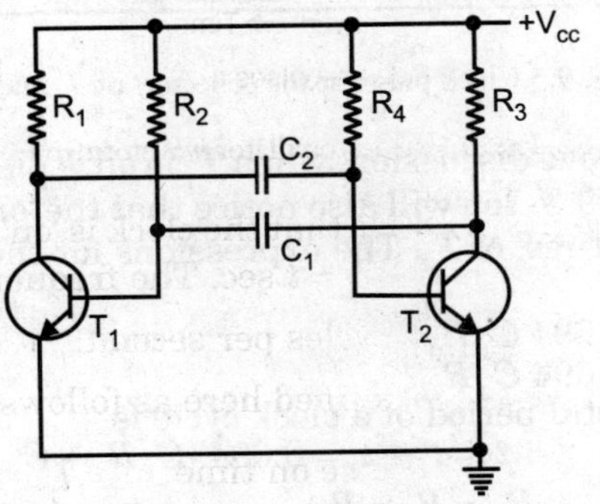

Fig. 9.2 Clock oscillator

For the sake of our analysis, we will assume that $R_1 = R_3$; $R_2 = R_4$; $C_1 = C_2$ and T_1 is similar to T_2. When power is switched on current flows from collector to emitter in both transistors. However, in spite of the symmetry we have assumed, one transistor will draw more current than the other. Let us suppose that T_2 draws more current than T_1. As more and more current flows through R_3, the collector of T_2 will gradually become more and more negative than the collector of T_1. This build up of negative voltage at the collector of T_2 is coupled to the base of T_1 via C_1, thus making the base of T_1 more and more negative, which causes a reduction in the forward bias of T_1. This has two consequences. It reduces the collector current of T_1 and makes the collector of T_1 even more positive. The build-up of positive voltage at the collector of T_1 is passed on to the base of T_2 via C_2, which has the effect of increasing the forward bias of T_2 and consequently its collector current increases further. In a short time this regenerative feedback causes T_2 to saturate while T_1 is cut off.

After T_2 has reached saturation, the resistance between the collector and emitter of T_2 approaches zero. Therefore C_1 starts discharging through T_2 and R_2. As C_1 discharges towards the positive supply line, the voltage at the base of T_1 begins to rise to a more positive value, which brings it out of cut off and into conduction. Collector current now starts to flow in T_1 and, as a result, the collector voltage of T_1 drops and this change is coupled via C_2 to the base of T_2, which reduces its collector current. The voltage at the collector of T_2 rises and this positive voltage change is coupled via C_1 to the base of T_1. The same sequence of events, as described earlier, follows and T_1 reaches saturation and T_2 is cut off. This process goes on indefinitely as long as power is supplied to the circuit. The waveforms at the collectors of T_1 and T_2 will be as shown in Fig. 9.3.

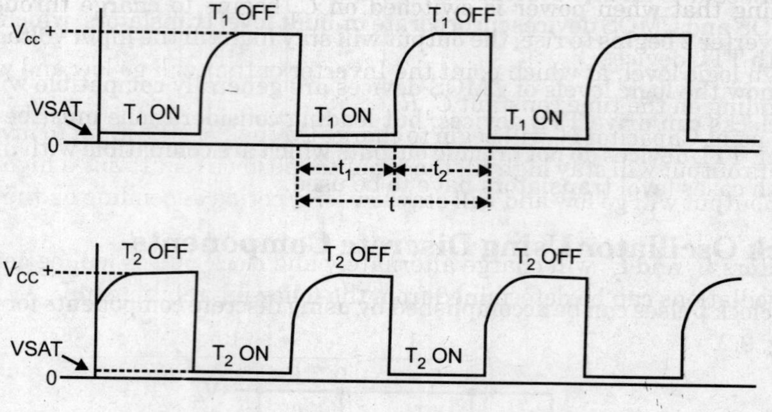

Fig. 9.3 Clock pulses at the collectors of T_1 and T_2

As is obvious from the above discussion, when T_1 is on, T_2 is off, and when T_2 is on T_1 is off, as has also been shown in Fig. 9.3. You will also notice that the 'on time' an 'off time' of T_1 are the same as the 'off time' and 'on time' of T_2. The expressions for the 'off times' of T_1 and T_2 are as follows:

For T_1, off time = $t_2 = 0.694\, C_1 R_2$
For T_2, off time = $t_1 = 0.694\, C_2 R_4$
The expression for the total period of a clock cycle is

$$t = t_1 + t_2 = 0.694\,(C_1 R_2 + C_2 R_4)$$

If we assume that $R_1 = R_2 = R$

and $C_1 = C_2 = C$, as is usually the case,

$$t = 1.4\,RC$$

and the clock frequency

$$f = \frac{1}{t} = \frac{0.7}{RC} \qquad \text{...(9.1)}$$

where f is in H_z,
R is in Megohms and
C is in Microfarads

9.2.2 TTL Clock Oscillator

A simple clock oscillator employing Inverters is shown in Fig. 9.4. It consists of two inverters 1 and 2, with the output of one connected to the input of the other. Inverter 3 is used as a buffer, which isolates the load from the frequency determining components. The circuit bears a close resemblance to the clock oscillator of Fig. 9.2 and it functions very much in the same way.

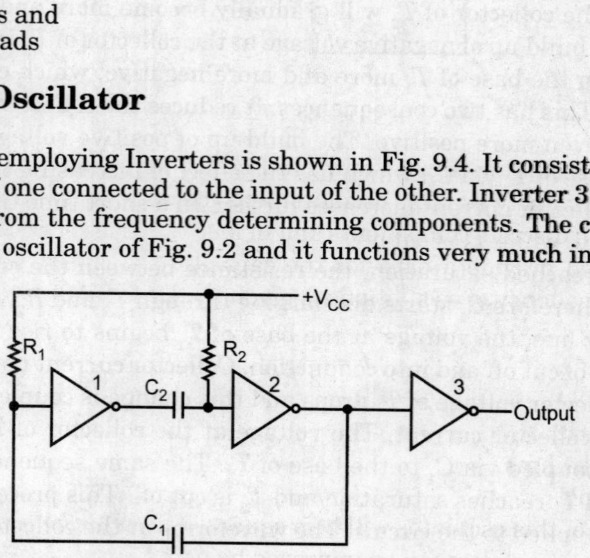

Fig. 9.4 TTL clock oscillator

Assuming that when power is switched on C_2 begins to charge through R_2, the input voltage of inverter 2 begins to rise, the output will stay high till the input voltage to the Inverter attains a high logic level, at which point the Inverter output will go low and will stay low for a period depending on the time constant $C_2 R_2$.

At this point Capacitor C_1 will begin to charge through R_1, the input to inverter 1 will begin to rise, and its output will stay high till the input to the inverter attains a high logic level, when the Inverter output will go low and will stay low for a period depending on the time constant $C_1 R_1$.

Capacitors C_1 and C_2 will charge alternately and clock pulses will be generated. The frequency of oscillations can be determined from the following relationship.

$$f = \frac{1}{t_1 + t_2} = \frac{1}{0.7\,R_1C_1 + 0.7\,R_2C_2}$$

If $R_1 = R_2 = R$ and $C_1 = C_2 = C$

$$f = \frac{1}{1.4RC} = \frac{0.7}{RC}$$ It is the same as Eqn. (9.1)

where R is in Megohms
C is in Microfarads
and f is in Hz

Another clock oscillator built with TTL Inverters, and very similar to the one shown in Fig. 9.4, is given in Fig. 9.5. The frequency stability of these two oscillators is not good, as it depends on the resistors and capacitors used in these circuits. Frequency stability can be improved by using quartz crystals.

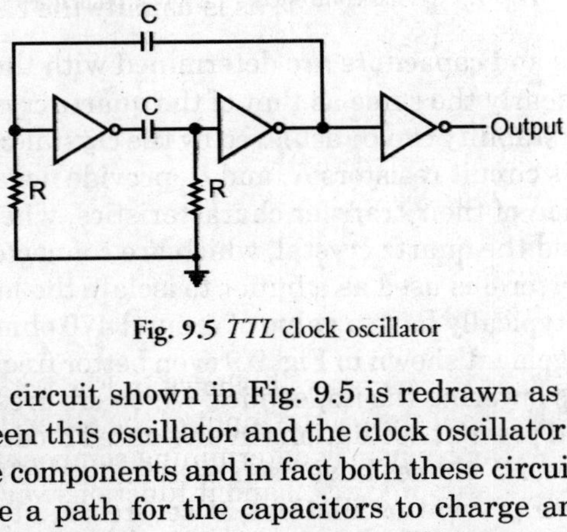

Fig. 9.5 *TTL* clock oscillator

If the clock oscillator circuit shown in Fig. 9.5 is redrawn as shown in Fig. 9.6, you will notice the similarity between this oscillator and the clock oscillator in Fig. 9.2, which has been implemented with discrete components and in fact both these circuits operate in the same way. The resistors used provide a path for the capacitors to charge and also provide bias to the Inverters. The frequency of oscillations is given by the following expression:

$$f \approx \frac{1}{2\,RC} \qquad ...(9.2)$$

where f is in kHz
R is in k ohms
and C is in μF

The output of this oscillator will be a square wave with nearly 50% duty cycle.

The frequency stability can be improved by using quartz crystals as shown in Fig. 9.7.

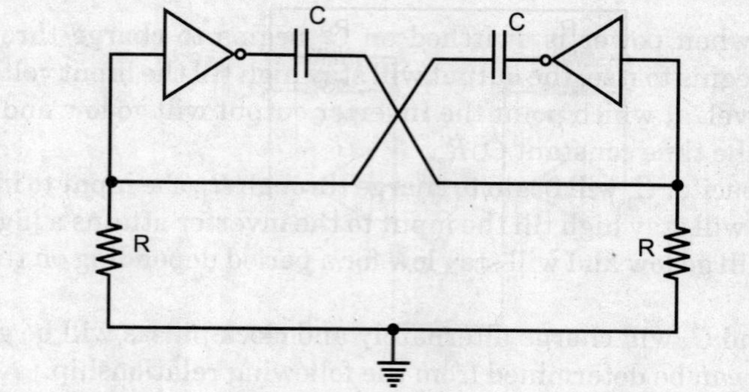

Fig. 9.6 TTL clock oscillator (buffer not shown in the diagram)

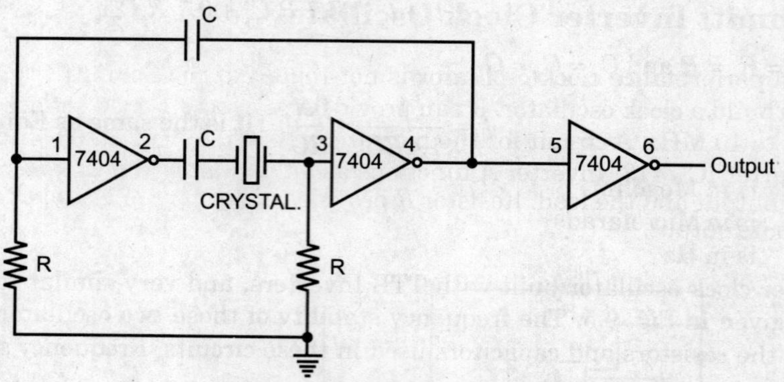

Fig. 9.7 Crystal-controlled TTL clock oscillator

The values of resistors and capacitors are determined with the help of Eqn. (9.2), so that the oscillator frequency is nearly the same as that of the quartz crystal being used.

Even better frequency stability can be achieved by the crystal-controlled TTL clock oscillator shown in Fig. 9.8. In this circuit resistors R_1 and R_2 provide negative feedback and bias the Inverters in the linear region of their transfer characteristics, when they work as amplifiers. The trimmer capacitor C and the quartz crystal, which are connected between the two Inverters, complete the loop. Inverter 3 is used as a buffer to isolate the load from the oscillator. The biasing resistors R_1 and R_2 typically have a value of around 470 ohms.

With the circuit arrangement shown in Fig. 9.9 even better frequency stability is achieved. Capacitors C_1 and C_2 help is lowering the impedance, which ensures that the crystal will oscillate in its primary mode and prevent oscillations in unwanted modes. In order to maintain the loop gain at high frequencies, *RF* chokes have been used instead of biasing resistors. Resistors R_1 and R_2 have been used to prevent oscillations at self-resonant frequencies of the chokes. Capacitor C is used as a series trimmer for fine adjustment of the resonant frequency.

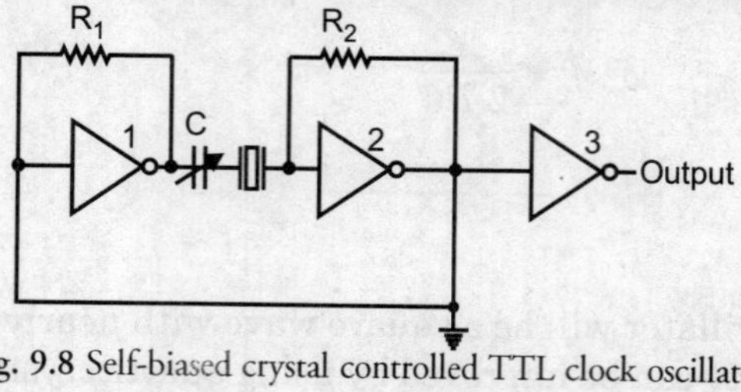

Fig. 9.8 Self-biased crystal controlled TTL clock oscillator

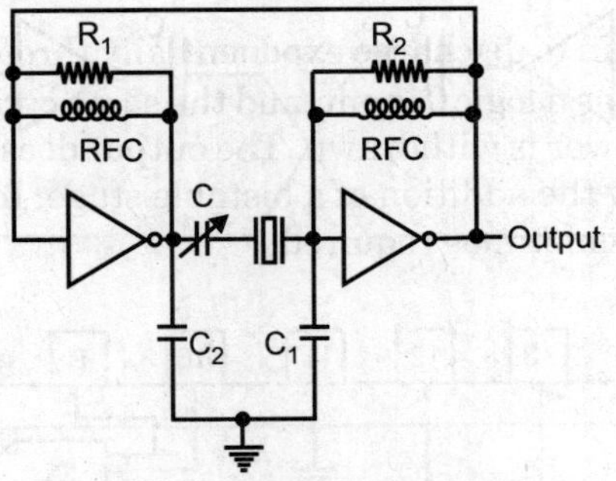

Fig. 9.9 Crystal-controlled TTL clock oscillator

9.2.3 Schmitt Inverter Clock Oscillator

When a high performance clock oscillator is not required, the Schmitt trigger offers a convenient way to build a clock oscillator. It can provide a reasonably good square wave output from about 10 Hz to 10 MHz. A circuit for the purpose is shown in Fig. 9.10, which is based on Hex Schmitt Inverter IC 7413. Inverter *A* functions as an oscillator and Inverter *B* acts as a buffer between the output and the load. Resistor *R* provides a measure of feedback from the output of Inverter A to its output.

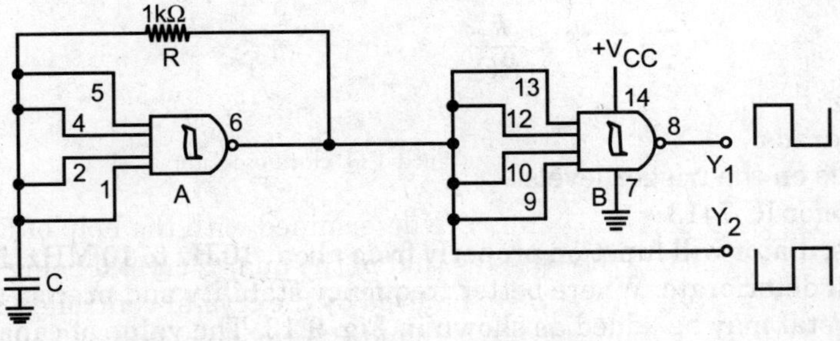

Fig. 9.10 Clock oscillator using Schmitt trigger IC 7413

The operation of this circuit depends on the fact that a Schmitt trigger exhibits hysteresis in the logic 0 and logic 1 threshold voltage levels. Let us assume that capacitor *C* is fully discharged, the input is low and the output is high. When power is switched on, capacitor *C* will begin to charge through resistor *R*. When the voltage across it reaches 1.7 V, which this Schmitt trigger (IC 7413) recognizes as a logic 1 input, the output of Inverter *A* will rapidly fall to about 0.2 V as shown in Fig. 9.11.

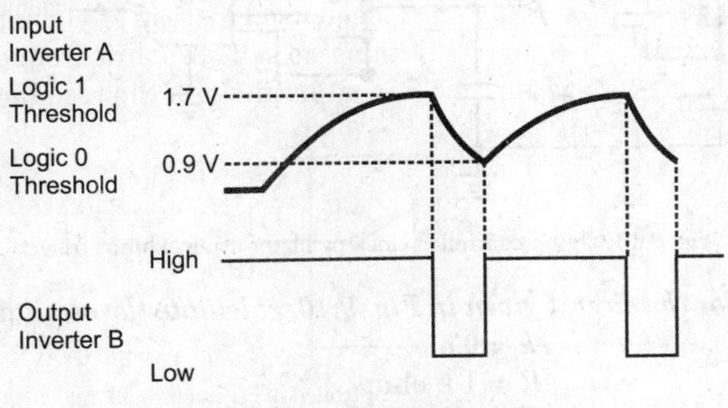

Fig. 9.11 Schmitt oscillator waveform

Capacitor C will now begin to discharge exponentially through R to about 0.9 V, which this Schmitt trigger will recognize as a logic 0 input, and the same cycle will be repeated. It will go on repeating indefinitely until power is withdrawn. The output does not have a 50% duty cycle, but that can be easily corrected by the addition of a bistable stage. Inverter B will produce complementary outputs, which are sometimes required.

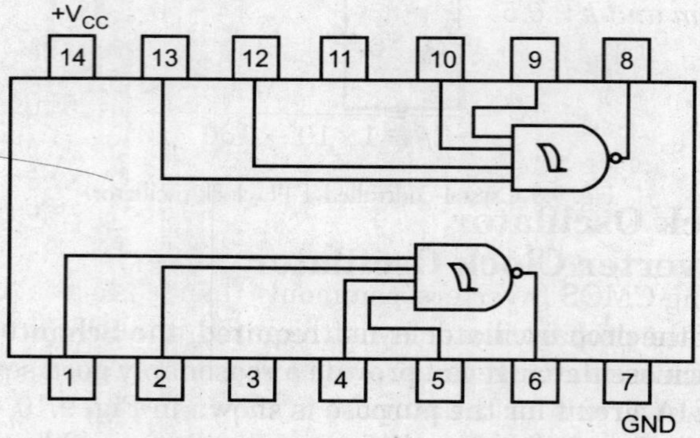

Fig. 9.12 Pin diagram for Schmitt trigger IC 7413

The frequency of oscillations is given by the following expression:

$$f = \frac{k}{RC} \quad \text{...(9.3)}$$

where f is in Hz
C is in Farads
and k depends on the trigger levels
k is = 0.5 for IC 7413

This clock oscillator will function properly from about 10 Hz to 10 MHz. Beyond this range the waveform will deteriorate. Where better frequency stability and precise timing are important, a quartz crystal may be added as shown in Fig. 9.13. The value of capacitor C should be chosen, so that without the crystal in place, the circuit operates at close to the desired frequency. For precise frequency adjustment, a trimmer capacitor of about 50 pF may be connected across the crystal.

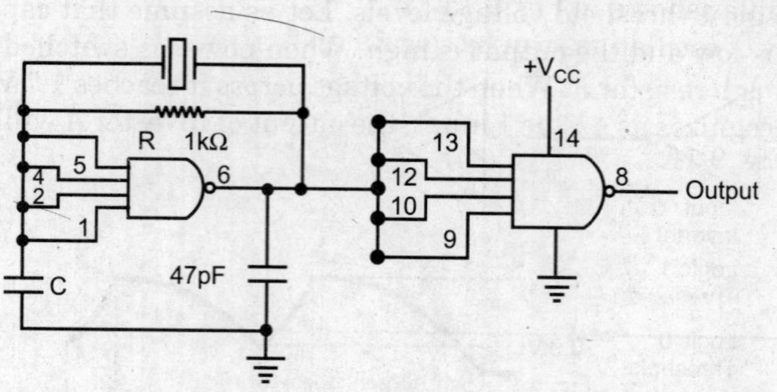

Fig. 9.13 Crystal-controlled clock oscillator using Schmitt trigger

Example 9.1: *For the circuit given in Fig. 9.10, calculate the oscillator frequency when*

$k = 0.5$

$R = 1$ k ohm

and $C = 470$ pF.

Solution:

$$f = \frac{k}{RC} = \frac{0.5}{1000 \times 470 \times 10^{-12}}$$

$$= 1\text{MHz}$$

Example 9.2: *For the same circuit, calculate the value of the capacitor required, when f = 100 kHz, R = 1 k ohm and k = 0.5.*

Solution:

$$C = \frac{k}{Rf} = \frac{0.5}{1 \times 10^3 \times 100 \times 10^3} = 5 \text{ nF}$$

9.2.4 CMOS Clock Oscillator

A simple oscillator, using CMOS Inverters, commonly referred to as a 'ring oscillator' is shown in Fig. 9.14. Because of the propagation delay in the gates, it takes a finite time before a change in the input logic level causes a change in the output logic level. As a result of this delay, a circuit with an odd number of Inverters has a natural tendency to oscillate. If each gate contributes a delay t_{pd}, the output waveform will have a period equal to $6t_{pd}$, and the oscillator frequency will be $1/6t_{pd}$. As the frequency of this oscillator also depends on the supply voltage and temperature, we will have very little control over the output frequency.

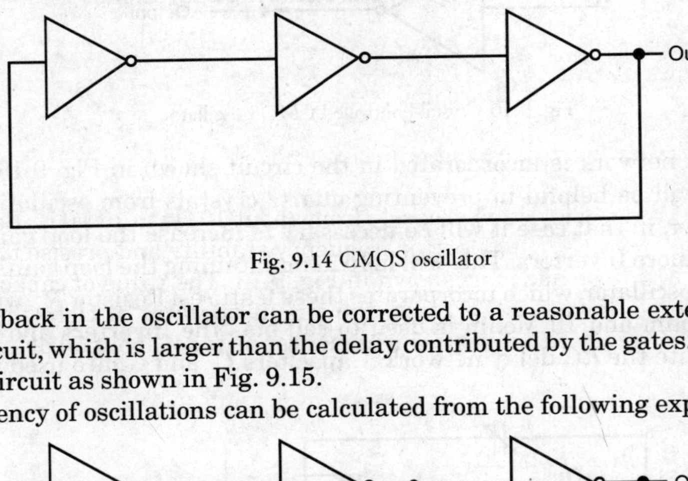

Fig. 9.14 CMOS oscillator

This drawback in the oscillator can be corrected to a reasonable extent by introducing a delay in the circuit, which is larger than the delay contributed by the gates. This can be done by adding an *RC* circuit as shown in Fig. 9.15.

The frequency of oscillations can be calculated from the following expression:

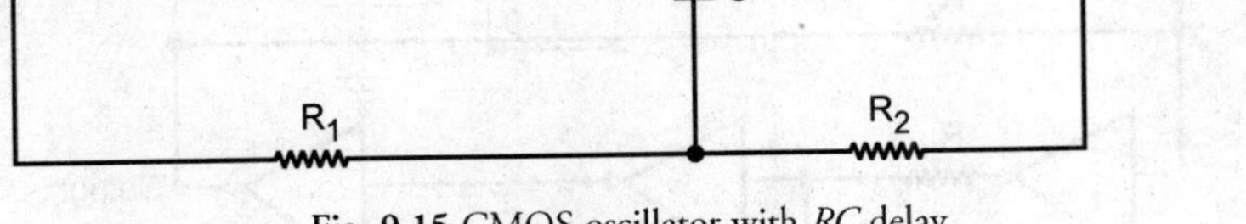

Fig. 9.15 CMOS oscillator with *RC* delay

$$f = \frac{0.559}{RC} \qquad ...(9.4)$$

where *f* is in Hz

C is in Microfarads

and R is in Megohms

The duty cycle is approximately 50%

9.2.5 Crystal-controlled CMOS Oscillator

CMOS Inverters, when biased in the linear region, can be used as amplifiers and oscillators. In these applications they offer very high input impedance, low power consumption, and high temperature stability. In the oscillator circuit shown in Fig. 9.16, resistor R is used to self-bias the Inverter in the linear region of its transfer characteristics. The quartz crystal, which is connected between the input and the output, enables the circuit to function as an oscillator. Capacitors C_1 and C_2 are intended for fine adjustment of the oscillator frequency.

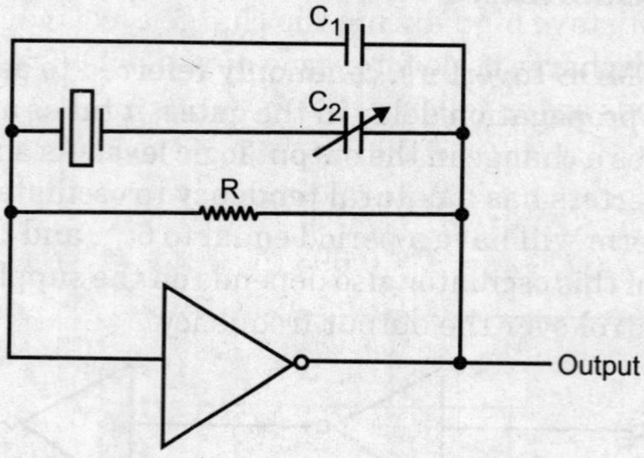

Fig. 9.16 Crystal-controlled CMOS oscillator

If an RC delay network is incorporated in the circuit shown in Fig. 9.16, this enhanced propagation delay will be helpful in preventing quartz crystals from oscillating at harmonic frequencies. However, in that case it will be necessary to increase the loop gain, which can be done by adding two more Inverters. This will help in maintaining the loop gain. Fig. 9.17 shows a crystal-controlled oscillator, which incorporates these features. Resistor R_2, which may have a value between 1 Mohm and 10 Mohm is used to self-bias the Inverters and resistor R_1 and capacitor C_1 constitute the RC delay network. Capacitors C_2 and C_3 are used to fine tune the oscillator frequency.

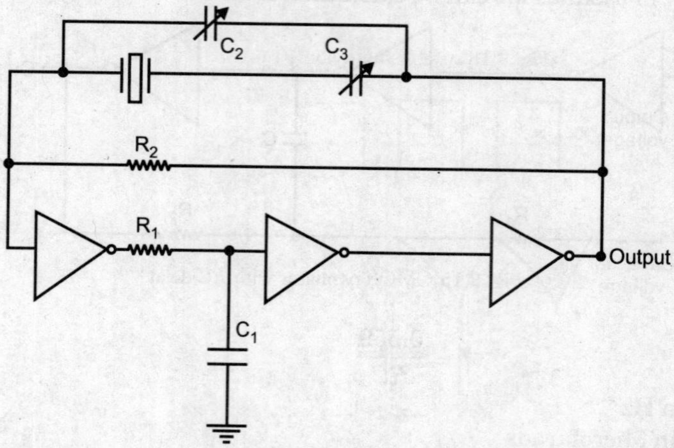

Fig. 9.17 CMOS cyrstal-controlled oscillator with self-bias and RC delay network

9.2.6 Timer 555 as Astable Multivibrator

Figure 9.18 shows Timer 555 connected as an astable multivibrator. The discharge transistor (pin 7) of the Timer is connected to the junction of two resistors R_A and R_B. A timing capacitor, C, is connected as shown in the diagram. When power is switched on, the timing capacitor begins to charge towards $2/3V_{cc}$ through resistors R_A and R_B. When, the capacitor voltage has reached this value, the upper comparator of the Timer triggers the flip-flop and the capacitor begins to discharge to ground through resistor R_B. When the capacitor voltage reaches $1/3\ V_{CC}$, the lower comparator is triggered and another charge cycle begins.

The waveforms generated by this astable multivibrator are shown in Fig. 9.19.

The waveforms also show that the charge and discharge cycles are repeated between $2/3\ V_{CC}$ and $1/3\ V_{CC}$. The output stays high during the charge cycle, which spans a time duration t_1 and stays low during the discharge cycle for a time duration t_2. The formulae applicable for the charge and discharge periods are as follows:

Charge time $\quad t_1 = 0.693\ (R_A + R_B)\ C$ second

Discharge time $\quad t_2 = 0.693\ R_B C$ second

Total period $\quad t_1 + t_2 = T = 0.693\ (R_A + 2R_B)\ C$ second

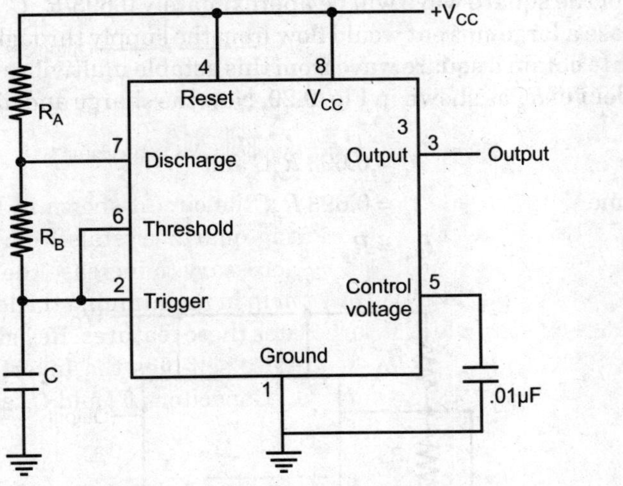

Fig. 9.18 Astable multivibrator using Timer 555

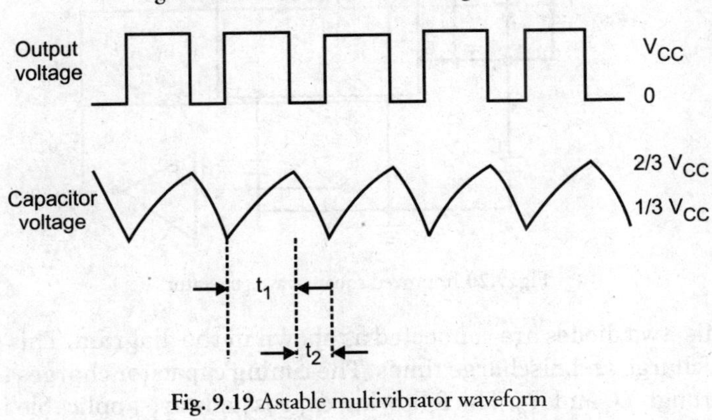

Fig. 9.19 Astable multivibrator waveform

The expression for the output frequency, f, and the duty cycle are as follows. Here the duty cycle has been defined as the ratio of t_2, low output time, to the total cycle time, T. It is often expressed as a percentage.

The expression for the output frequency, f, and the duty cycle, D, are as follows:

$$f = \frac{1}{T} = \frac{1.443}{(R_A + 2R_B)C} \quad ...(9.5)$$

$$D = \frac{\text{Low output time}}{\text{Total cycle time}} = \frac{t_2}{T} = \frac{R_B}{R_A + 2R_B} \quad ...(9.6)$$

where f is in Hz
C is in Farads
and R_A and R_B are is ohms

Since the capacitor charges through resistors R_A and R_B and discharges through resistor R_B only, the charge and discharge times are not equal. As a consequence the output is not a symmetrical square wave. This could have been possible if R_A was nearly zero, which is not possible. However, to obtain an output close to a square wave, R_A can be made much smaller than R_B and in that case the charge and discharge times will be essentially dependent on R_B and C. The frequency of the square wave will be approximately $0.693/R_B\,C$. R_A cannot be made very small, as in that case a large current would flow from the supply through pin 7, when it goes low.

Another way to obtain a square wave from this astable multivibrator is to make the charging path independent of R_B as shown in Fig. 9.20. Now the charge and discharge times will be as follows:

Charge time $t_1 = 0.693\,R_A C$ and

Discharge time $t_2 = 0.693\,R_B C$

If $R_A = R_B$

$t_1 = t_2$

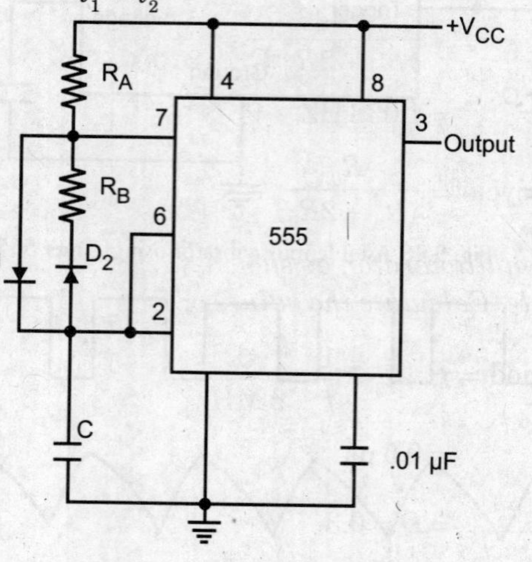

Fig. 9.20 Improved square wave generator

To achieve this, two diodes are connected as shown in the diagram. This gives an independent control of the charge and discharge times. The timing capacitor charges through D_1 and R_A and discharges through D_2 and R_B. The following expressions are applicable in this case.

$$t_1 + t_2 = T = 1.386\, R_A C$$

and $$f = \frac{1}{T} = \frac{0.722}{R_A C} \qquad ...(9.7)$$

An even better scheme to obtain a perfectly symmetrical square wave is to connect the timer output to a *JK* master-slave flip-flop, which will toggle at every cycle. This will give a two-phase clock output; but as shown in Fig. 9.21 the output frequency will be half of the input frequency. Since the duty cycle will be 50%, the output will be a perfectly symmetrical square wave.

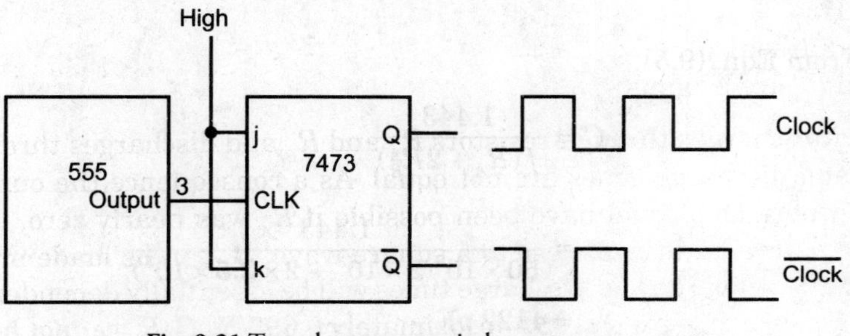

Fig. 9.21 Two-phase symmetrical square wave output

Example 9.3: *Calculate the frequency and the duty cycle of the output of an astable multivibrator using Timer 555. The relevant data is as follows:*

$$R_A = 27 \text{ K ohm}$$
$$R_B = 56 \text{ K ohm}$$
$$C = .01\ \mu\text{F}$$

Solution:

$$f = \frac{1.443}{(R_A + 2R_B)C} = \frac{1.443}{(27000 + 2 \times 56000) \times 0.01 \times 10^{-6}}$$
$$= 1{,}038 \text{ HZ}$$

$$\text{Duty cycle} = \frac{R_B}{(R_A + 2R_B)} = \frac{56000}{27000 + 2 \times 56000} = 40.3\%$$

Example 9.4: *An astable multivibrator, as shown in Fig. 9.18 is used to provide a 2 MHz clock frequency at 30% duty cycle. Calculate the values of R_B and C if R_A = 3000 ohms.*

Solution: Clock cycle period = $t_1 + t_2 = \frac{1}{f} = \frac{1}{2 \text{ MHz}}$

$$= 0.5\ \mu\text{s}$$

$$\frac{t_2}{t_1 + t_2} = D = 0.3$$

Therefore $$t_2 = 0.3 \times 0.5 = 0.15\ \mu\text{s}$$

From Eqn. (10.6), $$D = \frac{R_B}{R_A + 2\,R_B} = 0.3$$

or $$R_B = 0.3\, R_A + 0.6\, R_B$$

or $$0.4\,R_B = 0.3 \times 3000$$

$$R_B = 2250 \text{ ohm}$$

Discharge time $$t_2 = 0.693\,R_B C$$

Therefore $$C = \frac{t_2}{0.693\,R_B} = \frac{0.15 \times 10^{-6}}{0.693 \times 2250} \text{ Farad}$$

$$= 96 \text{ pF}$$

Example 9.5 : *Determine the value of the timing capacitor required for an astable oscillator as shown in Fig. 9.18, so that it delivers a clock frequency of 50 kHz when R_A = 2 kΩ and R_B = 2.5 k Ω.*

Solution: From Eqn. (9.5)

$$C = \frac{1.443}{f(R_A + 2R_B)}$$

$$= \frac{1.443}{50 \times 10^3 (2 \times 10^3 + 2 \times 2.5 \times 10^3)}$$

$$= 4122 \text{ pF.}$$

9.3 MONOSTABLE MULTIVIBRATORS

The monostable multivibrator, as its name implies, has a stable and a quasistable state, and for this reason it is also called a 'One Shot'. The Q, normal output, of a One Shot is normally logic 0 and it corresponds to the reset state of a flip-flop. Its $\overline{Q}$ output is normally logic 1, which corresponds to the set state of a flip-flop. The symbol normally used for a One Shot is shown in Fig. 9.22. You will notice that it has a trigger input which may respond to the positive going or negative going pulse. If the One Shot is responsive to the negative going pulse, the output will change state on the falling edge of the pulse as shown in Fig. 9.23. The diagram shows that the Q output changes form logic 0 to logic 1 on the falling edge of the pulse.

You will also notice from the diagram that the Q output, which normally rests in the logic 0 state, and switches to the logic 1 state when the One shot receives a trigger pulse, remains in the logic 1 state for a predetermined length of time, t, which defines the duration of the unstable state. The same sequence of events is repeated when subsequent trigger pulses arrive.

It will be evident to you from the diagram, that the trigger pulse generates a delayed pulse at the output, which stays there for a predetermined period. This is a very important feature of a One Shot which, for this reason, finds many applications in numerous fields. Before considering these applications we will refer to a simple One Shot circuit based on 555 Timer.

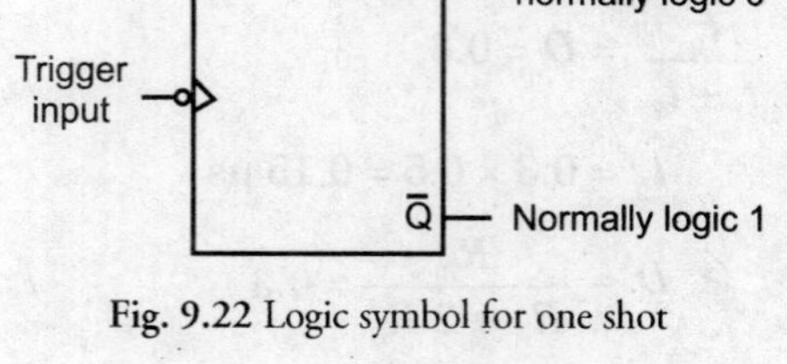

Fig. 9.22 Logic symbol for one shot

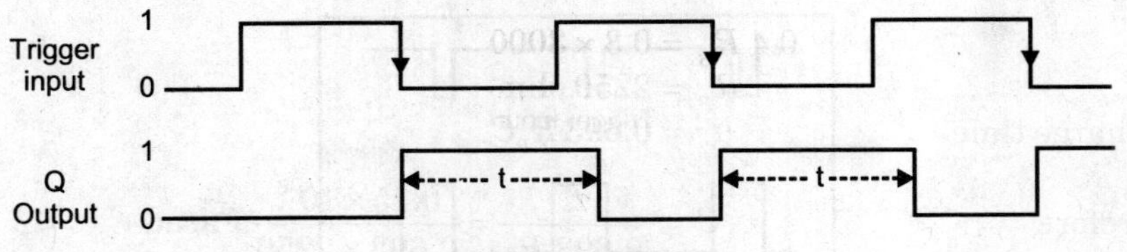

Fig. 9.23 Waveform

9.3.1 One Shot Using 555 Timer

Fig. 9.24 shows a 555 Timer wired for monostable operation. The waveforms generated by it are shown in Fig. 9.25.

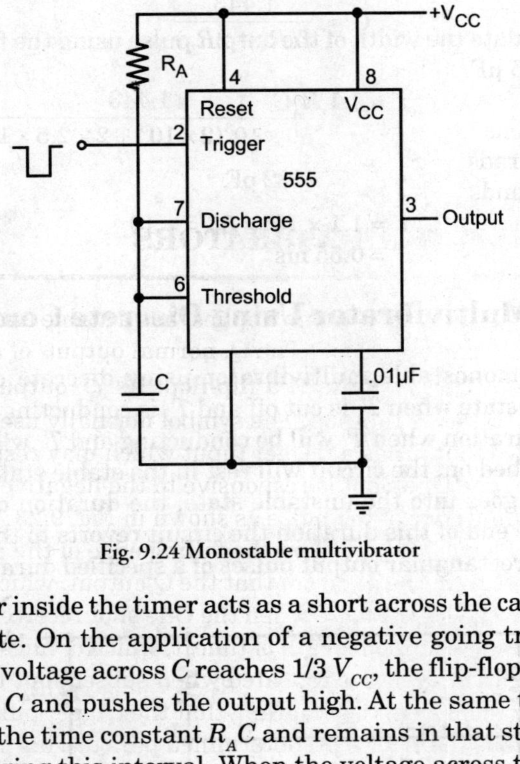

Fig. 9.24 Monostable multivibrator

Initially a transistor inside the timer acts as a short across the capacitor C which is, therefore, in a discharged state. On the application of a negative going trigger pulse at pin 2, the circuit triggers when the voltage across C reaches 1/3 V_{CC}, the flip-flop in the timer is set, which releases the short across C and pushes the output high. At the same time the voltage across C rises exponentially with the time constant $R_A C$ and remains in that state for a period $R_A C$ even if it is triggered again during this interval. When the voltage across the capacitor has reached 2/3 V_{CC}, the threshold comparator resets the flip-flop, which discharges C and the output is driven low. The circuit will remain in this state until the application of the next negative going pulse at pin 2.

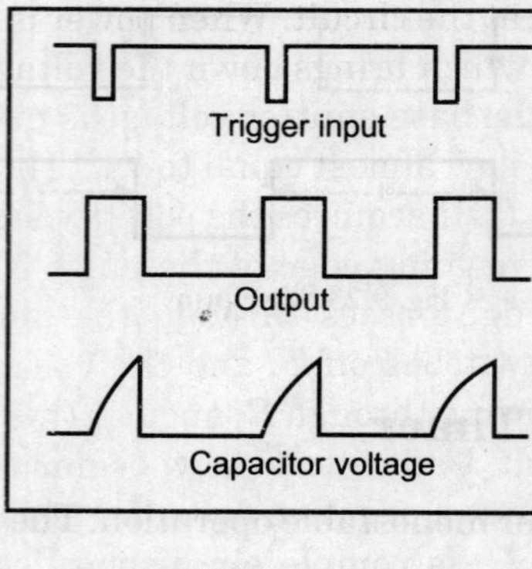

Fig. 9.25 Monostable waveforms

Example 9.6 : Calculate the width of the output pulse using the following equation, when R_A = 10 k ohm and C = .05 μF.

Pulse width $t = 1.1\,R_A C$ ...(9.8)

where R is in Ohms
C is in Farads
and t is in Seconds

$$t = 1.1 \times 10^4 \times 0.05 \times 10^{-6}$$
$$= 0.55 \text{ ms}$$

9.3.2 Monostable Multivibrator Using Discrete Components

A circuit diagram for a monostable multivibrator using discrete components is given in Fig. 9.26. It has its stable state when T_1 is cut off and T_2 is conducting. It can be triggered into the unstable state for a duration when T_1 will be conducting and T_2 will be cut off.

When power is switched on, the circuit will rest in the stable state until a trigger pulse is applied, when the circuit goes into the unstable state, the duration of which depends on the values of C_2 and R_3. At the end of this duration the circuit reverts to the stable state. Thus the monostable will generate rectangular output pulses of a specified duration, each time a trigger pulse is applied.

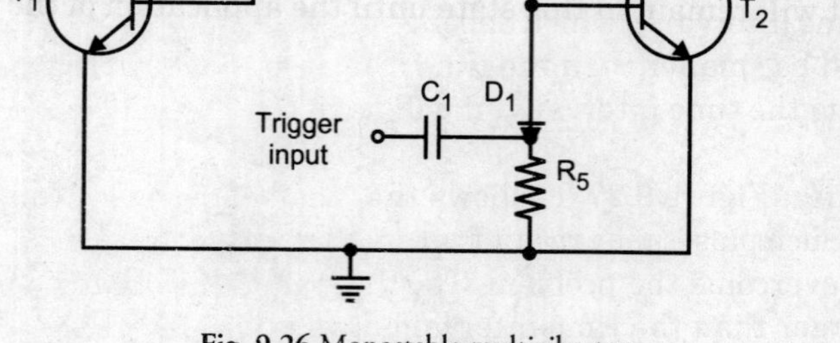

Fig. 9.26 Monostable multivibrator

We can now have a closer look at the circuit. When power is applied T_2 is forward-biased by resistor R_3, and T_2 soon saturates, which brings down the voltage at its collector to nearly zero volt. This cuts off transistor T_1 as the base-emitter voltage is not enough to allow it to conduct. The voltage at the collector of T_1 is now almost equal to V_{CC}. This charges capacitor C_2 through R_2 and the base-emitter junction of T_2. It acquires the polarity indicated in the diagram. When a trigger pulse is applied, the positive-going edge of the pulse is blocked by the diode, but the trailing edge or negative-going edge passes through the diode, which reverse-biases the emitter-base junction of T_2. This switches off T_2 and the voltage at its collector rises, which forward-biases T_1 by the current flowing through R_4 and R_1. This saturates T_1 and the voltage at its collector drops nearly to zero volt. Capacitor C_2 now begins to discharge through R_3 and T_1. Because one end of capacitor C_2 was at a negative potential at the commencement of the operation, T_2 will remain cut off until C_2 is completely discharged. After some time C_2 will be discharged and then charged in the opposite direction. When the voltage across C_2 is enough, it will forward-bias T_2, which will now conduct and T_1 will be cut off. As soon as T_2 begins to conduct, the output pulse is terminated.

The duration of the output pulse will depend on the value of C_2 and R_3 and is given by the following expression:

$$t_1 = 0.694\, C_2 R_3$$

The value of R_3 should be low enough to ensure that transistor T_2 saturates during operation. However the values of R_2 and C_2 should be such as would allow C_2 to recharge through R_2 and the base-emitter junction of T_2 between trigger pulses. This places a limit on the duty cycle, which should not exceed 90%. Since the value of R_2 cannot be made very small because of other circuit requirements, this places a limit on the maximum value of C_2.

9.3.3 Pulse Shaping with One Shot

We have already discussed how a delayed pulse can be produced with a One Shot. They can also be used for narrowing, widening and blocking of pulses. We will consider some basic ideas about pulse shaping before we take up specific applications. In the following examples non-retriggerable One Shots triggered by negative-going pulses have been discussed.

1. Pulse narrowing: Figure 9.27 (a) shows that to start with the Q output of the non-retriggerable One Shot is logic 0. When input pulses are applied, the Q output goes high every time the input pulse goes low and it stays high for a time interval t_2, which depends on the timing components of the One Shot, resulting in a train of narrow output pulses. The values of the timing components chosen will ensure that the output pulses are narrower than the input pulses (t_2 less than t_1).

2. Pulse Widening: Figure 9.27 (b) shows that the input to the One Shot are narrow pulses. The Q output, which is low to begin with, goes high every time the input pulse goes low and stays high for a time interval t_4, which depends on the timing components. It is necessary in this case that t_4 should be smaller than the time interval t_5 between input pulses. If any input pulse is received during the time interval t_4, it will have no effect on a non-retriggerable single-shot circuit.

3. Pulse Blocking: Figure 9.27 (c) shows that the trigger pulse consists of a number of short duration pulses. Such pulses may result from mechanical switches, when contact debouncers are generally used to overcome the problem. The diagram shows that if the time interval t_6 of the output pulse is larger than the time interval between trigger pulses, the resultant output will be a single pulse.

9.3.4 Non-retriggerable Monostable Multivibrator IC 74121

As IC 74121 is a non-retriggerable One Shot, it will respond to a trigger input only when it is in its stable (quiescent) state. This implies that if a second trigger pulse arrives while the Q output of the One Shot is still high, it will be ignored. The Q output of the monostable multivibrator will return to the low state after a period, which will be determined by the values of R and C, even while the trigger pulse is still active. Later on we will consider a retriggerable One Shot, which responds to a trigger pulse even when it is in the quasistable (On) state.

The logic diagram for IC 74121 is given in Fig. 9.28, and its pin connection is shown in Fig. 9.29.

This monostable multivibrator has three inputs, $\overline{A_1}$ and $\overline{A_2}$, which are active low, and B which is active high and triggers the device on a positive edge (or low to high transition). Arrows

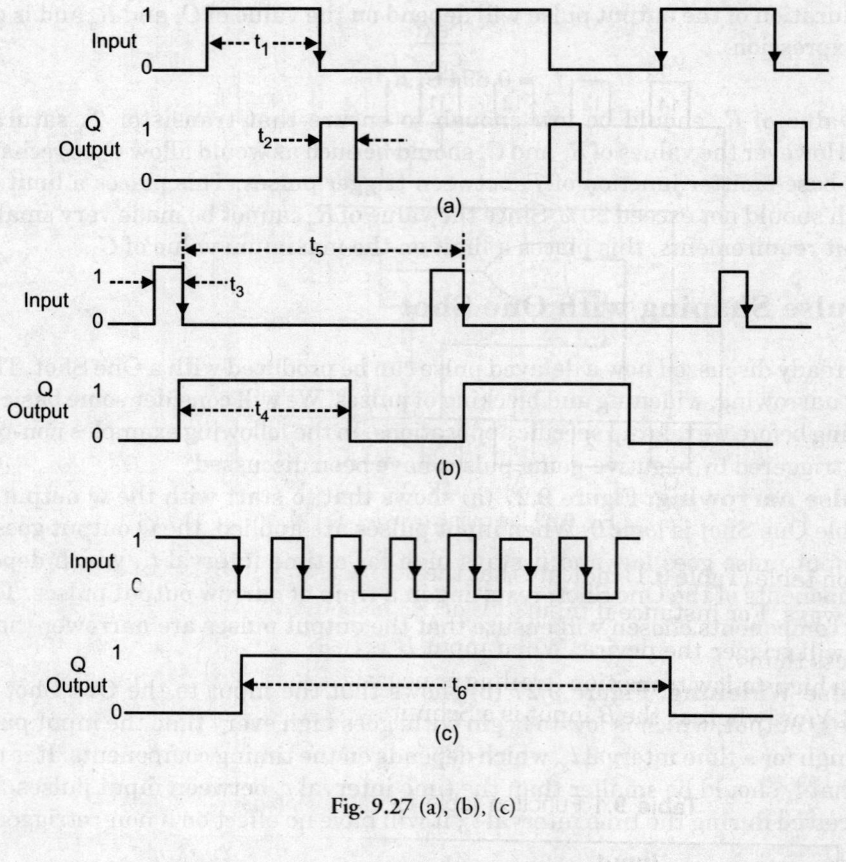

Fig. 9.27 (a), (b), (c)

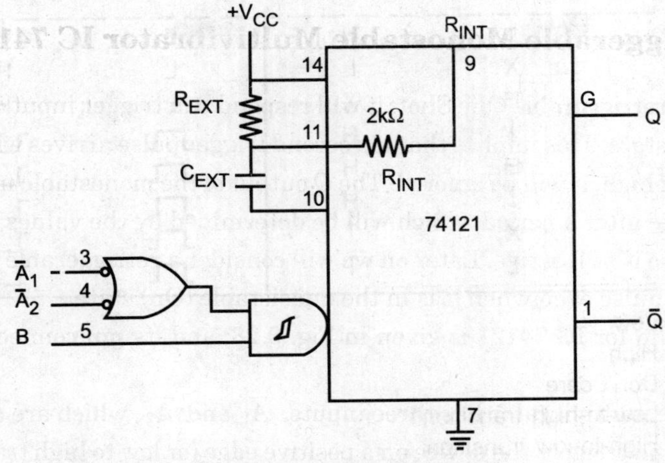

Fig. 9.28 Monostable multivibrator IC 74121

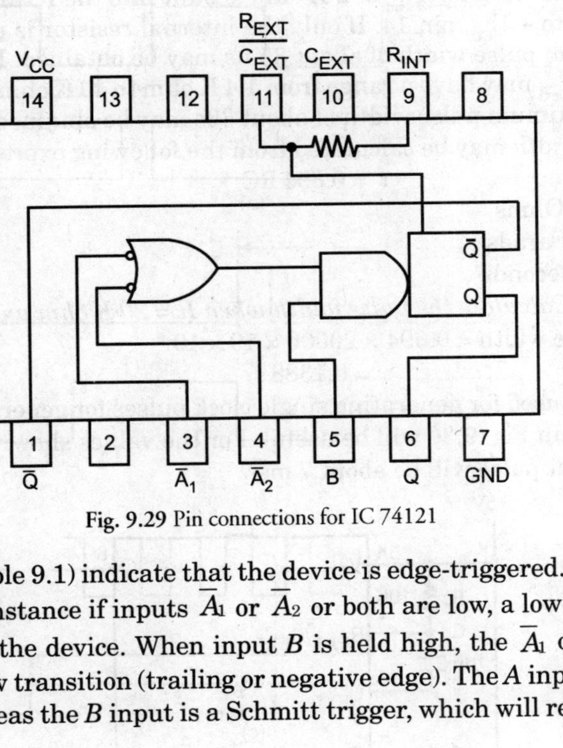

Fig. 9.29 Pin connections for IC 74121

in the function table (Table 9.1) indicate that the device is edge-triggered. It can be triggered in a number of ways. For instance if inputs $\bar{A}_1$ or $\bar{A}_2$ or both are low, a low-to-high transition on the B input will trigger the device. When input B is held high, the $\bar{A}_1$ or $\bar{A}_2$ inputs can also trigger it on a high-to-low transition (trailing or negative edge). The A inputs require rise times in excess of 1 V/µs, whereas the B input is a Schmitt trigger, which will respond to rise rates as low as 1 V/s.

Table 9.1 Function table for monostable multivibrator

Input			*Output*	
$\bar{A}_1$	$\bar{A}_2$	B	Q	$\bar{Q}$
L	X	H	L	H

X	L	H	L	H
X	X	L	L	H
H	H	X	L	H
H	↓	H	⊓	⊔
↓	H	H	⊓	⊔
↓	↓	H	⊓	⊔
L	X	↑	⊓	⊔
X	L	↑	⊓	⊔

L = Low
H = High
X = Don't care
↑ = Low-to-high transition
↓ = High-to-low transition

The duration of the output pulse will depend on the values of the resistor and capacitor in the circuit. An internal resistor, R_{int} of 2 K ohm is built into the IC and it can be made effective by connecting pin 9 to + V_{CC}, pin 14. If only the internal resistor is used without any external capacitor, a minimum pulse width of about 35 ns may be obtained. If an external resistor and capacitor are used, R_{ext} may have a range from 1.4 K ohm to 40 K ohm and C_{ext} may have a value up to 1000 μF. A maximum pulse width of about 30s may be obtained with maximum values of R_{ext} and C_{ext}. Pulse width may be calculated from the following expression:

Pulse width, $t = 0.694\text{ RC}$ ...(9.9)

where R is in Ohms,
C is in Farads
and t is in Seconds

Example 9.7: *Calculate the pulse width when R = 20 K ohm and C = 10 μF.*

Solution: Pulse width = $0.694 \times 20000 \times 10 \times 10^{-6}$

$= 0.1388\text{ s}$

This IC is often used for generating single clock pulses for general purpose work. For such use the circuit given in Fig. 9.30 will be useful. For the values shown in the diagram, the time duration of the output pulse will be about 7 ms.

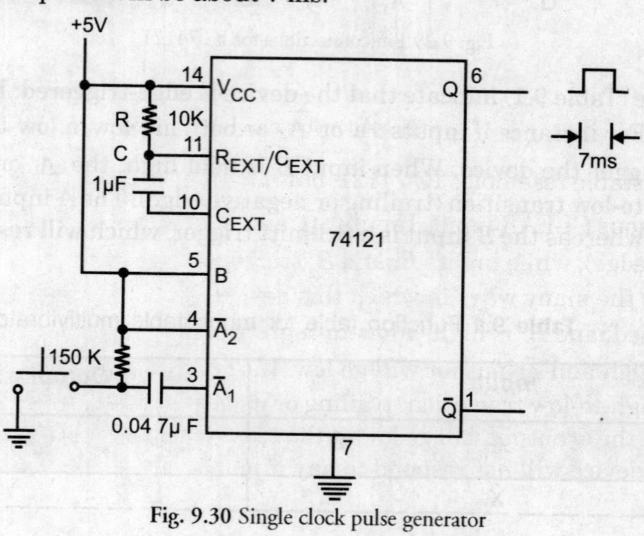

Fig. 9.30 Single clock pulse generator

Example 9.8: *If you are required to obtain a pulse 1 μs wide with IC 74121, calculate the value of the capacitor required if you are using the internal resistor in the device.*

Solution: From Eqn. (9.9)

$$C = \frac{1 \times 10^{-6} \times 10^{12}}{0.694 \times 2 \times 10^{4}} = 720 \text{ pF}$$

Example 9.9: *In the above example, if you want to obtain a pulse of the same width with a capacitor of 500 pF, what should be value of the resistor?*

Solution: $R = \dfrac{1 \times 10^{-6}}{0.694 \times 500 \times 10^{-12}}$

$= 2898$ ohm

9.3.5 Retriggerable Monostable Multivibrator : IC 74122

This is a retriggerable monostable multivibrator which, unlike IC 74121, will respond to a trigger pulse even when it is in the 'On' state. A functional diagram for this IC is given in Fig. 9.31.

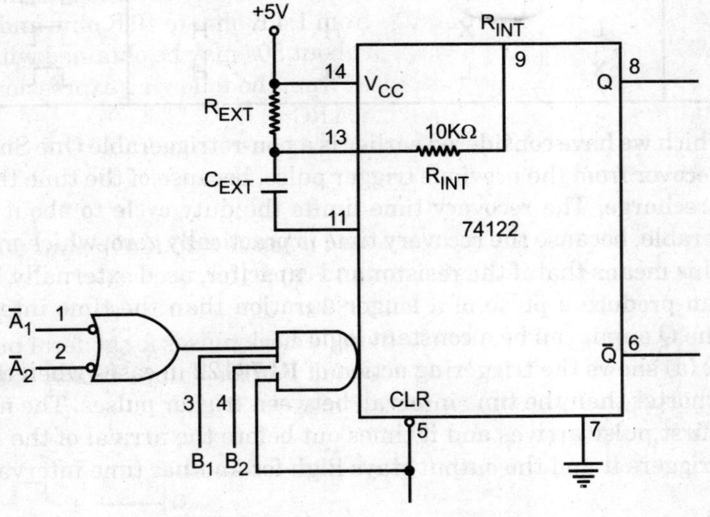

Fig. 9.31 Monostable multivibrator IC 74122

This monostable resembles IC 74121, but it has one more active high trigger input, as well as an asynchronous CLEAR input. Inputs $\overline{A_1}$ and $\overline{A_2}$ trigger on a high-to-low transition (trailing or negative edge), while inputs B_1 and B_2 trigger on a positive edge (low-to-high transition). Table 9.2 shows the many ways in which this device can be triggered. For instance if input $\overline{A_1}$ or $\overline{A_2}$ is grounded, and B_2 is high, a low-to-high transition on B_1 will trigger the device. The Q output will go high and $\overline{Q}$ output will go low. If B_1 and B_2 are high, $\overline{A_1}$ or $\overline{A_2}$ inputs can also trigger it on a high-to-low transition (trailing or negative edge). If the CLEAR input is activated by taking it low, the Q output will go low at the same time and will stay low. If the CLEAR input is held low, the device will not respond to any input.

Table 9.2 Function table for monostable multivibrator IC 74122

	Input				Output	
Clear	$\overline{A_1}$	$\overline{A_2}$	B_1	B_2	Q	$\overline{Q}$
L	X	X	X	X	L	H
X	H	H	X	X	L	H
X	X	X	L	X	L	H
X	X	X	X	L	L	H
H	L	X	↑	H	⊓	⊔
H	L	X	H	↑	⊓	⊔
H	X	L	↑	H	⊓	⊔
H	X	L	H	↑	⊓	⊔
H	H	↓	H	H	⊓	⊔
H	↓	↓	H	H	⊓	⊔
H	↓	H	H	H	⊓	⊔
↑	L	X	H	H	⊓	⊔
↑	X	L	H	H	⊓	⊔

IC 74121 which we have considered earlier is a non-retriggerable One Shot, which requires a finite time to recover from the previous trigger pulse, because of the time the capacitor in the circuit takes to recharge. The recovery time limits the duty cycle to about 90%. Monostable 74122 is retriggerable, because the recovery time is practically zero, which makes a 100% duty cycle possible. This means that if the resistor and capacitor, used externally, have the required values, which can produce a pulse of a longer duration than the time interval between two trigger pulses, the Q ouput can be a constant logic 1.

Figure 9.32 (a) shows the triggering action of IC 74122 in cases when the duration of the output pulse is shorter than the time interval between trigger pulses. The monostable is triggered when the first pulse arrives and it times out before the arrival of the second pulse. The second pulse retriggers it and the output stays high for another time interval and it times out again.

Figure 9.32 (b) shows the state of affairs when the duration of the output pulse is longer than the time interval between two trigger pulses. The monostable is triggered by the positive edge of the first pulse and an output is generated. When the positive edge of the next trigger pulse occurs, before the output pulse has completed its duration, the first timing interval is terminated and the second timing interval is initiated. Therefore there is no break in the output pulse. The output pulse has not completed its duration even when the third trigger pulse occurs, which retriggers the monostable. As there is no trigger pulse after the third, the output pulse terminates its normal duration following the positive edge of trigger pulse 3. Also notice that t_2 is greater than t_1.

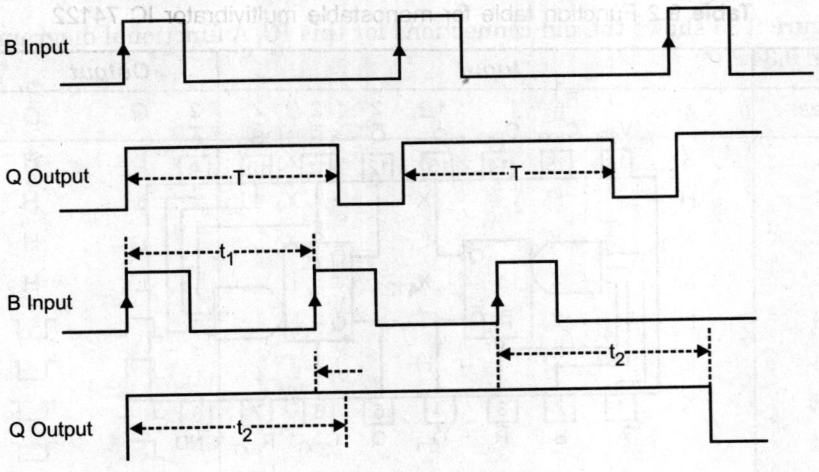

Fig. 9.32 (a), (b)

The duration for which the output will stay high depends on the values of R and C_{ext}. A 10 K ohm internal resistor is provided in the device. If this is used R_{int} pin should be connected to $+V_{CC}$. The connections for R_{ext} and C_{ext} are shown in Fig. 9.31. R_{ext} can have any value from 5 to 50 k ohms. There is no restriction on the maximum value of C_{ext}.

If the timing capacitor used is smaller than 1000 pF, the pulse width should be determined with the help of the chart recommended by the manufacturer of the device. Where the value of the capacitor used is larger than 1000 pF, the pulse width can be estimated from the following equation:

$$\text{Pulse width, } t = 0.35 \times R_{ext} \times C_{ext} \qquad ...(9.10)$$

where t is in Seconds

R is in Ohms

and C is in Farads

Example 9.10: *Calculate the pulse width for a 74122 monostable multivibrator, when R_{ext} = 15 K ohm and C_{ext} = 0.002 μF.*

Solution: From Eqn. (9.10)

$$t = 0.35\,(15 \times 10^3)\,(0.002 \times 10^{-6})$$
$$= 10.5\ \mu s$$

Example 9.11: *Calculate the value of C_{ext} required, so that a 74122 monostable multivibrator produces a pulse width of 200 ns when R_{int} is used.*

Solution: From Eqn. (9.10)

$$C_{ext} = \frac{t}{0.35 \times R_{int}}$$
$$= \frac{200 \times 10^{-9}}{0.35\,(10 \times 10^3)} \times 10^{12} \text{ pF}$$
$$= 57 \text{ pF}$$

9.3.6 Retriggerable Monostable Multivibrator IC 74123

This IC has two retriggerable monostable multivibrators in one package and it operates in the same way as IC 74122. The only difference is that IC 74123 does not have an internal timing resistor. Figure 9.33 shows the pin connections for this IC. A functional diagram for the IC is given in Fig. 9.34.

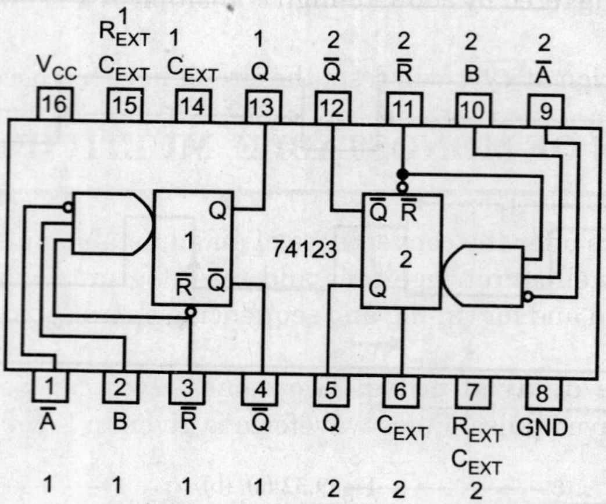

Fig. 9.33 Pin connections for IC 74123

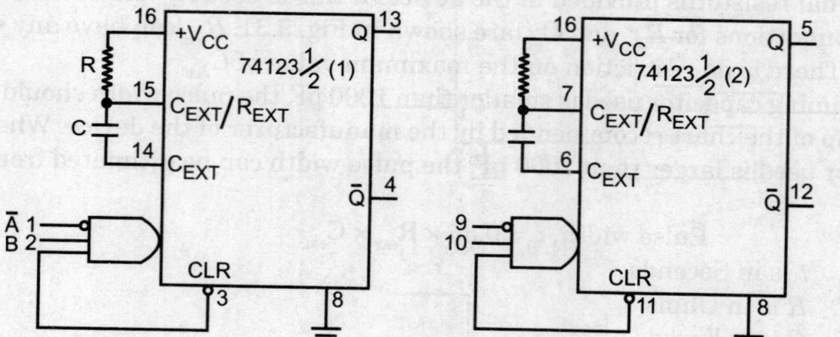

Fig. 9.34 Functional diagram for IC 74123

A function table for IC 74123 is given in Table 9.3.

Table 9.3 Function table for IC 74123

Input			Output	
$\overline{A}$	*B*	$\overline{CLR}$	*Q*	$\overline{Q}$
↓	H	H	positive pulse	negative pulse
L	↑	H	positive pulse	negative pulse
L	H	↑	positive pulse	negative pulse
X	X	L	negative pulse	positive pulse
X	X	↓	negative pulse	positive pulse

Table 9.3 shows that this monostable can be triggered by applying pulses at input $\overline{A}$, *B* or $\overline{CLR}$. A high-to-low transition at input $\overline{A}$ will trigger the circuit when inputs *B* and $\overline{CLR}$ are held high. The output at *Q* will become logic 1 from logic 0.

A low-to-high transition at B will also trigger the circuit when $\overline{A}$ is held low and CLR is held high. It can also be triggered by a low-to-high transition at CLR when $\overline{A}$ is held low and B is held high.

A high-to-low transition at $\overline{CLR}$ will reset the circuit irrespective of the values of $\overline{A}$ and B.

9.4 APPLICATION OF MONOSTABLE MULTIVIBRATORS

Monostable multivibrators offer the convenience of an adjustable pulse width with the help of external components as well as retriggerable and reset features, which makes it a versatile device for pulse generation and for timing and sequencing operations. We will consider some of these applications here.

1. Generation of a delayed pulse: Two monostables can be connected as shown in Fig. 9.35 to provide a delayed pulse. Pulse waveform is given in Fig. 9.36.

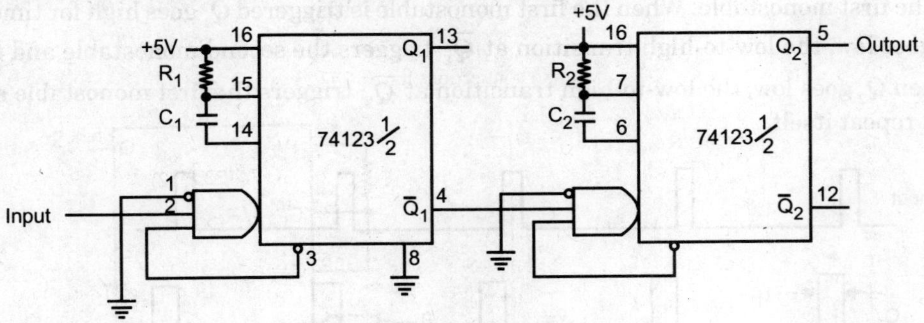

Fig. 9.35 Delayed pulse generator

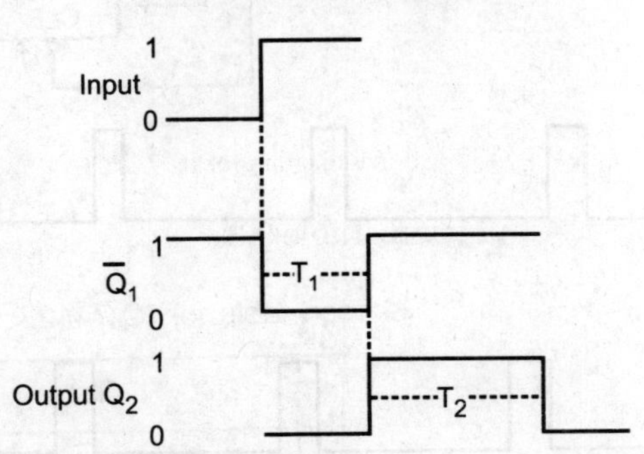

Fig. 9.36 Pulse waveforms for the circuit of Fig. 9.35

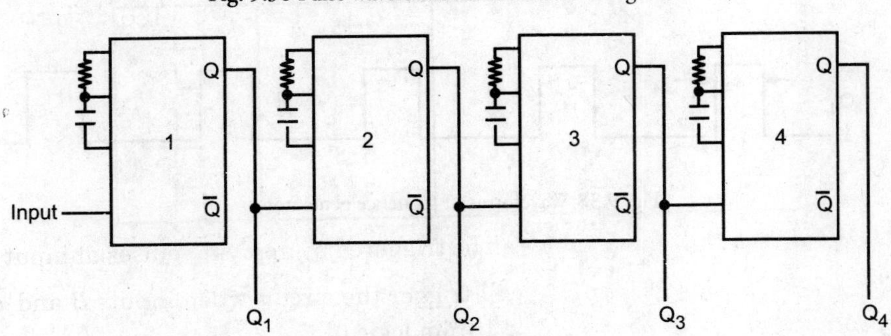

Fig. 9.37 Pulse sequence generator

2. Pulse sequence generator: The method that we have used for generating a delayed pulse can be extended to generate a sequence of timing pulses as shown in Fig. 9.37. Timing components are chosen for the required timing interval. The resultant waveforms are shown in Fig. 9.38.

3. Generation of long duration pulses: In Section 9.3.5 we have mentioned that a retriggerable monostable can be used to generate long duration pulses by making the pulse width of the monostable longer than the time interval between input trigger pulses. This enables the monostable to remain triggered during the sequence of input pulses. This set up can also be used for detecting missing pulses. If any of the input pulses should fail to occur, the monostable will time out and the output will go low.

4. Astable multivibrator using IC 74123: An astable multivibrator can be built by connecting IC 74123 as shown in Fig. 9.39.

You will notice that the $\overline{Q}_2$ output of the second monostable is connected to pin 2 of the input of the first monostable. When the first monostable is triggered Q_1 goes high for time t_1 and when it goes low, the low-to-high transition at $\overline{Q}_1$ triggers the second monostable and Q_2 goes high. When Q_2 goes low, the low-to-high transition at $\overline{Q}_2$ triggers the first monostable and the cycle will repeat itself.

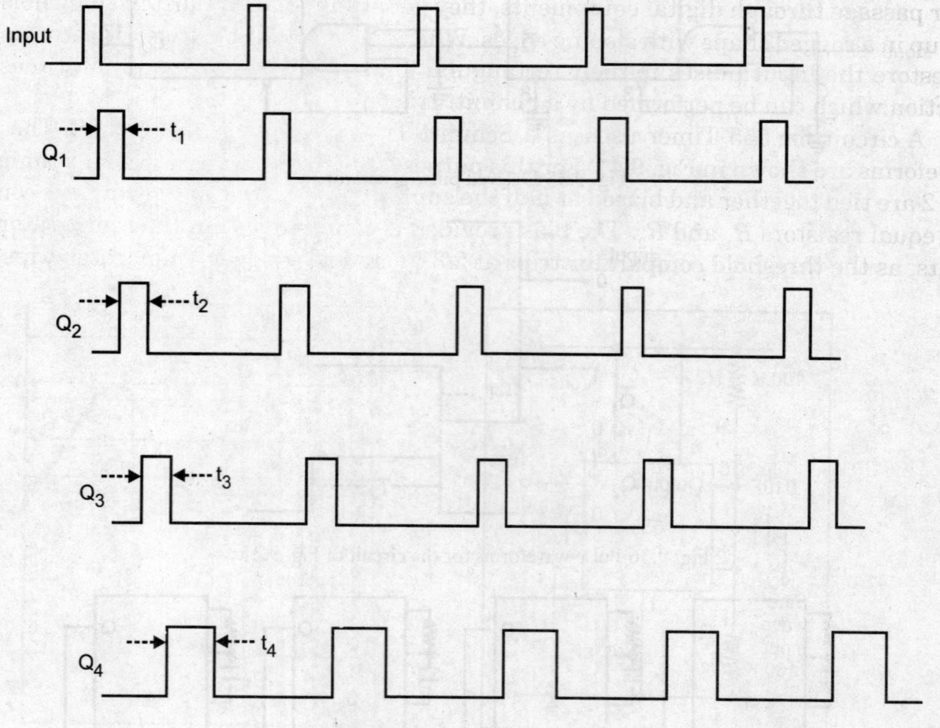

Fig. 9.38 Waveforms of sequence generator

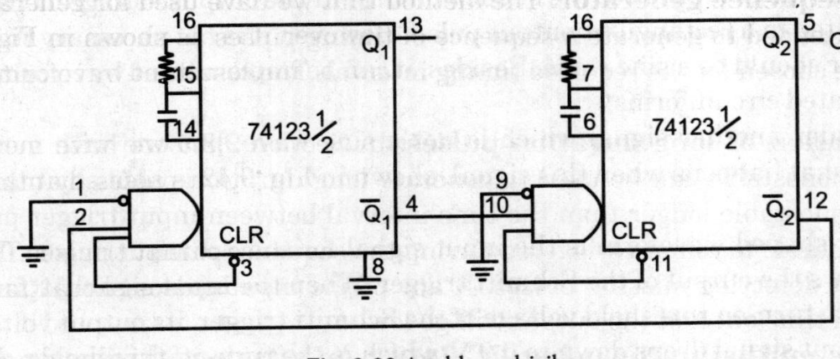

Fig. 9.39 Astable multivibrator

9.5 SCHMITT TRIGGER

For satisfactory operation, logic gates require input signals which change very fast from low to high and from high to low voltage levels. In short they require rectangular pulses with very sharp edges. However, even if we provide perfect inputs to logic devices, during the course of their passage through digital equipments, they get attenuated, are distorted by noise and may end up in a ragged shape with sloping edges. When such a situation arises, it becomes necessary to restore the input pulses to their rectangular shape with fast rise and fall times. This is a function which can be performed by a Schmitt trigger.

A circuit for 555 Timer used as a Schmitt Trigger is given in Fig. 9.40. The associated waveforms are shown in Fig. 9.41. For this purpose, the threshold and trigger terminals, pins 6 and 2 are tied together and biased at half the supply voltage, by a voltage divider comprising of two equal resistors R_1 and R_2. The bias provided is centered within the comparator's tripping limits, as the threshold comparator trips at 2/3 V_{cc} and the trigger comparator trips at 1/3 V_{cc}.

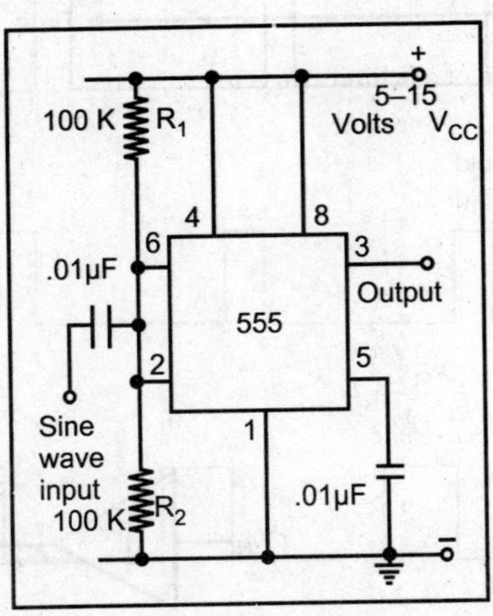

Fig. 9.40 Schmitt trigger

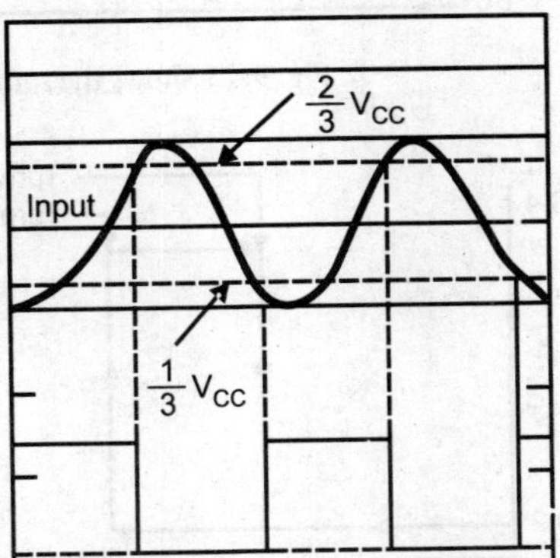

Fig. 9.41 Schmitt trigger waveforms

If a sine wave input is applied, having an amplitude greater than the comparator's reference levels, it will cause the timer flip-flop to set and reset. The input sine wave and the output waveforms are given in Fig. 9.41. The phase relationship between the two waveforms

can be seen from the diagram. Notice the sudden change in the output voltage at the threshold points, which resulted in a rectangular output pulse. However, it is not necessary that the input to a Schmitt trigger should be a sine wave. Besides, it can be implemented by circuits which are available in integrated circuit forms.

We will consider another signal which is not a sine wave, but one with very irregular shape. Let us see what happens when this signal, shown in Fig. 9.42 is applied at the input of a Schmitt trigger.

The irregular-shaped waveform is the input signal for the Schmitt trigger. The squared signal below it shows the output of the Schmitt trigger. When the input signal attains the level of 1.7 V, which is the turn-on threshold voltage of the Schmitt trigger, its output voltage rises to 3.4 V. When the input signal drops down to 0.9 V, which is the turn-off threshold voltage of the Schmitt trigger, its output voltage falls to 0.2 V. Thus the input signal, which had an irregular shape is converted into rectangular pulses. The difference between the turn-on and turn-off threshold levels is called 'hysteresis'. Figure 9.43 shows the threshold levels and the hysteresis voltage. Figure 9.44 shows the symbol for a Schmitt trigger.

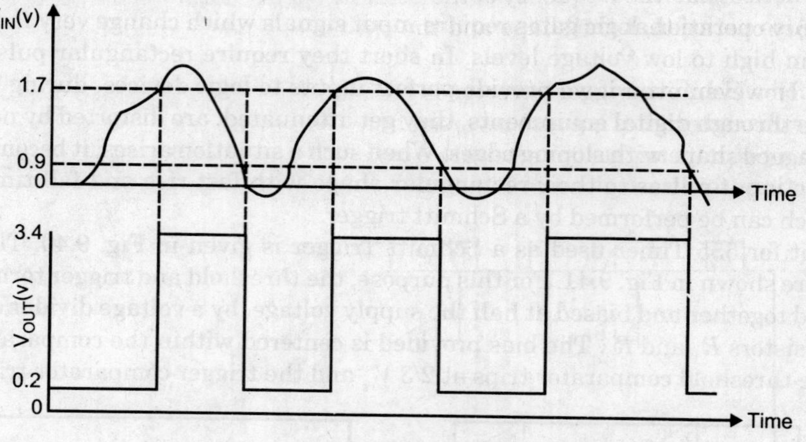

Fig. 9.42 Shows the squaring action of a Schmitt trigger

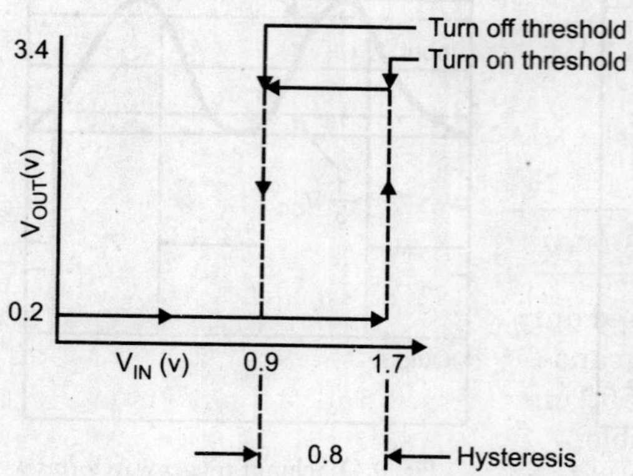

Fig. 9.43 Transfer characteristics of a Schmitt trigger

Fig. 9.44 Schmitt trigger symbol

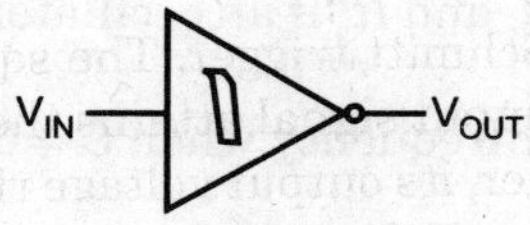

Fig. 9.45 Schmitt trigger inverter symbol

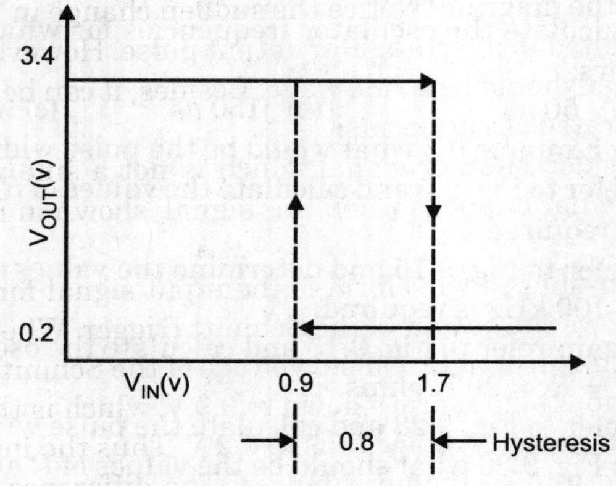

Fig. 9.46 Transfer characteristics of a Schmitt trigger inverter

You will also notice that the frequency of the Schmitt trigger output is the same as that of the input signal. Also notice that the shape and the output levels are compatible with output devices.

The symbol for a Schmitt trigger inverter is shown in Fig. 9.45. Because it inverts the signal, the transfer characteristics are also reversed from those shown in Fig. 9.43. The transfer characteristics for a Schmitt trigger inverter are given in Fig. 9.46. IC 7414 is a hex Schmitt trigger. Pin connections for it are given in Fig. 9.47.

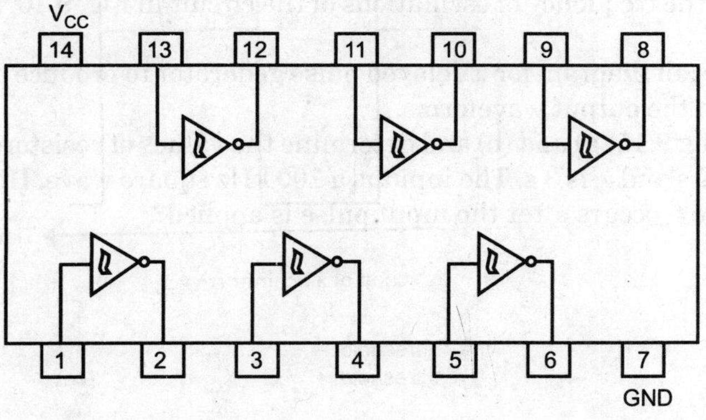

Fig. 9.47 Pin connections for hex Schmitt inverter IC 7414

Problems

9.1 Calculate the operating frequency and duty cycle for 555 Timer in the astable mode, when R_A = 10 K ohm, R_B = 47 K ohm and C = 0.01 μ F (Refer to Fig. 9.18).

9.2 Design an astable oscillator using 555 Timer to oscillate at a frequency of 1 kHz with a duty cycle as close to 50% as possible.

9.3 For a 555 Timer operating in the astable mode, as shown in Fig. 9.18, you require a clock cycle duration of 1 ms and a duty cycle of 40%. Calculate the oscillator frequency and the required values of R_A and C, if R_B = 28,800 ohm.

9.4 Calculate the duration of a clock cycle for the following frequencies:

(a) 8 MHz (b) 3 MHz (c) 100 kHz (d) 1 kHz

9.5 Calculate the oscillator frequencies for which the duration of clock cycles is as follows:

(a) 50 ns (b) 150 ns (c) 500 ns (d) 1000 ns.

9.6 In Example 9.3 what would be the pulse width of the output frequency?

9.7 Refer to Fig. 9.5 and calculate the values of R and C if an oscillator frequency of 1 kHz is required.

9.8 Refer to Fig. 9.15 and determine the values of C, R_1 and R_2 if an oscillator frequecny of 100 kHz is required.

9.9 Again refer to Fig. 9.15 and calculate the oscillator frequency when $C = 0.01$ µF and $R_1 = R_2 = 20$ K ohms.

9.10 Refer to Fig. 9.28 and calculate the pulse width if $R = 100$ K ohm and $C = 0.01$ µ F.

9.11 In Fig. 9.30 what should be the values of R and C if a pulse width of 5 ms is required.

9.12 Refer to Fig. 9.34. What will be the state of the output at $\overline{Q}$ under the following conditions?

(a) $\overline{A} = H : B = L :$ CLR $= L$

(b) $\overline{A} = L : B = H :$ CLR $= H$

(c) $\overline{A} = L : B = L :$ CLR $= H$

(d) $\overline{A} = H : B = H :$ CLR $= L$

9.13 Refer to Fig. 9.34 and calculate the pulse width if $R = 39$ K ohm and $C = 0.02$ µF.

9.14 Calculate the frequency of oscillations of the circuit in Fig. 9.10, if $C = 0.02$ µF and K is 0.5.

9.15 Draw a circuit diagram for a delayed pulse generator to produce three delayed pulses and sketch the output waveforms.

9.16 Refer to Fig. 9.15 (a) and (b) and determine the values of resistors and capacitors if t_1 is 1s, t_2 is 2 s and t_3 is 3 s. The input is a 100 kHz square wave. How much time will it take before t_1 occurs after the input pulse is applied?

10 Combinational Logic Circuits

10.1 INTRODUCTION

In this chapter we will consider combinational logic circuits, which differ from sequential circuits for the reason that they do not possess memory. Besides, in combinational systems, the output is the direct result of the state of the inputs at that moment and bears no relation to the prior state of the inputs, and the response of the output follows immediately after the inputs. As long as the input values are maintained, the output will undergo no change. Consider a 4-input AND gate. As soon as all the four inputs become 1, the output becomes 1 and remains in this state as long as the input is unchanged.

Combinational circuits are provided with a set of inputs which are connected to a logic network which operate on the inputs and produce a set of outputs. The logic network comprises of gates and possibly other components as well. Combinational logic circuits take many forms; but the ones most commonly used are decoders, encoders, multiplexers, demultiplexers, comparators and code converters, and are used to process binary data.

Most of these functional devices are available in MSI form. It is very often unnecessary to design your own system, as you may be able to locate one which meets your requirements. When you have found the right devices for your needs, your job is reduced to interconnect the devices so that the combination performs the required function. We will consider some of these devices in this chapter and see how they can be used to solve some digital problems.

10.2 DECODERS

Decoders are used to docode the binary state of the inputs. Suppose you have two inputs marked A and B as in Fig. 10.1. These two inputs will have four states, A, $\overline{A}$, B and $\overline{B}$.

As there are two variables, there will be four input states and, when you want to know the decimal value of any set of inputs, you will look at the output, which will indicate the decimal value of the binary inputs as shown in Table 10.1.

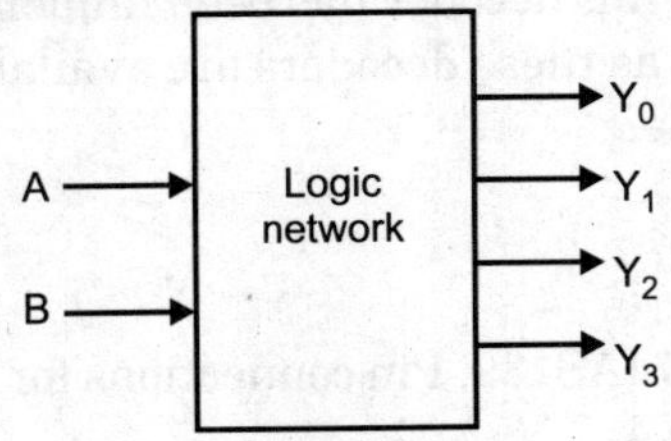

Fig. 10.1

Table 10.1

Input		*Output*			
A	*B*	Y_0 0	Y_1 1	Y_2 2	Y_3 3
L	L	L	H	H	H
L	H	H	L	H	H
H	L	H	H	L	H
H	H	H	H	H	L

If the outputs are connected to logic indicators, when an input is applied you can immediately know the decimal value of the inputs by looking at the logic indicators. If you use a bulb at the output with suitable circuitry to illuminate marked numerals, you can read the decimal value of the inputs. This decoder can be implemented by the circuit shown in Fig. 10.2.

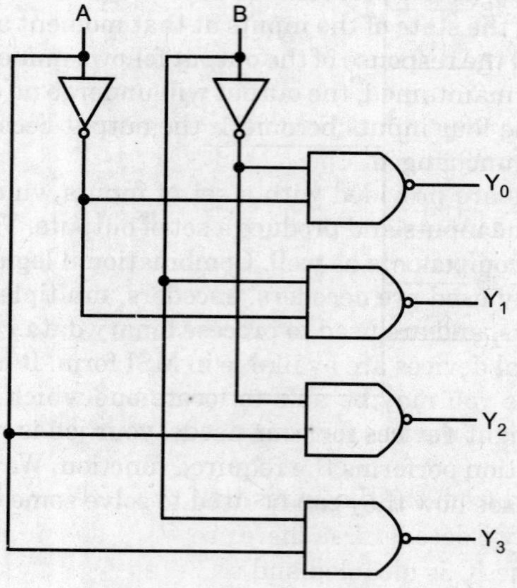

Fig. 10.2

Table 10.1 represents the truth table for this deoder. You will notice from this table that for any combination of the inputs, only one output is low and all the other outputs are high. Since NAND gates have been used at the output, a low value of Y represents the state of the inputs. The decoder selects only one of the outputs at a time and this decoder is, therefore, called a 1-of-4 decoder. In the same manner, as this decoder has been implemented, you can make a 1-of-8, 1-of-10 or 1-of-16 decoder. However, as these decoders are available in integrated circuit forms, it is really not necessary to build one.

10.2.1 1-of-4 Decoder

A 1-of-4 decoder is available as IC 74AS139. Pin connections for this IC are given in Fig. 10.3 and its logic symbol is given in Fig. 10.4.

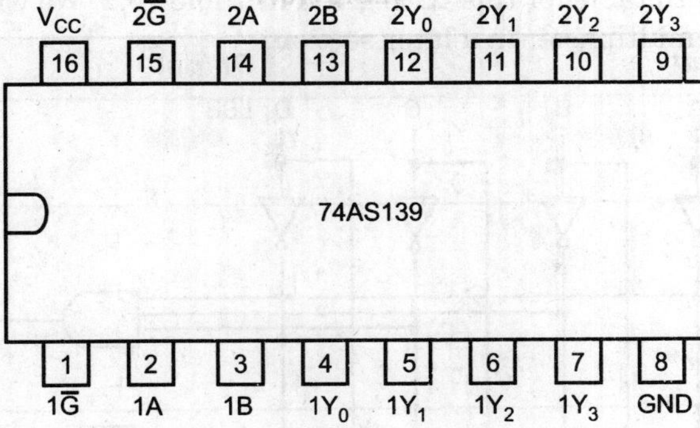

Fig. 10.3 Pin connections for IC 74AS139

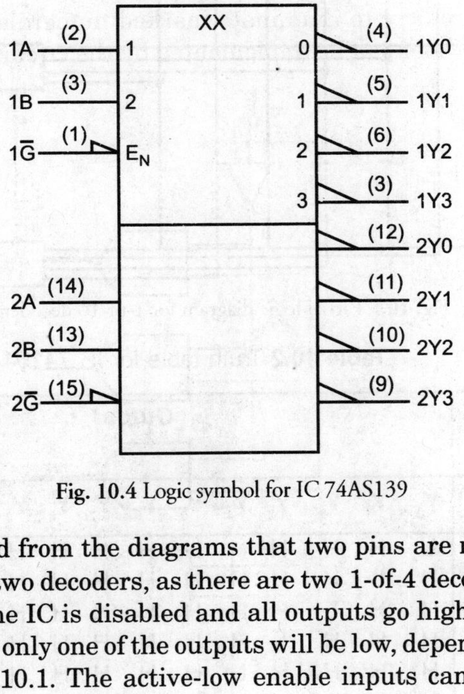

Fig. 10.4 Logic symbol for IC 74AS139

You must have noticed from the diagrams that two pins are marked $1\bar{G}$ and $2\bar{G}$. These are the enable pins for the two decoders, as there are two 1-of-4 decoders in one package. When these pins are held high, the IC is disabled and all outputs go high. When these pins are held low, the chip is enabled and only one of the outputs will be low, depending on the condition of the inputs as shown in Table 10.1. The active-low enable inputs can be used as a data line in demultiplexing applications.

10.2.2 1-of-16 Decoder

A 1-of-16 decoder can be implemented in the same way as a 1-of-4 decoder. A partial logic diagram for such a decoder is given in Fig. 10.5. It will accept four inputs and produce 16 outputs. For the decoder diagram shown here, only one of the 16 outputs will be high at a time. When the input is 0000, output Y_0 will be high and all other outputs will be low. When the input is 1111, output Y_{15} will be high and all other outputs will be low. Notice that the subscripts of the outputs represent the decimal value of the binary inputs.

A 1-of-16 decoder is available as IC 74154 and it is designated as a 4-line to 16-line decoder-demultiplexer, since it can also be used as a demultiplexer. Pin connections for this IC are shown in Fig. 10.6 and its logic symbol is given in Fig. 10.7. This is also called a binary-to-decimal decoder. The truth table for this IC is given in Table 10.2. We will consider its application as a decoder and demultiplexer in a later section.

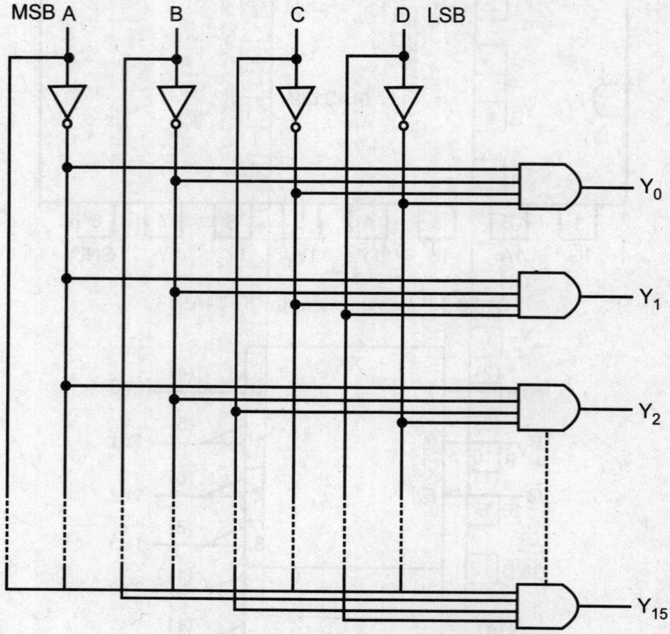

Fig. 10.5 Partial logic diagram for 1-of-16 decoder

Table 10.2 Truth table for IC 74154

Strobe	*Data input*	*Control input*				*Output*															
		A	*B*	*C*	*D*	Y_0	Y_1	Y_2	Y_3	Y_4	Y_5	Y_6	Y_7	Y_8	Y_9	Y_{10}	Y_{11}	Y_{12}	Y_{13}	Y_{14}	Y_{15}
L	L	L	L	L	L	L	H	H	H	H	H	H	H	H	H	H	H	H	H	H	H
L	L	L	L	L	H	H	L	H	H	H	H	H	H	H	H	H	H	H	H	H	H
L	L	L	L	H	L	H	H	L	H	H	H	H	H	H	H	H	H	H	H	H	H
L	L	L	L	H	H	H	H	H	L	H	H	H	H	H	H	H	H	H	H	H	H
L	L	L	H	L	L	H	H	H	H	L	H	H	H	H	H	H	H	H	H	H	H
L	L	L	H	L	H	H	H	H	H	H	L	H	H	H	H	H	H	H	H	H	H
L	L	L	H	H	L	H	H	H	H	H	H	L	H	H	H	H	H	H	H	H	H
L	L	L	H	H	H	H	H	H	H	H	H	H	L	H	H	H	H	H	H	H	H
L	L	H	L	L	L	H	H	H	H	H	H	H	H	L	H	H	H	H	H	H	H
L	L	H	L	L	H	H	H	H	H	H	H	H	H	H	L	H	H	H	H	H	H
L	L	H	L	H	L	H	H	H	H	H	H	H	H	H	H	L	H	H	H	H	H
L	L	H	L	H	H	H	H	H	H	H	H	H	H	H	H	H	L	H	H	H	H
L	L	H	H	L	L	H	H	H	H	H	H	H	H	H	H	H	H	L	H	H	H
L	L	H	H	L	H	H	H	H	H	H	H	H	H	H	H	H	H	H	L	H	H
L	L	H	H	H	L	H	H	H	H	H	H	H	H	H	H	H	H	H	H	L	H
L	L	H	H	H	H	H	H	H	H	H	H	H	H	H	H	H	H	H	H	H	L
L	H	X	X	X	X	H	H	H	H	H	H	H	H	H	H	H	H	H	H	H	H
H	L	X	X	X	X	H	H	H	H	H	H	H	H	H	H	H	H	H	H	H	H
H	H	X	X	X	X	H	H	H	H	H	H	H	H	H	H	H	H	H	H	H	H

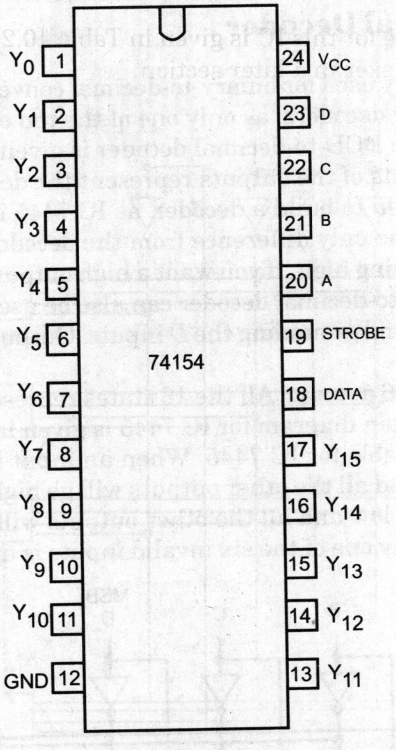

Fig. 10.6 Pin connections for IC 74154

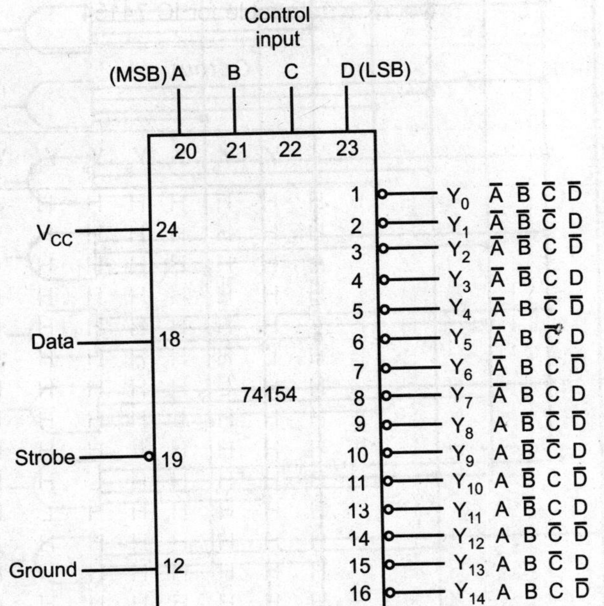

Fig. 10.7 Logic symbol for IC 74154

10.2.3 BCD-to-Decimal Decoder

Decoder circuits are commonly used for binary-to-decimal conversion. BCD-to-decimal decoders are also referred to as 1-of-10 decoders, as only one of the ten output lines in high (or low) at a time. A circuit to implement a BCD-to-decimal decoder is given in Fig. 10.8.

In Fig. 10.8 the subscripts of the outputs represent the decimal value of the inputs. However, it is not necessary for you to build a decoder, as IC 7445 is available, which is a BCD-to-decimal decoder. In this IC the only difference from the decoder in Fig. 10.8 is that the active output line is low instead of being high. If you want a high output in the active line, you will have to use an inverter. This BCD-to-decimal decoder can also be used as a 1-of-8 or octal decoder by using only *A*, *B* and *C* inputs and grounding the *D* inputs. Outputs Y_8 and Y_9 from pins 10 and 11 may be ignored.

A Hex decoder is a 1-of-16 decoder. All the 16 states represented by four input lines can be recognized by this decoder. A pin diagram for IC 7445 is given in Fig. 10.9.

Table 10.3 is the truth table for IC 7445. When an input is applied to this IC, the corresponding output will go low and all the other outputs will go high. For instance, when the input is 0100, output line Y_4 will go low and all the other outputs will go high, which you will notice from the truth table. When any one of the six invalid inputs is applied, all outputs will go high.

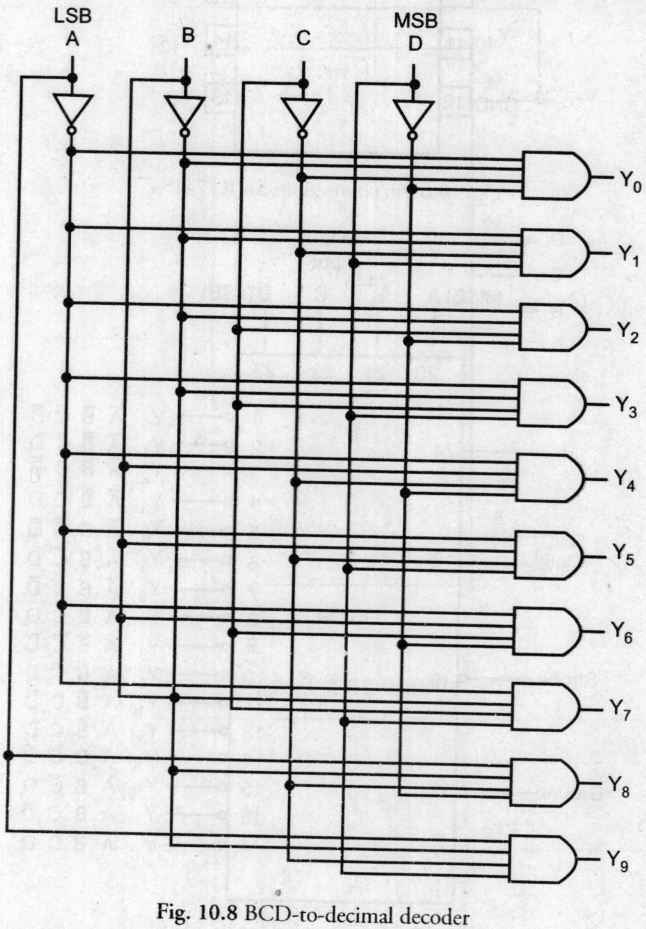

Fig. 10.8 BCD-to-decimal decoder

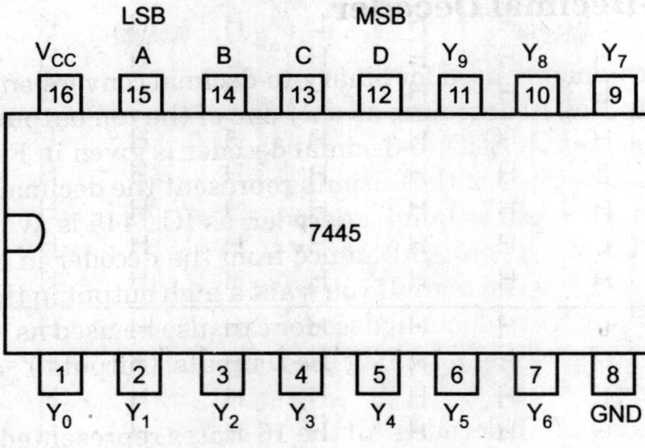

Fig. 10.9 Pin connections for IC 7445

The outputs of this decoder can be displayed by connecting LEDs at the outputs as shown in Fig. 10.10. A suitable resistor will have to be used in series with each LED to limit the current to a safe value.

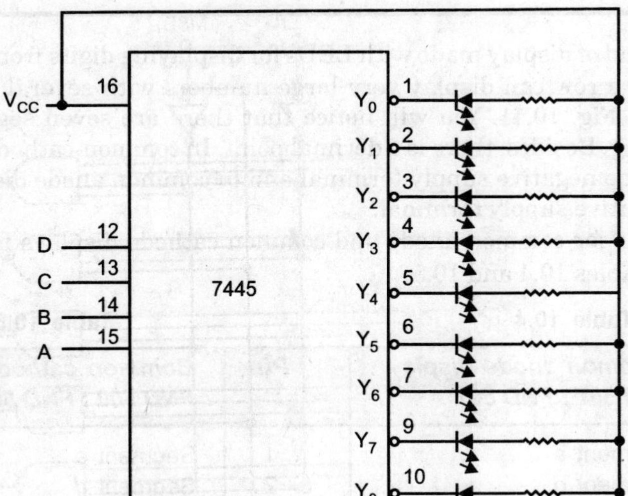

Fig. 10.10

Table 10.3 Truth table for IC 7445

No.	*Inputs* D MSB	C	B	A LSB	*Outputs* Y_0	Y_1	Y_2	Y_3	Y_4	Y_5	Y_6	Y_7	Y_8	Y_9
0	L	L	L	L	L	H	H	H	H	H	H	H	H	H
1	L	L	L	H	H	L	H	H	H	H	H	H	H	H

2	L	L	H	L	H	H	L	H	H	H	H	H	H	H
3	L	L	H	H	H	H	H	L	H	H	H	H	H	H
4	L	H	L	L	H	H	H	H	L	H	H	H	H	H
5	L	H	L	H	H	H	H	H	H	L	H	H	H	H
6	L	H	H	L	H	H	H	H	H	H	L	H	H	H
7	L	H	H	H	H	H	H	H	H	H	H	L	H	H
8	H	L	L	L	H	H	H	H	H	H	H	H	L	H
9	H	L	L	H	H	H	H	H	H	H	H	H	H	L
Invalid	H	L	H	L	H	H	H	H	H	H	H	H	H	H
	H	L	H	H	H	H	H	H	H	H	H	H	H	H
	H	H	L	L	H	H	H	H	H	H	H	H	H	H
	H	H	L	H	H	H	H	H	H	H	H	H	H	H
	H	H	H	L	H	H	H	H	H	H	H	H	H	H
	H	H	H	H	H	H	H	H	H	H	H	H	H	H

10.3 SEVEN-SEGMENT LED DISPLAY

There is a special kind of display made with LEDs for displaying digits from 0 through 9. A bank of these displays in a row can display very large numbers with several digits. A single digit display is shown in Fig. 10.11. You will notice that there are seven segments and they are designated from *a* to *g*. Besides, there is a decimal point. In common-cathode displays pins 3 and 8 are connected to the negative supply terminal and in common anode displays these pins are connected to the positive supply terminal.

Pin connections for common anode and common cathode displays for some types of displays are given in Tables 10.4 and 10.5.

Table 10.4

Pin	*Common anode display FND 507 : FND 567*
1	Segment *e*
2	Segment *d*
3	Common anode
4	Segment *c*
5	Decimal point
6	Segment *b*
7	Segment *a*
8	Common anode
9	Segment *f*
10	Segment *g*

Table 10.5

Pin	*Common cathode display FND 500 : FND 560*
1	Segment *e*
2	Segment *d*
3	Common cathode
4	Segment *c*
5	Decimal point
6	Segment *b*
7	Segment *a*
8	Common cathode
9	Segment *f*
10	Segment *g*

Table 7.10 gives the segments required to be illuminated for a given digit. The segments to be illuminated are marked 1 and those not required to be illuminated are marked 0. The table also gives the decimal numbers displayed as well as the BCD code for each decimal number. A BCD to 7-segment decoder driver is required to operate the LED display. The decoder driver decodes the decimal states of the input from 0 through 9 and develops the seven output signals, one for each segment of the display to operate the LED display.

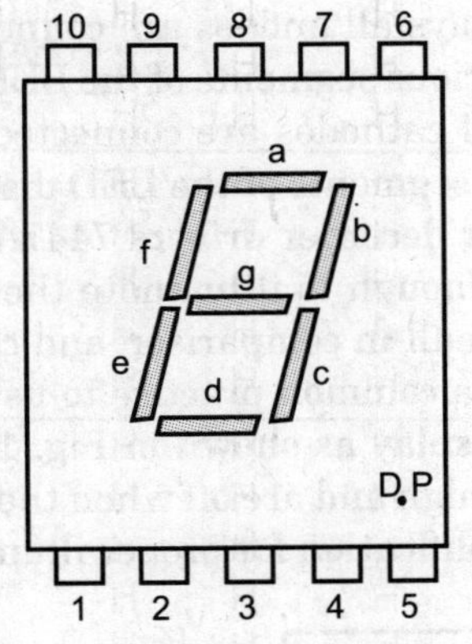

Fig. 10.11 Seven-segment LED display

10.4 BCD-TO-SEVEN-SEGMENT DECODER DRIVER

We will consider two decoder drivers ICs 7447A and 7448. They are used to drive seven-segment LED displays, which we have just considered. Pin connections for both these ICs are the same and have been shown in Fig. 10.12. The only difference is that IC 7448 incorporates voltage dropping resistors for the LED display, whereas external resistors are required for IC 7447A. Besides, IC 7448 is used with common-cathode displays, where as IC 7447 A is meant for use with common-anode displays. Tables 10.6 and 10.7 give the truth tables for decoder-drivers 7447A and 7448, respectively.

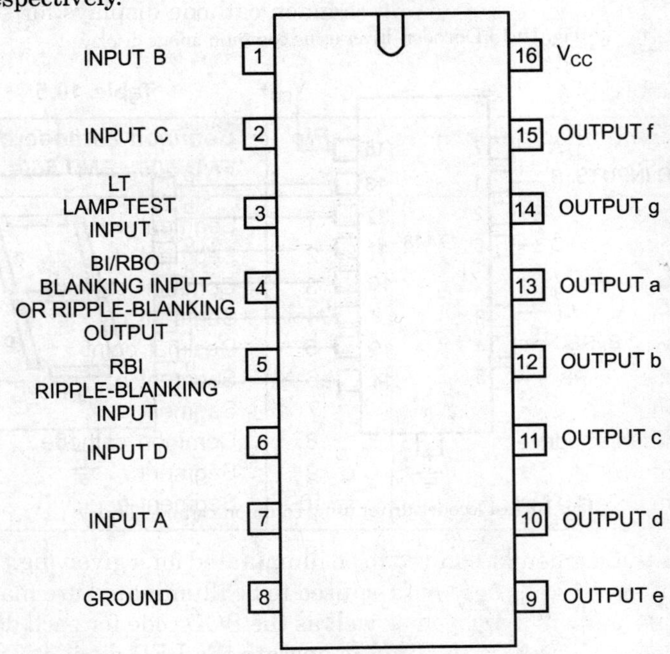

Fig. 10.12 Pin connections for ICs 7447A and 7448

In common anode LED displays all anodes are connected together to Vcc + and decoder driver outputs are connected to various segments of the LED displays as shown in Fig. 10.13. In common-cathode LED displays all cathodes are connected to ground and the decoder driver outputs are applied to the various segments of the LED display as shown in Fig. 10.14.

If you refer to data sheets for decorder drivers 7447A and 7448, you will notice that the output current of 7447A is large enough to illuminate the segments adequately, whereas the output current of 7448 is quite small in comparison and cannot therefore illuminate the segments adequately. It is, therefore a common practice to use buffer amplifiers between the decoder driver 7448 and the LED display as shown in Fig. 10.15. The buffer transistors are on when the decoder driver output is high and are off when the output is low. These buffer transistors provide adequate current amplification for proper illumination of the LED display.

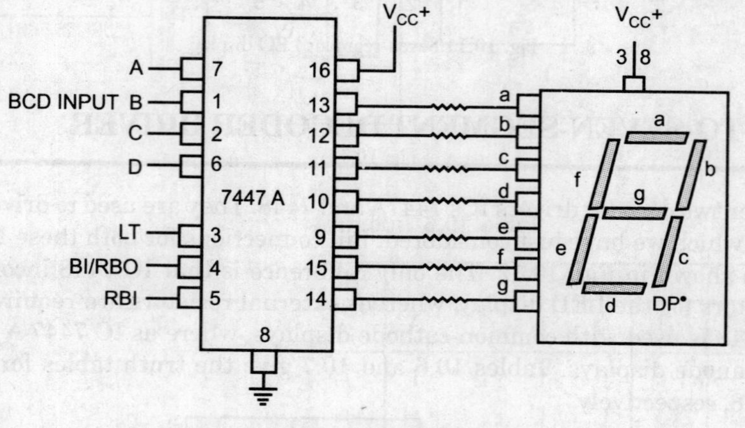

Fig. 10.13 Docoder-driver using common-anode display

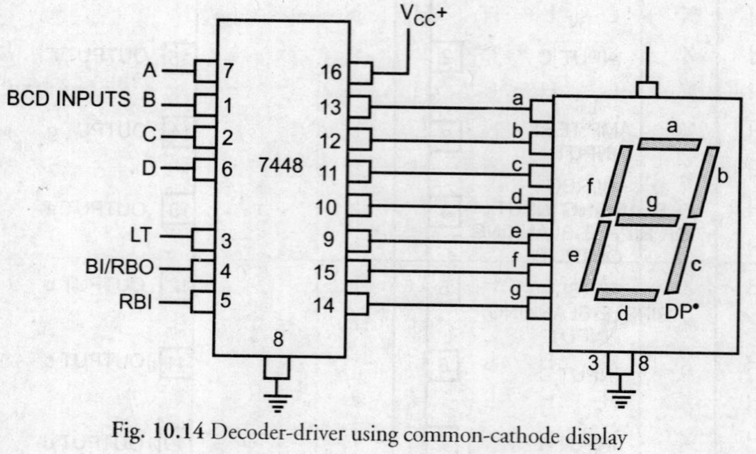

Fig. 10.14 Decoder-driver using common-cathode display

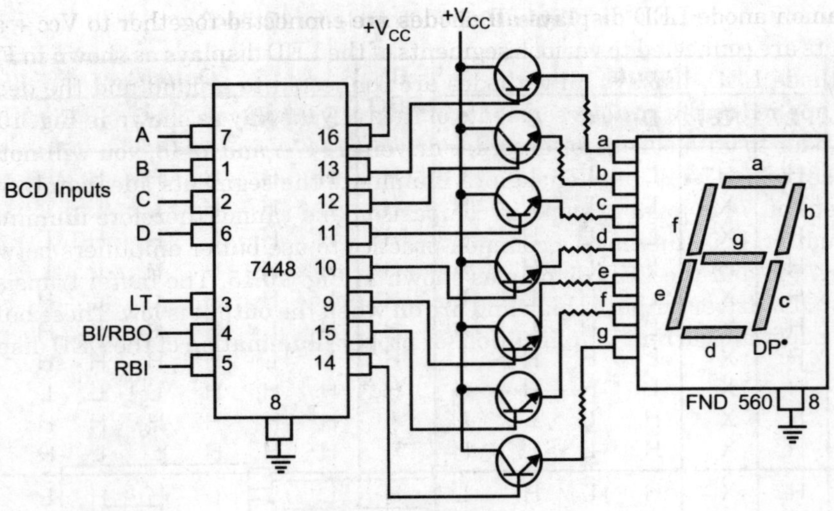

Fig. 10.15

Table 10.6 Truth table for IC 7447 A

Decimal or function	Inputs						BI/RBO	Outputs							Note
	LT	RBI	D	C	B	A		a	b	c	d	e	f	g	
0	H	H	L	L	L	L	H	L	L	L	L	L	L	H	
1	H	X	L	L	L	H	H	H	L	L	H	H	H	H	
2	H	X	L	L	H	L	H	L	L	H	L	L	H	L	
3	H	X	L	L	H	H	H	L	L	L	L	H	H	L	
4	H	X	L	H	L	L	H	H	L	L	H	H	L	L	
5	H	X	L	H	L	H	H	L	H	L	L	H	L	L	
6	H	X	L	H	H	L	H	H	H	L	L	L	L	L	
7	H	X	L	H	H	H	H	L	L	L	H	H	H	H	
8	H	X	H	L	L	L	H	L	L	L	L	L	L	L	
9	H	X	H	L	L	H	H	L	L	L	H	H	L	L	1
10	H	X	H	L	H	L	H	H	H	H	L	L	H	L	
11	H	X	H	L	H	H	H	H	H	L	L	H	H	L	
12	H	X	H	H	L	L	H	H	L	H	H	H	L	L	
13	H	X	H	H	L	H	H	L	H	H	L	H	L	L	
14	H	X	H	H	H	L	H	H	H	H	L	L	L	L	
15	H	X	H	H	H	H	H	H	H	H	H	H	H	H	
BI	X	X	X	X	X	X	L	H	H	H	H	H	H	H	2
RBI	H	L	L	L	L	L	L	H	H	H	H	H	H	H	3
LT	L	X	X	X	X	X	H	L	L	L	L	L	L	L	4

H = Logic 1 : L = Logic 0 : X = Don't care

Table 10.7 Truth table for IC 7448

Decimal or function	*Inputs*						*BI RBO*	*Outputs*							*Note*
	LT	*RBI*	*D*	*C*	*B*	*A*		*a*	*b*	*c*	*d*	*e*	*f*	*g*	
0	H	H	L	L	L	L	H	H	H	H	H	H	H	L	
1	H	X	L	L	L	H	H	L	H	H	L	L	L	L	
2	H	X	L	L	H	L	H	H	H	L	H	H	L	H	
3	H	H	L	L	H	H	H	H	H	H	H	L	L	H	
4	H	X	L	H	L	L	H	L	H	H	L	L	H	H	
5	H	X	L	H	L	H	H	H	L	H	H	L	H	H	
6	H	X	L	H	H	L	H	L	L	H	H	H	H	H	
7	H	X	L	H	H	H	H	H	H	H	L	L	L	L	
8	H	X	H	L	L	L	H	H	H	H	H	H	H	H	
9	H	X	H	L	L	H	H	H	H	H	L	L	H	H	1
10	H	X	H	L	H	L	H	L	L	L	H	H	L	H	
11	H	X	H	L	H	H	H	L	L	H	H	L	L	H	
12	H	X	H	H	L	L	H	L	H	L	L	L	H	H	
13	H	X	H	H	L	H	H	H	L	L	H	L	H	H	
14	H	X	H	H	H	L	H	L	L	L	H	H	H	H	
15	H	X	H	H	H	H	H	L	L	L	L	L	L	L	
BI	X	X	X	X	X	X	L	L	L	L	L	L	L	L	2
RBI	H	L	L	L	L	L	L	L	L	L	L	L	L	L	3
LT	L	X	X	X	X	X	H	H	H	H	H	H	H	H	4

H = Logic 1 : L = Logic 0 : X = Don't care

Note:

1. Input BI/RBO represent blanking input/ripple blanking output. These inputs are held open or at a high logic level for output functions from 0 through 15, which you will notice from Tables 10.6 and 10.7. This input can also be used for controlling the intensity of the display by applying a variable duty cycle pulse signal at this input.
   If it is desired that decimal 0 is not displayed, the ripple blanking input, RBI, must be held low.
2. When a low logic level is applied to the blanking input, BI, all segment outputs are off, irrespective of the state of the other inputs.
3. When the ripple blanking input, RBI, and inputs *A*, *B*, *C* and *D* are at a low logic level, with the lamp test input, LT, high, all segment outputs will go off, and the ripple blanking output, RBO, will go to a low level.
4. When the blanking input/ripple blanking output, BI/RBO, is open or high, and a low is applied to the lamp test input, LT, all segments will be on. This test can be applied at any stage to check if all the segments are in order.
5. When BCD inputs corresponding to functions 10 through 15 are applied, you will see displays as shown in Fig. 10.16.

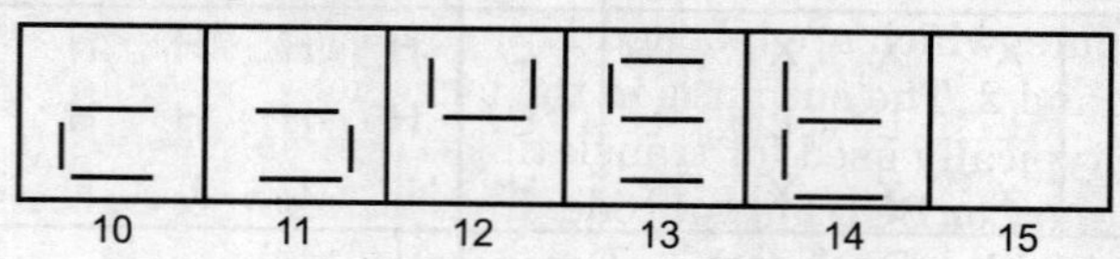

Fig. 10.16

10.5 TOTALIZING COUNTER

If a BCD counter is added to the circuit given in Fig. 10.14 and it is stepped up with a clock signal, it will automatically count the number of clock pulses applied to the circuit from 0 through 9. It will count in the standard 8421 BCD code. The output of the counter 7490 A is fed to the decoder, which drives the display. A clock signal applied at pin 14 of the counter steps up the counter. The counter can be reset by taking the reset pin, 2, temporarily high. When it has reached the count of 9, the counter will be reset to 0 and the same counting, cycle will be repeated. Notice that inputs LT, BI/RBO and RBI are left unconnected and are therefore at a high logic level (refer to the diagram Fig. 10.17).

If you add another decoder and display to the circuit in Fig. 10.17, you can count from 0 to 99. Notice that pin 11 of the first counter is connected to pin 14, input pin of the second counter. When the first counter has counted up to 9, and is automatically reset to 0, the second counter is stepped up and shows a count of 1. When the first counter has again counted up to 9, and is reset to 0, the second counter is stepped up and shows a count of 2. In this way when it has counted up to 99, both counters will show a count of 00 at the next input pulse.

The circuit for this expanded counter is given in Fig. 10.18. Notice that the reset inputs of both the counters are connected together. Before starting counting, the reset input is momentarily taken high, which resets both the counters.

The count capability can be further increased by adding more counting circuits.

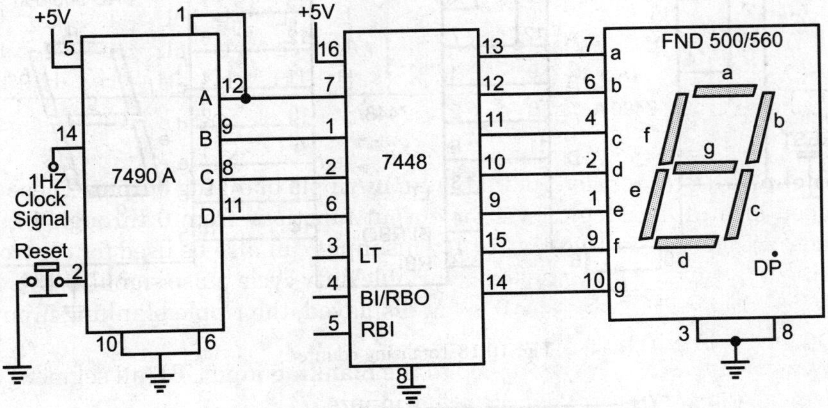

Fig. 10.17 Totalizing counter

10.6 ENCODERS

You are already familiar with decoders which can select a single output from binary inputs. On the other hand an encorder provides binary coded outputs from an input selected from a given number of inputs. Let us consider a very elementary encoder given in Fig. 10.19. This encoder has pushbutton inputs, which are labelled 1, 2, and 3. The encoder outputs are obtained from two NAND gates 1 and 2. The output is in the form of a 2-bit binary code.

Encoders are typically used for translating a decimal keyboard, like the one you see in a calculator, into a binary or BCD output code. In this circuit we have assigned decimal numbers 1, 2 and 3 to three pushbutton switches. For instance when switch 1 is depressed we conclude that the input to the encorder is decimal 1. When none of the switches is depressed the input to the encoder is considered to be decimal 0 and therefore the input to both the NAND gates is high. Consequently, outputs A and B are low, that is the output is 00. When switch 1 is depressed, that is the input is decimal 1, both inputs to gate 1 are high and so its output is low. Whereas only one input to gate 2 is high and the other is low. Therefore, its output is 1 and the output of the encorder is 01, which tallies with the input which is decimal 1. Figure out the outputs when keys 2 and 3 are depressed, that is when the decimal input equals 2 and 3.

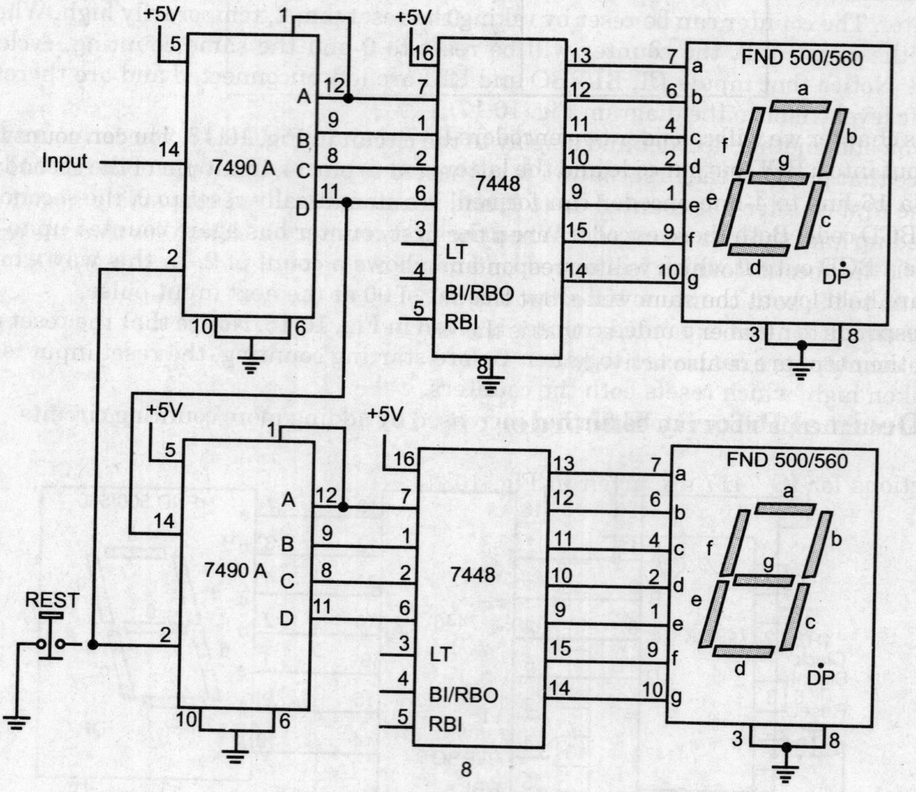

Fig. 10.18 Totalizing counter

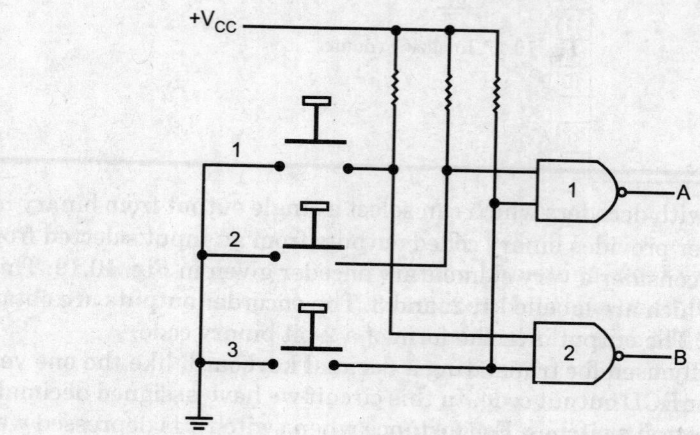

Fig. 10.19

Table 10.8

Decimal inputs	*Binary outputs*	
	A	*B*
0	0	0
1	0	1
2	1	0
3	1	1

In this chapter we will consider two encoders IC 74147 and IC 74148. The former coverts a decimal input into a BCD output code and the latter is an 8-bit encoder. When two ICs 74148 are combined, a 16-line to 4-line encoder can formed, which is useful in converting hexadecimal digits into BCD code. Both these encoders are priority encoders, which implies that the encoder will provide a BCD output which will correspond to the highest order digit. Suppose the inputs X_6 and X_7 are held low at the same time; but the priority encoder will produce a binary output which corresponds to number 7 only, as that is the higher order input. These ICs have active low inputs and the outputs are also active low.

10.6.1 Decimal Priority Encoder : IC 74147

Pin connections for IC 7417 are given in Fig. 10.20 (*a*) and its logic symbol is given in Fig. 10.20(*b*).

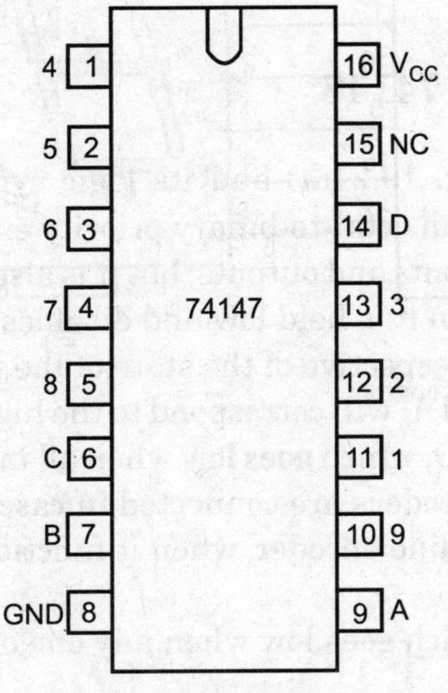

Fig. 10.20(a) Pin connections for IC 74147

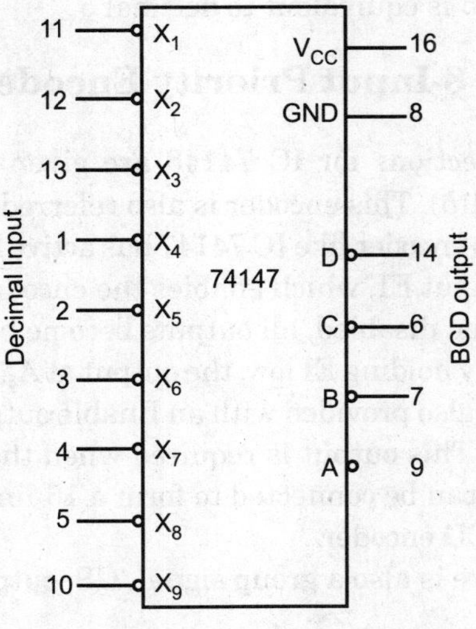

Fig. 10.20(b) Logic diagram for IC 74147

The logic diagram shows that inputs and outputs are active low as is indicated by the bubbles. Inputs are on the left hand side and are marked from X_1 to X_9.

The subscripts, indicate the decimal number of the inputs. The BCD outputs are marked *D*, *C*, *B* and *A*. As has been mentioned earlier, it is priority encoder which means that if more than one input is low at the same time, the highest of these inputs gets encoded in the output. For instance if X_4 and X_6 are low, the output will be 0 1 1 0, equivalent to decimal 6. The truth table for this encoder is in Table 10.9.

Table 10.9 Truth table for IC 74147

Inputs									*Outputs*			
X_1	X_2	X_3	X_4	X_5	X_6	X_7	X_8	X_9	*D*	*C*	*B*	*A*
H	H	H	H	H	H	H	H	H	H	H	H	H
X	X	X	X	X	X	X	X	L	L	H	H	L
X	X	X	X	X	X	X	L	H	L	H	H	H
X	X	X	X	X	X	L	H	H	H	L	L	L
X	X	X	X	X	L	H	H	H	H	L	L	H
X	X	X	X	L	H	H	H	H	H	L	H	L
X	X	X	L	H	H	H	H	H	H	L	H	H
X	X	L	H	H	H	H	H	H	H	H	L	L
X	L	H	H	H	H	H	H	H	H	H	L	H
L	H	H	H	H	H	H	H	H	H	H	H	L

H = HIGH logic level; L = Low logic level; X = Irrelevant

You will notice from this truth table that when all the inputs are high, that is none of them is active, the output is H H H H, which is equivalent to 0 0 0 0 as the outputs are active low. When input X_5 is low and all higher order inputs are high, the output as this table shows, is H L H L which is equivalent to decimal 5.

10.6.2 8-Input Priority Encoder: IC 74148

Pin connections for IC 74148 are given in Fig. 10.21(*a*) and its logic symbol is shown in Fig. 10.21(*b*). This encoder is also referred to as an octal-to-binary priority encoder.

This encoder like IC 74147 has active low inputs and outputs; but it is also provided with an Enable input EI, which enables the encoder when it is held low and disables it when it is held high. When disabled, all outputs become high irrespective of the state of the inputs. When it is enabled by holding EI low, the output at A_2, A_1 and A_0 will correspond to the highest active input.

It is also provided with an Enable output, EO, which goes low when all inputs from X_0 to X_7 are high. This output is required when these encoders are connected in cascade. Two of these encoders can be connected to form a 16-line to 4-line encoder, when it functions as a hexadecimal to BCD encoder.

There is also a group signal, GS, output which goes low when any one or more inputs are held low.

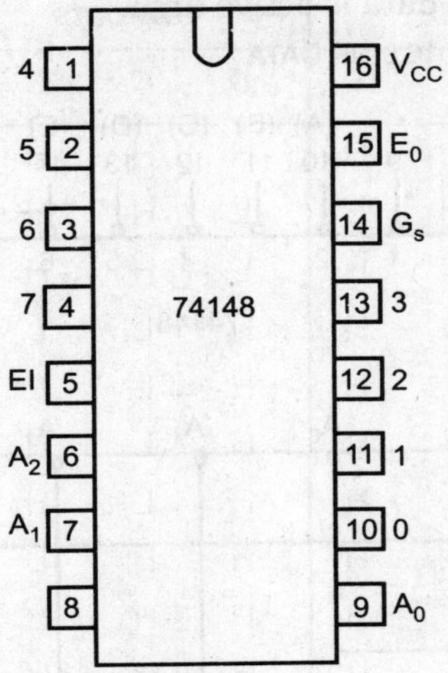

Fig. 10.21 (a) Pin connections for IC 74148

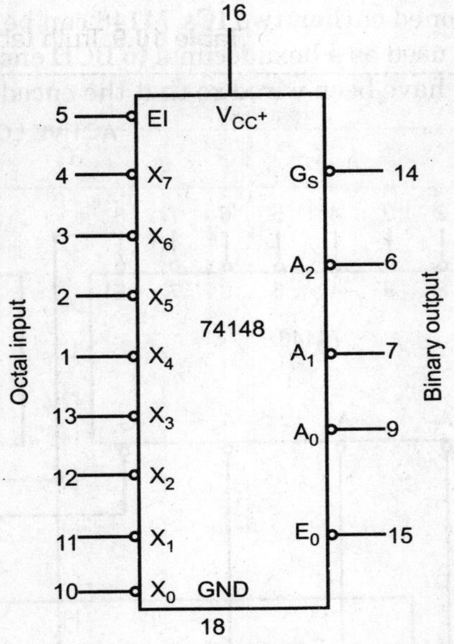

Fig. 10.21 (b) Logic symbol for IC 74148

This encoder has eight inputs from X_0 to X_7. The subscripts at the inputs refer to decimal values assigned to the inputs. As in the case of IC 74147, higher order inputs take priority over the lower order inputs. This means that input X_7 has the highest priority and X_0 the lowest. For instance, if a low input is applied at X_5, the output will be 101 which corresponds to decimal 5. If both inputs X_5 and X_3 are held low, the output will still be 101 as input X_5 takes priority over input X_3. Table 10.10 is the truth table for IC 74148.

Table 10.10 Truth table for IC 74148

Input									*Output*				
EI	X_0	X_1	X_2	X_3	X_4	X_5	X_6	X_7	A_2	A_1	A_0	**GS**	**E0**
H	X	X	X	X	X	X	X	X	H	H	H	H	H
L	H	H	H	H	H	H	H	H	H	H	H	H	L
L	X	X	X	X	X	X	X	L	L	L	L	L	H
L	X	X	X	X	X	X	L	H	L	L	H	L	H
L	X	X	X	X	X	L	H	H	L	H	L	L	H
L	X	X	X	X	L	H	H	H	L	H	H	L	H
L	X	X	X	L	H	H	H	H	H	L	L	L	H
L	X	X	L	H	H	H	H	H	H	L	H	L	H
L	X	L	H	H	H	H	H	H	H	H	L	L	H
L	L	H	H	H	H	H	H	H	H	H	H	L	H

H = High logic level; L = Low logic level; X = Irrelevant

As mentioned earlier, two ICs 74148 can be connected to form a 16-line to 4-line encoder, when it can be used as a hexadecimal to BCD encoder. A circuit for this purpose is given in Fig. 10.22. The ICs have been wired so that the encoded data is active high.

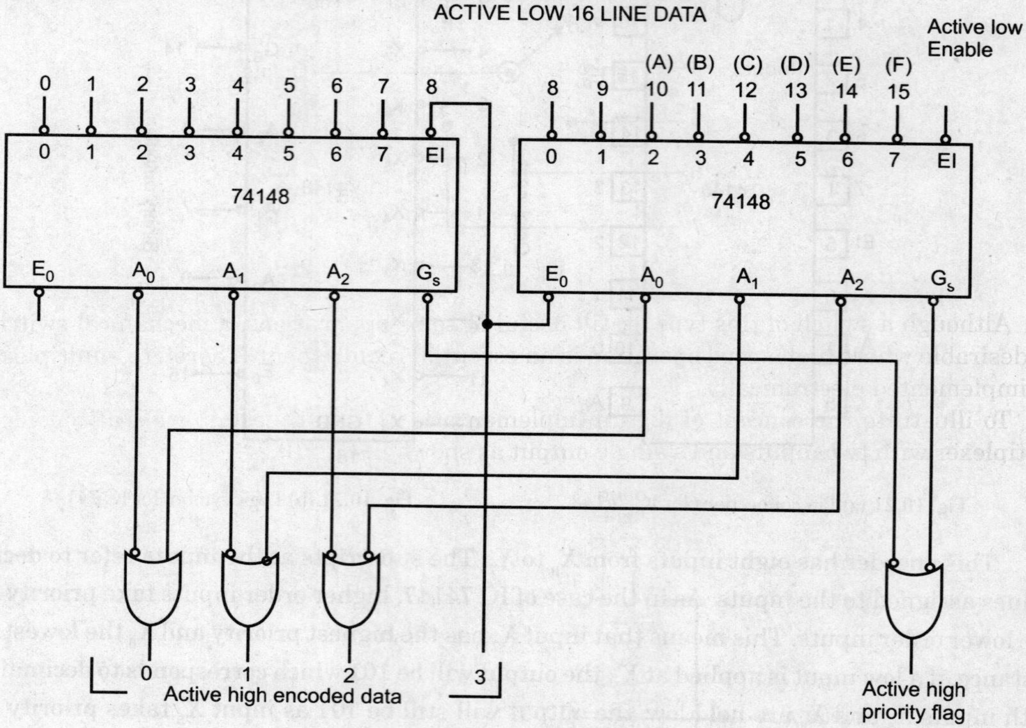

Fig. 10.22 16-line to 4-line encoder

The way this circuit functions is as follows. Since the enable input, EI, of the IC on the right is connected to ground, it is permanently enabled. If any input in this IC goes low, its EO goes high and since it is connected to the enable input, EI, of the IC on the left, it is disabled.

Also notice that the GS output of the IC which is enabled goes low when any of its input goes low. If no input of any of the ICs is low, the GS outputs of both the ICs will be high.

10.7 MULTIPLEXER

A multiplexer is a combinational logic circuit which can select any one of a number of inputs and route it to a single output. Multiplexers are available with 4, 8 and 16 inputs and a single output. A rotary switch with multiple contacts and a single rotor as in Fig. 10.23 is a mechanical multiplexing device. As the diagram shows the rotor, which is connected to the output, can make contact with any of the inputs. Thus it can route any input to the output line.

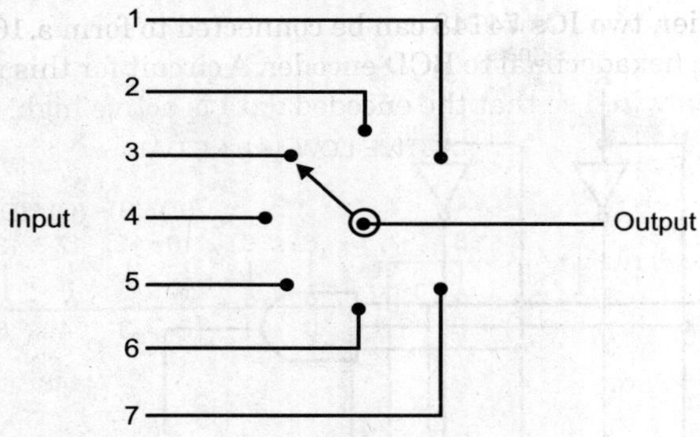

Fig. 10.23

Although a switch of this type is still useful in some applications, a mechanical switch is not desirable where high speed operation is an essential requirement. Therefore, multiplexers are implemented electronically.

To illustrate the concept of digital implementation of multiplexers, we will consider a multiplexer with two inputs and a single output as shown in Fig. 10.24.

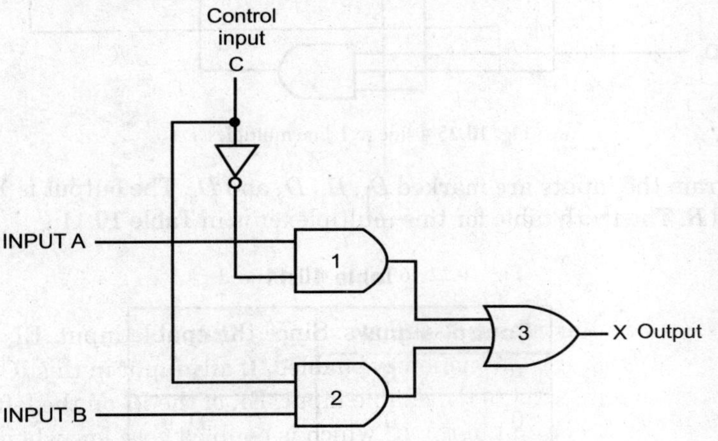

Fig. 10.24 Two-line to one-line multiplexer

In this diagram, A and B are the two inputs, X is the output and C is the control input. If input A is to be routed to the output line, the control input goes low, $C = 0$, which makes both inputs to AND gate 1 high. This enables AND gate 1 and its output passes through the OR gate 3 to the output. When input B is to be routed to the output, the control input is made high, $C = 1$, which enables AND gate 2 and its output passes through the OR gate 3 to the output. The output equation in this case is as follows:

$$X = A\overline{C} + BC$$

By using the same basic concept as in this multiplexer, more versatile multiplexers can be built. Incorporating the same technique a 4-line to 1-line multiplexer is shown in Fig. 10.25.

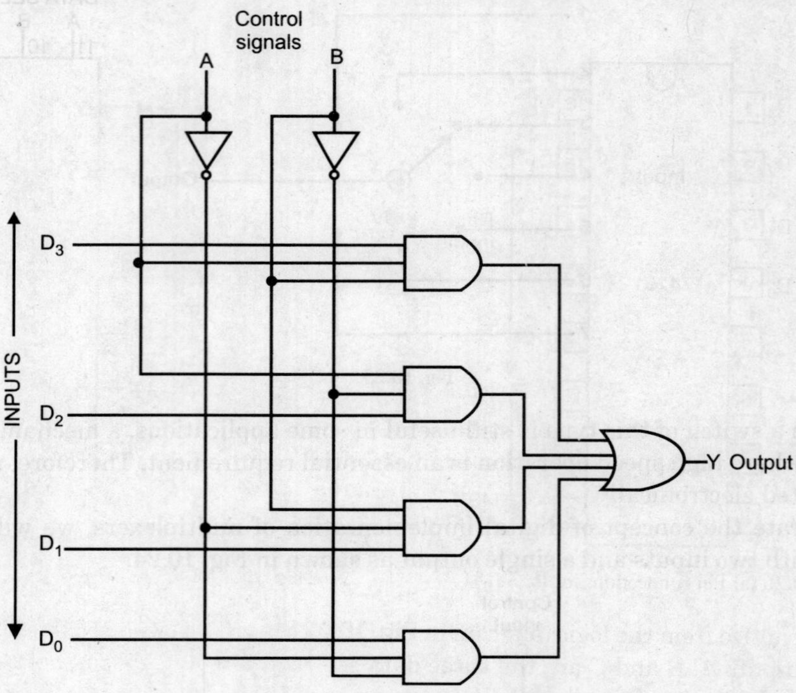

Fig. 10.25 4-line to 1-line multiplexer

In this diagram the inputs are marked D_0, D_1, D_2 and D_3. The output is Y and the control signals are A and B. The truth table for this multiplexer is in Table 10.11

Table 10.11

Control signal		Output
A	B	Y
0	0	D_0
0	1	D_1
1	0	D_2
1	1	D_3

This multiplexer has four 3-input AND gates and there is no provision for a strobe input. This improvement can be carried out by using 4-using AND gates. If all the four inputs are connected together to a strobe through an inverter, the multiplexer can be enabled by a logic 0 at the strobe and disabled by a logic 1 input. A dual 4-input multiplexer is commercially available and is designated IC 74153.

10.7.1 8-line to 1-line Multiplexer, IC 74151

This multiplexer has eight input lines and three select inputs. There is also provision for a strobe which is active low. When it is held low the multiplexer is enabled and when it is held high it is disabled. Pin connections for this multiplexer are given in Fig. 10.26(a) and its logic symbol is in Fig. 10.26 (b). The logic diagram for this multiplexer is in Fig. 10.27.

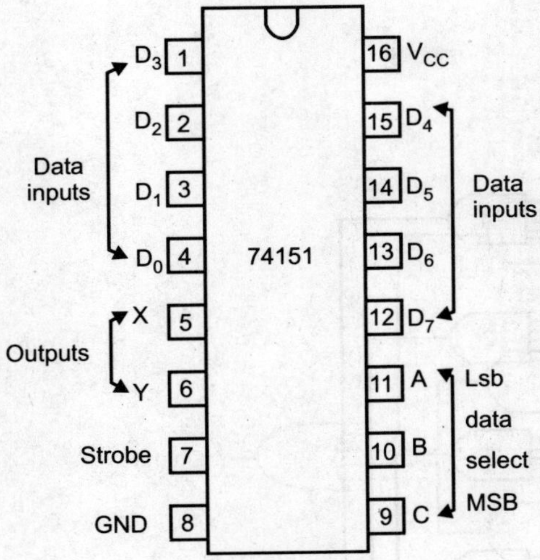

Fig. 10.26 (a) Pin connections for IC 74151

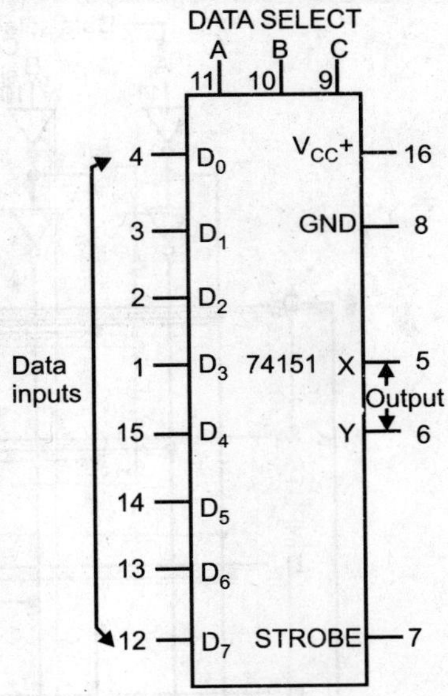

Fig. 10.26 (b) Logic symbol for IC 74151

You will notice from the logic diagram in Fig. 10.27 that IC 74151 has 8 data inputs from D_0 through D_7. Inputs *A*, *B* and *C* are the three data select inputs and they generate 3-bit binary words, which enable one of the eight AND gates depending on the code of the data select inputs. The binary word from the data select inputs is in fact an address code, which determines the data input line that will be routed to the output. Output *X* provides the normal output and the output at *Y* is the complement output. The strobe is active low. Therefore the multiplexer will be disabled when strobe is high and it will be enabled when the strobe is low.

The input lines have a subscript which correspond to the decimal value of the data select input *A*, *B* and *C*. For instance if the data select is 0 0 0, input line D_0 will be enabled and if strobe is low, AND gate 1 will be enabled and its output will be transmitted to the *X* and *Y* outputs. If D_0 is low, the *X* output will be low and if D_0 is high the output at *X* will be high. In either case the state of the output will depend on the state of the D_0 input line. If the data select input is $A\ \overline{B}\ C$ that is 101, the decimal value of the data select input will be 5 and this will enable input line D_5. As before the *X* output will follow the D_5 input. If D_5 is low X will be low and if D_5 is high *X* will be high.

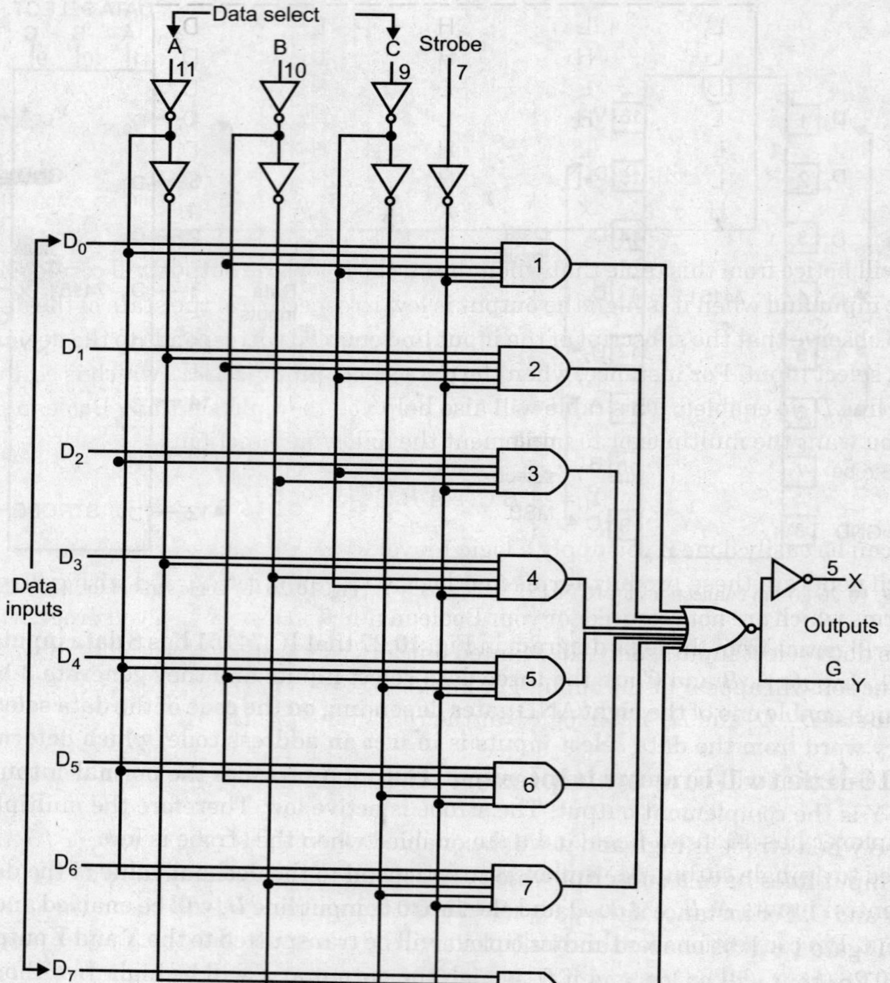

Fig. 10.27 Logic diagram for multiplexer IC 74151

In every case the output at X will follow the input at the input line, which has been enabled by the data select code. The output at Y will always be the complement of the X output. When the strobe is high, all AND gates will be disabled and the output at X will be low.

The output of the multiplexer has been summarized in Table 10.12.

Table 10.12 Truth table for IC 74151

Strobe	***Data select***			***Output***
	LSB A	***B***	***MSB C***	***X***
L	L	L	L	D_0
L	H	L	L	D_1

L	L	H	L	D_2
L	H	H	L	D_3
L	L	L	H	D_4
L	H	L	H	D_5
L	L	H	H	D_6
L	H	H	H	D_7
H	X	X	X	L

You will notice from this table that when the strobe is low the output will correspond to the data select input and when it is high the output is low irrespective of the state of the data select input. Also observe that the subscript of the input line enabled corresponds to the decimal value of the data select input. For instance, when the data select input is LHL, which is equivalent to decimal 2, line D_2 is enabled. This table will also help you to implement any Boolean function. Suppose you want the multiplexer to implement the following function:

$$Y = \overline{A}\,B\,\overline{C} + A\,\overline{B}\,\overline{C} + \overline{A}\,\overline{B}\,C$$

This can be easily done if you apply a logic 1 level to the inputs associated with those AND gates which generate these product terms and logic 0 to inputs associated with gates of those product terms which are not required for your Boolean function. Now when you progress through the various data select inputs, only the wanted outputs connected with product terms in your Boolean function will appear at the ouput. For implementing this function you will have to apply logic 1 inputs at D_1, D_2 and D_4 and a logic 0 at the remaining inputs.

10.7.2 16-line to 1-line multiplexer: IC 74150

This multiplexer has 16 input lines and a single output. It can select one out of 16 inputs for being routed to a single output. Multiplexers are, therefore, also referred to as data selectors. It has four control inputs *A*, *B*, *C* and *D* and the input data selected depends on the value of the control input. Pin connections for this multiplexer are given in Fig. 10.28(*a*) and its logic symbol is in Fig. 10.28 (*b*).

The 16 inputs to this multiplexer are from D_0 through D_{15} and the output is marked *Y*. The bubble at the output line indicates that the output is low when the data bit selected is high. In other words, the output is always the complement of the selected data bit. *A*, *B*, *C* and *D* are the data select inputs.

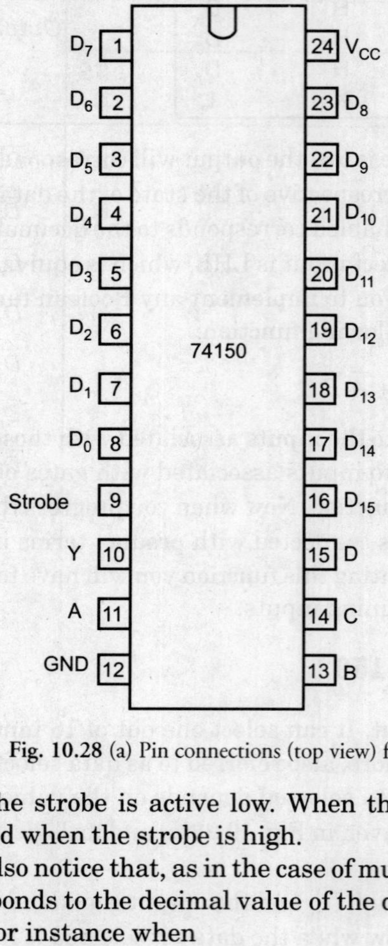

Fig. 10.28 (a) Pin connections (top view) for IC 74150

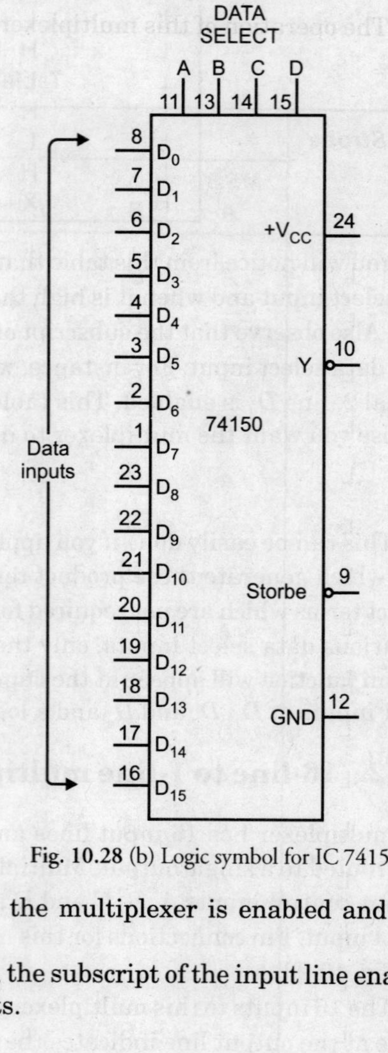

Fig. 10.28 (b) Logic symbol for IC 74150

The strobe is active low. When the strobe is low, the multiplexer is enabled and it is disabled when the strobe is high.

Also notice that, as in the case of multiplexer 74151, the subscript of the input line enabled corresponds to the decimal value of the data select inputs.

For instance when

$$\overline{A}\,\overline{B}\,\overline{C}\,D = 0\ 0\ 0\ 1 \text{ or decimal } 1$$

the selected input is D_1. When the data select input is

$$A\,\overline{B}\,C\,\overline{D} = 1\ 0\ 1\ 0 \text{ or decimal } 10$$

the selected input is D_{10}. The selected input is routed to the output and therefore

$$Y = \overline{D_{10}}$$

You must however remember that the output is always the complement of the data bit selected by the data select inputs. Also note that, as there are four bits in the data bit selected by the data select inputs. Also note that, as there are four bits in the data select input, it can produce 16 4-bit words. Each one of the 16 words will enable only one of the 16 input lines, which will be transmitted to the Y output. Thus in every case the output will be as follows:

$Y = \overline{D_n}$, where 'n' corresponds to the decimal equivalent of the data select input A, B, C, D.

The operation of this multiplexer is summarized in Table 10.13.

Table 10.13 Truth table for IC 75150

Strobe	***Data select***								***Output***
	MSB			***LSB***	***MSB***			***LSB***	
	A	***B***	***C***	***D***	***A***	***B***	***C***	***D***	***Y***
L	$\overline{A}$	$\overline{B}$	$\overline{C}$	$\overline{D}$	L	L	L	L	$\overline{D_0}$
L	$\overline{A}$	$\overline{B}$	$\overline{C}$	D	L	L	L	H	$\overline{D_1}$
L	$\overline{A}$	$\overline{B}$	C	$\overline{D}$	L	L	H	L	$\overline{D_2}$
L	$\overline{A}$	$\overline{B}$	C	D	L	L	H	H	$\overline{D_3}$
L	$\overline{A}$	B	$\overline{C}$	$\overline{D}$	L	H	L	L	$\overline{D_4}$
L	$\overline{A}$	B	$\overline{C}$	D	L	H	L	H	$\overline{D_5}$
L	$\overline{A}$	B	C	$\overline{D}$	L	H	H	H	$\overline{D_6}$
L	$\overline{A}$	B	C	D	L	H	H	H	$\overline{D_7}$
L	A	$\overline{B}$	$\overline{C}$	$\overline{D}$	H	L	L	L	$\overline{D_8}$
L	A	$\overline{B}$	$\overline{C}$	D	H	L	L	H	$\overline{D_9}$
L	A	$\overline{B}$	C	$\overline{D}$	H	L	H	L	$\overline{D_{10}}$
L	A	$\overline{B}$	C	D	H	L	H	H	$\overline{D_{11}}$
L	A	B	$\overline{C}$	$\overline{D}$	H	H	L	L	$\overline{D_{12}}$
L	A	B	$\overline{C}$	D	H	H	L	H	$\overline{D_{13}}$
L	A	B	C	$\overline{D}$	H	H	H	L	$\overline{D_{14}}$
L	A	B	C	D	H	H	H	H	$\overline{D_{15}}$
H	X	X	X	X	X	X	X	X	H

You will notice from this table that when the strobe is low, the output will respond to the data select inputs and when it is high, as in the last row, the output will be high irrespective of the state of the data select input. Also observe that the output Y will always be the complement of the input D_n. As has been mentioned earlier, the subscript of the input line enabled corresponds to the decimal value of the data select input. For instance when the data select input is $\overline{A}\,\overline{B}\,C\,\overline{D}$, corresponding to LLHL, which is equivalent to decimal 2, line D_2 is enabled. If D_2 is high the output will be low, since the output is the complement of the input.

As in the case of the IC 74151, you can implement any Boolean function or truth table with IC 74150 also. All that you have to do in implementing a truth table is to ground that input data line of the IC which corresponds to logic 1 in the truth table. Those input data lines which correspond to logic 0 in the truth table should be connected to $+V_{cc}$. Any truth table with four variables can be implemented with this multiplexer.

Example 10.1: *Implement truth Table 10.14 with IC 74150*

Table 10.14

Input	*MSB*		*LSB*		*Output*
D_n	*A*	*B*	*C*	*D*	*Y*
$\overline{D}_0$	0	0	0	0	1
$\overline{D}_1$	0	0	0	1	1
$\overline{D}_2$	0	0	1	0	0
$\overline{D}_3$	0	0	1	1	1
$\overline{D}_4$	0	1	0	0	0
$\overline{D}_5$	0	1	0	1	0
$\overline{D}_6$	0	1	1	0	0
$\overline{D}_7$	0	1	1	1	1
$\overline{D}_8$	1	0	0	0	1
$\overline{D}_9$	1	0	0	1	0
$\overline{D}_{10}$	1	0	1	0	1
$\overline{D}_{11}$	1	0	1	1	1
$\overline{D}_{12}$	1	1	0	0	0
$\overline{D}_{13}$	1	1	0	1	0
$\overline{D}_{14}$	1	1	1	0	0
$\overline{D}_{15}$	1	1	1	1	1

Solution: The last column of this table gives the required output, which represents the output required from the multiplexer. The first column gives the input and a high input produces a low output, all that you have to do is to connect those inputs to ground against which a high output is required and the remaining inputs to $+V_{cc}$ as shown in Fig. 10.29. Now when you sequence the data select inputs from 0000 to 1111, the required Boolean function will be generated at the output in a serial form.

10.7.3 Word (Nibble) Multiplexer : IC 74157

If we have to select one of two input words or nibbles, as they are sometimes called, the ideal solution is to use a word multiplexer. The inputs to a word multiplexer are two words of 4-bits each. The logic diagram of a word multiplexer is shown in Fig. 10.30.

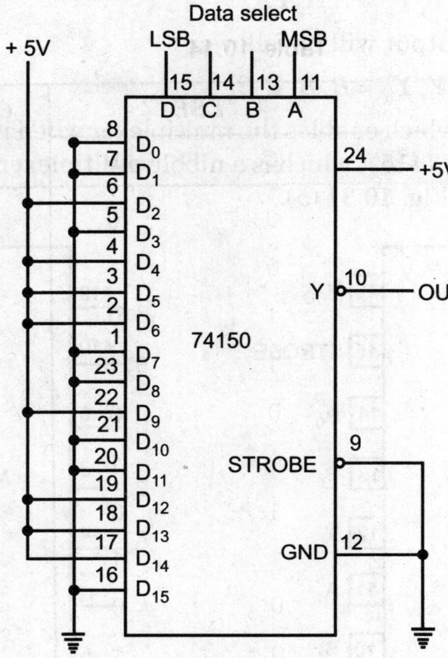

Fig. 10.29

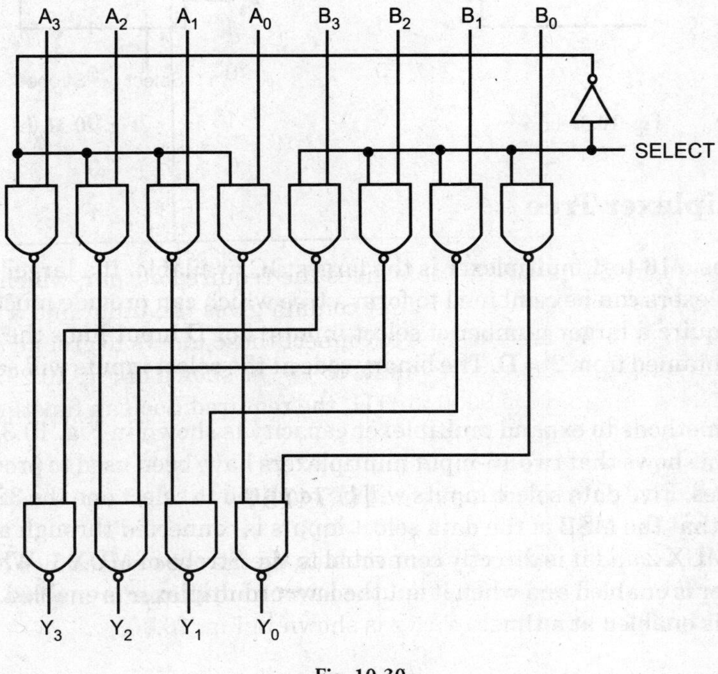

Fig. 10.30

The multiplexer diagrams shows two input words of 4-bits each. The word on the left is A_3, A_2, A_1, A_0 and the word on the right is B_3, B_2, B_1, B_0. The Select control determines which nibble will be transmitted to the output. When Select is low the output will be as follows:

$$Y_3 Y_2 Y_1 Y_0 = A_3 A_2 A_1 A_0$$

When Select is high the output will be follows:

$$Y_3 Y_2 Y_1 Y_0 = B_3 B_2 B_1 B_0$$

A Strobe is also provided, which enables the multiplexer when it is low and disables it when it is high. Pin connections for IC 74157, which is a nibble multiplexer, are shown in Fig. 10.31 (*a*) and its logic symbol is given in Fig. 10.31 (*b*).

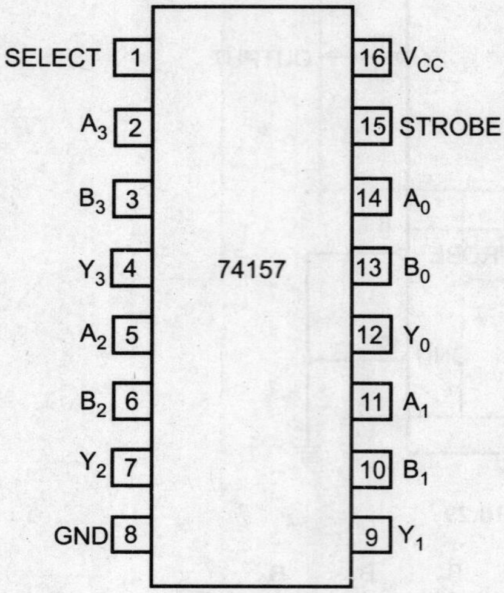

Fig. 10.31 (a)

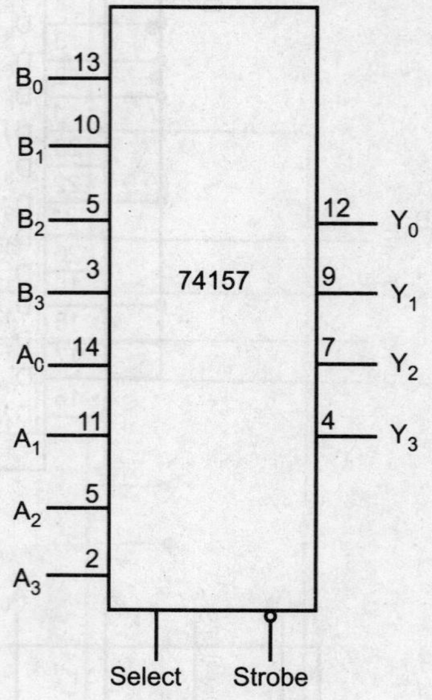

Fig. 10.31 (b)

10.7.4 Multiplexer Tree

IC 74150 which is a 16-to-1 multiplexer is the largest IC available. If a larger input capacity is required, multiplexers can be combined to form a tree which can provide much larger capacity. This will also require a larger number of select inputs. For D input lines the number of select inputs s can be obtained from $2^s = D$. The binary code at the select inputs will select the required input line.

One of the methods to expand multiplexer capacity is shown in Fig. 10.31 (*c*).

The diagram shows that two 16-input multiplexers have been used to provide provision for 32 data input lines. Five data select inputs will be required to select one the 32 data input lines ($2^5 = 32$). Notice that the MSB of the data select inputs is connected through an Inverter to the Strobe input of MUX 2 and it is directly connected to the Strobe of MUX 1. When MSB is 0, the upper multiplexer is enabled and when it is 1 the lower multiplexer is enabled. Thus only one of the multiplexes is enabled at a time.

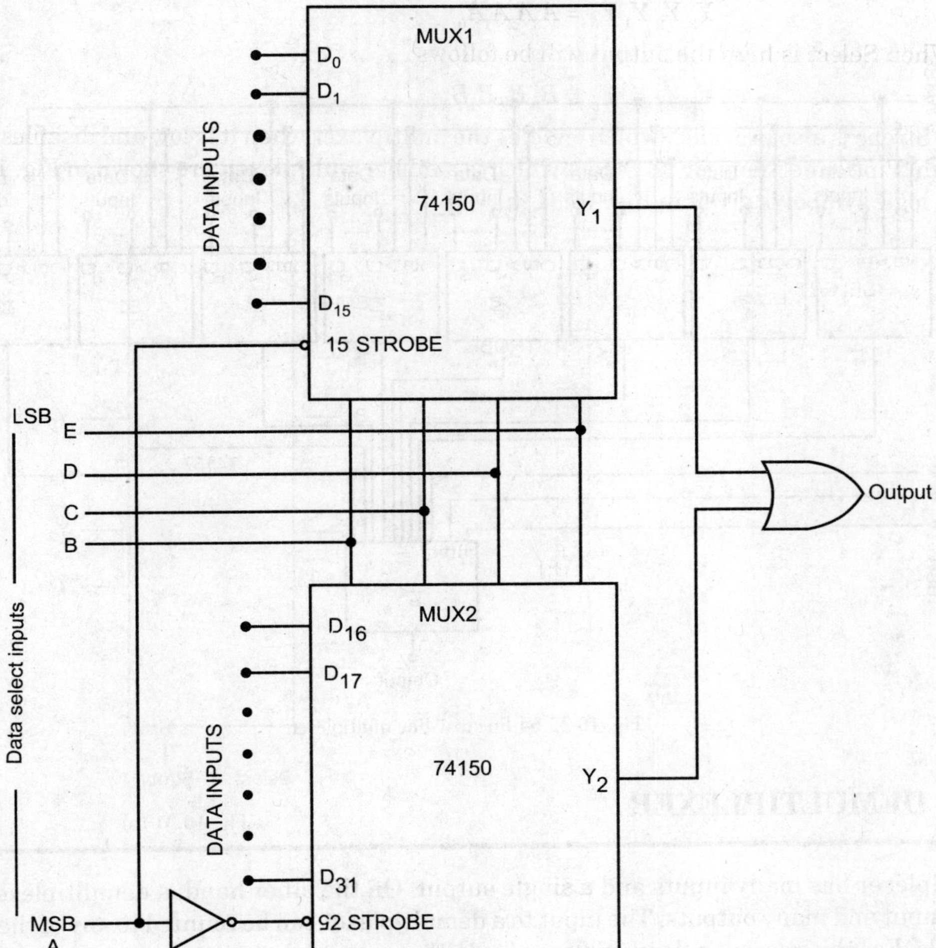

Fig. 10.31 (c)

When a much larger number of input lines have to be accommodated, the scheme shown in Fig. 10.32 can be adopted. This arrangement uses nine 8-input multiplexers to provide a 64-line to 1-line multiplexing capability. All the three data select inputs are connected to eight multiplexers arranged one above the other. These inputs $A_0\,A_1\,A_2$ select a data input from each of the eight multiplexers and route them to the output multiplexer. If the binary value of the data select input is 0 1 1, the data input line D_6 from each one of the multiplexers will be routed to the output multiplexer. The output multiplexer also has three data select inputs, which enables it to select any one of the eight inputs to it. For instance if the data select input of the output multiplexer is as follows:

$$\begin{matrix} A_3 & A_4 & A_5 \\ 1 & 1 & 0 \end{matrix}$$

data input D_6 from mutliplexer M_3 will be routed to the output.

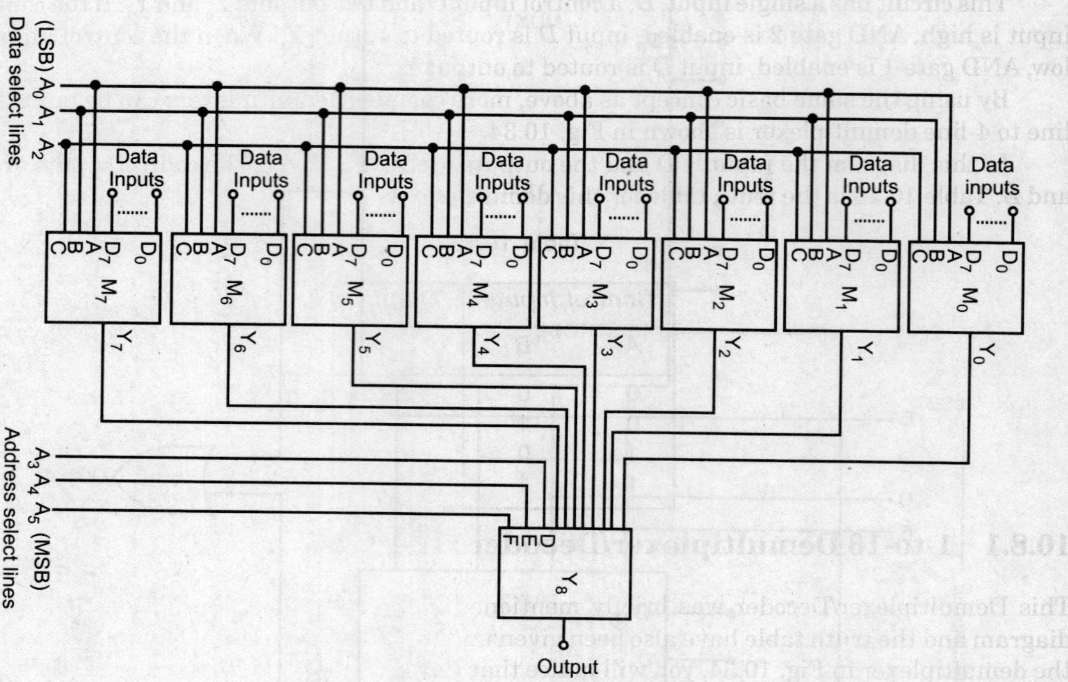

Fig. 10.32 64-line to 1-line multiplexer

10.8 DEMULTIPLEXER

A multiplexer has many inputs and a single output. On the other hand, a demultiplexer has a single input and many outputs. The input to a demultiplexer can be rounted to any of the output channels. For this reason, a demultiplexer is also known as a data distributor.

Consider the switch in Fig. 10.23. If the output is changed to input and the inputs to output, it will function as a demultiplexer. A demultiplexer can also be implemented by electronic circuits. Consider the circuit in Fig. 10.33, which is a 1-line to 2-line demultiplexer.

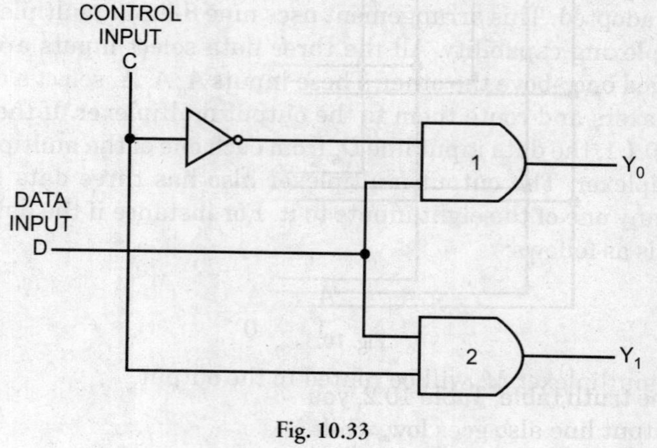

Fig. 10.33

This circuit has a single input, D, a control input C and two outputs Y_0 and Y_1. If the control input is high, AND gate 2 is enabled, input D is routed to output Y_1. When the control input is low, AND gate 1 is enabled, input D is routed to output Y_0.

By using the same basic concept as above, more complex demultiplexers can be built. A 1-line to 4-line demultiplexer is shown in Fig. 10.34.

In this diagram the input is D and the outputs are Y_0, Y_1, Y_2, Y_3. The control inputs are A and B. Table 10.15 is the truth table for this demultiplexer.

Table 10.15

Control Inputs		Output
A	B	
0	0	Y_0
0	1	Y_1
1	0	Y_2
1	1	Y_3

10.8.1 1-to-16 Demultiplexer/Decoder : IC 74154

This Demultiplexer/Decoder was briefly mentioned in Section 10.2.2. Pin connections, logic diagram and the truth table have also been given under than section. If you have a close look at the demultiplexer in Fig. 10.34, you will notice that the data input line D is connected to one of the inputs of all the AND gates. Similarly the data input line in IC 74154 is connected to all the decode gates. The input data bit is controlled by the control inputs A, B, C and D. The data bit is automatically steered to the output line, whose subscripts corresponds to the decimal equivalent of the control inputs. This IC also has a Strobe, which enables the IC when it is low and disables it when it is high.

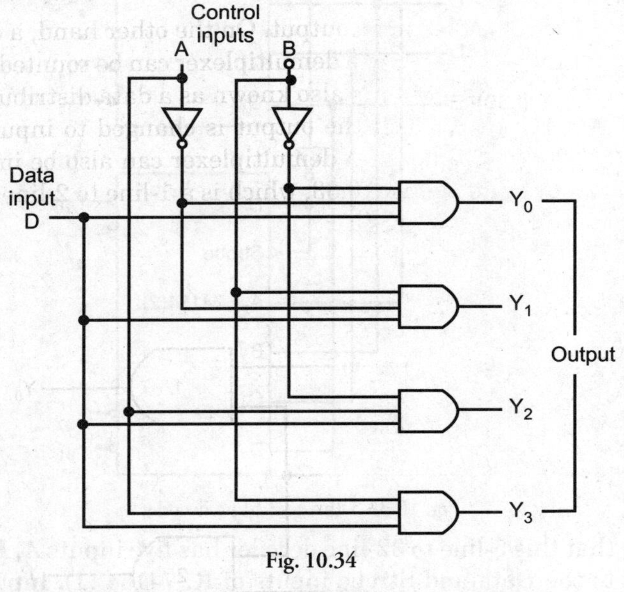

Fig. 10.34

If you refer to the truth table, Table 10.2, you will observe that when the data input is low, the corresponding output line also goes low, while the other output lines stay high. Bubbles on the output line indicate that the output is low. For instance, if the data input is low and the control input is LHLH, corresponding to decimal 5, output line Y_5 is enabled, its output goes low and all output lines stay high. Also observe that when the data input is high, all output lines go high irrespective of the state of the control inputs. When the Strobe is high, all output lines go high indicating that the IC is disabled.

In order to use IC 74154 as a decoder, the input to the decoder is applied at the control inputs *A, B, C* and *D*. The data and strobe inputs are connected to ground to enable all the 16 gates. In Fig. 10.7 the output lines are marked from Y_0 to Y_{15}. The output states in terms of the inputs have also been shown in the diagram. The diagram also shows that when the input is $\overline{A}\,B\,\overline{C}\,\overline{D}$, which is equal to decimal 4, output Y_4 is low. Table 10.2 also shows that with this input, output Y_4 is low. It also shows that all the other outputs are high. Similarly when the input is $\overline{A}\,B\,C\,D$, gate Y_7 is enabled. In every case you will notice that the subscript of the output enabled is equal to the decimal value of the input.

10.8.2 Demultiplexer Tree

Although 4-line to 16-line decoders are the largest decoders available, they can be combined to form decoders having larger capacity. Figure 10.35 illustrates how two 74154 demultiplexers can be connected to provide a 5-line to 32-line decoder.

5-line to 32-line Decoder

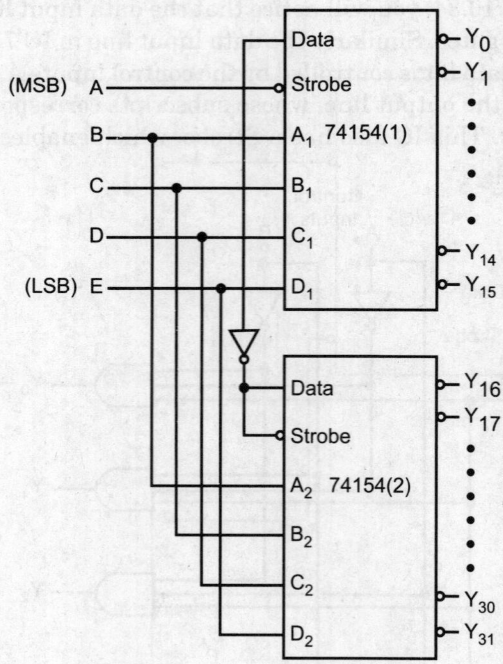

Fig. 10.35 5-line to 32-line decoder

You will notice that this 5-line to 32-line decoder has five inputs *A*, *B*, *C*, *D* and *E*. Input A (MSB) is connected to the Data and Strobe inputs of IC 74154 (1). Input A is also connected through an inverter to the data and strobe inputs of IC 74154(2). When input A goes low the upper IC is enabled, and the lower IC is disabled. When the upper IC is enabled, inputs *B*, *C*, *D*, and E drive the upper IC and only one of the output lines in the upper IC goes low, depending on the state of the B, C, D and E inputs. When input A goes high, the lower IC is enabled and the upper IC is disabled One of the outputs in the lower IC goes low depending on the state of the B, C, D and E inputs. Thus the combination functions as a 5-line to 32-line decoder.

8-line to 256-line Decoder

A decoder with a larger capacity than the one in Fig. 10.35 can be built using 17 4-line to 16-line decoders, as shown in Fig. 10.36. The four inputs of decoder 1 develop 16 outputs from Y_0 to Y_{15} and each one of these outputs is connected to the data input of sixteen 4-line to 16-line decoders. Thus each one of these sixteen decoders develop 16 outputs, making the total number of outputs 256 from Y_0 to Y_{255}. The combination thus functions as an 8-line to 256-line decoder. The enable and data inputs of each one of the decoders are connected together, which enables them when the data input goes low.

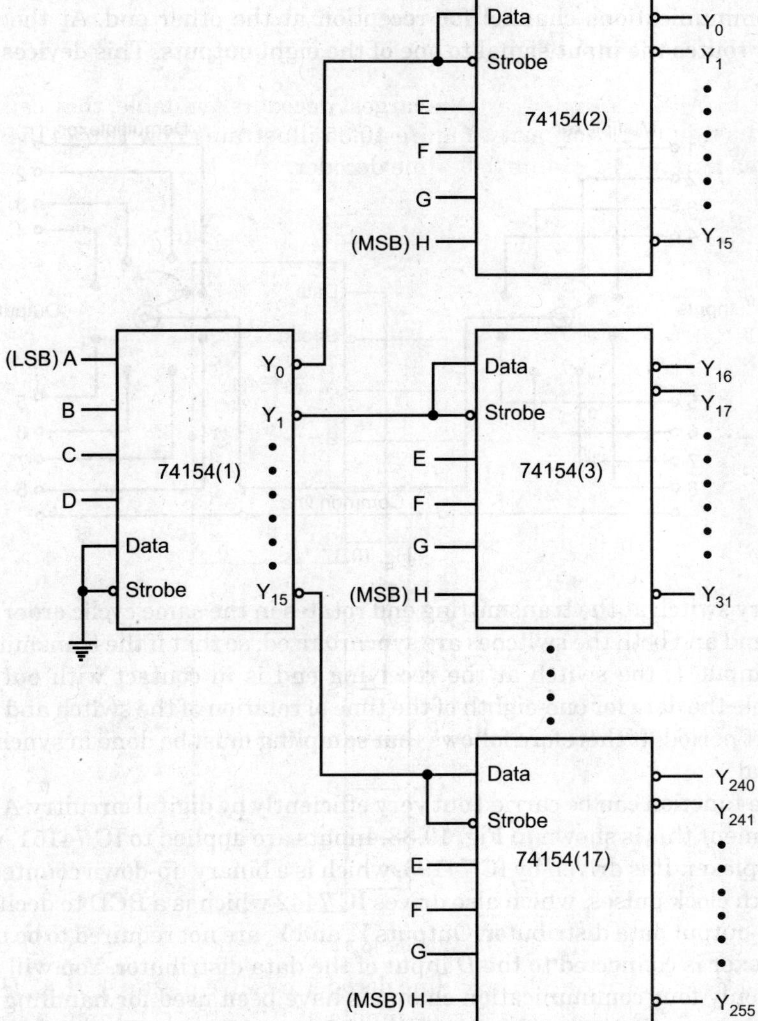

Fig. 10.36 8-line to 256-line decoder

Let us assume that the *ABCD* input of decoder 1 is 0000. Output Y_0 of this decoder will go low, which will enable decoder 2 and the other decoders will not be enabled as outputs Y_1 to Y_{15} of decoder 1 will be high. The *EFGH* inputs of decoder 2 will now be active and will activate the output line which corresponds to the input. In effect the combination will function as an 8-line to 256-line decoder.

10.9 MULTIPLEXING

Here we will consider briefly the multiplexing technique, which finds considerable application when a number of digital signals have to be processed in an identical manner, or are required to be transmitted over a significant distance. In such applications the multiplexing technique leads to a reduction in the number of processing circuits and communication channels. First we will consider a very simple mechanical device which can select one out of eight inputs, and route it to a single communications channel for reception at the other end. At the receiving end a demultiplexer routes the input signal to one of the eight outputs. This devices is illustrated in Fig. 10.37.

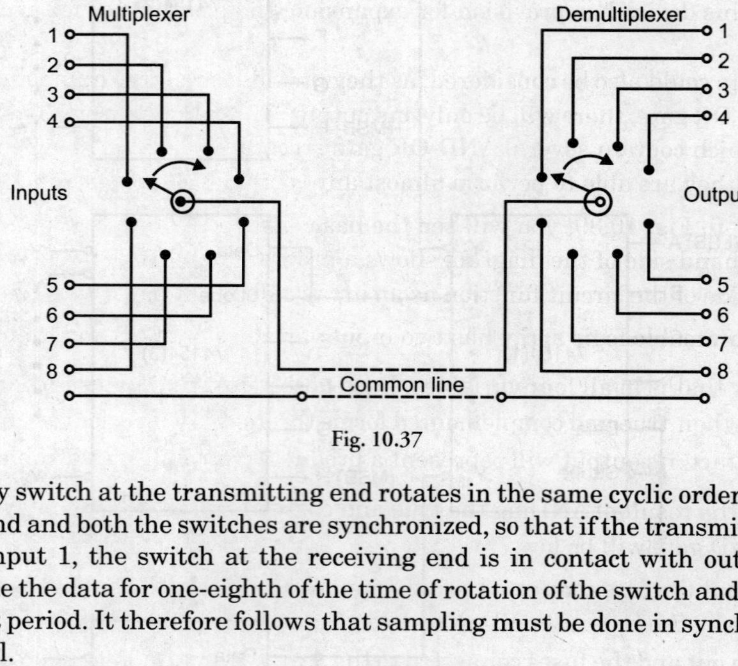

Fig. 10.37

The rotary switch at the transmitting end rotates in the same cyclic order as the switch at the receiving end and both the switches are synchronized, so that if the transmitting switch is in contact with input 1, the switch at the receiving end is in contact with output 1. Both the switches sample the data for one-eighth of the time of rotation of the switch and thus sample the data for a short period. It therefore follows that sampling must be done in synchronization with the input signal.

The same function can be carried out very efficiently by digital circuitry. A circuit arrangement to implement this is shown in Fig. 10.38. Inputs are applied to IC 74151, whic is an 8-line to 1-line multiplexer. It is driven by IC 74193, which is a binary up-down counter. The counter is stepped up with clock pulses, which also drives IC 7442 which is a BCD to decimal decoder and is used as an 8-output data distributor. Outputs Y_8 and Y_9 are not required to be used. The output of the multiplexer is connected to the *D* input of the data distributor. You will notice from this diagram that only four communication channels have been used for handling eight signal inputs. A 4-bit binary code is capable of handling 16 signal inputs. Therefore the utility of this system increases with an increase in the number of input lines.

10.10 PROGRAMMABLE LOGIC ARRAYS (PLAs)

Earlier on you have seen how combinational logic circuits is sum-of-products (SOP) and product-of-sum (POS) forms can be designed to perform many combinational logic function. To implement these circuits, you can use ICs incorparatin AND, OR and Invert gates. However, the problem with this approach is that, you have to use separate ICs containing these gates, connections for which have to be made outside the chips, which is likely to affect reliability, an increase in package size and power dissipation. This will, therefore, not result in an ideal circuit arrangement.

Another solution which we have considered earlier in Chap. 3 is the use of AND—OR-Invert gates; but again we face the limitation that our flexibility is confined to the given number of inputs and outputs in a package. Fo instance consider to the given number of inputs and outputs in a package. For instance consider the AND—OR-Invert gate in Fig. 3.31 which is a 2-input, 2-wide device, which means that there are two AND gates with two inputs each and there is only one OR gate. Another device given in Fig. 3.34 is a 2-2-4-4 input, 4-wide AND—OR-Invert gate. Although this device has provision for expansion, the possibilities for expansion are limited.

Multiplexers could also be considered, as they provide for a large number of inputs; but as there is only one OR gate, there will be only one output. These limitations have led designers to make devices which contain several AND-OR gate structures and can also be programmed in such a way that they are able to perform almost any combinational logic function.

If you refer to Fig. 10.39, you will see the basic structure of a programmable AND—OR circuit. The left hand side of the diagram shows a programmable array of four AND gates and the right hand side of the circuit function as an array of four OR gates with four inputs each.

This programmable logic array has two input variables A and B and their complemented forms $\overline{A}$ and $\overline{B}$, that is in all four variables. Each of the four AND gates is connected to all the four variables in their true and complemented forms through fuses. As long as all the fuses to an AND gate are intact, its output will represent a product term of all the variables, that is A, $\overline{A}$, B and $\overline{B}$. Since the result of ANDing the true and complemented form of any variable is 0, the output of the AND gate will be low.

If we blow out the fuse connected to any input of an AND gate, that input to the AND gate will be pulled up by the internal pull-up resistor. Suppose the fuses connected to the $\overline{A}$ and B inputs are blown out and the fuses connected to the A and $\overline{B}$ inputs remain intact, the output of the AND gate will be $A\overline{B}$. It follows that the output of an AND gate will contain those variables which have their fuses intact. When a particular term is not required in the output of an AND gate, we should blow out the fuse connected to that variable.

Which fuses should be blown out and which should be retained, depends on the product terms required at the output of the AND gates. These product term will appear in the final OR expression. We will see how that happens.

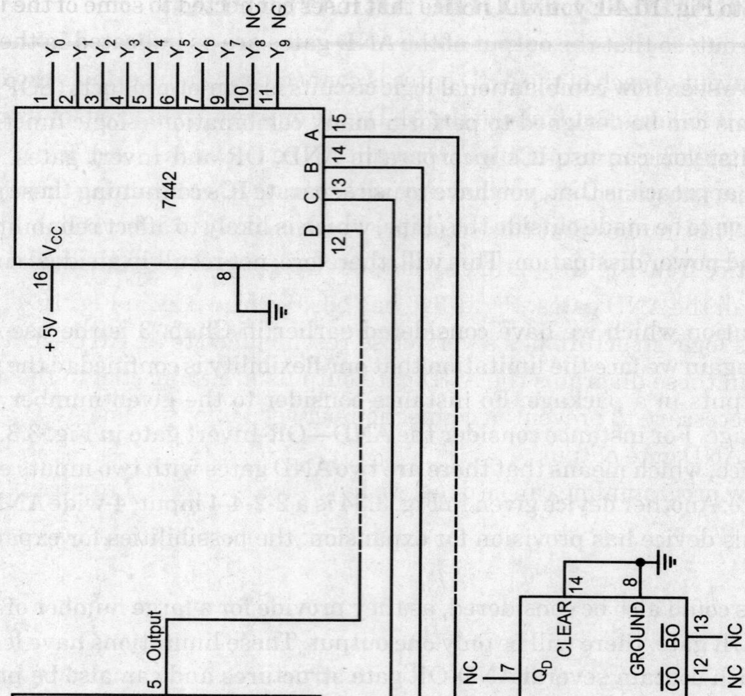

Fig. 10.38 Multiplexer-demultiplexer data link

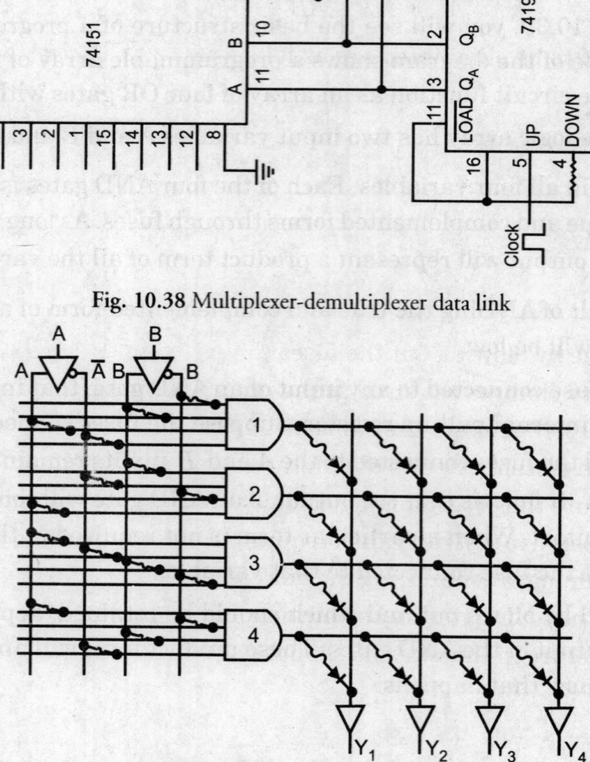

Fig. 10.39 Basic programmable AND-OR device

If you refer to Fig. 10.40, you will notice that fuses connected to some of the input variables have been blown out, so that the output of the AND gates are as indicated in the diagram. Also notice that the output of each of the AND gates is connected via a fuse and a diode to the output through a buffer. It follows that if any of the AND gate outputs, connected for example to output Y_1 is high, it will pull the Y_1 output high. Or if all AND gate outputs are low, it will pull the Y_1 output low. This in, substance, means that any one of the AND gate outputs, if it is high, can pull the output high. This implies that this structure functions as a 4-input OR gate.

You will notice from Fig. 10.40 that all outputs from Y_1 to Y_4 contain all the product terms in the output of all the AND gates. Fig. 10.40 has been redrawn as in Fig. 10.41 to bring out of the fact that this logic structure has a very close resemblance to an AND—OR structure. You will notice that in these diagrams the AND gate outputs are connected to the output through diodes. This is necessary to prevent a connection between a low on one AND gate output to a high on another AND gate output.

To show how programming can be done, we have assumed that the outputs required are as follows:

$$Y_1 = A\overline{B}$$

$$Y_2 = \overline{A}\,\overline{B}$$

$$Y_3 = B$$

$$Y_4 = A\overline{B} + \overline{A}B$$

The term required to be eliminated are as follows:

$Y_1 : \overline{A}\,\overline{B}, \overline{A}B, B$

$Y_2 : \overline{A}B, B, A\overline{B}$

$Y_3 : \overline{A}B, \overline{A}\,\overline{B}, A\overline{B}$

$Y_4 : \overline{A}\,\overline{B}, B$

This has been done by blowing out the fuses connected to these inputs and the associated OR gates. The necessary changes required at the inputs to the AND gates have been shown by blown fuses as in Fig. 10.42 and are the same as in Fig. 10.40. In Fig. 10.42 are shown all the inputs which have been disconnected to obtain the required logic function.

During manufacture the programming of logic arrays is done according to customers specifications. A mask is prepared to suit individual requirements to produce diodes, transistors, etc., on the silicon die. Programming is done during the process of manufacture by making connections to the required inputs of the AND gates and by putting diodes at the AND outputs where required. Subsequent to manufacture in this way, no changes can be made in these logic arrays and they are known as PLAs.

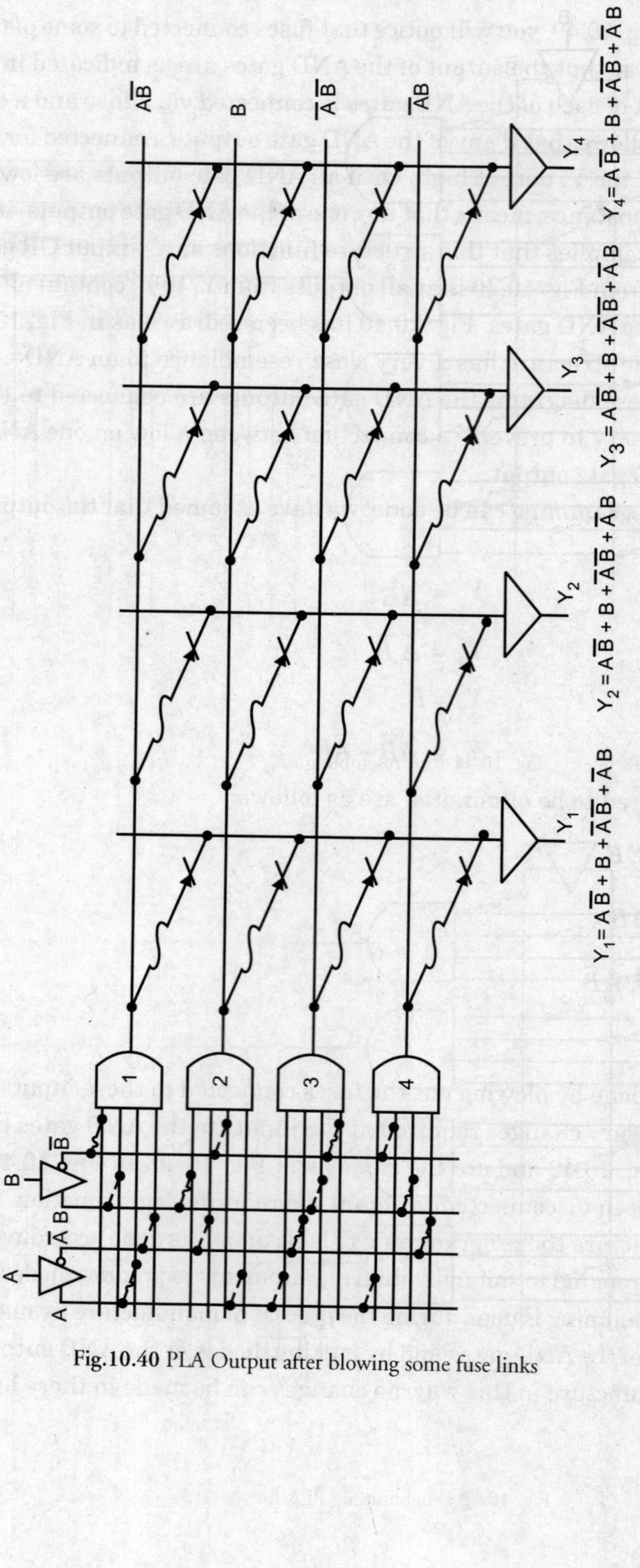

Fig.10.40 PLA Output after blowing some fuse links

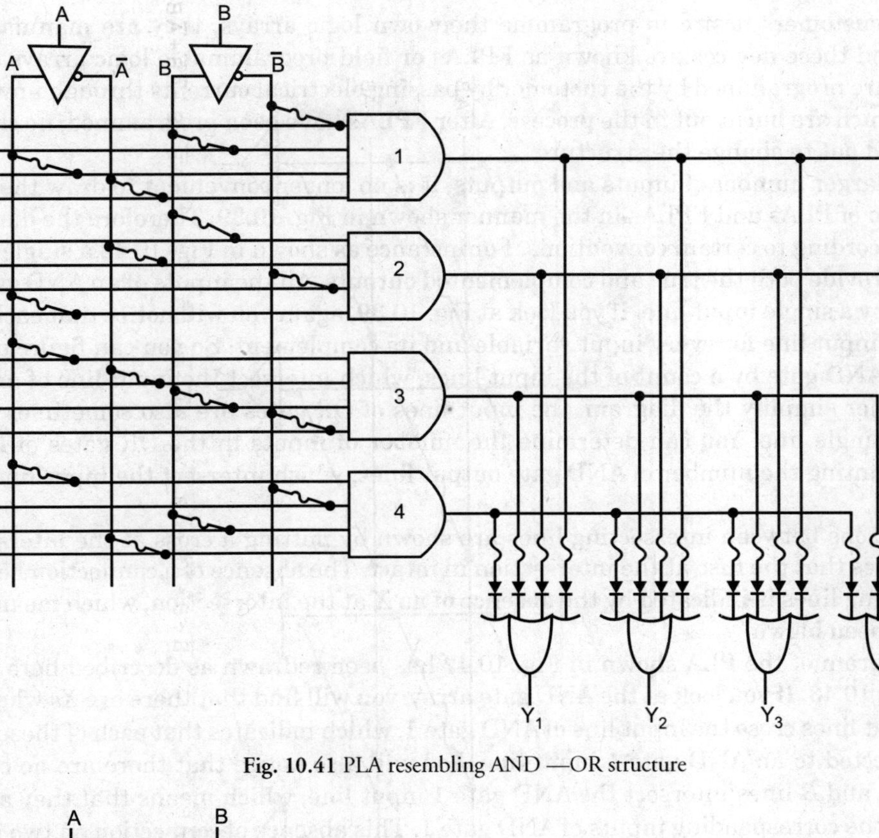

Fig. 10.41 PLA resembling AND —OR structure

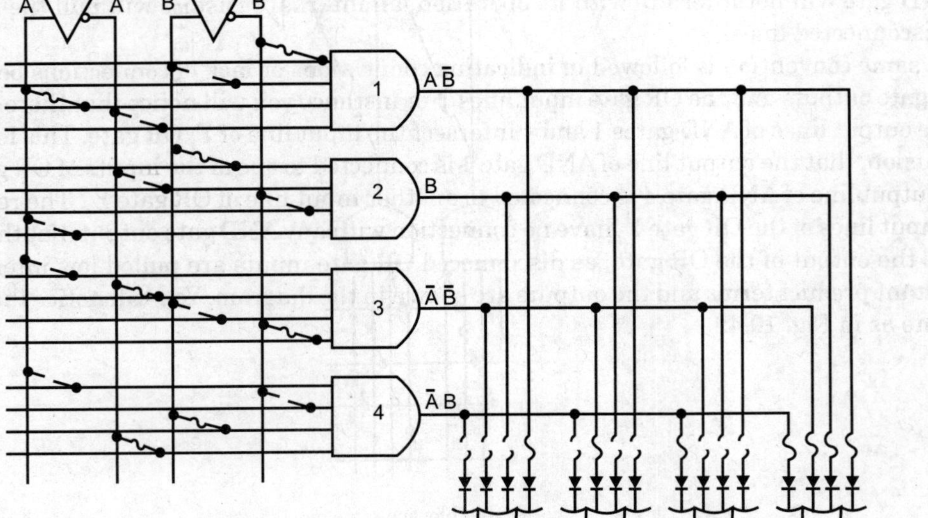

Fig. 10.42 Programming PLA for the desired output

Where customers desire to programme their own logic arrays, they are manufactured with fuses and these devices are known as FPLAs or field programmable logic arrays. These logic arrays are programmed by the customer by passing electrical currents through unwanted fuse links, which are burnt out in the process. After FPLAs have been programmed, no changes can be carried out to change the structure.

With a larger number of inputs and outputs, it is no longer convenient to draw the structural diagram of PLAs and FPLAs in the manner shown in Fig. 10.39. Therefore the diagrams are drawn according to certain conventions. For instance as shown in Fig. 10.43 a single buffer is shown to provide both the true and complemented outputs. All the inputs of an AND gate are represented by a single input line. If you look at Fig. 10.39, again you will notice that each AND gate has one input line for every input variable and its complement. So you can figure out the inputs of an AND gate by a count of the input lines, which intersect the input line of an AND gate. To further simplify the diagram, the input lines of OR gates are also sometimes represented by a single line. You can determine the number of inputs in the OR gates of FPLAs merely by counting the number of AND gate output lines, which intersect the input line of an OR gate.

Connections between intersecting lines are shown by putting a cross at the intersection which indicates that the fuse at the intersection in intact. The absence of a connection between two intersecting lines is indicated by the absence of an *X* at the intersection, which means that the fuse has been blown.

The diagram of the PLA shown in Fig. 10.42 has been redrawn as described here and is shown in Fig. 10.43. If you look at the AND gate array, you will find that there are *Xs* where the A and $\overline{B}$ input lines cross the input line of AND gate 1, which indicates that each of these input lines is connected to an AND gate 1 input line. You will also notice that there are no crosses where the $\overline{A}$ and B lines intersect the AND gate 1 input line, which means that they are not connected to the corresponding inputs of AND gate 1. This absence of connection on two inputs of the AND gate will not interfere with its operation, an internal resistors will pull the inputs high of disconnected lines.

The same convention is followed in indicating connections or lack of connections between the AND gate outputs and the OR gate input lines. For instance you will notice that there are *Xs* where the output lines of AND gates 1 and 4 intersect the input line of Y_4 OR gate. This leads to the conclusion, that the output line of AND gate 1 is connected to one of the inputs of OR gate Y_4 and the output line of AND gate 4 is connected to another input line of OR gate Y_4. The remaining two input lines of the OR gate Y_4 have no connection with any AND gate output; but this will not affect the output of the OR gate, as disconneced OR gate inputs are pulled low internally. The resultant product terms and the outputs are shown in the diagram. You will notice that this is the same as in Fig. 10.42.

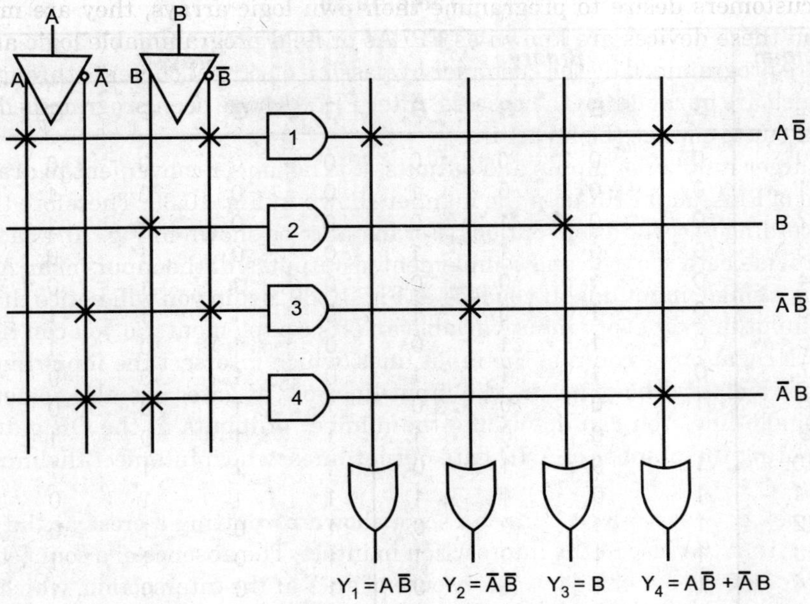

Fig. 10.43 FPLA diagram using standard conventions

10.11 GRAY CODE CONVERTERS

You are already familiar with binary and BCD codes as well as with Gray and XS3 codes, which have been discussed in Chapter 1 and 7. It is sometimes necessary to use two or more different codes in digital systems. To acquire compatibility between different circuits in a system, it becomes necessary to use code converters to convert code signals from one source to another code.

You are already familiar with some code converters such as BCD to decimal, decimal to BCD, octal to BCD, etc. The Gray code, XS3 code, ASCII code and some other codes are also in use in digital systems. We will now take up some more codes for further consideration.

10.11.1 Binary-to-Gray Code Converter

The Gray code has been given earlier in Table 1.12. However, it is reproduced here, with some modification, for your convenience.

Converting one code into another may require a lot of circuitry when the codes are complicated. In such cases read-only-memory (ROM) code converters may be found most convenient to use. Pre-programmed ROMs are also available for code conversion.

Table 10.16

Decimal	*Binary*				*Gray*			
	B_3	B_2	B_1	B_0	G_3	G_2	G_1	G_0
0	0	0	0	0	0	0	0	0
1	0	0	0	1	0	0	0	1
2	0	0	1	0	0	0	1	1
3	0	0	1	1	0	0	1	0
4	0	1	0	0	0	1	1	0
5	0	1	0	1	0	1	1	1
6	0	1	1	0	0	1	0	1
7	0	1	1	1	0	1	0	0
8	1	0	0	0	1	1	0	0
9	1	0	0	1	1	1	0	1
10	1	0	1	0	1	1	1	1
11	1	0	1	1	1	1	1	0
12	1	1	0	0	1	0	1	0
13	1	1	0	1	1	0	1	1
14	1	1	1	0	1	0	0	1
15	1	1	1	1	1	0	0	0

Here we will consider Binary-to-Gray and Gray-to-Binary code converters which use XOR gates. Table 10.16 shows that the MSBs of both the codes are the same and, therefore, the MSBs require no conversion. A Binary-to-Gray code converter based on XOR gates is shown in Fig. 10.44.

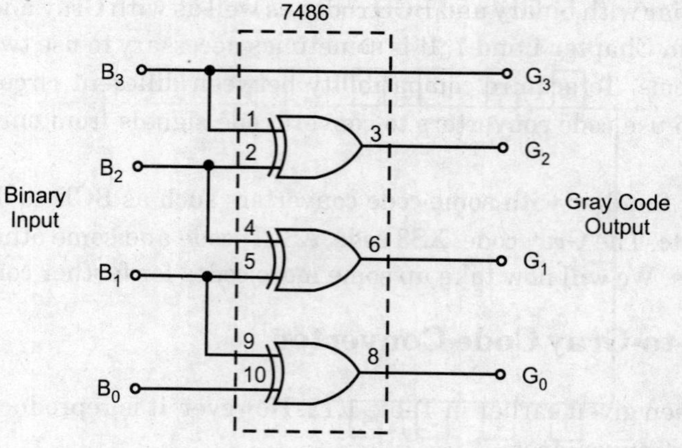

Fig. 10.44 Binary-to-Gray code converter

The operation of this circuit can be verified by connecting logic switches at the binary inputs and logic indicators at the output.

10.11.2 Gray-to-Binary Code Converter

A circuit diagram of a Gray-to-Binary code converter is given in Fig. 10.45. The operation of this circuit can be verified by connecting logic switches to Gray inputs and logic indicators to Binary outputs. When inputs in the Gray code are applied at the input, the output obtained will be in the Binary code.

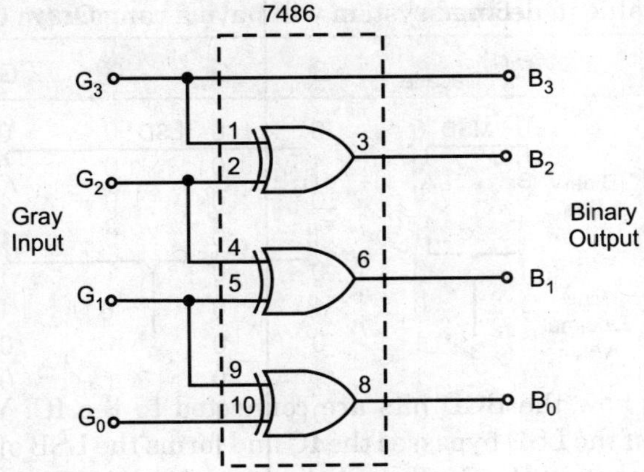

Fig. 10.45 Gray-to-Binary code converter

10.12 BCD-TO-BINARY CODE CONVERTER

There are two MSI ICs 74184 and 74185A, which are quite convenient to use when the words required to be converted are not very large. We will consider the application of these ICs for some common applications as well as for some conversions required in arithmetic operations. A pinout diagram for these ICs, which is the same for both, is given in Fig. 10.46.

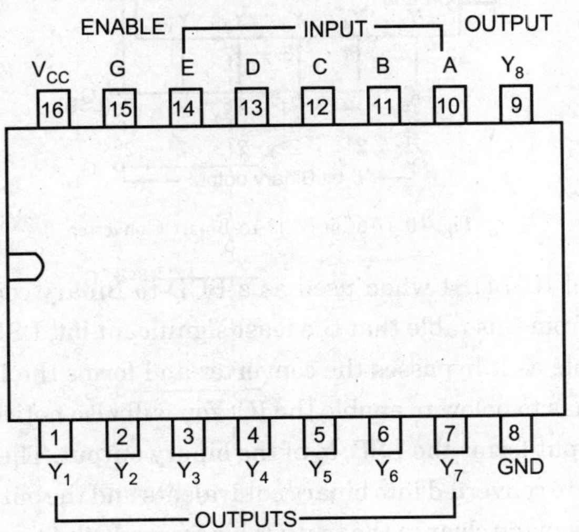

Fig. 10.46 Pinout diagram for ICs 74184 and 74185 A

When IC 74184 is used for BCD-to-Binary conversion, the BCD inputs are applied at pins A through E and the binary output is obtained at pins Y_1 to Y_5. Pins Y_6, Y_7 and Y_8 are not used for BCD-to-Binary conversion. A single IC 74184 will accept the LSD (least significant digit) consisting of four bits D_0, B_0, C_0, A_0 and two least significant bits, B_1, A_1, of the second digit (MSD), that is it will accept 1½ decade consisting of six BCD bits.

As shown below the decimal value of the ½ decade MSD cannot exceed 3 and the decimal value of the LSD cannot exceed 9. This implies that six BCD bits can be converted to the binary system, of which the value in decimal system will have a range from 00 to 39.

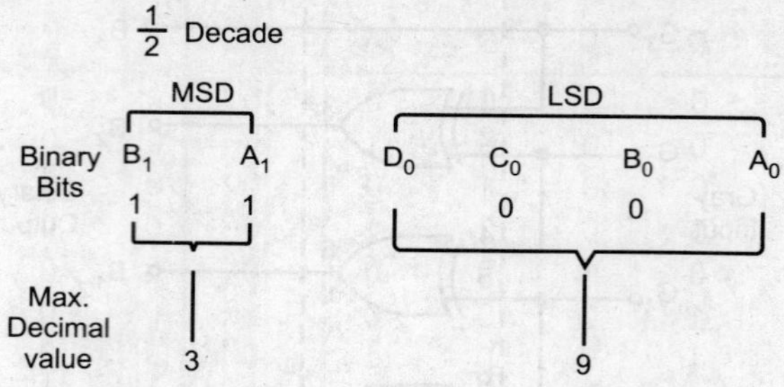

Fig. 10.47 shows how the BCD bits are connected to the IC. You will notice from the diagram that the LSB of the LSD bypasses the IC and forms the LSB of the binary number. The other bits of the LSD that is D_0, C_0, B_0 and the bits of the MSD that is B_1 and A_1 are also connected to the IC as shown in the diagram.

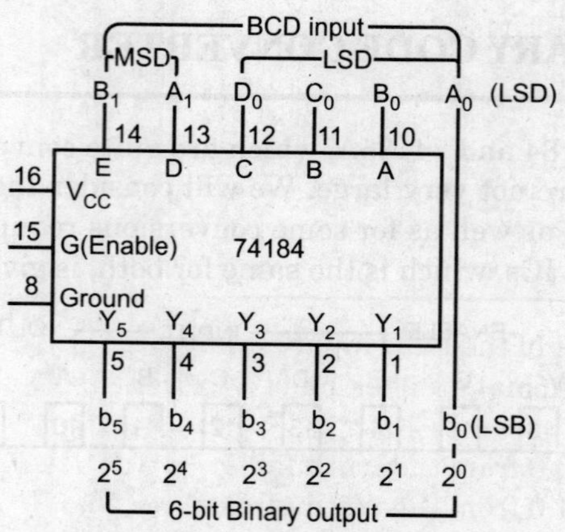

Fig. 10.47 6-bit BCD-to-Binary Converter

The truth table of IC 74184 when used as a BCD-to-Binary converter, is given in Table 10.17. You will notice from this table that the least significant bit, LSB, of the BCD input is not shown in the truth table as it bypasses the converter and forms the LSB of the binary output. The Enable input, *G*, has to below to enable the IC. You will also notice from Fig. 10.47 that the LSB, A_0, of the BCD input forms the LSB, b_0 of the binary output. The remaining five BCD bits shown in the diagram are converted into binary equivalents and the output appears at Y_1 through Y_5. The same position is made clear in the truth table from which you will notice that the output of the BCD inputs *EDCBA* is presented in binary form at Y_1 through Y_5 and the LSB is the same as in the BCD input.

Table 10.17 Truth table of BCD-to-Binary converter 74184

Equivalent decimal numbers	*BCD inputs*					*Enable*	*Binary outputs*				
	E	*D*	*C*	*B*	*A*	*G*	Y_5	Y_4	Y_3	Y_2	Y_1
0–1	0	0	0	0	0	0	0	0	0	0	0
2–3	0	0	0	0	1	0	0	0	0	0	1
4–5	0	0	0	1	0	0	0	0	0	1	0
6–7	0	0	0	1	1	0	0	0	0	1	1
8–9	0	0	1	0	0	0	0	0	1	0	0
10–11	0	1	0	0	0	0	0	0	1	0	1
12–13	0	1	0	0	1	0	0	0	1	1	0
14–15	0	1	0	1	0	0	0	0	1	1	1
16–17	0	1	0	1	1	0	0	1	0	0	0
18–19	0	1	1	0	0	0	0	1	0	0	1
20–21	1	0	0	0	0	0	0	1	0	1	0
22–23	1	0	0	0	1	0	0	1	0	1	1
24–25	1	0	0	1	0	0	0	1	1	0	0
26–27	1	0	0	1	1	0	0	1	1	0	1
28–29	1	0	1	0	0	0	0	1	1	1	0
30–31	1	1	0	0	0	0	0	1	1	1	1
32–33	1	1	0	0	1	0	1	0	0	0	0
34–35	1	1	0	1	0	0	1	0	0	0	1
36–37	1	1	0	1	1	0	1	0	0	1	0
38–39	1	1	1	0	0	0	1	0	0	1	1

The decimal equivalent of the BCD input is shown in the extreme left column of the truth table. Let us consider the decimal number 14, of which the BCD and binary equivalents are as follows:

BCD 0 1 0 1 0 0 from the truth table
Binary 0 0 1 1 1 0 from the truth table

Let us consider decimal number 15

BCD 0 1 0 1 0 1 from the truth table
Binary 0 0 1 1 1 1 from the truth table. Notice that the LSBs remain unchanged in both the cases.

When a BCD input consisting of two BCD decades is required to be converted to binary form, this can be done by conneting two 74184 ICs as shown in Fig. 10.48. As before the LSB A_0 of the LSD bypasses ICI and forms the LSB of the Binary number, b_0. Let us suppose that the BCD input required to be converted to binary form is as follows:

D_1	C_1	B_1	A_1	D_0	C_0	B_0	A_0
1	1	0	1	0	0	1	1

Since the LSB A_0 will appear as the LSB of the binary number, we will leave it as it is and convert B_1, A_1, D_0, C_0 and B_0 that is we convert to 0 1 0 0 1. From Table 10.17 we find that the binary equivalent is 0 0 1 1 0, which has been shown as the output of ICI in the diagram. Similarly, we can now convert the input to IC2, which is 0 1 0 0 1. According to the truth table the output of IC2 is 0 0 1 1 0. The final binary output of the BCD is as shown in the diagram.

Larger BCD numbers can be converted to binary form by adding more ICs, but the circuit will become complicated.

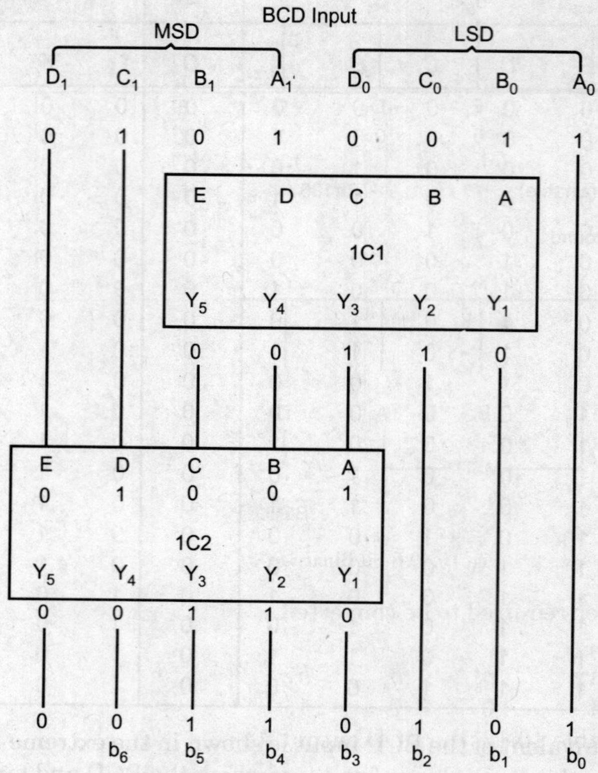

Fig. 10.48 BCD-to-Binary converter for two decades

10.13 BINARY-TO-BCD CODE CONVERTER

IC 74185 A can be used for conversion from BCD to binary form. As shown in Fig. 10.49 a 6-bit binary input is applied at pins. *E*, *D*, *C*, *B* and *A* and the LSB of the binary input bypasses the converter and appears as the LSB of the BCD output. Outputs are obtained at pins Y_1 through Y_6. Pin Y_7 and Y_8 are not used for this conversion and they will be at logic 1 output.

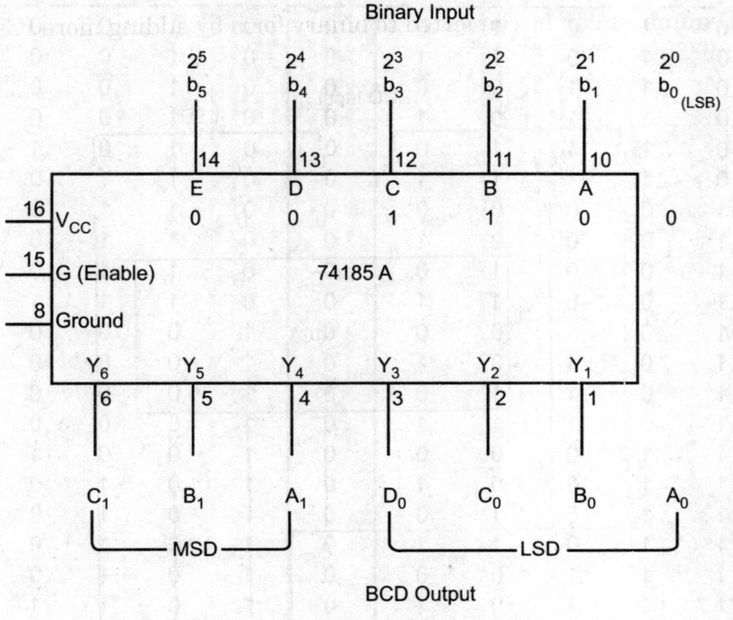

Fig. 10.49 6-bit Binary-to-BCD converter

The binary number required to be converted to BCD form is shown in the diagram and is as follows:

Binary	b_5	b_4	b_3	b_2	b_1	b_0
Input	0	0	1	1	0	0

From the Truth table 10.18, the BCD output for this binary number is as follows:

Y_6	Y_5	Y_4	Y_3	Y_2	Y_1	Y_0
0	0	1	0	0	1	0
MSD			LSD			
BCD Output						

Table 10.18 Truth table of Binary-to-BCD Converter 74185 A

Decimal number	Binary input						BCD output					
	E	*D*	*C*	*B*	*A*	*G*	Y_6	Y_5	Y_4	Y_3	Y_2	Y_1
0–1	0	0	0	0	0	0	0	0	0	0	0	0
2–3	0	0	0	0	1	0	0	0	0	0	0	1
4–5	0	0	0	1	0	0	0	0	0	0	1	0
6–7	0	0	0	1	1	0	0	0	0	0	1	1
8–9	0	0	1	0	0	0	0	0	0	1	0	0
10–11	0	0	1	0	1	0	0	0	1	0	0	0
12–13	0	0	1	1	0	0	0	0	1	0	0	1
14–15	0	0	1	1	1	0	0	0	1	0	1	0
16–17	0	1	0	0	0	0	0	0	1	0	1	1
18–19	0	1	0	0	1	0	0	0	1	1	0	0

20–21	0	1	0	1	0	0	0	1	0	0	0	0
22–23	0	1	0	1	1	0	0	1	0	0	0	1
24–25	0	1	1	0	0	0	0	1	0	0	1	0
26–27	0	1	1	0	1	0	0	1	0	0	1	1
28–29	0	1	1	1	0	0	0	1	0	1	0	0
30–31	0	1	1	1	1	0	0	1	1	0	0	0
32–33	1	0	0	0	0	0	0	1	1	0	0	1
34-35	1	0	0	0	1	0	0	1	1	0	1	0
36–37	1	0	0	1	0	0	0	1	1	0	1	1
38–39	1	0	0	1	1	0	0	1	1	1	0	0
40–41	1	0	1	0	0	0	1	0	0	0	0	0
42–43	1	0	1	0	1	0	1	0	0	0	0	1
44–45	1	0	1	1	0	0	1	0	0	0	1	0
46–47	1	0	1	1	1	0	1	0	0	0	1	1
48-49	1	1	0	0	0	0	1	0	0	1	0	0
50–51	1	1	0	0	1	0	1	0	1	0	0	0
52–53	1	1	0	1	0	0	1	0	1	0	0	1
54–55	1	1	0	1	1	0	1	0	1	0	1	0
56–57	1	1	1	0	0	0	1	0	1	0	1	1
58–59	1	1	1	0	1	0	1	0	1	1	0	0
60–61	1	1	1	1	0	0	1	1	0	0	0	0
62-63	1	1	1	1	1	0	1	1	0	0	0	1

10.14 DECIMAL NUMBER COMPLEMENTS

We have considered in Chap. 1 how 9's and 10's complements of decimal numbers can be obtained by simple arithmetic manipulation. The complements of these decimal numbers are useful in arithmetic operations like addition and subtraction. In this section we will consider how IC 74184 can be used for obtaining 9's and 10's complements of decimal numbers.

10.14.1 BCD 9's Complements Converter

Figure 10.50 gives the circuit arrangement for coverting BCD numbers into BCD 9's complement numbers with the help of IC 74184. The BCD input is applied at pins marked D, C, B and A. The BCD 9's complement is obtained from outputs marked N_D, N_C, N_B, N_A.

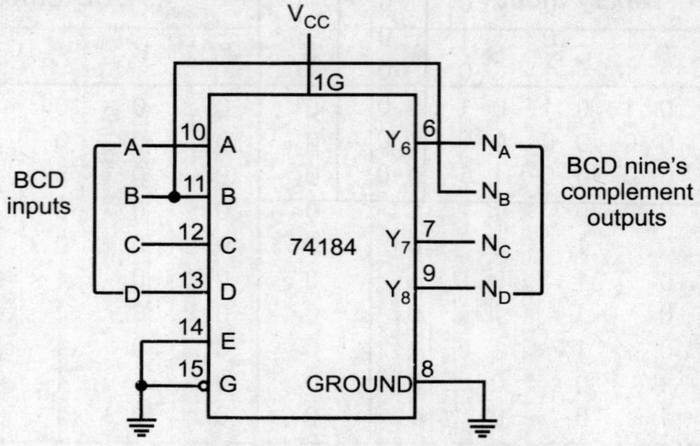

Fig. 10.50 BCD 9's complement converter

The truth table for IC 74184 when used as a BCD-to-9's complement converter is given in Table 10.19. Input G has to be held low to enable then IC.

Table 10.19 BCD 9's complement converter truth table of IC 74184

Decimal	Inputs						Outputs			BCD 9's complement			
	E	*D*	*C*	*B*	*A*	*G*	Y_8	Y_7	Y_6	N_D	N_C	N_B	N_A
0	0	0	0	0	0	0	1	0	1	1	0	0	1
1	0	0	0	0	1	0	1	0	0	1	0	0	0
2	0	0	0	1	0	0	0	1	1	0	1	1	1
3	0	0	0	1	1	0	0	1	0	0	1	1	0
4	0	0	1	0	0	0	0	1	1	0	1	0	1
5	0	0	1	0	1	0	0	1	0	0	1	0	0
6	0	0	1	1	0	0	0	0	1	0	0	1	1
7	0	0	1	1	1	0	0	0	0	0	0	1	0
8	0	1	0	0	0	0	0	0	1	0	0	0	1
9	0	1	0	0	1	0	0	0	0	0	0	0	0

10.14.2 BCD 10's Complement Converter

IC 74184 can also be used as a BCD-to-10's complement converter. A circuit for this purpose is given in Fig. 10.51. The truth table for this IC when used for this purpose is given Table 10.20. BCD inputs are applied at pins A through *D* and the 10's complement output is available at T_A, T_B, T_C, and T_D. The input labelled *E* has to be held at logic 1 level and the enable pin *G* has to be held low to enable the IC.

Table 10.20 BCD 10's complement converter truth table of IC 74184

Decimal	Inputs						Outputs			BCD 9's complement			
	E	*D*	*C*	*B*	*A*	*G*	Y_8	Y_7	Y_6	T_D	T_C	T_B	T_A
0	1	0	0	0	0	0	0	0	0	0	0	0	0
1		0	0	0	1	0	1	0	0	1	0	0	1
2	1	0	0	1	0	0	1	0	0	1	0	0	0
3	1	0	0	1	1	0	0	1	1	0	1	1	1
4	1	0	1	0	0	0	0	1	1	0	1	1	0
5	1	0	1	0	1	0	0	1	0	0	1	0	1
6	1	0	1	1	0	0	0	1	0	0	1	0	0
7	1	0	1	1	1	0	0	0	1	0	0	1	1
8	1	1	0	0	0	0	0	0	1	0	0	1	0
9	1	1	0	0	1	0	0	0	0	0	0	0	1

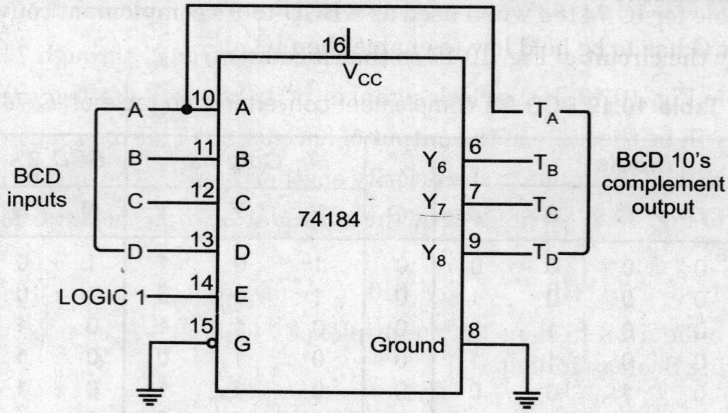

Fig. 10.51 BCD 10's complement converter

Problems

10.1 Modify the decoder circuit of Fig. 10.2 to incorporate an active low enable input.

10.2 Draw a truth table for the modified circuit in Prob 10.1.

10.3 What will be the maximum number of outputs for a decoder with a 6-bit data word?

10.4 Refer to Fig. 10.5. What should be the state of the BCD inputs when the outputs required are as follows?

(*a*) Y_0 (*b*) Y_9 (*c*) Y_{11} (*d*) Y_{14}

10.5 If the BCD inputs for the decoder circuit of Fig. 10.5 are as follows, what will be the outputs?

(*a*) 0101 (*b*) 1110 (*c*) 0010 (*d*) 0100

10.6 What will be the output of decoder 74154, if the strobe is high, the data input low and the control inputs are as follows?

(*a*) 1010 (*b*) 1101 (*c*) 1001 (*d*) 0000

10.7 Will the output of decoder 74154 in Prob 10.6 be different if the strobe is low, data input high and the BCD inputs are the same as in Prob 10.6?

10.8 What will be the output of decoder 74154 if the strobe and data are low and the BCD input is H H H H?

10.9 Refer to Table 10.3. Which output lines will be activated with the following inputs?

(*a*) 0110 (*b*) 1001 (*c*) 0000 (*d*) 1010

10.10 In a 7-segment LED display, which of the segments should be illuminated to display the following decimal numbers?

(*a*) 2 (*b*) 5 (*c*) 9 (*d*) 1

10.11 Draw a diagram showing how LED segments should be positioned and connected in a 7-segment LED display?

10.12 In Fig. 10.13 if the maximum current through each LED segment is required to be limited to 15 mA, what should be the value of the voltage dropping resistors when V_{cc} is +5V and the voltage drop for each LED segment is 2.2 V?

10.13 Modify the circuit of Fig. 10.17 so that it counts from 1 through 7.

10.14 Refer to Fig. 10.17. If the clock signal is 1kHz how will it affect the LED display?

10.15 What will be the state of the output of encoder 74147 if the inputs are X_3, X_7, X_5?

10.16 What will be the input to the priority encoder 74148 if the output is HLH?

10.17 Refer to Fig. 10.27. What will be the output at X when the data select inputs are as follows?

(*a*) 101 (*b*) 110 (*c*) 010 (*d*) 011

10.18 Draw a diagram to show how multiplexer 74151 should be used to implement the following Boolean function

$$F = \bar{A}\,B\,\bar{C} + A\,B\,\bar{C} + \bar{A}\,B\,C + A\bar{B}\,C$$

10.19 What should be the data select input to multiplexer 74151 if you want the output to represent the state of the D_5 input?

10.20 Draw a diagram using multiplexer 74150 to implement the truth table given in Prob 7.20.

10.21 Draw a diagram to show how IC 7445 can be used as an 8-output data distributor.

10.22 What should be the data select inputs in Prob 10.21 so that the output appears at Y_6?

10.23 Implement a hexadecimal-to-binary encoder using ICs 74148 and a nibble multiplexer IC 74157.

10.24 Refer to Fig. 10.31 (*c*). What should be the data select inputs if the following data input lines are to be routed to the output?

(*a*) D_0, (*b*) D_{12}, (*c*) D_{29}, (*d*) D_{30}.

10.25 Refer to Fig. 10.31(*c*). Which of the data inputs will be routed to the output when the data inputs are as follows?

	A	*B*	*C*	*D*	*E*
(*a*)	1	0	1	0	1
(*b*)	1	1	0	0	1
(*c*)	1	1	0	1	1
(*d*)	0	0	1	1	0

10.26 Refer to Fig. 10.32. What should be the data select and address select inputs if the following data inputs are to be routed to the output:

(*a*) Input D_2 from M_0

(*b*) Input D_3 from M_3

(*c*) Input D_5 from M_5

(*d*) Input D_7 from M_7

10.27 Refer to Fig. 10.32. If the select inputs are as follows which of the input lines will be routed to the output?

	A_0	A_1	A_2	A_3	A_4	A_5
(*a*)	0	1	0	1	1	0
(*b*)	1	0	0	0	0	0

(c) 1 1 0 1 0 1

(d) 0 0 0 1 1 1

10.28 Refer to Fig. 10.36. Which of the output lines will be activated when the decoder inputs are follows?

	A	B	C	D	E	F	G	H
(a)	0	0	0	1	1	0	1	0
(b)	0	1	0	0	0	1	1	0
(c)	1	1	1	0	1	0	0	1
(d)	1	1	0	1	1	0	0	0

10.29 Refer to Fig. 10.36. What should be the decoder inputs if the following output lines are to be activated?

(a) 31, (b) 15, (c) 149, (d) 255.

10.30 Draw a 3-input variable diagram for a PLA (as in Fig. 10.47) when the required outputs are as follows:

Y_1 $\overline{A}\,\overline{B}\,C$

Y_2 $\overline{A}\,B\,\overline{C}$

Y_3 $\overline{A}\,\overline{B}\,C$

Y_4 $\overline{A}\,\overline{B}\,\overline{C}$

Y_5 $A\,B\,C$

Y_6 $A\,B\,\overline{C}$

10.31 Determine the 9's complement of the following BCD numbers.

(a) 0 0 0 1

(b) 0 1 0 0

(c) 0 1 1 1

(d) 1 0 0 0

10.32 Draw a diagram to show the conversion of the following BCD number to binary from with the help of IC 74184:

0 1 1 0 0 0 1 1

10.33 Draw a diagram to show the conversion of the following binary number to BCD from with the help of IC 74185 A:

1 1 1 0 0 0

10.34 Draw a diagram to show the conversion of the following binary number to BCD form with the help of IC 74185 A:

1 0 0 0 0 1 1 1

10.35 Determine the 10's complement of the following BCD numbers:

(a) 0 0 1 0

(b) 0 1 0 0

(c) 0 1 1 0

(d) 1 0 0 0

11

Shift Registers

11.1 INTRODUCTION

Shift registers, like counters, are sequential circuits and, as they employ flip-flops, they possess memory; but memory is not the only requirement of a shift register. The function of storage of binary data can be very well performed by a simple register. Shift registers are required to do much more than that. They are required to store binary data momentarily until it is utilized, for instance, by a computer, microprocessor, etc. Sometimes data is required to be presented to a device in a manner which may be different from the way in which it is fed to a shift register. For instance, shift registers can present data to a device in a serial or parallel form, irrespective of the manner in which it is fed into the shift register. Data can also be manipulated within the shift register, so that it is presented to a device in the required form. These devices can also shift data left or right, and it is this capability which gives them the name of shift register. A look at Fig. 11.1 will show you the many ways in which data can be fed into a shift register and presented by it to a device.

Apart from the use of shift registers for data conversion, they have also found application as circulating shift registers, when the data can be kept circulating for storing data code for a number of clock signals. If only a few bits of data are required to be moved, this can be done by applying the required number of clock pulses. It is also possible to make changes at any point in the data, if these changes become necessary at a later stage or in any particular form for a different device. The Ring counter and Johnson counter, which are very useful devices, are also implemented with shift registers.

Shift registers have found considerable application in arithmetic operations. If you recall the binary number system you will at once notice that moving a binary number one bit to the left is equivalent to multiplying the number by 2 and moving the number one bit position to the right amounts to dividing the number by 2. Thus, multiplications and divisions can be accomplished by shifting data bits. Shift registers find considerable application in generating a sequence of control pulses. The applications are too numerous to mention. In this chapter, we will deal with the basic characteristics of shift registers and demonstrate their application in data manipulation.

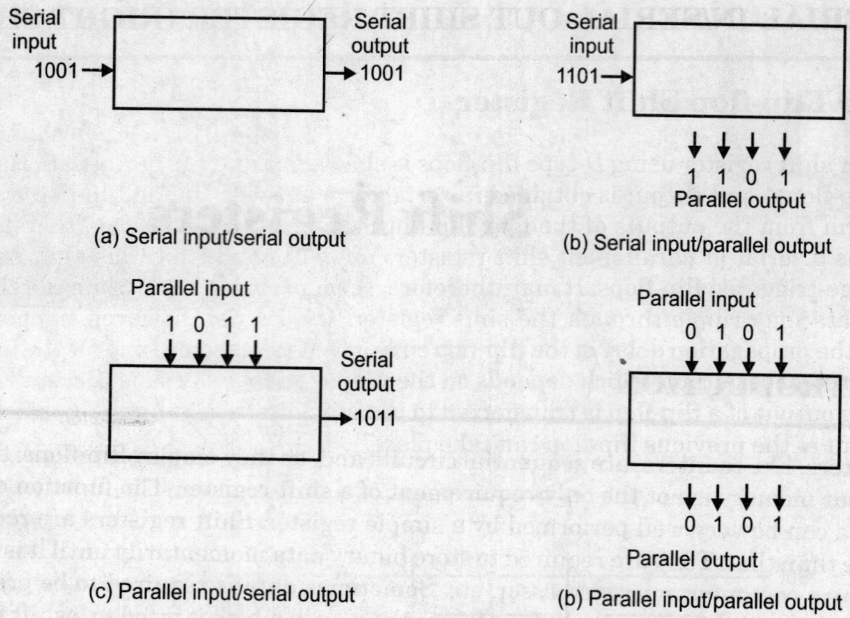

Fig. 11.1 Data conversion with a shift register

11.2 SHIFT REGISTER : MODES OF OPERATION

If you refer to Fig. 11.1, you will observe that shift registers can be operated in four different modes as indicated below:

1. *Serial input/serial output:* In this mode of operation data is applied at the input in serial form and, as clock pulses are applied at the clock input, the data moves by one position for every single clock input pulse. The output obtained is also in serial form. The data can be moved either to the left or to the right depending on the shift register configuration.

2. *Serial input/parallel output:* In this mode of operation the data is again applied at the serial input, but the output is obtained in parallel form after the full data word has been shifted in.

3. *Parallel input/serial output:* In this mode the data is located into the shift register in parallel form and it can be shifted out of the shift register to the left or to the right.

4. *Parallel input/parallel output:* In this case the data is loaded in parallel and is also read out in parallel at the outputs.

Shift registers employ binary storage elements and the most commonly used storage elements are flip-flops. Flip-flops in a shift register are so cascaded that the bits stored in them can be shifted from one flip-flop to the one adjacent to it. When clock pulses are applied simultaneously to all the storage elements, the data stored is moved by one position for every single clock pulse applied to the register.

We will consider how different types of flip-flops can be interconnected to form a shift register.

11.3 SERIAL-IN/SERIAL-OUT SHIFT REGISTER (RIGHT SHIFT)

11.3.1 D Flip-flop Shift Register

A 4-bit right shift register using *D*-type flip-flops is shown in Fig. 11.2. Serial data is fed at the *D* input of flip-flop *A* and output is obtained in serial form at the output of flip-flop *D* and also in parallel form from the outputs of the four flip-flops. This shift register can, therefore, also be classified as a serial-in parallel-out shift register. You will notice that this shift register uses positive edge-triggered flip-flops. It may, therefore, seem probable that, while the shift pulse is at 1, the data may ripple through the shift register. It does not, however, happen that way because of the propagation delay of the flip-flop circuitry. It takes some time for the input data to be transferred to be output, which depends on the propagation delay time. Because of its delay, the existing output of a flip-flop is transferred to the next flip-flop in the chain, before a change in the output of the previous flip-flop can take place.

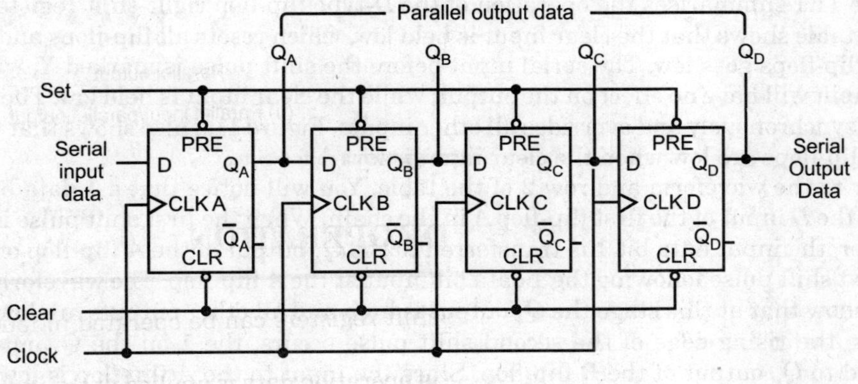

Fig. 11.2 Shift-right register using *D* flip-flop

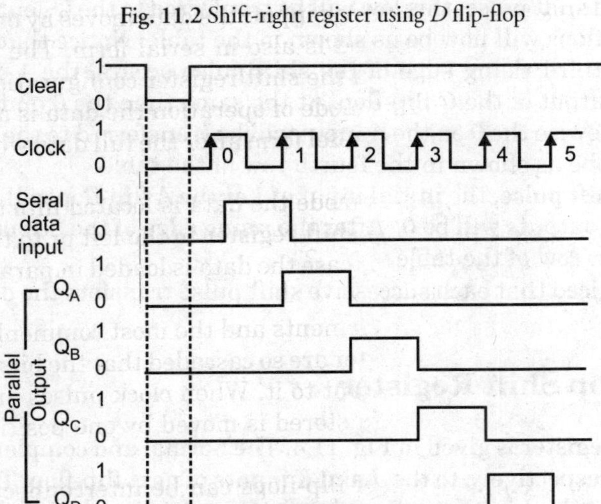

Fig. 11.3 Waveform for 4-bit serial-input shift-right register implemented with *D*-type flip-flops

Table 11.1 Truth table for *D* flip-flop shift-right register

Clear	*Input before shift pulse*	*Shift pulse*	*Output after shift pulse*			
			Q_A	Q_B	Q_C	Q_D
L	X	0	0	0	0	0
H	1	1	1	0	0	0
H	0	2	0	1	0	0
H	0	3	0	0	1	0
H	0	4	0	0	0	1
H	0	5	0	0	0	0

X = Irrelevant

Table 11.1 summarises the operation of the *D*-type flip-flop right-shift register. The first row of the table shows that the clear input is held low, which resets all flip-flops and the output of all the flip-flops goes low. The serial input before the shift pulse is marked *X*, which means that the input will have no effect on the output, while the clear input is held low. The clear input operates asynchronously and overrides all other inputs. Figure 11.3 also shows that the outputs of all the flip-flops are low when the clear input is low.

Refer to the waveform and row 2 of the table. You will notice that a 1 data bit has been applied to the *D* input of the first flip-flop *A* in the chain. When the first shift pulse is applied to the register, the input data bit 1 is transferred to the Q_A output of the *A* flip-flop on the rising edge of next shift pulse following the 1 data bit input at the *A* flip-flop. The waveform as well as the table show that at this stage the Q_A output is high and all other outputs are low.

When the rising edge of the second shift pulse occurs, the 1 on the Q_A output will be transferred to Q_B output of the *B* flip-flop. Since the input to the *A* flip-flop is low before the rising edge of the second shift pulse, this low will be tranferred to the Q_A output of the *A* flip-flop. The outputs of the flip-flops will now be as shown in the table. Notice that this tallies with the waveforms. When the third rising edge of the shift pulse occurs, the 1 on Q_B output will be transferred to the Q_C output of the *C* flip-flop. At the same time the 0 on the Q_A output will be passed on to the Q_B. Likewise the 0 on the *A* input will be transferred to the Q_A output. The state of the outputs will now be as shown in the fourth row of the table.

After the fourth shift pulse, the initial input of 1 at the *A* flip-flop will be transferred to the Q_D output and all other outputs will be 0. After the rising edge of the 5th pulse, the data will be lost as shown in the last row of the table.

You must have noticed that each successive shift pulse transfers the data bit by one step to the right.

11.3.2 JK Flip-flop Shift Register

A diagram of this shift register is given in Fig. 11.4. The normal and complement outputs of each flip-flop are connected respectively, to the *J* and *K* inputs of next flip-flop. The reset inputs of all the flip-flops are connected to a common reset input through an inverter, so that an input of 1 on the reset line will reset all the flip-flops. The preset inputs of all the flip-flops are also connected to a common line, so that all flip-flops in the register can be set at the same time. The shift pulse inputs are also connected to a common line, so that all the flip-flops are toggled simultaneously.

The serial input is connected to the J input of flip-flops A and its complement to the K input. Shift pulses are applied in synchronization with the input to the flip-flop and this shift register is, therefore, a synchronous circuit. When a shift pulse is applied, any data present at the input or in the flip-flops will be shifted by one bit position to the right. Also notice that the flip-flops used in this circuit are the negative edge-triggered type. This means that data will be shifted on the falling edge of the shift pulse.

We will now consider how serial data 1 1 0 1 can be loaded into the shift register. Figure. 11.5 shows the waveform diagram of the status of each flip-flop at the commencement of the operation and also after the trailing edge of each shift pulse. The serial input which feeds the data into the shift register is synchronized with the shift pulses. Shift pulse 1 occurs first and the other pulses follow one after the other. The serial inputs and the output states of all the flip-flops are given in a tabular form in Table 11.2.

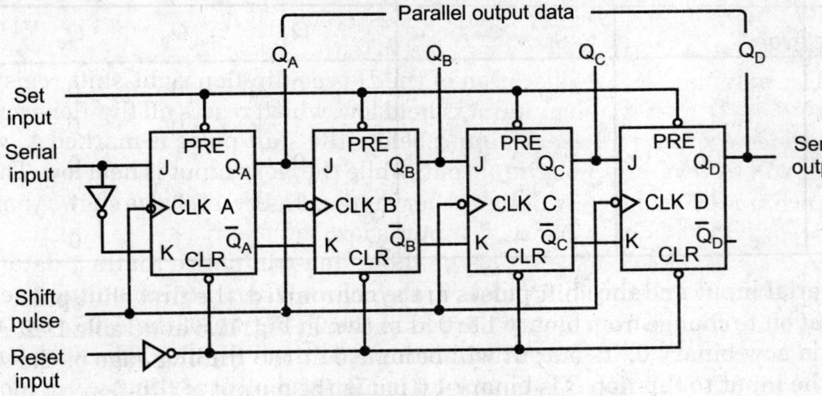

Fig. 11.4 Shift-right register using *JK* flip-flops

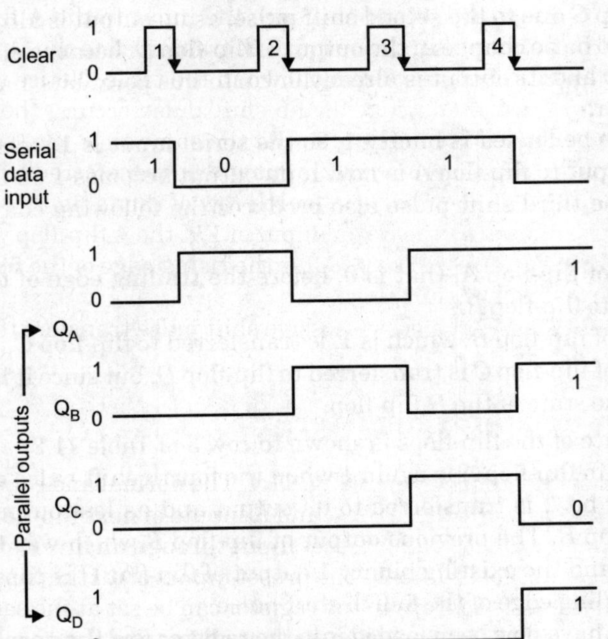

Fig. 11.5 Waveforms for *JK* flip-flop shift-right register

At the commencement of the loading operation all the flip-flops are reset as has been shown in Fig. 11.5. Since the first bit to be loaded is binary 1, the serial data input at this stage is binary 1. When the trailing of the first shift pulse occurs, the binary 1 is loaded into the *A* flip-flop. The first shift pulse is also applied to all other flip-flops and as such the binary bit 0 initially stored in the *A* flip-flop is transferred to the *B* flip-flip. Also the 0 bits stored in the *B* and *C* flip-flops will be transferred to the *C* and *D* flip-flops on the trailing edge of the first shift pulse. Since the bits stored in *B*, C and *D* flip-flops are already binary 0, there will be no change in the states of the *B*, *C* and *D* flip-flops. The state of the register at this stage is shown in row 2 of Table 11.2.

Table 11.2 Truth table for JK flip-flop shift-right register

Reset input	*Input before shift pulse*	*Shift pulse*	*Output after shift pulse*			
			Q_A	Q_B	Q_C	Q_D
H			0	0	0	0
L	1	1	1	0	0	0
L	0	2	0	1	0	0
L	1	3	1	0	1	0
L	1	4	1	1	0	1

As the serial input and the shift pulses are synchronized, the first shift pulse also causes the serial input bit to change from binary 1 to 0 as shown in Fig. 11.5 and Table 11.2. As the input to flip-flop *A* is now binary 0, its output will become 0 at the trailing edge of the second shift pulse. Since the input to flip-flop *B* is binary 1 (that is the output of flip-flop *A*), its output will change to 1 on the trailing edge of the second shift pulse. However, there will be no change in the output of flip-flop *C* due to the second shift pulse, as its output is already 0 and the input to it is 0. There will also be no change in the output of flip-flop *D*, because of the second shift pulse, as the input to it is 0 and its output is already 0. Up to this point bits 1 and 0 have been loaded into the shift register.

The third bit to be loaded is binary 1, so the serial input is 1 when the third shift pulse arrives. Since the input to flip-flop *A* is now 1, its output becomes 1 on the trailing edge of the third shift pulse. The third shift pulse also produces the following changes in the outputs of flip-flops *B*, *C* and *D*.

- The output of flip-flop *A*, that is 0, before the trailing edge of the third shift pulse is transferred to flip-flop *B*.
- The output of flip-flop *B*, which is 1, is transferred to flip-flop *C*.
- The output of flip-flop *C* is transferred to flip-flop *D*; but since it is already 0, there is no change in the state of the *D* flip-flop.

The present state of the flip-flops is shown in row 3 of Table 11.2.

The next input to flip-flop *A* is again 1 when the fourth shift pulse arrives. On its trailing edge the new binary bit 1 is transferred to its output and its last output which was also 1 is transferred to flip-flop *B*. The previous output of flip-flop *B* which was 0 is transferred to the output of flip-flop *C* and the existing binary 1 output of flip-flop *C* is passed on to the output of flip-flop *D* by the trailing edge of the fourth shift pulse.

All the four bits have now been loaded into the register and the parallel output is now 1101 as shown in Fig. 11.5 and Table 11.2 (fourth row).

11.3.3 RS Flip-flop Shift Register

Shift registers can also be built by using RS flip-flops. IC 7491 is an 8-bit shift register which uses *RS* flip-flops. Its logic diagram in given in Fig. 11.6 and its pin connections are as given in Fig. 11.7. You will notice from Fig. 11.6 that the inputs to the last seven flip-flops in the chain receive complementary inputs, that is if $S = 0, R = 1$ and if $S = 1, R = 0$. It is, therefore, obvious that they will behave exactly like *JK* flip-flops. The first flip-flop has complementary *S* and *R* inputs and, therefore, it behaves like a *D*-type flip-flop. Because of the inverter in the clock line, data will be transferred to flip-flop outputs on the positive going edge of the clock pulse. There are two inputs *A* and *B*. Any one of the inputs can be used. Since a 1 input at *A* or *B* will be a 1 input at *S* of the first flip-flop, as a result of double complementation, a positive going clock pulse will produce an output of 1 at *Q* of the first flip-flop. Normally both *A* and *B* inputs of the NAND gate are connected together when data is being fed and the NAND is not required to serve as a gate.

11.4 SERIAL-IN/SERIAL-OUT SHIFT REGISTER (LEFT SHIFT)

In previous sections, we have considered shift registers which can shift data to the right. For instance, if you refer to Fig. 11.5 and Table 11.2, you will see that we loaded data 1 1 0 1 (LSB) into the shift register and after the operation the contents of the flip-flops were as follows:

Q_A	Q_B	Q_C	Q_D	
1	1	0	1	(LSB)

Now if the input to the *A* flip-flop is a contant, binary 0 and four shift pulses are applied, the data will be shifted out of the register and it will be as follows:

1	1	0	1	(LSB)

You must have noticed from this example that a right-shift register shifts data from the high to the low order bits and the binary output number starts with the LSB, which in this case is binary 1 (output of flip-flop *D*). When additions are to be carried out, the first bit, that is the least significant digit is required to be shifted to the right. In such applications shift-right registers are found useful. However, there are certain other operations which require data to be transmitted in a certain given order. For instance, if data is required to be shifted from the low to the high order bits, shift-left registers have to be used. Shift registers can be built to shift data to the right or to the left and this operation is controlled by the direction of the control input.

11.4.1 D Flip-flop Shift Register

A shift register using *D* flip-flops is shown in Fig. 11.8.

You will notice from the diagram of the shift-left register that shift pulses are applied to all the flip-flops simultaneously, and the serial data is applied at the input of the first flip-flop in the chain. Output is available at the *Q* output of the last flip-flop. When a shift pulse occurs, the input data of each flip-flop is transferred to its output. For instance, if the input number is 1 1 0 1 (LSB) as before the MSB, bit 1 will constitute the input to flip-flop *A*. We will assume that all the flip-flops are reset to begin with. When the first shift pulse occurs at the MSB, bit 1 will be transferred to the output of *A*. The output of *A* which was initially 0 will be transferred to the output of *B* and so on. When subsequent shift pulses occur, data transfer will take place from one flip-flop to the other on its left as shown in Table 11.3. Each shift pulse shifts the data

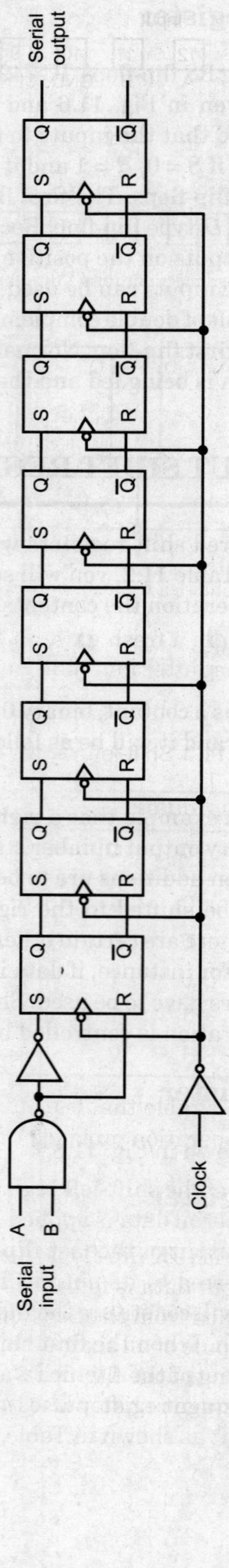

Fig. 11.6 *RS* flip-flop shift register (shift-right)

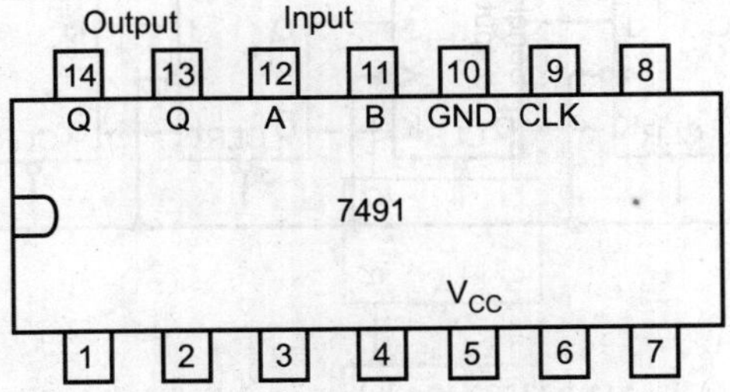

Fig. 11.7 Pin connections for *RS* flip-flop IC 7491

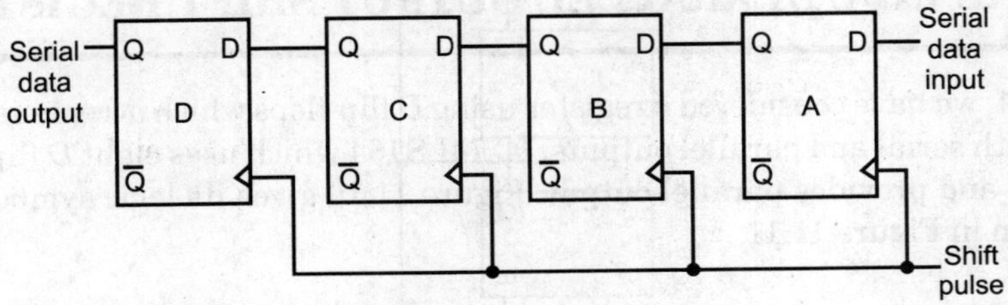

Fig. 11.8 Shift-left register using D flip-flops

stored in the register by one stage, while a fresh data bit is applied to the first flip-flop in the chain. You will notice from the table that after four shift pulse, the entire binary word will have been shifted to the register.

Table 11.3 Shift-left register operation

Shift pulse	*Flip-flop output*				*Input word*
	Q_D	Q_C	Q_B	Q_A	
0	0	0	0	0	1 1 0 1 (LSB)
1	0	0	0	1	
2	0	0	1	1	
3	0	1	1	0	
4	(MSB) 1	1	0	1	

You must have observed from this table that the shift-left operation provides data which begins with the MSB. The shift-right operation provided the same data beginning with the LSB.

11.4.2 JK Flp-flop Shift Register

A left-shift register can also be built with *JK* flip-flops. A circuit for this purpose which uses six *JK* flip-flops is shown in Fig. 11.9. Input data is fed at the *J* and *K* inputs of the flip-flop on the extreme right and the output is obtained from the flip-flop on the extreme left. Shift pulses are simultaneously applied to the clock inputs of all six flip-flops. The flip-flops can be reset with the help of a reset pulse prior to the loading of the flip-flops. Data is shifted to the left, one bit at a time, by applying shift pulses. A six-stage register like this one will require six shift pulses to shift in a 6-bit data word.

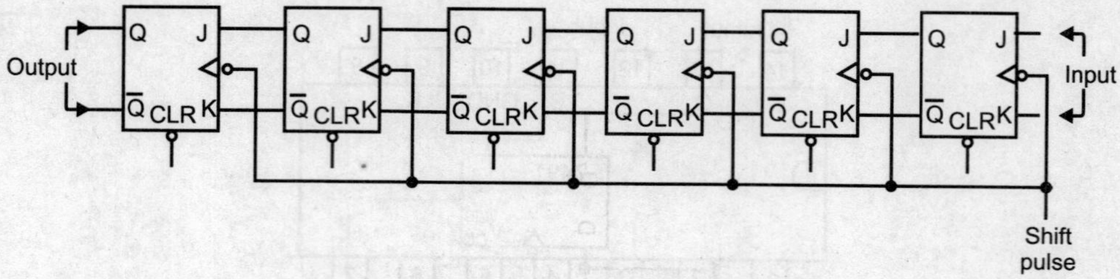

Fig. 11.9 Shift-left register using *JK* flip-flops

11.5 SERIAL INPUT/PARALLEL OUTPUT SHIFT REGISTER

In Section 11.3.1, we have considered a register using *D* flip-flops which accepts serial data input and provides both serial and parallel outputs. IC 74LS164 which uses eight *D* flip-flops, accepts 8-bit data word and provides parallel output. Figure 11.10 gives its logic symbol and the logic diagram is given in Figure 11.11.

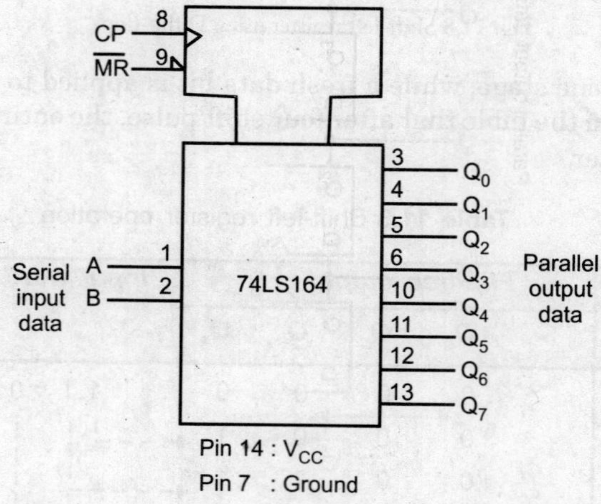

Fig. 11.10 Logic symbol for *IC* 74LS164

Before data is loaded into the register, it may be cleared by applying a low input at the master reset input MR. Input data may be applied at pins *A* or *B*, both of which are connected internally to a single serial data bit. Data may be shifted into the register by applying low-to-high transition at the clock input, CP. The output data is available at the parallel output pins.

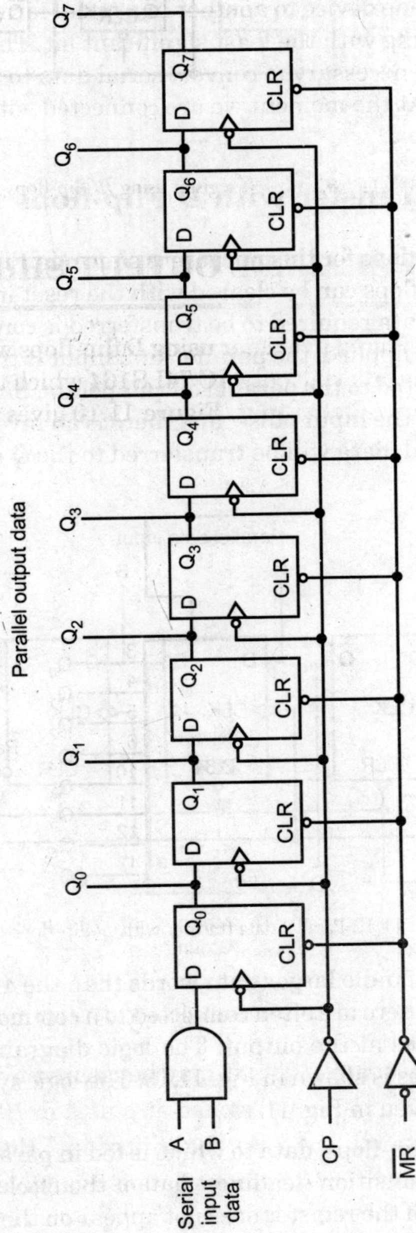

Fig. 11.11 Logic diagram of *IC74LS164*

11.6 PARALLEL-INPUT/PARALLEL-OUTPUT SHIFT REGISTER

Data can be transferred from one device to another in a serial form, but only one bit of data can be transferred at a time, starting with the least significant bit. This process is time consuming and it is, therefore, sometimes necessary to convert serial data to parallel from. This, however, we will consider a little later. At the moment we are connected with the transfer of the parallel data from one device to another.

11.6.1 Parallel Data Transfer with *D* Flip-flops

A circuit which employs *D* flip-flops for this purpose is shown in Fig. 11.12. Prior to the transfer of parallel input data, the flip-flops can be cleared with the reset input. The shift pulse input is common to all flip-flops. The data required to be transferred is connected to the *D* inputs of the flip-flops. When a clock pulse is applied, the parallel data input is transferred to the *Q* outputs of the flip-flops, which are connected to the parallel output points. Since the *D* flip-flops used here respond to the negative edge of the input pulse, and there is an inverter between the clock input of flip-flops and the clock signal, data will be transferred to the *Q* outputs on the rising edge of the clock signal input.

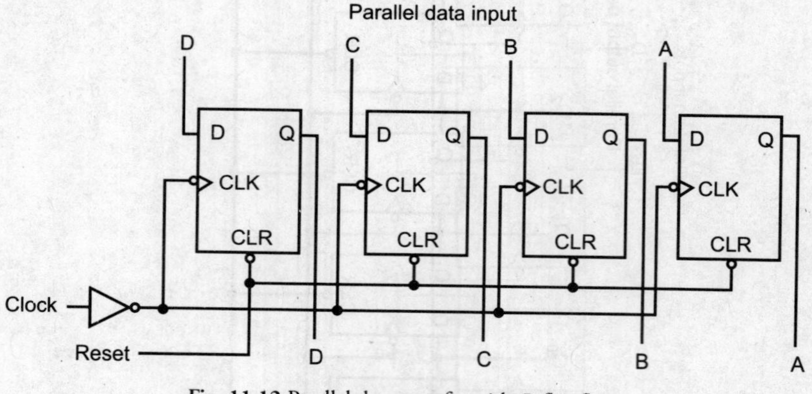

Fig. 11.12 Parallel data transfer with *D* flip-flops

Registers are required to handle larger data words than the 4-bit size we have considered in Fig. 11.12. Besides since registers are often connected to a common data bus, provision is also required for three-state switches at the output. The logic diagram of an 8-bit register which incorporates three-state switches is shown in Fig. 11.13. The logic symbol for this register which is available as IC 74LS574 is given in Fig. 11.14.

This register has eight *D* flip-flops, data to which is fed in parallel. The data is transferred to the output on the positive transition (leading edge) of the clock, *CP*. As long as the output enable (OE) is high, the output of the register does not appear on the output lines and the output pins continue to be in the high impedance state. If the output lines of the register are connected to a common data bus, the data bus remains free to handle data from other registers connected to the bus, as its normally high impedance does not interfere with the operation of other registers connected to the bus. When the output of the register is to be transferred to the bus, the output enable (OE) is driven low.

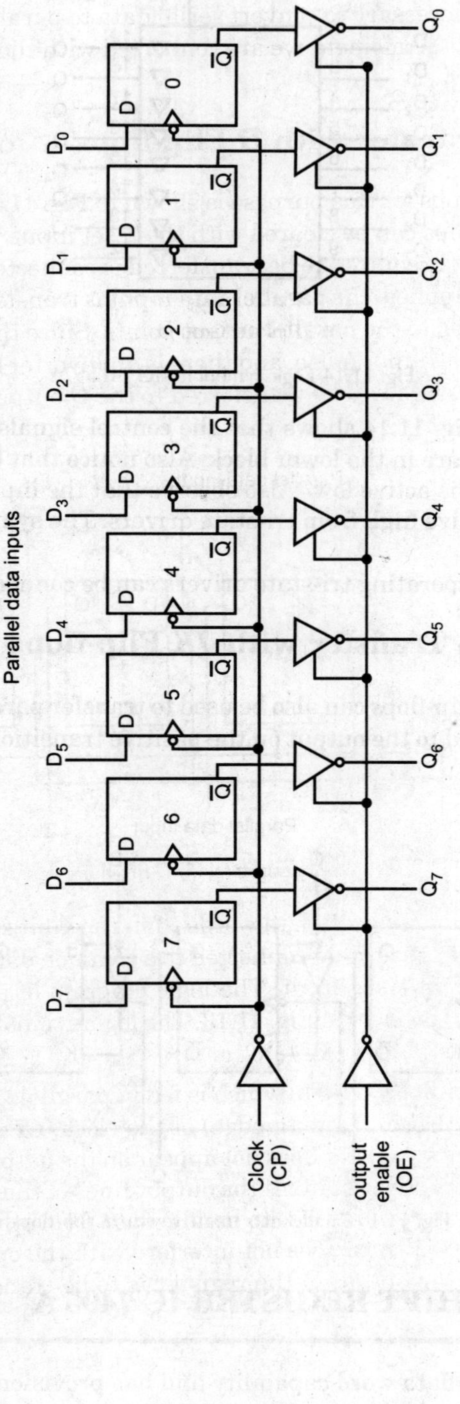

Fig. 11.13 Eight-bit D flip-flop register with tri-state outputs

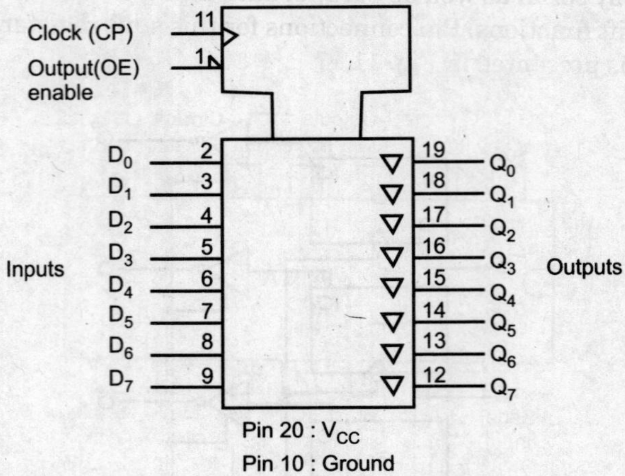

Fig. 11.14 Logic symbol for IC 74LS574

The block symbol in Fig. 11.14 shows that the control signals are in the upper rectangle and the inputs and outputs are in the lower block. Also notice that the clock (CP) is active high and the output enable (OE) is active low. Also observe that the input lines are active high and the output lines are also active high from tri-state drivers. The symbol for tri-state drivers is a triangle at the output pins.

Several registers incorporating tri-state drivers can be connected to a common data bus.

11.6.2 Parallel Data Transfer with *JK* Flip-flops

As shown in Fig. 11.15, *JK* flip-flops can also be used to transfer parallel data to parallel output. The input data is transferred to the output on the positive transition (leading edge) of the clock input.

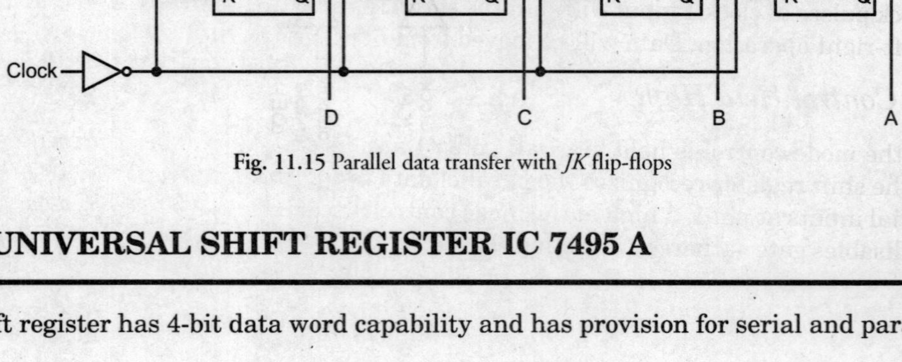

Fig. 11.15 Parallel data transfer with *JK* flip-flops

11.7 UNIVERSAL SHIFT REGISTER IC 7495 A

This shift register has 4-bit data word capability and has provision for serial and parallel outputs. It can be loaded by serial as well as parallel data inputs and has the capability to provide left-shift and right-shift functions. Pin connections for this shift register are given in Fig. 11.16 and its logic diagram is presented in Fig. 11.17.

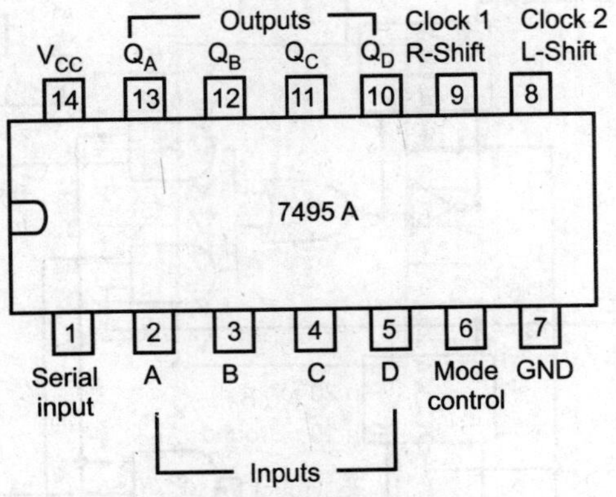

Fig. 11.16 Pin connections for IC 7495 A

The mode control and the two clocks determine the function which the shift register will perform. We will, therefore, first look into the function of these controls and see how they control the modes of operation of the shift register.

Mode Control Held Low

The setting of the mode control determines the function which will be performed by the shift register. The mode control input controls the input gating to the flip-flops as well as the operation of the two clocks. When the mode control is low all gates 1 are enabled, which enables the shift register to perform the shift-right operation. When serial input is applied at pin 1, it passes through gates 1 and 2 to flip-flop *A*. The output of the flip-flop *A* is connected in a similar manner to flip-flop *B*; *B* to *C* and *C* to *D*.

Low input on mode control disables gate 6, thereby disabling clock 2; enables gate 4, thereby enabling clock 1. A clock pulse applied to clock 1 passes through gate 5 and thus controls all the flip-flops. In this mode the shift register recognizes the serial input at pin 1 and ignores the parallel inputs at *A*, *B*, *C* and *D*.

Shift-right Function

With mode control low, as described above, the register will recognize the serial input at pin 1 and clock pulses at clock 1 input will shift the serial input data into the register and also perform the shift-right operation. Data will be moved from flip-flop *A* to *B*; *B* to *C* and *C* to *D*.

Mode Control Held High

When the mode control is held high, all gates 1 are disabled and gates 3 are enabled. In this mode the shift register recognizes the parallel data inputs at inputs *A*, *B*, *C* and *D* and ignores the serial inputs at pin 1. A high at the mode control also enables gate 6, thereby enabling clock 2 and disables gate 4, thereby disabling clock 1.

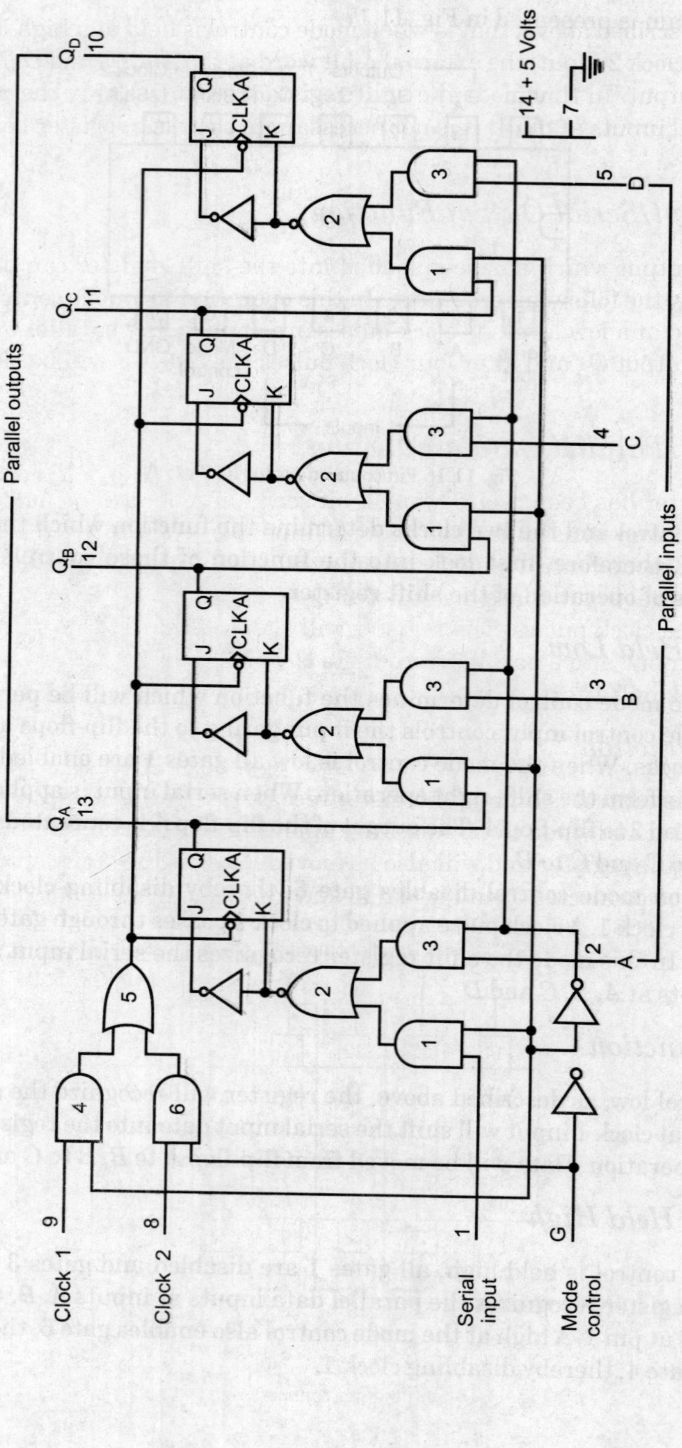

Fig. 11.17 Logic diagram of IC 7495 A

Parallel Input/Parallel Output Function

In the mode described above, that is when mode control is held at a high level, if a clock pulse is applied at the clock 2 input, the external 4-bit word at the *A*, *B*, *C* and *D* inputs will be loaded in the parallel output. In this mode the shift register recognizes only the parallel inputs and ignores the serial inputs at pin 1. It is not necessary to clear the register before loading a parallel word.

Parallel Input/Serial Output Function

Any parallel output which has been loaded into the shift register can be made available as a serial output by the following procedure. In this operation the mode control and the serial input control are held at a low level. As clock pulses are applied, the parallel word will be shifted out serially from output Q_D and after four clock pulses the register will be cleared, since the serial input is low.

Serial Input/Parallel Output Function

After the register has been cleared, any 4-bit serial number can be loaded into the register as described here. We will assume that the serial input word 0001 has to be loaded into the parallel output. Set the mode control input to low and the serial input to high. Apply a clock pulse which will shift the serial input 1 into the register. Q_A will now be 1. Return serial input switch to low and apply three clock pulses. The register will show an output of 0 0 0 1. This procedure converts a serial input into a parallel output. To clear the register, set the serial input to low and apply four clock pulses.

Left Shift Function

When the mode control is high, the register recognizes the serial input at *D*. At the same time clock 2 is enabled and when clock pulses are applied at the clock input, the serial input data will be shifted into the register and will also be moved left. For the shift-left operation, outputs and inputs should be connected as in Fig. 11.18 and input should be applied at pin 5.

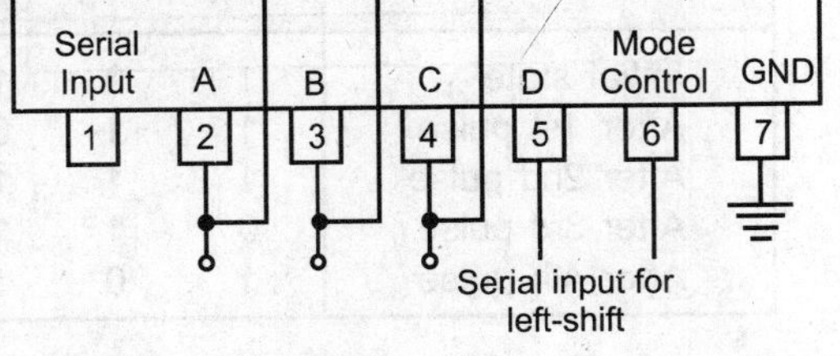

Fig. 11.18 Shift register connections for left-shift function

11.8 RECIRCULATING SHIFT REGISTER

When a large data code is required to be stored for a number of clock pulses, a recirculating shift register comes in very handy, as it can store the required data in its memory, which can be kept recirculating in the register for use as and when required. A diagram for a recirculating shift register is given in Fig. 11.19. If a 4-bit data word is fed into this register and its output is fed back into the serial input, as shown in the diagram, and shift pulses are applied, the contents of the flip-flops after each shift pulse will be as shown in Table 11.4. After exactly four shift pulses, the contents of the flip-flops will be the same as at the initial stage, as the number of flip-flops is four. If there are *N* flip-flops, it will require *N* shift pulses for the register to return to the original state.

To operate the recirculating shift register, all flip-flops must first be reset by applying a 1 input to the reset control. Data is entered at the serial input by first applying a logic 0 to the control input. After the each data bit entry, a shift pulse is applied to move the data to the right in the register. Since the register shown in the diagram has only four flip-flops, four data bits can be loaded in this way. When data has been stored in the register, the control input is set to high. This inhibits gate 1 and thereby prevents other data bits which may appear at the input from being recognized by the register.

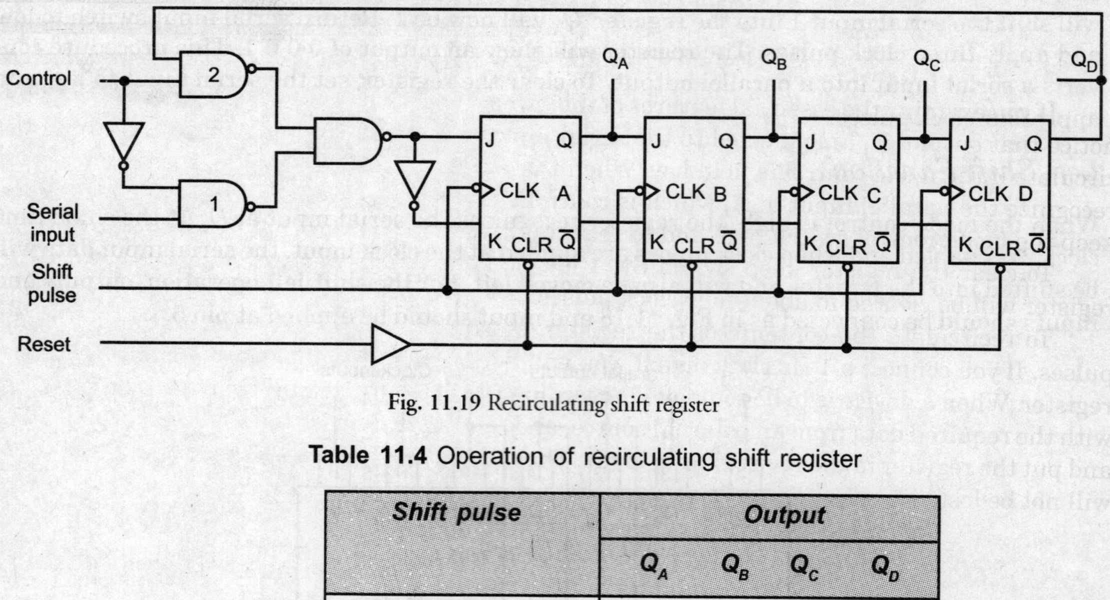

Fig. 11.19 Recirculating shift register

Table 11.4 Operation of recirculating shift register

Shift pulse	*Output*			
	Q_A	Q_B	Q_C	Q_D
Initial state	1	0	1	1
After 1st pulse	1	1	0	1
After 2nd pulse	1	1	1	0
After 3rd pulse	0	1	1	1
After 4th pulse	1	0	1	1

To circulate the data automatically within the register, the shift pulse input is connected to a clock generator and the control input to high. This enables gate 2 and at this gate is also connected to the output of the register, the data which is being shifted out serially also serves as the input to the register. The data shifted out can be used by an external circuit, the functioning of which depends on the data in the register's memory.

If fresh data is rquired for any application at a particular position in the binary code, this may be done by first circulating the data to the desired position and then entering the new data.

We will now consider the application of shift register IC 7495 A as a recirculating shift register. Figure 11.20 gives the required circuit connections for this purpose.

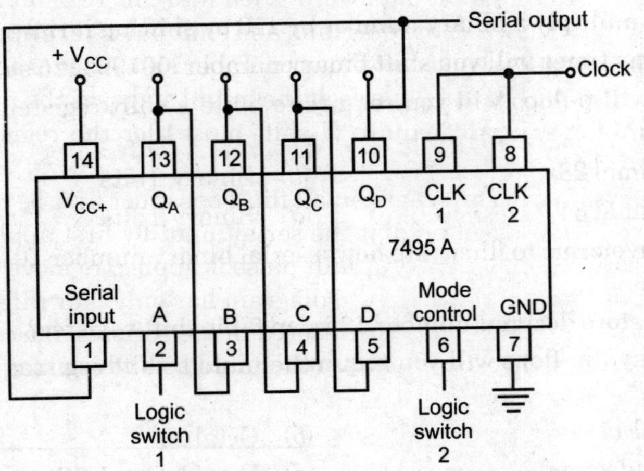

Fig. 11.20 Recirculating shift register using IC 7495 A

If you examine the essential features of this circuit and compare it with Fig. 11.17, you will notice that output Q_D is connected to the serial input to flip-flop A, which enables the data to circulate if the mode control is held low. When the mode control is held high, the register will recognize the parallel input at A, which is controlled by logic switch 1. Therefore to feed data keep the mode control switch high and to recirculate data keep it low.

To clear the register keep switch Sw 1 low and Sw 2 high and apply clock pulses. The register will be cleared in about four clock pulses.

To recirculate the contents of the register, keep the mode control low and apply clock pulses. If you connect a 1 Hz clock signal, you will notice how the data keeps circulating in the register. When a device is to be controlled according to a certain sequence, you load the register with the required data from an external source, and connect the device to the serial output at Q_D and put the register in the recirculating mode. The data in the register will keep circulating and will not be lost.

Problems

11.1 The inputs to a *JK* shift register are as follows:

(*a*) $J = 1 : K = 0$ (*b*) $J = 1 : K = 1$

(*c*) $J = 0 : K = 0$ (*d*) $J = 0 : K = 1$

What will be the complement outputs?

11.2 The complement output required from a clocked *RS* latch are as follows:

(*a*) No change (*b*) 0

(*c*) 1

What should be the inputs and the states of the clock?

11.3 What will be the complement output of a clocked D latch under the following conditions?

(*a*) Clock 0 : D = X (*b*) Clock 1 : D = 0

(*c*) Clock 1 : D = 1

11.4 A binary number is to be divided by 64. By how may positions will you shift the number and in what direction to achieve this?

11.5 Can you multiply a binary number by 118 by shifting it right or left?

11.6 How many times will you shift binary number .001953125 so that it equals 1?

11.7 How may flip-flops will you require to build a shift register to store the following numbers?

(*a*) Decimal 28 (*b*) Binary 6 bits

(*c*) Decimal 34 (*d*) Binary 3 bits

11.8 Draw waveforms to illustrate how a serial binary number 1011 is loaded into a shift register.

11.9 Can you store decimal number 12 in an 8-bit shift register?

11.10 How many flip-flops will you require to build a shift register, to store the following numbers?

(*a*) Octal 17 (*b*) Octal 20

(*c*) Hexadecimal *A* (*d*) Hexadecimal *FF*

11.11 If *RS* flip-flops are used instead of *JK* flip-flops in shift register 7945 A, will it affect its functioning?

11.12 How will you design a 4-bit shift register, if only serial input/parallel output and left-shift functions are required?

11.13 How will you obtain a serial output from a serial input with shift register 7495 A?

11.14 Draw the waveforms to shift binary number 101101 into the left-shift register given in Fig. 11.9.

11.15 Calculate the time it will take to shift the 6-bit number into the shift register in Problem 11.14, if the clock frequency is

(*a*) 2 MHz (*b*) 10 MHz

11.16 If in Problem 11.15 the transition times is not to exceed the following limits, what should be the maximum clock frequency?

(*a*) 25 ns (*b*) 15 ns

11.17 Draw a diagram to show how you will connect two registers IC 74LS574 to a common output data bus.

12

Counters

12.1 INTRODUCTION

We will now consider another class of sequential circuits, commonly known as counters, to which a brief reference was made in Chapter 11, which dealt with registers. Both counters and registers belong to the class of sequential circuits. In the present chapter we will mainly deal with counters and also consider design procedures for sequential logic circuits. As the important characteristic of these circuits is memory, flip-flops naturally constitute the main circuit element of these devices and, therefore, there will be considerable emphasis on their application in circuit design.

You must already be familiar with some sequential devices, in which operations are performed in a certain sequence. For instance, when you dial a phone number, you dial it in a certain sequence, if not, you cannot get the number you want. Similarly, all arithmetic operations have to be performed in the required sequence.

While dealing with flip-flops, you have dealt with both clocked and unclocked flip-flops. Thus, there are two types of sequential circuits, clocked which are called synchronous, and unclocked which are called asynchronous. As you have noticed in an earlier chapter on flip-flops, synchronous types are triggered by a clock oscillator, which produces regular timing pulses when flip-flop outputs can change only during the course of these timing pulses.

In asynchronous devices, a change occurs only after the completion of the previous event. A digital telephone is an example of an asynchronous device.

If you are dialing a number, say 6354, you will first punch 6 followed by 3, 5 and 4. The important point to note is that, each successive event occurs after the previous event has been completed.

Sequential logic circuits find application in a variety of binary counters and storage devices and they are made up of flip-flops. A binary counter can count the number of pulses applied at its input. On the application of clock pulses, the flip-flops incorporated in the counter undergo a change of state in such a manner that the binary number stored in the flip-flops of the counter represents the number of clock pulses applied at the input. By looking at the counter output, you can determine the number of clock pulses applied at the counter input.

Digital circuits use several types of counters which can count in the pure binary form and in the standard BCD code as well as in some special codes. Counters can count up as well as count down. In this chapter we will be looking at some of the counters in common use in digital devices.

Another area of concern to us in this chapter will be the design of sequential circuits. We will be considering both synchronous and asynchronous sequential circuits.

12.2 BINARY RIPPLE UP-COUNTER

We will now consider a 3-bit binary up-counter, which belongs to the class asynchronous counter circuits and is commonly known as a ripple counter. Figure 12.1 shows a 3-bit counter, which has been implemented with three *T*-type (toggle) flip-flops. The number of states of which this counter is capable is 2^3 or 8. This counter is also referred to as a modulo 8 (or divide by 8) counter. Since a flip-flop has two states, a counter having *n* flip-flops will have 2^n states.

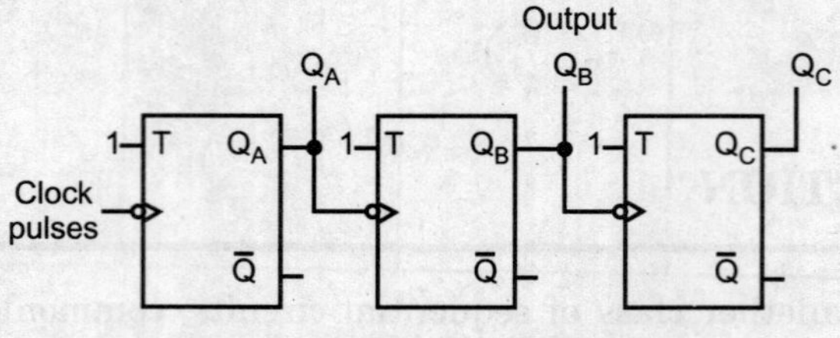

Fig. 12.1 3-Bit binary up-counter

When clock pulses are applied to a ripple counter, the counter progresses from state to state and the final output of the flip-flops in the counter indicates the pulse count. The cirucit recycles back to the starting state and starts counting all over again.

There are two types of ripple counters, (a) asynchronous counters and (b) synchronous counters. In asynchronous counters all flip-flops are not clocked at the same time, while in synchronous counters all flip-flops are clocked simultaneously.

You will notice from the diagram that the normal output, *Q* of each flip-flop is connected to the clock input of the next flip-flop. The *T* inputs of all the flip-flops, which are *T*-type, are held high to enable the flip-flops to toggle (change their logic state) at every transition of the input pulse from 1 to 0. The circuit is so arranged that flip-flop *B* receives its clock pulse from the Q_A output of flip-flop *A* and, as a consequence, the output of flip-flop *B* will change its logic state when output Q_A of flip-flop *A* changes from binary 1 to 0. This applies to all the other flip-flops in the circuit. It is thus an asynchronous counter as all the flip-flops do not change their logic state at the same time.

Let us assume that all the flip-flops have been reset, so that the output of the counter at the start of the count is 0 0 0 as shown in the first row of Table 12.1. Also refer to Fig. 12.2, which shows the output changes for all the flip-flops at every transition of the input pulse from 1 → 0.

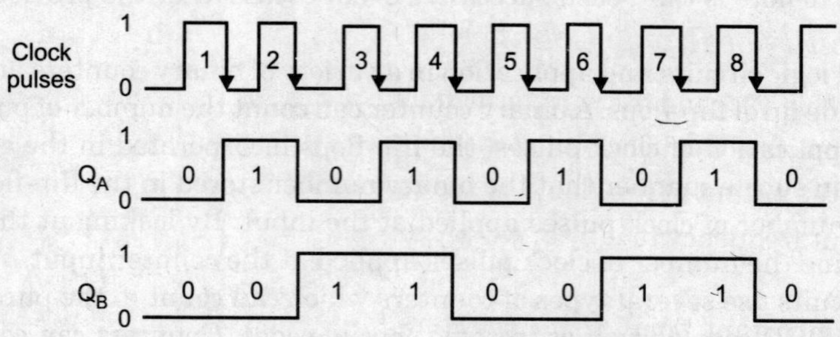

Fig. 12.2 Waveform for 3-bit binary ripple up-counter

Table 12.1 Count-up sequence of a 3-bit binary counter

Input pulse	*Count*		
	2^2 Q_C	2^1 Q_B	2^0 Q_A
0	0	0	0
1	0	0	1
2	0	1	0
3	0	1	1
4	1	0	0
5	1	0	1
6	1	1	0
7	1	1	1

Recycle

When the trailing edge of the first pulse arrives, flip-flop *A* sets and Q_A becomes 1, which does not affect the output of flip-flop *B*. The counter output now is as shown in row 2 of the table. As a result of the second clock pulse, flip-flop *A* resets and its output Q_A changes from 1 to 0, which sets flip-flop *B* and the counter output now is as shown in row 3 of the table.

When the third clock pulse arrives, flip-flop *A* sets and its output Q_A becomes 1, which does not change the state of the *B* or the *C* flip-flop. The counter output is now as shown in row 3 of the table. When the fourth pulse occurs, flip-flop *A* resets and Q_A becomes 0, which in turn resets flip-flop *B* and Q_B becomes 0, which sets flip-flop *C* and its output changes to 1.

When the 5th clock pulse arrives, flip-flop *A* sets and Q_A becomes 1; but the other flip-flops remain unchanged. The number stored in the counter is shown in the 6th row of the table. The 6th pulse resets flip-flop *A* and at the same time flip-flops *B* and *C* are set. The 7th pulse sets all the flip-flops and the counter output is nɔw shown in the last row of the table.

The next clock pulse will reset all the flip-flops, as the counter has reached its maximum count capability. The counter has in all 8 states. In other words, it registers a count of 1 for every 8 clock input pulses. It means that it divides the number of input pulses by 8. It is thus a divide by 8 counter.

Count Capability of Ripple Counters

If you refer to Table 12.1 and the waveform diagram, Fig. 12.2, it will be apparent to you that the counter functions as a frequency divider. The output frequency of flip-flop *A* is half the input frequency and the output of flip-flop *B* is one-fourth of the clock input frequency. Each flip-flop divides the input frequency to it by 2. A 3-bit counter will thus divide the clock input frequency by 8.

Another important point about counters is their maximum count capability. It can be calculated from the following equation:

$$N = 2^n - 1$$

where N is the maximum count number and

n is the number of flip-flops

For example if $n = 12$, the maximum count capability is

$$N = 2^{12} - 1 = 4095$$

If you have to calculate the number of flip-flops required to have a certain count capability, use the following equation:

$$n = 3.32 \log_{10} N$$

For example if the required count capability is 5000

$$n = 3.32 \log_{10} 5000$$

$$= 12.28$$

which means that 13 flip-flops will be required.

Counting Speed of Ripple Counters

The primary limitation of ripple counters is their speed. This is due to the fact that each successive flip-flop is driven by the output of the previous flip-flop. Therefore, each flip-flop in the counter contributes to the total propagation delay. Hence, it takes an appreciable time for an impulse to ripple through all the flip-flops and change the state of the last flip-flop in the chain. This delay may cause malfunction, if all the flip-flops change state at the same time. In the counter we have just considered, this happens when the state changes from 011 to 100 and from 111 to 000. If each flip-flop in the counter changes state during the course of a counting operation, and if each flip-flop has a propagation delay of 30 nanoseconds, a counter having three flip-flops will cause a delay of 90 ns. The maximum counting speed for such a flip-flop will be less than.

$$\frac{1}{90} \times 10^9 \text{ or } 11.11 \text{ MHz.}$$

If the input pulses occur at a rate faster than 90 ns, the counter output will not be a true representation of the number of input pulses at the counter. For reliable operation of the counter, the upper limit of the clock pulses of the counter can be calculated from

$$f = \frac{1}{nt} \times 10^9$$

where n is the number of flip-flops and

t is the propagation delay of each flip-flop.

12.3 4-BIT BINARY RIPPLE UP-COUNTER

A 4-bit binary ripple up-counter can be built with four *T*-type flip-flops. The diagram will follow the same pattern as for a 3-bit up-counter. The count-up sequence for this counter is given in Table 12.2 and a waveform diagram is given in Fig. 12.3. After the counter has counted up to 1111, it recycles to 0000 like the 3-bit counter. You must have observed that each flip-flop divides the input frequency by, 2 and the counter divides the frequency of the clock input pulses by 16.

Table 12.2 Count-up sequence of a 4-bit binary up-counter

Input pulse	*Count*			
	2^3 Q_D	2^2 Q_C	2^1 Q_B	2^0 Q_A
0	0	0	0	0
1	0	0	0	1
2	0	0	1	0
3	0	0	1	1
4	0	1	0	0
5	0	1	0	1
6	0	1	1	0
7	0	1	1	1
8	1	0	0	0
9	1	0	0	1
10	1	0	1	0
11	1	0	1	1
12	1	1	0	0
13	1	1	0	1
14	1	1	1	0
15	1	1	1	1
16 or 0	0	0	0	0

Recycle

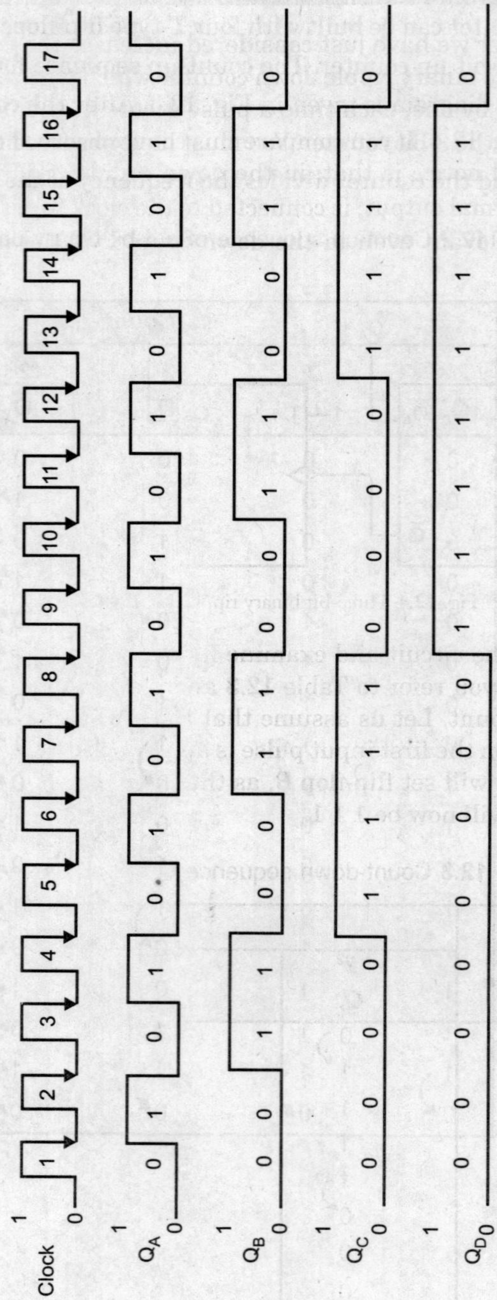

Fig. 12.3 Waveform for 4-bit binary up-counter

12.4 Three-BIT BINARY RIPPLE DOWN COUNTER

The binary ripple up-counter we have just considered increases the count by one, each time a pulse occurs at its input. The binary ripple down counter which we are going to consider in this section decreases the count by one, each time a pulse occurs at the input. A circuit for a 3-bit down counter is given in Fig. 12.4. If you compare this counter with the up-counter in Fig. 12.1, the only difference you will notice is that, in the down counter in Fig. 12.4 the complement output $\overline{Q}$, instead of the normal output, is connected to the clock input of the next flip-flop. The counter output which is relevant even in the down counter is the normal output, Q, of the flip-flops.

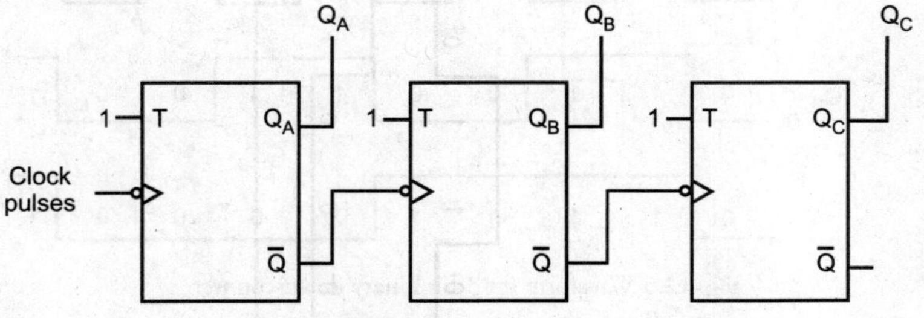

Fig. 12.4 Three-bit binary ripple down counter

We can now analyze the circuit and examine its operation. It will help you to follow the operation of the counter, if you refer to Table 12.3 and waveform of the counter given in Fig. 12.5 for each input pulse count. Let us assume that the counter is initially reset, so that the counter output is 0 0 0. When the first input pulse is applied, flip-flop A will set, and its complement output will be 0. This will set flip-flop B, as there will be a 1→ 0 transition at the clock input. The counter output will now be 1 1 1.

Table 12.3 Count-down sequence of a 3-bit binary counter

Clock pulse	*Count*		
	2^2 Q_C	2^1 Q_B	2^0 Q_A
0	0	0	0
1	1	1	1
2	1	1	0
3	1	0	1
4	1	0	0
5	0	1	1
6	0	1	0
7	0	0	1
8	0	0	0

Recycle

When the second clock pulse is applied, flip-flop A will reset and its complement output will become 1, which will not affect the other flip-flops. The counter output will now be 1 1 0 as shown in row 3 of the Table 12.3.

When the third clock pulse occurs, flip-flop *A* will set and its complement output will become 0, which will reset flip-flop *B*, its output becomes 0, and the complement output will be 1, which will not affect the other flip-flops. The counter will now show an output of 1 0 1, as in the fourth row of the table.

You will notice that every clock pulse decrements the counter by 1. After the eighth clock pulse, the counter output will be 0 0 0 and the counter will recycle thereafter.

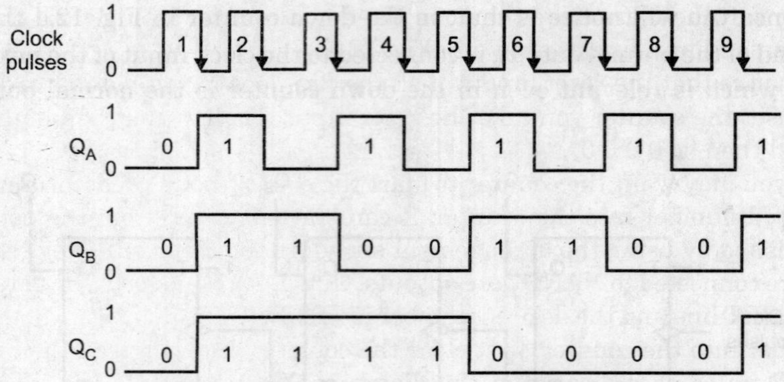

Fig. 12.5 Waveform for 3-bit binary down-counter

12.5 UP-DOWN COUNTERS

The counters which we have considered so far can only count up or down; but they cannot be programmed to count up or down. However, this facility can be easily incorporated by some modification in the circuitry. You might recall that in an up-counter the normal output of a flip-flop is connected to the clock input of the following flip-flop, and in a down counter it is the complement output which is connected to the clock input of the following flip-flop. The change from normal to complement connection to the clock input of the following flip-flop can be easily managed. A circuit for this purpose is shown in Fig. 12.6.

The normal and complement outputs of flip-flops are connected to AND gates *D* and *E* and the output of the AND gates goes to the clock input of the next flip-flop via OR gates *F*. When the up-down control is binary 1, gates *D* and *F* are enabled and the normal output of each flip-flop is coupled via OR gates *F* to the clock input of the next flip-flop. Gates *E* are inhibited, as one input of all these gates goes low because of the inverter. The counter, therefore, counts up.

When the up-down control is binary 0, gates *D* are inhibited and gates *E* are enabled. As a consequence the complement output of each flip-flop is coupled via OR gates. *F* to the clock input of the next flip-flop. The counter, therefore, counts down.

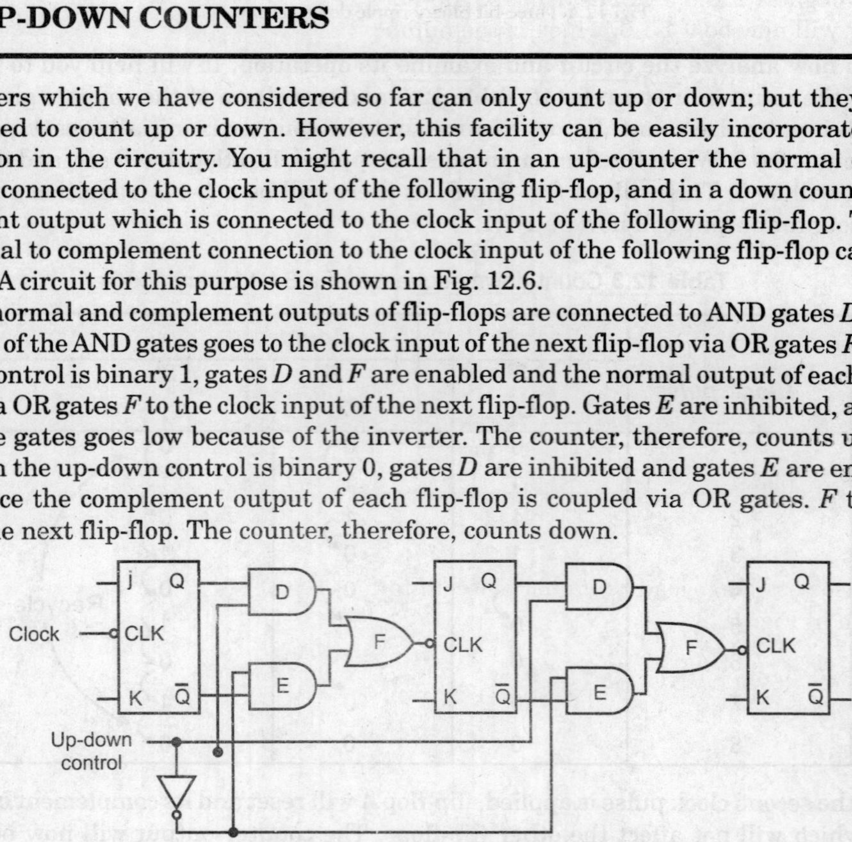

Fig. 12.6 Up-down counter

12.6 RESET AND PRESET FUNCTIONS

Reset and preset functions are usually necessary in most counter applications. When using a counter you would, in most cases, like the counter to begin counting with no prior counts stored in the counter. Resetting is a process by which all flip-flops in a counter are cleared and they are thus in a binary 0 state. *JK* flip-flops have a CLEAR or RESET input and you can activate them to reset flip-flops. If there are more than one flip-flop, the reset inputs of all flip-flops are connected to a common input line as shown in Fig. 12.7.

You will notice that the reset inputs of all the flip-flops in the counter are active low, and therefore, to reset the counter you take the reset input line low and then high. The output of the counter will then be 0 0 0 0.

At times you may want the counter to start the count from a predetermined point. If you load the required number into the counter, it can start counting from the point. This can be easily accomplished by using the arrangement shown in the diagram. The preset inputs of all the flip-flops are connected to NAND gate outputs. One input of each NAND gate is connected to a common PRESET line and the desired number is fed into the other inputs of the NAND gates. To load a number into the counter, first clear the counter and then feed the required number into the NAND gates as indicated in the diagram. When you take the PRESET line high momentarily, the output of NAND gates 1 and 4 will be 1, so flip-flops *A* and *D* will remain reset. The output of gates 2 and 3 will be 0 and so flip-flops *B* and *C* will be set. The number stored in the counter will now be 0 1 1 0, which is the number required to be loaded in the counter.

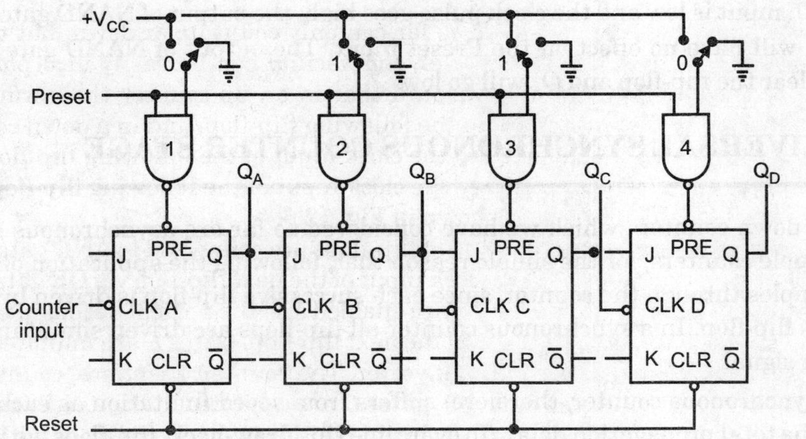

Fig. 12.7

It is also possible to load a number in a counter in a single operation, by using the arrangement shown in Fig. 12.8.

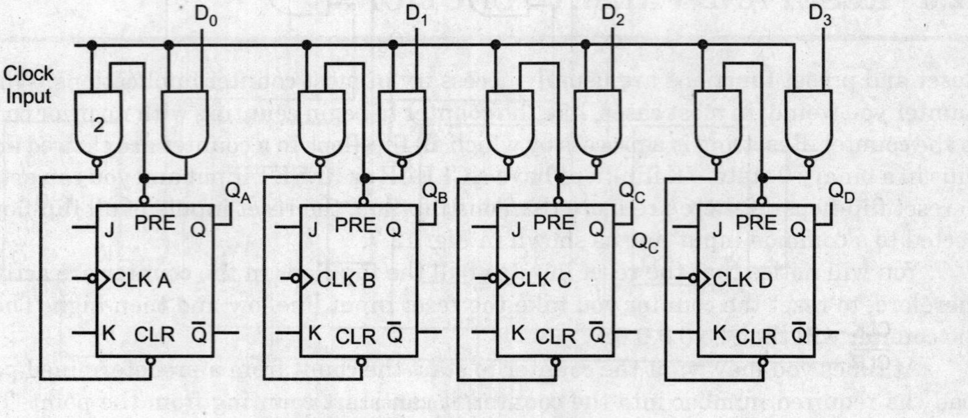

Fig. 12.8 Single pulse data transfer

The arrangement for data transfer, which is a single pulse operation, makes use of the Preset and Clear inputs of the flip-flops. When the clock pulse is low, the output of both NAND gates 1 and 2 is high, which has no effect on the Preset and Clear inputs of the flip-flop and there is no change in its output. If the D_0 inpult is high, the output of NAND gate 1 will go low when the clock pulse goes high. This will result in output Q_A going high at the same time. Since one input of NAND gate 2 will be low at this time, the clear input to the flip-flop remains high.

If the D_0 input is low and the clock pulse goes high, the output of NAND gate 1 will remain high, which will have no effect on the Preset input. The output of NAND gate 2 will go low, which will clear the flip-flop and Q_A will go low.

12.7 UNIVERSAL SYNCHRONOUS COUNTER STAGE

The up and down counters which we have considered so far are asynchronous counters, also known as ripple counters, for the simple reason that, following the application of a clock pulse, the count ripples through the counter, since each successive flip-flop is driven by the output of the previous flip-flop. In a synchronous counter all flip-flops are driven simultaneously by the same timing signal.

The asynchronous counter, therefore, suffers from speed limitation as each flip-flop contributes to the total propagation delay. To overcome this draw-back, flip-flops with lower propagation delay can be used; but the ideal solution is to use synchronous counters. In these counters the circuit is so arranged that triggering of all flip-flops is done simultaneously by the input signal, which is to be counted. In these counters the total propagation delay is the delay contributed by a single flip-flop.

The design concept used in the synchronous counter shown in Fig. 12.9(a) uses counter stage blocks and this design concept lends itself to building large synchronous counters. Counter modules of the type used in this circuit and also shown separately in Fig. 12.9 (b) can be interconnected to build counters of any length.

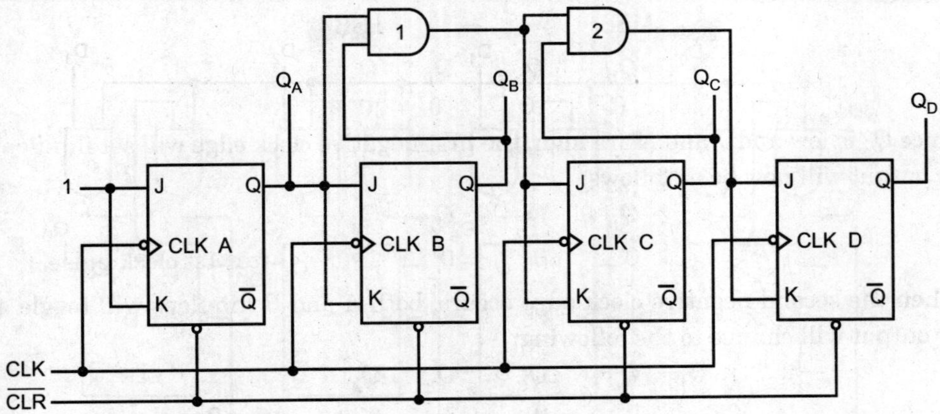

Fig. 12.9 (a) Synchronous counter

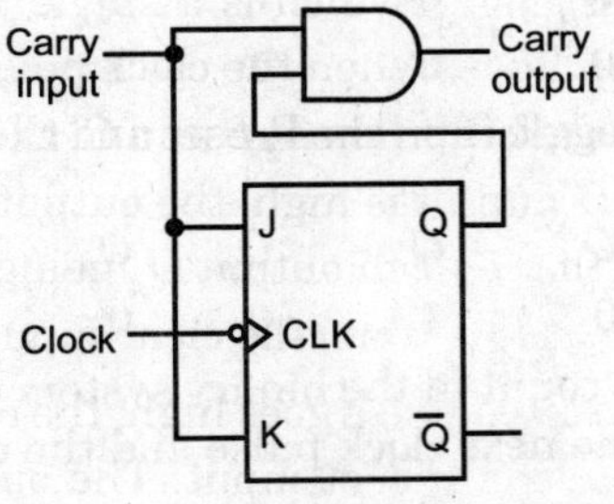

Fig. 12.9 (b) Universal counter stage block

Let us consider the synchronous counting circuit shown in Fig. 12.9(*a*). It is a 4-bit counter and the clock inputs of all the flip-flops are connected to a common clock signal, which enables all flip-flops to be triggered simultaneously. The Clear inputs are also connected to a common Clear input line. The *J* and *K* inputs of each flip-flop are connected together, so that they can toggle when the *JK* input is high. The *JK* input of flip-flop *A* is held high. Also notice the two AND gates 1 and 2, and the way they are connected. Gate 1 ensures that the *JK* input to flip-flop *C* will be binary 1 when both inputs Q_A and Q_B are binary 1. AND gate 2 ensures that the *JK* input to flip-flop *D* will be binary 1 only when outputs Q_A, Q_B and Q_C are binary 1.

We can now look into the output states required for the flip-flops to toggle. This has been summarized below:

1. Flip-flop *A* toggles on negative clock edge.
2. Flip-flop *B* toggles when Q_A is 1
3. Flip-flop *C* toggles when Q_A and Q_B are 1
4. Flip-flop *D* toggles when Q_A, Q_B and Q_C are 1

This means that a flip-flop will toggle only if all flip-flops preceding it are at binary 1 level.

We can now look into the counting process of this counter. We begin by resetting the counter, which is done by taking CLR temporarily low.

MSB			LSB
Q_D	Q_C	Q_B	Q_A
0	0	0	0

Since Q_A is low and J and K are high, the first negative clock edge will set flip-flop A. The counter output will now be as follows:

Q_D	Q_C	Q_B	Q_A	
0	0	0	1	After 1st clock pulse.

When the second negative clock edge occurs, both A and B flip-flops will toggle and the counter output will change to the following:

Q_D	Q_C	Q_B	Q_A	
0	0	1	0	After 2nd clock pulse.

When the third clock pulse arrives, flip-flop B will not toggle as Q_A is 0 but flip-flop A will toggle. The counter will show the following output:

Q_D	Q_C	Q_B	Q_A	
0	0	1	1	After 3rd clock pulse.

The fourth clock pulse will toggle flip-flop A, B and C, as both Q_A and Q_B are 1. The counter output is now as follows:

Q_D	Q_C	Q_B	Q_A	
0	1	0	0	After 4th, clock pulse.

The counter will continue to count in the binary system until the counter output registers 1 1 1 1, when it will be reset by the next clock pulse and the counting cycle will be repeated.

12.8 SYNCHRONOUS COUNTER ICs

Many types of counter ICs are avilable and it is very likely that one of these will meet you design requirements. You may not, therefore, find it necessary to design your own counter. However, should that become necessary, a variety of *JK* flip-flops are available, with which you can design one to meet your specific needs.

Some of the counter ICs available are listed below:

Counter type	*Parallel load*	*IC No*
1 Decade Up	Synchronous	74160
	Synchronous	74162
2 Decade Up/Down	Synchronous	74168
	Synchronous	74ALS568
	Asynchronous	74ALS190
	Asynchronous	74ALS192
3 4-bit binary Up counter	Synchronous	74161
	Synchronous	74163
4 4-bit binary UP/Down counter	Synchronous	74169
	Asynchronous	74191
	Asynchronous	74193
	Asynchronous	74ALS569

All the counters listed here have parallel load capability, which implies that a binary data input applied to the counter will be transferred to the output when the load input on the counter is asserted. The load operation may be synchronous or asynchronous. If it is asynchronous, the data applied will be transferred to the output as soon as the load input is asserted.

In case it is synchronous, the data will not be transferred to the output until the next clock pulse occurs. In either case the counters will begin to count from the loaded count when clock pulses are applied.

The decade up-counters count from 0000 to 1001. Decade up-and down-counters can be programmed to count from 0000 to 1001, or from 1001 to 0000. 4-Bit binary counters in the up-count mode count from 0000 and 1111 and in the down-count mode count from 1111 to 0000.

We will now discuss the facilities available in counter IC 74193 and its operating procedures. Pin connections for this IC are given in Fig. 12.10. Figure 12.11(a) gives its traditional symbol and Fig. 12.11(b) gives the IEEE/IEC symbol.

12.8.1 Counter Functions

Clear (Reset) Function

As the Clear input is active high, it is normally held low. To clear the counter it is taken high momentarily.

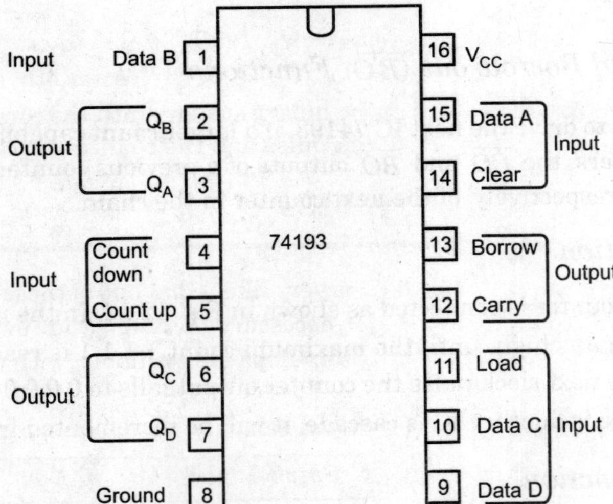

Fig. 12.10 Pin connections for IC 74193

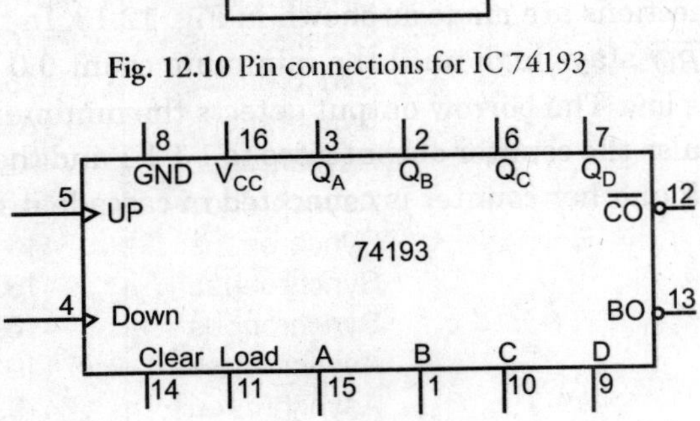

Fig. 12.11 (a) Traditional symbol for IC 74193

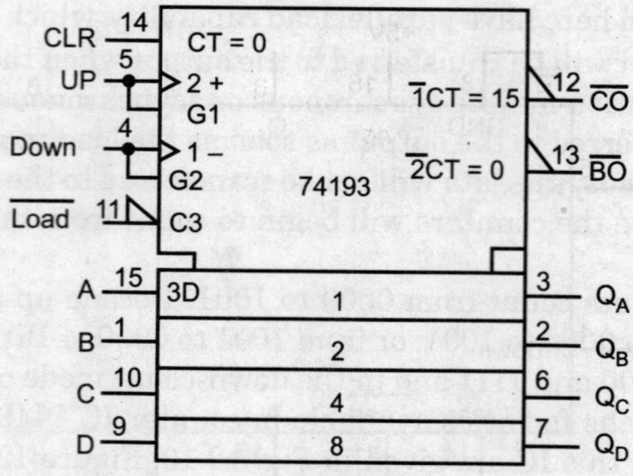

Fig. 12.11 (b) IEEE/IEC symbol for IC 74193

Load (Preset) Function

To load the counter with a predetermined 4-bit binary number, it is fed into the parallel data inputs *A*, *B*, *C* and *D*. The number is shifted into the counter by taking the LOAD input momentarily low. Both Clear and LOAD inputs are synchronous and will override all synchronous counting functions.

Carry out ($\overline{CO}$) *and Borrow out* ($\overline{BO}$) *Functions*

These inputs are used to drive the next IC 74193, if a larger count capability is required. While cascading these counters, the $\overline{CO}$ and $\overline{BO}$ outputs of a previous counter are connected to the UP and Down inputs respectively, of the next counter in the chain.

Up-counting Function

For counting up, the counter is connected as shown in Fig. 12.12. In the up-counting mode the carry output $\overline{CO}$ remains high, until the maximum count 1 1 1 1 is reached, when the carry output goes low. At the next clock pulse the counter output falls to 0 0 0 0 and the carry output $\overline{CO}$ goes high. If there is another IC is cascade, it will be incremented from 0 0 0 0 to 0 0 0 1.

Down-counting Function

For down-counting, connections are made as shown in Fig. 12.13. In the down-counting operation the borrow output $\overline{BO}$ stays high until the minimum count 0 0 0 0 is reached, when the borrow output $\overline{BO}$ drops low. The borrow output detects the minimum counter value.

At the next input pulse the counter output rises to 1 1 1 1 and there is a 0→1 transition at the borrow output $\overline{BO}$. If another counter is connected in cascade it will be decremented.

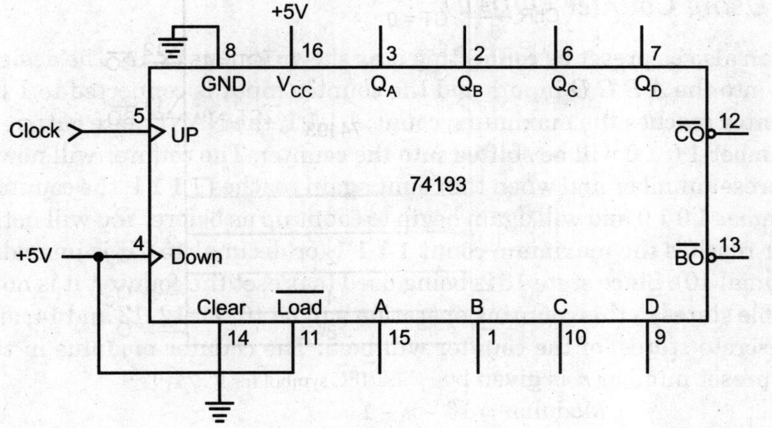

Fig. 12.12 Counter connected to count up

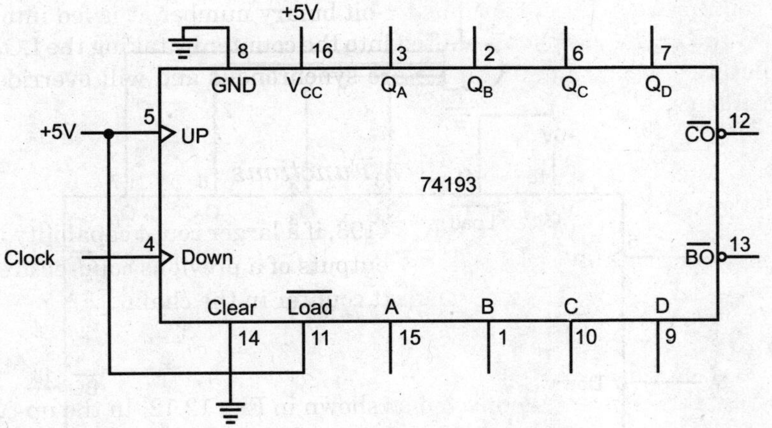

Fig. 12.13 Counter connected to count down

Presetting (Up-Counting Mode)

The counter can be preset to any 4-bit binary number, which is first fed into the parallel inputs *A*, *B*, *C* and *D*, and the load input is held low momentarily, which shifts the number into the counter. It is not necessary to reset the counter before presetting it. Let us suppose that the number shifted into the counter 1 0 1 0 and the counter is made to count up. The counter output will be stepped up after each input pulse and after the 6th pulse the output will be 0 0 0 0. The counting up begins from the number preset in the counter and the 6th pulse resets the counter and then it starts counting up from this point.

Presetting (Down-Counting Mode)

The counter is set up in the down-counting mode and, as before, suppose the number fed into the counter is 1 0 1 0 and the counter is made to count down. The 10th, input pulse will reset the counter to 0 0 0 0 and the 11th, pulse will show a count of 1 1 1 1 and then it will begin to count down from this number.

Presetting (Using Counter Output)

The counter can also be preset by connecting it as shown in Fig. 12.14. The desired number, say 1 0 1 0, is fed into the *A B C D* inputs and the counter input is connected to 1 Hz clock signal. When the counter reaches the maximum, count, 1 1 1 1, the NAND gate output will go low and the binary number 1 0 1 0 will be shifted into the counter. The counter will now begin to count up from this preset number and when the count again reaches 1 1 1 1, the counter will return to the preset number 1 0 1 0 and will again begin to count up as before. You will notice that as soon as the counter reaches the maximum count 1 1 1 1 (or decimal 15), it is immediately preset to 1 0 1 0 (or decimal 10). Since state 15 is being used to preset the counter, it is no longer a stable state. The stable states in this counting operation will be 10, 11, 12, 13 and 14, and the modulus (number of discrete states) of the counter will be 5. The counter modulus in the up-counting mode for any preset number n is given by

$$\text{Modulus} = 16 - n - 1$$

In this case $\quad \text{Modulus} = 16 - 10 - 1 = 5$

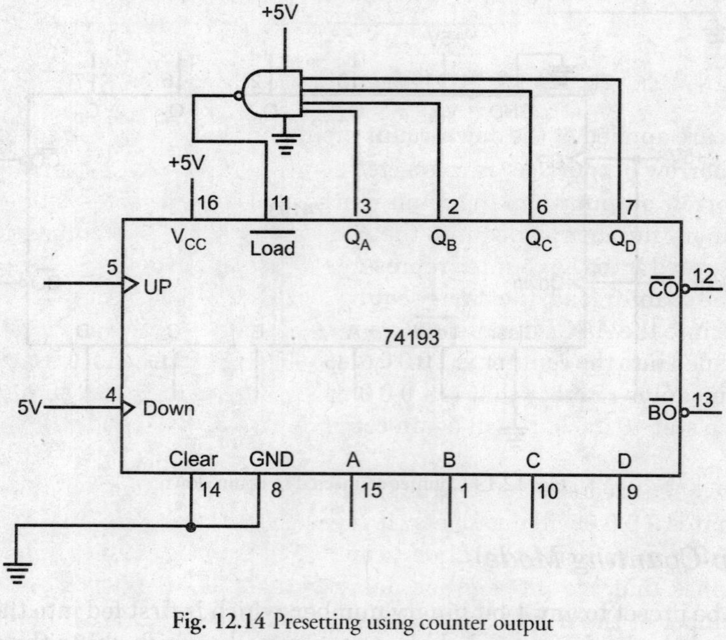

Fig. 12.14 Presetting using counter output

In the down-counting mode, the counter will count down from the preset number, 1010 (or decimal 10). As before the counter will count down as follows; 9, 8, 7, 6, 5, 4, 3, 2, 1, 0. In this case, the counter modulus will be as follows:

$$\text{Modulus} = n + 1$$

In this case $\quad \text{Modulus} = 10 + 1 = 11$

When the counter is preset in this manner, it should never be preset to number 15 as this is not a stable state, and it is likely to get latched up in this state.

Modulo N Counter Using IC 74193

In Section 12.8 you have seen how this IC can count up or down from a preset number. If fact, it can function as a modulo counter by using a NAND gate to preset the counter to the desired number. There is a simpler way of implementing a modulo counter with this IC, but it has some drawbacks which we will discuss shortly. A circuit for a modulo counter using this IC in the down-counting mode is given in Fig. 12.15.

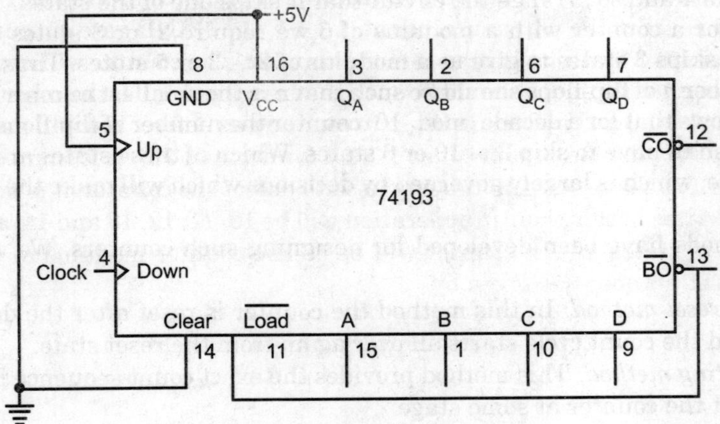

Fig. 12.15 IC 74193 connected as a modulus counter

Clock pulses are applied at the down-count input and the up-count input is held high. Also observe that the borrow output $\overline{BO}$ is connected to the load input. The borrow output detects the state of the borrow output when the count reaches 0 0 0 0. Since it is connected back to the load input, the binary number loaded into the *A B C D* inputs is shifted into the counter. The decimal number loaded into the counter represents its modulus.

To operate the counter load, the binary equivalent of the decimal number representing the required modulus into the *ABCD* inputs and apply clock pulses at the down-count input. If the binary number loaded into the counter is 1 0 0 0 (decimal 8) and the counter is decremented with clock pulses, the modulus number that is 1 0 0 0 will be loaded into the counter, as soon as the output reaches the state 0 0 0 0. It will again count down to 0 0 0 0 and will again be preset to 1 0 0 0.

You must have realized that as soon as the preset number is loaded into the counter, the borrow output, that is 0 0 0 0 will disappear. It is important, therefore, that the borrow output state, 0 0 0 0, must be of sufficient duration to enable the preset number to be shifted into the counter. This implies that the propagation delay of the gates responsible for presetting the counter to the number at the *A B C D* inputs must be of shorter duration than the duration of the clock pulse. To a certain extent this can be ensured by introducing some delay between the borrow output and the load input. This can be done by connecting an even number of inverters between the borrow output $\overline{BO}$ and the load input.

12.9 MODULUS COUNTERS

The modulus of a counter, as discussed before, is the number of discrete states a counter can take up. A single flip-flop can assume only two states 0 and 1, while a counter having two flip-flops can assume any one of the four possible states. A counter with three flip-flops will have 8 states and so on. In short the number of states is a multiple of 2. With n flip-flops the number of possible states will be 2^n. Thus by building counters which count in the normal binary sequence, we can build counter with modulus of 2, 4, 8, 16, etc. In these counters the count increases or decreases by 1 in pure binary sequence. The problem arises in building counters whose modulus is 3, 5, 7, 9, etc. For instance, if we need a counter with a modulus of 3, we have to use a counter with a modulus of 4 and so arrange the circuit that it skips one of the states.

Similarly, for a counter with a modulus of 5 we require 2^3 or 8 states and arrange the circuit so that it skips 3 states to give us a modulus of $2^n - 3$ or 5 states. Thus for a modulus N counter the number n of flip-flops should be such that n is the smallest number for which $2^n > N$. It, therefore, follows that for a decade (mod -10) counter the number of flip-flops should be 4. For this counter we shall have to skip $2^4 - 10$ or 6 states. Which of these states are to be skipped is a matter of choice, which is largely governed by decisions which will make the circuit as simple as possible.

Many methods have been developed for designing such counters. We will consider the following:

1. *Counter reset method:* In this method the counter is reset after the desired count has been reached and the count cycle starts all over again from the reset state.

2. *Logic gating method:* This method provides the exact count sequence required without any need to reset the counter at some stage.

3. *Counter coupling method:* This method is used to implement counters of the required modulus. For instance we can interconnect mod-2 and mod-3 counters to implement a modulus 3 × 2 or mod-6 counter.

12.10 COUNTER RESET METHOD (ASYNCHRONOUS COUNTERS)

Let us first consider the typical case of a counter which has 3 states as shown in Fig. 12.16.

12.10.1 Mod-3 Counter

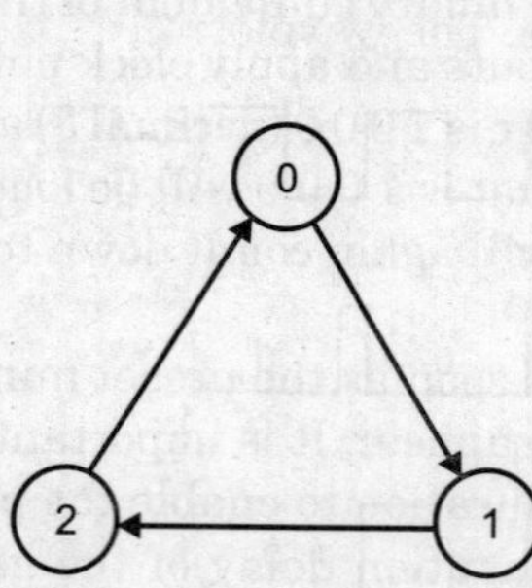

Fig. 12.16 State diagram for a mod-3 counter

It is obvious that a mod-3 counter will require two flip-flops which, when connected as a counter, will provide four states as shown in Table 12.4.

Table 12.4 States for a two flip-flop counter

Q_A LSB	Q_B	Count value (Decimal)
0	0	0
1	0	1
0	1	2
1	1	3
0	0	0

This counter counts in the binary sequence 0, 1, 2, 3 and then it returns to 0, the starting point. Each count is referred to as a state. If we are building a mod-3 counter, the most convenient solution is to skip state 3 and then return to state 0 from state 2 and then again go through states 0, 1, 2 before returning to state 0. What we need is a combinational logic circuit, which will feed a reset pulse to the counter during state 3, and immediately after state 2, which is the last desired state. This reset pulse is applied to the CLR inputs which resets the counter to 0 after state 2.

A circuit diagram for a mod-3 counter together with the required combinational logic is given in Fig. 12.17.

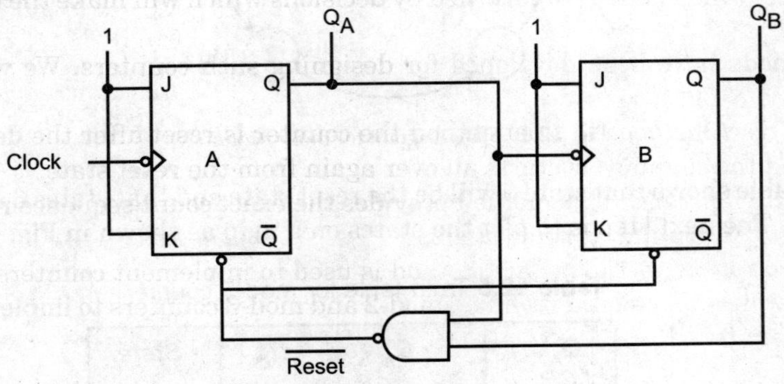

Fig. 12.17 Modulo-3 counter

When both outputs Q_A and Q_B are 1, the output of the NAND gate, which provides the reset pulse, goes low and both the flip-flops are reset. The counter returns to state 0 and it starts counting again in 0, 1, 2, 0 sequence. The waveforms for this counter are given in Fig. 12.18.

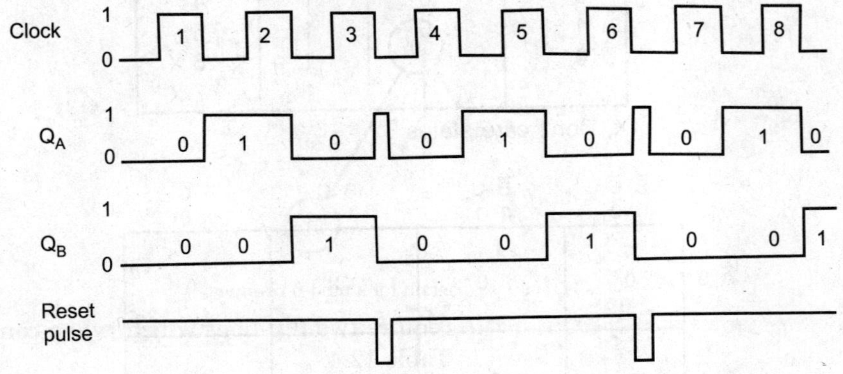

Fig. 12.18 Waveform for mod-3 counter

12.10.2 Mod-5 Counter

The minimum number of flip-flops required to implement this counter is three. With three flip-flops, the number of states will be 8. A modulo-5 counter will have only 5 states. A state diagram for this counter is given in Fig. 12.19. It will progress from state 000 through 100. The truth table for this counter, which will determine the state at which the reset pulse should be applied, is given in Table 12.5.

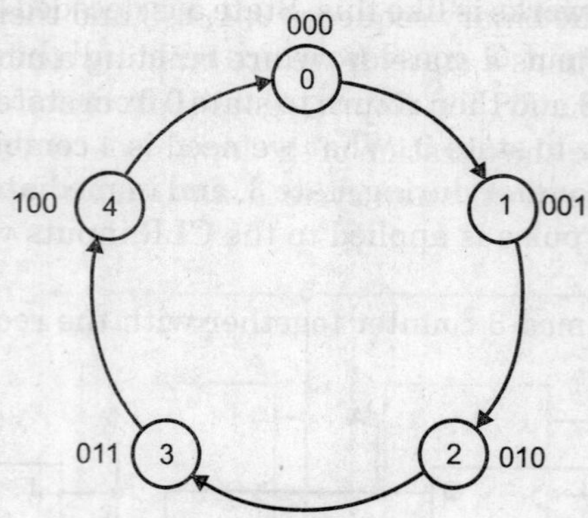

Fig. 12.19 State diagram for mod-5 counter

The truth table shows that state 5 will be the reset state and that states 6 and 7 will be the don't care states. The next step is to plot the states on a map as shown in Fig. 12.20.

Table 12.5 Truth table for mod-5 counter

Q_A LSB	Q_B	Q_C	*State*
0	0	0	0
1	0	0	1
0	1	0	2
1	1	0	3
0	0	1	4
1	0	1	5
0	1	1	6 X
1	1	1	7 X

X, Don't care states

	$\bar{B}\,\bar{C}$ 0 0	$\bar{B}$ C 0 1	B C 1 1	B $\bar{C}$ 1 0
$\bar{A}$ 0	0 [0]	0 [4]	X [6]	0 [2]
A 1	0 [1]	1 [5]	X [7]	0 [3]

Fig. 12.20

The map shows that the reset pulse is determined by $R = Q_A \cdot \overline{Q}_B \cdot Q_C$. The logic diagram for this counter is given in Fig. 12.21. The diagram shows that a reset pulse will be applied when both A and C are 1. You may have noticed that the reset pulse shown in Fig. 12.18 for the mod-3 counter was very narrow and in some cases it may not be suitable to control other logic devices associated with the counter. The mod-5 counter circuit Fig. 12.21 incorporates an RS flip-flop, which produces a reset pulse, the width of which is equal to the duration for which the clock pulse is low. The way it works is like this. State 5 is decoded by gate *D*, its output goes low, the *RS* flip-flop is set, and output $\overline{Q}$ goes low, which resets all the flip-flops. The leading edge of the next clock pulse resets the *RS* flip-flop, $\overline{Q}$ goes high which removes the reset pulse. The counter thus remains reset for the duration of the low time of the clock pulse. When the trailing edge of the same clock pulse arrives, a new cycle is started. The waverform for Mod-5 counter is given in Fig. 12.22.

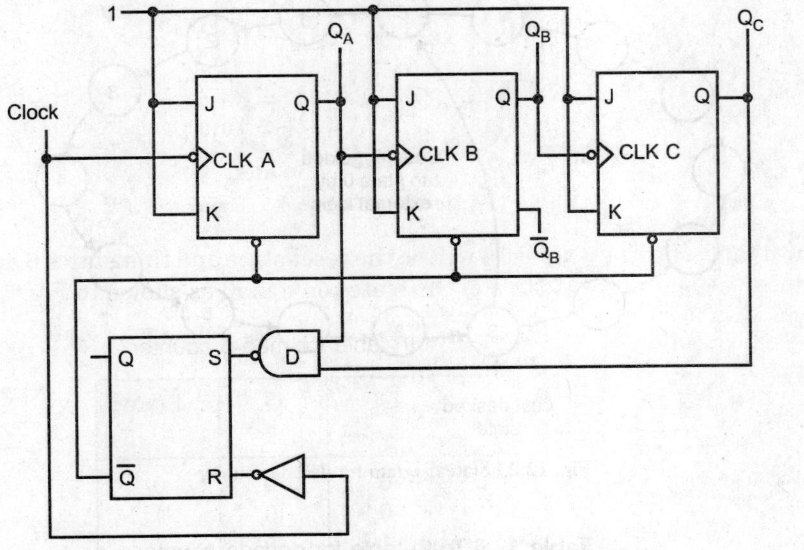

Fig. 12.21 Modulus-5 counter

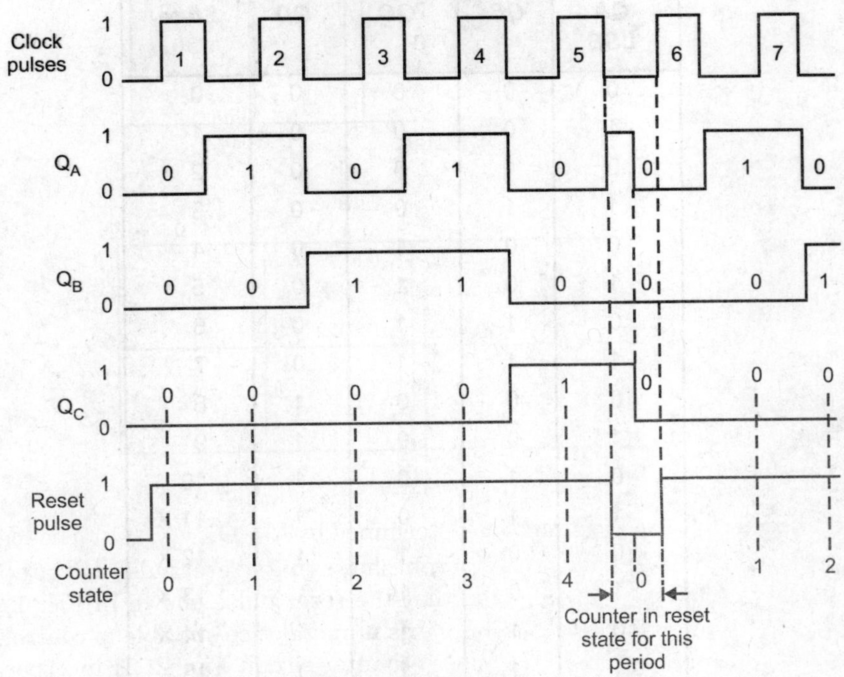

Fig. 12.22 Waveform for modulus-5 asynchronous counter

12.10.3 Mod-10 (Decade) Counter

The decade counter discussed here is also an asynchronous counter and has been implemented using the counter reset method. As the decade counter has ten states, it will require four flip-flops to implement it. A state diagram for this counter is given in Fig. 12.23 and the truth table is given in Table 12.6.

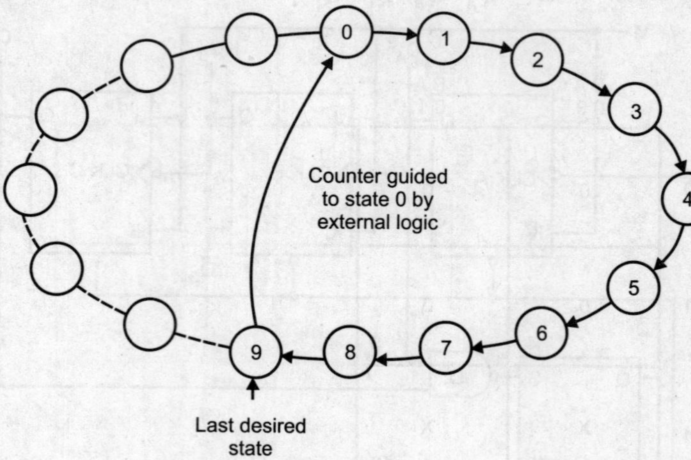

Fig. 12.23 State diagram for decade counter

Table 12.6 Truth table for decade counter

QA LSB	*QB*	*QC*	*QD*	*State*
0	0	0	0	0
1	0	0	0	1
0	1	0	0	2
1	1	0	0	3
0	0	1	0	4
1	0	1	0	5
0	1	1	0	6
1	1	1	0	7
0	0	0	1	8
1	0	0	1	9
0	1	0	1	10
1	1	0	1	11 X
0	0	1	1	12 X
1	0	1	1	13 X
0	1	1	1	14 X
1	1	1	1	15 X

The table shows that state 9 will be the last desired state and state 10 will be the reset state. State 11, 12, 13, 14 and 15 will be the don't care states. The next step is to plot the states on a map to determine the reset pulse. This has been done in Fig. 12.24.

The map shows that the reset pulse is determined by the following expression:

$$R = \overline{Q}_A \cdot Q_B \cdot \overline{Q}_C \cdot Q_D$$

	$\overline{B}\,\overline{A}$ 00	$\overline{B}A$ 01	BA 11	$B\overline{A}$ 10
$\overline{D}\,\overline{C}$ 00	0 (0)	0 (1)	0 (3)	0 (2)
$\overline{D}C$ 01	0 (4)	0 (5)	0 (7)	0 (6)
DC 11	X (12)	X (13)	X (15)	X (14)
$D\overline{C}$ 10	0 (8)	0 (9)	X (11)	1 (10)

Fig. 12.24

The decade counter circuit Fig. 12.25 is essentially a binary ripple counter, which can count from 0000 to 1111; but since a decade counter is required to count only from 0000 to 1001, a reset pulse is applied at count 10 when the counter output is $\overline{Q}_A \cdot Q_B \cdot \overline{Q}_C \cdot Q_D$. In order to have control over the reset pulse width, a 4-input NAND gate is used to decode state 10. To decode count 10, logic inputs that are all one at the count of 10, are used to feed the NAND gate. At this count the NAND gate output goes low providing a 1→0 change which triggers the one-shot unit. The $\overline{Q}$ output of the one shot unit is used, as it is normally high and it goes low during the one-shot timing period, which depends on the *RC* constants of the circuit. The timing period of the one-shot can be adjusted, so that the slowest counter state resets. Although only *A* and *D* flip-flops need to be reset, the reset pulse is applied to all the flip-flops to make doubly sure that all flip-flops are reset.

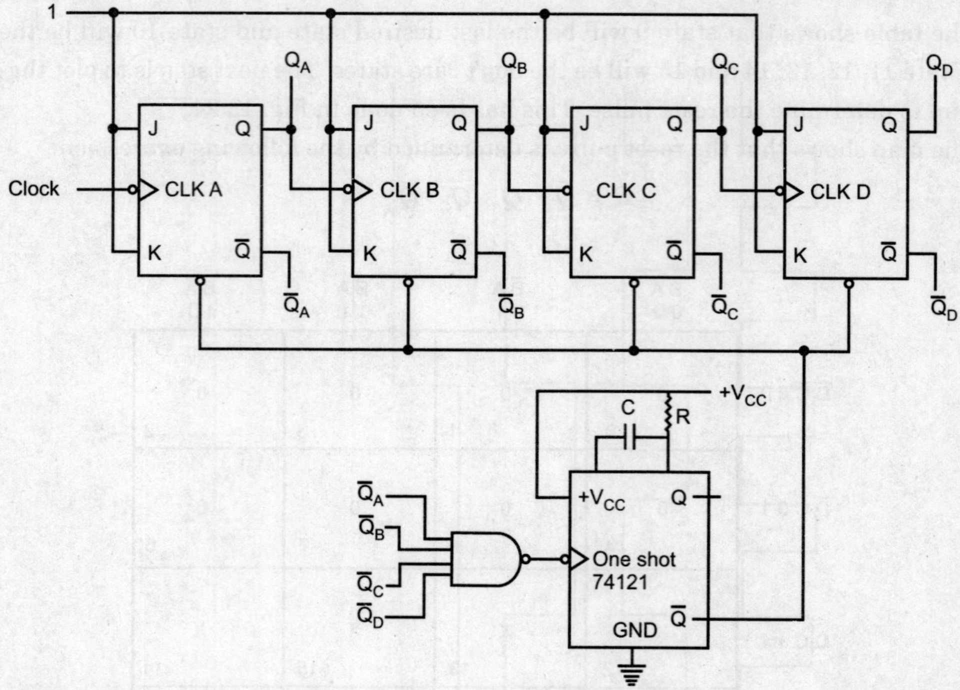

Fig. 12.25 Decade (Mod-10) asynchronous counter using count reset and pulse width control

Since decade (Moldulus-10) counters have 10 discrete states, they can be used to divide the input frequency by 10. You will notice that at the output of the *D* flip-flop, there is only one output pulse for every 10 input pulses. These counters can be cascaded to increase count capability.

The waverform for this counter is shown in Fig. 12.26.

12.11 LOGIC GATING METHOD

The counter reset method of implementing counters, which we have discussed in the previous section, has some inherent drawbacks. In the first place, the counter has to move up to a temporary state before going into the reset state. Secondly, pulse duration timing is an important consideration in such counters, for which purpose special circuits have to be incorporated in counter design.

We will now consider another approach to counter design, which provides for the exact count sequence. We will discuss the design of some modulus counters to illustrate the procedures.

12.11.1 Mod-3 Counter (Synchronous)

Let us suppose that we are required to design a modulo-3 counter which conforms to the truth table given in Table 12.7.

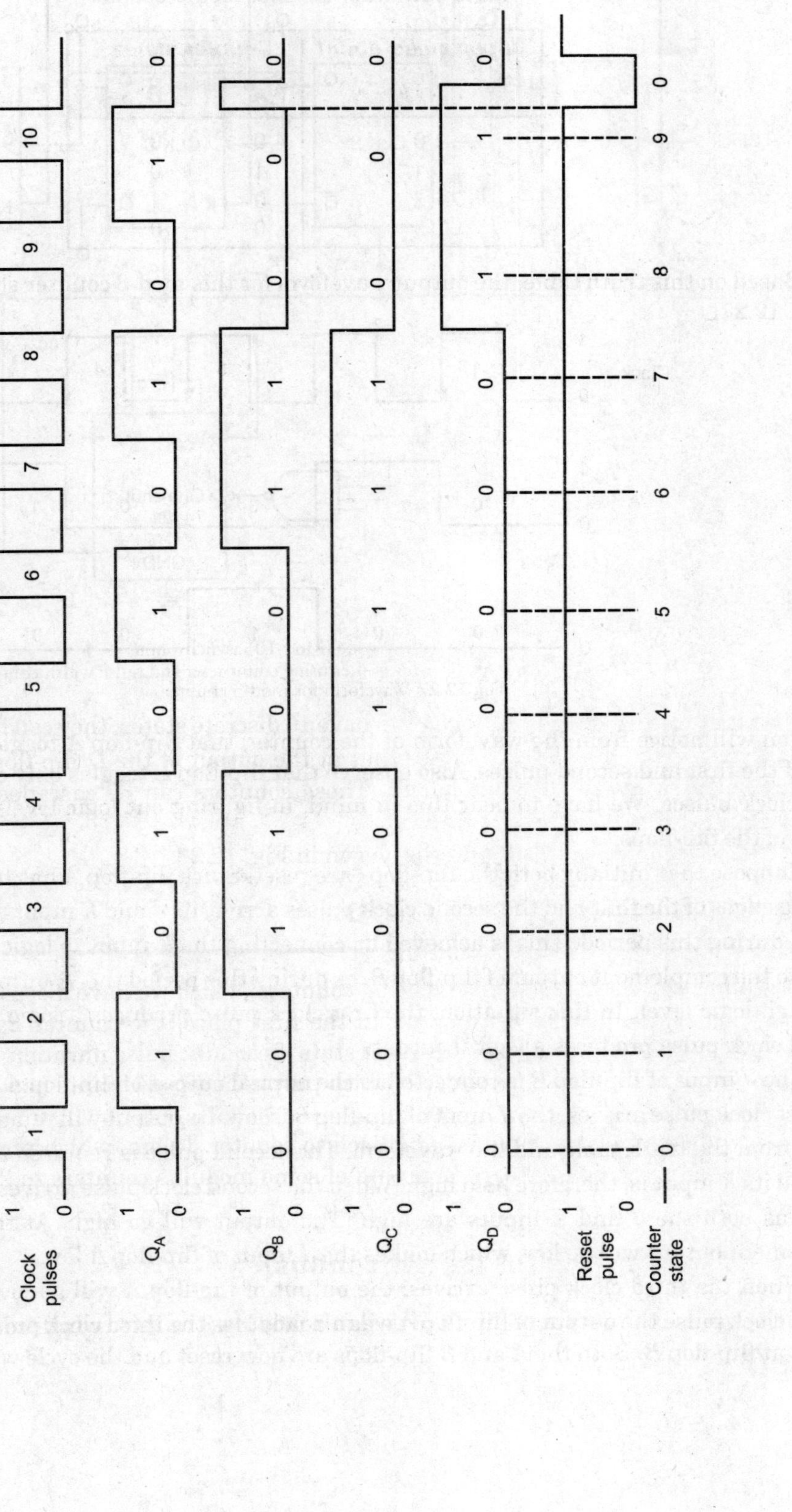

Fig. 12.26 Waveform for decade counter

Table 12.7 Truth table for mod-3 counter

Input pulse count	*Counter states*	
	A	*B*
0	0	0
1	1	0
2	0	1
3	0	0

Based on this truth table, the output waveform for this mod-3 counter should be as shown in Fig. 12.27.

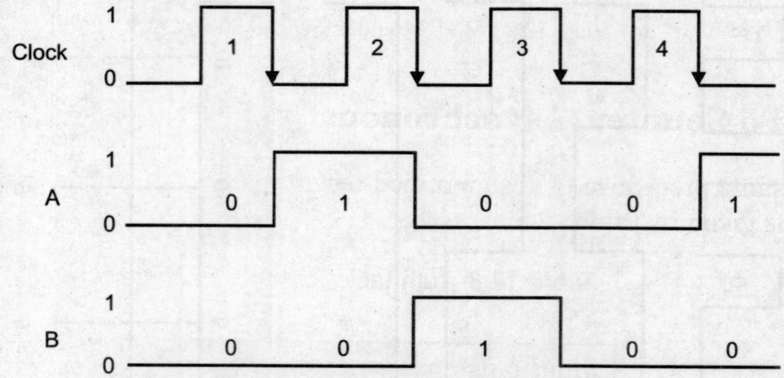

Fig. 12.27 Waveform for mod-3 counter

You will notice from the waveform of the counter, that flip-flop *A* toggles on the trailing edge of the first and second pulses. Also observe that flip-flop *B* toggles only on the second and third clock pulses. We have to bear this in mind, in figuring out logic levels for the *J* and *K* inputs of the flip-flops.

Suppose that initially both the flip-flops are reset. Since flip-flop *A* has to toggle when the trailing edges of the first and the second clock pulses arrive, its *J* and *K* inputs should be at logic 1 level during this period. This is achieved by connecting the *K* input to logic 1 level and the *J* input to the complement output of flip-flop *B*, as during this period the $\overline{B}$ output of flip-flop *B* is at a high logic level. In this situation, the first clock pulse produces a logic 1 output and the second clock pulse produces a logic 0 output.

The *J* input of flip-flop *B* is connected to the normal output of flip-flop *A*. Therefore, when the first clock pulse arrives, the *J* input of flip-flop *B* is low. Its output will remain low as you will notice from the truth table and the waveform. The second pulse is required to toggle this flip-flop and its *K* input is, therefore held high. When the second clock pulse arrives, the flip-flop will toggle as both the *J* and *K* inputs are high. The output will go high. At the same time its complement output will be low, which makes the *J* input of flip-flop *A* low.

When the third clock pulse arrives, the output of flip-flop *A* will go low. Since after the second clock pulse the output of flip-flop *A* was already low, the third clock pulse produces a low output at flip-flop *B*. Both the *A* and *B* flip-flops are now reset and the cycle will be repeated.

A logic diagram for the Mod-3 counter is given in Fig. 12.28.

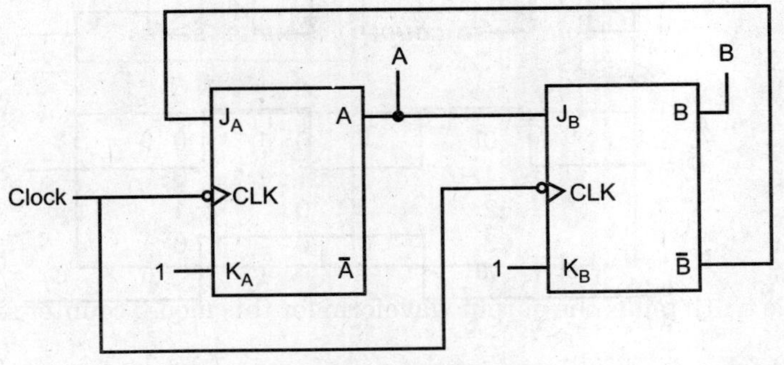

Fig. 12.28 Mod-3 counter (Synchronous)

12.11.2 Mod-5 Counter (Asynchronous)

We will use the same procedure to design a mod-5 counter as before. The truth table required for this counter is given in Table 12.8.

Table 12.8 Truth table for mod-5 counter

Input pulse count	*Counter states*		
	A	*B*	*C*
0	0	0	0
1	1	0	0
2	0	1	0
3	1	1	0
4	0	0	1
5	0	0	0

The waveform for this counter based on this truth table is given in Fig. 12.29. You will notice from the truth table and the wave form that the *A* flip-flop complements each input pulse, except when the normal output of flip-flop *C* is logic 1, which is so after the trailing edge of the 4th, clock pulse. It, therefore, follows that the *K* input of flip-flop *A* should be a constant logic 1 and the *J* input should be connected to the complement output of flip-flop will be 0 when *C* is 1, so that the output of flip-flop *A* remains low after the trailing edge of the 5th clock pulse.

If you observe the changing pattern of the output of the *B* flip-flop, you will notice that it toggles at each transition of the *A* output from 1→0. It is, therefore, obvious that the *A* output should be connected to the clock input of the *B* flip-flop and the *J* and *K* inputs of this flip-flop should be at logic 1 level.

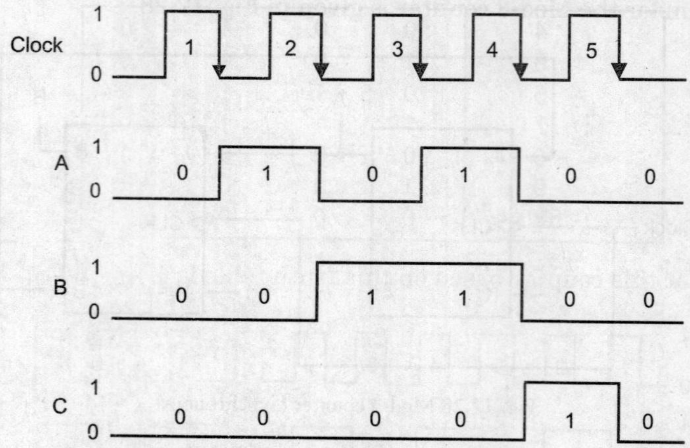

Fig. 12.29 Waveform for mod-5 counter

After the 3rd clock pulse, the outputs of *A* and *B* flip-flops are 1. An AND gate is used to make the *J* input to flip-flop *C* as 1 when both *A* and *B* are 1. The *K* input to flip-flop *C* is also held at logic 1 to enable it to toggle. The clock is also connected to the clock input to flip-flop *C*, which toggles it on the 4th, clock pulse and its output becomes 1. When the 5th, clock pulse arrives, the *J* input to flip-flop *C* is 0 and it resets on the trailing edge of this clock pulse. Thereafter the cycles are repeated. The logic diagram for the mod-5 counter is given in Fig. 12.30.

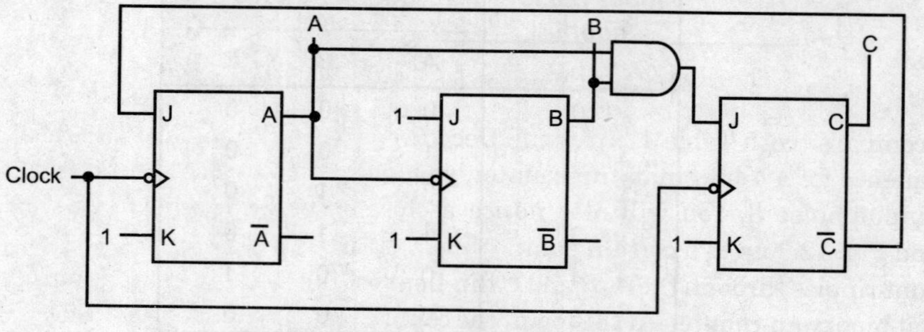

Fig. 12.30 Logic diagram for mod-5 counter

12.11.3 Mod-10 (Decade) Counter (Asynchronous)

The truth table for a Decade counter is given in Table 12.9.

Table 12.9 Truth table for decade counter

Input pulse count	*Counter states*			
	A	*B*	*C*	*D*
0	0	0	0	0
1	1	0	0	0
2	0	1	0	0
3	1	1	0	0

4	0	0	1	0
5	1	0	1	0
6	0	1	1	0
7	1	1	1	0
8	0	0	0	1
9	1	0	0	1
10(0)	0	0	0	0

The waveform for this counter based on this truth table is given in Fig. 12.31.

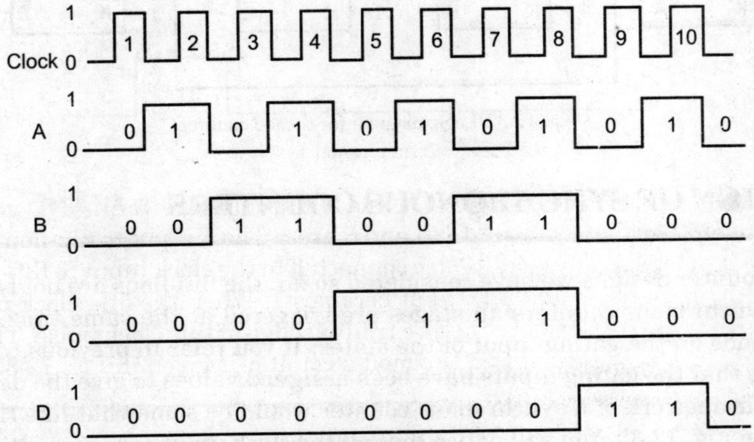

Fig. 12.31 Waveform for decade counter

If you compare truth Table 12.9 for the Decade counter with Table 12.2 which gives the count-up sequence for a 4-bit binary up-counter, you will notice a close similarity between the two, up to input pulse 8. You will also notice a close resemblance between waveforms of Fig. 12.31 and Fig. 12.3 up to a certain point.

The count ripples through the *A*, *B* and *C* flip-flops for the first seven input pulses, as in the standard 4-bit binary up-counter. At this point the counter will show an output of 1 1 1 0 (decimal 7). On the application of the 8th pulse, flip-flops *A*, *B* and *C* must reset and the *D* output should be 1, that is the counter state should change from 1 1 1 0 to 0 0 0 1. In order that the *J* input to flip-flop *D* is 1, so that when *K* is 1 the *D* flip-flop output goes from 0 to 1; *B* and *C* outputs are applied to the input of an AND gate and its output goes to the *J* input. In order that the *B* and *C* outputs are 0, when *D* output is 1 for the 8th and the 9th count, the complement output of the *D* flip-flop which will be 0 when *D* is 1, is connected to the *J* input of the *B* flip-flop.

After the trailing edge of the 8th pulse *D* becomes 1 and *A*, *B*, and *C* become 0, the 9th pulse is required to change the output from 0 0 0 1 to 1 0 0 1. Since no change is required in the *D* output, the *D* flip-flop is triggered by the *A* output. When the 9th pulse arrives, the *A* output changes from 0 to 1, but this causes no change in the *D* output. When the 10th input pulse arrives, it changes the *A* output from 1 to 0, which changes the *D* output from 1 to 0. The counter output changes from 1 0 0 1 to 0 0 0 0. During the 9th and the 10th pulses, the *B* and *C* outputs will remain unchanged.

A logic diagram for the Decade counter is given in Fig. 12.32.

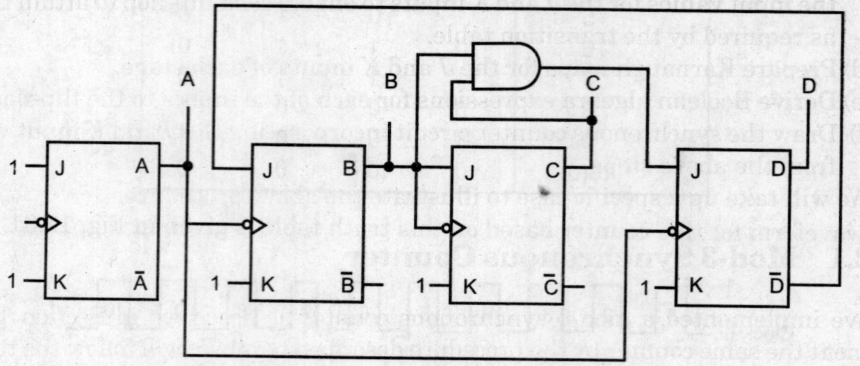

Fig. 12.32 Logic diagram for decade counter

12.12 DESIGN OF SYNCHRONOUS COUNTERS

In most of the counter designs we have considered so far, the flip-flops are not triggered simultaneously. In synchronous counters all stages are triggered at the same time. The output of each state depends on the gating input of the states. If you refer to previous counter designs, you will observe that the gating inputs have been assigned values to give the desired outputs.

The basic framework of a synchronous counter would be somewhat like the partial logic diagram given in Fig. 12.33. You will notice that all the clock inputs are connected to a common line and the *J* and *K* inputs of the flip-flops have been left open. They are required to have the values necessary to give the required outputs after each input pulse.

The *J* and *K* inputs of each flip-flop are therefore required to have the values which will produce the desired counter states at each input pulse. The entire purpose of the exercise is to determine the input values for each stage. A typical design procedure can be summed up in the following steps:

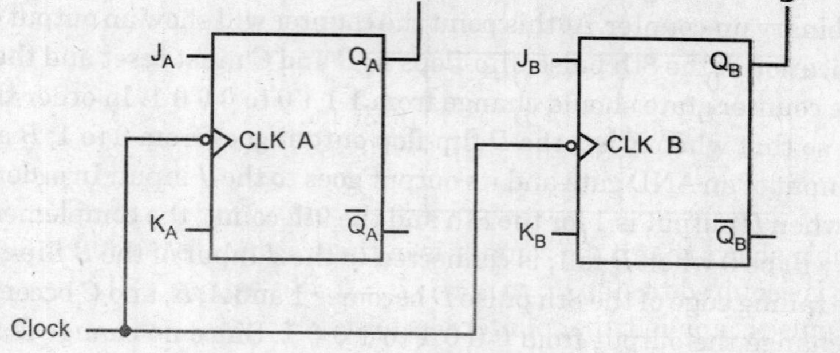

Fig. 12.33

(a) Write the desired truth table for the counter.

(b) Write the counter transition table which should list the starting state and the subsequent states the counter is required to take up.

(c) With the help of the excitation table and using the counter transition table, write down the input values for the *J* and *K* inputs to enable each flip-flop to attain the output state as required by the transition table.
(d) Prepare Karnaugh maps for the *J* and *K* inputs of each stage.
(e) Derive Boolean algebra expressions for each of the inputs to the flip-flops.
(f) Draw the synchronous counter circuit incorporating the *J* and *K* input values obtained from the above steps.

We will take up a specific case to illustrate the above procedure.

12.12.1 Mod-3 Synchronous Counter

We have implemented a mod-3 synchronous counter as described in Section 12.11.1. We will implement the same counter by the procedure described here. We will follow the truth table given in Table 12.7. The excitation table for *JK* flip-flops has been given earlier in Table 8.15 for *JK* and other flip-flops. For your convenience the excitation table for *JK* flip-flops is reproduced here.

Table 12.10 Excitation table for *JK* flip-flop

Present state	*Next state*	*J*	*K*
0	0	0	X
0	1	1	X
1	0	X	1
1	1	X	0

We now prepare a counter design table listing the two flip-flops (as only two flip-flops are required) and their states and also the four inputs to the two flip-flops as in Table 12.11.

Table 12.11 Counter design table

Counter state		*Flip-flop inputs*			
A	*B*	*A*		*B*	
		J_A	K_A	J_B	K_B
0	0	1	X	0	X
1	0	X	1	1	X
0	1	0	X	X	1
0	0				

The table shows that if the counter is in the state $A = 0, B = 0$ and a clock pulse is applied, the counter is required to step up to $A = 1, B = 0$. When the counter is in the state $A = 1, B = 0$ and a clock pulse is applied, the counter has to step up to $A = 0, B = 1$. Lastly when another clock pulse is applied the counter has to reset.

From the excitation table for *JK* flip-flops we can determine the states of the *J* and *K* inputs, so that the counter steps up as required. For instance for the *A* flip-flop to step up from 0 to 1, J_A should be 1 and K_A should be *X*. Similarly the *J* and *K* input values of both the flip-flops for the remaining counter states have been worked out as shown in the table.

The next step is to derive boolean algebra expressions for each of the inputs to the flip-flops. In the above exercise, our effort was to generate flip-flop inputs in a given row, so that when the counter is in the state in that row, the inputs will take on the listed values, so that the next clock pulse will cause the counter to step up to the counter state in the row below.

We now form boolean algebra expressions from this table for the J_A, K_A, J_B and K_B inputs to the flip-flops and simplify these expressions using Karnaugh maps. Expressions for these inputs have been entered in Karanaugh maps in Fig. 12.34 (a), (b), and (c) and (d). The simplified expressions obtained for the inputs are also indicated under the maps.

The counter circuit when drawn up with the following resultant data will be the same as worked out before in Fig. 12.28.

$$J_A = \overline{B}$$
$$K_A = 1$$
$$J_B = A$$
$$K_B = 1$$

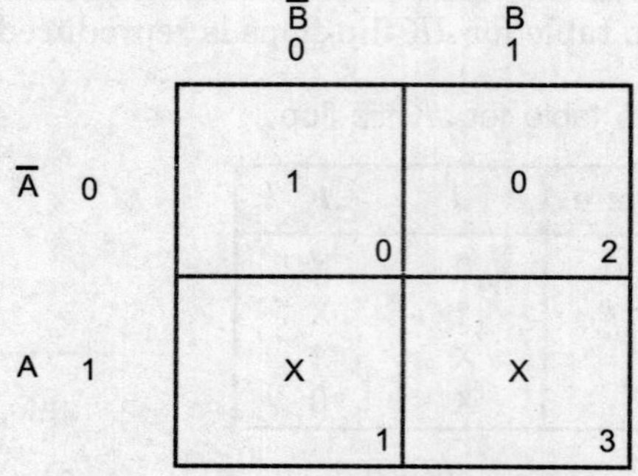

(a)
Map for J_A
$J_A = \overline{B}$

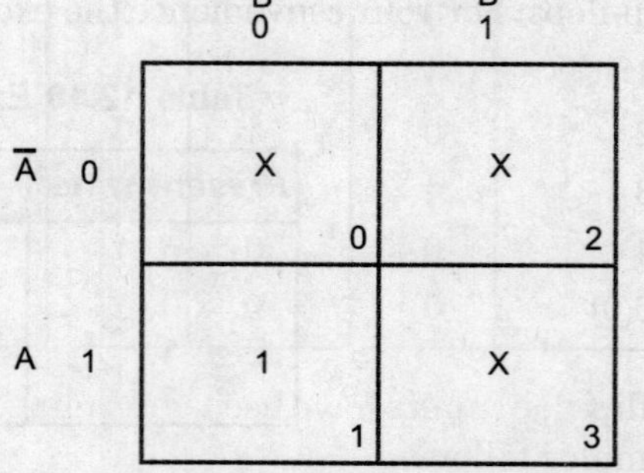

(b)
Map for K_A
$K_A = 1$

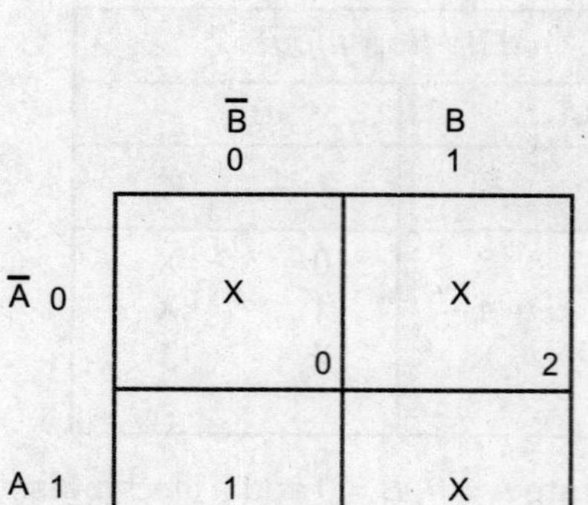

(c)
Map for J_B
$J_B = A$

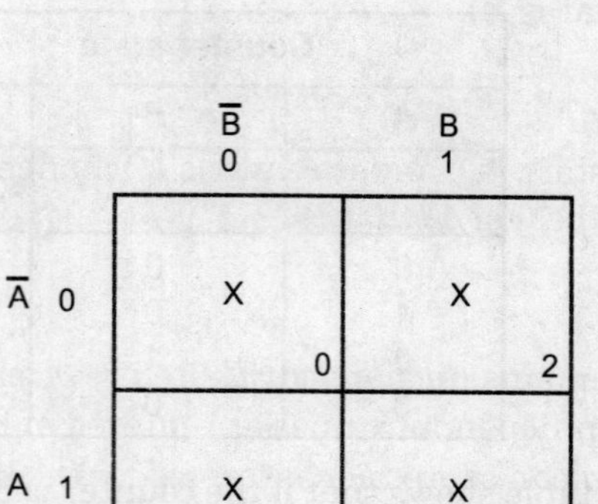

(d)
Map for K_B
$K_B = 1$

Fig. 12.34 (a), (b), (c) and (d)

12.12.2 Mod-5 Counter (Synchronous)

The Mod-5 counter we are going to implement will be a synchronous counter, but it will have the same counter states as given earlier in Table 12.8. The counter design table for this counter lists the three flip-flops and their states an also the six inputs for the three flip-flops. The flip-flop inputs required to step up the counter from the present to the next state have been worked out with the help of the excitation table (Table 12.10). This listing has been shown in Table 12.12.

Table 12.12 Counter design table for mod-5 counter

Input pulse count	*Counter states*			*Flip-flop inputs*					
	A	B	C	J_A	K_A	J_B	K_B	J_C	K_C
0	0	0	0	1	X	0	X	0	X
1	1	0	0	X	1	1	X	0	X
2	0	1	0	1	X	X	0	0	X
3	1	1	0	X	1	X	1	1	X
4	0	0	1	0	X	0	X	X	1
5(0)	0	0	0						

The flip-flop inputs have been determined with the help of the excitation table, Table 12.10. Some examples follow:

A flip-flop

The initial state is 0. It changes to 1 after the clock pulse. Therefore J_A should be 1 and K_A may be 0 or 1 (that is X).

B flip-flop

The initial state is 0 and it remains unchanged after the clock pulse. Therefore J_B should be 0 and K_B may be 0 or 1 (that is X).

C flip-flop

The state remains unchanged. Therefore J_C should be 0 and K_B should be X.

The flip-flop input values are entered in Karnaugh maps Fig. 12.35 [(a), (b), (c), (d), (e) and (f)] and a boolean expression is formed for the inputs to the three flip-flops and then each expression is simplified. As all the counter states have not been utilized, Xs (don't) are entered to denote un-untilized states. The simplifed expressions for each input have been shown under each map. Finally, these minimal expressions for the flip-flop inputs are used to draw a logic diagram for the counter, which is given in Fig. 12.36.

	$\bar{B}\bar{C}$ 00	$\bar{B}C$ 01	BC 11	$B\bar{C}$ 10
$\bar{A}$ 0	1 (0)	0 (4)	X (6)	1 (2)
A 1	X (1)	X (5)	X (7)	X (3)

(a) Map for J_A
$J_A = \bar{C}$

	$\bar{B}\bar{C}$ 00	$\bar{B}C$ 01	BC 11	$B\bar{C}$ 10
$\bar{A}$ 0	X (0)	X (4)	X (6)	X (2)
A 1	1 (1)	X (5)	X (7)	1 (3)

(b) Map for K_A
$K_A = 1$

	$\bar{B}\bar{C}$ 00	$\bar{B}C$ 01	BC 11	$B\bar{C}$ 10
$\bar{A}$ 0	0 (0)	0 (4)	X (6)	X (2)
A 1	1 (1)	X (5)	X (7)	X (3)

(c) Map for J_B
$J_{AB} = A$

	$\bar{B}\bar{C}$ 00	$\bar{B}C$ 01	BC 11	$B\bar{C}$ 10
$\bar{A}$ 0	X (0)	X (4)	X (6)	0 (2)
A 1	1 (1)	X (5)	X (7)	1 (3)

(d) Map for K_B
$K_B = A$

	$\bar{B}\bar{C}$ 00	$\bar{B}C$ 01	BC 11	$B\bar{C}$ 10
$\bar{A}$ 0	0 (0)	X (4)	X (6)	0 (2)
A 1	0 (1)	X (5)	X (7)	1 (3)

(e) Map for J_C
$J_C = AB$

	$\bar{B}\bar{C}$ 00	$\bar{B}C$ 01	BC 11	$B\bar{C}$ 10
$\bar{A}$ 0	X (0)	1 (4)	X (6)	X (2)
A 1	X (1)	X (5)	X (7)	X (3)

(f) Map for K_C
$K_C = 1$

Fig. 12.35

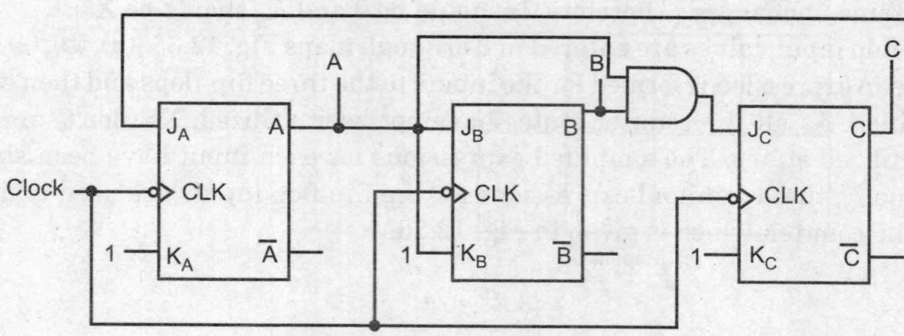

Fig. 12.36 Synchronous mod-5 counter

12.12.3 Mod-6 Counter (Synchronous)

The desired counter states and the *JK* inputs required for counter flip-flops are given in the counter design (Table 12.13).

Table 12.13 Counter design table for mod-6 counter

Input pulse count	*Counter states*			*Flip-flop inputs*					
	A	*B*	*C*	J_A	K_A	J_B	K_B	J_C	K_C
0	0	0	0	1	X	0	X	0	X
1	1	0	0	X	1	1	X	0	X
2	0	1	0	1	X	X	0	0	X
3	1	1	0	X	1	X	1	1	X
4	0	0	1	1	X	0	X	X	0
5	1	0	1	X	1	0	X	X	1
6(0)	0	0	0						

As before, the *JK* inputs required for this have been determined with the help of the excitation, (Table 12.10). These input values have been entered in Karnaugh maps Fig. 12.37 and a boolean expression is formed for the inputs to the three flip-flops and then each expression is simplified. *Xs* have been entered in those counter states which have not been utilized. The simplified expressions for each input have been shown under each map and finally a logic diagram based on these expressions has been drawn, as given in Fig. 12.38.

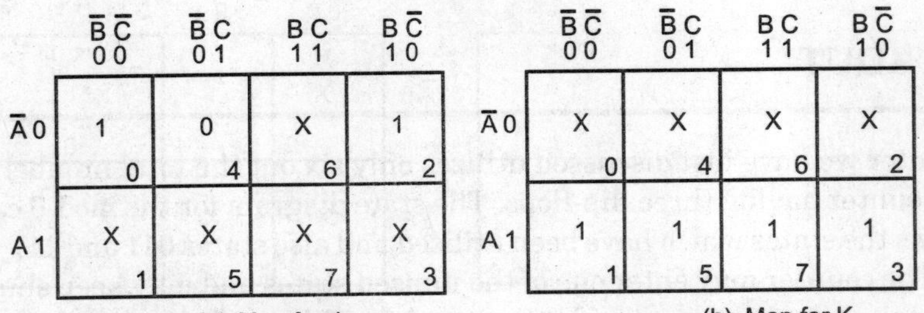

(a) Map for J_A
$J_A = 1$

(b) Map for K_A
$K_A = 1$

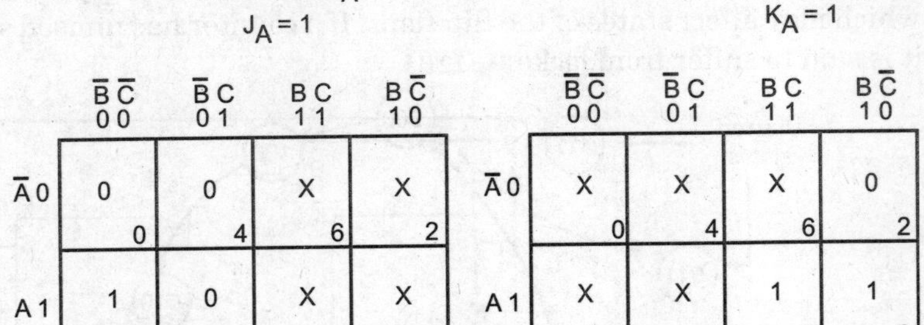

(c) Map for J_B
$J_B = A\overline{C}$

(d) Map for K_B
$K_B = A$

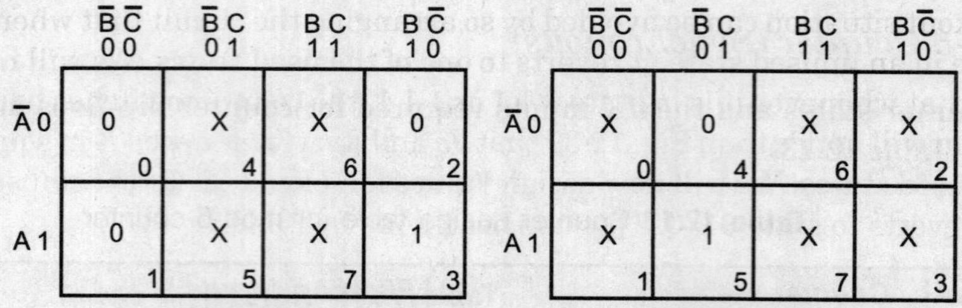

(e) Map for J_C

$J_C = AB$

(f) Map for K_C

$K_C = A$

Fig. 12.37

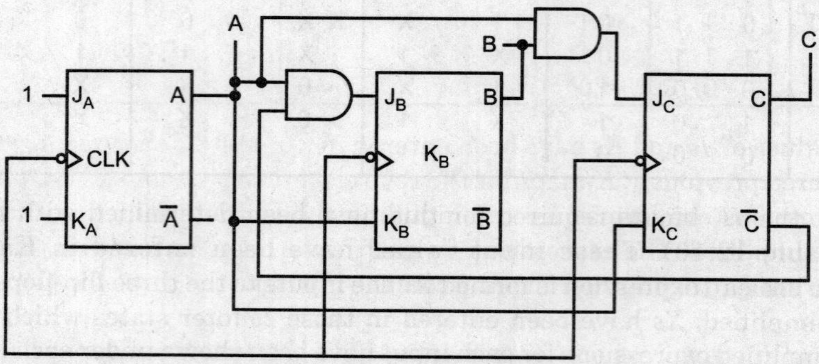

Fig. 12.38 Synchronous mod-6 counter

12.13 LOCKOUT

The mod-6 counter we have just discussed utilizes only six out the total number of eight states available in a counter having three flip-flops. The state diagram for the mod-6 counter given in Fig. 12.39, shows the states which have been utilized and also states 011 and 111 which have not been utilized. The counter may enter one of the unused states and may keep shuttling between the unused states and not come out of this situation. This condition may develop because of external noise, which may affect states of the flip-flops. If a counter has unused states with this characteristic, it is said to suffer from lockout.

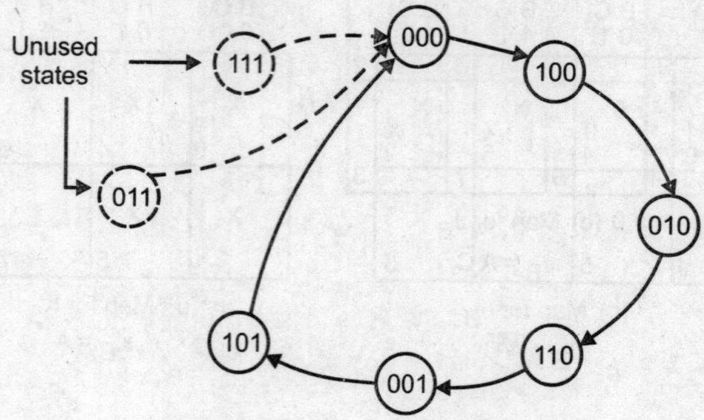

Fig. 12.39 State diagram for mod-6 counter

The lockout situation can be avoided by so arranging the circuit that whenever the counter happens to be in an unused state, it reverts to one of the used states. We will redesign the mod-6 counter so that whenever it is in state 0 1 1 or 1 1 1, the counter switches back to the starting point 0 0 0. You will notice from Fig. 12.37 that *Js* and *Ks* were marked *X* in squares corresponding to the unused states. We will now assign values for *Js* and *Ks* for the unused states, so that the counter reverts to state 0 0 0. This has been done in Table 12.14.

Table 12.14

Counter states			***Flip-flop inputs***					
A	***B***	***C***	J_A	K_A	J_B	K_B	J_C	K_C
0	1	1	0	X	X	1	X	1
1	1	1	X	1	X	1	X	1
0	0	0						

These values of *Js* and *Ks* have been entered in *K*-maps for those counter states where *Xs* had been entered previously. *K*-maps for the revised values of *Js* and *Ks* are given in Fig. 12.40. Boolean expressions are formed for the inputs to the three flip-flops and the expressions so obtained are simplified. The expressions for each input have been shown under each map and the logic diagram for the improved mod-6 counter is given in Fig. 12.41.

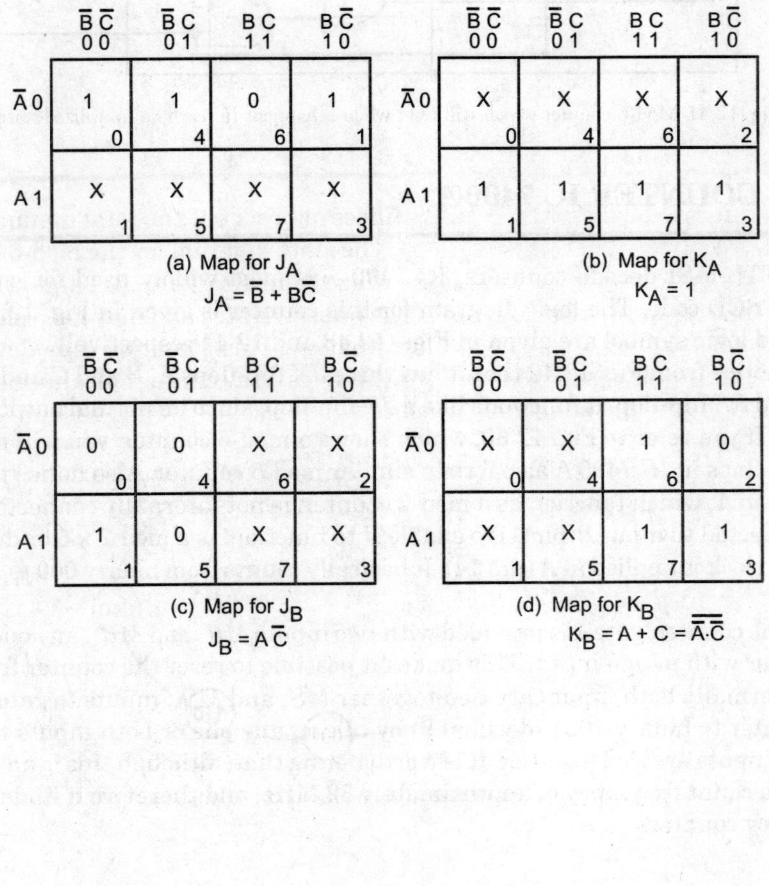

	$\overline{B}\,\overline{C}$ 00	$\overline{B}C$ 01	BC 11	$B\overline{C}$ 10
$\overline{A}$ 0	0 (0)	X (4)	X (6)	0 (2)
A 1	0 (1)	X (5)	X (7)	1 (3)

(e) Map for J_C

$J_C = AB$

	$\overline{B}\,\overline{C}$ 00	$\overline{B}C$ 01	BC 11	$B\overline{C}$ 10
$\overline{A}$ 0	X (0)	0 (4)	1 (6)	X (2)
A 1	X (1)	1 (5)	1 (7)	X (3)

(f) Map for K_C

$K_C = A + B = \overline{\overline{A}\cdot\overline{B}}$

Fig. 12.40

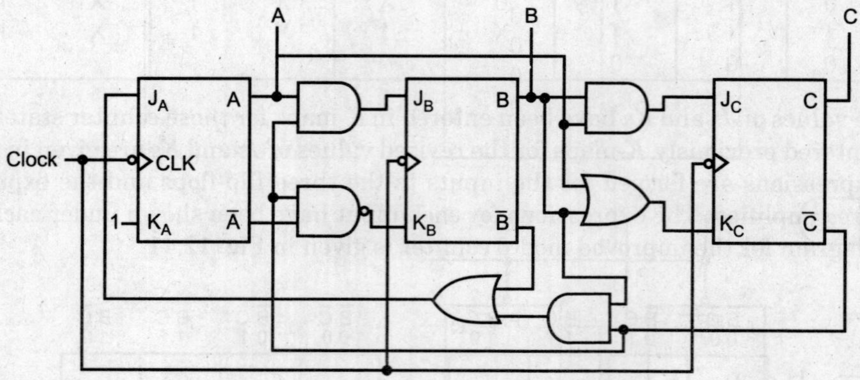

Fig. 12.41 Mod-6 counter which will reset when it happens to reach an unutilized state

12.14 MSI COUNTER IC 7490 A

Of the many TTL MSI decade counters, IC 7490 A is most widely used for counting in the standard 8421 BCD code. The logic diagram for this counter is given in Fig. 12.42 and its pin connections and logic symbol are given in Figs. 12.43 and 12.44 respectively.

You will notice from Fig. 12.42 that it has three *JK* flip-flops *A*, *B* and *C* and, although the *D* flip-flops is an *RS* flip-flop, it functions like a *JK* flip-flop, since its normal output is connected to the *R* input. If you refer to Fig. 12.30, which shows a mod-5 counter, you will notice that the *B*, *C* and *D* flip-flops in *IC* 7490 A also form a similar mod-5 counter. Also notice that output Q_A pin 12, of flip-flop *A*, which function as a mod-2 counter, is not internally connected. It has to be externally connected to input *B*(pin 1) to enable it to function as a mod 2 × 5 or decade counter, when the input clock is applied at *A* (pin 14). It basically counts from binary 000 to 1001 and back to 0000.

To reset the counter, gate 1 is provided with two inputs MR_1 and MR_2, any one of which will reset the counter with a high input. This makes it possible to reset the counter from any one of two sources. Normally both inputs are tied together MS_1 and MS_2, inputs to gate 2 are used to preset the counter to binary 1001 (decimal 9) by taking any one or both inputs to gate 2 high. Normally both inputs are tied together. It is worth noting that, although this is an asynchronous counter, it has a count frequency of approximately 32 MHz, and therefore it finds wide application in frequency counters.

As you will see later, this counter also finds application as a modulo counter and it can be used to divide the input frequency by 5, 6, 7, etc.

Table 12.15 Bi-quinary (5 × 2) sequence

Output			
Q_A	Q_D	Q_C	Q_B
0	0	0	0
0	0	0	1
0	0	1	0
0	0	1	1
0	1	0	0
1	0	0	0
1	0	0	1
1	0	1	0
1	0	1	1
1	1	0	0

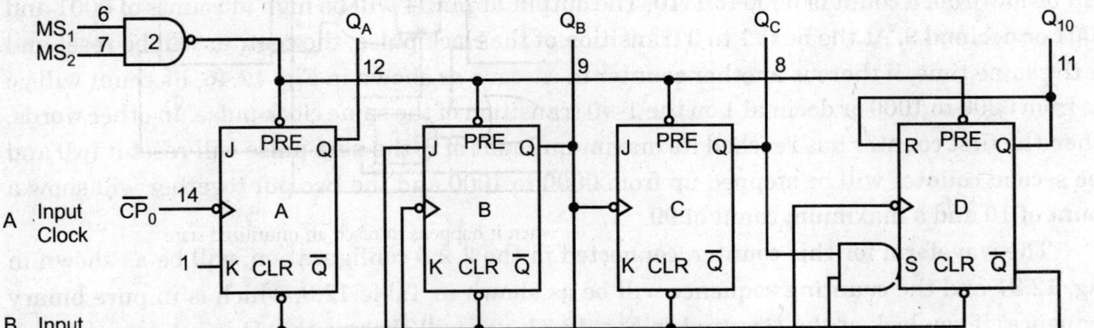

Fig. 12.42 Logic diagram for counter IC 7490 A

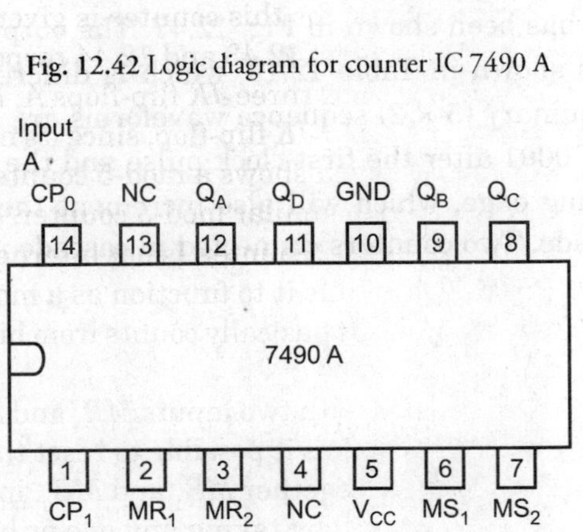

Fig. 12.43 Pin connections for counter IC 7490 A

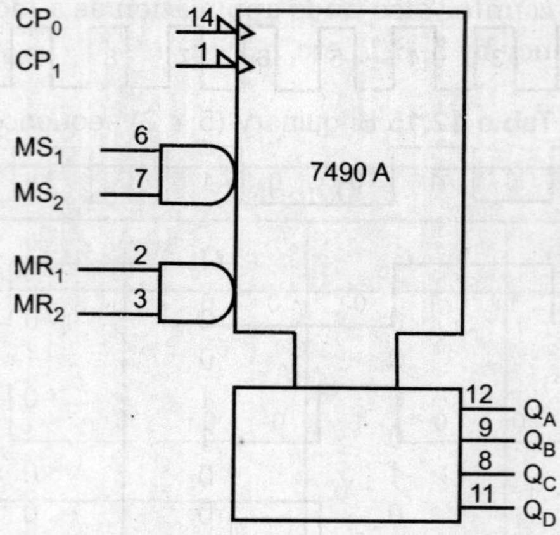

Fig. 12.44 Logic symbol for counter IC 7490 A

When this counter is used as a decade counter in the 2 × 5 configuration, Q_A (pin 12) is connected to pin 1 as in Fig. 12.45 and clock pulse are applied at pin 14. The output at Q_D (Pin 11) will be low from a count of 0000 to 1110. The output at pin 11 will be high at counts of 0001 and 1001 or decimal 9. At the next 1 to 0 transition of the clock pulse, the counter will be reset and at the same time, if there is another counter in cascade as shown in Fig. 12.46, its count will go up from 0000 to 1000 or decimal 1 on the 1→0 transition of the same clock pulse. In other words, when the first counter has reached its maximum count of 9, the next pulse will reset it to 0 and the second counter will be stepped up from 0000 to 1000 and the two put together will show a count of 10 and a maximum count of 99.

The waveform for this counter, connected in the 2 × 5 configuration, will be as shown in Fig. 12.31 and the counting sequence will be as shown in Table 12.9, which is in pure binary sequence. If you look at the *D* output in Fig. 12.31, you will observe that it is not symmetrical. If this counter is connected in the 5 × 2 mode, the output will have a symmetrical shape.

To operate this counter in the 5 × 2 mode, pin 14 is connected to Q_D (pin 11) and the clock signal is applied at pin 1 as has been shown in Fig. 12.47. The output will now follow the bi-quinary (5 × 2) sequence as shown in Table 12.15, which is different from the pure binary sequence in Table 12.9. Bi-quinary (5 × 2) sequence waveforms are shown in Fig. 12.48. The counter will show a count of 0001 after the first clock pulse and the 10th pulse will reset the counter to 0000 on its trailing edge, which will also increment the next counter if another counter is connected in cascade. Two counters connected in cascade in the 5 × 2 configuration are shown in Fig. 12.49.

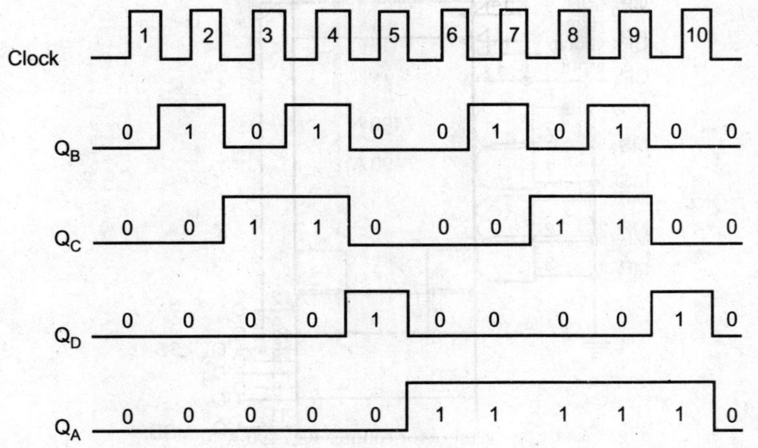

Fig. 12.45 IC 7490 A connected as a decade counter (2 × 5) configuration

For two decade counters connected in cascade, there will be only one output pulse for every ten input clock pulses, which shows that the frequency of the train of input pulses is scaled down by a factor of 10. In other words, if the input frequency is *f*, the output frequency will be *f*/10.

In digital instruments, it is often necessary to divide a frequency by a given factor and for this function scalers are used. Scalers will accept input pulses and output a single pulse at the required interval. A single decade scaler will divide a train of pulses by 10 and four decade scalers will divide the input frequency by 10^4.

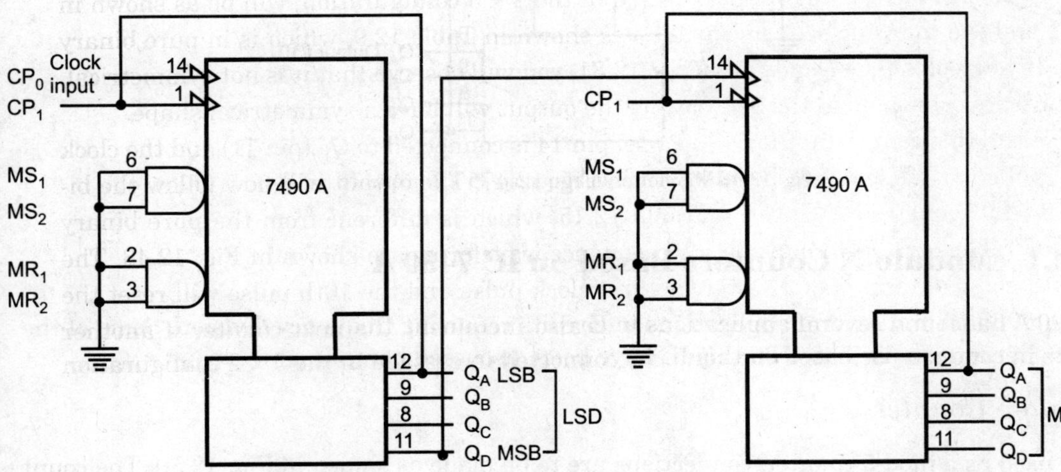

Fig. 12.46 IC 7490 A connected as a two-decade counter (00-99)

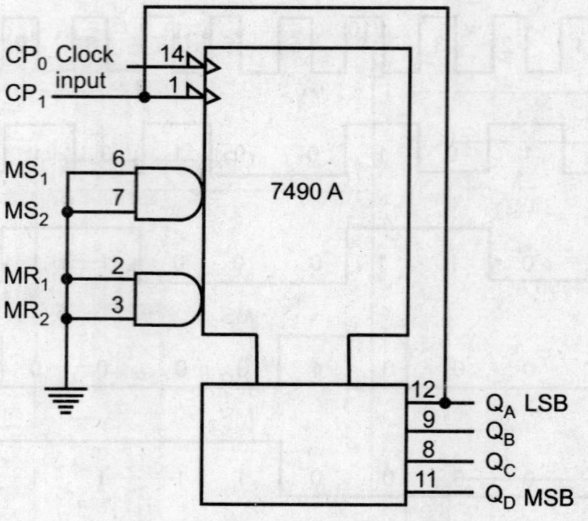

Fig. 12.47 IC 7490 A connected as a decimal scaler (5 × 2) configuration

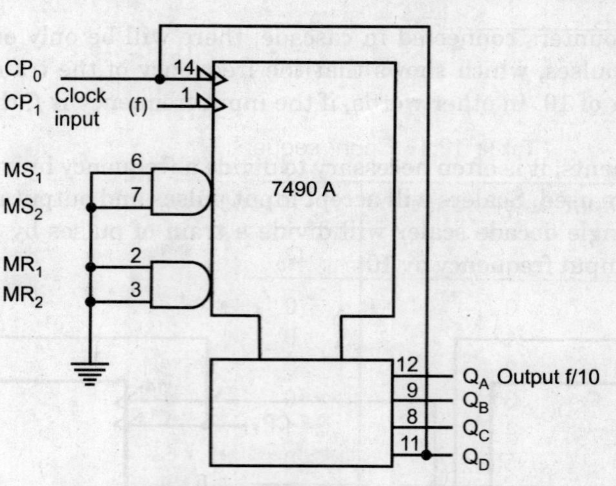

Fig. 12.48 Waveforms in bi-quinary (5 × 2) sequence

12.14.1 Modulo-N Counters Based on IC 7490 A

IC 7490 A has found several applications in circuits requiring frequency division. Some of the circuits in common use based on this IC have been discussed here.

Modulo-5 Counter

When used as a mod-5 counter, connections are to be made as shown in Fig. 12.50. The count sequency for this counter is as given in Table 12.16.

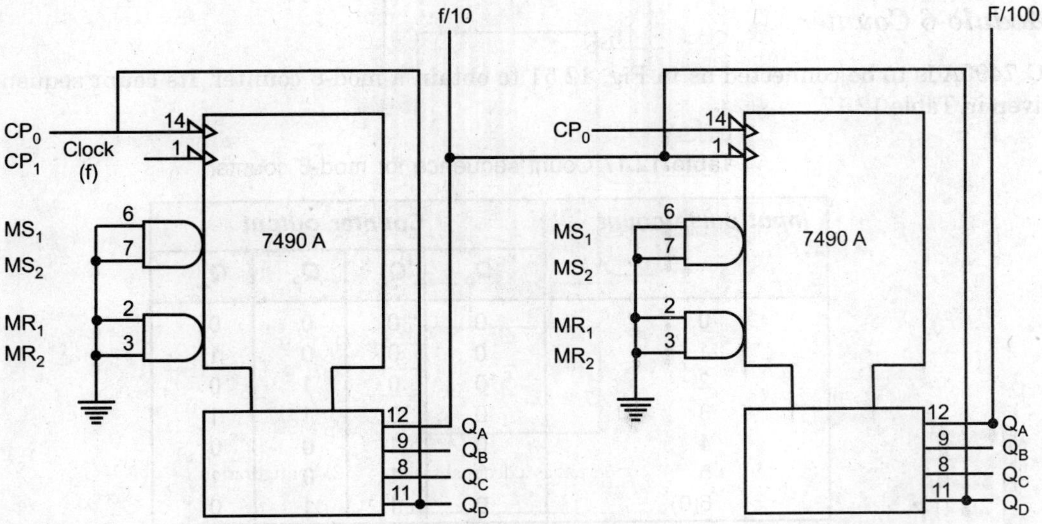

Fig. 12.49 Divide by 100 scaler

Table 12.16 Count sequence for Mod-5 counter

Input pulse count	*Counter output*		
	Q_D	Q_C	Q_B
0	0	0	0
1	0	0	1
2	0	1	0
3	0	1	1
4	1	0	0
5(0)	0	0	0

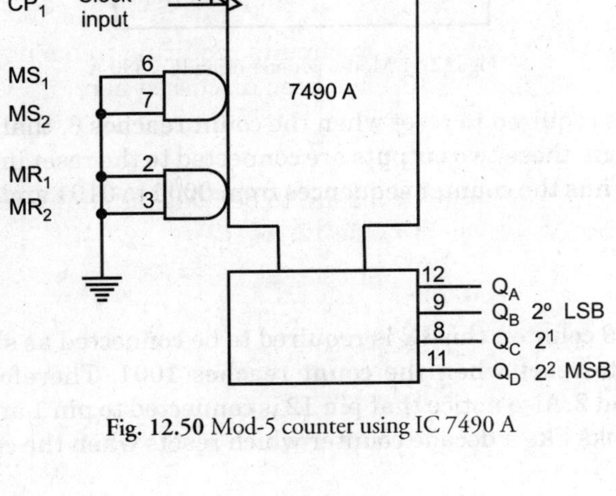

Fig. 12.50 Mod-5 counter using IC 7490 A

Modulo-6 Counter

IC 7490A is to be connected as in Fig. 12.51 to obtain a mod-6 counter. Its count sequence is given in Table 12.17.

Table 12.17 Count sequence for mod-6 counter

Input pulse count	*Counter output*			
	Q_D	Q_C	Q_B	Q_A
0	0	0	0	0
1	0	0	0	1
2	0	0	1	0
3	0	0	1	1
4	0	1	0	0
5	0	1	0	1
6(0)	0	1	1	0

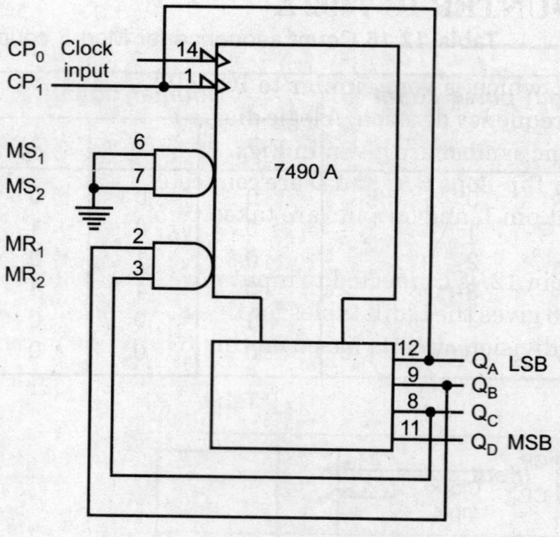

Fig. 12.51 Mod-6 counter using IC 7490 A

As the counter is required to reset when the count reaches 6, that is 0 1 1 0 when both Q_B and Q_C outputs are high, these two outputs are connected to the reset inputs so that the counter resets at this count. Thus the counter sequences from 0000 to 0101 and thereafter it resets and the cycle is repeated.

Modulo-9 Counter

When used as a mod-9 counter, this IC is required to be connected as shown in Fig. 12.52. The counter is required to reset when the count reaches 1001. Therefore pins 11 and 12 are connected to pins 3 and 2. Also notice that pin 12 is connected to pin 1 and clock input is applied to pin 14, so that it looks like a decade counter which resets when the count reaches decimal 9.

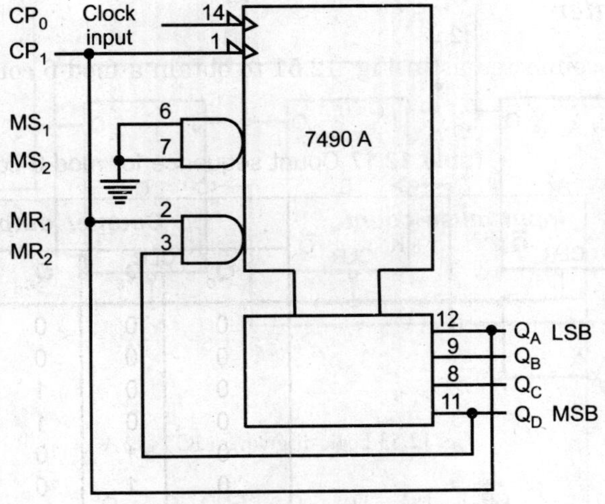

Fig. 12.52 Mod-9 counter using IC 7490 A

12.15 MSI COUNTER IC 7492 A

Counter IC 7492 A, which is very similar to IC 7490 A, also finds considerable application in circuits requiring frequency division. A logic diagram of this IC is given in Fig. 12.53 and its pin connections and logic symbol are given in Figs. 12.54 and 12.55 respectively.

In this counter flip-flops *B*, *C* and *D* are connected in the 3 × 2 configuration and, therefore, if input is applied at pin 1, and outputs are taken from Q_B, Q_C and Q_D, this counter will function as mod-6 counter.

If output Q_A, pin 12, is connected to input pin 1, this IC functions as a 2 × 3 × 2 or mod-12 counter. Table 12.18 gives the truth tables for this IC when Q_A, pin 12, is connected to input, pin 1. Some frequency division circuits based on this IC have been considered here.

Table 12.18

Input pulse count	*Counter output*			
	Q_D	Q_C	Q_B	Q_A
0	0	0	0	0
1	0	0	0	1
2	0	0	1	0
3	0	0	1	1
4	0	1	0	0
5	0	1	0	1
6	1	0	0	0
7	1	0	0	1
8	1	0	1	0
9	1	0	1	1
10	1	1	0	0
11	1	1	0	1
12	0	0	0	0

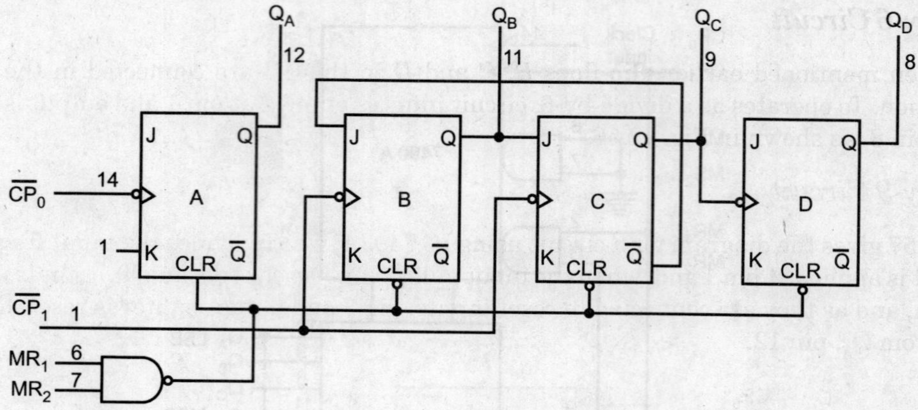

Fig. 12.53 Logic diagram for IC 7492 A

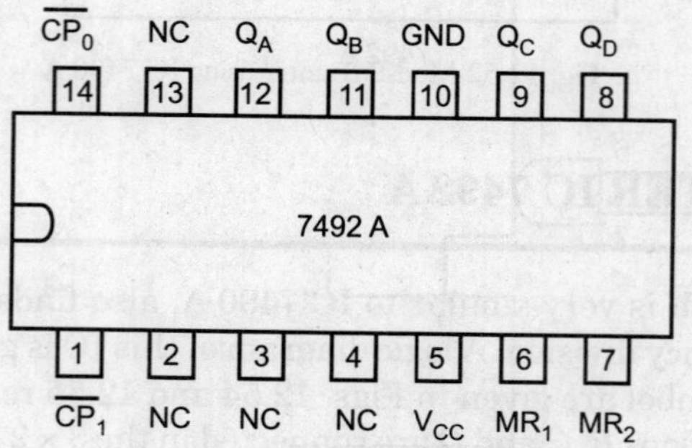

Fig. 12.54 Pin connections for IC 7492 A

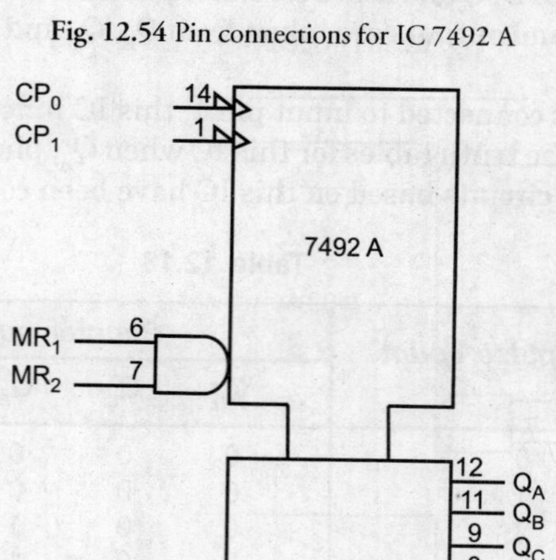

Fig. 12.55 Logic symbol for IC 7492 A

12.15.1 Divide-by-*N* Circuits Based on IC 7492A

This IC like 7490 A is also a useful tool for circuits which require frequency division. Some circuits based on the IC have been considered here.

Divide-by-6 Circuit

As has been mentioned earlier, flip-flops B, C and D in this IC are connected in the 3 × 2 configuration. To operates as a divide-by-6, circuit input is applied at pin 1 and output is taken from Q_D, pin 8, as shown in Fig. 12.56.

Divide-by-9 Circuit

Figure 12.57 gives the diagram for a circuit using IC 7492A, which divides the input frequency by 9. Input is applied at pin 1 and, when the input pulse count reaches decimal 9, outputs Q_D and Q_A go high, and as they are connected to reset inputs, pin 7 and 6, the counter is reset. Output is taken from Q_A, pin 12.

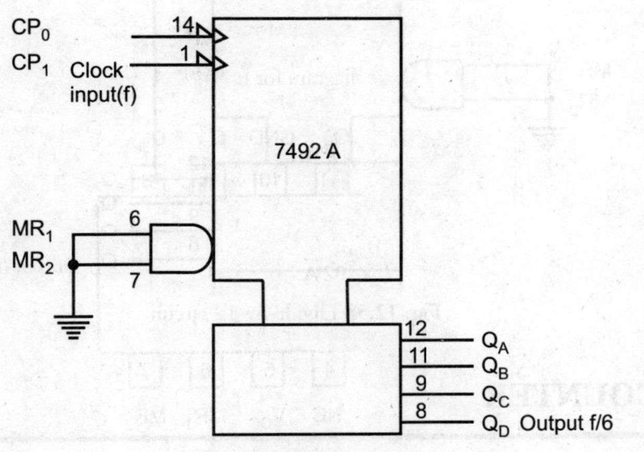

Fig. 12.56 Divide-by-6 circuit

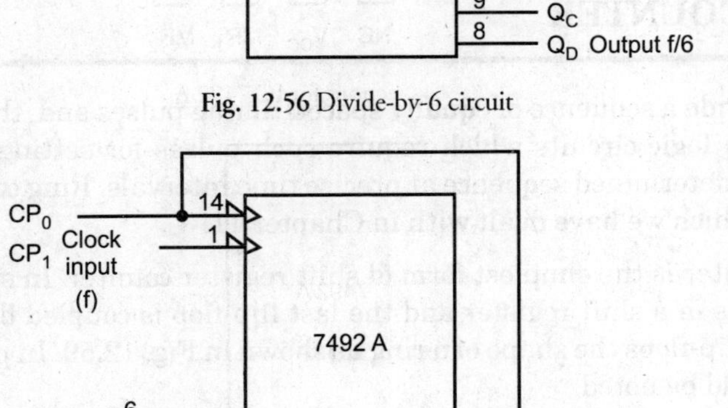

Fig. 12.57 Divide-by-9 circuit

Divide-by-12-Circuit

A circuit based on IC 7492 A which will divide the input frequency by 12 is given in Fig. 12.58. Clock input is applied at pin 1 and the output is taken from Q_D, pin 12. When the circuit reaches pulse count 12, it is automatically reset and it repeats the cycle all over again.

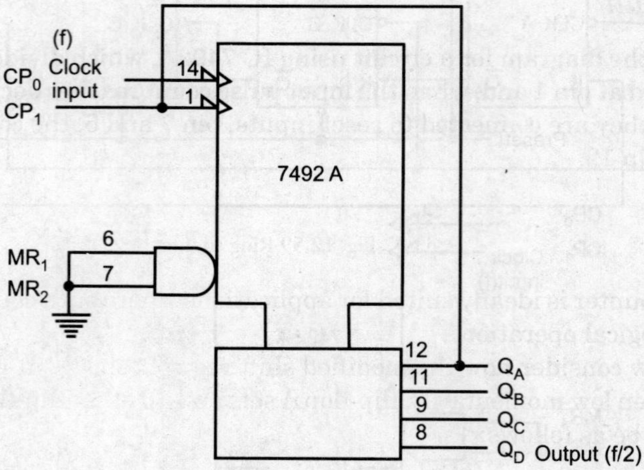

Fig. 12.58 Divide-by-12 circuit

12.16 RING COUNTER

Ring counters provide a sequence of equally spaced timing pulses and, therefore, find considerable application in logic circuits which require such pulses for setting in motion a series of operations in a predetermined sequence at precise time intervals. Ring counters are a variation of shift registers which we have dealt with in Chapter 11.

The ring counter is the simplest form of shift register counter. In such a counter the flip-flops are coupled as in a shift register and the last flip-flop is coupled back to the first, which gives the array of flip-flops the shape of a ring as shown in Fig. 12.59. In particular two features of this circuit should be noted.

1. The Q_D and $\bar{Q}_D$ outputs of the *D* flip-flop are connected respectively, to the *J* and *K* inputs of flip-flop *A*.

2. The preset input of flip-flop *A* is connected to the reset inputs of flip-flops *B*, *C* and *D*.

If we place only one of the flip-flops in the set state and the others in the reset state and then apply clock pulses, the logic 1 will advance by one flip-flop around the ring for each clock pulse and the logic 1 will return to the original flip-flop after exactly four clock pulses, as there are only four flip-flops in the ring. The ring counter does not require any decoder, as we can determine the pulse count by noting the position of the flip-flop, which is set. The total cycle length of the ring is equal to the number of flip-flop states in the counter. The ring counter has the advantage that it is extremely fast and requires no gates for decoding the count. However, it is uneconomical in the number of flip-flops. Whereas a mod-8 counter will require four flip-flops, a mod-8 ring counter will require eight flip-flops.

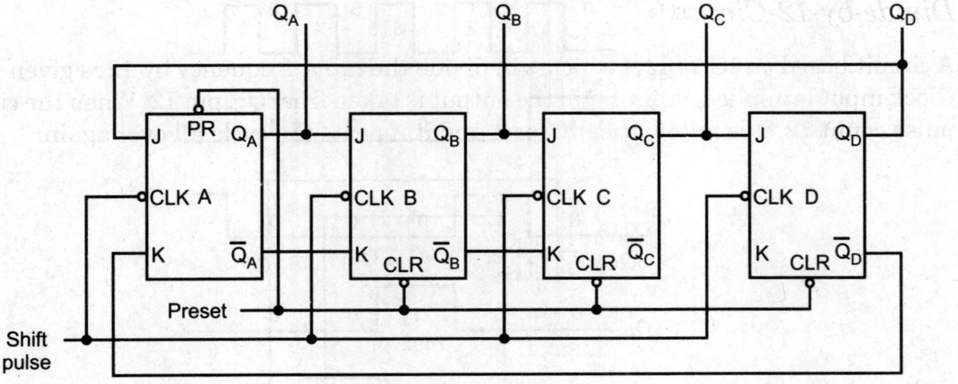

Fig. 12.59 Ring counter

The ring counter is ideally suited for applications where each count has to be recognized to perform some logical operation.

We can now consider how the modified shift register shown in Fig. 12.59 operates. When the preset is taken low momentarily, flip-flop *A* sets and all other flip-flops are reset. The counter output will now be as follows:

Q_A	Q_B	Q_C	Q_D
1	0	0	0

At the negative clock edge of the 1st pulse, flip-flop *A* resets Q_A becomes 0, Q_B becomes 1 and Q_C and Q_D remain 0. The counter output is now as follows:

Q_A	Q_B	Q_C	Q_D
0	1	0	0

After the 4th clock pulse, the counter output will be as follows:

Q_A	Q_B	Q_C	Q_D
1	0	0	0

You will notice that this was the position at the beginning of the operation, when the preset input was activated. A single logic 1 has travelled round the counter shifting one flip-flop position at a time and has returned to flip-flop *A*. The states of the flip-flops have been summarized in Table 12.19.

Table 12.19 Ring counter states

States	***Counter output***			
	Q_A	Q_B	Q_C	Q_D
1	1	0	0	0
2	0	1	0	0
3	0	0	1	0
4	0	0	0	1
5	1	0	0	0

The relevant waveforms are shown in Fig. 12.60.

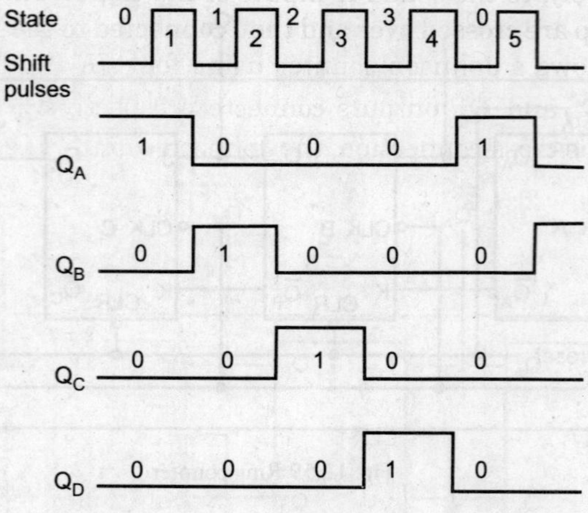

Fig. 12.60

If preset and clear inputs are not available, it is necessary to provide the required gating, so that the counter starts from the initial state. This can be simply arranged by using a NOR gate as shown in Fig. 12.61.

The NOR gate ensures tha the input to flip-flop A will be 0 if any of the outputs of A, B or C flip-flops is a logic 1. Now, on the application of clock pulses 0s will be moved right into the counter until all A, B and C flip-flops are reset. When this happens, a logic 1 will be shifted into the counter, and as this 1 is shifted right through the A, B and C flip-flops it will be preceded by three more 0s, which will again be followed by a logic 1 from the NOR gate when flip-flops, A, B and C are all reset.

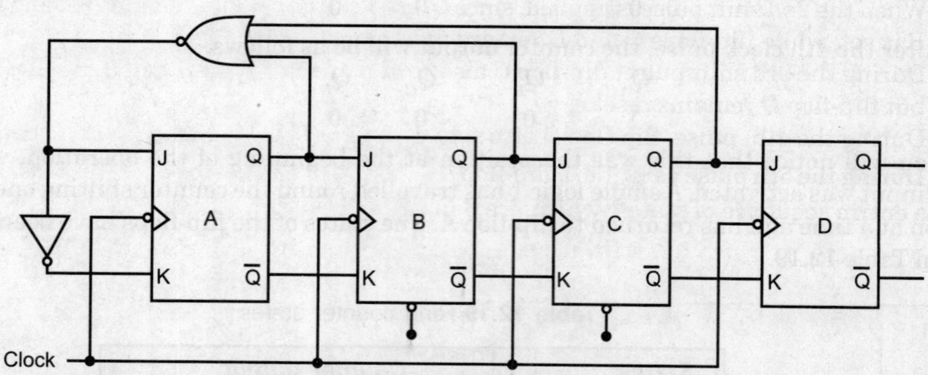

Fig. 12.61 Ring counter with correcting circuit

12.17 JOHNSON COUNTER

The ring counter can be modified to effect an economy in the number of flip-flops used to implement a ring counter. In modified form it is known as a switchtail ring counter or Johnson counter. The modified ring counter can be implemented with only half the number of flip-flops.

In the ring counter circuit shown in Fig. 12.59, the Q_D and $\bar{Q}_D$ outputs of the D flip-flop were connected respectively, to the J and K inputs of flip-flop A. In the Johnson counter, the outputs of the last flip-flop are crossed over and then connected to the J and K inputs of the first flip-flop. Figure 12.62 shows a Johnson counter using four JK flip-flops in the shift register configuration, showing Q_D and $\bar{Q}_D$ outputs connected respectively, to the K and J inputs of flip-flops A. Because of this cross-connection, the Johnson counter is sometimes referred to as a twisted ring counter.

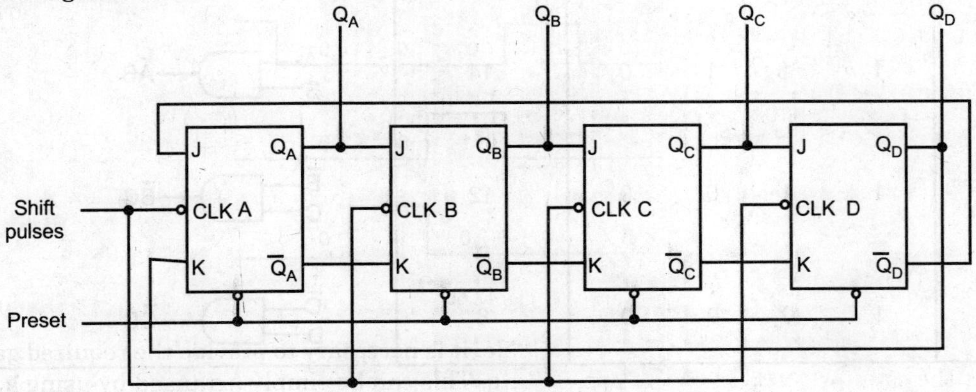

Fig. 12.62 Four state Johnson counter

To enable the counter to function according to the desired sequence, it is necessary to reset all the flip-flops. Initially therefore, Q_D is 0 and Q_A is 1, which makes the J input of flip-flop A logic 1. We will now study how shift pulses alter the counter output.

1. Since the J input of flip-flop A is 1, the 1st shift pulse sets the A flip-flop and the other flip-flops remain reset as the J input of these flip-flops are 0 and K inputs are 1.
2. When the 2nd shift pulse is applied, since Q_D is still 1, flip-flop A remains set and flip-flop B is set, while flip-flops C and D remain reset.
3. During the 3rd shift pulse, flip-flop C also sets, while flip-flops A and B are already set; but flip-flop D remains reset.
4. During the 4th, pulse, flip-flop D also sets while flip-flops A, B and C are already set.
5. During the 5th pulse as $\bar{Q}_D$ is 0, flip-flop A resets, while flip-flops B, C and D remain set.

The entire sequence of states, which are 8 in all, is as shown in Table 12.20.

Table 12.20

State	Q_D	Q_C	Q_B	Q_A	*Binary equivalent*	*Output decoding*
1	0	0	0	0	0	$\bar{A}$, $\bar{D}$ → $\bar{A}\cdot\bar{D}$
2	0	0	0	1	1	A, $\bar{B}$ → $A\cdot\bar{B}$
3	0	0	1	1	3	B, $\bar{C}$ → $B\bar{C}$

4	0	1	1	1	7	C, $\bar{D}$ — $C\bar{D}$
5	1	1	1	1	15	A, D — AD
6	1	1	1	0	14	$\bar{A}$, B — $\bar{A}B$
7	1	1	0	0	12	$\bar{B}$, C — $\bar{B}C$
8	1	0	0	0	8	$\bar{C}$, D — $\bar{C}D$

You will notice from Table 12.20 that Johnson counter with four flip-flops has eight valid states. Since four flip-flops have been used, the total number of states is 16, out of which 8 are invalid, which have been listed in Table 12.21.

The valid states require decoding, which is different from normal decoding used for standard pure binary count sequence. You will notice that state 1 is uniquely defined, when the outputs of flip-flops *A* and *D* are low. Thus a 2-input AND gate with inputs as shown in the table can decode state 1. State 2 is also fully defined by *A* high and *B* low. Similarly, the other outputs can be decoded by the gates with inputs as shown in Table 12.20.

Table 12.21 Invalid states

Q_D	Q_C	Q_B	Q_A	*Binary equivalent*
0	1	0	0	4
1	0	0	1	9
0	0	1	0	2
0	1	0	1	5
1	0	1	1	11
0	1	1	0	6
1	1	0	1	13
1	0	1	0	10

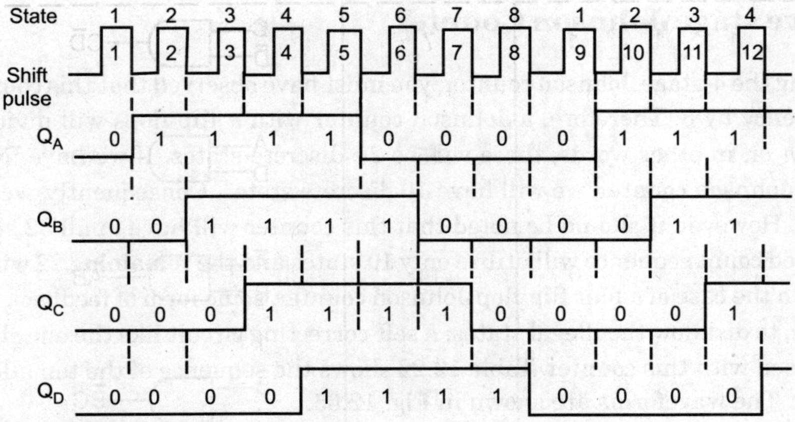

Fig. 12.63 Waveforms for a 4-state Johnson counter

In order to ensure that the counter counts in the prescribed sequence given in Table 12.20, an initial reset pulse may be applied, which will reset all the flip-flops. If this is not done, there is no surety that the counter will revert to the valid counting sequence. If the counter should find itself in an unused state, it may continue to advance from one disallowed state to another. The solution to the problem lies in applying extra feedback, so that the counter reverts to the correct counting sequence. For this purpose, the self-correcting circuit given in Fig. 12.64 may be used. The input to the AND gate is $Q_A \bar{Q}_B \bar{Q}_C Q_D$ and thus it decodes the word 1 0 0 1, which overrides the input, which is 0 and the counter produces an output of 1 1 0 0, which is a part of the allowed counting sequence. From then onwards the counter functions in the desired sequence.

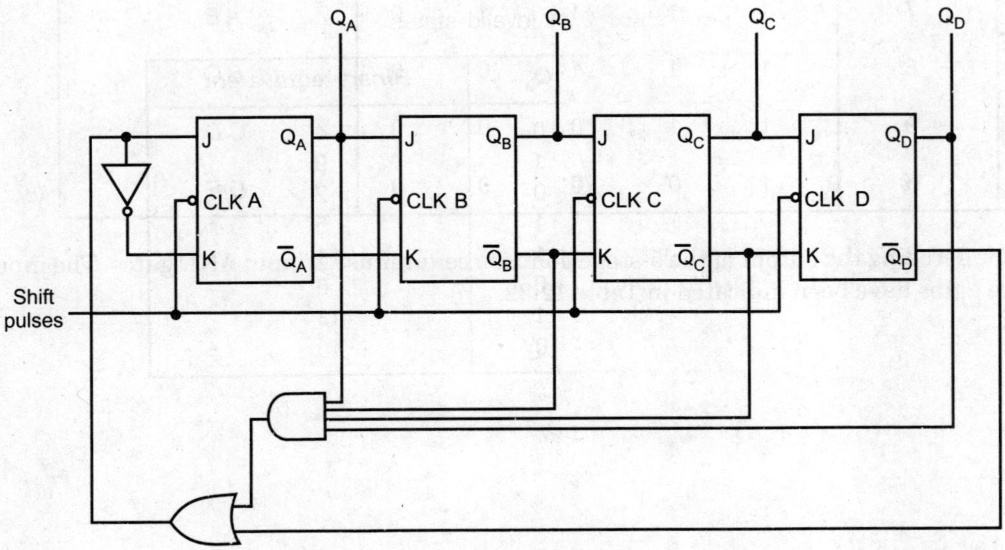

Fig. 12.64 Self-starting and self-correcting Johnson counter

12.17.1 Five stage Johnson Counter

While discussing the 4-stage Johnson counter, you must have observed that this counter divides the clock frequency by 8. Therefore, a Johnson counter with n flip-flops will divide the clock frequency by $2n$ or, in other words, there will be $2n$ discrete states. If we have five flip-flops connected as a Johnson counter, we will have 10 discrete states. Consequently, we will have a decade counter. However, it should be noted that this counter will have in all 32 states, out of which the desired count sequence will utilize only 10 states and the remaining 22 will have to be disallowed. As in the case of a four flip-flop Johnson counter, some form of feedback will have to be incorporated, to disallow the illegal states. A self-correcting circuit like the one shown in Fig. 12.64 may be used with this counter. Table 12.22 shows the sequence of the ten allowed states for this counter. The waveforms are shown in Fig. 12.65.

Table 12.22

State	*E*	*D*	*C*	*B*	*A*	*Output decoding*
1	0	0	0	0	0	$\bar{A}\bar{E}$
2	0	0	0	0	1	$A\bar{B}$
3	0	0	0	1	1	$B\bar{C}$
4	0	0	1	1	1	$C\bar{D}$
5	0	1	1	1	1	$D\bar{E}$
6	1	1	1	1	1	$A\,E$
7	1	1	1	1	0	$\bar{A}B$
8	1	1	1	0	0	$\bar{B}C$
9	1	1	0	0	0	$\bar{C}D$
10	1	0	0	0	0	$\bar{D}E$

For decoding the output of the 5-stage Johnson counter use 2-input AND gates. The inputs to these gates have been indicated in Table 12.22.

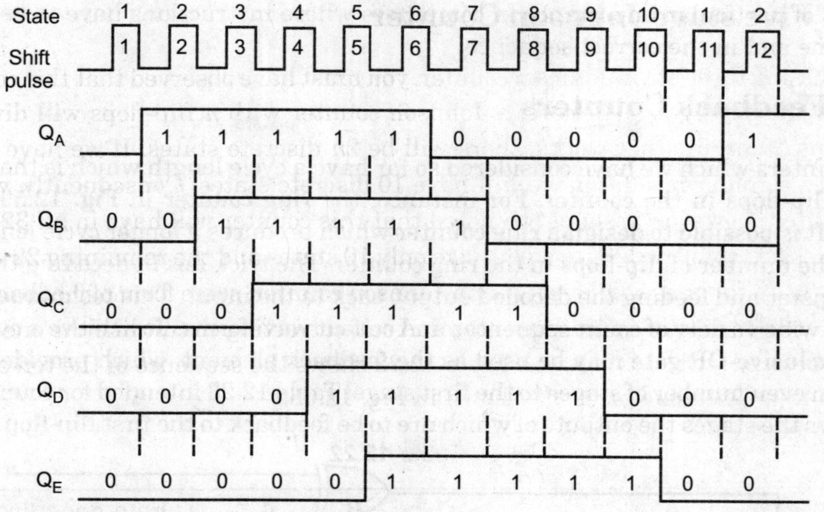

Fig. 12.65 Waveform for a 5-stage Johnson counter

12.18 RING COUNTER APPLICATIONS

Ring counters find many applications as

1. Frequency dividers,
2. Counters,
3. Code generators, and
4. Period and sequence generators.

Frequency dividers

If you look at the waveform Fig. 12.60 of the 4-stage ring counter shown in Fig. 12.59, you will notice that the *B* flip-flop produces one output pulse for two input pulses, that is it divides the frequency of the shift pulse by 2. Similarly, flip-flop *C* produces one output pulse for every three input pulses, that is it divides the input frequency by 3, and flip-flop *D* divides the input frequency by 4. If there are *n* flip-flops they will divide the shift pulse by *n*. Thus a shift register connected as a ring counter can be used as a frequency divider.

Counters

A shift register, when connected as a ring counter, can also be used as a counter. For instance, the flip-flop outputs of the ring counter in Fig. 12.59 also give an indication of the number of pulses applied and, therefore counting requires no decoding.

Sequence Generators

Sequence generators are circuits which generate a prescribed sequence of bits in synchronism with a clock. By connecting the outputs of flip-flops in a ring counter to the logic circuits whose operations are to be controlled according to a certain sequence a ring counter can perform a very useful function. Since ring counters are activated by fixed frequency clocks, the timing intervals between the logic circuits to be controlled can be very precise.

This is of particular importance in computers where instructions have to be executed at the right time and in the correct sequence.

12.18.1 Feedback Counters

The ring counters which we have considered so far have a cycle length which is the same as the number of flip-flops in the counter. For instance, the ring counter in Fig. 12.59 has a cycle length of 4. It is possible to design a ring counter which produces a longer cycle length of $2^n - 1$, where n is the number of flip-flops in the ring counter. The trick lies in decoding the outputs of the shift register and feeding the decoded output back to the input. This technique can be used to develop a wide variety of count sequences and output waveforms. To achieve a cycle length of $2^n - 1$, an exclusive-OR gate may be used as the feedback element, which provides a feedback term from an even number of stages to the first stage. Table 12.23 intended for counters up to 12 stages, shows the stages the outputs of which are to be feedback to the first flip-flop in the chain.

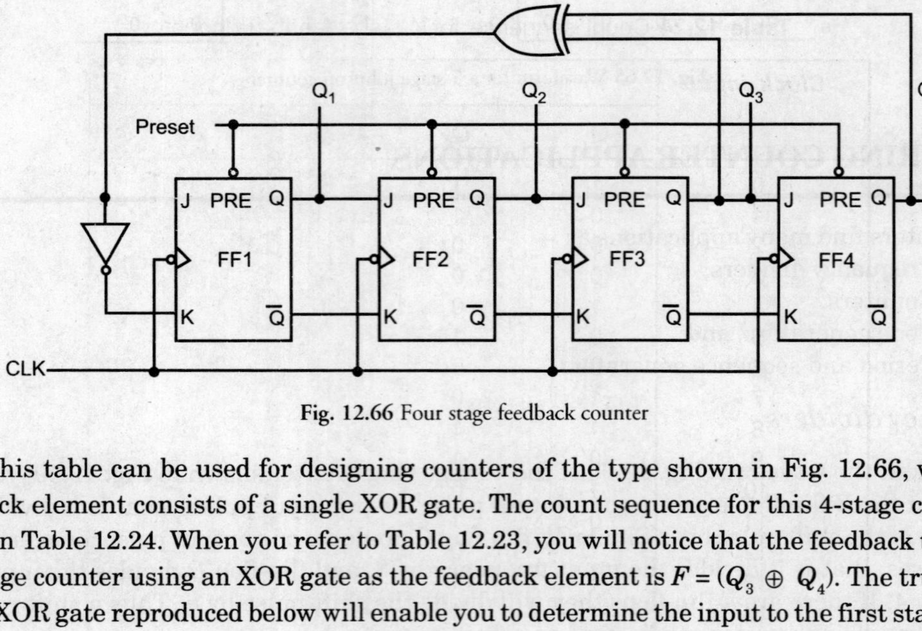

Fig. 12.66 Four stage feedback counter

This table can be used for designing counters of the type shown in Fig. 12.66, when the feedback element consists of a single XOR gate. The count sequence for this 4-stage counter is given in Table 12.24. When you refer to Table 12.23, you will notice that the feedback terms for a 4-stage counter using an XOR gate as the feedback element is $F = (Q_3 \oplus Q_4)$. The truth table for an XOR gate reproduced below will enable you to determine the input to the first stage in the counter.

Input		Output
A	*B*	*F*
0	0	0
0	1	1
1	0	1
1	1	0

Table 12.23 Feedback terms for counter design

No. of stage	*Feedback stage*			
2		Q_1	Q_2	
3		Q_2	Q_3	
4		Q_3	Q_4	
5		Q_3	Q_5	
6		Q_5	Q_6	
7		Q_6	Q_7	
8	Q_4	Q_5	Q_6	Q_8
9		Q_5	Q_9	
10		Q_7	Q_{10}	
11		Q_9	Q_{11}	
12	Q_6	Q_8	Q_{11}	Q_{12}

Table 12.24 Count sequence for 4-stage feedback counter

Clock input	*Output*			
	Q_1	Q_2	Q_3	Q_4
0	1	1	1	1
1	0	1	1	1
2	0	0	1	1
3	0	0	0	1
4	1	0	0	0
5	0	1	0	0
6	0	0	1	0
7	1	0	0	1
8	1	1	0	0
9	0	1	1	0
10	1	0	1	1
11	0	1	0	1
12	1	0	1	0
13	1	1	0	1
14	1	1	1	0
15	1	1	1	1

In determining the counter states, all that is necessary to determine the feedback input to the first flip-flop and, since *JK* flip-flops have been used, the input to the first flip will be the same as the output of the XOR gate, which depends on the outputs of FF3 and FF4. Table 12.24 has been prepared on this basis.

It is important to note that the 0 state of count sequence has to be excluded by additional gating or by using the preset input. If you refer to the first row of the table, you will observe that both outputs Q_3 and Q_4 are 1 and therefore $F = 0$. Consequently, the input of the first flip-flop is also 0, which will make its output on the first clock pulse 0. The outputs of FF2 and FF3 will remain unchanged on the first clock pulse. You can determine the outputs in the remaining rows on this basis.

A close look at the table will show you that the output of FF2 resembles the output of

FF1, but it is delayed by one clock pulse from that of FF1. Similarly, the output of FF3 and FF4 are also delayed by one clock pulse as compared to the outputs of the immediately preceding flip-flops.

This procedure can be used for designing counters which are required to cycle through a large number of states. For instance a counter which uses 8 flip-flops will cycle through $2^8 - 1$ or 255 states. We have used only a single XOR gate as the feedback element, but the feedback logic can be designed differently to sequence through any desired sequence or waveform.

12.18.2 Sequence Generators

Here we are concerned with pseudo-random sequence generators. They will be random in the sense that the output generated will not cycle through the normal binary count. The sequence is termed pseudo, as it is not random in the real sense, because it will sequence through all the possible states one every $2^n - 1$ clock cycles. The random sequence generator given in Fig. 12.67 has n stages and it will therefore sequence through $2^n - 1$ values before it repeats the same sequence of values.

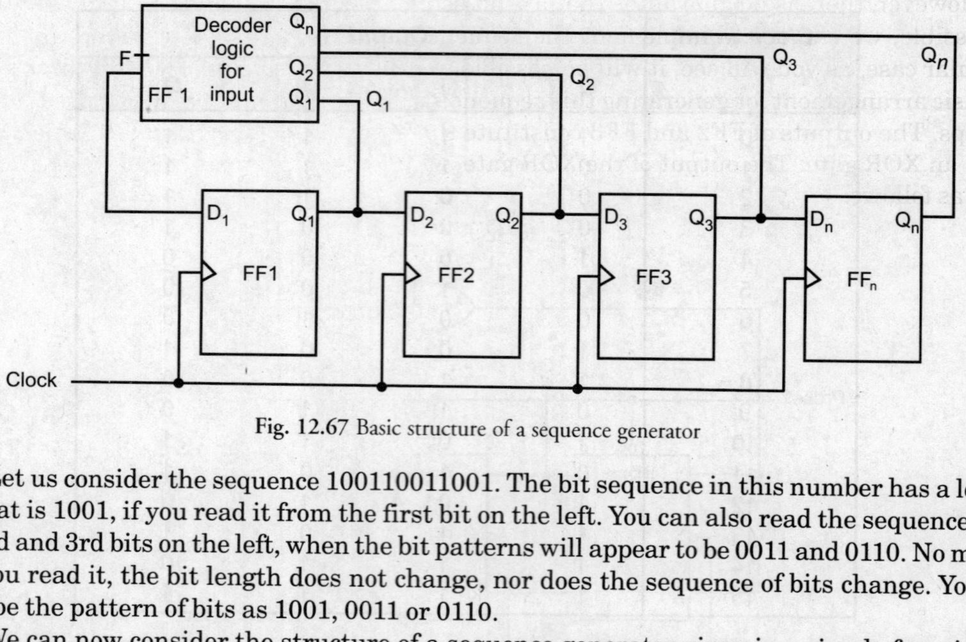

Fig. 12.67 Basic structure of a sequence generator

Let us consider the sequence 100110011001. The bit sequence in this number has a length of 4 that is 1001, if you read it from the first bit on the left. You can also read the sequence from the 2nd and 3rd bits on the left, when the bit patterns will appear to be 0011 and 0110. No matter how you read it, the bit length does not change, nor does the sequence of bits change. You can describe the pattern of bits as 1001, 0011 or 0110.

We can now consider the structure of a sequence generator given in a simple form in Fig. 12.67 using D-type flip-flops connected as in a shift register. The outputs of the flip-flops are connected through a feedback decoder to the input of the first flip-flop. The output of the decoder is a function of the flip-flop outputs connected to it and the decoder circuitry. We can state this as follows:

$$F = f(Q_1, Q_2, Q_3, Q_n)$$

The desired sequence of bits will appear at the output of each of the flip-flops, but the output of each of the successive flip-flops will show a delay in the appearance of the sequence by one clock interval over the one which precedes it.

The minimum number of flip-flops required to generate a sequence of length S is given by

$$S = 2^n - 1$$

where n is the number of flip-flops in the chain.

However, if the minimum number of flip-flops is used, it is not possible to say off hand, that it will be possible to generate a sequence of the required length; but for a given number of flip-flops there is invariably one sequence which has the maximum length.

It is important that in the generation of a sequence no state should be repeated, as that will put a limit on the number of states, because every state determines the development of the future sequence. Besides, the all 0 state has to be excluded, as in this case the input to the first flip-flop in the chain will be 0, which implies that the next state will also be 0, in which case the sequence generator would stop functioning.

We will now consider the steps in the generation of the sequence 1001001 of seven bits. The number of stages that will be required to generate this sequence can be deterined as follows:

$$S = 2^n - 1$$

Since $S = 7$; n should be 3, that is three flip-flops will be required.

However, there is no guarantee that a 7-bit sequence can be generated in 3 stages. If it is not possible, we can try to implement the sequence by using a 4-stage counter; but in this particular case, as you will see, it will be possible to generate this sequence with three stages. The basic arrangement for generating this sequence is shown in Fig. 12.68, which uses three *JK* flip-flops. The outputs of FF2 and FF3 constitute the inputs to the logic decoder, which in this case is an XOR gate. The output of the XOR gate, which constitutes the input F to FFI can be stated as follows:

$$F = (Q_2 \oplus Q_3)$$

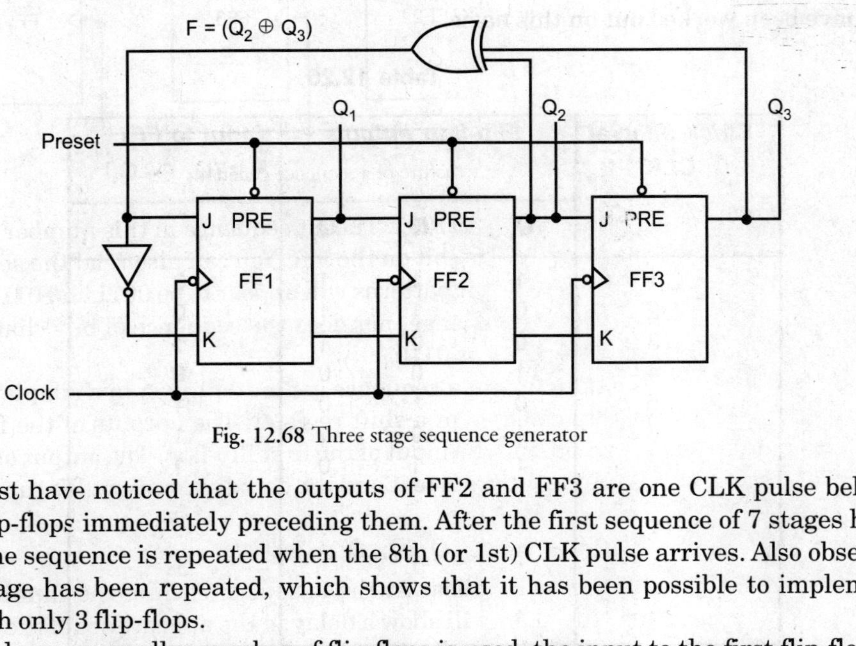

Fig. 12.68 Three stage sequence generator

You must have noticed that the outputs of FF2 and FF3 are one CLK pulse behind the outputs of flip-flops immediately preceding them. After the first sequence of 7 stages has been completed, the sequence is repeated when the 8th (or 1st) CLK pulse arrives. Also observe that no output stage has been repeated, which shows that it has been possible to implement the sequence with only 3 flip-flops.

When a large or smaller number of flip-flops is used, the input to the first flip-flop can be worked out on the same basis; but the feedback logic will be different as shown in Table 12.25 for sequence generators using up to 8 stages. For instance for a generator using four flip-flops, F will be as follows:

$$F = (Q_3 \oplus Q_4)$$

Table 12.25 Logic design table for shift register sequences of maximum length ($S = 2^n - 1$)

Clock n	*Feedback stage*
2	Q_1 Q_2
3	Q_2 Q_3
4	Q_3 Q_4
5	Q_3 Q_5
6	Q_5 Q_6
7	Q_6 Q_7
8	Q_2 Q_3 Q_4 Q_8

The implementation of sequence 1001011 has been presented in Table 12.26.

The count sequence has been developed as follows: You will notice from the table that at the commencement of the operation, the counter is set as shown against CLK 1. Before CLK 2 is applied at FF1 input, the *F* input to it should be 0, so that its output changes from 1 to 0. Since Q_2 and Q_3 are both 1, and *F* input to FF1 will be 0. This condition is, therefore, satisfied, the second clock pulse, therefore, changes Q_1 from 1 to 0 and Q_2 and Q_3 remain on 1 as the inputs to these flip-flops are 1. Since both Q_2 and Q_3 are again 1, the *F* input to FF1, before the arrival of the 3rd clock pulse will again be 0. Therefore, on the arrival the CLK pulse 3, the output of Q_1 will remain 0, as the input to it is 0. On the same CLK pulse Q_2 will change from 1 to 0 as the input to it is 0 and Q_3 will remain on 1 as the input to Q_3 is still 1. Successive changes in the outputs have been worked out on this basis.

Table 12.26

Clock interval CLK	*Flip-flop outputs*			*Input to FF1 $F = (Q_2 \oplus Q_3)$*
	Q_1	Q_2	Q_3	
1	1	1	1	0
2	0	1	1	0
3	0	0	1	1
4	1	0	0	0
5	0	1	0	1
6	1	0	1	1
7	1	1	0	1
.	.	.	.	.
.	.	.	.	.
.	.	.	.	.
1	1	1	1	1

Problems

12.1 A counter uses *JK* flip-flops of the type shown in Fig. 8.31(a). Will the counter state change on the leading or the trailing edge of the clock pulse?

12.2 The number stored in a 4-bit binary up-counter is 0101. What will be state of the counter after the following clock pulses?

(*a*) 3rd clock pulse (*b*) 5th clock pulse

(*c*) 8th clock pulse (*d*) 12th clock pulse

12.3 In a 4-bit ripple up-counter how many clock pulses will you apply, starting from state 0 0 0 0, so that the counter outputs are as follows?

(*a*) 0 0 1 0 (*b*) 0 1 1 1

(*c*) 1 0 0 1 (*d*) 1 1 1 0

12.4 Draw the logic diagram for a binary up-counter using four *JK* flip-flops and draw the truth table and the output waveforms.

12.5 Connect four edge-triggered *D*-type flip-flops to make an asynchronous up-counter.

12.6 How many *JK* flip-flops will you require to make the following modulo counters?

(*a*) Mod-4 (*b*) Mod-6

(*c*) Mod-9 (*d*) Mod-11

12.7 What will be maximum count capability of a counter having 12 *JK* flip-flops?

12.8 How many flip-flops will you require to attain a count capability of 8500?

12.9 An asynchronous counter has four flip-flops and the propagation delay of each flip-flop is 20 ns. Calculate the maximum counting speed of the counter.

12.10 A synchronous counter has four flip-flops and the propagation delay of each is 20 ns. What is its maximum couting speed?

12.11 By how much will a ripple down-counter having three flip-flops divide the input frequency?

12.12 Draw a logic diagram, truth table and output waveforms for a ripple down-counter with four flip-flops.

12.13 What will be the output states of a four-flop binary down-counter, after the following input clock pulses, if the initial state of the counter was 1111?

(*a*) 4 (*b*) 7 (*c*) 9 (*d*) 14

12.14 Draw the logic diagram of a presettable down counter with a maximum preset capability of 7.

12.15 What will be the modulus of IC 74193 in the up-counting mode, if the numbers preset in the counter are as follows?

(*a*) Decimal 5 (*b*) Decimal 7

(*c*) Decimal 9 (*d*) Decimal 12

12.16 What will be the modulus of IC 74193 in the down-counting mode, when the binary numbers preset in the counter are the same as in Problem 12.15?

12.17 A 74193 up-counter starts counting up from binary number 1 0 0 0. What will be the state of the counter after the 8th clock pulse?

12.18 Draw the logic diagram of a mod-6 counter using the counter reset method. Write its truth table and draw the output waveforms.

12.19 Show how you will connect two ICs 74193 to build an 8-bit up-down counter.

12.20 What is the maximum counting capacity of a chain of five BCD counters?

12.21 A BCD counter is required to have the following states. After how many clock pulses will these states be reached, if the counter was initially reset?

(*a*) 0 0 1 0 (*b*) 0 1 0 0

(*c*) 0 1 1 0 (*d*) 1 0 0 1

12.22 Connect two ICs 74193 to make a modulo-20 divider circuit.

12.23 Design a mod-10 (Decade) synchronous counter using *JK* flip-flops.

12.24 Draw decoding gates for the decade counter in Fig. 12.32.

12.25 Draw decoding gates for the counter of Fig. 12.30.

12.26 Redesign the synchronous mod-5 counter circuit discussed in Section 12.12.2, so that whenever the counter reaches the unutilized states 1 0 1, 0 1 1 and 1 1 1 the counter is reset.

12.27 Design a mod-7 counter using IC 7490 A.

12.28 Design a divide-by 120 counter using ICs 7490 A and 7492 A.

12.29 Design a correcting circuit for a 4-state ring counter using a NAND gate instead of a NOR gate as used in Fig. 12.61.

12.30 Determine the maximal length sequence, which can be generated using four *JK* flip-flops and draw the sequence generated by the first flip-flop in the chain.

13 Arithmetic Logic Circuits

13.1 INTRODUCTION

In Chapter 1, we have discussed how binary numbers can be added, subtracted and multiplied and we had restricted our discussion to positive numbers only; but all numbers, like decimal numbers, can be either positive or negative. However, if we are dealing either with positive or negative numbers only in a particular operation, there are fewer complications than when we have to deal with both positive and negative numbers at the same time. Since logic circuits recognize only binary inputs, we have to consider a method for representing positive and negative numbers in a manner which logic circuits can recognize. In this chapter we will consider how positive and negative numbers can be identified by binary methods without using positive and negative signs. We will also consider logic circuits which can carry out arithmetic operations.

13.2 UNSIGNED BINARY NUMBERS

As stated above, in actual operations, we have to deal with both positive and negative numbers. If your operations involve only positive or only negative numbers, they can be easily handled by logic circuits without complicated circuitry. In such operations we will be concerned only with the magnitude of the numbers, irrespective of their sign. In such cases all the bits of a binary number can be used to represent the magnitude of the number. For instance, decimal number 15 will be represented by 1111. Thus all the bits in a 4-bit system are used to represent the magnitude of the number. Similarly, in the BCD system binary numbers from 0000 0000 to 1111 1111 will represent decimal numbers from 0 to 225. You will observe that all the bits are utilized to represent magnitude. For this reason such numbers are called unsigned binary numbers.

13.3 SIGNED BINARY NUMBERS

When we are dealing with both positive and negative numbers, at the same time we have to devise a convention for indicating the magnitude as well as the sign of the numbers. In order to get rid of the minus sign for indicating negative numbers, we can use 0 as a prefix for positive numbers and 1 as a prefix for negative numbers. Thus we have the sign bit followed by the magnitude bits in these numbers, as shown in Fig. 13.1.

Sign		Magnitude Absolute value

0 ; Plus
1 ; Minus

Fig. 13.1 Representation of sign and magnitude of numbers

Let us consider decimal numbers 4, 5, 6 and –4, –5 and –6. The first thing to do is to represent them in binary form, as has been shown in column 2. We can now use 0 as a prefix for the positive numbers and 1 as a prefix for the negative numbers, as shown in the 3rd, column which incorporates the sign as well as the magnitude. When numbers are represented in this manner, they are called signed binary numbers or sign-magnitude numbers.

Decimal number 1	*Binary equivalent* 2	*Sign magnitude representation* 3 *Sign Magnitude*
4	1 0 0	0 1 0 0
5	1 0 1	0 1 0 1
6	1 1 0	0 1 1 0
7	1 1 1	0 1 1 1
–4	–1 0 0	1 1 0 0
–5	–1 0 1	1 1 0 1
–6	–1 1 0	1 1 1 0
–7	–1 1 1	1 1 1 1

A sequence of 4-bit sign magnitude numbers is shown in Table 13.1 along with the equivalent decimal numbers.

Table 13.1 Signed binary numbers

Decimal number	*Signed binary number*
+ 7	0 1 1 1
+ 6	0 1 1 0
+ 5	0 1 0 1
+ 4	0 1 0 0
+ 3	0 0 1 1
+ 2	0 0 1 0
+ 1	0 0 0 1
0	0 0 0 0
– 1	1 0 0 1
– 2	1 0 1 0
– 3	1 0 1 1
– 4	1 1 0 0

– 5	1 1 0 1
– 6	1 1 1 0
– 7	1 1 1 1

Large binary numbers can also be expressed in sign magnitude form. Some examples are given below:

Decimal number	Signed binary number	
+ 4	0000	0100
– 4	1000	0100
+ 8	0000	1000
– 8	1000	1000

In the signed binary number system, the only difference between positive and negative numbers is the sign bit. To figure out the equivalent decimal number, omit the sign bit and convert the remaining bits to decimal form. Mathematical operations are difficult to perform with signed binary numbers and, therefore, they have very little application, which is mainly in analog-to-digital (A/D) conversion.

13.4 1's COMPLEMENT REPRESENTATION

In the signed binary number system (sign-magnitude convention), which we have just considered, we have the sign bit followed by the magnitude bits, where sign bit 0 stands for a positive number and sign bit 1 stands for a negative number. Thus 0110 equals decimal number +6 and 1110 equals decimal number –6. You will notice that the magnitude bits are the same in both the numbers and the only difference is in the sign bits.

Another way to represent a negative number is known as 1's complement method. In this system, the bit-for-bit complement of a number is know as its 1's complement and it is taken to represent the magnitude of the negative number. Consider the following examples.

Given number Sign	Magnitude		1's complement Sign	Magnitude	
0	0 1 1	(+3)	1	1 0 0	(– 3)
0	1 0 1	(+5)	1	0 1 0	(– 5)

Using this convention, decimal numbers from + 7 to – 7 can be expressed by a 4-bit word as shown in Table 13.2.

Table 13.2

Decimal number	*Equivalent signed binary number*			
	Sign	*Magnitude*		
+ 7	0	1	1	1
+ 6	0	1	1	0

Number					
+ 5	0	1	0	1	Positive numbers in sign magnitude form. Sign bit 0 stands for positive numbers.
+ 4	0	1	0	0	
+ 3	0	0	1	1	
+ 2	0	0	1	0	
+ 1	0	0	0	1	
0	0	0	0	0	Equivalent negative numbers in 1's complement representation. Sign bit 1 stands for negative numbers.
− 1	1	1	1	0	
− 2	1	1	0	1	
− 3	1	1	0	0	
− 4	1	0	1	1	
− 5	1	0	1	0	
− 6	1	0	0	1	
− 7	1	0	0	0	

1's complement representation is suitable for arithmetic operations by electronic circuitry, as it can be easily implemented by using inverters as shown in Fig. 13.2. The diagram shows inverters connected to the output of an 8-bit register which complements the word bit-for-bit. However the 2's complement representation is ideally suited for arithmetic logic circuits, as you will see from the discussion that follows.

13.5 ARITHMETIC IN 1's COMPLEMENT REPRESENTATION

Since numbers can be conveniently represented in 1's complement system by electronic circuitry, this system would appear to be an obvious choice for arithmetic operations. We will consider all possible combinations of positive and negative numbers to illustrate the application of 1's complement method in carrying out additions. In our examples here, we will use a sign bit 0 to indicate positive numbers and a sign bit of 1 for negative numbers.

1. *Adding a positive to another positive number.*

Example 13.1: *Add + 3 to + 5.*

Solution:

		Number with sign bit
+ 3	+ 0 0 1 1	0 0 0 1 1
+ 5	+ 0 1 0 1	0 0 1 0 1
+ 8	1 0 0 0	0 1 0 0 0

In this case, since both sign bits are 0 no sign bit will be generated and the result of addition will be positive number.

2. *Adding a negative to a positive number*

Example 13.2: *Add – 7 to + 5.*

Solution:

		Number with sign bit	
+ 5	0 1 0 1	0 0 1 0 1	
− 7	− 0 1 1 1	1 0 1 1 1	1's complement
− 2	0 0 1 0	1 1 1 0 1	

Since the sign bit is 1 the answer is in the negative. The answer will be the 1's complement of the last four bits, that is – 0 0 1 0 or – 2.

When a positive and a negative number are added and the negative number is larger in magnitude than the positive number, the sum will be negative as in the above example. If the positive number is larger in magnitude than the negative number, the sum will be positive as in the example that follows:

Example 13.3: *Add + 7 to – 5.*

Solution:

		Number with sign bit	
+ 7	0 1 1 1	0 0 1 1 1	
– 5	0 1 0 1	1 1 0 1 0	1's complement
+ 2	0 0 1 0	1 0 0 0 1	
		1	
		0 0 0 1 0	

In this case the end-around carry, that is 1, has to be added to the LSB of the sum to get the correct answer, which will be 00010 . There will be a 0 in the sign bit indicating that the answer is positive.

3. *Adding two negative numbers*

When two negative numbers are added, an end-around carry is always generated. The sum obtained will be in the 1's complement form and the sign bit will be 1.

Example 13.4: *Add – 6 to – 2.*

Solution:

		Number with sign bit	
– 6	– 0 1 1 0	1 1 0 0 1	1's complement
– 2	– 0 0 1 0	1 1 1 0 1	1's complement
– 8	– 1 0 0 0	1 0 1 1 0	
		1	
		1 0 1 1 1	

The answer is 1's complement of 0 1 1 1 with 1 as the sign bit that is 11000 or – 8.

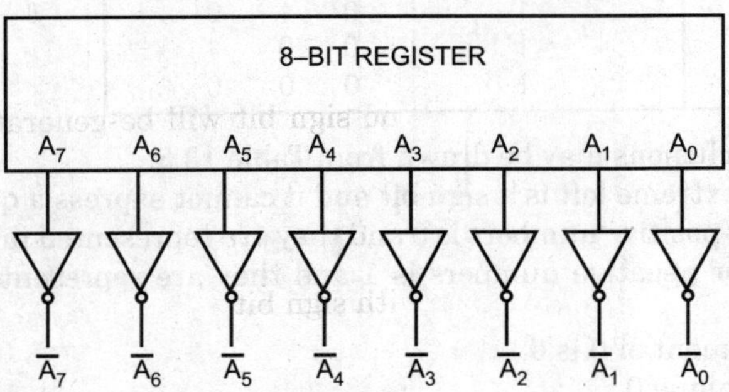

Fig. 13.2

13.6 2's COMPLEMENT REPRESENTATION

The 2's complement of a binary number is used to represent negative numbers and is obtained by adding 1 to the 1's complement of the binary number. In equation form it may be stated as follows:

2's complement = 1's complement + 1

Consider the following examples:

Signed binary number		*1's complement*	*Add*	*2's complement*	
Sign	Magnitude			Sign	Magnitude
0	1 1 0	1 0 0 1	+ 1 =	1	0 1 0
0	0 1 1	1 1 0 0	+ 1 =	1	1 0 1
0	0 0 1	1 1 1 0	+ 1 =	1	1 1 1

Table 13.3 present signed binary number using 2's complement representation.

Table 13.3

Decimal number	*Equivalent signed binary number*				
	Sign	*Magnitude*			
+ 7	0	1	1	1	Positive numbers in sign magnitude form. Sign bit 0 stands for positive number.
+ 6	0	1	1	0	
+ 5	0	1	0	1	
+ 4	0	1	0	0	
+ 3	0	0	1	1	
+ 2	0	0	1	0	
+ 1	0	0	0	1	
0	0	0	0	0	
– 1	1	1	1	1	Equivalent negative numbers from 0 to –8 in 2's complement representation. Sign bit 1 stands for negative number.
– 2	1	1	1	0	
– 3	1	1	0	1	
– 4	1	1	0	0	
– 5	1	0	1	1	
– 6	1	0	1	0	
– 7	1	0	0	1	
–8	1	0	0	0	

The following conclusions may be drawn from Table 13.3.

1. The bit at the extreme left is a sign bit and it cannot express a quality.
2. The sign bit for positive numbers is 0 and they are represented in sign magnitude form.
3. The sign bit for negative numbers is 1 and they are represented in 2's complement form.
4. The 2's complement of 0 is 0.
5. There is one unique 0.
6. There are 16 unique states, of which 7 are positive integers and 8 are negative integers.

It is worth noting that taking the 2's complement of a number amounts to a sign change or negation. Consider the following Examples:

1. 2's complement of 0001 (or 1) = 1111 (or –1)
   2's complement of 1111 (or – 1) = 0001 (or 1)
2. 2's complement of 0101 (or 5) = 1011 (or –5)
   2's complement of 1001 (or – 5) = 0101 (or 5)

The importance of this lies in the fact that if you have to change the sign of a number, all that you need to do is to take the 2's complement of the number. Since logic circuits that can produce the 2's complement of a number are easy to design, arithmetic logic circuits can be easily implemented, as you will see later on in this chapter.

Another important point that emerges from this table is the limit on the maximum number of positive and negative integers that are possible in a word of a given size. This requires special attention in arithmetic operations, as logic systems are so designed that the size of the word is fixed. If the size of the numbers being processed exceeds the capability of the logic system, errors are bound to arise. Let us now consider the formulae from which you can determine the limits mentioned above.

Number of positive integers = $2^{B-1} - 1$
where B is the number of bits
Number of negative integers = 2^{B-1}
We will now consider what limits are imposed on words of various sizes.

4-Bit Word

No. of + ve integers = $2^{4-1} - 1$ = 7 : 0 to + 7 :
0000 to 0111

No. of – ve integers = 2^{4-1} = 8 : 0 to – 8
0000 to 1000

8-Bit Word

No. of + ve integers = $2^{8-1} - 1$ = 127 : 0 to + 127
0000 0000 to 0111 1111

No. of – ve integers = 2^{8-1} = 128 : 0 to – 128 :
0000 0000 to 1000 0000

There is another system of representing negative numbers which we have dealt with Sec. 1.10.2 and it is commonly knows as the 10's and 9's complement system. This system has also been found useful in binary arithmetic operations.

13.7 ARITHMETIC IN 2's COMPLEMENT REPRESENTATION

We will now consider some examples of additions and subtractions to illustrate the applications of 2's complement representation.

Addition

Example 13.5: *What decimal number does 1010 1001 represent?*

Solution: 2's complement of 1010 1001 = 0101 0111
= + 87

Therefore 1010 1001 = – 87

Example 13.6: *What decimal number does 1000 0001 represent?*

Solution: 2's complement of 1000 0001 = 0111 1111

= + 127

Therefore 1000 0001 = – 127

Example 13.7: *Add + 3 and + 4.*

Solution: Convert to 2's complement representation and add as follows:

3	:	0011		2's complement augend
+ 4	:	0100		2's complement addend
7	:	0111	= + 7	

Example 13.8: *Add – 3 and – 4.*

Solution: Convert to 2's complement representation and add as follows:

– 3	:	1101		2's complement augend
+ (–4)	:	+ 1100		2's complement addend
– 7	:	11001	= – 7	

Disregarding the overflow, 2's complement of 1001 is 0111, which is equal to + 7. The sum is therefore – 7, which tallies with the result. The overflow can be disregarded as – 7, is in the range of 4- bit 2's complement convention.

Example 13.9: *Add + 57 and + 45.*

Solution: Convert to 2's complement representation and add as follows:

57	:	0011 1001		2's complement augend
+ 45	:	+ 0010 1101		2's complement addend
102	:	0110 0110	= + 102	

Example 13.10: *Add – 93 and – 25.*

Solution: Convert to 2's complement representation and add as follows:

– 93	:	1010 0011	2's complement augend
+ (–25)	:	+ 1110 0111	2's complement addend
– 118	:	1 1000 1010	

We can disregard the overflow as in Ex 13. 4 and take the 2's complement of 1000 1010, which is equal to decimal – 118. It tallies with the result as it is within the range of 8-bit arithmetic.

Example 13.11: *Add + 127 and – 50.*

Solution: Convert to 2's complement representation and add as follows:

+ 127	:	0111 1111	2's complement augend
+ (–50)	:	+ 1100 1110	2's complement addend
77	:	1 0100 1101	

Disregarding the overflow, 0100 1101 is equal to + 77 which tallies with the decimal addition.

Example 13.12: *Add + 27 and – 128.*

Solution: Convert to 2's complement representation and add as follows:

+27	:	0001 1011	2's complement augend
+ (–128)	:	+ 1000 0000	2's complement addend
–101	:	1001 1011 = –101	

2's complement of 1001 1011 is equal to – 101, which tallies with the decimal addition.

Example 13.13: *Add + 6 and + 5 in 4- bit arithmetic.*

Solution:

6	:	0110	2's complement augend
+5	:	+ 0101	2's complement addend
11	:	1011 = –5	

The result is – 5 although it should have been + 11. This is because the maximum number that can be represented in 2's complement convention is + 7. Therefore an error has occured.

Example 13.14: *Add – 7 and – 5.*

Solution: Convert to 2's complement representation and add as follows:

–7	:	1001	2's complement augend
+(– 5)	:	+ 1011	2's complement addend
– 12	:	1 0100	

We have to disregard the overflow of 1 as it is lost in 4-bit arithmetic. The remaining number 0100 is equal to + 4. Since 4-bit arithmetic cannot accommodate – 12, an error has occurred. Let us do the same calculation in 8-bit arithmetic and see what happens.

–7	:	1111 1001	2's complement augend
+(– 5)	:	+ 1111 1011	2's complement addend
– 12	:	1 1111 0100	

The overflow is ignored, as it is of no consequence in 8-bit arithmetic. 2's complement of 1111 0100 is equal to = + 12 and therefore 1111 0100 is equal to – 12, which agress with the result.

Example 13.15: *Add + 100 and + 30.*

Solution:

100	:	0110 0100	2's complement augend
+30	:	0001 1110	2's complement addend
130	:	1000 1110	

The sign bit is negative, although it should have been positive as two positive numbers have been added. The answer is wrong, because the decimal number 130 lies outside the range of 8-bit arithmetic.

Example 13.16: *Add – 87 and – 65.*

Solution:

–87	:	1010 1001	2's complement augend
+(–65)	:	1011 1111	2's complement addend
–152	:	0110 1000	

The sign bit is positive, although it should have been negative as two negative numbers are being added. The answer is wrong as the decimal number – 152 lies outside the range of 8-bit arithmetic.

In Examples 13.3 and 13.6, which deal with additions of both positive and negative numbers, you will notice that it was possible to express the sum with not more than three digits for 4-bit arithmetic, and not more than seven digits for 8-bit arithmetic. Therefore, the answer always tallied with the decimal addition. In other words, as long as the sum is within the range from – 8 to + 7 for 4-bit arithmetic and from – 128 to + 127 for 8-bit arithmetic, the answer will always be correct.

You will also notice from Examples 13.7 and 13.8 that when positive and negative numbers are added, the sum is always less than the larger of the two numbers being added. Since in this situation overflow is impossible, the answer is always correct.

The following cases require careful consideration as they may present problems:

1. When it is not possible to express fully the value of a sum with only three digits in 4-bit arithmetic or, in other words, when the sum lies outside the range from – 8 to + 7, overflow will occur, which will result in errors as in Examples 13.9 and 13.10.
2. When it is not possible to express fully the value of a sum with only seven digits in the case of 8-bit arithmetic or, in other words, when the sum lies outside the range from – 128 to + 127, overflow will occur, which will result in errors as in Examples 13.11 and 13.12.

Subtractions

We will now consider some examples of subtractions to illustrate the application of 2's complement arithmetic. If you add a negative number to a positive number, it amounts to subtracting the negative number from the positive number. All subtractions in 2's complement arithmetic are therefore performed by adding the 2's complement of the number to be subtracted (subtrahend) to the positive number.

Example 13.17: *Subtract + 1 from + 7.*

Solution: Convert to 2's complement representation and add as follows:

7	:	0111
+(–1)	:	+1111
+6	:	10110

The overflow is disregarded in 4-bit arithmetic. Since the MSB in the result is 0 the answer is positive and it is + 6.

Example 13.18: *Subtract – 2 from + 4.*

Solution: Convert to 2's complement representation and add as follows:

$$\begin{array}{rl} 4: & 0100 \\ -(-2): & 0010 \\ \hline & 0110 \end{array}$$

Since the MSB is 0 the answer is positive and is + 6.

Example 13.19: *Subtract 3 from – 4.*

Solution: Convert to 2's complement representation and add as follows:

$$\begin{array}{rr} -4: & 1100 \\ -(+3): & 1101 \\ \hline & 1\ 1001 \end{array}$$

The carry from the MSB is to be ignored. Since the MSB in the result is 1, the answer is negative and is in the 2's complement form. Two's complement of 1001 is 0111. The answer is, therefore, – 7.

Example 13.20: *Subtract – 1 from – 5.*

Solution: Convert to 2's complement representation and add as follows:

$$\begin{array}{rl} -5: & 1011 \\ -(-1): & 0001 \\ \hline & 1100 \end{array}$$

Since the MSB is 1, the answer is negative and is in the 2's complement form. Two's complement of 1100 is 0100. The answer is, therefore, – 4.

Example 13.21: *Subtract – 5 from – 6.*

Solution: Convert to 2's complement representation and add as follows:

$$\begin{array}{rl} 6: & 0110 \\ -(-5): & 0101 \\ \hline & 1011 \end{array}$$

In this case the answer is wrong as it is beyond the range of 4-bit arithmetic.

The correct solution for this problem can be obtained if we consider it in 8-bit arithmetic as follows:

$$\begin{array}{rl} 6: & 0000\ 0110 \\ -(-5): & 0000\ 0101 \\ \hline & 0000\ 1011 \end{array}$$

Since the MSB is 0 the answer is positive and it is 1011 or + 11.

Example 13.22: *Subtract + 67 from + 45.*

Solution: Convert to 2's complement representation and add as follows:

$$\begin{array}{rl} 45: & 0010\ 1101 \\ +(-67): & 1011\ 1101 \\ \hline & 1110\ 1010 \end{array}$$

Since the MSB is 1, the answer is in the negative and is the 2's complement of the sum which is 0001 0110 or – 22.

Example 13.23: *Subtract – 70 from – 45.*

Solution: Convert to 2's complement representation and add as follows:

$$\begin{array}{rl} -45: & 1101\ 0011 \\ +70: & 0100\ 0110 \\ \hline & 1\ 0001\ 1001 \end{array}$$

This overflow has to be disregarded in 8-bit arithmetic. Since the MSB of the sum is 0, the answer is positive and is equal to + 25.

From the above examples of subtractions which we have considered, the following conclusions are obvious.

- When the most significant bits generate a carry it has to be ignored.
- As a result of subtraction, if the MSB in the result is a '1' the answer is in the negative and is in the 2's complement form.
- The answer will be positive if the MSB in the result is a '0'.
- If the result of subtractions exceeds the limit of the 2's complement representation we are using, the result will be wrong. The range will be exceeded when the MSB of *A* and (–*B*) are of the same sign and the MSB of the result has the opposite sign.

13.8 ARITHMETIC CIRCUITS

Having considered arithmetic operation in 2's complement representation, we can turn our attention to arithmetic logic circuits capable of carrying out these operations. The problem will appear simple, if we break the operations into their constituent parts and then consider the design of building blocks for each individual operation. For instance, when we add two numbers and begin by adding the LSBs, initially there is no carry in to add and we need a circuit to add only two digits. A circuits which will do this is called a half-adder. As we proceed further in the addition process, we also have to add the carry in to the digits in the next column to the left, which means that we need a circuit which can add three digits at a time. A circuit which will do this is called a full-adder. Then there are some building blocks to implement subtractions. We will begin with the first building block called the half adder.

13.9 HALF-ADDER

We will have another look at the rules for binary addition, which you have already considered earlier in Section 1.3.4. For your convenience these rules are being reproduced here in Table

13.4. This table shows the sum and carry digits in the same column. In Table 13.5 the sum and carry digits have been shown in separate columns.

Table 13.4

Augend A		*Addend* B	*Sum* Σ
0	+	0	0
0	+	1	1
1	+	0	1
1	+	1	10 or 0; sum 1, carry

Table 13.5

Augend A		*Addend* B	*Sum* Σ	*Carry* C_o
0	+	0	0	0
0	+	1	1	0
1	+	0	1	0
1	+	1	0	1

We will now take up a very simple case of addition of two binary numbers merely to bring out some important points.

1 0 0 0 ← Carries

LSBs

X 1 1 0 0 ← A

X 1 0 1 0 ← B

0 1 1 0 Sum

You will notice that the digits in the two number being added follow the same order as digits *A* and *B* in Table 13.5. Since all additions and subtractions begin from the LSBs, that is the order we have to follow.

			Sum		Carry
Column 1	0 + 0	=	0	:	0
2	0 + 1	=	1	:	0
3	1 + 0	=	1	:	0
4	1 + 1	=	0	:	1

You will notice that there are no carries from the first three columns. There is a carry out from the fourth column, which is the carry in for the fifth column to the left. No digits have been shown in the fifth column.

You must have observed that when there is no carry in, as in the first four columns, only two digits are required to be added; but when there is a carry in, as in the fifth column, three digits are required to be added. For the present we will consider a circuit to add only two digits and later consider a circuit which will add two digits and a carry in. You will also realize that circuits should have two outputs, one to indicate the sum and the other to indicate the carry.

If the same two digits, *A* and *B*, as shown in Table 13.5, represent logic input for XOR and AND gates, the outputs will be as shown in Table 13.6. You will notice that XOR and AND gate outputs are the same as the sum and carry digits shown in Table 13.5.

Table 13.6

Input		*Output*	
A	*B*	*XOR gate*	*AND gate*
0	0	0	0
0	1	1	0
1	0	1	0
1	1	0	1

This leads to the inevitable conclusion that the sum of two binary digits can be represented by the output of an XOR gate and the carry output can be represented by the output of an AND gate. In short, if the same two inputs are applied to XOR and AND gates, the outputs of the XOR gate will represent the sum and the AND gate will represent the carry.

A circuit is shown in Fig. 13.3 (a) based on the above considerations,which will perform the functions required for adding two digits. The circuits is known as the half-adder and alongside is shown the block symbol for the half-adder in Fig. 13.3 (b).

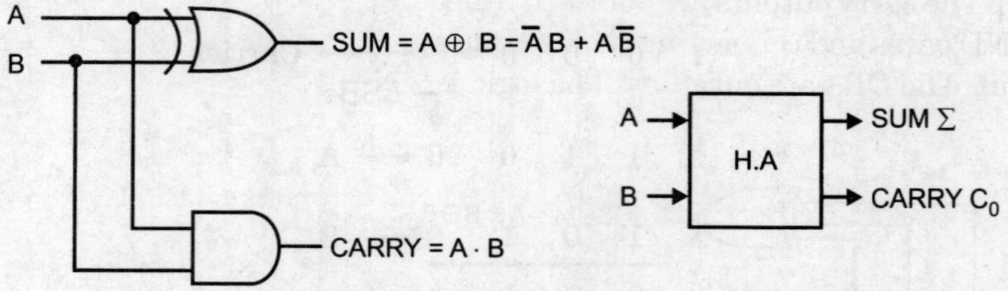

Fig. 13.3 (a) Half-adder(b) Block symbol for half adder

13.10 FULL-ADDER

A half-adder can add only two digits, while a full-adder should have provision for adding two digits plus a carry digit from a previous column. If you refer to the example of an addition in Section 13.7, you will notice that the fourth column had thrown up a carry which is required to be added to the other two digits of the fifth column. Even if there is no carry from a lower order column, which may happen in some cases, provision must exist in a full-adder for the addition of three digits.

Refer to Table 2.18, which is the truth table for a 3-input XOR gate. If you take the sum of the digits representing the input logic levels, you will find that the output column of this table truly represents the sum of the digits; but it does not represent the carry. Therefore, the sum of three digits, except the carry, can be represented by the output of a 3-input XOR gate. This has been shown in Table 13.7.

Table 13.7

S.No.	*Input*					*Output*	
	A		*B*		*C*	*XOR gate (Sum)*	*Carry out* C_o
1	0	+	0	+	0	0	0
2	0	+	0	+	1	1	0
3	0	+	1	+	0	1	0
4	0	+	1	+	1	0	1
5	1	+	0	+	0	1	0
6	1	+	0	+	1	0	1
7	1	+	1	+	0	0	1
8	1	+	1	+	1	1	1

It will appear from this table that if the digits to be added are taken to represent logic level inputs to a 3-input XOR gate, its output will represent the sum; but it will not represent the carry output. Both the sum and carry outputs can be realized by the full-adder circuit shown in Fig. 13.4(a). The carry outputs are obtained by feeding inputs *A* and *B*, *B* and *C*, *A* and *C* to three 2-inputs AND gates and connecting their outputs to a 3-input OR gate, which gives the required carry output. The OR gate output will be logic 1, whenever the output of any of the AND gates is logic 1.

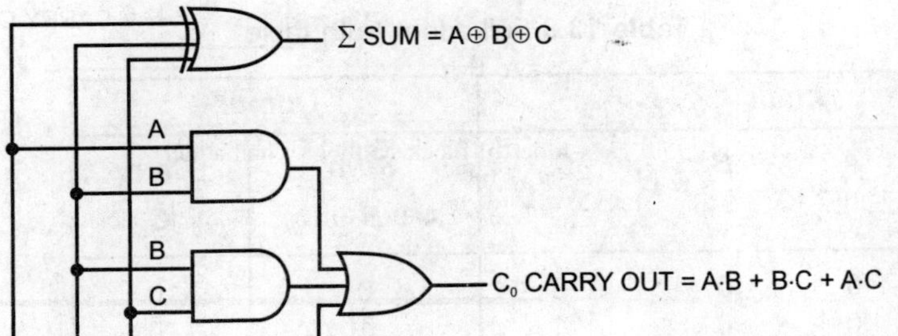

Fig. 13.4 (a) Full-adder

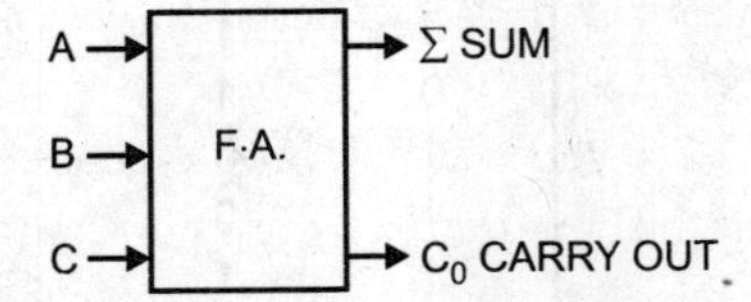

Fig. 13.4 (b) Full-adder symbol

The full-adder circuit can also be implemented by combining two half-adders as in Figs. 13.5 (a) and (b). Table 13.8 is the truth table for this full-adder circuit.

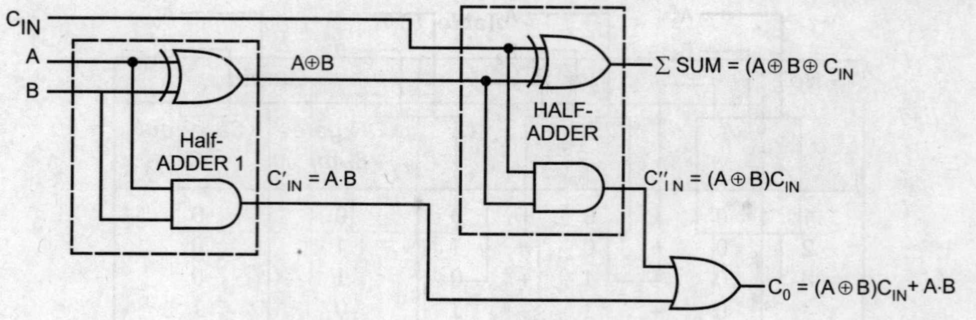

Fig. 13.5 (a) Logic diagram for full-adder

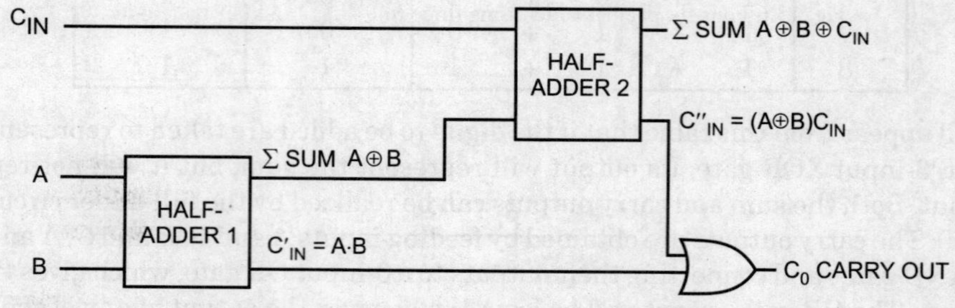

Fig. 13.5 (b) Full-Adder made from two half-adders and an OR gate (block diagram)

Table 13.8 Full-adder truth table

Input			***Output***	
A	***B***	C_{IN}	***Sum*** $A \oplus B \oplus C_{IN}$	***Carry*** C_0
0	0	0	0	0
0	0	1	1	0
0	1	0	1	0
0	1	1	0	1
1	0	0	1	0
1	0	1	1	0
1	1	0	0	1
1	1	1	1	1

13.10.1 Four-bit Adder

A four-bit adder can be built by combining three full-adders and a half-adder as shown in Fig. 13.6. This adder can add two 4-bit numbers. The addition sequence is as follows:

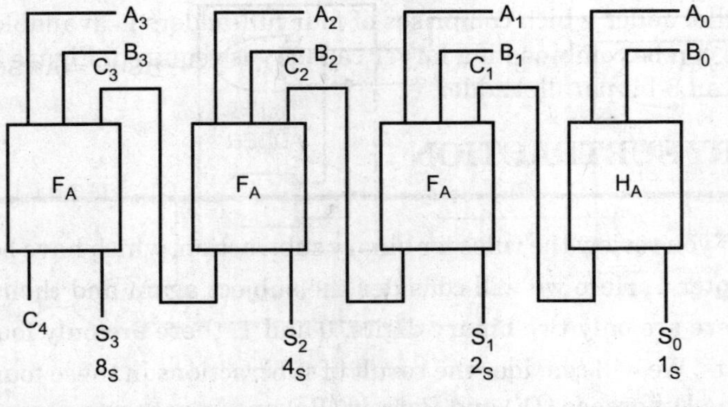

Fig. 13.6 Four-bit parallel adder using three full-adders and one half-adder

C_4	C_3	C_2	C_1	C_0	Carries
	A_3	A_2	A_1	A_0	
	B_3	B_2	B_1	B_0	
	S_3	S_2	S_1	S_0	Sum

The carry output of each adder goes to the carry input of the next adder to the left. There is no carry in for the first adder, as in this adder only two LSBs are being added. The addition of these two digits produces a sum S_0 and a carry out of C_1. The second adder will add digits A_1 and B_1 and carry out C_1 producing a sum S_1 and a carry out C_2. The third adder adds A_2, B_2 and C_2 producing a sum S_2 and a carry out C_3. In the last adder the addition of A_3, B_3 and C_3 produces a sum S_3 and a carry out of C_4. In 4- bit arithmetic, carry C_4 will be lost. In a similar manner 8-bit and 16-bit adders can be built.

In making a full adder shown in Fig. 13.6 we have used three full-adders and a half-adder. From the point of view of standardization of circuitry, it is more logical and convenient to use building blocks of the same logic design Fig. 13.7 shows a 4-bit adder implemented with four full-adders. In this configuration, the first full-adder functions as a half-adder as its carry input is held at logic 0 level.

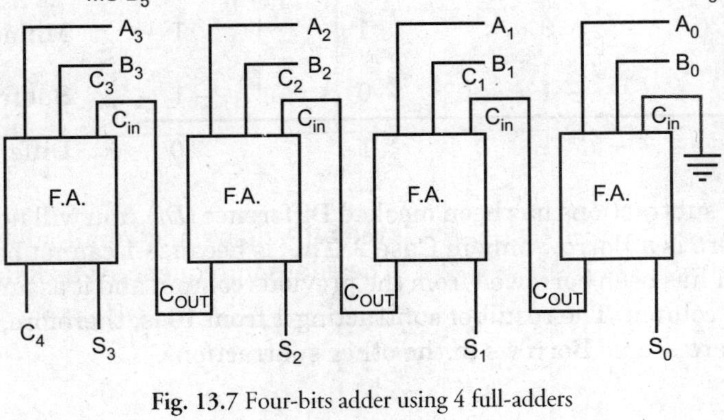

Fig. 13.7 Four-bits adder using 4 full-adders

A 4-bit parallel adder which comprises of four full-adders is available as IC 7483. Two or more of these ICs can be combined if a larger capacity is required. Figure 13.8 shows two such ICs used to make an 8-bit parallel adder.

13.11 BINARY SUBTRACTION

It will be helpful if you review the rules for binary subtraction, which have been dealt with in the Sec. 1.3.3 of Chapter 1. Here we will consider the subject again and their application to logic circuits. Since there are only two binary digits, 0 and 1, there are only four possible combinations of these digits. We will consider the result of subtractions in these four cases. Pay particular attention to the Difference (*Di*) and Borrow (*Bo*) and how they are generated as we will be dealing with these in greater detail later.

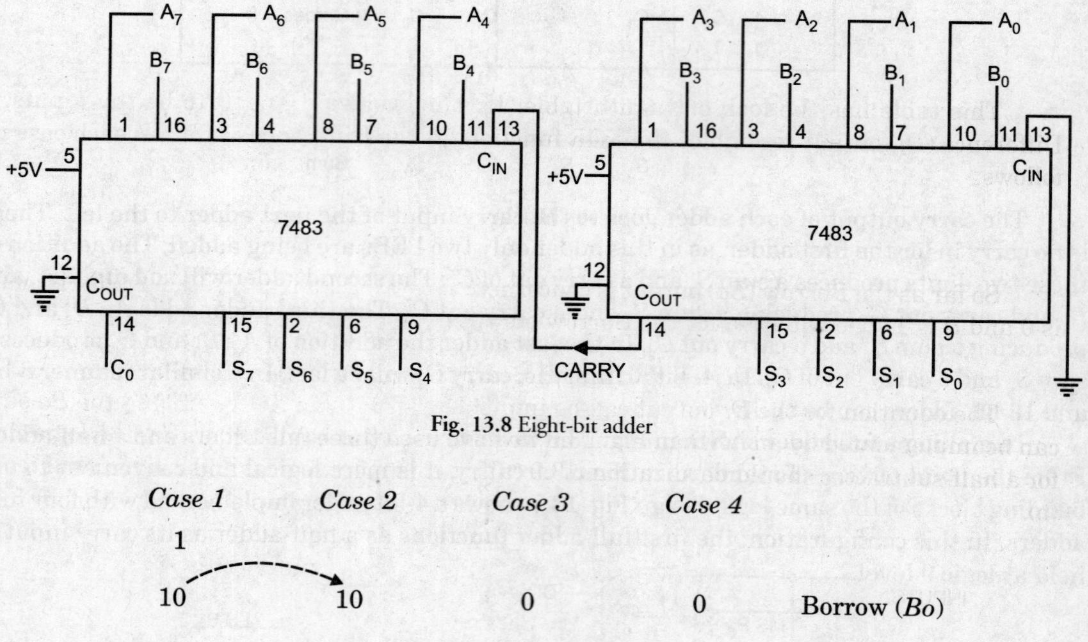

Fig. 13.8 Eight-bit adder

Case 1	*Case 2*	*Case 3*	*Case 4*	
1				
10	10	0	0	Borrow (*Bo*)
0	0	1	1	Minuend
– 0	– 1	– 0	– 1	Subtrahend
0	1	1	0	Difference (*Di*)

The result of subtractions has been marked Difference (*Di*). You will notice from the above examples that there is a Borrow only in Case 2. This is because 1 cannot be subtracted from 0 and that is why a 1 has been borrowed from the previous column and it assumes the value 10 (or decimal 2) in that column. The result of subtracting 1 from 10 is, therefore, 1, but there is also a Borrow of 1. There are no Borrows in the other subtractions.

13.12 HALF-SUBTRACTER

The four cases of binary subtraction which we have just considered lay down the ground rules for binary subtraction and have been summarised in Table 13.9.

Table 13.9

Inputs		*Outputs*	
Minuend	*Subtrabend*	*Difference*	*Borrow*
A	*B*	*Di*	*Bo*
0	0	0	0
0	1	1	1
1	0	1	0
1	1	0	0

This table has the look of a truth table. If you consider *A* and *B* to be the inputs, the Difference (*Di*) output resembles the XOR function, as the Difference output in each case is as follows:

$$Di = A \cdot \overline{B} + \overline{A} \cdot B = A \oplus B$$

So far as the Borrow (*Bo*) output is concerned, Borrow is 1 only in one case, that is when *A* is 0 and *B* is 1. The equation for the Borrow output is, therefore as follows:

$$Bo = \overline{A} \cdot B$$

The equation for the *Di* output can be implemented with an XOR gate and the *Bo* output can be implemented by an AND gate and an inverter. On these considerations, the logic circuit for a half-subtracter should be as in Fig. 13.9 (a). The logic symbol for this is given in Fig. 13.9 (b).

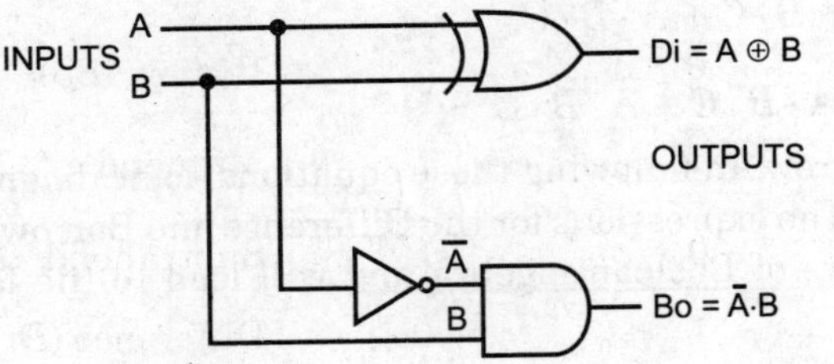

Fig. 13.9 (a) Half-subtracter

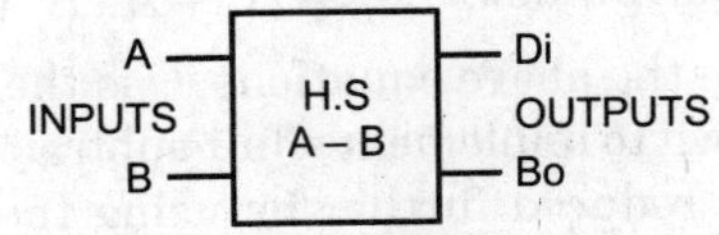

Fig. 13.9 (b) Logic symbol

13.13 FULL-SUBTRACTER

In a full-adder we have to take into account inputs *A* and *B* and the carry in. Similarly, in a full-subtracter we will require a logic circuit which will take into account the Minuend *A*, Subtrahend *B* and generate the Difference and the Borrow outputs. Therefore, we need a logic circuit with three inputs and two outputs. The first step is to draw up a truth table to conform to our rules of subtraction, taking into account all the inputs. We will now draw up a truth table based on the following sequence of subtraction:

Table 13.10 *A* – *B* – Borrow In

Input			Output	
A	***B***	***Borrow In***	***Difference***	***Borrow Out***
0	0	0	0	0
0	0	1	1	1
0	1	0	1	1
0	1	1	0	1
1	0	0	1	0
1	0	1	0	0
1	1	0	0	0
1	1	1	1	1

The correctness of the truth table for a full-subtracter given in Table 13.10 can be verified by applying the rules for binary subtraction. In order that you may understand how this can be done, we will consider row 2 of the table.

$A = 0$

$B = 0$

Difference $= 0$

Borrow in $= 1$

Difference $= 1$ Borrow Out $= 1$

The result is the same as given in the table.

The equations required for the Difference and Borrow outputs can be derived from Table 13.10 and are as follows:

Difference : $\overline{A} \cdot \overline{B} \cdot C + \overline{A} \cdot B \cdot \overline{C} + A \cdot \overline{B} \cdot \overline{C} + A \cdot B \cdot C$

Borrow out $= \overline{A} \cdot \overline{B} \cdot C + \overline{A} \cdot B \cdot \overline{C} + A \cdot B \cdot C + \overline{A} \cdot B \cdot C$

In the above equations, *C* is the Borrow. In following these equations, logic diagrams can be drawn to implement a full-subtracter. The expressions for the Difference and Borrow outputs can be reduced further by using the laws of Boolean algebra and will lead to the following simplified expressions:

Difference $= \overline{C}\,(\overline{A} \cdot B + A \cdot \overline{B}) + C\,\overline{(\overline{A} \cdot B + A \cdot \overline{B})}$

Borrow out $= \overline{A} \cdot B + C\,\overline{(\overline{A} \cdot B + A \cdot \overline{B})}$

The expression $(\overline{A} \cdot B + A \cdot \overline{B})$ represents the outputs of an XOR gate. If this is expressed by *D*, the expression for the Difference take the following form:

Difference $= \overline{C} \cdot D + C \cdot \overline{D}$

This expression again represents the output of an XOR gate. It, therefore, follows that the inputs of the 1st half-subtracter will be A and B and the inputs of the 2nd half-subtracter will be C (Borrow In) and $(\overline{A} \cdot B + A \cdot \overline{B})$. The output of the 2nd half-subtracter will represent the Difference output of the full-subtracter.

So far as the Borrow Out output is concerned, the expression $\overline{A} \cdot B$ resembles the Borrow output of a half-subtracter and the second term is the inverted Difference output of the 1st XOR gate.

So far as the borrow Out output is concerned, it represents the output of ORing two inputs. One of the inputs, that is $\overline{A} \cdot B$ resembles the Borrow output of a half-subtracter and the other input to the OR gate is the result of ANDing the Borrow In input C and the inverted Difference output of the 1st XOR gate.

Based on this analysis, a logic diagram for the full-subtracter is shown in Fig. 13.10. Full-subtracter using logic symbols is shown in Fig. 13.11. Logic symbol of full-subtracter is shown in Fig. 13.12.

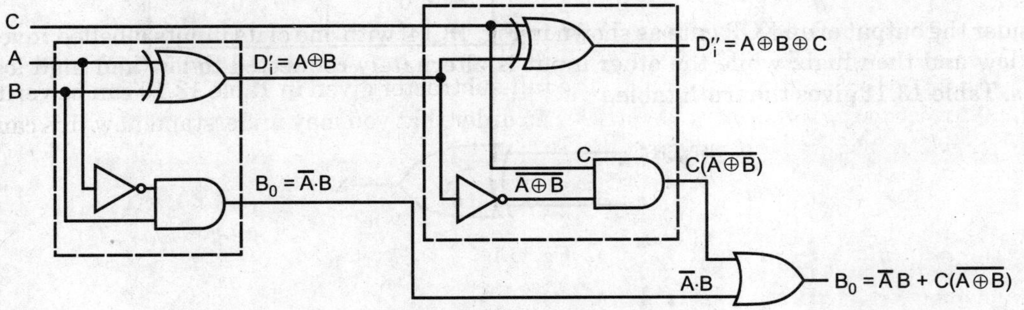

Fig. 13.10 Full subtracter logic diagram

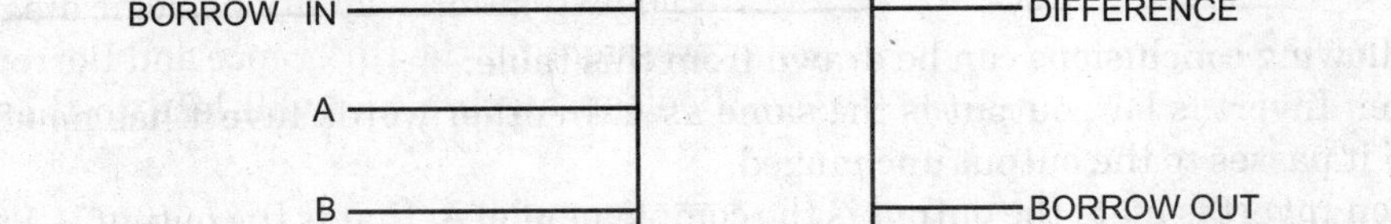

Fig 13.11 Full-subtracter using logic symbols

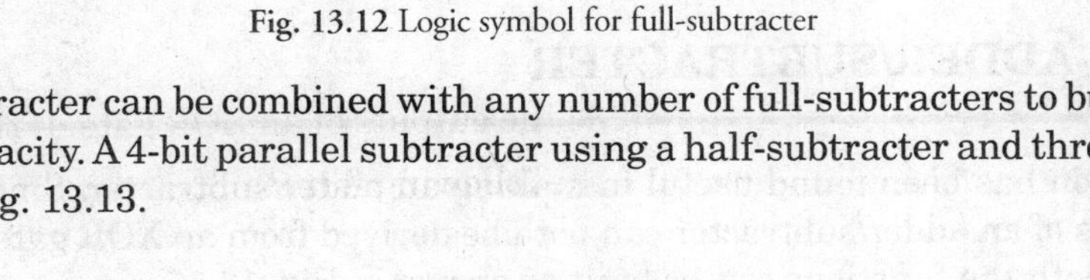

Fig. 13.12 Logic symbol for full-subtracter

A half-subtracter can be combined with any number of full-subtracters to build subtracters with a larger capacity. A 4-bit parallel subtracter using a half-subtracter and three full-subtracters is given in Fig. 13.13.

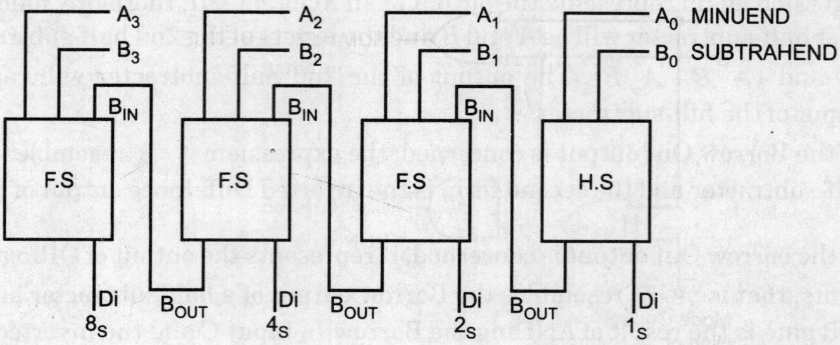

Fig. 13.13 Four-bit parallel subtracter

13.14 CONTROLLED INVERTER

Consider the output of an XOR gate as shown in Fig. 13.14, with one of its inputs labelled Invert, held low and then high, while the other input is alternately connected to low and high logic levels. Table 13.11 gives the truth table.

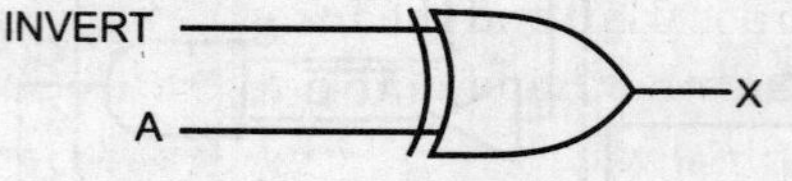

Fig. 13.14

Table 13.11

Input		*Output*	*Comment*
A	*Invert*	*X*	
0	0	0	Output same as A
1	0	1	
0	1	1	Output is the complement of A
1	1	0	

The following conclusions can be drawn from this table:

1. When Invert is low, output is the same as *A*. In other words Invert has no effect on *A* and it passes to the output unchanged.
2. When Invert is high, the output is the complement of *A*, that is the output is 1's complement of the input *A*.

13.15 HALF-ADDER/SUBTRACTER

The invert function has been found useful in making an adder/subtracter. Since the sum and difference outputs of an adder/subtracter can both be derived from an XOR gate, a logic circuit which combines both the functions can be built as shown in Fig. 13.15.

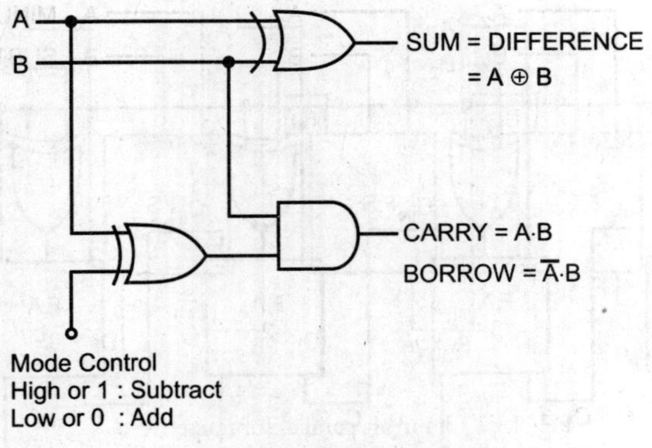

Fig. 13.15 Half-adder/subtracter

13.16 2's COMPLEMENT ADDER/SUBTRACTER

If we connect four XOR gates as shown in Fig. 13.16, the 4-bit output word will be bit-for-bit complement of the input word. All the four invert inputs are connected together and are held high. For instance if the input word is 0110 and the invert is high, the output word will be 1001, which is its 1's complement. On the other hand, if the invert is low, the output will be the same as the input word, that is 0110.

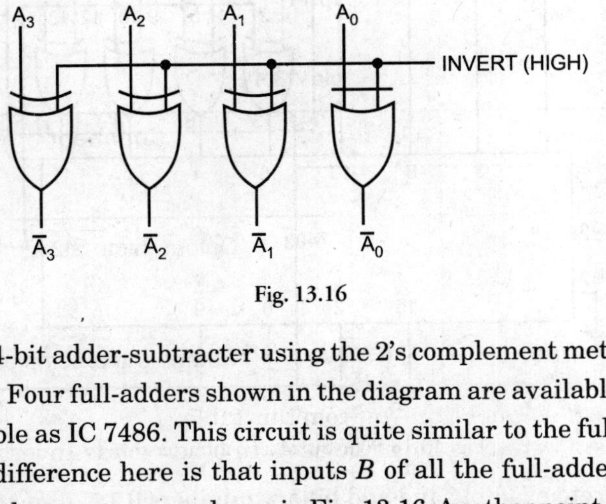

Fig. 13.16

A diagram for a 4-bit adder-subtracter using the 2's complement method of representation is shown in Fig. 13.17. Four full-adders shown in the diagram are available as IC 7483, and four XOR gates are available as IC 7486. This circuit is quite similar to the full-adder shown in Fig. 13.7. The important difference here is that inputs *B* of all the full-adders are connected to a controlled inverter, in the same way as shown in Fig. 13.16. Another point worth nothing is that, the invert input of the XOR gates, which are connected together, are also connected to the carry in input of the first full-adder. The reason for this will be explained shortly.

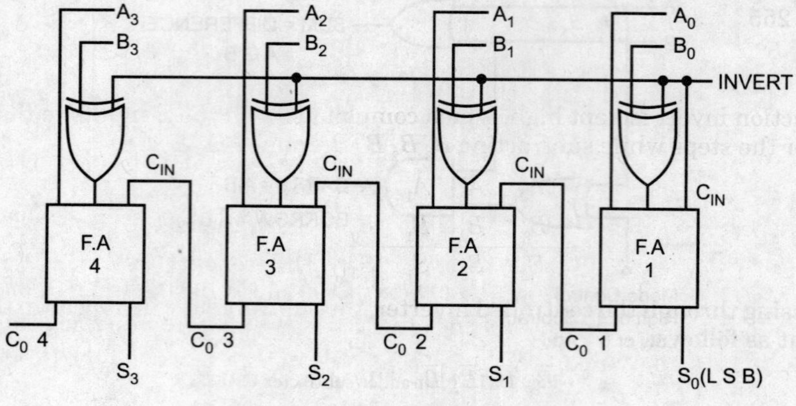

Fig. 13.17 Four-bit adder/subtracter

A 4-bit adder/subtracter using ICs 7483 and 7486 is shown in Fig. 13.18.

Addition

When addition is carried out the invert is kept low, so that bits $B_3B_2B_1B_0$ pass on to the full-adder without any change and take part in the addition process in the normal way. The four bits are added up as follows:

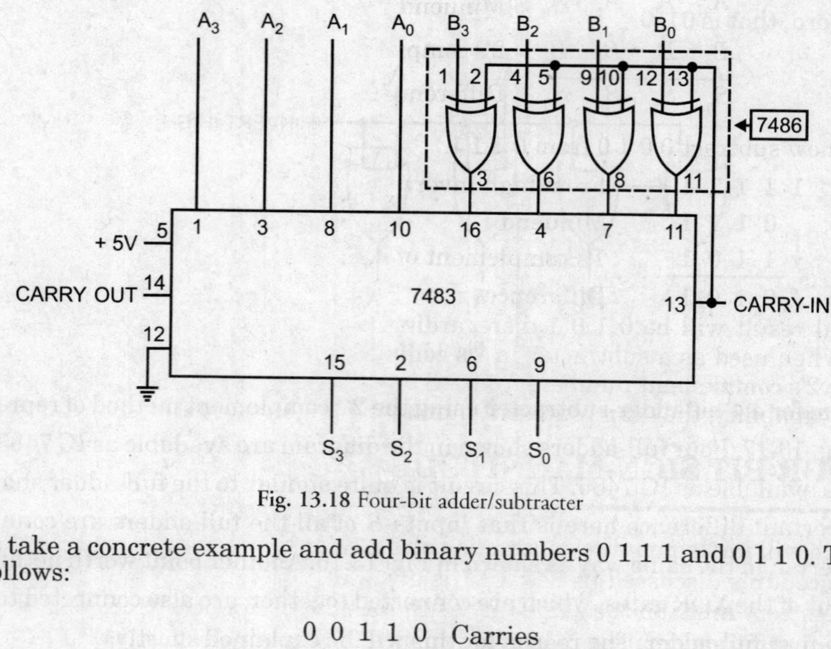

Fig. 13.18 Four-bit adder/subtracter

Let us take a concrete example and add binary numbers 0 1 1 1 and 0 1 1 0. The addition will be as follows:

$$
\begin{array}{ll}
0\ 0\ 1\ 1\ 0 & \text{Carries} \\
\ \ 0\ 1\ 1\ 1 & A_3\ A_2\ A_1\ A_0 \\
\ \ \underline{0\ 1\ 1\ 0} & B_3\ B_2\ B_1\ B_0 \\
\ \ 1\ 1\ 0\ 1 & \text{Sum}
\end{array}
$$

When the 4-bit adder-subtracter is used for carrying out additions, it can add unsigned binary numbers and the output can accommodate unsigned numbers from 0 to 15 only. If two such adders are in tandem, the adder will acquire 8-bit capability and represent unsigned numbers from 0 to 255.

Subtraction

During subtraction invert is kept high, which complements all the *B* inputs to the full-adders. Let us consider the steps while subtracting $B_3\ B_2\ B_1\ B_0$ from $A_3\ A_2\ A_1\ A_0$.

$$\begin{array}{rcccl} & A_3 & A_2 & A_1 & A_0 \quad \text{Minuend} \\ - & B_3 & B_2 & B_1 & B_0 \quad \text{Subtrahend} \\ \hline & S_3 & S_2 & S_1 & S_0 \quad \text{Difference} \end{array}$$

After passing through the controlled inverter, the subtrahend will appear in the form of its 1's complement as follows:

$$\overline{B}_3\ \overline{B}_2\ \overline{B}_1\ \overline{B}_0 \quad \text{1's complement}$$

High invert will now add 1 to the 1's complement of the Subtrahend as follows:

$$\begin{array}{cccccl} & & & & 1 & \text{From high invert} \\ & \overline{B}_3 & \overline{B}_2 & \overline{B}_1 & \overline{B}_0 & \text{1's complement of } B_3\ B_2\ B_1\ B_0 \\ \hline & \hat{B}_3 & \hat{B}_2 & \hat{B}_1 & \hat{B}_0 & \text{2's complement of } B_3\ B_2\ B_1\ B_0 \end{array}$$

Subtraction is carried out by adding $\hat{B}_3\ \hat{B}_2\ \hat{B}_1\ \hat{B}_0$ to the Minuend $A_3\ A_2\ A_1\ A_0$ as follows:

$$\begin{array}{ccccl} A_3 & A_2 & A_1 & A_0 & \text{Minuend} \\ \hat{B}_3 & \hat{B}_2 & \hat{B}_1 & \hat{B}_0 & \text{2's complement of } B_3\ B_2\ B_1\ B_0 \\ \hline S_3 & S_2 & S_1 & S_0 & \text{Difference} \end{array}$$

We can now subtract 0 0 1 0 from 0 1 1 1.

```
Carries   1 1 1 1 1 ←—— From high invert
            0 1 1 1     Minuend
          ↓ 1 1 0 1     1's complement of subtrahend
          ---------
          1 0 1 0 1     Difference
```

The final result will be 0 1 0 1 disregarding the carry of 1, which will be lost in 4-bit arithmetic. When used as a subtracter in 2's complement representation, the 4-bit adder can accommodate 2's complement numbers from – 8 to + 7. When two such 4-bit adders are used to acquire 8-bit capability, they can represent numbers in 2's complement from – 128 to + 127.

13.17 FOUR-BIT SIGN-MAGNITUDE BINARY SUBTRACTER

A circuit which will implement the subtraction of 4-bit sign-magnitude binary numbers according to the procedures discussed in Sec. 13.7 is given in Fig. 13.19. With minor changes, this circuit operates very much in the same way as the 4-bit adder-subtracter shown in Fig. 13.18. The 4-bit sign-magnitude binary numbers are applied at inputs *A* and *B* of IC1 and the difference of the two numbers is obtained at outputs S'_3, S'_2, S'_1 and S'_0 of IC2. Output S'_3 also serves as input to IC4 and as the sign bit of the final output. If S'_3 is a 1, IC3 and IC4 again generate the 2's complement of the output of IC2 and the final output magnitude is obtained at $S_2\ S_1$ and S_0. If S'_3 is a 0, the output of IC2 remains unchanged, as it should, and appears at the final output. The final output gives the sign and the magnitude of the result of subtraction.

13.18 ONE DIGIT BCD ADDER

We have discussed the rules for BCD addition in Section 1.4.2 which you may review before considering the one-digit adder circuit given here in Fig. 13.20. The two BCD inputs to be added are applied at inputs *A* and *B* of IC1, which is a binary adder. The sum output of IC1 is passed on to the *B* inputs of IC2. The carry output and the sum outputs S_1, S_2 and S_3 are connected through an inverter and two NAND gates to a 3-input NAND gate 3. In this arrangement of the circuit, if the addition of the four digits results in a carry out of 1, or if the result of addition produces an illegal code at the output of IC1, the output of NAND gate 3 goes high. The results in the addition of 0 1 1 0 (6) to the *B* input of IC2. The output of IC2 thus gives the correct result of 1's digit. The output of NAND gate 3 constitutes part of the 10's digit.

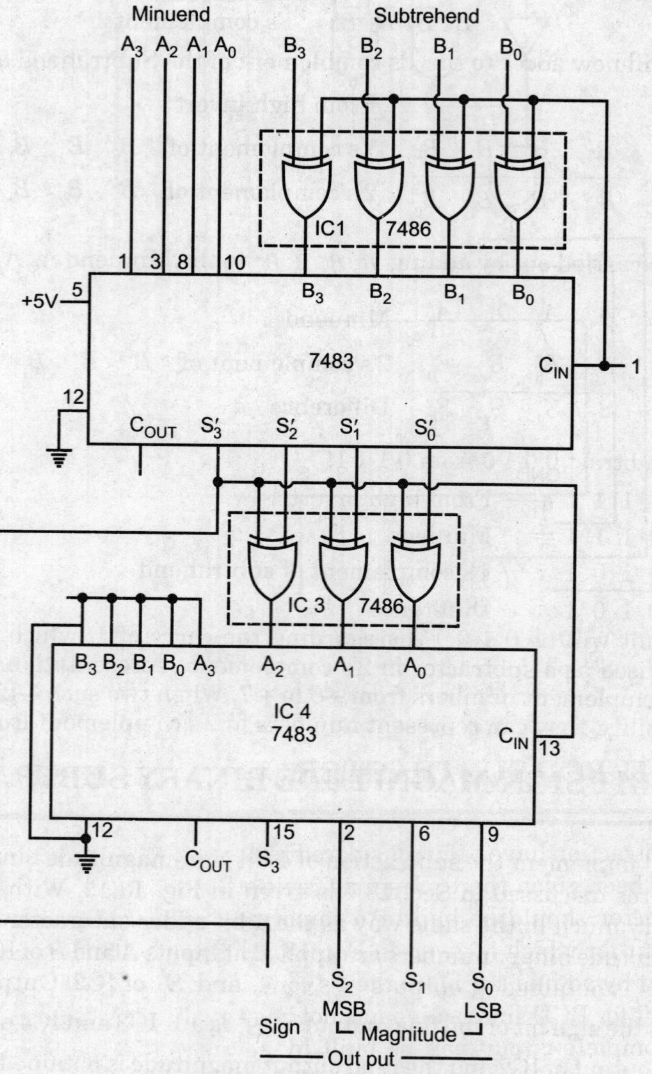

Fig. 13.19 4-bit sign-magnitude binary subtracter

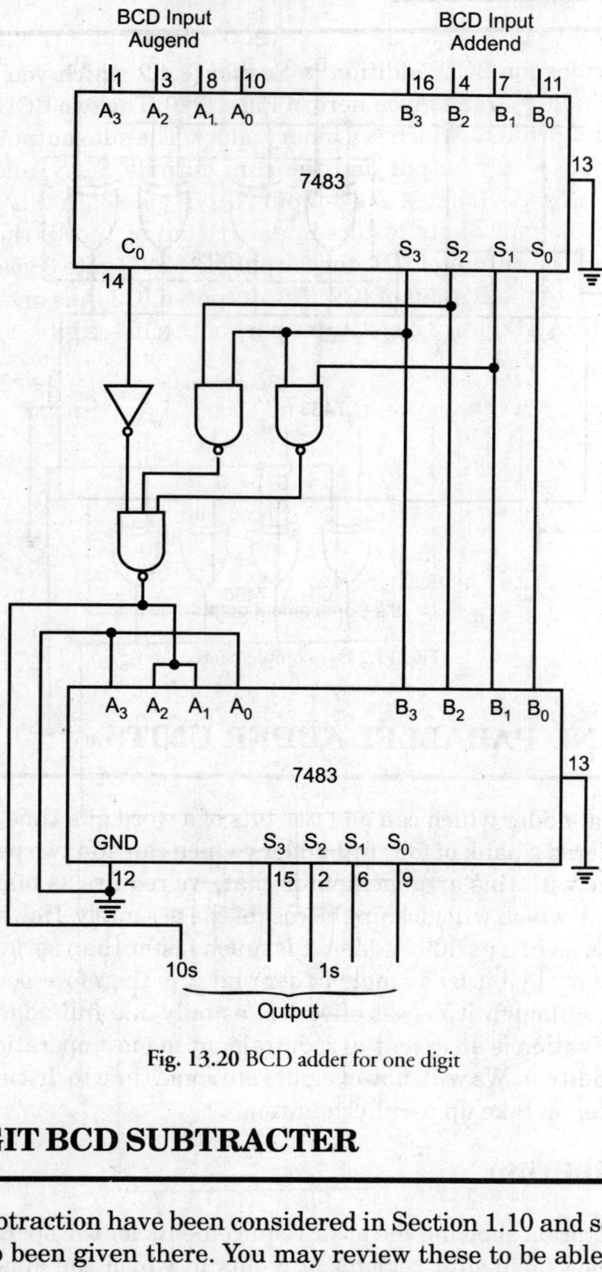

Fig. 13.20 BCD adder for one digit

13.19 ONE DIGIT BCD SUBTRACTER

The rules for BCD subtraction have been considered in Section 1.10 and some examples of BCD subtraction have also been given there. You may review these to be able to understand how a one-digit BCD subtracter should be built. An important part of this circuit would be a 9's complementer, a circuit for which is given in Fig. 13.21. This circuit produces the 9's complement of the BCD input by adding 1 0 1 0 to the 1's complement of the BCD input.

A complete circuit for BCD subtraction has not been given and has been left as an exercise for the students. A complete circuit can be built by adding on to the 9's complementer, the necessary circuit to implement the various stages of the subtraction process given in Examples 1.54, 1.55 and 1.56.

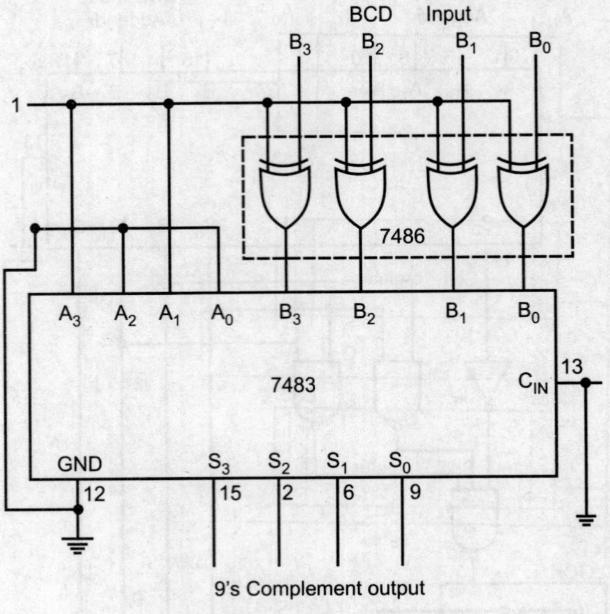

Fig. 13.21 9's complementer

13.20 SERIAL AND PARALLEL ADDER UNITS

We have discussed a full-adder which can add two bits of a word at a time, as well as the carry-in. We have also considered a bank of four full-adders which can add two parallel words of 4-bits each. The disadvantage with this arrangement is that, we require as many full-adders as the number of bits in a word, which will jack up the cost of the assembly. However, if all the bits are added at the same time, as in a parallel adder, it is much faster than serial addition. In a serial adder, addition is done bit-by-bit by a single adder and it is therefore bound to take longer to carry out an addition, although it is cost effective, as only one full-adder is required in this process. As speed of operation is an essential requirement in most operations, parallel addition is preferred to serial addition. We will, however, devote some time to discuss the serial addition technique and then later on take up parallel addition.

13.20.1 Serial Addition

The set-up for serial addition showing the basic requirements for the operation is shown in Fig. 13.22. The diagram shows one shift register of N-bits in which the augend is loaded from a register; another shift register of N-bits in which the addend is loaded and a shift register of $N + 1$ bits, into which the sum of each operation is transferred. When clock pulses are applied, the shift registers shift data one bit position to the right on each clock pulse. The same clock pulse also triggers the D-type flip-flop, the D-input of which is connected to the carry output of a full-adder and its Q output is connected to the carry-in input of the full-adder. The data stored in the A and B shift registers go to the A and B inputs of the full-adder, LSBs moving out first.

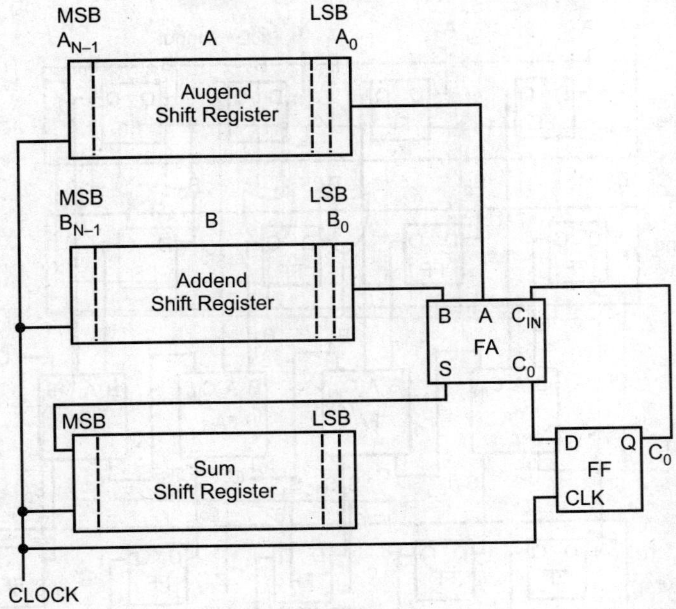

Fig. 13.22 Serial adder

The operation of the serial adder can be described as follows. To begin with the flip-flop is reset, so that at the commencement C_{in} is 0. Since the LSBs of the A and B registers are already connected to the full-adder, the sum output will be $S_0 = A_0 \oplus B_0$, which will constitute the input to the sum register and C_0 will be the input to the flip-flop. Now when a clock pulse is applied, S_0 will be shifted to the MSB position of the sum register: bits A_1 and B_1 will move into the full-adder and C_0 will move into the C_{in} position of the full-adder. The sum and carry outputs will now be S_1 and C_1. The second clock pulse will move S_1 to the MSB position of the sum register and bit S_0 will be shifted one bit position to the right and at the same time carry output C_1 will move into the full-adder. The sum and carry outputs of the full-adder will now be S_2 and C_2.

Subsequent clock pulse will continue to transfer the sum and carry outputs as before, until all the bits have been added. At that stage, registers A and B will be empty and the sum register will contain the sum of the augend and the addend. Notice that the sum register has one bit more than the A and B registers. The last carry will appear at the S output of the full-adder, which will be transferred into the sum register by the $(N + 1)$st clock pulse.

13.20.2 Parallel Addition

We have considered a 4-bit parallel adder in Section 13.10.1. It has been implemented with three full-adders and a half-adder. A more flexible arrangement is to use only full-adders, as that will make it possible to add on more full-adders when the words are longer than four bits in length. Since in parallel addition all orders of augend and addend are added simultaneously, they are faster than serial adders. The bare essentials of a parallel adder system are shown in Fig. 13.23.

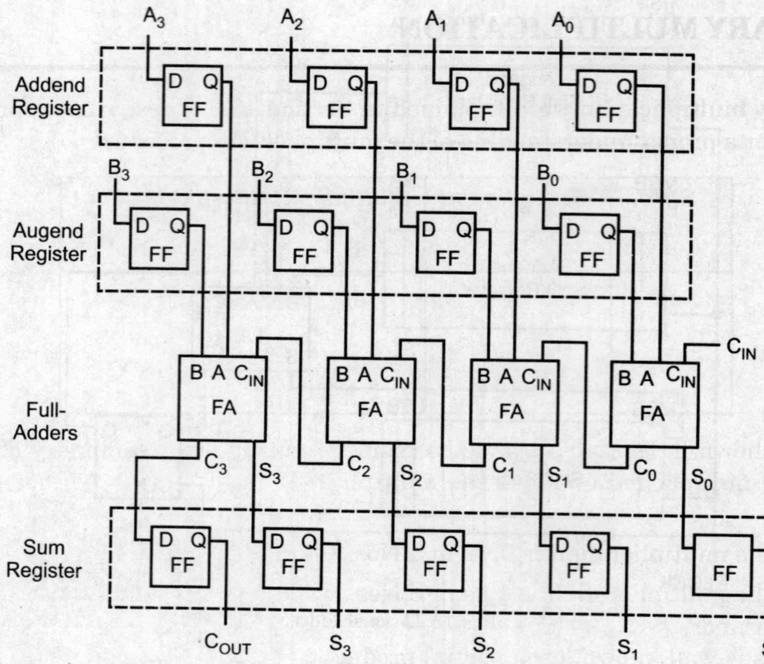

Fig. 13.23 Parallel adder configuration

To begin with, the addend, which is stored in a memory register, is transferred to an addend register, which consists of as many flip-flops as the number of digits in the addend. When a clock pulse is applied to the addend register after the memory register present the data input to the flip-flop inputs, the data appears at the outputs of the flip-flops.

Similarly the augend is also stored in a memory register and the data is transferred to the flip-flop output of the augend register, after the application of a clock pulse to the augend register. Unlike the serial adder, the addend and augend registers are storage registers and not shift registers. The data from the addend and augend registers is presented to the full-adders and their output is presented to the sum register, which is also a storage register and consists of the required number of flip-flops. On the application of a clock pulse to the sum register, the sum output appears at the output of the flip-flops.

Parallel adders suffer from speed limitation, since the carries generated have to travel to the last adder in some cases and the time taken in these cases will amount to the sum of propagation delay of the full-adders. Some fast adders incorporate circuits referred to as look-ahead carry, which use gates to look ahead for a carry, rather than wait for the carry to ripple through to all the adders.

The arrangement shown in Fig. 13.23 can also be used to add more than two numbers, if successive numbers are presented at the inputs of the addend register in synchronization with clock waveforms. The first clock transition will add the first number to the word in the augend register and the second clock transition will register this in the sum register and at the same time present the second number to the augend register. The procedure can be repeated until all the numbers have been added.

13.21 BINARY MULTIPLICATION

Rules for binary multiplication were explained in Section 13.3. These rules reproduced below are important for a proper understanding of the multiplication procedure.

S.No.	*Multiplicand* A	*Multiplier* B	*Partial product* A × B
1	0	0	0
2	0	1	0
3	1	0	0
4	1	1	1

We have shown in the table above the result of multiplying two binary digits *A* and *B*, where *A* is the multiplicand and *B* is the multiplier. The conclusions can be summed up as follows:

1. When the multiplier digit is 0, as in S.Nos. 1 and 3, the partial product is 0.
2. When the multiplier digit is 1 as in S.Nos. 2 and 4, the partial product is equal to the multiplicand.

Besides, as is well known, each partial product is shifted one step to the left to give due consideration for the differing numerical significance of each digit of the multiplier.

The sum of the partial products gives the result of multiplication. We will take up an example of multiplication and consider the application of these rules.

		1 1 1 0	Multiplicand
		1 0 1 0	Multiplier
		0 0 0 0 0	Partial product 1
Sum 1 + 2	1 1 1 0 0	1 1 1 0	Partial product 2
Sum 1 + 2 + 3	0 1 1 1 0 0	0 0 0 0	Partial product 3
		1 1 1 0	Partial product 4
Sum 1 + 2 + 3 + 4		1 0 0 0 1 1 0 0	Final product

Since the 1st and 3rd, digits in the multiplier are 0, partial products 1 and 3 are 0 0 0 0. As the 2nd, and 4th, digits of the multiplier are 1, partial products 2 and 4 are the same as the multiplicand. Also notice another important feature. Every successive partial product is shifted by one position to the left. You will notice that on the left hand side partial products 1 + 2 and 1 + 2 + 3 have been shown. In machine operation it is not necessary that addition should be done after all the partial products have been entered. As and when a partial product has been formed, the sum can be shown as has been done here. It is easier for logic circuits to add two binary numbers at a time, rather than all partial products in a single operation.

The same multiplication, which we have considered for manual operation has been rewritten here, which follows the add-and-shift method commonly used in machine operation (Fig. 13.24).

Multiplicand	1 1 1 0	
Multiplier	1 0 1 0	
1st partial product	0 0 0 0	Multiply 1 1 1 0 by 1's bit 0
	0 0 0 0 0	Shift left
2nd partial product	1 1 1 0 0	Multiply 1 1 1 0 by 2's bit 1
	1 1 1 0 0	Add 1st & 2nd partial products
	1 1 1 0 0 0	Shift left
3rd partial product	0 0 0 0 0 0	Multiply 1 1 1 0 by 4's bit 0
	1 1 1 0 0	Add 1st, 2nd and 3rd partial products
	1 1 1 0 0 0 0	Shift left
4th partial product	1 1 1 0 0 0 0	Multiply by 8's bit 1
	1 0 0 0 1 1 0 0	Add 1st, 2nd, 3rd and 4th partial products

Fig. 13.24

The multiplier shown in Fig. 13.25 is also based on the add-and-shift method used in the calculation given in Fig. 13.24. The multiplier shown in the diagram can multiply a 3-digit multiplicand by a 3-digit multiplier. To begin with, the multiplicand is loaded in FFs 1, 2 and 3, of the multiplicand shift register, the LSB occupying FF1. The multiplier is loaded in FFs 1, 2 and 3 of the multiplier shift register, the LSB being in FF1. Multiplication is accomplished by the AND gates and addition of the partial products is done by the six full-adders. The sum of all the partial products accumulates in the accumulator register.

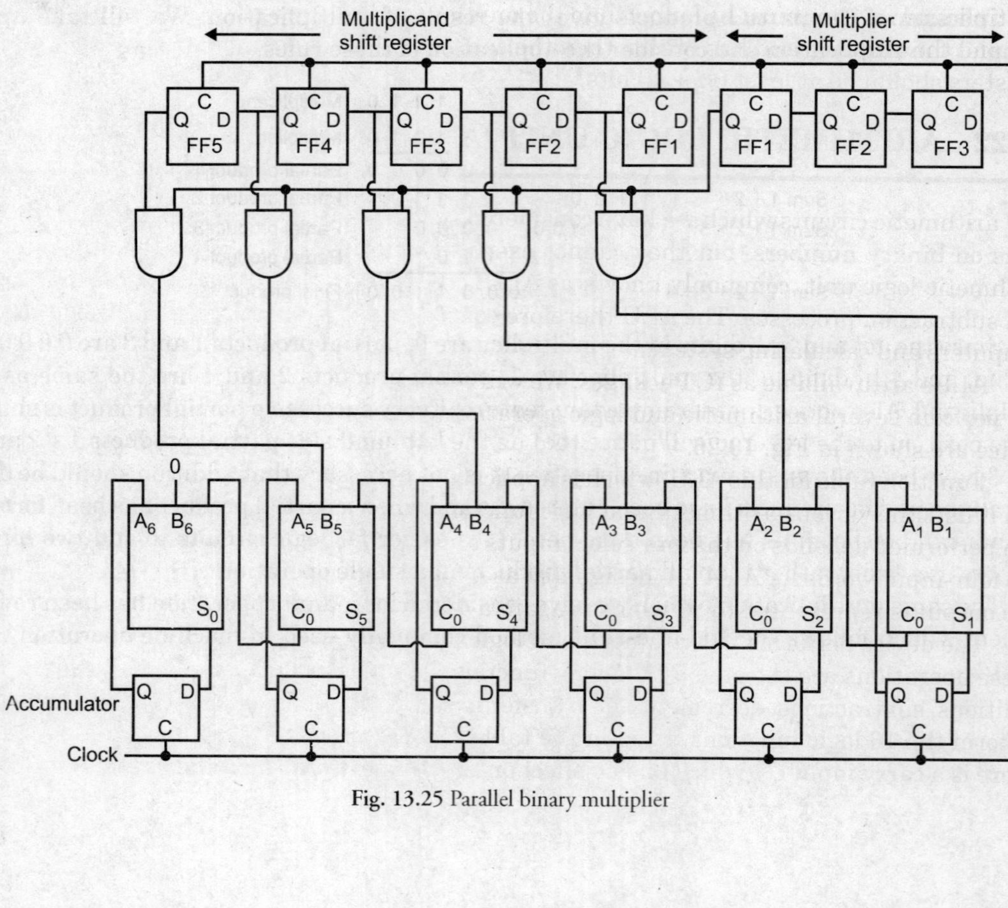

Fig. 13.25 Parallel binary multiplier

Before the application of any clock pulse, the following action takes place:

1. The multiplier bit in FF1 appears at the input of all the AND gates which copy the multiplicand bits in FFs 1, 2, and 3.
2. Consequently, the three bits of the multiplicand appear at the adder inputs B_3, B_2 and B_1.
3. Since initially the accumulator is cleared, adder inputs A_3, A_2 and A_1 will be 0. The adder output will appear at S_3, S_2 and S_1.

On the application of the first clock pulse, the following action will be initiated:

1. The partial product S_3, S_2, S_1 is registered in the accumulator FFs 3, 2 and 1, and subsequently it also appears at inputs A_3, A_2, A_1 of the full adders.
2. The multiplier bit in FF2 is shifted to FF1 of the multiplier register.
3. Each of the multiplicand digits in the multiplicand shift register is shifted one step to the left in this register.
4. Now the second multiplier digit multiplies the multiplicand digits in FFs 4, 3 and 2 and, as before, the second partial product appears at the adder inputs B_4, B_3 and B_2.
5. The sum of the first and second partial products will now appear at the adder outputs S_5, S_4, S_3, S_2 and S_1.

On the application of the second clock pulse, the same sequence of operations will follow. There will be in all three partial products, the sum of which will appear at the six adder outputs. When the third clock pulse is applied, the sum of all the partial products will be registered in the accumulator.

As in this multiplier set-up the multiplicand digits are required to be shifted left, the multiplicand register must be larger than the multiplicand number, that is if a multiplier has M bits and the multiplicand has N bits, then the capacity of the multiplicand, the adder and sum registers should be at least $(M + N)$ bits.

13.22 ARITHMETIC LOGIC UNIT (ALU)

The arithmetic circuits which we have considered so far can perform certain arithmetic operations on binary numbers, but they cannot execute logical operations. On the other hand an arithmetic logic unit, commonly known as ALU, can execute many variations of the addition and subtraction processes. The ALU therefore constitutes the central part of microprocessors, computers and calculating systems.

ALUs are available as IC Packages. We will consider a TTL ALU device 74AS181B, which can perform several arithmetic and logic operations. Pin connections for the N package of this device are shown in Fig. 13.26.

Function table for this ALU, which is applicable for active-high data is given in Table 13.12 and it lists the various arithmetic and logic functions which this device can perform. The function performed depends on the four select inputs and the mode input signal. This device accepts two four-input words A_3, A_2, A_1, A_0 designated as A in the table and B_3, B_2, B_1, B_0 designated as B. The output is represented by F, which is again a 4-bit word F_3, F_2, F_1, F_0.

The device performs 16 arithmetic and logic functions on two 4-bit binary words A and B. These operations are selected by the four-function select lines S_3, S_2, S_1, S_0 and can carry out additions, subtractions, decrement and transfer in the arithmetic mode. In the logic mode it can perform the 16 logic functions listed in the table, plus some more which have not been listed. There is a carry input C_n, which has no effect on the output word when the device is in the logic

mode. There is a mode control, which has to be low in the arithmetic mode and high in the logic mode. The select and the mode inputs determine the exact operations being performed.

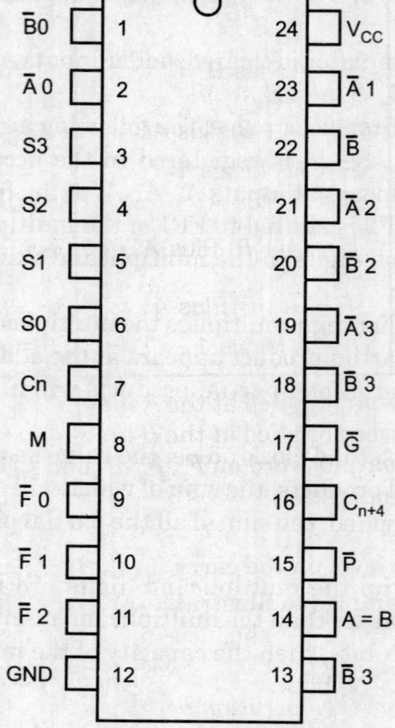

Fig. 13.26 Pin connections for ALU IC 74AS181B (N package)

Table 13.12

Select input	Logic functions $M = 1$	Active-high data: Arithmetic and logic functions $M = 0$, $C_N = 1$ (No carry)	Active-high data: Arithmetic and logic functions $M = 0$, $\overline{C_N} = 0$ (With carry)
S_3 S_2 S_1 S_0	F	F	F
0 0 0 0	$F = \bar{A}$	$F = A$	$F = A$ Plus 1
0 0 0 1	$F = \overline{A + B}$	$F = A + B$	$F = (A + B)$ Plus 1
0 0 1 0	$F = \bar{A} \cdot B$	$F = A \cdot \bar{B}$	$F = (A + \bar{B})$ Plus 1
0 0 1 1	$F = 0$	F = Minus 1(2's Compl)	$F = 0$
0 1 0 0	$F = \overline{A \cdot B}$	$F = A$ Plus $A\bar{B}$	$F = A$ Plus $A\bar{B}$ Plus 1
0 1 0 1	$F = \bar{B}$	$F + (A + B)$ Plus $A\bar{B}$	$F = (A + B)$ Plus $A\bar{B}$ Plus 1

0 1 1 0	$F = A \oplus B$	$F = A$ Minus B Minus 1	$F = A$ Minus B
0 1 1 1	$F = A \cdot \overline{B}$	$F = A\overline{B}$ Minus 1	$F = A \cdot \overline{B}$
1 0 0 0	$F = \overline{A} + B$	$F = A + AB$	$F = A$ Plus AB Plus 1
1 0 0 1	$F = \overline{A \oplus B}$	$F = A$ Plus B	$F = A$ Plus B Plus 1
1 0 1 0	$F = B$	$F = (A + \overline{B})$ Plus AB	$F = (A + \overline{B})$ Plus AB Plus 1
1 0 1 1	$F = AB$	$F = AB$ Minus 1	$F = AB$
1 1 0 0	$F = 1$	$F = A$ Plus A	$F = A$ Plus A Plus 1
1 1 0 1	$F = A + \overline{B}$	$F = (A + B)$ Plus A	$F = (A + B)$ Plus A Plus 1
1 1 1 0	$F = A + B$	$F = (A + \overline{B})$ Plus A	$F = (A + \overline{B})$ Plus A Plus 1
1 1 1 1	$F = A$	$F = A$ Minus 1	$F = A$

A : Represents 4-bit long word applied at the A inputs
B : Represents 4-bit long word applied at the B inputs
F : Represents 4-bit long output word on F_3, F_2, F_1 and F_0 outputs
+ : Represents logical OR operation
Plus : Represents addition
$\overline{C}_n$: Represents the logic level on the carry input. It is active low.

We will consider some examples to illustrate the operating procedures for this device.

Logic Operations

Example 13.24: *Determine the operation being performed when the control and data inputs are as follows:*

Select inputs 1011
Mode input M = 1

Word	*A*	A_3	A_2	A_1	A_0	1 0 0 1
Word	*B*	B_3	B_2	B_1	B_0	1 0 1 1
Output	*F*	F_3	F_2	F_1	F_0	1 0 0 1

With the given selects inputs, the two words will be ANDed. ANDing or ORing or any other logic operation is done on a bit-by-bit basis by this device. In this case the output will be $F = 1\,0\,0\,1$.

You will find this operation easier to comprehend, if you consider that the two bits in each position are being processed by a 2-input AND gate.

Example 13.25: *Determine the operation being performed when the control and data inputs are as follows:*

Select inputs 0 1 1 0
Mode input M = 1

Word	*A*	A_3	A_2	A_1	A_0	1 1 0 0
Word	*B*	B_3	B_2	B_1	B_0	0 1 1 0
Output	*F*	F_3	F_2	F_1	F_0	1 0 1 0

This is a case of XOR operation. Again the two bits in each position are XORed. The result will be $F = 1\,0\,10$

Arithmetic operations

Additions of 4-bit Words—Addition of inputs at A and B can be performed by making the mode input low and programming the select inputs with 1 0 0 1 logic levels. The F output will now be A plus B.

If there is a carry-in from the lower order of four bits, C_n will be low, indicating a carry-in and a 1 will be added to the sum. If this addition also produces a carry, the C_{n+4} output will go low. This addition of four bits is carried out at high speed as this device incorporates a look-ahead-carry scheme.

Addition of larger words at low speed—If words larger than four bits are not required to be added at high speed, two such devices can be cascaded by connecting the C_{n+4} output of the lower order device to the C_n input of the higher order device.

Addition of larger words at high speed—For addition of larger words at high speed, the propagate carry output $\overline{P}$ and the generate carry output $\overline{G}$ can be connected to another device which provides for a look-ahead-carry generator and uses the $\overline{P}$ and $\overline{G}$ signals to anticipate and generate carry input signals.

Decrementing Words—If the select inputs are programmed with 1 1 1 1 and the input M is kept low and the C_n input high, the output word will be A minus 1.

Incrementing Words—If the select inputs are programmed with 0 0 0 0, the mode input is held low and C_n high, the word on the output will be A. If C_n is made low, the word on the output will be A plus 1.

Subtraction—If the select inputs are programmed with 0 1 1 0, the mode input is held low and C_n high, the word on the output will be A minus B minus 1. This subtraction is performed by the device by generating the 1's complement of B and adding the result to the A word. This subtraction yields a result which is 1 less than true result. To obtain the correct result, C_n is held low, which adds 1 to the previous result.

Magnitude Comparison—The $A = B$ output is used for the comparison of the magnitudes of two words A and B. The programme select inputs are programmed with 0 1 1 0, the mode input and C_n are held low. This procedure subtracts the B words from the A word. Now

If $A = B : A = B$ output will be high
If $A > B : C_{n+4}$ output will be high : $A = B$ output will be low
If $B > A : C_{n+4}$ output will be low.

Eight-bit adder-subtracater

Two 74AS181B ICs can be connected in cascade to implement an 8-bit adder-subtracter. Connections are required to be made as follows:

1. The lower order of 4 bits of words A and B should be connected to the A and B inputs of the lower order ALU.
2. The higher order 4 bits of words A and B should be connected to the A and B inputs of the higher order ALU.
3. The C_{n+4} output of the lower order ALU should be connected to the C_n input of the higher order ALU.
4. The select input lines of both the ALUs should be connected together.

The output will be available on the eight F outputs of the two ALUs. The logic levels for the select input lines, mode control and carry-in inputs should be as follows:

For additions: $S = 1\ 0\ 0\ 1$
$M = 0$

$C_n = 1$ for lower order ALU

For subtractions: $S = 0110$

$M = 0$

$C_n = 0$ for the lower order ALU.

Problems

13.1 Convert the following sign-magnitude numbers into decimal forms:

(a) 0010 (b) 1011
(c) 1100 (d) 0001 1010
(e) 1000 1100 (f) 1001 0100

13.2 Convert the following decimal numbers into sign-magnitude form:

(a) – 6 (b) + 4
(c) + 16 (d) – 15

13.3 Derive the 1's complement of the following numbers:

(a) 0101 (b) 1101
(c) 0100 1101 (d) 1010 1110

13.4 Derive the 2's complement of the following numbers:

(a) 0010 (b) 1110
(c) 1011 (d) 0001 1110
(e) 0010 1111 (f) 0101 0110

13.5 Derive the decimal equivalent of the following numbers, which are in 2's complement form:

(a) 1101 (b) 1001
(c) 1001 0101 (d) 1101 1011

13.6 Add the following numbers using 2's complement representation:

(a) + 50 : + 43 (b) – 90 : – 20
(c) + 125 : – 45 (d) + 25 : – 120

13.7 Carry out the following subtractions using 2's complement representation:

(a) + 45 from + 60 (b) + 70 from + 20
(c) – 75 from – 40 (d) + 60 from + 30

13.8 Draw circuit for a half-adder using only NAND gates.

13.9 Draw a circuit diagram for a full-adder using only NAND gates.

13.10 Show how you will programme IC 74AS181B to performs the following arithmetic functions ?

(a) A PLUS B (b) AB PLUS A
(c) $\overline{AB}$ (d) B PLUS $A\overline{B}$
(e) B PLUS 1 (f) B MINUS A
(g) B PLUS AB PLUS 1 (h) BA MINUS 1

13.11 Show how you will programme IC 74AS181B to perform the following logic functions?

(*a*) $\overline{A}B$ (*b*) $\overline{A \oplus B}$

(*c*) $A + \overline{B}$ (*d*) $A + B$

13.12 Show how you will connect ICs 7483 and 7486 to implement an 8-bit parallel adder-subtracter?

13.13 What output words will be produced by the following logic operations of two words using IC 74AS181B?

(*a*) 1 0 1 0 AND 0 1 1 0 (*b*) 1 1 0 0 OR 0 1 0 1 (*c*) 1 0 0 1 XOR 0 0 1 0

13.14 Show a pencil multiplication of binary numbers 1 0 1 0 1 by 1 1 0 1 0 by the add-and-shift method.

13.15 Show how you will connect IC 7483 and some gates to implement a 4-bit parallel subtracter?

14 Memory Devices

14.1 INTRODUCTION

Data storage devices are an essential requirement of computer systems, and many other electronic devices depend on memories for their functioning. Memories are required to store data as well as to make it available for processing as and when required. Data and programmes required for computer operations are commonly stored on magnetic bulk storage devices like tapes and discs. Where memory requirements are not so large, a bank of semiconductor circuits can serve the purpose of memory storage and retrieval.

Semiconductor memories consist of an array of memory cells arranged in a rectangular pattern and are fabricated on a silicon wafer using bipolar, MOS, or CMOS technology. Each memory cell can store one bit of data and a number of memory cells put together can store an immense amount of data. Memory chips using bipolar technology are capable of high speed operation; but for low power consumption, small size and low cost, MOS and CMOS technologies are preferred.

Some memory requirements are met from memories from which data can only be read. These memories are dedicated to perform a particular task and quite a few such memories are required in computers. The memories are known as ROMs, or read-only-memories. The storage capacity of a memory depends on the number of memory cells which it incorporates. For instance ROM 74S370 can store 512 words of 4-bits each, which requires 2048 (512 × 4) memory cells.

Data is permanently stored in the memory cells of an ROM. For this reason ROMs are manufactured according to uses requirements. Therefore, the memory contents are specified by the user for manufacture according to his specific needs. Data once stored in a ROM cannot be changed: it can only be read.

There are some programmable read-only memories known as PROMs which are usually programmed by the user according to his own needs. Data once stored in PROMs cannot be altered. However, there are some erasable PROMs known as EPROMs, in which data can be erased and the EPROM reprogrammed. ROMs are classified as non-volatile devices, because data stored in them is not lost when power is shut off.

In some applications data storage is of a temporary nature and the data keeps changing according to operational requirements. Devices which provide this facility are known as RAMs, random access or read-write memories. In these devices data can be written into and read from their outputs. For deciphering whether a memory cell has stored a binary 0 or a binary 1, logic circuits are used for reading the contents from the memory outputs. The output is buffered, which ensures that the memory contents are not lost during the read operation. RAMs are referred to as volatile memories, since the memory contents are lost when power is shut off.

Apart from memory devices which we have mentioned here using bipolar MOS and CMOS technologies, there are other memory devices which depend on more recent innovations; but we will discuss them at a later stage. For the present we will confine our discussion to a study of the characteristics of memories which we have already mentioned so far. The memory structure of some of the memory devices is given in Fig. 14.1.

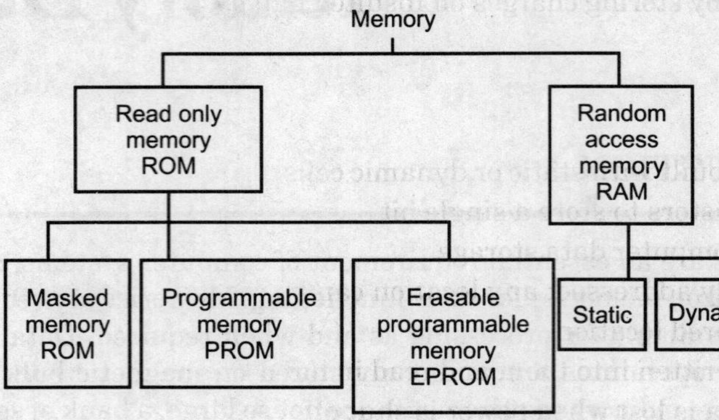

Fig. 14.1 Memory classification

The important features of these memories have been summarized below.

ROMs

- Mask programmed during manufacture
- Cannot be reprogrammed
- Nonvolatile; retain data even when power is shut off
- Cheaper than programmable devices
- Generally used to perform specific functions
- Useful for fixed programme instructions
- Nondestructive readout devices

PROMs

- Programmed by blowing built-in fuses,
- Cannot be reprogrammed
- Occupy more space; leads to low memory density
- Nonvolatile
- Useful for small volume data storage
- User programmable

EPROM

- Erasable, programmable ROM
- Programmed by storing charge on insulated gates

- Erasable with ultraviolet light
- Reprogrammable after erasure
- Nonvolatile

EEPROM

- Electrically erasable programmable ROM
- Programmed by storing charges on insulted gates
- Nonvolatile

RAM-Static

- IC RAMs are built with static or dynamic cells.
- Use 5-6 transistors to store a single bit
- Suitable for computer data storage
- Can be directly addressed; any location can be read; no need to shift data bit-by-bit to reach the desired location
- Data can be written into them and read in nanoseconds
- Generally data is lost when power is shut off
- Available in TTL, ECL, NMOS and CMOS technologies

RAMs-Dynamic

- Use a single transistor memory cells; occupy less space
- Consume less power than static RAMs
- Slower than static RAMs
- Charge is stored in tiny capacitors, which drains off after a short time
- To retain data every cell has to be refreshed after every 6-8 milliseconds.

14.2 READ-ONLY-MEMORY (ROM)

ROMs are used to permanently store binary information and are implemented with electronic devices. Data stored in ROMs can be read or recalled for use in digital devices. In the reading process the contents of the memory appear at the output and, as the output is buffered, the memory contents are not lost while the memory contents are being read. ROMs use memory cells which are fabricated by using bipolar or MOS technology. Data is written into the memory at the time of manufacture to meet specific user requirements.

Memory cells in ROMs are organized in rows and columns as shown in Fig. 14.2. The diagram shows that each row of 4 bits constitutes a word and there are eight such rows which makes the number of memory cells 8 × 4 or 32. Each word can be addressed, one at a time, by an address decoder with eight outputs. The address decoder has three inptus C, B and A which provide 8 (2^3) addresses for access to each word in the memory. Any word can be addressed at random, depending on the BCD input to the address decoder. Notice that the subscripts of the address decoder output Y_0 through Y_7 are the same as the memory locations of the words in the ROM.

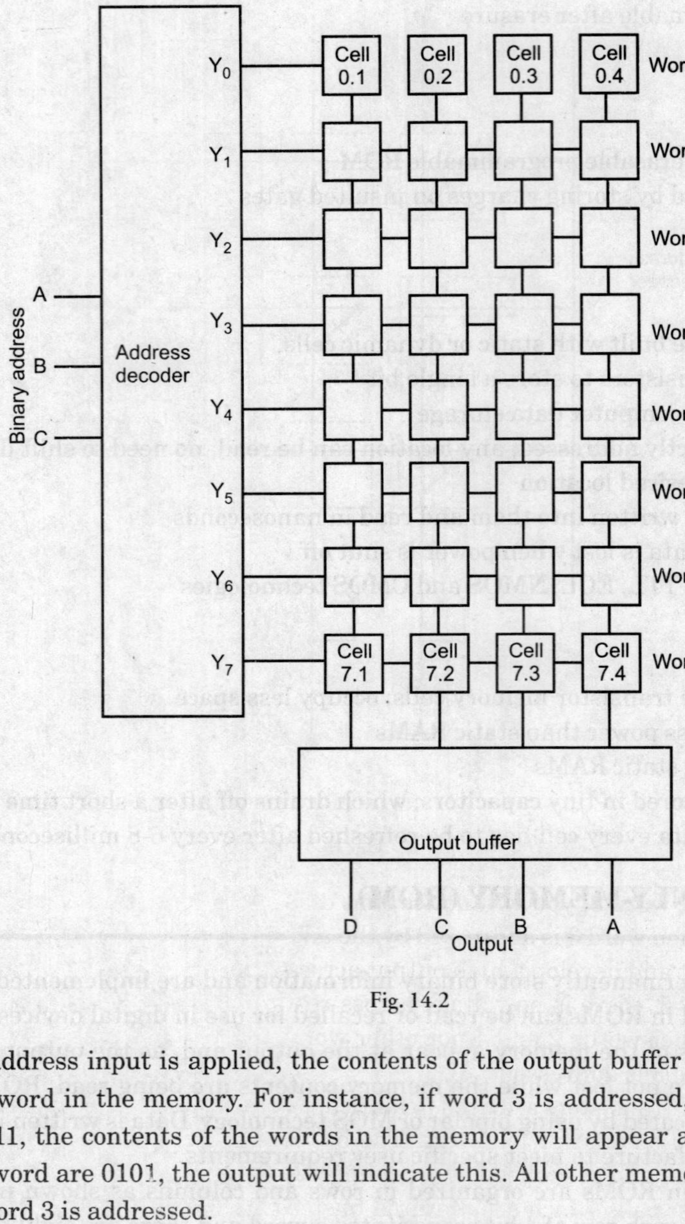

Fig. 14.2

When an address input is applied, the contents of the output buffer indicate the binary contents of the word in the memory. For instance, if word 3 is addressed, the BCD input for which will be 011, the contents of the words in the memory will appear at the output. If the contents of the word are 0101, the output will indicate this. All other memory locations will be ignored when word 3 is addressed.

ROMs use both bipolar and MOS technologies. The information contained in each cell of a ROM is stored in them during the manufacturing process by using photolithographic masks. These ROMs are also known as mask-programmed ROMs. For programming a memory cell with a 1 or 0, diodes may be used; but normally single NPN transistors are used, which are connected as emitter followers. We will first see how ROMs can be made by using diodes. Figure 14.3 shows how a word 0101 can be programmed.

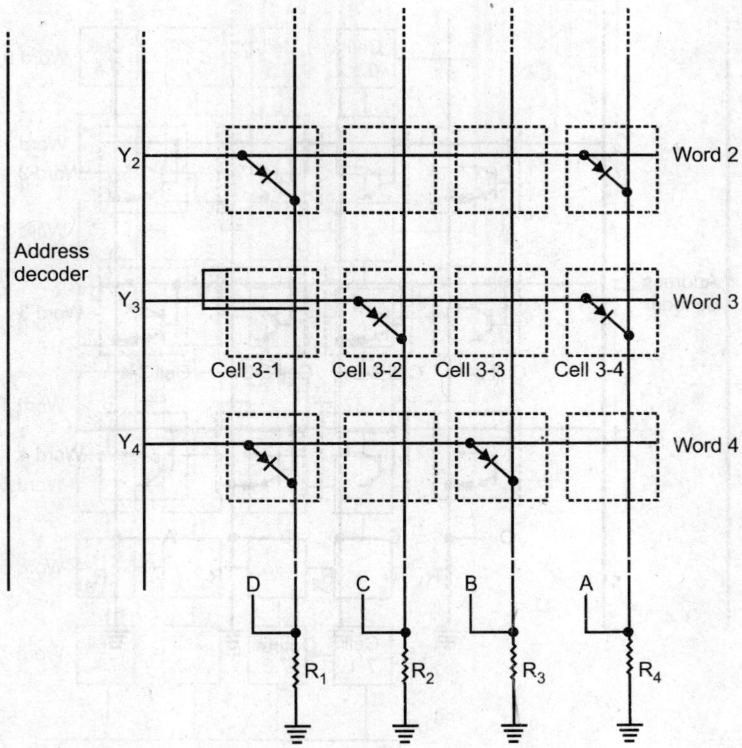

Fig. 14.3

If you look at word 3, you will notice that diodes are connected as shown in cell marked 3 – 2 and 3 – 4. When word 3 is addressed by the address decoder, output Y_3 goes high, diodes in these cells conduct and develop a high output across resistors R_2 and R_4. As there are no diodes in cells 3–1 and 3–3, there is no voltage across resistors R_1 and R_3. The output will therefore read 0 1 0 1. Neither words 2 and 4 nor other words in the ROM receive any output from the decoder when word 3 is addressed.

When bipolar transistors are used to fabricate ROMs, single NPN transistors are used and they are connected as emitter followers. The bases of these transistors are connected to the decoder output lines and the collectors are connected to the positive supply rail. The emitters of transistors in those cells which are required to store a binary 1 are connected to output lines, while in those cells which are required to store a binary 0, the emitters are left open. These ROMs are programmed using a custom mask which determines the binary contents of the memory cells. Figure 14.4 shows how the partial ROM diagram shown in Fig. 14.3 can be implemented by this technique.

You will notice from this diagram that emitters of transistors are connected to output lines only in those cells which are required to store a binary 1. These are the same cells in which diodes were connected in Fig. 14.3.

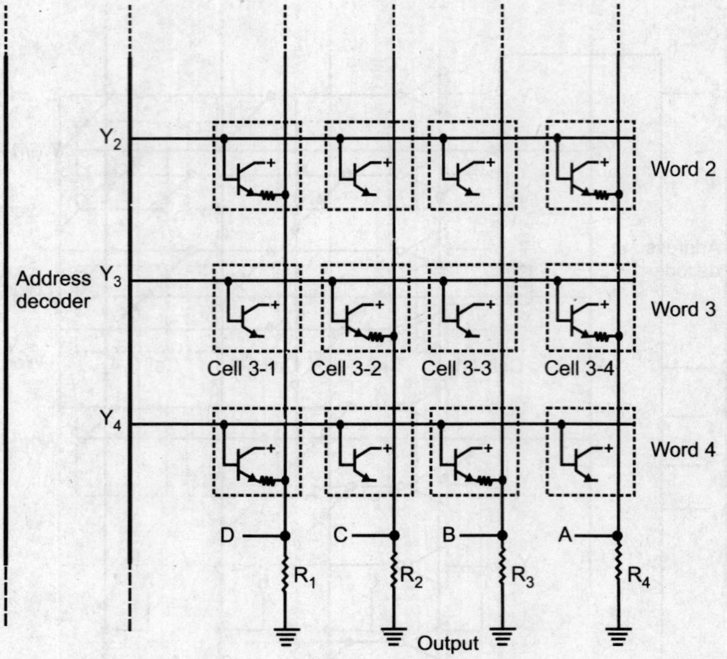

Fig. 14.4

14.2.1 Diode Matrix ROM

Figure 14.5 shows the circuit of a 40-bit ROM using diodes. The memory cells are arranged in 10 rows and 4 columns, so that there are 10 words of 4 bits each. The word locations are numbered from 0 through 9, which are addressed by a 1-of-10 decoder. Each column is connected to the output circuitry, so that when any word is addressed its contents will appear at the output. The decoder will activate only the word which has been addressed and produce an output corresponding to the memory contents of the row which has been activated.

Suppose word 1 has been addressed by the decoder. The diodes connected to output lines *D*, *B* and *A* will conduct and develop a high output across the associated resistors. Since no diode is connected to output line *C*, it will remain low. The output will read 1 0 1 1 which tallies with the contents of word 1 as given in Table 14.1. If you compare this table with Fig. 14.5, you will notice that where a bit is a binary 1 in the table, a diode is connected in the corresponding memory cell.

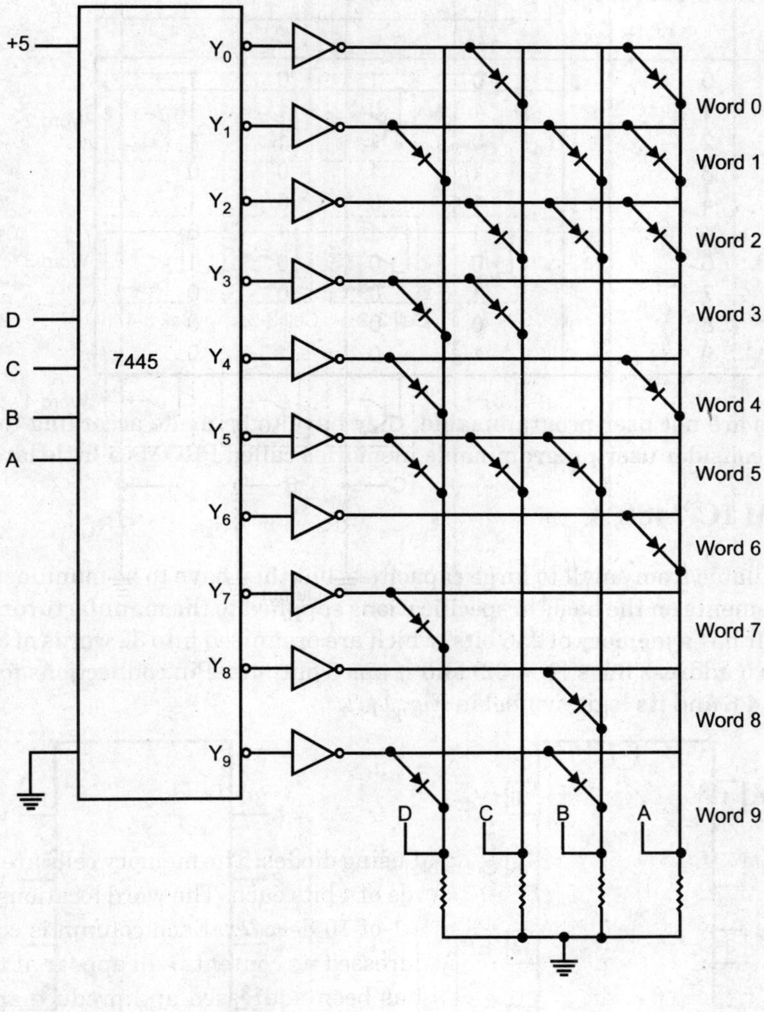

Fig. 14.5 ROM with decoder

ROMs can be implemented with diodes or with bipolar or MOS devices. However, generally MOSFETS are used for fabricating ROMs, as they have an access time between 10 and 200 ns. Bipolar ROMs have an access time which is almost twice as much. The underlying idea is always the same. There are as many address lines as there are words and as many output lines as the number of bits in the words. If there are 10 input lines and the words are 4-bit words, there will be 10 × 4 or 40 memory cells.

Table 14.1

Word address	*Output*			
	D	*C*	*B*	*A*
0	0	1	0	1
1	1	0	1	1
2	0	1	1	1
3	1	1	0	0
4	1	0	0	1
5	1	1	1	0
6	0	0	0	1
7	1	0	0	0
8	0	0	1	0
9	1	0	1	0

As ROMs are not user programmable, they have to be made according to user specifications. We will consider user-programmable memories called PROMs a little later.

14.2.2 ROM IC 7488 A

ROMs are available from small to large capacities, but they have to be manufactured according to user requirements on the basis of specifications supplied to the manufacturer. ROM 7488 A is a TTL device. It has a memory of 256 bits, which are organized into 32 words of 8 bits each. This ROM requires 5 address lines ($2^5 = 32$) and it has 8 outputs. Pin connections for this ROM are given in Fig. 14.6 and its logic symbol in Fig. 14.7.

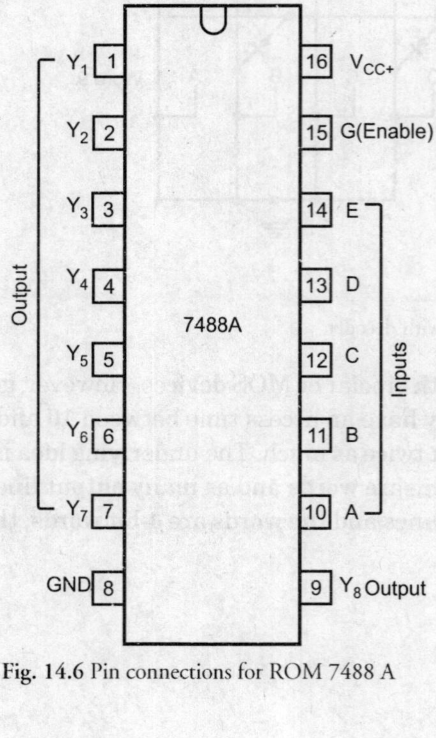

Fig. 14.6 Pin connections for ROM 7488 A

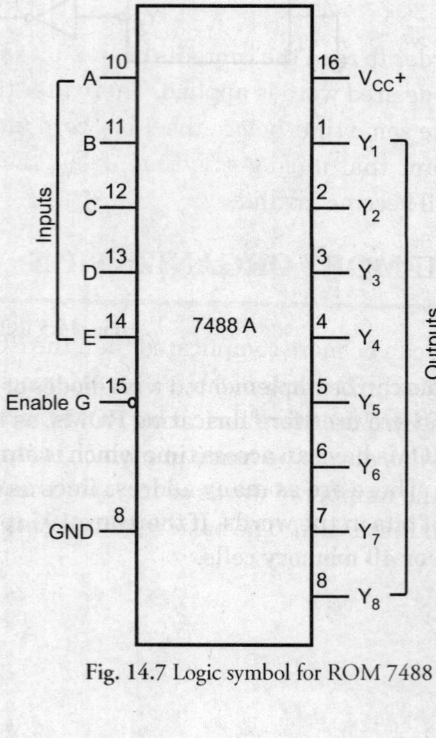

Fig. 14.7 Logic symbol for ROM 7488 A

In this ROM memory consists of 32 words of 8 bits each, from Y_1 through Y_8. This requires 32 addresses which are provided by 5 address lines ($2^5 = 32$) from A through E, which select 1 of 32 words in the momory.

G is the enable input, which can be used to enable or disable all the decoding gates. When G is high, all the decoding gates are disabled and all the output lines go high. When G is low, the ROM is enabled and one of the 32 words in the memory is selected which corresponds to the input address. The enable input G also helps in expanding the memory by combining the ROM with other similar ROMs. The enable input is also referred to as the chip-enable line and can be used as an extra bit when memory is expanded.

The ROM has a buffered output as shown in Fig. 14.8. Since each output buffer has an open collector output, as shown for output Y_1, a pull-up resistor of between 510 ohm and 5.1 k ohm is required to be connected from each output pin to V_{CC} +.

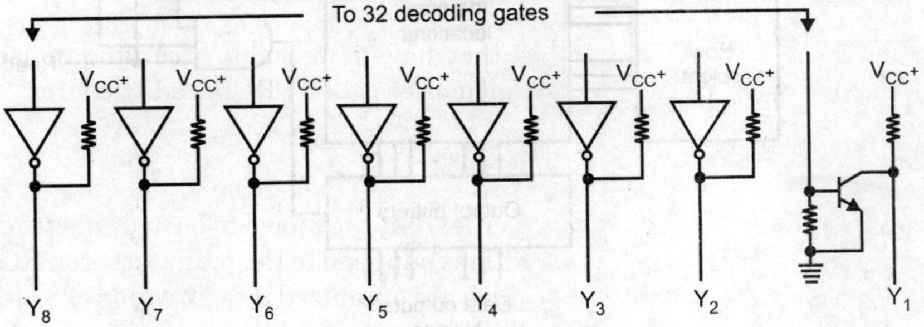

Fig. 14.8

In order to read the contents of an 8-bit word in the memory an input address corresponding to the desired word is applied. Thereafter the enable input is taken low to enable the ROM. It will take some time before the 8-bit word in the memory becomes available at the output. It is important that during this time delay, the address bus remains stable, as otherwise the output will become invalid.

14.3 MEMORY ORGANIZATION

Memories can be more complicated than the ROM memory we have discussed in Section 14.2.2, which had only 32 words of 8 bits each. Memories may have many more words and in read-write memories (RAMs) there has to be provision to read data from a location or write data into. Provision has also to be made in memories, so that a number of memories can be combined to increase the number of words or increase the word size. We will consider all these aspects here during our discussion. The basic requirements of memory organization have been brough out in Fig. 14.9.

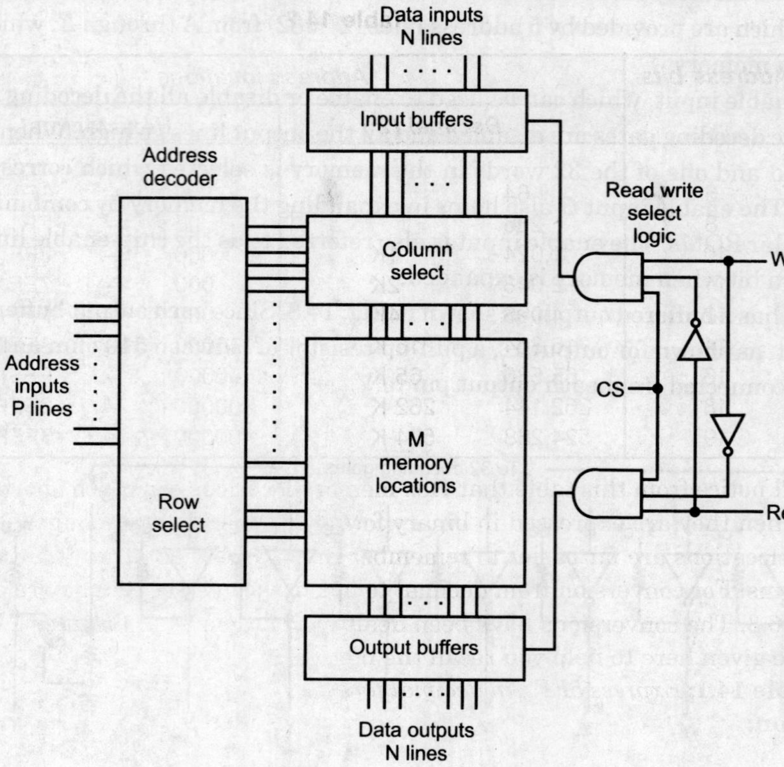

Fig. 14.9 Memory structure

The diagram shows a memory with M locations and N bits in each location. The total number of bits in the memory will, therefore, be $M \times N$ bits. Each memory location has a unique address, which can be used to access any of the M memory locations. All the locations can be accessed by P inputs, where

$$2^P = M$$

The address inputs are applied to an address decoder, which decodes the P input lines and activates the memory location depending on the address. As you will see later the memory cells are organized to enable the address bits to select a word or a group of bits of data.

If a word is required to be written into a desired location, the word to be loaded is applied at the data input and the address of the desired location is applied at the address inputs. A logic 1 level is applied at the chip select input CS, and the write command is applied at the write input terminal. With these commands, the input buffers are enabled, the output buffers are disabled, the memory is cleared and the word is loaded into the memory at the desired location.

To read data from a particular location in the memory, a high logic level input is applied at the CS input and the address of the desired memory location is applied at the address inputs. Now when the read control input is activated, the data at the addressed location in the memory becomes available at the data output.

The number of address locations in a memory depends on the number of address input bits. The following table will give you an idea of the number of address bits required for a given number of locations.

Table 14.2

Address bits	*Address locations*				
	Decimal (2^n)		*Hexadecimal*		
6	64		00	–	3F
8	256		00	–	FF
10	1,024	1K	000	–	3FF
11	2,048	2K	000	–	7FF
12	4,096	4K	000	–	FFF
14	16,384	16 K	0000	–	3FFF
16	65,536	65 K	0000	–	FFFF
18	262,144	262 K	00000	–	3FFFF
19	524,288	524 K	00000	–	7FFFF

You will notice from this table that Hex memory locations are much shorter than in decimal form. When they are expressed in binary form, they become unmanageable. For this reason memory locations are far easier to remember in hexadecimal form rather than in decimal or binary forms. For conversion from decimal to hex or vice versa, you may refer to Table 1.10 in Section 1.6.3. The conversions have been dealt with at length in Chapter 1. However some examples are given here to help you recall the method.

Example 14.1: *Express $5FF_{16}$ in decimal form.*

Solution:

$$\begin{aligned} 500 &= 5 \times 16^2 = 1280_{10} \\ F0 &= 15 \times 16 = 240_{10} \\ 0F &= \quad 15 = 15_{10} \\ \hline 5FF & \quad\quad\quad = 1535_{10} \end{aligned}$$

You will get the same result if you consult the table.

Example 14.2 : *Express 3320_{10} in Hex*

Solution: From the table

$$\begin{aligned} 3072_{10} &= 0C00 \\ 240_{10} &= \quad F0 \\ 8_{10} &= \quad 08 \\ \hline 3320_{10} &= CF8_{16} \end{aligned}$$

14.4 ROM IC 74S370

The ROM that we have just discussed had 32 words of 8 bits each. It had 32 rows and 8 columns. The 32 rows were accessed by 5 address inputs ($2^5 = 32$). Larger memories are organized differently.

For instance ROM 74S370 is a 2048-bit memory, which has 512 words of 4 bits each. You would expect a 512 × 4-bit memory matrix; but this ROM is organized as an array of 64 × 32-bit memory matrix, that is 64 rows and 32 columns. The 32 columns are divided into 8 groups of 4 bits each. You will notice from Fig. 14.10 that there are 6 address lines A_3 through A_8 to select one of the 64 rows and 3 address lines, A_0, A_1 and A_2, which select one of the eight 4-bit groups for which 3 address lines ($2^3 = 8$) are sufficient. If the address inputs are as follows, it will select row 25 and 4 bits (four columns) in group 5.

Row select input						Group select input		
A_8	A_7	A_6	A_5	A_4	A_3	A_2	A_1	A_0
0	1	1	0	0	1	1	0	1

The input address lines A_0 through A_8 are buffered. There are 3-state buffers on outputs D, C, B and A. When input EI goes low, the stored data will appear at the output. Pin connections for this ROM are given in Fig. 14.11.

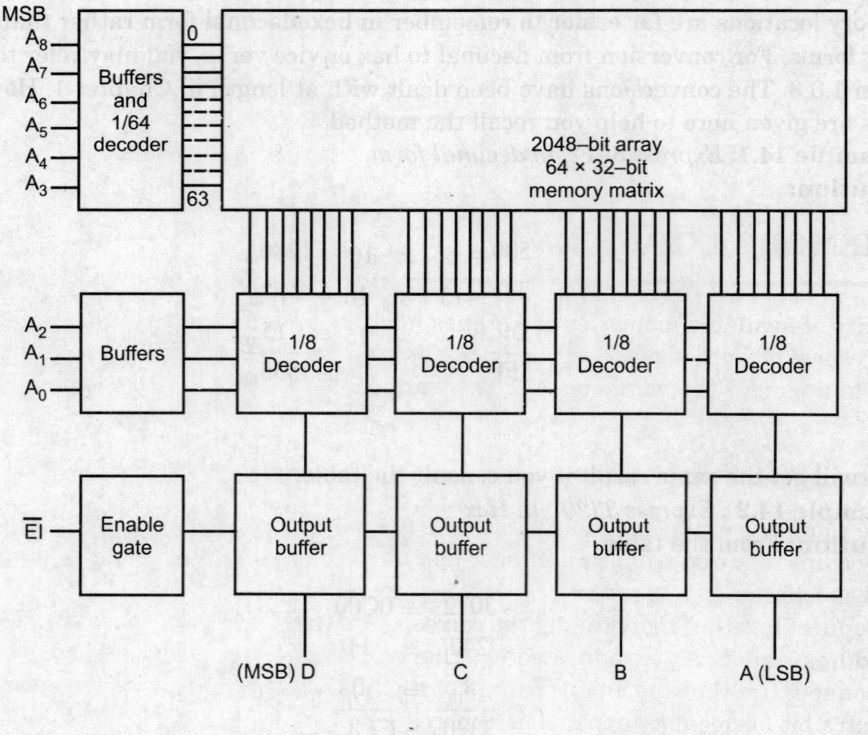

Fig. 14.10 Block diagram of ROM 74S370

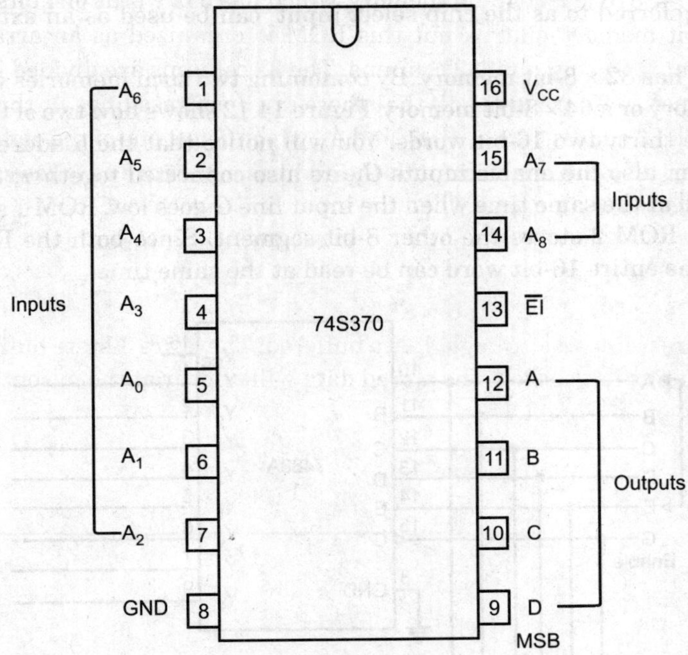

Fig. 14.11 Pin connections for ROM 74S370

14.5 MEMORY EXPANSION

The capacity of available memories is at times found to be inadequate to meet specific needs, either in respect of word size or word capacity or both. In these situations memory ICs can be combined to augment the word size and the word capacity. We will consider how this can be done.

Expansion of word size

If the word size in the available memory is N and the required word size is n, the number of memory chips required will be an integer just bigger than n/N. The memory chips should be connected as follows:

1. Connect together individually the corresponding address input lines of the ICs. So that address inputs A are connected together as also inputs B and C, etc.
2. Connect together the enable inputs of the ICs. This input can also now be used as an extra bit for memory expansion, if necessary.
3. The number of output lines will be equal to the original word size multiplied by the number of ICs used. If, for instance, each IC had an 8-bit word and two ICs were used, the combination will produce a 16-bit word, half of each word will be stored in each IC.

We will consider expansion of the memory capability by combining ROMs 7488A. If you refer to Fig. 14.7, you will notice that there is an enable input G, which is used to enable or disable the ROM. This input helps in combining it with other similar ROMs in implementing a memory with many more locations, or a bigger word size. In expanded memories the input line

G, which is also referred to as the chip select input, can be used as an extra bit for memory expansion.

ROM 7488A has 32 × 8-bit memory. By combining two such memories we can form either a 32 × 16-bit memory or a 64 × 8-bit memory. Figure 14.12 shows how two of these ROMs can be combined to store thirty-two 16-bit words. You will notice that the 5 address input lines are connected together, also the enable inputs *G*, are also connected together; therefore both the ROMs are enabled at the same time when the input line *G* goes low. ROM 1 stores one of the 8-bit segments and ROM 2 stores the other 8-bit segment. Since both the ROMs are enabled simultaneously, the entire 16-bit word can be read at the same time.

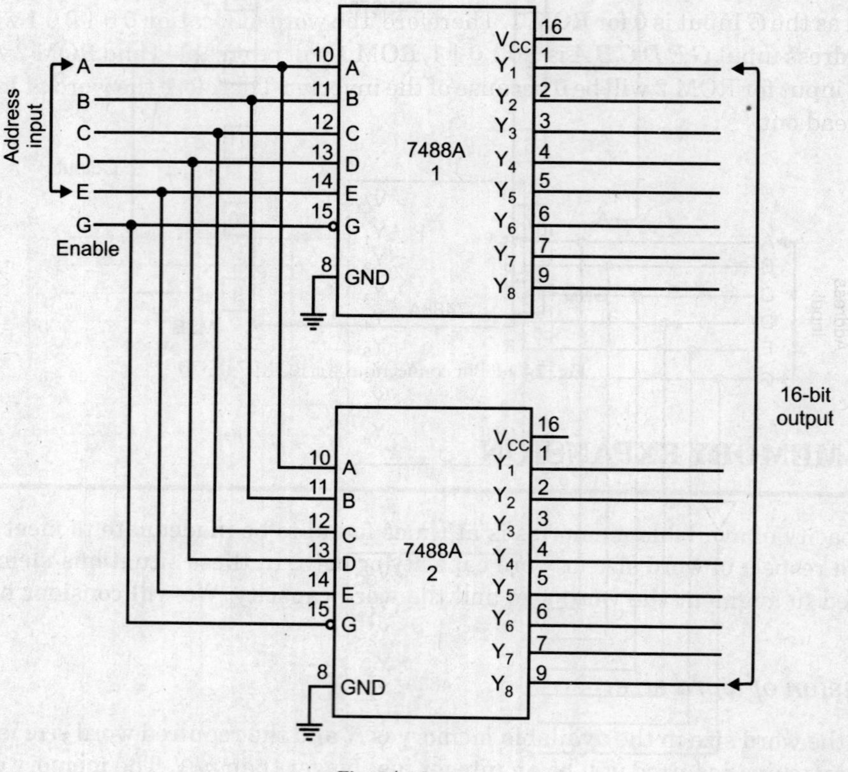

Fig. 14.12

Expansion of word capacity

Memory ICs can also be combined to produce a larger memory. If the memory requirement is *m* words and the memory IC is available has a capacity of *M* words, the number of ICs required will be a whole number just larger than m/*M*. Similar ICs can be connected as follows:

1. Connect the corresponding address input lines together, so that the *A* inputs are connected together so also the *BCD* etc., inputs.
2. If only two ICs are used, connect the enable input of one to the enable input of the other IC through an inverter, so that only one of the ICs is enabled at a time.
3. If more than two ICs are used, connect a decoder output to the enable inputs of the ICs, so that only one of the ICs is enabled at a time.

4. Connect together the corresponding output lines of the ICs, so that output Y_1's are connected together, so also outputs Y_2, Y_3, etc.

Figure 14.13 shows how these ROMs can be combined to form a memory which will store sixty four 8-bit words. ROM 1 stores the bottom half of the 64 × 8 memory locations from 0 to 31 and ROM 2 stores the top half of the memory, that is locations from 32 to 63. You will notice from the diagram that address lines *A* through *E* are connected in parallel. The chip enable line *G* is used as the 6th address input to provide 64 (2^6) address lines. Address input lines *A* through *E* are available to both the ROMs and both the ROMs are addressed simultaneously by these address inputs. However, because of the inverter, which is connected between the *G* inputs of the ROMs, only one of the ROMs will be enabled by the *G* input at a time.

If the address input *G E D C B A* is 0 0 1 0 0 1, ROM 1 will be enabled and ROM 2 will be disabled as the *G* input is 0 for ROM 1. Therefore, the word at location 0 0 1 0 0 1 will be read out. If the address input *G E D C B A* is 1 0 1 0 1 1, ROM 1 will be disabled and ROM 2 will be enabled as the *G* input for ROM 2 will be 0 because of the inverter. Therefore the word at location 101011 will be read out.

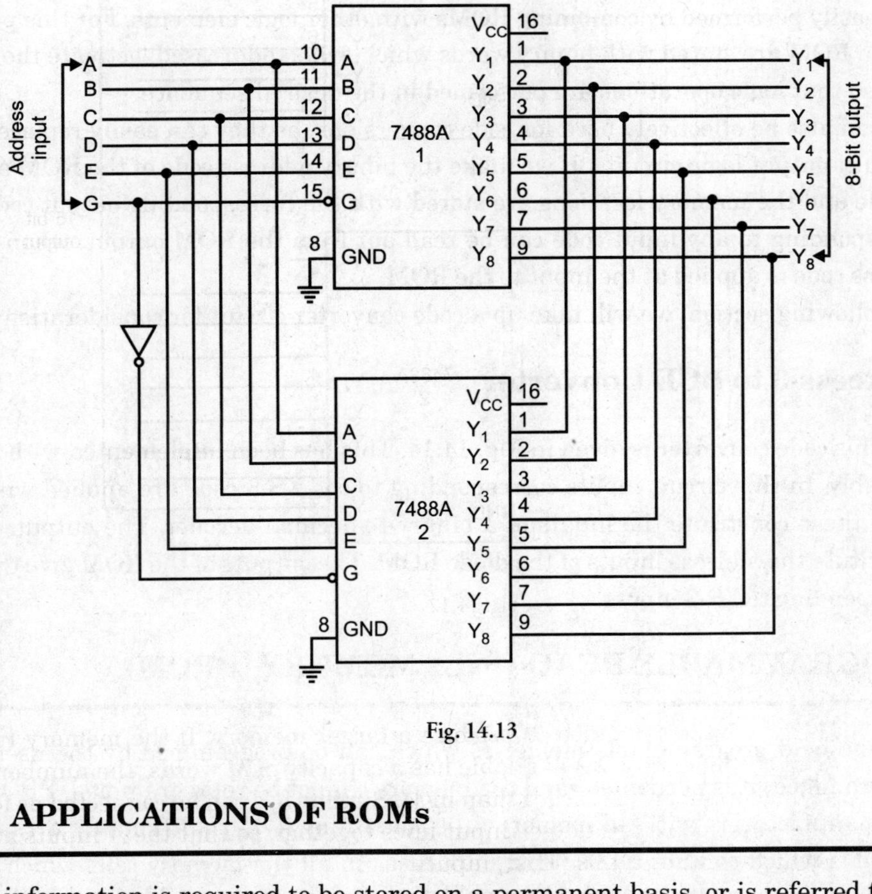

Fig. 14.13

14.6 APPLICATIONS OF ROMs

Where information is required to be stored on a permanent basis, or is referred to frequently, ROMs find considerable application. They also serve a very useful purpose in computer systems, for storing utility programs like assemblers, compilers, etc.

ROMs are very useful when semi-permanent or reference data like logarithmic tables, tables of complex mathematical functions, sine, cosine, etc., value of angles are required to be referred to frequently.

When you have to design complex logic circuits with multiple inputs and outputs, ROMs will be found very useful. When you design such a circuit using discrete components, you will first draw up a truth table, from which a Boolean equation is developed and later minimized and it is then translated into a logic circuit. Ultimately, it is implemented with discrete components. This is a lengthy process.

The same capability can be easily acquired by using a ROM. For this purpose, the input logic states are treated as address inputs of the ROM and the memory locations, which correspond to these address inputs, are stored with binary words, which represent the required output state for the corresponding address inputs. Thus the outputs corresponding to any input logic state can be read out from the output of the ROM.

ROMs also perform a very useful function in a digital computer. Sequential logic operations can be easily performed by combining ROMs with other logic elements. For this purpose, memories in a ROM are stored with binary words which, when addressed, activate the associated devices so that logic operations are performed in the desired sequence.

ROMs can also be effectively used for code conversions, as they can easily replace multi-input and multi-output logic circuits. If we make the binary address code of the ROM equal to the input code and the memory locations are stored with the corresponding output codes, the output corresponding to any input code can be read out from the ROM output, when the required address code is applied at the input to the ROM.

In the following section, we will take up a code converter circuit for consideration:

14.6.1 Excess-3 to BCD Converter

A circuit for this code converter is given in Fig. 14.14. This has been implemented with a diode matrix assembly. In this circuit inputs corresponding to the XS-3 code are applied with logic switches and these constitute the inputs of a binary-to-decimal decoder. The outputs of this decoder constitute the address inputs of the diode ROM. The outputs of the ROM give the BCD output corresponding to XS-3 inputs.

14.7 PROGRAMMABLE READ-ONLY MEMORY (PROM)

There are some field programmable memories which can be programmed by the user. Once they are programmed, it is permanent and the memory cannot be reprogrammed. PROMs are supplied by manufacturers with all memory cells containing a 0, or alternately a 1. We will consider PROMs which contain all 0s. There are fuses in all the memory cells which can be blown open if a memory cell is required to store a 1.

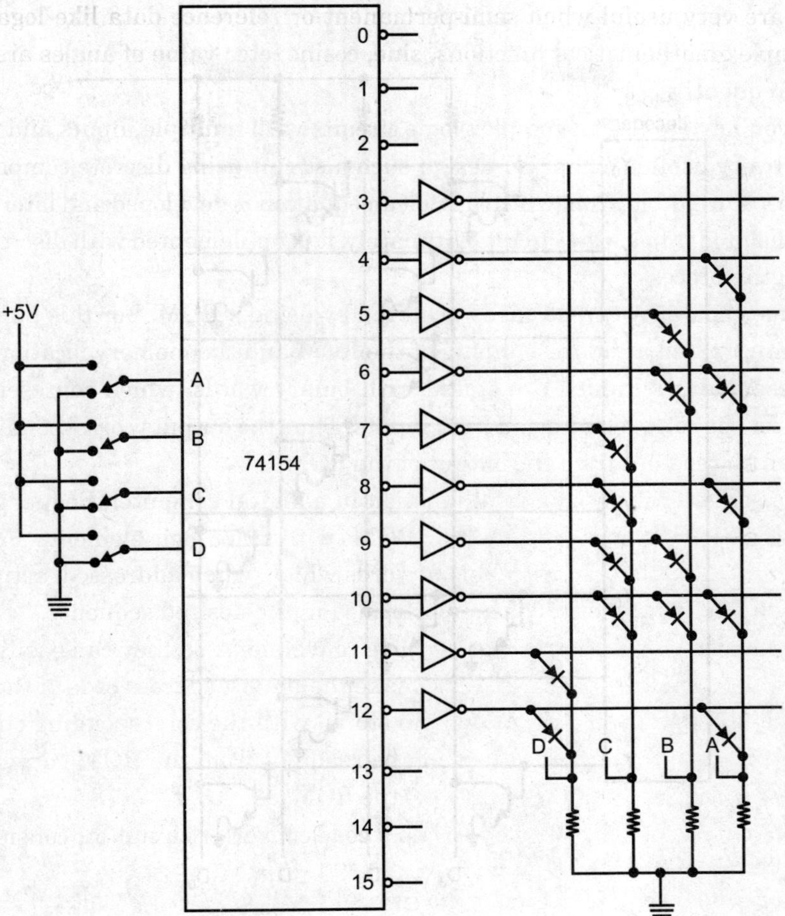

Fig 14.14 Excess-3 to BCD converter

PROMs with fusible links commonly use bipolar technology. They are programmed by applying high current pulses to fusible links. A bipolar PROM will have transistors in each cell and will look somewhat like Fig. 14.15. The diagram shows that the emitters of all the transistors are connected to earth through fusible links.

In the diagram transistors have been shown only in some of the cells. However, the PROMs supplied by manufacturers have transistors in all the cells. Let us suppose that output Y_3 of the decoder is high. As a consequence the D_1 output will go low. Thus if there are transistors in all the cells, all the outputs for all the decoder inputs will be low. The cells which do not have transistors will produce a high output. Therefore, when we have to program a PROM all that we have to do is to blow out the fuses in those cells which are required to give a logic 1 output.

Let us suppose that at address 1 0 1, that is Y_5, the word required to be put into the memory is

D_0	D_1	D_2	D_3
1	1	0	1

To program this word, we have to apply electric pulses at outputs D_0, D_1 and D_3 after the required address, that is 101 has been fed into the decoder. Links will be fused open in the corresponding cells and these cells will now store binary 1s.

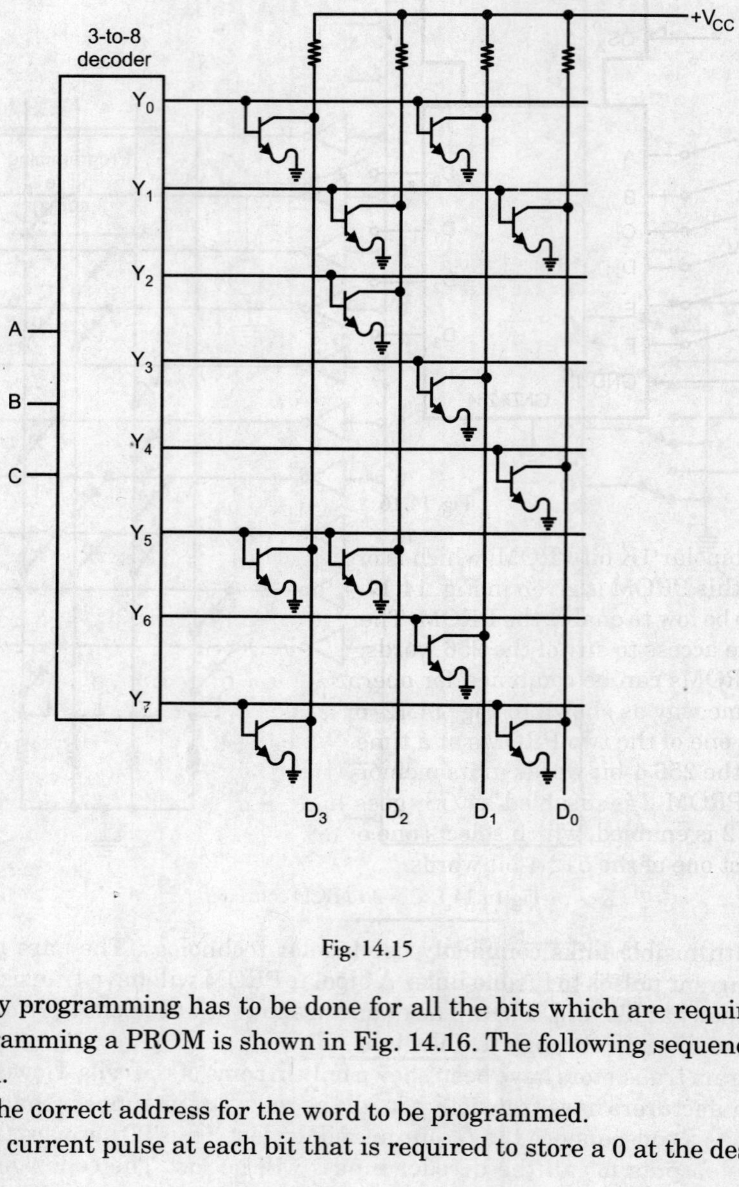

Fig. 14.15

In this way programming has to be done for all the bits which are required to be low. A circuit for programming a PROM is shown in Fig. 14.16. The following sequence of operations may be followed.

1. Apply the correct address for the word to be programmed.
2. Apply a current pulse at each bit that is required to store a 0 at the desired data positions.
3. These steps have to be repeated for all the words to be stored in the memory.

Manufacturer's data sheets should invariably be consulted for information regarding voltage levels, current pulses, etc., before any programming operation is undertaken. Once a PROM has been programmed, no changes can be made in the memory contents. Since manual programming is quite a tedious process and mistakes are not unlikely, most fusible link PROMs are normally automatically programmed with the help of mini-or microcomputers.

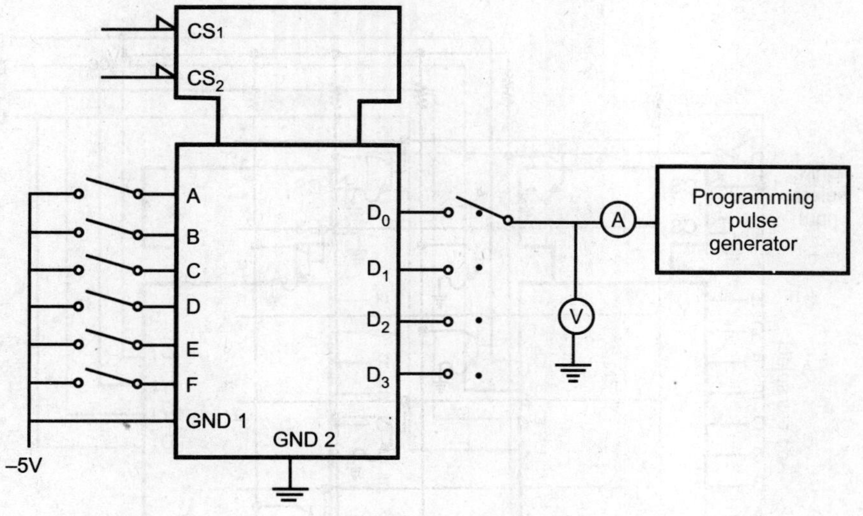

Fig. 14.16

IC 74S387 is a bipolar 1K bit PROM, which is organized as a 256 words by 4-bits memory. The logic symbol for this PROM is given in Fig. 14.17. It has two chip select inputs CS_1 and CS_2, both of which have to be low to enable the PROM. There are four data outputs and eight address inputs, which provide access to any of the 256 words.

Two of these PROMs can be combined for operation as a 512 words by 4-bit memory by connecting in the same way as shown in Fig. 14.12, or as shown in Fig. 14.18.

Input I enables one of the two PROMs at a time. When input I is low, PROM 1 is enabled and it selects one of the 256 4-bit words in its memory with the help of the 8-bit address select input. At this time PROM 2 is disabled as CS_1 goes high. When input I is high, PROM 1 is disabled and PROM 2 is enabled, which selects one of the 256 4-bit words in its memory. Thus the two PROMs select one of the 512 4-bit words.

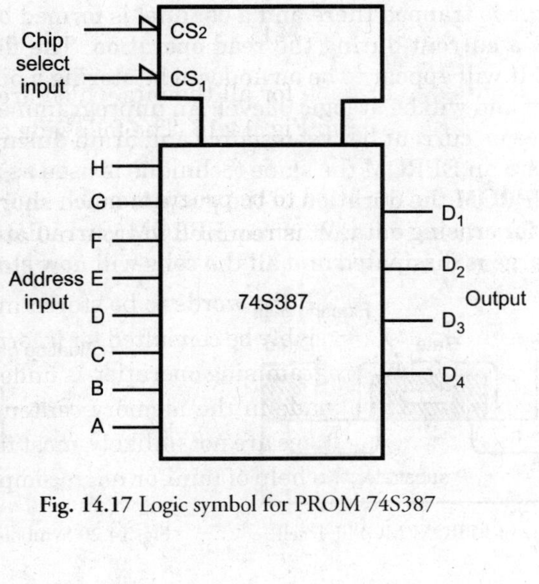

Fig. 14.17 Logic symbol for PROM 74S387

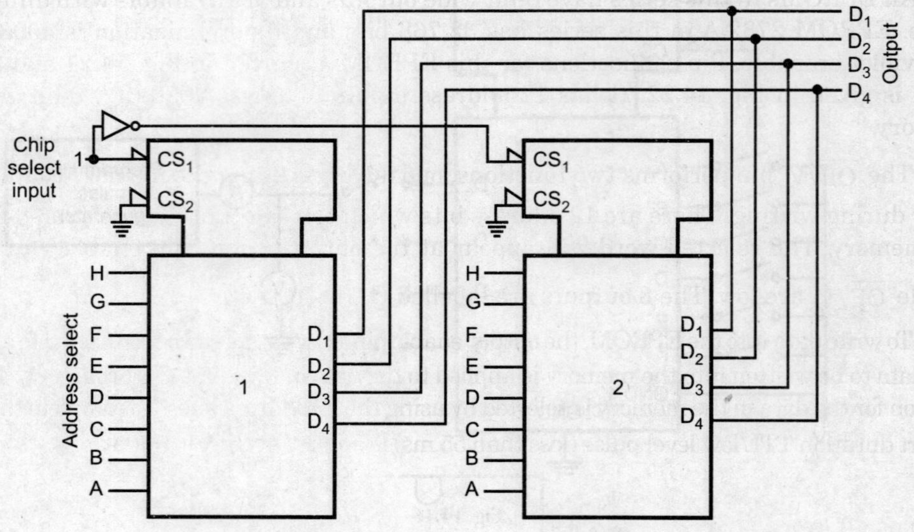

Fig. 14.18 Two PROMs connected in the 512 word × 4-bit configuration

14.8 ERASABLE PROM (EPROM)

This is another variety of a programmable read-only-memory, in which memory can be recorded and erased any number of times. Figure 14.19 shows the basic structure of the cell of an EPROM. A *p*-substrate enhancement type MOSFET is used and an additional floating gate is formed within the silicon dioxide. Symbol for floating gate MOSFET is presented in Fig. 14.20. Data is recorded in these insulated gate MOSFETs by applying a high voltage pulse to the insulated gate. Charge is thus passed on to the gate and is lodged there. As there is no connection to the floating gate, the charge is trapped there and a channel is formed between the source and the drain, which produces a current during the read operation. The floating gate will retain the charge for a long time. It will appear to be on and will be storing a binary 1. When the charge is dissipated, it will be off and will be at logic 0 level. An unprogrammed cell will also be at logic 0 level and it will produce no current between source and drain during a read operation.

In order to program an EPROM the same technique is used as for programming a PROM; but in the case of an EPROM the duration of the pulse is much shorter. EPROMs are provided with a quartz window for erasing data. When an EPROM is irradiated with ultraviolet light on top of the chip, the charge is dissipated and all the cells will now store a binary 0.

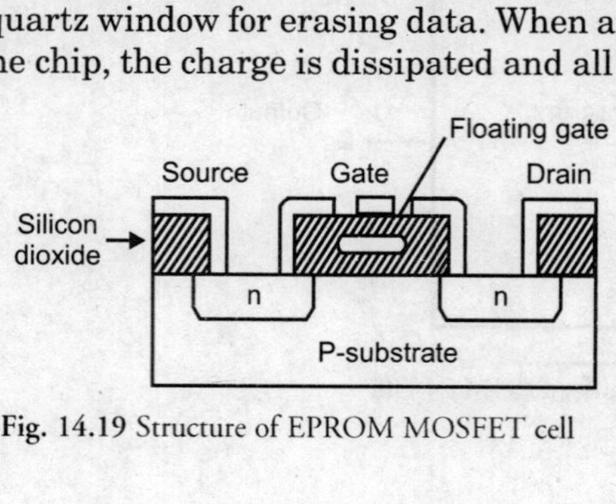

Fig. 14.19 Structure of EPROM MOSFET cell

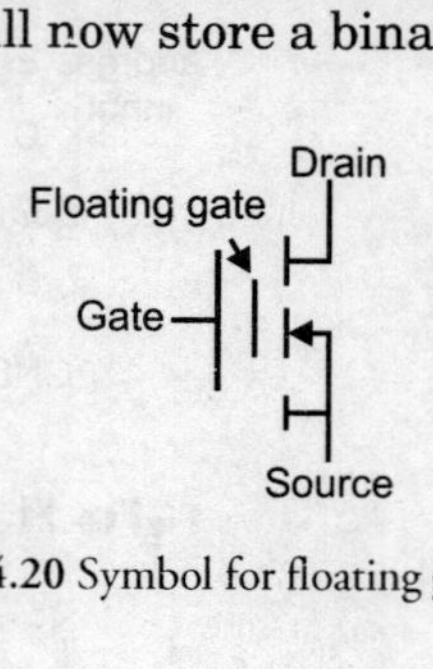

Fig. 14.20 Symbol for floating gate MOSFET

EPROMs in the 27XX series are available with very large storage capacities up to 524288 bits. All EPROMs in this series have 8-bit wide outputs and are available with different access times. EPROM 2732 A in this series has 32,768 bits and its organization is 4096 × 8 and is ultraviolet erasable. Pin connections for this EPROM are given in Fig. 14.21 and a block diagram is given in Fig. 14.22. It has 12 address inputs to access 4096 (2^{12}) 8-bit words in the memory.

The $\overline{OE}/V_{pp}$ pin performs two functions, one during reading the memory contents and the other during writing. There are 12 address bits which can select one of the 4096 8-bit words in the memory. The selected word will appear at the output when chip enable $\overline{CE}$ and output enable $\overline{OE}/V_{pp}$ are low. The 8 outputs are labelled O_0 through O_7.

To write data into the EPROM, the output enable pin OE/V_{pp} should be connected to a 21 V supply. The data to be written into the memory is applied to the data output pins O_0 through O_7. The required location for the data in the memory is selected by using the 12 address lines. To complete the procedure, a short duration TTL low level pulse (less than 55 ms) is applied at the $\overline{CE}$ input.

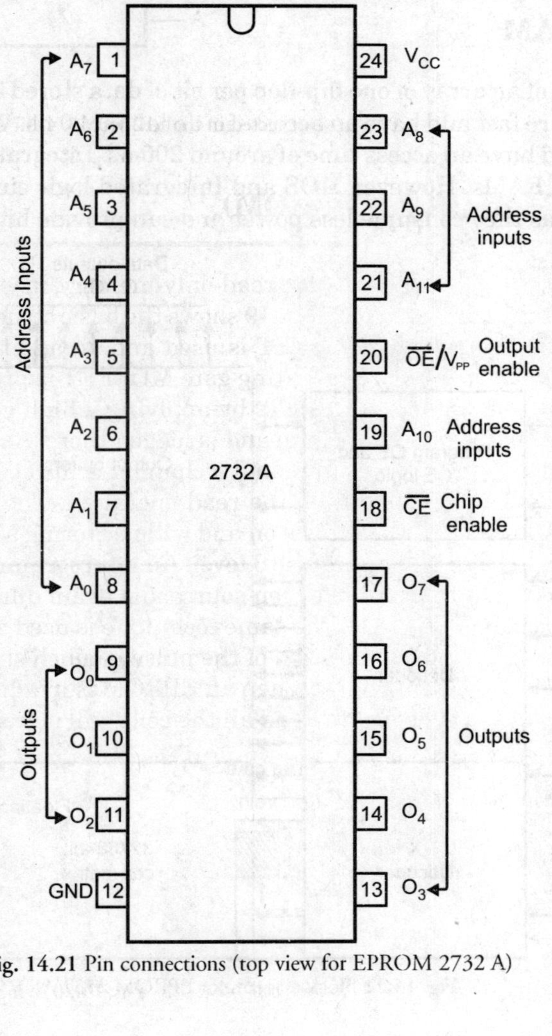

Fig. 14.21 Pin connections (top view for EPROM 2732 A)

Special equipment is available for EPROM erasing and programming. The EPROM window should be covered with an opaque sticker to protect the memory from unwanted exposure to ultraviolet light. It is best to avoid exposure to sun light and fluorescent lights.

14.9 RANDOM ACCESS MEMORY (RAM)

Read-only-memories which we have discussed in the previous sections are used only for reading data stored in the memory ROMs can be programmed only once and, as you have seen, data once recorded cannot be erased. In a RAM, data can be written into its memory as often as desired and the data stored in a RAM can be read without destroying the contents of the memory.

There are two types of RAMs, static and dynamic. The basic memory cell in a static RAM is a flip-flop, bipolar or MOS. After a bit has been stored in the flip-flop of a memory cell, it will remain there while power is available. Dynamic RAMs called DRAMS are based on charge which is stored by using MOS devices. Since this charge is dissipated by passage of time, DRAMS need periodical recharging or refreshing. You will now realize why both RAMs and DRAMS are classified as volatile devices.

14.9.1 Static RAM

A static RAM consists of an array of one flip-flop per bit of data stored in the memory. RAMs built with bipolar devices are fast and have an access time of about 20 ns. Whereas RAMs using MOS devices are slower and have an access time of around 200 ns. Integrated injection logic circuitry is also used for static RAMs. However MOS and Integrated logic circuitry have an advantage over bipolar devices, as they consume less power and can provide higher packing density.

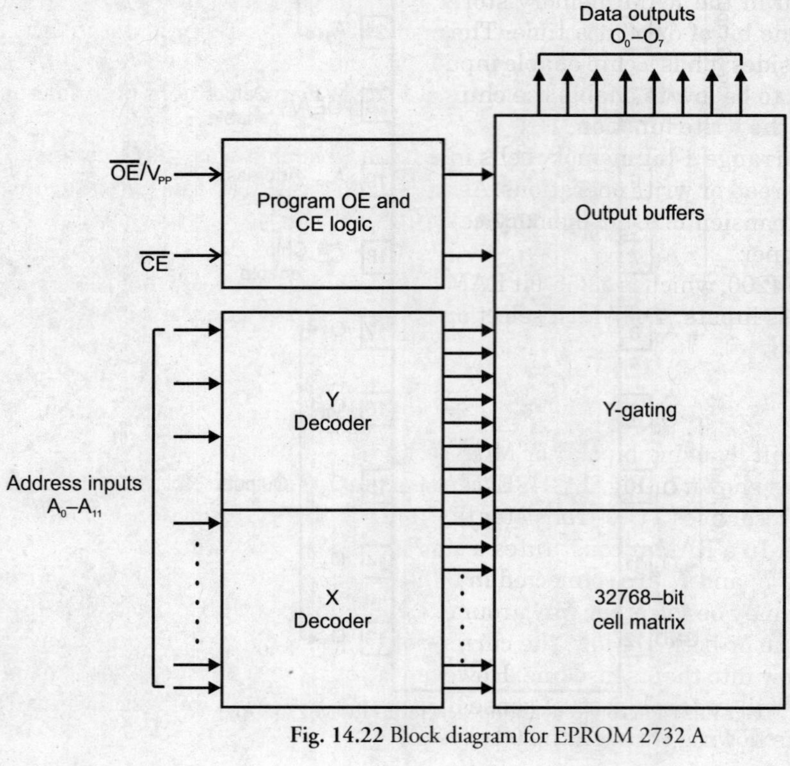

Fig. 14.22 Block diagram for EPROM 2732 A

It will be easier to follow the organization of memory in a RAM, if you consider how a single memory cell is read or written into. This has been shown in Fig. 14.23.

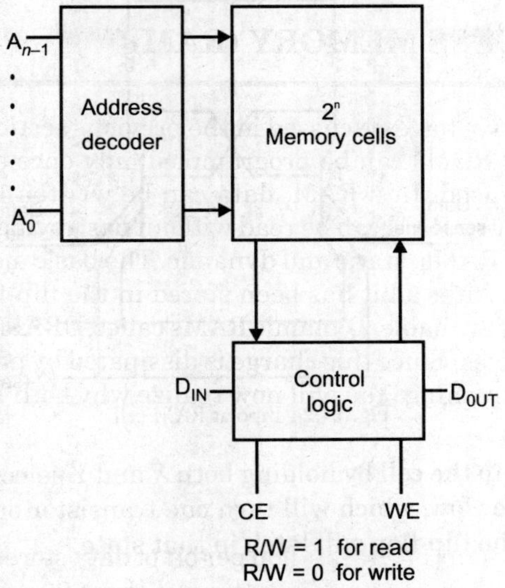

Fig. 14.23 Block diagram for static RAM

The diagram shows that n address input lines are used to select one of the 2^n memory cells in the array. Each cell in the RAM memory stores a single data bit. Therefore, the address decoder selects only one bit of data at a time. The control logic has a single data input and a single data output. Besides it has a chip enable input, CE, and a read and a write input WE. The chip enable input has to be low to enable the chip and the WE input is held high for the read operation and low for the write function.

It is possible to arrange 1-bit memory cells in a RAM in such a way that any one of them can be selected for the read or write operations. As we will discuss later, this can be achieved by serial and parallel expansion of 1-bit memory cells. RAMs with very large memories can be assembled in this manner.

For instance IC 74200, which is a 256-bit RAM has 256 words, each of which is only 1-bit in length. It has 8 address inputs, 4 of which select one of the 16 rows and the remaining 4 select one of the 16 columns.

Bipolar RAM cell

RAM cells are built by using bipolar or MOS technology. The basic structure of RAM cell using bipolar devices is shown in Fig. 14.24. Except for the multi-emitter transistors, you will notice that the circuit resembles a two-transistor flip-flop and in fact it functions as a flip-flop for storing one-bit of data. In a RAM it constitutes a single memory cell.

Since transistors T_1 and T_2 are connected in a flip-flop configuration, if T_1 is 'on' (conducting), T_2 will be off or it may be the other way around. Let us suppose that T_1 is conducting and if either X or Y select line or both are low, the current of transistor T_1 will find an easy path to ground and will not flow into the 1 sense line. However, if both X and Y select lines are high, the collector current of T_1 will go through the 1 sense line, which will be an indication of a stored 1-bit, while no current is flowing through the 0 sence line.

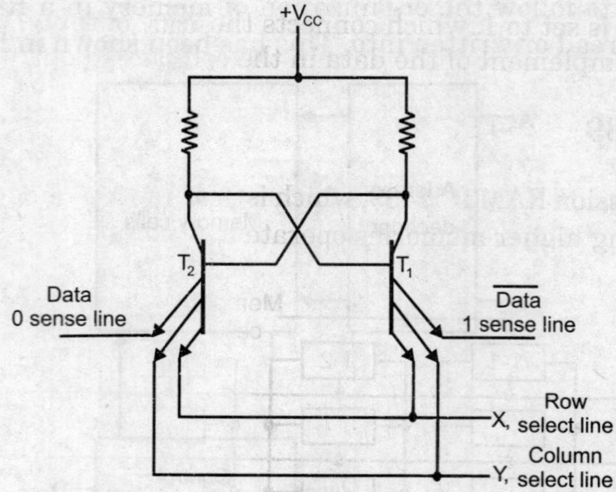

Fig. 14.24 Bipolar RAM cell

Data can be written into the cell by holding both X and Y select lines high and holding one sence line high and the other low, which will turn one transistor on and the other off. X and Y are now returned low and the flip-flop will latch in that state.

Static MOS RAM Cell

The structure of a static MOS RAM cell is shown in Fig. 14.25. Like the bipolar RAM cell the MOS cell is also a flip-flop with transistors T_1 and T_2, which are always in opposite states. Transistors T_3 and T_4 function as active pull-up resistors. Transistors T_5 and T_6 are used to connect the cell to bit lines. When transistor T_1 is on, its drain voltage is almost 0, which cuts off transistor T_2, or if T_2 is on, T_1 will be off.

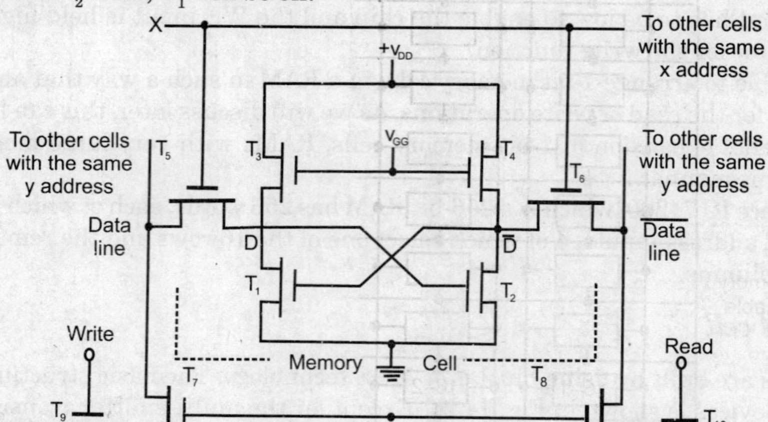

Fig. 14.25 Static MOS RAM cell

The memory cell is addressed by setting X and Y to logic 1. When X is logic 1, the cell is connected both to the data and $\overline{\text{data}}$ line. Taking Y to logic 1 switches on transistors T_7 and T_8. To write data into the cell, the write control is set to 1, which switches on T_9. If the data input is 1, the voltage at D will correspond to level 1, which will switch on T_2 and the logic level at $\overline{D}$ will be 0.

If the data input is logic 0, T_2 will be off and the $\overline{D}$ logic level will be 1. To read the data in the cell, the read control is set to 1, which connects the data output $\overline{D}$ as T_6, T_8 and T_{10} are on at this time. Thus the complement of the data in the cell is read out.

14.9.2 RAM IC 7489

We will take up for discussion RAM IC 7489, which is very representative of this class of devices, since other RAMs offering higher memories operate in a more or less similar fashion. A block

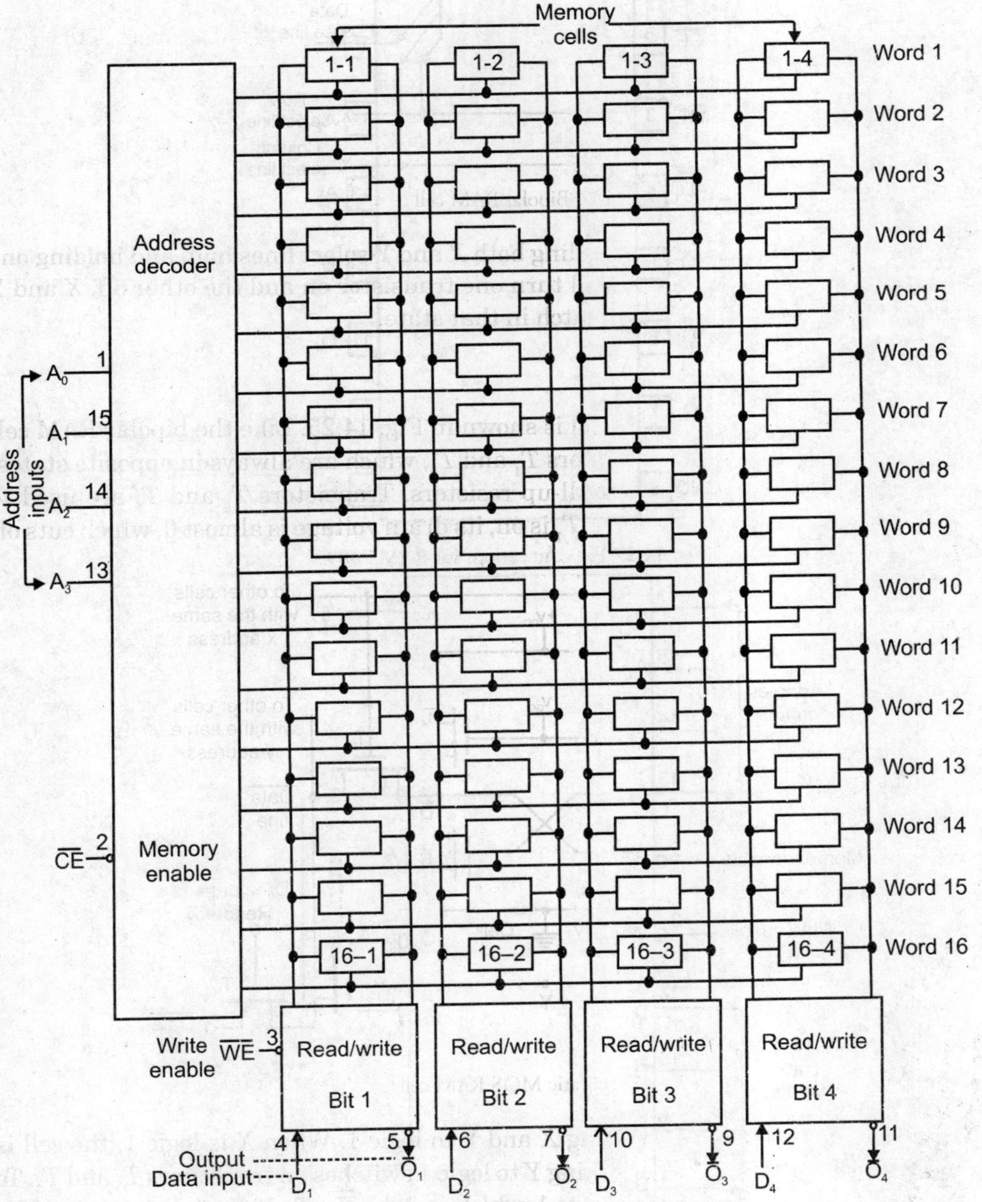

Fig. 14.26 Block diagram of 64-bit RAM 7489

diagram of RAM 7489 is given in Fig. 14.26 and its pin connections and logic symbol are given in Figs. 14.27 and 14.28. It has 64 memory cells arranged in 16 rows and four columns. Each of the 16 words has 4 bits each, which are accessed by 4 address data inputs. There are 4 data input lines from 1 through 4 into which data is fed for being written into the memory. There are 4 outputs from O_1 through O_4 and remember that the data at the output is the complement of the data in the memory.

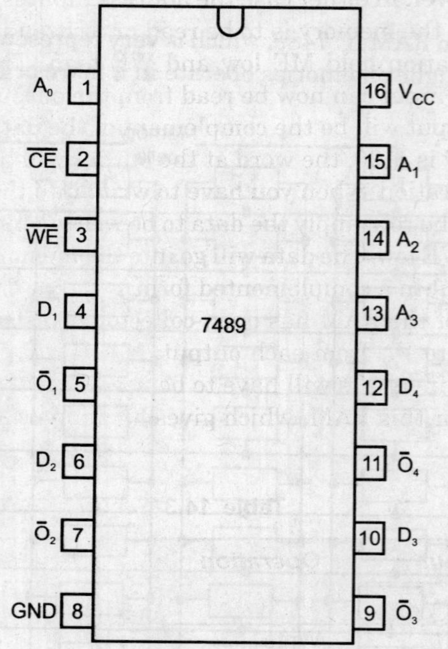

Fig. 14.27 Pin connections for RAM 7489

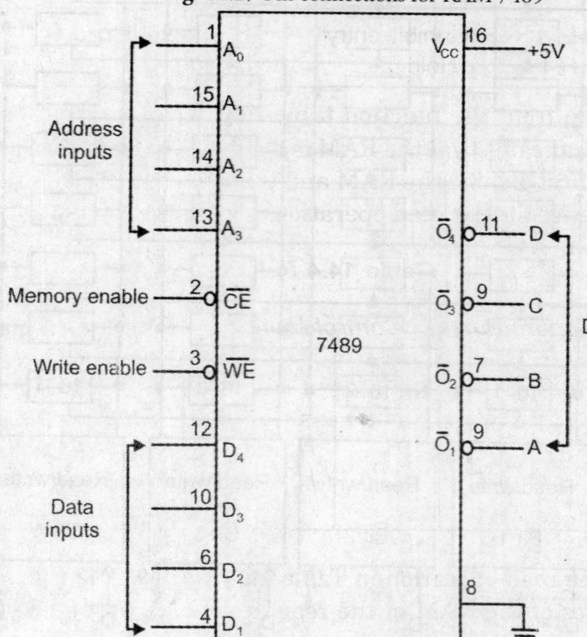

Fig. 14.28 Logic symbol for RAM 7489

The memory has open-collector outputs, which may by wired-AND connected to permit expansion up to 4704 words without additional output buffering. Access time is about 33 ns.

There are two enable inputs which are labelled memory enable, $\overline{CE}$, and write enable, $\overline{WE}$. Memory enable is held low both for reading data from the memory as well as for writing into the memory. Moreover, in either case the address input is used to select one of the 16 rows, from which the word in the memory is to be read or written into.

For the read operation hold ME low and WE high. The 4-bit data word from the row selected by the address input can now be read from the output. However, you must remember that the data at the output will be the complement of the data in the memory. For instance, if the word in the memory is 1100, the word at the output will be 0011.

As in the read operation, when you have to write into the memory, select the appropriate input address to select the row, apply the data to be written into the memory at the data inputs, and hold both ME and WE low. The data will go into the memory at the selected address and will also appear at the output in a complemented form.

Since the output of the RAM has open-collector transistors, pull-up resistors will be required to be connected to V_{CC} from each output. If you want the output to be available in an uncomplemented form, inverters will have to be used at each output.

A function table for this RAM, which gives a summary of what has been stated above is given in Table 14.3.

Table 14.3 Function table

Input		***Operation***	***State of output***
$\overline{CE}$	$\overline{WE}$		
L	*L*	Write	Complement of data inputs
L	*H*	Read	Complement of selected word
H	*L*	Inhibit entry	Undetermined
H	*H*	Hold	High

You will also notice from the function table that when both $\overline{CE}$ and $\overline{WE}$ go high, the outputs go high, which indicates that the RAM is disabled. In fact, the right way to begin a read or write operation is to first disable the RAM and then take the further necessary steps to read or write. A proper sequence for the read operation is given in Table 14.4.

Table 14.4 Read sequence

	Sequence of operation	***Control inputs***		***State of output***
		$\overline{CE}$	$\overline{WE}$	
1	Disable RAM	*H*	*H*	All outputs go high
2	Select address	*H*	*H*	All outputs are still high
3	Read data	*L*	*H*	Data at the selected address in the memory appears at the output

While following the read operation in Table 14.4 also refer to Fig. 14.29, which gives the switching characteristics of the RAM in the read cycle. As a first step you should disable the RAM by holding both $\overline{CE}$ and $\overline{WE}$ high. The next step is to select the address of the word in the memory to be read. You will notice from Fig. 14.29 that the memory enable is brought low at the same time. However, it takes some time for the data to appear at the output. This propagation delay, t_{PHL}, is the period of time it takes for stable data to appear at the output after the transition of $\overline{CE}$ from high to low level. The maximum time delay is 50 ns and it is typically 33 ns. You will also notice from the diagram that the memory enable and address input lines are held stable during the entire read operation. This diagram also shows that the output is the complement of the data word stored in the memory. There is another significant time delay, t_{PLH}, which indicates the time it takes for the outputs to return to the high state after the transition of $\overline{CE}$ from low to high level. The RAM is now disabled at both $\overline{CE}$ and WE are high and you can now proceed to read the next word in the memory. This delay period t_{PLH} is typically 26 ns although the maximum value as listed in data sheets is 50 ns.

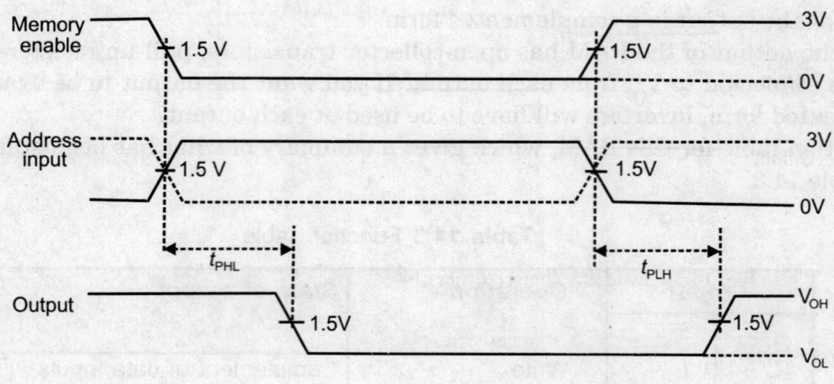

Fig. 14.29 Switching characteristics of RAM 7489 in the read cycle

The proper sequence to be followed for the write operation is given in Table 14.5.

Table 14.5 Write sequence

	Sequence of operation	***Control inputs***		***State of output***
		$\overline{CE}$	$\overline{WE}$	
1	Disable RAM	*H*	*H*	All outputs go high
2	Select address	*H*	*H*	All outputs are still high
3	Apply at the data inputs the word to be stored in the memory	*H*	*H*	All outputs are still high
4	Write data into the memory	*L*	*L*	Data is written into the memory and it also appears at the output

While following the write sequence given in Table 14.5 also refer to Fig. 14.30, which gives the switching characteristics of the RAM in the write cycle. Explanation of the several time parameters in this diagram have been explained below.

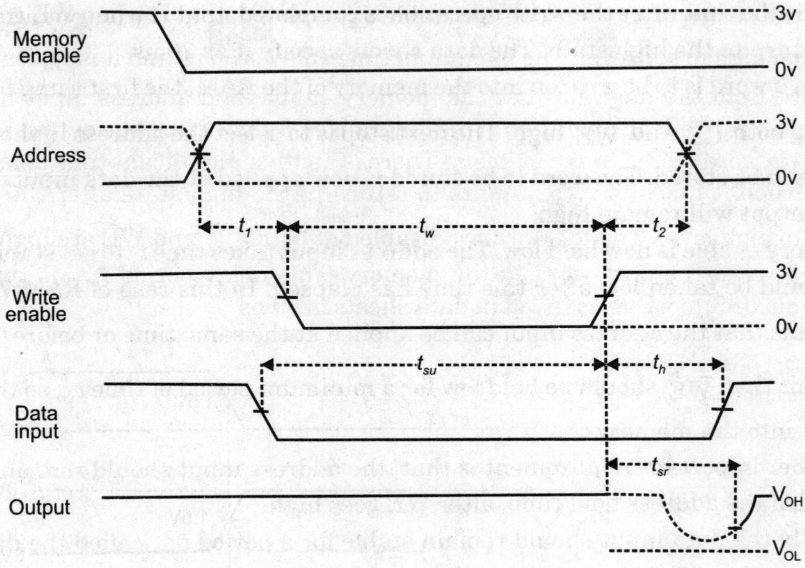

Fig. 14.30 Switching characteristics of RAM 7489 in the write cycle

Address set up time t_1

This is the minimum period after the address gets stabilized and before WE goes low. For RAM 7489 the minimum time required is 0.0 ns, that is the two events may occur at the same time.

Address hold time t_2

This is the minimum period of time for the address input to remain stable after WE goes high. The minimum time for this RAM is 5 ns.

Write enable low state t_w

This is the minimum period of time for which WE should be held low for the data to be stored in the memory. According to data sheets it is 40 ns.

Data set up time t_{SU}

It is measured from the point when the data becomes stable up to the point when WE goes high. (The data input should get stabilized for a minimum period of time prior to WE going low.) In this case t_{SU} is the same as t_w.

Data hold time t_h

It is the time for which the data must remain stable for a period after WE goes high. It is about 5 ns (minimum).

Sense recovery time t_{SR}

This is the time after the write operation is completed, that is when WE goes high, and the outputs return to the high state. The data sheets specify it as 70 ns.

When a word is to be written into the memory of the RAM, the first thing to do is to disable it by taking both $\overline{CE}$ and $\overline{WE}$ high. The next step is to select the address in the memory, where the word is to be stored. The word to be stored is now applied at the data inputs. During all this time the output will remain high.

Memory enable is now held low. The address input takes time t_1 to get stabilized. The write enable should be taken low after this time has elapsed. In this case of RAM 7489 t_1 is 0.0 ns, which means that the address input can be applied at the same time or before $\overline{WE}$ goes low. It is important that $\overline{WE}$ should be held low for a minimum period of time t_W, so that the data can be written into the memory.

Another important requirement is that, the address input should remain stable for a period t_2, called the address hold time, after WE goes high.

Finally the data input should remain stable for a period t_{SU}, called the data set-up time, before $\overline{WE}$ goes high, and for a period t_h, called the data hold time, after WE goes high.

Lastly, after the write operation has been completed and $\overline{CE}$ goes high, it will take time t_{SR}, called the sense recovery time, for the outputs to return to the high state.

14.9.3 Expansion of Capacity: RAM 7489

The word capacity and word size normally possible with RAM 7489 can be increased by adopting the same technique as was used earlier for IC 7488 A. By using two ICs 7489 as shown in Fig. 14.31, it is possible to extend the capacity to 16 words of 8-bit length. The input data is applied at inputs D_0 to D_7 and the desired address is chosen with address inputs A_0 to A_3. $\overline{CE}$ is held low to enable both the ICs.

Word capacity can be increased to 32 words of 4-bit each as shown in Fig. 14.32. The input marked CE is used to enable only one of the ICs at a time. Since the IC has open-collector outputs, it is necessary to use pull-up resistors at the output. By using a larger number of these ICs, memory can be extended to 4704 words.

14.10 RAM MEMORY ORGANIZATION

A basic RAM memory cell can accommodate only 1 bit of data; but a number of cells can be put together to provide large storage capacity. Data can be written into or read from these memory cells by following the procedures already explained while dealing with RAM 7489. To increase data storage capacity, single cells can be arranged in serial or parallel form or in a combination of both as will be discussed here.

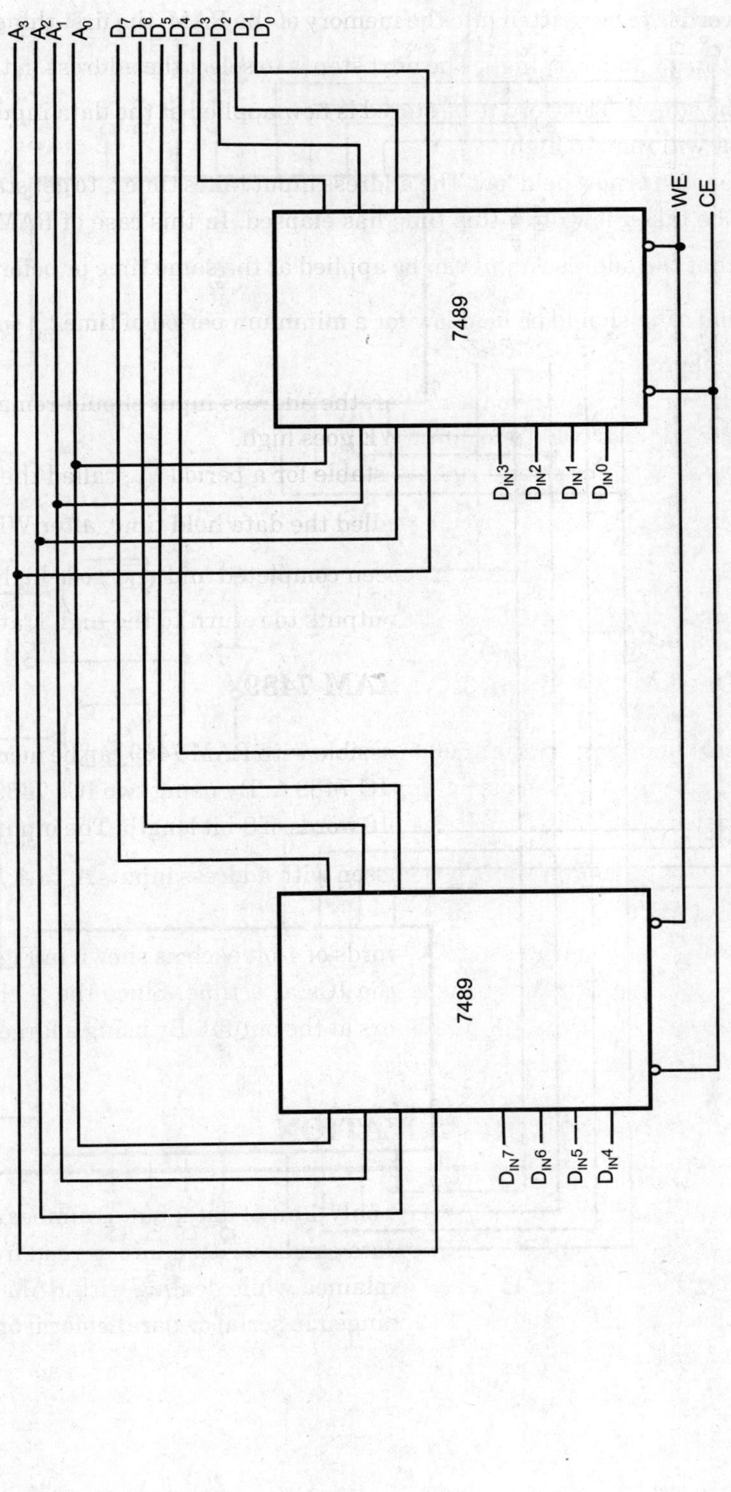

Fig. 14.31 RAM IC 7489 connected to function as a 16-word, 8-bit memory

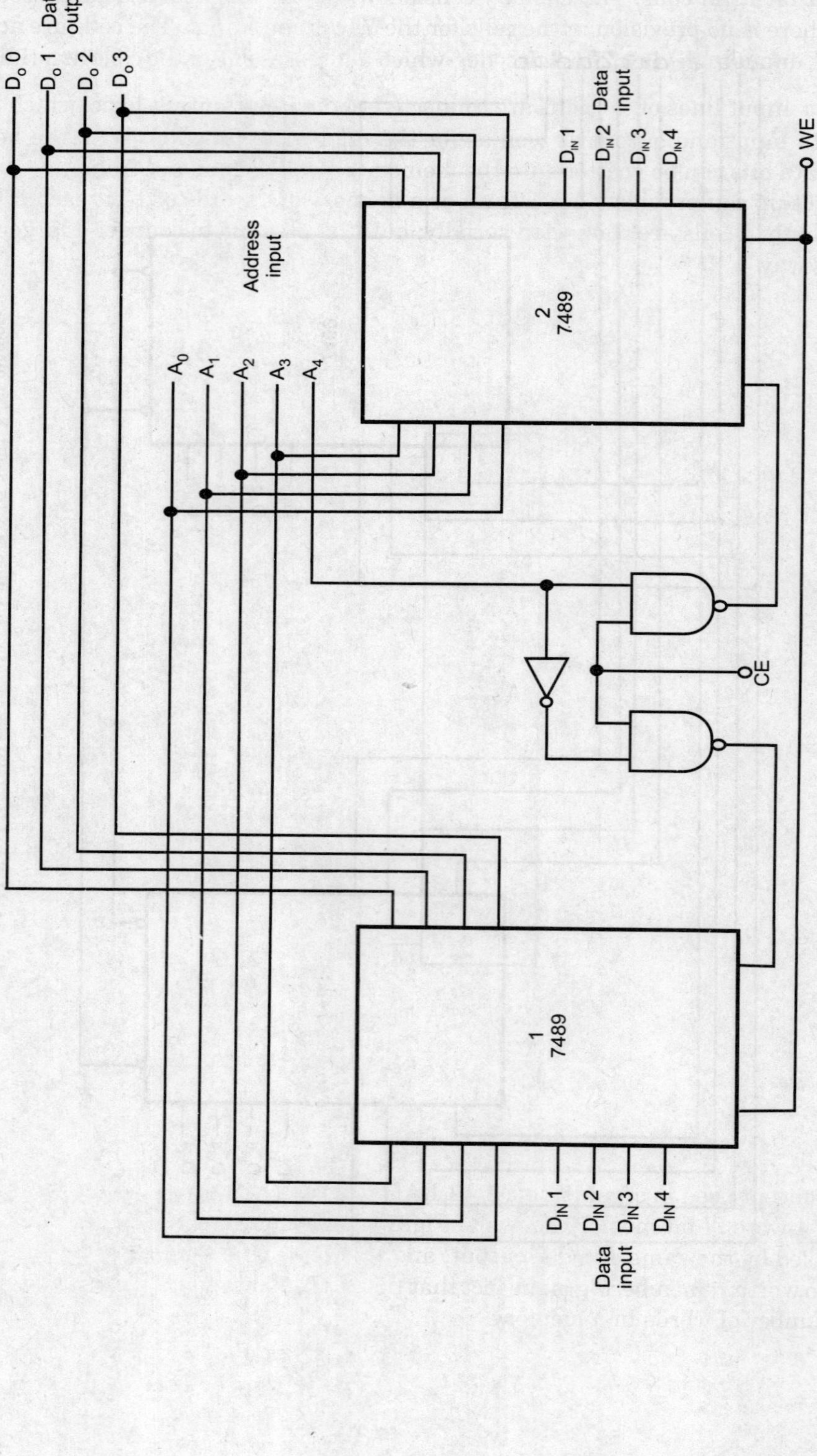

Fig. 14.32 RAM IC 7489 connected to function as a 32-word, 4-bit memory

14.10.1 Serial Expansion of RAM Memory

Figure 14.33 shows how a RAM memory consisting of 4 words of 1-bit each can be realized by using four 1-bit RAM cells. The memory cells shown in the diagram are addressed via the *X*-input and there is no provision in the cells for the *Y* (column) input. The cells are addressed by taking the *X*-input high via a 2-to-4 decoder, which addresses one of the cells at a time. The data and the $\overline{\text{data}}$ input lines of the cells are connected to the input-output logic, which have provision for data input and output as well as for the read-write function. With the help of these functions data bits can be written into the memory as well as read out from it.

This set-up can provide a 4 × 1 RAM or a memory of 4 words of 1-bit each. The diagram shows that only 4 cells are connected serially; but it is possible to connect a larger number of cells in this way.

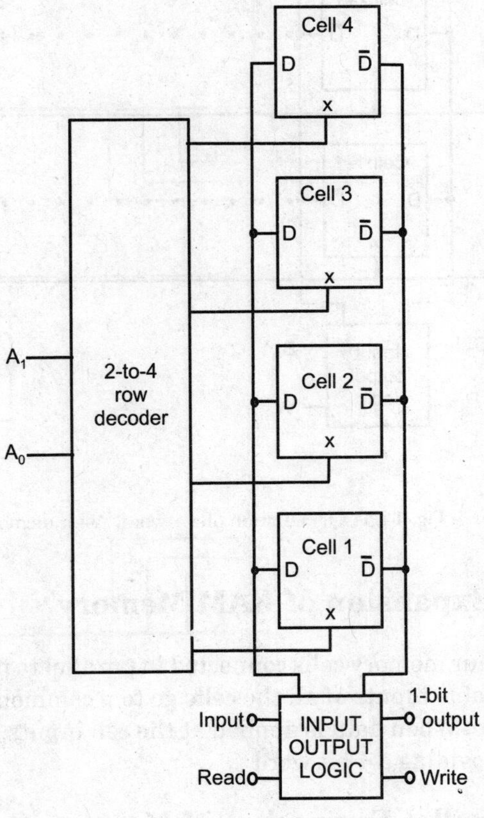

Fig. 14.33 Serial expansion of memory cells to function as a 4 × 1 RAM

The concept used in organizing a 4 × 1 RAM has been carried a step further in the organization of a 4-word *N*-bit memory shows in Fig. 14.34. Notice that all the cells in the same row are addressed by the same decoder output, and, therefore, the number of bits in each word is also *N*. Also worth remembering is the fact that the group of bits which are separately addressed give the number of words in a memory.

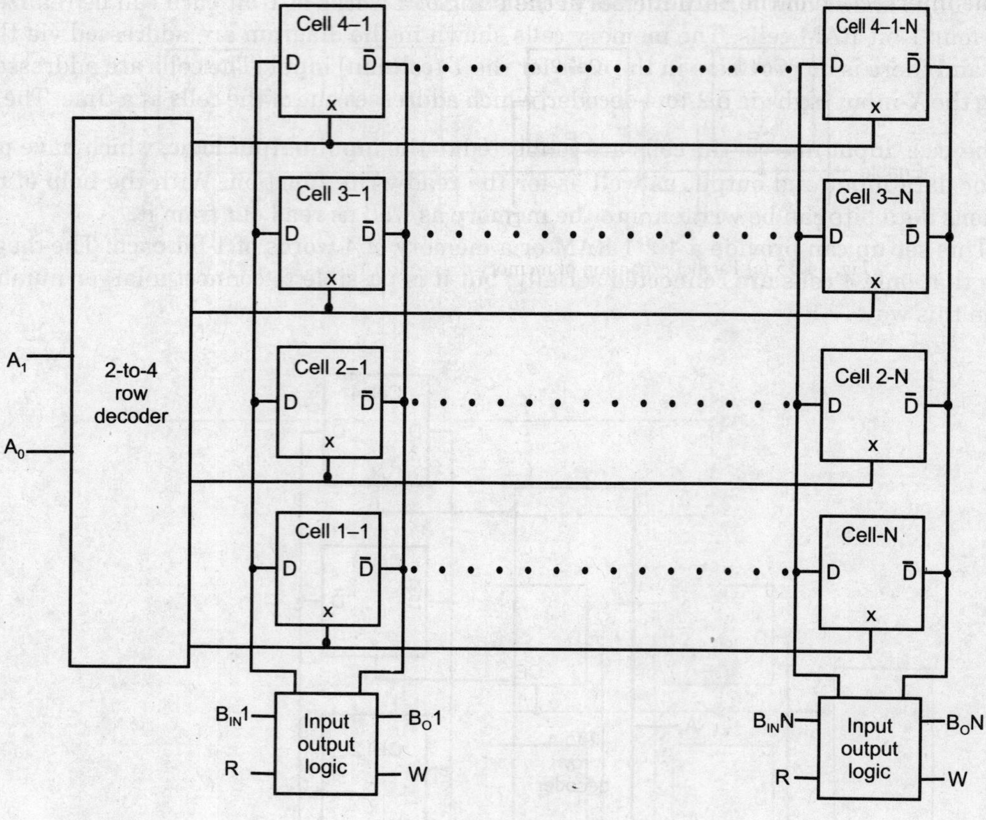

Fig. 14.34 Organization of a 4-word, N-bit memory

14.10.2 Parallel Expansion of RAM Memory

Figure 14.35 (a) shows four memory cells connected in parallel to provide a single word memory having four bits. The enable inputs of all the cells go to a common line, so that all the cells are enabled at the same time. When data is applied at the cell inputs, the corresponding 4-bit data appears at the output providing a 4-bit word.

14.10.3 Serial-parallel Expansion of Memory Cells

If we connect M groups of memory cells in series following the general arrangement shown in Fig. 14.35 (a), very large memories can be built. Figure 14.35 (b) shows how groups of the 4 cells can be connected in series to provide a 4-word memory with 4-bit in each word. The cells in each group are connected to a common enable input, so that all the cells in each group are enabled at the same time. The four-chip enable inputs are connected to a 2-to-4 decoder, so that any of the groups can be enabled at a time. The cells in each group are connected to a 2-to-4 decoder, which

can enable any cell in each group. With this arrangement only that cell can be accessed which lies at the intersection of the output lines of the two decoders.

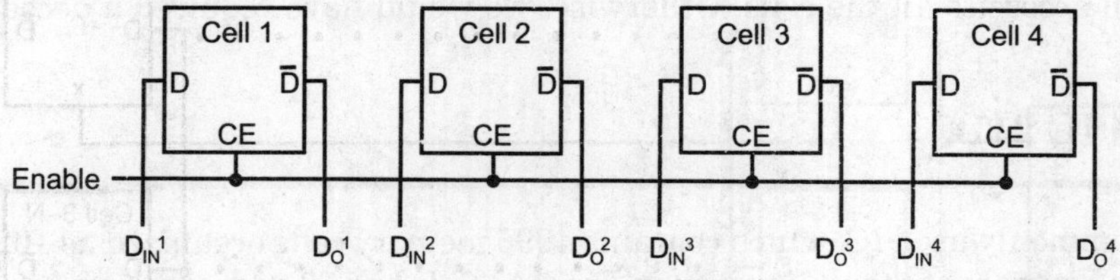

Fig. 14.35 (a) Parallel expansion of memory cells to function as a 1 × 4 RAM

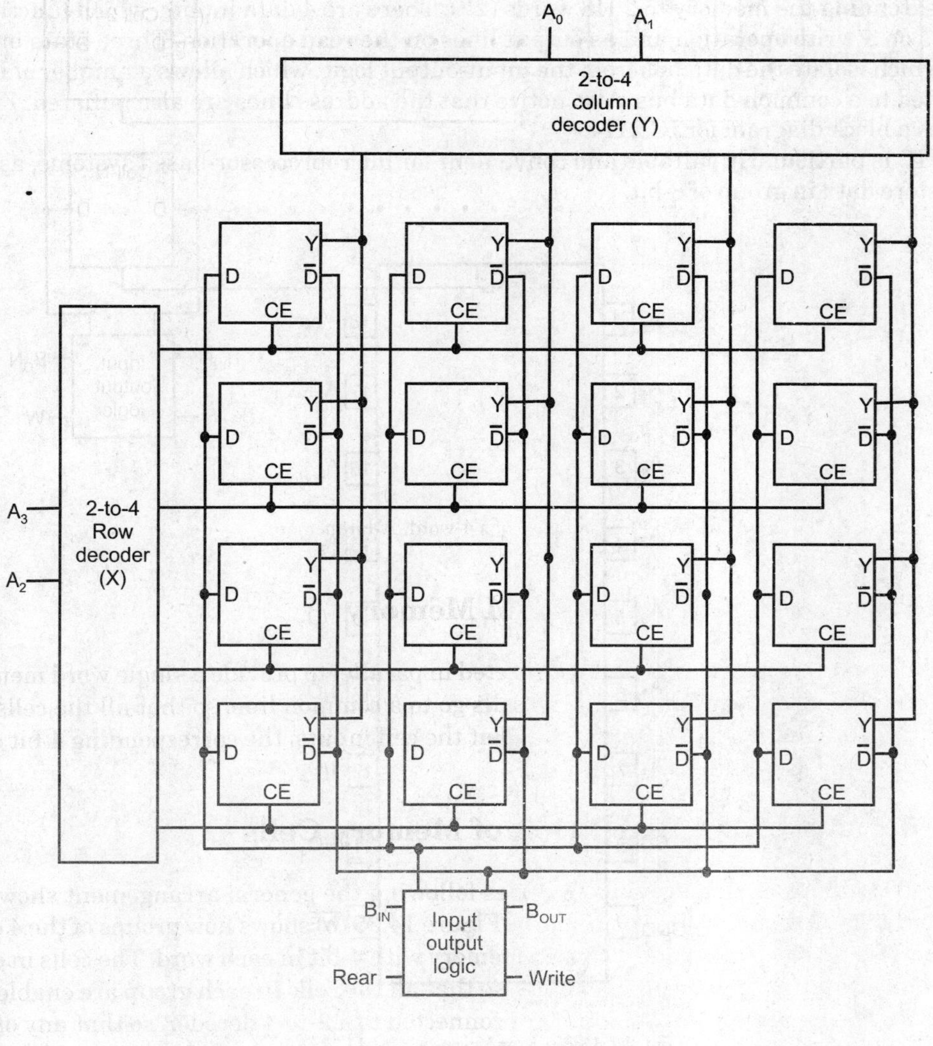

Fig. 14.35 (b) Serial-parallel expansion of memory cells to function as a 4 × 4 RAM using 1 × 4 RAMS

It should also be noted that as access is available to only one cell at a time, the data input-output lines of all the cells have been connected in parallel, which enables a single input-output logic to handle all the functions. Because of this arrangement only 4 address inputs A_0 to A_3 are required to gain access to all the cells. Otherwise, we would have required a decoder with 16 outputs.

14.11 RAM IC 2114

This is a very commonly used IC, which contains 4096 memory cells organized as 1024 words of 4-bit each. A pin diagram of this IC is given in Fig. 14.36. It has 10 address lines, which provide access to 1024 (2^{10}) words. It has a chip-select input, which can be used for the expansion of memory as will be demonstrated later. It has a write-enable control input, which permits selection between the read and write modes. Further, the CS input can be used as the 11th, address input for extending the memory to 2048 words (2^{11}). There are 4 data inputs, which function as input lines on a write operation and as output lines on the read operation. Three-state buffers are used which isolate the data bus from the input-output logic, which allows a number of ICs to be connected to a common data bus. Also notice that the address lines are also buffered. Figure 14.37 gives a block diagram for IC 2114.

This IC is particularly suitable and convenient for microprocessor-based systems, as they typically store data in group of 8-bit.

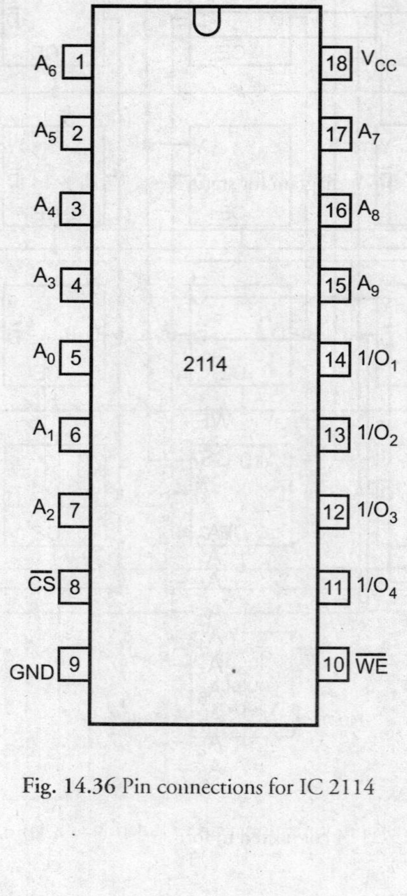

Fig. 14.36 Pin connections for IC 2114

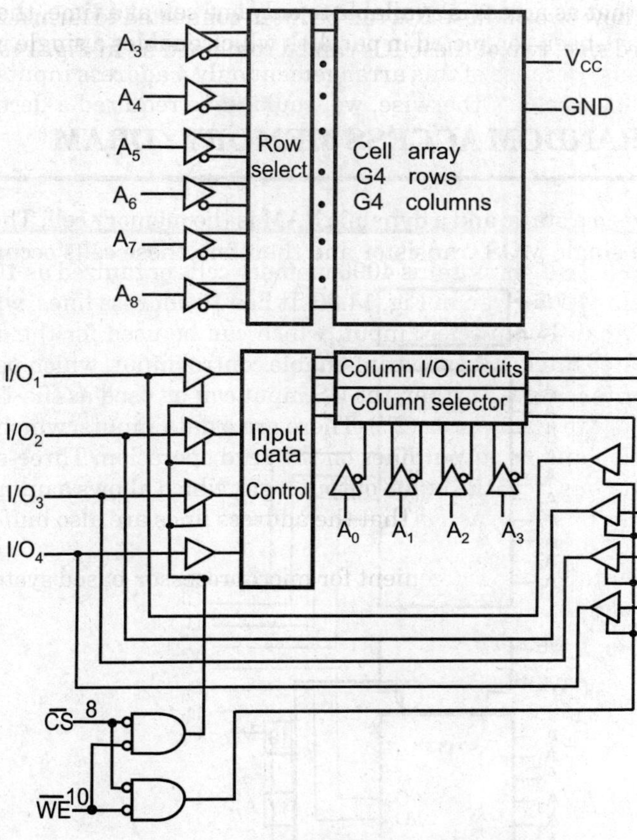

Fig. 14.37 Block diagram for static RAM IC 2114

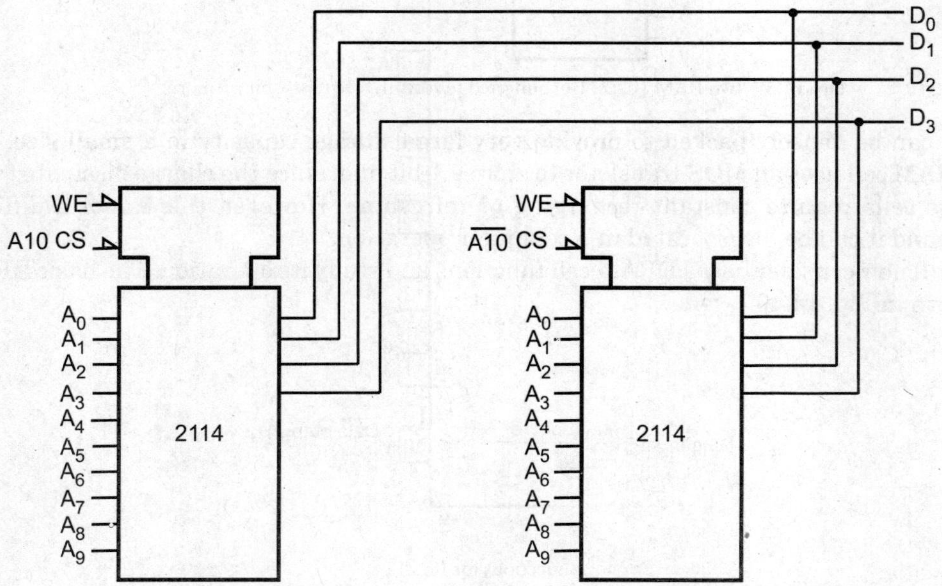

Fig. 14.38 Two RAM ICs 2114 connected to form a 2K byte × 4-bit memory

Figure 14.38 shows how two of these ICs can be inter-connected to form a 2 K byte by 4-bit memory. For an 8-bit word size, two of these ICs can be combined as in Fig. 14.39 to form a 1 K byte by 8-bit memory.

14.12 DYNAMIC RANDOM ACCESS MEMORY : DRAM

The main difference between a static and a dynamic RAM is the memory cell. The dynamic RAM memory cell uses only a single MOS transistor and therefore these cells occupy a very small

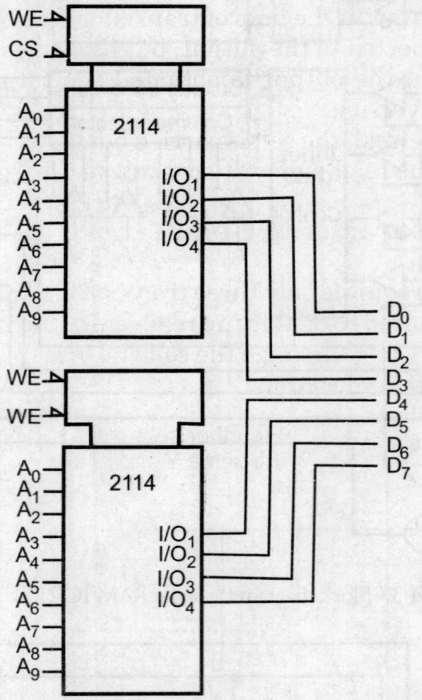

Fig. 14.39 Two RAM ICs 2114 connected to form 1 K byte × 8-bit memory

space and can be densely packed to provide very large storage capacity in a small size. The dynamic RAM cell uses an MOS transistor to store a 1-bit and, since the charge dissipates with time, these cells require constant recharging or refreshing. However, this is not a difficult procedure and it can be incorporated in a computer operation.

We will now consider how a DRAM cell functions and study its operation. The basic DRAM cell is shown in Fig. 14.40.

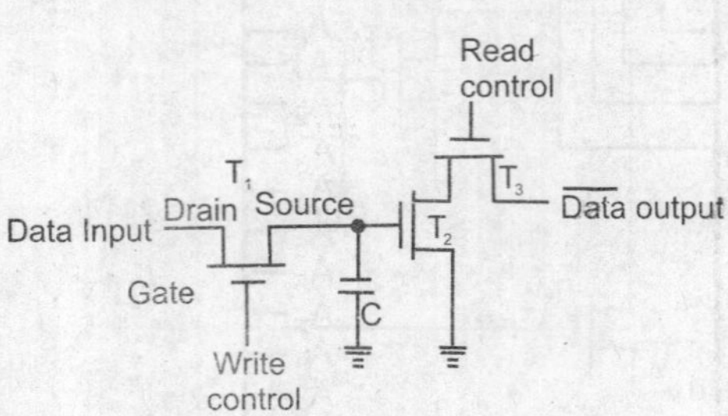

Fig. 14.40 Basic DRAM memory cell

The DRAM cell consists of a single MOS transistor T_1, and capacitor C_1. The capacitor has a very small value roughly 0.040-0.070 pF, which is connected between the source of the transistor and the substrate of the chip. The memory cell also requires two MOSFET transistors for read and write functions. Transistor T_1 functions essentially as a switch, which connects the data input to the capacitor C, when the row containing the cell is addressed. The data input switches on T_1 and, if the data input is high, the capacitor is charged when the write control is on. When the data input is low, the capacitor is discharged by the write operation. There is no problem in maintaining a stored low in the cell; but a stored high can be maintained only as long as the capacitor retains the charge. Since the capacitor will get discharged quickly through the gate-source resistance of T_2, it is necessary to periodically rewrite the data at least every 2 ms.

The stored data is read out with the help of transistor T_3. When transistor T_3 is turned on, the data in the memory is connected to the output, but the output is inverted because the data is stored at the gate of T_2 and the output is obtained from its drain. An external circuit is required to correct the data inversion.

Rewriting of the data to refresh the cell is carried out by writing back into the cell the data which is read out while both the read and write controls are turned on.

14.12.1 Three-transistor DRAM Cell

Although the basic DRAM cell requires only three transistors as shown in Fig. 14.40, some more supporting transistors are required to enable the read, write the refresh functions to be incorporated into it. It is also necessary to so arrange the cells into rows and columns, that a cell can be accessed from a particular memory location.

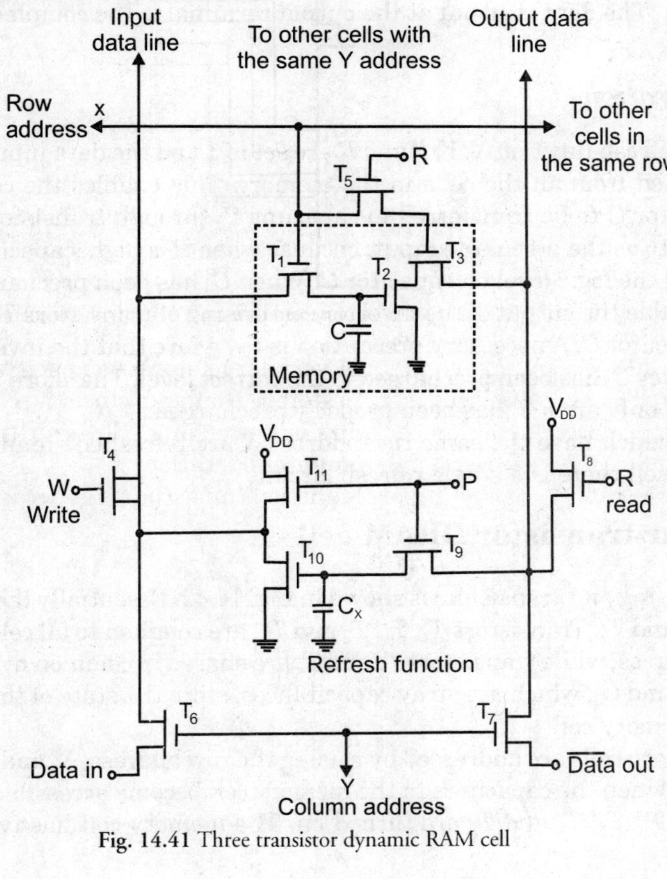

Fig. 14.41 Three transistor dynamic RAM cell

A memory configuration which satisfies some of these basic requirements is given in Fig. 14.41. In this diagram transistors T_1, T_2 and T_3 perform the same function as transistors bearing the same numbers in Fig. 14.40. Transistor T_4 is used for the write operation and transistors T_5 and T_8 are used for the read function. Transistors T_6 and T_7 are required for data input and output, respectively. Transistor T_8 functions as the load for transistor T_2.

Memory cells having the same X address are connected to lines marked XX and similarly cells having the same Y address are connected to lines marked YY. This enables any cell to be accessed by feeding the appropriate address at the row select input X, and the column select input Y, both of which should be held high to obtain access to a cell.

Write Operation

For the write operation, the required cell is accessed by applying the appropriate address at the row select input, X, and the column select input, Y, when both X and Y become 1. The refresh circuit is disconnected by setting P to 0 and W is set to 1 for the write operation. As T_6 is already on and T_4 and T_1 are also turned on, this operation enables capacitor C to charge to the same state as the data input.

Read Operation

For the read operation R is set to 1 and W to 0, which turns on transistors T_3, T_5 and T_8, which connects the drain of T_2 to the $\overline{\text{data}}$ output terminal. T_8 functions as the load for T_2 in the read operation. The data read out at the output terminal is the complement of the level stored on C.

Refresh Operation

For the refresh function X, Y, P and R are set to 1 and the data input and output terminals are disconnected from all the cells in the memory. This enables the complement of the logic level of capacitor C to be transferred to capacitor C_r through transistor T_9. The terminal P is often referred to as the precharge input, because when P is high, capacitor C_r precharges to the complement of the logic level on capacitor C. When C_r has been precharged W is set to 1 and R to 0, which enable the output of the inverter comprising of transistors T_{10} and T_{11} to refresh the charge on capacitor C. A necessary precaution is to ensure that the inverter amplifier does not load C until after C_r has been precharged to the correct level. Therefore, the refresh amplifier is connected to C only after C_r has been properly precharged.

All cells which have the same row address X are refreshed simultaneously and for each column of the cell there is a single refresh circuit.

14.12.2 Four-transistor DRAM cell

A DRAM cell using four transistors is shown in Fig. 14.42. Essentially the cell consists of transistors T_1, T_2, T_3 and T_4. Transistors T_5, T_6, T_9 and T_{10} are common to all cells which have the same column, Y, address, while transistors T_7 and T_8 are shared in common by all cells in the memory. Capacitors C_1 and C_2, which are stray capacitances, store the state of the cell and are the backbone of the memory cell.

The memory cells are addressed by raising the row address, X, and the column address, Y, to logic 1 level when the capacitors in the memory cell become accessible to the data terminals, as transistors T_3, T_4, T_5 and T_6 are turned on. The memory cell has two states. In one of the states the voltage across C_1 is large which turns T_1 on and the voltage across T_2 is zero which turns T_2 off. In the other state this position is reversed.

After the cell has been accessed, the state of the memory stored in the cell can be read by setting $R = 1$. Writing in the cell can be done by setting $W = 1$.

As data stored in the cell cannot be retained for long because of leakage problems, these cells require constant refreshing. This is achieved by allowing brief access to the cell from the supply voltage V_{DD}. This is done by simultaneously raising the logic levels of X address and the refresh terminal to logic 1 level, which turns on transistors T_3, T_4, T_9 and T_{10} at the same time. If at the start of the refresh operation T_1 is on and T_2 is off, the voltage across C_1 will be large and zero across C_2. Since T_2 is off, the current from the supply will flow through C_1 to replenish its charge. As T_1 is on C_2 will not charge as rapidly as C_1. Similarly, when T_1 is off and T_2 is on, the V_{DD} supply charges C_2 faster than C_1.

While the cell is being refreshed T_4 and T_{10} serve as load for T_2; while T_3 and T_9 serve as load for T_1. Hence during the refresh interval, the cell functions as a conventional flip-flop consisting of two cross-coupled inverters. However, whatever the state of the cell during the refresh interval, this initial state is reinforced by the refresh operation.

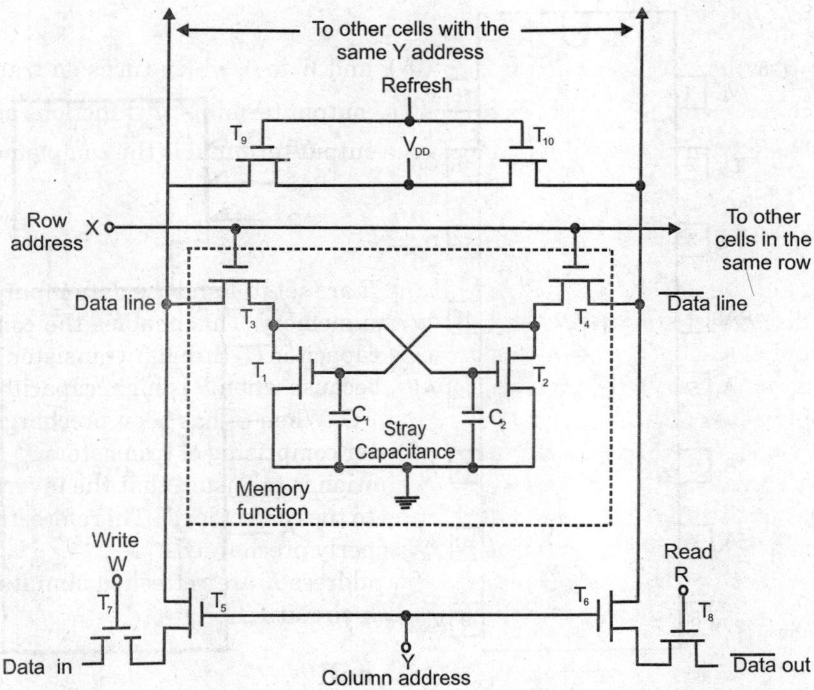

Fig. 14.42 Four-transistor dynamic RAM cell

14.13 DYNAMIC MEMORY ORGANIZATION

The main difference between a static and a dynamic RAM memory lies in the memory cell they use. The dynamic cell uses much less space and, therefore for the same memory capacity, dynamic RAMs take much less space on a chip. The other difference will be noticed in the support circuitry required for dynamic RAMs. However, even then the small size of a dynamic cell cancels the disadvantage of a large support circuitry.

Dynamic RAM 4116, which is widely used, is a typical example of a dynamic RAM. It has 16, 384 memory cells oranized as a 16K × 1-bit memory. The cells are arranged in a square array with 128 rows and 128 columns. There is a single input line D_{IN} and a single data output line D_{out}. It has seven address inputs A_0 to A_6. Its pin and logic diagrams are given in Figs. 14.43 (a) and (b).

To gain access to cells in a memory having 16,384 cells, normally 2^{14} (16,384) address lines would be required; but IC 4116 has only 7 address lines. The capability to access all the memory cells is achieved with the control inputs $\overline{RAS}$ and $\overline{CAS}$. First the 7 address bits A_0 to A_6 are provided for the row address selection bits, which are latched by the internal circuitry of the memory when the $\overline{RAS}$ control input goes low. Next the same 7 address lines are provided for the column address selection bits, which are now latched by the internal circuitry when the $\overline{CAS}$ control input goes low. This procedure makes it possible to select one of the 2^7 (128) rows and one of the 128 columns. Thus it is possible to select one of the 128^2 or 16,384 memory locations.

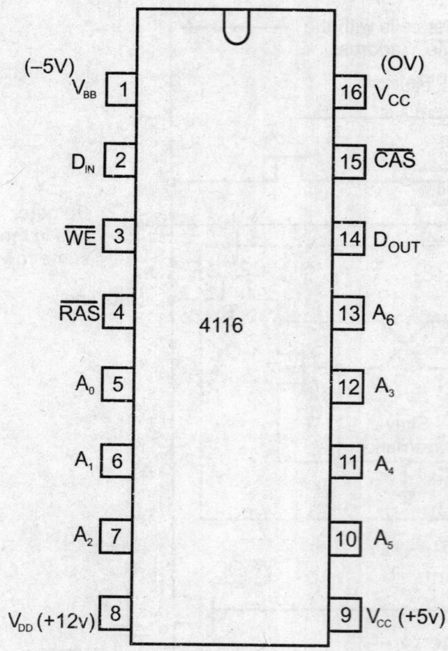

Fig. 14.43 (a) Pin diagram for DRAM IC 4116

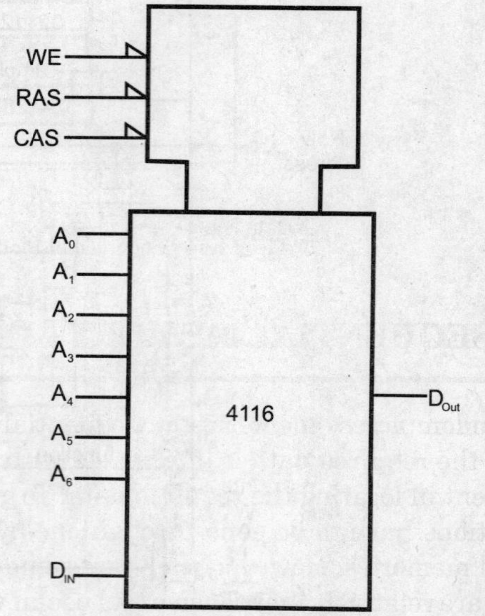

(b) Logic diagram for DRAM IC 4116

Figure 14.44 gives a functional block diagram of the IC 4116. You will notice that the memory cells are arranged in two groups of 64 rows and 128 columns. When the memory is addressed, as indicated, the row address bits select one of the 64 rows in the top or bottom half of the memory and the column bits are decoded to select one of the 128 columns.

In this way, during the read operation, one of the 16,384 memory cells is latched as the output data bit with the help of the CAS control input. If $\overline{WE}$ is held low, the data bit present at the input D_{in} will be stored in the selected bit position on a write operation.

You will notice that there are two latches associated with D_{in} and D_{out}, which are required to hold the data for storage and read out.

Since all the operations are carried out in a prescribed sequence, the timing requirements are very important and have to be strictly observed.

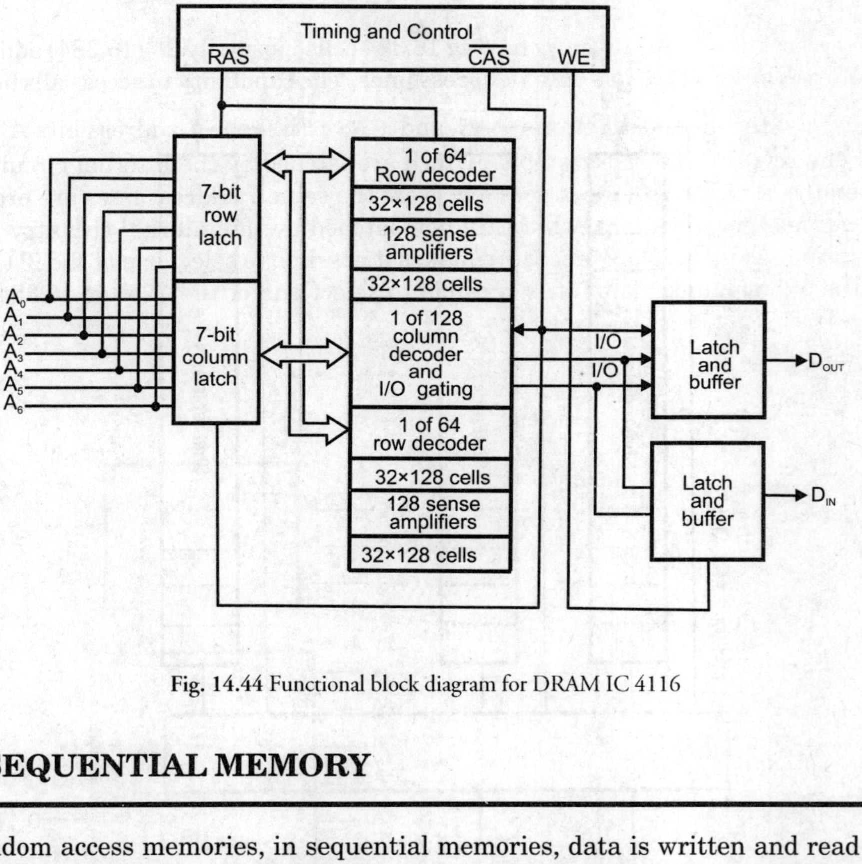

Fig. 14.44 Functional block diagram for DRAM IC 4116

14.14 SEQUENTIAL MEMORY

Unlike random access memories, in sequential memories, data is written and read out in sequence. If the required data is intermixed with other data, as is usually the case, a lot of time may be spent in locating the required data. To gain access to the relevant data all the intermediate locations have to be gone through one-by-one in sequence. Herein lies the limitaion of sequential memories. However, there are some plus points also in favour of sequential memories. They are relatively inexpensive and useful when data is to be read out in the order in which it is written into the memory.

14.14.1 Static Shift Register Memory

The essential features of a sequential shift register memory are shown in Fig. 14.45. The diagram shows N shift registers, each with M stages which are implemented with flip-flops. This sequential memory will provide storage for M words each having N bits. Each register will contain one of the N bits of each of the M words. When clock input is applied, bits in all the registers will advance by one step. Thus all the bits in each word will advance in step to the right and the words will be available at the output.

The register outputs may be connected to their inputs, when they can function in the manner of the circulating shift register. It is, therefore, possible to circulate the register contents endlessly. A logic input control is shown at the extreme left of the diagram, which can be used to recirculate the register contents, to erase certain words in the memory, as well as to fill up the erased spaces with fresh data. The write enable control enables new data to be entered.

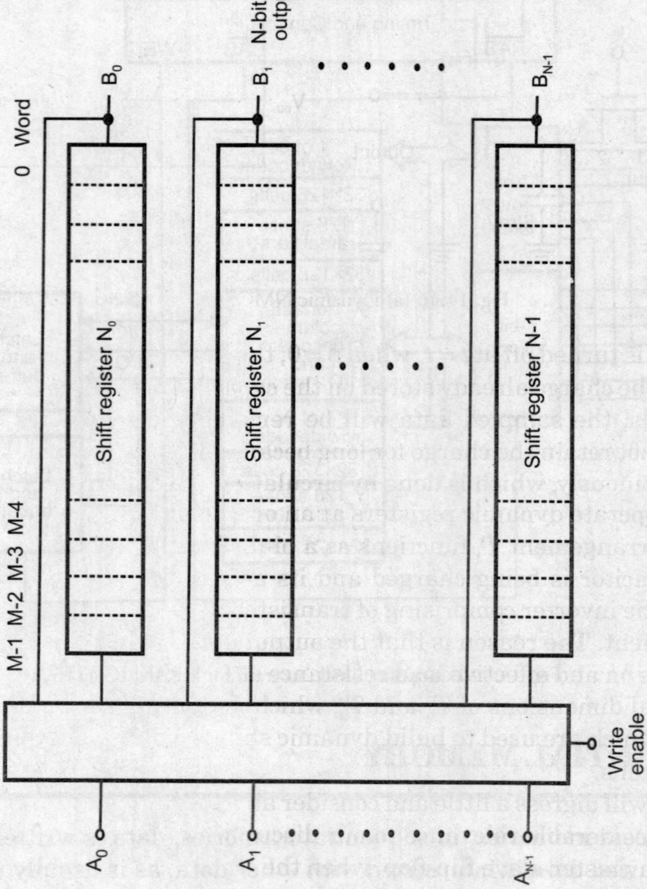

Fig. 14.45 Sequential shift register memory

14.15 DYNAMIC SHIFT REGISTER

Sequential shift register memories can be implemented using bipolar devices; but it is inconvenient to use them for large-scale memories, as bipolar devices take up a lot of space on a chip. It is therefore more desirable to use MOS devices for sequential shift register memories.

Like bipolar flip-flops, MOS devices can also be cascaded to implement sequential shift register memories. We will consider a dynamic MOS cell, given in Fig. 14.46(a), which forms the basis of dynamic MOS memories. When the gate input of T_1 is at logic 1 level at $t = t_1$, T_1 will be turned on and will charge capacitor C to the same logic level as the input for the duration of the interval, when $\phi = 1$. You will notice that in this arrangement T_1 functions only as a transmission gate.

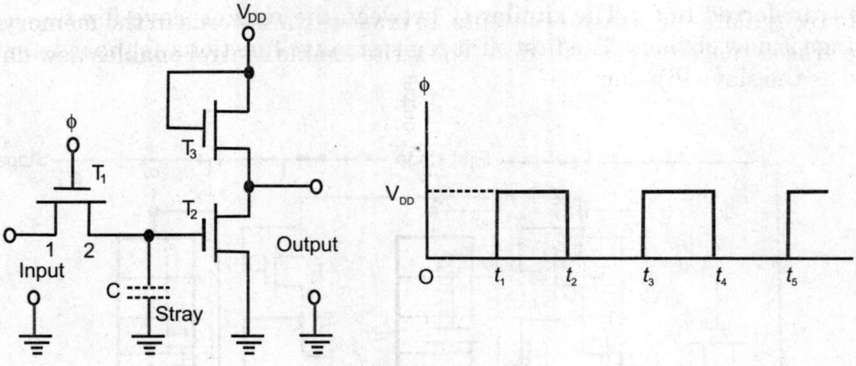

Fig. 14.46 (a) Dynamic NMOS cell (b) Clock waveform

When T_1 is turned off at $t = t_2$ when $\phi = 0$, the inverter comprising of T_2 and T_3 will continue to respond to the charge already stored on the capacitor, as long as the charge has not leaked off. In other words, the sampled data will be remembered by the inverter. However, since the capacitor cannot retain the charge for long because of leakage problems, they are required to be refreshed continously, which is done by circulating the data held in the register. It is therefore necessary to operate dynamic registers at an operating frequency of not less than 10 kHz.

In this arrangement T_1 functions as a bi-directional switch. Terminal 1 acts as the drain when the capacitor is being charged and its acts as the source when the capacitor is being discharged. The inverter comprising of transistors T_2 and T_3 is referred to as a ratio inverter in this arrangement. The reason is that the output of the inverter is dependent on the resistance of T_2 when it is on and effective load resistance of T_3. The ratio of these two resistances depends on the physical dimensions of T_2 and T_3, which is typically 1 : 5. This leads us to two types of storage cells which are used to build dynamic shift registers. They are referred to as ratio cells and ratioless cells.

Here we will digress a little and consider an important feature of the master-slave flip-flop, which is of considerable relevance to our discussion of dynamic shift register stages. You will recall that in a master-slave flip-flop, when the output of the flip-flop is responding to the existing data, the data at the input of the flip-flop must not in any way affect the output. In our design of a dynamic shift register stage, this will have to be taken care of.

14.15.1 Two-phase Ratio NMOS Dynamic Shift Register Stage

A dynamic shift register stage consisting of two inverter stages is shown in Fig. 14.47. It requires two gating voltages ϕ_1 and ϕ_2 to control the two transmission gates T_1 and T_4. The two gating waveforms are shown in Fig. 14.48. These waveforms are so phased that T_1 and T_4 will not be on at the same time. When T_1 is on, T_4 will be off and when T_4 is on, T_1 will be off. Let us consider the situation at $t = t_1$, when θ_1 is 1, which turns on T_1. At this time the input data bit to the stage will be transferred to C_1. Simultaneously as T_1 is also turned on, the complement of the data bit stored on C_2 will be transferred to C_1', which is the input storage capacitor of the second stage.

Also observe that when $\phi_1 = 1$ and $\phi_2 = 0$ at the moment when the input data bit is being stored on C_1, this input bit will in no way interfere with the output stage or with the bit which is being transferred to the second stage. Later on when $\phi_2 = 1$, the complement of the bit stored on C_1 will be transferred to C_2. The similarity between the master-slave flip-flop and this shift register stage is now obvious. The first shift register stage functions as the master flip-flop and the second as the slave flip-flop.

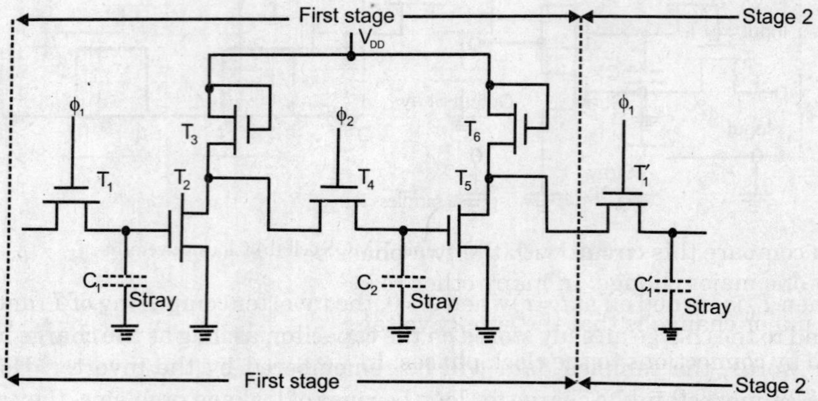

Fig. 14.47 Two-phase ratio NMOS dynamic shift-register stage

It is important that the time duration for change of ϕ_1 from 0 to 1 and 1 to 0 should not be too large, for otherwise the charge stored on capacitor will leak off. For this reason these shift registers are operated dynamically, and are therefore classified as dynamic shift registers.

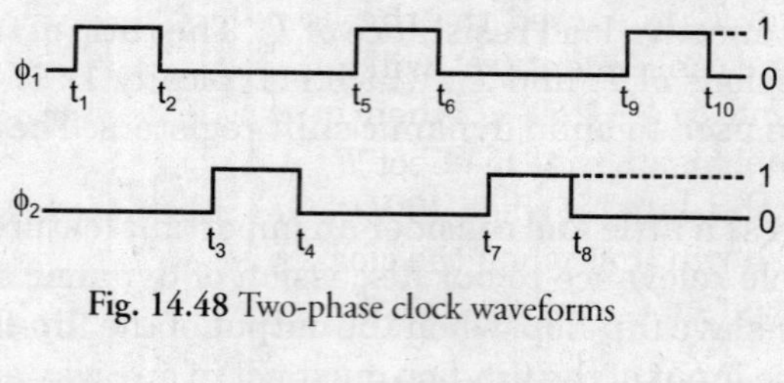

Fig. 14.48 Two-phase clock waveforms

14.15.2 Two-phase Ratioless Shift Register

In the two-phase ratio dynamic shift register, we have just considered the channel resistance of the load has to be large in comparison with the channel resistance of the driver. This implies that the length-to-width ratio (L/W) of the load must be larger than the corresponding dimensions of the driver. It follows, therefore, that the load will occupy a larger area on the chip than the driver, which would seriously affect the storage capacity of the chip. Another important consideration is the speed of operation, which will be seriously affected by an increase in the load resistance.

To a very large extent these problems can be overcome by using low resistance MOS devices, which have the same geometry. The resultant dynamic shift register is referred to as a two-phase ratioless shift register. A ratioless shift register is given in Fig. 14.49.

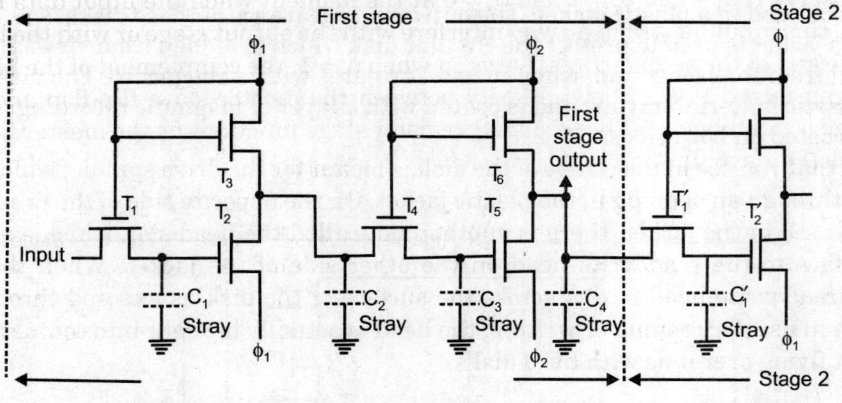

Fig. 14.49 Two-phase ratioless dynamic shift register stage

If you compare this circuit with the two-phase shift register shown in Fig. 14.47, you will notice only one major change. In many other respects the two circuits have considerable similarity. The major change is that the supply voltage V_{DD} and the ground connections have been substituted by connections to the clock phases. In the discussion that follows, we will refer to 0 V as $\phi = 0$ and V_{DD} as $\phi = 1$.

To begin with let us assume that as $t = t_1$, when ϕ_1 goes to 1 (V_{DD}), transistors T_1 and T_3 are turned on and if the data input bit is at V_{DD}, C_1 will be charged to V_{DD} through T_1; and C_2 will also be charged to V_{DD} through T_3 as that will also be on. It is to be noted that while C_2 is being charged, T_2 will be off as at no time during this period will the gate voltage of T_2 exceed the source voltage by T_2's threshold voltage V_T.

When ϕ_1 drops to 0 (0 V), T_3 is turned off and T_2 is turned on, since the charge stored on C_1 causes the gate voltage of T_2 to exceed the threshold voltage, and as a consequence, C_2 discharges to 0 through T_2 and consequently C_2 will now store the bit which will be the complement of the input bit at the end of ϕ_1, that is when it has returned to 0. The net effect of these operations leads to the conclusion that in effect T_2 and T_3 are functioning as an inverter. It can be shown that if initially the data bit was 0 (0 V), the same inversion will take place.

Similarly, it can be shown that when the clock phase ϕ_2 changes from 0 to 1 and returns to 0, the complement of the bit on C_2 will be transferred to C_4.

14.16 MAGNETIC DISK MEMORY

While data and programs are normally stored in computer systems by using ROMs, RAMs, EPROMs, etc., these devices cannot meet the requirement for large amount of data storage. These devices are, therefore, classified as internal storage devices. When a large amount of data is required to be stored, computer systems depend on external storage systems. One such system in common use is storage on magnetic disks. Here again there are two classes of disk storage systems, known as hard disks and floppy disks, also known as diskettes. We will consider these in some detail in the following sections.

14.16.1 Floppy Disks (Diskettes)

Floppy discs normally come in the following sizes; 3½ inch, 5¼ inch and 8 inch. Currently the standard for small computer systems is 5¼ (5.25) inch. They are very thin and circular and are permanently enclosed in a plastic jacket. The outward appearance of these disks is as shown in Fig. 14.50. The jacket is used to protect the circular disk which is hidden from view. The disk is never removed from the jacket and, when in use, it rotates within the jacket. The disk is made of very thin plastic material (mylar) and is coated with a layer of magnetic recording oxide and are normally coated on both sides.

The hole that you see in the centre of the disk is meant for the drive spindle, which clamps on to the disk through an opening in the plastic jacket. On the opposite side of the pressure pad slot, which you see in the jacket, there is another slot called the head slot, which exposes the recording surface to the read/write head on the other side of the jacket. When the disk is spinning, the read/write head moves across the surface of the disk as exposed through head window. When in use, for reading or writing, the head is actually brought into contact with the disk and is not flying over it as with hard disks.

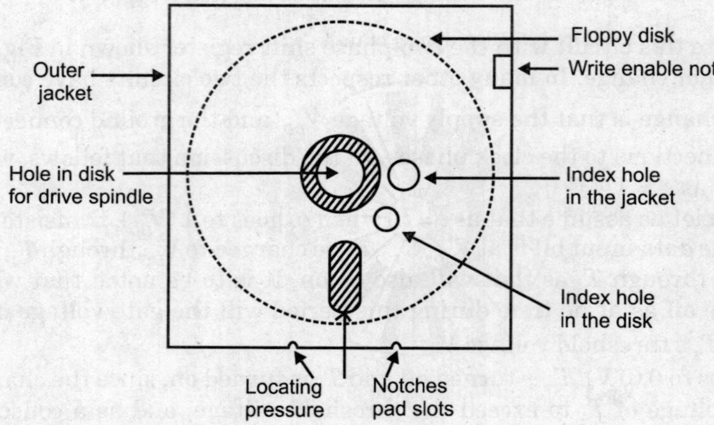

Fig. 14.50

There is an index hole in the jacket near the centre of the disk, which enables the drive electronics to detect whenever the index hole in the disk crosses this point. This produces an index mark pulse which passes on the necessary timing and positioning information to the drive control mechanism.

To prevent the data recorded on the disk from accidental erasure, there is a write enable notch which, when convered with a tab, ensures against erasure of the data on the disk. Also notice two locating notches on the front edge of the jacket, which assist in positioning of the disk correctly in the drive.

Disk formats

In order that data recorded on the disk may be located or written into an allotted slot, it is necessary to organize the disk into tracks and tracks into sectors. There are two standards which are in common use with 5.25 inch disks. One of the standards has 40 tracks and the other 80 magnetic tracks. Figure 14.51 shows the outside track which is numbered 00 and the inside track which is numbered 39 (or 79 in the case of the 80 track standard). The number of usable tracks on a disk depends largely on the quality of the disk and the drive mechanism. Both these should have a high standard to enable a larger number of tracks to be employed.

In the case of the 40 track disk, the number of tracks is about 48 to an inch, which are positioned as close to the outside edge of the disk as possible. Although the outer tracks are longer than the inner ones, it is so arranged that both contain the same amount of information.

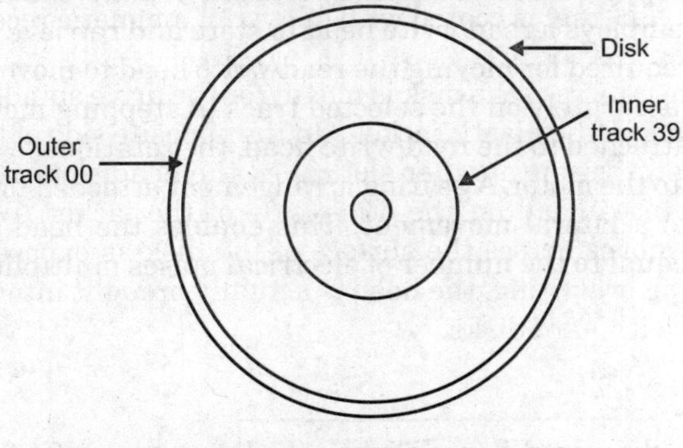

Fig. 14.51 Positioning of tracks on disk

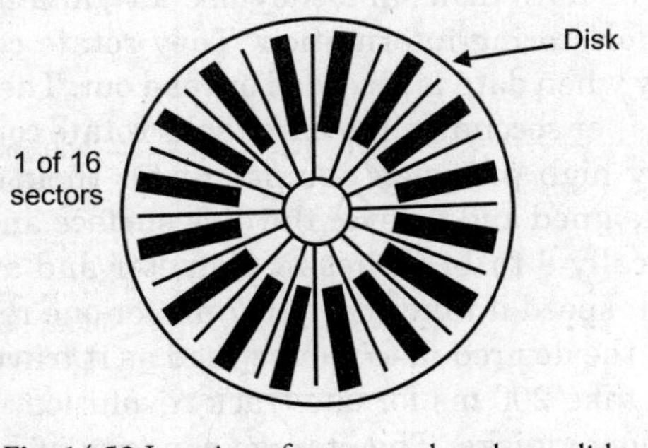

Fig. 14.52 Location of sectors and tracks on disk

Each track is now divided into an equal number of sectors. In Fig. 14.52 we have divided the tracks into sixteen sectors but the number may be more or less than 16. The standard capacity chosen for a disk sector is 256 bytes. We now have 40 × 16 or 640 sectors, each capable of accommodating 256 bytes. The total storage capacity for a single side of a disk will therefore be 640 × 256 or 163, 840 bytes.

Disk formatting

Before we start recording data on a disk it is necessary to impose the disk format we have just described on to a blank floppy disk. This is done with the help of a program known as a formatter. In this process the concentric magnetic tracks are imposed on the disk and the sectors are marked out and numbered. The tracks are numbered from 00 (the outermost track) to 39 (the innermost track). The sectors in each track are numbered from 0 to 15, if there are 16 sectors.

In order to facilitate cataloging of the data recorded on the disk, so that the required data may be retrieved or fresh data may be recorded in the place allotted to it, some sectors are reserved on disks to be used for cataloging. In this space, so reserved, the computer records the names, locations and other relevant information for all the files recorded on the disk. It is also necessary to reserve some more space for cataloging for later expansion when required. In short, the formatting of a disk is like preparing a register and allotting columns and rows for a variety of data to be entered into it.

If the disk being used is doubled-sided, both sides of a disk can be formatted and used for storing information. This, however, requires not only a disk coated on both sides, but also a double-sided disk drive. A floppy disk drive basically consists of a drive motor which rotates the disk within the jacket and employs a read/write head to store and retrieve data. The other part of the drive mechanism is required for moving the read/write head to move it radially along the disk and also to position it accurately on the selected track. A stepping motor is used to control the rotation of the spindle attached to the read/write head, the rotation of which is controlled by electrical impulses applied to the motor. A gearing arrangement attached to the spindle converts the rotational movement to a lateral movement. This enables the head assembly to move a distance radially, which is equal to the number of electrical pulses multiplied by the track spacing.

14.16.2 Hard Disks

In the last section, we have discussed floppy disks, which are made of a flexible material. Another class of disks is known as hard disks and they use a rigid aluminium platter, on which recording oxide is deposited for storing information. They rotate continuously as opposed to floppy disks, which rotate only when data is recorded or read out. The speed of rotation of floppy disks is 300 rpm (4 revolutions per second) while hard disks rotate continuously at 2400 or 3000 rpm. Hard disks require very high precision equipment for their operation. The read/write heads are aerodynamically designed and fly over the disk surface and never touching it.

The hard disks are typically 8 to 14 inches in diameter and at 3600 rpm they make 60 revolutions per second. At that speed it takes only 16.7 ms for one revolution. If the read/write head is over the desired data, the desired data can be read as it traverses that region. A floppy disk rotating at 300 rpm will take 200 ms for one track revolution. Hard disks are capable of storing far more data than floppy disks. The storage capacity of hard disk drives runs into megabytes per drive.

14.16.3 Winchester Disk Drives

These disc systems can hold a number of hard disks and are contained in a sealed assembly. These disks are kept rotating continously, are coated with a magnetic material and are stacked one beside the other with space between them. Information is recorded on the surface of disks by magnetic heads which are mounted on access arms. On each side of a disk there are several thousand data tracks. The density of bits recorded along a track can vary from 500 to 24,000 bits per inch. The disks normally rotate at a speed of 3600 rpm.

Most Winchester disk drives use 14,8,5¼ or 3½ inch disks. The storage capacities also vary from about 5 megabytes to very large capacities. Bit densities along a track also vary from about 300 bits per inch to 20,000 bits per inch.

14.17 MAGNETIC TAPE DATA STORAGE SYSTEM

You must be familiar with cassette tape-recorders which use tapes coated with a magnetic material for recording speech and music. Magnetic tapes are also being used for recording data in a coded form. Consider the following advantages of recording data on tapes.

1. Very large quantities of data can be recorded on tapes.
2. Data recorded on tapes can be erased and rewritten.

3. Tape reels can be changed and thus the same drive mechanism can be used.
4. Data stored on tapes does not fade away.

However, there are some drawbacks in this system. In the first place the access time is more than for other systems in use. Secondly, data stored on tapes does not provide random access capability. These drawbacks are, to a certain extent, offset by the low cost of storing data on tapes.

The tape transport mechanism for data storage has to operate at high speeds and should be able to start and stop in a very short time, even at high speeds. The requirements are met by specially designed tape transport mechanisms.

Tape read/write heads used in data storage systems have a read gap and a write gap and the read gap is positioned after the write gap, so that the data recorded can be checked for accuracy.

Tapes used in magnetic tape storage systems have width varying from ½ inch to 3 inch. Tapes in common use are ½ inch wide. Data is recorded on tapes in rows as shown in Fig. 14.53. Normally there are 7 or 9 tracks, and one of these tracks is used to store a parity bit. The parity bit is added if necessary, so that the number of 1s in every row is an odd number. Data is recorded in blocks with gaps between every two blocks. Every block of data has start and stop indicators. Tapes are provided with metallic coating at the beginning and end of tapes, which activate photocells to prevent tape overruns.

Codes are used for recording on tapes and they differ from one another in some respects. One commonly used code is an IBM code as shown in Fig. 14.53. The tape used is ½ inch wide and has seven tracks. Another IBM standard code is also ½ inch wide, but it has nine tracks. The seven track code in the diagram shows only part of the code. The codes for digit 3 and alphabet *A* have been indicated, in this code 0s are blank spaces and 1s are indicated by a vertical line.

14.18 CHARGE-COUPLED DEVICES (CCDs)

In memory storage systems which are required to store millions of bits of data, the cost input is a very important consideration. Suppose 500 million bits of data are required to be stored and the cost per bit of data is 0.05 cent; the cost of the memory storage system would be 250,000 $, which may be prohibitive in some cases.

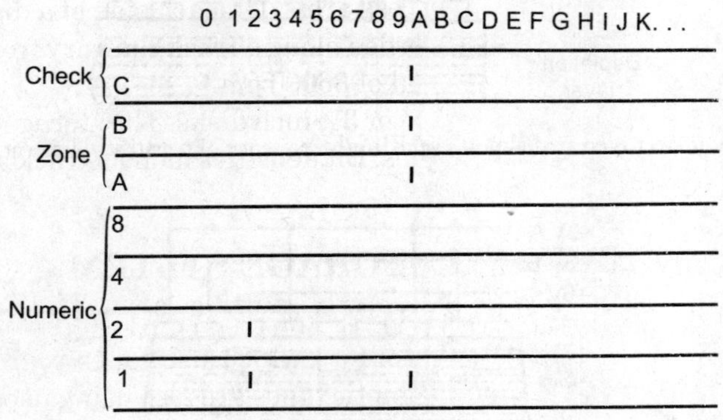

Fig. 14.53 Seven-track BCD code

Besides, reliability of the data storage system as well as power requirements are the other important factors. Generally electromechanical devices, which have moving parts, consume more power and are not as reliable as semiconductor memories.

The speed of operation and ease of access are the other important requirements. Therefore, in any memory storage system, a compromise has to be evolved between the different requirements. For instance, random access memory devices are generally used only in those areas of a memory system where speed of operation and easy accessibility are the determining factors. In other areas, where these considerations are not so important, lower cost memory systems which have only serial access capability are generally acceptable.

Scientists have therefore been busy for some time in search of memory devices, which will cost less and be more reliable. In 1970 two scientists Willard S. Boyle and George E. Smith of Bell Laboratories in New Jersey developed the charge-coupled device technology for memory devices.

CCD devices are to a certain extent based on the MOS technology. A CCD memory chip consists of a homogeneous region of *N*-type or *P*-type doped semiconductor material. There is a layer of silicon dioxide on top of the semiconductor material. Metal electrodes are deposited on the silicon dioxide surface. This strcuture has been shown in Fig. 14.54 (a). You will notice from this diagram that the semiconductor material is of *N*-type, in which the majority current carries are electrons. The electrodes are connected in groups of three to a bias line. For instance, electrodes 1, 4 and 7 are connected to the same bias line. All the three bias lines in this diagram are at 0 V. The voltages marked in these diagrams only represent the relative magnitudes of the various bias voltages and should not be confused with the actual voltages used in the operation of this device.

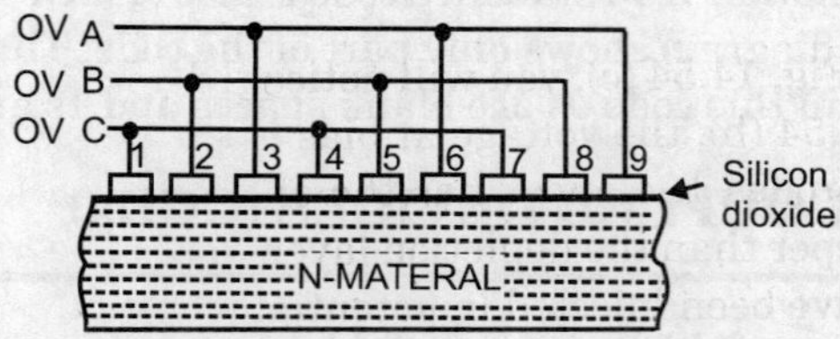

Fig. 14.54 (a) Majority current carrier are evenly distributed in the absence of negative voltage at the electrodes

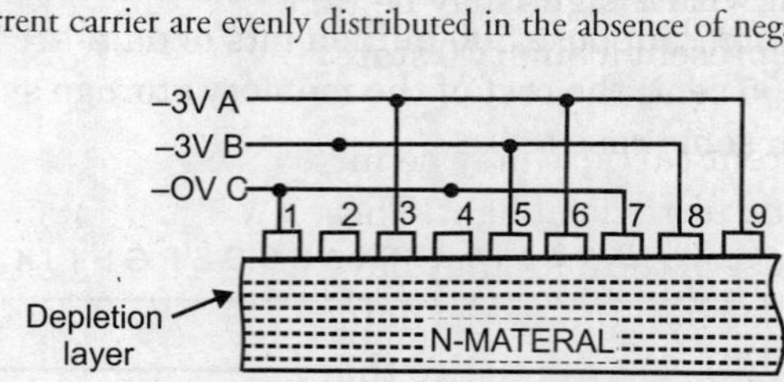

Fig. 14.54 (b) A depletion layer is created almost evenly in the presence of negative voltage at most of the electrodes

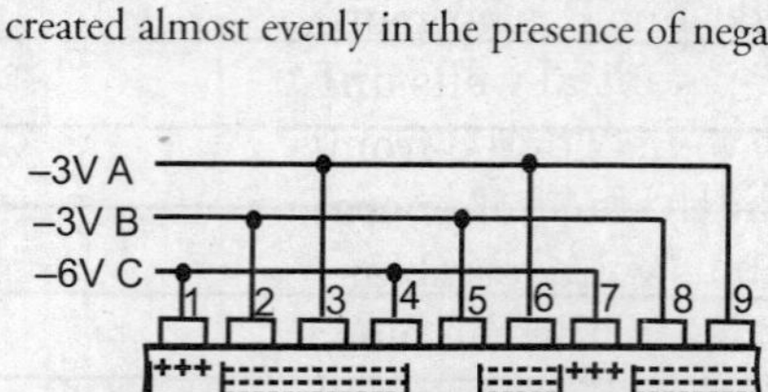

Fig. 14.54 (c) A higher negative voltage at electrodes 1, 4 and 7, than at other electrodes, creates potential wells near these electrodes, which are deeper than the depletion layer

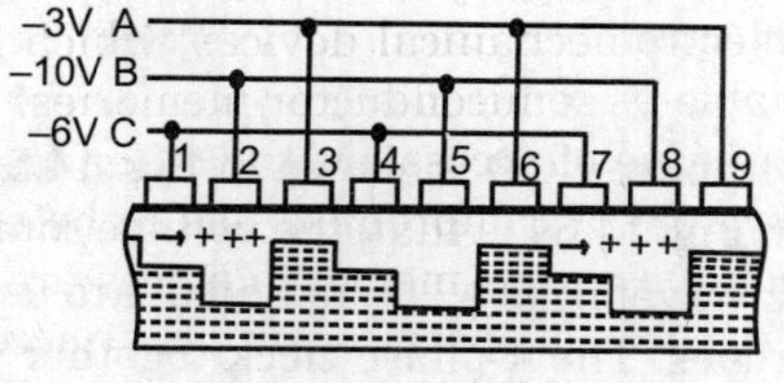

Fig. 14.54 (d) The voltage at electrodes 2, 5 and 8 is more negative than the voltage at the rest of the electrodes which deepens the potential wells under these electrodes and therefore the minority carriers shift to the right under these electrodes

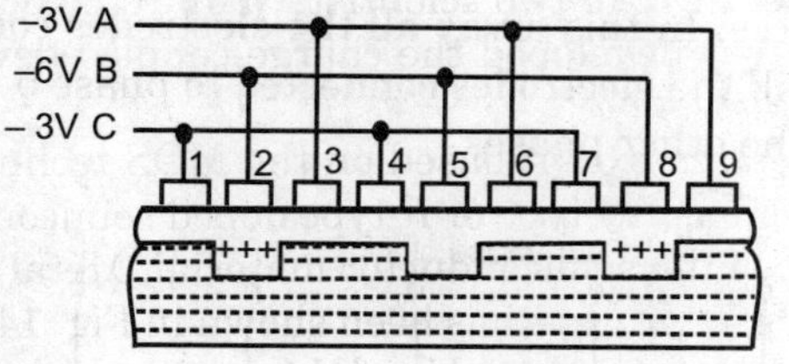

Fig. 14. 54 (e) The electrode voltages are now in the storage mode. The charge packets, compared to Fig. 14.54(c) are now under the adjacent electrodes to the right

Refer now to Fig. 14.54(b). You will notice that bias voltage lines *A* and *B* are at –3 V while bias line *C* is still at 0 V. Because of the negative bias voltage on most of the electrodes, a depletion layer is formed, which is deprived of the majority current carriers, just below the silicon dioxide layer.

If you refer now to Fig. 14.54 (c), you will notice that, whereas the bias voltage at *A* and *B* is the same as in Fig. 14.54 (b), the voltage at bias line *C* is much lower, that is –6V. A higher negative voltage at electrodes 1, 4 and 7 has the effect of creating potential wells near these electrodes, which are deeper than the depletion layer. You will also notice that minority current carriers, that is holes, have been injected in potential wells under electrodes 1 and 7, and none under well 4. A potential well with + signs may be taken to represent a binary 1 state and an empty well may be taken to represent a binary 0 state or vice versa, depending upon the convention adopted.

Packets of minority current carriers may be introduced in potential wells by a process of injection or by irradiation using ultraviolet light. These wells are now representative of the data bits stored in them. To make use of the data they have to be moved, so that they can be detected by some device. We will now see how the stored data is moved within the chip.

If you refer to Fig. 14.54 (d), you will notice that bias voltage at bias lines *A* and *C* is the same as in Fig. 14.54 (c), but the bias line *B* is far more negative than bias lines *A* and *C*. This has the effect of creating much deeper potential wells under electrodes 2, 5 and 8. As a consequence the minority carriers move under wells 2 and 8 from wells 1 and 7.

Figure 14.54(e) shows the next stage of operation, which is the storage state. You will notice from this diagram that the bias voltage at bias lines *A* and *C* maintain the depletion layer level under the respective electrodes, while the bias voltage at bias line *B*, being lower, maintains the normal depth of potential wells to provide storage for the minority carriers. If you compare Fig. 14.54 (e) with Fig. 14.54 (c), you will notice that the potential wells along with their charge packets have moved by one electrode position to the right. This movement can take place at very high clock rates in the region of megacycles.

Operation of CCDs

The basic structure of a 4-phase CCD is shown in Fig. 14.55. The difference between this structure and the one shown in Fig. 14.54 is that, the voltage sources have been replaced by a 4-phase clock. The 4-phase clock waveforms ϕ_1, ϕ_2, ϕ_3 and ϕ_4 are used to drive the device through the four adjacent metal electrodes. The 4-phase clock together with the device is designed to give this dynamic flip-flop the essential features of a master-slave flip-flop. This feature enables the device to move the data in one direction only.

While the diagram shows only one dynamic flip-flop, the shift register assembly consists of an array of such MOS devices. In this array all the electrodes connected to phase ϕ_1 are connected together. Similarly, all the electrodes connected to phase ϕ_2 are connected together, and so also those connected to the other phases.

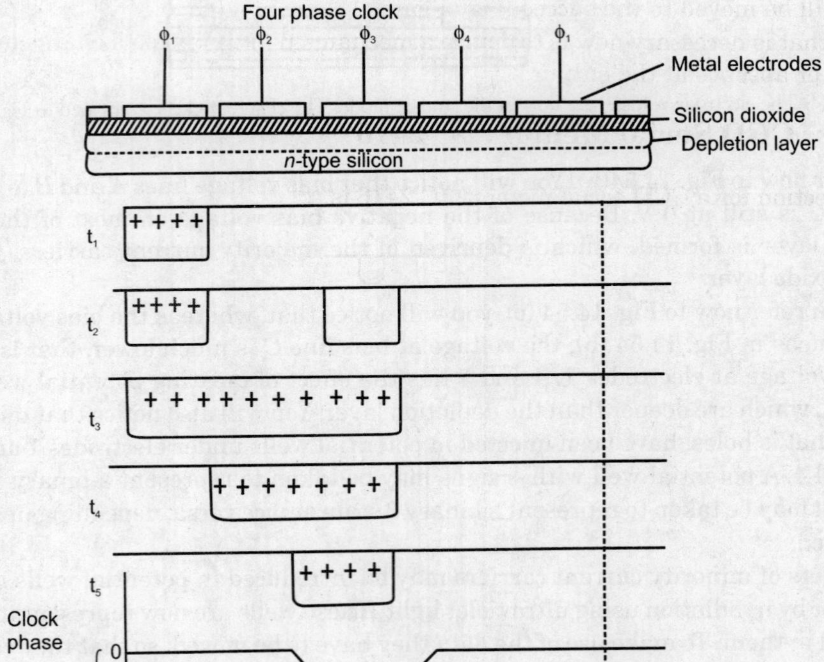

Fig. 14.55 Basic structure of a CCD device, also showing the transfer of charge under a 4-phase clock waveform

If you look at the diagram, you will notice that during the time interval t_1 only ϕ_1 is at a negative voltage, which enables a depletion region to be created under ϕ_1. The diagram also shows that we have somehow injected a positive charge in the depletion region under ϕ_1 from an outside source, or from the gate immediately preceding it. We may assume here that a logic 1 is stored when a positive charge is being held in the depletion region and a logic 0 is stored when the depletion region is empty.

During the time interval t_2 as ϕ_1 is still at a negative voltage, the depletion region under the ϕ_1 gates remains unchanged, while at the same time new depletion regions are created under the ϕ_3 gates as ϕ_3 is at a negative voltage. During the time interval t_3 phase ϕ_2 also goes negative while ϕ_1 and ϕ_3 are already at a negative voltage. Therefore, the depletion region now extends from gate ϕ_1 to ϕ_3. This enables the positive charge to spread throughout this extended depletion region.

During the time interval t_4, ϕ_1 goes positive, which eliminates the depletion region under ϕ_1 gates. During the interval t_5, ϕ_2 also goes positive, the depletion region under ϕ_2 gates also vanish. Thus the charge which was originally under gate ϕ_1 is pushed to the right under ϕ_3 gates. Following a few time intervals from t_6 to t_8, the positive charge which was initially under gate ϕ_1 will be moved to the succeeding ϕ_1'gate.

All that is necessary now is to device a mechanism for injecting a charge and detecting its presence or absence at the output.

14.18.1 CCD Serial Memory IC 2416

Pin connection for a CCD serial memory IC 2416 is presented in Fig. 14.56.

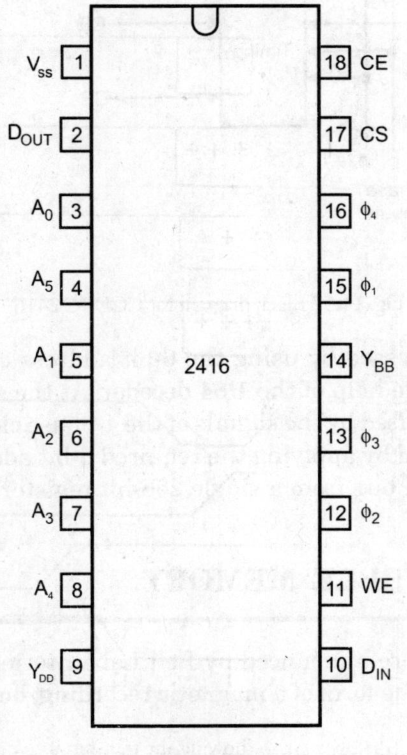

Fig. 14.56 Pin connections for CCD IC 2416

A block diagram for CCD serial memory IC 2416 is given in Fig. 14.57.

The CCD memory device IC 2416 shown in Fig. 14.57 is organized as a 16384 × 1 bit serial memory, consisting of 64 registers each of 256 bits.

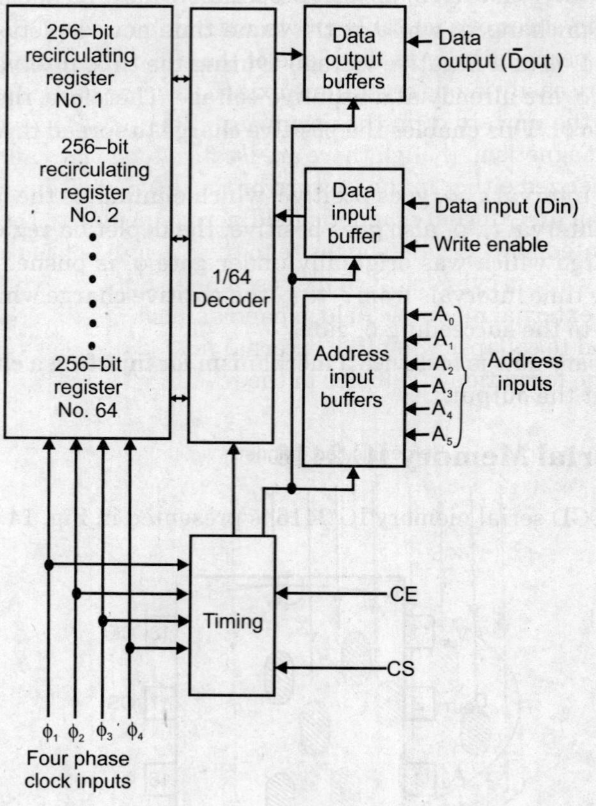

Fig. 14.57 Block diagram for CCD IC 2416

The registers can be accessed by using the 6-bit address code, which selects one of the recirculating registers with the help of the 1/64 decoder. At the same time, the data in the 64 registers is simultaneously shifted by the signals of the 4-phase clock. After a shift cycle, each of the 64 registers can be selected by applying the required 6-bit address code. If the address bits remain unchanged, sequential bits from a single 256-bit register will be presented serially for reading or writing.

14.19 MAGNETIC BUBBLE MEMORY

Magnetic bubble memories were announced by Bell Laboratories in 1967. Like tapes, data is stored in bubble memories in the form of a magnetic recording; but otherwise there is not much similarity in other respects.

Magnetic bubble memory devices depend on the magnetic properties of materials, such as single crystalline garnets, orthoferrites, hexaferrites and amorphous intermetallics. The choice of the material is made keeping in mind the necessity for high mobility, a small bubble size and a large operating temperature range. This is so for the simple reason, that bit density is dependant on bubble size and accessibility depends on the bubble propagation velocity.

These materials have some very special properties which makes magnetic bubble memories possible. Very thin slices of a suitably grown magnetic material is produced with its preferred magnetization perpendicular to the plane of the slice. These magnetic materials can be magnetized much more easily in one crystalline axis than in the other. Besides, this thin slice is magnetized either in the upward or in the downward direction. However, the slice as a whole does not exhibit any magnetism, though there are localized regions, called domains, within the slice, which are magnetized either in the upward or the downward direction.

In the presence of an external magnetic field perpendicular to the plane of the slice, domains which are oriented in a direction opposite to the direction of the external magnetic field shrink, and eventually attain cylindrical shape resembling bubbles, while those oriented in the same direction as the external magnetic field expand and merge to occupy the remainder of the slice. The bubbles tend to collapse when the external field is increased beyond a certain point. Figure 14.58 shows the formation of bubbles in the presence of external magnetic field.

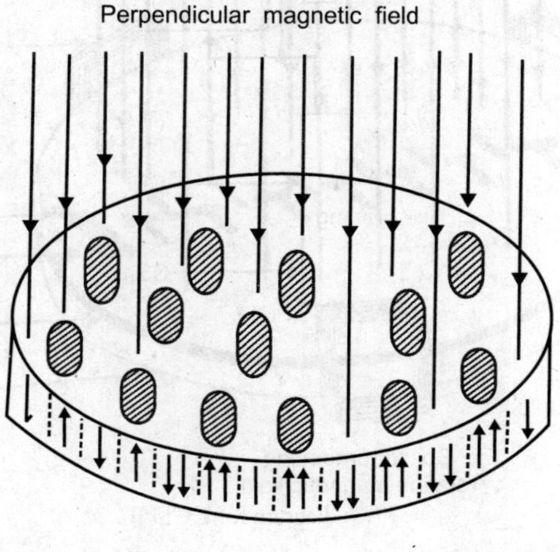

Fig. 14.58 Magnetic bubbles formed in a thin film in the presence of an external magnetic field

New bubble domains can be created in the slice by passing current through a loop of conductor on the surface of the slice, so that it creates a localized field, the direction of which is opposite to the main magnetic field. The bubbles present in the slice can also be manipulated in order to store data.

We can now consider the basic structure of a memory device. A thick slice of a non-magnetic rare earth garnet is used as a substrata. On this substrata a very thin layer of a magnetic garnet is grown epitaxially. To produce a perpendicular magnetic field a permanent magnet is used, which is required to maintain the bubbles. As long as this magnetic field is maintained, the bubbles will continue to exist. A small loop of a conductor is located at one side of the slice on its surface to produce bubbles. This conductor loop acts as the device input. To manipulate the bubbles and move them around, another magnetic field is required, which is meant to rotate in the field of the slice.

To produce this magnetic field, a set of coils is used. A pattern of magnetically soft permalloy is deposited over the garnet slice, along with a silicon dioxide layer for isolation and passivation. The rotating magnetic field acts on the magnetic bubbles via this pattern of permalloy pole pieces.

The permalloy pole pieces are in the shape of arrow heads or as alternate bars and Ts. The latter arrangement is referred to as the T-bar system. These pole pieces are arranged in the form of a chain and act as magnets in the presence of the rotating magnetic field.

The magnetic bubbles at the device input are carried along the chain of permalloy pole pieces. Each full rotation of the rotating magnetic field moves a bubble across one T-bar pattern.

The T-bar pattern on the surface of the slice therefore functions as a register, which can store data that is carried by the bubbles. The register clocks at the same rate as the frequency of the rotating magnetic field.

This basic structure of magnetic bubble memory device is shown in Fig. 14.59.

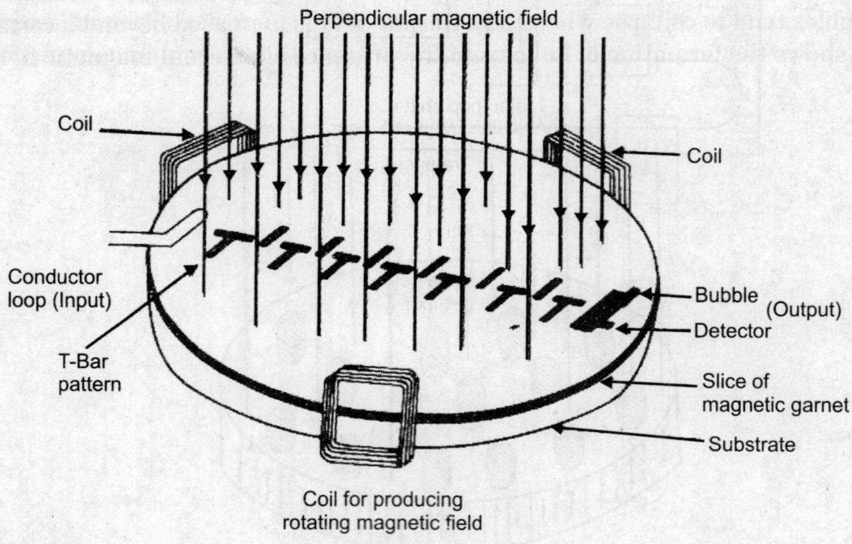

Fig. 14.59 Basic structure of magnetic bubble memory

The presence or absence of bubbles at the end of the magnetic bubble register can be detected by electromagnetic induction, Hall effect, direct optical sensing, or by measurement of magnetic reistance of a permalloy strip. The last method depends on change in the resistance of a permalloy strip in the presence of an external magnetic field. This change can be easily detected to read the information at the register output.

For storing and processing information in magnetic bubble memories, the binary format is used. The presence of a bubble may represent binary 1 and its absence may represent a binary 0.

To write data into the bubble memory, a bubble representing the data bit is created either by nucleating a new bubble, by the input coils, or by replicating a bubble, which is already present, by dividing a bubble domain present near the permalloy propagation channel into parts and propagating the new bubble into the channel. If a bit of data is to be cleared, it can be done by raising the bias field above the collapse field level, which will clear the data bit.

Figure 14.60 shows how bubble memories are organized. The bubble memory chips are organized into major and minor loops. Serial information is fed into the major loop register and the stored information is also read out from the major loop register. The actual function of storage is assigned to a number of minor loops, which are of the recirculating type. The major loop has access to all the minor loops.

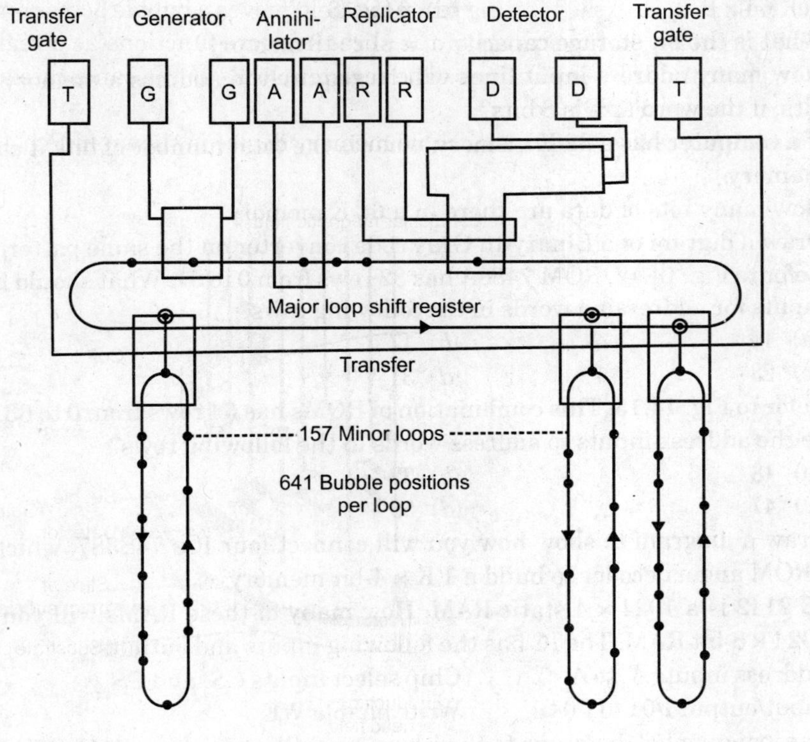

Fig. 14.60 Bubble memory organization

In short, the minor loops are used for storage of data, while the major loop is used for input and output functions. The bits of words required to be stored are distributed among the various minor loops. When a word is selected, the corresponding bits in the minor loops are transferred to the major loop, where they are assembled into a word which is carried to the detector circuit.

In the bubble memory organization shown in Fig. 14.60, there are 157 minor loops and each of the loops has 641 bubble positions. Thus it has a potential storage capacity of 100637 bits of data. This device is housed in a 14 pin DIP package, which comprises of the bubble memory chip, permanent magnet to provide the required bias, coils to provide the rotating field and a device to protect the memory from external magnetic fields.

Problems

14.1 Refer to Fig. 14.5 and write the addresses of the following words in binary form:
(*a*) Word 3 (*b*) Word 5
(*c*) Word 8 (*d*) Word 9

14.2 What is the word size in the following ROMs?
(*a*) 16 × 8 (*b*) 32 × 4
(c) 64 × 8 (d) 64 × 16

14.3 What is the bit storage capacity of a 512 × 8 memory?

14.4 How many address input lines will be required to address a memory with 524,288 bits, if the word size is 8 bits?

14.5 If a computer has a 32 K memory, what is the total number of bits it can store in the memory.

14.6 How many bits of data are there in a 64 K memory?

14.7 Draw a digram of a Binary-to-Gray code converter on the same pattern as Fig. 14.5.

14.8 Refer to Fig. 14.12. ROM 7488A has 32 rows from 0 to 31. What should be the address inputs for addressing words in the following rows?
(a) 11 (*b*) 17
(*c*) 23 (*d*) 31

14.9 Refer to Fig. 14.13. This combination of ROMs has 64 rows from 0 to 63. What should be the address inputs to address words in the following rows?
(a) 18 (*b*) 32
(*c*) 47 (*d*) 59

14.10 Draw a diagram to show how you will connect four ICs 74S387, which is a 256 × 4 PROM and a decoder to build a 1 K × 4-bit memory.

14.11 IC 2142 is a 1024 × 4 static RAM. How many of these RAMs will you require for a 1024 × 8-bit RAM. The IC has the following inputs and outputs:
Address inputs A_0 to A_9 Chip select inputs CS_1 and CS_2
Input/output I/01 to I/04 Write enable WE

14.12 Use logic symbol diagrams to show how you will connect two 4116 DRAM ICs to build a 16 K × 2-bit memory.

14.13 IC 2114 is a 1K × 4-bit memory. How many of these ICs will you require for a 8K × 4-bit memory?

15

Analog-Digital Conversion

15.1 INTRODUCTION

The nature of analog and digital signals has been discussed in Chap 1. An analog signal varies smoothly and continously, whereas a digital signal is a series of pulses of rapidly changing levels of voltage or current, in which change in level occurs in discrete steps or increments.

Most signals are analog in nature. For instance, temperature varies smoothly and continuously, so also sound and so many other signals. For instance, consider a communication system which requires transmission of signals over a long distance. In this process it is likely to pick up a lot of noise, which can be overcome by converting the analog input signal into a digital one. At the receiving end the signal can be reconverted from digital to analog form. This is known as pulse code modulation system.

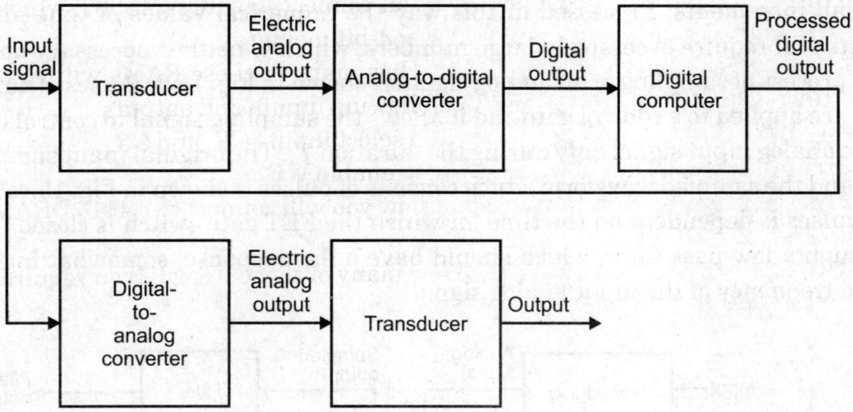

Fig. 15.1 Digital processor

There are many systems where digital computers are used to control or monitor the functioning of devices. In a processing plant, the computer will receive analog signals from the devices it is required to control and process these inputs to generate the necessary inputs for the devices it is required to control. If these signals are converted to digital form, any numerical operation can be performed on them, which is not possible if the signal is in an analog form. After processing the signal can be converted back to analog form to provide an input for the device under control.

For processing signals it is, therefore, necessary to convert analog signals into equivalent digital signals, which can be very easily processed. To accomplish this we need an analog-to-digital converter. After the digital signals have been processed, we have to convert them again into analog signals and thereafter use a transducer to obtain an output which will be capable of interpretation by the human mind. For this we will require a digital-to-analog converter followed by a transducer. We will have two interfaces, the first one between analog and digital circuits and the other between digital and analog circuits. A block diagram given in Fig. 15.1 gives a general idea of the requirements of signal processing.

At the input end of this digital processor, we require a transducer which will convert the input signal into an electric analog output. This is followed by an analog-to-digital converter, the operation of which can be considered under four sequences, commonly referred to as sampling, holding, quantizing in amplitude and time, and encoding. Some of these sequences are performed in a single operation. After the signal has been digitally processed, it is required to be reconverted into analog form. This operation is performed by a digital-to-analog converter. In this chapter we will discuss all these operations.

15.2 SAMPLING

An analog signal is a continuous signal which has smooth variations in voltage and current with respect to time. It follows that there are no breaks in amplitude or in time. It can change from a low to high level, but it must pass through all the intermediate values. At every point in time it has an exact value of amplitude. It follows that if the time axis is resolved into small increments, the amplitude axis can be resolved into corresponding small increments. If we resolve the time axis into infinitely small increments, the amplitude axis will have corresponding infinitely small increments. Processed in this way the numerical values of time and amplitude increments will require excessively large numbers, which is neither necessary nor desirable.

The process of sampling of an analog signal is shown in Fig. 15.2. Pulses of duration T_1 and period T_2 are applied to a control gate and it allows the sampling signal to control the transmission of the analog input signal only during the duration T_1. The original input signal is shown in Fig. 15.3 and the sampled waveform which consists of pulses is shown in Fig. 15.4. The duration of these pulses is dependent on the time for which the FET gate switch is closed. These pulses pass through a low-pass filter, which should have a flat response, somewhat higher than the maximum frequency of the input analog signal.

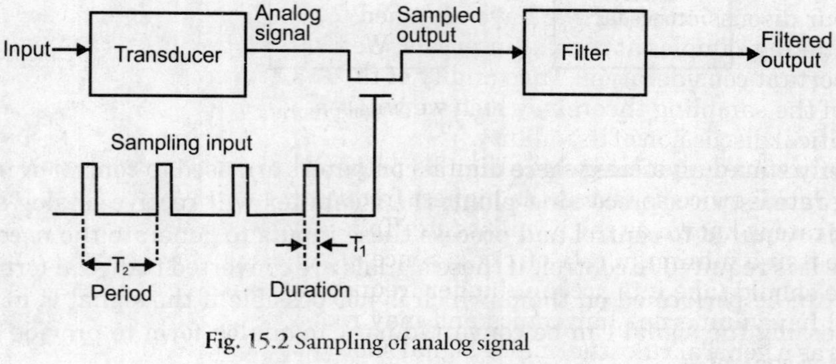

Fig. 15.2 Sampling of analog signal

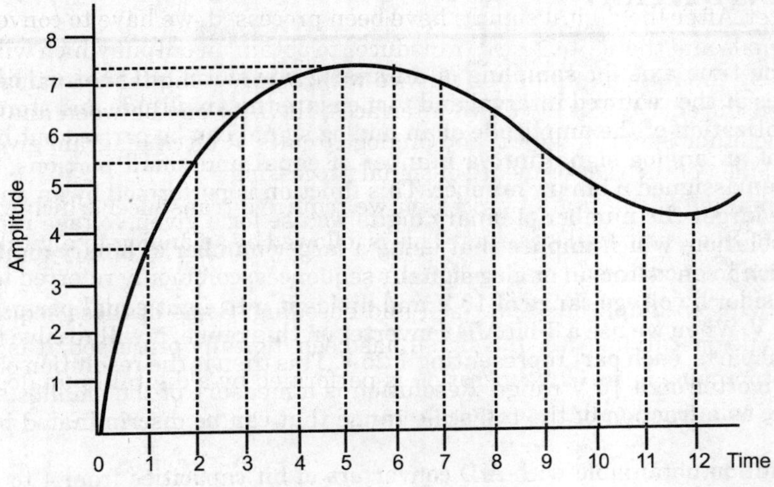

Fig. 15.3 Waveform sampling at regular intervals showing signal values in decimal numbers at the time of sampling

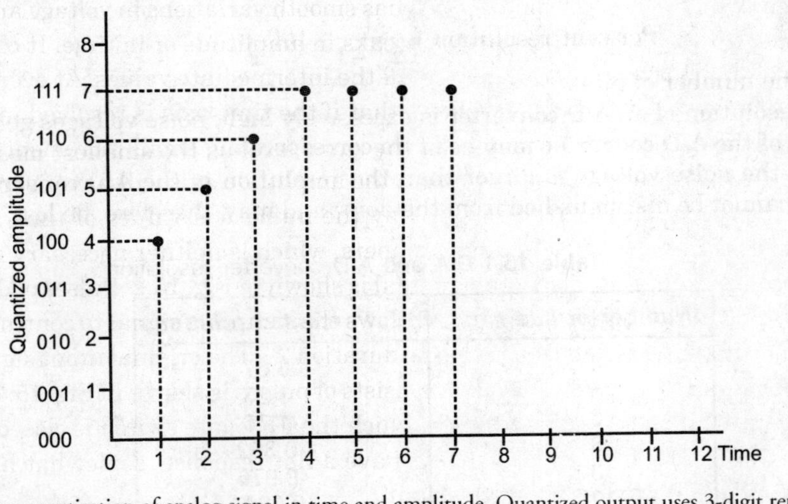

Fig. 15.4 Shows quantization of analog signal in time and amplitude. Quantized output uses 3-digit representation

In our discussion so far, we have assumed that the analog signal can be perfectly reproduced by taking samples at regular intervals. We have not discussed the rate of sampling which is an important consideration. The validity of the sampling process depends essentially on the validity of the sampling theorem, which we will state in a very few words without going into a mathematical discussion of its validity.

Briefly stated an analog signal can be properly reproduced from its sample points, if the sampling rate is twice as fast as the highest frequency component of the signal. This minimum sampling rate is known as the Nyquist rate. To perfectly reproduce a 1kHz sine wave, we have to sample it at a minimum rate of 2kHz. Since all analog signals are not sine waves, the sampling rate should take into account higher frequency components. For instance a 1kHz square wave will have numerous harmonics and may require sampling at a minimum rate of 8kHz. However, as a general rule, the analog signal should be sampled at a minimum rate of about ten times of the maximum frequency component.

15.3 QUANTIZATION

To quantize the time axis for sampling of an analog waveform, all that we have to do is to generate pulses at the required interval and to measure the amplitude and store it.

The quantization of the amplitude of an analog signal can be carried out by dividing the entire range of an analog signal into a number of equal and small portions. Each of these intervals is then assigned a binary number. This function is performed by an analog-to-digital converter. The larger the number of binary digits we use for a given voltage range, the better will be the resolution, which implies that using a larger number of binary digits will provide greater precision in encoding an analog signal.

If we consider a voltage range of 10 V and divide it into eight equal parts, each part will represent 1.25 V. When we use a 3-bit A/D converter on this range, it will resolve the 10 V range into eight equal parts, each part representing 1.25 V. This then is the resolution obtainable with a 3-bit A/D converter on a 10 V range. Resolution is a measure of the smallest change in the output voltage, as a fraction of the full scale range that can be discriminated by an A/D converter.

The resolution obtainable with A/D converters of bit capacities from 4 to 16 is given in Table 15.1.

The per cent resolution of a converter can be determined from the following equation:

$$\text{Per cent resolution} = \frac{1}{2^N - 1} \times 100$$

where N is the number of bits.

If the resolution of an A/D converter is excessively high, noise voltages generated within the circuitry of the A/D converter may be of the same level as the smallest measurable increment. When the noise voltage is larger than the resolution of the A/D converter, the signal information cannot be distinguished from the noise and may, therefore, be lost.

Table 15.1 D/A and A/D converter resolution

Number of bits	*Percent resolution*
4	6.67
5	3.23
6	1.75
8	0.392
10	0.976
12	0.0244
14	0.00610
16	0.00153

15.4 BINARY DIGIT WEIGHT

Earlier on in Chap 1, we have considered the weight assigned to binary digits. Figure 1.6 gives the positional weights and values of binary numbers. We will again review it in brief. Let us consider a four-digit binary number given in Fig. 15.5.

Binary digit position	3	2	1	0
Binary digit	1	1	1	1
Digit weight	2^3	2^2	2^1	2^0
Digit value	8	4	2	1

Fig. 15.5

You will notice from the diagram that the weight of each successive bit to the left is twice the weight of the preceding bit. It follows that since 1 represents the value of the LSB, the weights of the other digits will be as shown in the diagram. From this we can draw very important conclusions, which are very relevant for analog/digital conversions.

In a 4-bit binary system, each successive binary count represents 1/15 th of the entire range of binary numbers from 0000 to 1111. The binary equivalent weight of the 4 bits will therefore be as follows:

	MSB			LSB
Binary bit	2^3	2^2	2^1	2^0
Binary equivalent weight	8/15	4/15	2/15	1/15

The weight of the LSB is $\dfrac{1}{(2^4-1)}=\dfrac{1}{(16-1)}=\dfrac{1}{15}$ and this increases by 1 for every binary count as is shown in Table 15.2.

Table 15.2

Binary number				Binary equivalent weight
D	*C*	*B*	*A*	
0	0	0	0	
0	0	0	1	1/15
0	0	1	0	2/15
0	0	1	1	3/15
0	1	0	0	4/15
0	1	0	1	5/15
0	1	1	0	6/15
0	1	1	1	7/15
1	0	0	0	8/15
1	0	0	1	9/15
1	0	1	0	10/15
1	0	1	1	11/15
1	1	0	0	12/15
1	1	0	1	13/15
1	1	1	0	14/15
1	1	1	1	15/15

In the present case, per cent resolution will be as follows:

$$\text{Per cent resolution} = \frac{1}{2^4-1}\times 100 = 6.67$$

If a higher resolution is required, a larger number of bits will have to be used. For instance with 8-bit words the resolution can be increased to 0.39%. However, there is a practical limit to the number of bits, which depends, among other things, on component tolerances which should be much better than the desired per cent resolution. Cost is another important factor.

Table 15.3 shows how voltages from 0 to 15 V can be represented by 4-bit binary words. The same representation has been shown in a graphical from in Fig. 15.6. In this case binary number 0001 represents 1 V and 0010 represents 2 V. We had chosen the range 0–15 V for the sake of convenience of representation by 4-bit binary words. If the range was 0–10 V, binary number 0001 would have represented 10 × 1/15 or 0.666 V and binary number 0010 would have represented 10 × 2/15 or 1.333 V.

If you have a close look at Table 15.2, it will show the way to express an analog quantity in terms of a binary word. For instance, if voltages from 0 to 15 V are to be expressed in terms of a 4-bit binary word, what we have to do is to express 0 V by binary word 0000 and 15 V by binary word 1111. Since each successive binary count represents 1/15th of the entire voltage, the voltages assigned to each word will be as follows:

Table 15.3

Binary number	***Equivalent weight***	***Voltage***
0 0 0 0	0	0
0 0 0 1	1/15	15 × 1/15 = 1
0 0 1 0	2/15	15 × 2/15 = 2
0 0 1 1	3/15	15 × 3/15 = 3
0 1 0 0	4/15	15 × 4/15 = 4
⋮	⋮	⋮
1 1 0 0	12/15	15 × 12/15 = 12
1 1 0 1	13/15	15 × 13/15 = 13
1 1 1 0	14/15	15 × 14/15 = 14
1 1 1 1	15/15	15 × 15/15 = 15

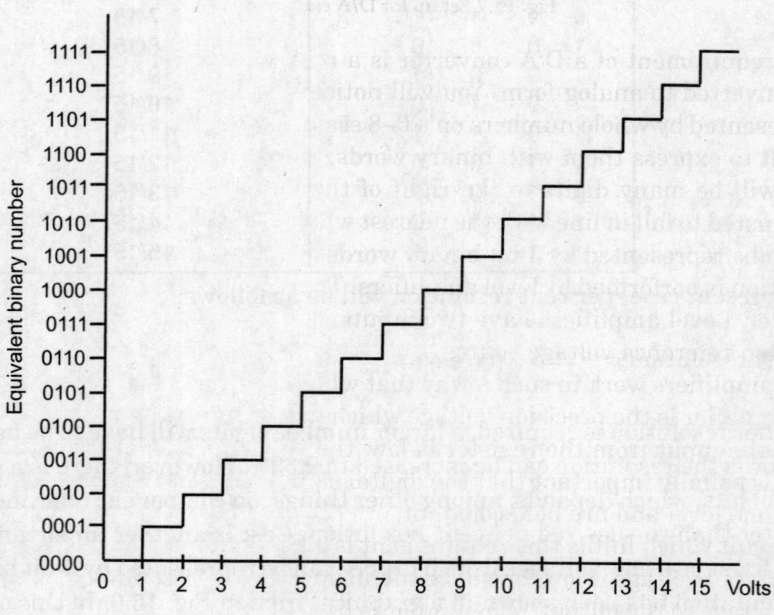

Fig. 15.6 Analog voltage expressed in binary form

You will notice from this table that a span of 15 V range can be resolved into discrete numbers by using a 4-bit binary word. Since the resolution possible in this case is only 1 V, fractions of 1 V cannot be represented with 4-bit words. A larger number of bits will be required to express fractional parts.

15.5 DIGITAL-TO-ANALOG CONVERSION

A block diagram of a set-up required for digital-to-analog conversion is shown in Fig. 15.7.

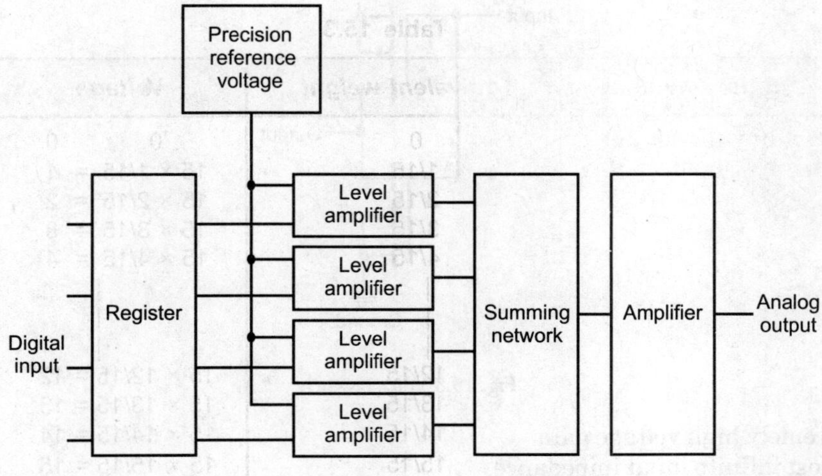

Fig. 15.7 Set up for D/A conversion

The first requirement of a D/A converter is a register which stores the digital input required to be converted to analog form. You will notice from Fig. 15.3 that the sampled pulses cannot be represented by whole numbers on a 0–8 scale, as they have fractional parts. It will be equally difficult to express them with binary words, since this will require a large number of bits, as there will be many digits to the right of the binary point. However, if the sampled outputs are adjusted to fall in line with the nearest whole number, as has been done in Fig. 15.4, the outputs can be represented by 3-bit binary words on a 0–8 scale.

This function is performed by level amplifiers. There is a level amplifier for every input bit from the register. Level amplifiers have two inputs, one of which goes to the register and the other to precision reference voltage source.

The level amplifiers work in such a way that when the input from the register is high, the output of the amplifier is the precision voltage which will be interpreted as logic 1 level by logic circuits. When the input from the register is low, the output of the level amplifiers will be at logic 0 level. It is equally important that the digital signals presented to the summing network are all of the same level and are held constant.

A basic circuit which fulfils this requirement is given in Fig. 15.8.

When the input voltage is low, T_2 will be cut off and T_1 will be turned on, which will connect the reference voltage to the output. When input is high, T_1 will be cut off and T_2 will be turned on, which will result in grounding of the output.

Before considering the summing network and the amplifier, we will discuss the operational amplifier which plays a very important function in D/A conversion as you will see later.

15.6 OPERATIONAL AMPLIFIERS

The important characteristics of the operational amplifier (Op-amp) are as follows:

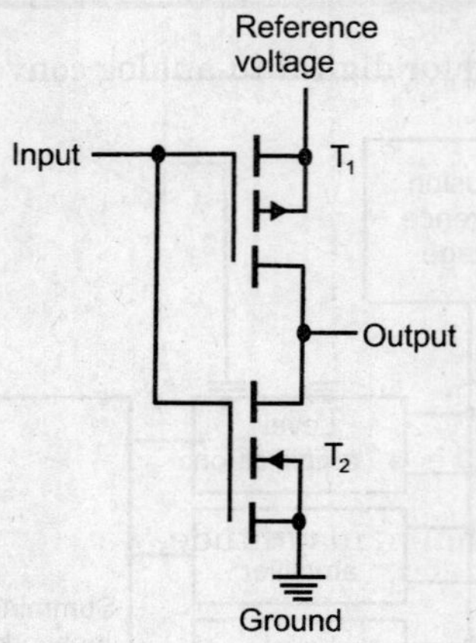

Fig. 15.8 Voltage switch

- Extremely high voltage gain
- Almost infinite input impedance
- Very low output impedance

The voltage gain of Op-amps is very high, which permits its use with negative feedback. The current drawn from the input source is negligible as it has very high input impedance. At the same time the output impedance is so low that it can directly drive a load.

In a D/A converter, it is used for current summation and it incorporates a resistive network. It adds currents which represent the weight of binary digits. The current after summation is converted to voltage by the operational amplifier, which also scales the voltage to the desired level.

Here we will consider in brief how it functions as an amplifier and current summer. The operational amplifier has an inverting (–) and a non-inverting (+) input as shown in Fig. 15.9. We will consider how it performs in the inverting mode. We have grounded the non-inverting (+) input and the input voltage is applied to the inverting input terminal through a resistor R_s. A feedback resistor R_f is connected between the output and the inverting input to provide a feedback path for the output.

The input voltage V_s forces a current through R_s into the inverting input terminal of the op-amp. However, the current that flows from the input through R_s is negligible, because of the infinite input impedance of the op-amp. This flow of current tends to raise the voltage V_i, which causes a decrease in the output voltage V_0. As V_0 falls, it pulls the voltage V_i down to oppose the change in V_0. This is a property of negative feedback circuits, which tend to oppose any change in the output, resulting from a change at the input.

Another important point to be noted is that, as no current flows into the op-amp, the current flowing through R_s from the input must be the same as the current flowing through R_f

to point A. These two currents meeting at point A tend to cancel each other and, therefore, a state of almost zero potential is formed at point A. This phenomenon is called a 'virtual earth' and is shown by dotted lines in the diagram.

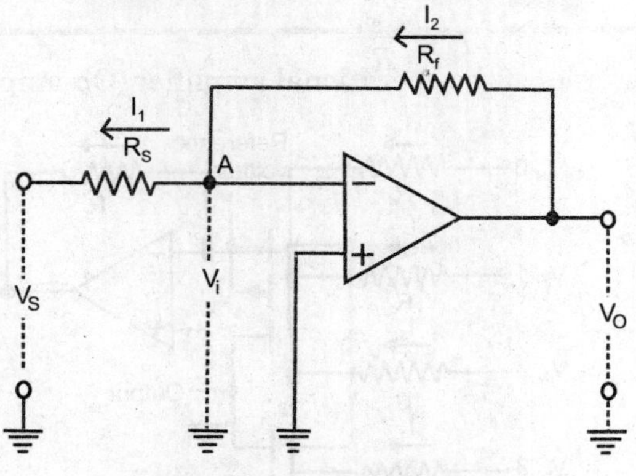

Fig. 15.9 Operational amplifier

Knowing that I_1 and I_2 are equal in magnitude, we can now develop an expression for the voltage gain of the op-amp:

$$I_1 = \frac{V_s}{R_s}$$

$$V_0 = -I_1 R_f$$

$$= \left(-\frac{V_s}{R_s}\right) . R_f$$

Therefore $$A_v = \frac{V_0}{V_s} = \frac{R_f}{R_s} \text{ (Voltage gain)}$$

15.7 CURRENT SUMMING NETWORKS

Current summing networks are used in D/A converters to sum up the current resulting from binary inputs. We will consider how an op-amp can function as a current summer.

15.7.1 OP-AMP Current Summer

A simple arrangement which illustrates the principle of current summation with the help of an op-amp is shown in Fig. 15.10.

There are four inputs which feed current to the op-amp. The current in each branch is as follows:

$$I_1 = \frac{V_{in_0}}{R_1}$$

$$I_2 = \frac{V_{in_1}}{R_2}$$

$$I_3 = \frac{V_{in_2}}{R_3}$$

$$I_4 = \frac{V_{in_3}}{R_4}$$

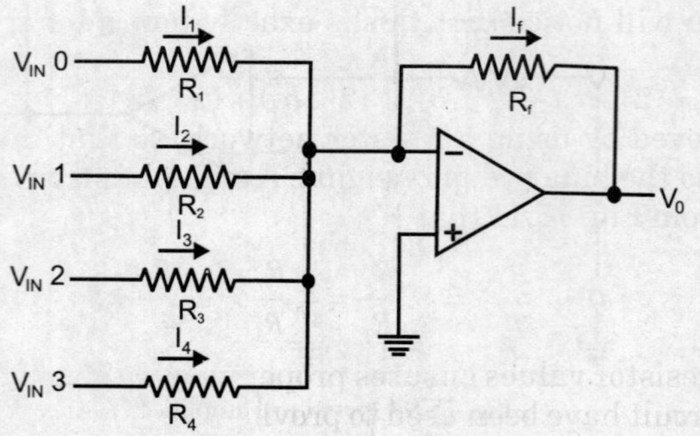

Fig. 15.10 Op-amp current summer

Since the sum of these currents is equal to the feedback current I_f

$$I_f = I_1 + I_2 + I_3 + I_4$$

Therefore

$$-\frac{V_0}{R_f} = \frac{V_{in_0}}{R_1} + \frac{V_{in_1}}{R_2} + \frac{V_{in_2}}{R_3} + \frac{V_{in_3}}{R_4}$$

$$-V_0 = \frac{R_f}{R_1} V_{in_0} + \frac{R_f}{R_2} V_{in_1} + \frac{R_f}{R_3} V_{in_2} + \frac{R_f}{R_4} V_{in_3} \quad ...(15.1)$$

This shows that the output voltage reflects the weighted sum of the input voltages. The factor by which it is weighted is a function of the ratio of the feedback resistor to the input resistor in each case. Notice that the output is inverted because the inputs are connected to the inverting input of the op-amp.

Example 15.1: *Determine the output voltage for the current summer given in Fig. 15.10. The values of the voltages and resistors are as follows:*

$V_1 = -2$ V : $R_1 = 1\,2$K ohm
$V_2 = +6$ V : $R_2 = 2$ K ohm
$V_3 = -4$ V : $R_3 = 2$ K ohm
$V_4 = -3$V $R_4 = 10$ K ohm
$R_f = 15$ K ohm

Solution:

$$\begin{aligned} I_1 &= -2/2000 \text{ mA} = -1 \text{ mA} \\ I_2 &= 6/2000 \text{ mA} = 3 \text{ mA} \\ I_3 &= -4/2000 \text{ mA} = -2 \text{ mA} \\ I_4 &= -3/10{,}000 \text{ mA} = -0.3 \text{ mA} \\ V_0 &= -(I_1 + I_2 + I_3 + I_4)\, R_f \\ &= -(-1 + 3 - 2 - 0.3) \times 15000 \\ &= -(-0.30) \times 15000 \text{ mV} \\ &= 0.3 \times 15 \text{ V} = 4.5 \text{ V.} \end{aligned}$$

15.8 WEIGHTED RESISTOR DIGITAL-TO-ANALOG CONVERTER

We have considered binary digit weights in an earlier section, and we will make use of it now in order to convert digital inputs to analog outputs. For instance, if we have a 4-bit digital input, we have to devise a circuit which will weight the four binary digits with weights $8(2^3)$, $4(2^2)$, $2(2^1)$ and $1(2^0)$, and sum the currents (or voltages), and thus produce an analog output. If you look at Eqn. (15.2) given below, you will notice that this is exactly how a binary number is converted into decimal form.

$$\text{Decimal number} = (2^3 \,.\, b_3) + (2^2 \,.\, b_2) + (2^1 \,.\, b_1) + (2^0 \,.\, b_0) \quad ...(15.2)$$

This can be achieved by using a resistor network, so that the resistors are weighted inversely in proportion to the binary digit weights. A summation circuit is shown in Fig. 15.11.

You will notice from Fig. 15.11 that

$$\frac{R_f}{R_1} = 8, \frac{R_f}{R_2} = 4, \frac{R_f}{R_3} = 2, \frac{R_f}{R_4} = 1$$

The selection of resistor values ensures proper weightage to bits in a 4-bit binary number. The switches in this circuit have been used to provide logic level inputs which will tally with the digits of the binary number. The circuit produces an output voltage which is proportional to the binary input.

Let us consider the output of this circuit when V_{ref} is 1 V and the binary input is 1111. Since R is 10 K ohms, the MSB will contribute a current of 0.1 mA and the other bits will contribute currents of 0.05,0.025 and 0.0125 mA. The total current through R_f will be 0.1875 mA and the output voltage will be –0.1875 × 80 V, which will be –15 V. It is obvious that this circuit can output voltages from 0 to 15 V in steps of 1 V. We can also write the expression for the output voltage as follows:

$$V_0 = -\left(V\frac{R_f}{R_1} + V\frac{R_f}{R_2} + V\frac{R_f}{R_3} + V\frac{R_f}{R_4}\right) \quad ...(15.3)$$

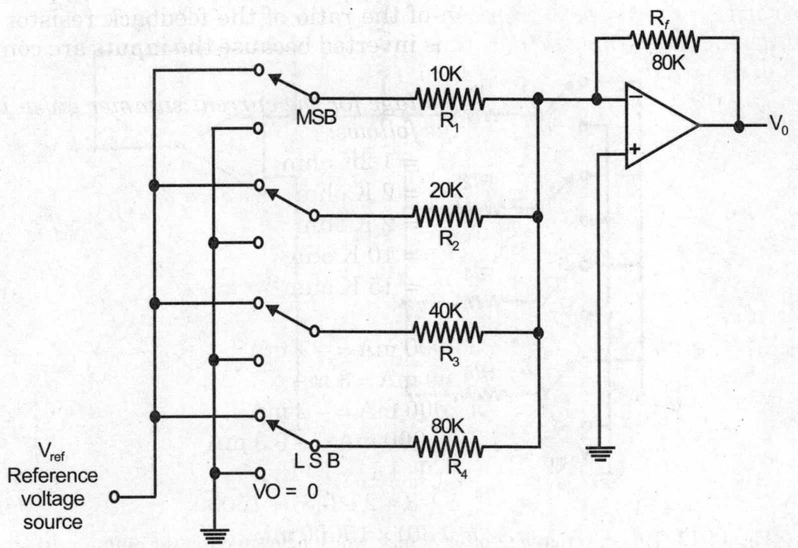

Fig. 15.11 4-bit D/A converter

In this expression, we have assumed that all bits are at logic 1 level. However, this is not always the case. We therefore, need an expression for the output voltage which will take into account the reference voltage as well as the values of the binary bits. An expression which takes this into account, is given in Eqn. (15.4).

$$V_0 = -V_{\text{ref}}\left(\frac{R_f}{R}b_{n-1} + \frac{R_f}{2R}b_{n-2} + \frac{R_f}{2^2\,R}b_{n-3} + \ldots \frac{R_f}{2^{n-1}\,R}b_0\right) \quad \text{...(15.4)}$$

This resistor network for digital-to-analog conversion has some serious drawbacks for more than one reason. In the first place, it require high precision resistors of many different values. The accuracy of the analog output depends a great deal on resistor tolerance. Besides, the values of the resistors are also limited by the input and output impedances of the op-amp. Another limitation on the values of resistors is imposed by the switching transistor, which is used in place of mechanical switches, because it is neither a perfect open nor a perfect closed switch. Because of these limitations, a kind of ladder network is used which we will discuss shortly.

The D/A converter circuit which we have considered swings the output voltage in one direction only and we describe this output as unipolar. To convert the digital data into bipolar format, $V(1)$ is set a 1/2 V and $V(0)$ is $\neq 0$ and is set at –1/2 V. Then in the case of a 4-bit converter, the output will swing about 0V from –7.5 V to + 7.5 V.

Another method of producing an offset in the output voltage is shown in Fig. 15.12. The offset voltage produced is given by the following expression:

$$\frac{R_f}{R_{\text{off}}}\,.\,V_{\text{off}}$$

These methods for representing negative numbers are very useful in certain applications, for instance when the output is required to swing in either direction.

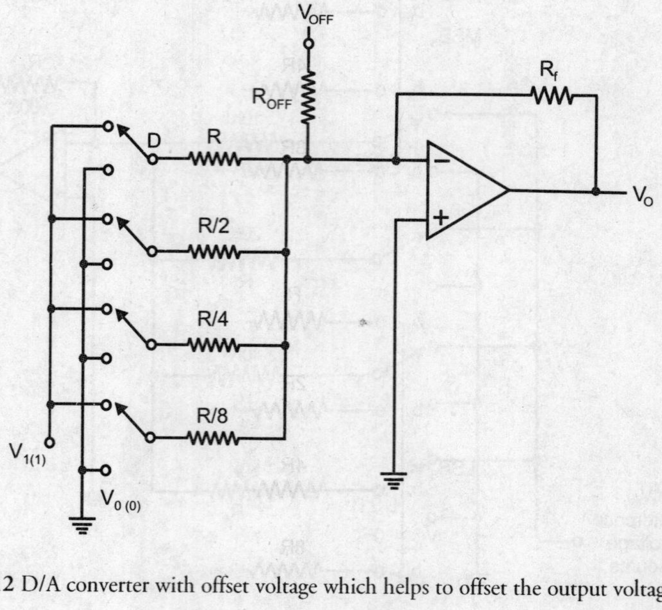

Fig. 15.12 D/A converter with offset voltage which helps to offset the output voltage

We will consider the application of this offset device to produce a symmetrical output voltage in a 4-bit D/A converter given in Fig. 15.11. With the resistor values and the voltages indicated, this D/A converter produces an output of 15 V. With a binary input of 1 0 0 0, the output in this D/A converter is 8 V. Therefore, to produce a bipolar output, we need an offset voltage of –8 V, so that the output is 0 with a digital input of 1 0 0 0. The values of V_{off} and R_{off} can be determined from the following expression:

$$-\frac{R_f}{R_{off}} \cdot V_{off} = -8 \text{ V; Required offset}$$

Since R_f is 80 K ohm, we can make R_{off} = 10 K ohm and V_{off} = 1 V. The output voltage will now swing about 0 V from + 7 V to – 8 V.

15.9 EXTENDED CAPACITY BINARY D/A CONVERTERS

We have so far considered a binary D/A converter, which has the capacity to handle four binary bits. The capacity of a weighted-resistor D/A converter to handle a larger number of bits is limited, because of the inevitable spread in resistor values. However, with slight modification in the circuitry a larger number of bits can be accommodated. The modification has been indicated in Fig. 15.13. The input resistors are divided into groups of four resistors each. The least significant group of resistors is connected to the op-amp through a resistor R_x, which is in addition to the weighted resistors. The value of R_x is determined so that the corresponding bits in the two groups of resistors have the following ratios:

$$\frac{b_7}{b_3} = \frac{b_6}{b_1} = \frac{b_5}{b_1} = \frac{b_4}{b_0} = 16$$

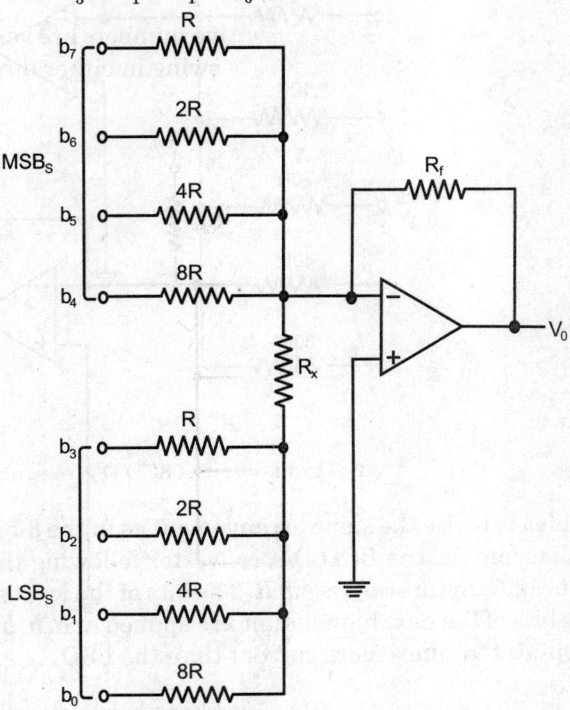

Fig. 15.13 8-bit binary D/A converter

For this ratio to hold good, R_x should be 8 R. You will notice that resistors of only two values have been used in this arrangement and the spread in resistor value has, therefore, been contained. It is possible to use this arrangement with a large number of bits than eight, provided the same scheme of things is repeated for additional groups of 4-bit each.

15.10 BCD D/A CONVERTER

Where high resolution is not required, a BCD D/A converter can be made as shown in Fig. 15.14. This uses weighted resistors; a group of four resistor for the LSD and another group of four resistors for the MSD. The weight of the 10's resistors is one-tenth the weight of the unit's resistors. It is not desirable to extend it any further because of the large spread in resistor values.

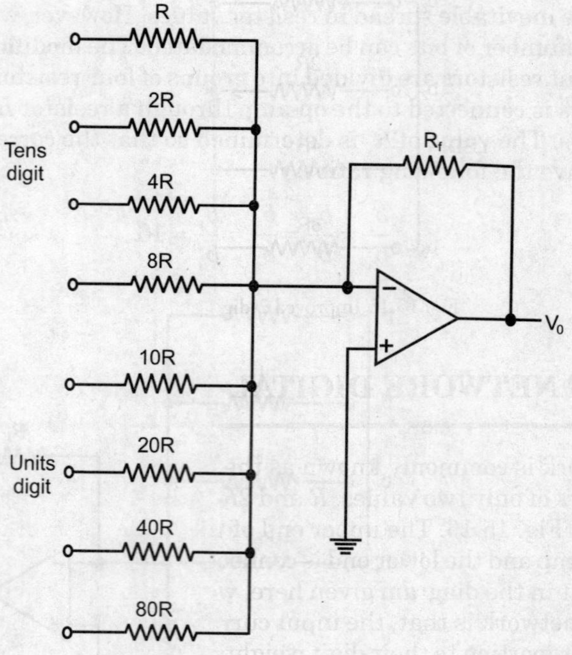

Fig. 15.14 Two-digit BCD D/A converter

A better idea is to use the same arrangement as in the 8-bit binary D/A converter shown in Fig. 15.13. A diagram for the BCD D/A converter following this arrangement is given in Fig. 15.15. The value of R_x in this case is 4.8 R. The bits of the least significant digit are applied at b_3 b_2 b_1 b_0 and the bits of the next higher digit are applied at b_7 b_6 b_5 b_4. With the value of R_x = 4.8 R, =the MSD supplies ten times more current than the LSD.

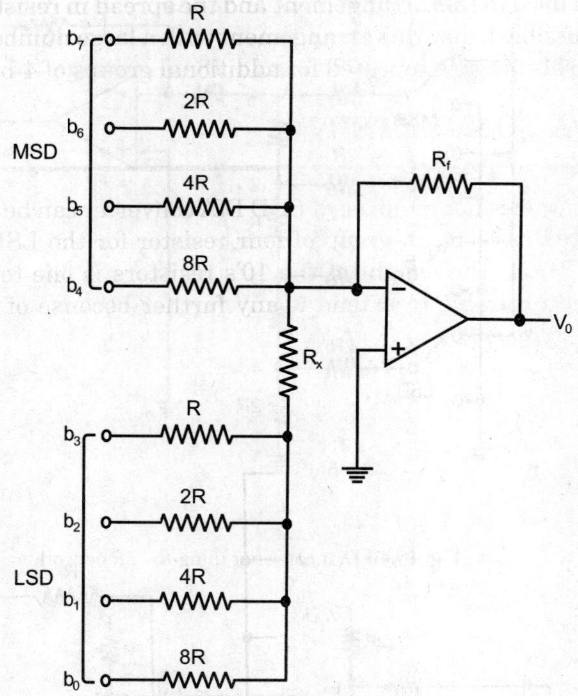

Fig. 15.15 Improved 2-digit BCD D/A converter

15.11 LADDER NETWORK DIGITAL-TO-ANALOG CONVERTER

This resistor network is commonly known as the $R - 2R$ ladder network, for the simple reason that it uses resistors of only two values, R and $2R$. A 4-bit digital-to-analog converter using this network is given in Fig. 15.16. The upper end of the ladder network is connected to the inverting input of an op-amp and the lower end is connected to ground. Binary inputs are applied using level amplifiers; but in the diagram given here, we have used switches to explain its operation. The beauty of this network is that, the input current provided to the op-amp by the four binary inputs is in direct proportion to their digit weights. Thus the MSB provides eight times as much current as the LSB. This is due to the fact that looking up or down from the four nodes 1,2,3 and 4, the resistance is $2R$ ohm. We will reduce the network to its equivalent circuit to prove this (Fig. 15.17).

The output of the circuit in Fig. 15.17 depends on the combined effect of all the four inputs. However, we will consider the output when only the D input, that is the MSB, is at logic 1 level and the remaining three inputs are at logic 0 level. Consider the circuit in Fig. 15.17 (a), which shows that only the D input has been activated while inputs C, B and A are grounded. You will notice that circuit (*d*) is equivalent to circuit (*a*), which proves that looking up or down from node 1, the resistance is $2R$ ohm. This, in other words, means that the current supplied by the D input (MSB) is divided equally between two portions, half of it goes to the op-amp and the other half goes directly to ground.

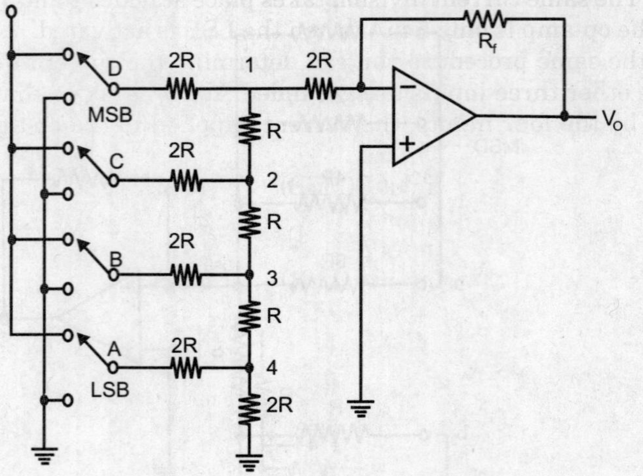

Fig. 15.16 D/A converter using $R - 2R$ network

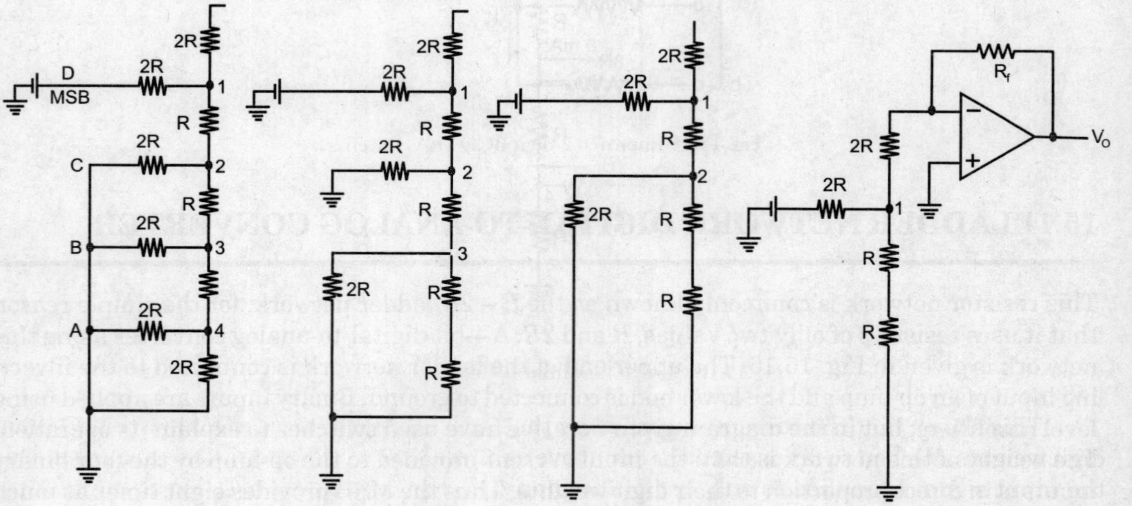

Fig. 15.17 Equivalent circuit for ladder network

If in a similar manner you determine the resistance from any other node, while the remaining inputs are connected to ground, you will find that looking up or down from any node, the resistance will be $2R$ ohm, that is the same as from input D.

In Fig. 15.18 we have shown the current division when input is applied to the LSB, while inputs B, C and D are grounded. We have assumed that the current from the LSB is 80 mA. The resistance from node 4 looking up or down will be $2R$ ohm. Therefore 40 mA, of current flows up and the same quantity flows directly to ground. Now, coming to node 3, the resistance looking up or down is also $2R$ ohm. Therefore 20 mA or current flows up and the same quantity flows down to ground. The same current division takes place at nodes 2 and 1. Ultimately, the current that flows into the op-amp is only 5 mA, when the LSB is activated.

Following the same procedure you can determine the current division from inputs B, C and A, when the other three inputs are grounded. You will notice that whereas the same current is supplied by the four inputs, the current supplied to the op-amp by these inputs is as follows:

Input D(MSB)	40 mA
Input C	20 mA
Input B	10 mA
Input A (LSB)	5 mA

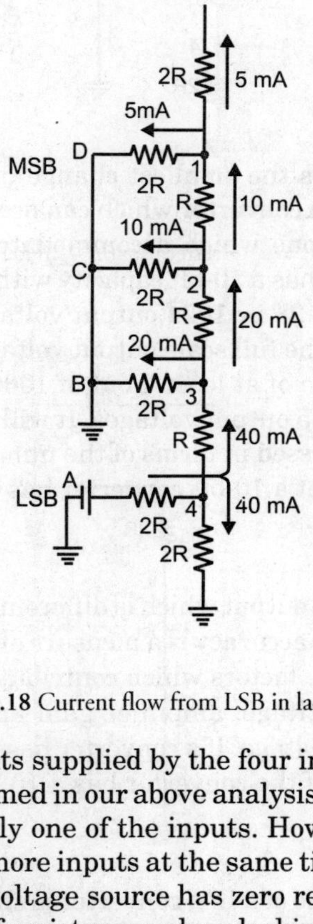

Fig.15.18 Current flow from LSB in ladder network

This shows that the currents supplied by the four inputs are in direct proportion to their digit weights. We had so far assumed in our above analysis that while three inputs are grounded, the input signal is applied to only one of the inputs. However, this is not the case in practice. Signal may be applied to one or more inputs at the same time. However, our analysis holds good in these cases also, as an ideal voltage source has zero resistance. It is, therefore, immaterial, for the purpose of our analysis of resistance values looking up or down from any node, whether an input is connected to ground or is at logic 1 level.

If the input signal voltage is V volt, we can now calculate the current supplied by each of the inputs to the op-amp. The D input, like all other inputs, sees a total resistance of 3 R ohm. Therefore, the current supplied by it is $V/3R$. Of this current half of it flows into the op-amp and thus the current supplied to the op-amp is $V/6R$. The currents supplied by the four input bits to the op-amp will be as follows:

Input D(MSB)	$V/6R$
Input C	$V/12R$

Input B	$V/24R$
Input A (LSB)	$V/48R$

This again shows that the current supplied by the four inputs is in direct proportion to their digit weights.

15.12 D/A CONVERTER SPECIFICATIONS

The performance of a D/A converter is judged on the basis of the following criteria:

- Resolution
- Accuracy
- Linearity
- Settling time
- Temperature sensitivity.

Resolution

The resolution capability determines the smallest change in the analog input, which can be discriminated by the D/A converter. A converter which can accommodate a large number of bits, will have a better resolution than one which accommodates a smaller number of bits. For instance, compare a converter which has a 10-bit capacity with another which has 8-bit capacity. The converter with 10 bits will have 2^{10} or 1024 output voltages. The smallest voltage change which it can detect will be 1/1024 of the full scale output voltage. If the full-scale output voltage is 1000, it is said to have a resolution of at least 1 out of 1000, or 0.1%. A converter which can accommodate 8 bits will have 2^8 or 255 output voltages. It will have a resolution of 1 part in 225, or 0.4%. Resolution can also be expressed in terms of the number of bits a converter can accommodate. For instance, we can say that a 10-bit converter has 10-bit resolution.

Accuracy

If a D/A converter produces an analog output which is different from what it should be in an ideal case, it is said to be inaccurate. The inaccuracy is a measure of the difference between the actual and the expected output voltage. The factors which contribute to inaccuracy are non-linearity, lack of precision in the reference voltage, amplifier gain and offset, etc. It is specified as a percentage of the maximum output voltage. If a converter has an accuracy of ± 0.5% it will cause an error of 0.5 × 10/100 or ± 50 mV, if the converter has a 10 V full-scale output voltage range.

Linearity

The output versus input characteristic of a D/A converter is shown in Fig. 15.19. This shows the analog output obtained from a given digital input. The digital input is marked along the X-axis with equal intervals. The output is marked along the Y-axis. The relationship between the input and output is represented by the diagonal. The actual output for each input in indicated by dots on the graph. If the converter was ideal, the dots would have fallen on the diagonal. The error due to non-linearity is represented by the differences between the actual voltage and the ideal voltage. It has been indicated by $\in$. The Δ in the diagram represents the analog output change corresponding to digital input change equivalent to the LSB. The linearity of a converter is specified in terms of Δ. It is commonly specified as ± 1/2 LSB, which implies that $|\in| < 1/2\ \Delta$.

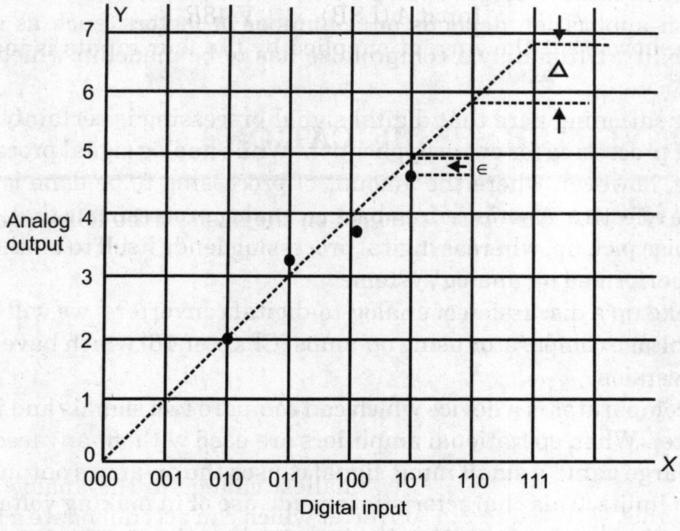

Fig. 15.19 Output-input characteristic of a D/A converter

Settling time

Since a D/A converter consists of switches, active and passive devices, there are always some stray capacitances and inductances associated with these devices and as a result transients occur in the output voltage when a digital input is applied to a converter. It, therefore, takes a finite time for the output to reach a stable state and sometimes oscillations may also occur. The time that elapses after the input change and when the output is stabilized, is called the 'settling time'. Typically the settling time may be around 500 ns. However, if a converter is operated at a very high frequency, the analog output voltage may not reach a stable state before the application of the next digital input.

Temperature sensitivity

D/A converters like may other devices are temperature sensitive. Even when the digital input remains unchanged, the analog output will vary with temperature. Sensitivity to temperature ranges from about 50 ppm/°C in a general purpose converter, to as small as 1.5 ppm/°C in a better quality device.

15.13 ANALOG-TO-DIGITAL CONVERSION

Analog-to-digital conversion is just the reverse of digital-to-analog conversion. However, analog-to-digital conversion requires a lot more circuitry and besides it takes up a lot of time. While we have considered only two methods of digital-to-analog conversion, there are many ways of converting analog signals to digital form; but all these methods depend on complicated systems and therefore it is not possible to give detailed schematic diagrams of their circuitry. In our discussion, therefore, we will use digital and analog blocks, with which you are familiar, to describe their operation.

Each system has its advantages and disadvantages and the choice of a particular system to be used in a given application depends on a number of factors, such as speed of operation, accuracy and stability. Ultimately a compromise has to be made, in which cost also plays an important part.

It is worth mentioning here that digital signal processing is certainly not more advantageous than analog processing for every application. While analog signal processing is faster than digital processing, however, where the amount of processing to be done is significant, digital processing is more effective. A serious drawback in analog processing is that, analog systems are highly prone to noise pick up, whereas digital processing lends itself to mathematical operation, which cannot be performed on analog systems.

Before we take up a discussion of analog-to-digital converters, we will briefly mention the functioning of a voltage comparator using op-amps (Chapter 16) which have considerable application in A/D conversion.

Basically a comparator is a device which can compare two signals and indicates which one of the two is greater. When operational amplifiers are used without any feedback (that is when they have a very large gain), a small input signal causes the op-amp's output to switch between its two saturation limits. This characteristic is made use of in making voltage comparators.

When used as a voltage comparator, the two inputs of the op-amp are connected to the two signal sources to be compared. The result of comparison is shown by the output. The truth table for its operation as a comparator is given in Table 15.4.

Table 15.4 Truth table for op-amp comparator

Signal input voltage	***Output***
$V_a > V_b$	$F = 1$
$V_a < V_b$	$F = 0$
$V_a = V_n$	Previous value

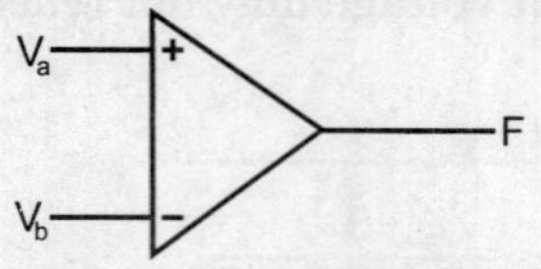

Fig. 15.20 Op-amp voltage comparator

15.13.1 Flash A/D Converter

In a D/A converter we know the number of digital inputs which are required to be converted into analog form, whereas in an A/D converter the analog input may have any value over a wide range. However, the digital output can have only 2^N discrete values when the A/D converter has N bits. This makes it necessary to represent the entire range of analog values using only 2^N intervals. Each interval is then required to correspond to a digital output.

We will consider how a 3-bit digital representation can express an analog voltage having a range from 0 to V. The entire range of analog voltage has been divided into eight intervals as shown in Fig. 15.21. The middle six ranges are at an interval of $V/7$. The top and bottom ranges have an interval of $V/14$. The diagram also shows the digital value assigned to each interval. In each interval the entire range of analog voltages in a system will be represented by only one digital value. Therefore, an element of error is built into this quantization; but that is unavoidable since the number of bits must have a limit. For instance, consider the range extending from $5V/14$ to $7V/14$, which will be represented by the digital output of 011. This entire range will represent the analog voltage of $3V/7$ or $6V/14$. The quantization error in this range, like all the other ranges, will not be larger than $P/2$. The error in the top and bottom ranges will also not be larger than P/2, irrespective of where the analog input falls in the range.

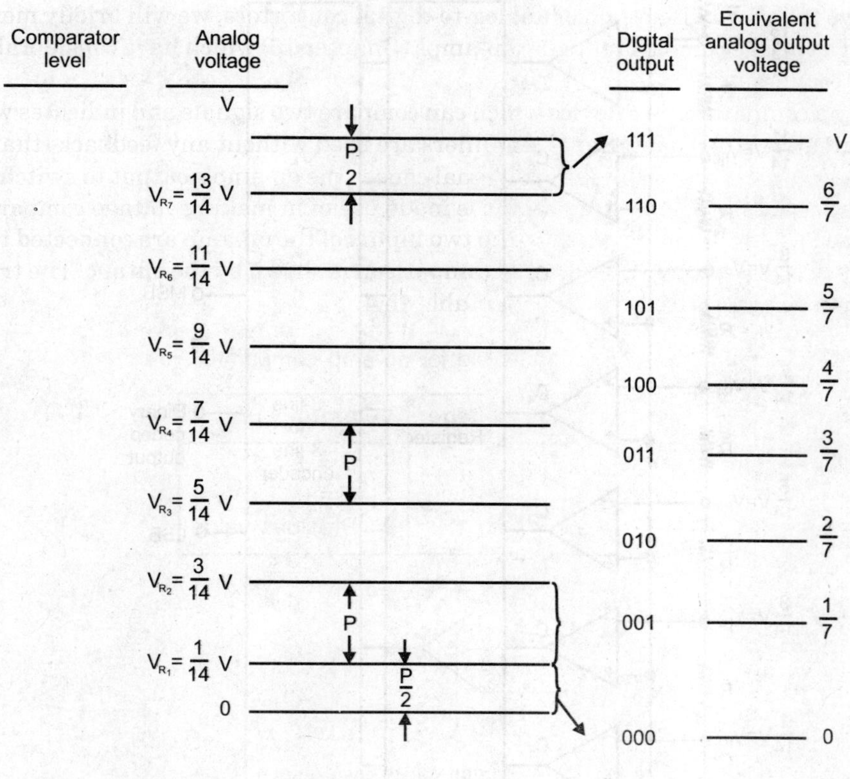

Fig. 15.21 Analog voltage divided into levels and levels assigned digital values to ensure quantization with a maximum error of $P/2$

The A/D converter using this concept has been given in Fig. 15.22. This circuit uses a resistive divider to divide the reference voltage into equally spaced voltage intervals between the reference voltage and the ground. Thus at each node of the voltage divider, a comparison voltage is available. The basic idea is to compare the analog input voltage with each of the node voltages. For this purpose there are op-amp voltage comparators, which compare the analog input voltage with voltage at the nodes. The result of this comparison has been shown in Table 15.5. You will notice from this table that when the analog input lies between V_{R2} and V_{R3}, comparator outputs C_2 and C_1 are 1 and C_3 is 0, which indicates that while analog input is larger than

V_{R2} and V_{R3}, it is smaller than V_{R4}. The comparator outputs are stored in a register, which feeds an 8-line to 3-line encoder to produce a 3-bit digital output. This table clearly indicates that when the output voltage is less than the reference voltage, the comparator output is 0 and when the analog input is greater than the reference voltage, the comparator output is 1.

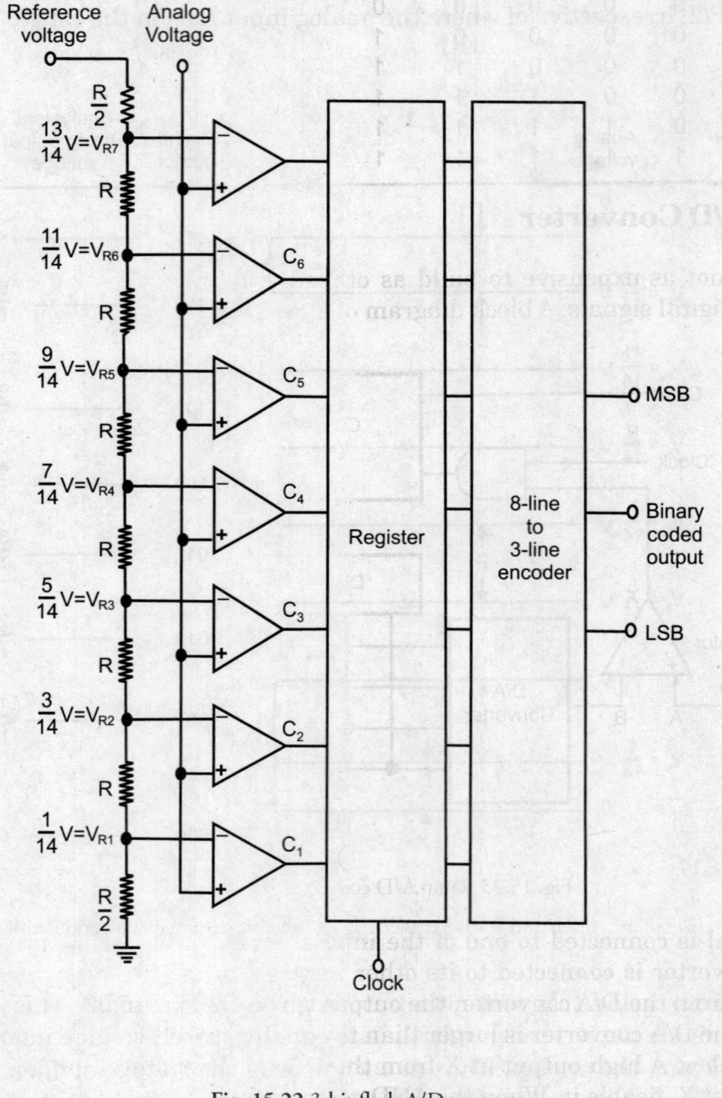

Fig. 15.22 3-bit flash A/D converter

For this converter we have used 2^N-1, that is 8 – 1 or 7 comparators from C_1 to C_7. However, a much larger number of comparators will be required for a larger number of bits, and this method, therefore inspite of its speed is not practical, where higher resolution is required.

Table 15.5 Analog input and digital output for flash converter

Analog input	***Comparator output***							***Digital output***		
V_a	C_7	C_6	C_5	C_4	C_3	C_2	C_1	B_2	B_1	B_0
0 to V_{R1}	0	0	0	0	0	0	0	0	0	0
$V_{R1} - V_{R2}$	0	0	0	0	0	0	1	0	0	1
$V_{R2} - V_{R3}$	0	0	0	0	0	1	1	0	1	0
$V_{R3} - V_{R4}$	0	0	0	0	1	1	1	0	1	1
$V_{R4} - V_{R5}$	0	0	0	1	1	1	1	1	0	0
$V_{R5} - V_{R6}$	0	0	1	1	1	1	1	1	0	1
$V_{R6} - V_{R7}$	0	1	1	1	1	1	1	1	1	0
$V_{R7} - V_R$	1	1	1	1	1	1	1	1	1	1

15.13.2 Ramp A/D Converter

A ramp converter is not as expensive to build as other devices; but it is a slow method of converting analog to digital signals. A block diagram of a ramp converter is given in Fig. 15.23

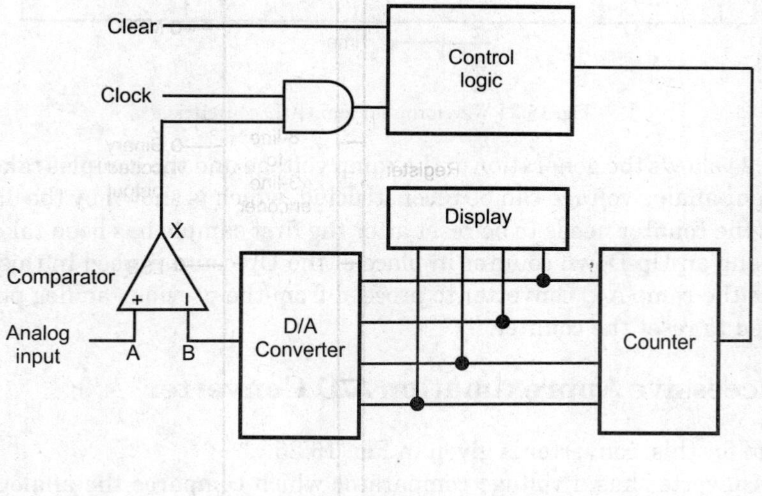

Fig. 15.23 Ramp A/D converter

The analog signal is connected to one of the inputs of the voltage comparator and the output of the D/A converter is connected to its other input. When the analog input signal is larger than the input from the D/A converter, the output of the voltage comparator is high and when the input form the D/A converter is larger than the analog input signal, the output of the voltage comparator is low. A high output at *X* from the voltage comparator enables the AND gate and a low output at X disable it. When the AND gate is enabled, the clock signal can enter the control logic, and when it is passed on to the counter it is stepped up.

We can now consider how the circuit as a whole performs analog-to-digital conversion. When a clear signal is applied, the counter is reset and its output at this stage will be 0000 and the output of the D/A converter will also be 0. When the analog input signal is larger than the input form the D/A converter, the AND gate is enabled and the clock steps up the counter to

0001. As long as the output of the D/A converter is small than the analog signal, the clock signal will continue to step up the counter. As soon as the input from the D/A converter exceeds the analog input signal, the AND gate is disabled and the clock is inhibited from stepping up the counter. The counter output recorded by the display at this stage represents the digital equivalent of the analog input signal.

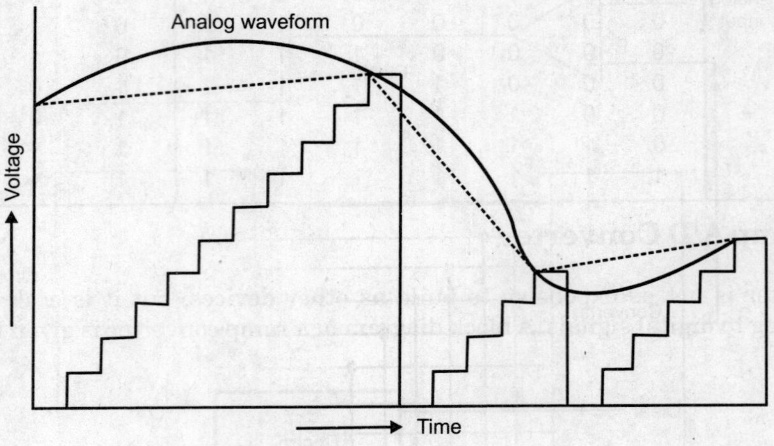

Fig. 15.24 Waveforms for ramp A/D converter

Figure 15.24 shows the generation of the ramp voltage and the samples taken. From these samples the input analog voltage can be reconstructed, which is shown by the dashed line. You will notice that the counter needs to be reset after the first sample has been taken. This can be overcome by using an Up-Down counter in place of the Up-counter used in this arrangement. This will enable the ramp A/D converter to proceed from the previous analog point to the next without the need to reset the counter.

15.13.3 Successive Approximation A/D Converter

A block diagram for this converter is given in Fig. 15.25.

This A/D converter has a voltage comparator which compares the analog input voltage with the output of a D/A converter. The voltage comparator is followed by control logic, which feeds the successive approximation register. The output of the register feeds the D/A converter. The register is also connected to a display which shows the digital equivalent of the analog input voltage.

The operation of this converter is best explained by an example. We will consider an 8-bit device which will have a resolution of 1/255 (2^8–1) of the full-scale reading. A TTL converter of this type can accept an analog voltage of 5V. Since the resolution will be 0.02 V, whenever the voltage increases by 0.02 V the digital output will increase by 1. The following analog voltages will therefore be represented by the binary words given against them.

Analog voltage, V	Binary word
0.0	0000 0000
0.02	0000 0001

0.1	0000	0101
1.08	0011	0110
5.00	1111	1111

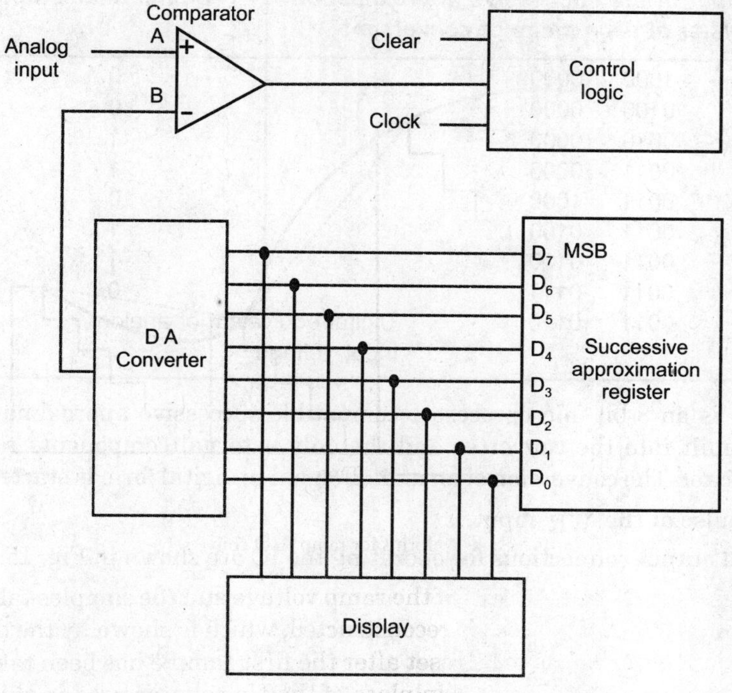

Fig. 15.25 Successive approximation A/D converter

We will now see how an analog voltage of 1.08 V can be converted into digital form using this converter. The required procedure follows:

1. Reset the register to 0 with the clear input.
2. Applya voltage of 1.08V (0011 0110) at input *A* of the voltage comparator.
3. Place a 1 in the MSB (D_7). The register output will now be 1000 0000. This will be converted by the D/A converter into an analog value and the voltage comparator will compare the two voltages. Since in this case the D/A converter output will exceed the input voltage of 1.08 V (0011 0110), the voltage comparator will set the D_7 bit to 0.
4. Now place a 1 in the D_6 bit. The register output will now be 0100 0000, which is also larger than the input voltage. After comparison by the comparator, the D_6 bit will also be set to 0.
5. Next place a 1 in the D_5 bit. The register output will now be 0100 0000, which is smaller than the input voltage. After comparison by the voltage comparator, the 1 bit in the D_5 position will be retained.

The entire sequence of operations is shown in Table 15.6. Follow the sequence remembering that if the D/A converter ouput to the voltage comparator is smaller than the analog input, a 1 will be retained in the register and if it is larger, it will not be retained. The final output displayed by the register will be 0011, 0110, which represents 1.08 V.

Table 15.6

Output of the successive approximation register at each stage of conversion	*Comparator output*
1000 0000	0
0100 0000	0
0010 0000	1
0011 0000	1
0011 1000	0
0011 0100	1
0011 0110	1
0011 0111	0
0011 0110	Digital equivalent of analog input voltage

IC ADC 0804 is an 8-bit microprocessor compatible successive approximation A/D converter. A clock is built into the converter and the only external components required are a resistor and a capacitor. The conversion of an analog signal to digital form is started by applying a low-going clock pulse at the $\overline{WR}$ input.

The input and output connections for operating the IC are shown in Fig. 15.26.

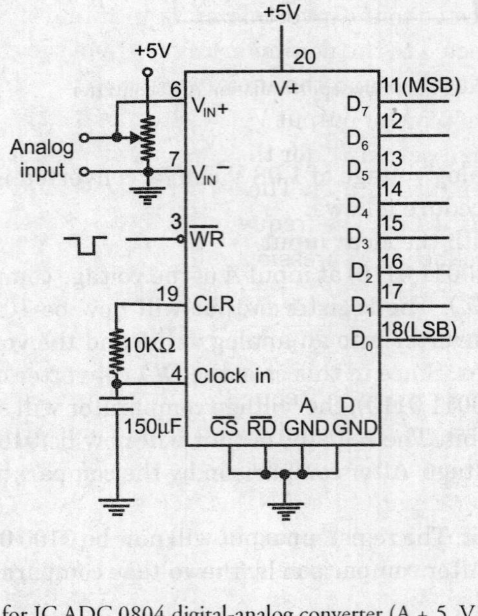

Fig. 15.26 Pin connections for IC ADC 0804 digital-analog converter (A + 5 V supply for test purposes may be connected instead of the analog signal.)

15.13.4 A/D Converter Based on Voltage/Frequency Conversion

The voltage-to-frequency conversion technique can be used as the basis for converting analog signals to digital form. As a starting point, the analog voltage is used to produce pulses, the frequency of which is proportional to the analog voltage. The pulses are counted by a counter and the count will be proportional to the pulse frquency; it will also be propotional to the input analog voltage.

A voltage-to-frequency converter can be built as shown in Fig. 15.27.

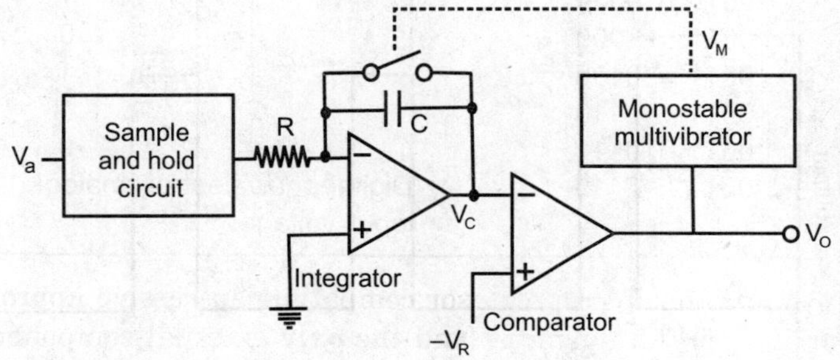

Fig. 15.27 Voltage-to-frequency converter

The analog voltage is supplied to the integrator through a sample and hold circuit, which should hold the sample long enough for the analog voltage to be formed at the integrator input. The integrator output V_c is connected to the inverting input terminal of the voltage comparator. A reference voltage $-V_R$ is connected to the non-inverting input of the comparator. At the start of the operation, switch S is held open and the integrator output V_c falls linearly with time. When it falls down to $-V_R$, the comparator output V_0 goes high, which is used to close the switch of the integrator for a long enough period T_2, for the capacitor to discharge fully. The period T_2 is controlled by the monostable multivibrator. The switch reopens after a period T_2 when the integrator output V_c again begins to fall. The frequency of the waveforms shown in Figs. 15.28 (a) and (b) is obtained from the following expression:

$$f = \frac{1}{T_1 + T_2} \frac{1}{\tau} \cdot \frac{V_a}{V_R}$$

This expression clearly shows that the frequency of the waveform is proportional to the analog input voltage. To obtain the digital equivalent of the analog input, the output of the voltage-to-frequency converter is connected through an AND gate to the clock input of a counter, as shown in Fig. 15.29. The other input to the AND gate is the same as the sampling voltage, which is at logic 1 level for a fixed duration. During this period V_a is held at the same level, as it was at the commencement. The counter output is read when the sampling voltage is 0.

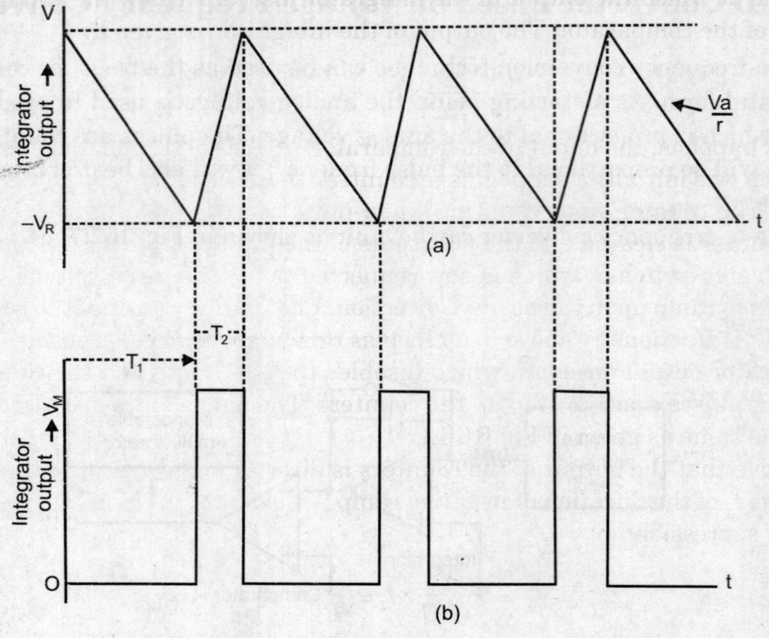

Fig. 15.28 Voltage-to-frequency converter waveforms

15.13.5 Dual Slope A/D Converter

A dual slope digital voltmeter has been discussed in Section 16.4 of Chap. 16. The dual slope A/D converter operates on the same principle as this voltmeter. It is suggested that the operation of this device be studied first, as that will lead to a better understanding of the operation of this A/D converter.

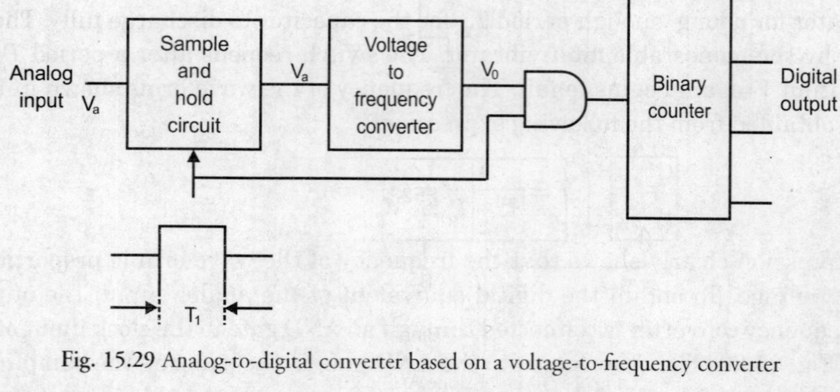

Fig. 15.29 Analog-to-digital converter based on a voltage-to-frequency converter

A circuit diagram for this converter is given in Fig. 15.30. At the commencement of the conversion process switch S is connected to the input analog voltage. The output of the integrator is given by the following expression, where $\tau = RC$, is the time constant of the RC network and t_1 is the time at which the output of the integrator just falls below the voltage of the non-inverting input of the comparator. The output of the integrator is given by

$$V_0 = -\frac{V_a}{RC} \times t_1$$

When that happens, the ouput of the comparator, V_0 goes high, the AND gate is enabled, the counter which was initially clear begins to count, as the clock pulses are now enabled to step up the counter. The counter stops counting when pulse count reaches 2^{N-1}. At the next clock pulse, 2^N, the counter is cleared and the Q outputs of the flip-flop goes high. This transition of the flip-flop activates switch S, which is now connected to the reference voltage V_{ref}. The integrator now starts to ramp up in the positive direction. The counter continues to count and stops counting when V_0 is fractionally above 0. As soon as this happens and V_0 becomes slightly positive, the comparator output goes low, which disables the AND gate and the counter will stop counting as clock pulses cease to step up the counters. The shape of the negative and positive ramps will be the same as given in Fig. 16.13.

We can prove that the output of the counters is directly proportional to the analog input voltage. The time t_1 of the duration of negative ramp is related to the period of the clock pulses by the following expression:

$$V_0 = -\frac{V_a}{RC} \times t_1 = \frac{V_a}{RC} \times 2^N t_p$$

where t_p is the period of the clock pulses.

Since V_0 was 0V at the commencement of the operation, it is 0 again at the end of the operation.

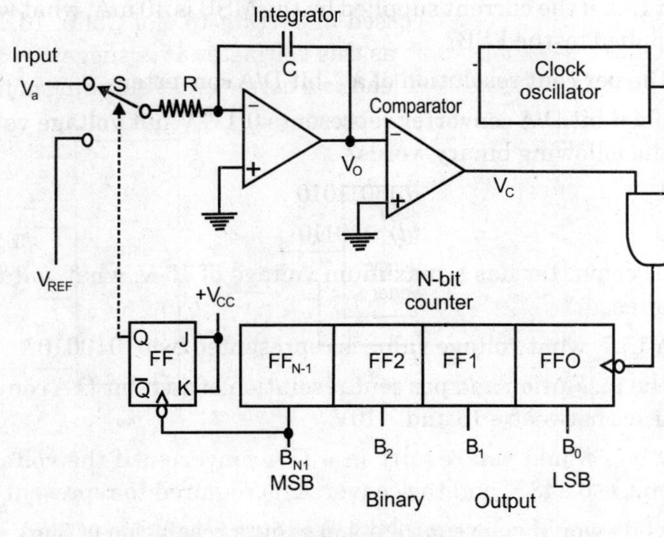

Fig. 15.30 Dual-slope A/D converter

Therefore $$\frac{V_r}{RC} \times t_2 = \frac{V_a}{RC} \times t_1 = \frac{V_a}{RC} \times 2^N t_p$$

since $$t_1 = 2^N t_p$$

It follows that $$t_2 = \frac{V_a}{V_r} \times 2^N t_p$$

Now if the read out in the flip-flops is n at the end of time t_2

$$t_2 = \frac{V_a}{V_r} \times 2^N t_p = nt_p$$

Therefore, $$n = \frac{V_a}{V_r} \times 2^N$$

This shows that the counter output is directly proportional to the input analog voltage V_a. The counter can be made direct reading if $V_r = 2^N$. In that case the count recorded in the counter will be numerically equal to the input voltage V_a. A fresh cycle can be started after discharging capacitor C.

Problems

15.1 What will be binary equivalent weight of each bit in the following cases?

(*a*) 3-bit resistive divider (*b*) 4-bit resistive divider

(*c*) 5-bit resistive divider (*d*) 6-bit resistive divider

15.2 Draw a *R*-2*R* ladder network for 6 bits.

15.3 By how much will the output of the following D/A converters increase, with an increase of 1 in the binary count?

(*a*) 4-bit (*b*) 8-bit

15.4 In Problem 15.2 if the current supplied by the MSB is 40 mA, what will be the value of current supplied by the LSB?

15.5 Calculate the per cent resolution of a 7-bit D/A converter.

15.6 The LSB of a 6-bit D/A converter represents 0.1V. What voltage value will be represented by the following binary words?

(*a*) 110101 (*b*) 011010

(*c*) 101010 (*d*) 110110

15.7 At 8-bit A/D converter has a maximum voltage of 15 V, what voltage change would each bit represent?

15.8 In Problem 15.7, what voltage value is represented by 01010010?

15.9 Calculate the resolution and per cent resolution of an 8-bit D/A converter, the output of which varies between +10 and – 10V.

15.10 How many bits would you require in a D/A converter, if the voltage increment required per bit is 0.048 V and the converter is required to represent 0 –50 V.

15.11 How many bits would you require if you want a resolution of 5 mV and the full-scale voltage is 15V?

15.12 For successive approximation converter ADC 0804, draw up a table like Table 15.6, when the analog voltage required to be converted into digital form is 2.1V. What would be the digital equivalent of the analog voltage?

16 Digital Equipment

16.1 INTRODUCTION

Digital techniques have found extensive application in test equipment, process control systems, medical electronics, microprocessors, computers, etc. With digital measuring equipment, much better accuracy and resolution can be achieved than with analog instruments, which use meter-type indicators as there is always some reading error when meters are used.

The most commonly used digital instrument is the digital multimeter, which can measure voltage, current and resistance. A digital multimeter is essentially an analog-to-digital converter. This technique can also be extended for the measurement of the capacitance, inductance, etc.

In this chapter, we will be trying to bridge the gap between theory and practice and guide the students of electronics to apply the knowledge he has gained so far in designing some basic systems.

Before considering any equipment as a whole, we will pay our attention to some of the basic building blocks, which are common to many of these devices. A digital display is one of them, but there are some other common factors as well.

16.2 DIGITAL BUILDING BLOCKS

All instruments require an input circuit of some kind and digital instruments are no exception. The other requirements are a clock, a time base a wave shaper and a digital display. In this section we will consider these building blocks.

16.2.1 Input Circuit

The basic essential of an input circuit have been shown in Fig. 16.1. The first requirement of an input circuit is a resistive attenuator, which is required to step down the input voltage level, so that it is compatible with the rest of the circuit. In some cases a frequency compensated attenuator may be required. Besides the attenuation provided by the resistive attenuator, protection is also required from signals of very large amplitude. For this purpose clamping diodes are generally used as shown in the diagram.

In order to increase the sensitivity of the input circuit, some amplification is necessary to enable the instrument, of which the input circuit forms a part, to be able to measure very weak signals. The impedance looking into the input circuit should be high, so that the circuit being tested is not unduly loaded. At high frequencies the loading due to the input capacitance also assumes importance and should be kept low.

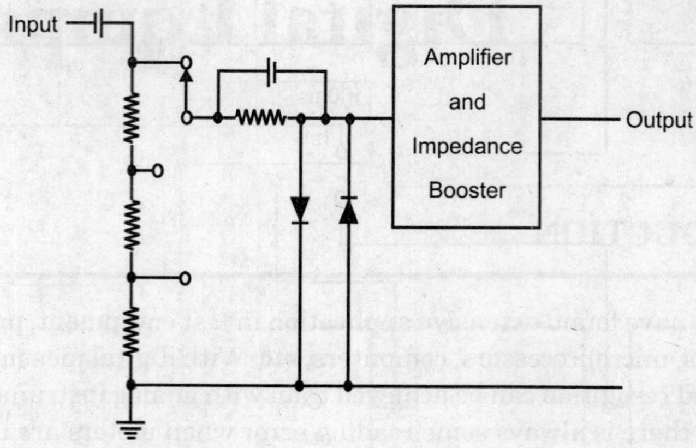

Fig. 16.1 Input circuit

A very important part of the input circuit is the wave shaper, which is required when the input is an alternating current signal, as for instance when audio or radio frequencies are being measured. Since input signals may be of irregular shapes, it is necessary to shape them into square waves. This is done by using a Schmitt trigger, which has been discussed earlier in Sec. 9.2.3. The Schmitt trigger performs another important function. It provides an output which is compatible with the rest of the circuit, as has been explained earlier. The Schmitt trigger does not alter the input frequency, which remains the same as that of the input signal.

The frequency response of the input circuit, to a large extent, determines the frequency characteristics of the instrument. The low frequency response is mainly determined by the coupling capacitor at the input and the input resistance. If the input capacitance is large in proportion to the input resistance, the low frequency response will be good. The high frequency response of the circuit depends not only on the characteristics of the amplifier in the input circuit, but also on the propagation delay contributed by gates and decade counter, etc.

16.2.2 Clock and Time Base

Clocks are an essential requirement of most digital circuits. We have discussed clocks in Sec. 9.2. In precision instruments, it is necesary to use crystal-controlled clocks. Crystal oscillators are generally designed to run at 1MHz or 10 MHz. High precision instruments commonly use temperature compensated crystal oscillators. In instruments where precision is not an essential requirement, the ac power line can be used, which has a frequency of 50 Hz and is normally accurate to within 0.1%.

For the generation of decade sub-multiples of oscillator frequencies, BCD counters are used as frequency dividers. These signals are than used as a standard for carrying out frequency and other measurements. A circuit for a time base is given in Fig. 16.2. This circuit can generate a time base from 1μs to 1s. The time base uses a 1MHz crystal oscillator and monostable to produce pulses of predetermined width and a precisely known time interval between the leading edge of pulses.

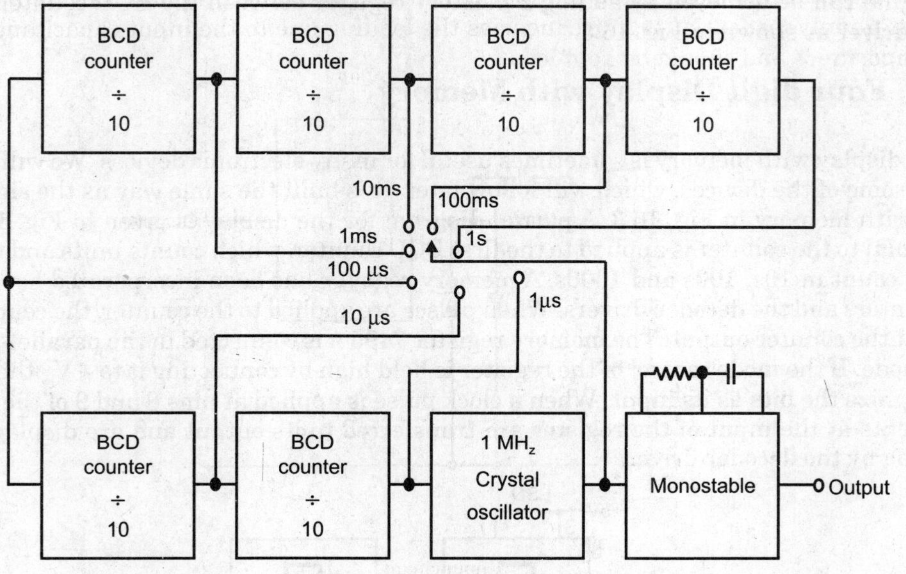

Fig. 16.2 Clock and time base

16.2.3 Digital Display

A digital display which can display two digits has been given earlier in Fig. 10.18. This display uses a BCD counter followed by a decoder-driver, which drives a seven-segment display. A number of these units can be connected to display more digits.

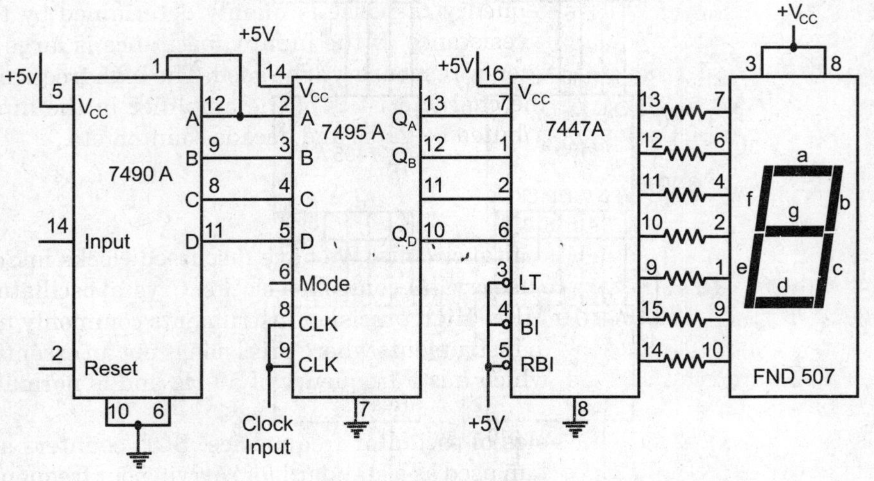

Fig. 16.3 Single digit display with memory

A counter of this type is suitable for some devices, but in applications where the input has to be sampled continually, some changes have to be made in this counter, especially when the input frequency or voltage are being monitored. This capability for repeated monitoring of the input signal can be achieved by adding a memory register between the BCD counter and the decoder driver as shown in Fig. 16.3.

16.2.4 Four digit Display with Memory

A 4-digit display with memory is sometimes useful for many electronic devices. We will be using these in some of the devices, which will follow later. It is built the same way as the single digit display with memory in Fig. 16.3. A partial diagram for the display is given in Fig. 16.4. The input signal to the counter is applied to the first BCD counter, which counts units and the other counters count in 10s, 100s and 1000s. A memory register has been incorporated between the BCD counters and the decoder-drivers. When pulses are applied to the counter, the count output appear at the counter output. The memory register 7495 A is connected in the parallel-in/parallel-out mode. If the mode control of the register is held high by connecting it to + V_{cc} the register will recognize the bits as its input. When a clock pulse is applied at pins 8 and 9 of the register, the contents at the input of the register are transferred to its output and are displayed after processing by the decoder-driver.

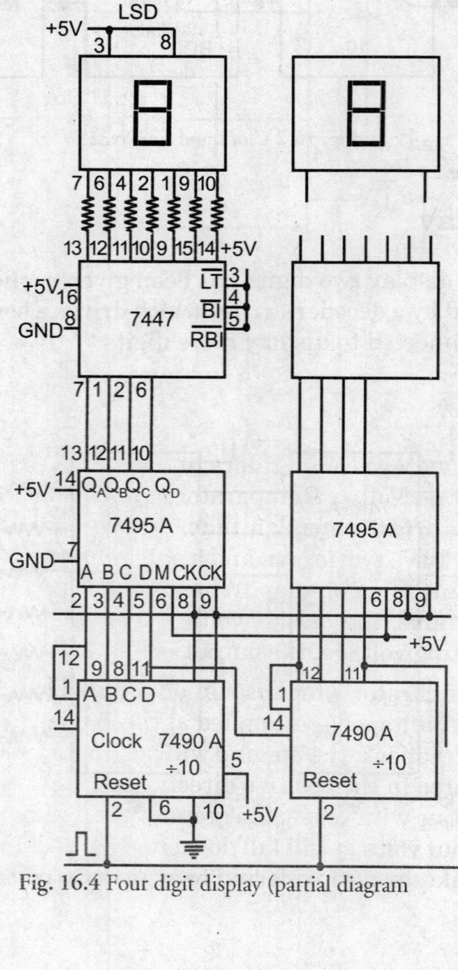

Fig. 16.4 Four digit display (partial diagram

As the counters are connected in cascade, the same sequence follows in the rest of the counters, registers and decoder-drivers.

At the commencement of a counting operation, the BCD counters are reset by applying a low going pulse at rest pin 2.

16.2.5 Totalizer

A totalizing counter counts the total number of pulses applied at its input and it will display the count as it progresses. A circuit for this counter is shown in Fig. 16.5. You will notice from the block diagram of the display, that it is almost the same as the one shown in Fig. 16.4, with the only differences that it has no memory register as it is not required. A NAND gate has been connected between the input and the first BCD counter. The operation of the counter is controlled by the start-stop switch, which can enable or disable the NAND gate.

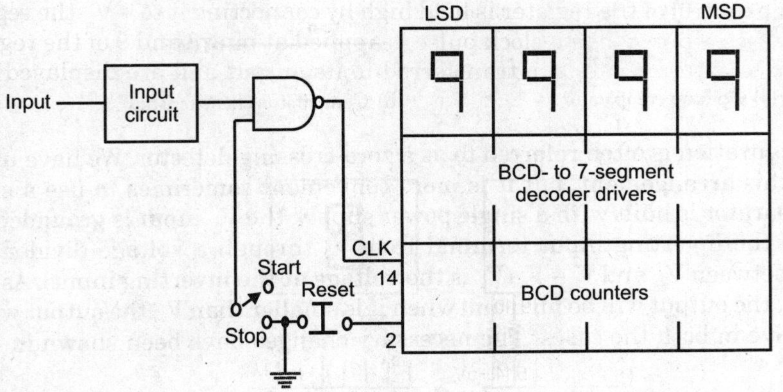

Fig. 16.5 Totalizer

16.2.6 Comparators

We had briefly mentioned voltage comparators in Sec. 15.13. We will now look into their functioning in a little more detail. Voltage comparators are used when we compare two voltages to find out which of the two is greater in magnitude. Operational amplifiers function very well as voltage comparators. They have two inputs and a single output. The two signals to be compared are applied at the two inputs of an op-amp. When the non-inverting voltage is larger than the voltage at the inverting input, the output voltage goes high. When the inverting voltage is larger than the non-inverting voltage, the output is low.

We will discuss a comparator which is run on a dual power supply and has its inverting input terminal grounded. A voltage V_{in} is applied at the non-inverting terminal as shown in Fig. 16.6 (a). Since there is no feedback, the op-amp will be saturated by the smallest increase in V_{in}. The op-amp will be saturated in the positive direction and the output voltage will jump to $+V_{cc}$. If V_{in} is even slightly negative with respect to ground, the op-amp will be saturated in the negative direction and the output voltage will fall down to $-V_{sat}$ as shown in Fig. 16.6 (b). The voltage at which switching over takes place is referred to as the trip point. In this case, the trip point is

0 volt. When V_{in} is larger than the trip point, the output voltage is high and when it is less than the trip point, the output voltage is low.

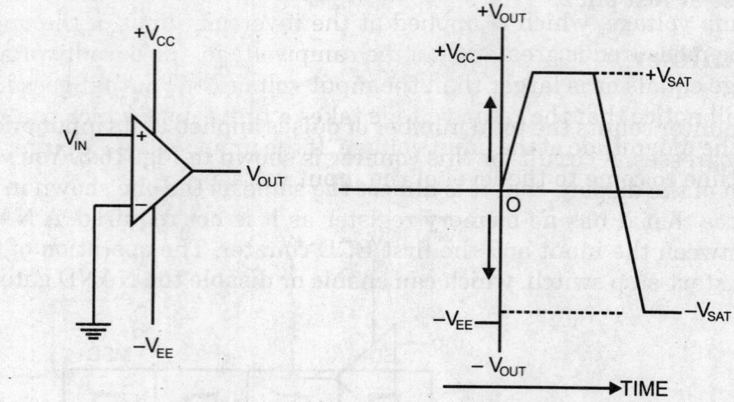

Fig. 16.6 (a) Op-amp comparator (b) Comparator characteristics

This op-amp configuration is often referred to as a zero-crossing detector. We have used a dual power supply in this arrangement, but it is more convenient sometimes to use a single power supply. If a comparator is built with a single power supply, the V_{ee} input is grounded and a voltage is applied to the inverting input terminal from V_{cc} through a voltage divider. The output can now swing between V_{cc} and $V_{cc} - V_r$ (V_r is the voltage at the inverting input). As long as V_{in} is greater than V_r, the output will be high and when it is smaller than V_r, the output will be low, but it will be positive in both the cases. The necessary changes have been shown in Figs. 16.7(a) and (b).

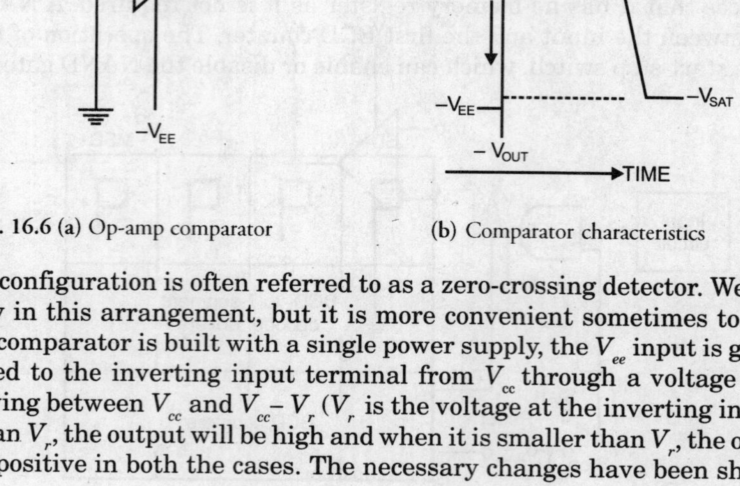

Fig. 16.7 (a) Comparator using a single power supply (b) Transfer characteristics

Voltage comparators find considerable application for measurement of voltage in digital multimeters. Figure 16.8 shows how op-amps are used in digital meters. The input voltage is applied at the non-inverting input of the op-amp and it is compared with a staircase (ramp) voltage, which is generated internally in the input circuit of the voltmeter. The diagram shows a rising ramp voltage, which is applied at the inverting input of the op-amp. As long as the voltage to be measured is greater than the ramp voltage, the output voltage is high. When the ramp voltage equals or is larger than the input voltage, the output goes low.

You will notice that the ramp voltage takes a finite time, which can serve as a measure to determine the magnitude of the input voltage. If the input voltage is large, the ramp voltage will take more time to come to the level of the input voltage.

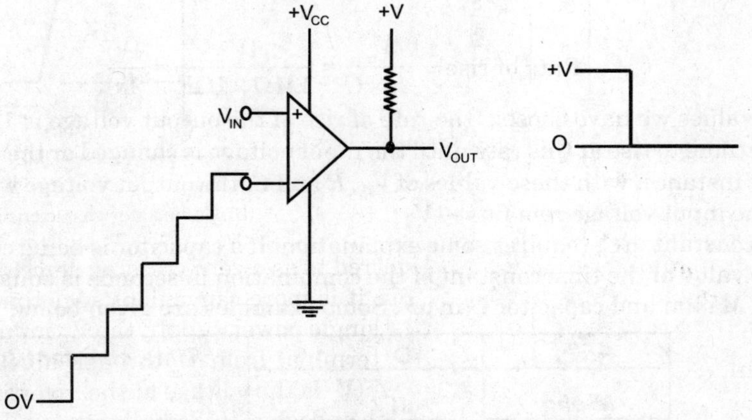

Fig. 16.8. Using an op-amp for comparison of the input voltage with a ramp voltage

16.2.7 Integrators

Integrators can convert fast rising and falling waveforms into linearly rising and falling ones and find useful application in digital voltmeters for producing rising or falling waveforms. For the present we will consider how a rising waveform can be generated by using an op-amp. A circuit for this purpose is given in Fig. 16.9.

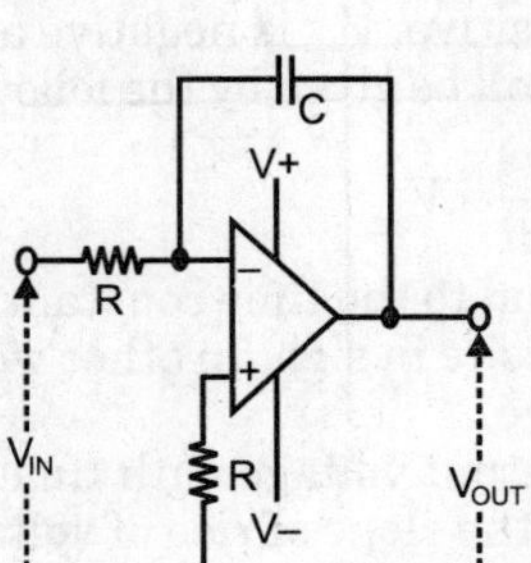

Fig. 16.9 Integrator

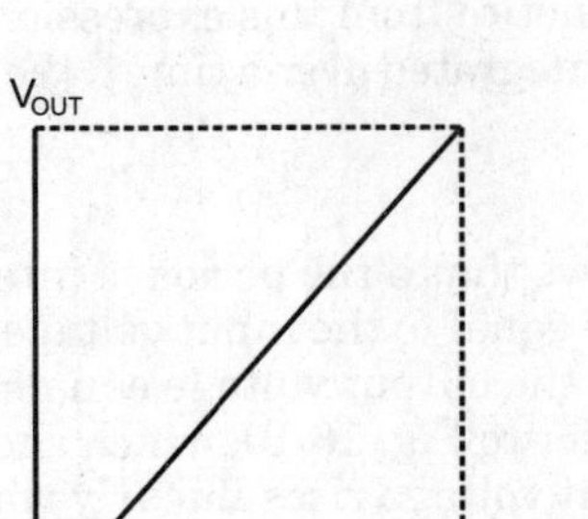

Fig. 16.10

The diagram shows an op-amp as an inverting amplifier. Input to the op-amp is applied through a resistor R and feedback is applied via capacitor C, which enables the op-amp to perform as an integrator. Another resistor R of the same value as the input resistor is connected between ground and the non-inverting input to reduce drift due to bias currents.

If a voltage of – 1 V is now applied at the input and the input resistor R is 1M ohm, a current of 1μA will flow through this resistor. Because the inverting input terminal is virtually at ground potential, a current of 1μ A will flow from the output through capacitor C to maintain the inverting input at ground potential.

This current takes time to attain the value of 1μA, because a capacitor charges or discharges exponentially. In order to supply this current a continuously rising voltage has to be generated at the output. The rate of rise of the output voltage is given by the following expression:

$$\text{Rate of rise} = \frac{V_{in}}{R \times C} = \frac{1V}{1M\Omega \times 1\Omega F} = \frac{1V}{1s}$$

With the values we have chosen, the rate of rise of the output voltage is 1V/s. The output voltage will continue to rise at this rate until the input voltage is changed or the op-amp reaches saturation. For instance, with these values of V_{in}, R and C, the output voltage will be 1V after a lapse of 1s, if the input voltage remains –1V.

The time constant, RC, requires some explanation. If a capacitor is being charged through a registors, the value of the time constant of the combination in seconds is equal to the product of resistor R in M ohm and capacitor C in μF. Some examples are given below.

R	C	Time constant (τ)
M ohm	μF	
1	1	1s
0.1	0.1	10 ms (millisecond)
0.1	0.01	1 ms (millisecond)

The output voltage of the circuit which we have just considered can be calculated from the following equation:

$$V_{out} = -\frac{1}{CR}\int_0^t V_{in}\, dt$$

You will notice from this expression that if V_{in} in positive, V_{out} is negative and vice versa. If the output is integrated over a time t, the output voltage will be given by the following expression:

$$V_{out} = \frac{1}{CR} \times V_{in}\, t \text{ or } \frac{t}{CR} \times V_{in}$$

This shows that if the period of integration, t, is equal to the time constant, CR, the output voltage will be equal to the input voltage, but will be opposite in sign. In other words, during one time constant the output voltage equals the input voltage.

If you refer to Fig. 16.10, which shows the rise of output voltage with time, you will notice that the output voltage rises linearly with time. That is the slope of rise of voltage with time is constant. This is important, because we cannot build a digital voltmeter if the rise of the output voltage with time is not linear.

We will consider a few examples of the rise of output voltage with time. Let us suppose that the input voltage is 1V and the time constant is 1ms. The output voltage will rise at the rate of 1 Vms. Consider the following examples:

Table 16.1

Rate of voltage increase	Input (V)	Time duration, μs	Output (V)
1V/10ms	0.0009	9	0.0009
	0.0099	99	0.0099
	0.0999	999	0.0999
	0.9999	9999	0.9999
	0.0596	596	0.0596
	0.4529	4529	0.4529

In Table 16.1, we have calculated the time taken for the output voltage to reach the level of the input voltage, when the rate of voltage increase for the integrator is 1V in 10 ms.

You will notice that at this rate of voltage increase, a voltage of 0.0009 V at the input produces the same voltage at the output in 9μs. If the input voltage is 0.0596V, it will take 596μs for the output to be the same as the input. For a time constant of 10ms, the input resistor should be 0.1 M ohm if the feedback capacitor has a value of 0.1 μF.

16.3 DIGITAL VOLTMETER

A circuit diagram for a digital voltmeter is given in Fig. 16.11. You will notice that the display portion of the circuit diagram is the same as has been given earlier and functions in the same way.

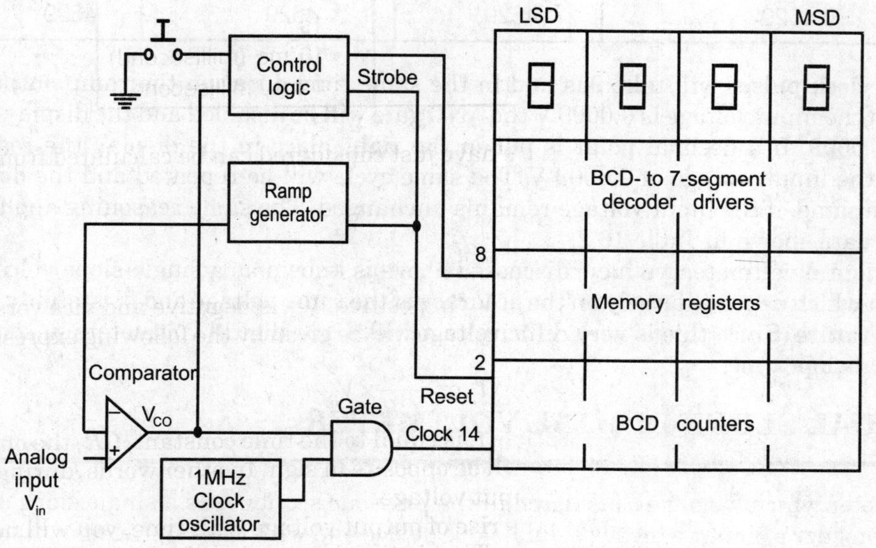

Fig. 16.11 Single slope digital voltmeter

The manual reset control is used to reset the decade counters to 0. The reset pulse also resets the ramp voltage to 0. The analog voltage being measured, which should be positive, is applied at the non-inverting input of the comparator. Since the ramp is at 0.0V, the output, V_{CO}, of the comparator will be high. This enables the AND gate to pass on the clock pulses of the 1 MHz clock oscillator to the BCD counters. The counters begin to count the pulses of the clock oscillator and the ramp output voltage begins to rise upward. After some time when the ramp output equals the input voltage, the output of the comparator, V_{CO}, goes low. The AND gate is disabled, and the counters stop counting. At the same time, the high-to-low transition of the comparator output, V_{CO}, generates a strobe signal in the control logic, which transfers the counter output from the memory to the decoder-drivers for display. The strobe signal is followed by a reset pulse from the control logic and the same cycle is repeated.

Since the clock oscillator is set at 1 MHz, it generates clock pulses at the rate of one pulse in 1μs. Let us suppose that the ramp used has a rate of voltage increase of 1.0V in 10ms. It has the same characteristics as have been shown in Table 16.1. The display used can accommodate decimal numbers from 0000 to 9999.

If the counter is initially set to 0000, the display will show 0009 after 9 clock pulses, which will be generated in 9μs. Consider Table 16.2 which shows the input voltage. V_{in}, clock pulses, time duration and the count shown in the display.

Table 16.2

Input voltage V_{in}	*Clock pulses*	*Time duration μs*	*Display*
0.0009	9	9	0009
0.0099	99	99	0099
0.0999	999	999	0999
0.9999	9999	9999	9999
0.0596	596	596	0596
0.4529	4529	4529	4529

Nine clock pulses will take 9μs and in the same time duration the ramp output will be 0.0009 V. If the input voltage is 0.0009 V the AND gate will be disabled and the display will show a count of 0009. If a decimal point is put in the right place in the display the reading will represent the input voltage of 0.0009 V. The same cycle will be repeated and the display will remain the same, if the input voltage remains unchanged. The same reasoning applies for the rest of the data shown in Table 16.2.

The digital voltmeter we have discussed above is known as a single-slope voltmeter, the accuracy of which depends largely on the accuracy of the ramp voltage and its stability with time and temperature. Since this is very difficult to achieve, the digital voltmeters in common use are the dual-slope type.

16.4 DUAL SLOPE DIGITAL VOLTMETER

The voltmeter which we have considered in the previous section was a single slope device. We will now consider a circuit which is a dual-slope device and with this improvement it overcomes the problem which arises due to temperature variations in the values of R and C. The circuit of a dual slope voltmeter is given in Fig. 16.12.

At the integrator input, there is a switch which can connect the voltmeter either to the analog input voltage or to a reference voltage – V_{ref}. The logic control circuit takes care of the switching at the appropriate time. The input is connected through a resistor R of 20 K ohm to the inverting input terminal of the integrator, of which the non-inverting input is grounded. The integrator output is fed back to the input via capacitor C of 0.05 mF. The integrator output is also connected to the inverting input terminal of the comparator and its output goes to one of the inputs of an AND gate. The other input of the AND gate goes to the 1MHz clock input. The clock will generate 1000 pulses every millisecond. The AND gate output is connected to the clock input of the first BCD counter of a 4-digit digital display. The memory register as well as the AND gate and comparator outputs are acces sible to the logic control circuit.

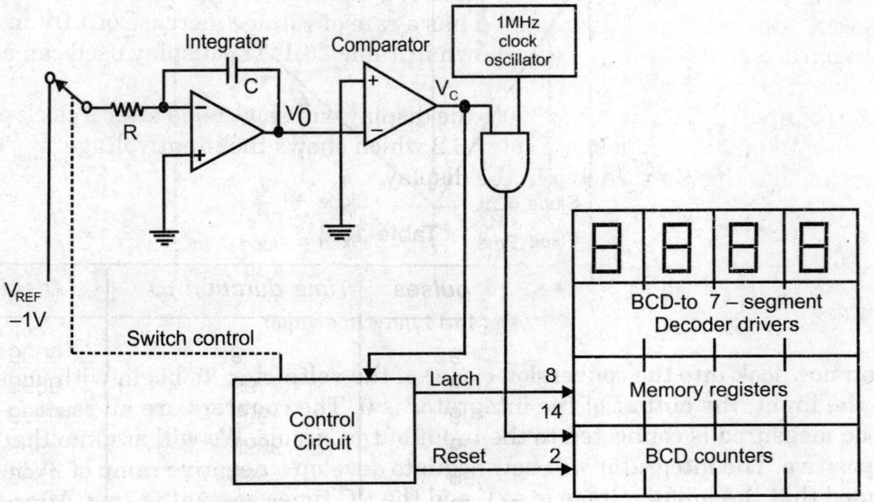

Fig. 16.12 Dual-slop digital voltmeter

Now, as you know how the circuit is organized, we will consider its operation. According to the values of R and C, we have used, the time constant of the R and C combination is 1ms. We will suppose that the input analog voltage is + 2 V. This will inject a current of 0.1 mA through the 20K ohm resistor in the direction of the op-amp. Since the inverting input terminal of the integrator has to be at ground potential, and it has very high input impedance, this current cannot flow into the op-amp. It therefore flows into one plate of the capacitor. As the non-inverting input of the integrator has to be at 0V, because it is virtually at ground potential, the op-amp output has to draw an equal amount of current from the other plate of the capacitor. In the process the capacitor acquires a charge and, as a consequence, the op-amp output falls to a more negative voltage to ensure flow of current from the capacitor. Since the capacitor is being charged by a constant current positive voltage source from the input, it gives rise to a negative linear ramp as shown in Fig. 16.13. When we apply a negative voltage from the reference voltage $-V_{ref}$, there will be a ramp in the positive direction as shown in Fig. 16.13. The slope of the negative ramp of the integrator output will be as follows:

$$\text{Negative ramp slope} = \frac{V_{in}}{RC} = -\frac{+2}{1\,\text{ms}} = -2\,\text{V/ms}$$

when the input voltage is + 2V.

$$\text{Positive ramp slope} = \frac{V_{ref}}{RC} = \frac{1V}{1\,\text{ms}} + 1\text{V/ms}$$

where $V_{ref} = -1\text{V}$

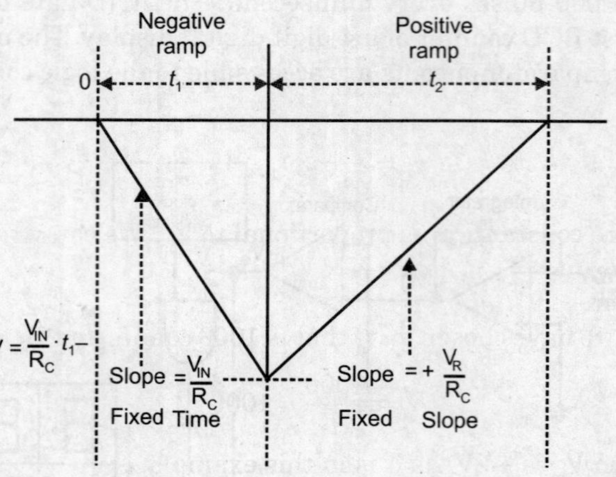

Fig. 16.13 Integrator output

We can now look into the conversion cycles of the voltmeter. To begin with, as there is no voltage at the input, the output of the integrator is 0. The counters are all reset to 0 and the voltage to be measured is connected to the input of the circuit. We will assume that the input voltage is positive. The integrator will now begin to develop a negative ramp of 2V/ms since we have assumed that the input voltage is +2V and the RC time constant is 1ms. After time t_1 the output of the integrator will fall below 0 V and as soon as that happens the comparator output will go high, which will enable the AND gate and allow the 1MHz clock signal to step up the counters. The integrator continues to ramp negative for a predetermined number of counts, at the end of which the logic control initiates the following action:

- The counters are reset to 0.
- The integrator is switched on to the reference voltage V_{ref} which is –1V.

Since the input voltage to the circuit is now negative, the integrator will develop a positive ramp as shown in Fig. 16.13. When the integrator output goes a fraction of a volt above 0, the comparator output will go low, which will disable the AND gate and the clock will be disconnected from the counters. At that stage, as the logic control circuit notices this transition, the count which is stored in the registers is latched, the counters are reset to 0 and the circuit input is connected back to the voltage source being measured and another conversion cycle is commenced.

At this point the count stored in the registers bears a definite proportion to the unknown voltage. We will consider why that is so.

In the fixed time t_1 during which the integrator is allowed to ramp negative for a known number of pulses from the clock oscillator, the output of the integrator falls down to

$$V_0 = \frac{V_{in}}{RC} \times t_1$$

So that the integrator output may return to 0 V, when the input is connected to the reference voltage source, the integrator is required to inject enough voltage during the positive ramp period t_2, The voltage that is injected into the integrator during t_2 is

$$\frac{V_{ref}}{RC} \times t_2$$

Since the change in the output voltage during the two ramp durations t_1 and t_2 has to be the same

$$\frac{V_{in}}{RC} \times t_1 = \frac{V_{ref}}{RC} \times t_2$$

Therefore $$t_2 = \frac{V_{in}}{V_{ref}} \times t_1$$

As t_1 and V_{ref} are constants, t_2 is proportional to V_{in}. We can write the equation as follows:

$$t_2 = K \times V_{in}$$

where K is a constant.

For the values we have chosen for t_1 that is 1000 counts and V_{ref} which is –1V, this constant

$$K = \frac{1000}{1} = 1000$$

Therefore, when V_{in} is + 2V, as it is in this example,

$$t_2 = 1000 \times 2 \text{ or } 2000 \text{ counts.}$$

The display will show a count of 2000. If a decimal is properly placed after 2, the display will read 2V. It follows that if K is properly chosen, the t_2 count in the display will show the correct voltage every time.

So far as the values of R and C are concerned, they should be so chosen that the op-amp integrator does not go into saturation when the input voltage being measured has the maximum recommended value.

A voltage divider is a necessary requirement for all voltmeters, more so for digital voltmeters, to scale down the input voltage to an acceptable level. The voltage dividers use precision metal film resistors. Their values should be chosen for proper scaling of the input voltage to a level suitable for digital devices as shown in Fig. 16.14. The voltage at the lowest range should not exceed above 0.5 V, as any voltage above that level may be outside the capability of a converter. Besides, a series resistor and clamping diodes are also necessary to provide necessary protection to the device, when the input exceeds the limited capability of about ± 4V.

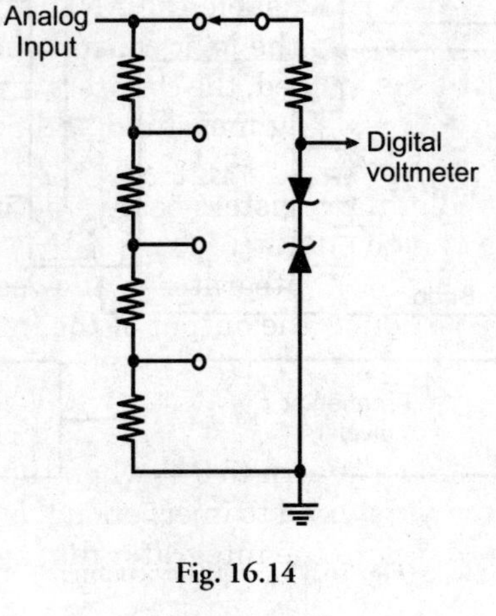

Fig. 16.14

16.5 FREQUENCY COUNTER

The circuit for a frequency counter is given in Fig. 16.15. The input circuit has been discussed earlier; but what was not mentioned is the amplifier. The amplifier used is an op-amp, which is connected as a Schmitt trigger. The output of the op-amp are square waves, which are at the same frequency as the input signal. Another advantage in using an op-amp as an amplifier is that, its output levels are compatible with logic devices. The op-amp output goes to an AND gate, which steps up the counter when the gate is enabled by the output of the *JK* flip-flop. The flip-flop is connected in the toggle mode. When clock pulses are applied to it, the output frequency of the flip-flop is half the input frequency. If the input frequency produces a 1s cycle, the *Q* output will produce a frequency with a period of 2*s*. This, in other words, means that the Q output will be high for 1*s* and low also for 1*s*. The *JK* flip-flop can be clocked by clock pulses from a frequency divider, which produces pulses with periods of 0.1, 1 and 10s.

Let us suppose that a 1Hz square wave is being used to trigger the *JK* flip-flop. The *Q* output of the flip-flop will produce a 1/2 Hz square wave. As mentioned before, its output will be high for 1s and also low for 1s. When the output is high the AND gate is enabled, which steps up the counter and its count goes up by 1. When the high output of the flip-flop is followed by a low output the counter stops, while the negative transition at the *Q* output triggers the one shot 74121. At the same time the $\overline{Q}$ output of the flip-flop goes high, which strobes the contents of the register into the display. After a propagation delay of about 30 ns in the one shot (74121), a negative reset pulse appears at its $\overline{Q}$ output. This delay is necessary to ensure that before the counters are reset by the low output of the one shot at its $\overline{Q}$ output, the contents of the register are transferred to the display.

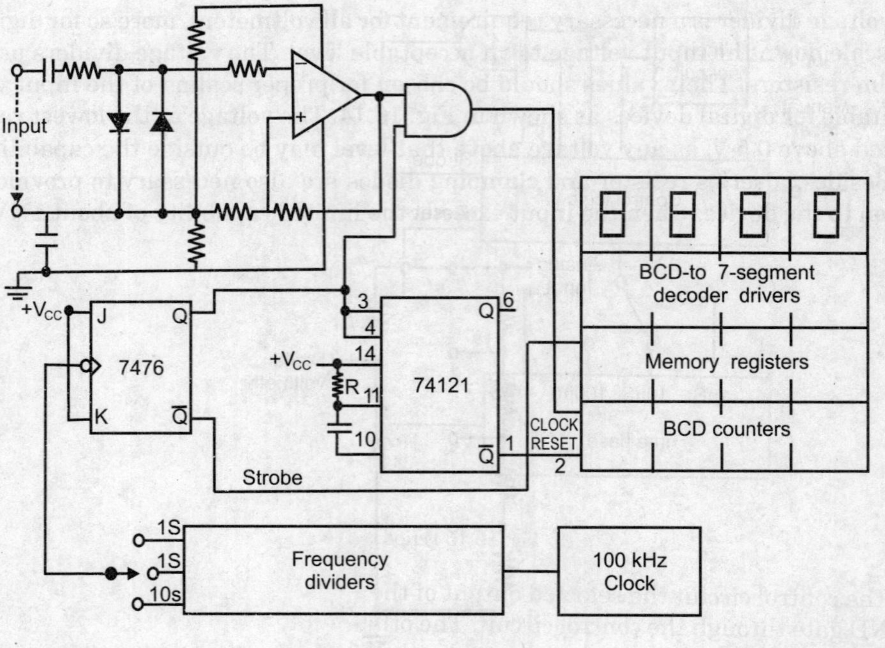

Fig. 16.15 Frequency counter

The width of the reset pulse of the one shot can be set by a suitable choice of the values of *R* and *C*. The end of each pulse from the one shot indicates the end of one measurement period.

When the time base is set at 1s and the display is 4573, this will represent a frequency of 4573 Hz. If the time base is set at 1ms, the display will represent the frequency in kHz. If the display is the same as before and the time base is 1ms, the frequency will be 4573 kHz or 4.573 MHz. When the time base is set, the decimal point is positioned at the proper place. The time base, therefore, serves as a range indicator.

16.6 PERIOD COUNTER

The frequency counter which we have discussed in the last section gives satisfactory results when high frequencies are measured. This counter is not suitable for low frequency measurement. In the latter case better results are obtained if the period of one cycle of the frequency is measured. If this period is *t* seconds, the number of cycles is one second is $1/t$, which gives the frequency.

This can be done by slightly modifying the frequency counter circuit given in Fig. 16.15. In fact many frequency counters can function in both the modes. The circuit diagram of a period counter is given in Fig. 16.16. The display portion of the circuit is the same as in Fig. 16.15 and it functions also in the same manner.

In this mode of period measurement, the counter counts the number of time base pulses during the period of one complete cycle of the input frequency being measured. If the number of pulses counted during this period is *N* and the duration of each time base pulse is *t* seconds, the time duration of a cycle of the frequency being measured is $N \times t$ seconds. The frequency will be given by $1/Nt$.

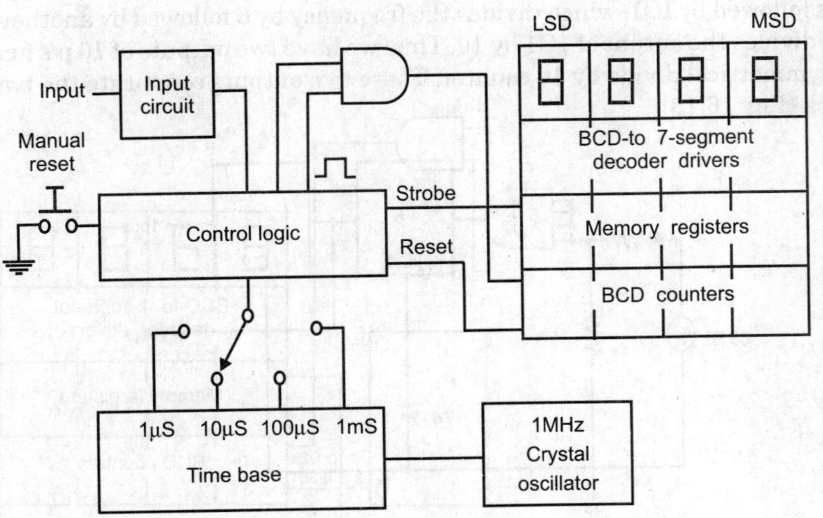

Fig. 16.16 Period counter

In the control circuit the selected output of the time base is connected to one of the inputs of the AND gate through the control circuit. The other input of the AND gate is connected to the input through the control circuit, which enables the input signal to operate the AND gate for the period of one cycle of the input signal, after the counter has been first reset by the control circuit. After the counter has counted the number of time base pulses during the period of one cycle of the input signal, the control circuit signals the memory registers to transfer the contents to the decoders for display. Shortly thereafter, the counters are reset by the control circuit and the cycle is repeated.

If the time base is set at 10 μs and the display count records 2485 pulses during one cycle period of the input signal, the frequency of the input signal can be calculated as follows:

Time duration of one cycle of the input signal = 2485 × 10 μs

Number of cycles in 1s (1000, 000 μs) $= \dfrac{1000,000}{2485 \times 10} = 40.24\,\text{Hz}$

The frequency of the input signal is therefore 40.24 Hz.

This method of measuring the frequency of the input signal gives better accuracy and resolution. The time base settings provide different ranges for the measurement of low frequencies.

16.7 DIGITAL CLOCK

The first requirement for a digital clock is an oscillator which will generate 1pps (pulse per second). A crystal oscillator will provide great accuracy; but where extreme accuracy is not the primary consideration, the mains frequency of 60p/s or 50p/s, which is normally quite accurate can also be used. A circuit for this purpose based on a mains frequency of 60 C/s is given in Fig. 16.17. After rectification, the input from the mains is shaped into square waves by a Schmitt trigger. This is followed by IC1, which divides the frequency by 6 followed by another frequency divider, which divides the output of 1C1 by 10. Thus we have two outputs of 10 p/s and 1p/s. IC2 is wired as a symmetrical divide by 10 counter. These two outputs constitute the two inputs to the digital clock (Fig. 16.18).

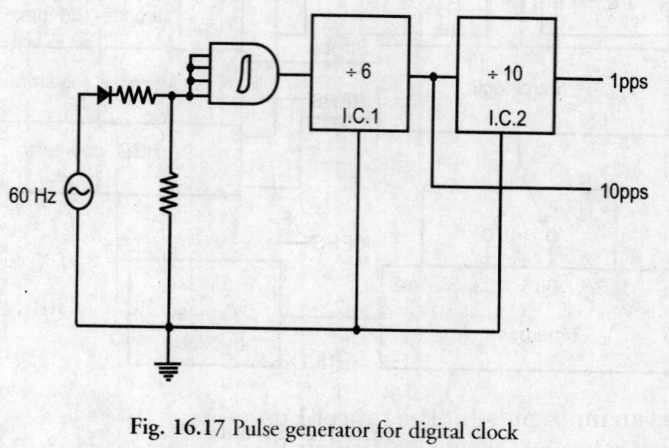

Fig. 16.17 Pulse generator for digital clock

The1 p/s signal goes to a logic control circuit which is used for running the clock and also for setting the time. When time is required to be set, Switch S_1 is held at the 'fast' position, when the 10 p/s signal runs the clock by closing switch S_2.

For normal operation, the 1p/s signal drives the decade counter IC 3. This counter drives the display in the ones position of the seconds display through a decoder driver. Decade counter IC3 also divides the 1p/s signal by 10 and provides this input to IC4, which is a Mod-6 counter. IC 4 drives the digit in the tens position of the seconds display. After the seconds display has reached a count of 59, the next pulse which is a 1p/m pulse drives IC 5, which together with IC 6 drive the digits in the minutes column through two decoder drivers.

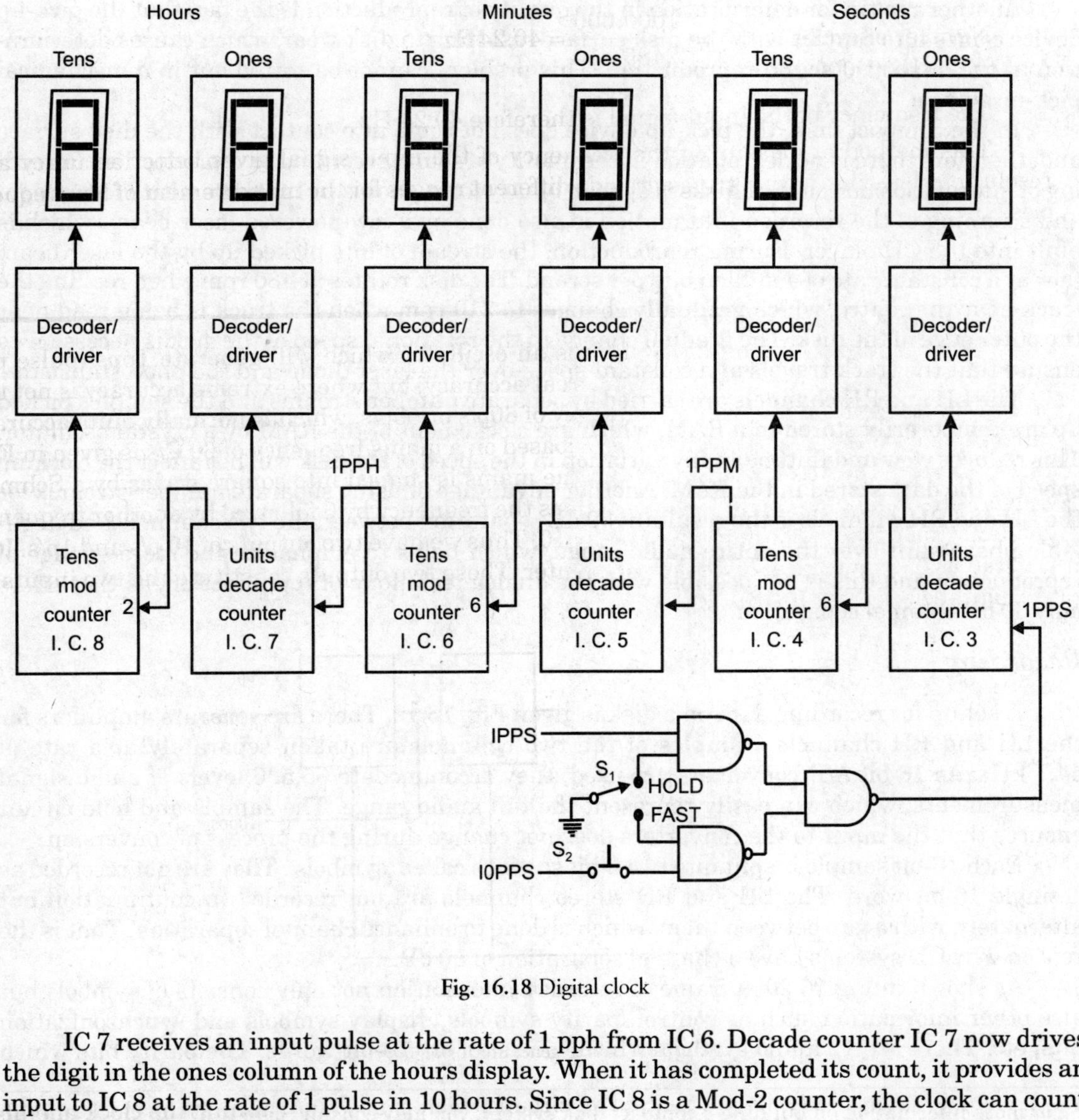

Fig. 16.18 Digital clock

IC 7 receives an input pulse at the rate of 1 pph from IC 6. Decade counter IC 7 now drives the digit in the ones column of the hours display. When it has completed its count, it provides an input to IC 8 at the rate of 1 pulse in 10 hours. Since IC 8 is a Mod-2 counter, the clock can count up to 24 before it is reset.

A complete diagram for the digital clock has been left as an exercise for the student.

16.8 DIGITAL AUDIO (COMPACT DISK)

We had become so used to LP disks for the reproduction of music, that it took us some time to realize the value of digital recording and reproduction, which became available on compact disks* in late 1982. LP disks depended on analog signal processing for recording and reproduction. However, in this system the signal gets distorted in many ways and it may not entirely correspond to the original signal. Besides the circuitry could cause spurious harmonics and noise. This could happen both in recording and reproduction.

Another reason for deterioration in the quality of reproduction is the fact that the pick-up device comes into contact with the disk surface resulting in disk wear, which causes deterioration in the quality of sound reproduction. This problem cannot be sorted out in a mechanical pick-up system.

In the compact disk, the pick-up device does not come into contact with the disk surface and, therefore there is no degradation in the quality of sound recording or reproduction. Recording of information on compact disks is done in binary form, that is in 1s and 0s with a laser beam and scanning of the recorded information is also done by a low-powered laser beam, which is built into the CD player. During reproduction, the stream of bits picked up by the laser beam flow at a constant rate of 4 million bits per second. The disk rotates at 480 rpm when reading the track near the centre, which gradually changes to 210 rpm when the track is being read near the outer edge of the disk. The gradual change in the rotational speed of the disk is necessary to ensure that the track travels at a constant speed over the laser diode and the phototransistor.

The LH and RH channels are carried by separate number streams and the samples picked up are temporarily stored in a RAM, which are clocked out of the RAM by a crystal oscillator. This reduces wow and flutter, as any variation in the speed of the disk will not affect the clocking speed of the data stored in the RAM. Another advantage of using separate number streams for the LH and RH channels is the resultant 90 dB separation between the two channels and negligible phase shift over the entire audio range, which helps to emphasize the stereo image of reproduction and this is not possible with the analog technique of reproduction, as that offers only 30 dB channel separation.

Recording

A set up for recording data on a disk is given Fig. 16.19. There are separate amplifiers for the LH and RH channels. Samples of the two channels are taken separately at a rate of 44.1 kHz. As 16-bit A/D converters are used, they accommodate 65,536 levels of audio signal measurements, which can easily represent the full audio range. The sample and hold circuit ensures that the input to the converters does not change during the process of conversion.

Each 16-bit sample is split into two 8-bit sections called 'symbols'. They are not recorded as a single 16-bit word. The LH and RH stereo channels are not recorded in continuation but alternately, with a gap between them, which is done to enhance channel separation. That is the reason why CD systems have a channel separation of 90 dB.

As shown in Fig.16.20, a frame of recorded information not only consists of symbols but also other information such as control, parity symbols, display symbols and synchronization bits, etc. There are 12 audio symbols which consist of six 16-bit words. The parity bits which

---

* For more information on building a compact disk system, you may consult Signetics data sheets for the TDA photo-diode signal processor SAA 7210 decoder, TDA 1541 dual 16-bit D/A converter and the SAA 7220 digital filter.

follow the audio symbols are required for error correction. These are again followed by 12 audio symbols, four parity bits and synchronization data, which provide information about the beginning and end of each frame. A complete frame has 33 symbols of 8 bits. Each frame is divided into six sampling zones. Each sample provides 16 bits of data for each channel.

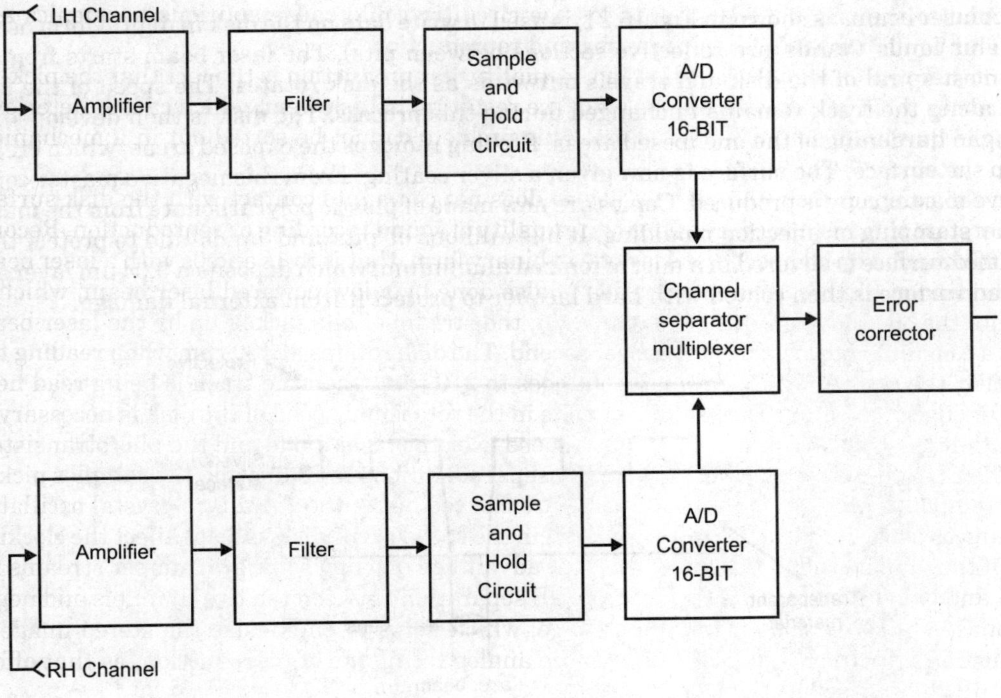

Fig. 16.19 Set up for disk recording

Control and Display	12 Audio symbols: Each of six 16-bit words	4 Parity bits	12 Audio symbols: Each of Six 16-bit words	4 Parity bits	Synch. data

Fig. 16.20 Sequence of information recorded in one frame

While recording, the audio samples are interlaced with those of an adjacent frame by a delay time of 1, known as CIRC (cross interlaced Solomon code). Interlacing ensures that mistakes are spread out and are not jumbled up in any one position. The error-correction circuit is thus in a better position to take care of the errors by averaging from the adjacent symbols to make up for the lost information. The output of the A/D converters for the LH and RH channels goes to a chennel separator (multiplexer), which performs two functions. In the first place it converts parallel data into serial data, as recording on the disk is done in serial form. Secondly, it inter-leaves data bits from the two channels. The 32 bits of data in the audio channels are divided to make 4 symbols in the audio bit stream. The channel separator is followed by an error correction circuit, which feeds a modulator. The modulator output goes to a laser head, which records data on the disk.

A laser beam, as shown in Fig. 16.21, is used to write data on the disk in digital form as tiny 'pits' and 'lands' ('lands' are reflective sections between pits). The laser beam starts from the innermost spiral of the disk and travels outwards as the disk rotates. The speed of the laser beam along the track remains unchanged during this process. The disk is then developed, resulting in hardening of the unexposed areas. Etching removes the exposed areas, which creates pits in the surface. The surface is now given a silver coating. From this negative master copy a positive master copy is produced. Copies are now made of plastic polycarbonate from the master copy by stamping or injection moulding. It has millions of 'pits' and 'lands' and to protect them the pitted surface is silvered in a mist of ionized aluminium, which deposits a 0.04 μm layer. The silvered surface is then coated with hard lacquer to protect it from external damage.

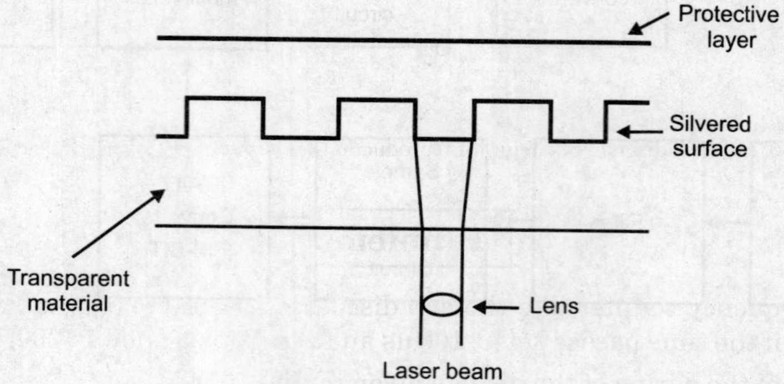

Fig. 16.21

Reproduction

For reading information recorded on the disk, it has to be read from the side opposite to that on which data are recorded and, therefore, pits appear as humps. Humps in the disk are about a quarter wavelength of light source higher (0.12 μm) from the adjoining area as shown in Fig. 16.22. The light reflected back from the surface travels half a wavelength further than the light reflected from the steps and this results in cancellation, which is detected to reproduce the information read out from the disk. The light reflected from the disk is focussed on photodiodes, from which the audio information is recovered and converted into audio signals by the set-up shown in Fig. 16.23.

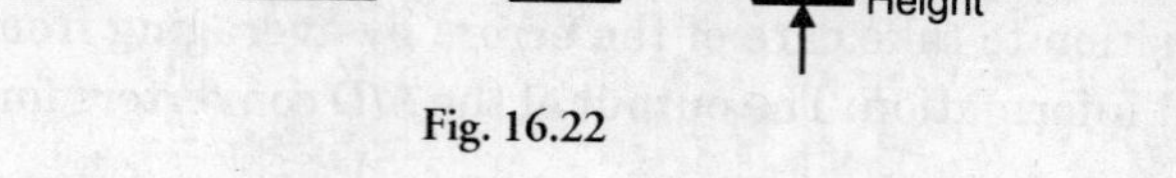

Fig. 16.22

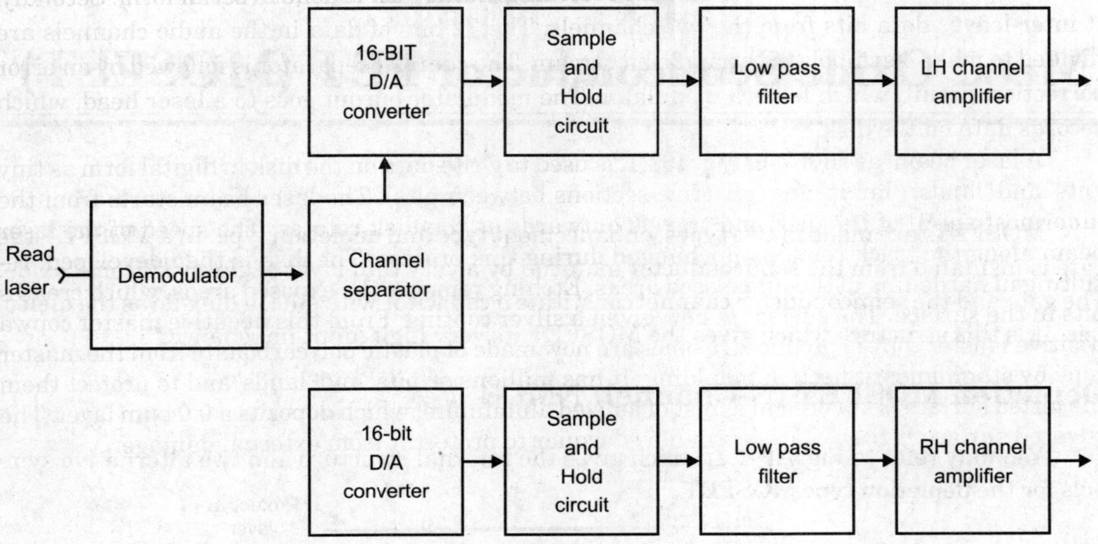

Fig. 16.23 Block diagram of circuit for reproduction of information from a compact disk

Problems

16.1 In a frequency counter like the one discussed in Sec. 16.5, what will be input frequency if the time base is set at 100 μs and the display shows 4290?

16.2 Complete the wiring of the display given in Fig. 16.4.

16.3 What time base will you use to measure frequency which lies between 5 MHz and 9 MHz and a frequency counter having a 4-digit display?

16.4 What will a 4-digit display of a frequency counter read, if the frequency is 74.23 MHz and the time base is 100 ms?

16.5 The frequency being measured on a frequency counter is 4.590 MHz and the time based is 100ms. What will be the display?

16.6 Draw a complete circuit diagram for the digital clock given in Fig. 16.18. Also indicate the changes necessary for a 12 hour display.

Appendix 1

Metal Oxide Semiconductor FET (MOSFET)

MOSFETs are made in two types, enhancement type and depletion type. In a MOSFET the gate is insulated from the semiconductor material by a very thin layer of glassy silicon dioxide. The gate and the semiconductor channel constitute a capacitor with silicon dioxide as the dielectric. It is this structure which gives the MOSFET its very high input impedance.

Depletion MOSFET (N-Channel) NMOS

You may refer to Fig. AP-1.1, which gives the internal structure and two alternative symbols for the depletion type MOSFET.

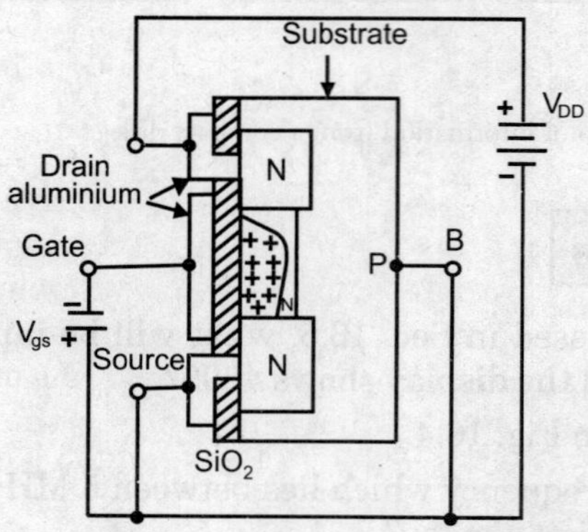

Fig. AP-1.1(a) Structure of depletion MOSFET (*N*-channel)

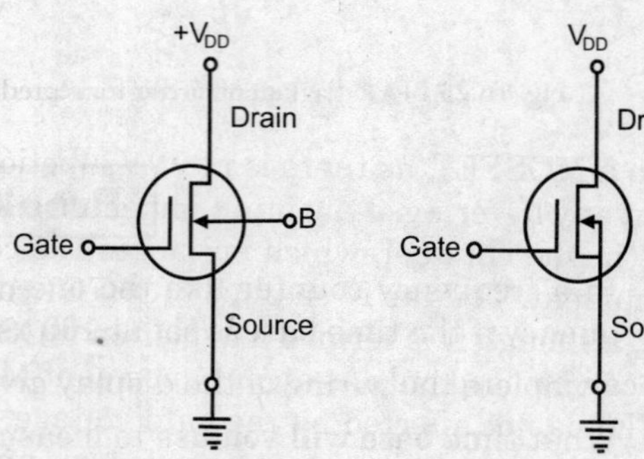

Fig. AP-1.1(b) Symbols for *N*-channel depletion MOSFET

You will notice that the gate and the *N*-channel form a capacitor with a thin film of silicon dioxide (SiO_2) serving as the dielectric. There is no *P-N* junction like one in an FET and it is this construction which gives the MOSFET very high input impedance. Biasing is as shown in Fig. AP-1.1 (a). The symbol shows that the gate is insulated from the channel. In some types the substrate is connected to the source and in others it is brought out as a separate terminal, which is desirable in some applications.

The drain current characteristics are shown in Fig. AP-1.2. If the gate is connected to ground, the drain current will be limited only by the resistance of the *N*-channel for a given V_{DS}. Up to a point the drain current will increase with increasing V_{DS} and thereafter it will level off as the gate-to-channel voltage becomes more negative near the drain, due to the voltage drop across the bulk of the channel, as a consequence of which the channel gets more depleted near the drain. The result will be a drain current curve as shown in Fig. AP-1.2 for $V_{GS} = 0$. When a negative potential is applied to the gate, a positive charge is induced in the channel, which is the other plate of the capacitor. This is shown in Fig. AP-1.1(a). The induced charge causes a depletion of majority carriers in the channel. The conductivity of the channel decreases resulting in a decrease of the drain current, which will be cut off with reverse high bias.

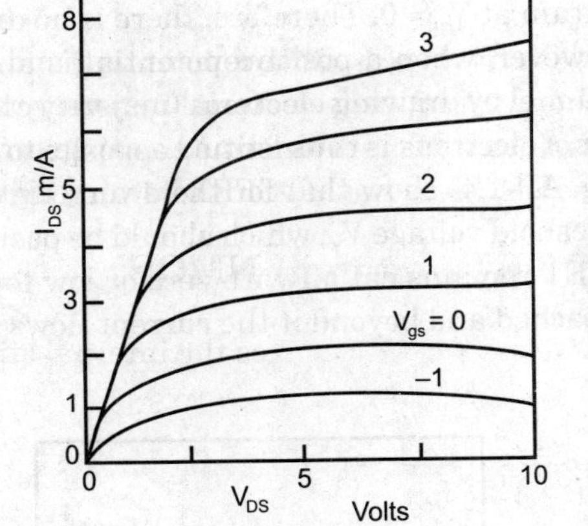

Fig. AP-1.2 Drain current characteristics for *N*-channel depletion MOSFET

In a MOSFET, as there is no *P-N* junction, the gate can also be given a positive potential without any lowering of the input impedance. A positive potential at the gate induces a negative charge in the channel, which enhances the conductivity of the channel and thereby also the drain current. Thus an *N*-channel MOSFET can be used both in the enhancement and depletion modes, although it is termed a depletion MOSFET, which differentiates it from the other type, which can be used only as an enhancement MOSFET. As the input impedance of the depletion MOSFET is not affected by the gate voltage, it may be used with zero gate bias without any deterioration in performance when used as an amplifier for ac signals.

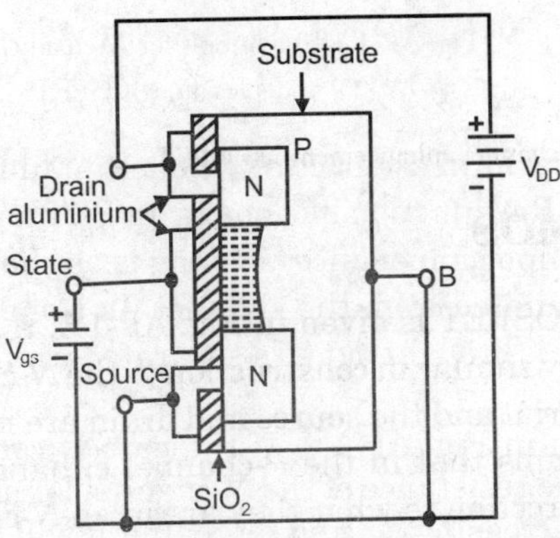

Fig. AP-1.3(a) Structure of enhancement MOSFET (*N*-channel)

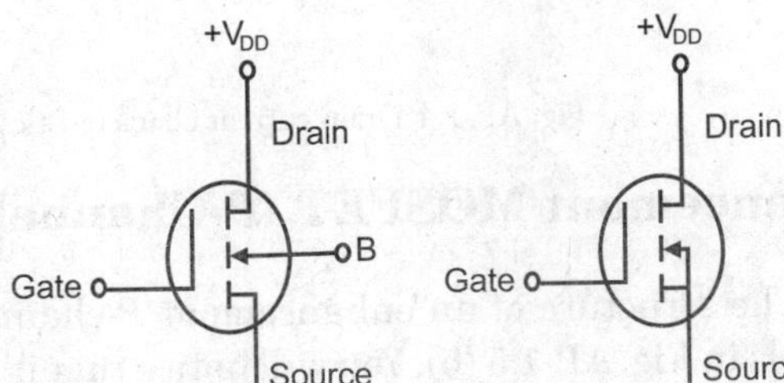

Fig. AP-1.3(b) Symbols for enhancement MOSFET (*N*-channel)

ENHANCEMENT MOSFET (N CHANNEL) NMOS

The structure and symbols for an *N*-channel enhancement MOSFET are shown in Fig. AP-1.3. Current carriers are electrons as in *N*-channel depletion MOSFET and it flows from source to drain; therefore the conventional flow of electric current is from drain to source within the device. It is for this reason that the drain is kept positive with respect to the source. You will notice from the diagram that unlike the *P*-channel MOSFET, there is no continuous channel between the source and drain at $V_{GS}= 0$. Therefore, there is no drain current without a positive potential at the gate. However, when a positive potential is applied at the gate, it induces a negative charge in the channel by drawing electrons (majority current carriers) from the *P*-type bulk. A concentrated layer of electrons is thus formed opposite to the gate. Typical drain current characteristic curves (Fig. AP-1.4) show that for the drain current I_{DS} to flow, the gate-source voltage must exceed a threshold voltage V_T, which should be positive with respect to the source. The enhancement MOSFET remains cut off with zero or low forward bias at the gate, until a threshold voltage V_T is reached and beyond it the current flows freely.

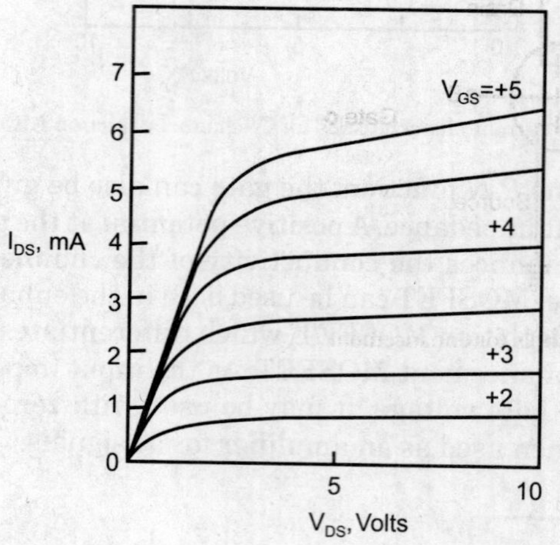

Fig. AP-1.4 Drain current characteristics for *N*-channel enhancement MOSFET

Enhancement MOSFET (*P*-Channel) PMOS

The structure of an enhancement *P*-channel MOSFET is given in Fig. AP-1.5(a) and its symbols in Fig. AP-1.5 (b). You will notice that it is very similar in construction to the *N*-channel MOSFET. Here the substrate is made of *N*-type material and the source and drain are made of *P*-type material. You will also notice from the diagrams that in the *P*-channel enhancement MOSFET all voltages and currents are opposite in direction to what they are in an *N*-channel enhancement MOSFET. In all other respects the *P*-channel device functions in the same manner as an *N*-channel device.

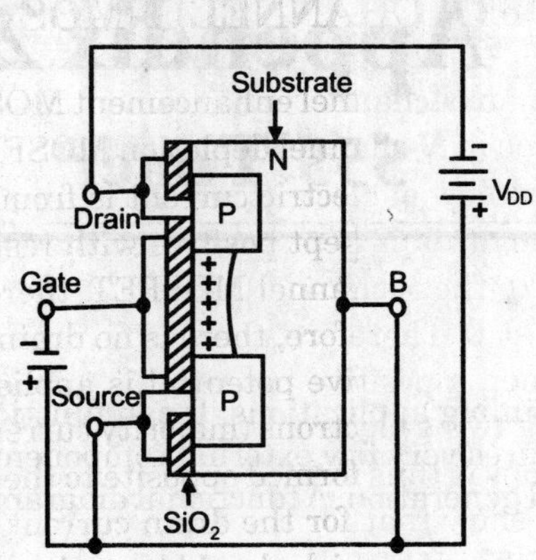

Fig. AP-1.5(a) Structure of enhancement MOSFET (*P*-channel)

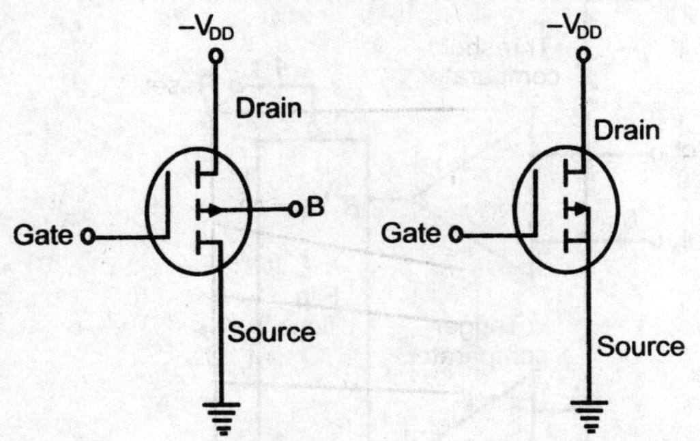

Fig. AP-1.5(b) Symbols for enhancement MOSFET (*P*-channel)

Appendix 2
555 Timer

This timer is useful in timing applications. It can function as an astable, monostable and bistable oscillator and it requires very few external components. It finds application in sequential timing, pulse shaping and generation. A functional diagram for this timer is given in Fig. AP-2.1.

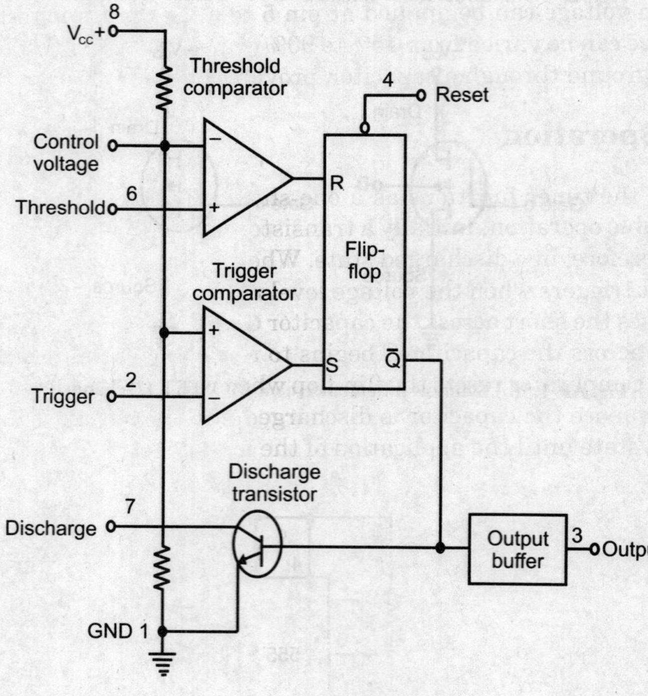

Fig. AP-2.1 Functional diagram for timer 555

This timer can be used on supply voltages from 5 to 15V and it has a maximum rating of 18V. It can handle power dissipation up to 600 mW. Its output is compatible with CMOS and TTL devices when used on a 5V supply. It consists of a flip-flop which is controlled by two comparators. Three resistors of 5 K ohm connected across the supply provide internal reference voltages of 2/3 V_{cc} for the threshold comparator and 1/3 V_{cc} for the trigger comparator. In standby condition the output at pin 3 is low and the discharge transistor is conducting providing a short (low impedance) to ground at pin 7.

With the input at pin 2 high, the trigger comparator is held biased at 1/3 V_{cc}. A negative going pulse at pin 2, when it goes low below 1/3 V_{cc} activates the trigger comparator, sets the flip-flop, drives the output high and cuts off the discharge transistor, thus raising the impedance at pin 7. If the trigger pin 2 is held low, the output would stay high until the trigger is driven high again.

A rising pulse on pin 6 resets the flip-flop as the signal crosses the threshold comparator bias of 2/3 V_{cc}, the output is driven low and the impedance at pin 7 goes low as the discharge transistor goes into conduction.

The reset input provides a facility which enables the flip-flop to be reset, overriding any instructions from the trigger comparator to set, whenever the reset input is less than 0.4V. The reset input, pin 4, is normally connected to + V_{cc} when this overriding facility is not in use. The output buffer is only intended to serve as buffer between the flip-flop and the output. If the reset input is below 0.4V, the output is forced to go low and would remain low even on release, until a trigger pulse is applied.

A modulation voltage can be applied at pin 5 to alter the timing independent of the *RC* network. Its voltage can be varied from 45% to 90% of V_{cc} in the monostable mode. Normally the pin is returned to ground through a capacitor, providing immunity from false triggering.

Monostable Operation

In this mode the timer functions as a one-shot multivibrator. Figure. AP-2.2 shows the circuit for monostable operation. Initially a transistor in the timer acts as a short across capacitor *C*, which is, therefore, in a discharged state. When a negative-going trigger pulse is applied at pin 2, the circuit triggers when the voltage level reaches 1/3 V_{cc} and the flip-flop in the timer is set, which releases the short across the capacitor *C* and the flip-flop in the timer is set, which releases the short across the capacitor *C* begins to rise exponentially, the time constant being *RC*. The threshold comparator resets the flip-flop when the voltage across the capacitor reaches 2/3 V_{cc}. As a consequence the capacitor is discharged and the output is driven low. The circuit will remain in this state until the application of the next negative going pulse at pin 2.

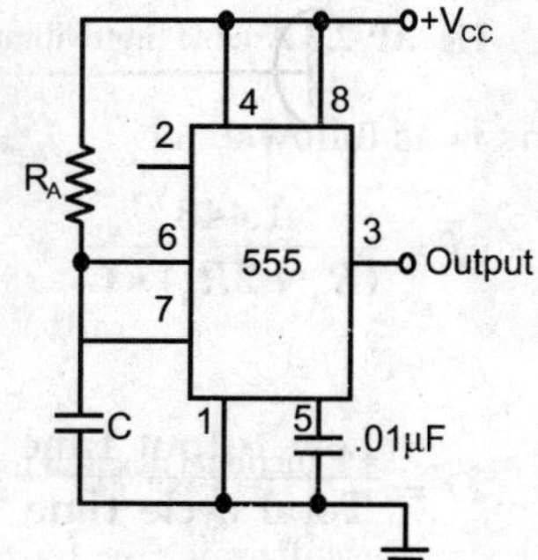

Fig. AP-2.2 Monostable multivibrator

After the circuit has been triggered, it will continue in this state for a period dependent on the values of *R* and *C*, even if it is triggered again during this interval of time. The duration for which the output remains in the high state is given by 1.1 *RC*.

Example 2.1: *Calculate the width of the output pulse when R = 10 K Ohm and C = 0.05 μF*

Solution: Pulse width = 1.1 RC

$= 1.1 \times 10{,}000 \times 0.05 \times 10^{-6}$

$= 0.00055$

$= 0.55$ ms

If a negative pulse is simultaneously applied to reset pin 4 and trigger pin 2 during the timing cycle, capacitor *C* will get discharged and the cycle will start all over again. This timing cycle will commence on the positive edge of the reset pulse. When not in use, the reset pin should be connected to + V_{cc} to avoid false triggering.

Astable Operation

Figure AP-2.3 gives the circuit for an astable multivibrator. Capacitor *C* charges through R_A and R_B and discharges through R_B only. The capacitor charges and discharges between 1/3 V_{cc} and 2/3 V_{cc}. The frequency as well as the charge and discharge times are independent of the supply voltage.

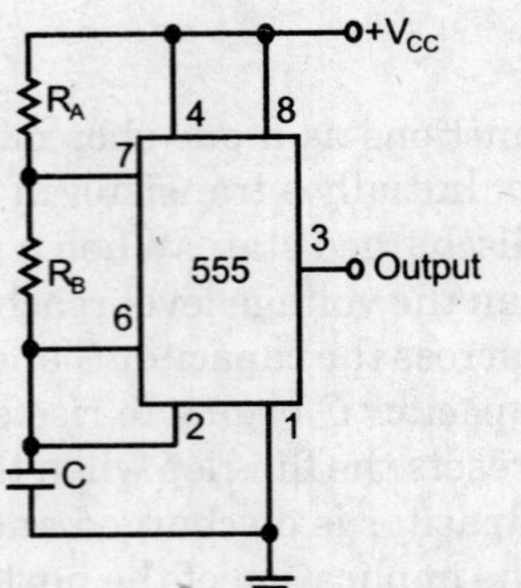

Fig. AP-2.3 Astable multivibrator

The frequency of oscillations is as follows:

$$f = \frac{1.443}{(R_A + 2R_B) \times C}$$

The duty cycle is given by

$$D = \frac{\text{Low output time}}{\text{Total cycle time}} = \frac{t_2}{T} = \frac{R_B}{R_A \times 2R_B}$$

as in Section. 9.2.6.

Bistable Operation

Timer 555, functioning as a bistable multivibrator finds application as a compatible driver in TTL circuits. Its output is adequate to drive relays directly from its output pin. A circuit for this purpose is given in Fig. AP- 2.4. When a negative going pulse is applied at its trigger input, pin 2, the flip-flop in the timer is set and its output goes high. When a positive going pulse is applied at the threshold input, pin 6, the flip-flop in the timer is reset and drives the output low.

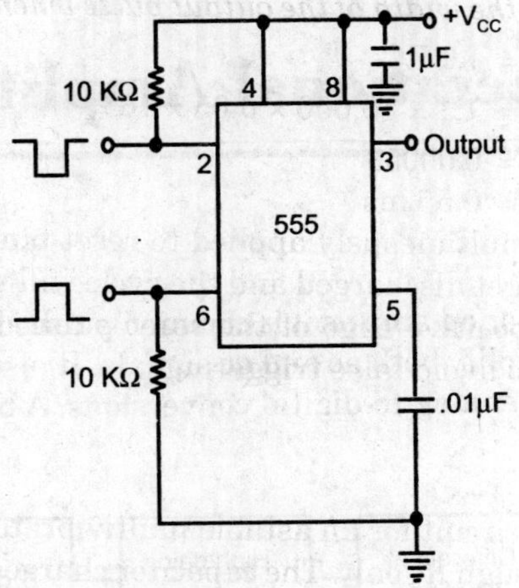

Fig. AP-2.4 Bistable flip-flop

Appendix 3

Operational Amplifier

An operational amplifier, or op-amp as it is commonly called, is essentially a very high gain linear amplifier, which can amplify both ac and dc signals. It also possesses special features for mathematical operations and analog-to-digital conversions. A block diagram for an op-amp is given in Fig. AP-3.1.

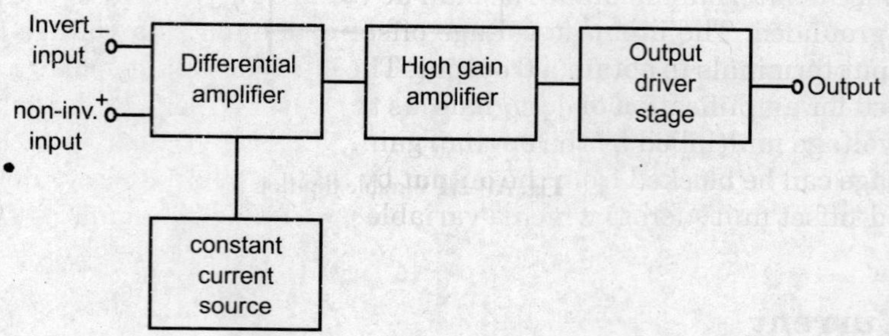

Fig. AP-3.1 Op-amp block diagram

The differential amplifier is so designed that only the difference of two input signals is amplified and their similarities are rejected. The basic circuit for a differential amplifier is given in Fig. AP-3.2.

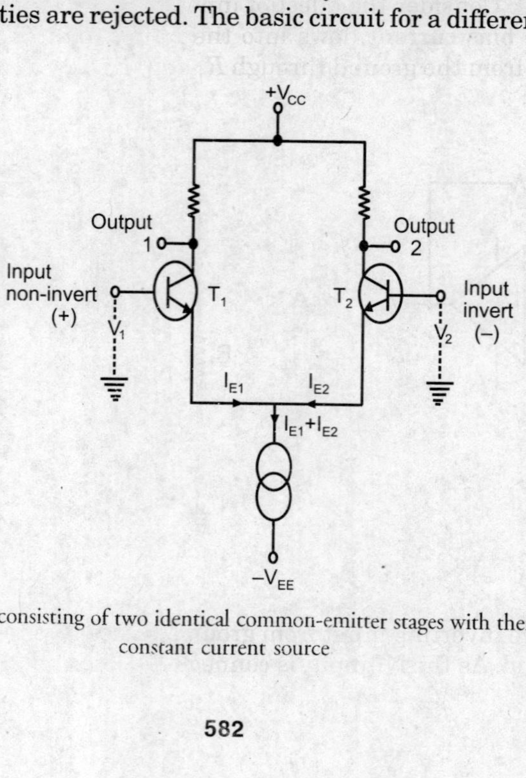

Fig. AP.3.2 Differential amplifier consisting of two identical common-emitter stages with their emitters connected to a constant current source

If a positive signal V_1 is applied to the base of T_1, its collector current will increase and at the same time the collector current of T_2 will decrease by the same amount, since both T_1 and T_2 are connected to a constant current source. If the common emitter gain of T_1 and T_2 is A, a voltage AV_1 will appear at output 2. Notice that a positive signal at the input of T_1 produces a positive output. This, therefore is a non-inverting input.

Following the same reasoning, a positive signal V_2 at the input of T_2 will produce an output of $-AV_2$ at output 2. The negative sign indicates that this is an inverting input. If both V_1 and V_2 are applied simultaneously, the output at V_2 will be $A(V_2 - V_2)$. It follows that the differential amplifier amplifies the difference of the two input signals.

Input DC Offset Voltage

Op-amps are designed in such a manner that when both inputs are grounded, the output is 0. However, because of internal imbalance a small dc voltage may appear at the output, even if both inputs are grounded. The input dc voltage offset is defined as a voltage that should be applied to the input terminals to obtain a 0 output. The offset dc voltage poses a problem when the op-amp is used for amplification of dc signals, as the offset voltage at the output is equal to the input offset voltage multiplied by the op-amp gain. There is no problem with ac signals, as the offset dc voltage can be blocked from the output by a capacitor. Some op-amps are provided with pins marked 'offset null', across which a variable resistor can be connected for nulling the offset voltage.

Input Bias Current

Another factor which contributes to the offset error results from the input bias current. The op-amp input requires a biasing current. This gives rise to a dc output voltage even in the absence of an input signal. Consider the effect of input bias current in an inverting amplifier given in Fig. AP-3.3. The bias current flows into the NI (+) input from ground and into the inverting (–) input partly from the ground through R_1 and partly through R_2 from the output.

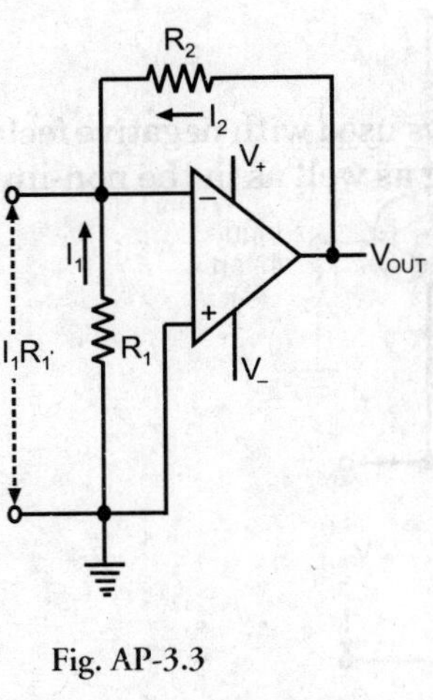

Fig. AP-3.3

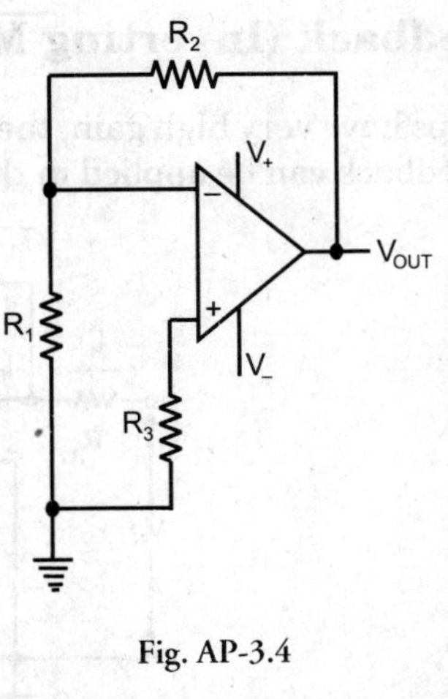

Fig. AP-3.4

Current I_1 flowing into the inverting input from ground causes a voltage drop I_1R_1 between the inverting input and ground. As the NI input is connected to ground, this voltage drop appears between the inverting and NI inputs. On amplification by the op-amp, this appears as a much larger voltage at the output. This voltage is equal to the product of the bias current and R_2. This problem assumes importance when the feedback resistor is large. The solution lies in ensuring that the op-amp input circuits are symmetrical. This can be achieved by connecting a resistor R_3, so that

$$R_3 = \frac{R_1 \times R_2}{R_1 + R_2}$$

as shown in Fig. AP-3.4.

In the presence of a signal between R_1 and ground having internal resistance R_s, R_3 should be computed as follows:

$$R_s = \frac{(R_s + R_1) \times R_2}{R_s + R_1 + R_2}$$

In the case of a non-inverting amplifier, it is not easy to compensate for the effect of the bias current. However, in such cases the normal practice is to use a signal source having an internal resistance R_s, so that

$$R_s = \frac{R_1 \times R_2}{R_1 + R_2}$$

Gain-Bandwidth Product

The gain of an op-amp without feedback, referred to as open loop gain, is very high. For instance for IC741, the dc gain is about 200,000. The gain is not the same when an op-amp is used for the amplification of ac signals. Besides, the gain begins to drop as the frequency increases. The gain-bandwidth product for op-amps is fixed. Some have a very high gain-bandwidth product and they can be used at frequencies in the region of several megacycles. For op-amp 741, it is 1 MHz. The realizable bandwidth up to which amplification is possible, is 1 MHz/gain. For instance, for a gain of 100, the bandwidth obtainable is 10 kHz.

Negative Feedback (Inverting Mode)

Since op-amps have very high gain, they are always used with negative feeback to stabilize gain. Negative feedback can be applied in the inverting as well as in the non-inverting mode. A

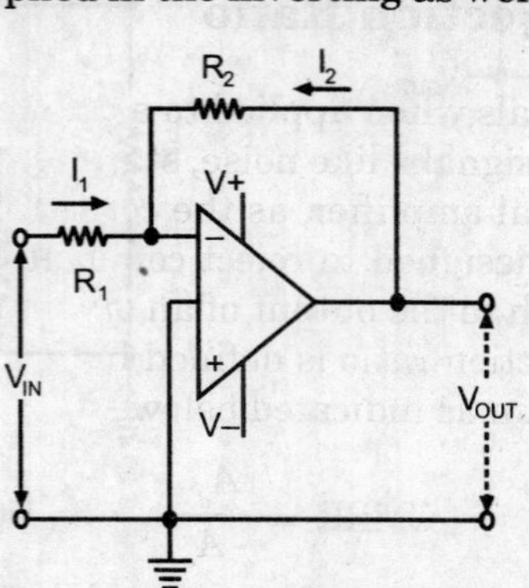

Fig. AP-3.5 Op-amp with negative feedback in the inverting mode

circuit for the inverting mode is given in Fig. AP-3.5. Since the signal is connected to the inverting input, if voltage V_z at the op-amp input increases, V_{out} will decrease and when V_{out} falls, it has the effect of pulling V_z down. In other words, whenever a change occurs, the output voltage is fed back, which opposes the change in the input.

As has been mentioned, the op-amp gain is $R_2 R_1$. By using resistive and capacitive networks in the feedback path, an inverting amplifier can be built to give the desired frequency response.

Power Supply Requirements

Op-amp circuits are generally designed to operate from a dual symmetrical power supply, one delivering positive voltage with respect to ground and the other negative voltage. When a dual power supply is used, the application of bias becomes simple. However, op-amps can also be operated from a single power supply as shown in Fig. AP-3.6 for an inverting amplifier.

Two resistors R_3 and R_4 of equal value are connected across the power supply and the centre tap is connected to the NI input. Thus the NI input is at half the supply voltage and accordingly the output is also at half the voltage.

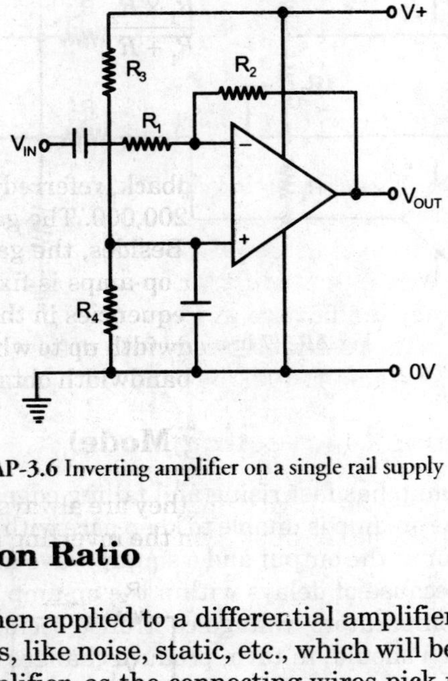

Fig. AP-3.6 Inverting amplifier on a single rail supply

Common-Mode Rejection Ratio

Common mode signals when applied to a differential amplifier will drive both amplifiers equally. There are many signals, like noise, static, etc., which will be picked up equally by both the inputs of a differential amplifier, as the connecting wires pick up these signals equally. A differential amplifier is designed to reject common mode signals and thus a lot of unwanted signals do not get through to the output of an op-amp.

Common mode rejection ratio is defined in terms of the differential voltage gain and the common mode voltage gain as indicated below:

$$\text{CMRR} = \frac{A_d}{-A_c}$$

The minus sign is used so that the ratio is a +ve number. Data sheets list CMRR in decibels, and can be determined as follows:

$$\text{CMMR}' = 20 \log \text{CMRR}$$

$$\text{If CMRR is 300 CMRR}' = 20 \log 300 = 49.5 \text{ dB.}$$

Instrumentation Amplifier

Figure. AP-3.7 gives the circuit for an instrumentation amplifier. The input op-amps are optimized for high input impedance and provide some amplification for the input signal. The circuit as a whole provides good common-mode rejection. The op-amp at the output further amplifies the input signal and converts the differential signal to a signal with reference to ground. The output can be determined from the following equation:

$$V_{out} = (V_1 - V_2) = \frac{R_1 + R_2 + R_3}{R_3} \times \frac{R_f}{R_4}$$

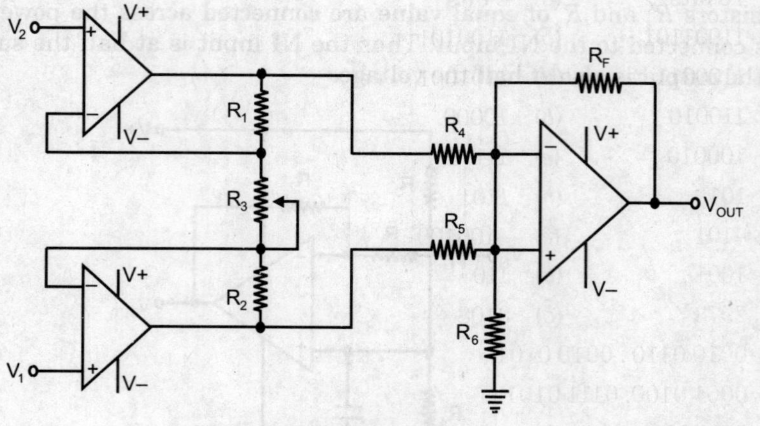

Fig. AP-3.7 Instrumentation amplifier

Slew Rate

If the input to an op-amp has fast rising and falling edges, we have a problem called the 'slew rate'. The output of the op-amp is unable to keep pace with fast changes in the input and as a result phase changes occur at the output and a square wave may get converted into a triangular shape. This happens because of delays within the op-amp. This is of great significance in applications like voltage comparators, voltage-controlled oscillators, sensors, etc., where error voltages are produced which should, in turn, produce changes in the op-amp output as fast as errors are sensed.

Let us consider the slew rate of op-amp 741, which is 0.5 Vμs. If the input to the op-amp is triangular wave having a frequency of 20 kHz and the peak-to-peak output voltage is 2V, the output has to change 2V, in half the period of the input waveform. The half period of this waveform is 25μs. This means that the output is required to change by 2V in 25 μs or 0.08 V in 1μs. This is within the capability of this op-amp. If the required peak-to-peak voltage change at the outut is 30V, the output will have to change by 30V in 25 μs or 1.2V in 1 μs. This is not within the capability of this IC. Even if the peak-to-peak voltage requirement remains unchanged at 30V but the input frequency is raised substantially, it will still be out of reach for this op-amp.

Therefore both frequency and amplitude are important design considerations.

Appendix 4
Answers to Odd Numbered Problems

CHAPTER 1

1.1	(*a*) 3897	(*b*) .263	(*c*) 302.57	
1.3	(*a*) 256	(*b*) 65536		
1.5	(*a*) 16 bits	(*b*) 8 bits		
1.7	(*a*) 11001101	(*b*) 1100101		
	(*c*) 1100011	(*d*) 1101001		
1.9	(*a*) 110010	(*b*) 10000	(*c*) 1010111	
	(*d*) 100010	(*e*) 11110	(*f*) 1010010	
1.11	(*a*) 101	(*b*) 1101	(*c*) 100000	
	(*d*) –101	(*e*) –100100	(*f*) –10010	
1.13	(*a*) 1001	(*b*) 110	(*c*) 1011	(*d*) 10100
1.15	(*a*) 2973	(*b*) 3108	(*c*) 7089	(*d*) 2591
1.17	(*a*) 0010 0110 . 0010 0101		(*b*) 0010 0011. 0101	
	(*c*) 0001 0100. 0111 0101		(*d*) 0001 0001.0101	
1.19	(*a*) 0111 0111		(*b*) 0001 0100 1000	
	(*c*) 0001 0011 0100		(*d*) 0001 0011 0000	
1.21	(*a*) 15	(*b*) 26	(*c*) 27.3	(*d*) 13.5
1.23	(*a*) 507	(*b*) 1362	(*c*) 2701	(*d*) 1751
1.25	(*a*) 26	(*b*) 51	(*c*) 661	(*d*) 471
1.27	(*a*) 52	(*b*) 30	(*c*) 144	(*d*) 1750
1.29	(*a*) 1111 . 1111 0100		(*b*) 1101 . 0100 1100 1101	
1.31	(*a*) 41980	(*b*) 19418	(*c*) 21754	(*d*) 62427
1.33	(*a*) 56.59	(*b*) 7A . 1B		
1.35	(*a*) 35		(*b*) 120	
	(*c*) 0010 1111 1100 0110		(*d*) 11100010	
	(*e*) 1111111000000000		(*f*) 11001011	(*g*) D001
	(*h*) FBC		(*i*) 62148	
1.37	(*a*) 2835		(*b*) 7450	
1.39	(*a*) 0101		(*b*) 1001	
	(*c*) 1110		(*d*) 1000	

1.41 (*a*) 0100 (*b*) 1001 (*c*) 0110

1.43 (*a*) 0111 1000 (*b*) 1001 0110

(*c*) 1000 1000 (*d*) 0111 1011

1.45 (*a*) 82 (*b*) 61 (*c*) 33 (*d*) 78

1.47 (*a*) 58 (*b*) 54 (*c*) 18 (*d*) 27

1.49 – 47

1.51 Acknowledge message

CHAPTER 2

2.1 (*a*) $\overline{A}$ (*b*) A (*c*) $\overline{A}$

2.3

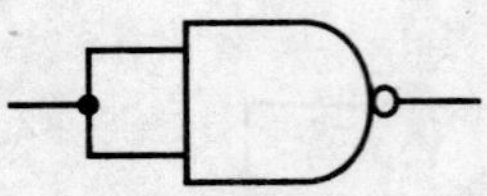

Fig. A-2.3 (a)

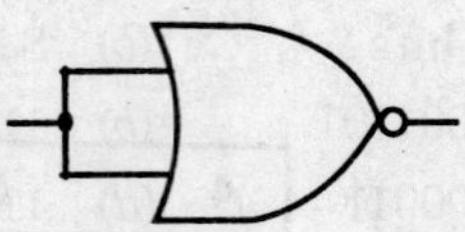

Fig. A-2.3(b)

2.5 A

2.7

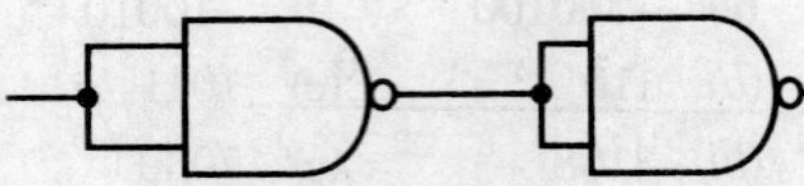

Fig. A-2.7

2.9

Truth Table 3- input AND gate

Inputs			*Output*
A	*B*	*C*	*Y*
0	0	0	0
0	0	1	0
0	1	0	0
0	1	1	0
1	0	0	0
1	0	1	0
1	1	0	0
1	1	1	1

2.11 See Figs 2.13 and 2.14

2.13 See Fig. 2.1 : OR gate

2.15 All inputs should be high : OR gate

2.17 16

2.19

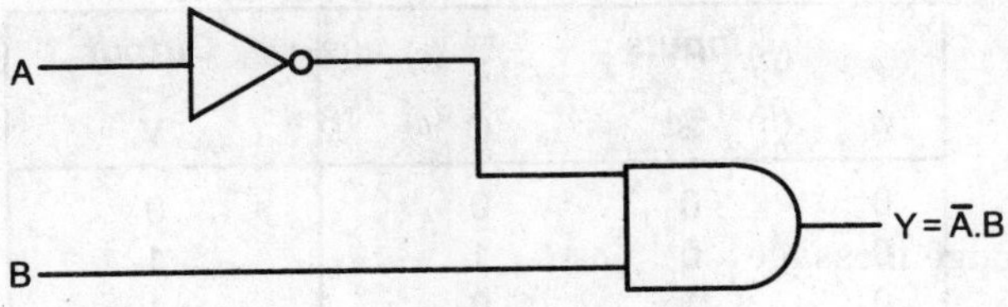

Fig. A-2.19

Truth Table

A	*B*	$\bar{A}$	*Y*
0	0	1	0
0	1	1	1
1	0	0	0
1	1	0	0

2.21 $\overline{A \cdot B}$

2.23

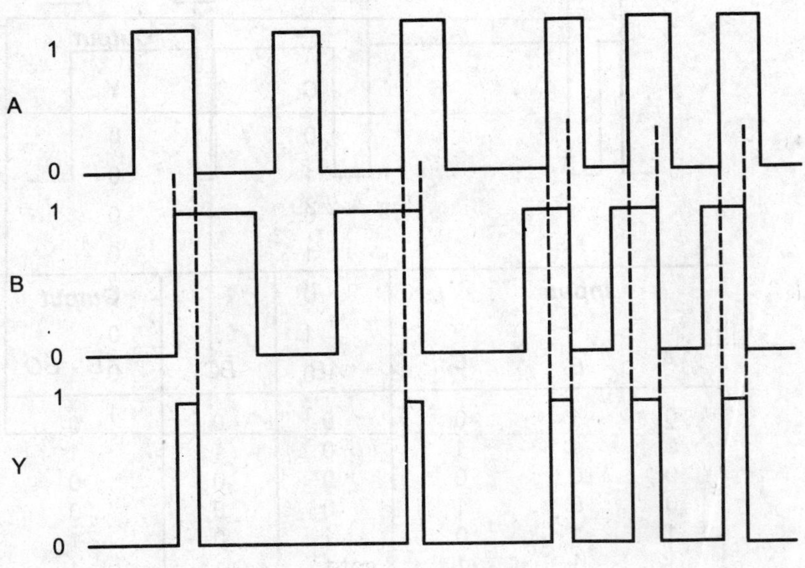

Fig. A-2.23

2.25

Truth Table

Inputs			Output
A	*B*	*C*	*Y*
0	0	0	0
0	0	1	1
0	1	0	1
0	1	1	1
1	0	0	1
1	0	1	1
1	1	0	1
1	1	1	1

2.27 Will function as an AND gate

2.29

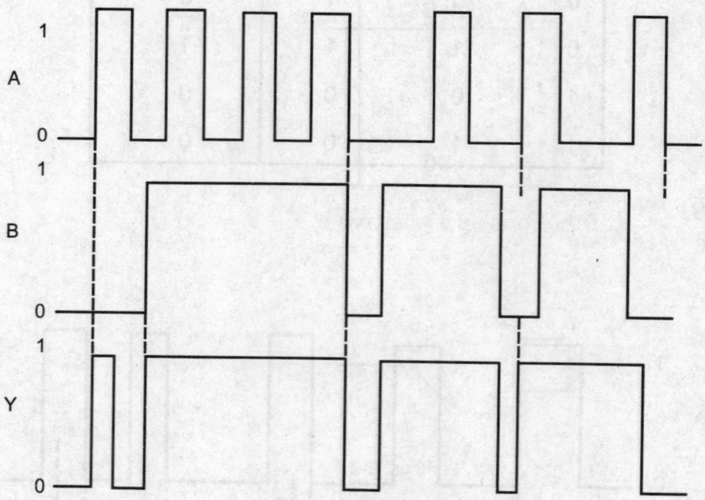

Fig. A-2.29

2.31

Inputs					Output
A	$\overline{B}$	*C*	$A\overline{B}$	$\overline{B}C$	$A\overline{B}+\overline{B}C$
0	1	0	0	0	0
0	1	1	0	1	1
0	0	0	0	0	0
0	0	1	0	0	0
1	1	0	1	0	1
1	1	1	1	1	1
1	0	0	0	0	0
1	0	1	0	0	0

2.33 (*a*) OR (*b*) NAND

(*c*) NAND (*d*) AND

2.35

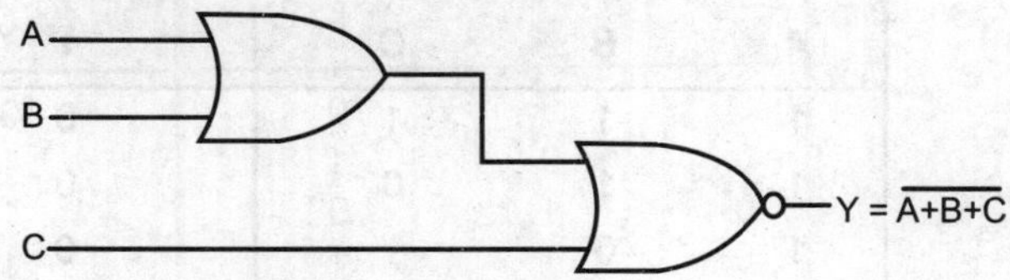

Fig. A-2.35

2.37 One or more inputs should be high

2.39

Inputs		Output
A	B	Y
1	1	0
1	0	1
0	1	1
0	0	1

It functions as a positive NAND gate

2.41

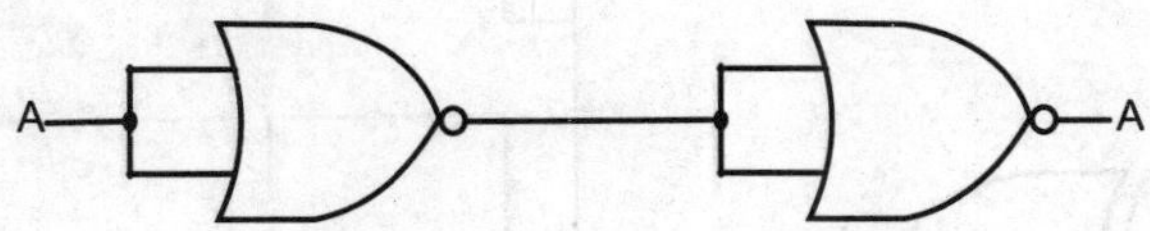

Fig. A-2.41

2.43

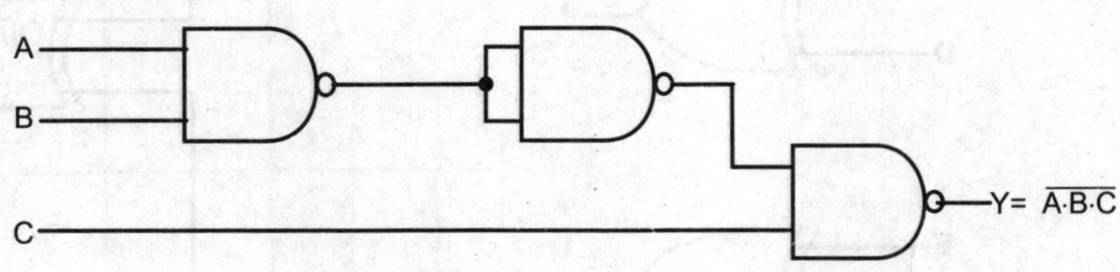

Fig. A-2.43

2.45

Truth Table

Inputs			Output
A	*B*	*C*	*Y*
1	1	1	0
1	1	0	0
1	0	1	0
1	0	0	0
0	1	1	0
0	1	0	0
0	0	1	0
0	0	0	1

Preforms the NOR function

2.47

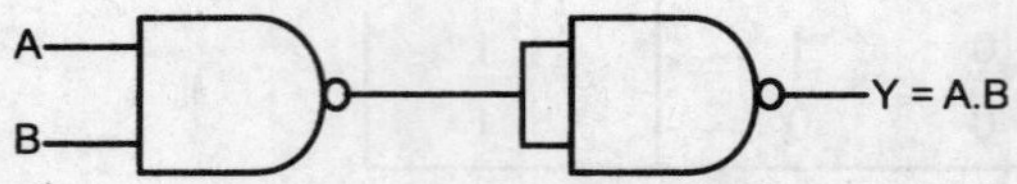

Fig. A-2.47

2.49 One or more inputs should be high

2.51

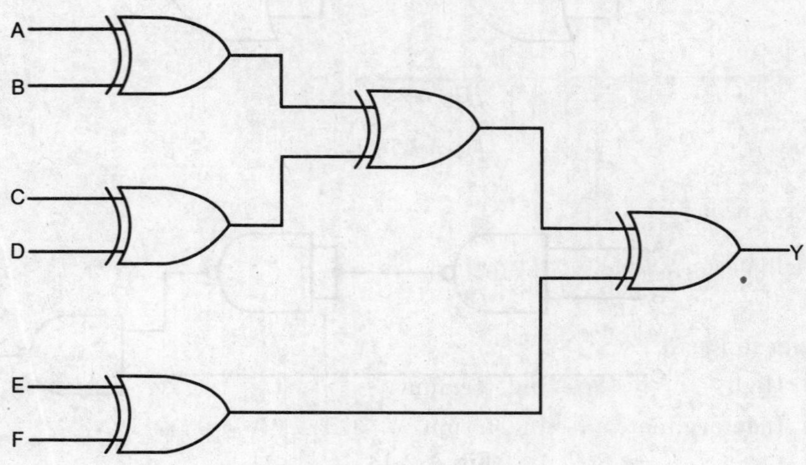

Fig. A-2.51

2.53 Both inputs should either be low or high

2.55

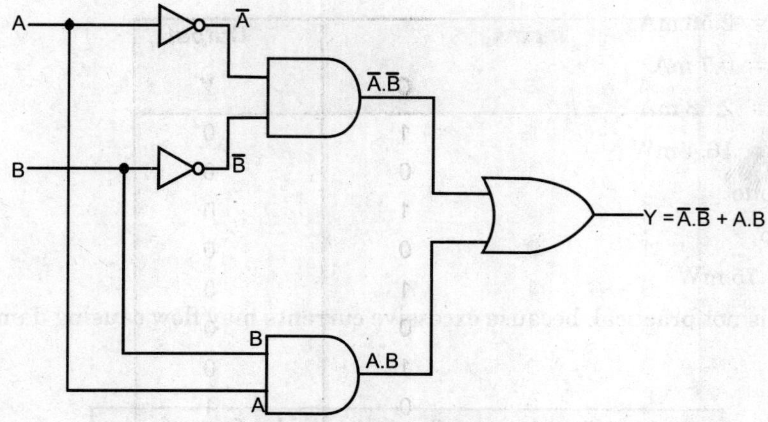

Fig. A-2.55

2.57

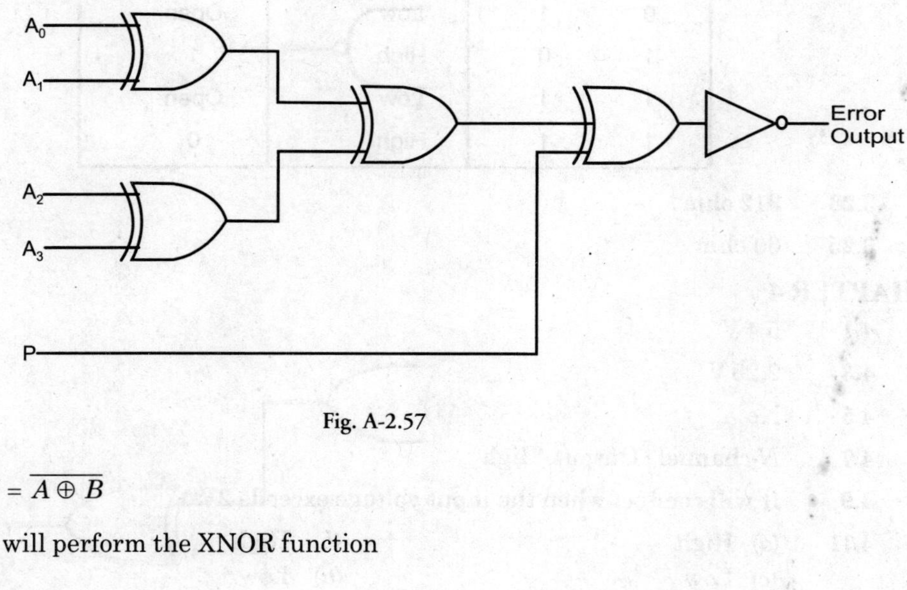

Fig. A-2.57

2.59 $Y = \overline{A \oplus B}$

It will perform the XNOR function

CHAPTER 3

3.1 Refer to Fig. 3.1

3.3 (*a*) High (*b*) Indeterminate

(*c*) Indeterminate (*d*) Indeterminate

(*e*) Low (*f*) High

3.5 1.07 mA

3.7 12.8 mA

3.9 10

3.11 $I_1 = 0.725$ mA

$I_2 = 2.56$ mA

$I_3 = 0.7$ mA

$I_4 = 2.58$ mA

$P = 16.4$ mW

3.13 None

3.15 No

3.17 31.75 mW

3.19 It is not practical, because excessive currents may flow causing damage.

3.21

Inputs		Control	Output
A	*B*	*C*	*Y*
0	0	Low	Open
0	1	Low	Open
1	0	High	1
1	1	Low	Open
1	1	High	0

3.23 312 ohm

3.25 60 ohm

CHAPTER 4

4.1 5.4 V

4.3 2.25 V

4.5 No

4.7 *N*-channel : Output, High

4.9 It will conduct when the input voltage exceeds 2V.

4.11 (*a*) High (*b*) High

(*c*) Low (*d*) Low

4.13 2.9 *V*

4.15 0.6 *V*

4.17 Inverter

4.19 15 ns

4.21 (*a*) Sink current 3.33 mA

(*b*) Voltage drop. 60 mV

CHAPTER 5

5.1

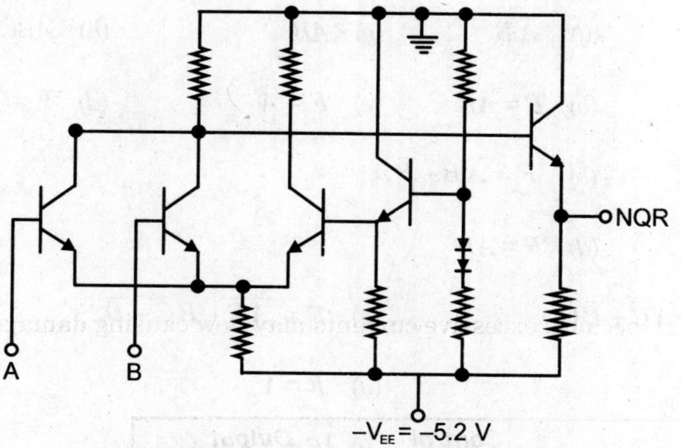

Fig. A-5.1

5.3

A	*B*	*C*	*Y*
0	0	0	1
0	0	1	0
0	1	0	0
0	1	1	0
1	0	0	0
1	0	1	0
1	1	0	0
1	1	1	0

5.5

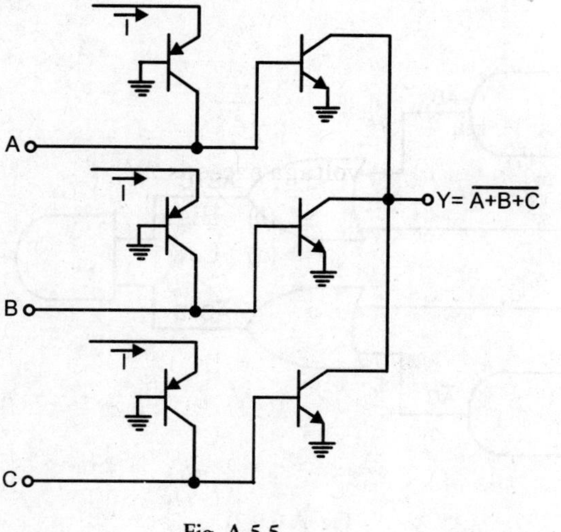

Fig. A-5.5

CHAPTER 6

6.1 (*a*) A (*b*) 0 (*c*) A (*d*) 0

(*e*) AB (*f*) $\overline{A}\,\overline{B}$ (*g*) AB (*h*) ABC

6.3 (*a*) $F = A$ (*b*) $F = AB$ (*c*) $F = A$ (*d*) $F = \overline{A}\,\overline{B}$

6.5 (*a*) $F = \overline{A}\,\overline{B}\,\overline{C}$ (*b*) $F = \overline{A}\,B + \overline{B}\,A$

(*c*) $F = \overline{A}\,B$ (*d*) $F = AB$

6.7 (*a*) $F = A\overline{B} + A\,\overline{C} + \overline{B}\,\overline{C}$ (*b*) $F = \overline{A}\,\overline{C} + B\,\overline{C} + \overline{D}$

(*c*) $F = AB\overline{C}$ (*d*) $F = 1$

(*e*) $F = 1$ (*f*) $F = A + B + \overline{C}$

6.9 (1)

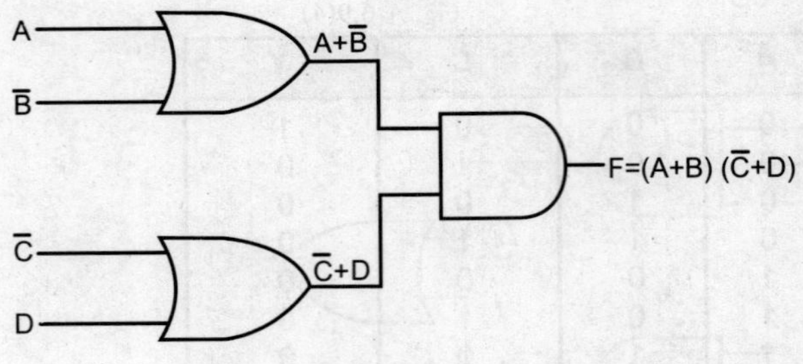

Fig. A-6.9(1)

(2)

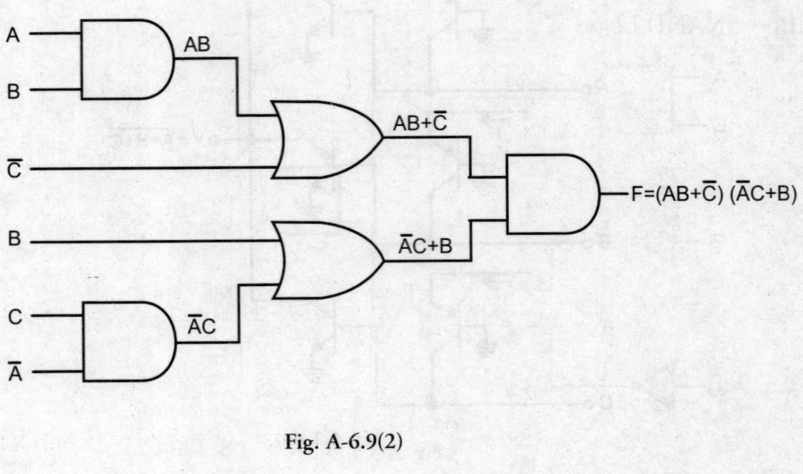

Fig. A-6.9(2)

(3)

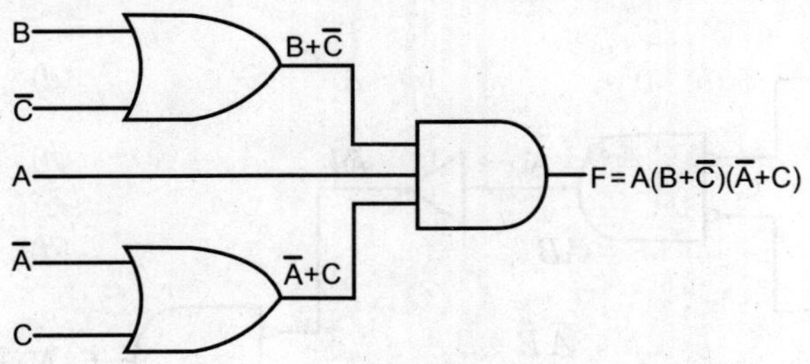

Fig. A-6.9(3)

(4)

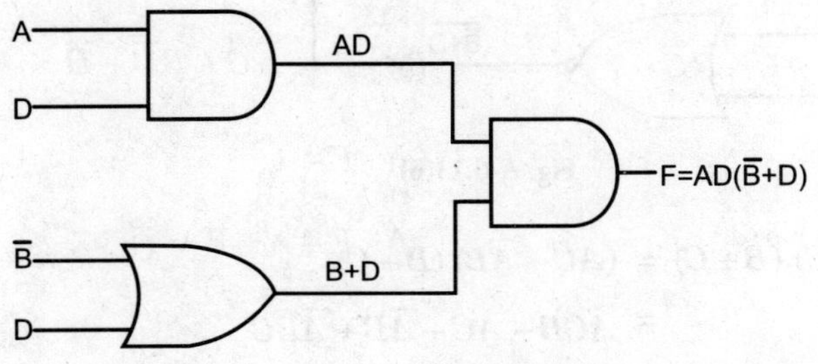

Fig. A-6.9(4)

6.11

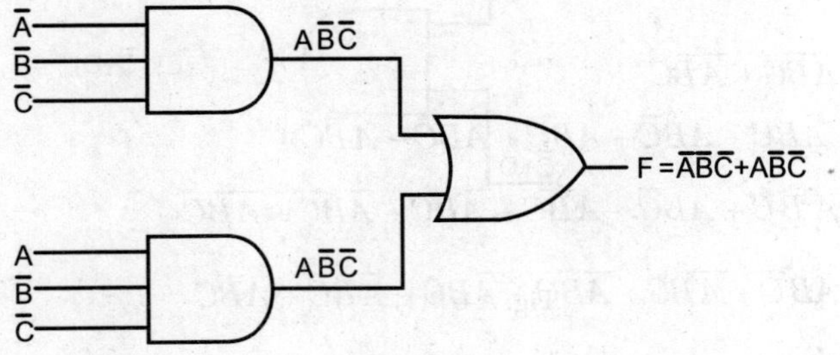

Fig. A-6.11

6.13 NAND Logic

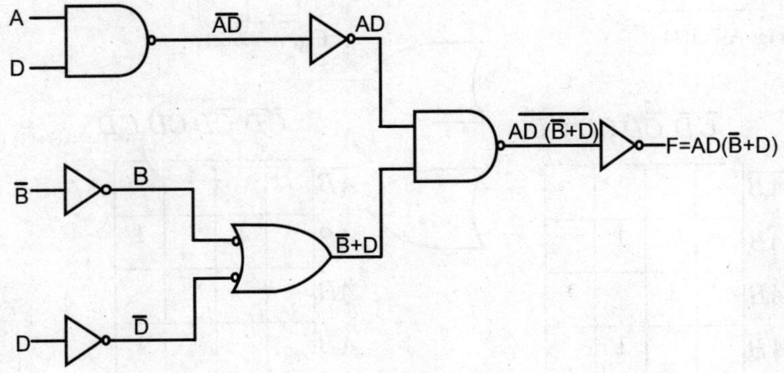

Fig. 6.13(a)

NOR Logic

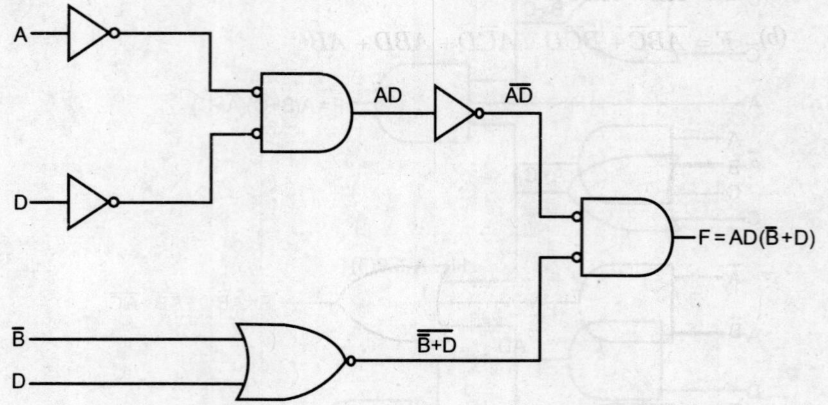

Fig. A-6.13(b)

6.15 $(A+B)(\overline{A}+C)(B+C) = (AC+\overline{A}B)(B+C)$

$$= ACB + AC + \overline{A}B + \overline{A}BC$$

$$= AC + BC + \overline{A}B$$

$$= (A+B) + (\overline{A}+C)$$

CHAPTER 7

7.1 (*a*) $ABC + A\overline{B}C + \overline{A}\overline{B}C$

(*b*) $\overline{A}\,\overline{B}C + \overline{A}BC + AB\overline{C} + \overline{A}B\overline{C} + ABC + A\overline{B}C$

7.3 (*a*) $ABC + A\overline{B}C + AB\overline{C} + A\overline{B}\overline{C} + \overline{A}BC + \overline{A}B\overline{C} + \overline{A}\overline{B}\overline{C}$

(*b*) $ABC + AB\overline{C} + \overline{A}\overline{B}C + \overline{A}B\overline{C} + \overline{A}BC + \overline{A}\overline{B}\overline{C} + A\overline{B}C$

7.5 (1)

	$\overline{B}$	B
$\overline{A}$	1	
A	1	1

Fig. A-7.5(1)

(2)

	$\overline{B}$	B
$\overline{A}$		1
A	1	

Fig. A-7.5(2)

7.7 (1)

	$\overline{C}\overline{D}$	$\overline{C}D$	CD	$C\overline{D}$
$\overline{A}\overline{B}$				
$\overline{A}B$			1	
AB		1		1
$A\overline{B}$			1	

Fig. A-7.7(1)

	$\overline{C}\overline{D}$	$\overline{C}D$	CD	$C\overline{D}$
$\overline{A}\overline{B}$			1	
$\overline{A}B$		1		1
AB				
$A\overline{B}$				1

Fig. A-7.7(2)

7.9 (*a*) $F = AB + A\overline{B}C\overline{D}$

(*b*) $F = \overline{A}B\overline{C} + B\overline{C}D + A\overline{C}D + ABD + ABC$

7.11

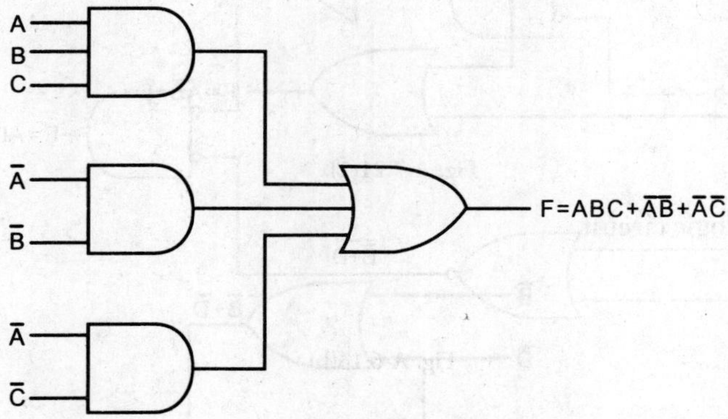

Fig. A-7.11

7.13 $F = \pi M\ (0, 2, 4, 6)$

7.15 $F = \pi M\ (0, 2, 4, 5)$

$\overline{F} = \pi M\ (1, 3, 6, 7)$

7.17 $F = \overline{A}\,\overline{E} + \overline{D}\,\overline{E} + \overline{A}B\overline{D} + \overline{A}\,\overline{B}\,\overline{C}D + BC\overline{D}E$

7.19

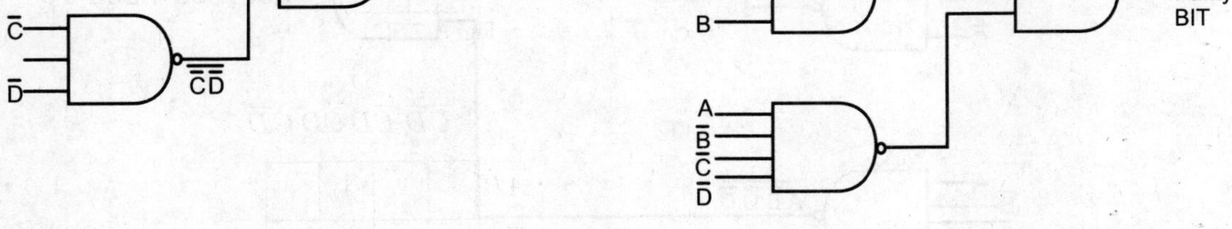

Fig. A-7.19

7.21 (1) SOP Logic circuit

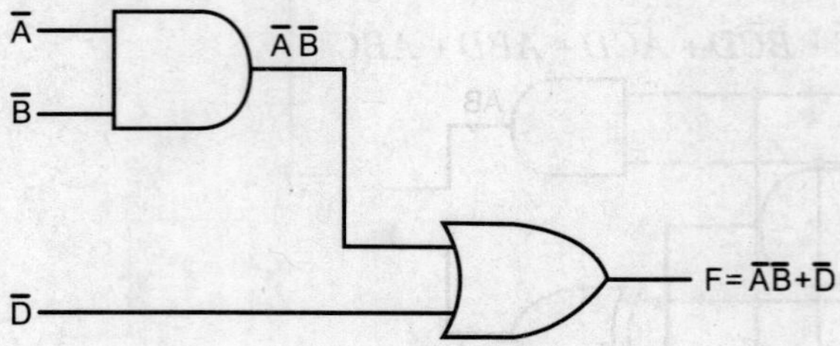

Fig. A-7.21(1)

(2) POS logic circuit

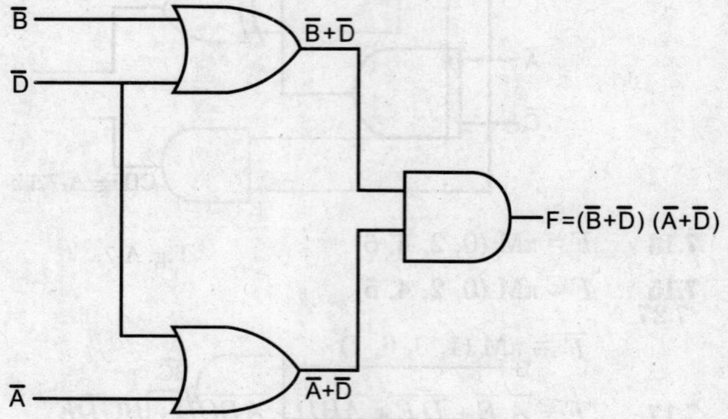

Fig. A-7.21(2)

7.23

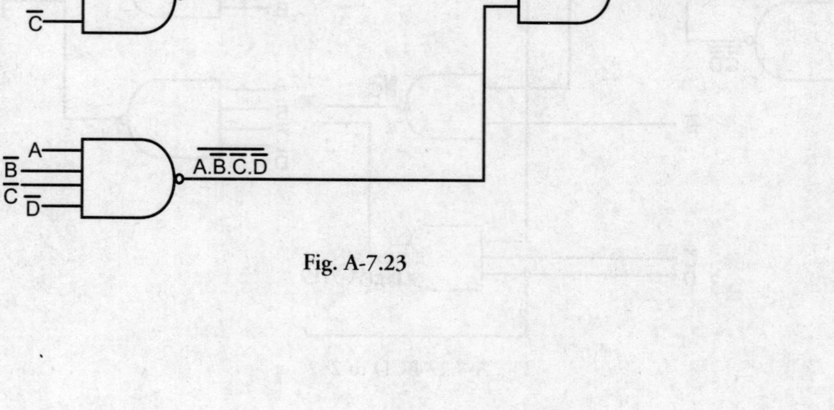

Fig. A-7.23

7.25

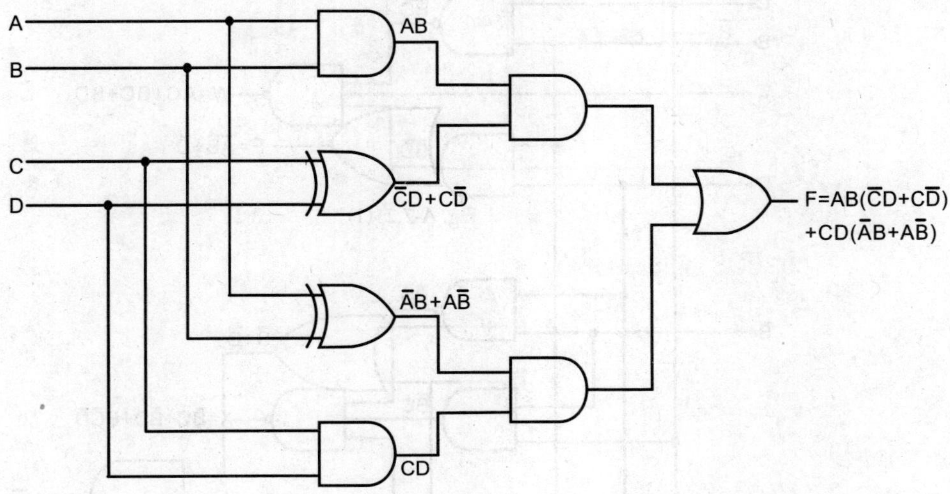

Fig. A-7.25

7.27

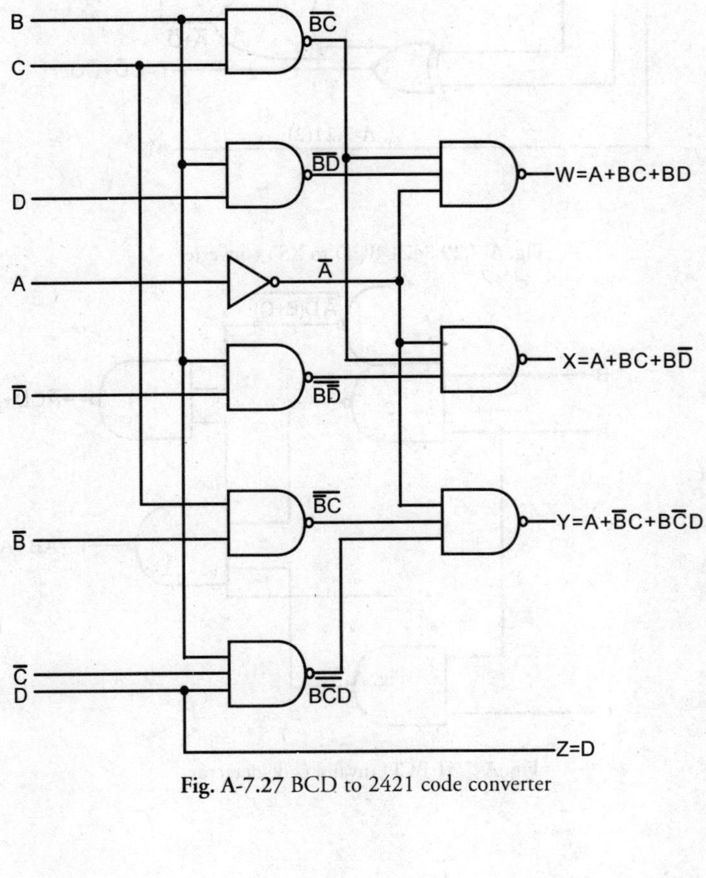

Fig. A-7.27 BCD to 2421 code converter

7.29

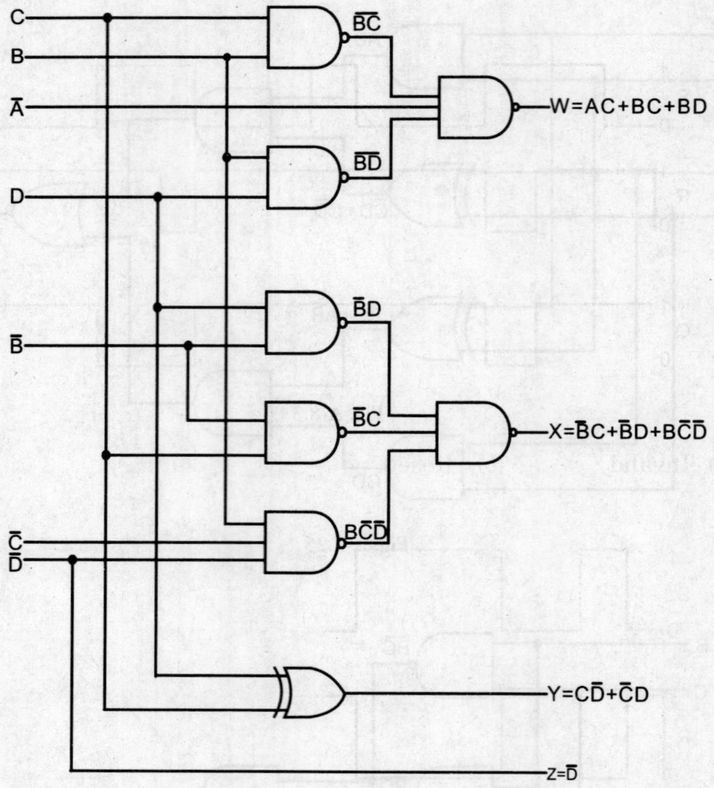

Fig. A-7.29 8421 BCD to XS3 converter

7.31

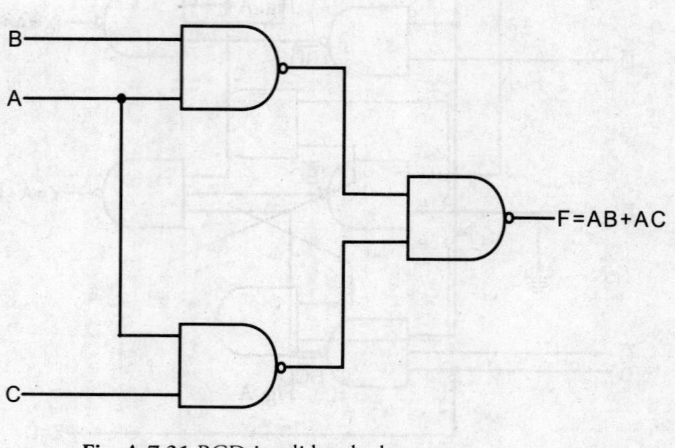

Fig. A-7.31 BCD invalid code detector

CHAPTER 8

8.1 (*a*) Set (*b*) Invalid (*c*) No change (*d*) Reset

8.3

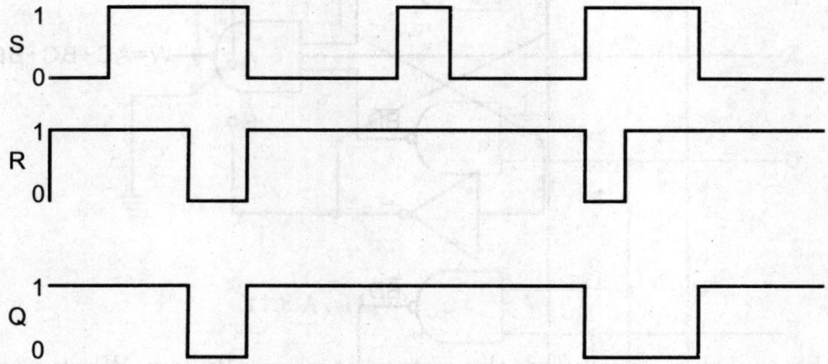

Fig. A-8.3

8.5 (*a*) Invalid (*b*) Reset (*c*) No change (*d*) Set

8.7

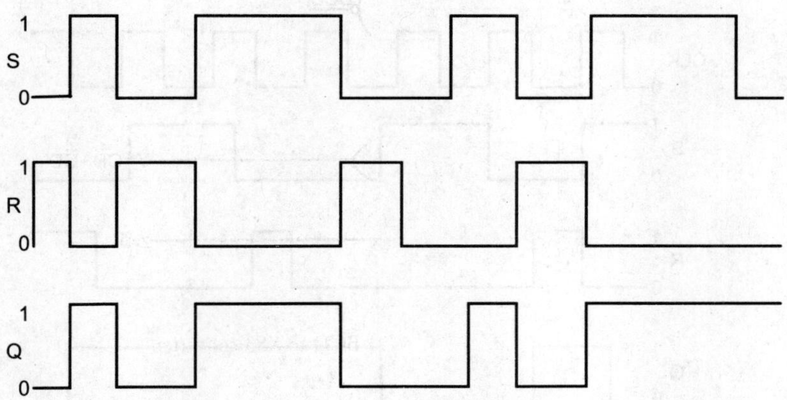

Fig. A-8.7

8.9

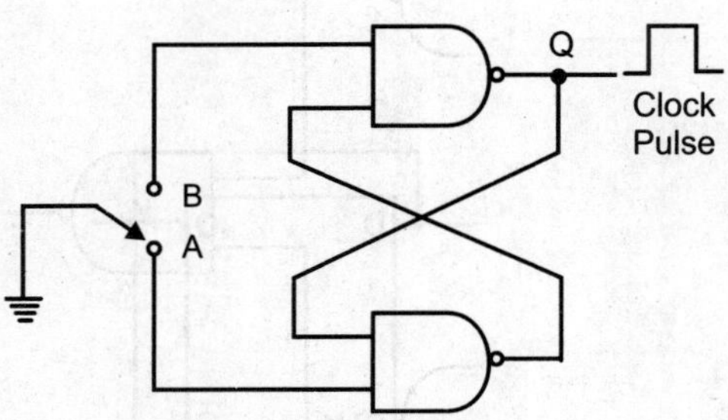

Fig. A-8.9

Truth table

Switch Position	*Q*
A	0
B	1

8.11

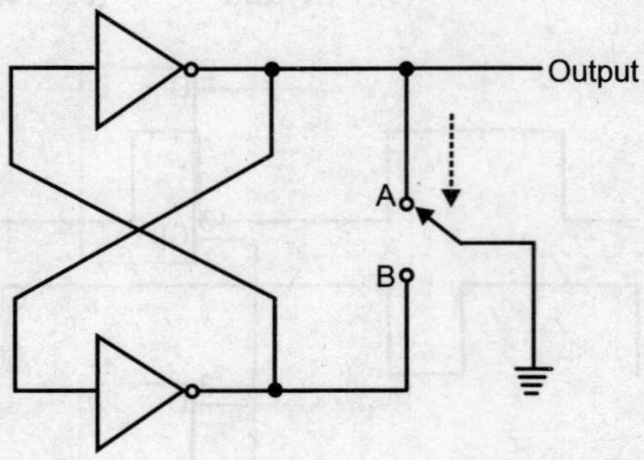

Fig. A-8.11

As the switch is grounded, the output is normally low. When pressed the output goes high.

8.13 (*a*) Reset (*b*) No change
(*c*) Reset (*d*) No change

8.15

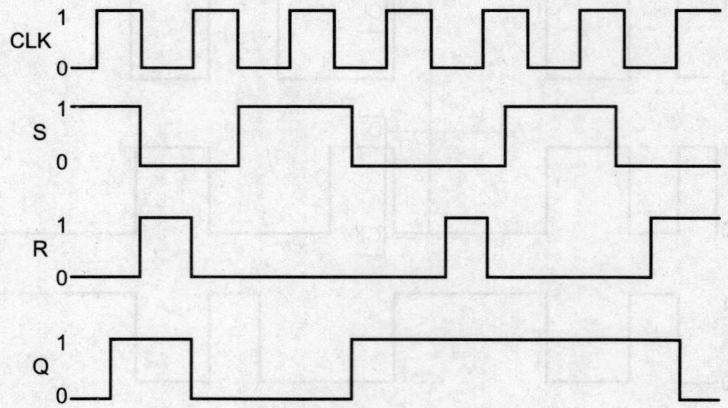

Fig. A-8.15

8.17 Will be reset

8.19

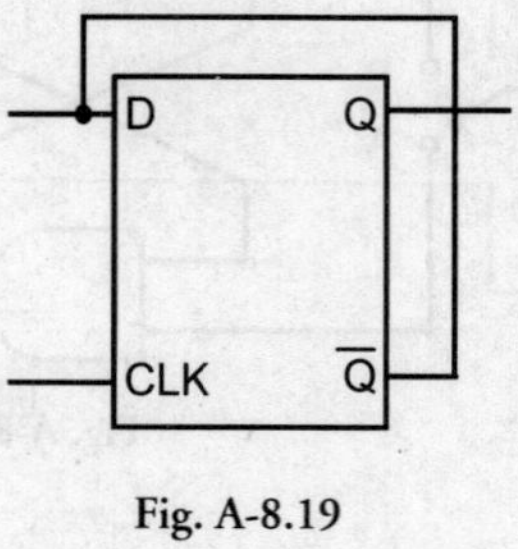

Fig. A-8.19

8.21

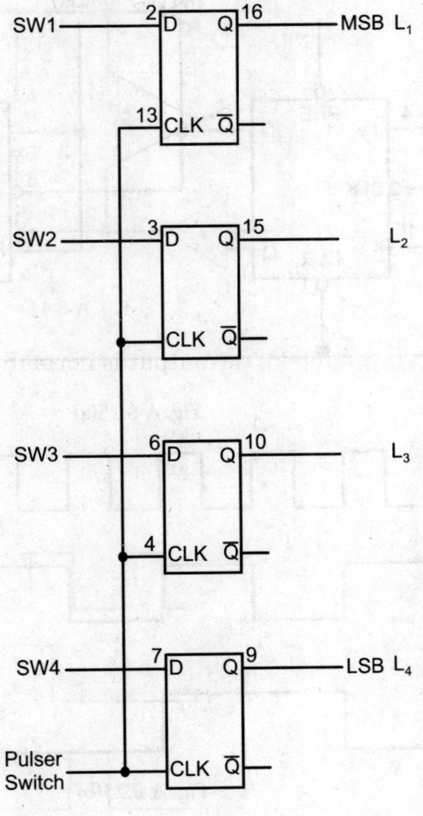

Fig. A-8.21

8.23

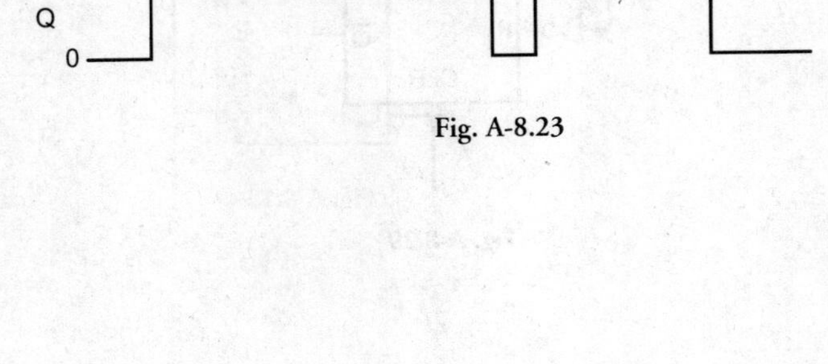

Fig. A-8.23

8.25

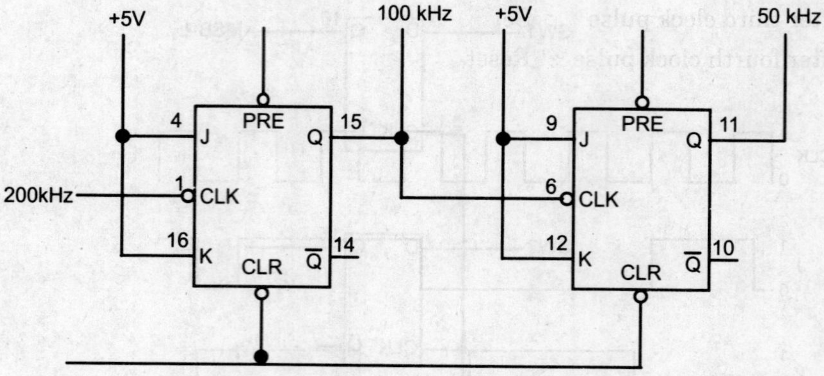

Fig. A-8.25(a)

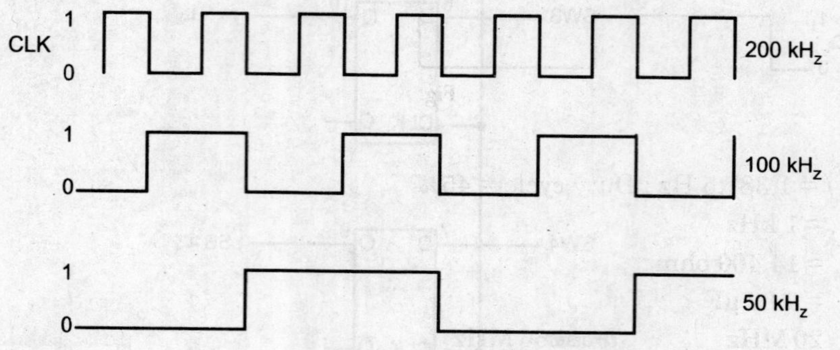

Fig. A-8.25(b)

8.27 The frequency is 500 kHz. Since the flip-flop toggles only once during each cycle, its duty cycle will be 50% and it will be independent of the duty cycle of the clock signal input. A *JK* flip-flop can, therefore, be used to produce a symmetrical clock output.

8.29

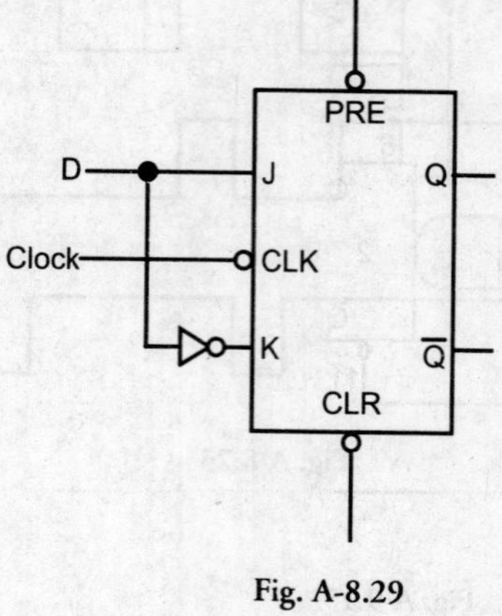

Fig. A-8.29

8.31 After first clock pulse : Set

After second clock pulse : Reset

After third clock pulse : Set

After fourth clock pulse : Reset

8.33

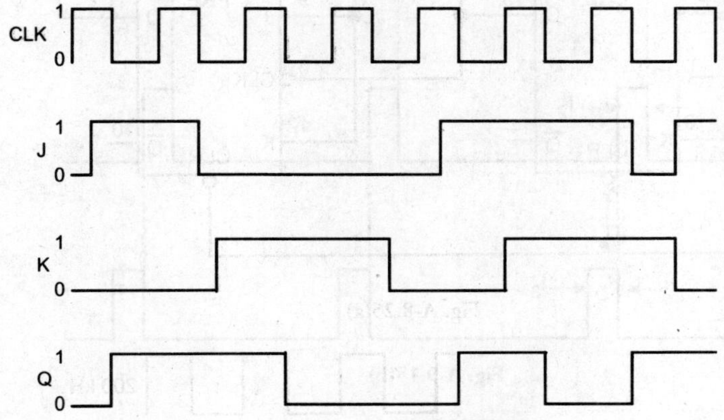

Fig. A-8.33

CHAPTER 9

9.1 $f = 1{,}387.5$ Hz : Duty cycle = 45%

9.3 $f = 1$ kHz

$R_A = 14{,}400$ ohm

$C = 0.02\ \mu F$

9.5 (*a*) 20 MHz (*b*) 6.66 MHz (*c*) 2MHz (*d*) 1MHz

9.7 $R_A = 5$ K ohm, $C = 0.1\ \mu F$

9.9 2250 Hz

9.11 R=15 Kohm, $C = 0.47\ \mu F$

9.15

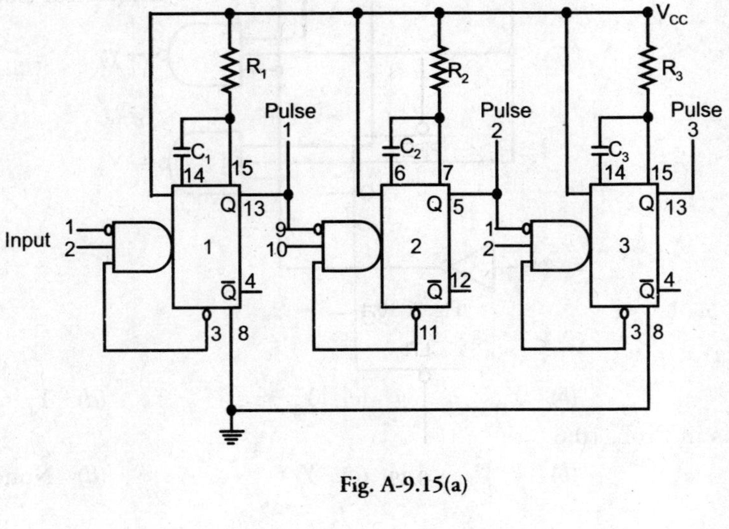

Fig. A-9.15(a)

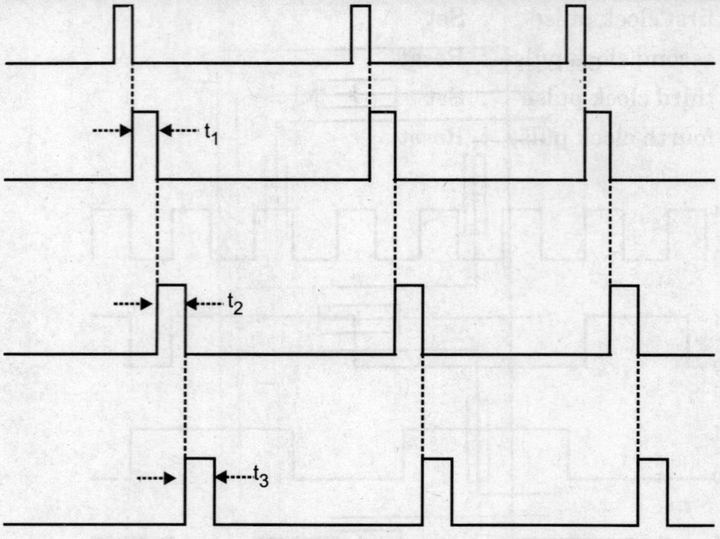

Fig. A-9.15(b)

CHAPTER 10

10.1

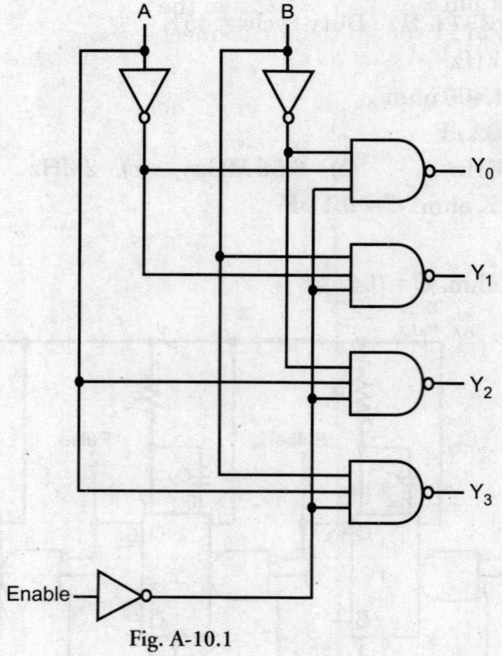

Fig. A-10.1

10.3 $2^6 = 64$

10.5 (*a*) Y_5 (*b*) Y_{14} (*c*) Y_2 (*d*) Y_4

10.7 Same as in Prob. 10.6

10.9 (*a*) Y_6 (*b*) Y_9 (*c*) Y_0 (*d*) None

10.11

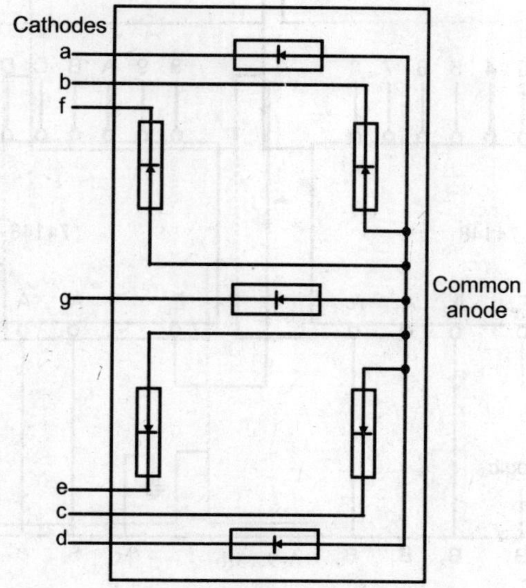

Fig. A-10.11

10.13 Disconnect pin 2 of IC, 7490 A from the reset switch and connect to pin 11 of the same IC. Pin 11 should remain connected to pin 6 of IC 7448.

10.15 HLLL

10.17 (*a*) D_5 (*b*) D_6 (*c*) D_2 (*d*) D_3

10.19 101

10.21

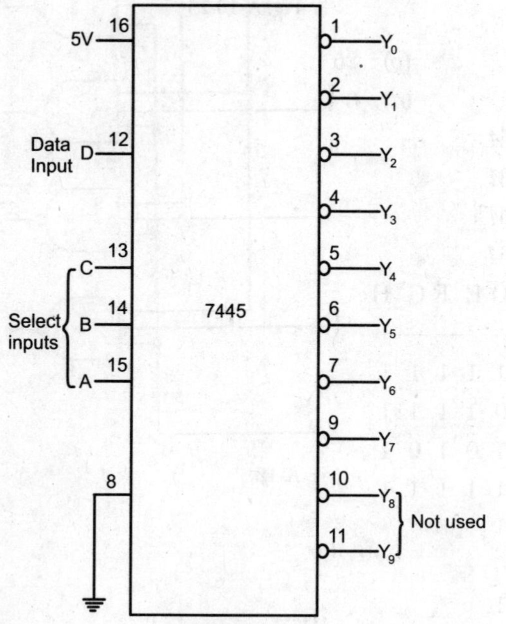

Fig. A-10.21

10.23

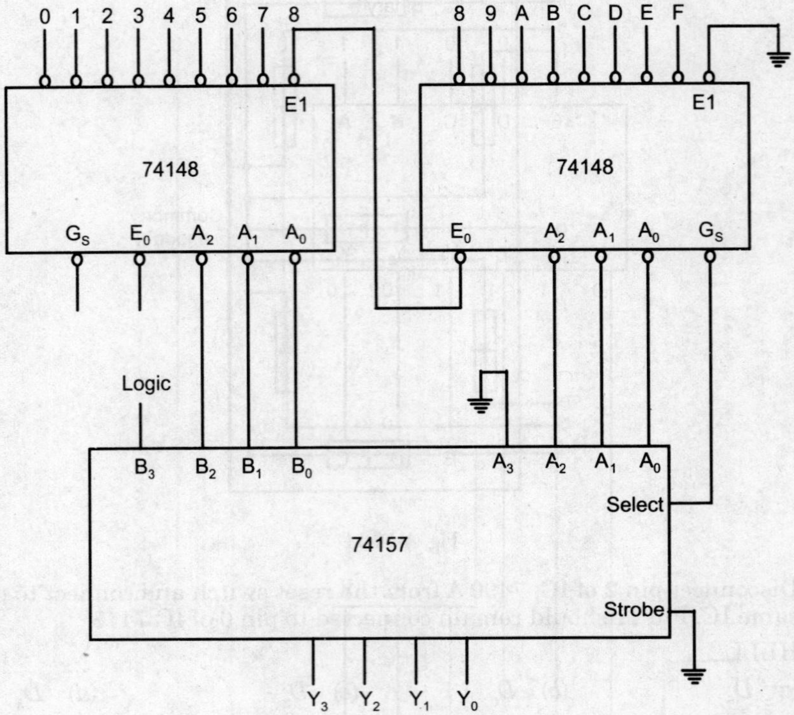

Fig. A-10.23

10.25 (*a*) 21 (*b*) 25
(*c*) 27 (*d*) 6

10.27 (*a*) 2 from M_3
(*b*) 1 from M_0
(*c*) 3 from M_5
(*d*) 0 from M_7

10.29

	A	B	C	D	E	F	G	H
(*a*)	0	0	0	1	1	1	1	1
(*b*)	0	0	0	0	1	1	1	1
(*c*)	1	0	0	1	0	1	0	1
(*d*)	1	1	1	1	1	1	1	1

10.31 (*a*) 1 0 0 1
(*b*) 0 1 1 0
(*c*) 0 0 1 1
(*d*) 0 0 1 0

10.33

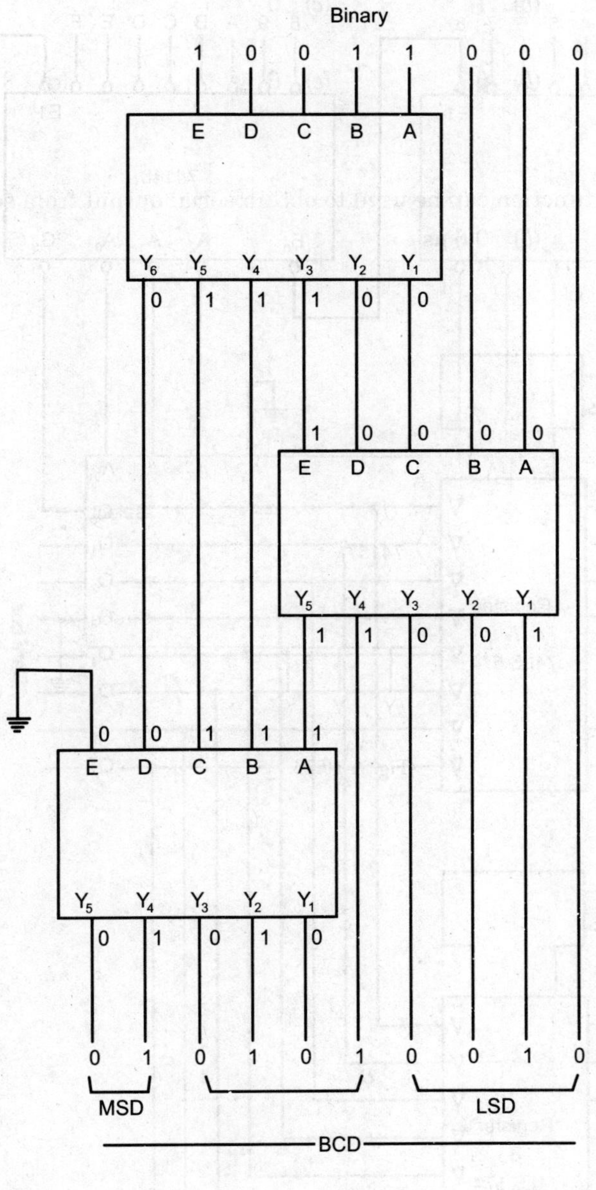

Fig. A-10.33

10.35 (*a*) 1 0 0 0
(*b*) 0 1 1 0
(*c*) 0 1 0 0
(*d*) 0 0 1 0

CHAPTER 11

11.1	(*a*) Q	(*b*) Toggle	(*c*) No change	(*d*) 1
11.3	(*a*) X	(*b*) 1	(*c*) 0	
11.5	No			
11.7	(*a*) 5	(*b*) 6	(*c*) 6	(*d*) 3
11.9	Yes			
11.11	No			

11.13 The shift-right function can be used to obtain serial output from serial input.

11.15 (*a*) 3 μs (*b*) 0.6 μs

11.17

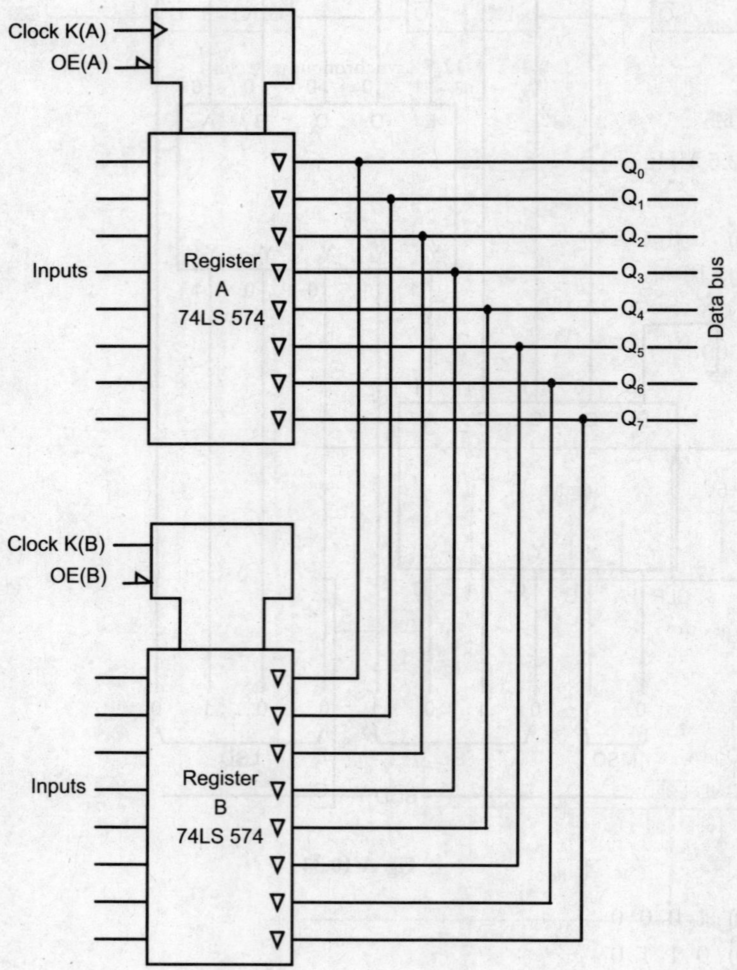

Fig. A-11.17

CHAPTER 12

12.1 Trailing edge

12.3 (*a*) 2 (*b*) 7 (*c*) 9 (*d*) 14

12.5

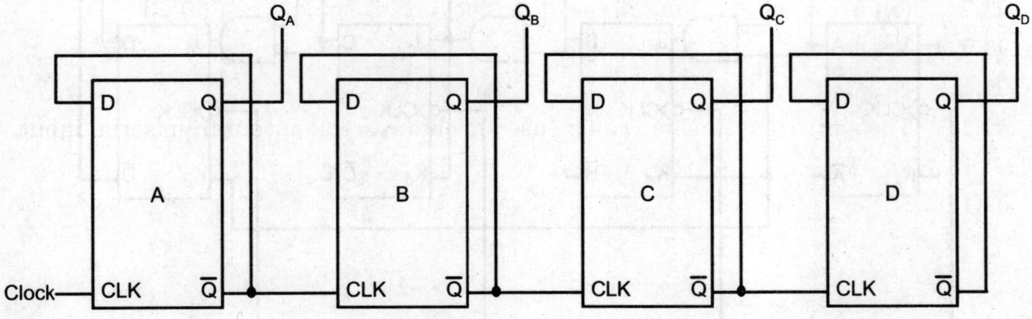

Fig. A-12.5 Asynchronous up-counter

12.7 4095

12.9 12.5 MHz

12.11 8

12.13 (*a*) 1 0 1 1 (*b*) 1 0 0 0 (*c*) 0 1 1 0 (*d*) 0 0 0 1

12.15 (*a*) 10 (*b*) 8 (*c*) 6 (*d*) 3

12.17 0000

12.19 0000

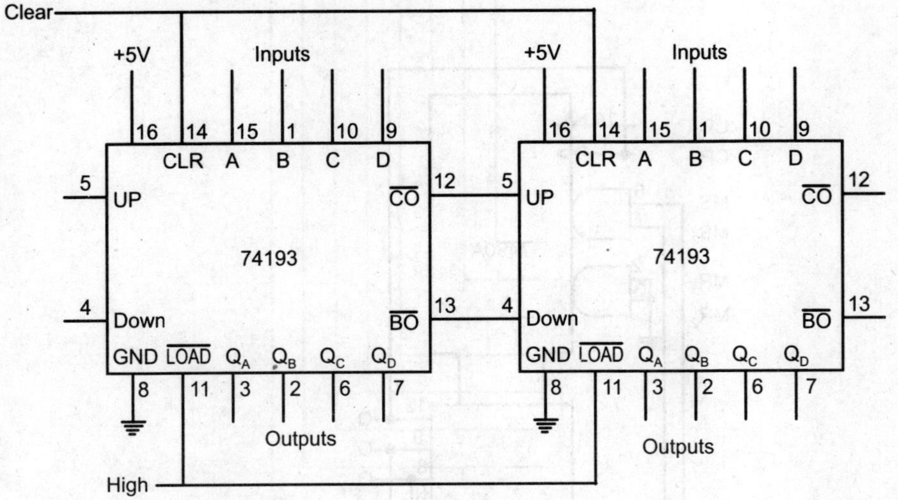

Fig. A-12.19

12.21 (*a*) 2 (*b*) 4 (*c*) 6 (*d*) 9

12.23

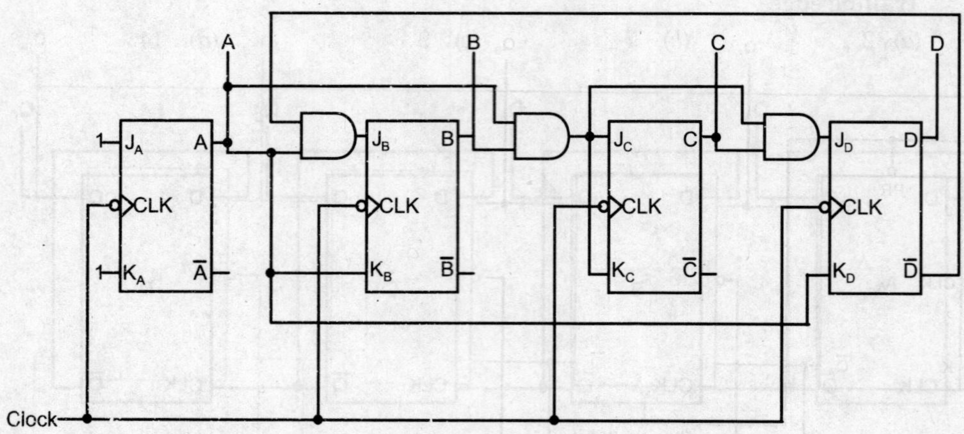

Fig. A-12.23 Synchronous decade counter

12.25

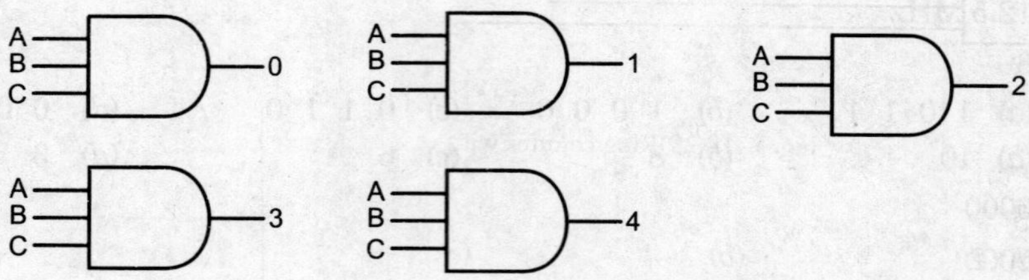

Fig. A-12.25

12.27

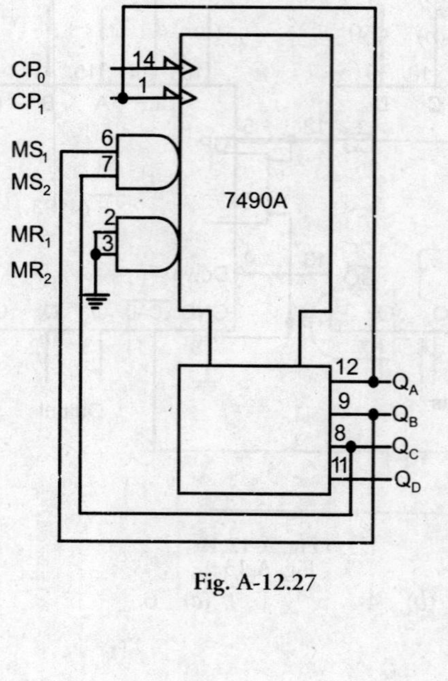

Fig. A-12.27

12.29

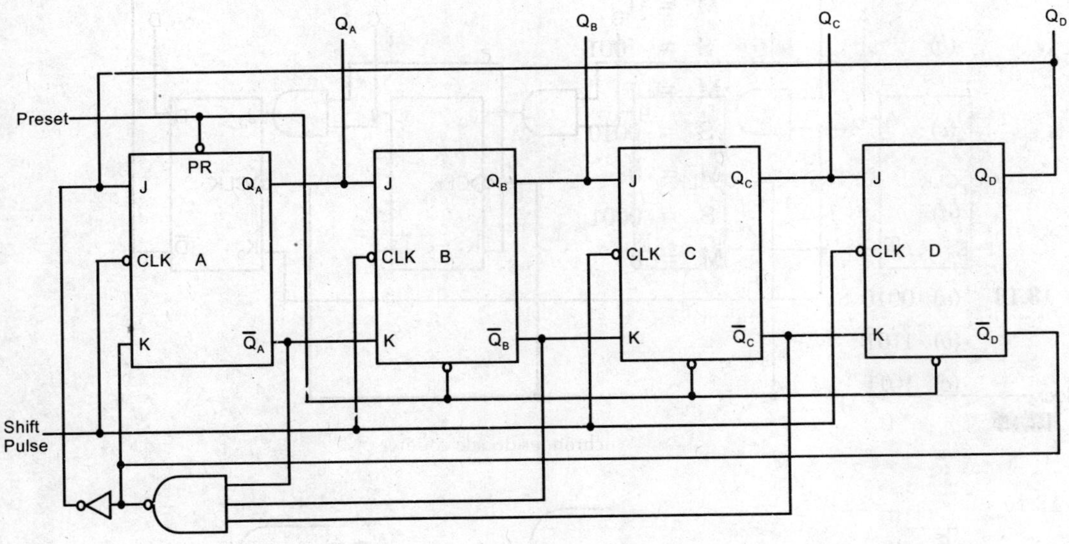

Fig. A-12.29 Ring counter with correcting circuit

CHAPTER 13

13.1	(*a*) 2	(*b*) –3	(*c*) –4	
	(*d*) 26	(*e*) –12	(*f*) –20	
13.3	(*a*) 1010	(*b*) 0010		
	(*c*) 10110010	(*d*) 01010001		
13.5	(*a*) –3	(*b*) –7	(*c*) –107	(*d*) –37
13.7	(*a*) 15	(*b*) –50	(*c*) 35	(*d*) –30

13.9

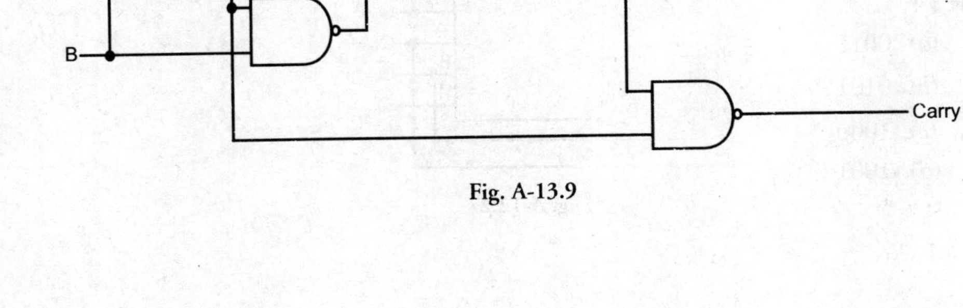

Fig. A-13.9

13.11 (*a*) Connect word *A* to *B* inputs and word *B* to *A* inputs

S = 0111

M = 1

(*b*) S = 1001

M = 1

(*c*) S = 0010

M = 0

(*d*) S = 0001

M = 0

13.13 (*a*) 0010

(*b*) 1101

(*c*) 1011

13.15

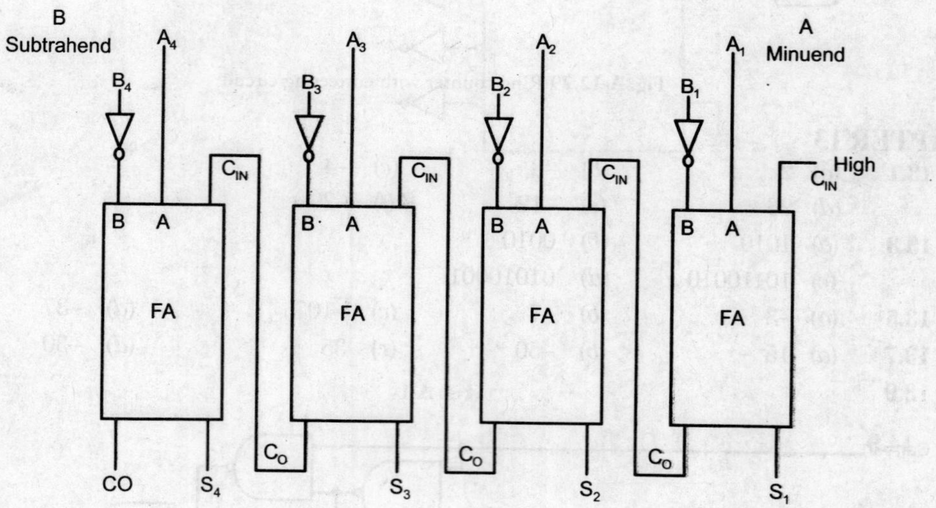

Fig. A-13.15

CHAPTER 14

14.1 (*a*) 0011

(*b*) 0101

(*c*) 1000

(*d*) 1001

14.3 4096 bits

14.5 262,144 (32768 × 8)

14.7

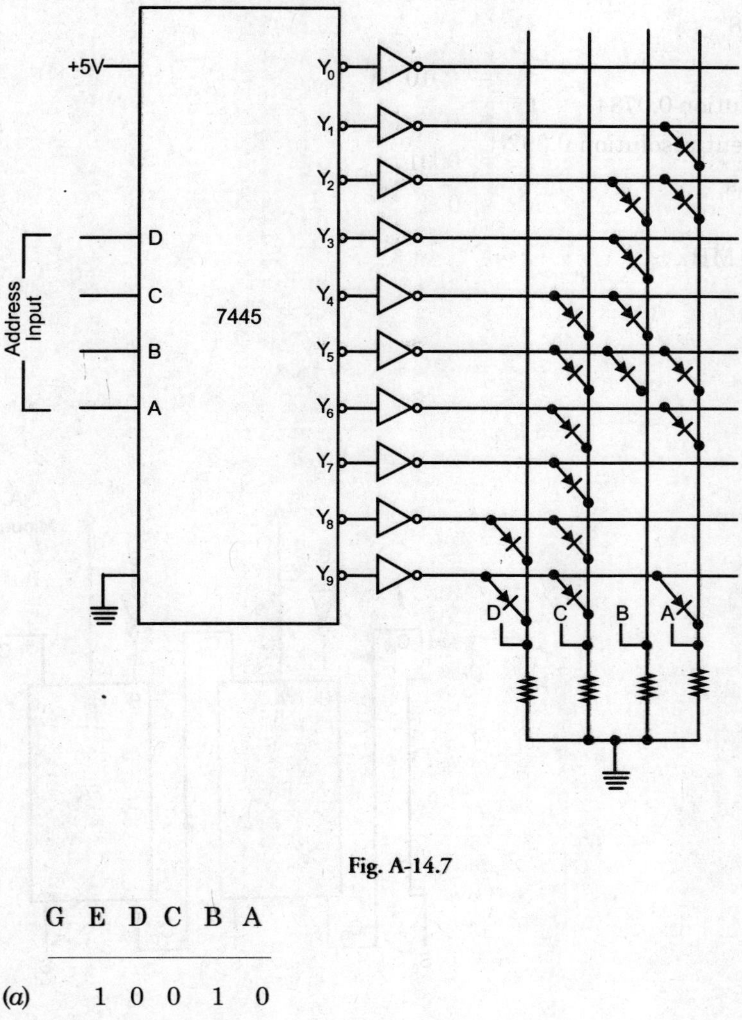

Fig. A-14.7

14.9

	G	E	D	C	B	A
(*a*)		1	0	0	1	0
(*b*)	1	0	0	0	0	0
(*c*)	1	0	1	1	1	1
(*d*)	1	1	1	0	1	1

14.11 Four RAM ICs and a 2-to-4–decoder

14.13 81Cs

CHAPTER 15

15.1 (*a*) 1/7, 2/7, 4/7

(*b*) 1/15, 2/15, 4/15, 8/15

(*c*) 1/31, 2/31, 4/31, 8/31, 16/31

(*d*) 1/63, 2/63, 4/63, 8/63, 16/63, 32/63

15.3 (*a*) 1.15 of the maximum output voltage

(*b*) 1/255 of the maximum ouptut voltage

15.5 0.0078

15.7 0.058

15.9 Resolution 0.0784

Per cent resolution 0.392

15.11 12 bits

CHAPTER 16

16.1 42.90 MHz

16.3 1ms

16.5 9000

Bibliography

Belove-Schilling, *Digital & Analog Systems, Circuits and Devices* : McGraw Hill Book Co.

Blakeslee, T.R., *Digital Design with Standard MSI & LSI* : John Wiley and Sons.

Fletcher, W.L., *An Engineering Approach to Digital Design* : Prentice Hall Inc.

Greenfield, J.D., *Practical Digital Design Using ICs*: John Wiley & Sons.

Greiner, *Semiconductor Devices & Applications* : McGraw Hill Book Co.

Heiserman, D.L., *Handbook of Digital IC Applications* : Prentice Hall Inc.

Hnatek, E.R., *User's Handbook of Semiconductor Memories* : John Wiley & Sons.

Hnatek, E.T., *User's Handbook of Integrated Circuits* : John Wiley & Sons.

Intel Corporation, *Memory Design Handbook.*

Levine, M.E., *Digital Theory & Practice Using Integrated Circuits:* Prentice Hall Ins.

Malvino, A.P. and Leach, D.P., *Digital Principles & Applications* : McGraw Hill Book Co.

National Semiconductor, *CMOS Integrated Circuits,* 1975.

National Semiconductor, *TTL Data Book,* 1976.

Oberman, *Disciplines in Combinational & Sequential Circuit Design* : McGraw Hill Book Co.

Oliver-Cage, *Electronic Measurements & Instrumentation:* McGraw Hill Book Co.

Signetics, *Logic TTL Data Manuel,* 1978.

Terman & Petit, *Electronic Measurements* : McGraw Hill Book Co.

Texas Instruments Inc., *The TTL Data Book for Design Engineers,* 1976.

Texas Instruments Staff, *Designing with TTL Integrated Circuits:* McGraw Hill Book Co.

Tocci, R.J., *Digital Systems, Principles and Applications* : Prentice Hall Inc.

Tokheim, *Digital Electronics* : McGraw Hill Book Co.

Triebel, W.A. & CHU, A.E., *Handbook of Semiconductor & Bubble Memories:* Prentice Hall Inc.

INDEX